Texts in Computer Science

Editors
David Gries
Fred B. Schneider

For further volumes:
www.springer.com/series/3191

Kenneth P. Birman

Guide to Reliable Distributed Systems

Building High-Assurance Applications and Cloud-Hosted Services

 Springer

Kenneth P. Birman
Department of Computer Science
Cornell University
Ithaca, NY, USA

Series Editors
David Gries
Department of Computer Science
Cornell University
Ithaca, NY, USA

Fred B. Schneider
Department of Computer Science
Cornell University
Ithaca, NY, USA

ISSN 1868-0941   e-ISSN 1868-095X
Texts in Computer Science
ISBN 978-1-4471-5842-4   ISBN 978-1-4471-2416-0 (eBook)
DOI 10.1007/978-1-4471-2416-0
Springer London Dordrecht Heidelberg New York

British Library Cataloguing in Publication Data
A catalogue record for this book is available from the British Library

Printed on acid-free paper

Springer is part of Springer Science+Business Media (www.springer.com)

Preface

Setting the Stage

The *Guide to Reliable Distributed Systems: Building High-Assurance Applications and Cloud-Hosted Services* is a heavily edited new edition of a prior edition that went under the name *Reliable Distributed Computing*; the new name reflects a new focus on *Cloud Computing*. The term refers to the technological infrastructure supporting today's web systems, social networking, e-commerce and a vast array of other applications. The emergence of the cloud has been a transformational development, for a number of reasons: cost, flexibility, new ways of managing and leveraging large data sets. There are other benefits that we will touch on later.

The cloud is such a focus of product development and so associated with overnight business success stories today that one could easily write a text focused on the cloud "as is" and achieve considerable success with the resulting text. After all, the cloud has enabled companies like Netflix, with a few hundred employees, to create a movie-on-demand capability that may someday scale to reach every potential consumer in the world. Facebook, with a few thousand employees, emerged overnight to create a completely new form of social network, having the importance and many of the roles that in the past one associated with vast infrastructures like email, or the telephone network. The core Google search infrastructure was created by just a few dozen employees (by now, of course, Google has tens of thousands, and does far more than just search). And the cloud is an accelerator for such events: companies with a good idea can launch a new product one day, and see it attract a million users a week later without breaking a sweat. This capability is disruptive and profoundly impactful and is reshaping the technology sector at an accelerating pace.

Of course there is a second side to the cloud, and one that worries many corporate executives both at the winners and at other companies: the companies named above were picked by the author in the hope that they would be success stories for as long as the text is in active use. After all this text will quickly seem dated if it seems to point to yesterday's failures as if they were today's successes. Yet we all know that companies that sprang up overnight do have a disconcerting way of vanishing just as quickly: the cloud has been a double-edged sword. A single misstep can spell doom. A single new development can send the fickle consumer community rushing to some new and even more exciting alternative. The cloud, then, is quite a stormy place! And this book, sadly, may well be doomed to seem dated from the very day it goes to press.

But even if the technical landscape changes at a dizzying pace, the cloud already is jam-packed with technologies that are fascinating to learn about and use, and that will certainly live on in some form far into the future: BitTorrent, for example (a swarm-style download system) plays key roles in the backbone of Twitter's data center, Memcached (a new kind of key-value store) has displaced standard file system storage for a tremendous range of cloud computing goals. MapReduce and its cousin Hadoop enable a new kind of massively parallel data reduction. Chubby supports scalable locking and synchronization, and is a critical component at the core of Google's cloud services platform. ZooKeeper plays similar roles in Yahoo!'s consistency-based services. Dynamo, Amazon's massively replicated key-value store, is the basis for its shopping cart service. BigTable, Google's giant table-structured storage system, manages sparse but enormous tabular data sets. JGroups and Spread, two commercially popular replication technologies, allow cloud services to maintain large numbers of copies of heavily accessed data. The list goes on, including global file systems, replication tools, load balancing subsystems, you name it. Indeed, the list is so long that even today, we will only touch on a few representative examples; it would take many volumes to cover everything the cloud can do, and to understand all the different ways it does those things. We will try and work our way in from the outside, identifying deep problems along the way, and then we will tackle those fundamental questions. Accordingly, Part I of the book gives a technical overview of the whole picture, covering the basics but without delving deeply on the more subtle technology questions that arise, such as data replication. We will look at those harder questions in Parts II and III of the text; Part IV covers some additional technologies that merit inclusion for reasons of completeness, but for which considerations of length limit us to shallow reviews.

Above, we hinted at one of the deeper questions that sit at the core of Parts II and III. If the cloud has a dark side, it is this: there are a great many applications that need forms of high assurance, but the cloud, as currently architected, only offers very limited support for scalable high assurance computing. Indeed, if we look at high assurance computing in a broad way, and then look at how much of high assurance computing maps easily to the cloud, the only possible conclusion is that the cloud really does not support high assurance applications at all. Yes, the cloud supports a set of transactional-security features that can be twisted this way and that to cover a certain class of uses (as mentioned earlier, those concerned with credit card purchases and with streaming copyright-protected content like movies and music from the cloud to your playback device), but beyond those limited use cases, high assurance technologies have been perceived as not scaling adequately for use in the cloud, at least in the scalable first tier that interacts with external clients.

The story is actually pretty grim. First, we will encounter two theorems about things we cannot do in cloud settings: one proves that fault-tolerant distributed computing is impossible in standard networks, and the second that data consistency cannot be achieved under the performance and availability requirements of the cloud. Next, we will find that the existing cloud platforms are designed to violate consistency as a short-cut towards higher performance and better scalability. Thus: "High assurance in the cloud? It cannot be done, it cannot scale to large systems, and even if it could be done and it could be made to scale, it is not the way we do it."

The assertion that high-assurance is not needed in most elements of most modern cloud computing applications may sound astonishing, yet if one looks closely, it turns out that the majority of web and cloud applications are cleverly designed to either completely avoid the need for high-assurance capabilities, or find ways to minimize the roles of any high assurance components, thereby squeezing the high-assurance side of the cloud into smaller subsystems that do not see remotely as much load as the main systems might encounter (if you like, visualize a huge cache-based front end that receives most of the workload, and then a second smaller core system that only sees update transactions which it applies to some sort of files or databases, and then as updates commit, pushes new data out to the cache, or invalidates cached records as needed).

For example, just to pick an example from the air, think about a massive government program like the Veteran's Administration Benefits program here in the United States. This clearly needs strong assurance (all sorts of sensitive data moves back and forth), money changes hands (the VA system is, in part, a big insurance system), sensitive records are stored within the VA databases. Yet if you study such a system carefully, as was done in a series of White House reviews during 2010 and 2011, the match with today's cloud is really very good. Secure web pages can carry that sensitive data with reasonable protection. The relatively rare transactions against the system have much the same character as credit card transactions. And if we compare the cost of operating a system such as this using the cloud model, as opposed to having the Veteran's Administration run its own systems, we can predict annual savings in the tens of millions hundreds! Yet not a single element of the picture seems to be deeply at odds with today's most successful cloud computing models.

Thus, our statements about high-assurance are not necessarily statements about limitations that every single high assurance computing use would encounter. E-commerce transactions on the web work perfectly well as long as the transactional system is not down, and when we use a secured web page to purchase a book or provide a credit card number, that action is about as secure as one can make it given some of the properties of the PCs we use as endpoints (as we will see, many home computers are infected with malware that does not do anything visibly horrible, yet can still be actively snooping on the actions you as the user take, and could easily capture all sorts of passwords and other security-related data, or even initiate transactions on its own while you are fast asleep!) Notice that we have made a statement that does not demand continuous fault-tolerance (we all realize that these systems will sometimes be temporarily unavailable), and does not expose the transactional system to huge load (we all browse extensively and make actual purchases rarely: browsing is a high-load activity; purchasing, much less so). The industry has honed this particular high-assurance data path to the point that most of us, for most purposes, incur only limited risks in trusting these kinds of solutions. Moreover, one cannot completely eliminate risk. When you hand your credit card to a waiter, you also run some risks, and we accept those all the time.

Some authors, knowing about the limitations of the cloud, would surely proclaim the web to be "unsafe at any speed;" Indeed, I once wrote an article that had this title (but with a question mark at the end, which does change the meaning). The bottom line is that even with its limitations today, such a claim would be pure hyperbole. But it would be quite accurate to point out that the vast majority of the web makes do with very weak assurance properties. Moreover, although the web provides great support for secure transactions, the model it uses works for secure transmission of a credit card to a cloud provider and for secure delivery of the video you just licensed back to your laptop or Internet-connected TV, not for other styles of high-assurance computing. Given the dismal security properties of the laptops, the computing industry views Web security as a pretty good story. But could we extend this model to tackle a broader range of security challenges?

We can then ask another question. Is it possible that *scalable* high-assurance computing, outside what the cloud offers today, just is not needed? We emphasized the term "scalable" for a reason: the cloud is needed for large-scale computing; the methods of the past few decades were often successful in solving high-assurance computing challenges, but also limited to problems that ran on more modest scales. The cloud is the place to turn when an application might involve tens of thousands of simultaneous users. With six users, the cloud could be convenient and cheap, but is certainly not the only option. Thus unless we can identify plenty of important examples of large-scale uses that will need high assurance, it might make sense to conclude that the cloud can deal with high-assurance in much the same way that it deals with credit card purchases: using smaller systems that are shielded from heavy loads and keep up with the demand because they aren't really forced to work very hard.

There is no doubt that the weak-assurances of the cloud suffice for many purposes; a great many applications can be twisted to fit them. The proof is right on our iPads and Android telephones: they work remarkably well and do all sorts of amazing tricks and they do this within the cloud model as currently deployed, and they even manage to twist the basic form of web security into so many forms that one could easily believe that the underlying mechanism is far more general than it really is. Yet the situation would change if we tried to move more of today's computing infrastructure as a whole to a cloud model. Think about what high assurance really means. Perhaps your first reaction is that the term mostly relates to a class of very esoteric and specialized systems that provide services for tasks such as air traffic control, banking, or perhaps management of electronic medical records and medical telemetry in critical care units. The list goes on: one could add many kinds of military applications (those might need strong security, quick response, or other kinds of properties). There is a lot of talk about new ways of managing the electric power grid to achieve greater efficiency and to share power in a more nimble way over large regions, so that we can make more use of renewable electric generation capacity. Many government services need to be highly assured. And perhaps even non-politicians would prefer that it was a bit harder to hack their twitter, email and Facebook accounts.

So here we have quite a few examples of high assurance applications: systems that genuinely need to do the right thing, and to do it at the right time, where we're defining "right" in different ways depending on the case. Yet the list did not include very many of what you might call bread-and-butter computing cases, which might lead you to conclude that high assurance is a niche area. After all, not many of us work on air traffic control systems, and it is easy to make that case against migrating things like air traffic control to cloud models (even privately operated cloud models). Thus, it is not surprising that many developers assume that they do not really work on systems of this kind.

We're going to question that quick conclusion. One reason is that the average enterprise has many high assurance subsystems playing surprisingly mundane roles; they operate the factory floor equipment, run the corporate payroll, and basically keep the lights on. These are high assurance roles simply because if they are not performed correctly, the enterprise is harmed. Of course not many run on the cloud today, but perhaps if cloud computing continues to gain in popularity and continues to drop in cost (and if the reliability of the cloud were just a touch higher), operators may start to make a case for migrating them to cloud settings.

This is just the area where scalability and high assurance seem to collide: if we imagine using the cloud to control vast numbers of physical things that can break or cause harm if controlled incorrectly, then we definitely encounter limitations that today's cloud cannot easily surmount. The cloud is wonderful for scalable delivery of insecure data, and adequate for scalable delivery of certain kinds of sensitive data, and for conducting relatively infrequent purchase-style transactions. All of this works wonderfully well. But the model does not fit nearly so well if we want to use it in high-assurance control applications.

This is a bit worrying, because the need for high assurance cloud-hosted control systems could easily become a large one if cloud computing starts to displace other styles of computing to any substantial degree, a trend the author believes to increasingly probable. The root cause here is the tendency of the computing industry to standardize around majority platforms that then kill off competitors simply for economic reasons: lacking adequate investment, they wither and die. As cloud computing has flourished, it has also become the primary platform for most kinds of application development, displacing many other options for reasons of cost, ease of development, and simply because the majority platform tends to attract the majority of developers.

Some of the most exciting future uses of computing presume that computers will penetrate into the home and car and office to such a degree that we will be able to start to do intelligent, environmentally aware, dynamic control of those kinds of systems. Traffic lights and water heaters will begin to be cloud-controlled systems. Fragile, elderly patients will manage to live at home for many years, rather than in assisted living settings, because computing systems will play vital monitoring and assistance roles. Cars will literally drive themselves on densely packed highways, at far higher speeds and with tighter spacings than today's human drivers can manage. Those kinds of visions of the future appear, at least superficially, to presume a new kind of high assurance cloud computing that appears, at least superficially, to be at odds with what today's cloud platforms are able to do. Indeed, they appear, again superficially, to be at odds with those theorems we mentioned earlier. If fault-tolerant computing is impossible, how can we possibly trust computing systems in roles like these? If the cloud cannot offer high assurance properties, how can the US government possibly bet so heavily on the cloud in sensitive government and military applications?

Accordingly, we must pose a follow-on question. What are the consequences of putting a critical application on a technology base not conceived to support high assurance computing? The danger is that we could wander into a future in which computing applications, playing critical roles, simply cannot be trusted to do so in a correct, secure, consistent manner.

This leads to the second and perhaps more controversial agenda of the present text: to educate the developer (be that a student or a professional in the field) about the architectures of these important new cloud computing platforms and about their limitations: not just what they can do, but also what they *cannot* do. Some of these limitations are relatively easily worked around; others, much less so.

We will not accept that even the latter kind of limitations are show-stoppers. Instead, the book looks to a future well beyond what current cloud platforms can support. We will ask where cloud computing might go next, how it can get there, and will seek to give the reader hands-on experience with the technologies that would enable that future cloud. Some of these enablers exist in today's commercial market place, but others are lacking. Consequently, rather than teaching the reader about options that would be very hard to put into practice, we have taken the step of creating a new kind of cloud computing software library (all open source), intended to make the techniques we discuss here practical, so that readers can easily experiment with the ideas the book will cover, using them to build applications that target real cloud settings, and could be deployed and used even in large-scale, performance-intensive situations. A consequence is that this text will view some technical options as being practical (and might even include exercises urging the reader to try them out him or herself using our library, or using one of those high-assurance technologies), and if you were to follow that advice, with a few hundred lines of code and a bit of debugging you would be able to run your highly assured solution on a real cloud platform, such as Amazon's EC2 or Microsoft Azure. Doing so could leave you with the impression would be that the technique is perfectly practical. Yet if you were to ask one of those vendors, or some other major cloud vendor, what they think about this style of high-assured cloud computing, you might well be told that such services do not belong in the cloud!

Is it appropriate to include ideas that the industry has yet to adopt into a textbook intended for real developers who want to learn to build reliable cloud computing solutions? Many authors would decide not to do so, and that decision point differentiates this text from others in the same general area. We will not include concepts that we have not implemented in our Isis^2 software library (you will hear more and more about Isis^2 as we get to Parts II and III of the book, and are welcome to download it, free of any charges, and to use it as you like) or that someone we trust has not worked with in some hands-on sense—anything you read in this book is real enough that someone has built it, experimented with it, and gained enough credibility that the author really believes the technique to be a viable one. Just the same our line in the sand does not limit itself to things that have achieved commercial acceptance on a large-scale. You can do things with a technology like Isis[2] (and can do them right on cloud platforms like Amazon's EC2 or Microsoft's Azure) that, according to the operators of those platforms, are not currently available options.

What is one to make of this seeming disconnect? After all, how could we on the one hand know how to do things, and on the other hand be told by the operators and vendors in the cloud area that they do not know how to do those same things? The answer revolves around economics. Cloud computing is an industry born from literally billions of dollars of investment to create a specific set of platforms and tools and to support some specific (even peculiar) styles of programming. We need to recognize the amazing power of today's cloud platforms, and to learn how the solutions work and how to adapt them to solve new problems. Yet today's platforms are also limited: they offer the technologies that the vendors have gained familiarity with, and that fit well with the majority of their users. Vendors need this kind of comfort level and experience to offer a technology within a product; merely knowing how to solve a problem does not necessarily mean that products will embody the solutions the very next day. For the vendor, such choices reflect economic balancing acts: a technology costs so much to develop, so much more to test and integrate into their product offerings, so much more after that to support through its life style. Doing so will bring in *this* much extra revenue, or represent *such-and-such* a marketing story. Those kinds of analyses do not always favor deploying every single technical option. And yet we should not view cloud computing as a done deal: this entire industry is still at in its early days, and it continues to evolve at a breathtaking pace. The kinds of things we offer in our little library are examples of technologies that the author expects to see in common in use in the cloud as we look a few years out into the future.

This somewhat personal view of the future will not necessarily convince the world's main cloud providers to align their cloud platforms with the technologies covered in this text on day one. But change is coming, and nothing we cover in this text is impractical: everything we will look at closely is either already part of the mainstream cloud infrastructure, or exists in some form of commercial product one could purchase, or is available as free-ware, such as our own Isis[2] solution. A world of high-assurance cloud computing awaits us, and for those who want to be players, the basic elements of that future are already fairly clear.

Acknowledgements

Much of the work reported here was made possible by grants from the U.S. National Science Foundation, the Defense Advanced Research Agency (DARPA), the Air Force (specifically, the offices of the Air Force CIO and CTO, the Air Force Research Laboratory at Rome NY (AFRL), and the Air Force Office of Scientific Research (AFOSR)). Grants from a number of corporations have also supported this work, including Microsoft, Cisco, Intel Corporation, Google and IBM Corporation. I wish to express my thanks to all of these agencies and corporations for their generosity. The techniques, approaches, and opinions expressed here are my own; they may not represent positions of the organizations and corporations that have supported this research. While Isis^2 was created by the author, his students and research colleagues are now becoming involved and as the system goes forward, it seems likely that it will evolve into more of a team effort, reflecting contributions from many sources.

Many people offered suggestions and comments on the earlier book that contributed towards the current version. I remain extremely grateful to them; the current text benefits in myriad ways from the help I received on earlier versions. Finally, let me also express my thanks to all the faculty members and students who decide to use this text. I am well aware of the expression of confidence that such a decision represents, and have done my best to justify your trust.

Ithaca, USA   Ken Birman

Trademarks

Unix is a Trademark of Santa Cruz Operations, Inc. CORBA (Common Object Request Broker Architecture) and OMG IDL are trademarks of the Object Management Group. ONC (Open Network Computing), NFS (Network File System), Solaris, Solaris MC, XDR (External Data Representation), Jaa, J2EE, Jini and JXTA are trademarks of Sun Microsystems, Inc. DCE is a trademark of the Open Software Foundation. XTP (Xpress Transfer Protocol) is a trademark of the XTP Forum. RADIO is a trademark of Stratus Computer Corporation. Isis Reliable Software Developer's Kit, Isis Reliable Network File System, Isis Reliable Message Bus, and Isis for Databases are trademarks of Isis Distributed Computing Systems, Inc. Orbix is a trademark of Iona Technologies Ltd. Orbix+Isis is a joint trademark of Iona and Isis Distributed Computing Systems, Inc. TIB (Teknekron Information Bus), Publish-Subscribe and Subject Based Addressing are trademarks of TIBCO (although we use these terms in a more general sense in this text). Chorus is a trademark of Chorus Systems, Inc. Power Objects is a trademark of Oracle Corporation. Netscape is a trademark of Netscape Communications. OLE, COM, DCOM, Windows, Windows XP, .NET, Visual Studio, C#, and J# are trademarks of Microsoft Corporation. Lotus Notes is a trademark of Lotus Computing Corporation. Purify is a trademark of Highland Software, Inc. Proliant is a trademark of Compaq Computers, Inc. VAX-Clusters, DEC MessageQ, and DECsafe Available Server Environment are trademarks of Digital Equipment Corporation. MQSeries and SP2 are trademarks of International Business Machines. PowerBuilder is a trademark of PowerSoft Corporation. Ethernet is a trademark of Xerox Corporation. Gryphon and WebSphere are trademarks of IBM. WebLogic is a trademark of BEA, Inc.

Among cloud computing products and tools mentioned here, Azure is a trademark of Microsoft Corporation, MapReduce, BigTable, GFS and Chubby are trademarks of Google, which also operates the GooglePlex, EC2 and AC3 are trademarks of Amazon.com, Zookeeper is a trademark of Yahoo!, WebSphere is a trademark of IBM, BitTorrent is both a name for a technology area and standard and for a product line by the BitTorrent Corporation, Hadoop is an open-source implementation of MapReduce.

Other products and services mentioned in this document are covered by the trademarks, service marks, or product names as designated by the companies that market those products. The author respectfully acknowledges any that may not have been included.

Contents

Part II   Reliable Distributed Computing

Introduction

1

1.1 Green Clouds on the Horizon

Any text concerned with cloud computing needs to start by confronting a puzzling issue: There is quite a bit of debate about just what cloud computing actually means! This debate isn't an angry one; the problem isn't so much that there is a very active competition between the major vendors and cloud data center operators, but rather that so many enterprises use the cloud in so many ways that any form of computing accessible over a network, and almost any kind of activity that involves access to massive data sets, falls into the cloud arena.

Thus for some, the cloud is all about web search, for others social networking, while still others think of the cloud as the world's most amazing outsourcing technology, permitting us to ship data and computation to some remote place where computing and storage are dirt cheap. All of these visions are absolutely correct: the cloud is all things to all users, and even more uses and meanings of the term are emerging even as you read these lines.

Individual cloud-based platforms have their own features and reflect different priorities and implementation decisions, but the federation of systems that comprises the cloud as a whole offers a rich and varied spectrum of capabilities and technologies, and many are turning out to be incredibly popular.

Traditional computing systems made a distinction between client computers and servers, but both tended to be owned by your company, situated in the same rooms that you and other employees are working in, and managed by the overworked folks in the administrative suite up the hall (a group that you probably rely on in more ways that you would care to admit). We also own personal computers of various kinds, connected to the Internet and giving us access to a wide array of web-based services. Add up all of this and you are looking a staggering amount of computing hardware, people to manage that hardware and the software that runs on it, power to keep them running, and cooling. If your family is like mine, even the computing systems in your own home add up to a considerable investment, and keeping them all functioning properly, and configured to talk to one-another and to the Internet, can be a real chore.

K.P. Birman, *Guide to Reliable Distributed Systems*, Texts in Computer Science,
DOI 10.1007/978-1-4471-2416-0_1, © Springer-Verlag London Limited 2012

We will not get rid of computers anytime soon; they are surely the most important and most universal tool in the modern world. Nor will we have fewer of them around: the trend, indeed, seems to run very strongly in the other direction. But this traditional way of computing can be incredibly wasteful, and cloud computing may be the first really promising opportunity for slashing that waste without losing the benefits of computing. Moreover, cloud systems offer some real hope of a world with far fewer computer viruses, fewer zombie-like bot computers enslaved to remote, malicious hackers, and the day may soon arrive when the kind of hands-on system configuration that we have all learned to do, and to hate, will be a thing of the past.

Consider power. When a computer in your office consumes 200 watts of power, that power needs to be generated and transported from the power plant to the building in which you work. Quite a bit is lost in this process; certainly, a factor of 10, and perhaps as much as 100 if your office is far from the generating station. So to ensure that you will be able to consume 200 watts of power when you decide to plug in your laptop, someone may need to generate 2000 or even 20,000 watts, and most of power will simply be wasted, dissipating as heat into the environment. Worse still, to the extent that generated power actually reaches your office and gets used to run your computer, the odds are good that your computer will just be sitting idle. Most computers are idle most of the time: the owners leave them running so that the responses will be snappy when they actually need to do something, and because of a widely held belief that powering machines up and down can make them failure prone. So we are generating huge amounts of power, at a huge cost to the environment, yet most of it is simply wasted.

But this is not even the whole story. The 200 watts of power that the computer consumes turns into heat, and unless one actually wants a very warm office, air conditioners are required to bring things back to a comfortable temperature. There is some irony here: in the past, a hot computer tended to fail, but today many computers can safely be operated at relatively high temperatures—100°F (about 40°C) should not be any problem at all, and some systems will operate correctly at 120°F (50°C), although doing so may reduce a machine's lifetime. But obviously, we are not about to let our offices or even our machine rooms get that hot. And so we use even more power, to cool our offices.

A natural question to ask is this: why not just turn these idle computers off, or replace them with very energy-efficient screens that take minimal power to operate, like the ones used in eReaders like the Kindle or the Nook? The obvious answer is that power-efficient computers are pretty slow. But networks are fast, and so we arrive at the cloud model: we do some simple work on the client's computer, but the heavy lifting is done remotely, in a massive shared data center.

Cloud computing is not just about where the computer runs. The style of computing differs in other ways as well. One difference concerns the sense in which cloud computing is powerful. Past computing systems gained speed by speeding up the clock, or through massive parallelism and very high-speed multiprocessor interconnections: desktop computers were headed towards becoming small supercomputers until as recently as 2000. But modern computing favors large numbers of less powerful individuals cores: a typical modern machine might have two or four cores, each of which is individually weaker than a single-core but cutting edge gaming computer system might have been just a few years ago. The cloud is about marshalling vast numbers of "medium speed" machines (but with huge amounts of memory and disk space) to subdivide big tasks into easy smaller pieces, dole out the pieces, and collect up the responses. If you know anything about the famous SETI@Home project (a search for signs of extraterrestrial life), you might want to think of the cloud as a new form of SETI platform that searches not for aliens, but rather for the very best buy on home appliances! As a result, in this text we will be learning a lot about ways of dividing big tasks into small tasks. In fact this is one of the problems with the cloud: for all the power of cloud data centers, they are relatively poor choices for problems that demand vast amounts of raw computing cycles and that *do not* subdivide nicely into separate tasks that can run whenever the cloud has a chance to schedule them. This is not the only limitation of the cloud, but it is a limitation that can be quite constraining for some uses.

When you run a full-featured computer system at home, or in the office, and install all sorts of applications on it, you often run into screens full of options that you probably leave set to the default values. This can result in mistakes that leave your machine open to compromise; indeed, as we will see, many home and office computing systems are infected by viruses or covertly belong to "botnets". Such systems are wide open to hackers who might want to steal your identity, or to use your computer to host various kinds of inappropriate material, or even to force it to send out waves of emails about cheap medications, unbelievable investment opportunities, and dubious body-part enhancements. With a little bad luck, your home computer may already have played a small part in taking some country off the network entirely. This has happened a few times; for example, in 2008 and 2009 first Estonia and then Ukraine found themselves in disputes with Russia. Within a few days massive distributed denial of service (DDoS) attacks were launched from computers worldwide, overwhelming both countries with such massive floods of nonsense messages that their computing infrastructures collapsed. Yet very few of the individuals whose machines were involved in sending those messages had any idea that they did so, and in fact many of those same machines are still compromised in the same ways!

What this adds up to is that we have been working with computers in a remarkably inefficient, failure-prone, and insecure manner. The approach is wasteful of power, wasteful of computers, and even wasteful of money. While privately owned computers may seem private and secure, the reality is exactly the opposite: with today's model insecurities are so pervasive that there is little hope of ever getting that cat back into the bag. And anyone who believes that modern technology protects privacy has not been following the tabloid press. Even without knowing when you will read this paragraph, I can say with absolute confidence that this week's newspapers will be reporting in lurid detail on the bad behavior of some actor, actress or politician. Even if the story does not say so, many of these events are first uncovered by unscrupulous reporters or investigators who specialize in illegally breaking into the computing systems and mobile phones of their targets; the information then gets sold to a newspaper or some other organization, and the story finally leaks out, with no real chain of events leading back to the computer break-in. But the bottom line is that anyone who attracts enough attention to lure the hackers is wide open to even very unsophisticated intrusion tools. Our desktop and laptop computers, mobile phones, iPads: all of them are at risk from malefactors of many kinds. Someday, we will all look back and wonder what in the world we were thinking, when we entrusted so much personal and sensitive information to these insecure, unreliable devices!

1.2   The Cloud to the Rescue!

Although they have many limitations, which we will be looking at closely in this text, today's cloud systems are far more environmentally friendly, far less prone to configuration issues, and far more secure against these sorts of hijacking exploits, than the machines they are displacing. Thus the more we move to the cloud, the better for everyone: for us personally, for the environment, and even for small countries (at least, those which might find themselves on the wrong side of a dispute with a cyber warfare unit).

Cloud systems are implemented by massive data centers that can be surprisingly inexpensive to operate (economies of scale), in which the machines are shared by many kinds of application and kept busy (reducing waste), located close to power generators (saving power transmission losses), and running at relatively high temperatures (no air conditioning). Best of all, someone else manages all of those cloud computers; if an application needs to be installed and launched, it gets done automatically and often by automated scripts. These include powerful ways of protecting themselves against viruses and other kinds of malware.

With all of this remote computing power, the machines we carry around can be slimmer, less prone to virus infections, cooler, less power-hungry... and yet in many ways even more powerful than the ones they are displacing. Cloud systems will not reduce the numbers of computers we have around us, but they could make those systems far easier to own and operate, and far less power-intensive, and they will be able to do things for us that we would never be able to implement on a dedicated personal computer.

It would be an understatement to say that cloud computing data centers have been expanding rapidly. As recently as a few years ago, data centers rarely had more than a few hundred computers. Today, a state-of-the-art data center might contain hundreds of *thousands* of machines, spanning surfaces that can be as large as a dozen football fields. yet for all this growth, the cloud computing area still seems to be in its infancy. It may not be long before we see individual centers with millions or servers. Moreover, each of those servers is like a miniature computer network on a chip, with configurations having 16 or more cores already common, and talk of substantially larger numbers down the road.

The machines themselves are packed into racks, and those racks are packed into shipping containers: a typical cloud installation can literally buy and install machines a truckload at a time. Cloud computers run hot and busy, and they wear out faster than the ones in your office. So, perhaps just two or three years later, another truck backs up, pulls the container out, and off it goes to be recycled. But if this sounds wasteful, just think about all those idle, hot machines that the cloud is replacing. If we are going to use computers, we might as well put them where the power is cheap and keep them working 24x7. And it actually makes sense to talk about recycling a whole container of machines, which permits far better rates of recovery of the materials than if the same machines were disposed of individually.

When you add it all up, cloud computing seems to be a genuinely greener, more intelligent way to handle both small and large-scale computing tasks. A few friends with a cool new idea for a web application might, in the past, have been blocked from exploring it by the cost of the computers that would be needed. Now they can put their application together on their laptops, using powerful cloud-computing tools, and then launch the system by filling in a form. If the idea is a huge success, the cloud operator (perhaps Facebook, Amazon, Google, Force.com, IBM) just provides more machines on which to run it. If it fails, little money was lost. All sorts of enterprises are doing this analysis and seeing that cloud computing changes the equation. And many in the computing field believe that we are really just at the beginning of the revolution. As Berkeley professor David Patterson, who heads Berkeley's new cloud computing laboratory, puts it: "The future is in the clouds." To which one might add: ". . . and those clouds are going to be green."

This book is about building the applications that run on the cloud, or that run in the web and talk to the cloud. We will see that with care, one can create scalable, flexible ("elastic" is a popular term) applications that are reliable, secure, consistent and self-managed. But getting there has not been easy for the developers of the early cloud systems, and unless we take the time to learn from their experiences, we will just make the same mistakes. Size brings huge economies of scale, but also creates challenges: with each new expansion, we are discovering that some of the things we thought we understood just do not work anymore!

The issue is that as you scale a system up costs can grow in a non-linear manner, a situation somewhat analogous to the one we see when a single machine is used to solve a problem like searching, or sorting, or computing the shortest path in a graph. Algorithm designers, of course, have long been familiar with the complexity hierarchy, and we teach entire courses about the analysis of complexity and the associated theory. Cloud computing poses complexity issues too, but they very often take a different form.

1.3   A Simple Cloud Computing Application

Let us think about a very simple cloud computing application: a video playback application that might be deployed by a company like YouTube. Such an application would need a way to upload new videos, and to search for videos, but we will focus on the playback side of the problem. The obvious, simplest, way to scale such a system is to just create huge numbers of copies of the video playback application; when a user's request comes in, it can then be routed to some copy of the player, which would then find the file containing the video and stream it over a TCP connection to the client's computer system or television set.

Readers who have taken courses on multithreading would probably guess that a successful content delivery company would want to build its own, very powerful, parallel video servers, but this is not necessarily the case. Many cloud computing systems take a simpler path to obtain scalability. Rather than grapple with the complexities of building a multithreaded playback application that can take full advantage of multicore parallelism and other features of the hardware, the developers typically start by looking for the simplest possible way to build a scalable solution, and that often does not involve building any new software at all.

For example, operating systems like Linux and Windows offer reasonably efficient ways to run multiple copies of an application on a single machine, and if that machine is a multicore server, the different applications will each run on different cores. When one runs many applications on one machine there is always some risk that they will interfere with one-another, hence an increasingly common approach is to create a "virtual machine" that wraps an application and any helper files it needs into what seems like a dedicated, private computer. Then the virtual machine can be executed on any physical machine that hosts a virtual machine monitor (VMM), and if the physical machine has enough capacity, the VMM can just run many copies of the VM containing the application. The effect is to create a whole virtual network operating within a single multicore server.

Thus, at least until all the cores are fully loaded, if we just run one copy of the playback application per client, we will get a very efficient form of scalability. In fact, this approach can outperform a multithreaded approach because the copies do not share memory, so they do not need to do much locking; a multithreaded application typically has a single shared memory pool, and ends up wasting a surprising amount of time on locking.

What we are left with is a strikingly simple application development path. The developer needs to create a program that accepts a single TCP connection (probably one coming from a web browser that runs the HTTP or HTPPS protocol), reads in a video request in encoded as a web page (there are libraries to handle that part), open the appropriate file (for this the Linux remote file system is quite adequate: it does a good job of supporting remote access to files that rarely change, and videos of course are write-once, read-many objects) and stream the bytes down the TCP connection, again using a web page representation (and again, that part is automatic if you use the right libraries). These returned web pages would carry embedded objects with an extension registered to some player application—perhaps, .mpg, shorthand for MPEG (a major video compression standard). The client's browser, seeing such an object, would pass it to the mpeg player, and voilà! Movies on demand. Figures 1.1 and 1.2 illustrate these two approaches.

As it happens, we would not even need to create this particular program. Mature, very efficient video playback applications already exist; Windows and most versions of Unix (Linux) both have vast numbers of options for simple tasks of this sort, and many are unfettered open source versions that the development team can download, experiment with, and even modify if needed.

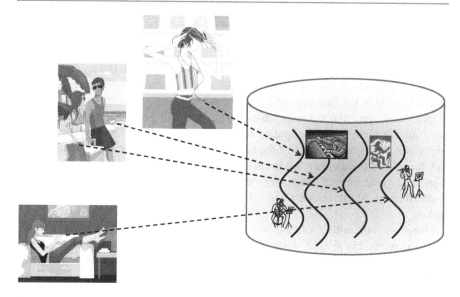

Fig. 1.1   A multithreaded video player: Each thread handles a distinct user. Design is potentially complex and any single failure could impact many users

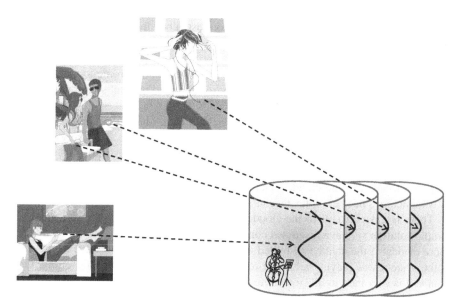

Fig. 1.2   A simpler design in which a single-threaded video server is instantiated once per user, perhaps by running each in a virtual machine. If a player crashes, only a single user is impacted

So how would the team deploy this solution, and ensure that it can scale out? The first step involves registering the application with a cloud-computing load balancing service, such as the Amazon EC2 management layer. That service asks a few simple questions (for example, it will want to know where to find the executable virtual machine). Click a few times, enter your credit card information, and the service will be up and running. The hardest work will turn out to be finding the video content and making business deals so that the solution will actually earn money (hopefully, by the bucket load). No wonder companies like YouTube sprang up overnight: cloud computing makes the first steps in our challenge trivial!

Obviously, once the solution scales out, things will get more complex, but it turns out that many cloud computing teams get very far before hitting any sort of limitations. The usual story is that the first few factors of ten are easy, although later, each factor of ten scale increase starts to demand major redesigns. By the time this happens, a typical cloud computing enterprise may be highly profitable, and able to afford the skilled developers needed to push the scalability envelope further and further.

Moreover, our initial solution will probably be quite robust. First, the code needed is incredibly simple—dramatically simpler than if we had set out to create a home-brew scalable server with multithreading and its own fancy file representations. In effect, our solution is little more than a script, and indeed, many applications of this sort are literally built as scripts. The approach lets us take advantage of operating system features that have existed for decades, and the solution will probably be far robust than a home-made one, since a bug that crashes one playback server might not bring down the others on that same machine, especially if they are running in distinct virtual machines. In contrast, a bug in a multithreaded server would presumably crash that server, and if one server handles many clients, all of them would lose their video feeds. Readers who once sweated to learn to program in a highly threaded, and concurrent model will surely find it ironic to realize that with this approach, we end up with a highly scalable and parallel solution without writing a line of concurrent code.

One major insight, then is that while the cloud is all about reliability and scalability through massive parallelism, these properties can come from very simple mechanisms. In other settings you have learned about scalability through sophisticated data structures, clever ways of organizing information, and precomputed (or cached) answers. In the cloud, scalability is still the most important goal, but we only sometimes need complex mechanisms to achieve this objective.

There is a darker side to the cloud. It may not be obvious, but the sort of very simple solution we have discussed conceals some weaknesses that would be much more evident if the data being pulled into the system were of a sensitive nature, or if the system was playing a critical role in some kind of life or death setting. Of course it is very hard to imagine a life-or-death video playback scenario, although I suppose it certainly can be upsetting to if you planned to watch the decisive game of the World Series on your network-based TV system, only to discover that the service is not working. But we will see examples later in which a system is doing air traffic control, or managing medical care for patients who need very close monitoring, or running the electric power grid; in those settings, seemingly minor mistakes such as pulling up a stale version of something that was recently updated without realizing that the data are no longer valid might be enough to put two airplanes on a collision course, cause a patient's insulin pump to administer the wrong dose, or trigger a rolling blackout. The very simple ways of building a cloud computing system do not provide guarantees that would address these sorts of needs.

But even without pointing to applications with extreme requirements, there might still be some issues hidden in our video service as we have described it. For example, suppose that our playback applications are spread within the data center in such a way that they happen to share some network link—perhaps, a link to the outside world, perhaps a link to the file server, or perhaps even a network link associated with something else, like checking to make sure that the user is logged in under a valid account, or that this user has permission to see that particular video. Well, this shared link could become a bottleneck, with the whole data center grinding to a halt because the overloaded link is unable to handle the traffic.

Carrying this kind of story further, here is a more subtle version of the same kind of problem. Think about driving at rush-hour on a highway that has ample capacity for the normal rush hour peak traffic as long as cars are evenly spaced and each maintains a steady 50 mph. Now, some driver opens a window, and a fly gets into his car. This startles him, and he touches the brakes, which startles the cars around him, and they brake too. The cars behind those slow down even more, and a kind of wave of slowdown spreads back along the highway. In no time at all, a little jam has formed.

Notice that even though the highway had ample capacity to handle the peak traffic as long as vehicles maintained average behavior, it may require much more than average capacity to avoid the risk of jams forming, because if the cars are close enough to one-another, any minor event can trigger this sort of ripple effect. In effect, we have watched a bottleneck form, all by itself, and that bottleneck could linger for a long time, propagating steadily backwards up the highway. This is one way that rush-hour jams can form even when there are no accidents to explain them.

It turns out that the same problem can occur in a cloud computing system such as our little video playback site. Even if the system has adequate capacity so long as all the components are working at a steady, average load, sometimes conditions create a load surge in one corner, while everything else runs out of work to do and becomes idle (in between the traffic jams, your favorite highway could have stretches that have no traffic at all—that are idle, in the same sense). The cloud computer system stops working at the average pace: some parts are overworked, and others are not doing anything at all. The total amount of work being completed plunges.

Spontaneous traffic jams are just one example in a long list. Cloud computing systems can become overloaded in ways that create avalanches of messages, triggering huge loss rates that can drive the applications into failure modes not seen in other settings. Cloud systems can develop strange, migrating bottlenecks in which nothing seems to be happening at all. They can even enter oscillatory states in which loads rise to extreme levels, then fade away, then rise again. Seemingly minor problems can trigger cascades of secondary problems, until the entire data center is overwhelmed by a massive storm of error messages and failures. Components that work perfectly well in test settings can break inexplicably only when deployed in the real data center. Worse, because we are talking about deployments that may involve tens of thousands of application instances, it can be very hard for the developer to make sense of such problems if they arise. The creation of better cloud computing performance tuning and management tools is very much a black art today.

Phenomena such as this sometimes cannot be triggered on a small scale, so to build cloud-scale systems that really work well, we need to understand what can cause such problems and (even more important), how to prevent them. Otherwise, we will spend a fortune, and yet our sparkling new cloud computing facility just will not deliver an acceptable quality of service! Indeed, if you talk to the major developers at the world's biggest cloud computing systems, to a person you will hear the same thing: each new factor of ten brought major surprises, and very often, forced a complete redesign of the most heavily used applications. Things that optimize performance for a system running on one node may hurt performance when you run it on ten; the version that blazes at ten may be sluggish at one hundred. Speed a single-node application up, and you may discover strange oscillations that only arise when it runs on a thousand nodes, or ten thousand day you finally scale to ten thousand you may learn that certain kinds of rare failures are not nearly as rare as you thought. And the story just goes on and on.

How, then, do developers manage to create scalable cloud solutions? Today the usual picture is that a great deal of effort has gone into stabilizing certain elements of the standard cloud platforms. For example, any cloud system worth its (low) fees will offer a scalable file system that lets applications share data by sharing files. Generally, the file system will come with a warning: updates may propagate slowly, and locking may not even be supported. Yet if one designs an application to be tolerant of update delays, modern cloud file systems enable remarkable scalability. This picture is an instance of a general pattern: well designed, scalable infrastructures on which applications can scale provided that they put up with limitations, generally of the kind just mentioned: stale data, slow update propagation and limited use of locking (or no locking at all). Departing from this model is a tricky proposition, and developing new infrastructure services is very difficult, but in this text, we will consider both options. For applications that are not embarrassingly easy to match to the standard model, there simply isn't any other way to build secure, reliable cloud applications today.

1.4   Stability and Scalability: Contending Goals in Cloud Settings

The scalability goal that we end up with is easy to express but potentially much harder to achieve, particularly because the application developer may not have any idea what the topology of the data center will be, or how the application will be mapped to the nodes in the data center, or how to answer of a dozen other obvious questions one might pose. In effect, we need a way to build applications so that no matter how the cloud platform deploys them or scales them out, they will continue to run smoothly. Networks can exhibit strange delays: communication between nodes might normally be measured in the milliseconds, and yet sometimes spike into the seconds. We even need to know that if a few nodes out of the ten thousand virtual ones we are running on are half broken, with malfunctioning disks, high network packet loss rates, or any of a dozen other possible problems, that the other nine thousand, nine-hundred ninety nodes or so will be completely unaffected. All of this will be a big challenge as we tackle the technical options in the remainder of this book.

Once our application is running, we will need smart ways to distribute client requests over those machines. Often, this routing task has application-specific aspects: for example, it can be important to route requests from a given client to the server it last talked to, since that server may have saved information that can be used to improve response quality or times. Or we might want to route searches relating to books to the servers over here, and searches for garden supplies to the servers over there. This implies that the applications should have a way to talk to the data center routers. Indeed, more and more cloud platforms are reaching out into the Internet itself, leveraging features that allow Internet routers to host wide-area virtual networks that might have data center specific routing policies used within, but that then tunnel traffic over a more basic Internet routing infrastructure that employs a standard Internet routing protocol such as BGP, IS-IS or OSPF for routing table management.

Load can surge, or ebb, and this can happen in a flash; this implies that the infrastructure used to manage the cloud will need to be rapidly responsive, launching new instances of applications (or perhaps tens of thousands of new instances), or shutting down instances, without missing a beat. But it also implies that cloud applications must be designed to tolerate being launched suddenly on new nodes, or yanked equally suddenly from old ones. Hardest of all, cloud applications do not know what the cloud infrastructure will look like when they are launched, and yet they need to avoid overloading any element of the data center infrastructure, including communication links, other kinds of hardware, and the data center services that glue it all together.

These considerations can interplay in surprising ways. Let us peer into one kind of particularly troublesome data center malfunction that was first witnessed in big financial computing systems in the early 1990s and lives on even now in modern cloud computing data centers: the *broadcast storm*, a term that will cause even the most seasoned cloud computing operator to turn pale and sweaty. We will see that the community memory of this issue lives on: modern cloud computing platforms do not allow users to access several highly valuable communication options because vendors fear repeat episodes (as the saying goes, "Fool me once, shame on you. Fool me twice, shame on me!"). The story thus will illustrate our broader point in this introduction: there are many things that cloud systems do today, or reject today[1], several of which might re-emerge as options in the future, provided that cloud vendors relax these policies, developers see a good reason to use them, and systems that do use them take the necessary measures to prevent malfunctions.

---

[1]More accurately, they do not let the typical developer use these technologies; internally, most do get used, carefully, by the platforms themselves.

As you know, that there are three basic Internet protocols: TCP, IP and IP Multi-cast (IPMC):

1. TCP is used to make connections between a single source and a single destina-tion, over which a stream of data can be sent. The protocol automatically over-comes packet loss, delivers data in order, and does automatic flow control to match the sender rate with the receiver rate.

2. UDP provides point-to-point messages: individual messages are transmitted without any prior connection and delivered if the destination node has an open UDP socket bound to the appropriate IP address and port number. UDP does not guarantee reliability: in cloud computing settings, the network would almost never lose UDP packets, but they can easily be lost if the receiving node gets overwhelmed by too high an incoming data rate, or if the application falls behind and its sockets run out of space to hold the incoming traffic. UDP imposes size limits on packets, but the developer can increase the value if the default is too small.

3. IPMC generalizes UDP: rather than one-to-one behavior, it offers one-to-many. From the user and O/S perspective, the underlying technology is really the same as for UDP, but the receivers use a special form of IP address that can be shared among multiple processes, which also share the same port number. The network router is responsible for getting data from senders to the receivers, if any. Like UDP, no reliability guarantees are provided, but the network itself will not nor-mally drop IPMC packets.

Today, all cloud platforms support TCP. Cloud platforms run on hardware and software systems that include support for UDP and IPMC, but most cloud platforms restrict their use, for example by limiting non-TCP protocols to applications created by their own infrastructure services teams.

What are the implications of this choice? TCP can be slow for some purposes, and has poor real-time properties, hence one consequence is that applications cannot make use of the fastest available way of sending a single message at a time from a sender to some receiver. When everything is working properly, UDP is potentially *much* faster than TCP, and whereas TCP will slow down when the receiver falls behind, UDP has no backpressure at all, hence new messages continue to arrive (they will overwrite older ones, causing loss, if the receiver does not catch up before the O/S socket queues overflow). If one wants fresher data even at the cost of potentially dropping older data, this makes UDP very appealing.

As noted above, studies have shown that within the cloud, almost all UDP packet loss occurs in the receiving machine. The issue is fundamentally one of application-level delays that cause overflows in the incoming UDP socket buffers. Of course, only some of those delays are ones the developer can easily control. Even an appli-cation designed to pull data instantly from their buffers might still find itself virtu-alized and running on a heavily overloaded physical system, and hence subjected to long scheduling delays. Thus one can see why UDP is a risky choice in the cloud.

A similar case can be made in favor of IPMC. If UDP is the fastest way to get a packet from one sender to one receiver, IPMC is the fastest way to get a packet from one sender to potentially huge numbers of receivers. Yet IPMC is banned. Why has this happened?

To understand the issue, we need to understand how IPMC really works. The mechanism is really very simple: all the receivers register themselves as listeners on some shared IPMC address (by binding IPMC addresses to sockets created for this purpose). Those registration requests trigger what are called IGMP messages that announce that the sender is interested in the IPMC address. The network routing technology used in the data center listens for IGMP messages, and with them builds one-to-many forwarding routes. When a router sees an IPMC packet on some incoming link, it just forwards a copy on each outgoing link that leads to at least one receiver, namely the ones on which it saw an IGMP message recently announcing that some receiver is interested in that address (the entire mechanism repeats every few seconds, hence if the receiver goes away, the IGMP messages cease, and eventually the route will clear itself out of the system). Data centers also use network *switches* with more limited functionality; if IPMC is enabled, these typically just forward every IPMC message on every link except the one it came in on.

Now the question arises of how the router should do this one-to-many forwarding task. One option is to keep a list of active IPMC addresses, look them up, and then send the packet on each outgoing link that has one or more receivers. This, however, can be slow. To speed things up, modern routers more often use a faster hash-based mechanism called a *Bloom Filter*.

A filter of this kind supports two operations: *Set* and *Test*. The Set operation takes a key (in our example, an IPMC address) and includes it into the filter, and Test returns true if the value is in the filter; false if not. Thus the filter functions as a tool for determining set inclusion. The clever twist is that unlike a true set, Bloom Filters do not guarantee perfect accuracy: a test is permitted to sometimes give a false "yes, I found it" response, when in fact the tested-for value was not in the set. The idea is that this is supposed to be rare, and the benefit of the specific implementation is that Bloom filters can do these tests very rapidly, with just two or three memory references (accurate set lookup has cost $O(\log(N))$ in the size of the set). To build a Bloom filter for routing, one maintains a vector of b bits in association with each link in the router (so: if the router has l attached network links, we will have l filters). For each link, when an IGMP message arrives, indicating that some receiver exists on that link, we will do an Add operation on the associated filter, as follows. Given the IPMC address a, the router computes a series of hashes of a that map from a to $[0 \ldots b - 1]$. Thus, if we have k hash functions, the router computes k integers in the range $0 \ldots b$.

Then the router sets these k bits in the bit vector. Later, to test to see whether or not a is in the filter, it does the same hashing operation, and checks that all the bits are set. The idea is that even if a collision occurs on some bits, the odds of collisions on all of them are low, hence with a large enough value of b we will not get many false positives. This enables routers that support IPMC packet forwarding to make a split-second decision about which network links need copies of an incoming multicast packet.

Over time applications join and leave, so the filter can become inaccurate. Accordingly, this scheme typically operates for a few tens of seconds at a time. The idea is to run in a series of epochs: during epoch t, the router forwards packets using Bloom filters computed during epoch $t - 1$, but also constructs a Bloom filter for each link to use during epoch $t + 1$. The epoch length is programmed into the receivers: each receiving machine reannounces its multicast interests (by sending duplicate IGMP messages that effectively "reregister" the machine's interest in the IPMC address) often enough to ensure that in any epoch, at least one subscription request will get to the router.

Bloom filters work well if b is large enough. A typical Bloom Filter might use $k = 3$ (three hash functions) and set b to be a few times the maximum number of receivers that can be found down any link. Under such conditions, the expected false positive rate will be quite small (few messages will be forwarded on a link that does not actually lead to any receivers at all). As a result, for the same reason that UDP is relatively reliable at the network layer, one would expect IPMC to be reliable too. Unless many senders try to talk to some single receiver simultaneously, or some receiver experiences a long delay and can't keep up with the rate of incoming messages on its UDP and IPMC sockets, a cloud computing network should have ample capacity to forward the messages, and network interface cards should not drop packets either. When nothing goes awry, the protocol is as efficient as any protocol can possibly be: the "cost" of getting messages from senders to receivers is minimal, in the sense that any message traverses only the links that lead towards receivers, and does so exactly once.

Of course, hardware router manufacturers cannot know how many distinct IPMC addresses will be in use in a data center, and the IPMC address space is large: 2^{24} possible addresses in the case of IPv4, and 2^{32} for IPv6. Thus most router vendors arbitrarily pick a value for b that would work for a few thousand or even tens of thousands of IPMC addresses. The kind of memory used in this part of a router is expensive, hence it is not feasible to use extremely large values.

Nonetheless, given the very fast and inexpensive nature of the technology, you might expect IPMC to be appealing in cloud computing settings, where data often must be replicated to vast numbers of machines. For example, if our YouTube system happens to have a really popular video showing, say, the winning goal in Superbowl XLIV, tens of millions of football fans might want to play it (and replay it, and replay it) simultaneously for hours. We will need a *lot* of copies of that particular file, and an IPMC-based protocol for file replication would seem like an obvious choice; with TCP and UDP, which are both one-to-one protocols, that system would pay a network-level cost linear in the number of playback systems that need a copy. Of course this does require some careful application design work (to make sure the application reads packets with high probability, for example by posting large numbers of asynchronous read requests so that packets arriving while the application is sleeping can be delivered even if the application cannot be scheduled promptly), but with such tricks, one could design applications that use IPMC very effectively even in cloud settings.

Thus it may be surprising to learn that many data center operators have rules *against* using IPMC, and often against UDP as well. Today, to build an application that sends an update to a collection of n machines that have replicas of some file or data item, the update would often need to be sent in n point-to-point messages, and very often, over TCP connections, and some data centers go ever further and require

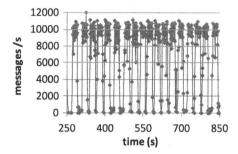

Fig. 1.3 During a *broadcast storm*, a router malfunction caused by excessive use of IPMC addresses causes the normal network destination filtering to fail. All the nodes in the entire data center are overwhelmed by huge rates of undesired incoming messages. Loads and loss rates both soar, causing a complete collapse of the center. This temporarily causes loads to drop, but as components restart, the problem also reemerges

the use of the web's HTTP protocol too: HTTP over TCP over the underlying IP protocol. Obviously, this is very slow in comparison to sending just one message. Indeed, these approaches are slow enough that they motivated the emergence of some very fancy solutions, such as the parallel downloading scheme implemented by BitTorrent, a technology we will look at closely in Chap. 4.

So, why have data center operators ruled out use of a network feature that could give them such huge speedups? It turns out that they have been seriously burned by IPMC in past systems: the protocol is definitely fast, but it has also been known to trigger very serious data center instabilities, of the sort illustrated in Fig. 1.3. This graph was produced by an experiment that emulates something that really happened. As the developers at one major eTailer explain the story (we were told the story on condition of anonymity), early in that company's evolution an IPMC-based product became extremely popular and was rolled out on very large numbers of machines. The product malfunctioned and caused the whole data center to begin to thrash, just as seen in the figure: first the network would go to 100% load, associated with huge packet loss rates; then the whole system would come to a halt, with no machine doing anything and the network idle, then back to the overload, etc. Not surprisingly, that particular cloud computing player was very quick to outlaw IPMC use by that product! Worse still, until recently the exact mechanism causing these problems was a mystery.

But by understanding the issue, we can fix it. In brief, when large numbers of applications make heavy use of distinct IPMC addresses, the Bloom Filters associated with the routers can become overloaded. As mentioned above, the value of b is a vendor-determined constant (Tock et al. 2005): a given router can handle at most some maximum number of IPMC addresses. Thus if a data center uses many IPMC addresses, its network router will learn about many receivers on each link, and eventually, all the bits in its Bloom Filter will be set to ones due to a kind of collision of addresses in this hashed bit-space. But think about the consequences of this particular form of collision: normally, IPMC is very selective[2], delivering packets to precisely the right set of receivers and not even forwarding a packet down a link unless it has (or recently had) at least one receiver. With this form of collision, the router will start to forward *every* IPMC message on every link! Worse, a similar issue can arise in the network interface cards (NICs) used by machines in the data center. If a lot of IPMC addresses are used, those can start to accept every IPMC message that shows up on the adjacent link (the O/S is expected to discard any unwanted messages in this case).

Put these two design flaws together, and we get a situation in which by scaling up the use of IPMC, a data center can enter a state in which floods of messages, at incredible data rates, will be delivered to every machine that uses IPMC for any purpose at all! Even IPMC packets sent to groups that have no receivers would suddenly start to be forwarded down every network link in the data center. The resulting avalanche of unwanted messages is called a broadcast storm, and poses a costly challenge for the machines that receive them: they need to be examined, one by one, so that the legitimate traffic can be sorted out from the junk that was delivered purely because of what is perhaps best characterized as a hardware failure. That takes time, and as these overburdened machines fall behind, they start to experience loss. The loss, in turn, disrupts everything, including applications that were not using IPMC. So here we see the origin of the 100% network loads and the heavy packet losses.

Next, applications began to crash (due to timeouts) and restart themselves. That takes time, so a period ensues during which the whole data center looks idle. And then the cycle resumes with a new wave of overload.

By now you are probably thinking that maybe outlawing IPMC is a very good idea! But it turns out that this kind of meltdown can be prevented. Notice that the root cause was router overload: routers and NICs have limits on the numbers of IPMC addresses they can handle. If these limits are respected, no issue arises; what causes problems is that nothing enforces those limits, and we have described a case in which the aggressive scaling of an application causes an overload.

To solve this problem, we need to modify the data center communication layer, adding logic that lets it track the use of IPMC throughout the entire data center, and then arranges for machines to cooperate to avoid overloading the routers. The basic idea is simple: it suffices need to count the number of IPMC addresses in use. Until the hardware limit is reached (a number we can obtain from the router-manufacturer's hardware manuals) nothing needs to be done. But as we approach the limits, we switch to a mode in which IPMC addresses are doled out much more carefully: groups with lots of members and lots of traffic can have such an address, but for other IPMC groups, the operating system just emulates IPMC by sending point-to-point UDP packets to the group members, silently and transparently. Obviously, such an approach means that some groups that contain n receivers will

---

[2]In fact some systems have used this feature for debugging: applications send IPMC packets on "debugger trace" addresses. If nobody is using the debugger, the network filters out the packets and they "vanish" with no load beyond the network link where the sender was running; when the debugger is enabled, the IPMC routing technology magically delivers these packets to it.

require n unicast sends. We can also go further, looking for similar IPMC groups and merging them to share a single IPMC address.

The solution we have described is not trivial, but on the other hand, nothing about it is prohibitively difficult or expensive. For example, to track IPMC use and group membership we incur a small background overhead, but later in this text we will see that such things can be done efficiently using *gossip* protocols. Moreover, although the best ways of deciding which applications get to use IPMC and which need to use UDP involve solving an NP complete problem, it turns out that real data centers produce unexpectedly "easy" cases: a simple greedy heuristic can solve the problem very effectively. But proving this requires some heavy-duty mathematics. The whole solution comes together in a research paper by Ymir Vigfusson and others (Vigfusson et al. 2010).

We see here cloud-computing distilled into a nutshell. First, some business plan had a big success and this forced the company to scale up dramatically: a rich person's problem, if you wish, since they were making money hand over foot. But then, as scale got really dramatic, the mere scaling of the system began to have unexpected consequences: in this case, an old and well-understood feature of IP networking broke in a way that turned out to be incredibly disruptive. Obviously, our eTailer was in no position to debug the actual issue: every time that load oscillation occurred, huge amounts of money were being lost! So the immediate, obvious step was to ban IPMC. Today, years later, we understand the problem and how to solve it. But by now IPMC is considered to be an unsafe data center technology, used only by system administrative tools, and only with great care. The cloud, in effect, "does not support IPMC" (or UDP, for that matter). And yet, by looking at the question carefully, we can pin down the root cause, then design a mechanism to address it, and in this way solve the problem. The mystery we are left with is this: now that we can solve the problem, is it too late to reverse the trend and convince data center operators to allow safe use of IPMC again? After all, even if IPMC must be used with care and managed correctly, it still is a very efficient way to move data from one source to vast numbers (perhaps millions) of destinations, and far simpler than the slower solutions we mentioned earlier (chains of relayers operating over TCP, or BitTorrent).

This vignette really should be seen as one instance of a broader phenomenon. First, IPMC is not the only technology capable of disabling an entire cloud computing data center. Indeed, stories of entire data centers being crippled by a misdesigned application or protocol are surprisingly common in the cloud computing community. If you have ever wondered what stories data center operators tell when they find themselves sitting around campfires late at night, they do not involve monsters lurching around the Pacific Northwest forests; it is stories about poisonous data center applications and broadcast storms that really make their blood run cold. But of course, when a billion-dollar data center grinds to a halt, the lessons learned tend to be taken to heart.

It all comes down to scalability. Cloud computing is about scalability first, performance next, and everything else comes after these two primary considerations. But as we have seen, scalability can revolve around some really obscure issues. We have elaborate theories of single-machine complexity, but lack tools for understanding scalability of cloud computing solutions, and the theoretical work on scalability of distributed protocols and algorithms seems very disconnected from the settings in which the cloud runs them, and the cost-limiting factors in those settings. Certainly, if we pin down a particular deployment scenario, one could work out the costs. But cloud systems reconfigure themselves continuously, and the number of possible layouts for a set of applications on such a huge number of machines may be immense. Short of actually running an application in a given setting, there are very few ways to predict its likely behavior or to identify any bottlenecks that may be present.

1.5   The Missing Theory of Cloud Scalability

Our example highlights another broad issue: while we know that scalability is of vital importance in cloud systems, surprisingly little is understood about how to guarantee this key property. Obviously, today's cloud solutions are ones that scale well, but it would be inaccurate to say that they scale well because they were designed to scale, or even that data center operators understand precisely how to account for their scalability properties in any crisp, mathematically sound way. A better way to summarize the situation is to say that lacking a "theory of scalability", cloud computing operators have weeded out things that do not work at scale (such as IPMC in the absence of a management layer of the kind we have outlined) in favor of mechanisms that, in their experience, seem to scale well. They start with some basic goals, which generally center on the need to support really massive numbers of clients in a snappy and very decentralized way (in a nutshell, no matter where you issue a request, and no matter which data center it reaches, once it gets to a service instance, that instance will be able to respond instantly based on its local state). And with this as their basic rule of thumb, the cloud has achieved miracles.

We have already seen that those miracles do not extend to every possible feature or property. For example, our IPMC example illustrates a sense in which clouds sometimes sacrifice performance (by adopting a slower data replication approach), in order to gain better stability at scale. And we have noted that in other ways, clouds relax a number of trust and assurance properties, again to encourage stability and snappy responsiveness at massive scale.

Yet while these statements are easily made, they are harder to formalize, and they also run counter to the traditional notion of scalability as explored in theory textbooks and research papers. For more classical notions of scalability, one typically asks how the rate of messages in a service will be impacted as one adds members to the service, or even how the number of members should relate to the number of failures a service needs to tolerate. Thus, one might see a theoretical paper showing that whereas traditional "atomic broadcast" protocols send $O(n^2)$ messages to replicate an update within a set of n members under worst-case failure assumptions, "gossip" protocols send only $O(n \log(n))$ messages. Another paper might show that for certain kinds of system, it is possible to overcome f failures provided that the system includes $3f + 1$ or more members. Still another paper might show that with a slightly different definition of failures, this requirement drops; now perhaps we only need $n \geq 2f + 1$. And yet a cloud operator, having read those papers, might well react by saying that this kind of analysis misses the point, because it does not talk about the characteristics of a system that determine its responsiveness and stability; indeed, does not even offer a theoretical basis for defining the properties that really matter in a crisp way amenable to analysis and proofs.

In some sense, one would have a dialog of apples and oranges: the theoretician has defined scalability in one way ("to be scalable, a protocol must satisfy the apple property") and shown that some protocol achieves this property. The cloud operator, who has a different (and very vaguely formalized) notion of scalability objects that whatever that apple proof may show, it definitely is not a proof of scalability. For the operator, scalability is an "orange" property. This will probably frustrate our theoretician, who will want the operator to please define an orange. But the operator, who is not a theoretician, might be justified in finding such a request a bit passive-aggressive: why should it be the operator's job to find a formalism for the cloud scalability property acceptable to the theory community? So the operator would very likely respond by inviting the theoretician to spend a year or two building and operating cloud services. The theoretician, no hacker, would find this insulting. And this is more or less where we find ourselves today!

Meanwhile, if one reads the theory carefully, a second concern arises. While this is not universally the case, it turns out that quite a number of the classic, widely cited theory papers employ simplifying assumptions that do not fit well with the realities of cloud computing: one reads the paper and yet is unsure how the result maps to a real cloud data center. We will see several examples of this kind. For example, one very important and widely cited result proves the impossibility of building fault-tolerant protocols in asynchronous settings, and can be extended to prove that it is impossible to update replicated data in a fault-tolerant, consistent manner. While terms like "impossibility" sound alarming, we will see that these papers actually use definitions that contradict our intuitive guess as to what these terms mean; for example, these two results both define "impossible" to mean "not always possible."

That small definition has surprising implications. For example, suppose that you and I agree that if the weather is fine, we will meet for lunch outside; if the weather looks cold and damp, we will meet in the cafeteria. But your cubicle is in the basement, and I have a window, so I will email you to let you know how things look. Now, we know that email is unreliable: will this protocol work? Obviously not: I see sunshine outside, so I email you: "What a lovely day! Let us eat outside." But did you receive my email? I will worry about that, so you email back "Great! See you under that flowering cherry tree at noon!". Well, did I get your confirmation? So I email back "Sounds like a plan." But did you receive my confirmation? If not, you might not know that I received your earlier confirmation, hence you would worry that I'm still worried that you did not get my original email. Absurd as it may seem, we end up sending an endless sequence of acknowledgments. Worse, since we can never safely conclude that we will both realize that we should eat outside, we will end up in the cafeteria, despite both knowing full well that the weather has not been nicer the whole year! We will be victims of a self-inflicted revenge of the nerds, and will probably enjoy a depressing lunch conversation about Gödel's incompleteness theorem, which basically says that there are true things that cannot be proved with logic.

Now, this example illustrates a thing we can solve, and a thing we cannot, side by side. In fact, is there some way to run a protocol of this kind that would let us safely meet for lunch outside? Obviously, normal people would quickly reach a point at which both of us can deduce that this is a safe thing to do. Indeed, any normal couple would get to that point after my second email; only real logicians or the truly deranged would ever send endless sequences of acknowledgments.

Yet with just three emails, can we actually prove that both of us will turn up for lunch under that lovely tree? As it turns out there is no sound protocol that exchanges messages and leaves us in the identical knowledge state about a decision such as this one. If we insisted on waiting for a perfectly symmetric knowledge state (a notion that can be formalized very elegantly), we will never achieve it: it is "impossible" to achieve common knowledge on a new decision in a standard message-passing system (Halpern and Moses 1990). With our three-message exchange, the scenario to imagine is this: having sent my third email, I leave and head out to the cherry tree. But it never reaches you. So you received my first email, but saw no response to your acknowledgment confirming it. Gosh, perhaps I never saw the acknowledgment at all! In that case I might not realize you ever saw my email about having lunch outside, and am waiting down in the cafeteria. So off you go... to the cafeteria. Our friendship will probably be tested once we finally sort this out!

What you can see here is that, as humans, we often reason in a way that is not really entirely sound, if reduced purely to logic. We could do much better if we added probabilities to this sequence; in each of these steps there was a high-probability event (the email gets through), and then a second low-probability one (the email does not); working out the numbers would allow each of us to realize that meeting outside is the better bet. Yet we would not derive the *same* probabilities for each of the possible outcomes, because we do not have identical data: each of us is working with different certainties and different uncertainties. In particular, each is uncertain about the state of the other!

In a similar sense, we can show that it is impossible to build a fully asynchronous fault-tolerant decision-making protocol, or a replicated data update protocol, but what such a statement really means is less easily explained. Very much in the same sense just outlined, impossible does not mean that we cannot ever solve the problem; indeed, for these goals, we can almost always solve the problem: an asynchronous fault-tolerant decision protocol can almost always reach a decision; a replicated update protocol can almost always complete any requested update. Impossible simply means that there will always be some sequence of events, perhaps vanishingly improbable, that could delay the decision or the update endlessly.

The distributed systems that operate today's cloud tackle impossible problems all the time, and usually, our solutions terminate successfully. To say that something is impossible because it is not always possible seems like an absurdist play on words, yet the theory community has often done just this. No wonder, then, that the theory community has not been taken terribly seriously by the cloud community. But this cuts both ways, because in some ways, things the cloud community views as impossible may well turn out to be completely feasible, but simply needing new ideas, or perhaps a complex implementation. For the cloud practitioner, impossible too often means "I do not know how to do that" or even "I prefer that you not do that." To the author of this textbook, neither way of defining impossibility is satisfying. In this text, unless otherwise noted, a thing is only "impossible" if it genuinely cannot be done, for scientific and engineering reasons that hold up under scrutiny and that do not hinge on technicalities in the definitions, or on arbitrary conventions accepted but not questioned by the practitioners who operate today's cloud.

Accordingly, we need to approach many cloud computing questions with an open mind, and cannot entirely trust the things we might read in certain kinds of research paper, or in certain kinds of popular-press article on cloud computing. We will need to understand precisely what a question is asking, and precisely what the terminology means, before drawing any conclusions.

Returning to the FLP result (the impossibility of fault-tolerance in asynchronous systems), we can apply this way of thinking. So, before judging the meaning of this result, we should ask the obvious question: Are cloud computing systems "asynchronous"? You are probably ready with a quick answer, but in fact the right response is to ask precisely how that term is defined. And as it turns out the definition is quite technical and includes some oddities. In this particular theorem, asynchronous systems are ones that have no clocks and make no use of time, and in which networks never lose messages but can delay them arbitrarily long. There are no timeouts, and a protocol that terminates correctly after running for 1000 years is considered to be absolutely fine. Fault-tolerance has a very technical definition as well, revolving around a form of decision making called the consensus problem, and it too has a highly technical definition.

We could explain all of these but in fact, it turns out that cloud systems are not asynchronous in the precise sense of the definition used in the FLP theorem. This, then, raises the puzzling question of whether the impossibility results would still apply in a more realistic communication model. But what is this more realistic model? We see that to answer such a question, we would need a very precise and detailed model of cloud computing. In some sense, it's turtles all the way down, as in Stephen Hawking's famous joke about Bertrand Russell. Further complicating the task, we lack that model, today: the theory community has not been very engaged in exploring cloud computing as a first-class topic.

For example, cloud computing systems are very prone to long scheduling and communication delays and to bursts of packet loss, yet delay-tolerant protocols have been viewed as an oddity and received little direct attention. Thus one of the most prominent features of the cloud isn't properly captured by today's models. Similar comments could be made about several other aspects of cloud computing as currently deployed.

How does this situation impact us in this text? Clearly, since we are concerned with reliability, at a minimum we will be forced to ask what we mean by reliability; to the extent that we seek fault-tolerance, we will need to define precisely what is meant by a fault-tolerant protocol. We will do that in Part II. Having done so, we will certainly want to visit the FLP result. We have already noted that impossible does not necessarily mean "impossible" in the sense you might use in a normal conversation with a friend. But even so, is fault-tolerance of the practical kind possible? We will discover that the answer is usually affirmative: normally, we can solve such problems. Sometimes, however, when the cloud is experiencing really serious disruptions, we might be unable to do so.

But the theory for our area is not very complete and lacks answers for many of the most important questions. For example, it would be very hard to find theoretical results that shed much light on the overload problem outlined in the prior section and the form of oscillation we have described in connection with broadcast storms. One could claim that these problems have been studied by researchers interested in stochastic phenomena, queuing systems and self-synchronization, and indeed they do resemble problems that have been examined carefully in those settings. Yet nobody really knows how to apply that preexisting theory to these specific settings and these specific kinds of question. The match is not nearly as close as one would hope.

We will not try to fill those gaps in this text, although when can derive a clearer understanding of a problem by drawing on the theory, we will do so. To keep the tone of the text even, the book as a whole will be light on theory, but because some topics demand a more rigorous exposition, we will sometimes dive a bit deeper; an example is seen in Appendix A, which offers a more rigorous treatment of an important idea about reconfiguring an active system that we will study in Part II. The hope is to strike a balance: the book strives to maintain a fairly practical engineering focus, rather typical of cloud computing as portrayed by those who do it. Since our goal is reliability, we will obviously be forced to look at the theory, selectively, as a tool to better understand the forms of consistency and fault-tolerance cloud computing can offer. But those who love the mathematical side of computing will probably find that even when we do get rigorous, we do not go far enough. If it comes as any consolation, this is really more of a research opportunity than a weakness of the textbook: the author is not the right person to invent a comprehensive theory of cloud computing, and hence can only present the results that have been published and gained enough "traction" to be accepted as valid in a practical sense. There is a fairly complete theory of distributed computing on smaller scales, and we will include many results from that work, but the scalability and responsiveness needs of the cloud shift the terrain enough to reveal many new questions.

1.6   Brewer's CAP Conjecture

Let us have a closer look at another famous negative result, this time concerning the scalability of data replication methods that seek to guarantee *consistency*. The theorem in question asserts that in cloud computing settings, an application that replicates data can have just two out of three from {Consistency, Availability and Partition Tolerance}. It was advanced by Berkeley Professor Eric Brewer, who dubbed it the CAP Principle (Brewer 2000); a CAP Theorem was soon thereafter proved by MIT researchers Seth Gilbert and Nancy Lynch (Gilbert and Lynch 2002).

As we will see now in a broad overview, and more carefully later, CAP is widely accepted in the modern cloud, especially for services that will run in the most

- First tier: web page with associated request processing logic.
- Second tier: highly scalable key-value storage, caches, used to support the first tier. The term *sharding* is often used to refer to the process of breaking a data set into smaller replicated data sets so that the data associated with each key value (a *shard*) is replicated on just a few nodes.
- Inner tiers: Databases and index files used by the first and second tiers
- Back-end: Batch processing applications that run out-of-band to create precomputed index files and analyze large data collections

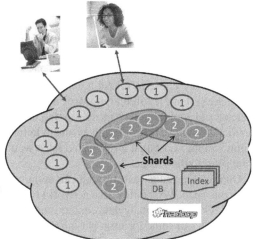

Fig. 1.4 Tiers in a cloud computing system

scalable layers of modern cloud computing data centers (see Fig. 1.4). These layers, called the first and second tiers, consist of the applications that handle incoming client requests, and services that directly support those applications such as scalable caches and key-value stores. They definitely are not the whole story: the requests that cannot be handled directly in the first tiers are routed to inner services that hopefully see less extreme loads and less extreme scalability/elasticity demands, and can therefore use methods that might be slightly more costly. But in the first and second tiers, we are limited to very lightweight styles of computing. CAP is a statement about what these kinds of application can, and cannot, do.

We've seen how important can be to look closely at definitions for the terms used in stating and proving theoretical results. As Brewer defines the terms in CAP, *consistency* means that any data item has a value reached by applying all the prior updates in some agreed-upon order. Consistency also has a durability dimension: a consistent service must never forget an update once it has been accepted and the client has been sent a reply. *Availability* is really a mixture of performance and fault-tolerance: our service should keep running and offer rapid responses even if a few replicas have crashed or are unresponsive, and even if some of the data sources it needs are inaccessible. No client is ever left waiting, even if we just cannot get the needed data right now. By *partition tolerance*, Brewer means that a system should be able to keep running even if the network itself fails, cutting off some nodes from the others (here the failure left those other nodes running, but we just cannot talk to them right now).

Here we should perhaps pause an note that in fact, partitioning is not an issue within modern data centers, because they use very resilient data center networking hardware. Obviously one could still have a network outage that cuts off some nodes, such as a container of machines, but if this happens those machines would also be disconnected from their external clients and would probably lose power. Thus the kinds of partitioning event that occur tend to isolate and "kill" a small number of machines, leaving the remainder of the data center connected and healthy. Indeed, modern cloud management systems have features that will detect the kinds of partitioning events just listed (those that somehow isolate a few nodes) and will force the impacted nodes to restart. If the node states may have been damaged in the crash, the cloud may chose to reload a completely clean state before permitting them to rejoin the system: it will literally wipe away any old state and reload fresh operating systems and application instances running in a new and empty file system. Thus, the cloud maps internal partitioning events to failure, and in some cases, to "permanent failure" in the sense that a re-imaged node would not have any memory of its state from prior to the outage.

On the other hand, partitioning can definitely occur if a cloud provider has services that span WAN (wide area network) links. For example, companies like Amazon and Google run many data centers, and one can easily have a situation in which a data center in some location is running, yet has temporarily lost contact with the others. Although the Internet is highly resilient as well, WAN disruptions occur frequently and sometimes do not heal for several minutes. Configuration mistakes have sometimes created WAN outages that lasted for hours. Thus, partitioning is a rare but legitimate worry in services that span WAN links, but not a requirement within cloud data centers, where one would only have local area networks (LAN links). In these LAN settings, if a partition were to happen, we would not need to guarantee that the service remains available on both sides of the broken link.

Brewer's conjecture was that cloud systems will need to guarantee availability and partition tolerance, and hence would need to accept a weakening of consistency. As stated, this is clearly a WAN conjecture, because of the partition tolerance aspect. But from the very start Brewer noted that sometimes even if a system is not partitioned we might want to act as if it was. He pointed to situations in which some inner service is either faulty (perhaps, restarting from a crash) or even just very slow. In such cases, he suggested, we would like our first-tier cloud service to remain available, using cached data (he calls this it *soft state*) so as to respond rapidly to requests that arrive during periods when some needed inner-tier services might be unresponsive. Brewer argued that the value of quick responses is so high that even a response based on stale data is often preferable to leaving the external client waiting. In effect, he said, cloud systems should *always return a rapid response*, even if the required data could be stale, incorrect, or are partially missing.

This principle of rapid response even at the cost of some small but tolerable inconsistencies has been widely accepted. When a web page renders some content with a small red "x" to designate missing or unavailable content, we are seeing CAP in action. Hopefully, most readers will agree that this is far preferable to seeing the entire web page timeout and not render at all. If we return to the definitions, we can summarize CAP: it posits an *inescapable* tradeoff between consistency (and durability) on the one hand, and availability (or responsiveness) and partition-tolerance (or fault-tolerance) on the other.

CAP comes in two forms. Brewer stated it more or less as a design principle: a kind of rule of thumb (Brewer 2000). Gilbert and Lynch then proved a CAP theorem (Gilbert and Lynch 2002). We will not delve into to the CAP theorem right now, except to say that in proving it, Gilbert and Lynch first restated it more formally. As part of this restatement, they adopted a somewhat narrower set of definitions than the ones we have given above, focusing on the question of maintaining availability during true network partitioning. As a result, the CAP theorem they proved is somewhat narrower than what Brewer actually intended.

The intuition behind Brewer's rule-of-thumb argument is entirely pragmatic. Basically, he imagines some popular, heavily loaded service that needs to scale out very aggressively. Think, for example, of that first tier of Amazon on the day the new X-Box first is released, ten weeks before Christmas. Within seconds, hundreds of thousands of dutiful parents and hopeful children visit the X-Box web page; some just to check pricing, while thousands of others attempt to place orders simultaneously. Amazon does not want to miss a single sale. Under these conditions, Brewer argues that if we want to track information with perfect accuracy (here, the inventory of remaining X-Boxes), we will delay the responses by forcing a parent to wait while the web-page builder (a tier-one service) asks the inventory service (an inner service) to reserve an X-Box prior to finalizing each sale. Since far more people get to the last step and then do not click the purchase button than do click it, many of these temporary reservations will need to be cancelled. Yet this means that quite a few real buyers may be told that all of the inventory is currently reserved. In overall balance, we end up with a solution that will not make any mistakes, but could run slowly and lose a great many sales.

Instead, Brewer argues, it would be better to initially run in an optimistic mode, booking the sale without checking the remaining inventory stock. We skip the reservation step: there were 10,000 units in inventory twenty seconds ago, so some are probably still available now. This leads to a highly responsive solution that runs some risk of overselling the product: every single one of Amazon's front-tier service replicas is eager to book sales, without checking that inventory remains. But the end-user experience is better, on average, than in the more conservative approach. Broadly, Brewer argues that the scenario exposes a question of priorities: scale and performance on the one hand, and absolute accuracy on the other. Because Amazon earns more money by being highly responsive, it makes sense to run some risk of errors. Moreover, one can easily reduce the risk of mistakes: as we run low on X-Box systems, we can just switch to a more cautious approach while selling the last few hundred units. The only risk would then arise if the demand is so much higher than we anticipated that we do not switch modes quickly enough and oversell our stock. This, of course, can happen, but a big company like Amazon would certainly find some other way to fill any orders beyond their target, so the risk is manageable. And this is the deeper sense of the CAP theorem: sometimes, a system should run acceptable risks if by doing so it can offer far better responsiveness and scalability.

To take CAP to a slightly deeper level, we will need to understand exactly what consistency means here; after all, while we all know what this property means in an intuitive sense, we have just seen how sensitive a theorem can be to the definitions used. Accordingly, imagine a cloud computing service accessible over the network: it sees a series of requests (queries and updates), and it responds with replies. Suppose that these events occur one by one: the service, as a whole, only sees a single request at a time. The service never fails and is correct, so it will not forget a completed operation. Let us call this a sequential service.

Now suppose that someone builds a scaled-out cloud version of the same service, with tens of thousands of components, but implemented in such a manner that from the requests and replies alone, *there is no way to distinguish the cloud solution from the original single, non-faulty, server.* If you know much about database transactions, you might recognize this as a kind of one-copy serializability property. Let us say that a cloud system offers a strong consistency property if it achieves the behavior we have just described. In effect, it achieves a high level of parallelism and scalability, but always looks like a single entity (one that performs updates sequentially) when accessed by external users.

This is basically what Brewer means by consistency in CAP: he makes reference to the database ACID model (we will discuss this in more detail in Chap. 14), and other cloud researchers have echoed his reasoning. This is the sense in which consistency in CAP is really a short-hand for two properties: an order-based consistency property (namely, updates to data replicated in the system will be applied in the same order at all replicas), and a durability property (namely, once the system has committed to do an update, it will not be lost or rolled back). Later we will see that this conflation of consistency with durability may be important, because durability is expensive, and yet turns out to be of limited value in the first tier of the cloud, where services are not allowed to keep permanent state (if a tier-one service instance fails, or is shut down by the cloud management system, any files it created are discarded: these services can only store things in a durable way by passing them to inner-tier services). However, the implications of this point will need to wait until Part II of this text.

CAP applies to inner-tier services, too, but not in such a clear-cut way. In fact many inner-tier services in today's cloud scale well and are highly available while offering consistency and durability guarantees. For example, Google's GFS file system guarantees that when an application reads a file the version will be current. GFS thus offers consistency plus durability, provided that only one application tries to write the file at a time. To provide synchronization for concurrent writers, GFS comes with a locking service, called Chubby. Using Chubby together with GFS, applications can achieve all sorts of mixtures of consistency and durability. Chubby even lets the application that requests a lock script out the actions that Chubby should take if a failure occurs: should Chubby release the lock if the holder crashes? Hold it until that process recovers? Run some sort of command that, in effect, notifies the application that a problem occurred? There are also policy options that tell Chubby how to handle its own failures, although the basic rule is that unless the application specifically wants very lightweight locking, locks will be preserved across Chubby crashes, including crashes that knock an entire Chubby service out entirely for some period of time. This property, called *strong durability*, is one we will be looking at closely in Part II of the text.

The story seen at Google has counterparts in any of the major cloud computing platforms. Yahoo!'s ZooKeeper (a kind of consistency-preserving file system), is extremely popular in cloud settings, and has similar functionality but wrapped into a single solution presented as a file system, but in which files can be used as locks (an old Unix trick). Call this one consistency plus durability. Microsoft Azure has consistency-preserving services, including a file system similar to GFS and a locking infrastructure similar to Chubby. Database products offer consistency (in the cloud, the most popular model is *snapshot isolation*, a variation on database serializability that treats read transactions using a timestamp-based versioning scheme, while handling writes using a locking approach). Anyone who would claim that the major products in this area do not scale just has not tracked the database literature! Consistency even extends to the open-source version of the MapReduce technology, Hadoop: these systems allow large problems to be split into smaller parts, distributed for parallel execution, and then recombined is a tremendous success. When a MapReduce execution ends, one can be quite sure that it reflects all the subresults of the computation, each counted exactly once. We could go on and on, listing database products for cloud use, management tools, fast key-value storage technologies: cloud consistency is a very common guarantee. MapReduce falls into a consistency-without-durability case: if it gives a result, the result is correct, but if some kind of major failure occurs, it simply cleans up.

This text will not focus on database systems for the cloud; that topic is a huge one that deserves a volume of its own. But we should certainly all understand that database systems do offer strong consistency, as noted, and that they scale extremely well. Many have their own multi-tier infrastructures: the important products all offer first-tier application-building tools that are closely integrated with the inner tier database services, and these solutions work extremely well. No modern cloud platform could exist without them.

So we have quite a list of consistency-guaranteeing cloud services. Notice, however, that our list is mostly composed of datacenter infrastructure components, not the kinds of service replicas that face the end-user; the one exception we cited here is really an automated way of building first-tier front-ends to database products, not a general methodology for building arbitrary services. Moreover, across the board, these examples took years to develop, and all of them reflect at least tens of millions of dollars of corporate investment; the number rises to billions of dollars if we include the major database products.

So the correct way to understand Brewer's point definitely is not to assume that he's convinced that the cloud cannot offer scalability and consistency, at the same time. The CAP theorem does not really say that, and neither did Eric Brewer. Rather, he argued that we need low-effort, inexpensive options for building scalable, elastic applications for the first tier. And then he argued that the easiest path to this end is to accept the idea that by weakening consistency in those services it becomes much easier to achieve amazing scalability and speed. Few of us have pockets as deep as those of Google or Oracle. Thus, the average reader of this text is probably in the community to which Brewer's advice was aimed. In effect, we want CNN.com to be amazingly fast. If this comes down to not waiting to fetch the most current version of the score in an NBA basketball game, then perhaps we should just used a cached score from a few seconds ago. The end user can always refresh the web page, and sooner or later, the cached score will be updated. In contrast, to give you the perfect, most accurate answer, we would need to pull up the most current data available, and that would introduce a non-local delay.

The nutshell takeaway, then, is that Brewer argues against locking and in favor of using cached data and sending updates out asynchronously, because he believes that using locking to read a value that definitely is not being updated at the moment the read occurs, or waiting until updates have committed, will be too slow. The locking point, as it happens, is precisely why database systems use snapshot isolation: they want reads to run without delay even if writes have locked up the current state of the database and will keep that current state busy for a while. Brewer sees this kind of delay as being contrary to a more important goal, namely local responsiveness. And so he argues that instead of casually building a first-tier cloud service that offers consistency, one should spend a bit more time thinking about whether that service can get away with a weaker guarantee. Hopefully, the reader of this text will agree that Brewer's point is a sound one.

Cloud operators and platform vendors have accepted this point. Development tools like Azure make it easy to build very lightweight, scalable, soft-state services for the first tier. They offer prebuilt technologies that can help the developer carry out Brewer's approach, and they lack the kinds of tool that might lead typical developers into the thicket of issues associated with trying to make stronger forms of consistency scale well enough to work in the first tier (tools and issues we will be discussing throughout the entire remainder of this text). To the extent that these existing platforms offer a systematic methodology for first-tier service development, it seems to be one inspired by an approach that eBay research Dan Pritchett calls BASE. BASE, as the name suggests, is the opposite of ACID; the acronym is short for Basically Available services that run on Soft-State and offer Eventual Consistency. Think about that CNN.com scenario. The idea behind BASE is to write cloud applications that run using cached data, do not obtain locks, are highly pipelined, and respond to the user as quickly as possible. Lacking locks, and with updates issued asynchronously, all sorts of consistency issues can arise: CNN.com might show the user a stale page for that NBA game in progress. The E, for eventual consistency, reflects the idea that things do catch up: refresh the page a few times, and you will finally see that Kobe just scored the 3-pointer and tied the game. But it may take a few tries: eventually, you do see updates, but right this second, you might see stale data. In BASE, the assumption is that when an inconsistent result is served up, in many cases nobody will notice. Meanwhile, various background mechanisms labor to catch up, and the cloud system is expected to eventually converge towards a consistent state. So if refreshing that CNN.com page is starting to give you tendonitis, just go get a cup of coffee. By the time you get back, your local cloud service replica should have the story right.

1.7   The Challenge of Trusted Computing in Cloud Settings

Can trusted applications that demand high-assurance guarantees run in a cloud setting, given all of this fuss about CAP and BASE and the general lack of a theory for building scalable, high-assurance solutions? To assist ourselves in thinking about the role of consistency in cloud settings, let us explore a concrete scenario that at a glance seems to need strong trust properties. Then we can ask ourselves whether the problems that arise could safely be solved in a cloud setting with weak consistency properties.

In recent years many countries have struggled with rising health-care costs, and it seems natural to turn to improved automation as a productivity tool that might cut these costs. Here in the United States, the 2009 Health Care Reform Act was predicated on huge savings from productivity improvements; those savings are programmed into the budget projections that underlie the cost estimates for the initiative. Thus, health care on the web is supposed to become a reality in the fairly near future. Indeed in some countries this step has already been taken.

Very often, this concept of improved productivity centers on switching the industry from today's mix of paper and computerized records to a future in which all medical health records would have an electronic form. There is no doubt that this step would be beneficial, if taken far enough to completely eliminate paper records, and if there is a single national standard. But the medical world has many kinds of health records. In what follows, let us imagine a realistic scenario in which the records in question are more like database records and where computing systems use them in an active way for patient management.

Accordingly, consider someone who has diabetes and depends on a *continuous insulin infusion pump* to control his or her blood sugars. These are small devices, about the size of a mobile telephone, which can be programmed to provide microscopic doses of insulin throughout the day and night, coming much closer to the way that a healthy human pancreas would behave. For individuals with severe type I (inherited) diabetes, continuous insulin infusion devices are literally life savers, and also tremendously improve quality of life. Not only is the patient freed from endless injections, often many times daily, but the steady small doses are apparently handled by the body more efficiently, so less insulin is required and the patient is far less likely to develop complications such as blindness or cardiac disease. Patients with type II diabetes often move to pumps as well, for exactly the same reason.

Today's insulin pumps are not simple devices: users need to be able to do some simple mathematics, are expected to have a degree of manual dexterity, and must be able to follow instructions carefully. For example, it is important to measure blood sugars regularly. But there has been progress on sensors that could do this and we will assume that such a device exists and that the home-care patient is wearing one, probably integrated right into the insulin pump itself. The basic task now becomes the following: Since insulin is the body's way of regulating blood sugars after consuming food, a diabetic patient needs to track their diet and activity level rather carefully, estimate the caloric content and the ratio of carbohydrate calories to fat calories in foods, and then estimate the rate at which they are burning calories (for example, when jogging versus sleeping). Then this information is used to tell the pump what it should do. Someday, perhaps it will be possible to do this the way a healthy person's body does it working purely from the measured blood sugar levels, but such a step would be too far in the future. So the task falls to the pump wearer who can factor in food consumption, level of activity, and other background factors that can impact the body's response to insulin.

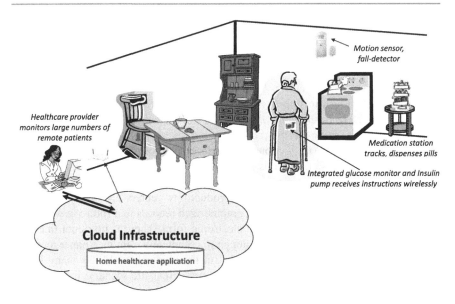

Fig. 1.5 As society ages, we face a growing need to use technology to assist frail patients who will prefer to live at home, and yet may need close medical supervision

Unfortunately, more and more diabetic patients fall into a category that might be broadly described as in need of help. For example, there are huge numbers of elderly diabetic patients, living at home, but who lack the ability to deal with the complexities of keeping their insulin pump configured correctly, or who may not be able to physically manipulate the controls. These individuals end up needing some form of help: from family members, or visiting nurses, or other individuals, and they may need several such visits daily. The cost of that form of care is quite steep, simply because these visits take time.

Let us assume that this is the (very large) category of patients your new startup company has decided to focus upon as potential clients. For a fee, your company plans to handle the semi-automated task of adjusting insulin dosages, over the Internet, on the basis of the physicians targets and recommendations, using blood sugar information captured through online devices as your input source, and implementing a variety of mechanisms to protect against error (after all, a blood sugar reading requires that the device be used correctly, etc.). Your company will have humans in the loop, but the goal will be to automate what can be automated safely, reducing this hands-on activity to a minimum.

Figures 1.5, 1.6, and 1.7 illustrate three scenarios that might arise in this context. In Fig. 1.5 we see a home-care patient who is being monitored remotely; the system is watching her blood sugars and other parameters (we will say more in a moment), adjusting her insulin pump, and posting data to monitoring interfaces that humans watch. In Fig. 1.6, a home visit is underway, and the visiting nurse has become aware of some issues that require her to consult with a doctor, who ends up adjusting medications. In Fig. 1.7 the doctor's actions have also caused us to adjust the

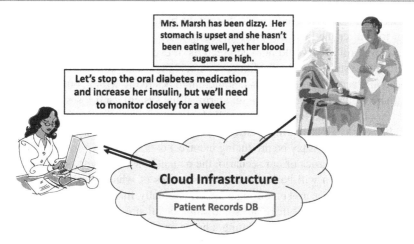

Fig. 1.6 For certain kinds of interactions with the remote patient, hard-state records are created or modified. In these cases a cloud-hosted solution would need to guarantee very strong assurance properties, including privacy, durability, consistency

parameters that control the cloud-hosted monitoring system. Not shown but implicit in these scenarios are the updates to the patient's healthcare records (the privacy of which is guarded by law, for example the United States HiPPA regulations), and

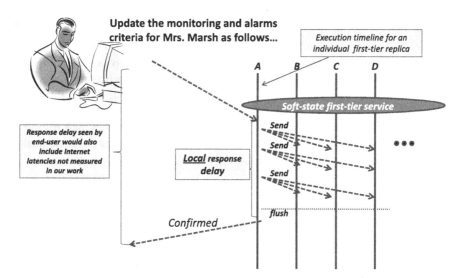

Fig. 1.7 Other tasks might have weaker requirements. In this monitoring scenario, a cloud-hosted monitoring infrastructure is being configured with new parameter settings. In many cloud settings, we would use soft-state services running in the first tier for such purposes, benefiting from the scalability and quick responsiveness of that tier, but also accepting the limitation that durable state must be stored elsewhere. Yet even in these soft-state use cases, privacy and consistency may be of great importance

the associated long-term audit trails that might be maintained to track actions the system took after the fact. But not everything is tracked in fine-grained detail; for example, we probably would not keep records of every single parameter change in a monitoring system. Finally, the figures do not show whatever failsafe mechanisms might be in place to trigger alarms if something goes really wrong, but without any doubt there would be several of these: alarms if the system itself loses contact with the devices being monitored and controlled, alarms if the patient's vital signs drift out of the healthy zone, alarms if the software for adjusting the insulin pump senses that the control policy may be producing incorrect data, etc.

So we have the basics of our scenario: the patient's insulin pump needs periodic dose updates, which will be based on our estimates of what the patient has been eating and on her measured blood sugar levels. Normally, this is a routine matter that can be done remotely, but there are some situations that might require other kinds of medical intervention, like scheduling a home or office visit, or even sending the patient to the emergency room. Your target is to create a cloud computing solution that will assist in caring for this kind of patient, dramatically increase the number of at-home patient's that a given care provider can manage, while simultaneously improving the average quality of care. You will develop the needed software and the devices (the insulin pumps and blood sugar monitoring units) and will make its money by operating the technical side of the system on behalf of the medical offices that sign onto the new technology. Those local medical offices would access the system through the network on normal machines, probably PCs or Macs (the two most common platform choices in medical settings).

Notice that we are not trying to cut the human out of the loop. Instead, the big win here would be that a much smaller team could handle a much larger patient population, and by having better data at its fingertips, provide better care than this kind of patient could achieve on his or her own. In fact, the scenario we have outlined is one of the major reasons that elderly patients often have to move into managed care facilities: they lose their ability to deal with the complexities of operating a device like an insulin pump, and this puts them at grave risk. So if this problem can be solved, a tremendous number of patients might be able to live out their lives at home, who would otherwise be forced into a nursing facility at huge psychological (and economic) price. It might even make sense to put frail patients with type II diabetes (a much larger group) on insulin pumps: although the pump is a costly technology, the benefits of being able to control it remotely could outweigh those costs. Such a step would open an immense market for your company, with literally tens of millions of potential patients in the United States alone.

But the new system will need to be trustworthy in several senses of the term. Any medical system must respect the relevant health information system guidelines with respect to security and privacy: the HiPPA requirements. These boil down to two principles. First, only authorized individuals can access medical records (obviously, there is a concept of emergency authorization that bypasses normal restrictions). And second, no matter who accesses a record, an audit record is maintained and an oversight policy ensures that if an inappropriate access occurs, someone can step in very promptly to address the situation.

With respect to reliability, the situation is really in flux, and will depend upon a legal question that, to the author's knowledge, has not yet been answered in the law: is a medical computing system of the sort we have outlined "practicing medicine" (in which case it would be subject to very stringent FDA oversight), or is it really just a tool used strictly under human control (in which case the FDA would not play a primary role)? Let us bet that the latter is the more likely interpretation. Just the same, because our system does play central roles in medical decision making, it clearly has to be reliable enough to justify the trust that patients and health-care workers are going to place in it.

For example, the system needs to ensure that it gets the right information to the right place at the right time: the health-care worker in the local endocrinology office needs *accurate* information to make insulin dose decisions, and also to detect abnormal conditions that require a face to face visit, as can easily happen (for example, if an insulin pump needs adjustment, which is not common but does occur, or if the patient develops some sort of secondary condition that requires hands-on treatment). The issue comes down to not basing decisions on stale data, and ensuring that when some component needs to raise an alarm, that alarm will definitely go off. Beyond this are secondary issues: considering the nature of our customer base, this system really needs to be very reliable in the normal day to day sense of keeping itself running without a lot of hands-on care. Our elderly patients probably will not be happy if they constantly need to reboot their network modems or run through diagnostic screens on their insulin pumps! And our health-care team will probably be so small, and with such a large number of patients, that any kind of serious outage could overwhelm them.

To keep the story short: even this little scenario highlights the dilemma. On the one hand are the compelling economic advantages of the cloud model, coupled with cutting edge development tools that will certainly reduce the cost of creating, testing and deploying your solution. And on the other hand, a laundry list of worries. But we can make the story even shorter: right now, many projects would go with a cloud solution.

In fact, when we solve problems using technology, we are always forced to grapple with these kinds of questions. Clearly, computing cannot safely be used in medical settings, or air traffic control, or other purposes without taking that step. Given that we know things can fail, our job is to make systems that are as self-healing as possible, and that fail in a safe way when they cannot overcome the damage caused by a crash. Knowing that the world has a lot of hackers (and more than a few cyber terrorists), we need to make these systems as secure against attack as we can. A perfectly secure, reliable technology could still be misused to create an insecure, unsafe medical system. Our task here runs the other way: we just need to create a reasonably secure, reasonably safe solution on a somewhat insecure, somewhat unreliable infrastructure.

Let us summarize some of the concerns that this solution raises, and just sketch some ideas for how we might deal with each. Later, we will cover these same topics in the body of the textbook, but in a more thoughtful, detailed way.

- *Security.* Our system has many attributes one associates with typical web applications, and seems like a good match to the cloud computing model. Yet it will be constructed using normal machines running normal operating systems and programming languages. Can we harden it sufficiently so that virus or other attacks will not run a significant risk of harming patients? After all, viruses and other problems are common on today's Internet.
- *Data privacy.* Google and Microsoft and Amazon may not be evil, but none of them allow data subject to HiPPA regulations to be uploaded to their cloud systems. We will either need to operate a private cloud just for the medical community, but using the same cloud technologies that make Microsoft and Amazon such inexpensive providers, or we will need to somehow encrypt all sensitive data so that we can upload it to a third-party cloud platform without risking some sort of disastrous compromise by intruders. Which ever way we go, we will need to build an audit mechanism to track access to the data, and to sound the alarm if someone seems to be nosing around. If we go with a third-party cloud, our audit system will need to record access by the people operating the cloud, not just accesses from within our medical application.
- *Consistency.* Here the issue is that modern cloud technologies, even when used to build a private cloud, do not necessarily guarantee that data updates will be visible in a timely manner. Thus if a blood sugar reading is taken and the cloud data store is updated to reflect that new reading, cloud applications might see stale data for a long time. There are ways to obtain stronger properties, however, and we will focus on them. One option is to use a transactional database to store our patient data; these do not scale to Internet scale, but could get us pretty far, particularly if we find a way to partition the data into smaller databases so that the load on any one database is limited. Another option will be to adopt a replication package that uses the *virtual synchrony* model, or one that implements *state machine replication.* If we are concerned about attacks or other compromises we could even opt for *Byzantine Agreement.* So we have some good options. But will they be scalable enough for use in cloud settings?
- *Fault tolerance.* Cloud systems demand various forms of application fault-tolerance: cloud platform design is such that management software can shut down machines unexpectedly, for example, when a truck backs up and unplugs a container of cloud servers. This kind of shutdown will often be indistinguishable from a crash failure. The typical assumption is that while the server may crash, the application running on the client's computer will probably not go down, and is expected to ride out these glitches. The problem is that doing so is not always possible: as we will see, there are conditions under which the client platform may be unsure what state the cloud service was left in, and hence may be unable to resume uninterrupted operation without help either from the server itself (assuming that it recovers and remembers its state), or even from a user with systems administration privileges. Stronger forms of fault-tolerance are possible but require extra measures by the cloud computing service itself, which may be incompatible with scalability. Today, the bias is definitely on client-side failure handling, and thus when one uses an Internet radio or watches a TV show on a streaming

channel, there are problems now and then—the screen might freeze up, or seem bursty, or you might even have to reboot your computer. These kinds of options will not work in our health-care setting; as we have seen, our home-care patient population just will not be able to deal with such things. But as we will see, future systems will surely need other options, and those exist, provided that we base them on sufficiently scalable versions of the underlying platform software.

- *Fail-safe behavior.* We have reduced several goals to a simpler objective, which can be paraphrased as "try to keep the system healthy when some form of self-defense or self-repair is possible." But when other remedies can no longer handle an issue, the critical need is for a fail-safe solution in which any component that might cause harm by virtue of being unable to do the right thing (or to be sure it is doing the right thing) instead sounds an alarm, takes itself offline, or otherwise protects the real user—the patient—from ill effect. The certainty that if a component shuts itself down, the system will still be safe can be a huge relief to the application designer. For example, in air traffic control, or in a medical setting, sometimes it is better for the system to announce that it cannot make progress and shuts down, than for the system to try and try to overcome a failure while valuable time elapses. The air traffic controller has other options, such as the direct radio link from the ATC center to the plane, and the medical provider can, similarly, pick up the phone or dispatch a medical aide to have a look at the patient's insulin pump.

Focusing on our medical scenario again, one can now review these properties one by one. Although the discussion above merely touches on the issues, such a review leads to the conclusion that a cloud solution definitely might be possible, and even quite appropriate and safe. But one also finds that the application itself needs to be conceived with the limitations of the cloud in mind, and that even so, the solution might need to include some non-standard functionality. It will surely need security tools different from those seen in most cloud settings today, will almost certainly need to do something about data consistency, and the HiPPA audit requirement could be particularly hard to address (how ironic to realize that we might be able to build a solution, only to discover that regulations formulated more than two decades ago could then step in and prevent us from operating it!) But assuming that these issues can all be addressed, it may be possible to create a solution that could safely operate on cloud platforms.

1.8   Data Replication: The Foundational Cloud Technology

Up to now, we have discussed the reliability issue in rather broad terms, but to make this more concrete, let's try to be a bit more specific about data replication and the properties one can assume in an application that needs to base some action on a replicated object or record.

Replication, as we will see, is a nearly universal mechanism in distributed systems, and it is not hard to see why this should be the case. After all, if a distributed system has no replicated state at all, its components would all be independent little (or big) subsystems, running by themselves. More often we want a distributed system to act like a single entity that performs extremely well, but also to conceal its inner structure from the user. In effect, the user should not become aware that the system is really composed of millions of smaller parts operating with only a loose form of coordination.

Many cloud-computing applications require access to some form of replicated and consistent state: a patient's medical records and current insulin dose and schedule, the updates to a Twitter feed or a Facebook page, the remaining inventory of X-Box game controllers. All of these are examples in which information changes, and in which those changes need to reach the system components that handle web requests: in effect, data must be *replicated* so that every component that needs to access it, or update it, can do so.

Earlier, when discussing CAP, we suggested that one should sometimes build cloud systems to run in two (or more) distinct modes. At that time, we argued that if we have, say, 10,000 X-Box systems and want the Amazon web pages that sell such things to respond rapidly, it might make sense to just book the sales without tracking the detailed inventory: nobody cares if there are 9,751 units still in stock, as opposed to 9,157. But we also suggested that one might switch modes and sell more cautiously, by insisting on reserving an actual inventory item, as the remaining stock dwindled. In this cautious mode some sort of replicated, consistent, inventory counting service would play the key role: replicated because it needs to be fault-tolerant, and consistent because it needs to give a correct answer. Thus a cloud system might opt for weak consistency in some situations or in some respects, while using stronger forms of consistency in other subsystems. Part of our challenge as cloud designers will be to make these choices intelligently; a second part of the job will be to build the fastest and most scalable replicated, consistency-preserving, services possible.

Such decisions can sometimes require debate and the right answer could require a bit of thought about priorities. For example, should Twitter be reliable and consistent? A Tweet that does not reach some of the followers of a popular feed might not harm anyone or result in a revenue loss, but it certainly could reduce confidence in the Twitter service and cause confusion among the follows of that Twitter feed. A physician who is preparing a patient's revised care plan and encounters old, stale data could make a serious mistake, or might realize that the data just cannot be correct, but either way his or her confidence in the medical system will be seriously eroded. But one could imagine categories of twitter feeds, or situations in medical monitoring, where the right thing to do is to omit data. For example, suppose that it is taking a very long time to track down a missing Tweet, or to recover some EKG data that were lost in the communication system. Even if one wants Tweets to normally get through, and one normally wants a continuous EKG feed, it could easily make more sense to skip forward in these cases, just to keep up with the current updates.

While such actions may sound like recipes for confusion, it often is possible to "fix" the system to make these behaviors into features. For example, if the medical records carry unique dates and times, many kinds of mistake can be avoided simply by checking those timestamps and suppressing old data. The physician may be annoyed if the system complains that a network outage that began at 9:11 am has left the data center disconnected from the patient's monitoring unit, but at least no errors are likely to result, and when he sees a blood sugar measurement from last night, he will realize that the data are old. This, then, is a way to potentially take an inconsistent underlying mechanism (one that might sometimes report old, stale data) and then to layer a fail-safe mechanism over it. Indeed, described in this way, it may seem almost inconceivable that a medical system of this sort could be designed in any other way!

Broadly, we are starting to see that cloud computing will require a new style of design and thinking in which rather than resolving each system down to one set of functionality that you will implement in one way, some solutions should be implemented in somewhat circuitous ways that bias for rapid response over guarantees (but then compensate if any errors result), while others might even be implemented using multiple side-by-side functionalities, with the system switching between modes based on application-specific criteria such as the relative importance of keeping up with current data, versus being absolutely consistent and complete in the way data are reported. Clever designs will often give far better performance but at the price of added cases that the developer needs to think through. If the short-cuts that this requires then force us to find a way to present anomalous events to the end-user as part of the normal behavior of the system, well, those extra steps might simply be the key to achieving really ambitious scalability.

On the other hand, it is not a good idea to take things for granted when designing software solutions in which a great deal is riding on the behavior of the system. There have been too many examples of thoughtless or naive systems, sometimes used in extremely sensitive settings, in which no effort was made to verify that the solution has the needed properties. Some of these were later caught; others proved to be dangerously flawed when they actually caused harm. Software technology has always been littered with mistakes of these sorts, and the insight one gains is that what seems obvious to one person can trigger a serious oversight or error for another. Mistakes can reflect fuzzy thinking, but can also arise when a person is transferred off a project (or falls ill) before the job was finished, when people work long hours without much sleep, or when a very large team is assembled without adequate thought to how the parts will interface. Cloud systems invite these kinds of mistakes because many applications are constructed by gluing preexisting components together and then scaled out by simply running huge numbers of application instances on different nodes, with the size of the replica set varying elastically as new copies are launched to handle more load, or shut down to free up unused resources. The developer of such an application has very little insight into how it will really behave under all the possible deployment scenarios. Faced with this reality, there is no alternative to a systematic, careful design and validation process that leaves no stone unturned; sometimes this process might be a little boring, but those dull design reviews can greatly increase confidence that things will work as required.

The other key insight from these examples is that even when an application needs replicated data and strong consistency guarantees, these do not necessarily represent a huge barrier to successful cloud computing. We simply need to ask how we can provide those guarantees. We will only hit a real barrier to a cloud solution if we encounter a scenario that combines a mixture of needs, such as rapid response to updates, consistency, and very high availability, and if that mixture somehow runs afoul of the existing platform support for data replication. And even then, there may be ways to push beyond what cloud platforms do today, so as to achieve the desired properties.

Replication underlies other functionality, too. Suppose a request needs to be carried out even if something crashes. We might replicate the request and arrange for a backup machine to step in and take over if the primary handler crashes while doing the operation (of course if the backup crashes too, that can pose other kinds of issue; we will explore them, but not now!) Indeed, pushing this even further, we might replicate data about the health of the machines in our data center, which would permit agreement on their status (operational, failed, overloaded, etc.). By having every machine track the status of the other machines with which it interacts by looking at this form of replicated database, we avoid the free-for-all that occurs if each machine makes such decisions on its own, for example using timeouts to sense failure or to infer loads.

The reader might wonder why we are singling out replication rather than distributed synchronization. After all, for many kinds of concurrent system, locking and other forms of synchronization or coordination are the core around which everything else gets built. And few systems have more concurrency than cloud platforms, with their thousands or hundreds of thousands of servers, each of which will often be a multi-core processor, each running what will probably be a multi-threaded application! Indeed, synchronization *does* turn out to be fundamental: at Google, for example, a locking service called Chubby lives at the core of the entire consistency hierarchy of the GooglePlex. Yet Chubby itself is build as a replication mechanism, which runs on several nodes (for fault-tolerance) and tracks the lock state as locks are requested, granted, and released: in effect, this translates locking into the language of fault-tolerant replication.

Indeed, even cloud computing security reduces to a replication and data consistency question. Viewed in very abstracted terms, a secure system is one that uses some set of policy rules to decide, for each action, whether that action should be permitted or blocked. These decisions occur all over the system, and at high rates. Moreover, the security rules evolve as new users join the system, new objects are created or destroyed, and as permissions change. Thus, deciding whether a particular entity should be permitted to take some action on some object reduces to a question of (securely) replicating the information on which decisions are based. If we replicate these inputs correctly, our security system will make appropriate, correct decisions. If our underlying replication technology makes errors, those will manifest not just as data inconsistencies, but also as potential security flaws. And while it may sound like a tautology to assert that in general, security questions reduce to secure data replication, one can see that in fact the latter problem is a much narrower one.

In summary, one can make a pretty good case for replication as a universal tool: the single most useful technology in our cloud computing toolbox. But replication comes in many flavors, and not every form of replication is really universally pow-

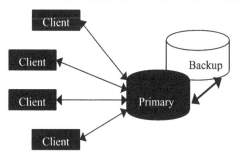

Fig. 1.8 An idealized client/server system with a backup server for increased availability. The clients interact with the primary server; in an air traffic application, the server might provide information on the status of air traffic sectors, and the clients may be air traffic controllers responsible for routing decisions. The primary server keeps the backup up to date, so that if a failure occurs, the clients can switch to the backup and resume operation with minimal disruption

erful. In particular, recall the discussion of CAP from earlier in this chapter. CAP, as we saw, is a kind of cloud-computing design principle, very widely accepted in modern cloud computing platforms, and what it does it to warn the developer that to achieve very high levels of availability (quick response) even in scalable systems, it may be necessary to weaken data consistency guarantees. Is CAP, then, the enemy of secure and consistent data replication?

1.9   Split Brains and Other Forms of Mechanized Insanity

To appreciate the sense in which CAP may be at odds with our goals, it will help to look at the system illustrated in Fig. 1.8. This shows an element of an air traffic control system on which the author has worked (it was initially rolled out in France and continues to be used quite heavily in Europe). Here we see two machines cooperating to help a group of air traffic controllers make decisions about routing airplanes through some region of airspace. There is a server in the system, with a backup, and it warns the controller if a potential danger is sensed.

A controller who depends on a system such as this needs an absolute assurance that if the service reports that a sector is available and a plane can be routed into it, this information is correct and no other controller has been given the same information in regard to routing some other plane. An optimization criterion for such a service would be that it minimizes the frequency with which it reports a sector as being occupied when it is actually free. A fault-tolerance goal would be that the service remains operational despite limited numbers of failures of component programs, and perhaps that it takes a component off-line if it somehow falls out of synchronization with regard to the states of other components.

Goals of the type just enumerated would avoid scenarios such as the one illustrated in Fig. 1.9, where the system state has become dangerously inconsistent as a result of a network failure that fools some clients into thinking the primary server has failed, and similarly fools the primary and backup into mutually believing one another to have crashed.

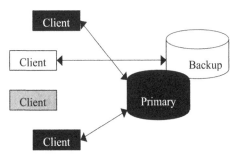

Fig. 1.9 This figure represents a scenario that will arise in Sect. 6.8, when we consider the use of a standard remote procedure call methodology to build a client/server architecture for a critical setting. In the case illustrated, some of the client programs have become disconnected from the primary server, perhaps because of a transient network failure (one that corrects itself after a brief period during which message loss rates are very high). In the resulting system configuration, the primary and backup servers each consider itself to be in charge of the system as a whole. There are two clients still connected to the primary server (*black*), one to the backup server (*white*), and one client is completely disconnected (*gray*). Such a configuration exposes the application user to serious threats. In an air traffic control situation, it is easy to imagine that accidents could arise if such a situation were encountered. The goal of this book is two-fold: to assist the reader in understanding why such situations are a genuine threat in modern computing systems, and to study the technical options for building better systems that can prevent such situations from occurring. The techniques presented will sometimes have limitations, which we will attempt to quantify and to understand any reliability implications. While many modern distributed systems have overlooked reliability issues, our working hypothesis will be that this situation is changing rapidly and that the developer of a distributed system has no choice but to confront these issues and begin to use technologies that respond to them

Why might inconsistency arise? Obviously, if the developers were big believers in the CAP principle, this kind of inconsistency might be a basic feature of the system. One would not want to use CAP-based platforms for air traffic control without somehow compensating for the lower level inconsistencies CAP deliberately embraces. But even if we set out to build our solution on the basic elements offered by the network: message passing, perhaps unreliable, and machines that can crash, it turns out that split-brain behavior such as this can arise quite easily, unless real care is taken to prevent it!

The central issue turns out to reflect the difficulty of detecting a failure. If a computer crashes, attempts to communicate with applications running on it will time out. But this can also happen if the network experiences a transient disconnection, or for any number of other reasons. Thus a failure might be "erroneously" reported: our failure detector is itself somewhat unreliable. But this kind of very low-level inconsistency can give rise to all sorts of higher level issues, because replication schemes typically struggle to update operational replicas, but give up if a replica seems to have crashed. Thus, if a replica is incorrectly reported as crashed, it will not see some updates and yet (since it was not really down) will continue to respond to inquiries. Moreover, in situations like the ones in the two figures, a backup might take over when the primary is still running.

We could evade these issues by just making the rule that (1) an application will retry requests indefinitely until a response is received; and (2) any failed component will be restarted, eventually. But it is easy to see that while this might give us a form of reliability, it will not work in an air traffic control system where we need to take actions within fractions of a second; restarting a crashed computer could take hours and certainly will not take less than minutes. Thus when reliability also entails *high availability* we are in trouble. This illustrates the converse of CAP: if we do want strong consistency, we may lose availability under some conditions. An air-traffic control system would solve this using a fail-safe mechanism: some design or feature intended to ensure that if the system cannot make progress (if it *hangs*), the controller will be warned in a visible, unmistakable way. Then he or she can use a backup technology to keep the planes safe until normal function is restored.

In the remainder of this text we will see other ways of approaching this problem. Surprisingly, we will discover that even in services that need to scale very ambitiously and hence seem to be governed by CAP and perhaps forced to use a BASE methodology, there may be ways to accept CAP and follow BASE that still achieve stronger forms of consistency. For example, we will discover a way to implement sequential consistency for soft-state that actually performs just as well as any eventual consistency system and in some situations, dramatically outperforms the usual eventual consistency approaches! It may seem paradoxical to claim that CAP and BASE could still lead to systems that have strong consistency, and that such systems might actually win the performance face-off, but this is precisely what we will discover, at least for certain kinds of system. Other kinds of system might be perfect matches for the version of BASE that leads to solutions like Amazon's Dynamo shopping cart, an an example of a service we'll study in Sect. 5.7.3. The key will relate to that hidden "D" mentioned earlier in CAP: the role of durability in the way that CAP defines consistency. But again, that story will need to wait.

And while it may be unlikely that the world will ever need to have hundreds of thousands of ATC controllers sharing a cloud-hosted safety service, keep in mind that there are other applications with very similar structures that will need to scale ambitiously. For example, Google has invested heavily to create a new technology of self-driving automobiles; each of those cars might be a bit like an air traffic control, getting routing advice from the cloud. Fleets of robots performing tasks like farming could fit the bill. And in fact, as you push further on the example, you will realize that all sorts of relatively mundane applications may share at least some of the high-assurance needs seen in our ATC case, and that many of those would benefit from a cloud-hosted deployment, if only we could do so with adequate assurance properties.

The upshot of this way of thinking is that we will want to study ways that one might create cloud-hosted solutions for large, complex applications like medical care systems and air traffic control systems and even payroll and accounting systems: systems that need to work correctly, and need to work when needed, and yet that we might want to run on a cloud platform in a scaled-out, inexpensive way. We will discover ways of systematically breaking complex tasks into simpler subtasks and of understanding which one can safely be done using weak forms of convergent consistency, which ones need hard-state services with sequential consistency, and which ones fall in the middle ground: soft-state services for which scalable consistency is needed nonetheless. And in each case, we will study the best of breed options. Everything we look at closely will be hands-on and practical: either in major products commercially integrated with today's cloud platforms, or in less widely known but still commercial products aimed at specialists, or (in the limit) in our own Isis[2] software, available for you to download and play with from the author's web site.

1.10   Conclusions

This introduction has touched on some of the major themes that underlie the present version of this textbook. We did so with a dual agenda: on the one hand to survey the content that will follow, but at the same time to make sure that the reader embarks on the study of reliable cloud computing with an awareness of just how peculiar cloud computing can be, and the extent to which reliability has really been rejected as a cloud computing property. Our mission will not be a trivial one: while much is known about reliability and other forms of assurance, there has not been remotely enough work on scalability for those well-known techniques. Worse, cloud computing vendors and operators, if asked, assure us that one can easily be badly burned by reliability and that to first approximation, the things that scale best are the things that promise the least.

Yet we will also see that this is in many ways a symptom of a very young area: one born almost overnight under intense commercial and competitive pressures, in which the urgency of scaling up outweighed any other considerations. That intense pace was a good thing in many ways: it freed the cloud computing developers from the shackles of decades of distributed computing theory and practice, opening their minds to other ways of solving problems, and they have achieved something astonishing almost overnight.

But not every decision made in this race to the clouds should be accepted as if it were engraved in stone, and not every reliability or security technique needs to be rejected out of hand as non-scalable and irrelevant. We will try to strike a balance: first learning the standard stories and the officially accepted rules of the road, but then asking how one could take the next step or two. Those are steps that will soon be necessary, because high assurance applications are coming to the cloud, like it or not, and the cloud platforms that are in widest use today are just not capable of dealing with high assurance computing, without a bit of help. But the good news is that we will not need to depart all that far from the prevailing solutions to get where we need to go. We can accept CAP, and BASE, and still end up with scalable forms of consistency. We will just need to show a bit of sophistication about what works, what does not, and about how we validate the scalability and stability of the key ideas in realistic cloud computing environments.

Part I
Computing in the Cloud

The place to start any inquiry into cloud computing is with a more careful look at a typical interaction between a client computing application and a cloud service. In this first chapter of the text we will briefly survey the origins of the cloud computing concept, and will look at how today's client to cloud interactions differ from the styles of client-server computing that were common even a few years ago. Then we will drill down to understand some of the basics of cloud computing: the key elements of the overall picture, some consisting of generally accepted standards that are relatively mature (such as the options for representing a web page and rendering it); others that are easily programmed and hence almost arbitrarily extensible.

The Way of the Cloud

2

2.1 Introduction

2.1.1 The Technical and Social Origins of the Cloud

Cloud computing is a new term, but not really such a new idea. What we call cloud computing today can be traced to the 1990s, when researchers at Xerox PARC published papers on a new idea that they called *ubiquitous computing*: a world in which computing devices would surround us, and in which we would rely upon them as casually as electric lights or tapwater.

At the time, many sober-minded computing professionals viewed this idea as being a bit over the top: in those days, *distributed computing* was still a relatively new phenomenon, and the earlier networked but relatively loosely connected computing systems were only just becoming common. It did not help that some of the early researchers in the field came across as being a bit quirky. For example, one fellow decided to capture all the events in his life digitally; he went about with cameras strapped to his head, microphones, location tracking devices, etc. These were the days when cameras and microphones and other networked devices were all big bulky things, and the photos of this skinny researcher with all those components strapped on did not exactly inspire imitation. Newspaper editorials debated the pros and cons of building systems that by their very nature intrude into what normally had been private interactions. And many of the core technologies did not even work very well. Ubiquitous computing seemed very unrealistic and over-ambitious, and very unlikely to become a reality anytime soon.

Yet however fanciful the Xerox vision may have seemed in its heyday, cloud computing has to be seen as a realization of that vision and indeed, one that goes far beyond what the Xerox research team anticipated. It turns out that your cell phone, buried in your pocket or in your purse, does track your location rather accurately, unless you disable that feature. And even if you disable GPS tracking, the phone may still know your location to very high accuracy simply by virtue of the wireless networks it can sense in the vicinity: there are growing numbers of high-resolution maps that identify the locations of wireless basestations; a mobile device can often situate itself to an accuracy of several meters by triangulating with respect to the

K.P. Birman, *Guide to Reliable Distributed Systems*, Texts in Computer Science, DOI 10.1007/978-1-4471-2416-0_2, © Springer-Verlag London Limited 2012

availlable wireless systems (even ones that are secured and hence not really accessible). A telephone's microphone is not supposed to be listening to you unless you are making calls, but countless movies revolve around the idea that a spy organization (or even an obsessive ex-boyfriend) might find a way to turn the phone on covertly, and apparently this is not even all that hard to do. Few people videotape their lives as they move around, but crowded public places in the UK often have video cameras trained on the crowd, and there are more and more in the United States as well.

We are putting all kinds of information online; including data of kinds that the early Xerox Parc researchers could never have imagined. For example, who could have anticipated the success of social networking sites such as Facebook and Twitter and YouTube? Using the cloud as an intermediary, people are sharing ideas and experiences and photos and videos and just about everything else in a casual, routine way; maintaining close contact with friends and family nearly continuously; and trusting our the cloud to recommend the best prices on product, to offer hints about good local restaurants, and even to set up impromptu dates with people in the vicinity who might be fun to meet. As we move about and interact, the devices around us collect data and those data enter the cloud, often being stored and indexed for later use. Not much is ever really erased, in part because this can be hard to do. Consider email: suppose a friend sends you a private email, and you read it and then delete it. How sure can you be that the data are gone? If an email-provider erases your email, does this mean it cannot also offer a recovery feature to recover precious emails that might accidentally be erased, or would that violate the policy? The question makes sense because many cloud-hosted email systems do have ways to recover deleted emails. But if deleted emails are recoverable, in what sense were they deleted? What if some index was computed and a deleted email somehow lingers within the computed result: must we recompute every such index? Again, a sensible question, because indexing occurs all the time. And what if the email provider has a backup technology in place: does erasing the email also erase the backups? Probably not: backups are typically "write once" data.

Realistically, it makes sense to just assume that *any* data that find their way online have a good chance of ending up indexed, filed away, and retained (perhaps in a derived form) for use in enhancing your web search experience and to optimize advertising placement. This is not limited to data we deliberately upload; it includes data about credit card purchases, telephone calls, the car we drive and how fast we drive it, speeding and parking tickets, common destinations and routes. It includes angry letters you exchanged with your "ex" in the period before the breakup. The cloud tracks home ownership and mortgage data, and property value trends. Any kind of public records, insurance records, marriages, divorces, arrests: it all gets collected, correlated, stored; entire companies have sprung up to play precisely this role.

Cloud providers make their money by matching your queries to the right web sites, placing advertising likely to appeal to you personally, and trying to "understand" who you are and what motivates you, so as to shape your experience positively. These goals motivate them to capture more and more information. Obviously, some limits do apply (medical records, for example, are covered by HiPPA regulations in the United States, and other countries, such as Israel, have very strong privacy rules around digital data). Yet up to the limits allowed by the law, you can be quite sure that cloud computing companies are doing anything technically feasible that might offer even the slightest edge in the battle for screen space on your mobile device and user interest. In some cases, by accepting a user agreement, you agree to waive your rights under these kinds of data collection laws. Yet many people click to accept without reading such agreements (and only some people have the legal experience to understand them, in any case).

Even in the early days, the Xerox ubiquitous computing crowd worried about the ways that computing systems capable of capturing huge amounts of data might transform society itself, notably by eroding privacy and, in the more dystopian visions, creating a kind of smothering Big Brother society. Today, for all the fretting about privacy, most cloud users feel liberated, not oppressed by these technical trends. If someone were to assert that the cloud is becoming Big Brother, they would be viewed as being especially paranoid. There isn't even one cloud: the cloud is a world within which multiple companies compete, with no clear single winner. Moreover, those companies need to maintain customer trust. Google's "Don't be Evil" corporate motto is just one of the ways that these companies constantly remind their developers and employees of the central importance of being trusted by the user. And they are right to put trust front and center: Every major cloud company understands how easy it can be to fall from dizzying success to utter failure. Serious invasions of privacy could wipe out a major player overnight.

Of course the cloud does cut both ways, but the darker side has not been all that visible in Western society. There is no question that politicians and other public figures are finding the cloud troublesome; it seems very likely that at least some of the recent spate of "outings" of bad behavior originated with politically motivated hackers who broke into email or Twitter accounts, turned up damning information, and then found ways to arrange to leak that information to the public. Yet there has not been much outrage at the idea this might be going on: the public seems to have a real appetite for tawdry news and clearly enjoys watching the rich and famous taken down a notch or two.

Perhaps a bit more of a concern is the degree to which the cloud has simultaneously been a liberating technology in repressive countries (for example, making it easier to organize protests) but also a tool for those same governments to spy on their citizens and to identify signs of dissent, thus enabling further waves of repression. This was very visible during the so-called Arab Spring, when protesters in Iran and Egypt used Twitter and Facebook to orchestrate demonstrations, but then saw their leaders rounded up by the military a few weeks or months later, to be forcefully reminded about who was really in charge. For those working in cloud computing, the societal penetration of their technologies represent a complex and paradoxical phenomenon: leaders within the community are often proud to talk about the cloud as a powerful vehicle for individual expression, and yet how could they not also feel anxious when they see these same technologies helping the military or other repressive forces identify the most troublesome of the protesters. It is not at all clear how this will play out, and how history will view cloud technologies and their roles in repressive societies, over the long term.

This text will not have much more to say about those kinds of issue (readers wishing to learn more might read Laurence Lessig's work on the topic (Lessig 1999)), but it is interesting to think about how the cloud has transformed our contemporary notion of privacy. In 1890, Justices Warren and Brandeis famously defined privacy as the "right to be left alone" and ultimately authored a Supreme Court decision that firmly recognized the Constitutional basis of this right. How quickly the very notion has been confused and eroded by technology, and by the collective behavior of the world's email, Twitter and Facebook users! How could one really be left alone today, short of moving to a cabin in the woods and never touching technology at all (and even then, would not the cloud preserve information about your life up to that moment, and your ownership of that cabin (perhaps even a satellite photo), and maybe even your purchases in the local store)? Professor Lessig is often quoted for his observation that technology often gets far ahead of the law, but here we see a situation in which technology has actually gotten far ahead of our societal norms, literally reshaping the way we live.

But let us return to the early days of the cloud, this time with a more technical focus. When the Xerox Parc group first conceived of ubiquitous computing, most systems were personal ones. These personal computing systems were highly autonomous: they had their own operating systems, private copies of whatever applications you wanted to run and were prepared to pay for, and used the network mostly to exchange email and data files.

The term networking was used as a catchall covering the computer network itself together with those limited kinds of network application: email, early versions of blogs, file transfer (it evolved into the Internet, but the Xerox work on ubiquitous computing actually predated what we would call the Internet today). This book will try to use networking as a term focused on connectivity that enables these kinds of application, as distinct from the way we will use the term *distributed computing*, which for us is concerned with collections of computers, connected to one-another by networks, that collaborate to jointly carry out tasks. That is, for our purposes here, a networked computing system is a machine with its own roles and objectives, which obtains data from servers (with their own roles and objectives) via network connection. Distributed computing, in contrast, is concerned with what teams of collaborating computers can jointly accomplish. The distinction is analogous to shopping as an individual (this would be the networked case), versus dividing up the work and shopping in a collaborative way with friends (the distributed case). In both cases we interact with stores (services), but in the former case the client is on his or her own. In the latter one, the clients talk to one-another and share the job.

In the earliest days of cloud computing, networking was the bread and butter from which most applications were created. Distributed computing was the nec-plus-ultra of systems at the time. As Leslie Lamport[1], a researcher at Digital Equipment Com-

---

[1]Lamport's comment about distributed system may have been somewhat pessimistic, but as we will see later in this book, he was in the midst of developing what we now think of as the theo-

pany's SRC laboratory put it, distributed systems were ones in which your personal computer could become unusable because of a failure in some other computer that you had never heard of, playing a role that you were unaware that you depended upon: not really the most positive or flattering way to characterize the technology. In contrast, if the network was down, you could not read your email, but could still use your computer to write software (or play Tetris).

Although some Xerox Parc researchers expected that Lamport's style of distributed system would turn out to be the key to ubiquitous computing, most Xerox researchers were of the roll-up-one's sleeves and solve the problem mold; when they encountered a problem, they were more likely to dream up a clever engineering solution than to head for Leslie's office for a lesson on the nascent theory. As a result, Xerox pioneered on the practical side of the field, and many of the ideas we will be studying in this text had early forerunners that were developed at Xerox Parc, but never commercialized. By the time the web really picked up steam, the Xerox group had already broken up, although many of those same researchers became leaders in developing today's cloud platforms.

With the benefit of hindsight, one can now see that cloud computing is different from all of these earlier forms of Internet-based computer systems. The cloud reflects a dramatic recent evolution relative to the technologies that predated it, and this evolution has gone in two somewhat opposing directions. On the one hand, the cloud is very elaborate in some ways: servers can send programs over the network for execution within your browser, and there are all sorts of subtle ways for a cloud platform to control the routing of requests and to federate with other cloud provided services, including ones implemented by other companies. And the cloud is massively larger than any prior distributed computing infrastructure: even a few years ago, one rarely saw clustered computing systems with more than 128 or 256 machines; suddenly, we are casually talking about hundreds of thousands and anticipating millions. The Xerox Parc people certainly did not expect this, even though many of the technologies their team created can now be seen as having evolved into key elements of the modern cloud.

Yet the cloud has simultaneously pulled back in some respects relative to distributed computing. As we saw in the introduction, it is not clear that the cloud can safely support applications like air traffic control, or medical computing systems; if it can, it will not do so in the identical way that earlier distributed systems did so. Cloud computing systems, indeed, often guarantee even less than the early networked systems did, and far less than the distributed systems of the 1990s. The evolution to the cloud, in effect, has been a mixture: expansion of things that work, but also a retrenchment from things that did not scale well, even if this entailed a loss of desirable properties.

For example, in the early days of the cloud one tended to view the network as a separate technology from the data centers and clients it linked: the network moved

---

retical foundations that side of the field. Today, Lamport's theories of distributed computing are widely recognized as foundational steps towards solving problems of consistency, fault-tolerance and coordination. Few people have had more impact on any part of computer science.

the bits; the applications made sense of them. Cloud computing has revamped this thinking in many ways: today, the network is controlled to a growing degree by the cloud applications that depend on it, and those applications actively reprogram the network so as to route traffic, filter unwanted messages, and to host content in ways optimized for what the cloud applications need to do. Thus the network has become a true partner of the cloud, and this has begun to force a rapid evolution of network routing protocols and hardware.

In contrast, the weakening of guarantees and consistency properties that we discussed earlier would be an example of a retrenchment: in these areas, the cloud does less than the massive transactional data centers it emerged from were doing ten years ago. Those platforms had simply expanded as much as they could, and when cloud developers realized that they needed to expand by factors of hundreds or thousands of times more, they decided that if trying to provide strong guarantees was turning out to be hard, they would simply have to weaken the guarantees and find ways to live with the consequences.

2.1.2 Is the Cloud a Distributed Computing Technology?

Reduced to the simplest terms, a distributed computing system is a set of computer programs, executing on one or more computers, and coordinating actions by exchanging *messages*. A *computer network* is a collection of computers interconnected by hardware that directly supports message passing and implements routing protocols, so that the messages have a reasonable likelihood of reaching their destinations.

Most distributed computing systems operate over computer networks, but one can also build a distributed computing system in which information flows between the components by means other than message passing. For example, as the relentless advance of computer architectures shifted from raw speed to multi-core parallelism in recent years, a realization emerged that even a single computer is more and more like a small distributed (clustered) computer system of a few years ago. Future operating systems for multi-core processors may turn out to have more in common with Lamport's style of distributed systems than with the single-core operating systems that of just a few years ago, because when those single-core systems are modified to run on multi-core hardware, they turn out to waste huge amounts of time on synchronization and shared memory management. A distributed system architecture can potentially avoid both problems.

In the introduction we used the term *client-server* to refer to a situation in which one computer requests services from another. The client computing system is just your laptop, desktop, pad computer or even your mobile telephone: whatever device is running the application that you, the user, interacts with. The server, of course, is the application that runs at Amazon or Google or Microsoft or any of a dozen other companies and handles your requests. In fact, as we will see, even a simple request might require cooperation by many servers, and those might not even be running at any single place or controlled by any single company. Moreover, for most kinds of request you can initiate, there are vast numbers of server systems that can field

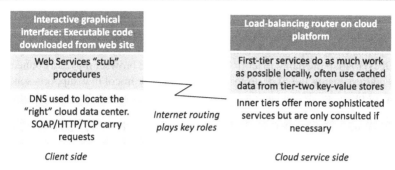

Fig. 2.1   Overall architecture of a cloud computing application

Load-balancing router: Role is to spray requests over available first-tier service instances. Desirable properties include proximity (use the right data center for this user), *affinity* (if possible, requests from a given client should route to the same server), load balancing, effective use of elasticity.

First-tier services are limited to using soft-state or running without any state at all: on restart, any temporary files or data will be wiped away. They make extensive use of key-value stores and caches running at similar scale in the second tier of the cloud.

Inner tiers offer more sophisticated services but are only consulted if necessary. These often include databases, large precomputed index files, etc. Some inner tier services use strong consistency models, such as the ACID model or snapshot isolation, but these are costly and hence the first-tier shields the inner ones from load.

Infrastructure services manage the ensemble, launching new services or shutting down active ones in response to shifting load patterns and failures. They may do this without warning, especially for services in the first-tier.

Back-end applications run batch-style, often on very large numbers of machines with very large data sets. Using tools like MapReduce or Hadoop, they analyze those data sets and create helper files that will be used later by the first-tier.

Fig. 2.2   Elements found within a cloud computing data center (see also Fig. 1.4)

the request; an important part of cloud computing involves routing each request to a good server that has a chance of responding rapidly and, one hopes, correctly.

Let us walk through a simple example to see how this client-server pattern plays out, and to better understand whether we are looking at networked applications or true distributed computing systems. Suppose that you use your mobile phone or a web browser to query the Google Maps service. While the mobile phone "app" may not look much like a web browser, in fact both of these cases do involve web browsers; they simply have different configurations that determine whether or not the web navigation buttons are displayed. So, in either case, we are looking at an application defined by the combination of the browser on the client's computer, and the Google Maps server.

Figures 2.1 and 2.2 illustrate the software layers and protocol stacks that are used on the client and data center sides of the application (Fig. 2.1), and the way that the cloud data center breaks the application into a series of *service tiers* (Fig. 2.2). We'll look at both perspectives in much greater detail in the pages that follow.

These interact through a fairly typical client-server protocol. The browser starts by parsing the URL (http://maps.google.com/maps). It extracts the name of the server, in this case, maps.google.com, and then asks the local Domain Naming System (DNS) to map the name to an IP address. Next, the browser makes a connection to this address, using the TCP protocol: the Internet protocol that supports sending streams of bytes reliably, meaning that no data are lost and that data are delivered in exactly the same order as they were sent. TCP has other features too, such as flow control, security, failure detection, but we do not need to worry about those right now.

So, the browser makes a connection to the server. The server sends back a web page back, which it renders. Of course web pages can be quite elaborate, and Google Maps uses some very sophisticated features. Thus these map pages have subpages, parts that can zoom and otherwise interact with the user, pushpins that open up to reveal photos of various sites, etc. Some pages have blanks that the user can fill in: in the case of maps, these let you type in your home address so that you can click to ask for driving directions. What happens here is that the browser creates a little web page that encodes the address you typed in, and then sends it to the server, which sends back a new page: take a left as you leave your driveway, drive 0.3 miles to the entrance of Route 81 North, etc.

Moreover, browsers are getting more and more elaborate; recent innovations allow a server to send a small program to the browser (using packages like Adobe Flex, Silverlight, Java Fx and others). These programs can run animations or interact with the user in very flexible fast ways, which would obviously not be feasible if the server had to compute each new image. Thus the distinction between a web page that the cloud generates, sends to the client, and that gets displayed passively on the client; and a program that runs on the client consuming data from a server has begun to vanish: to a growing degree, the cloud is able to put computation where computing is the sensible thing to do, data where data are most conveniently stored, and to move data to the computation or computation to the data in very flexible, easily implemented ways. Developers focus on functionality and think in terms of speed and responsiveness, and the technologies needed to map their best ideas into working applications are readily available.

This trend towards increasing sophistication is evident in other ways, as well. We are seeing that a client system may be a very elaborate platform, with data of its own (perhaps preloaded, perhaps downloaded and cached, or perhaps captured from cameras, microphones, or other devices), rendering web pages but also capable of running elaborate programs that might be embedded into (or linked to) web pages, and accessing data not just from the main server platform but also from other web sites, such as web sites maintained by content hosting companies or advertising intermediaries. The client could also be mobile, which can have important implications too: a mobile system might experience varying connectivity, and could even see its IP address change over time (for example, if you take your laptop from your office to the coffee shop up the street, the IP address assigned to it would change each time it rebinds to a different access point).

Let us think for a moment about how client mobility impacts our basic Google Maps scenario. Suppose that you are using Google Maps, but doing so as you move about. Google Maps needs a way to recognize that the same machine is involved in this series of requests. It cannot just use the IP address for that purpose, since that changes. Accordingly, it does the obvious thing: the application leaves a small file on your computer, called a *cookie*. The file can contain pretty much anything, but generally is kept small to minimize transmission costs: when you connect to the Google Maps service, the cookie (if any is available) is included with the initial connection request. But now think about the role of the network: previously, we described the job of the network in simple terms: it connects this IP address to that IP address, trusting the DNS to map host names to addresses, and moves bytes back and forth. Our mobility story is revealing extra complexities: the IP address of the mobile device may be changing as you move about; the cookie uniquely identifies you, but is buried in the application data stream. A seemingly simple networking role suddenly starts to look unexpectedly complex!

To appreciate the implications of these issues, let us briefly drill down on precisely how cloud computing systems and network routing interplay. As we do this, keep in mind that many cloud applications maintain some form of continuous connection to the servers, so that as you move about, they can update the information shown to the end-user. Thus, your mobile device is moving, and yet there is a form of continuity to the connection. We will see that the combination of issues that arises leads to a really complicated picture of network routing, and one that can come as a real surprise to readers who learned how IP networks operate even as recently as a five years ago.

Notice that from the perspective of the network, the IP address of the mobile device could change abruptly as the device moves around: first, it had an IP address assigned by the user's company, then suddenly it became an IP address assigned by Gimme! Coffee. And now the IP address is one assigned by T-Mobile. The application-specific cookie does establish continuity here, yet the network router will not see those cookies; it only sees the IP addresses.

In fact, the end-host addressing issue is even more complex than we are making it sound, because of the prevalence of what are called *network address translation* or NAT technologies. Many devices, such as wireless routers, have a single outward-facing IP address but support a small interior network, and when this occurs, they often use their own IP addressing space for the interior machines. What this means is that if I sit down in Gimme! Coffee in Ithaca, and then check my IP address, there is a good chance it will be 192.68.1.x, where x is some small number like 2 or 3. Yet the Google system sees a very different IP address, perhaps 176.31.54.144: that assigned to Gimme! Coffee by its ISP. The NAT box translates back and forth: when a packet is sent from an interior machine to the outside, the box replaces the IP address and port number in the packet with the IP address of the NAT box and a dynamically selected port number that it associates with the original sender. Later, when a reply packet is received, the NAT box maps in the other direction. NAT functionality and is very common today, and runs so quickly that we are completely unaware of it. Indeed, we would have run out of IPv4 addresses long ago if we did not have NAT capabilities. With NAT, each router can be a gateway to a huge range of IP addresses—perhaps, a whole cloud computing data center full of them.

In newspaper articles about the Internet one reads that an IP address is like a street name and house address, but here we can see that a single IP addresses might be in use by a great many computers. For example, as just noted, the local Gimme! Coffee here in Ithaca assigns IP addresses that look like 192.68.1.x. Well, it happens that the computer on which this chapter was being written *also* thinks its IP address is 192.68.1.2, even though I am nowhere near Gimme! Coffee right this minute. The reason is that 192.168.1.2 is perhaps the world's most heavily reused address: most wireless routers are preset to assign addresses starting with 192.68.1.1, which the router uses for itself. My router works this way, and it assigned my laptop computer the next address in the sequence. All over the world there must be millions of wireless routers, each of which uses 192.68.1.1 for itself and each of which has assigned 192.68.1.2 to some local user's laptop. The situation is similar to a world in which every town has a Main Street, and every Main Street has a building at number 2.

With NAT-enabled routers on the path, the Internet route between two points is really an implicit part of the address. If we trace a packet from your machine to Google Maps, we will see that your machine first routed it to the wireless router at Gimme!, which replaced the source address with its own address. Next it forwarded that packet through the Gimme! cable modem, which may even have done a second remapping very similar to the first one. Now your packet is inside the local Internet Service Provider (ISP), which maintains routing tables telling it that to get from here to Google.com, packets should be passed to the AT&T network, and so forth. Step by step, the packet advances (just as you were taught to expect a few years ago), but the source and destination addresses and port numbers potentially change each time the packet passes through an active routing element. The route from Gimme! in Ithaca to the nearest Google Maps data center probably involves 15 to 20 hops, and as many as five or six of these could remap the addresses as part of their routing functionality.

The sense in which the route is "part" of your computer's address is that for Google's servers to respond to your request, packets need to be sent back using the sender address in the IP header. This, of course, will have been modified by each NAT box in the route. Thus, the Google response travels to the last NAT box that your packet traversed on its way into Google, then from that box to the next one closer to you, and so forth until we get back to the router at Gimme!, which replaces the address with the internal IP address for your machine on the Gimme! wireless network. If you were to move your machine to a setting with a different wireless router, you might actually be assigned the same IP address (192.61.1.x) and yet packets sent by Google to your previous address will not get to you anymore. RSS feeds and Internet radio feeds and movie streams and podcasts will all fail, and need to be restarted from the new location.

So we have traced the route from Gimme! to Google and back. But two more questions arise: which Google data center was used? And which machine? The former question matters because Google.com is a single name by which all of Google's infrastructure is named, yet Google operates hundreds of data centers, worldwide. Obviously, the company would typically map a particular user's request to the nearest data center, which it does by forcing the DNS to hand out different IP addresses to different users, depending on where they originate—something it learns by looking at their IP addresses! Given the ubiquity of NAT boxes, one suddenly appreciates just how complex that determination can be: a million distinct machines, all over the globe, may claim that their IP address is 192.68.1.2, and that they need to send a packet to Google.com—meaning, the nearest Google data center.

As it happens, this localization problem is solvable, but not in a trivial way. Any textbook needs to limit its scope and this one will not cover networking technologies in great detail. In a nutshell, researchers have found ways to correlate delay to path length, and cloud computing data centers take advantage of this to create a kind of network coordinate system a bit like a GPS coordinate; two widely cited examples of systems offering this functionality are Vivaldi (Dabek et al. 2004) and Meridian (Wong et al. 2005). The basic idea is to establish some set of *landmarks*. The client system measures its round-trip times and perhaps some aspects of the route used to estimate its distance from each landmark, then encodes these data into a tuple that functions much like a 3-dimensional map coordinate in the real world. Given two such tuples, one can estimate the network latency between the machines at each location. And this functionality can also be embedded into the DNS name resolution mechanism: based on observations of timing, a company like Google can localize your DNS to at least some degree, and then use that localization to instruct that particular DNS server to give out this particular IP address as the mapping of Google.com. Thus Google is able to direct your machine to the closest data center, with one or two other options offered as good backup possibilities (DNS mappings typically resolve to a primary IP address but list some number of backup options as well). Notice that we've arrived at a definition of "closest" that minimizes network latency and maximizes bandwidth; the best choice of data center might not be the one that is physically nearest to your location.

So you launch your mapping application. It needs to map Google Maps to an IP address, and asks the DNS for help. The DNS does a quick request to Google, asking for the IP address to which your requests should be directed. From then on, at least until this DNS record expires, the DNS will give the same answer repeatedly. This, then, gives Google a way to direct queries from Chinese users to its Hong Kong data center, queries from India to a data center in Hydrabad, and queries from Ithaca to a data center somewhere in New Hampshire, or Canada: Google likes to place data centers in settings that are remote, where power is cheap, where the weather is as cool as possible, and with good networking capabilities.

Google can play with the expiration values on these DNS records: to exert very fine-grained control over the DNS mapping, it hands out DNS records that expire instantly; in such cases, every single host-to-IP-address mapping for machines at Google.com will need to be forwarded to Google. That can be slow, but gives Google total control. If Google's servers believe that it is safe to do so, on the other hand, they can hand out DNS records with much longer expiration times. Performance for DNS mapping will be much improved, but Google cannot retract those mappings other than by waiting for them to expire.

What happens after a packet reaches Google in New Hampshire? Here, a further complication arises: Google has its own specialized routers to handle incoming traffic; they look at each packet and select a Google server to handle it on the basis of a wide range of criteria: the requested service, the current configuration of the data center, load estimates, which server you last talked to, etc. A single data center can also host many .com names: YouTube.com and Google.com could route to the same data center. In some sense, we should understand the IP addresses and machines as being a virtual overlay, superimposed on the physical network and physical data center hardware, but accurately *emulating* a collection of networks and a collection of distinct, dedicated computers. This facilitates creation of new cloud computing applications. In one of the more common ways of creating a service, the developer implements the service on a development system but then uploads a virtual machine image, and the cloud deploys as few or as many copies as it likes, spraying incoming requests over the replicas to spread load.

Google, then, as a company hosting large numbers of virtualized services (including these kinds of virtualized web site), has a great deal of control over routing, and it needs that control in order to ensure that you as the end-user will have an acceptable experience and that it, as the provider, will make the best possible use of its data center resources. Part of this is determined by IP addresses, but because those are virtual, other factors also come into play: the actual route that was used from a client into the DNS hierarchy, the route from the DNS server that translated the address to Google, and even the cookies that identify the actual client. Ideally, Google needs to use all of these elements to control routing so as to optimize such aspects as performance, cost of the solution and security against disruption by malfunctioning applications. Moreover, Google will make an effort to route the stream of requests originating in your mobile device to some single server that will handle them all, unless a failure or some other kind of management event happens to force a reconfiguration. This way, if that server maintains state on your behalf, you get a continuous evolving story from your mobile application. And yet because the network does the routing, the only parts of this story that the IP network itself observes are the source and destination IP addresses and port numbers in use on each leg of the current path.

Here we encounter an example of a current cloud computing challenge. Today, Google is not able to inspect the contents of incoming packets until they actually reach one of its data centers. Thus, suppose your mobile application loses its connection and tries to reconnect. Perhaps its IP address has changed, and very likely it will find itself talking to a different DNS server than it was using moments earlier. That server may not have any knowledge of which Google data center you were talking to. Thus, your reconnect might show up at a very different Google data center than your previous packets were talking to.

When the reconnect arrives, the load-balancing component of the data center can inspect the packet, find the cookie, and perhaps make an association to the prior activity, in which case the end-user experience will be nearly seamless. But it may also be too late to preserve application continuity, and that seems especially likely if because of the changing IP address used by your mobile, the reconnection request was routed to a different data center. In that case, you'll experience a very annoying loss of continuity. If your friend were to tell you about some other mapping system that never breaks down this way, you might switch.

Let us compare the way this works today with the ways it might be improved, as an opportunity to peer into the way that cloud computing makes tradeoffs right now. To be concrete, assume that the client was watching a movie and that it was streaming from a server S in Google's YouTube system, and that just as we reached time 10:27 in the movie, the connection broke. What are the options for masking this problem?

Notice that there can be many reasons for a connection failure: the client may have lost connectivity to the Internet or been shut off, the server may have failed or been "elastically" shut down or migrated (really, the same thing, since the cloud migrates a server by killing one instance and starting a different one), the Internet routing system may be having issues, etc. In our toy scenario, the client is still up. So it issues a completely new connection request to YouTube, but now the URL encodes the offset into the stream. Ideally, the player resumes seamlessly; now some server S′ is probably handling the request, and playing back starting at time 10:28.

How long will this take? To mask the outage the new connection would need to be up and running within a few seconds. But of course S′ may not have a cached copy of the movie, in which case it would need to fetch a copy from the global file system. S′ might also need to recheck the client's credentials, something S would have done during the initial connection. Thus the client probably will see at least some delay during this process: very likely long enough to exceed the few seconds of tolerance. Thus it is not uncommon to need to restart that sort of transfer manually today.

One could do better. For example, if the cookie the client presents to S′ has some sort of "recently validated" token in it, S′ could cut that step short. But this still would not eliminate delays associated with the film not being locally available.

Suppose that S is still running, and we lost the connection entirely because of mobility: one of those changing IP address scenarios. In this case, if the protocol used between the cloud and the video player includes some kind of ticket representing the original server, S, the player could reconnect to S under some sort of server name: S.YouTube.com. Your local DNS would not know how to resolve this name, so it would be passed to YouTube (that is, to Google.com as the host for YouTube.com), where an attempt could be made to reconnect you to your original server, S. Thus with a bit of DNS trickery, the client ends up talking to the original server, which has a warm cache, and we get playback more or less instantly. Notice that "S" doesn't have to be a name bound to a specific physical server, either: in modern computing settings, a computer can have more than one name, and those names can be moved around. So "S.YouTube.com" is really more of a logical name for a virtual server, not necessarily the physical name of a specific machine in a specific location.

In fact one can even get this behavior when a server migrates. Suppose that S failed but that our cloud system assigned its roles to S′ prior to S shutting down, so that S′ has a chance to prefetch the movie and copy the credentials. In such cases, one can actually splice a new TCP connection to an old one seamlessly, so that the connection never breaks at all. The same techniques can also support IP address migration on the client side (we will discuss this in more detail in Chap. 4). These schemes can be surprisingly lightweight (the former approach is transparent but a bit more expensive, the latter requires some help from the endpoint application (the video player in the client, or the server), but imposes almost no additional cost at all, and can reestablish connections in tens of milliseconds. Thus one could actually imagine systems that completely mask disconnection and offer continuous streaming availability so long as the outage was one of these recoverable cases.

We do not see such mechanisms in use today, for purely pragmatic reasons. First, as noted, even if we did use these techniques, there would still be cases they cannot handle: for example, if a client vanishes, how long should its server wait before giving up on the connection? Thus the disruption scenario would need to be pretty common relative to these unrecoverable ones in order for the schemes we have cited to be beneficial: if they could overcome 99% of all crashes, they would make obvious sense; if they only cover 6% of them, far less so. One can guess that the benefit must not be all that high since today's cloud platforms are quick to embrace improvements that end-users would notice.

Thus, rather than use fancy failover schemes, today we see other sorts of reconnection hacks. For example, right now video playback is the dominant case where such issues arise, and realistically, video playback works reasonably well without needing these fancier reconnection solutions. Applications that need better behavior, such as voice-over-IP telephone connections, avoid relaying data through the cloud: Skype, for example, uses a cloud platform to make the initial phone connection, but after that tries to use direct point-to-point connectivity between the callers. Internet conferencing solutions are just not all that popular. But if use of such technologies grows, the cloud could easily evolve to mask disruptions more effectively.

Our example illustrates a pattern we will see throughout this textbook. Today's cloud is a world of tradeoffs that optimize certain kinds of applications; tomorrow's cloud is likely to make these same tradeoffs in different ways, depending on the way that demand in the marketplace evolves, and on the kinds of application that are bringing in the lion's share of the revenue. One reason for learning about techniques like recoverable TCP connections is that even if they are not widely used today, they could be the key to success in some important setting tomorrow. Moreover, while it made sense in the past to talk about distributed systems as distinct from networked ones, the cloud is so complex that these simple distinctions no longer can be applied. Recalling Lamportis point, in the cloud we all "depend" on a great many components. If any fails, our computers could become unusable.

Figure 2.3 shows the overall architecture of a typical cloud computing application, highlighting the various routing and address translation layers we have discussed. Sophisticated applications control the DNS mapping from host name to IP address, typically seeking to direct each user to the nearest data center, and then as the request reaches that data center, redirecting it again to reach a lightly loaded machine in the first tier.

Figure 2.4 shows some elements one might find inside a typical cloud computing data center. Here we see the router and DNS at the top left, vectoring requests to the highly scaled and elastic row of first-tier services. The elements of this layer can be spun up or shut down very abruptly as demand varies A second row of staleful services runs behind the first-tier applications providing somewhat greater functionality, but at higher cost and with less ability to scale up or down as quickly. These

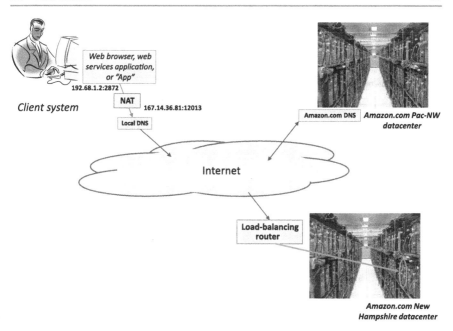

Fig. 2.3 Overall architecture of a cloud computing system focusing on the routing of a user's request to a data center. The user's initial request to Amazon.com is vectored by the local Domain Name Service (DNS) to a DNS service managed by Amazon, which selects a data center to which the user's traffic should be routed. In this illustration, the DNS that receives the mapping request happens to be the one running at one of Amazon's Pacific NorthWest data centers, but the user will be redirected to an Amazon data center in New Hampshire, where a load-balancer will in turn redirect it to a specific server. There may be one or more network address translation devices on the path; these convert between an internal IP address and port number and an external IP address and port number, with the effect of greatly enlarging the address space

in turn are supported by various databases and files. In the back-end of the system, a variety of offline applications collaborate to maintain those databases and files, manage the infrastructure, share data over large numbers of nodes, etc. The most dramatic level of scaling occurs in the first tier, which absorbs as much of the work as possible, seeking to offer locally responsive behavior even if this may entail running on stale data or not waiting for a slow component to respond, which are just two of the many cases in which a cloud system might behave in an inconsistent and perhaps insecure manner.

Notice that any particular data center will have its own set of services and that many cloud systems would look quite different from the one shown in the figure. Cloud systems share an overall style, but the details depend very much on the particular applications being supported and the platform developer's design choices. Indeed, most cloud systems evolved independently to solve specific problems: the Amazon.com system to support its e-commerce web sites, the Facebook system to support its social networking applications, Google's to support search. Then as time passed, they grew more and more general and began to host third-party content.

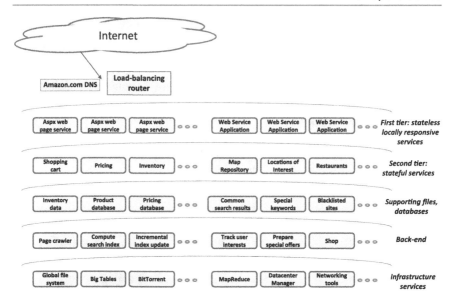

Fig. 2.4 Interior of a cloud computing system, showing some of the major functional tiers on which the textbook will focus

Today, there are a few dozen major cloud computing platforms, each with its own specialties, and while there is a great deal of functional overlap between the resulting systems, there are also big differences.

In this text we will not focus on any specific cloud platform but will try to abstract major questions and look at the fundamental issues that are posed. On the other hand, we will look closely at some of the most widely discussed cloud technologies, such as cloud computing file systems (GFS for Google, Zookeeper from Yahoo!, as well as others), key-value stores (BigTable in the case of Google, Dynamo for Amazon), locking services (Chubby, which uses the Paxos protocols), compute engines (MapReduce, also widely used through the Hadoop open-source version), data distribution tools (BitTorrent), and others. Our hope is to strike a balance: to expose the reader to some of the "big name" technologies that are best known and most widely deployed, while also pushing to deeper questions such as just how one offers consistency in a data replication service, or a locking service.

2.1.3 What Does Reliability Mean in the Cloud?

We have been fairly informal about our terminology. let us pin things down. When computer systems exchange messages over a network, we say that a *protocol* is running between the applications that participate. More formally, we will use the term "protocol" in reference to an algorithm governing the exchange of messages, by which a collection of processes coordinate their actions and communicate information among themselves. Much as a *program* is a set of instructions, and a *process* denotes the execution of those instructions, a *protocol* is a set of instructions governing the communication in a distributed program, and a distributed computing system is the result of executing some collection of such protocols to coordinate the actions of a collection of processes in a network.

We keep using the term *reliability* but this needs a bit more precision too. After all, reliability can have many meanings. Here are a few that matter here:

- *Fault tolerance*: The ability of a distributed computing system to recover from component failures without performing incorrect actions. (Of course, the application designer gets to define correct and incorrect behavior.)

- *High availability*: In the context of a fault-tolerant distributed computing system, the ability of the system to restore correct operation, permitting it to resume providing services during periods when some components have failed. A highly available system may provide reduced service for short periods of time while reconfiguring itself.

- *Continuous availability*: A highly available system with a very small recovery time, capable of providing uninterrupted service to its users. The reliability properties of a continuously available system are unaffected or only minimally affected by failures.

- *Recoverability*: Also in the context of a fault-tolerant distributed computing system, the ability of failed components to restart themselves and rejoin the system, after the cause of failure has been repaired.

- *Consistency*: The ability of the system to coordinate related actions by multiple components, often in the presence of concurrency and failures. Consistency underlies the ability of a distributed system to emulate a non-distributed system. Later, though, we will see that there are many ways to implement this kind of emulation—many ways to implement consistency guarantees. Thus when we commented that consistency is an issue in the cloud, and talked about CAP, that really relates to one particular consistency model (the one used in database settings that support ACID guarantees). One can accept that this form of consistency will not work in the cloud, and yet still build cloud-scale solutions that have strong consistency properties.

- *Scalability*: The ability of a system to continue to operate correctly even as some aspect is scaled to a larger size. For example, we might increase the size of the network on which the system is running—doing so increases the frequency of such events as network outages and could degrade a "non-scalable" system. We might increase numbers of users, or numbers of servers, or load on the system. Scalability thus has many dimensions; a *scalable system* would normally specify the dimensions in which it achieves scalability and the degree of scaling it can sustain.

- *Security*: The ability of the system to protect data, services, and resources against misuse by unauthorized users.

- *Privacy*: The ability of the system to protect the identity and locations of its users, or the contents of sensitive data, from unauthorized disclosure.

- *Correct specification*: The assurance that the system solves the intended problem.

- *Correct implementation*: The assurance that the system correctly implements its specification.

- *Predictable performance*: The guarantee that a distributed system achieves desired levels of performance—for example, data throughput from source to destination, latencies measured for critical paths, requests processed per second, and so forth.
- *Timeliness*: In systems subject to real-time constraints, the assurance that actions are taken within the specified time bounds, or are performed with a desired degree of temporal synchronization between the components.

Underlying many of these issues are questions of tolerating failures. Failure, too, can have many meanings:

- *Halting failures*: In this model, a process or computer either works correctly, or simply stops executing and crashes without taking incorrect actions, as a result of failure. As the model is normally specified, there is no way to detect that the process has halted except by timeout: It stops sending "keep alive" messages or responding to "pinging" messages and hence other processes can deduce that it has failed.
- *Fail-stop failures*: These are accurately detectable halting failures. In this model, processes fail by halting. However, other processes that may be interacting with the faulty process also have a completely accurate way to detect such failures— for example, a fail-stop environment might be one in which timeouts can be used to monitor the status of processes, and *no timeout occurs unless the process being monitored has actually crashed*. Obviously, such a model may be unrealistically optimistic, representing an idealized world in which the handling of failures is reduced to a pure problem of how the system should react when a failure is sensed. If we solve problems with this model, we then need to ask how to relate the solutions to the real world.
- *Send-omission failures*: These are failures to send a message that, according to the logic of the distributed computing systems, should have been sent. Send-omission failures are commonly caused by a lack of buffering space in the operating system or network interface, which can cause a message to be discarded after the application program has sent it but before it leaves the sender's machine. Perhaps surprisingly, few operating systems report such events to the application.
- *Receive-omission failures*: These are similar to send-omission failures, but they occur when a message is lost near the destination process, often because of a lack of memory in which to buffer it or because evidence of data corruption has been discovered.
- *Network failures*: These occur when the network loses messages sent between certain pairs of processes.
- *Network partitioning failures*: These are a more severe form of network failure, in which the network fragments into disconnected sub-networks, within which messages can be transmitted, but between which messages are lost. When a failure of this sort is repaired, one talks about *merging* the network partitions. Network partitioning failures are a common problem in modern distributed systems; hence, we will discuss them in detail in Part III of this book.
- *Timing failures*: These occur when a temporal property of the system is violated— for example, when a clock on a computer exhibits a value that is unacceptably far

from the values of other clocks, or when an action is taken too soon or too late, or when a message is delayed by longer than the maximum tolerable delay for a network connection.

- *Byzantine failures*: This is a term that captures a wide variety of other faulty behaviors, including data corruption, programs that fail to follow the correct protocol, and even malicious or adversarial behaviors by programs that actively seek to force a system to violate its reliability properties.

Readers might want to pause at this point and consider some cloud computing application that they often use: perhaps, our map-based applications, or perhaps some other application such as Shazam (a mobile application for recognizing music from small samples), or Twitter. Look at these notions of reliability, and imagine yourself in the role of a lead developer creating that application. Which forms of reliability would matter most, if you want to ensure that clients can count upon your solution as a reliable mobile tool that would play a big role in their mobile lives? What obstacles to that form of reliability can you identify, and where would be your best hope of addressing the resulting requirements? The client system? The Internet itself? Or the cloud computing system? You'll see that even without knowing how cloud computing systems really work, you actually can reason about a question like this. Moreover, you can probably convince yourself that the answer necessarily involves many moving parts: for any sophisticated cloud functionality, the client can (and probably must) provide some of the needed functionality, the network others, and the cloud system itself has its own role to play. The cloud solution may be the conductor of the orchestra, but without ways to control each of these components, it would not be possible to build reliable cloud applications.

2.2   Components of a Reliable Distributed Computing System

So, at the end of the day, where does reliability really come from? There isn't any single magic answer. Reliable distributed computing systems are assembled from basic building blocks; in general, those building blocks can experience failures, and depending on the nature of the problem and its severity, the system may be able to overcome the issue, or it may shut down or malfunction. Thus, the Google Maps service can tolerate the crash of a cloud server running the map application: if this happens, the client requests will be reissued and routed to a different server. Of course, some information might be lost, but the map application is designed so that such events have minimal disruptive impact. But suppose that a recent accident has closed a bridge on the route you are taking. Will your Google Maps unit know? This is less certain: while mapping systems track such events, to get this information to you the server you are talking to will need to see the update promptly; your mobile device will need to talk to that server; the network will need to be stable enough to let it download the relevant data. Over time, the cloud can certainly do all of these things. If split-second decisions are involved, however, we run into a situation for which the cloud as currently designed just is not ideal (obviously, some systems, like Twitter, are specialized in replicating some forms of information, but those are specialized and not typical of the platforms in the widest use). The point here is that even if a map application is perfectly reliable, you might perceive it as unreliable if it fails to warn you of a closed bridge. Reliability must be judged by the end-user experience, not in terms of any kind of narrower, more technical definition focused purely on the reliability of individual subsystems.

Staleness of underlying data is just one of many issues of this kind. Cloud systems are also at risk of being confused by data that were incorrect in the first place, or that became corrupted once they entered the system. Moreover, systems like the ones we have described sometimes turn into targets for hackers or other kinds of intruder, such as foreign intelligence organizations or corporate espionage teams. Attacks can come from the outside or the inside: not every single employee at the company necessarily buys into the "do not be evil" motto. One can only protect against some of these kinds of issue, and even when we can, the mechanisms are sometimes expensive or use techniques that do not scale very well. Some forms of reliability, in effect, go beyond what a cloud platform is designed to do.

Your job, as the designer of a reliable cloud computing application, will be to start by thinking hard about what reliability needs to mean for the end-user, taking a holistic approach: you need to think about what the end-user is trying to accomplish, and to view your system as a black box, thinking about its properties without rushing to make decisions about how it will be built. You'll need to set reasonable goals: a system might be able to protect itself against some forms of problems, but perhaps not others; some properties may even be mutually exclusive. Moreover, you need to strike a balance between the costs of the reliability properties you desire to offer and other properties, such as the speed and scalability of your solution. Even the complexity of the solution should be viewed as an issue: a complex reliability-enhancing technique could actually decrease reliability by being hard to implement. A simpler solution that offers less coverage may still be more reliable if it can be completed on schedule and on budget, tested more carefully, and if the limitations do not pose frequent and grave problems for its users.

Our job in this text will not be to address this software engineering task. Instead, we will take up the challenge at the next step: given sensible reliability goals, we will focus here on the technical options for achieving them. In effect, we will create a menu of options, within which the savvy designer can later pick and chose. Reliability will not turn out to be a one-size-fits-all story; for any given purpose, it demands choices and often requires compromises. Indeed, sometimes reliability comes as much from steps taken outside of a system as it does from the ones we take within it. For example, when designing health-care systems and air traffic control systems, one explicitly recognizes that even the most reliable system will sometimes fail. Accordingly, we use a fail-safe mindset: we design the solution with safeguards that will ensure the safety of the end-user no matter what may happen within the system. Thus, if a cardiac monitoring system goes offline, one wants it to somehow signal that the technology has failed; this is far preferable than trying to engineer a system that can never fail.

2.3   Summary: Reliability in the Cloud

Our simple example leads to several kinds of insight. First, we have seen that cloud computing systems need to be understood in terms of three distinct components, each of which has a distinct role (and each, of course, is itself structured as a set of components). The first component is the client application: perhaps a browser, or perhaps some sort of program that uses the same protocols employed by browsers, issuing requests to cloud-hosted services and receiving replies from them. These requests and replies take the form of web pages, but in a very simple format intended for machine consumption, not humans. The second component is the network itself, which moves the data, and is built as a complex assemblage of routers, together with a small set of network-hosted technologies like DNS (to map host names to IP addresses) and BGP (one of the protocols used by routers to maintain routing tables). Indeed, while we often think of the Internet as a kind of fancy wire carrying data from our laptops to the data centers that provide services like email, the better mental image would be more akin to those very fancy Swiss watches stuffed with springs and gears and all sorts of strange looking twisty things, all moving in a completely implausible ballet. But this Swiss watch is vastly larger and has far more moving parts! Finally, the third major component of a cloud computing system is the cloud computing data center itself. That data center reaches out to control the routing from your computer to its point of ingress, and then the ingress router examines your packets and redirects them to some server. That server, talking to other servers, builds a response for you: you're a client of the server, but it is a client of other servers and services.

Next, we have seen that the system per-se is really a part of a bigger story. The end-user is concerned with that bigger story, not the minutia of how the system works internally. Reliability is an end-user property; the end-user's goals and perception should shape the technical goals and decisions we make as we look more closely at each of the three components of the solution.

When we ask about reliability, we have seen that we are being sloppy: many people have an intuitive sense that reliability is about availability and quick response, but we might have any of a number of other properties in mind; moreover, some settings actually require some mixture of properties for safety (for example, a controller for an insulin pump should either operate properly, or it should go offline and a warning should sound), while others intend the term in a looser sense. Speaking broadly, we have seen that reliability in the cloud as it exists today is of this latter kind: it can be hard to pin down a precise meaning for the term, and the kind of reliability we are offered comes from many separate mechanisms, each working to overcome certain kinds of issue. These can add up to a convincing illusion of reliability, but can also break down in visible ways, without anything in the cloud realizing that anything has "gone wrong." After all, what does "wrong" mean for a system that does not really define "right?"

To the extent that a reliability property in question is pinned down, there may be many ways to obtain the desired behavior. Among these, we might change the application to require a different property (this can be a good idea if the original property is unreasonably costly or even infeasible), we might manage to show that a standard cloud service can achieve the desired property, or we might find a non-standard way to implement what we seek, hosting the resulting system on a cloud platform (and taking steps to confirm that the cloud will not do anything that might prevent our implementation for working correctly).

Depending on the situation, not all of these options will be applicable. For example, modifying an application is not always feasible; there are often serious requirements that we just cannot hack around. Building an entire home-brew infrastructure is not a minor undertaking: you will have a big job, and your solution, however good it may be at guaranteeing whatever you set out to promise, may seem to be lacking all sorts of basic features that users have come to expect. Moreover, the experience in the field makes it clear that any approach that deviates too far from the main-stream will later seem hard to maintain, expensive and ultimately will fail. When feasible, the best choice is to just find some way to run the needed solution on a standard cloud infrastructure, but to take steps to confirm that it does what we really need from it—to prove, in effect, that the solution will really solve the problem.

This approach does raise questions, however. First, building a cloud-hosted application that pushes beyond the limits of the standard cloud is not a minor undertaking. As we have observed, and will see in upcoming chapters, the cloud has bought heavily into the end-to-end principle and the CAP conjecture, leaving reliability and security and other similar properties to the client and the server, and leaving the Internet to play one role: moving packets as rapidly as possible. But we will see that sometimes, one can strengthen these kinds of behavior in ways that respect the standards, and yet give us more than the standards can provide. Second, even if our solution works on day zero, we need to worry that as the cloud evolves, something that was implicitly assumed in the application might cease to hold.

A second question really relates to a stylistic choice for this textbook. Would it make more sense to dive deep on specific questions, such as the network routing control problem we discussed above? Or should we focus on design patterns: paradigms that one can study in a more abstracted way, and then later translate back to practice when working on specific applications. On this the author of this text feels conflicted: having built cloud computing services of his own, it is absolutely clear that a book of cloud computing recipes could be hugely successful. Right now, the best way to find out how to do many things is just to issue enough web search queries to stumble on an example in which someone else did the thing you are trying to do, and then copy the code. This is definitely not the best way to learn, and seems certain to propagate mistakes from the random web pages you stumble upon into your own software. Yet this is how one does it today.

Nonetheless, this will not be a book of recipes. Instead, we will opt for the second approach, teasing out abstracted questions that we can focus upon in a clean way, solve, and then either implement as needed, or perhaps package within the Isis^2 library (Appendix B), if the technique is a bit tricky. In the chapters that follow, we will often pose important questions that admit many kinds of answer. Sometimes we will lay the options out one by one; in other cases we will just focus on the best known answer, or the approach actually used in cloud computing standards and platforms. As a reader of this text, you will need to think these questions out on your own: is this the right way to pose my application goals? Can my goals be realized in a low-cost way? Given multiple possible realizations, which is the best choice? There will not be any simple formula to guide you to the answers, but an approach that focuses on scalability and simplicity will rarely steer you wrong.

Einstein is said to have remarked that one should strive to make things as simple as possible... but not simpler. Cloud computing systems are unavoidably complex, because they have so many components, connected in such elaborate and dynamically evolving ways. We could lose ourselves within this complexity and not learn very much at all. Within the cloud, we work with a vast array of mechanisms and normally, those mechanisms are working and doing a wonderful job; this is why cloud computing has taken off. Yet our overarching theme in this text is reliability, and the real challenges arise not when all works as hoped, but when something goes wrong: how, then, will the application behave? Today's cloud often opts for the simplest solution that will not trigger a crash and a blue screen. But if we need to make a cloud application more reliable than what you get in the standard way, we should expect that in some cases, there will not be any easy way to avoid grappling with fairly complex issues. Oversimplifying would simply be a recipe for unreliability.

2.4 Related Reading

The slide set used by Eric Brewer for his 2000 PODC keynote talk on cloud computing scalability (Brewer 2000), and the slide sets and remarks of speakers at the 2008 ACM Workshop on Large Scale Distributed Systems (LADIS) are well worth looking at. LADIS, in particular, featured a number of cloud computing experts (see http://www.cs.cornell.edu/projects/ladis2008).

Stanford law professor Lawrence Lessig has written several fascinating books on the growth of the Internet and the impact of technology on society (see Lessig 1999).

On the topic of fail-safe application design (see Leveson 1995).

General discussion of network architectures and the OSI hierarchy (see Architecture Projects Management Limited 1989, 1991a, 1991b; Comer 1991; Comer and Stevens 1993; Coulouris et al. 1994; Cristian and Delancy 1990; Tanenbaum 1988; XTP Forum).

Pros and cons of layered architectures (see Abbott and Peterson 1993; Braun and Diot 1995; Clark and Tennenhouse 1987, 1990; Karamcheti and Chien 1994; Kay and Pasquale 1993; Ousterhout 1990; van Renesse et al. 1988, 1989).

Reliable stream communication (see Comer 1991; Comer and Stevens 1991, 1993; Coulouris et al. 1994; Jacobson 1988; Ritchie 1984; Tanenbaum 1988).

Failure models and classifications (see Chandra and Toueg 1991; Chandra et al. 1992, Cristian 1991b; Cristian and Delancy 1990; Fisher et al. 1985b; Gray and Reuter 1993; Lamport 1978a, 1978b, 1984; Marzullo 1990; Sabel and Marzullo 1994; Skeen 1982a; Srikanth and Toueg 1987).

Client Perspective

3

3.1 The Life of a Cloud Computing Client

In this chapter, we drill down on some of the major issues that a cloud computing client system must handle. The client application itself will not be our focus; it might be a web browser (perhaps running a sophisticated application coded in a language like SilverLight or Caja), an "App" (these are really just a category of web browser pages designed to run without the usual task bars and buttons), or it could be some arbitrary program that uses Web Services protocols to issue requests to services running in the cloud. Whatever the application, it faces the challenge of connecting to an appropriate server (some machine within the cloud running the desired service), preparing and sending requests in the format favored by the cloud (an encoding called SOAP, which is actually a dialect of XML—a form of very structured web page), handling disruptions such as server failures or connectivity problems, running downloaded code safely (assuming that the application is one that can run downloaded code; this is not always the case), copying with mobility, and dealing with some of the annoyances created by the modern web, such as ISPs that aggressively insert hyperlinks to their commercial partners in situations where they believe that doing so will not break anything.

Our goal here is to provide an overview, although some of the functionality we will touch upon is quite complex. The decision to not go deep reflects a question of balance: a comprehensive treatment of these topics could easily consume an entire textbook. At the end of the chapter we suggest some additional readings that could be explored to learn more about the network layer and the ways client systems use them, the details of the Web Services standards, and some of the many products available for application development in this space.

K.P. Birman, *Guide to Reliable Distributed Systems*, Texts in Computer Science, DOI 10.1007/978-1-4471-2416-0_3, © Springer-Verlag London Limited 2012

3.2   Web Services

3.2.1   How Web Browsers Talk to Web Sites

Cloud computing systems adhere to a collection of *Web Services* standards (some readers may have encountered these under an alias: the US government and military use the web services standards, but with a different acronym: they refer to these as Global Information Grid or GIG standards). The web services area is a large and active one and very much a moving target: it includes a huge collection of standards that evolve regularly as existing ones are revised and new sub-standards are agreed upon by the web services consortium, a group called W3. Here, we will discuss just a few of its many components.

A Web service is most easily imagined as a program that runs in a data center, accepting requests for web pages in the form of URLs (perhaps with additional parameters), and then generating and sending back web pages to the web browser that initiated the session. The basics are very simple: the browser starts by making a connection to the server, typically using TCP. TCP engages in the three-way handshake for which it is so famous, and establishes a two-way stream over which data can be sent reliably: in order and without loss. TCP also takes care of matching data rates: it gradually ramps up the size of its sliding window using the so-called *slow start* policy until it reaches a point at which some router, or the remote machine (in this example, the server) signals overload by dropping a packet. The upshot of this is that TCP bandwidth varies continuously, but ideally will track the maximum possible rate of the connection (a small example is seen in Fig. 3.1). Protocols that run on unusual versions of TCP, UDP or even through very non-standard pathways like files, shared memory, email, etc., are also possible, although one sees them less commonly.

The data transmitted on these connections will be text strings: commands that the browser sends to the web site to specify the request, together with arguments and other contextual data, such as the content of browser cookies maintained for that site. The web site responds, also in text, with the web page corresponding to this request.

Fig. 3.1 TCP bandwidth traces out a sawtooth as the protocol dynamically adjusts data rates to seek the highest possible rate, using a linear increase/multiplicative decrease rate scheme in which packet loss triggers the backoff (decrease) events

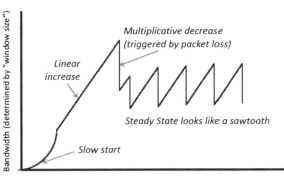

The commands exchanged between a web site and a web browser use a language called HTTP (the Hypertext Transfer Protocol) to request web pages, and HTTP in turn is defined over a more general encoding standard called HTML, which uses a notation called XML (short for Extensible Markup Language). The way to understand this sort of layering is to think in terms of higher level layers that are specialists, running on lower levels that are general purpose. Thus, in our particular scenario, TCP can carry any kind of data stream; its job is to make sure data are delivered in order without loss or duplication. Were one to look down, toward the network, we would find that TCP is really a layer built over the Internet's IP protocols, and those in turn run over various hardware message-passing layers.

Looking up toward the end-user, we first find that TCP is carrying XML objects. XML is a very general encoding language that represents objects in text form and can be used in many contexts; its role is to define a way to represent information together with markups and tags. HTML uses XML to define a way of representing pages that can be displayed in a browser; you have probably seen HTML versions of web pages when fooling around with your web browser. But other technologies use XML too, without using the HTML documentation standards. For example, an early draft of this text was edited using Word, which employs a representation called ".docx" for its files: XML, but not HTML. In effect, XML defines the notation and HTML uses that notation to represent the properties of pages: the fonts to use, the width of the pages, etc. The language is recursive: it supports web pages that contain other web pages. Moreover, since some of these pages can contain executable objects, there is a sense in which "web scripting" is Turing complete: anything that can be computed can, potentially, be computed using XML provided that these features are enabled. As this text was being prepared, the implications of cross-site web scripting were still largely unnoticed. Yet it would not be surprising if by the time the book reaches its readers, the most widely used applications (such as social networking systems) were not already making heavy use of these features.

Moving up the hierarchy we arrive at HTTP: an even higher-level language that represents commands exchanged between a browser and a data center as HTML pages. HTTP defines a few simple commands (*get, put, poll, ...*) whereby the web browser can either request a web page, send information encoded as a web page to the server, or ask about the current version number for a web page without fetching it. The protocol is quite flexible, offering several ways that the browser or server can specify additional arguments, for example to pass information in cookies that the client system may have stored on behalf of this web site. The responses to these HTTP requests are also represented as XML web pages, and are passed back from the server to the client to be rendered.

Notice that because the server is a program, and the web page request is really just a string that can include arguments encoded through the name of the web page or as optional additional arguments on the URL after the web page name, it is not actually necessary that web page exist before the request was made. Thus, while some web pages are relatively unchanging (like the author's home page), others can be highly dynamic, with the content generated on demand, for example by retrieving information from a database and then formatting it to respect the HTTP formatting rules. When you fetch a web page from CNN.com or Amazon.com, everything you see was assembled, on the fly, by a CNN or Amazon web server, although images and other large objects within the page will often be passed using URLs that point to so-called *content hosting servers* from which they can be rapidly downloaded; several companies provide content hosting services and specialize in ensuring that the biggest downloads required to render a web page will be from a server very close to your point of access and with outstanding latency and bandwidth to your machine.

Web development has become a very well-supported technology area. For example, because many companies maintain their most important information in databases, today's most popular database products can function as web servers, allowing developer to provide rules for mapping requests to web pages. A good example of a product that works this way is PHP, a specialized and very powerful database solution designed specifically for use in building web sites. However, PHP is just one of many options. In cloud settings this is a common phenomenon: so important and popular are cloud systems today that there are many products for any particular role (competing in terms of functionality, ease of use, performance and scalability, etc.).

A web server can also use more general logic to respond to incoming requests (that is, without necessarily interacting with a database). A widely popular technology for this purposes is Microsoft's .ASP framework. Using .ASP (short for Application Service Page), arbitrary code written in any of the 40 or so programming languages supported by Microsoft .NET can interpret the incoming request, slice it into parts to be handled by concurrently running subservices, and then assemble the results into any form that makes sense for the application.

We mentioned that many web pages contain embedded minipages that will fetched and rendered, concurrently, even as the remainder of the main page is downloaded and rendered. This approach allows the user to leverage powerful third-party solutions without needing to know much about them. For example, many web sites earn revenue by placing advertising, yet few developers are expert in rendering third-party content. It turns out that this entire task is standardized: one can simply embed a frame (a mini-page) that will download and display content retrieved from other platforms, and by pointing such a frame to an advertising site, revenue will flow each time a user visits your site. The company that provides the advertising content selects the right advertising to display and tracks the click-through rates to determine how much you will be paid. A similar approach is used when a page needs to contain large, relatively static forms of content, such as high-resolution images or videos. Rather than burden your web site with the need to serve up these kinds of data, which might overload your network link, a web site can subscribe to services that will copy the content once, then cache it and deliver it on demand, often from a location near the end-user (Akamai, a well known player in this space, is said to have hundreds of content-hosting sites, placed worldwide to ensure rapid data delivery no matter where the end-user might be located). These kinds of features reduce Internet loads, speed web page display, and shield the developer from all sorts of complexities. We could go deeper and deeper, giving examples, but to do so would require much more space than this text can budget for any single technology.

Notice the many ways concurrency (parallelism) enters the picture. In the cloud, even simple tasks such as fetching data and rendering pages routinely run as concurrent activities, with the goal of ensuring the fastest possible response from the perspective of the user. Parallel computation of the subframes of a web page represent just one example of a very common motif: a great deal of thought and engineering has been expended on ensuring that user requests will get rapid responses, with caching and embarrassing[1] parallelism used very aggressively. For example, we noted earlier that downloads of complex web pages (those structured as a hierarchy of frames) are issued concurrently, and rendered as the content is received. But this is also done when updates are triggered by a request to a cloud computing system: rather than do the update first and then return a result only when it finishes, cloud platforms often issue the response first (often by optimistically applying the update to a local copy of the underlying data), and then leave the "real" update running in the background after the response has already been sent.

A natural question to ask is how early responses can possibly guarantee correctness, since the approach lacks locking and hence could result in inconsistency, e.g. if a crash were to cause the update to be forgotten, or if two conflicting updates were to run concurrently. The short answer is that the cloud simply accepts the risk of these kinds of inconsistency. The longer answer is that web applications are expected to tolerate such issues, to automatically repair any inconsistencies they encounter, and thus to embrace these risks as unavoidable complications of cloud computing!

Caching is taken to extremes as well. For example, in addition to caching recently accessed data and files (often, both on the client system and on the server system), browsers typically leave the TCP connection open for a while. The value of caching connections is that if a new request needs to be sent to the same server, no connection delay will occur and the data rates may already have stabilized close to whatever the peak rate possible for the connection might be. All of these forms of caching can be sources of inconsistency: rather than limiting caching to *coherent* caches, meaning those that are guaranteed to reflect a correct and current version of the underlying data, many cloud systems work with potentially inconsistent cached data, namely data that could be stale or otherwise incorrect. The concern even applies to cached TCP connections, since by reusing an existing connection, we deprive the cloud management infrastructure of the chance to use what it might consider to be the ideal mapping. For example, the reused connection might direct a request to a server in a way that is inconsistent with the internal mapping policies the cloud might be

---

[1] We say that parallelism is embarrassing if the method of subdividing the computation and performing it is extremely simple. This is in contrast to methods of achieving parallelism that employ complex algorithms and are correspondingly complex to reason about.

trying to implement. Such errors are viewed as just an unavoidable cost that one tolerates to achieve massive scalability and high speeds.

Notice the way that the cloud balances decisions in favor of using simple ideas, such as HTML web page encodings, and then overloading them with fancier mechanisms that run on top of the same basic infrastructure. This is partly historical: if one looks at the evolution of the area, we have seen the web generalize from simple web page rendering in the early days, to rendering of program-generated content, to client-side Javascript program execution. With each new development the web became dramatically more programmable. Yet each new step also leveraged the scalability features of the existing infrastructure that supported the prior technology, and this was definitely not a historical accident: the key insight is that scalability has been hard to achieve, and has come first for the simplest things. Rather than throw away hard-won performance and scalability, by finding a way to layer a more complex behavior over a simple existing mechanism, we can get the best of both cases: fancy behavior, but great scalability and performance.

Developers in the cloud community often comment that the wisdom of this approach grew on them slowly. In academic settings, students are taught to think system designs through from the ground up, making the best decision at each step. So, as students enter the professional world of cloud computing they often assume that rather than learning how some existing but overly simplistic technology works, the best way to implement a fancy new feature is to start from scratch. Yet the team that finds a way to layer the fancy feature on some existing fast, scalable mechanism will probably win the race even if the resulting architecture is a bit ungainly. In the cloud, there is real value in backward compatibility because the existing systems were really hard to build even if the things they do are simple. In some sense, the complexity is not really in the applications, per se, but rather in the scale at which they need to run. So while academic purists might look at the resulting jerry-rigged, incrementally created technology stack and groan, the engineers who really built the web have learned that this is just the "way of the cloud."

One sees this again in the case of web pages. Initially, web pages were static, but not long into the web revolution two contending options for supporting dynamic web pages emerged: one approach using web pages that have an expiration time and then must be refreshed; the other based on a kind of stream of pushed notifications encoded using a special representation called ATOM (this is how RSS feeds work). Still more features allow a web page to instruct the client's browser to connect to some other web site and download content from there. In the early days, this was seen as a security loophole, but it soon gained mainstream acceptance because it simplified the insertion of advertising onto pages and made it possible for specialized companies to track click-through rates. Today, one might still argue that the feature is a security loophole, but it is much too late to roll it back.

Fanciest of all are the new technologies that allow a web server to send a full program (typically in Javascript or Flash) to your browser, which will then execute it in a kind of virtual machine (despite the name, Javascript is not Java, and this is not the JVM, but the idea is similar). These programs are closer and closer to full-featured, general purpose applications. They even have sophisticated access to your file system: again, a feature that has obvious security implications, but that ultimately won out because it permits web pages to upload files, photos, videos and other content that you might wish to post to the web. Thus, we have gone from web pages with images on them to web frames that run substantial programs, downloaded over the web, with only the security features of Javascript or Flash protecting us from a hijacking of our machines. Yet each of these steps has represented a huge advance in the flexibility and power of the cloud experience, and those advances have been irresistible to the companies that are ultimately paying the bill for all of this technology, namely the ones advertising and doing e-Commerce using the web.

The fundamental driver in each of these cases was customer demand for features: slicker web page interfaces, more flexibility in terms of what the web can do, and better performance. It would be a mistake to visualize hoards of evil technology companies waving large checkbooks at the main cloud-computing platform vendors, demanding that they rush to deploy immature technologies lacking critical assurance and security properties. We have ended up with a technology base that suffers from those deficiencies, but nobody ever intended that this be the case.

The real problem is that better web experiences have been rewarded by crowds of users who flock to web sites that leverage the cutting edge options. Browsers slow to support popular technologies have been abandoned by a fickle end user community demanding richer feature sets. This has been counterbalanced, but only to a limited degree, by a fear of bad press on issues of security, but it would be hard to find a case in which a vendor has delayed a new feature for security reasons. More typical has been a trend to introduce desired features as quickly as possible, and then to follow on with upgrades that patch specific security holes or that sandbox those features, to limit the risk of exploits.

Thus today we have a web that offers very solid protection for credit card transactions over the Internet: we would not be able to make e-purchases otherwise. One certainly reads of large losses of credit card information, but these typically involve exploits targeting database systems storing credit card data, and often reflect some form of insider help. All other forms of security are far weaker: anyone who keeps sensitive data on a home or office computer is placing unwarranted trust in a porous infrastructure that seems to get leakier by the day. The trends, indeed, favor cloud storage as the safer option: a well managed cloud storage system should be far less prone to computer virus infections or cross-site scripting attacks than our personal machines. On the other hand, it defies common sense to upload one's most sensitive digital possessions to an infrastructure operated by third parties dominated by commercial objectives that may be very remote from our own.

Thus, at the end of the day, the shape of the web is very much determined by the end-user; if the web lacks properties we might wish it had, before complaining too loudly we should pause to think of the many ways that our own actions are responsible for the form the web has taken. And when we accept this context, together with the obvious motivation of cloud developers to leverage their best scalability and performance successes, it becomes very easy to understand how the web might have followed what has to be seen as an unusually haphazard evolutionary path.

3.2.2   Web Services: Client/Server RPC over HTTP

While all of this activity was happening on the client side of the traditional browser/server infrastructure, a second trend began to play out (again anticipated in many ways by the ubiquitous computing visionaries at Xerox Parc). Not long after web browsers were invented, it became clear that the web had the potential to function as a universal standard. Whereas previous standardization attempts of this kind had faltered, the low price of web services technologies made it possible to inexpensively modify all sorts of things to support web protocol interfaces: television sets, air conditioners, radios, microwave ovens, cameras, wireless routers. Thus the same thinking that evolved web pages with images on them into animated interactive gecko lizards applies equally to all of these other technologies: what some have referred to as the *Internet of Things*.

Prior to the emergence of the modern web, we used *remote procedure calls* to access services offered by a remote computer over the network. In an RPC system, we say that the server defines a set of procedure call stubs, which look to the client system much like a library to which it can link. Type checking and so forth work normally, and a protocol such as TCP or UDP is used to connect the client to the server when the client process starts up.

With Web Services, exactly the same ideas apply, except that one talks to a Web Service using the same standards that a web browser uses to talk to a web site: HTTP, typically running over TCP. To facilitate this style of application the web services standards include a special web page format, called the Simple Object Access Protocol (SOAP), which uses the HTML representation but (just as in our other layered examples) defines a very specific style of HTML page. To exploit this capability, the client computer encodes requests as a SOAP page and ships the resulting pages to the server. The server decodes the page, does a procedure call internally to perform the requested action, and then uses SOAP again to encode the result, shipping it back. In effect, SOAP allows an active program to generate specially formatted web pages that encode their requests, and allows servers to encode results to those requests, again in special web pages. Indeed, one can use a web browser to display these SOAP pages. They include the name of the request being issued, the argument names and types that were supplied, the values being passed (again, encoded into an text format), etc. Obviously, this is not a tremendously efficient representation, but it works well enough for all but the most performance-intensive uses. For those purposes, other, more optimized options exist (for example, one can switch to a binary XML standard).

Web Services requests function very much like remote procedure calls, but it is important to remember that they are not identical to method invocations on objects: arguments need to be passed "by value", obviously, and type checking is not very elaborate. But this is to be expected, since the client and server often run on different machines and are often coded in different programming languages. There may not be any real object involved, either: MyFavoritePhotoOfBiscuit.jpg could be a real photo stored in the file system, but could also be generated on demand. (For example, upon receipt of the request, a little robot could zip outside, snap a photo of

Biscuit nicely posed on the porch, and then transmit it back to you.) The approach turns out to be incredibly flexible.

This vision of a cloud that can reach out and do something, or touch something, leads back to the notion of the Internet of things, although the topic is not one we can afford to cover in in much detail. Once one opens the door to using web services as a way to talk to devices, a tremendous variety of opportunities, and challenges, are uncovered. Unfortunately, however, that world of opportunity also reflects some fairly basic core assumptions different enough from the assumptions underlying our treatment here to make it hard to cover both topics in a single coherent way. There is some irony in this: our focus here is on relatively powerful client systems that talk to cloud-hosted services over a network, and that is also the bigger story today. Yet the Internet of (little) things, fusing computation with the real world in a way mediated by the cloud could easily become the much bigger story in the long run.

Let us explore this story very briefly, but then return to our main themes. When the web is used between a client's computer system and a cloud platform, one has a certain set of expectations: a client's computer has memory, storage, substantial computing capabilities, unlimited power from the nearest power outlet, some limited degree of mobility and autonomy, are continuously connected to the Internet, etc. Even mobile devices like telephones actually are surprisingly close to this model; obviously, power is more of an issue, but on the whole the model is very similar to that for the desktop you use at the office.

These assumptions are called into question if the web services device we are looking at is a teakettle or a microwave oven. Such devices have very limited roles and even if we could transmit arbitrary Javascript programs to them, it is not at all clear what an animated gecko designed to sell cheaper automobile insurance would do once it got there. The location and roles of these devices are important: this light switch controls the lights in the basement; that switch controls the ones in the bathroom, and this other device controls the hot water heater. Indeed, so important are these questions of physical location and physical role that one could argue that we are wrong to use the term "Internet" of things, because "Internet" sounds too network-centric; better, perhaps, would be "universe" of things: accessible on a network, but occupying physical locations and functioning as sensors or actuators in some narrow way. Moreover, however eager web vendors might be to display advertising on a teakettle, it is not obvious that consumers would embrace that sort of thing: who would want to live in a home filled with online advertising devices? Thus this universe of things is ultimately very different from the Internet that gave rise to cloud computing, and the economic drivers that will push it forward may be more end-user driven and a bit less advertising driven than what we have seen for the client-server side of the cloud.

Similarly, the ways that a cloud computing system might manage and exploit vast numbers of very lightweight, limited devices differ from the ways a cloud deals with a heavy-weight, full-functionality client system. With a client-server situation, one can reasonably expect the client to do much of the work. With a cloud controlling your home, the responsibilities clearly tilt toward the cloud. And finally, the demands that these very different styles of applications might put on network protocols or operating systems are also different from the patterns that dominate in today's client-server cloud. While the teakettle might not require very much from the cloud, as one spins out stories of this future universe, all sorts of safety and timing challenges arise not seen in traditional cloud settings (Lee and Seshia 2011).

Yet while these sorts of issues represent challenges that will need to be solved, perhaps ultimately distancing the universe of things from the client-server cloud as we know it today, that universe also offers some incredibly exciting opportunities. As we reach the point of exploiting those opportunities, the resulting capabilities could transform the world in very positive ways.

One especially appealing direction involves the automation of some of the more human-intensive and expensive aspects of today's healthcare infrastructure. Recall the healthcare scenarios we touched upon in the introduction. As we saw, there are more and more at-home patients who need some degree of remote monitoring and help managing their medications and other devices, and hence who could bene-fit from techniques to automate some of these roles. Consider our elderly diabetic patient who needs to periodically measure his or her blood sugars and adjust the dosages of insulin being administered by an insulin pump. Errors could cause a nasty fall, hospitalization or even death. Yet if the technology is handled correctly, that patient's health prospects would be greatly enhanced. To what extent might we view this as an instance of the universe of things, and how can that scenario help us understand the properties such applications would require?

Clearly the universe of things, if capable of offering the right properties, repre-sents a very powerful and exciting possibility for healthcare. By connecting small devices to the cloud, it becomes possible to imagine a future in which a small team of medical experts, amplified by a cloud-hosted monitoring infrastructure, could keep an eye on a very large population of home-care patients. This would require some home visits by skilled nursing aids, but the network and cloud could offload a great deal of the burden. Basically, we would use devices in the home to monitor blood sugars and track food consumption (that part might be tricky but it seems feasible to solve it, either by just asking the patient how much they ate, or in a fancier scenario, perhaps by using RFID chips on frozen meals to figure out what the patient picked for lunch). One would then upload the data into the cloud, build a model of how this particular patient metabolizes meals, and use that to compute the right corrective dose of insulin. The physician's office would oversee the big picture, looking for signs of trouble: perhaps, some patient's sugars are running higher than the model predicts (a possible sign of infection), or running unexpectedly low (a sign that the patient might have lost her appetite). Then the office could phone or schedule a visit. A technology like this could also watch for signs that the patient is developing balance problems, notice if she leaves a teakettle on the burner unattended, and so forth.

Yet here we also see a constellation of challenges. Can medical devices of these kinds support web services interfaces, given the stringent rules imposed on medical technology by the various regulatory authorities that would be involved? Can we operate the cloud and the network in a sufficiently secure and reliable way to be able to trust it as the intermediary in this setting? What about power: people wear insulin pumps and continuous glucose monitors, and wireless networking consumes power. Thus one must ask if there are aspects of the web services protocols that are wasteful in their use of network bandwidth; if so, we would need to adapt those to work more effectively with devices running on very limited batteries. Failures will surely occur in any case, so we would need to make sure these systems only fail in safe modes; for example, if an insulin pump is running but has lost its network connection, we need to ensure that no harm will occur and that someone will look into the cause of the failure (this is not as simple as turning off the insulin pump: that could leave the patient with very high blood sugars and, in a short time, hospitalization or worse). All of what we have described involve "electronic health records," but whereas much of the trade press on this subject assumes that such records are just electronic versions of the records kept in doctor's offices today, we can see here that they might also include other kinds of data generated or obtained in any kind of medical situation, and hence span a very broad range of forms of data and use cases. In this larger view, an electronic health record is any form of data that might be stored in a computing system and used in connection with healthcare decision making or treatment. Can we build solutions that respect the HiPPA requirements for protecting this kind of sensitive, private data?

Beyond these basics, one must worry about more extreme questions. How would we ensure that computer viruses or hackers can't somehow gain control over medical devices playing, literally, life-or-death roles? Will CSI episodes of the near future feature endless "murder by Internet" scenarios? (The black-sheep nephew hacks his rich uncle's insulin pump, knocking him off with a text message sent from some very public place a thousand miles away.... but the brilliant, fashion-conscious CSI investigators notice a blinking error code on the insulin pump interface, figure out that the device has been hacked, and finally uncover the trail of digital forensic evidence that leads directly to the remote cell phone....)

Yet if all of those problems can be solved (and this author believes that with effort, every single issue we are raised could be resolved, except perhaps the predictability of that future CSI script), the resulting technology could slash medical expense in carrying for a very expensive kind of patient, and greatly improve quality of care! The benefits here far outweigh the risks that we might not be able to solve some element of the needed technical story. Indeed, students reading this text who are wondering what to do with their careers after school might want to consider founding start-up companies in this or one of the other universe-of-things sectors. It is not hard to predict that they could become the next really big thing, and fairly soon, too: the technical enablers "almost" exist (after decades during which they were lacking), and the demand is almost unlimited. Take the last step or two, and you could literally save lives and make a fortune doing it!

Similar stories can be imagined in many settings. A second opportunity, perhaps even more important than the medical one, would be to use cloud computing technologies as an enabler to help in the creation of a much smarter electric power grid. The idea here starts by recognizing the absurd inefficiencies we routinely tolerate in power distribution and utilization today: we are burning coal and running nuclear power plants that contribute to pollution and global warming, and yet much of the power vanishes entirely: nothing actually used it. Moreover, it has been incredibly difficult to integrate green power sources into the grid because of its irregular and unpredictable production properties: solar panels do not put out much power on cloudy days, turbines do not turn if there is no wind, etc. One needs to find ways to share power over large distances to smooth these irregularities enough to exploit these kinds of power source.

Now imagine a new kind of smart power grid in which small devices, like our mobile telephones, are used on a vast scale to monitor and control the use of power in every way you could dream up. These could include running the hot water heater and the dishwasher at times convenient to the power grid, turning out the lights in rooms that have nobody in them, and maybe even diminishing the power supply to entire regions that are currently generating their power using local solar or wind technologies. The scale of the undertaking would be comparable to the scale of today's cloud enabled web, hence it makes sense to conclude that the smart electric power grid will turn out to be a new kind of cloud computing platform.

Smarter power management, controlled through the cloud, could certainly contribute in big ways to energy efficiency. Yet once again, we see that the required model departs in important ways from what one sees for hard-wired desktop machines, or for mobile telephones. The smart grid will end up with its own safety and reliability requirements, its own security challenges, and all sorts of real-time responsiveness requirements. These are solvable problems, but they take us in directions sufficiently distinct from today's cloud computing solutions that to treat them in a fair and thorough way would require a different kind of textbook.

The list goes on. Think about how the universe of things could impact other aspects of daily life. Could your car direct you around a local traffic jam to a parking space right next to your office? Could we go even further and somehow use the cloud to create cars that safely drive themselves home in ways that reduce the risk of traffic jams or accidents, or that drive themselves to a parking lot when you reach your destination, then drive back to pick you up when you are ready to leave? What about a personal cloud hosted assistant, ever prepared to help you plan your life, with instant answers to all of life's persistent questions?

These kinds of question are not all that new: the embedded computing community has debated similar problems for decades and speculated about how a cloud-computing style of computing could respond, over time, to these and other concerns, yielding a very different world in which technology would partner with human users to improve life in many ways. The ubiquitous computing folks at Xerox also ran into questions that, today (20 years later) remain unclear: are these technologies ultimately anathema to personal privacy and security? Yet we run into the same bottom line mentioned above: doing justice to this speculative technology base would be difficult in a text that also tries to do a good job of covering reliability issues for the existing client-server version of the cloud.

Hence our decision to steer away from the universe of things (however promising a future it may represent). It seems very likely that the expansion of web services into the universe of things will make all of the ideas tossed out above feasible in a surprisingly short period of time; market forces will then determine which ones become real and which ones fade away. But our role in this textbook will be more limited: we will limit our attention to the network and data center side of the story, leaving the universe of things to await some other book.

3.3   WS_RELIABILITY and WS_SECURITY

3.3.1   WS_RELIABILITY

Our discussion of the universe of things led us to a collection of issues centered on the reliability and security of client-server applications in which the things are the clients and the servers live in the cloud. To what extent are today's cloud standards adequate to address these kinds of needs? To answer this question, we need to look closely at the web services guarantees for client-side applications that require reliability and/or security, such as banking systems that permit transactions against one's bank account over a secured connection from a secured web page. As we will now see, the good news is that the web services standards do include ones defining reliability and security protocols. The bad news is that security and reliability are very broad terms, and these standards have much narrower, more specific meanings that might surprise some readers.

As one might expect, the role of WS_RELIABILITY is to standardize the handling of failures that occur while a web service is handling a client request. Given that the Internet itself is not a perfectly reliable platform, and that the cloud "uses" failure as a platform management option (e.g. to elastically vary the number of first-tier service instances in response to changing load, or to migrate services off nodes that need to be physically serviced), failure arises surprisingly often in the cloud.

The basic issue addressed by WS_RELIABILITY, is that sometimes, a client will issue a request to a server, but then receive a timeout before the request has been completed. This is a common event when a server crashes or is migrated, and as we have noted, those kinds of server problem are surprisingly common in cloud settings. Indeed, it would not be an exaggeration to say that the cloud is an environment in which failure must be viewed as part of the normal life cycle of any application. Failures in which the client remains healthy but a request is interrupted are thus something that one simply must deal with in the cloud.

The web services standard starts by requiring that each SOAP request contain an identifier that, in association with some form of client identifier, will uniquely identify the request. The client identifier is tricky: we can't use the IP address of your computer for this because of the NAT and mobility issues mentioned earlier; instead, some form of client-id would typically be assigned by the server at an early stage of registering the client and then stored in a cookie or retrieved during a login-sequence. To this the client would then append a counter that increments for each request it issues. The rule defined by WS_RELIABILITY, the Web Services reliability standard, is that if the client and server both implement the reliability protocol, the client can resubmit the same request as often as it wishes, and the server will only perform the request once (or not at all, if the request never reaches it). On the other hand, if either of the two does not implement the standard, no exceptions will be thrown: the client that wants to use WS_RELIABILITY is expected to make sure that the services it talks to implement the standard. As it turns out, not many do, but we will defer that question of technology uptake for a moment and return to it later.

As you read this, you probably have a good idea of how a server could implement WS_RELIABILITY: it would need to maintain a table indexed by request-id listing, for each completed request, the reply that was sent. Then, if a request turns out to be a duplicate of one that was received earlier, the identical reply can be transmitted back to the client. But of course in cloud settings, this is much more complex than meets the eye. First, there is an issue of garbage collection; some services are very busy. Should they keep old request id's and replies indefinitely? And if not, for how long? Then one might worry about the size of these old replies: could not they be very large in some cases? What if the reply had time-sensitive content that needs to be refreshed for the old reply to remain valid?

WS_RELIABILITY is silent on such questions: apparently, a service should keep this information indefinitely and deal with such issues on its own. On the other hand, recall our discussion of cloud consistency. The nature of the cloud limits the degree to which any cloud system can really guarantee anything, and a close reading of the WS_RELIABILITY standard makes it clear that even when using WS_RELIABILITY, the user should anticipate that sometimes, a service will violate the standard (presumably, by performing some requests more than once without noticing that they are duplicates, but doing so very rarely).

But there are additional, even more serious, issues. Recall that a cloud platform might deploy clones of a service on thousands of machines. WS_RELIABILITY does not cut any slack for such cases: if any one machine receives and performs a reliable request, every other machine that sees the identical request had better skip the execution step and return a copy of the result. But now if you think back to Brewer's CAP principle, you should be able to see that we are talking about functionality at odds with the CAP approach. WS_RELIABILITY requires a form of consistent behavior cutting across the full set of first-tier servers, while CAP warns that such behaviors may scale poorly.

Very likely this conflict explains why so few cloud-scale services support WS_RELIABILITY. Indeed, the author is only aware of one specific case in which the standard does get used, namely in services that enqueue requests for later processing. These services function like mailboxes: the client (in effect) emails the request to the service, and it enters a mailbox that automatically senses and discards duplicated requests. Now and then the service checks for new mail and, if it sees any requests, processes them and mails back the reply. Sooner or later the client checks for replies, and finding that one of its pending requests has been handled, downloads the answer. And then, days later, the email system automatically cleans up the old requests and old replies. Such services have many names, but are most commonly called Message Oriented Middleware systems, Message Queuing Middleware, or Enterprise Message Bus systems (in the latter case, there are actually two subcategories: we are describing what one would call *durable* behavior, but there is also a non-durable mode that would not support WS_RELIABILITY). Any of a dozen products fall into this overall category of solutions, and they are extremely common in cloud computing settings. Indeed, it would not be any exaggeration at all to say that these are the most important form of glue used to assemble cloud computing reliability stories today, with transactional database reliability a close runner-up (we will discuss that topic later).

3.3.2   WS_SECURITY

What about WS_SECURITY? Here we encounter a much more elaborate set of specifications. The technology underlies the little lock-and-key icon seen on many web pages (namely those with HTTPS prefixes in the URL), and implements what are called secure-socket-layer (SSL) connections, which are just normal TCP connections, but on which data are sent purely in encrypted form. A detailed discussion would take too much space, but a brief summary should be adequate to leave the reader with a good sense of the options.

The Basics of Distributed Systems Security

Before we look at the cloud security standard, it may be helpful to lay the foundations by discussing the basic mechanisms for achieving security in distributed systems. These revolve around secret keys, which are typically said to fall into two categories: *symmetric* keys and *asymmetric* ones. A key, of course, is simply some sort of large number. A symmetric key is one that would be held (only) by the endpoints of a communication session; a sender uses the symmetric key to encrypt any sensitive data it transmits, and the same key is then used by the receiver to decrypt the data. There are a number of symmetric encryption standards with high-quality implementations; Isis[2], for example, uses AES-256 (Advanced Encryption System with 256-bit keys). The Digital Encryption Standard (DES) is also a popular option.

An asymmetric cryptographic system is one in which the sender and receiver have different keys: the sender uses one key to encrypt, and the receiver must use the other key to decrypt. One popular asymmetric key implementation is called RSA (named for its three inventors: Rivest, Shamir and Adelman). This scheme has the interesting property that the two keys can both be used in either role: the sender can use key K to encrypt data and the receiver $K - 1$ to decrypt it, but it is also possible to use $K - 1$ as the encryption key and K as the decryption key. Moreover, knowledge of $K - 1$ does not reveal K.

These properties make it possible to use RSA keys in support of what we call *public key* cryptography: one can publish $K - 1$ in a completely public way. Anyone who looks up $K - 1$ (in a trusted manner) can use the key to encrypt a message that only the holder of K can read, and the process holding K can send messages that must have come from it, since no other process knows K, and since $K - 1$ will correctly decrypt those messages. On the down side, asymmetric public-key cryptography is rather slow in comparison to symmetric key cryptography.

Let us look at an idealized interaction between a client and a server and ask how it can be secured using these tools. We will say that our client is C, and the server S. The server, for example, might be the Bank of America web site, and the client, C, might be your computer, accessing the site to pay your monthly credit card bill using an electronic transfer from your checking account. C wants to be sure that it is talking to S, and not some sort of fake site, so it starts by looking up the Bank of America public key. This is done by contacting a credential-management service, such as Verisign, which provides the certificate, encrypted using the Verisign secret key. Of course, this means that C must find Verisigns public key, which involves the exact same process. The recursion ends when C reaches a "root of trust". If your computer runs Microsoft Windows, that root would be Microsoft, which builds its corporate public key into every Windows system it ships. This yields a *chain of trust:* Microsoft vouches for Verisign, and Verisign provides Bank of America's public key to you.

With the Bank of America public key, C can safely send a message that only Bank of America can decipher. For example, C could send an encrypted message containing your login name and password and the transfer request. Of course this would defeat our security goals: it would be vulnerable to *replay attacks,* where an intruder just captures traffic between C and S, then resubmits the same packets without even trying to decrypt the contents. A protocol this simple would be at risk of repeatedly transferring money until finally, your checking account was emptied into your visa account.

Accordingly, C and S would normally do something a bit more sophisticated. In support of this it would be common to use the initial session to negotiate a secret symmetric key with which the two can securely exchange web pages. Symmetric security is very fast, and represents the core goal of the HTTPS standard. The necessary protocol standard is called SSL: the secured socket layer.

Notice that in our example, C authenticates that S really represents Bank of America in a way that depends on knowing first that Verisign is the correct certificate repository to consult, and secondly that the bank uses Bank of America as its online name (as opposed, say, to BOA.com, or Banque d'Amerique, etc.). Had C been tricked into using BadCreds.com as the certificate repository, it might have used a bad certificate, and if it requested the certificate of some other site than Bank of America, even if it used the right credentials authority, it might receive a certificate for something else entirely. So one issue we have here is that while C is able to make a secure connection to S, we need to be sure that S is the correct site. The problem occurs in the other direction too: while the bank knows that some computer C is talking to it using a secured channel, it has no way to know that C corresponds to such-and-such a person; it learns this from the login dialog.

The problem we see here is basic: even if C is a computer used only by Bill Gates, we can't be sure that Bill was physically in control of that computer at the time of the interaction. Thus before allowing any kind of transaction against Bill's accounts, the Bank of America server will want additional proof that C is being used by the right person. The converse problem arises as well: if Bill was tricked into clicking a fake link for Bank of America, he will find himself talking security to a site that might be a very complete and convincing replica of the Bank of America site, created specifically to trick him into revealing his personal credentials. Can we push beyond these superficial guarantees to achieve deeper security?

Banks have taken some limited steps to work around such issues. For example, Bank of America uses a two-step validication procedure. The first page you encounter asks for your login name but not your password. Given your login name, a second page appears; it does request your password but also shows a personalized graphic on it. Thus, perhaps when Bill set up the account, he picked the dragon from a set of possible graphics. His password page will always show the dragon. But here is the tricky step. The picture turns out to be managed in an unusual way: part of the data for displaying it comes from the bank, but part is stored on the customer's computer, and the two are combined only at the last moment. Moreover, the dragon was one of a huge number of possible images, and inspection of the portion of the image on the client computer, or on the bank, reveals nothing about the choice: separately, the images are just noise. Thus if Bill were tricked into talking to a faked Bank of America web site, the login dialog would not look normal: the fake site would not be able to replicate the dragon picture. It would somehow need to deviate from the normal sequence, perhaps by asking for both his login and his password in a single step. The hope is that Bill would notice the departure from the norm and realize he is interacting with a fake site.

Now, in fact, we can go a bit further by baking secret keys right into the computer's hardware, in a device called a Trusted Computing Base (TCB) or a Hardware Root of Trust (HRT) (two names for the same technology). With a TCB, one can specifically identify a piece of hardware: this is a particular computer, manufactured by Dell Computer, sold to Bill Gates on such-and-such a date, etc. The idea is very similar to the one we used above, to obtain a security certificate, except that here, one queries Dell and it responds with a certificate testifying to the identity of the computer in which that particular TCB was installed, with the corresponding public key. There is no way to steal the key because the TCB is designed to carry out cryptographic operations without revealing it. Similarly, some computers have special card readers and one can plug into them a card that essentially plays the TCB role, holding keys that can be used, but not read or copied. Some systems go even further, using digital identity cards, iris scanners, thumbprint checks, or other verification methods.

Taken jointly, these mechanisms can support a wide variety of security protocols and models, although they also have limitations, such as the ones just mentioned (namely, the bank can never be sure it is really talking to Bill, and Bill's confidence that he is really talking to the bank turns out to revolve around a shared secret, namely that dragon image—a lot of trust to place in a single step of the protocol). But given these tools, we could easily create other security solutions. For example, we could turn our point-to-point security scheme into one that would work for groups, In what follows, we will see that the cloud uses roughly the same client-server protocol just outlined. On the other hand, it stops there: we can design all sorts of security technologies, but there is really only one option for cloud security, aimed at solving one particular security problem. Worse, as an accident of the way the cloud evolved, it also supports a second security standard, and that second option is not secure at all! Caveat emptor: when using the cloud, one must understand which security standard a given system is using, and precisely what form of security is offered!

3.3.3 WS_SECURITY

With this as our goal, let us look at the WS_SECURITY standard. As in the case of WS_RELIABILITY, the first question to ask is precisely what the standard actually proposes to secure. It turns out that the focus is rather narrow. Most importantly, WS_SECURITY provides a way for clients to connect to a server with reduced risk that an intruder might hijack the connection or "spoof" (mimic) the server. That is, the first role is to support secured connections. The second role is authentication: the technology offers a way for the server to gain enhanced certainty that this computer is acting on behalf of user so-and-so, and (as noted) for the user to gain some certainty that this is really Bank of America and not a hacker web site using the Bank of America logo and layout.

The two forms of security supported by WS_SECURITY are called *basic* security and HTTPS security. Basic security is really very weak: when a connection to a web site is first established, this scheme sends the user's login and password in the first web request, in plain text. Thus, any intruder in a position to see the bytes on the wire or in the air can potentially grab the account access information, then connect to the same site later using the same credentials. Unfortunately, many web sites use this scheme, and because many users employ the same login and password for all sites, a single compromise can result in all sorts of intrusions.

The stronger security model operates in precisely the manner described earlier for our Bank of America scenario, using HTTPS and running over SSL. We will not repeat that discussion here, except to remind the reader that a web page can be a complex object with many subpages (frames) that contain content from multiple sources. HTTPS really makes sense only for a single page coming from a single source, and this presents a problem, since so much of the web revolves around third-party hosting services, ad-placement services, and request redirection. Moreover, as we saw above, allowing C to connect to S did not really secure anything; Bank of America ends up using a fairly elaborate secondary scheme on top of the basic SSL security and only this combination can be trusted. A bank skipping that secondary step would be at much greater risk of being spoofed, SSL or not!

There are also forms of security that are easy to describe but hard to achieve with cloud systems. An example would be medical consultation: suppose that Doctor Smith needs to ask Doctor Jones for advice on a difficult case, and only the two are authorized to participate in the dialog. It is not hard to design a secure key exchange protocol, like the one we discussed above, for this purpose; with shared secret keys, everything Dr. Smith says can be encrypted so that only Dr. Jones can understand the contents. But in the cloud, there are no standards for client-to-client security, this while nothing blocks us from implementing such a solution, it is not likely that we would find cloud computing tools to help in such an interaction.

In fact the situation is really somewhat worse than this makes it sound, because in cloud computing applications, one normally places data within the cloud. The expectation is thus that Dr. Smith will upload the data, so that Dr. Jones can pull it out. This suddenly exposes those data to many other potential viewers: other users, other applications, etc. If the cloud is operated by a third party that cannot be trusted, we would need to encrypt the data we upload, but this prevents us from using the cloud to compute on those data (for example, if the medical record was some form of image, such as a CT scan, we might want to use cloud computing tools to rotate and enhance the image or to highlight possible abnormalities. Decrypting the data to run such applications would expose it to the prying eyes of cloud operators and, potentially, other users. While there has been some work on techniques for computing directly on encrypted data, at present these methods have very limited reach.

In summary, cloud computing certainly offers some useful security guarantees, provided that the developers understand what these technologies actually seek to do, and how they work. Yet one must not assume that security actually means security in an end-user sense. This is obvious with the old "basic" web (in)security standard, but as our Bank of America example showed, can even be an issue when using HTTPS and SSL in a completely correct manner. The bottom line is that the cloud offers a secure way to move data into and from a cloud platform, and a means of obtaining security certificates for web sites. Beyond that we, as developers, need to start thinking very hard about our goals, how we plan to achieve them, and how the resulting solution might be attacked.

3.4   Safe Execution of Downloaded Code

WS_SECURITY focuses on the authentication of the client to the server, making sure that hackers cannot spoof servers, and establishing connections that cannot be wiretapped or tampered with. Yet this is just part of the client-side of the cloud security question, and in many ways, the minor part. The core problem is this: a secure client-server protocol presupposes that the client system and the server system are themselves secure. Yet as we will see, there are serious reasons to doubt that modern client systems *can* be secured. This being the case, the game may be up before it even begins! The situation is slightly better on servers, although this could change as time passes and hackers make inroads on attacking cloud operating systems and software tools.

Focusing on the client system, we will see that there are two basic sources for concern, both arising from deep within the model. First, the hardware itself might be compromised, or the firmware loaded into it. Few of us give much thought to the origins of the chips and other components in our computers, or to the device drivers and firmware that operates things like disks, graphics displays and networks, yet all of these represent very substantial technologies. They are as complex in their respective ways as the operating systems we use, or the Internet. Moreover, they have been "handled" by third parties all over the world: the disk in my desktop computer was fabricated in Malaysia, the machine itself in China, and several chips come from India and Indonesia. The display technology originated in Japan. My wireless network has components in it from Sri Lanka but was designed and mostly built in India. The various integrated circuit boards were mostly assembled in China and India. Thus only the design occurred in the United States, and even here, only some aspects of design were really entirely controlled by United States firms. Those companies, in fact, employ huge numbers of overseas workers.

Computing, in effect, has become highly globalized. This has driven costs down and brought us a huge leap forward in terms of product quality, steady supplies and even time to market, but on the down side means that organizations intent on penetrating our computing infrastructure, including some major countries with governments that compete with the Unitied States government, have a very wide range of options available if they want to design "back doors" into our computing systems. As we will see, one can imagine ways of building components such as these that operate completely normally and yet have additional, stealthy, behaviors hidden within them: almost as if there was a computer within the computer. These would be essentially undetectable because the normal computer itself might be quite unaware of the intrusion. For example, if a keyboard was silently recording every single keystroke typed since it was first shipped, saving this into a flash memory, how would I know this had happened? Short of reverse engineering the entire keyboard chipset, it might be completely impossible to do so.

Even if we trusted the hardware, one has the problem of backdoors or security deficiencies in the software. This includes things like device drivers for cameras and smart phones and GPS units and iPads, the applications that bring them up to date and let us customize them (including photo editors, etc.), web extensions for our browsers, computer games, and so forth. Each time we patch a system we download and install new code or new programs. Indeed, it has become so important to be able to run applications locally on client systems that for many purposes, the cloud will routinely and even automatically download software into the browser, which then runs it. The idea of extending computing systems by adding new software systems is really central to what makes computing systems useful.

This capabilities also presents all sorts of issues, and many just cannot be resolved in any simple way. As noted, cloud computing trends are making the issue more and more fundamental to the whole cloud model. Javascript-based languages like Caja and Silverlight, and proprietary ones like Adobe Flash, are becoming so common as to be universal. It will not be long before the great majority of web pages uses one or more of these technologies.

The problem, of course, is that any of this huge stack of technologies and components can represent an attack vector for a sophisticated hacker. There are powerful attack tools available, free, for download from the Internet, and if one of those is used to probe a typical computer it will find all sorts of vulnerabilities, no matter who manufactured the computer, which operating system it runs, and how you use it. One can reduce the risks by better management of the installed technology base and by using high-quality virus scanners, but even so, we only manage to protect against the known risks. The more sophisticated kinds of intrusion often use vulnerabilities that the wider hacking community is just not aware of. Hence, most computers are at risk, and probably *all* are at risk if the attacker is from a corporate or military espionage team.

These attacks happen all the time, and have many kinds of goals. One important goal is to simply hijack a computer by installing so-called "botnet" software on it, which allows a remote control system to send it commands. Such a computer can then be ordered to email waves of spam, launch distributed denial of service attacks on targets selected by that remote operator, search the disk drive for sensitive materials such as bank account logins, etc. Anger one of these people and your computer just might download a huge pile of child pornography and then set itself up as a web site for others to stumble upon. (Just imagine trying to explain such a event to the local judge!) There are even tools that can reconstruct deleted files on a disk and turn them back into files that an intruder could read.

Thus, hijacking a system isn't all that hard. Moreover, a hijacked system can seem perfectly healthy and normal. While some viruses are damaging, to a growing degree they are designed to hide inside what seem to be normal device drivers or programs or files, and to stay in the background. All of which adds up to trouble, because it suggests that the machines we use at home for personal correspondence, social networking and other non-work tasks are particularly vulnerable.

If this all seems like wildly paranoiac speculation, you might want to read Richard Clarke's book, *Cyber War*. Clarke, a former national security advisor who knows his stuff, describes real intrusions into a vast range of systems, accomplishes through just the kinds of attack we have been describing. He explains how easy it would be to break into power generators, and how an experimental attack called El-igible Receiver not only succeeded in this kind of break-in, but even demonstrated (without taking the very last step) that the attackers could trigger a serious blackout or damage generating equipment in ways that might be very hard to repair, among other things. That exercise was carried out nearly 20 years ago; while research has yielded solutions to some problems since then, the incredible evolution of the tech-nology base over the ensuring period has created many new vulnerabilities. Indeed, studies and experiments have revealed vulnerabilities in just about every kind of enterprise that the "red teams" involved have been asked to attack. And it is not just military systems that need to work. Banks and other institutions have suffered serious break-ins. We read about theft of credit card data almost daily.

One might think that state-of-the-art system management and monitoring would offer some defense. For example, military computer systems are locked down into standard configurations and closely monitored, as are military networks. Theoret-ically, even the smallest deviation from the norm triggers alarms. Nonetheless, Clarke reports that in 2006, a foreign spy organization (probably Chinese) pene-trated US military networks (some of the world's most closely watched and pro-tected systems) and managed to download *terabytes* of data over the very network links that the monitoring systems scrutinize most closely. He then outlines how such attacks could escalate into a kind of war, conducted through computers but with impact on the physical world, because computers control so much of the physical world.

The New York Times also carried articles about some of these exploits, including the attack on the American military networks. While the details are classified, even without knowing precisely how it was done, these articles and Clarke's book to make it clear that these and other events involved the kinds of mechanisms outlined above.

Clarke explains how the first steps of one major break-in occurred, and the example instructive because it involved machines for which the users were not permitted to install their own software, and that did not even have browsers connected to the public Internet (although they were connected to military networks and were hosting military versions of standard office software: email, documented editing, spreadsheets, etc.). Apparently, spies scattered new, very high-capacity USB storage keys in public locations frequented by military staff: the parking area near the Pentagon, restrooms in that building, etc. They bet (successfully) that someone would pick one of these up, and plug it into a USB port. Now, there was nothing obviously wrong with the USB itself: it was just what it looked like, namely an empty large-capacity USB, and worked wonderfully for storing and retrieving data. The problem was that it also had some extra features that most USBs lack: Any machine to which these malicious USBs were connected to was instantly compromised by a virus cleverly hidden on the device. That virus was designed to hide itself on the targetted machine, and to begin monitoring disks, networks and keyboards.

So this got the virus a toehold into some very sensitive, highly classified computers. But how in the world did it manage to transmit terabytes of data over classified networks? Here, Clarke is silent, hence we can only speculate. This author's guess would center on the ideas mentioned at the outset. Suppose that the network the military was monitoring was not the "real" network, but rather some form of virtualized view of the network. In that case, one would not see anything out of the norm, but only because the virus has concealed the abnormal traffic from the monitoring system.

Even more extreme is the following thought. Today's optical network links and interfaces can run at 10 Gbits/second, yet most PCs still use the 100 Mbit ethernet standard. Could one perhaps build a stealth dual network that runs 100 Mbits side-by-side with a hidden 10 Gbit network, so that the monitoring system knows about and sees one network, but the virus has access to the other network. One would not want to rule out that it could be done, particularly if there was a way to compromise the network chip set itself. Indeed, once one begin to speculate along these lines, all sorts of covert channel ideas come up. It would not be hard for a sufficiently well-funded team to get away with just about anything it sets out to do, whether that might be corporate espionage, theft of national intelligence secrets, or simply intrusion into whatever we keep on our personal machines.

Thus even a tightly monitored military network can be at risk. But of course most networks are not remotely so tightly monitored. Thus, in 2011 as this text was being revised, we learned from the McAfee security company that a foreign country, which they suspect to be China, had engaged in what McAfee refers to as "Project Shady RAT" (the acronym is a reference to a remote access tool) over a 5-year period, breaking into a minimum of 72 global organizations ranging from government and UN facilities to major corporations. "Even we were surprised by the enormous diversity of the victim organizations and were taken aback by the audacity of the perpetrators" McAfee's vice president of threat research, Dmitri Alperovitch, wrote in a 14-page report released in August 2011. "What is happening to all this data . . . is still largely an open question. However, if even a fraction of it is used to build better competing products or beat a competitor at a key negotiation (due to having stolen the other team's playbook), the loss represents a massive economic threat" Alperovitch later went on to comment that "This is the biggest transfer of wealth in terms of intellectual property in history. The scale at which this is occurring is really, really frightening."

Thus anyone who doubts that the problem is real, or thinks of it as a paranoid fantasy of the military intelligence community, is simply wrong. Our computers are under massive, systematic attack, for all sorts of reasons, and by all sorts of actors. This is happening today, and it is eroding the competitiveness of our companies, exposing military vulnerabilities that could be exploited in future confrontations, and even to harass individuals with political beliefs that the perpetrators dislike.

This author once attended an unclassified briefing by an expert in this area, who works with a major law enforcement organization. He started his briefing by telling a story (a parable, if you like) about a very rich village up on the hill, where all the residents loved to keep golden bowls full of jewels on their dining room tables. A rash of thefts occurred, and a security expert was summoned by the mayor: what should be done? The first suggestion, namely that the residents just lock up the golden bowls with the jewelry, was rejected out of hand: in this town, one's most precious valuables simply belong on the table in the living room! "In that case," suggested the expert, "you might consider closing the doors to your homes. Locks on the doors and windows would help too."

This probably came as a shock to the residents, who were in the habit of keeping their doors and windows wide open. But they did not much like losing their treasure to thieves, so they took the advice, and for a while it helped. The robbers focused on the stubborn residents who ignored the expert advice, and those who took the advice began to relax.

The story does not end very well, unfortunately. Each new security suggestion only reveals the next set of issues. So once the residents finally closed and locked all their first floor doors and windows, the thieves simply showed up with ladders and climbed into the ones on the second floor. The locks were not iron-clad and could be picked. In the limit one could break a window pane, reach in, and unlock a door or window. For each security improvement, a dozen new issues were revealed.

However paranoid it may sound, our computers genuinely live in a very unsafe world. The vast majority of machines are at risk in many ways, and nobody knows the percentage that have already been compromised. Your machine is at risk no matter what company you bought it from, and no matter what browser and operating system you use.

The usual advice certainly helps. If you employ cutting edge virus protection software, you can reduce the threats substantially. Applying security patches really helps. Downloading software only from known sources is helpful. Picking good passwords helps (short catchy phrases with punctuation and numbers in them work far better than single words, I am told: "I met Mary on the Eiffel Tower on 1/3/92, and it was love!" will not easily be guessed by attackers.

Yet whatever you do, be under no illusions: virus scanners only offer limited protection, because they cannot protect against exploits that have not yet been noticed by the good guys, and yet are being used by the bad guys! And it might be wise to pay for the virus scanning solution you install: at least one major "free" anti-virus product is now known to have been a kind of virus itself, kicking off *other* viruses, but at the same time, installing your machine on a botnet operated by the developer. This illustrates the adage that in reality, nothing is ever really free!

While there has been some work on protecting client computing systems from attacks, progress is mixed. On the positive side, there are ways to reduce the attack options that these programs use to compromise your machine. Poorly configured applications are a big issue; with cloud computing we can run fewer applications on the client machine and, one hopes, do a better job of administering the ones that remain. A new technique called stack randomization can be used by the operating system; this makes programs less predictable, so that a virus designed to overrun a particular buffer and to leverage that to cause a jump into arbitrary downloaded code is more likely to trigger a crash than to take over the computer. Downloaded systems can be run in virtual machines, so that they do not have direct access to your real file system or your real devices; when the program finishes executing, we discard the virtual machine and any compromises that occurred while it was running should vanish too.

But one must be wary of false security. Earlier we talked about the very weak basic form of web security. Here is a second example, illustrating either that the early cloud computing architects were very weak security students, or simply that complex mechanisms can have unintended flaws. The Web Services standards impose a rule that if an application is downloaded from some site, say Amazon.com, then it can only establish connections to Amazon.com. This is intended to offer protection: if a hacker somehow spikes Amazon.com with a virus application, people who have the misfortune to download it do not see their bank account data emailed to Moscow because the application can only connect back to the same Amazon.com server from which it came.

Can you see the flaw in this reasoning? Think back to our discussion of IP addresses. When we say "only connect back to Amazon.com", how much of a restriction is that? If you read the introduction and Chap. 2, you should see that Amazon.com is a shorthand for any of a dozen massive data centers, and each of those may have hundreds of thousands of servers. That application is being limited all right: it can only connect back to a couple of million places. Moreover, if a web page includes frames that define sub-pages, the download restriction rule does not apply. Those subpages can and routinely do download content from servers managed by other companies. Thus your Amazon web page might easily have pointers to content hosted on Akamai.com, or to advertising that will be supplied by DoubleCick.com.

Why should it matter that the "downloads only from the same site" rule is not applied to embedded frames? After all, embedded frames were intended to support content hosting and advertisement placements, and in any case, the word frame makes it sound as if each frame would show up as a distinct web page with a heavy black border. The problem is that these frames are formatted under complete control of the web site that defined the parent page, hence *anything* you see on a web page could be part of an embedded frame and hence subject to its own (different security policy). A frame will only have a border around it if the web page indicates that it should. Moreover, if Amazon's web page defines a minipage supplied by DoubleClick, then an intruder who manages to penetrate the DoubleClick cloud computing system could hide frames of his own in the DoubleClick advertising content; thus, even without breaking into Amazon, a hacker could potentially compromise an Amazon-supplied web page. Moreover, unless an embedded frame uses HTTPS, it may be relatively easy for a hacker to trick the DNS into routing those subpage requests to some other site than the originally intended one. Thus, a frame that Amazon redirects to DoubleClick could, at least potentially, be redirected again by a hacker to a web site he controls. The technique is called web-site hijacking, and while it is not easy to accomplish on a large scale (e.g. one could not easily gain control over *all* DoubleClick.com traffic), it can be relatively easy to confuse a specific user's system for a short period of time; hackers make casual use of these techniques, and have sophisticated tools available to help them do so. All of this adds up to a huge security exposure.

You might not notice any of this. A frame can be completely invisible, with no borders at all, and there are ways to float a frame over some other part of the page, so that what you see on a web page could actually have more than one frame associated with it. The invisible frame can still intercept your keystrokes send copies back home (wherever that might be), and there are ways to do this without blocking those keystrokes from reaching the underlying page.

To conclude this somewhat depressing section, the bottom line is that client-side security is deeply compromised today, at every level. The cloud computing security model is good in some respects and weak in others; it introduces at least one new glaring issue (namely that "basic" security model we mentioned), yet also brings a reasonably solid option to the table, in the form of SSL security used to support HTTPS. But it would be foolish to blame cloud computing for eroding security, because the broader security issue predates cloud computing and is so deep and so far-reaching that cloud computing is merely the latest in an endless line of events.

At the end of the day, the fact is that our client systems can be attacked at every level from the chipset used to build them, up through drivers and the operating system, applications, and most recently, cross-site web scripts. There are bright spots, such as the stack randomization technique mentioned earlier, and good management can really help reduce the attack exposure of an individual machine, at least relative to run-of-the-mill attackers. But if you have genuinely valuable data, and fear genuinely professional attacks, it may be wise to just not put that data on a computer in the first place. The technology base we use today is just not capable of protecting information in a really serious way. Scott McNealy, then CEO of Sun Microsystems, put it this way in an interview he gave to Wired Magazine some years ago: "There is no privacy anymore. Get over it." At the time, some journalists were shocked. But Scott was simply being honest. Fifteen years later, Eric Schmidt, then CEO at Google, basically repeated Scott's point, commenting that if you use computers, just do not do anything you would not want other people to know about. And this is the world we live in, like it or not.

Where cloud computing does bring a new issue is in the ability of cloud computing operators to aggregate vast amounts of information and to cross-index it. Prior to the cloud, if one wanted to learn all about Princess Diana's private life, one had to pay a private investigator to hack into her personal computer and telephone (as we have learned, British newspapers did just that). This was illegal, and risky, and in the process one might easily be discovered.

Today, so much data find its way into the cloud that even without hacking into someone's personal computing system, the very same information might also be replicated into the massive data stores at Microsoft Live, Google, Yahoo!, Facebook, Twitter, YouTube and other major networking sites, along with all the other kinds of data mentioned in the introduction. Thus the main new thing that the cloud has done is to enable corporations to do a kind of massive-scale data mining on our personal information: the same kind of thing that happened to Princess Diana, but now on hundreds of millions of individuals in parallel, albeit with more benign goals tied mostly to placing advertising or supporting social networking services. Moreover, while it was illegal to hack Princess Di's phone and computer, we are granting explicit permission to these cloud computing companies and essentially trading them the right to troll through our data in exchange for very low pricing on devices like mobile phones or social networking technology. Thus one must really think hard about which is the bigger and more real security risk: the weak security of our personal computing platforms, or the ability of the cloud providers to review our lives in such detail for these purposes? Indeed, the question to ask seems to be this: does anyone actually care about security today?

Laurence Lessig, mentioned earlier in this book, suggests that when all the technical options are inadequate, we need to turn to the law. This seems to be the right answer to computing security on the client side of the cloud. We need to make it absolutely clear that corporate espionage and misuse of private data without permission is illegal and punishable with huge fines, prison terms, or other appropriate sanctions. Cloud providers need to help us customize our desired security profiles and to enforce those preferences. But then, knowing that intrusions will still occur, we should also reward those who blow the whistle when large, serious intrusions occur. And this would then be the best remedy to a situation that just cannot be controlled in a technical way. Remember our security consultant? His advice would now be quite simple: "Why not offer a reward for information about this gang, arrest the thieves and then jail them?" And that might be the best response possible, given the times in which we live and the technologies available today.

3.5   Coping with Mobility

Not all client-side challenges are completely hopeless. One important class of such issues involves mobility. Modern computing systems evolved from desktop and laptop systems that did not get moved around very much, or when they were moved, tended to go from the office to an airport to a hotel. Thus we have only had a few years of experience with machines that move almost continuously, as do our mobile phones and GPS map devices. How does extreme mobility challenge the client platform, and what might be done to ease these issues?

Recall that as you move a machine around (be it a cell phone, a laptop, or any other device), it will get a new IP address from each router to which it binds. Even if two routers give out what may look like the identical IP address, such as 192.64.168.3, the address really means different things, because by the time any server sees requests that originate on your machine, network address translation will have replaced that address (and your session's port number too) with some other address and port number corresponding to the outward facing side of some NAT box, and this might even happen multiple times on the route from your machine to the services it uses.

Thus, if we have an open TCP connection to a web service, we need to expect that the IP address associated with your endpoint will change. TCP cannot tolerate such events, so those connections will break. And because of the end-to-end and CAP mindset of the cloud, your system is supposed to reconnect and deal with the disruption on its own. Sometimes one can do that; for example, a video player might manage to reconnect to the Fox Online web site and reset itself to the exact spot at which your episode of Fringe Science was interrupted when you closed your machine. More often, though, video streams, RSS feeds and all sorts of other web services and content would be disrupted, forcing the user to reconnect manually.

In fact the situation is worse than we are making it sound, because even if the IP address stays fixed, mobile machines need to cope with periods of during which connectivity can be very poor (like tunnels on a highway), or disrupted by static (for example, when a train triggers a shower of electric sparks), or signal fade (like when your car drives down into a valley and the local cell phone tower vanishes behind the hill).

How might we avoid such problems? Readers who have taken a good networking class will be familiar with the concept of *tunneling*. What this means is that we take network packets, perhaps generated by a cloud computing application, and treat them as data, running them through some *other* network connection that has no idea that the inner data consist of network data. This is how virtually private networks work, and because VPN technology is widely deployed, the very same features offer some hope for virtual connections that do not break quite so often.

One approach runs as follows. We can tunnel the cloud traffic through some sort of private network operated by the ISP that gives you your mobile connectivity, perhaps using UDP or additional TCP connections. Basically, Verizon or AT&T or T-Mobile would write software that implements a kind of tunnel, with one end on your machine (the cloud end), one end out in the web (the cloud service end), and a dynamic route in between, designed to very rapidly sense connectivity issues and to compensate by resending packets aggressively, acquiring new IP addresses for use by the tunnel layer, etc. Your mobile machine ends up having two IP addresses at any given time: one stable IP address, which it thinks of as its IP address for cloud computing purposes, and a series of temporary IP addresses used by the tunneling software to preserve the illusion of continuous connectivity. The key point is that the cloud client and cloud server never see disruptions, and hence mobile services can ride through the periods of slow performance without actual connection resets.

This idea can be taken further and further. As you may know, many cloud computing systems are already multi-homed: companies such as Amazon buy Internet connections from multiple ISPs, hence any data center is accessible by at least two different primary IP addresses. We talked about how Amazon controls the DNS mapping from Amazon.com to an IP address, but in fact the mapping is to a list of IP addresses. Any are equally good choices, and the client system is told to switch from one to another at its preference; they lead to the same place.

Well, tunneling lets us do the same thing on the client side. The cloud server thinks of your mobile platform as having a specific, unchanging IP address. However, as your machine moves about, it can potentially bind itself to more than one network (picky readers will object that network interface cards only bind to one wireless channel at a time, but there is a work-around called MultiNet now, allowing one card to multiplex itself over two or more channels, each bound to a distinct base station). In this manner, your machine might actually have three active IP addresses: the one seen by the cloud services it talks to, and then two different IP endpoints used for tunneling, connected to distinct base stations. If one connection goes bad, the other might ride the disruption out, giving the illusion of continuous connectivity. Obviously, each packet will need to be sent once per connection, but packet duplication is a well known phenomenon in the Internet, and protocols such as TCP automatically filter out and discard the extra copies. Thus the cloud service won't miss a beat!

In fact, many ISPs already do a form of tunneling, for a different reason: ISPs often have so many mobile devices in a given region that they are at risk of running low on IPv4 addresses, even with NAT. Thus, they have become early adopters of IPv6, which has no real limits on the IP address space. Yet the major cloud services run on the normal, IPv4 Internet. The solution is just what you might expect: we can tunnel IPv4 over IPv6 within the ISP, switching to pure IPv4 once we traverse the ISPs NAT box and enter the public network.

What we have described is really just the tip of an approaching iceberg. ISPs are discovering a wide variety of services that they can implement on behalf of the cloud, and that the cloud providers would love to see. For example, it is currently quite hard to cache content on behalf of mobile devices, particularly if the content is changing rapidly and has a short lifetime. Examples would include computer games, conference calls, or data associated with sporting events: in all of these cases one might have large numbers of receivers for the same data, yet our current model seems to require that each make its own stream connection to a server and stream its own copy (perhaps over a tunnel, as just outlined). Thus many researchers are working on schemes for caching transient information, and because mobile access has become such a common model, doing so in ways that can tolerate endpoint mobility. It is very likely that the network providers will need to play some roles in supporting such a model: as a user moves from place to place, the right place to cache rapidly changing data on that person's behalf will also change, and only a solution that coordinates the handling of movement with the handling of caching would succeed. There is every reason to anticipate that this sort of thing will succeed, and that we will see steady progress in the capabilities and quality of the mobile experience for many years to come.

3.6   The Multicore Client

A final source of rapid change on the client side results from the emergence of multicore parallelism in the form of low-power chips that have multiple side-by-side CPUs on a single platform. The issue here relates to Moore's law, which holds that the density and capacity of computing chips, memory chips rises exponentially over time (the exponent is somewhere in the range between 1.5 and 1.8 depending on the study; it was closer to 2.0 when Moore first made the prediction). Networks are tracking this performance curve as well.

Around the year 2000, Moore's law seemed to hit a wall: chips dissipate heat roughly as the square of the clock speed, hence as chips got faster they also got much hotter, reaching a point at which they literally began to melt down. Medical journals reported cases of heavy computer users showing up at hospital emergency rooms with burn marks on their thighs. Consumer watchdog groups warned that some computing systems were at risk of catching fire if their cooling fans broke. These developments shocked the computing hardware industry and resulted in a massive industry-wide push toward lower power solutions. The winning idea involving putting multiple CPUs side by side on the same chip, but to run them somewhat slower. These could be specialized CPUs, such as graphics processors or network accelerators, or standard general-purpose CPUs; most future systems will probably include a mix of both. It turns out that with one CPU running 4 times as fast on a single chip, we use roughly the same amount of space on the chip as would the circuitry for 4 CPUs. Yet the $4\times$ faster chip generates $16\times$ as much heat, and consumes $16\times$ more power. Thus we gain the desired speed, but without consuming so much power or heat.

Multicore clients offer many potential benefits: we just need to find ways to use those cores to better understand what the end user is doing. With enough computing power we can potentially run programs that could listen to human speech, track gestures, and capture more of the end-user's intent and environment, hence offering a better interactive experience. Because each of those tasks would involve different programs, one could potentially do this without writing explicitly parallel code, and hence without stumbling over concurrency-related issues or other problems. Up to the present, the main impact of multicore clients on the cloud has been to drive vendors toward parallel download technologies and browsers that can run multiple windows concurrently, but these are still very early days.

Many researchers are working actively on ideas in this space. For example, we have talked about the issues associated with viruses and other kinds of damaging download. One group of researchers are combining multicore parallelism with virtualization to tackle such questions. The idea is to run a system in a speculative manner: they create a virtual machine, launch the application within it, and allow the application to download the web page and run it. If a fault occurs, they can roll back the results by just terminating the virtual machine, then relaunch the application in a safer, more limited mode, and replay the web page more cautiously. This works because the signs of a virus attack are sometimes detectable through side-effects visible in the speculated state, even though it may not be obvious what caused the side effect. For example, many viruses trigger cause at least some system services to crash and restart. Thus by noticing these things and rolling the speculative execution state back, one might protect against a virus without even knowing precisely what it was doing. A technique like this might be too slow on an older single-core machine, but with a multicore platform one has CPU cycles to expend. Moreover, notice that this sort of idea requires no special programming on the part of the developer at all. It illustrates a point we made in the introduction: sometimes the best way to use a technology is not to invent a completely new programming style, but rather to look for ways to extend the existing technology base by taking advantage of the new capability in other ways that require less development effort and yet bring obvious benefits.

Thus the client platform of the future is likely to be mobile, web enabled and multicore, yet probably will not be drastically different in any deep sense form the client systems we use today. Instead, we are likely to see evolution of an incremental form that starts here, and then builds to work around limitations in ways that require minimal change to the existing code base, and yet enhance the user experience. One can certainly imagine ways of using multicore platforms that would be far more disruptive to the code base, but embracing them would require rebuilding a huge amount of technology that works fairly well. Far better would be to just sneak these new capabilities into existing systems, improving them without needing to rebuild from scratch.

3.7   Conclusions

In summary, we have looked a bit more closely at the client side of the cloud and discovered a rich and evolving world. The client system is inevitably a key partner in the cloud: only it can interact directly with the end user, sense the end-user's environment, and take actions that ultimately lead to revenue for the cloud provider. Yet all of this occurs in a client environment complicated by a diversity of very complex challenges: mobility, a very porous security model in which the hardware itself, the software that runs it, downloaded content and downloaded code are all fundamental to the experience, and yet all might be undetectably tainted. The client desires a reliable experience, and yet we must work with a weak reliability model that throws many kinds of reliability concerns into the hands of the client, even if that client might be unable to deal with the resulting issues.

Meanwhile, many things are driving progress on the client side. Multicore parallelism and mobility are pushing for rapid evolution of the computing model. The promise of a universe of things is nearly certain to focus a new wave of innovative product development on client systems and, in so doing, to thrust these client platforms into increasingly sensitive roles. Security and privacy hang in the balance: if trends continue to play out in the same directions currently seen, basic societal guarantees will surely be eroded. Yet we are gaining powerful capabilities, and perhaps could compensate for the technical deficiencies in these areas using legal mechanisms: if we cannot secure private data adequately with the tools cloud platforms offer us, we can at least jail those who steal private data and misuse it in ways that harm the individual. Like so many things in the modern world, these sorts of compromises are often the best we can do, and are also often adequate to address all but the most extreme concerns.

David Patterson, a cloud computing researcher summed it up by remarking that the "The future is cloudy", and it would be hard to better capture the message of this chapter. Cloud computing will dominate and will reshape many things, sometimes for the better, sometimes for the worse. Yet one should not be pessimistic about where this will lead. On the contrary, as technologists, we need to recognize the issues as opportunities to innovate, and to keep in mind that just when things seem to have reached an impasse, a revolutionary new hardware concept can sometimes break through into completely uncharted territory. The bottom line is this: if you want to have a big impact today, just jump into the client side of cloud computing, grab one of these big challenges, and see what you can do!

3.8   Further Readings

Readers interested in learning more about the ramifications of the cloud for personal privacy and security are referred to Laurence Lessig's books (see Lessig 1999), the book by Diffie and Landau (see Diffie and Landau 2007), or Jeffrey Hunker's recent treatment (see Hunker 2011). Richard Clarke's wonderful book is Clarke and Knake (2010).

For more information on the Web Services model and standards, visit http://www.w3.org.

For more information on the Internet of Things, see http://en.wikipedia.org/wiki/Internet_of_Things.

A good treatment of client-side security issues can be found in http://ows.microsoft.com/en-US/windows7/Laptop-security-basics.

Recent work on integrating client computing systems with distributed communication tools has yielded many interesting solutions and systems, although uptake of these by industry has been limited. But we highly recommend that readers look at the approach used in BAST (Guerraoui et al. 1998; Garbinato and Guerraoui 1997), which proposed an object oriented programming language, intended for use in large computing deployments, and in which the ideas of group communication are encapsulated into a base object class, from which the developer creates new applications by refinement (creating specialized subclasses). Also of interest in this connection is Ostrowski's work on the Live Distributed Objects platform (Ostrowski and Birman 2009; Birman et al. 2010), in which a drag-and-drop paradigm is used to compose communication-enabled components into live applications that run on the client system and update themselves dynamically as new events occur. Both BAST and Live Distributed Objects are available for free download, are either would be an outstanding basis for student projects in the areas touched upon in this text.

Network Perspective

4

4.1 Network Perspective

The previous chapter looked at cloud computing from a client's perspective. Late in the discussion we touched on one of the ways that cloud computing is forcing the Internet itself to evolve. In this chapter, we will say more about that topic.

4.2 The Many Dimensions of Network Reliability

Although our overarching theme in concerned with the assurance properties of distributed systems, it is important to realize that not every component of a system needs to guarantee every property. Sometimes, a lower layer should not even try to do so. This insight can be seen as a generalization of one of the most deeply held beliefs about the Internet: the so-called End-to-End Principle. First formulated in a 1981 conference paper by Saltzer, Reed, and Clark, the end-to-end argument (the "proof" of the principle) shows that the best way to achieve network reliability is not necessarily to make the lowest layers of the network reliable. Instead, one might actually achieve *higher* reliability by just making the lower layers of the network extremely fast and mostly reliable, then running a reliability protocol between the endpoints of our connection.

The basic analysis runs as follows. Suppose that we have a network linking endpoint A to endpoint B, and we want to send data reliably from A to B. And now suppose that the path takes several hops to get from A to B: X–Y–Z. Should we try to make each hop reliable?

Obviously, we could do so: we *could* run the traffic over the X link on a TCP connection from the router that sends on X to the router that receives on X. Similarly, we could use TCP on Y and Z. But would this make the A–B route reliable? Hopefully, you can see why it would not: after all, one of those routers could crash and reboot with amnesia; if so, any packets that were in it at the time of the outage would be dropped. Routing could also change while a session is active: perhaps, while packets are moving from A to B we will suddenly switch from the X–Y–Z route to route W–Z, and packets might be dropped or arrive out of order as a result. Moreover, routers explicitly drop packets to signal that they are becoming overloaded; this causes TCP to back off, as we saw in Fig. 3.1 (the famous TCP sawtooth bandwidth curve). Obviously, if we make the lowest layers reliable, we lose that signaling option.

From this we reach a preliminary conclusion: no matter how reliable we make the individual hops in the network, we will need to do some kind of packet loss-recovery and ordering-recovery at the endpoints. Only the endpoints are in a position to guarantee reliability for the connection. Moreover, the reliability role and the flow-control roles of the endpoints are tightly related. We will pay that cost no matter what the network does. Thus, any property the network tries to offer, beyond its basic role of moving packets rapidly, entails a cost that will have to be paid over and above the basic costs of the basic end-to-end reliability, flow-control, and ordering protocol. The end-to-end principle argues that in most settings, the network should not try to do more than move packets because the incremental improvement in reliability will be negligible, and because the costs associated with that improvement might reduce the performance of the network. This analysis could be applied to security too: security on a hop-by-hop basis in the network will not give us end-to-end security. If we want the client-server session to be secure, we will need to negotiate the security keys directly between the client and the server: the endpoints.

Thus the end-to-end principle teaches that in many situations the best way to get a reliable end-to-end behavior is to optimize lower levels for high performance, generally high reliability (but without absolute promises), and very low overheads. The end-to-end approach does not preclude exceptions: one certainly might consider tunneling through a reliability protocol when running over a noisy wireless link (Balakrishnan et al. 1999), or encoding recovery information into the data flow on a WAN link that sometimes overloads its receivers by delivering packets faster than they can accept them due to bursty flow dynamics (Balakrishnan et al. 2008; Freedman et al. 2010). These are cases in which high loss occurs on some individual link or some individual component, and for that sort of localized, higher frequency loss, local recovery makes good sense. But the key is the analysis: before blindly assuming that every component of a reliable system needs to be reliable, we need to ask what reliability buys us, layer by layer. In some cases we gain better high-level reliability by not paying for an unnecessary reliability guarantee in a lower layer.

What does this tell us about the modern network in a world of reliable cloud computing? The cloud certainly embraces an end-to-end philosophy, on the whole. But just as we might make exceptions on wireless networks or WAN networks that sometimes generate such high data rates that receivers cannot keep up, necessitating an in-network response, what we will see in this chapter is that there are other situations that also require some form of network-level remedy or mechanism. The first sections will focus on cloud-computing applications that depend upon steady data flows, such as systems that stream video or other media content. For these cases, we run into a design issue with the Internet: from its earliest days, the Internet was viewed as a distinct technology relative to voice telephony and television, and had no need to guarantee smooth delivery of the data streams used for VOIP or other media-over-IP uses. We will see that improving the network to better support these uses is entirely feasible, but requires that we migrate what may seem like data-center reliability ideas right down into the router itself. Then we will look at other opportunities, associated with mobility and caching short-lived dynamically created data. Each of these will reveal a need, and a way that by innovating in the network, the network can be a better partner for the future reliable cloud. The perspective that emerges is one of a kind of co-evolution: the cloud is evolving in ways that are changing the roles and pressures on the network, which as a result must also evolve. But we should also keep the end-to-end insight in mind: even if our goal is to achieve a reliable cloud computing function, doing so does not necessarily mean that we should blindly push the desired end-to-end properties into the network itself.

4.2.1   Internet Routers: A Rapidly Evolving Technology Arena

Perhaps the best place to start our review of networking in the age of cloud computing is with a close look at Internet routers, and particularly the category called "core" Internet routers. Until fairly recently, routers tended to be available in three basic sizes, at steadily increasing price, but all best viewed as black boxes that do their magic in ways that the customer (in our case, the cloud computing developer) had very limited ways to influence or control. These three categories include network switches, enterprise routers (sometimes called "edge" routers), and core Internet routers. We will say a few words about each category, then drill down on some of the reasons that developments in the enterprise and core Internet areas that have especially important implications for those of us interested in cloud computing. Unfortunately, enterprise routing is currently in flux to such an extreme degree that as this text was being revised, one could not really discuss the category in any degree of detail: anything true in 2011 could be invalidated by developments in 2012. Accordingly, we will focus on the core.

In our three broad categories, *network switches* are the simplest and in many ways, least functional kind of devices, although even switches are becoming much more elaborate. However, at least for the time being, a switch should be understood as a very simple device that would typically be used to link a set of optical network segments with a few machines on each segment into a larger virtual ethernet LAN. Switches route traffic between the segments, generally employing hardware MAC addresses as the basis for their switching decisions, and have a limited capability forward traffic "up" towards a core router if the destination that does not match the MAC address range used in the virtual ethernet LAN. Switching policies are normally very simple ones and are defined in manually constructed configuration tables that do not change while the network is in use. Although there are IP switching devices, which function in very much the same manner just described but use IP addresses as the basis for their actions, even these switches do not run routing protocols.

Routers, in contrast, make forwarding decisions on the basis of IP addresses and offer much more flexibility in terms of how the routing tables that control those decisions are maintained. Typically, a router will load routing tables from configuration files, but then update those while active by running one or more routing protocols, each concerned with some category of routing behavior: for example, an ISP might use BGP (the Border Gateway Protocol) to interact with other ISPs, but OSPF (the Open Shortest Path First protocol) for decisions about routing within its region. We will say more about this category of devices in a moment.

Modern cloud computing data centers contain both kinds of networking devices. A typical cloud computing data center is constructed in a modular manner, from machines that slot into racks, with 32 or 64 machines per rack. Each rack will have a 10 Gbit ethernet interconnecting the machines within it (along with power, cooling and perhaps some form of rack management software), and these ethernet segments connect to a switch. The role of the switch is thus to link some number of racks into a larger LAN network, and then to shunt traffic that needs to leave the group towards the core data center network. Many data centers are constructed from container-trucks packed with computing systems (as opposed to storage systems), and in these one finds many densely packed racks. Thus a single container could contain a few thousand machines in total (and each of those might have 12 or more cores), together with the equipment to power them, cool them, detect faults, etc. The in-container network would consist of multiple optical ethernet segments, linked into a virtual ethernet by the container switch. Data centers are often designed to resemble warehouses, with bays into which 18-wheel trucks can back up, drop off or remove a container of machines, and where those containers will reside while in use. The owner plugs the container into the dock, supplying power, cooling and network access, and the container boots much in the way that a device boots when connected to your PC at home: the data center manager becomes aware of the machines, configures them, and starts running applications on them.

This way of building data centers results in a kind of tree in which the machines at the leaves are themselves basically clusters (modern multi-core architectures are very similar to small clusters). These machines are in turn clustered into racks of perhaps 32 nodes, and the racks are interconnected into containers with perhaps 5,000 machines in one container. At all of these levels switches handle most network traffic. The containers are interconnected to one another and to the data center management infrastructure, in contrast, by a more traditional routed network, with routers talking to the containers and to one-another in some sort of topology. These routers determine routing by a mixture of policy (configured by the data center owner) and protocols (running between the routers and used to adapt dynamically as links are brought up or down).

In a modern data center some applications generate extremely high loads that could crowd out other traffic. To handle such cases, a switch can be programmed to isolate the heavy traffic flows and redirect them over network links that other traffic cannot access. This feature is often used when the layout of applications results in a predictable and long-term load from one side of a data center to another (for example, a data center might have some set of containers each maintaining a mirrored copy of part of its file system). By sending all that traffic (in our case, file system updates) on a dedicated set of links, the data center owner achieves better performance, and also spares the enterprise router from needing to deal with the associated load.

Moreover, since the network would otherwise be roughly tree-like, shortcuts that can divert these steady, high-volume data flows avoid overwhelming the network links near the core, which otherwise see excessive loads. In effect, we end up with a data center network that still looks like a tree, but now it has additional high-load optical cables interconnecting some of its branches. Data center application management software will typically be programmed to know about this topology, and will try to place applications in such a way that as much of the traffic generated as possible follows short routes: between two neighboring blades in the same rack, for example, or between two adjacent racks. Again, this avoids overloading the core of the network, which could easily see far too much traffic if layout was indifferent to data center network topology.

Management of such an elaborate infrastructure can become very difficult, particularly when one considers that cloud computing systems also have firewalls (both software and hardware versions, employed to prevent third-party applications from malfunctioning in disruptive ways), network address translators, load balancers and other kinds of configurable device within them. In the recent past, each such device used to be hand-configured; any reader who has ever set up their home network firewall to accept incoming TCP connections[1] will be aware of the manner in which this is done (basically, by filling out a table on a web page implemented directly by the firewall). In response, the enterprise networking community has begun to develop standards for controlling switches and other enterprise network routing devices remotely, and software to automate the needed actions. The standard, called OpenFlow, is quite simple: it defines an interface between the switch and the remote controlling logic but says almost nothing about how that logic might use this functionality. A wide variety of products are now emerging in this space, each with its own specialized ways of managing switches, firewalls, NAT boxes, etc. In the simplest uses, the OpenFlow technology allows the data center operator to centralize the management of the configuration tables for all of those devices. However, fancier

---

[1]Network address translators and firewalls often allow connections to be established in just one direction: from the "inner" network towards the external one. Thus, from Gimme! Coffee in Ithaca, my laptop can connect to a server at Amazon.com, but were Amazon.com to try and connect to my laptop, that second option would not work. It should be easy to see why this happens: although my machine has a unique IP address assigned by the DHCP protocol within the Gimme! wireless network, from the outside, all of the machines currently in use at Gimme! seem to share a single IP address, namely that assigned to Gimme! by the ISP from which the coffee shop gets its network connectivity. For connections from my machine to Amazon, all of this poses no issue at all: my machine picks a port number and tries to connect to Amazon, and the Gimme! wireless router simply replaces my IP address with its own IP address, and my port number with one it selects to be unique. When packets come back from Amazon, it does the reverse translation. But in contrast, had Amazon tried to connect to me directly, the connection establishment packets would have the IP address of Gimme!'s wireless router (or perhaps, firewall) in them, and the port number would seem to identify a service running on the router, not on my machine within the wireless subnetwork. Thus, short of assigning a static IP address and port range to my machine and somehow exposing that address to the outside world, incoming connections cannot be supported because the wireless router will not know what to do with them. There have been some proposals to work around this limitation, but to date, none has been widely adopted by the Internet community.

OpenFlow technologies are rapidly entering the marketplace. These maintain a kind of dialog with the devices they control, installing one set of rules, running for a while, but then receiving a form of interrupt or exception when something out of the rule coverage space occurs, at which point the OpenFlow control system can step in and modify the rule set. It is easy to see that over time, this will create a new kind of enterprise routing capability. In mid 2011, the Open Networking Foundation was created to advance the standard and reduce the barriers to commercialization issues. The technology press reports very rapid adoption of technologies in this space, and a huge commercial investment in these kinds of technology.

The second two categories of routers are the ones concerned with enterprise routing and core Internet routing, and both involve true routers that form routes under software control through peer-to-peer protocols that run between the routers and implement any of a variety of routing algorithms. Enterprise routers are sometimes also referred to as "edge" routers; these terms had more meaning in the past than they do today, and we will not worry much about the old distinctions that were implied. Basically, core network routers run more complete sets of routing protocols; edge routers more typically limit themselves to a smaller set of routing protocols. Moreover, while core network routers often have connectivity to large numbers of other routers ("peers"), edge routers would generally have connectivity to core routers running "above" them, and to switches or other enterprise routers running "below" them. To reiterate, though, these distinctions mean much less today than they did even five years ago.

As noted at the start of this chapter, enterprise routing is in turmoil today. Data center operators are finding existing routing options inadequate for their demanding needs, and this is forcing rapid evolution of data center enterprise routers; so much so, in fact, that anything we could say about them would be invalidated in a very short time. It seems likely that the architecture of these kinds of router will be utterly transformed by this process. Core Internet routers, in contrast, are also evolving under pressure from the cloud, but in a way that seems to reflect a more stable, more incremental process. Thus while we are seeing these devices transform from very big, very expensive black boxes into much more open architectures, those underlying architectures are not changing drastically from what has been the norm over the past decade or so. In particular, it seems clear that for at least a decade or two into the future, a core Internet router will consist of a collection of computers that control clusters of router "blades", interconnected by some form of internal routing fabric. The routing per se occurs in hardware: a network link enters the router, and the router hardware reads packets off that link and then decides where to send each packet next. The hardware is controlled by a routing table, which can be downloaded into it by routing software. And this routing software consists of what we call router daemons: programs dedicated to running some particular routing protocol, which compute updates to the routing tables and then tell the hardware to revise its behavior accordingly, by pushing those updates down into the fabric layer.

The routers used in the core of the Internet send and receive data on optical fibers, which are typically engineered to an extremely high quality standard. Loss rates of less than 1 bit in 10^{19} are not uncommon. With modern laser technology, under the physical constraints imposed by signal power and by the transmission properties of optical cables, a single fiber cannot carry more than about 25 Gbits/second of traffic, and 10 Gbits currently represents a practical limit over longer distances (this reflects the Shannon coding theory for optical networking technology: there are only so many dimensions in which an optical bit can be encoded, and only certain optical wavelengths that can be used in this manner). As a result, when we talk about routers that already run at speeds of 40 Gbits/second and will soon reach 100, then 400, and then a Terabit/second, parallelism represents the main option for improved speed. For example, today a 40 Gbit router might operate over 4 side-by-side strands of optical fiber, each carrying 10 Gbits/second of traffic. We can reach 100 Gbits by deploying 25 Gbit technology on the fiber links, but beyond that step, speedups will come mostly from running multiple fibers side-by-side.

Similar issues arise within the router itself. Routers, like other computing devices, seem to have reached a peak clocking speed and even with the help of hybrid optical/electrical hardware, the clocking speed limits their ability to switch data. Faster clocks would result in excessive heat, leaving the switching circuits at risk of meltdown. Thus, just as servers and even desktop machines are now shifting towards multicore architectures, so too are routers. The routers at the core of the Internet used to be elaborate but largely single-core machines; over the past decade, the balance has shifted dramatically and now these machines are massively parallel.

How will a typical core Internet router look during the coming decade or two, and why is the architecture of such importance? The answers may surprise the reader: a modern router looks more and more like a small data center, consisting of racks of switching cards (each will typically have 16 to 32 optical ports, for cables running to other routers at geographically remote locations). Associated with each switching card one typically sees a coprocessor dedicated to running the device driver for the card (this will have the job of installing the low-level routing tables on which the switching fabric itself operates), and one or more additional co-processor cards that will often run a standard operating system, such as Linux or QNX, and can support standard applications.

A high-capacity core Internet router might have tens of units of this sort, each with its switching card and co-processors, resulting in a single router that consists of perhaps 50 or more machines, and the industry is talking about routers that might include thousands of CPUs in the future. One can think of such a structure as a kind of high-performance parallel computer dedicated to controlling massive numbers of specialized devices (the individual line cards, and the hardware "fabric" of the switch that allows the cards to talk to one-another at line rates). At the data rates we are talking about, the actual work of switching data must occur within a few tens of clock cycles, and will often have a performance "budget" limiting the logic to just three or four memory references.

This has all sorts of implications. An implication for routing, per-se, is that modern routing algorithms do not have time to search tables or perform other kinds of classification that might require memory references: there is time for a single lookup but not much more. The solution to this problem is to use very large hashed tables: a router receives a packet, pulls the destination address[2] into a high-speed hardware register, and uses the value as an index into the routing table, from which it immediately learns the outgoing queue to which the packet can be copied and the corresponding port (link). Unless there is some level of congestion on the link, the hardware barely needs to touch the packets as they flow through the device: it just forwards the packet, decrementing the TTL count as it does so, and then appends a new checksum if needed (this is because when we decrement the TTL we also invalidate the previous checksum; fortunately, the computation can be performed incrementally from the previous value).

The hardware-dominated process we have outlined here is very much in contrast to traditional store-and-forward routing, where the entire packet would typically have been read into some form of router memory, then enqueued for output on the appropriate network link. A modern core Internet router will have some limited store-and-forward queuing ability, but even when packets do get queued up, software will not necessarily be involved. IP multicast operates in a similar manner. The IPMC address is pulled off the incoming packet, and now a parallel processing task occurs: for each outgoing link, in parallel, a Bloom Filter test is performed to see if the packet should be forwarded on that link. Recall that a Bloom Filter will typically operate with $k = 3$, and hence 3 memory references may be required, but this is a perfect opportunity for parallelism.

With this background out of the way, we can ask what the main reliability issues associated with modern Internet routing turn out to be. Such a question quickly leads to a great deal of complexity, because core routers run a great many different routing protocols. Some routers run more than one at a time: one might see a single router on which daemons for BGP (the Internet Border Gateway Protocol), IS-IS (Intermediate System To Intermediate System), OSPF (Open Shortest Path First) are all in use, side-by-side, with their routing decisions then merged to create a single routing table. Moreover, cloud computing companies are increasingly eager to create virtual corporate networks that span sections of the core Internet, each with its own internal routing policies. But if we try to discuss reliability against this full picture, we will just confuse ourselves. Accordingly, let us pretend that we only care about BGP: almost every router runs this protocol, and the issues turn out to be similar for other routing protocols, so what we can say about BGP will generalize easily to other protocols. In what way does BGP contribute to network reliability? How do current implementations of BGP interfere with our goals, and what can be done to improve those aspects?

---

[2]This could be an IPv4 address or an IPv6 address; one hears a great deal of discussion about the two as if they were dramatically different standards, but in fact as currently defined, the only major difference is that IPv6 addresses are twice as long as IPv4 addresses. In particular, routing algorithms and routers are essentially unchanged by the move towards IPv6.

4.2.2 The Border Gateway Protocol Under Pressure

Until recently, a protocol such as BGP would have been coded to run on a single machine (perhaps a multicore machine on which a multithreaded programming language would be an especially good choice), using TCP connections to BGP peers running in neighboring routers or neighboring ISPs, and updating the BGP routing table according to the rules laid out in the document that standardizes the BGP protocol. But times have changed, and today's BGP is a rather different beast.

First, the BGP protocol itself has been evolving, under pressure triggered partly by the sheer size of the Internet, partly to defend against routine mishap such as operator errors in remote locations that might disrupt BGP routing, and partly by the worry that hackers (or cyber warriors under control of some foreign government) might attack the BGP protocol. The size issue is this: as the Internet has grown, the size of BGP routing tables has also grown, particularly because so many companies operate multi-homed networks, with two primary IP addresses obtained from two distinct ISPs, as a protection against failures that take one of the ISPs entirely off the Internet (studies have shown that at any time, the global Internet has 60 to 100 regions in which some form of brownout is occurring, preventing applications in those regions from establishing connections to some other major region, even though all the end-hosts are healthy). As customers push back because of disruptions triggered by mobility, the pressure to consider some form of tunneling or multihoming solution for the mobile endpoint will grow, too.

Secondly, just because the number of ISPs involved is growing so sharply, more and more opportunities exist for someone to make a minor mistake that would result in the spread of erroneous BGP routing advertisements. For example, suppose that the folks at InformationWantsToBeFree.com, a small ISP based in Freedonia happen to have a corrupted entry in their BGP routing tables, claiming that the best possible route to the US military network leads into their network, and then out on a link that happens to be shut down. This is called a black-hole mistake: if this BGP route is accepted, traffic to the military network will vanish into nowhere.

BGP configuration mistakes such as this happen all the time. What prevents them from spreading, and destabilizing the Internet in some basic, long-lasting way? Nothing, really, except that ISPs have learned to defend themselves against implausible BGP updates. Incoming BGP routing updates are passed through a kind of sanity check, and an updated route will not be accepted unless it passes the test. This also offers some degree of protection against a sudden decision by the government of, say, North Caledonia to disable the entire Internet by transmitting nonsense BGP routing tables, thereby precipitating a world-wide collapse of Western governments and clearing the tables for the installation of the Beloved Father of North Caledonia as the new and permanent world visionary. To some extent, existing sanity checks would probably catch such BGP routing packets in their tracks; should one slip past the checks, the operators of the impacted ISPs would quickly notice that traffic is suddenly pouring towards Freedonia New York, or New Caledonia, and would realize that an errant BGP routing table entry was responsible, at which point they could update their filtering policy and defend against the problem.

Another problem is caused by upgrades. A core network router needs to be running 24x7, yet each time we patch or otherwise modify the BGP daemon software, we will need to switch from the currently active version to the new one. Similarly, migrating the BGP daemon from whatever node it happens to be running on to a new node will force it to shut down and restart, and we may need to do this for any of a number of reasons. Today, vendors tend to patch and pray: they set up the new BGP, then issue a command that abruptly shuts down the old copy and enables the new version. It would be nice to have a way to run multiple BGP instances side by side, just to test out the new version before putting it in the driver's seat, but this is not yet an option.

Here we encounter a major network reliability challenge. Think about what happens if a BGP daemon shuts down, and then instantly restarts. There turn out to be two behavior, neither of which is all that good. In the basic BGP mode, if BGP shuts down on a router, that router's peers will begin to route traffic around it, on the assumption that the router itself may be down. So, we were using route X–Y–Z, but suddenly Y seems to be down, hence we need to come up with some other option, perhaps X–U–V–W–Z. These routing changes are disruptive: they need time to stabilize (during which traffic may route in cycles or even vanish into black holes), and secondary routes are sometimes inferior in other ways: they may be longer, more loss-prone, etc. Now, the new BGP starts to connect to its peers and they send routing data to help it resynchronize. After what can be several minutes in a core-Internet setting, the new BGP is finally back into sync and we are back to using route X–Y–Z. Yet in the meanwhile, any users with traffic flowing through the impacted area could see huge disruptions.

The second mode of BGP operation is similar, except that BGP signals to its peers that it wants to use "graceful restart", a special BGP option. Recall that our router does the real heavy lifting in hardware, not software. The idea behind graceful restart is to leave that hardware routing table in place and hence basically to leave the router on auto-pilot while the new BGP synchronizes with its peers. The peers keep using the same routes they were using previously, and the hope is that the sorts of disruptions we have mentioned will not occur. Yet here a different problem arises: in the core Internet, BGP updates may occur at rates of tens or even hundreds per second. Thus within a short time, our router may have drifted out of sync with respect to its peers because until the new BGP daemon is running and in sync with them, the router will not be responding properly to those updates. Once again we end up with the potential for routing loops and black holes, and again, the end-user sees a reliability issue.

A widely cited 2004 study of router availability yielded the data shown in Fig. 4.1, and stands as a kind of blueprint for what needed to be done back then to achieve better routing behavior. The table reveals several main sources of router downtown, and as we will see, one can attack pretty much all of them. The most important problems as of 2004 involved network link failures. Over the ensuing period, ISPs have begun to deploy redundant network links: rather than depending on a single connection from Freedonia to Ithaca, the ISPs in the region use two or more links and balance the load. If a storm takes out one link, the other is still available.

Fig. 4.1 Availability
breakdown of a typical
network router, from a 2004
study by the University of
Michigan

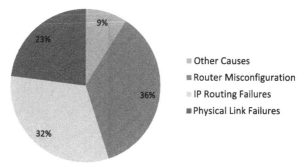

Source: University of Michigan and Sprint, October 2004

Similarly, the 2004 picture showed a huge contribution from hardware failure, but of course in 2004, most routers were still single, monolithic devices. Today routers contain redundant hardware: in a cluster, one rarely sees large numbers of blades crash simultaneously; more often, an individual machine goes down or needs to be replaced. Thus, the main forms of hardware failure can be tolerated provided that the component that failed was not playing some sort of unique, irreplaceable role. Continuing to work from the figure, we can see that as of 2004, we really needed much better router management software; this has evolved enormously.

In fact, whereas the 2004 reliability picture was pretty dire (routers back then were achieving what could be called 3-nines availability, meaning that over long periods of time, the router was up 99.9% of the time: not such an impressive number; telephone networks aim for 5-nines), the situation today is dramatically different. Right now the big remaining issue is to improve the software availability of the routing protocols themselves, or more accurately, the daemons running them, such as the BGP daemon that implements the BGP protocol. Such a daemon is a large, complex software system (readers might want to read about the open-source Quagga routing daemon to learn more). If a BGP daemon crashes or has to be migrated, the resulting several-minute periods of BGP confusion (the delay depends on whether or not the router enables graceful restart) represent the largest obstacle to modern router reliability!

Could we do better? Recent research has focused on this question, with very encouraging results. For example, Princeton's networking group (led by Jennifer Rexford and Mike Freedman) has explored virtualization as a tool for rapidly migrating BGP (Wang et al. 2008). In this approach, a BGP image can be moved from node to node without ever disconnecting it from its peers, even briefly. Part of the trick is to recall that an IP address is not necessarily tied to a specific machine in a modern network. Thus one can literally freeze BGP, move it, and move its IP address too. BGP resumes execution on the new node in the identical state to the one it was in before the migration!

On the other hand, migrating BGP will not help if we needed to restart BGP for some other reason, such as a node or software crash, or to do a BGP upgrade. For this we need a way to get the new BGP rapidly into the same state as the old BGP, and then to somehow hide the event from the remote peers: if the TCP connections

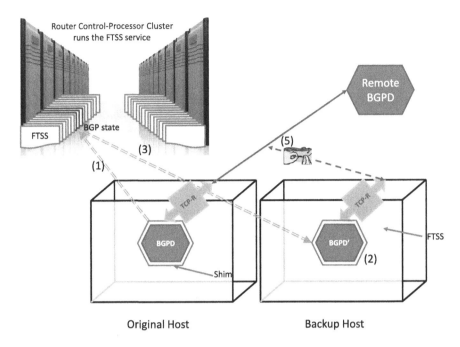

Original Host   Backup Host

Fig. 4.2 The fault-tolerant Border Gateway Protocol daemon (BGPD) architecture. The architecture runs on a router constructed as a cluster of host computers that control racks of network line cards, with the actual routing done mostly in the hardware. The shim (a) replicates BGPD's runtime state into the fault-tolerant storage service (FTSS), which is implemented as a distributed hash table (DHT; shown as an oval). The figure portrays the BGPD state as if it resided at a single node, but in fact the solution spreads it over multiple nodes for fault tolerance and also to speed things up by enabling parallel PUT and GET operations. After a failure, (b) BGPD can restart on some healthy node, (c) recover its precise state, and (d) resume seamlessly. The TCPR layer (e) splices connections from the new BGPD to the still-open end points its remote peers hold, masking the BGPD failure/recovery event

they use are in any way disrupted, they will insist on running the basic or graceful BGP restart protocol, with all the disruptions this can cause. Yet this problem can be solved, too (Agapi et al. 2011), as illustrated in Fig. 4.2.

The basic idea starts by storing the BGP routing table directly in the memory of all those nodes that make up the cluster, in a redundant (3-replicated) manner designed to survive almost any likely failure pattern. In this manner, when BGP dies on node A and is relaunched on node B, reloading its state takes as little as hundreds of milliseconds even for very large routing tables. We will be looking at these kinds of collaborative in-memory storage schemes later; they fall into the general category of "distributed hash tables" and are implemented as key-value stores supported by daemon programs running on each of the participating nodes. Checkpointed restart can be completely seamless: by ensuring that the BGP state is checkpointed as each incoming update is received, and before any outgoing update is sent, we can ensure that the recovering version of BGP will behave in a way that is byte-by-byte identical to that of the failed copy it replaces. The performance of the approach centers on the extremely low latencies and high bandwidths of the network that runs within the cluster, which makes it only slightly slower to access data in some other node's memory than it is to access it from a node's own memory (and orders of magnitude faster than disk accesses would be). The particular DHT used in the work on BGP is called the Fault-Tolerant Storage System, FTSS, and was developed by Agapi and Kielmann, at the Vrije Universiteit in Amsterdam.

Thus we can potentially get our new BGP instance running and into the right state in milliseconds, by storing an in-memory checkpoint and playing it back very rapidly when the new instance is launched. But, to avoid needing to run the graceful restart protocol, we also need to prevent the BGP peers from wasting time trying to resynchronize with this restarted BGP. Having gone to the trouble of making the fail-over seamless, it would be pointless for the remote peers to still think that BGP experienced a failure. Here we run into a second issue: BGP is defined to treat a TCP connection reset as a sign that the remote BGP peer failed. Thus, our solution runs afoul of the need to reconnect BGP on node B to all the peers that BGP had sessions to when it ran on node A! One could change the BGP standard, but (inspired by our insight into how cloud computing evolved), might there not be a way to solve this without forcing anyone to modify their existing BGP implementations?

The technical challenge that arises in implementing this scheme is that it requires a special kind of TCP session that somehow hangs in a frozen state when the end-point originally using the protocol fails. Then, when the new instance of BGP takes over from the failed one, we need a way to *splice* a new TCP endpoint to the old, active, TCP session, without any disruption at all being visible to Verizon. Figure 4.2 illustrates the desired sequence of events. As it turns out, this is a solvable problem; we will look at it in Part II, and will see several ways of solving it. One uses replication to replicate the entire TCP stack in the AT&T data center; this method, due to Zagorodnov et al. (2009) treats the TCP endpoint as a kind of object, used by but distinct from the application process that receives data on that endpoint. A second method was developed more recently by Surton (Agapi et al. 2011) and is dramatically simpler: rather than replicate the TCP stack itself, Surton leverages the knowledge held by the old BGP application and by the new instance that took over from it and works a little like a firewall or network address translator, editing some fields in the IP packet header to graft the restarted BGP to the old TCP session in a manner invisible to the Verizon side of the connection. The overhead for this scheme, which Surton calls TCP-R, is remarkably low: it requires just 350 microseconds for BGP to reestablish all the connections that were in use prior to the fail-over event, in a manner completely invisible to the remote peers. This is such a short delay that it falls well within the norms for BGP peer-to-peer communication under regular operating conditions. In effect, the peers just do not notice that anything happened.

By combining a version of BGP modified to use collaborative in-memory checkpointing with this TCP-R solution, we can completely hide the BGP failure and restart from neighboring routers. Referring back to Fig. 4.1, this eliminates the last major source of availability issues identified in that old 2004 study of router availability! Not a single of the major categories identified in the study remains unaddressed. Indeed, taken jointly, the industry has made such dramatic progress since 2004 that one really would have to redo the study to understand the availability routers built this new way could achieve: we seem to be out of the 3-nines or less availability levels and into some totally new regime. Such studies await further research, but a back-of-the-envelope analysis suggests that the Internet could be heading for the 5-nines reliability level associated with the older telephone network. Indeed, it may even be possible to push beyond 5-nines.

From this we arrive at several kinds of insight. One is that tomorrow's Internet could achieve availability levels of a kind we normally associated with wired telephone networks, with very low frequency of disruptions. Today we are not quite there yet (the approach just outlined, for example, has been demonstrated in research labs, but no products offer these capabilities yet). Even so, they presage a tremendous change in the way the Internet behaves. For more than 40 years, we have lived with an Internet that was built to move email and files and seems poorly matched to such uses as VOIP telephony or media streaming. In the near future, we will start to see a new kind of high availability Internet, motivated by customer pull from both the end-user (who wants a more seamless networking experience) and from cloud-providers (for whom market share revolves around that same question of customer experience). Moreover, higher availability would accelerate the shift of television and radio and voice telephony to the Internet: a trend that is already underway, but up to now has been limited by inadequate availability levels, manifesting as connections that freeze up or break for no obvious reason.

A second insight is that the cloud style of incremental technology evolution can apply in the network too. By setting the goal of masking BGP failures, and insisting that we do not want to change BGP itself in deep ways, we have found a path that lets us achieve higher BGP availability but treats the BGP daemon itself, and the TCP stack, as black boxes. None of the technologies mentioned above require that TCP be modified, and while they do require some changes to the way BGP behaves, it turns out that rather than modifying BGP one can simply build a kind of "wrapper" that runs a legacy BGP instance but handles such tasks as talking to TCP-R and storing data in the DHT on its behalf. Moreover, we arrived at a solution one could deploy incrementally (meaning one router at a time), with benefits to users who send traffic over the region using our technique, and yet without any kind of disruption to organizations that prefer not to use and that would rather not see changes to the BGP protocol specification. Finally, although we have used BGP as our target here, everything we discussed would be equally applicable to a daemon running IS-IS or OSPF, or even some other routing scheme invented by Amazon.com or Google.

A final insight is that the cloud and the Internet are ultimately partners, each playing its role in the overall cloud enterprise. Moreover, the same technologies are needed within the cloud data center, and within the router. We solved our BGP fault-tolerance problem by using what sounds like a cloud computing reliability technique, yet we used it right in a core Internet router. In doing so, we ended up with a new network option that might be useful for things other than high availability routing. Given unbreakable TCP connections, why not also use them when a web client talks to a service, especially in settings like our medical scenarios, or in the control of the electric power grid, or in other settings where continuous connectivity might be important? The basic methodology would seem to apply in any situation where the two end-points maintain notions of their respective states, and where loss of a connection can trigger an extended and disruptive resynchronization.

4.2.3   Consistency in Network Routing

One interesting topic that has gained increasing attention in the research community concerns the question of *consistency* as applied to routing. We will say that a set of routers are in mutually consistent states if all are using local routing tables that combine seamlessly into a single global routing policy. The routing protocols we have mentioned all settle into consistent states if a network experiences disruption but then settles down.

During periods when a routing update is being propagated, however, routing can briefly become inconsistent. As we saw, this poses risks: perhaps node X thinks the best route to node Z is via node Y, but node Y thinks the best route is via W, and W is still routing via X. Thus packets intended for Z end up on a cycle: X–Y–W–X and loop until their time-to-live (TTL) values decrement to zero. Black holes can also form: traffic from X to Z might be forwarded into Y, and yet Y might have no outgoing paths leading to Z except the one back to X; if this occurs, Y drops all the traffic to Z.

Inconsistency is a serious problem in the Internet; it causes all sorts of outages: services may become unreachable, traffic may come to a sudden halt, data could arrive out of order, or duplicated, etc. The end-user will be seriously impacted if such issues occur on routes that some important application depends upon.

There have been a few proposals to develop new forms of consistent routing protocols. For example, at the University of Washington, Arvind and Anderson have explored a scheme they call *consensus* routing, in which new routes are installed through a kind of two-phase dialog with the routers that need to adapt their paths (BGP paths, in this particular case). The scheme is such that when a router does switch to a new routing table, the other routers that will also need to switch do so in what looks like a single atomic action. Of course, this needs to be done in a fault-tolerant manner, and it needs to be very fast. We will be looking at ways of solving such problems in Part II of this text. Indeed, the Isis[2] system that we will use for some exercises in this text could be used as a consensus routing tool, and doing so raises fascinating research questions.

Routing consistency issues are of even greater importance within data centers and other large enterprises, where the OpenFlow standards have made it possible to treat the full set of routing equipment within a data center as if they were all components of a single massive, distributed, routing technology. Two kinds of issue arise. First, for scalability, one needs solutions that have costs local to the equipment involved in an actual routing change. Thus if Amazon's data center has 10,000 switches but some event should only cause routing updates in 35 of them, one wants any performance impacts to be local to those 35 devices, not the full data center. Second, we still want to be able to make global statements about consistency; ideally, we would like to be able to assert that any given packet traverses a series of routers and switches that are in mutually consistent states. Lacking that, we might accept a slightly weaker property, such as a statement that any given route sees a series of switch and router states that are in temporally monotonic states: they reflect the same "route-table time", or increase in this time metric, but never travel from a switch that is using routing table t to one using routing table $t - 1$.

Stating such a problem can make it sound easy to solve, but in fact this is very far from the case. The question we have just posed is a good example of a topic that could earn PhD theses for future graduate students in the area. Achieving a solution that scales well, performs well, and that has minimal impact on data center performance when routes change will be a hard engineering challenge. That solution must also be fault-tolerant and secure against intrusion or attack: a tall order!

Yet there is every reason to believe that these questions are solvable, and that solving them will enable big advances in the capabilities of the cloud platforms that they support. After all, today's cloud platforms, just like the Internet WAN, are at constant risk of severe data center wide disruptions each time routing changes in a big away. When that happens, every single application hosted on the center could be impacted, perhaps in severe ways. Thus the first company to offer a really good solution stands to revolutionize the field and, in the process, to make a real killing in the data center network management market, which is expanding at a white-hot pace. It would be hard to imagine a better PhD research topic!

4.2.4 Extensible Routers

If a router has ample processing capacity, and supports the software needed to build reliable services that can survive faults in ways invisible to their users, it makes sense to think about ways of extending the ability to control routing decisions so that the customers themselves might be able to determine routes that will apply to their own traffic. The customers we have in mind here are big cloud providers, and they would pay for the use of these customization services. But on the other hand, companies like Google and Microsoft and IBM and Facebook each have "opinions" about the very best place to route each packet that enters their data centers. If they can impose control over the Internet routers themselves, they may be in a position to offer higher reliability, new kinds of service and to reduce the costs of doing so. And they may also be able to reduce the load on the Internet as a whole, by making smarter routing choices than the network itself would have made.

Today, this kind of extensibility is difficult and requires contracts between the cloud provider and the ISPs carrying the traffic in question. Those ISPs would convert the cloud provider's routing desires into policy that would then shape the routing tables they produce, for example by sending traffic generated by some Amazon.com data center over a particular route to some other Amazon.com data center. There are obvious advantages for the ISP in making such deals: the traffic will be predictable, hence they can assign a specific optical link with a known capacity, and can otherwise provision their networks intelligently to handle the load. On the other hand, Amazon.com would need to engage the ISP in dialog over every routing change they need that could impact the ISP.

Better, but still out of reach at the time this text was being revised, would be an ability for the router to host what might be viewed as a virtualized corporate router managed directly by Amazon itself, but operating purely within a virtual LAN that carries Amazon's traffic. In effect, the ISP would classify Amazon.com traffic—think of this traffic as being tagged with some color, like yellow. Google traffic might be tagged blue, etc. Now, the yellow traffic would be routed within yellow links using routing table entries from a yellow routing table *managed by Amazon itself.* In effect Amazon would gain a great deal of policy control, but only for decisions in which Amazon lives at one or both endpoints of the communication session. Then Amazon could run whatever routing policy it likes for these internal decisions. Readers familiar with a concept called a virtualized LAN or VLAN will recognize that what we are describing would generalize the way that VLANs work today, taking what is currently an enterprise networking concept used purely within a data center and extending it to also run between data centers. On the other hand, doing so would raise many technical questions.

The intense pressure to move in these directions makes it relatively likely that something along these lines will become common during the next decade or so. The resulting network might look very different from today's Internet, as discussed more fully in "The League of Supernets" (Birman 2003). In a fully deployed solution, we would basically have a set of networks that share the same hardware and can share links or even route traffic through one-another (consistent with whatever policies the owners and operators impose), but with each network potentially routing in a completely different manner. The most obvious use is the one we have described, in which a company like Amazon or Google takes control of how traffic from its clients, or between its data centers, will be routed.

Taken to the extreme, however, one could imagine deployments in which the network links and routing bandwidth would not necessarily be shared between such uses at all. Suppose that some ISP that already operates a very big router were willing to buy a bit more hardware. The ISP could then lease part of its router to a company with deep pockets, like Netflix or Amazon, perhaps along with some guaranteed link bandwidth or even a set of dedicated but currently unused fibers. The lease arrangement would promise that the company leasing the fibers and router hardware has the right to control routing over those links or through those line cards. This type of incremental expansion of an existing router is cheaper than buying one outright, so Netflix would save money by renting rather than owning. Netflix ends up in a position not merely to design its own routing protocols, but even to design network policies that might be very different than those seen in today's normal Internet. Obviously, the packet format would need to be IPv6: these routers bake the IPv4 and IPv6 packet formats into hardware. But the routing *policies* used could be customized to an almost arbitrary degree. Thus Netflix, which transmits video streams, could come up with video routing policies and even network queuing and prioritization policies optimized for their kind of traffic. Yet these links would be side by side with the standard IP network operated by the ISP, hence Netflix would also have the ability to use IPv4 or IPv6 as a normal transport protocol on the same links. The ISP ends up playing a role a bit like a cloud computing provider does today: it owns technology that is not used as effectively as it could be right now. With such a virtualized leasing option in place, the ISP suddenly is in a position to make money by renting its space capacity to cloud providers, who spend less to rent than they would to build from scratch.

The value would not be limited to a company like Netflix. A secure medical computing system could implement its own wire-level protocols and routing on behalf of the new medical communication services it offers: perhaps, those would be secure, robust against even extreme disruption, and offer timing guarantees, for example. Once again, the ISPs willing to run this new router add-on could charge for doing so, but the medical records cloud company might be willing to pay those fees rather than put patients at risk by trying to give similar behaviors over the shared, public Internet. A military network might reserve hardware components and links of intelligence traffic. Thus, we end up with what seem to be side by side Internets, yet in each case, can leverage the powerful cost incentives for renting rather than owning.

The League of Supernets paper cited above imagines how such a process might look after it entered wide use. We end up with a set of side-by-side networks that can talk to one-another, share resources, and cooperate in other ways, and yet can also do things that are very non-Internet-like on their dedicated infrastructures. The paper envisages a series of *super networks:* perhaps, a security network, a fault-tolerance network, a video-data delivery network. Each of these networks would need to be designed and operated and perhaps even "invented". On the other hand, the new networks could still reuse functionality associated with the existing Internet, to the extent that the existing solution has adequate properties. For example, that Netflix video streaming network could use the standard Internet to configure itself, employing streaming protocols only within the video network layer. Thus the Netflix solution would end up grafting something new to something old, and whole thing would run on something borrowed. The ISP would find itself in the cloud-like role of owning infrastructure (router hardware and optical fiber) and renting those resources, on demand, to big cloud customers, Today's ISPs do not participate fully in the cloud revenue stream, but such a vision suggests that perhaps tomorrow's ISPs will find themselves in a much more interesting place, commercially.

4.2.5 Overlay Networks

We have discussed the idea of application-specific routing, but all our examples related to standard routing protocols such as BGP, IS-IS and OSPF. This might leave the reader with a misimpression, because many of the most interesting application-layer routing options are not at all similar to the routing protocols used to manage the Internet itself. In this section, we will look at several examples of novel routing structures that researchers have worked with during the past decade or so, and that might fit this model. As we will see, while one could imagine putting these schemes on routers, they were designed for use directly by the end-host systems that use them; in some sense, they tunnel over the Internet but are implemented in user-space by the end-points themselves.

We will start with the simplest and best known example: MIT's Resilient Overlay Network (RON) system, which basically routes around Internet slow spots, adapting much faster than the Internet itself, which (by design) is slow to change its routing tables. Next, we will look at what are called *Distributed Hash Tables* (DHTs), which are distributed data structures offering quick ways to find things even in massive networks. These actually play a big role within today's cloud computing systems too, but they emerged from work on peer-to-peer file sharing and we will focus on that application when we discuss them here. Finally, we will discuss Berkeley's *Internet Indirection Infrastructure*, a novel way to use DHT structures in support of completely new Internet functionality.

In this subsection we will also look at some applications that run on top of these kinds of overlay infrastructure. The examples on which we will focus are just two among many: BitTorrent, the well-known protocol (and system) for rapid downloads of files and other large objects, and Sienna, a content-based routing infrastructure for sharing information in wide-area environments. Later we will revisit some of these technologies in cloud settings, where they play distinct roles. For example, BitTorrent is used for downloads of big files such as software patches in the Internet WAN, but has an important role for internal file copying at YouTube, which runs it within its own data centers. DHTs were invented in connection with peer-to-peer file sharing, but today, Amazon's shopping cart service, called Dynamo, uses a DHT technology invented by Amazon. These in-house network solutions sometimes can take advantage of special information, like network topology data, not available in the WAN. Yet they still have a great deal in common with the WAN versions, and we can gain a lot of insight by starting in the WAN and then looking at the cloud uses of these solutions later.

4.2.6   RON: The Resilient Overlay Network

MIT's Resilient Overlay Network (RON) system is a great place to start our tour of application-layer networking tricks because the concept is easy to understand, works remarkably well, and offers several important insights that we will apply in other contexts, too.

The RON effort started when researchers at MIT noticed that Internet routing sometimes picked very poor network routes relative to what the end-user (for us, a cloud provider talking to a client) might have wanted. Suppose that a client C is talking to a cloud platform S, and for simplicity, assume that S would seem to be the ideal cloud center to support C: nearby, with cached data for C's requests etc. Is C guaranteed to have a good network route to S?

The RON project studied this question and discovered that surprisingly often, the Internet route from a node (perhaps the server at S) to the client was very slow, lossy, or showed higher than predicted latencies. Many factors can explain such observations: congestion within the Internet, routing focused on the cost to the ISP for sending traffic (ISPs often enter into agreements with one-another, hence S's traffic might be routing through an ISP that finds it cheaper to send data via some second ISP even though the resulting route is not ideal from the perspective of the S-to-C data), etc.

Most students in networking classes are taught that the whole point of Internet routing is to adapt as conditions evolve, but in fact really quick adaptive routing is a thing of the past. Today, routing is managed carefully and routing decisions often have business ramifications for ISPs. Special pricing agreements, path capacity and many other considerations have given us a modern Internet that will certainly adapt to route around failures (although perhaps not all that quickly; two or three minutes would be a typical delay), but in which most routing is relatively static most of the time. Thus, the problems noted by RON are really a symptom of competing economic interests. While the data center servers and customers would like to see the fastest possible routes for data from S to C, the Internet routes actually used also need to give very strong weight to the interests of the ISPs carrying the traffic.

RON takes routing into the application's own hands. The work starts with the realization that many services run at multiple locations. For example, our cloud provider could easily have multiple data centers, call them S, T, U, V... The basic idea of RON is to take a set of endpoints (we would add the client systems to the set, so: C, S, T, U, V), compute the pairwise performance statistics using a simple probing technique that runs every minute or two, and then calculate the best route from S to C within this matrix of speeds and latencies. Sometimes the ideal choice may be to just use the S-to-C route offered by the Internet. But RON is also open to routing from S-to-U-to-C if that gives better performance. We call the resulting scheme an *overlay network* because in effect, it overlays a network managed by the cloud provider on the Internet. Sometimes the term "application layer" is also included just to stress that the Internet layer itself was unaware that RON implemented this higher level overlay.

It turns out that even a single indirect hop can have a dramatic impact. This highlights the issues we discussed in the previous section, illustrating precisely why today's cloud providers (which, after all, lose revenue if the network path is unreasonable slow or lacks adequate capacity) might want to control network routing.

RON is not a panacea, and some have argued that it risks a phenomenon that Adam Smith, an early American economist, would have called a *crisis of the commons*. The term arose from a classic economics dilemma. Suppose that we live in a small village and share a commons: a grassy central space that our houses surround, and where the community enjoys picnics and sporting events. Our village is famous for its wool—all of us raise sheep—and has been a prosperous and happy place. But one day, John Higgens, local wool entrepreneur has a sudden insight. Rather than having his sheep graze in the fields on the edge of the village, he can save himself a great deal of walking back and forth by letting them graze on the commons. So John moves his flock and gains a few hours of leisure.

The rest of us, exhausted by the trek to and from our fields, become jealous. So we move our sheep too. But the commons did not have enough grass for so many animals, and in a short while has been completely denuded. Sheep poop litters the whole area and nobody would dream of setting out a picnic. What was good for the individual has turned out to be bad for the community. So this is the essential nature of a crisis of the commons.

How would Adam Smith's argument map to the way that RON does routing? The commons is the Internet, and the place to start is by recognizing that there are good economic reasons that Internet routing, without RON in use, takes the form it currently has. In some ways the economics of the Internet shape the preferred routes: the routes the network uses are necessarily pretty close to being best money can buy (averaging over a long timescale, obviously: no company can react instantly when conditions evolve). In the long term, any ISP offering inferior routes and spending more of its revenue to run the network would lose out to its competitors.

So in this self-optimized situation, we suddenly start to deploy RON. The first company to do so might easily get a big win, assuming that the company itself is not one of the really big players. But if we all start to use RON (or if Facebook, Google, Amazon and other big players do), a kind of arms race has emerged. Now the optimization decisions the ISPs are making are backfiring because the traffic they had planned to send over such-and-such a high-capacity link, perhaps at a bargain rate, vanishes and tries to crowd itself onto some other lower capacity, expensive path that the ISP was not eager to use. Each time the ISP changes its routing, RON adapts and counters that decision with some other decision optimized for the RON users, but perhaps harmful to the whole network ecosystem.

Not surprisingly, it turns out that while RON is ignored for small-scale use (you can download the free software from MIT, compile it against your code, and start using it just like that). But for large users the situation is different. ISPs have rules prohibiting the use of RON-like overlay techniques unless their customers first request and are given permission to do so. In the eyes of an ISP, RON might be acceptable if it does not trigger the sort of struggle for optimization we outlined above, but ISPs have no tolerance at all for big customers who try and cheat to gain an advantage over other paying customers!

Although Adam Smith did not realize it at the time, his crisis of the commons idea eventually led to a Nobel Prize in economics, but much later. A Princeton mathematician, John Nash, became fascinated with the instability we see in these cases, where there are competing societal and individual interests. He showed how one can formalize these problems (doing so involves writing down *utility functions* that compute the value of a scenario to a participant; here one would need a utility function for the client, for the servers, and for the ISPs). We then express the global utility of the system as a combination of the individual utilities for the participants. This lets us ask what policy strikes the best balance among the competing options: in effect, which policies earn the most utility for each kind of player?

Nash showed that not all situations are stable. The ones that do have stable solutions are said to permit Nash Equilibria: a policy having the property that any change of strategy causes all the participants to lose utility—to be less satisfied. When operating using the Nash Equilibrium policy, there is no incentive to try and game the system. By using RON without dialog with an ISP, we run a substantial risk of the sorts of instabilities that Nash predicted: a duel of wits between the ISP, with its routing objectives and constraints, and the application, bringing a distinct set of objectives and constraints. But with dialog, it may sometimes be possible to find a mutually beneficial compromise: a Nash Equilibrium solution.

As we read about other tricks one can play within the Internet, it turns out to be useful and important to keep these perspectives on RON in mind. RON was not the first system to create network overlays, but it uses them in an elegant, easily appreciated way. We will want to keep this idea in mind, because it can be useful in other settings too. Next, RON highlights the sense in which the application might want to gain control over things that are traditionally thought of as black boxes one uses, but cannot control. And finally, we need to think beyond the initial stage: a technology cannot benefit its users in ways that could harm the community. The Internet is a shared resource, and applications need to be mutually respectful, and also respectful of the fact that someone is paying for each element of the system. If we build systems that behave selfishly to the detriment of others, or that hurt the economic interests of the network providers, we will just find those solutions blacklisted.

4.2.7 Distributed Hash Tables: Chord, Pastry, Beehive and Kelips

What else can overlay networks be used to do? Our next topic arose in the late 1990's when a wave of illegal movie and music sharing systems suddenly gained popularity. Most readers will be familiar with some of them (Napster was probably the best known, others include Gnutella, and Freenet). Several of these live on even now, although inexpensive legal solutions like the Apple iTunes store for music, and the Netflix and Amazon video streaming sites, are gaining ground steadily.

Systems like Napster, at least at first, offered a tool to assist in what was called peer-to-peer file sharing. The idea was simple: Sally happens to own a copy of the latest Lady Gaga album, and she uploads the songs to her computer. She allows Napster to catalogue this new music. Now Tom, a person Sally does not know and who does not even live in the area, searches for Lady Gaga's hit "Born this Way." Napster offers Tom a list of sources that includes Sally's machine (no personal information is offered). Tom clicks one of the links and his browser connects to Sally's system. Assuming the request is not blocked, Tom's music player will fetch the music from Sally's machine and play it for him. At this point Tom will also have a copy he can share, etc. Of course the request might be blocked by a firewall and the connection could be slow, but Tom is always free to click one of the other links. Usually, within a few tries, he will find one that works.

This type of music sharing is illegal, and we are not going to venture into the pros and cons of the underlying notion of digital property and control. The author happens to believe in the protection of intellectual property, but his experience trying to convince students first, that this is the correct position, and second, that they should actually live that way has not been all that good. But hopefully, we can all agree that the technical challenges are interesting.

A system like Napster has several components. One involves a server; it helped Tom's system find Sally's system. Such a server could track the actual music available at each user's machine, or it could just help the computers form a connected overlay within which search could be done in a more distributed, symmetric way. Thus we see an issue of overlay formation, and a second question of search. The third component is one that can download content when we find what we are looking for.

In fact Napster had other components too. Naturally, it was out to make a buck; Napster did this by placing advertising on its web pages (and it made a *lot* of money that way, a reminder of where the money really is in the Internet today). Because the recording industry felt threatened by Napster, the company found itself under attack: the industry had a strong incentive to upload Frank Sinatra songs and then to label them as Lady Gaga, in the hope of making the Napster experience so erratic that users would abandon the service. The industry also used virtualization to create fake servers that just performed very poorly (so Tom would perhaps find a virtual Sally, wait a very long time, and then hear Frank's rendition of Bim Bam Baby). This is called a Sybil attack, a reference to the famous novel about a woman suffering from multiple personality disorder. And finally, the industry sometimes attacked servers: so many Napster users were behind firewalls (and hence unreachable) that by attacking the few users who, like Sally, could actually accept incoming connections, the whole system could be destabilized. Napster, for its part, did all it could to defend itself and blacklist bad players. At the end of the day, of course, a judge settled the question, ruling that what Napster was doing was clearly illegal and shutting the service down, at least in this free sharing form. Obviously, that did not end the matter (dozens of other services soon sprang up to replace Napster, and Napster itself resurfaced in a new and legal form), but again, let us not go there.

There has been research on all aspects of this, including defending against the kinds of attack just listed (in effect, research on better ways of supporting illegal file sharing), but the topic we will focus on here starts with the idea of abstracting a few of the key steps in what Napster was doing and supporting those as clean functions.

Chord

The systems that emerged from this idea implement what is called *distributed hash tables* (DHTs), and there are many examples; we will look at just a few. Although it was not the first project to explore the topic, the first widely used DHT was Chord, a system created at MIT (Stoica et al. 2001). Chord takes a set of machines and organizes them as a cooperative online memory system, capable of storing information and retrieving it. The programming interface could not be simpler: Chord lets the user *put* a (key, value) tuple into the store, or *get* the value associated with some key. Fancier DHTs allow multiple values associated with a single key and ways of removing a (key, value) mapping, and there has even been work on doing full database searches using patterns (queries) on the keys or values, but we will not follow the idea quite so far; we will focus just on the basic *get* and *put* operations.

Chord works by creating a kind of distributed binary search tree. As a first step, we take some form of unique machine identifier for each node in the system. Let us not worry about firewalls and network address translation, which complicate things

Fig. 4.3 Chord, a widely
used distributed hash table
(DHT) organizes nodes into a
ring, using hashed ids to
place each node. (key, value)
tuples are then stored at the
node with hashed key closest
to but less than or equal to the
hash of the tuple's key and
replicated on it successors.
Any value can be located
within at most $\log(N)$ hops,
where N is the size of the ring

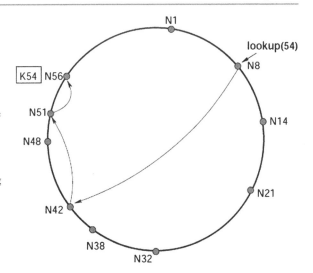

quite a bit, and just assume that we have a set of machines that all have unique IP
addresses; we will use these as the id's. Chord defines a *hashing* function; this takes
a value (an id, for example) and maps it in a deterministic way into a range of values,
ideally in a way that looks relatively random. Let us assume that the range of values
is just the unsigned 32-bit integers. Thus if Chord has a good hashing function, and
we have a set of perhaps ten participating nodes, we would ideally hope that even if
they have very similar IP addresses, each maps to a unique value in the 32-bit range,
and those values are relatively evenly spread out within the range. Chord will work
properly if something goes wrong, but it works best if these properties hold.

One good way to hash a value in this manner is to use MD5, a so-called cryptographic hash function. MD5 takes an input value, crunches it in various ways, and
returns a number that depends on the input but in a way that looks very random.
MD5 has good mathematical properties and can be computed rapidly, which is also
important in systems like Chord.

Next, we think of our 32-bit addressing space as a ring, in which positions on the
ring are identified by value. Figure 4.3 illustrates the idea.

To implement *put*, Chord takes the given key and applies the hashing function to
map it to a location on the ring. The rule is that a given computer owns any (key,
value) pairs that happen to map to its own hashed id, or to any hashed value up to
the id of the next node in the ring. Thus, if computer S maps to hashed location 1000
and computer T maps to hashed location 25000, and there are no other machines in
between, S owns the keys that map into [1000, 24999]. For example, if some user
(e.g. some computer using Chord) does a *put* of (K, V) and K maps to 3000, then
S will be asked to hold a copy of (K, V). Later if any computer does a *get* with the
same key K, the requestor will recompute the mapping, again obtain hashed value
3000, and the request will be directed to S. S will find the tuple in its local memory,
and return V.

How does Chord implement the lookup that gets us from whoever did the *put* or *get* to machine S? There are two ways to do this, and Chord supports both. One is to just have each node track its predecessor and successor on the ring. Thus if we happen to have machines S, T, U, V and W on our ring in that order, S will know that its predecessor is W and that its successor is T. If W needs to find the owner of key K, it can just forward the *put* or *get* in either direction, probably favoring the direction that seems numerically closer. If N is the number of machines in the ring, after (on average) $N/2$ hops we should reach the machine that owns key K. Of course, that machine can respond directly to node W without needing to route hop-by-hop back. Node W would then cache the node id that was involved, and the (K, V) pair; if a subsequent request arrives for the same information, it would be in a position to respond immediately.

Notice that we are acting as if the DHT treats these (K, V) tuples as *immutable*: once a value is written, it remains in the DHT. In practice Chord and other DHTs are generally fancier; they may support expiration times for tuples, deletion operations, and ways to do updates. But none of those features really change the basic idea.

Chord also has a kind of optimization that speeds all of this up. Each machine keeps a small table containing log(MAXINT) entries, assuming that MAXINT is the largest possible hashed key. In this table, entry i tracks the node that owns key $myHashedKey + 2^i$, where myHashedKey is the hashed key of the node owning the table. The tables will differ, of course, because each node has a different value for myHashedKey. Thus if Chord hashes into a 64-bit address space, the table might have 64 entries, listing 64 nodes. We call these *finger pointers*, and the table a *finger table*.

Now, suppose that W needs to *put* some value at the hashed location corresponding to key K. Rather than routing the (K, V) pair hop by hop around the ring, W can just find the finger with the largest value less than or equal to the hash of K and forward the (K, V) pair directly to that ring member. The receiving machine repeats this process using its own finger table. It should be easy to see that in a system with N nodes, following a search pattern very much like a binary search, our (K, V) pair reaches the right destination in at most $\log(N)$ hops. In practice, W would also cache some recently contacted target nodes, so that if the same key is used again, it can reach the right owner in just a single hop.

Of course our scheme, so far, will not tolerate failures. To deal with this, Chord replicates information. Rather than having a member track just its immediate predecessor and immediate successor, Chord tracks $\log(N)$ predecessors and $\log(N)$ successors. And rather than storing data at just one machine, Chord replicates each (K, V) pair at $\log(N)$ successive locations. When a computer fails, the neighbors notice this and make extra copies of any (K, V) pairs that are no longer sufficiently replicated; when a member joins the ring, the (K, V) pairs it should hold are copied to it by its predecessor and successor, and any (K, V) pairs that are now overly replicated are discarded by the ring member having the $N + 1^{st}$ copy.

Finally, we have the question of how to maintain all of these pointers. The basic idea in Chord is to have a very careful scheme for managing the predecessor and successor pointers. All the other pointers are periodically discarded and recomputed, but in an unsynchronized manner. Thus, every few seconds machine W might select some finger table entry, look up the key to which it corresponds, and update the finger table to reflect the correct id (if it changed). This type of highly randomized algorithm can be shown to converge after almost any imaginable failure, with one important exception: a network partitioning failure.

Imagine a Chord that has half its nodes at MIT, and half at Cornell. Now imagine that the Cornell to MIT link fails. As the two Chords repair themselves, they will converge towards a configuration with two distinct rings, slowly breaking one cross-link after another as the automated ring repair algorithms run. Eventually, the two rings will be completely disjoint, with no nodes in common, and no cross-ring links. To prevent this from happening, Chord has a notion of landmark nodes that members attempt to contact at some regular frequency, together with a ring merge scheme that kicks in if two partitioned rings happen to discover each other (as might occur if the Cornell to MIT connection is repaired). The merge is done by having nodes remove themselves from whichever ring they are on, and then reinsert themselves into the ring that the landmark nodes are on; the idea is that one of the rings (presumably the one at Cornell) will fade away, with its nodes reappearing in the MIT ring, and then replicating their (K, V) tuples through the normal process of replicating data to successors.

This merge algorithm is a weak point for Chord: while it is not very likely, one can "design" a failure pattern that would leave us with two rings, one at Cornell and one at MIT, having a few lingering connections between them. If we repair the network partition just at this instant, Chord can remain in this sort of stable but mostly split brain state, and will not recover from it. Yet to provoke such a situation would be very difficult; one needs a nearly omniscient adversary with perfect knowledge of the system state and perfect control over when the various links will break, or be refreshed. Thus, Chord is an example of a system that in some technical sense cannot guarantee correct behavior, but that does have a very high probability of correctness.

Pastry

Pastry, developed by a large collaborative team led by researchers at Microsoft Research Labs in Cambridge England and Rice University, is very much like Chord, but built using a slightly different short-cut method. The idea here is to pick some radix (some numeric representation base), perhaps 16 or 10. We still use a ring, as in Chord, and a hash function. But now we think of hashed values as *numbers* expressed using this radix. For example, a given key might hash to 000000000000A43D in radix 16. In practice Pastry limits itself to radix values that are powers of 2.

Pastry maintains finger pointers as a 2-dimensional table (a structure called a Plaxon tree); one dimension tells us which digit we are looking at in the key (we just number digits 0 to $\log_{\text{radix}}(MAXINT)$, from the high-order digit down). Thus 000000000000A43D has 0 in digits 0 through 11, an A in digit 12, a 4 in digit 13, a 3 in digit 14, and a D in digit 15. We will have a row in this table for each possible digit (hence 16 rows), and for each possible value that the digit could have (hence, 16). Had we used radix 8 (3 bits per digit), we end up with 11 rows, each with 8

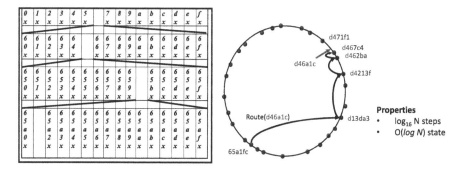

Fig. 4.4 The Pastry DHT uses a radix-based finger-table organization to gain greater flexibility in the choice of peers. Because Pastry will often have several candidate peers to pick from at each level (each "hop"), the system can select a node that is accessible (with no firewall or network addressing obstacles) and will offer high performance (low latency, high bandwidth)

columns for the possible bit values. Using radix 1 (binary), Pastry would need 32 rows, but each row would have just 2 possible values, 0 or 1.

Now, let us think about machine W in our ring, with an id that hashes to some value KW. For simplicity, let us assume that KW is the same value, 000000000000A43D, we used in our example in the prior paragraph. With this information, W populates its table as follows. Row r corresponds to the first digit of hashed keys. Notice that KW has a 0 in this first digit. So it puts its own node-id in column 0 of row 0. Then, for each of the other columns, Pastry puts the address of the closest known peer for keys matching in the prior rows and having the corresponding value in that column. Thus, if we were to jump down and look at row 13, we are talking about keys that start with 000000000000A and then have values $0, 1, \ldots, F$ in the next digit, and each column gives the address of the closest known peer for keys with the corresponding next digit. Figure 4.4 illustrates this example.

The forwarding rule is just as you might expect: When dealing with a hashed key that does not fall into the range you own, match the hashed key against your own key up to the first point at which the keys differ. Look in the column for that digit and forward to the machine you find listed there. You will always have some option because you always know of at least 3 nodes: yourself, your predecessor on the ring, and your successor. So in the worst case, you just forward to the successor or predecessor, whichever is closer to the desired key.

With radix 2, Pastry will actually behave exactly like Chord. The advantage is that with other radix values, Pastry gains some flexibility. Chord members are required to forward messages to a particular peer, namely the one you get to by looking up the hashed value of a key plus 1, 2, etc. Pastry can potentially use any of a number of peers as its finger partners because there may be many machines that match the first r digits of a key and that have a particular value as their next digit: it must find one that matches the key up to that point, but then picks the one that is closest in a latency sense if it still has a few to select among. For example, suppose W is trying to forward a (K, V) pair with a key that hashes to 7000000000000000. Any node with a 7 in the first digit of its hashed key is a legal possible peer. Thus, within this set, Pastry is free to look for a machine that happens to be nearby, using measured round-trip times to improve the choice of finger table partner. Studies of this strategy show that where Chord might often end up with very high latency "hops" in its searches, Pastry can often completely avoid that risk.

We have not said much about how Pastry initially populates the table, or how it deals with machines that join, leave, or fail; the details do not really matter for our treatment here and in any case, are basically similar to what Chord does. Thus Pastry is a more general formulation of the Chord concept, with a twist that gives Pastry a useful degree of freedom, namely the ability to chose the best among a set of possible partners so as to optimize performance. This idea is one used in many peer-to-peer systems. After all, why send a request from MIT to Kenya if there is a machine at Cornell that could forward it for you, especially if the actual destination machine turns out to be at Harvard?

Beehive

The researchers who developed Beehive, Rama Ramasubramanian and Gun Sirer, asked themselves what would happen if Chord replicated popular (K, V) tuples so that the system would have many copies rather than just the minimum needed for fault-tolerance. As an extreme case, suppose that some (K, V) tuple was replicated to the entire Chord ring. Since every node would have a copy, every query will return immediately: Chord becomes a 0-hop DHT. Of course, storing new (K, V) tuples on all N nodes in the ring will be costly, but the payoff would be an instant lookup.

Next, let's imagine that we replicate just half as much: a given (K, V) tuple will be replicated to $N/2$ nodes (those with key values between K and K−MAXINT/2). Consider a lookup for some particular key K.

With probability 0.5, the node doing the lookup will be in the range of nodes on which the (K, V) pair was replicated. If so we're in luck and have an instant answer with delay 0. The other possibility is that the node issuing the lookup falls into the other half of the Chord ring: the keys between K+1 and K+MAXINT/2. In such a case, Chord uses its finger-table to jump closer; in particular, the first hop will be of distance MAXINT/2, and hence will take us to a node that falls into the replication range and will therefore have a copy of the (K, V) tuple. Thus, with probability 0.5 we have a reply in 0 hops, and with probability 0.5, in 1 hop: on average, the delay will be 0.5 hops. Figure 4.5 illustrates this case.

Generalizing, the Beehive researchers found that they could replicate tuples to produce any desired average lookup latency between 0 and $\log(N)$. Next, they designed a simple popularity-tracking mechanism: for each (K, V) tuple, each access increments a counter at the node where the access succeeded, and then periodically, these counters are summed up over all the copies in the Chord ring. This enables Beehive to form a popularity ranking, at which point the system computes an optimal replication factor proportional to (K, V) tuple popularity: a popular item is replicated heavily; an unpopular one, only enough to satisfy fault-tolerance requirements. This yields a tunable optimization scheme with whatever average lookup delay the system desires. In practice Beehive is normally used with an average 1-hop delay, a value that trades off between replication cost (due to storage consumed) and speed.

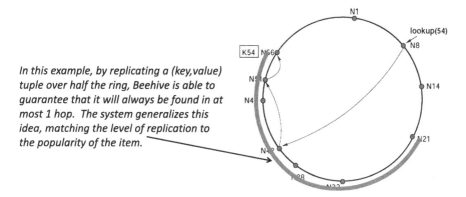

In this example, by replicating a (key,value) tuple over half the ring, Beehive is able to guarantee that it will always be found in at most 1 hop. The system generalizes this idea, matching the level of replication to the popularity of the item.

Fig. 4.5 The Beehive system, built over a Chord-like infrastructure, replicates (key, value) pairs to reduce the delay in finding popular values. By matching the replication factor to popularity achieves constant popularity, Beehive average delay O(1-hop). One application area was to support a faster version of the Internet DNS (the CoDNS project)

We will see other uses for this form of optimization, hence it may be useful to point out that "optimal" might not have the precise meaning one would expect here. The issue is that some node needs to compute this optimal data replication policy, and will do so using whatever data it has available. Those data could easily include stale membership data and stale information about item popularities and the relative ranking of those popularities. We would then optimize, but do so relative to a non-optimal approximation of the true values. Generalizing, when we see optimization used in distributed systems, we will always want to think about how the proposed scheme might work if the underlying data become stale or skewed. Beehive has been tested under conditions that include these kinds of staleness scenarios, and has shown itself to be very robust.

Kelips

The next DHT to consider here is Kelips (Gupta et al. 2003), a system created at Cornell to highlight the value of a technology called *gossip* communication. We will have much more to say about gossip protocols later in the text, so for now we will limit ourselves to a brief glimpse of the idea.

A *gossip state exchange* is said to occur when two machines in a network (two peers, in the terminology used above) come into contact and share information, much as humans do when they meet friends and spread a rumor. So, for example, node A contacts node B and asks if B has heard the story about node C making a killing in the stock market. Well, B certainly has heard the story now. Now A contacts D while B contacts E. The rumor spreads exponentially quickly, eventually reaching all nodes.

Gossip actually comes in several flavors: push gossip (the version we have just described), pull gossip (A asks B if B has any news to report; B responds with a hot story about C losing its fortune on a bad bet in the commodity markets...), and push-pull, which combines both patterns.

Notice that to use gossip, A needs to have a way to get into contact with B. Typically, this is done using a rendezvous server that hands out a few initial contacts; A boots, downloads those contact names from the server, and from then on runs gossip. Thus, when a gossip system starts up, each node would typically be in touch with some small set of nodes already in the system. If a machine is the very first one to launch the gossip application, the rendezvous service just tells is so, and it starts in an empty state, or perhaps loads an initial state from some form of checkpoint maintained by the application.

Once launched, most gossip systems start to gossip about multiple kinds of information concurrently, including membership in the system. Thus, if we launch node B it might be given A as an initial contact, and the first gossip exchange it does with A will include a long list of other members. From then on B will quickly become a full-fledged participant, catching up very quickly with everyone else. As membership changes, word will spread: perhaps node C joins, and first A learns (as an initial contact), but soon B learns too, perhaps directly from C (if C happens to gossip with B), perhaps via A, etc.

To deal with failures, many gossip systems track the last time anyone in the system heard of each node, and gossip that information just as they gossip anything else. The idea is that if B is healthy and gossiping in a normal way, these "last heard from" times for B will tend to spread through the system, tracking the current time (we are assuming clocks are synchronized well enough for this kind of thing, and they normally should be). So while C may be slightly out of date—perhaps it thinks that the last time anyone heard from B was at time 10:01.251 and the true last time was 10:02.020, these numbers will advance fairly steadily, lagging the exact number by varying amounts, but never by a lot. If B fails, on the other hand, the last-heard-from time will become fixed at some value and we can then declare it faulty after a suitable delay.

As mentioned, gossip can include many kinds of information; in general, one thinks of the message as a list of elements, each having an information category (membership, data, etc.), identifier, value and perhaps other attributes such as the member-id that contributed this value. There is no fixed rule: the developer of a gossip application would normally design the content of their gossip messages to fit the way the data will be used. For use in a DHT, gossip messages could include a list of (K, V) tuples, each giving the key and value of some tuple that forms part of the DHT state.

One might wonder how the actual message passing should work. On this gossip systems are extremely flexible. Obviously, they do need some form of communication infrastructure: TCP, perhaps, or UDP: in the latter case messages can get lost in the network (leading to partial or completely failed gossip rounds), but it turns out that the exponential spread of rumors is such a powerful force that we do not actually need ordering or reliability or other guarantees (for example, we can use UDP messages and not wait for acknowledgements, or even retransmit lost packets). The insight is that even if a large percentage of messages are dropped, the gossip protocol will not slow it down much. In fact, very little can stop a gossip protocol, short of an outright network partitioning failure.

Most gossip protocols take advantage of these observations and just run over UDP with no attempt to ensure reliability. They often run at a fixed but unsynchronized pace: each node picks some peer and gossips with it every t milliseconds. And it is common to bound the size of gossip messages to whatever UDP packets can hold, typically 8 K bytes. This makes these protocols extremely stable and predictable.

Gossip protocols need to make a section of the gossip partner. For now, assume this is just random: node B has a list of other nodes, and at some frequency just picks a node, gossips with it, and then sleeps until it is time to do another round of gossip, at which point it picks again. One can build more elaborate solutions here, such as to track just a subset of the members of the system (in a very big system, there is not much value in tracking every single member, hence many solutions keep just a limited peer-set at each member, taking care to pick them in a way that will not cause a partitioning of the nodes). Kelips puts these mechanisms together in an elegant way to implement a DHT that exists purely as a kind of virtual entity, materialized by a gossip protocol. In doing so, it avoids the need to construct a ring, manage predecessor and successor pointers, track levels of replication to deal with membership changes, or even to build finger tables.

The basic idea is as follows (see Fig. 4.6 for an illustration). Given a node id, or a key, Kelips hashes it, just as we do in Chord or Pastry. But now the system maps the hashed values into sqrt(N) bins, so that on average each bin will contain sqrt(N) members of the system, and 1/sqrt(N) of the (K, V) tuples. Each (K, V) tuple is replicated within the bin to which it fell, so that all the members of that bin have a copy. In this way, a get can be performed by just finding one member of the appropriate bin and asking for a copy: a 1-hop lookup.

How does gossip help us implement this scheme? First, Kelips gossips about the system membership in a continuous, steady manner. Each member hears about all other members this way, over time.

As member W hears about other members, it separates the member id's into two sets: those that are in the same bin as W is in (over time there will be sqrt(N) such members, more or less), and those that are in other bins. W tracks all the members of its own bin, and maintains a list of contacts for each of the other bins, picking contacts that seem to be healthy, reachable, and that have good round-trip delays. Members age out of these lists if W has not heard from them in a while or repeated attempts to gossip with one of them fail.

We can think of Kelips as doing two side by side gossip state exchanges. One of them, which runs between members of the same bin (e.g. when W picks one of the peers in its own bin as a gossip target) is used to replicate both membership data and any (K, V) tuples that mapped into the bin. The other, running to members of other bins, only carries membership data.

To put a new (K, V) tuple into the system, W simply maps K to the appropriate bin, then sends it to its contact within that bin. This will be a nearby node and should be fast. Then gossip will spread the tuple through the whole bin. To perform a get W does the same thing, but now it queries its contact, which returns the current value associated with the specified key.

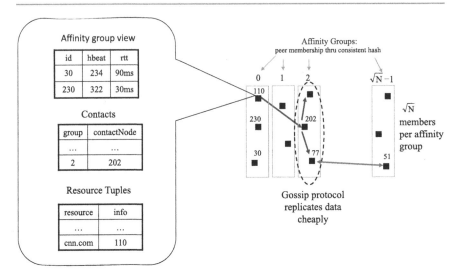

Fig. 4.6 Kelips uses gossip techniques to construct a DHT that emerges purely from the structure of the gossip epidemic and offers O(1-hop) lookups. The approach requires $O(\sqrt{N})$ space to keep replicated (key, value) tuples and to track membership information; the state of a typical node is shown on the left (that of node 110 in affinity group 0). Like Pastry, Kelips can select peers so as to optimize for low latency and high speed. In this example, node 110 stores a (key, value) tuple into affinity group 2 (that is, the key hashes to 2). Later node 51, in affinity group $\sqrt{N} - 1$, fetches the same (key, value) tuple from node 77: its preferred peer within affinity group 2. Only one hop is needed, and the only protocol required is a gossip epidemic

Kelips trades simplicity and speed for larger amounts of space: the list of contacts, the list of members of its own bin, and the list of replicated (K, V) tuples will all be $O(\text{sqrt}(N))$ in size. But for this it gains a very fast way to do lookups: unlike Chord and Pastry, which will require a log(N) delay in the worst case, Kelips always finds the value for a given K in one hop. Put has a comparable cost: it takes log(N) time to put a new (K, V) tuple into any of these systems.

Fireflies

In their work on the Fireflies DHT, Van Renesse and others explored robustness of these solutions to outright attack (Johansen et al. 2006). The issue this group raised is as follows: with very large numbers of participating nodes, and often with open-source software that does not specifically protect itself against misuse, one could imagine a form of attack in which some malicious user would download the software for the DHT and then run a modified version designed to cause disruption. The issue is not as fanciful as it may sound: the recording industry is known to have paid hacking organizations to do precisely this, in the hope that your attempt to listen to Lady Gaga would repeatedly trigger system crashes or keep pulling up Frank Sinatra's music instead of Lady Gaga's new hit.

Fireflies combats such problems by running multiple copies of a Chord-like DHT side-by-side. These multiple rings are superimposed on the identical set of nodes but in such a way that any given node has distinct sets of neighbors in the various rings. The effect is that even if an attacker were to isolate a node in one particular ring, it would still have a good chance of learning updates and handling lookup requests properly through one of those other rings. Obviously, such a scheme can only tolerate a limited number of attackers; in Part II of the text, when we discuss Byzantine Agreement, we will see precisely what the limits turn out to be. But the basic hope would be that if the attacker can be outnumbered by the good guys, we can still serve up a legitimate Lady Gaga hit song even though the compromised node is eagerly trying to defeat this outcome. As an aside, we should perhaps mention that there are many legal and important uses for DHTs in the modern cloud: the music sharing role is not really their only purpose. Moreover, for these legitimate uses, resilience is often cited as a main reason for employing a DHT: these structures will self-organize and self-heal even under attack or huge stress. Thus work of the kind done by the Fireflies group is important because it enhances the viability of the solution relative to these kinds of potential use cases.

Peer Selection Tools

Gossip peer selection turns out to be of such universal value and importance that the question deserves a few further comments. Notice that several of the DHTs we have reviewed need to select peers in non-random ways. Kelips and Pastry attempt to optimize performance by selecting subsets of peers to optimize criteria such as round-trip latency and bandwidth. Fireflies needs a way to lay out the peers into k disjoint rings, hence cannot use a completely standard random hashing function: needed are k side by side hashing functions that will give independent random locations on the various rings. A natural question to ask is whether, in imposing these kinds of special biasing policy, those systems risk partitioning themselves into multiple disjoint subregions: one would worry that Kelips running at Cornell could, in effect, deliberately decide to disconnect itself from Kelips running at Berkeley! We will encounter the same question again much later in the book, in Chap. 21, where we introduce probabilistic reliable replication and multicast protocols; indeed, those actually predated the DHT topic and were the first systems in which this issue of peer selection was encountered. But the core question is identical.

Let us first review the reasons a mesh creation scheme might not want to use purely random peer selection. Imagine that we are deploying Chord world-wide, and that two nodes in Ithaca happen to need to connect with one another, perhaps one is looking up a (key, value) tuple that resides on the other. The nodes are physically close to one-another, yet Chord will map them to random locations on the ring; very likely they will be $O(\log(N))$ hops away from one-another in a logical sense. Thus to connect from one system at Cornell to another in the next room, messages might easily be sent to South Africa, then to Moscow, then to Palo Alto, etc. Chord would perform poorly in such a situation.

A second reason was the one seen in Fireflies: we may want to be sure that peer selection picks failure-independent peers, so that a node will not somehow become dependent on just a small subset of the peers or network links, since such situations could put it at risk of a network isolation outage: a so-called network partitioning failure.

And a third reason for biased peer selection may be to optimize relative to some higher level objective. While this text will not explore the topic in any great depth, some systems do things like searching for data in ways that are highly sensitive to the mesh topology. As we have seen, Pastry and Kelips both have peer selection mechanisms that should reshape the mesh so that by and large, nodes use nearby peers for successive hops. In fact these kinds of mechanism are nearly universal: peer-to-peer systems that have the ability to do so will almost always bias their peer selection to optimize performance. Thus Pastry might still need $\log(N)$ hops to find the desired key, but hopefully all of those occur between nodes that are close to one-another. Kelips might easily find the specific one-hop lookup path leading directly to our target node (of course, in Kelips, any given data item is replicated on $\mathrm{sqrt}(N)$ nodes, so there are many candidates).

Broadly, *self-optimizing* mesh construction solutions are ones that seek to select neighbors with good connectivity and in such a way as to avoid unnecessary barriers, such as firewalls or NAT translation systems that might prevent full round-trip communication. Barriers of these kinds can be a serious problem in practice: Quema and Kermarrec have shown that failing to account for such issues can leave members in confused states, with lists of peers that are unreachable because communication is blocked in one or both directions; this results in confusion about node status (unreachable nodes can be declared as faulty), and also frustrates the gossip algorithms that run over the resulting damaged mesh. They recommend an indirection scheme to avoid this problem (Kermarrec et al. 2009).

A purely practical response has been to build general purpose mesh creation tools, over which algorithms such as Pastry or Kelips might run, thus separating the issue of peer selection and treating it as a distinct function that should yield high quality meshes. For example, Kermarrec and her collaborators have created a whole series of peer-selection algorithms (Voulgaris et al. 2004, 2007; Voulgaris and van Steen 2005; Jelasity et al. 2007). Particularly interesting among projects in this area was the network topology management service T-Man, developed by Jelasity in collaboration with Babaoglu and others at the University of Bologna (Jelasity and Babaoglu 2005; Jelasity et al. 2009). T-Man is a programmable infrastructure within which one can create whole families of peer-to-peer mesh construction algorithms simply by specializing a general-purpose infrastructure using per-mesh decision logic. Some very elegant videos illustrating the power of this approach can be found on the University of Bologna web site (see http://www.cs.unibo.it/~babaoglu/projects/index.html). One could potentially combine a system like T-Man with a system such as Pastry so as to "shape" the overlay on which Pastry will end up running. Today, many peer-to-peer systems are created by taking one of these peer-selection libraries as a starting point and then adding application-specific logic that imposes the DHT application structure, or some other structure, over the mesh created by the library.

The theory for this area has been explored by a number of researchers. Two findings are central to our modern understanding of the topic. The first was a result in which Jon Kleinberg developed a theoretical treatment of the problem and showed that there is an optimal solution to the question, which involves maintaining what are called *small worlds graphs* (Kleinberg 2000a, 2000b, 2001, 2004). The broader underlying theory is that of random walks on what are called expander graphs. For example, Broder et al. (1999) presents a theory from which one can show that as long as a gossip peer list is an *expander graph*, nodes can track a subset of peers and yet any algorithm proved correct for a fully random gossip model will also run correctly on the resulting subset mesh. It turns out that the expander property is easily achieved and most of the real systems discussed above are extremely likely to satisfy this requirement.

I3: How the Internet Indirection Infrastructure Uses DHTs to Route Network Traffic

The prior subsection pushed from the idea of a DHT down to a question of mesh construction. Also of interest are ideas that go in the other direction, building fancier structures *over* a DHT. We will see a number of such solutions throughout this text: Amazon's Dynamo shopping cart, for example (Chap. 5), or the Astrolabe system (Chap. 21). An example that fits well with the networking themes of the present chapter is Berkeley's *Internet Indirection Infrastructure* (I3) project, a system that uses a distributed hash table as the basis for a variety of other technologies. The basic idea is very simple and elegant.

I3 assumes a DHT (any of the ones we have discussed would work, but I3P is based on Chord: the leader of the project, Ion Stoica, was one of the inventors of that system). Applications that define services, such as printing or storage, use a standard naming convention for those services, and *put* (K, V) pairs in which the key, K, is the service name, and the value, V, is the IP address for the service. To use a service, one simply looks it up and then contacts the given IP address. I3P defines a variety of services: storage, message queuing, printing, etc. The system also explores the idea of data transformation through services, for example to transcode from the Windows mpv format into the Apple iTunes media format. A variety of mobile applications were also proposed, in which the DHT is used as a way for a mobile device that may have erratic connectivity to track down and load content that can be temporarily stored on its behalf.

As these examples suggest, I3P is amazingly powerful, for such a simple idea. Moreover, performance was shown to be quite good, and I3P enables many things that are hard to do today. For all of these reasons, the author of this text has always been puzzled that I3P did not become one of those smash hits that seem to transform the world every few years right now. Yet the market somehow has not embraced the concept. On the other hand, nobody every gets the last word, in the cloud technology space. Perhaps I3P was just a bit ahead of the time, and its day will come sometime in the near future!

4.2.8 BitTorrent: A Fast Content Distribution System

The BitTorrent system uses a peer-to-peer overlay to solve a different problem: rapid cooperative download of information. Before explaining how this works, we should just comment that BitTorrent defines a protocol, as well as a standard way of implementing that protocol. As a result, BitTorrent can and has been implemented in many ways. At the time of this writing there were several open-source BitTorrent clients, as well as at least one product implementing the scheme and professionally supported. The discussion below is intended to apply to any of these.

In the period prior to the introduction of BitTorrent, data center operators faced a challenging problem when an object, such as a video of a major news event or an upgrade to a popular software product, needed to be send to a very large number of clients with minimal delay. If all of those clients were to simultaneously contact a server and request a download, the data center would be overwhelmed; if they do so just a few at a time, some might wait for weeks. Clearly, parallelism offers an answer, and this is the angle explored by BitTorrent. The approach deals with very large objects as a series of moderately large pieces (perhaps, 1 Mbyte each); here, we'll describe its behavior in a simpler case: downloading a single piece. A larger download would simply repeat the process we describe below multiple times.

The first step of the BitTorrent scheme involves publishing small *torrent description* files, which clients can download. Somewhat like we saw in Kelips, this process leaves each client with contact information for some number of other clients. Bit-Torrent gives these out in a way that creates a fairly dense graph of peers: each client ends up knowing of some relatively random set of other clients, mostly nearby, but if we were to draw a picture of the connections, the graph would be a highly connected.

To carry out the actual piece dissemination, BitTorrent uses what we call a *swarm* protocol. First, the protocol *seeds* the segment into the torrent by sending copies to some random set of nodes. Each node with a complete copy of the piece becomes a new seed, so that over time, the number of seeds will grow until the piece is fully downloaded.

A participant lacking a piece of the file uses a peer-to-peer protocol to find a seed or seeds with copies and that are willing (and able) to send them. At this step an optimization problem arises: if a node can only find one such source, it will obviously need to ask that source for a copy, but what if it finds a large number of possible sources: which one should it ask?

BitTorrent favors a scheme that rewards a swarm participant for cooperation and punishes self-centered behavior. The system implements a mechanism that allows a participant to present another participant with a proof of its behavior in the torrent: evidence that it helped other participants by uploading data to them, in the form of unforgeable digital receipts confirming the upload. The idea is to use these receipts to reward altruism and punish greedy behavior: a node is more likely to request a piece from a peer that has uploaded copies to other peers successfully, and a peer functioning as a seed that receives multiple requests will favor requests from participants with a good track record of altruistic behavior. The receipts themselves are generated using a cryptographic signature scheme in the following simple way: each seed uploads data in an encrypted form, sharing the required decryption key only after the receiver sends a digitally signed hash of the data which will later be used as a receipt. A peer only sends data to uncooperative peers if there are no other requests pending, and it only contacts the Torrent server itself if it is unable to obtain the pieces it needs in this concurrent, peer-to-peer manner.

When BitTorrent works as intended, the effect is similar to the gossip behavior we described earlier: the first seeds rapidly propagate, so that the majority of clients manage to download pieces concurrently from one-another in a cooperative manner, and much faster than if the data center servers had to handle the majority of the workload. In principle, the system also tends to seed data rapidly at nodes that have good upload capabilities and that are not blocked by NATs or firewalls, leaving isolated nodes that can download but are unable to upload data until the end. BitTorrent does not always work as intended, however: although the scheme was designed to anticipate firewalls, network address translators, and slow network links, all of these are known to disrupt torrent behaviors to some degree. Moreover, Steve Gribble at the University of Washington in Seattle showed that many BitTorrent downloads fail to exploit the tit-for-tat scheme because many swarms are active for such a short period of time that there is not enough time to learn about the behaviors of participants (he proposed an extension to BitTorrent aimed at keeping history around a bit longer so that the outcome of one swarm could be used as data in a subsequent swarm). Yet these issues mostly arise when the actual number of participants is small. With a genuinely large crowd of downloaders active concurrently, the BitTorrent approach has been highly effective, for example to download large objects in the Internet WAN, and even more so within data centers. For example, YouTube replicates videos *within* its data centers using a BitTorrent system, and is reportedly very pleased with the performance obtained this way.

4.2.9   Sienna: A Content-Based Publish Subscribe System

We end this section by touching on another example of a peer-to-peer technology: wide-area publish-subscribe implemented as a network overlay. Publish-subscribe systems implement a kind of network-level broadcast service, in which client systems *subscribe* to data and servers *publish* it. The role of the system is to match publications to subscriptions so that any message published will reach every client that has a matching subscription.

There are several models for how subscriptions of this kind should work. The simplest is seen in very high speed publish-subscribe systems: these label each publication with a list of *topics*, and allow clients to subscribe to lists of topics; matching is exact. Thus, if a client were to subscribe to IBM and METALS, it would receive a message posted that lists IBM as the topic, and a message that lists ALCOA,METALS,ALUMINUM, but would not receive a message posted to PURINA,PETS,ANIMALFOODS. Examples of well known systems that use this topic-list model for subscriptions include the original Isis "News" facility (Birman and Joseph 1987a) and the Teknekron Information Bus (TIB) (Oki et al. 1993).

A second model generalizes this same idea, but allows subscriptions to be predicates over the topic list (which is often called a *tag* or *attribute* list in this case). In effect, the topics are treated as binary valued logic variables, and the predicates are logical expressions. The best known example of this kind of system was IBM's Gryphon system (Strom et al. 1998; Aguilera et al. 1999).

The last model goes one step further and eliminates topics in favor of the content of the messages themselves. In what are called *content based* publish-subscribe systems, subscriptions are predicates over the contents of the messages, which are assumed to be blocks of text annotated with standard keywords. Thus, one could design a query that would watch for news reports describing discoveries of oil, for example. The Sienna system is a good example in this category: it constructs a peer-to-peer overlay network and then routes messages within the network over trees which it maintains, from sources to matching destinations (Carzaniga et al. 2001).

The complexity of these last two kinds of system resides in the management of subscription information and the construction of the associated overlay forwarding trees. In a large system with many clients, each posting many subscriptions, it is easy to see how very large databases of pending subscriptions could arise. Forwarding a message will become slow because of the need to evaluate all of these subscriptions against each possible message; indeed, a single complex client could easily bring the entire forwarding infrastructure to its knees just by posting immense numbers of queries, since each message will need to be checked against each query.

But notice also that one can always err by simplifying queries in ways that result in overly conservative forwarding decisions. Thus a subscription table with a million entries posing "deep" content questions could always be collapsed into a single rule that just forwards every single message. Here, every message ends up reaching every client, and the clients (which must filter incoming traffic) end up with huge amounts of undesired data. The challenge turns out to be to automatically collapse subscriptions in ways that remain selective yet also result in compact forwarding tables suitable for rapid evaluation. Gryphon and Sienna both implement algorithms for doing this kind of merging, then layer on top of that basic ability the needed logic to maintain overlay forwarding trees that will adapt as new subscriptions come, old ones are cancelled (or the associated clients depart), and topology changes.

How effective are these optimizations? To understand the answer, it helps to start by recalling that most systems are structured hierarchically: often, as major data centers interconnected by WAN links, within which various services are running, each replicated to some extent, and finally supporting various groupings of clients. This hierarchy is reflected into the queries and thus one sees that "most" messages end up routing to most data centers, with filtering reducing the loads only as we get closer to the leaves.

Moreover, in cloud computing systems structured into WANs there are often subsystems that need to collect a copy of every data item. With respect to Sienna, if there are a cluster of Sienna users in New York, there would often also be a New York archive of past publish-subscribe messages, available to let those users datamine the history of the system and establish initial context when joining an active session. These archives will need to subscribe to everything.

The observation leads to an interesting insight: although Gryphon and Sienna go to quite a bit of effort to create sophisticated forwarding structures, one could probably do almost as well by just forwarding every message over every WAN link (hence all data centers would see all messages), and then filtering at the last hop, when messages are about to be delivered to client systems. After all, if some machine in each data center wants everything, there will not be any opportunity to do WAN filtering: the WAN will replicate everything. Thus as a New York user, any useful filtering would end up occurring in the link relaying from the data center to me.

This in turn suggests that a purely peer-to-peer implementation of the kinds of complex filtering technology seen in systems such as these last ones is perhaps just not the right way to go. In fact, the filtering role might better be handled by a database: we would view the communication task challenge as that of replicating all data to all archival systems over the WAN, and then employ a database as the archive of postings, and to filter incoming ones for delivery to clients. Those knowledgable about databases will realize that we are viewing subscription as *materialized queries*. The challenge of combining subscriptions becomes a form of query optimization. Cornell's Cayuga system is a widely cited example of a database system designed for this style of use: subscriptions can operate over temporal sequences of events: a client can ask to be shown messages that demonstrate a 10% rise in the price of any technology stock over a period of twenty minutes or less, for example.

We mention this last example to make the following point: even if a technology has an obvious mapping to the network, as for publish-and-subscribe behavior, it is not always obvious that the best way to implement it is to do so within network routers. Cloud computing systems impose structure in many ways, and this includes "shaping" the traffic flows and patterns that one will observe. One could go to great lengths to build a sophisticated solution, as occurs in these distributed data flow filtering schemes, only to discover that in real deployments, the problem either does not arise at all, or that it arises only in a narrower way that lends itself to a different solution.

To summarize the analysis here: If Sienna or Gryphon will end up forwarding every message to every cloud data center in some group of centers, there is really no need to even use Sienna or Gryphon at that WAN level: far easier would be a simpler replication technology that does not even look at the messages. Indeed, given the insight that all messages will enter a database in any case, we should really define our problem as a database query problem, despite the fact that the user thinks in terms of networks and messages and publish-subscribe query patterns. And once we have a database with the right properties and performance, there may not really be any role left for enhanced routers implementing these kinds of overlay network technology! In the case of content-based publish-subscribe, this indeed seems to be the way things have played out.

4.2.10 The Internet Under Attack: A Spectrum of Threats

It would not be right to wrap up a chapter on the Internet in the face of the cloud without at least commenting on the emergence of cyber war as a serious threat to the future of the cloud, and indeed of Western society.

Like it or not, the evolution of technology, and the co-evolution that this can trigger for society, is a one-way process. Facebook emerges, and some people fret, but in no time at all, Facebook announces that it has a billion users and predicts a second billion within just a year or two. Enterprises such as medical care and running the power grid or the military, or banking, or the transportation system, or the phone system, which one might never have imagined on the Internet, are poised to leap into the cloud, and completely new enterprises that did not even exist a few years ago, may soon be revealed as nationally critical: we lived without them until now, but may soon discover that we can no longer live without them!

In Chap. 3 we mentioned several national-scale examples: real cases in which countries have attacked other countries through the network, downloaded massive amounts of information, and conducted corporate espionage on a scale that boggles the mind. At McAfree, the Vice President for threat research, Dmitri Alperovitch put it this way in a 2011 interview: "In fact, I divide the entire set of Fortune Global 2000 firms into two categories: those that know they have been compromised and those that do not yet know." In the same article he detailed the massive Shady RAT intrusion, which penetrated hundreds of government, political and corporate systems, downloading data that were transmitted to locations in China. While Alperovitch stopped short of suggesting that the government of China was behind these exploits, the possibility certainly exists.

But it is not just about China. Our world has become deeply dependent upon the Internet. And for this reason, one simply has to look at the various forms of hacking, whether they involve a jealous boyfriend installing a keystroke logger, or an unethical country plotting to cripple its adversaries through the network, as very serious matters.

And we should be honest: despite some tough laws, very little has been done to prosecute cyber criminals or to clean up the mess.

Some studies suggest that as much as 60% of the world's computers are infected with viruses or other forms of malware. Vast numbers of machines have been captured by so-called botnets, which harness them to send advertising, sell drugs or pornography, to hunt for bank and credit account numbers that can potentially be broken into, etc. Criminals are starting to threaten companies: pay us off, or we will take you off the Internet, and if those companies turn to the law for help, they discover that the elite cyber crime units are mostly illusory: a few dusty machines in a corner, and a few police who have been assigned to run the investigations, but with minimal resources.

Meanwhile, the threat is growing. Recent books have documented episodes in which the United States, Israel, China, North Korea and Russia each apparently used the network for forms of cyber warfare, and we are talking here about genuine acts of war involving destruction of property and loss of life, not merely spying or causing minor disruptions. Some episodes were fairly minor; others had the potential to escalate into major conflicts. For example, there is some reason to believe that at least some of these actors would be in a position to physically destroy the electrical power grids and communication networks of their adversaries if a serious conflict broke out. Our societies can no longer function without power, telephones and transportation, and such an event would trigger massive civil disorder, huge numbers of civilian deaths, and perhaps a complete breakdown of government. It is not impossible to imagine such an event escalating into a military clash in the real world.

At the root of such fears one finds a basic technical reality: we have invested in various forms of research and development aimed at securing the Internet and securing critical computing systems for decades now, but the target seems to be moving much faster than the solutions. Thus, while we can definitely do a great deal to protect against the threats that mattered most in the year 2000, when the world anxiously awaited the roll-over of digital clocks and speculated fretfully about the risk that planes would fall from the sky and computers would fail, all the good things we have created have not given us any real protection against the new generation of threats, or the many security loopholes and errors embodied in the latest generations of systems. Each new operating system, and each new application, seems to create new security flaws.

Faced with the seeming impossibility of solving this problem, governments have begun to weaken in their resolve to even study it. While claiming that ever more funding is being invested in research on computer systems, security and reliability, in fact there has been a global collapse in funding for these areas. Meanwhile research on the web and social networks (not the kind we are studying here) has boomed. The message is clear: yes, it may rain, but until it does, let's party!

This stance may someday be revealed, in retrospect, as a deeply flawed one. If automobiles had a tendency to fall apart at highway speeds, there is no question we would do something about it. And simply because ten or fifteen years of research on computer security has not yet given us a solution does not really justify a decision to ignore the question. Perhaps what we really need most are taxes on the Internet: if the government's own revenue streams were directly threatened by the insecurities of the cloud and the Internet, it might be easier to persuade politicians to invest a bit of that revenue to try and find new protective options.

The irony, though, is that the rapid evolution of the cloud, and the Internet, may finally be giving us new opportunities to do something about the issues. We have discussed the potential for router enhancements. Why not explore ways of enhancing routing that also enhance security, denying attackers the opportunity to compromise Internet routing? Perhaps law enforcement tools hosted in the Internet could help us identify the operators of those massive botnets and cyber warfare systems (and even better would be to do so without compromising privacy to an even greater degree). Perhaps we can create the Internet equivalent of what some have dubbed the Great Internet Wall of China. China uses a barrier to block its citizens from seeing what it considers to be inappropriate web content, but why could not the Internet itself be used to block attacks even as they are launched?

As this book was going to press, it would have been possible to list a dozen or more ambitious, very active research efforts focused on just this opportunity. Will some clever student come up with a way to layer security over the Internet in a way that scales and performs well, defends against attack, and can be trusted? Only a very pessimistic reader with little experience in technology would want to bet against real progress. Change is coming, and we may finally be on the verge of a move to a much more secure network.

4.3   Summary and Conclusions

In this chapter we have skimmed the surface of a vast and very active research area concerned with extending modern computer networks to offer new guarantees of reliability and security, new functionality, and greater flexibility. Much of the impetus for network evolution comes from cloud computing, reflecting the eagerness of customers to gain access to powerful new options such as streaming downloads of movies, voice over IP telephony, and an increasingly rich mix of media content with social networking. Yet, as we have seen, even if cloud computing may seem to be a well-defined area, the area proves to be a rich one that confronts us with multiple challenges, reflecting the multiple perspectives that arise in cloud settings.

If we focus on the network from the familiar perspective of the client system, we encounter a mixture of issues dominated by addressing (and address translation), firewalls and bandwidth pinch-points, and complications due to client mobility. These issues, jointly with the desire for a reasonably seamless client experience, have shaped today's client-side of the cloud and will continue to do so as the technology base evolves into the future. And the client-side, in turn, places very specific requirements and pressures on the network. Mobility for sophisticated, mostly connected, client platforms seems poised to trigger the next major development in this space.

If we instead center attention on the role of the network as the routing infrastructure for data moving between cloud servers and clients, we encounter another collection of issues that now center on the options available to cloud providers for managing routing. We did not look closely at the network within individual data centers, but the same point could be made about trends in that space (our coverage was skimpy precisely because of this rapid evolution).

Last, we can look at the needs of applications that share the scalability and performance needs of cloud systems, and yet do not match the simple client-to-server model that prevails in the cloud. As we have seen, these applications have their own special needs, and those needs have driven the development of a wave of peer-to-peer mechanisms that effectively work around limitations stemming from the way that the cloud uses the standard infrastructures. Of course, some of these applications are entirely motivated by an illegal goal, namely unauthorized sharing of movies and other forms of intellectual property. But others use peer-to-peer methods for purposes that mesh more closely with the legitimate cloud, such as parallel downloads.

Down the road we will see even more opportunities as we move applications such as medical care, the smart power grid, and urban traffic control to networked platforms. A secondary driver for change comes from the network operators (ISPs), who are looking for ways to participate in the cloud computing revenue stream, and a third force reflects the cloud vendors themselves, who need to better control the network in order to improve cloud performance and flexibility. All of this makes the network an exciting area for innovation today and far into the foreseeable future.

4.4 Further Readings

To learn more about the Internet, we recommend Doug Comer's multi-volume book on this topic (Comer 1991; Comer and Stevens 1993).

Gun Sirer and Fred Schneider have done very interesting work on security first by an operating system kernel (Nexus) and then, using that secure kernel, creating a highly assured BGP-based edge router (Schneider et al. 2011; Shieh et al. 2011).

The Open Flow Consortium maintains an active web site with extensive links to papers related to the new Open Flow standards and how those can be used to control enterprise networks.

The Structure of Cloud Data Centers

5

Clouds
I've looked at clouds from both sides now
from up and down and still somehow
it's clouds illusions I recall
I really don't know clouds at all.—Joni Mitchell

In previous chapters we looked at cloud computing from the outside; here, we will do so from the inside, within the data center. Many technologies play important roles, but it would not be satisfying to do a very broad but very shallow overview, and we will also want to avoid getting bogged down in proprietary details: each cloud vendor has its own technologies, yet at the end of the day, they tend to fall into a few categories. Accordingly, we will focus on some well known cloud components in enough detail to appreciate the basic ideas, why they work (and when they might not work), and we will speculate a bit about how they might be generalized for use in other settings. This will not necessarily be enough background to wander into a cubicle at Google and start hacking new technologies for the GooglePlex, but should give you a foundation to work from, if you ever take such a job.

For readers who are in the habit of learning every aspect of a technology, top to bottom, the cloud can be frustrating. As Joni Mitchell put it, you can look at clouds from many sides, and yet still not really know clouds at all! The important insight is that this is not a topic for which one needs to know every single detail to work effectively at the highest levels. By understanding how some of the major success stories were achieved, we can learn the major patterns underlying scalability and responsiveness, and also understand the way that major cloud platforms accomplish the delicate balancing act required. This collection of overarching principles turn out to matter more, in the cloud, than the precise details of how each and every component technology operates.

K.P. Birman, *Guide to Reliable Distributed Systems*, Texts in Computer Science, DOI 10.1007/978-1-4471-2416-0_5, © Springer-Verlag London Limited 2012

5.1   The Layers of a Cloud

Prior chapters looked first at client computing systems and then at the process by which packets are routed through the network until they arrive at the gateway into a cloud computing data center. What happens next?

Most of today's cloud platforms are structured in a layers ("tiers"). Application developers tend to focus on just a subset of these tiers. For example, in Chap. 2 we focused on the client tier. The counterpart of that tier within the cloud is the first tier, which runs services that receive incoming client requests and are responsible for responding as rapidly as possible. Directly behind this is a tier of developer-configured and services, which include databases and other applications used by the components of the first tier. Beyond these tiers cloud platforms have other recognizable layers as well, and we will discuss them too: those concerned with infrastructure and platform management, for example, and the tier of systems running in what some call the "back end", doing offline work that can be performed in batches.

A good example of a back-end application would be the programs Google and Microsoft employ to precompute answers to common web queries: search engines use the output of last-night's indexing when responding to today's queries. But of course this is not the only thing they use: incremental updates also play a big role, particularly for fast-changing web pages like news web sites. Thus many first-tier systems depend on a mixture of sources: we would view those fast-moving updates as the output of a service living in the second tier, while the search index computed yesterday would end up in the file system and be treated as a kind of infrastructure resource. Notice the relative difference in size: the fast-changing index data can probably be represented in a few hundred gigabytes. But the offline analysis needs to index every web page in the world, pre-computing answers for every one, two or three word query (more complex queries are usually solved by breaking them down into several smaller ones and combining the results). The English language alone has perhaps 100,000 vocabulary words in active use (a million if one counts the less actively used ones), so these files will be enormous, literally petabytes in aggregate. Thus one can think of the tiers not just in terms of roles but also in terms of the size of the information managed: the first tier works from information it caches or holds in memory; the second tier deals with quick responses from "larger" information sources, and the back-end systems cope with the genuinely heavy lifting. But all of these tiers involve very large numbers of machines. Those petabyte index files are computed by marshaling tens of thousands of machines to jointly carry out the required computation. In effect, roles differ and assumptions differ, but all tiers of the cloud share an emphasis on massive scale and parallelism.

5.2   Elasticity and Reconfigurability

Applications and services running in the first tier of the cloud are often very heavily replicated: if a service is popular, it might have hundreds of thousands of replicas, each providing services to some number of clients whose requests were routed to it.

Yet perhaps that same service was a sleepy backwater just last night (think of the pattern of accesses to web services used to by sports fans to track popular Olympic events, or the web page of a Hollywood star who was arrested for drunk driving, and you can easily get a sense of why this sort of flash crowd might arise). To support the necessary degree of *elasticity*, a special programming style is needed: loads can shift on a dime, and cloud platforms need to be able to react by reconfiguring the first tier so quickly that the end-user is generally completely unaware that it happened. Thus at one instant we might have 50 instances of some service running, but seconds later, could see 1000, or 10,000. For the developer, this means that first-tier services need to be extremely simple, lightweight tasks that maintain no persistent state; by and large, they run out of cached data or parcel out subtasks to second-tier services. The idea is to end up with executable images that the cloud platform can shift around without any setup, launch without any long delays, and shut down abruptly without any prior negotiation. Yet lightweight though they may be, these services do need to soak up as much load as possible. Ideally, they respond to every request the instant it arrives, leaving an asynchronous stream of updates behind that gradually find their way into the deeper tiers of the cloud, where updates occur. We call this *rapid local responsiveness*; the property is the single most important property of tier-one cloud components.

Reconfiguration also has implications for the cloud infrastructure itself. For example, as deployments expand or shrink, the cloud needs to be able to route requests to the service instances in robust manner, so that clients will not find themselves abruptly cut off or exposed to long delays. Because caching is employed throughout the first tier, there is high value in routing follow-up requests to the same service instance that handled prior ones, and hence might have warm caches. Thus, routing emerges as an important challenge in modern cloud systems, and they offer many ways to optimize the routes that will be selected. One approach, very simple, is to just let the cloud platform use its default policies; those are typically based on periodic load measurements, and attempt to balance load by favoring lightly loaded replicas and reducing the frequency with which requests are sent to heavily loaded ones. Even this kind of simple policy is not as trivial as it may sound: routing often occurs in a cluster of gateway nodes, each making independent decisions, and obviously if some replica had a very light load, it would be unwise to just route every single incoming request to it. Thus, load-balancing is always randomized, and while it may be slightly weighted to favor lightly loaded nodes over heavily loaded ones, all nodes will see at least some requests.

Fancier policies are also possible. We mentioned the importance of *affinity*, namely the benefits of sending requests from the same client to the same replica, if feasible. So-called *packet inspection* techniques go even further: these look within the packet, routing requests on the basis of their contents. Thus, requests to such-and-such a service (perhaps the product-inventory service), accessing such-and-such an item identifier (perhaps, items coded A-XXXX to C-XXXX) might be sent to one replica, requests for items D-XXXX through G-XXXX to another replica, etc. This kind of fine-grained packet inspection can be slow, however: packets must be parsed, the relevant data extracted and converted into an appropriate representation, and then the desired pattern applied; at very high speeds, such elaborate processing is not always feasible. Moreover, as we get more and more fine-grained, we also run into the risk that the data being used to make these decisions might be stale: the load information available to the routers could be out of date, the affinity patterns may be ones that have been superseded by new data, etc. Failures or the launch of new replicas may have changed the available options. All of these complications argue for simpler policies that are less likely to get confused as conditions evolve dynamically: optimal routing, in effect, can be an unrealistic objective because the true dynamic conditions of the data center are simply not available when routing decisions must be made.

This observation is just the tip of an iceberg: cloud management platforms need to be able to rapidly reconfigure not just the software but also the physical hardware in the cloud; in many modern systems, one can literally back up an 18-wheel truck with a container of new machines, plug it into a bay of the data center, then yank out some other container and drive it back to the factory to be refurbished or recycled! A trucker on a tight schedule cannot sit around waiting for the cloud management system to gracefully spin things down. Thus, while the management layer obviously does have the *ability* to shut things down somewhat gracefully, by and large, such systems reject this in favor of a more abrupt approach: if they want to shut down a node, they just tell the operating system to shut it down, and the applications may have little or no warning at all (in particular, they would rarely have time to make a final checkpoint or to migrate large amounts of data in a graceful way to some other node). That 18-wheeler pulls up, plugs in its load, yanks some other container out, and off the driver goes.

Many systems also shut nodes down to deal with evidence of problems: if a node seems slow, or is reporting errors, rather than have a human operator look at, the management system will often reboot, then perhaps reimage the node (e.g. install a clean version of the operating system and a clean, empty file system), and then just take it offline, all in an automated process. Users would object if this happened in their offices, but in the cloud, where we may have tens of thousands of applications running, it just is not practical to deal with such issues in any other way. All of these kinds of problem are handled in a fully automated manner.

5.3   Rapid Local Responsiveness and CAP

By requiring that the first tier be composed of services that can safely handle abrupt reconfiguration events, cloud systems gain an important kind of flexibility: the management platform can be very aggressive about reconfiguring the data center as loads vary. And while abrupt shutdown may seem a bit harsh, the ability to dramatically expand a deployment is considered to be a key requirement in modern cloud platforms, and often cited in advertising materials. Thus, our intuition as we think about first-tier services needs to assume a very dynamic notion of cloud computing, with very rapid changes in configuration, numbers of replicas, etc.

Some first-tier cloud services parcel work out to an active service layer, which comprises the second tier of a typical cloud system. For example, to respond to a search request, Amazon might send the product search query itself to a service that will look up the requested book, but it could also send information about the user to dozens or even hundreds of other services that could look up the user's preferences, product popularity for products in the same category, special deals, etc. Many second tier services will also be stateless, but statelessness ceases to be a hard and fast rule in the second tier, and at least some services maintain forms of memory of their actions, their client lists, and what those clients requested or were told.

First and second tier services do extensive caching. To achieve the local responsiveness property mentioned above, a service must process requests with the minimum possible delay, and hence there are huge benefits to using data available locally such as cached copies of popular data items. For example, if a product popularity index is consulted by a service instance that has a cached copy of the desired data, a locally responsive implementation will not need to touch bases with other replicas before responding. Indeed, these benefits are so large that in many cloud services, one uses cached data even if those data are known to be stale, or at potentially stale. The value of a snappy response is simply judged to be higher than the value of a slower but correct response.

Local responsiveness rules out certain common styles of data replication. For example, in many popular data replication schemes, reading a single copy of a replicated object involves consulting $f + 1$ copies, where f is a bound on how many failures the replication scheme is expected to tolerate. Updates require access to $N - f$ copies, where N denotes the replication factor. Such schemes are not able to be locally responsive, and hence are considered inappropriate in the front-line of the cloud. One does find these methods in second-tier services and in the back end infrastructure, but throughout the cloud there is a very noticeable skepticism where guarantees of any kind are involved. Instead, the onus tends to be on the client computing system, which is expected to tolerate responses based on stale data, resubmit updates if a timeout occurs, and otherwise step in to achieve whatever guarantees may be desired. The term *eventual consistency* is popular: cloud services offer rapid local responses that may be inconsistent, but then are expected to somehow heal themselves of any inconsistencies that arise, gradually moving towards a more consistent state.

Not every layer of the cloud follows this principle. For example, deeper in the cloud one finds back-end services that work from files and databases; the front tiers consult these back-end layers if a cache-miss occurs or when a request just cannot be handled locally. And these might offer much stronger guarantees. A good example of a back-end service might be a transactional database system used to track purchases by end-users: we want such services to maintain consistency and to provide guarantees of durability, hence they normally are implemented using databases that provide the standard ACID properties. We will hear more about this model later, but the acronym stands for Atomicity (transactions never see other transactions midway through execution), Consistency (if the database was in a consistent state when the transaction started, it should be when it commits), Isolation (two transactions running concurrently will not interfere with one-another), and Durability (a committed transaction will not be forgotten by the data center).

Recall our mention of Brewer's CAP principle, in the Introduction of this text. What Brewer really said was that to guarantee availability (the "A" in CAP, which corresponds to the property we are calling "rapid" responsiveness), a first-tier service element may not have time to wait for locks or other forms of synchronization: the "local" part of our objectives. For Brewer, the "P" in CAP stands for partition-tolerance, but is really about this guarantee that components do not end up stuck, waiting for actions by other components that may be overloaded, unreachable or even in the process of recovering from failure. Thus, Brewer argues that first tier services will need the AP properties. To achieve them, he reasons that "C" will need to be relaxed; for him, this notion of consistency is a short-hand for the ACID properties. Thus CAP, in a nutshell, suggests that if we want rapid local responsiveness, we may not be able to simultaneously offer ACID guarantees. On the other hand, his focus was on the first-tier; in the inner tiers of the cloud, one might accept ACID guarantees at the price of losing some elements of local responsiveness. Brewer has no issue with the use of database systems *internal* to the cloud; he simply cautions against viewing the first-tier systems as database components.

Database vendors, it should be noted, strongly disagree with Brewer on this point, and back their arguments with technology: many database systems work perfectly well in the first tier. But pulling that trick off is hard, and expensive, and what Oracle is able to do in its first-line cloud computing products may be beyond what a more typical development team could achieve while creating first-tier applications for use in a medical computing platform. Thus, one sees debate about CAP, with database vendors arguing that they have the whole story, but many cloud providers arguing that some applications are more natural to code directly in language like Java, and that for these applications, CAP applies. It is not clear who will win this debate, but at the time of this writing, the prevailing view seemed to be that the first-tier needs to be locally responsive even at the price of weakening consistency, and that because not all first-tier systems can be built over Oracle's scalable database product line (sometimes for cost reasons, and sometimes simply because the application model does not match the one favored in database settings), CAP ultimately dominates. Indeed, there are some who argue that if one builds the identical first-tier application using a commercial database product and then using very lightweight solutions that accord with the CAP principal (for example, using the BASE approach (Basic Availability using Soft State with Eventual Consistency)), that the latter will be far more elastic and will perform much better than the former. The author is not quite so sure; we will look more closely at this point in Part II of the text.

Returning to our discussion of responsiveness in the various tiers, we now arrive at the innermost tier: the seventh circle of the cloud, as Dante might view it. Here, one finds services that run offline to build the indices and other rapid-lookup data structures employed by the client-facing side of the cloud. These work ceaselessly to scrape copies of the entire world-wide-web, organize the data for fast access, precompute inverted search indices to do rapid lookups, etc. Such systems are not really focused on local responsiveness, and yet in fact they have a very similar need, because they break big jobs into small pieces and each small piece needs to be completed as quickly and as autonomously as possible. Back-end systems often concern themselves with computing on genuinely massive data sets, employ massive parallelism, and Brewer's points also can be applied here: a component that can run locally and get an acceptable answer will outperform a component that strives for a slightly stronger guarantee on its answer, yet needs to pause periodically for purposes such as synchronization or to find the most current copy of a data item within a collection of replicas. In effect, CAP might even be relevant at the back end of the cloud!

Figure 2.4 illustrated these tiers and gave a few examples of services one might find in each.

This multitiered infrastructure is supported by hardware and managerial software systems. Very often the operating system will be one that supports virtualization, so that these servers can run multiple virtual machines. The effect is that a cloud data center could easily have 150,000 machines, each having 16 cores, and each hosting 10 or more virtual machines. User's submit jobs using batch scripts that can do things like requesting 1000 machines to run such-and-such an indexing application. Thus, it would not be unusual for a cloud system to have what seem to be millions of machines running in it, and these numbers will only rise as the technology continues to grow in popularity.

5.4   Heavily Skewed Workloads and Zipf's Law

Any large system runs up against scalability issues, and cloud platforms, which need to run on massive scale, must be conscious of scalability considerations at every step of the application or service design process (we will use "application" to denote the entire application from client to cloud and "service" to mean some subsystem that runs on the cloud and solves what may be just a narrow sub-problem within some larger scope). Scalability shapes the properties of cloud services: even very simple mechanisms can behave oddly when replicated onto thousands or tens of thousands of tier-one nodes, hence things that work well and seem obvious often break once a service becomes popular. Yet debugging such issues is extremely hard; we lack the right tools and even getting a vague sense of where the problem is located can be a huge challenge.

In fact, it turns out to be rare that a service can scale out, even in a dumb way, without requiring any attention at all to the myriad the stress points that can potentially malfunction as we scale up. For example, suppose that a service responds to requests by reading data from pre-computed files and using that data to construct a suitable web page. While the service itself will be easy to replicate, it could easily place stress on the cloud file system, which might degrade under concurrent load, particularly if file system caching cannot shield the core of the file system from the majority of the requests. Thus even this trivial style of scaling poses a hard question: can we count on caching to scale up and out?

What saves the day both for cloud file systems and for many other kinds of cloud service is that cloud platforms are so highly structured. We have seen that these are hierarchical systems with heavy replication, and there is a great deal of repetition and commonality in what clients do, too. Thus, almost any statistic one might wish to measure reveals cloud platforms to be heavily skewed. Expressed in terms of our file caching scenario, it will turn out that even with modest sized file caches can often achieve remarkably high cache hit rates: some of the files will magically turn out to be very popular and will quickly find their way into many caches, while the unpopular and poorly cacheable ones will turn out to be accessed at a low enough rate that the cloud file system has some chance of keeping up, although obviously it too must be designed to scale out.

The term "skew" used here relates to the shape a graph of file popularity would have if we were to graph frequency of access on the Y axis and list files from most to least popular on the X axis. We will see a peak on the left: the most popular files will be very frequently accessed, and then the distribution will quickly tail off. While that tail will be very long (indeed, many of these distributions are "heavy tailed", meaning that in absolute terms, a substantial percentage of all file accesses are to unpopular items), the files in the tail will not benefit from caching because they are accessed so rarely.

It turns out that situations like the one seen with file system access are very common in the cloud, and indeed scientists who have studied the statistics of other situations involving very large populations in other settings—pretty much every setting ever investigated—discover very similar patterns of popularity. If one measures the popularity of some category of objects, one will probably find a few very popular objects and then vast numbers of rarely accessed ones. This phenomenon was first documented by a linguist named George Kingsley Zipf, who plotted word occurrences in written texts for a variety of languages. The general form of a Zipf distribution is what we call a *power-law*: one ranks the objects by popularity, and then finds that the probability that the object with a given rank will be accessed is proportional to $1/rank^\alpha$ (we will favor this form of the equation for a positive value of α but should probably mention that some published papers prefer the form $rank^\alpha$, with a negative value of α). The same distribution is also called a Pareto distribution, and in fact forms just one member of a larger class called the *generalized Pareto* or GP class.

We have illustrated a simple example of this class in Fig. 5.1: it shows the frequency with which various problems were reported for preprinted shipping cartons at a large e-Tailer. Similar graphs arise if one looks at frequency of access to files, or typical sizes of files, or rates of message sending, etc. The rough form of the curve shown is exponential: the most common cases are quite frequent, but as we move away from the common ones we see what can be a very long tail of rarely reported "one time issues." The tail can be so long, in fact, that it might include the majority of all problems (a so-called "heavy-tailed" situation). It is important to realize that a number of distributions can give rise to very similar curves; other well known examples include the exponential, beta and power-law distributions (the latter are one class of Pareto functions). For many cases, these different models yield nearly

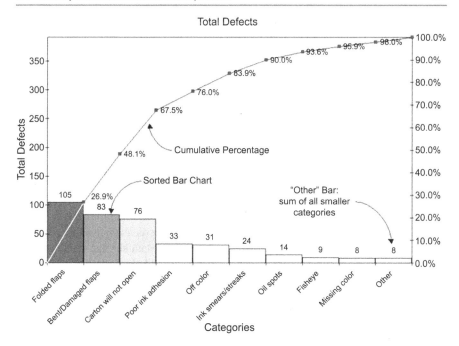

Fig. 5.1 A Pareto distribution graphing frequency of various problems with cardboard shipping cartons

identical curves, although there are parameter values they reveal them as being extremely different. This illustrates a risk that arises when trying to model phenomena observed in the cloud: often, very different models will seem to fit the data, and yet precisely because the models differ in a deeper mathematical sense, conclusions one might draw with one model may be invalidated if some other model is employed!

In distributed systems research, we generally assume that measured properties of real systems fit a power-law distribution. The larger the value of α, the steeper the tail-off effect, and what one finds in cloud settings is that these exponents can be very large: values of 2–3 are common and even larger values are reported in some situations. That is, we see some small percentage of objects that are very active (no matter what you mean by "object" and by "active"), and vast numbers that are very rarely accessed. This is quite a striking effect, and it tells us that even in a cloud system managing some huge amount of data, if we can do a great job of handling the common cases, we will often discover that we have soaked up most of the load. We often plot power-law distributions on using a log scale for the Y axis; doing so should yield a straight line. The slope of that line, if you fit it using a linear regression, will let you estimate α.

This is perhaps a good place to caution the reader about a common error that one sees frequently in research papers, or even when testing a cloud service in the lab. Suppose you had invented a new cloud service: how would you evaluate its scalability? Very likely you would fuss with a paper and pencil, but at some point you will need to run your code. But on what data set?

Lacking real data from a real cloud setting in which your application will run, it would be very common to just create a synthetic data set by looking up previous research papers and mimicking the shape of the data sets they described. Thus with many measurements of Zipf-like and other power-law distributions of access to objects in cloud settings, one frequently sees papers that look up a value of α and then create a purely synthetic data set with the desired statistics. If this seems confusing, think about how you might create a trace of file accesses in which the file with popularity rank r is accessed with frequency proportional to $r/rank^{\alpha}$. This is pretty easily done. Thus, you could create a trace of accesses to, say, a billion fake files, feed them into your new file caching software, and see how it does.

This exact sequence of steps is often followed by people developing new cloud computing technologies. So where does it go wrong? The issue is that when one uses a random number generator to create some new random data set that matches the power-law statistics of the original data set, we will very likely replace the "noise" in the original data set with random noise. The problem here is that the original data may not have incorporated real noise. Instead, one often sees that data such as file access statistics have a dominant behavioral trend, such as fitting a power-law file popularity curve, perhaps with $\alpha = 2.5$, but then may have a very structured residual distribution if we subtract out the power-law component. In replacing this structure with random variability of the kind seen in synthetic data, we often depart much further from reality than one would expect.

Furthermore, when one fits a power-law curve to measure α, it often turns out that the power-law portion of the curve "explains" only parts of the original data set: normally, the portion with higher-ranked data items. That is, if we use a randomized method to create a new synthetic data set with power-law distributions of access and the same value of α, we will often end up with data that has a tail with very different structure than the tail of the original data extracted from the real system. This matters because in a power-law distribution of accesses, a substantial percentage of accesses still fall into the tail: individual low-ranked items may be rarely accessed, yet in aggregate, many accesses are to low-ranked items.

Heavy-tailed distributions can be confusing to work with for many reasons. First, it turns out that simple statistics like averages often are meaningless when working with a heavy tailed distribution: whereas getting more and more data will give us better and better estimates of Gaussian distributions, with more and more data the mean and standard deviation just grow without limit in a heavy-tailed scenario. A remarkable number of papers and products in the cloud computing area are riddled with statistical mistakes for this reason: they quote properties that just do not mean anything at all for the category of data being analyzed!

Next, there can be a lot of structure in the data within the tail, but synthetic data will often lose that structure. For example, in studies of file system access one often sees very steep power-law popularity distributions in which, just to pull a number from the air, 80% of the accesses are to 3% of the files. But in the cloud, 20% of the accesses may still be a huge number. Synthetic data traces will probably treat those as purely random. In practice, though, even those accesses to rare files will turn out to be structured: many fine-grained studies of file access have shown high levels of correlation in the patterns of access to rarely touched files. In effect, some file is almost never accessed, but when it is accessed, it tends to be touched as part of a group that also involves access to these ten other files.

This matters a great deal. It explains why the *access affinity* property is so important in the cloud (we discussed it in Chaps. 2 and 3), and it really sheds a great deal of light on how big a file system cache needs to be, and what quality of cache-hits to expect.

Thus, the cloud can be a confusing environment for those of us who design services intended to run in it. Superficially, we find huge levels of correlation and dramatic usage patterns that clearly could shape the development approach for many kinds of scalable service. Yet we rarely know enough to model the data accurately, and if one skips that step and uses synthetic data in testing a new cloud service, big surprises await when it finally gets rolled out. The synthetic trace will probably miss the correlation patterns in the tail, giving very unrealistic workloads. Far better is to collect real user traces and play those into the new service in an emulation framework. Yet in doing so we run into a different problem: however bad privacy and security protection may be in the cloud, this particular privacy issue (trace collection and research on traces) has gained a lot of popular attention. Any kind of trace-driven research invites unwanted attention from the press!

5.5   A Closer Look at the First Tier

Armed with the overall picture we have developed, let us now look more closely at the tasks performed by components running in the first tier. As we saw earlier, two typical roles for services that run in the first tier of a cloud would be to construct web pages on behalf of clients accessing the cloud through a web browser, or (in the case of the Web Services remote method invocation model), to function as gateways between remote applications and the services implementing the methods those applications access. What challenges do we face?

It turns out that there are several basic issues even when building these very simple front-end services. First, services running in the first tier are expected to be *stateless*: they can communicate with other stateful services, but any storage they maintain is expected to be purely temporary and local, and cloud platforms are very relaxed about launching additional service instances or shutting instances down, typically without any form of warning. Second, as we saw earlier, they need to scale out to massive degrees without overloading in any serious way. Third, as much as possible, they need to soak up requests, shielding inner tiers from the immense loads they might otherwise encounter. Finally, they must be elastic: suitable for snap deployment and able to handle abrupt shutdowns.

Statelessness turns out to pose the main challenge to the developer. Suppose that some application issues requests that one would normally think about in terms of a transaction that performs a sequence of actions on underlying data: we would ideally like an atomic, all-or-nothing behavior. But how can one achieve that behavior in a stateless manner?

Earlier we mentioned a methodology called BASE: Basic Availability, Soft State Replication, Eventual Consistency. BASE emerged from precisely the issues just raised. The papers in this field, particular one by eBay cloud researcher David Pritchett, advocate starting with a transactional mental model for your first-tier cloud service, but then transforming it, step by step, into a non-transactional solution, in order to promote better scalability. With BASE one forgets about begin-transaction, abort, commit and locking operations. Instead, the first step is to deliberately break up that transaction into pieces, accepting as you do so that it will not execute atomically and will not necessarily even see a consistent underlying data set. We want the parts to run in parallel if possible; when impossible, we aim for short pipelines of operations. Thus a typical first-tier service becomes a series of side-by-side pipelines: the application is transformed into a kind of graph consisting of small steps that will be sequential only if one step depends on the output of the prior one. Each step would do one thing: access a piece of data, add it to the web page under construction, and so forth. Any updates that need to occur are often broken into a step that optimistically guesses at what the update will do, and a separate step that fires off the real update asynchronously. Of course the guess (the optimistic step) may have been wrong. But in BASE the recommendation is to simply conceal such issues, as much as possible: to embrace the asynchronous nature of the first tier and to make these oddities part of the normal behavior of the application.

Similarly, whereas a transaction automatically rolls back if a crash occurs, BASE recommends that if possible your application do nothing at all if a crash interrupts execution midway through one of these graph-like executions. Instead, it should tolerate that outcome as a normal one. Thus, if (for example) our application were booking a complex travel plan with hotels and cars and flights, a crash might leave us with some parts booked and some unreserved. In BASE one tries to compensate: perhaps, if the booked hotel is not paid for within 24 hours, the booking vanishes on its own (this is what eventual consistency really means: built-in mechanisms that will clean up, eventually, if anything goes wrong!).

Transactions use locking to guarantee serializability, but in BASE, we eliminate as much locking and synchronization as possible. And finally, to the extent that some steps simply must complete even if a failure occurs, we use what are called *durable message queuing systems* to store the steps in the form of messages containing scripts that describe the actions needed. A bit like an email system, a message queuing layer will do its best to deliver each such message just once. In this particular case some form of batch processing logic would periodically check for work to do, load the stored scripts, and run them.

With BASE, applications that might have seemed stateful and might normally require locking can often be transformed into ones that run in a highly parallel, locally responsive, stateless manner (that is, the only state ends up being the set of scripts stored in the message queuing layer). Yet one also loses guarantees that the original ACID formulation of the application would have offered. This weakening of consistency is pushed right to the end-user: one literally modifies the front-end application to tolerate or hide inconsistencies, with the goal that the end-user just should not be aware that anything odd has happened. The whole mindset does not fit well with applications like the financial, medical and process control scenarios we talked about earlier. But for browsing the eBay auctions, buying things from Amazon, or hunting for news articles about Mel Gibson's latest outburst, it works perfectly well. The first tier of the cloud is dominated by applications buildt in this manner.

5.6   Soft State vs. Hard State

Another important feature of the first tier is that it generally runs on soft-state to the greatest extent possible. As Eric Brewer, the U.C. Berkeley researcher and entrepreneur who pioneered the approach, explains, *hard-state* corresponds to durable data (i.e. files and databases), while soft-state is derived from other sources. Most readers of this book are already hard-state experts. *Soft-state*, in contrast, is cached data or other kinds of reconstructible data that can be discarded if a node managing it were to crash and restart. Thus when we say that the first tier is stateless, what we really mean is that first-tier systems maintain no local hard-state. But they do maintain soft-state all the time, in caches and in other forms.

The value of soft-state is that one can replicate it massively and, if a first-tier application uses it, the inner tiers are shielded from the associated load. For example, if we create a huge number of tier-one caches each holding the contents of a popular database, all the read requests encountered by first-tier applications can potentially be satisfied from the cache. Under the BASE approach, we will not use coherent caching: we might allow these caches to sometimes contain stale data, and even serve that data up to the external user, to avoid synchronizing against the real database. But in doing so we gain scalability: the first-tier gets to be a more and more independent computer that can handle the majority of incoming requests on its own. In effect it soaks up all the reads, optimistically guesses at what updates will do, and on that basis responds to the end-user. Then, asynchronously, any updates are dispatched into the inner tiers of the cloud, where they will eventually be executed. Obviously, this oversimplifies (sometimes one simply must interact with a hard-state service even from a first-tier application). But the basic idea is one of the key insights that have shaped today's cloud solutions.

Vogels, the CTO of Amazon.com, goes even further. He recommends that his development team think hard about changing the end-user results so that minor inconsistencies and other minor violations of a transactional model will be considered correct, normal behavior. In some sense, he suggests, a traditional transactional development model promises the end-user that they are getting a glimpse of an underlying system at an instant frozen in time, when it seemed as if no other users were active. Vogels and Pritchett are both fine with starting the tier-one development process by imagining such a service. But then one systematically weakens not just the implementation, but even the promises being offered to that external user. Now we slowly move towards a service that deliberately acknowledges the dynamic, temporarily inconsistent, elastic nature of the cloud, in such a way that nothing breaks when these kinds of event are noticeable. As these leaders explain, one can either labor heroically to build a cloud with strong assurance properties, or one can embrace the asynchronous, dynamic nature of the thing. The former is doomed, in their view. But the latter approach can work remarkably well, if a team simply sets its mind to anticipating all the things that can go wrong, and then find ways to paper over them!

5.7   Services Supporting the First Tier

First-tier services that need to store state, or need other forms of stronger guarantees, typically do so by interacting with second-tier services designed to play those roles. In this section, we will discuss a few of the best known and most popular examples. What quickly becomes evident is that these services are mostly storage/retrieval systems of various kinds, each optimized for a kind of storage/retrieval task that arises within the cloud on a truly massive scale.

5.7.1   Memcached

Memcached is a general purpose cache API backed by a widely used open source implementation and a growing array of commercial products. Products supporting this API (there are several) offer in-memory storage of data indexed by keys. The developer accesses the system through a small set of simple interfaces: `memcached_fetch` to fetch the value associated with some key, `memcached_add` to insert a new (K, V) tuple and `memcached_set` to modify the value associated with some existing key. This API can be implemented in many ways: with a simple in-memory data structure such as a hash table or tree, using some form of hardware such as an array of storage devices (see FAWN (Anderson et al. 2009)), or using a more sophisticated mix of larger servers connected by high speed networks (see Chockler et al. 2011). In distinction to some of the other options in this category that we will examine below, memcached servers normally operate independently from one-another: each server maintains a cache on behalf of its clients, but the servers do not cooperate in any way. For example, if a client-request cannot be satisfied by the server it sends the request to, that server will not forward the request to other memcached servers; indeed, the servers have no information about one-another at all.

    In a typical use of memcached, an application needing to fetch data associated with key K might call `memcached_fetch(K)` to see if a cached copy is available and, if not, retrieve it from a backend database system, calling `memcached_add` to save a copy. With the most common, open source, implementation, the data would be held in memory. Each copy of memcached is independent of every other copy, so a `memcached_add` performed on one node will have no impact on the results returned by `memcached_fetch` if the fetch is performed on some other node. However, some memcached products are implemented as more sophisticated distributed systems, in which the cache servers collaborate and a `memcached_fetch` performed on one node might be forwarded to memcached on some other node. This distributed memcached approach leverages the observation that fetching data from memory, even on a remote node, is often two or three orders of magnitude faster than fetching it from a tier-two server. The end-user API is unchanged.

Memcached has become a big business. According to the Wikipedia article on this topic, memcached technology is used by YouTube, Reddit, Zynga, Facebook and Twitter. Heroku (now part of Salesforce) offers a NorthScale-managed memcached add-on service as part of their platform. Google App Engine offers a memcached service through a proprietary API. Memcached is also supported by some popular content management systems such as Drupal, Joomla and WordPress. Finally, IBM research recently published a series of papers on a new memcached technology that operates as a distributed system, with the memcached servers collaborating to respond to requests in the manner outlined above (Chockler et al. 2011).

5.7.2   BigTable

Whereas Memcached is fundamentally a non-distributed service, in the sense that its components do not cooperate with one-another to present any sort of unified single-system image, BigTable is a *distributed* service for storing data in massive clusters and data centers: it can run at many locations, but users see a single coherent behavior. That is, BigTable is a living proof that CAP does not necessarily apply in all cases: this is a system that actually provides consistency, availability and fault-tolerance in a cloud setting. BigTable would not be able to offer symmetric availability if a network partitioning event split it into two halves within a single data center, but Google never experiences such failures within any single data center. But on WAN links (where such faults do occur), BigTable would not try to offer that guarantee: Google runs BigTable separately in each data center (e.g. there may be many servers in a single data center, but they jointly make up a single BigTable service per data center). These services are then linked by running separate services that read certain categories of BigTable data from one data center and then mirror the data over the WAN network by reinserting it into the BigTables at remote locations. So if anyone ever tells you that CAP rules out systems of this kind, just point out that Google published the first papers on BigTable nearly simultaneously with the earliest papers on CAP!

BigTable was originally created by Google developers who were finding that the Google file system (another large-scale system offering consistency) was too unstructured for many uses, but that databases were overly general and scaled poorly. BigTable was designed to implement a compromise: the system is file-like in many ways, yet it has an organizational structure similar to a very simple kind of database (the functionality is very limited, however, in comparison to a full-fledged database). There are a number of open-source technologies and products with similar functionality today, but we will limit ourselves to a closer look at BigTable itself. Readers interested in a detailed discussion of the technology should consult (Chang et al. 2008).

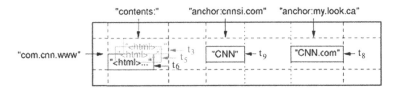

Fig. 5.2 Google's BigTable system implements a (key, value) store that looks to the user like a giant table, but one in which many of the entries aren't present: the data is sparse. In this system the column names are the keys, but each machine can contribute its own value, giving multiple rows, one per node. This figure is drawn from the primary BigTable publication, and illustrates case in a which various web page attributes are being stored for the page "com.cnn.com". Notice the column name notation, which provides a flexible and powerful grouping option. The system tracks versions (hence the timestamps shown in the figure), and has a variety of locking and atomicity mechanisms

BigTable organizes data into a conceptually massive but sparse 2-dimensional table in which the rows and columns are each named by arbitrary strings—*keys*, in the terminology of a DHT system. Each (K, K′, V) tuple is understood to have an additional temporal dimension: a value has a creation time and remains current until it is overwritten by an update or remove operation at some subsequent time. Queries specify the time and hence can retrieve any version of a desired value still in the system. BigTable garbage collects data under two conditions: the user can explicitly delete items, but can also provide expiration times, in which case they will silently be aged out by the BigTable system itself. This latter approach has the advantage of being very robust: even if the code that should have done a delete never runs, BigTable will not fill up with garbage.

The design of BigTable was motivated by some concrete examples; we will quote one that was described in the original OSDI publication on the system. In this scenario, Google was seeking a way to keep a copy of a large collection of web pages and related information shared by many applications and a large number of different projects. The solution involves having those projects share information through the table, which they call the Webtable. In Webtable, URLs are employed row keys, various aspects of web pages as column names. Columns are grouped into families. For example, Google stores the actual contents of the web pages in a column named by the key "contents:". As a page evolves over time, the contents get overwritten, giving a structure of the sort illustrated in Fig. 5.2.

One reason that this works is that in BigTable, row keys are of arbitrary size, although the research team that created BigTable comments that few keys exceeded a few hundred bytes in practice. Thus, any URL can be a row key.

As mentioned, columns are organized into *families*. A column name takes the form "family:name", although the name can be omitted if the family has just one column associated with it (as in the case of the "contents:" column we saw in Fig. 5.2). Family names must be registered in advance, and the system uses the names as a tool to physically organize table storage; in general, the system will cluster data so that data in the same row and same family will be grouped in the underlying storage structure, for fast access. Registration also avoids a potential problem: designers at Google could easily pick the same column names for completely different purposes, creating conflicts. But they would notice these conflicts when they try to register the family names for their application. Thus family names play several roles: one internal to the system (as an organizational hint) but a second that is external to the system and very social in nature (avoiding accidental conflicts over the meaning of row and column names).

It is important to appreciate that BigTable is a very sparse data representation. By this we mean that only a small subset of the possible (row, column) pairs will actually be in use at any time. The insight behind this sparseness property is a simple one: many different applications use BigTable, and each application can create its own rows, or define its own columns (or even its own column families). Thus WebTable defines one set of columns, while some other application might use an entirely disjoint set of columns. We end up with a conceptually huge table, but only some blocks of the table have data. Null entries are not stored (so no space is wasted), and attempts to access them return null strings.

We will not delve into the BigTable API in any detail; as one might expect it offers operations to create or delete families and individual columns, to add data, update data, query data, set (or reset) entry expiration times, etc. Iteration operators allow a program to scan the columns within a column family, or to look at just certain rows, columns, or timestamp ranges.

We commented earlier that whereas tier-one services typically avoid locking, this policy does not extend beyond the first tier. BigTable is an example of a rather synchronized, strongly consistent, scalable second-tier service. The system employs a powerful locking mechanism, which it uses to support a form of transaction: a set of columns within a single row can be updated as a group, so that any other client of the system will either see all of the updates, or none of them. This behavior is very similar to a database *atomicity* guarantee, and to implement it, BigTable uses synchronization, so as to ensure that reads are blocked while updates are underway, together with durability mechanisms to ensure that if a failure occurs, the table will not be left in a partially updated state.

A second built-in synchronization mechanism involves a way of using cells as shared counters, for example to generate a sequence of unique version numbers. Again, the scheme satisfies database transaction guarantees: if one application reads value 17 from a counter, no other application sees the same value.

The key to success for BigTable revolves around a question we will not be studying in any real depth in this section, namely the steps taken to ensure that related data will be clustered and packed for efficient access. In a nutshell, the development team created a series of mappings (one can think of these as being analogous to the hashing mechanisms used in DHTs) that have a high likelihood of placing data that a user might try to iterate over onto a small set of servers, in a way that ensures fault-tolerance (through replication) and promotes parallelism (multiple machines can cooperate to support parallel iterations). This set of features match nicely with a second set of design decisions, namely those that determined the query API: BigTable only allows applications to access data in ways that the implementation can efficiently carry out. In contrast, had BigTable allowed a full range of relational database operations, clients of the system could easily design query or update operations that might look quite innocent, but would perform extremely poorly. Thus the co-design of the API and the implementation turn out to be central innovations and jointly, make BigTable a successful technology at Google. Had either step failed, BigTable users could easily stumble into non-scalable modes of operation.

5.7.3   Dynamo

Amazon's development team confronted a problem very much like the one seen in BigTable, but solved it in a completely different way that requires far less synchronization: Dynamo is often cited as the hallmark example of CAP put into practice. Yet the solution, which they call Dynamo, is used in many of the same settings where a Google developer might use BigTable.

Like BigTable, Amazon's Dynamo system is a type of DHT managing collections of (K, V) tuples. Dynamo's main role is to support shopping carts and other services that Amazon uses to track actions by its customers. As readers will know, a shopping cart is a temporary form of storage that holds items the customer has selected while browsing the Amazon store. Browsing is basically a read-only operation[1]. Thus the shopping cart deals with the main stateful aspect of the browsing experience. A transactional database is employed when a user makes a real purchase, but not needed until that point is reached. As a result, the shopping cart was designed for rapid response and scalability, but not required to provide absolute reliability or extreme forms of synchronization.

For its intended purposes, Amazon concluded that the best fit would be a key-value structured storage technology, but rather than using databases as their mental model the way that the BigTable developers did, the Amazon team felt that a more weakly convergent style of solution might better match their intended use cases. This led them to select a DHT (a system much like Chord) and then ask how it might be extended to play the roles needed for a shopping cart. At first glance the match is rather close: Chord stores (K, V) tuples, replicating them for fault-tolerance, hence one could just use the DHT out of the box and would already have a reasonable shopping cart technology. On the other hand, such a solution might lack a few desired properties. Amazon pinned down these points of divergence, then enhanced their solution to address them, and Dynamo resulted from this incremental process.

First, it is important to be able to rapidly list the items in a shopping cart; this argues that for any given user, all his or her items should be grouped under the same key. But Chord-like systems usually require a unique key for each item. Additionally, Dynamo extends the Chord model by allowing a single key to index multiple objects, which are distinguished by unique object id's, timestamps, etc. The system also allows objects to be deleted.

Second, we run into an issue of fault-tolerance: when storing a value under time-pressure, suppose that some node is slow to respond. For Dynamo, as for Chord, this entails ensuring that $\log(N)$ nodes have copies. But which nodes? In Chord, the

---

[1]Obviously, Amazon does track browsing histories and takes actions to ensure that if a user clicks the back button to return to a page, the content will not have changed, but this is a relatively simple matter and can even be solved using browser cookies, hence we will not worry about it here.

nodes are required to be sequential ones along the ring starting with the successor of the node to which the key K was mapped. In Dynamo, a concern arose: what if those particular nodes include some unresponsive ones? Delay is costly at Amazon and the Dynamo team was unwilling to risk solutions that might be expensive in this sense. Instead, Dynamo tries to store copies of the (K, V) tuple on those nodes, but if a delay occurs, will retry using nodes further out along the ring.

This creates some risk: one could imagine a situation in which a (K, V) tuple should be stored on nodes a, b, and c, but because b and c are slow to respond, ends up stored on a, d and e. Now the user queries her shopping cart. If b has recovered and that query request happens to be serviced by b, the cart will appear to be lacking an item. The user could easily decide to re-add it, and end up purchasing two copies of the same thing.

Amazon accepts this risk, but to minimize the possibility of such an outcome, implemented a continuous self-repair mechanism within Dynamo. In a manner similar to the gossip protocols we mentioned in Chap. 4, Dynamo strives to shuffle (K, V) tuples until they are hosted on the right nodes. This is the model that gave rise to the BASE development methodology we mentioned previously: Dynamo prioritizes availability over all else, then replicates soft-state (in fact the (K, V) tuples are soft in the sense of Brewer's definitions), and then uses a self-repair protocol to ensure that the shopping cart will erase any inconsistencies that might be caused by transient failures such as a slow node, a failure, or a join event. Should our user end up with an unwanted second copy of the purchased object, Amazon's customer service team steps in to work out a suitable resolution of the error. In effect, Dynamo risks making mistakes (at low probability) in exchange for better availability properties.

At the end of the day, should developers favor the strong consistency of a solution like BigTable, or the more convergent style of consistency of Dynamo? This question hints at a deeper a puzzle, much debated in the cloud computing community: is CAP really a rule that applies in a universal way? If CAP was a universal rule, one would have expected that every development team facing the same large-scale questions would end up with similar large-scale answers. Here, that clearly is not the case: Google and Amazon were looking at similar questions, yet arrived at very different solutions, and one of them (BigTable) seems to defy the CAP principle.

If CAP is more of a convenience than a hard-and-fast requirement, there might still be an issue here. Perhaps the level of effort needed to build BigTable was so enormous, compared to that needed to build Dynamo, that CAP could still be valid even if no in an iron-clad way. Or perhaps applications layered over one or the other technology are harder to debug, or harder to maintain over their long-term life cycles. Researchers who believe in CAP in the strongest, most general sense, would presumably believe that this must be the case: that Google's approach must have a gottcha concealed within it. People who do not really accept CAP, and as we have already commented, CAP is more of a principle than a theorem in a formal sense (the theorem associated with CAP covers a fairly narrow case), might argue the other way, insisting Dynamo, because of its weak consistency, will leave developers at risk of all sorts of lingering bugs that occur but with low probability.

Unfortunately, at the time of this writing there was absolutely no data on that question at all. Perhaps there never will be: Amazon and Google compete and each company is fiercely loyal to its own technologies. Thus, as a practical matter, we have the CAP theorem, and we have Dynamo as an example of how this plays out in a second-tier service. Yet we also have large-scale technologies such as BigTable and the underlying Google File System, which work perfectly well in the same roles, and there is simply no hard evidence that either is really better than the other approach.

5.7.4   PNUTS and Cassandra

As noted in the introduction, brevity forced some decisions upon the author, and one of those was a decision to not spend much time on transactional and database systems. Accordingly, we will limit ourselves to two very brief notes about important examples of key-value storage systems created specifically to support database systems or programming models.

The Yahoo PNUTS system (Cooper et al. 2008), created by Raghu Ramakrishnan, is an extremely well known key-value store used in that company's SQL (and noSQL) platforms, both of which support forms of database-style queries against very large datasets. PNUTS is often cited as the system that invented *sharding*, which, as we have seen previously, is the process of fragmenting a data set so that any particular value is replicated to a small set of nodes, with the overall dataset stored in a much larger full set of nodes. For example, a database might assign some sort of unique tuple identifier to each tuple in a large relation, using that as a key, and then shard the data so that a set of n nodes will contain the full collection of tuples, but with each tuple replicated on perhaps 3 of the nodes. Those three would be the shard associated with the corresponding key. Notice that each node will probably hold a replica for a very large number of shards. We illustrated this idea in Fig. 1.4.

The notion of sharding is really distinct from the rules used to actually carry out the replication step. PNUTS uses a DHT-like scheme for this, but one could imagine other ways of mapping from keys to node identifiers. Moreover, debate rages around the important question of just what properties, if any, a PNUTS-like solution should offer. As we have mentioned, database and transactional systems normally use some variation on the ACID model, with the so-called snaphot-isolation model being especially popular in cloud settings. (Recall that with this model, reads are executed at a virtual instant in time against versions of the database that were valid at that period in time, while writes create new versions and are ordered using locking, but not necessarily using the same "serialization ordering" used for the reads). Should PNUTS itself directly implement such a model?

Early versions of the PNUTS system did offer strong consistency properties, but over time, the Yahoo research team discovered that these strong properties were at odds with their ambitious scalability goals: PNUTS runs in tier 2 of the cloud, where elasticity and scalability needs often preclude strong consistency (the CAP theorem). Thus modern versions of PNUTS offer a spectrum of options and encourage the user to work with weak models, such as a gossip-style of convergent consistency in which updates might not immediately reach all replicas of the relevant shard, but where the replicas themselves continuously exchange state and work to reconcile any inconsistencies as soon as the opportunity to do so arises.

Cassandra (Lakshman and Malik 2009) is a distributed storage system for managing structured data that is designed to scale to a very large size across many commodity servers, with no single point of failure. The system is structured as a peer-to-peer overlay, and aims to achieve scalability, high performance, high availability and applicability. In many ways Cassandra resembles a database and shares many design and implementation strategies with databases. Like PNUTS, however, Cassandra embodies a tradeoff between the model and properties offered and the speed and flexibility of the system, opting to support just a subset of the relational data model: it provides clients with a simple data model that supports dynamic control over data layout and format, but with weaker consistency guarantees that center on eventual, rather than immediate, propagation of updates across replica sets.

5.7.5 Chubby

This is probably the right place to at least mention the core technology used in BigTable to achieve consistency: a locking service called Chubby (Burrows 2006) We will have a great deal to say about totally ordered reliable multicast protocols in Part II of this text. Chubby is an application of one such protocol, namely the Paxos protocol designed by Lamport as a very simple (but not terribly efficient) solution to that problem, but then steadily refined over the subsequent decade into a more and more efficient, scalable technology. In Chubby, ordered multicasts are used to replicate lock state-changing events: lock grants and releases. Users see an API that allows them to request locks (again, using arbitrary-length keys to name them), and to release them. Chubby does a callback when a lock is granted. A somewhat complex mechanism is provided to handle cases where a lock holder crashes while holding a lock: breaking such a lock might not be wise (since whatever it protected may be in an inconsistent state), yet never breaking the lock is a guarantee of trouble! Chubby's form of replication does not scale all that well (you cannot just keep adding more and more members to a Chubby service; it slows down as you increase the number). But you can run multiple Chubby instances, each handling disjoint sets of locks, and scale up in this manner.

5.7.6 Zookeeper

The Zookeeper system is Yahoo!'s answer to the problems we have described (Junqueira and Reed 2009; Junqueira et al. 2009). Zookeeper looks like a file system: one can view it as a key-value store, but in this case the file names are playing the role of keys. It offers standard file system operations: file open, read, write, close, create. But it also offers a strong, built-in form of file locking that was very carefully thought out, and has ways to create file version numbers that are guaranteed to be unique. As a result, Zookeeper can do everything we have discussed above: it can be shared by large applications, can be used for synchronization, can create counters, etc.

Internally, Zookeeper is a replicated system that keeps any given portion of the file system on multiple nodes, using a form of atomic broadcast (more similar to an approach we will describe in Part II called *virtual synchrony* than to Paxos, for reasons of performance). Thus operations issued to Zookeeper translate to ordered multicasts, which are basically echoed by the Zookeeper server that first receives the request, then applied by individual service instances to maintain consistency across their replicated states. Notice that once again, we are looking at a tier two service with very strong consistency properties, in seeming defiance of CAP. Scalability of Zookeeper is tied to the hierarchical structure of the file system name space: each Zookeeper service handles some subtree of the overall name space, in the sense that all requests within that subtree are handled by that Zookeeper. And each of these services are typically replicated modestly, perhaps on three to five nodes. As they scale out, the capacity to handle read-only requests rises, but the cost of writes slowly grows.

Zookeepers can be interconnected using a kind of file-system mount that associates one Zookeeper file system with a file name in some other Zookeeper file system: that name becomes the root of the file system handled by the second Zookeeper. Thus one can scale Zookeeper without limit: any given service is rarely replicated on more than 5 nodes, but one could still run Zookeeper on thousands of nodes, divided into groups of 3 to 5 each, with each owning some subset of the overall file system.

Zookeeper does not need a separate service (like Chubby) for synchronization: because it uses reliable, ordered multicast as the basis for its file replication scheme, the system already has a strong enough primitive within it to do locking. Thus, the solution is basically a freestanding service covering several needs in a single package. This has made Zookeeper popular with the cloud computing research community, many members of which have gained access to it (Yahoo! is willing to release it for research uses) and then layered other solutions over it.

5.7.7 Sinfonia

In Aguilera et al. (2009a, 2009b), a team of researchers at Hewlett Packard Research Labs reported on a novel system that fuses storage and communication to achieve a very high speed and scalable data replication technology. The core idea is to push issues of consistency and fault-tolerance down into a shared data replication subsystem, Sinfonia, by mapping various application functionalities down to reads and writes against the shared storage abstraction, which in Sinfonia takes the form of an extensible log of memory versions. A built-in garbage collection layer recovers memory once there are no further needs to access it. The scheme is quite fast, and extremely general. However, we will not present it in any detail here; in Part II of the text, where we will look at group communication (multicast) with strong durability, we will see that this category of functionality really generalizes into a broader topic, namely a model called *state machine replication*, in which some set of replicas are maintained in a consistent state by applying the same updates in the same order and synchronizing the handling of failures with the delivery of updates. The model is extremely flexible; Sinfonia, in this sense, is a powerful demonstration of the practicality of this model and its value in the modern cloud.

5.7.8 The Smoke and Mirrors File System

The SMFS system (Weatherspoon et al. 2009) is a full cloud file system implementation that offers automatic data mirroring across multiple cloud computing data centers. The basic API offered to the user is completely standard: files that can be created, read, written, etc. Under the surface, SMFS uses a log-structured file system implementation in which updates are always performed as log appends. This facilitates replication, since the log updates can simply be streamed across a WAN link and then applied to a remote replica in the identical order.

In creating SMFS, the development team faced a difficult performance challenge: WAN networks are very fast (10 Gbit/s being common), but round-trip latencies are still slow enough (often 50–100 ms for a cross-country network route) that waiting for the remote data center to acknowledge successfully logging an update imposes too much delay. However, modern optical networks are reliable, dropping no more than one bit in 10^{-19}. Thus, once data has been *transmitted* it will almost surely be received by the remote mirror site, even if the sender does not wait for an acknowledgment.

Error correcting codes can drive these numbers down to an even greater extent: with such a coding scheme, if a packet is dropped now and then, for example because of congestion or receiver overload, it can be recovered from an error correcting packet later in the data stream.

If we combine these insights, we can achieve a solution that delays only until data and the associated error correction codes have been transmitted on the sending side. SMFS is able to offer performance nearly identical to that of a standard log-based file system, but still has the reliability assurances of a fully mirrored solution.

Experiments with SMFS made it clear that these error correcting codes were actually necessary: when the team ran SMFS over even completely dedicated local area networks, they observed episodic bursty packet loss. This inspired the creation of a new coding solution, called Maelstrom (Balakrishnan et al. 2008), that works by sending XORs of blocks of data in a manner designed to be rapidly computable and yet suitable for overcoming rare, bursty packet loss. Maelstrom does this by XORing blocks 0..9, 10..19, etc., then blocks 0, 10, 20, … and then 0, 1000, 2000, etc. The scheme is inexpensive and was shown to precisely match the needs of SMFS. Recovery of a lost packet is easy when using these forms of XORed data.

But why should an otherwise idle 10 Gbit network that drops so few bits on its optical links experience bursty loss in the first place? Resolving this puzzle led the SMFS team deep into the timing properties of ultra-high-speed WAN networks. In a project called BiFocals, the group designed an extremely accurate measurement apparatus with which it was possible to produce packet streams with highly precise inter-packet timing and to observe the timing properties when those streams emerged from a WAN network. By negotiation with the operators of the National Lambda Rail experimental WAN network, they were able to obtain a series of looped WAN data routes so that packets sent at Cornell would traverse various distances within the NLR, then reemerge at Cornell again (on a distinct IP address, of course).

What they discovered, as documented in Freedman et al. (2010), is that when data are transmitted on even a nearly idle optical network at these speeds, it rapidly forms into convoys of closely spaced packets that emerge in bunches. This explains the bursty loss problem that the SMFS experiments revealed: while the network receivers that system used could keep up with as much as 1 Gbit/s of traffic arriving on a 10 Gbit network link, these convoys caused 1 Gbit/s packet streams to bunch into 10 Gbit/s packet convoys with minimal inter-packet spacing, separated by longer idle period. The average rate was whatever the sender used, but the instantaneous rate could be 10 Gbit/s for a long period of time (some packet chains were as long as 10 packets in a row). These long chains of packets would overwhelm the receiver network interface card, causing packet loss in the receiver! Moreover, with modern multicore receiver platforms this problem gets worse: many such platforms have relatively slow internal bus speeds between the network interface and any individual core. This works well if packets show up at the rate they were transmitted, but if packets show up in big bursts, loss is a certainty. There simply is no place to put the incoming data.

The root cause of these bursts is not yet known with certainty, but seems likely to reflect mundane network congestion effects triggered by routine background traffic. Even an idle 10 Gbit network will still have some link management traffic on it, generally at a level of 1–3% of the network capacity. Thus when SMFS streams data at, say, 1 Gbit/s, although its packets may depart with very even spacing, as they travel through multiple router hops they are very likely to encounter at least some delays. Each such delay potentially allows some packet to catch up with the delayed packets, forming a chain that will grow in length for each successive delay. Other possible causes include routers configured in ways that aren't ideal for this data pattern, links that tunnel over MPLS (a second high-speed data transmission standard), and these are really just a few possibilities.

Most cloud computing systems offer file mirroring options over WAN links, although not all work in the manner of SMFS. A very common approach is to offer some form of queuing and transmission service. Outbound files are enqueued, and when the service gets a chance, it uses FTP to copy file by file to the remote destination. By having very large numbers of side-by-side file transfers underway, the sorts of delays that pose an issue for SMFS are hidden: the network stays busy even if some individual file transmission has paused to recover missing data. Services of this kind often break big files into multiple smaller chunks, to gain further parallelism. Thus, if one were to look at a WAN link connecting one Google or Microsoft data center to another, one would often see thousands of side-by-side TCP sessions, each copying chunks of files from source site to destination. While individual files might arrive with some delay for the reasons SMFS and Maelstrom encountered, the aggregated activity will still saturate the full WAN link.

5.7.9   Message Queuing Middleware

Earlier, in connection with BASE, we touched upon the idea of a Message Oriented Middleware (MOM) or Message Queuing Middleware (MQ) system. These are basically email systems used at a program-to-program level. Applications can place messages into the system, and they will be delivered to services that later read messages out.

The closest analogy to a mailbox arises when using a topic-oriented MQ system: the "topic" is just the name of the mailbox, and one often uses the term "publisher" for programs that generate messages, and "subscriber" for the program or programs that read data out. As one might expect, these systems offer a wide range of functionality: they can accommodate multiple publishers on one topic, multiple subscribers, they can be used in a transient storage mode that does not actually save messages for long periods, but merely relays them (e.g. a message published "now" is delivered to the servers "currently subscribing" to the topic), or a persistent one (messages live within the mailbox until they expire, or are removed by a subscriber).

In Chap. 3, we discussed the Sienna system. How might we rate Sienna relative to the MQ model? First, recall that whereas MQ systems are generally topic (mailbox) based, Sienna matches publishers to subscribers on the basis of patterns that can query the contents of messages, not just the source and destination. Second, Sienna only operates in a transient store-and-forward, then delete manner. Hopefully, however, one can see that these are all variations on a common theme. A good example of a modern publish-subscribe system is Corona (Hall et al. 1996); it provides scalable high-speed publish-subscribe and peer-to-peer application communication group support in moderately large network deployments. On the other hand, Corona was never applied in cloud-scale settings. Indeed, while there has been growing interest in offering this sort of functionality within the cloud, doing so poses some daunting research challenges.

At the highest data rates, MQ systems can sometimes be treated as *message busses*, a term picked to evoke the image of a memory bus in a computer's backplane. Just as a memory bus ferries data between CPUs and memory, a message bus ferries messages from publishers to subscribers. Often these busses run in the non-durable mode: messages are relayed as fast as possible directly between publishers and subscribers; if a published message is sent to a topic that has no current subscribers, that message is just dropped. Products in this area often offer both functionalities; the API has some form of flag that the publisher sets or disables to indicate whether or not durability is required. Of course, durability is slower, but with durability, applications can potentially replay old messages as a way to catch up with activity that occurred before the application was started. Without durability, the message bus may run at much higher speeds, but a new application instance would only receive subsequent postings to the topics it subscribes to; past history is not available. To work around this one sometimes sees non-durable message bus systems linked to database systems that subscribe to every possible topic, then archive all incoming published messages. A new subscriber can then subscribe to new postings, but can also search the database for past context. On the negative side, synchronization can be tricky in this case, e.g. in applications that need to see every single message, since the start of the system, without any duplications, omissions or misorderings.

Some cloud systems have used this model very aggressively; for example, it was extremely popular at Amazon.com in the early stages of its ramp-up. Advantages of the model are simplicity of addressing (one uses higher level topics to address messages rather than IP addresses, which decouples the logical function of the target from the physical node on which the target system might currently be running), speed and scalability. In principle, a well-implemented message bus could scale without limit, support any pattern of publishing and subscriptions, and would efficiently select the best message transport options dynamically: perhaps, IP multicast to send these transient messages from this publisher to those ten-thousand subscribers, UDP for this other relationship here, TCP over on that side where IPMC and UDP are not permitted.

In practice, one finds that these sorts of technologies are hard to automate to the necessary degree and hence work better in more predictable, constrained situations. While there are many message bus products that do their best to automatically shape behavior to the configuration of the data center in which they find themselves, and to the use patterns that arise in production, the wide variations in load and topology seen in the industry today pose a hugely complex challenge that can be hard to automatically optimize against. Thus while message bus solutions will often work well when load is light, care must be taken as they scale up and loads rise. The broadcast storms that were mentioned early in the book are a good example of how an innocent message bus technology decision (in that case, a product that made casual use of IP multicast without attention to the total number of IPMC addresses it was using) can go wrong.

To visualize how such an event might occur, we will close by just recapping that story as it really played out (without naming anyone, of course). The reader should recall from the Introduction that a large web e-Tailer was using a message bus heavily for many purposes. As it turned out, these even included debugging: the company realized that if a typical point-to-point connection was actually implemented not over TCP, but rather as a publication of a stream of messages on a topic that only the subscriber would listen to, one could simulate TCP and yet also have the ability to tap in later (by attaching an extra subscriber to the topic) if something seemed abnormal. Moreover, by publishing messages to *unsubscribed* topics, one could, in effect, print debug data to virtual consoles that do not exist unless someone attaches a subscriber to the topic. (Imagine that your program for tracking product inventories printed a stream of information to the topic inventory-debugging, for example).

The message bus vendor in our example could potentially have implemented logic to optimize the choice of transport, but in fact took a short-cut: the company used IP multicast for almost everything. The company reasoned that with a single robust IPMC-based transport solution, their software would reliably deal with patterns of 1-to-1 through 1-to-n communication, and that the IPMC hardware could filter out messages in this debugging case, where there would often be no receivers at all. Ideally, those messages would be emitted on the local optical network link but would not be routed beyond it because lacking IGMP subscription messages, the higher level routers would realize that they have no other destinations, hence would not forward them.

We saw earlier how this went wrong: with too many IPMC addresses in use, this simple concept breaks catastrophically at large scale. Suddenly even those debugging messages that should have gone into black holes start to be relayed to every link in the whole data center! Everything melts down.

Thus we see here in a nutshell the danger of scalability in cloud settings. A simple, seductively easy to use technology is adopted, with great success, by a company in its early days of growth. Everything works wonderfully for a long time. Yet one day, just because the data center needed to grow to support more load, a core component collapses. Now a panic occurs: everything in the entire organization depended upon this basic component—the message bus, in our example. We cannot trust it anymore, and there is not time to understand what was going wrong. After all, the entire data center just melted down! Money is being lost by the second.

There isn't really any moral to our little story. The people involved in this episode all remember it with a shudder, but if asked, none has any particularly good advice on how to avoid such events. Indeed, if pressed, individuals who worked at Amazon, Google and Yahoo will tell similar stories about the times that Dynamo, BigTable, the Google File System, Chubby, and Zookeeper malfunctioned and brought their data centers to a standstill. The bottom line is that *any* infrastructure service that ends up in a sufficiently key role is a risk factor in the cloud, and that *any* technology can melt down if used in ways sufficiently different from the ones that were tested. These hardened cloud researchers offer just one form of advice: to expect things to break, and to expect that every new factor of 10 scaleup will break some things very badly. Thus, one should not misunderstand such stories as being stories about the risks of any particular technology.

When things do break, there are often ways to resolve the problems. In the particular case, the eTailer resolved the issue by shifting all communication to point-to-point TCP, including patterns that look more like IPMC or UDP. This put an end to the broadcast storms and permitted the company to continue to scale, and even to continue to use the message bus "design pattern" internally. Today, we know of a second way this could have been fixed, from Chap. 1: managing the IP multicast address space might have prevented the hardware malfunction that apparently was at the root of this particular instability.

Given this choice of paths, it might seem as if fixing the IPMC layer would have been the better option. At a glance, TCP is not the best way to distribute messages in the 1-to-n cases that arise. Very likely the owners of this particular data center would agree with that sentiment, but they would also point out that having fixed the IP multicast hardware issue, one still faces a multicast flow control problem; TCP, at least, automatically handles that issue. Thus, any given technology raises layers and layers of issues. What API should we offer, and how can we best match the API to the style of desired use? By now we have seen several tier-two examples that overlap heavily in terms of all being able to support similar uses. Is it meaningful to say that one is better than another?

Even so, if one pins down cloud computing experts at today's conferences, they tend to agree on one thing. Almost all of them feel that stories like this are a reminder that TCP itself is a miracle in many senses, and that even at age 30, IP multicast is a very immature and ofen unruly cousin. While TCP can also malfunction, e.g. by slowing down when packet loss is occurring, even if the packet loss is due to a noisy link and sending faster might be a better remedy, TCP scalability has been a genuinely astonishing story that has taken us further and further into the Internet and cloud era with hardly a hitch. Some simple things really do scale remarkably well. When the message bus technology in question was reimplemented over TCP, the API that its users liked so much remained unchanged. Of course, performance suffered in some ways. Yet performance also improved in other ways; after all, the system used to melt down, and now it does not. This may not seem like a terribly deep insight to carry away from the story, but apparently, those who know these stories best feel that any deeper insight would just be a misunderstanding of what happened here, how it was fixed, and why the fix was a good one.

Thus if you ask these same folks whether they could ever imagine switching back from TCP to an IPMC-based solution, they actually agree that this could certainly happen. What they tell you is that today, at this scale, they see no reason to do so. But that perhaps tomorrow, at the next scale of ten, they won't have any other choice, and if that were to happen, will just cross that bridge when they come to it!

Second tier systems often are built around database or transactional products, and it is important for cloud computing researchers to learn about these technologies. The area is a deep, rich, and fascinating one. But it is also beyond our scope here.

5.7.10 Cloud Management Infrastructure and Tools

In this text, will not look closely at cloud management systems and tools, beyond the broad overview offered earlier by way of explanation for what might otherwise have seemed like strange constraints on the cloud application developer, such as the rule that first-tier applications be stateless and prepared for sudden and extreme rescaling or failures. The issue is simply that there are too many management systems and while all have similar roles, they differ widely in terms of details. Moreover, the APIs available differ greatly depending on whether the application shows up as a virtual machine, an Azure task, a PHP script, etc.

5.8   Life in the Back

The deeper layers of a typical data center (what we earlier referred to as the back-end) are somewhat more typical of the kinds of computing system familiar to many readers from their prior non-cloud experiences. As we move away from the front line services that deal directly with clients in an interactive mode, the cloud becomes dominated by what might be thought of as batch computing applications and more standard services, often built over high-end commercial database products. Here, the big change from a more standard distributed computing environment is one of speed and scale, but not necessarily in the sense the reader might expect. Whereas a desktop computer might have perhaps 4 cores and a few tens of gigabytes of disk storage, cloud applications often need to process petabytes of data scraped from web pages or other sources. Yet they do so on machines that often have substantially less available resources than a heavily provisioned desktop platform! The key insight here is that cutting edge machines are often disproportionately costly: cloud systems buy machines in bulk and optimize for price, hence there is a notable tendency to buy large numbers of mid-range servers, because in aggregate these offer more CPU and storage space per dollar, even if they may be slower than the top-of-the-line systems we often select for our desktop platforms. Cloud systems achieve scalability and speed not by just optimizing the performance of the individual application on a single machine, but also by finding ways to divide tasks so as to run them in a massively parallel manner, perhaps on hundreds of thousands of machines over thousands of CPU hours. The tools one encounters at this layer favor this parallel scalability model.

Parallel performance can be achieved in many ways. Perhaps the most common option is to program solutions using a tool designed for massive parallelism, such as a modern database platform. However, not every application fits a database model. A second option is to explicitly design a service to spread itself over hundreds or thousands of nodes and to orchestrate their behavior so that they run in a coordinated manner; we will spend a great deal of time in the pages to follow on that model, and the Isis[2] system (Appendix B) is designed specifically to support such uses. Finally, a number of cloud systems work in a looser version of this coordinated model, employing a technology such as MapReduce (or Hadoop, the open source implementation of the same technology).

MapReduce offers a rather simple and stylized batch processing model, programmed using scripts, in which the application runs in phases. Each phase starts by first *mapping* the job to some large number of processes (for example, by running some application multiple times and parameterizing each copy differently, e.g. to search different files), then *reducing* the size of the outputs by combining them into some smaller number of files, and then perhaps iterating the process.

For example, suppose that we wanted to create a list of two or three-word phrases that contain the word "dyskinesia", within some large corpus of medical documents. One might start by writing a simple program that looks for the word in question, then prints out the associated phrases. MapReduce would offer a way to run that program in parallel on our document collection: if the collection contains, for example, ten million documents, we might break the search down into perhaps ten thousand sub-tasks (each would search one thousand documents). MapReduce would, in essence, schedule the ten thousand jobs on some collection of machines: perhaps one per machine (if MapReduce happens to have ten thousand idle machines), perhaps 30 per machine (if only 333 were available), etc. If some tasks run slower than others, MapReduce just schedules a few extra copies, discarding any duplicate results. This compensates for machines that might be overloaded, faulty, or misconfigured and can even work around some kinds of application bugs. If the subtask was simply harder, a bit of work is wasted, but this tradeoff is viewed as one cost of scalability.

The map operation yields ten thousand separate results. A typical reduce operation might combine such result sets. For our little example, this is easily done: would just merge the result files, perhaps discarding rare phrases in favor of more common ones (thus, the reduce operation would also keep a count). Notice that we could merge all our result files into one big one, but we could equally well merge them into, say, one hundred partial result files. If we needed a single answer, the former is the way to obtain it, but if we plan to do additional computing using these files as intermediate results, the hundred partial solutions might be quite adequate, and by *not* combining them into a single file, we have the option of a more parallel next step. Obviously, one could also just do a two-phase reduction operation to create a single file; for reduction steps that are costly, such a splitting of the job could let us achieve a more parallel execution.

Many MapReduce applications are created incrementally, by building something basic, then extending it. For example, we could now expand on our basic solution. Perhaps rather than looking for phrases associated with just the single word "dyskinesia", we might modify the solution to take a list of words and to list phrases associated with each. We might do so by developing a second phase that takes the most common phrases that involve the "dyskinesia", then looks for phrases that are similar but in which "dyskinesia" is replaced by some word *similar* to dyskinesia, such as "fyskinesia" or "dyskenesia": such an approach would yield common spelling variants (and also common misspellings).

While the MapReduce model is very simple, one can do amazing things with it, and we are seeing the emergence of a whole engineering discipline concerned with transforming big problems into MapReduce implementations. The one constraint to keep in mind here is that MapReduce is really intended for what might be thought of as read-only applications: the files produced by a given run obviously become part of the cloud system state, but the data read during a phase of MapReduce is not modified by the map or reduce operations. Thus MapReduce implements a kind of functional programming model: it reads a state, then produces output that is a function of that state. This simplifies fault handling (MapReduce just relaunches any interrupted work), and also scheduling, since the subtasks can run independently and on any mix of machines that happens to be available.

General purpose database technologies can do the same things as MapReduce, and with less limitations; after all, a database can also modify data in place, whereas this is very risky to do in MapReduce because it often reexecutes individual steps multiple times, and sometimes (if some step fails repeatedly) aborts entire executions without offering any opportunity to roll things back, since the system is explicitly not intended for update transactions. The most powerful commercial databases could do this with very competitive performance too. Databases, though, are not optimized for the kind of batch processing, massively parallel execution model MapReduce offers: MapReduce is easily customized by the developer, who just scripts out the desired execution and supplies the desired mapping and reduction modules, often picking from preexisting ones (companies like Google have vast repositories of prebuilt modules of this kind, created over nearly a decade now). Thus we arrive at another example similar to the one we saw earlier in the case of second-tier storage systems: multiple ways of accomplishing more or less the same thing, with each different technical option having similar "power," and yet with each behaving rather differently in a purely practical sense. The best choice becomes a pragmatic engineering decision, not one that centers on fundamental questions such as the power of the underlying model.

Should we store data in Dynamo, BigTable, or Zookeeper? Should we use MapReduce for massive parallel search, or the cutting edge Oracle database product? There are no hard-and-fast answers to such questions; ultimately, the right choice comes down to the specific properties of the application, and the specific behavior of the technologies available to the team solving the problem. Cloud computing demands a kind of smart, street-wise decision making. Purely abstract thinking, of the kind one might use to derive theoretical predictions of asymptotic scalability for example, just does not turn out to have a major role.

5.9   The Emergence of the Rent-A-Cloud Model

Moving beyond the first tier, we arrive at the back-end of the cloud, which is very much like any massive data center one might have seen in past settings, although much more actively shared than a traditional massive data center might have been. This sharing reflects an economic reality, coupled with a technical problem.

Let us start by appreciating the nature of the problem. Early cloud platforms faced a problem: even when used just for proprietary purposes (for example, when Amazon.com's computers supported only Amazon-developed applications), a cloud often had so many applications running that the risk of interference between applications emerged as a major annoyance. For example, if two applications happen to store files in the temporary file area on the disk, then if one was carelessly designed to remove all temporary files at the end of each run, it might end up removing files created by the other. In a normal data center this sort of thing is not uncommon and leads to sharp exchanges between the development teams. But in the cloud, where applications might run on huge numbers of machines very remote from where the developers work, these sorts of confusions quickly escalated to become a major headache.

An obvious solution is to just encapsulate each application into a lightweight virtual machine, complete with its own virtual network (a form of virtually private network, combined with a form of virtual LAN or vlan), and its own virtual storage area within the file system. One can do this easily: modern operating systems permit the developer to package almost any application setup on any O/S configuration as a virtual machine, which can then be executed on some other machine just like any other executable: in effect, the machine (including your file system, network configuration and applications) becomes a big application program that pretends to be a physical machine, but might actually run side-by-side with other virtual machines on a shared physical platform. Virtualization even allows one to run Linux on Windows, Windows on Linux, etc. Today's cloud platforms have embraced this form of virtualization to the degree that non-virtualized ("bare metal") computing is becoming quite rare.

Virtualization can permit the cloud management layer to *pack* multiple virtual machines onto a single physical one. For example, suppose that a video player application is single-threaded and we run it on a mid-range machine that happens to have 8 CPU cores. The management layer will quickly discover that the machine never keeps more than 1 core busy (perhaps, 2 cores, if one also counts the activities of the O/S itself, which will often run on a different core than the application uses). In a fully automated manner the cloud management system, or *hypervisor*, can sense that there is unused capacity and if elasticity argues for running more copies of the video server, might launch as many as 7 more copies, aiming for a steady state that keeps the physical machine busy but not overloaded.

Obviously, virtualization and packing can go awry; not every packing decision is wise and mistakes will trigger resource contention or other kinds of performance problem. Ideally, these are eventually detected by the management layer, which will reduce load by killing some of the virtual machines and perhaps, if needed, launching new instances elsewhere. The resulting architecture realizes a concept that was first discussed decades ago, in which computing is available as a service, on demand, much as electric power or networking bandwidth are available for us on an as-needed basis. Today, a developer who creates an application that needs to run for five hours on ten thousand cores can purchase the needed resources from any of a number of companies, often for a tiny fraction of what it would cost to own the same infrastructure. After all, Amazon amortizes load over many users, whereas that developer might only need to do a run like this very rarely.

Of course, virtual machine models have their limitations. When we do experiments with physical computers in the lab or in the corporate data center, we generally can count on a given level of service: we know how the machines are configured, what other loads they may be experiencing, etc. In contrast, virtual machines are often very flaky: since the physical machine could be overloaded, an allocation of ten thousand virtual machines might include a few hundred running on bare metal, a few thousand on lightly shared machines, and a few hundred more on machines that are suffering extreme overloads or even hardware problems. Thus the developer who creates large-scale cloud applications cannot assume that all the participating machines will perform in comparable ways and either is forced to use a *delay-tolerant computing model*, or to somehow adapt the application to live with the available resources.

This can be a surprisingly difficult problem, depending on the programming style one favors. The developers who find it easier to deal with are those working on embarrassingly parallel applications (like those supported by MapReduce), since in these cases the tasks do not talk to one-another and it does not really matter how long each step takes to complete. The ones who struggle are those building tightly coupled applications such as parallel database systems, or the various tier-two subsystems we discussed above. The core teams who built the Google File System, BigTable, Chubby, Zookeeper and Dynamo are all battle-worn veterans with far more expertise in delay tolerant computing than anyone should ever need to gain!

In fact we are heading down this path too. For our purposes in this textbook, this kind of extreme variability will be a problem. In the second half of the book we will be exploring distributed protocols that can tolerate failures, but in which healthy machines have more or less predictable behavioral profiles. Obviously, if some healthy machines will be extremely slow, this forces us to be very conservative in our profile definitions: rather than assuming that messages arrive within 10 microseconds, for example (a typical datacenter internal network latency), we might need to assume that messages between healthy nodes sometimes take as long as 1 second to be delivered (a not-unreasonable worst case in a heavily loaded virtual situation). We can view this sort of thing as a research challenge (and should), but as a purely practical matter, it represents a serious obstacle to reliability in the existing cloud.

Fortunately, there is evidence of a positive trend: companies like Amazon are beginning to offer gold-service cloud options that provide guarantees that the virtualization they do will not cause these kinds of extreme overload. Obviously, Amazon cannot protect the developer against his or her own mistakes: an application that overloads a machine will do so whether or not it shares that machine with other applications. Amazon charges extra exchange for targeting a lighter average load: perhaps, rather than trying to load its servers at 90% capacity, the management platform might target 50%. This will allow us to design and run highly reliable services on the cloud, at a modest but not extreme cost premium relative to what we might see for very lightweight tasks that run on similar numbers of nodes but with no guarantees, and eliminates the need for complex work-arounds such as self-monitoring infrastructures that adaptively sense and shed nodes that seem to be underperforming.

5.9.1   Can HPC Applications Run on the Cloud?

Given such a cheap way to rent cycles, it makes sense to ask if cycle-hungry applications should migrate, en-masse, to the cloud. In particular, High-performance computing (HPC) systems have traditionally run on massive but dedicated supercomputing platforms; the cost per cycle of such systems is far higher than the cost of a cloud solution which might offer far more storage and far more cycles. Today, even a single large cloud-computing data center will often contain as much computing and storage as all the world's HPC systems combined. Thus a natural question to ask concerns the feasibility of migrating from traditional HPC settings to cloud ones, renting resources and running them in the back-end tier of the cloud. Yet as we saw earlier, the back end of the cloud is subject to some of the same pressures that gave rise to Brewer's CAP principle: applications run in virtual machines that may be scheduled unpredictably, nodes can fail without warning, and because resources are shared, contention between applications (for disk or network bandwidth, or CPU time) can yield very erratic run times. Can HPC applications adapt to run under this sort of model?

The obvious angle, well worth pursuing, starts by focusing on embarrassingly parallel HPC applications that read but do not modify some underlying data source. The match is especially good if the data files involved are enormous. To visualize how such an application might look, think about the model used in the SETI (Search for Extraterrestrial Intelligence) project, or about programs written to run under MapReduce. The steps in such a computation are *idempotent:* one can run each step just once, or a dozen times; each completed step with identical input parameters yields the identical result. The cloud is a great match for applications that fit this approach, and it matches the local-responsiveness goals of CAP. The big win, fundamentally, centers around tolerating the unpredictable performance of virtualized execution environments, coupled with the lower performance of the data center networks used in cloud settings relative to the ones used in HPC settings. In an embarrassingly parallel, highly decomposed mode, one achieves solutions in which each node can compute "on its own" and even can restart steps that run unexpectedly slowly.

Thus, researchers who work on such problems as reconstructing particle tracks from data sets collected at Cern's Large Hadron Collider, or on climate modeling, are flocking to cloud platforms. The biggest win is for applications that only run now and then: a team can access much larger amounts of equipment at much lower cost than if they needed to own the same systems. In contrast, if the application runs continuously, a private cloud or simply a private data center can be more cost-effective. Still, these applications do seem to match the cloud model fairly well.

But many HPC systems are very lock-step, are not decomposable this way, and depend on a great deal of inter-node communication. Subtasks may need to modified shared data structures in a fine-grained manner, and while such applications do typically have ways to checkpoint themselves and restart from the checkpoints, they may be intolerant of failures—often, even a single failure triggers a rollback of the whole application, and if this happens a few times without progress being made, the HPC system may stop the whole run. Obviously, this second style of HPC is ill-matched to today's cloud, with its aggressive management policies, high rate of node failures (both for physical and logical reasons), and the difficulty of running collections of nodes in anything approximating lock-step.

Over time, these physical considerations may fade away: continued popularity of the cloud model may yield such large data centers that one could reasonably request raw metal deployments even for hours at a time and even with hundreds of thousands of cores, at a relatively low cost compared to owning similar systems but leaving them idle a substantial percentage of the time (owning systems and keeping them busy is quite a different matter; no cloud will compete very well with that option in the near future, except in the sense that cloud computers do tend to be upgraded often).

Similarly, while today's HPC systems benefit from ultra-high speed interconnects such as Infiniband, one has to wonder whether tomorrow's data center interconnects might not seize the upper hand simply because they cater to a much larger market and hence can afford much greater investments in speed and latency. Cloud interconnects are evolving at an astonishing pace, far faster than HPC interconnects.

Perhaps the larger issue, for these reasons, centers on whether HPC systems that operate in a tightly coupled manner can cope with the failure rates seen in very large cloud settings. Recall that cloud computing management systems, for many reasons, have very high perceived node failure rates compared to other platforms. Just as a reminder, this reflects their handling of elasticity, their use of rebooting and reimaging as a fault-repair strategy, the way that nodes are brought online or taken offline for maintanence purposes, and even the tendency to run massive data centers at high temperatures to reduce cooling costs: doing so increases failure rates. If one works out the numbers, a higher rate of failures turns out to be the price of a dramatically reduced cooling and power bill. Thus, cloud systems embrace failure as a feature.

Today's HPC systems are notorious for not handling failures gracefully. Early in the history of HPC, a form of master/slave model emerged in which many applications were configured with a single master process running on some single machine that farmed out work to a large collection of slave processes. Standard packages like PVM and MPI use this model, and if a node fails, such packages generally cannot recover. Instead, as we saw above, the entire application is restarted from the most recent checkpoint.

How does this HPC model scale, particularly in a fault-prone setting? Suppose that we have a set of nodes that tend to fail at a rate of $1/t$ time units: one failure for every t elapsed seconds. A collection of n such nodes will experience one failure every t/n seconds: an expected time to failure that drops linearly as a function of the number of nodes on which we run. When a failure occurs we will lose the work done since the last checkpoint. The more nodes we have, the less work we are able to do before the next failure. This will motivate us to make a checkpoint before the next expected failure: thus more and more frequently, as we increase n. Eventually, there just won't be enough time to make a checkpoint before the next one is needed. Worse, making a checkpoint often has cost (delay) that rises as a function of n.

From this we see that the most standard forms of HPC will hit a wall: we can scale them by creating large numbers of separate HPC applications (embarrassing parallelism), but not by just throwing more and more nodes into a single HPC instance; the cloud may be a cheap place to rent lots of nodes, but is not a very good option if we need rock-solid stability. HPC may simply need to migrate to new computing models, designed to be more tolerant of failures, in order to take full advantage of this new and inexpensive computing option. Such a trend is already well established, with a growing HPC community using the cloud for applications that break up nicely into smaller chunks, leaving a smaller and smaller community to shoulder the costs of massive, super-reliable HPC platforms.

As this book was being prepared, the United States had just lost the world record for HPC performance. Quite possibly, this testifies not to some sort of technical weakness by US computing researchers, but rather to the massive shift away from traditional HPC and towards the cloud. Yes, we may not be building the fastest traditional supercomputers anymore. But perhaps the more important competition for the future just will not involve that sort of computing!

5.10   Issues Associated with Cloud Storage

A good place to end our architectural review of the cloud is by looking at storage. Obviously, cloud systems exist in part because of storage: many cloud vendors are focused on amassing truly staggering data sets and cross-correlating them to develop profiles of their users, so as to better place advertising and to optimize other services. Thus the cloud is a world of massive storage systems, and the storage capacity of modern cloud-hosting data centers is rising at an amazing rate. With so much storage available, the same thinking that led companies like Amazon to rent out spare CPU cycles is pushing for a rental storage model. And for activities involving really massive data centers, it can be extremely appealing to think about using that rented storage option. The cost savings are often very striking.

Yet cloud storage also creates a conundrum for many enterprises. Imagine that your company has created some form of very specialized, proprietary database. The database is becoming huge and the cost of ownership has been soaring. Along comes CloudStorageGuys.com and offers to host your system for pennies on the dollar. Is this a risk worth taking?

More and more organizations confront just this problem today: cloud computing really can be ten or a hundred fold cheaper, and cloud storage even more so, hence migration from a dedicated to a cloud solution has obvious appeal. Indeed, one might think about moving all sorts of storage-intensive applications to the cloud: email, corporate spreadsheets, customer-contact databases, etc. Yet consider the downside risks: if CloudStorageGuys.com were to fail, would your company even be able to access its sensitive corporate data? After all, once assets enter bankruptcy, they often cannot be accessed at all, and even operating a storage system to allow its users to copy their data off can be quite costly. Some cloud platforms cost millions of dollars per day to operate, and while you might imagine that only a tiny part of the cloud needs to be running for you to copy your data off, there is no way to know that this will be the case; it may actually be an all-or-nothing infrastructure.

What if a competitor purchased a big stake in CloudStorageGuys.com? Without even knowing it, you might find that your most delicate corporate secrets were being stored in your competitor's data center! Even a sharp rise in storage costs could pose a serious threat to your company's well being. For that matter, suppose that some minor bug or mistake by the cloud operator knocks your company off the network for a few days. Who should be responsible for the loss of revenue, and the lost clients? Read your cloud computing and storage user agreements closely if you have any doubts: it probably will not be the cloud provider! Those contracts often guarantee a certain level of service per year, but 99% uptime, over a year, is still more than three days of downtime: a big issue if the outage occurs all at once rather than being spread over the year in tiny, barely noticeable, events.

Further risks arise when we consider applications in which there are sensitive legal issues associated with the data, such as medical record management. If TrustedMedicalStuff.com builds a state of the art medical record system and runs it on its own private servers, the cost of using their solution could be sharply higher than the cost of the system offered by CheapMedicalRecords.com, which hosts their platform on a cloud. To make the comparison fair, let us assume that the product literature for both platforms brags about their state of the art, HiPPA-compliant technologies for record access and audit control. Yet notice that CheapMedicalRecords.com is not really a master of its own fate. Whereas TrustedMedicalStuff.com knows the whole story, CheapMedicalRecords.com can only be as trustworthy as the cloud on which it runs. Thus if they rent data store from CloudStorageGuys.com, and some employee of that cloud hosting company happens to be engaged in inappropriate activities, all the HiPPA guarantees in the world might not mean much.

Moreover, the story does not even end with CloudStorageGuys.com. Even the handling of cloud backups and recycled hardware emerges as an issue: what if a disk fails and is shipped away to be recycled, but the company doing so manages to repair it. Could they then access your sensitive data? A backup could pose risks: while hospitals keep data indefinitely, banks are under a legal obligation to keep records for certain amounts of time (often five years), yet are also under an obligation to destroy them after that time expires. How can a cloud computing record be destroyed, with any confidence at all? One does not even know where it physically resides, much less where the backups might be!

This kind of thinking leads to further worries. The scenarios we have outlined could easily lead to lawsuits. But who would be liable if a lawsuit were to occur? Such cases end up in court, but as of this writing there is very little case law to point to. Such questions will not be answered for many years; perhaps decades.

Yet if the situation creates uncertainties, it also has some very obvious elements that favor CheapMedicalRecords.com over TrustedMedicalStuff.com. After all, as stated, the solutions are similar in power and the former is sharply cheaper. The worries we have expressed all sound fairly abstract: what if CloudStorageGuys.com were to crash? What if some evil employee were to sneak in at night and steal data? A corporate executive making a budget decision might not believe that these worries (they do sound pretty paranoid) make all that much sense. Thus simple economics could drive us towards less trustworthy, less secure solutions that are at much higher risk of overnight "events" that could kill companies nearly instantly, leaving their customers with nowhere to turn.

The good news is that both researchers and even the cloud computing vendors recognize that these issues frighten potential customers, and much work is being done to resolve them. For example, all the major cloud storage providers offer backup and other redundancy features; they can protect against events localized to a single data center. There are tools that can create mirrored copies of files or other forms of application state, and some of those can even run across multiple cloud providers, for example shadowing your Force.com application on Amazon's AC3 storage system, so that if you ever need to migrate from Force.com to some other setting, you will have an accurate backup of the system state as of the time you made that decision.

Some ideas go much further but are still speculative. For example, many readers of the preceding section might have the idea of using data encryption: if we encipher data before uploading it to the cloud most of our worries evaporate. Then we can just provide the decryption key to the application accessing the data, and unless the cloud hosting company is genuinely corrupt, we can run our medical applications on the decrypted data, yet anyone who manages to get their hands on a disk will be blocked from the sensitive content. Short of breaking into a virtual machine image and stealing the key (entirely feasible, but only with root access to the physical machines), such a model is pretty secure. On the other hand, since we are dealing with *distributed* systems, we do run into the risk that decrypted medical data might be transmitted on the network and hence could be visible to anyone who manages to get their network interface card to listen on the appropriate addresses.

The more speculative idea is this: what if one could compute directly on the encrypted data without decrypting it first? In effect, we would encrypt the data using some sort of a function, and then support a full range of arithmetic and logical computing on that data, provided that the application doing the computing has access to the needed keys. Then, if those keys could (for example) be kept in hardware, we might have a fairly solid cloud computing security story for data of these kinds. The idea is very appealing, but nobody knows how feasible this might be. Much investment is going into this topic today and there is some hope the problem might be solved, but as of the time this chapter was being edited, the solutions were still quite limited in scope.

Today, there are some who believe that public models of cloud computing will simply not be viable options for the most sensitive uses: government and military cloud applications, for example, or the kinds of medical and banking example given above. These analysts generally argue that the cloud model either will not be accepted by those kinds of user, or that they will be ready to pay more for stronger guarantees. In that case one could imagine that some company might step up to the plate with a more specialized high-assurance cloud platform that could mimic the more standard shared clouds in many ways, but in which these sorts of questions have been resolved at the cost of a somewhat higher cost of operation.

Others, though, believe that the basic public style of cloud will win at the end of the day, attracting not just the low-security users but the ones with stronger needs too. These analysts basically argue that lower costs *always* win, even if the cheapest option is somehow inadequate. They also point out that no technology is frozen in time. Thus, if a small set of companies somehow win the cloud storage market and dominate, the huge cash flows that come from being a near monopoly might permit quite a bit of investment. Indeed, if we look at the overall history of the computing industry, there is no question that the companies that win in each sector do tend to respond (eventually) by enhancing their offerings both to maintain competitive advantage, and also to protect against any legal exposures that their cheap but inadequate solutions might create. Thus one can imagine a pattern in which we actually do end up with our medical records on CheapMedicalRecords.com, hosted in turn on CloudStorageGuys.com. Yet precisely because this style of use emerges, over time, it might motivate CloudStorageGuys.com to come up with better options for applications that host sensitive data. We would see a period of risk, perhaps a decade or so, but the longer term story might be a better one. After all, many of the issues raised above could be solved. Only time will tell us whether the pessimists or the optimists will win. But if the author of this text had to place a bet, he would not be too quick to bet against the cloud computing industry. We are still in the early days, and better technologies could plug many of the gaps.

5.11 Related Reading

Although we have included related readings sections in many other chapters in this text, the best way to learn more about the technologies covered in Chap. 5 is just to read the published papers about the technologies we touched upon. Google set a very high standard by publishing wonderfully detailed papers on the Google File System, BigTable, Chubby and MapReduce. Amazon has published extensively on Dynamo and its interpretation of CAP and BASE. One can read all about the implementation of Zookeeper in papers available from the development team at Yahoo. There are dozens of papers about Memcached technologies and products. Accordingly, we will end this chapter by recommending that interested readers consult those and other academic publications that lay out the details and design choices in careful systematic ways for these and related cloud technologies. A wonderful emerging source of this kind of paper would be the top cloud computing research conferences from ACM and IEEE, such as the ACM Symposium on Cloud Computing. These events bring experts in the field together, and often make a point of including both the most successful cloud technology developers from industry, as well as academic researchers. As a result, one sees the best work, learns of the open challenges, and gets a much more balanced perspective on where trends might lead than is possible from just reading purely academic papers (which are sometimes less than fully realistic about the realities of deployment in cloud settings), or purely trade press (which can be overly focused on the products of the moment).

Remote Procedure Calls and the Client/Server Model

6.1 Remote Procedure Call: The Foundation of Client/Server Computing

Up to now we have looked at cloud computing from a fairly high level, and used terms such as "client" and "server" in ways intended to evoke the reader's intuition into the way that modern computing systems work: our mobile devices, laptops and desktop systems operate fairly autonomously, requesting services from servers that might run in a machine up the hall, or might be situated in a massive cloud-computing data center across the country. Our overall plan, as outlined in the Introduction, is to keep this higher level perspective through the remainder of Part I of the book, then diving deeper in Part II as we look at more fundamental questions. However, even here in Part I, we need to have a sufficient sense of the details to understand some of the overall issues in a really concrete way.

Accordingly, we will pause in our overall review to look at one of the most basic building blocks of the cloud and other distributed systems: the client–server computing model. Our goals here will be to understand exactly how this model works, what its abilities and limitations are, and how modern computing systems use it. We will see that although cloud computing systems implement the client–server model in a different way than previous generations of systems did so, the basic properties and issues are really the same, and the solutions used in the cloud are really the same ones that were used in earlier client–server architectures. As we return to our broader Part I agenda, having this material under our belts will make it possible to look closely at an important and widely supported architecture for client–server systems, called CORBA (the Common Object Request Broker Architecture). One might wonder why we are interested in CORBA, given that CORBA is really a general-purpose distributed computing architecture, and not one specific to the cloud. But as noted earlier, except for the Web Services standards, we really lack a cloud architecture today. Thus while CORBA is not an architecture for cloud-computing, per-se, at least it does offer important insights into what such an architecture might someday look like. Moreover, many cloud platforms make extensive use of CORBA-like infrastructures.

K.P. Birman, *Guide to Reliable Distributed Systems*, Texts in Computer Science, DOI 10.1007/978-1-4471-2416-0_6, © Springer-Verlag London Limited 2012

With this in mind, let us start with the basics. The emergence of real distributed computing systems is often identified with the *client/server* paradigm and a protocol called *remote procedure call* (RPC), which is normally used in support of this paradigm. The basic idea of a client/server system architecture involves a partitioning of the software in an application into a set of *services*, which provide a set of operations to their users, and *client programs*, which implement applications and issue requests to services as needed to carry out the purposes of the application. In this model, the application processes do not cooperate directly with one another, but instead share data and coordinate actions by interacting with a common set of servers and by the order in which the application programs are executed.

There are a great number of client/server system structures in a typical distributed computing environment, be that the enterprise system in an office complex, a cloud computing data center, or even a single laptop talking to a line printers. Some examples of servers include the following:

- *File servers*: These are programs (or, increasingly, combinations of special-purpose hardware and software) that manage disk storage units on which file systems reside. The operating system on a workstation that accesses a file server acts as the client, thus creating a two-level hierarchy: The application processes talk to their local operating system. The operating system on the client workstation functions as a single client of the file server, with which it communicates over the network.

- *Database servers*: The client/server model operates in a similar way for database servers, except that it is rare for the operating system to function as an intermediary in the manner that it does for a file server. In a database application, there is usually a library of procedure calls with which the application accesses the database, and this library plays the role of the client in a client/server communication protocol to the database server.

- *Network name servers*: Name servers implement some form of map from a symbolic name or service description to a corresponding value, such as an IP address and port number for a process capable of providing a desired service.

- *Network time servers*: These are processes that control and adjust the clocks in a network, so that clocks on different machines give consistent time values (values with limited divergence from one another). The server for a clock is the local interface by which an application obtains the time. The clock service, in contrast, is the collection of clock servers and the protocols they use to maintain clock synchronization.

- *Network security servers*: Most commonly, these consist of a type of directory in which public keys are stored, as well as a key generation service for creating new secure communication channels.

- *Network mail and bulletin board servers*: These are programs for sending, receiving, and forwarding e-mail and messages to electronic bulletin boards. A typical client of such a server would be a program that sends an e-mail message or that displays new messages to a user who is using a newsreader interface.

- *Web servers*: As we learned in the introduction, the World Wide Web is a large-scale distributed document management system developed at CERN in the early 1990s and subsequently commercialized. The Web stores hypertext documents, images, digital movies and other information on *Web servers*, using standardized formats that can be displayed through various browsing programs. These systems present point-and-click interfaces to hypertext documents, retrieving documents using Web document locators from Web servers, and then displaying them in a type-specific manner. A Web server is thus a type of enhanced file server on which the Web access protocols are supported. Most of the "apps" on today's mobile platforms depend upon these kinds of service.

• *Web Services*: This is the standard we discussed briefly in Chap. 3, used between a client system running a browser or a web client system, and a Web server that handles documents or responds to other forms of requests. Web Services, at a minimum, have a description of the available services encoded as a WSDL document and support access via a protocol called SOAP, the Standard Object Access Protocol. They may also advertise themselves using forms of name services and with a protocol called UDDI employed to represent naming information.

In most distributed systems, and especially in cloud systems, important services are often instantiated multiple times—for example, a distributed system can contain multiple file servers or multiple name servers. We saw this in Chap. 5, where tier-one cloud services were often instantiated huge numbers of times, and many tier-two services replicated at least moderately, to handle heavy read-only loads and to provide fault-tolerance. Accordingly, in line with the language we used in Chap. 5, we will be using the term *service* to denote a set of *servers*, and a server will be our term for a single instance of some service. Thus, the *network file system service* consists of the network file servers for a system, and the *network information service* is a set of servers, provided on UNIX and Linux systems, that maps symbolic names to ASCII strings encoding values or addresses.

We say that a *binding* occurs when a process that needs to talk to a distributed service becomes associated with a specific server that will perform requests on its behalf. Various binding policies exist, differing in how the server is selected. For an NFS distributed file system, binding is a function of the file path name being accessed—in this file system protocol, the servers all handle different files, so that the path name maps to a particular server that owns that file. A program using the UNIX network information server (NIS) normally starts by looking for a server on its own machine. If none is found, the program broadcasts a request and binds to the first NIS that responds, the idea being that this NIS representative is probably the least loaded and will give the best response times. (On the negative side, this approach can reduce reliability: Not only will a program now be dependent on availability of its file servers, but it may be dependent on an additional process on some other machine, namely the NIS server to which it became bound.)

Within the cloud, binding has become a very complex problem. Earlier we saw some elements of this problem: the routing issues that determine which data center a client's request might be sent to, the gateway choice that routes the request to a first-tier server that handles that category of requests, be they web page construction or web services invocation. But now a final step in binding occurs: the client must actually bind itself to the specific server. What issues arise, particular in applications that might not be using the web services infrastructure, but could be talking "directly" to a service? For example, suppose that some application within the cloud uses memcached. How do we connect that application to the memcached server? Or, suppose that an external application uses the web services primitives to issues requests to a cloud-hosted service. How exactly do its requests get translated into a form that match the expectations of the service? What happens if things go awry?

6.2   RPC Protocols and Concepts

The most common communication protocol for communication between the clients of a service and the service itself is a Remote Procedure Call. The basic idea of an RPC originated in work by Birrell and Nelson in the early 1980s (see Birrell and Nelson 1984). Birrell and Nelson worked in a group at Xerox PARC that was developing programming languages and environments to simplify distributed computing. At that time, software for supporting file transfer, remote login, electronic mail, and electronic bulletin boards had become common. PARC researchers, however, had ambitious ideas for developing other sorts of distributed computing applications, with the consequence that many researchers found themselves working with the lowest-level-message-passing primitives in the PARC distributed operating system, which was called Cedar.

Much like a more modern operating system, message communication in Cedar supported three communication models:
- Unreliable datagram communication, in which messages could be lost with some (hopefully low) probability
- Broadcast communication, also through an unreliable datagram interface
- Stream communication, in which an initial connection was required, after which data could be transferred reliably

Programmers found these interfaces hard to work with. Any time a program, p, needed to communicate with another program, s, it was necessary for p to determine the network address of s, encode its requests in a way that s would understand, send off the request, and await a reply. Programmers soon discovered that certain basic operations needed to be performed in almost any network application and that each developer was developing his or her own solutions to these standard problems. Some programs used broadcasts to find a service with which they needed to communicate; others stored the network address of services in files or hard-coded them into the application, and still others supported directory programs with which services could register themselves, supporting queries from other programs at run time. Not only was this situation confusing, it turned out to be difficult to maintain the early versions of PARC software: A small change to a service might break all sorts of applications that used it, so that it became hard to introduce new versions of services and applications.

Surveying this situation, Birrell and Nelson started by asking what sorts of interactions programs were really needed in distributed settings. They concluded that the problem was really no different from a function or procedure call in a non-distributed program that uses a pre-supplied library; that is, most distributed computing applications would prefer to treat other programs with which they interact much as they treat pre-supplied libraries, with well-known, documented, procedural interfaces. Talking to another program would then be as simple as invoking one of its procedures—a *remote procedure call*, or RPC for short.

The idea of remote procedure call is compelling. If distributed computing can be transparently mapped to a non-distributed computing model, all the technology of non-distributed programming could be brought to bear on the problem. In some sense, we would already know how to design and reason about distributed programs; how to show them to be correct; how to test, maintain and upgrade them; and all sorts of preexisting software tools and utilities would be readily applicable to the problem.

Unfortunately, the details of supporting a remote procedure call turn out to be nontrivial, and some aspects result in visible differences between remote and local procedure invocations. Although this was not evident in the 1980s when RPC really took hold, the subsequent ten or 15 years saw considerable theoretical activity in distributed computing, out of which ultimately emerged a deep understanding of how certain limitations on distributed computing are reflected in the *semantics*, or properties, of a remote procedure call. In some ways, this theoretical work finally lead to a major breakthrough in the late 1980s and early 1990s, when researchers learned how to create distributed computing systems in which the semantics of RPC are precisely the same as for local procedure calls (LPC). In Part II of this book, we will study the results and necessary technology underlying such a solution, and we will see how to apply it to RPC. We will also see that such approaches involve subtle tradeoffs between the semantics of the RPC and the performance that can be achieved; the faster solutions also weaken semantics in fundamental ways. Such considerations ultimately lead to the insight that RPC cannot be transparent, however much we might wish that this was not the case.

Making matters worse, during the same period of time a huge engineering push behind RPC elevated it to the status of a standard—and this occurred *before* it was understood how RPC could be made to accurately mimic LPC. The result of this is that the standards for building RPC-based computing environments (and, to a large extent, the standards for object-based computing that followed RPC in the early 1990s) embody a nontransparent and unreliable RPC model, and this design decision is often fundamental to the architecture in ways that the developers who formulated these architectures probably did not appreciate. In the next chapter, when we study stream-based communication, we will see that the same sort of premature standardization affected the standard stream technology, which as a result also suffers from serious limitations that could have been avoided had the problem simply been better understood at the time the standards were developed.

In the remainder of this chapter, we will focus on standard implementations of RPC, with two specific standards in mind—the SOAP standard used in Web Services systems and the CORBA standard, which predates and serves as a form of template for RPC in industry platforms such as .NET and J2EE. As it happens, the details of these varied standards will not enter into the remainder of this chapter, because our interest is primarily in the basic steps by which a program RPC is coded in a program, how that program is translated at compile time, and how it becomes bound to a service when it is executed. Then, we will study the encoding of data into messages and the protocols used for service invocation and for collecting replies. Finally, we will try to pin down a semantic for RPC: a set of statements that can be made about the guarantees of this protocol and that can be compared with the guarantees of LPC. The details of exactly how a piece of data is represented in a message, or exactly how the RPC specifies that the client wants to invoke the "database lookup" function of the server as opposed to some other function, are examples of the sort of aspect for which the standards are very different, but that we will not be looking at in any detail. Interested readers, however, will find SOAP particularly easy to understand because the encoding is entirely in ASCII, and all aspects are accessible from a standard Web browser. Thus one can literally walk through every step by which a client finds a Web Services system, binds to it, sends it requests and decodes the replies, using a browser to inspect the information that would normally be hidden inside packets exchanged directly from an application on one computer with an application on a second one. Doing so is a useful exercise in demystification of this important class of technologies.

It should be noted that, while SOAP is rapidly stealing the stage, CORBA (the Common Object Request Broker Architecture) really deserves the credit for introducing many of the basic mechanisms used today. Web Services-oriented platforms such as .NET and J2EE actually trace more of their functionality to CORBA than to any other prior technology, and precisely because SOAP is verbose and very general, it is also a very slow performer. CORBA is more representative of the kinds of RPC that can really be used to build complex, high-speed applications.

The use of RPC leads to interesting problems of reliability and fault handling, shared among all major RPC platforms. As we will see, it is not hard to make RPC work if most or all components within a system are working well. When a system malfunctions, however, RPC can fail in ways that leave the user with no information at all about what has occurred and with no evident strategy for recovering from the situation. There is nothing new about the situations we will be studying—indeed, for many years, it was simply assumed that RPC was subject to intrinsic limitations, and since there was no obvious way to improve on the situation, there was no reason that RPC should not reflect these limitations in its semantic model. As we advance through the book, however, and it becomes clear that there *are* realistic alternatives that might be considered, this point of view becomes increasingly open to question. To this author's taste, it is a real shame that modern RPC platforms, such as .NET, J2EE and SOAP, have missed the boat by failing to take advantage of some of the options available to us today. Doing so would not be very difficult and might lead to big reliability benefits in applications hosted on the technology.

The good news is that the Web Services community has launched a whole series of projects aimed at developing a new set of standards for distributed computing. But the bad news is that there is absolutely no evidence that these standards will actually fix the problems, because the communities developing them have not approached the underlying issues in a systematic way, at least at the time of this writing in 2011. For example, we will see that a central issue underlying almost every aspect of reliability concerns the manner in which a system detects failures and reports them. Standard ways of solving this problem could have a huge impact and can transform the options for solving other problems. However, the Web Services community has tended to accept the basic Web architecture as a given, and as any user of a Web browser can confirm, failure detection and reporting in the Web is very haphazard. This, then, feeds into an overall mindset in which Web Services are expected to cope with (rather than to overcome) a great many problems associated with the unreliability and inconsistency of lower-level event reporting. Overall, the only conclusion one can draw is that existing standards are flawed, and the failure of the standards community to repair these flaws has erected an enormous barrier to the development of reliable distributed computing systems. In a technical sense, these flaws are not tremendously hard to overcome—although the solutions would require some reengineering of communication support for RPC in modern operating systems. The challenge is more of an educational one: a wider range of leaders from the relevant industry sectors needs to come to grips with the nature of the problem and the most promising options.

Interestingly, were these conceptual blocks overcome, one could build a greatly improved RPC environment that would have few, if any, user-visible incompatibilities with the usual approaches—it would look similar but work better. The issue then is one of education—the communities that control the standards need to understand the issue better, and they need to understand the reasons that this particular issue represents such a huge barrier to progress in distributed computing. They would also need to recognize that the opportunity vastly outweighs the reengineering costs that would be required to seize it. With this goal in mind, let us take a close look at RPC.

6.3 Writing an RPC-Based Client or Server Program

The programmer of an RPC-based application employs what is called a *stub-generation* tool. Such a tool is somewhat like a macro preprocessor: It transforms the user's original program into a modified version, which can be linked to an RPC run-time library. Different systems come with different forms of stub generators. Thus, on a UNIX or Linux system running CORBA, a stub generator is a program that one runs separately, whereas in Microsoft's .NET framework, users of Visual Studio C# automatically obtain the needed stubs simply by declaring that their applications are using external objects.

From the point of view of the programmer, a server or client program looks much like any other program, although it may be necessary to code the program in a somewhat stylized manner. Normally, the program will *import* or *export* a set of interface definitions, covering the remote procedures that will be obtained from remote servers or offered to remote clients, respectively. A server program will also have a name and a version, which are used to connect the client to the server. Once coded, the program is compiled in two stages: First the stub generator is used to map the original program into a standard program with added code to carry out the RPC, and then the standard program is linked to the RPC run-time library for execution.

RPC-based application or server programs are coded in a programming style very similar to certain kinds of non-distributed program, namely those written to interact through some form of graphical user interface (GUI). There is no explicit use of message passing, and the program is structured to register a variety of "callback" procedures, which will be invoked by the runtime system as events occur and need to be handled (this is a familiar model for anyone who has written a program using a standard GUI package). However, there is an important aspect of RPC programming that differs from programming with local procedure calls: the separation of the service interface definition, or IDL[2], from the code that implements it. In an RPC application, a service is considered to have two parts. The interface definition specifies the way that the service can be located (its name), the data types used in issuing requests to it, and the procedure calls that it supports. A *version number* is included to provide for evolution of the service over time—the idea being that if a client is developed to use version 1.1 of a service, there should be a way to check for compatibility if it turns out that version 1.0 or 2.3 is running when the client actually gets executed. These checks are often automated, and in some systems (notably the Microsoft .NET environment) there are mechanisms for automatically downloading versions of services needed by an application, and even for running two different versions of the same service side-by-side in support of a set of clients having varied requirements.

The basic actions of the RPC library were described earlier. In the case of a server program, the library is responsible for registering the program with the RPC directory service program, which is normally provided as part of the RPC run-time environment. An RPC client program will automatically perform the tasks needed to query the directory to find this server and to connect to it, creating a client/server binding. For each of the server operations it invokes, code will be executed to marshal a representation of the invocation into a message—that is, information about the way that the procedure was called and values of the parameters that were passed. Code is included to send this message to the service and to collect a reply; on the server side, the stub generator creates code to read such a message, invoke the appropriate procedure with the arguments used by the remote caller, and to marshal the results for transmission back to the caller. Issues such as user-id handling, security and privacy, and handling of exceptions are often packaged as part of a solution. Finally, back on the caller side, the returning message will be demarshaled and the result made to look like the result of a local procedure.

Although much of this mechanism is automatic and hidden from the programmer, RPC programming differs from LPC programming in many ways. Most noticeable is that most RPC packages limit the types of argument that can be passed to a remote server, and some also limit the size (in bytes) of the argument information—for

---

[2]It is common to call the interface to a program its IDL, although IDL actually is a shorthand for Interface Definition Language, which is the name of the language used to write down the description of such an interface when using CORBA. Thus one often reads about the "IDL" of a Web Services application, despite the fact that such applications describe their interfaces as part of the WSDL document.

Fig. 6.1   Remote procedure
call involves creating a
message that can be sent to
the remote server, which
unpacks it, performs the
operation, and sends back a
message encoding the result

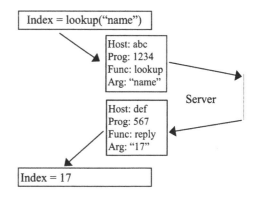

example, suppose that a local procedure is written to search a list, and an LPC is
performed to invoke this procedure, passing a pointer to the head of the list as its
argument. One can ask whether this should work in an RPC environment—and, if
so, how it can be supported. If a pointer to the head of the list is actually delivered
to a remote program, that pointer will not make sense in the remote address space
where the operation will execute. So, it would be natural to propose that the pointer
be de-referenced, by copying the head of the list into the message. Remotely, a
pointer to the copy can be provided to the procedure. Clearly, however, this will only
work if one chases *all* the pointers in question—a problem because many programs
that use pointers have some representation for an un-initialized pointer, and the RPC
stub generator may not know about this.

In building a balanced tree, it is common to allocate nodes dynamically as items
are inserted. A node that has no descendents would still have left and right pointer
fields, but these would be initialized to *nil* and the procedure to search nodes would
check for the nil case before dereferencing these pointers. If an RPC marshalling
procedure were to automatically make a copy of a structure to send to the remote
server (see Fig. 6.1), it would need to realize that for this particular structure, a
pointer value of nil has a special meaning and should not be chased.

The RPC programmer sees issues such as these as a set of restrictions. Depending
on the RPC package used, different approaches may be used to attack them. In
many packages, pointers are simply not legal as arguments to remote procedures. In
others, the user can control some form of argument-copying mechanism, and
in still fancier systems, the user must provide general-purpose structure traversal
procedures, which will be used by the RPC package to marshal arguments. Further
complications can arise if a remote procedure may modify some of its arguments.
Again, the degree to which this is supported at all, and the degree to which the
programmer must get involved, varies from package to package.

Perhaps ironically, RPC programmers tend to complain about this aspect of RPC
no matter how it is handled. If a system is highly restrictive, the programmer finds
that remote procedure invocation is annoying, because one is constantly forced to
work around the limitations of the invocation package—for example, if an RPC
package imposes a size limit on the arguments to a procedure, an application that

works perfectly well in most situations may suddenly fail because some dynamically defined object has grown too large to be accepted as an RPC parameter. Suddenly, what was a single RPC becomes a multi-RPC protocol for passing the large object in chunks, and a perfectly satisfied programmer has developed distinct second thoughts about the transparency of RPC. At the other extreme are programming languages and RPC packages in which RPC is extremely transparent. These, however, often incur high overheads to copy information in and out, and the programmer is likely to be very aware of these because of their cost implications—for example, a loop that repeatedly invokes a procedure having one changing parameter as well as others (including a pointer to some large object) may be quite inexpensive to invoke in the local case. But if the large object will be copied to a remote program on every invocation, the same loop may cost a fortune when coded as part of a distributed client/server application, forcing the program to be redesigned to somehow pass the object to the remote server prior to the computational loop. These sorts of issues make programming with RPC quite different from programming with LPC.

RPC also introduces error cases that are not seen in LPC, and the programmer needs to deal with these. An LPC would never fail with a binding error, or a version mismatch, or a timeout. In the case of RPC, all of these are possibilities—a binding error would arise if the server were not running when the client was started. A version mismatch might occur if a client was compiled against version 1 of a server, but the server has now been upgraded to version 2.

The resulting issues are not necessarily minor. For example, in 1996, a French Adrianne rocket crashed immediately after launch. It turned out that there was a version mismatch between the telemetry and guidance units; the powerful rocket motor managed to produce acceleration beyond the maximum value the telemetry unit could represent, and it overflowed, producing a value that confused the guidance unit. One could have fixed this by switching to a larger field for the acceleration data, but to do so, the guidance unit would need to be upgraded to accept those larger values, and retested. Here we see a kind of interface failure at several levels: between the guidance and telemetry systems, but also in some sense, between the rocket motor and the telemetry system. In another famous case, a Nasa mission to Mars crashed because one unit was outputting data in a metric unit (meters/second), but the unit reading those data expected it to be in non-metric format (feet/second). One would have preferred for all such problems to be caught either during compilation or testing, as binding-time interface mismatch exceptions. This sounds more like a type-checking problem, a bit like trying to pass a floating point value to a procedure that expects an integer argument.

Broadly, such issues highlight the sense in which client–server systems can encounter failures not seen in other settings, and may need new mechanisms to deal with them: at a minimum, we clearly need to realize that type checking may not be possible until the client actually finds the specific server version to which it will be bound, and even than suggests that we may need two separate notions here: one concerned with the version of the interface, and the other, distinct, the version of the client and server. This way, we could patch a bug in a server without needing to recompile the client, unless the bug fix changes the interface expected by the client in a way that requires changes on the client side.

In the cloud these issues are especially important because cloud systems need to be highly automated and will run for long periods of time. We will need to upgrade clients and servers on a regular basis, and may not be in a position to test every possible client against every possible server. Ideally, the client–server infrastructure should help in ways that reduce the risk of an unnoticed mistake.

Failure handling also poses problems. In RPC systems, failures are normally sensed using timeout mechanisms. A timeout could result from a server crash, a network problem, or even a problem on the client's computer. Many RPC applications would view these sorts of problems as unrecoverable errors, but fault-tolerant systems will often have alternative sources for critical services and will need to fail-over from a primary server to a backup. The code to do this is potentially complex, and in most RPC environments, it must be implemented by the application developer on a case-by-case basis.

The worst error-handling case arises when an application needs to know the precise outcome of a request in order to take the next step after a failure incapacitates the server with which it was communicating. For example, suppose that an application process requests that a ticket-selling server check for a seat in the orchestra of the local opera is available and, if so, record the sale. When this request fails by timing out, the application has no way to know whether or not a seat was purchased. Although there may be other servers to which the request can be reissued, doing so runs some risk that the client will be sold two orchestra seats instead of one. This is typical of a situation in which RPC's "semantics" are too weak to address the needs of the application.

6.4   The RPC Binding Problem

The RPC *binding* problem occurs when an RPC client program needs to determine the network address of a server capable of providing a matching instance of some service it requires: a service instance compatible, that is, with the particular version of the client. Binding can be approached from many perspectives, but the issue is simplified if issues associated with the name service used are treated separately, as we do here.

The first step in binding involves asking the naming service for a form of "handle" that can be used to contact the server. This interaction is highly specific to the platform: naming in CORBA is quite different from naming in .NET, J2EE or Web Services. However, the basic principle is the same: a library procedure is provided and the client application invokes this procedure with the name of the desired service, the host on which it is running, a list of properties it should have, or some other form of pattern that can be used to find the best matching server within a potentially longer list. Back comes a handle (in practice, an IP address and port number) or an error code. At this stage binding takes place, and consists primarily of a protocol for establishing a connection to the server and verifying compatibility between the client and server version numbers.

The compatibility problem is important in systems that will operate over long periods of time, during which maintenance and the development of new versions of system components will inevitably occur. Suppose that a client program, c, was developed and tested using server s, but that we now wish to install a new version of s, c, or both. Upgrades such as these create a substantial risk that some old copy of c will find itself talking to a new copy of s, or vice versa—for example, in a network of workstations it may be necessary to reload c onto the workstations one by one, and if some machines are down when the reload occurs, an old copy of c could remain on its disk. Unless c is upgraded as soon as the machine is rebooted—and this may or may not occur, depending on how the system is administered—one would find an old c talking to an upgraded s. It is easy to identify other situations in which problems such as this could occur.

Life would be greatly simplified if all possible versions of s and c could somehow communicate with all other versions, but this is not often the case. Indeed, it is not necessarily even desirable. Accordingly, most RPC environments support a concept of *version number*, which is associated with the server IDL and distinct from the notion of the service revision level, which changes each time the service is patched or otherwise upgraded. The idea is that a patch sometimes changes the interface, but not always. When a client program is compiled, the server IDL version is noted in software. This permits the inclusion of the client's version of the server interface directly in the call to the server. When the match is not exact, the server could reject the request as being incompatible, perform some operation to map the old-format request to a new-format request, or even preserve multiple copies of its functionality, running the version matched to the caller.

Connection establishment is a relatively mechanical stage of binding. Depending on the type of client/server communication protocol that will be used, messages may be transmitted using unreliable datagrams or over reliable communication streams such as TCP. Unreliable datagram connections normally do not require any initial setup, but stream connections typically involve some form of open or initialization operation. Having identified the server to which a request will be issued, the binding mechanism would normally perform this open operation.

The binding mechanism is sometimes used to solve two additional problems. The first of these is called the factory problem and involves starting a server when a service has no currently operational server. In this approach, the first phase of binding looks up the address of the server and learns that the server is not currently operational (or, in the connection phase, a connection error is detected and from this the binder deduces that the server has failed). The binder then issues a request to a "factory", namely a service in which the system designer has stored instructions for starting a server up when needed. The factory will now manufacture an instance of the desired object. After a suitable pause, the binder cycles back through its first phase, which presumably succeeds.

The second problem arises in the converse situation, when the binder discovers multiple servers that could potentially handle this client. The best policy to use in such situations depends very much on the application. For some systems, a binder should always pick a server on the same machine as the client, if possible, and should otherwise pick randomly. Other systems require some form of load-balancing, while still others may implement an affinity policy under which a certain server might be especially well suited to handling a particular client for reasons such as the data it has cached in memory or the type of requests the client is expected to issue once binding has been completed.

Binding is a relatively expensive operation—for example, in a Web Services RPC environment, binding can be more than ten times as costly as RPC. However, since binding only occurs once for each client/server pair, this high cost is not viewed as a major problem in typical distributed computing systems.

6.5   Marshalling and Data Types

The purpose of a data marshalling mechanism is to represent the caller's arguments in a way that can be efficiently interpreted by a server program. Since the client and server will often be coded in different programming languages and perhaps running in different operating systems or on different hardware, marshalling also seeks to provide universal representations that can be understood by any platform. In the most general cases, this mechanism deals with the possibility that the computer on which the client is running uses a different data representation than the computer on which the server is running.

Marshalling has been treated at varying levels of generality. Web Services, for example, make use of the Extensible Markup Language (XML) to represent data and data types. XML leads to a verbose representation, but a very general one. In contrast, major vendors have adopted data representations of their own, such as Sun Microsystem's External Data Representation (XDR) format, which is used in the widely popular Network File System (NFS) protocol. Indeed, some vendors, such as Microsoft, support multiple marshalling mechanisms in order to provide compatibility with a variety of "foreign" platforms while also offering the highest possible performance when Windows platforms interact.

The basic issues that arise in a data marshalling mechanism are as follows. First, integer representations vary for the most common CPU chips. On some chips the most significant byte of an integer is also the low byte of the first word in memory, while on others the most significant byte is stored in the high byte of the last word of the integer. These are called little endian and big-endian representations. At one point in the 1980s, computers with other representations—other byte permutations—were on the market, but at the time of this writing I am not aware of any other surviving formats.

A second representation issue concerns data alignment. Some computers require that data be aligned on 32-bit or even 64-bit boundaries, while others may have weaker alignment rules—for example, by supporting data alignment on 16-bit boundaries. Unfortunately, such issues are extremely common. Compilers know about these rules, but the programmer is typically unaware of them. However, when a message arrives from a remote machine that may be using some other alignment

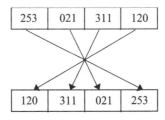

Fig. 6.2 The same number (here, a 32-bit integer) may be represented very differently on different computer architectures. One role of the marshalling and demarshalling process is to modify data representations (here, by permuting the bytes) so that values can be interpreted correctly upon reception

rule, the issue becomes an important one. An attempt to fetch data directly from a message without attention to this issue could result in some form of machine fault, or it could result in retrieval of garbage. Thus, the data representation used in messages must encode sufficient information to permit the destination computer to find the start of an object in the message, or the sender and destination must agree in advance on a packed representation that will be used for messages on the wire even if the sender and destination themselves share the same rules and differ from the standard. Needless to say, this is a topic capable of generating endless debate among computer vendors whose machines use different alignment or data representations.

A third issue arises from the existence of multiple floating-point representations. Although there is an IEEE standard floating point representation, which has become widely accepted, some older computers used nonstandard representations for which conversion would be required. These still live on, hence their representations remain relevant. Even within computers using the IEEE standard, byte-ordering issues can still arise.

A fourth issue concerns pointers. When transmitting a complex structure in which there are pointers, the marshalling mechanism needs to either signal that the user has requested something illegal, or somehow represent these pointers in a way that will permit the receiving computer to fix them upon reception of the request. This is especially tricky in languages that use pointers heavily, such as Java or C# or Lisp. In such cases the marshalling system must distinguish cases where data can be passed safely by value (by making a copy of the underlying values) from cases in which the application truely requires pointers (e.g. **out** or **ref** parameters), and hence cannot safely be used in an RPC. Researchers have explored ways of implementing pointers in RPC settings, but the general consensus is that even if this problem can be solved to a degree, it makes more sense to just limit RPC to call-by-value semantics.

Finally, a marshalling mechanism may need to deal with incompatibilities in the basic data types available on computers (see Fig. 6.2)—for example, a pair of computers supporting 64-bit integers in hardware may need to exchange messages containing 64-bit integer data. The marshalling scheme should therefore be able to represent such integers. On the other hand, when this type of message is sent to a computer that uses 32-bit integers the need arises to truncate the 64-bit quantities so that they will fit in the space available, with an exception being generated if data would be lost by such a truncation. Yet, if the message is merely being passed through some sort of intermediary, one would prefer that data not be truncated, since precision would be lost. In the reverse direction, sign extension or padding may need to be performed to convert a 32-bit quantity into an equivalent 64-bit quantity, but only if the data sent is a signed integer. Thus, a completely general RPC package needs to put a considerable amount of information into each packet, and it may need to do quite a bit of work to represent data in a universal manner. On the other hand, such an approach may be much more costly than one that supports only a very limited set of possible representations, or that compiles the data marshalling and demarshaling operations directly into in-line code.

The approach taken to marshaling varies from RPC package to package. The Web Service XML approach that underlies the cloud computing standards is extremely general, but this generality comes at a high cost: although there exists a binary option, in most cases data are converted to a printable ASCII representation for transmission and converted back on reception. This creates very large messages. The binary approach, in contrast, is less flexible. Thus one sees a tradeoff: less general schemes can gain efficiency, but only at the price of certain kinds of cross-platform incompatibility.

6.6   Associated Services

No RPC system lives in isolation. As we will see, RPC is always with additional mechanisms, such as security subsystems that employ keys and validate access, and that often employ timestamps that, in turn, depend upon a clock synchronization mechanism. For this reason, one often talks about distributed computing *environments* that include tools for implementing client/server applications such as an RPC mechanism, security services and time services. The most elaborate environments, such as J2EE and Microsoft .NET, go well beyond this, including system instrumentation, management interfaces and tools, fault-tolerant tools, and so-called Fourth-Generation Language (4GL) tools for building applications using graphical user interfaces (GUIs). These tools are often so powerful that a developer who knows almost nothing about programming can still create useful services in a kind of point-and-click style, in effect operating a complex machinery without having the slightest idea how it really works.

Cloud computing systems are even fancier: they build on top of distributed computing environments, layering in additional functionality associated with replication of the first-tier services that handle client requests. Some of these distributed environments are familiar ones; for example Microsoft's Azure cloud builds on that company's powerful .NET infrastructure, which provides a wide range of distributed computing functionality. Others are equally powerful but more proprietary. For example, Google's AppEngine runs over an infrastructure designed from scratch by Google's engineering team in the early days of that company's history. Force.com runs on the infrastructure SalesForce.com built up in its own early growth period, Amazon has yet another set of solutions, etc. Someday, perhaps we will see a winner in this space and some single distributed computing environment will sweep the others to the side. At the time of this writing, however, the best we can do is to look at some representative examples of what one finds in them, recognizing that any specific system on which a reader of this text might work will deviate from our examples in a great many ways.

6.6.1   Naming Services

A naming service maintains one or more *mappings* from some form of name (normally symbolic) to some form of value (normally a network address). Naming services can operate in a very narrow, focused way—for example, the Domain Naming Service of the TCP/IP protocol suite maps short service names, in ASCII, to IP addresses and port numbers, requiring exact matches. At the other extreme, one can talk about extremely general naming services, which are used for many sorts of data, allow complex pattern matching on the name, and may return other types of data in addition to, or instead of, an address. The Web Services standard specifies a whole language for "naming," called UDDI (the Universal Description, Discovery and Integration language). One can even go beyond this to talk about secure naming services, which could be trusted to only give out validated addresses for services and dynamic naming services, which deal with applications such as mobile computing systems in which hosts have addresses that change constantly.

In standard computer systems at the time of this writing, three naming services are widely supported and used. As previously mentioned, the Domain Name Service (DNS) offers limited functionality, but is very widely used. It responds to requests on a standard network port address, and for the domain in which it is running can map ASCII names to Internet port numbers. DNS is normally used for static services, which are always running when the system is operational and do not change port numbers at all—for example, the e-mail protocol uses DNS to find the remote mail daemon capable of accepting incoming e-mail to a user on a remote system. Although there are a number of extensions to the basic DNS functionality, and some applications have tried to use DNS in a very dynamic way (notably, the Akamai web hosting system), not all implementations of DNS comply with these more "esoteric" uses, and they have consequently found limited uptake in the field. Indeed, some members of the governing organization of the Internet, IETF, have complained about the Akamai use of DNS, arguing that DNS was not really designed to support rapid updates and that Akamai's pattern of use was disrupting DNS for other purposes and also imposing an unreasonably high load.

On UNIX and Linux systems, the Network Information Service (NIS), previously called Yellow Pages (YP), is considerably more elaborate. NIS maintains a collection of maps, each of which has a symbolic name (e.g., hosts, services, etc.) and maps ASCII keywords to an ASCII value string. NIS is used on UNIX systems to map host names to Internet addresses, service names to port numbers, and so forth. Although NIS does not support pattern matching, there are ways for an application to fetch the entire NIS database, one line at a time, and it is common to include multiple entries in an NIS database for a single host that is known by a set of aliases. NIS is a distributed service that supports replication: The same data are normally available from any of a set of servers, and a protocol is used to update the full set of servers if an entry changes. However, NIS is not designed to support rapid updates: The assumption is that NIS data consists of mappings, such as the map from host name to Internet address, which change very rarely. A 12-hour delay before NIS information is updated is not unreasonable given this model—hence, the update problem is solved by periodically refreshing the state of each NIS server by having it read the contents of a set of files in which the mapping data are actually stored. As an example, NIS is often used to store password information on UNIX and Linux systems.

Microsoft obtains NIS-like functionality from a very elaborate naming service called the "active registry." Within a local area network running Windows, the registry functions as a vast database, storing everything from the list of documents a user most recently opened to the location on the display where Word's window was most recently positioned. The application is notified when this information changes.

There are a number of standards for naming services such as DNS. The community that gave us the ISO standards defined X.500, an international standard that many expect will eventually replace NIS. This service, which is designed for use by applications running the ISO standard remote procedure call interface and ASN.1 data encoding, operates much like an NIS server. No provision has been made in the standard for replication or high-performance update, but the interface does support some limited degree of pattern matching. As might be expected from a standard of this sort, X.500 addresses a wide variety of issues, including security and recommended interfaces. However, reliability issues associated with availability and consistency of the X.500 service (i.e., when data are replicated) have not yet been tackled by the standards organization.

The more successful standard is called LDAP. LDAP is supported by most platforms and vendors, and is flexible enough to be compatible with emerging naming mechanisms, such as the UDDI naming scheme employed by Web Services. X.500, in contrast, probably cannot be stretched quite so far. Nonetheless, there is considerable interest in using LDAP or X.500 to implement general-purpose White-Pages (WP) servers, which would be explicitly developed to support sophisticated pattern matching on very elaborate databases with detailed information about abstract entities. Rapid update rates, fault-tolerance features, and security are all being considered in these proposals. At the time of this writing, it appears that the Web will require such services and that work on universal resource naming for use in the Web will be a major driving force for evolution in this overall area. One might speculate that LDAP will ultimately prevail in the battle to be the successful standard for naming services, but X.500 cannot be ruled out, and it is also possible that Web Services will give rise to new kinds of naming service and new, even more general, standards.

Last but (someday) most important in this list are name services for Web Services applications. As this book was being written, there was a tremendous amount of commercial competition to offer such services and each of the major vendors

(IBM, BEA, Microsoft, etc.) had its own proprietary product line with a specialized, high-value feature set. Eventually, it seems likely that a small set of winners will emerge to dominate this space, and that a new naming standard will then be defined, combining best-of-breed features from the most popular solutions.

6.6.2   Security Services

In the context of an RPC environment, security is primarily concerned with the *authentication* problem. The issue is similar to but not identical to the one discussed in Chap. 3, where we touched upon Web Services security for cloud systems. The reader will recall that in Chap. 3, the focus was on SSL security: a handshake used to compute a symmetric session key with which data on a TCP connection could be enciphered by the sender and deciphered by the receiver so as to hide the contents from intruders. In the process, that scheme gave the sender some confidence that it was really talking to the intended destination, but the receiver (the bank, in the example we used then) learned less.

Security for an RPC protocol would normally operate at a lower level and seek to mutually authenticate the client and server to one-another, while leaving the question of how data are encrypted for transmission (if at all) for the application to determine, through transport-level options that can be selectively enabled or disabled. Thus, we take the authentication question further, and at the same time leave the lower-level behavior requested from the RPC transport to be determined by the designer of the application. On the other hand, the RPC messaging layer does the encryption, if requested, in an automated manner: the developer provides the key but is not forced to actually encrypt or decrypt the bytes. Still all of this is complicated enough that whereas SSL security for web pages is common, RPC security is much less often enabled.

Briefly stated, an RPC security infrastructure solves the problem of providing applications with accurate information about the user-ID on behalf of which a request is being performed, but in a way that also authenticates the service to the client system as a kind of side-effect of the protocol structure. Obviously, one would hope that the user-ID is related in some way to the user, although this is frequently the weak link in security architecture. Given an accurate source of user identifications, the basic idea is to avoid intrusions that can compromise user-ID security through break-ins on individual computers and even replacements of system components on some machines with versions that have been compromised and hence could malfunction. As in the case of clock services, we will look more closely at security later in the textbook (Chap. 18) and hence limit ourselves to a brief review here.

To accomplish authentication, a typical security mechanism (e.g., the Kerberos security architecture for DCE (see Schiller 1994; Steiner et al. 1988)) will request some form of password or one-time key from the user at login time, and periodically thereafter, as keys expire on the basis of elapsed time. This information is used to compute a form of secure user identification that can be employed during connection establishment. When a client binds to a server, the security mechanism authenticates both ends, and also (at the option of the programmer) arranges for data to be encrypted on the wire, so that intruders who witness messages being exchanged between the client and server have no way to decode the data contained within them. (Unfortunately, however, this step is so costly that many applications disable encryption and simply rely upon the security available from the initial connection setup.) Notice that for such a system to work correctly, there must be a way to trust the authentication server itself: The user needs a way to confirm that it is actually talking to the authentication server and to legitimate representatives of the services it wishes to use. Given the anonymity of network communication, these are potentially difficult problems.

In Chap. 18, we will look closely at distributed security issues (e.g., we will discuss Kerberos in much more detail) and also at the relationship between security and other aspects of reliability and availability—problems that are often viewed as mutually exclusive, since one replicates information to make it more available, and the other tends to restrict and protect the information to make it more secure. We will also look at emerging techniques for protecting privacy, namely the true user-ID of programs active in a network. Although the state of the art does not yet support construction of high performance, secure, private applications, this should be technically feasible within the not-too-distant future. Of course, technical feasibility does not imply that the technology will become widely practical and therefore useful in building reliable applications, but at least the steps needed to solve the problems are increasingly understood.

6.6.3   Transactions

Later in this book we will discuss a programming model from the database community, in which applications are structured as "transactions" that operate on databases or other forms of persistent data storage. Databases are extremely important in commercial computing settings, and transactions are often closely integrated with RPC environments. For example, the J2EE system was developed as a very general purposed Java runtime environment, but has gradually become more and more popular for database applications encapsulated as "Java Beans." In support of this style of programming, J2EE provides an elaborate transactional package. Similarly, Microsoft's .NET system has a very comprehensive database subsystem called ADO.NET. Applications using this package gain automatic access to a transactional mechanism integrated with the basic .NET remote procedure call.

The Web Services standards that underlie cloud computing systems includes perhaps the most elaborate transactional mechanisms ever, supporting two forms of transactions. One form matches the "operation on a database" model just mentioned. The other is aimed at a broader problem, namely support for applications that will do a series of the basic style of transactions over a long period of time. These so-called "business transactions" raise all sorts of additional reliability issues. For example, suppose that a travel agent wants to book a request for a plane ticket, a rental car and a hotel. In the abstract this is a single transaction, but in practice each involves talking to a separate application and those applications are not likely to cooperate.

Accordingly, each request will probably be performed as a separate transaction—an RPC to the appropriate kind of Web Service with "transactional properties"—but the set will be treated as a business transaction—a series of transactions that should all be performed. If one fails, for example because no hotel rooms are available, it may be necessary to back the others out and return control to the user.

Later we will be looking closely at transactional mechanisms, and this is not the place to launch into that discussion. However, it is important for RPC programmers to be aware that many packages are designed with a model in mind. Developers should always be attentive to the styles of examples provided by the vendor or organization promoting a given package and, even before starting to use that package, confirm that those examples are very closely matched with the needs of the application being constructed.

6.7   The RPC Protocol

The discussion up to this point has focused on client/server computing and RPC from the perspective of the user. A remote procedure call *protocol* is concerned with the actual mechanism by which the client process issues a request to a server and by which the reply is transmitted back from the server to the client. We now look at this protocol in more detail. We will focus on RPC as it arises in systems like J2EE and .NET rather than in Web Services, where RPC (SOAP) runs over HTTP which in turn runs on TCP—the resulting layering is very complex, and because TCP lives at the bottom of the stack, many issues seen in other RPC settings simply do not arise for Web Services systems. On the other hand, Web Services run like molasses when compared with these other "native" implementations.

Abstractly, the remote procedure call problem, which an RPC protocol undertakes to solve, consists of emulating LPC using message passing. LPC has a number of properties—a single procedure invocation results in exactly one execution of the procedure body, the result returned is reliably delivered to the invoker, and exceptions are raised if (and only if) an error occurs.

Given a completely reliable communication environment, which never loses, duplicates, or reorders messages, and given client and server processes that never fail, RPC would be trivial to solve. The sender would merely package the invocation into one or more messages and transmit these to the server. The server would unpack the data into local variables, perform the desired operation, and send back the result (or an indication of any exception that occurred) in a reply message. The challenge, then, is created by failures.

Were it not for the possibility of process and machine crashes, an RPC protocol capable of overcoming limited levels of message loss, disorder, and even duplication would be easy to develop (Fig. 6.3). For each process to which it issues requests, a client process maintains a message sequence number. Each message transmitted carries a unique sequence number, and (in most RPC protocols) a time stamp from a global clock—one that returns roughly the same value throughout the network, up to clock synchronization limits. This information can be used by the server to

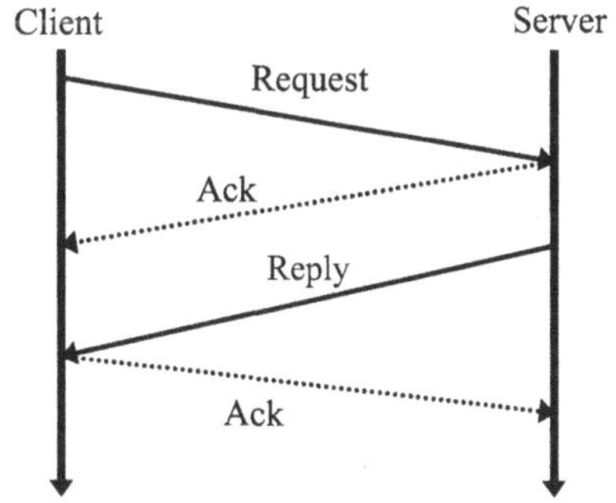

Fig. 6.3 Simple RPC interaction, showing packets that contain data (*thick*) and acknowledgements (*dotted*)

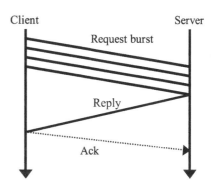

Fig. 6.4 RPC using a burst protocol; here the reply is sent soon enough so that an acknowledgement to the burst is not needed

detect very old or duplicate copies of messages, which are discarded, and to identify received messages using what are called *acknowledgment protocol messages.*

The basic idea, then, is that the client process transmits its request and, until acknowledgments have been received, continues to retransmit the same messages periodically. The server collects messages and, when the full request has been received, performs the appropriate procedure invocation. When it transmits its reply, the same sort of reliable communication protocol is used. Often, the acknowledgement is delayed briefly in the hope that the reply will be sent soon, and can be used in place of a separate acknowledgement.

A number of important optimizations have been proposed by developers of RPC-oriented distributed computing environments—for example, if one request will require the transmission of multiple messages, because the request is large, it is common to inhibit the sending of acknowledgments during the transmission of the burst of messages. In this case, a *negative acknowledgement* is sent if the receiver detects a missing packet; a single acknowledgement confirms reception of the entire burst when all packets have been successfully received (Fig. 6.4).

Process and machine failures, unfortunately, render this very simple approach inadequate. The essential problem is that because communication is over unreliable networking technologies, when a process is unable to communicate with some other process, there is no way to determine whether the problem is a network failure, a machine failure, or both (if a process fails but the machine remains operational the

Fig. 6.5 If an old request is replayed, perhaps because of a transient failure in the network, a server may have difficulty protecting itself against the risk of re-executing the operation

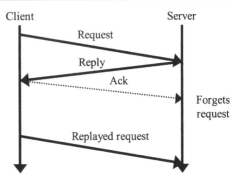

operating system will often provide some status information, permitting this one case to be accurately sensed).

When an RPC protocol fails by timing out, but the client or server (or both) remains operational, it is impossible to know what has occurred. Perhaps the request was never received, perhaps it was received and executed but the reply was lost, or perhaps the client or server crashed while the protocol was executing. This creates a substantial challenge for the application programmer who wishes to build an application that will operate reliably despite failures of some of the services upon which it depends.

A related problem concerns the issue of what are called *exactly once semantics*. When a programmer employs LPC, the invoked procedure will be executed exactly once for each invocation. In the case of RPC, however, it is not evident that this problem can be solved. Consider a process, c, that issues an RPC to a service offered by process s. Depending upon the assumptions we make, it may be very difficult even to guarantee that s performs this request *at most* once. (Obviously, the possibility of a failure precludes a solution in which s would perform the operation exactly once.)

To understand the origin of the problem, consider the possible behaviors of an arbitrary communication network. Messages can be lost in transmission, and as we have seen this can prevent process c from accurately detecting failures of process s. But the network might also misbehave by delivering a message after an unreasonably long delay—for example, suppose that a network router device fails by jamming up in such a manner that until the device is serviced, the software within it will simply wait for the hardware to be fixed. Obviously, there is no reason to simply assume that routers will not behave this way, and in fact it is known that some routers definitely could behave this way. Moreover, one can imagine a type of attack upon a network in which an intruder records messages for future replay.

One could thus imagine a situation in which process s performs a request from c, but then is presented with the same request after a very long delay (Fig. 6.5). How can process s recognize this as a duplicate of the earlier request?

Depending upon the specific protocol used, an RPC package can use a variety of barriers to protect itself against replays of long-delayed messages—for example, the package might check timestamps in the incoming messages, rejecting any that are very old. Such an approach, however, presumes that clocks are synchronized to a reasonable degree and that there is no danger that a message will be replayed with a modified timestamp—an action that might well be within the capabilities of a sophisticated intruder. The server could use a connect-based binding to its clients, but this merely pushes the same problem into the software used to implement network connections—and, as we shall see shortly, the same issues occur and remain just as intractable at that level of a system. The server might maintain a list of currently valid users, and could insist that each message be identified by a monotonically increasing sequence number—but a replay could, at least theoretically, re-execute the original binding protocol.

Analyses such as these lead us to two possible conclusions. One view of the matter is that an RPC protocol should take reasonable precautions against replay but not be designed to protect against extreme situations such as replay attacks. In this approach, an RPC protocol might claim to guarantee *at most once semantics*, meaning that provided that the clock synchronization protocol has not been compromised or some sort of active attack been mounted upon the system, each operation will result in either a single procedure invocation or, if a communication or process failure occurs, in no invocation. An RPC protocol can similarly guarantee at least once semantics, meaning that if the client system remains operational indefinitely, the operation will be performed at least once but perhaps more than once. Notice that both types of semantics come with caveats: conditions (hopefully very unlikely ones) under which the property would still not be guaranteed. In practice, most RPC environments guarantee a weak form of at most once semantics: Only a mixture of an extended network outage and a clock failure could cause such systems to deliver a message twice, and this is not a very likely problem.

A different approach, also reasonable, is to assume a very adversarial environment and protect the server against outright attacks that could attempt to manipulate the clock, modify messages, and otherwise interfere with the system. Security architectures for RPC applications commonly start with this sort of extreme position, although it is also common to weaken the degree of protection to obtain some performance benefits within less hostile subsets of the overall computing system. We will return to this issue and discuss it in some detail in Chap. 18.

At the start of this subsection, we commented that Web Services support SOAP RPC over TCP and hence avoid many of the issues just mentioned. It is important to realize that this positioning does not eliminate those issues. For example, TCP is a "reliable" protocol in the sense that it checks for and retransmits lost messages, but this form of reliability has limits. TCP cannot detect endpoint failures and cannot distinguish host crashes from transient network outages. Thus while TCP tries to be reliable, as a practical matter it is not able to be any more reliable than a hand-coded protocol running directly on UDP. In effect, all of the same issues just cited arise in Web Services RPC too, although the sources of the problems are buried in layer upon layer of abstractions.

Fig. 6.6 Idealized
primary-backup server
configuration. Clients interact
with the primary and the
primary keeps the backup
current

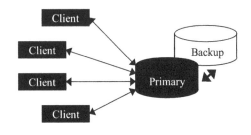

6.8   Using RPC in Reliable Distributed Systems

The uncertainty associated with RPC failure notification and the weak RPC invocation semantics seen on some systems pose a challenge to the developer of a reliable distributed application.

A reliable application would typically need multiple sources of critical services, so that if one server is unresponsive or faulty the application can re-issue its requests to another server. If the server behaves as a read-only information source, this may be an easy problem to solve. However, as soon as the server is asked to deal with dynamically changing information, even if the changes are infrequent compared to the rate of queries, a number of difficult consistency and fault-tolerance issues arise. Even questions as simple as load-balancing, so that each server in a service spanning multiple machines will do a roughly equal share of the request processing load, can be very difficult to solve.

Suppose that an application will use a primary-backup style of fault tolerance, and the requests performed by the server affect its state. The basic idea is that an application should connect itself to the primary, obtaining services from that process as long as it is operational. If the primary fails, the application will fail-over to the backup. Such a configuration of processes is illustrated in Fig. 6.6. Notice that the figure includes multiple client processes, since such a service might well be used by many client applications at the same time.

Consider now the design of a protocol by which the client can issue an RPC to the primary-backup pair such that if the primary performs the operation, the backup learns of the associated state change. In principle, this may seem simple: The client would issue an RPC to the server, which would compute the response and then issue an RPC to the backup, sending it the request it performed, the associated state change, and the reply being returned to the client. Then the primary would return the reply, as shown in Fig. 6.7.

This simple protocol is, however, easily seen to be flawed if the sorts of problems we discussed in the previous section might occur while it were running (see Birman and Glade). Take the issue of timeout (see Fig. 6.8). In this solution, two RPCs occur, one nested within the other. Either of these, or both, could fail by timeout, in which case there is no way to know with certainty in what state the system was left. If, for example, the client sees a timeout failure, there are quite a few possible explanations: The request may have been lost, the reply may have been lost, and either the primary or the primary and the backup may have crashed. Fail-over to the

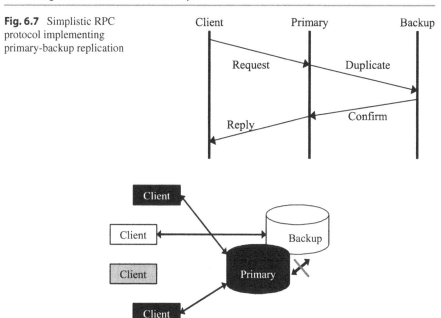

Fig. 6.7 Simplistic RPC protocol implementing primary-backup replication

Fig. 6.8 RPC timeouts can create inconsistent states, such as this one, in which two clients are connected to the primary, one to the backup, and one is disconnected from the service. Moreover, the primary and backup have become disconnected from one another—each considers the other faulty. In practice, such problems are easily provoked by transient network failures. They can result in serious application-level errors—for example, if the clients are air traffic controllers and the servers advise them on the safety of air traffic routing changes, this scenario could lead two controllers to route different planes into the same sector of the airspace! The matter is further complicated by the presence of more than one client. One could easily imagine that different clients could observe different and completely uncorrelated outcomes for requests issued simultaneously but during a period of transient network or computer failures. Thus, one client might see a request performed successfully by the primary, another might conclude that the primary is apparently faulty and try to communicate with the backup, and yet a third may have timed out both on the primary *and* the backup! We use the term "inconsistent" in conjunction with this sort of uncoordinated and potentially incorrect behavior. An RPC system clearly is not able to guarantee the consistency of the environment, at least when the sorts of protocols discussed above are employed, and hence reliable programming with RPC is limited to very simple applications

backup would only be appropriate if the primary were indeed faulty, but there is no accurate way to determine if this is the case, except by waiting for the primary to recover from the failure—not a "highly available" approach.

The line between easily solved RPC applications and very difficult ones is not a clear one—for example, one major type of file server accessible over the network is accessed by an RPC protocol with very weak semantics, which can be visible to users. Yet this protocol, called the Network File System protocol, is widely popular and has the status of a standard, because it is easy to implement and widely available on most vendor computing systems. NFS is discussed in some detail in Sect. 6.3 and so we will be very brief here.

One example of a way in which NFS behavior reflects an underlying RPC issue occurs when creating a file. NFS documentation specifies that the file creation operation should return the error code EEXISTS if a file already exists at the time the create operation is issued. However, there is also a case in which NFS can return error EEXISTS even though the file did not exist when the create was issued. This occurs when the create RPC times out, even though the request was in fact delivered to the server and was performed successfully. NFS automatically re-issues requests that fail by timing out and will retry the create operation, which now attempts to re-execute the request and fails because the file is now present. In effect, NFS is unable to ensure at most once execution of the request, and hence can give an incorrect return code. Had NFS been implemented using LPC (as in the local file system), this behavior would not be possible.

NFS illustrates one approach to dealing with inconsistent behavior in an RPC system. By weakening the semantics presented to the user or application program, NFS is able to provide acceptable behavior despite RPC semantics that create considerable uncertainty when an error is reported. In effect, the erroneous behavior is simply redefined to be a feature of the protocol.

A second broad approach that will interest us here involves the use of agreement protocols by which the components of a distributed system maintain consensus on the status (operational or failed) of one another. A rigorous derivation of the obligations upon such consensus protocols, the limitations on this approach, and the efficient implementation of solutions will be discussed later in this book (Sect. 10.2). Briefly, however, the idea is that any majority of the system can be empowered to vote that a minority (often, just a single component) be excluded on the basis of apparently faulty behavior. Such a component is cut off from the majority group: If it is not really faulty, or if the failure is a transient condition that corrects itself, the component will be prevented from interacting with the majority system processes, and will eventually detect that it has been dropped. It can then execute a rejoin protocol, if desired, after which it will be allowed back into the system.

With this approach, failure becomes an abstract event—true failures can trigger this type of event, but because the system membership is a self-maintained property of the system, the inability to accurately detect failures need not be reflected through inconsistent behavior. Instead, a conservative detection scheme can be used, which will always detect true failures while making errors infrequently (discussed in more detail in Sect. 11.3).

By connecting an RPC protocol to a group membership protocol that runs such a failure consensus algorithm, a system can resolve one important aspect of the RPC error-reporting problems discussed above. The RPC system will still be unable to accurately detect failures; hence, it will be at risk of incorrectly reporting operational components as having failed. However, the behavior will now be consistent throughout the system: If component a observes the failure of component b, than component c will also observe the failure of b, unless c is also determined to be faulty. In some sense, this approach eliminates the concept of failure entirely, replacing it with an event that might be called exclusion from membership in the system. Indeed, in the case where b is actually experiencing a transient problem, the resulting execution is much like being exiled from one's country: b is prevented from communicating with other members of the system and learns this. Conversely, the concept of a majority allows the operational part of the system to initiate actions on behalf of the full membership in the system. The system now becomes identified with a rigorous concept: the output of the system membership protocol, which can itself be defined formally and reasoned about using formal tools.

As we move beyond RPC to consider more complex distributed programming paradigms, we will see that this sort of consistency is often required in non-trivial distributed applications. Indeed, there appears to be a dividing line between the distributed applications that give nontrivial coordinated behavior at multiple locations, and those that operate as completely decoupled interacting components, with purely local correctness criteria. The former type of system requires the type of consistency we have encountered in this simple case of RPC error reporting. The latter type of system can manage with error detection based upon timeouts, but is potentially unsuitable for supporting any form of consistent behavior.

6.9   Layering RPC over TCP

Recall that when we discussed the interaction of cloud computing client systems with cloud servers, we described a layering that puts the marshalling (SOAP) over HTTP which runs, in turn, over TCP. In fact this pattern is quite common: one often sees systems that run RPC protocols over stream protocols such as TCP, an approach intended to simplify the implementation of the RPC interaction itself. In this approach, the RPC subsystem establishes a stream connection to the remote server and places it into an urgent transmission mode, whereby outgoing data are immediately transmitted to the destination. The reliability mechanisms built into the TCP protocol now subsume the need for the RPC protocol to implement any form of acknowledgement or retransmission policy of its own. In the simplest cases, this reduces RPC to a straightforward request-response protocol. When several threads multiplex the same TCP stream, sending RPCs over it concurrently, a small amount of additional code is needed to provide locking (so that data from different RPC requests are not written concurrently to the stream, which could interleave the data in some undesired manner) and to demultiplex replies as they are returned from the server to the client.

Beyond the SOAP scenario just mentioned, the most important example of a layering of RPC over TCP arises in object-oriented architectures such as CORBA and Web Services. In CORBA, this is part of the "inter-ORB" protocol by which one CORBA system can talk to another CORBA system. Web Services use SOAP RPC over HTTP over TCP to transport most of its requests. Thus the reliability of the RPC protocol becomes a question of the reliability of TCP. A CORBA "remote" request or a Web Services object invocation will fail if the TCP connection breaks or times out, and neither architecture is very clear about what the application programmer should do in this situation.

It is important to appreciate that the reliability associated with TCP will not normally improve (or even change) the reliability semantics of an RPC protocol superimposed upon it. A TCP stream would report a broken connection under essentially the same conditions where an RPC protocol would fail by timing out, and the underlying acknowledgement and retransmission protocol will not affect these semantics in any useful way. The major advantage of running RPC over a stream is that by doing so, the amount of operating system software needed in support of communication is reduced: Having implemented flow control and reliability mechanisms for the stream subsystem, RPC becomes just another application-level use of the resulting operating system abstraction. Such an approach permits the operating system designer to optimize the performance of the stream in ways that might not be possible if the operating system itself were commonly confronted with outgoing packets that originate along different computational paths. On the other hand, the user is left in a confusion situation: if a request fails, just as we saw earlier, it is unclear what state the server was left in. Generally, the application will either toss up its hands and let the (human) user sort things out, or engage in some sort of application-specific resynchronization whereby connection to the server (or to a backup) is cautiously reestablished, and then the state of the interrupted request is determined by some form of interrogation of the server. This is not trivial, and standards for reconnecting after a disruption are sorely needed.

To reiterate a point made earlier, the situation need not be such a mess. In work with Brad Glade, some years ago, we discovered that if RPC and TCP failure reporting was "rewired" to use a failure detection and agreement service, a considerable degree of consistency could be superimposed on the RPC layer. This could have widespread benefits throughout the system, and is not all that hard to do—TCP's timeout mechanism is controlled by a parameter, the so-called KEEPALIVE value, and can be disabled by the user, at which point some other failure sensing mechanism can be introduced. Nonetheless, even if the mechanism is available, such a change would not be minor, and unless the vendors who build the major operating systems platforms decide to take this step, we will all have to live with the very confusing outcomes that arise when doing RPC to a service over a protocol that employs timeout for failure detection.

In some situations, standards are intentionally designed to leave vendors room to innovate, and that is a good thing. Here, though, we see a situation where the standard in some sense defines the only acceptable behavior for the protocol. An ill-considered and yet absolute standard can be very dangerous, and the rather careless introduction of the TCP timeout mechanism into the Internet (David Clark has told the author that it was added "one night" by a developer at Berkeley and that many IETF members would have preferred an end-to-end solution) is a case in point! If Professor Clark's recollection is accurate, we have a good instance here of a poorly considered mechanism, tossed into the system rather thoughtlessly, which has now emerged as central source of unreliability for the entire Internet!

6.10   Stateless and Stateful Client/Server Interactions

Up to now, this book has focused on the communication protocols used to implement RPC, architectures for integrating RPC into larger applications (Chap. 7 tackles this in greater detail), and on the semantics provided when a failure occurs. Independent of the way that a communication technology is implemented, however, is the question of how the programming paradigms that employ it can be exploited in developing applications, particularly if reliability is an important objective. In this chapter, we examine client/server computing technologies, assuming that the client/server interactions are by RPC, perhaps implemented directly; perhaps issued over TCP. Our emphasis is on the interaction between the architectural structure of the system and the reliability properties of the resulting solutions. This topic will prove particularly important when we begin to look closely at the Web, where both browsing and the more recent Web Services architecture employ a stateless client/server computing paradigm, implemented over TCP connections to Web servers. The weakness of this model poses significant challenges to the programmer—challenges that browsers more or less ignore, but that demand much greater effort from the Web Services programmer, who may need to "overcome" problems emerging from deep within the system in order to achieve the strong guarantees required by a mission-critical application.

6.11   Major Uses of the Client/Server Paradigm

The majority of client/server applications fall into one of two categories, which can be broadly characterized as being the file server, or *stateless*, architectures, and the database-styled transactional, or *stateful*, architectures. Although there are a great many client/server systems that neither manage files nor any other form of database, most such systems share a very similar design with one or the other of these. Moreover, although there is an important middle ground consisting of stateful distributed architectures that are not transactional (including stateful file servers). These kinds of application can usually be understood as "enhanced stateless" architectures.

For example, Microsoft's NTFS file system looks stateful to the user, but is implemented as a "mostly stateless" system using event notification mechanisms to warn the client when events occur on the server that might be important to it; the client quickly rereads the changed data and, with any luck at all, applications running on it will not even notice the temporary inconsistency. If one understands the basic ideas behind stateless system designs, a file system such as this can be understood as starting from a stateless approach and then cleverly adding mechanisms that hide many of the usual issues encountered in stateless designs—an approach that gives the Microsoft system substantial robustness, and that readers of this book might want to think of as an especially good model to follow when building applications of their own. For example, the Web Services architecture invites one to follow a similar development path.

This chapter focuses on extreme cases: purely stateless file systems, and strongly stateful database systems. By doing this, we will gain familiarity with the broader technology areas of which each is representative and of the state of practice at the time of this writing. Part III of this book, starting with Chap. 10, discusses distributed systems architectures in more general terms and in much more detail, and will look at some systems that do not fit quite so cleanly into one category or the other, but in doing so will also move away from the sorts of technologies that one finds prepackaged into modern application builder tools into a class of technologies that are not as widely supported, and hence can only be exploited by sophisticated developers who are prepared to do quite a bit more of the nuts-and-bolts implementation.

A *stateless client/server architecture* is one in which neither the clients nor the server needs to maintain accurate information about one another's status. This is not to say that the clients cannot cache information obtained from a server; indeed, the use of caches is one of the key design features that permit client/server systems to perform well. Moreover, the server might include some form of call-back or event notification mechanism to warn its clients that information has changed and should be re-read. However, even without such a notification mechanism, cached information must *always* be understood as potentially stale, and any time an operation is performed on the basis of data from the cache, some sort of validation scheme must be used to ensure that the outcome will be correct even if the cached data has become invalid.

More precisely, a stateless client/server architecture has the property that servers do not need to maintain an accurate record of their current set of clients and can change state without engaging in a protocol between the server and its clients. If a server does track its clients, it may view that information as a kind of cache as well: the list of clients is understood to be an "approximation," and could list some machines that have since become disconnected from the network or that have been shut down. In a stateless architecture, when state changes occur on the server, even though the client systems will have data that lags the changes, their "correct behavior" must not be affected. That is, the client system can only used the cached data in ways that are cautious enough to avoid problems if those data turn out to be stale.

The usual example of a stateless client/server architecture is one in which a client caches records copied from a name server. These records might, for example, map from ASCII names of bank accounts to the internal account numbers and branch identification for the bank server maintaining that account. Should the account be reassigned to a different branch (i.e., if the customer moves to a different city but stays with the same bank), requests that access that account will be directed to the wrong server. Since the transfer of the account is readily detected, this request will fail and the client will realize that its cached branch record has become stale. It can then refresh its cache record by looking up the account's new location. The request can then be reissued and should now reach the correct server. This is illustrated in Fig. 6.9. Notice that the use of cached data are transparent to (concealed from) the application program, which benefits through improved performance when the cached record is correct, but is unaffected if an entry becomes stale and must be

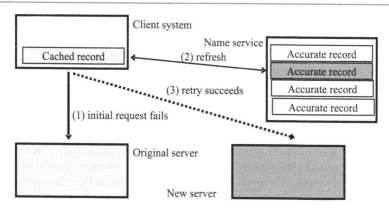

Fig. 6.9 In this example, a client of a banking database has cached the address of the server handling a specific account. If the account is transferred, the client's cached record is said to have become stale. Correct behavior of the client is not compromised, however, because it is able to detect staleness and refresh the cached information at run time. Thus, if an attempt is made to access the account, the client will discover that it has been transferred (step 1) and will look up the new address (step 2), or it will be told the new address by the original server. The request can then be reissued to the correct server (step 3). The application program will benefit from improved performance when the cached data are correct, which is hopefully the normal case, but it never sees incorrect or inconsistent behavior if the cached data are incorrect. The key to such an architecture lies in the ability to detect that the cached data has become stale when attempting to use this data, and in the availability of a mechanism for refreshing the cache transparent to the application

refreshed at the time it is used. This style of caching is extremely common; indeed, one unpublished study of Web Services by C. Mohan and G. Cuomo, senior technical leaders in the Web Services area for IBM, concluded that a typical commercial Web Services application might include as many as ten to fifteen different caches, all needed to accelerate performance, and with each differing slightly from the others. The authors concluded that caching plays a central role in modern architectures, but also found tremendous variability in the mechanisms used to detect staleness and recover when stale data are accessed. Moreover, while most of the validation mechanisms are simple, a small subset of them are remarkably complex.

One implication of a stateless design is that the server and client are independently responsible for ensuring the validity of their own states and actions. In particular, the server makes no promises to the client, except that the data it provides was valid at the time they were provided. The client, for its part, must carefully protect itself against the risk that the data it obtained from the server subsequently became stale. Applications that cannot be designed to behave this way should not use a stateless approach.

Notice that a stateless architecture does not imply that there is no form of state shared between the server and its clients. On the contrary, such architectures often share state through the cache, as seen in Fig. 6.9. The server might keep an approximate list of its clients, and that is also a form of shared state. The fundamental property of the stateless paradigm is that correct function does not require that such shared information be *accurate*.

The reader familiar with what are called "race conditions" in concurrent operating system code may recognize that stateless architectures embody a kind of race condition. Suppose that a client tries to access a record x by first checking to make sure that the cached copy, x', is still valid, and then permitting the client operation to proceed. On the server, x will not be locked against changes during the period between the validation operation and the completion of the client's operation, hence x could change just as this protocol executes. The client will then validate the record, and yet will access stale data, perhaps resulting in some sort of visible misbehavior in the eyes of an end-user. This is fundamental to stateless designs: they lack strong synchronization mechanisms (such as locking) and for that reason, applications may glimpse inconsistencies. The approach can only be used when the consequences of such anomalies are felt to be minor.

Despite its limitations, the stateless client/server paradigm is one of the most successful and widely adopted tools for building distributed systems. File servers, perhaps the single most widely used form of distributed system, are typically based on this paradigm, with the caveat noted earlier: arguably the most important file system, Windows NTFS, uses a stateless underpinning but then layers various callback and notification mechanisms over it to give the illusion of a fairly tightly coupled, stateful approach. The Web is based on stateless servers, and this is often cited as one of the reasons for its rapid success. Moreover, many of the special-purpose servers developed for individual applications employ a stateless approach.

However, as we will see momentarily, stateless architectures also carry a price: Systems built this way often exhibit strange reliability or consistency problems under what one hopes will be unlikely scenarios. Moreover, there is rarely any way to be sure that the troublesome scenarios will always be rare. For example, many stateless systems malfunction during network partitioning events. Networks normally work well, hence this kind of malfunction might never be experienced during development and may also be uncommon in practice. Even a developer aware of the risk could conclude that these events just do not occur. However, if something occurs to make network partitioning more common (a transient hardware failure, for example), the associated application-level problems could suddenly be both common and costly. An application that was perceived as working well will now be seen as buggy. Such considerations often preclude stateless architectures in settings where correct behavior is really important, such as medical systems or applications where human life or property could be placed at risk. As corporations move new generations of increasingly vital applications to computers, it seems likely that the stateless approach to server design will be less and less adequate.

A *stateful architecture* is one in which information is shared between the client and server in such a manner that the client may take local actions under the assumption that this information is correct. In the example of Fig. 6.9, this would have meant that the client system would never need to retry a request. Clearly, to implement such a policy, the database and name mapping servers would need to track the set of clients possessing a cached copy of any record that is about to be transferred. The system would need to somehow lock these records against use during the time of the transfer or invalidate them so that clients attempting to access the transferred record would first look up the new address. The resulting protocol would guarantee that if a client is permitted to access a cached record, that record will be accurate; however, it would do so at the cost of complexity (in the form of the protocol needed when a record is transferred) and delay (namely, delays visible to the client when trying to access a record that is temporarily locked, and/or delays within the servers when a record being transferred is found to be cached at one or more clients).

Later in this text we will see that stateful systems are, at their core, systems which depend upon replicated data, although the nature of the replicated information may not be immediately obvious. In effect, "state" really comes down to shared state, and what distinguishes these systems from the stateless ones is that we want the shared (replicated) state to mimic the behavior of a system in which the data in question is not replicated but instead resides at a single, highly available, server. A stateful system, then, replicates certain aspects of application state so as to mimic the behavior of a system that uses the identical information but does not replicate it.

To achieve this mimicry, stateful architectures invariably require locking mechanisms or other distributed synchronization protocols, permitting them to tightly synchronize the client with the server. If a client of a stateful system is modifying data, it must lock the data (potentially waiting until any pending readers or prior writers have finished), read an accurate copy, modify it, and check it back in. This behavior may be hidden from the developer or embedded into higher level mechanisms, such as transactions, but the core functionality is invariably present. Stateful systems thus embrace a more complex style of interaction between client and server and may need to accept reduced server availability as part of the price: if the client is temporarily unreachable but has locked some data, the server cannot allow other client systems to access those data. Such systems often work around the resulting limitations, for example by having the client ship operations to the server (the so-called "three-tier" architecture); by doing so, any availability issues that arise are shifted into the server, where it may be possible to use special hardware to minimize the impact of outages. But of course the application designer is now working in a model remote from more familiar distributed object and remote method invocation approaches. Existing platforms lack a widely accepted, well-supported, solution for the case where the application programmer needs high availability and consistency, and yet is not able to move to a transactional model.

Our comments on the Windows NTFS file server made it clear that a stateless system can become fairly complex, with layers of mechanisms designed to minimize the scenarios in which clients might realize that the system is ultimately not providing guaranteed consistency. Nonetheless, these mechanisms are often simple ones: caching, perhaps some form of event notification to warn clients that data have changed, etc. In contrast, stateful architectures often become extremely complex, because they really *do* provide strong guarantees. They also require a different style of application development. This is a cost we accept in situations, like a hospital or an air traffic control application, where those guarantees matter and make the complexity seem like a reasonable price to pay.

Stateful systems can also be associated with "coherent caching," in which the client system can cache data with confidence that the cached copy will not become stale. As we will see, this problem is solvable, although necessary mechanisms are rarely available to developers. The issue turns out to reflect a tradeoff between performance and properties. It is clear that a client system with a coherently cached data item will obtain performance benefits by being able to perform actions correctly using local data (hence, avoiding a round-trip delay over the network) and may therefore be able to guarantee some form of real-time response to the application. However, the system as a whole will see reduced performance because locking and other forms of synchronization are typically conservative, preventing some actions even when they would have been legal. Moreover, the associated mechanisms make the underlying platform more complex. Platform developers have apparently concluded that most users value higher performance more than they value strong guarantees and hence have opted for a simpler, faster architecture.

For applications in which the cost of communicating with a server is very high, or where there are relatively strict real-time constraints, coherent caching could offer extremely useful guarantees—for example, an air traffic controller contemplating a proposed course change for a flight would not tolerate long delays while checking with the database servers in the various air sectors that flight will traverse, but also cannot run the risk of giving out the wrong answer. Such a system accepts performance that may be quite a bit slower "on average" to avoid these very costly penalties. Similar issues are seen in many real-time applications, such as computer-assisted conferencing systems and multimedia playback systems. But these kinds of example are atypical, and the "usual" client/server system would not have such stringent requirements. Vendors tend to follow the majority of the market, hence until we see large-scale demand for coherent caching, the necessary mechanisms will probably remain non-standard.

There is one way to offer clients some of the benefits of stateful architecture, but without requiring that remotely cached data be maintained in a coherent state. The key is to use some form of abort or backout mechanism to roll back actions taken by a client on a server. Rollback occurs if the server detects that the client's state is inconsistent with its own state. This forces the client to roll back its own state and, presumably, retry its operation with refreshed or corrected data. This is sometimes called an "optimistic" replication or caching approach, because its benefits are achieved primarily when the optimistic assumption that the cached data has not become stale turns out to be valid. Optimistic caching is common in transactional database systems, perhaps the most common of the stateful client/server architectures.

The basic idea in a transactional system is that the client's requests are structured into clearly delimited transactions. Each transaction begins, encompasses a series of *read* and *update* operations, and then ends by *committing* in the case where the client and server consider the outcome to be successful or *aborting* if either client or server has detected an error. An aborted transaction is backed out both by the server, which erases any effects of the transaction, and by the client, which will typically restart its request at the point of the original begin, or report an error to the user and leave it to the user to decide if the request should be retried. A transactional system is one that supports this model, guaranteeing that the results of committed transactions will be preserved and that aborted transactions will leave no trace.

The connection between transactions and statefulness is as follows. Suppose that a transaction is running, and a client has read a number of data items and issued some number of updates. Often it will have locked the data items in question for reading and writing, a topic we discuss in more detail in Chap. 20. These data items and locks can be viewed as a form of shared state between the client and the server: The client basically trusts the server to ensure that the data it has read is valid until it commits or aborts and releases the locks that it holds. Just as our cached data were copied to the client in the earlier examples, all of this information can be viewed as knowledge of the server's state that the client caches. And the relationship is mutual: The server, for its part, holds an image of the client's state in the form of updates and locks that it maintains on behalf of the partially completed transactions.

Now, suppose that something causes the server's state to become inconsistent with that of the client, or vice versa. Perhaps the server crashes and then recovers, and in this process some information that the client had provided to the server is lost. Or, perhaps it becomes desirable to change something in the database without waiting for the client to finish its transaction. In a stateless architecture we would not have had to worry about the state of the client. In a transactional implementation of a stateful architecture, on the other hand, the server can exploit the abort feature by arranging that the client's transaction be aborted, either immediately, or later when the client tries to commit it. This frees the server from needing to worry about the state of the client. In effect, an abort or rollback mechanism can be used as a tool by which a stateful client/server system is able to recover from a situation where the client's view of the state shared with the server has been rendered incorrect.

In the remainder of this chapter, we review examples of stateless file server architectures from the research and commercial community, stateful file server architectures (we will return to this topic in Chap. 20), and stateful transactional architectures as used in database systems. As usual, our underlying emphasis is on reliability implications of these architectural alternatives.

6.12 Distributed File Systems

We have discussed the stateless approach to file server design in general terms. In this section, we look at some specific file system architectures in more detail, to understand the precise sense in which these systems are stateless, how their statelessness may be visible to the user, and the implications of statelessness on file system reliability.

Client/server file systems normally are structured as shown in Fig. 6.10. Here, we see that the client application interacts with a cache of file system blocks and file descriptor objects maintained in the client workstation. To illustrate these points, let us briefly review the implementation of the Network File System (NFS) client/server architecture. NFS was not the first network file system, but it was surely one of the most successful. The basic idea is to emulate the way that a UNIX operating system handles mounted disk file systems, but to do so in a way that does not require that the disk be attached to the client's computer.

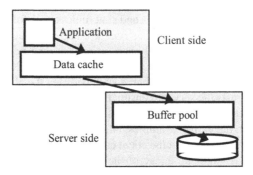

Fig. 6.10 In a stateless file system architecture, the client may cache data from the server. Such a cache is similar in function to the server's buffer pool, but is not guaranteed to be accurate. In particular, if the server modifies the data that the client has cached, it has no record of the locations at which copies may have been cached and no protocol by which cached data can be invalidated or refreshed. The client side of the architecture will often include mechanisms that partially conceal this limitation—for example, by validating that cached file data are still valid at the time a file is opened. In effect, the cached data are treated as a set of hints that are used to improve performance but should not be trusted in an absolute sense

A UNIX file system can be understood in terms of several basic data structures. An *inode* is a small data structure representing the on-disk information by which a file is defined. The inode contains identification information for the file's owner, a small access control vector, dates of file creation and last modification, file size, the file "type," and pointers to the data (depending on the size of the file, the inode may simply list the data blocks containing the file data, or may be "indirection" blocks that themselves list the data blocks). A disk has a *freelist* listing the blocks that are available for allocation. A *directory* is a type of file containing a list of file names and associated inode numbers.

To access a file system on a local disk, a UNIX user first issues a *mount* operation that associates the root directory of the mounted file system with some existing pathname. The user then issues the file operation; perhaps, a file *create* followed by a *write*. To perform the *create* operation, UNIX first searches the file system to ensure that the desired file does not already exist; if it does, an error (EEXISTS) is returned to the user. This behavior is widely exploited by applications that need a simple way to obtain locks in a UNIX setting: they *create* a "lock file," interpreting EEXISTS as an indication that the file is already locked, and otherwise performing the desired task and then releasing the lock by deleting the file. A successful *create* causes the file inode to be loaded into kernel memory, its reference counter to be incremented, and a file handle returned to the application. The application then specifies the file handle when issuing write operations.

The remote case is designed to closely parallel the local case. A remote *mount* operation is implemented by forming a message that encodes the parameters of the *create* into a standard byte order. NFS uses a self-describing representation called XDR (external data representation) for this purpose (NFS was designed in the early

1980's, long before the emergence of the SOAP and XML standards). The request is then transmitted to the server on which the file system resides.

On the server system, a *mount* request is checked for validity: the requested file system must be available and the client's user-id must be one permitted to perform a mount operation. NFS has two mechanisms for checking user-id's; one is based on a cryptographic authentication protocol, and provides fairly strong protection. The other, more commonly used, mechanism simply trusts the client operating system to set the client-id and group-id fields of the message correctly. In this mode, if my computer wishes to access a file system on your computer, I simply tell you what user-id I am using, and you check to see if that user is permitted to perform the operation. Nothing stops a client from cycling through user id's until one is found that will be accepted by the server, and indeed some virus programs exploit this as a way to break into UNIX file systems. As it turns out, the stronger authentication mechanism is rarely enabled, in part because it employs proprietary protocols and hence is incompatible with hardware and software from certain vendors. A result is that UNIX file systems are often poorly protected. We will see more examples of this momentarily.

It is interesting to realize that nothing requires the "server" to be a vendor-supplied UNIX implementation of NFS. A mount operation can be handled by *any* application, and in fact it is common for applications to implement the NFS proto-col, running in user-mode and perhaps even running on the same machine where the client doing the mount is active! This feature is very convenient for researchers who are developing new NFS-like file systems; they can build a user-level file server and debug it, and yet client software will see what appears to be a completely standard file system no different from any disk-resident one. Students using this textbook have often seized upon this ability to mount a fake file system implemented by an application as a "hook" enabling the introduction of sophisticated functionality without changing the operating system. For example, one can implement file sys-tems that construct data on demand, file systems that use replication to obtain high availability, and so forth.

At any rate, a successful mount operation returns a file-handle to the client sys-tem, which stores it in the remote mount table. The client is now ready to issue file system operations, such as file *open* or *create* requests. Let us consider a *create* in order to maintain the similarity between our local and remote cases. The arguments to a *create* request are the pathname of the file to be created and the access rights that should be used. The client file system will recognize that the desired file is on a remote-mounted disk while scanning the pathname, by encountering a pathname prefix that leads to a file system mount point. When this occurs, the suffix of the pathname and the access permission information are marshalled into an XDR mes-sage, which is sent with the mount handle to the remote server. Again, there are two modes; in one, the XDR request is signed cryptographically (permitting the re-mote server to protect against attacks); in the other more common mode, any request with a valid mounted volume handle is trusted, and no attempt is made to verify the user-id or group-id information. The remote server will receive the *create* request, perform the operation, package up the result into an XDR reply message, and send the reply back to the client system.

Remote procedure calls are not transported reliably, leading to one of the more peculiar issues seen with a stateless file system architecture. If our *create* operation times out, the client system will reissue it, and if that happens, no action occurs on the server side to detect repeat requests. Thus, a scenario can arise in which a *create* is issued, is performed successfully, and then the reply is lost. Should this happen, the request will be issued a second time, but will now fail, since the file was created on the first try! If we are using files as locks, the user's application would incorrectly conclude that the file is locked, when in fact the lock request succeeded. This is a good example of a case where a stateless approach sometimes malfunctions, but where the problem is normally rare enough to be ignored. When it does occur, however, a part of the system could go down until an administrator takes remedial action. In UNIX, this problem is sometimes seen when using printer spooling software, and an administrator may need to manually remove the lock file to unjam the printer.

If successful, operations like *create* and *open* return what is called a *virtualized inode* or *vnode* structure, providing the client operating system with basic information about the file and also a file handle that can be used in subsequent *read* or *write* requests. The client system will typically cache vnodes and also some subset of the blocks of the file itself, using what is called a *write through* policy under which writes modify the client cache (hence client applications will "see their own writes" instantly), then are written back to the server as bandwidth permits. A substantial time lag can easily arise, with the client system knowing about great numbers of updates that have yet to reach the server, and hence would be lost if the client system crashes or becomes disconnected from the network.

When performing NFS *read* and *write* operations, the split between authenticated and non-authenticated operations mentioned earlier arises again: in the non-authenticated case, any request with a valid file mount handle and vnode handle will be accepted by the server, which keeps no records of which clients have mounted the volume or opened a given file. Thus, an intruder can easily "spoof" the file system into permitting a mount operation and permitting file access with falsified user-id and group-id credentials. It is child's play to build the client-side software needed to exploit this form of UNIX attack, and unless the site administrator enables file system authentication, UNIX offers no real defense against the attacker.[3]

For example, suppose that a hospital system were to use a mixture of NFS-based file servers and client systems from many vendors, and for this reason found it impractical to use NFS authentication. Any teenage patient with a laptop and some time to kill could potentially connect the laptop to the hospital network, use a packet "sniffer" application to capture and examine some packets passing by, discover the identity of the hospital file servers and a few common user-ids, and then construct faked file system requests for those same servers using these same user-ids. He or

---

[3]The author describes this means of attacking an NFS system with some trepidation. Yet the security problem outlined here is so well known, and NFS deployments that disable strong security are so common, that only the most naïve hacker would be unaware of the issue. With this in mind, it seems more important to warn the next generation of system architects about the risk, even knowing that some particularly uninformed hackers could learn of this security hole from this textbook!

she would be granted unrestricted access to the hospital's files, and could even modify records. It is disturbing to realize that there must be literally hundreds of hospitals (and other similarly sensitive systems) exposed to such attacks. Even worse, administrators are often forced to deploy NFS insecurely, because the industry has been unable to reach agreement on cryptographic security standards, making file system security a largely proprietary matter. Small wonder that we read of major security intrusions on a regular basis!

Lest this all seem very dire, it is important to realize that file systems such as NFS with authentication enabled, Microsoft NTFS, or Carnegie Mellon's Andrew File System and CODA file system all use stronger authentication protocols and are far more secure. In these systems, the client system must authenticate itself and obtain cryptographic credentials, which are used to sign subsequent requests. The file server is able to reject falsified requests because they lack appropriate credentials, and to detect and rejected tampered requests because they will not have a correct signature. It is unfortunate that these stronger authentication protocols have not been unified into a single standard; had this occurred, file system security would today be far stronger than is commonly the case. Microsoft NTFS, Andrew and CODA are also more stateful than UNIX NFS: the server tracks the files open on clients, using this information to prevent inconsistency when a file is modified while some client systems have it open for reading and may have cached the contents. As noted earlier, NTFS ultimately treats such information as a hint, presumably because the designers did not want to leave files locked on a server in the event that a client using them crashes or becomes disconnected from the network. Andrew and CODA, in contrast, *do* leave such files locked, although administrative commands can be used to manually release locks if necessary.

Notice that statelessness and a relaxed approach to authentication are two separate issues, although in practice they often go hand-in-hand. What makes NFS stateless is a server design in which the server does not worry about copies of vnodes or file blocks on client systems. The UNIX client protocol is responsible for noticing staleness (in practice, applications are expected to use locking if they want to avoid potential problems). Even when NFS runs with authentication enabled, it remains a stateless architecture. Microsoft's file system, and the two CMU-developed file systems, employ not just stronger authentication mechanisms, but also forms of statefulness. One "sees" the statelessness of the NFS file system in many situations: when a *create* operation returns EEXISTS and yet the file did not exist before the request was issued, when a file read returns a stale cached file block rather than the most recently updated version, or when a change visible on a client system is nonetheless not seen by the server, perhaps for a long time.

NFS does what it can to conceal its statelessness from the client. As we have seen, client-side cached file blocks and vnodes in the cache represent the main form of state present in an NFS configuration. The approach used to ensure that this information is valid represents a compromise between performance objectives and semantics. Each time a file is opened, NFS verifies that the cached vnode is still valid. The file server, for its part, treats a request as invalid if the file has been written (by some other client system) since the vnode and its associated file handle was issued. Thus, by issuing a single open request, the client system is able to learn whether the data blocks cached on behalf of the file are valid or not and can discard them in the latter case.

This approach to cache validation poses a potential problem, which is that if a client workstation has cached data from an open file, changes to the file that originate at some other workstation will not invalidate these cached blocks, and no attempt to authenticate the file handle will occur. For example, suppose that process q on client workstation a has file F open, and then process p on client workstation b opens F, writes modified data into it, and then closes it. Although F will be updated on the file server, process q may continue to observe stale data for an unlimited period of time, because its cache subsystem has no occasion to check for staleness of the vnode. Indeed, short of closing and reopening the file, or accessing some file block that is not cached, q might *never* see the updates!

One case where this pattern of behavior can become visible to a UNIX NFS user arises when a pipeline of processes is executed with each process on a different computer. If p is the first program in such a pipeline and q is the second program, p could easily send a message down the pipe to q telling it to look into the file, and q will now face the stale data problem. UNIX programmers often encounter problems such as this and work around them by modifying the programs to use *fflush* and *fsync* system calls to flush the cache at p and to empty q's cache of cached records for the shared file.

NFS vendors provide a second type of solution to this problem through an optional locking mechanism, which is accessed using the *flock* system call. If this optional interface is used, the process attempting to write the file would be unable to open it for update until the process holding it open for reads has released its read lock. Conceptually, at least, the realization that the file needs to be unlocked and then relocked would sensitize the developer of process p to the need to close and then reopen the file to avoid access anomalies, which are well documented in NFS. At any rate, file sharing is not all that common in UNIX, as demonstrated in some studies (see Ousterhout et al. 1985), where it was found that most file sharing is between programs executed sequentially from the same workstation.

The NFS protocol is thus stateless but there are quite a few situations in which the user can glimpse the implementation of the protocol because its statelessness leads to weakened semantics compared to an idealized file system accessed through a single cache. Moreover, as noted in the previous chapter, there are also situations in which the weak error reporting of RPC protocols is reflected in unexpected behavior, such as the file *create* operation of Sect. 6.8, which incorrectly reported that a file could not be created because a reissued RPC fooled the file system into thinking the file already existed.

Similar to the basic UNIX file system, NFS is designed to prefetch records when it appears likely that they will soon be needed—for example, if the application program reads the first two blocks of a file, the NFS client-side software will typically fetch the third block of that file without waiting for a read request, placing the result in the cache. With a little luck, the application will now obtain a cache hit and be able to start processing the third block even as the NFS system fetches the fourth one. One can see that this yields performance similar to that of simply transferring the entire file at the time it was initially opened. Nonetheless, the protocol is relatively inefficient in the sense that each block must be independently requested, whereas a streaming style of transfer could avoid these requests and also handle acknowledgements more efficiently. In the following text, we will look at some file systems that explicitly perform whole-file transfers and that are able to outperform NFS when placed under heavy load.

For developers of mission-critical applications, the reliability of the file server is of obvious concern. One might want to know how failures would affect the behavior of operations. With NFS, as normally implemented, a failure can cause the file server to be unavailable for long periods of time, can partition a client from a server, or can result in a crash and then reboot of a client. The precise consequences depend on the way the file system was being used just prior to the crash. For the situations where a server becomes unreachable or crashes and later reboots, the client program may experience timeouts, which would be reported to the application layer as errors, or it may simply retry its requests periodically, for as long as necessary until the file server restarts. In the latter case, an operation will be reissued after a long delay, and there is some potential for operations to behave unexpectedly, as in the case of *create*. Client failures, on the other hand, are completely ignored by the server.

Because the NFS client-side cache uses a write-through policy, in such a situation a few updates may be lost but the files on the server will not be left in an extremely stale state. The locking protocol used by NFS, however, will not automatically break locks during a crash—hence, files locked by the client will remain locked until the application detects this condition and forces the locks to be released, using commands issued from the client system or from some other system. There is a mode in which failures automatically cause locks to be released, but this action will only occur when the client workstation is restarted, presumably to avoid confusing network partitions with failure/reboot sequences.

Thus, while the stateless design of NFS simplifies it considerably, the design also introduces serious reliability concerns. Our discussion has touched on the risk of processes seeing stale data when they access files, the potential that writes could be lost, and the possibility that a critical file server might become unavailable due to a network or computer failure. If you are building an application for which reliability is critical, any of these cases could represent a very serious failure. The enormous success of NFS should not be taken as an indication that reliable applications can in fact be built over it, but rather as a sign that failures are really not all that frequent in modern computing systems and that most applications are not particularly critical! In a world where hardware was less reliable or the applications were more critical, protocols such as the NFS protocol might be considerably less attractive.

Our discussion has focused on the case of a normal NFS server. There are versions of NFS that support replication in software for higher availability: R/NFS and Deceit (see Siegel et al. 1989), HA-NFS (see Bhide et al. 1991), and Harp (see Ladin et al. 1990, 1992; Liskov et al. 1991), as well as dual-ported NFS server units in which a backup server can take control of the file system. The former approaches employ process-group communication concepts of a sort we will discuss later, although the protocol used to communicate with client programs remains unchanged.

By doing this, the possibility for load-balanced read access to the file server is created, enhancing read performance through parallelism. At the same time, these approaches allow continuous availability even when some servers are down. Each server has its own disk, permitting tolerance of media failures. And, there is a possibility of varying the level of the replication selectively, so that critical files will be replicated and non-critical files can be treated using conventional nonreplicated methods. The interest in such an approach is that any overhead associated with file replication is incurred only for files where there is also a need for high availability, and hence the multiserver configuration comes closer to also giving the capacity and performance benefits of a cluster of NFS servers. Many users like this possibility of paying only for what they use.

The dual-ported hardware approaches, in contrast, primarily reduce the time to recovery. They normally require that the servers reside in the same physical location, and are intolerant of media failure, unless a mirrored disk is employed. Moreover, these approaches do not offer benefits of parallelism: One pays for two servers, or for two servers and a mirror disk, as a form of insurance that the entire file system will be available when needed. These sorts of file servers are, consequently, expensive. On the other hand, their performance is typically that of a normal server—there is little or no *degradation* because of the dual configuration.

Clearly, if the performance degradation associated with replication can be kept sufficiently small, the mirrored server and/or disk technologies will look expensive. Early generations of cluster-server technology were slow, hence software performed relatively poorly when compared with mirroring. However, the trend seems to be for this overhead to become smaller and smaller, in which case the greater flexibility and enhanced read performance, due to parallelism, would argue in favor of the NFS cluster technologies.

Yet another file system reliability technology has emerged into prominence over the past decade or so. It involves the use of clusters or arrays of disks to implement a file system that is more reliable than any of the component disks. Such so-called RAID file systems (see Patterson et al. 1988) normally consist of a mixture of hardware and software: the hardware for mediating access to the disks themselves, and the software to handle the buffer pool, oversee file layout, and optimize data access patterns. The actual protocol used to talk to the RAID device over a network would be the same as for any other sort of remote disk: It might be the NFS protocol or some other remote file access protocol. The use of RAID in the disk subsystem itself would normally not result in protocol changes.

RAID devices typically require physical proximity of the disks to one another (this is needed by the hardware). The mechanism that implements the RAID is typically constructed in hardware and employs a surplus disk to maintain redundant data in the form of parity for sets of disk blocks; such an approach permits a RAID system to tolerate one or more disk failures or bad blocks, depending on the way the system is configured. A RAID is thus a set of disks that mimics a single more reliable disk unit with roughly the summed capacity of its components, minus overhead for the parity disk. However, even with special hardware, management and configuration of RAID systems can require specialized software architectures (see Wilkes et al. 1995).

Similar to the case for a mirrored disk, the main benefits of a RAID architecture are high availability in the server itself, together with large capacity and good average seek time for information retrieval. In a large-scale distributed application, the need to locate the RAID device at a single place, and its reliance on a single source of power and software infrastructure, often means that in practice such a file server has the same distributed reliability properties as any other form of file server. In effect, the risk of file server unavailability as a source of downtime is reduced, but other infrastructure-related sources of file system unavailability remain to be addressed. In particular, if a RAID file system implements the NFS protocol, it would be subject to all the limitations of the NFS architecture.

6.13   Stateful File Servers

The performance of NFS is limited by its write-through caching policy, which has led developers of more advanced file systems to focus on improved caching mechanisms and, because few applications actually use the optional locking interfaces, on greater attention to cache validation protocols. In this section, we briefly discuss some of the best-known stateful file systems. Breakout 6.1 discusses the Andrew File System.

6.1 The Andrew File System (AFS)

Although the Andrew File System (AFS) was developed roughly two decades ago, the system continued to be widely cited for the innovative way that it combined a strong security architecture with file consistency guarantees, and was something of a model for the Windows file system, which uses a very similar approach to achieve comparable guarantees. Andrew was developed at Carnegie Mellon University and subsequently used as the basis of a worldwide file system product offered by Transarc, Inc. (see Satyanarayanan et al. 1985, 1989; Spasojevic and Satyanarayanan 1996), a company that was ultimately acquired by IBM. The basic ideas are easily summarized.

AFS was built with the assumption that the Kerberos authentication technology would be available. We present Kerberos in Chap. 18, and therefore limit ourselves to a brief summary of the basic features of the system here. When a user logs in (and, later, periodically, if the user remains connected long enough for timers to expire), Kerberos prompts for a password. Using a secure protocol, which employs DES to encrypt sensitive data, the password authenticates the user to the Kerberos server, which will now act as a trustworthy intermediary in establishing connections between the user and the file servers he or she will access. The file servers similarly authenticate themselves to the Kerberos authentication server at startup.

In Andrew, file system access is by whole-file transfer, except in the case of very large files, which are treated as sets of smaller ones. Files can be cached in the AFS subsystem on a client, in which case requests are satisfied out of the cached information whenever possible (in fact, there are two caches—one of file data and one of file status information—but this distinction need not concern us here). The AFS server tracks the clients that maintain cached copies of a given file, and, if the file is opened for writing, uses callbacks to inform those clients that the cached copies are no longer valid. Additional communication from the client to the server occurs frequently enough so that if a client becomes disconnected from the server, it will soon begin to consider its cached files to be potentially stale. (Indeed, studies of AFS file server availability have noted that disconnection from the server is a more common source of denial of access to files in AFS than genuine server downtime.)

AFS provides a strong form of security guarantee, based on access control lists at the level of entire directories. Because the Kerberos authentication protocol is known to be highly secure, AFS can trust the user identification information provided to it by client systems. Short of taking over a client workstation, an unauthorized user would have no means of gaining access to cached or primary copies of a file for which access is not permitted. AFS destroys cached data when a user logs out or an authorization expires and is not refreshed (see Bellovin and Merritt 1990; Birrell 1985; Lampson et al. 1992; Satyanarayanan et al. 1985, 1989; Schiller 1994; Steiner et al. 1988).

At its peak level of use, AFS functioned as a wide area file system, that included perhaps 1,000 servers and 20,000 clients in ten countries—all united within a single file system name space (see Spasojevic and Satyanarayanan 1996). Approximately 100,000 users used the system on a regular basis. Obviously, today we would not call this particularly large scale, but at the time, it was the largest scale file system deployment in steady use, and was therefore a topic of great interest and careful study. Interestingly, it turned out that in AFS, more than 96 percent of file system accesses were successfully resolved through cache hits, and server inaccessibility (primarily due to communication timeouts) was as little as a few minutes per day. Moreover, this was true even when a significant fraction of file references were to remote files.

Today's Windows file system is much like AFS in many ways, and achieves similar success. Of course, the cloud has brought us much larger file systems: user's who store data on a cloud platform such as GoogleDocs or who use Amazon's AC3 storage infrastructure are effectively accessing file systems literally millions of times larger than AFS. Yet many of the lessons learned in building AFS shaped these systems, and if AFS itself has faded into history, its impact remains large. Moreover, whereas we can learn a great deal about AFS at the most detailed levels, these more contemporary large-scale systems are proprietary products that compete in a very hotly contested arena for cloud computing. The vendors who built and operate them are thus loath to reveal a similar level of detail.

Work on stateful file systems architectures can be traced in part to an influential study of file access patterns in the Sprite system at Berkeley (see Baker et al. 1991). This work sought to characterize the file system workload along a variety of axes: read/write split, block reuse frequency, file lifetimes, and so forth. The findings, although not surprising, were at the same time eye-openers for many of the researchers in this field. In this study, it was discovered that all file access was sequential, and that there was very little sharing of files between different programs. When file sharing was observed, the prevailing pattern was the simplest one: One program tended to write the file, in its entirety, and then some other program would read the same file. Often (indeed, in most such cases), the file would be deleted shortly after it was created. In fact, most files survived for less than ten seconds or longer than 10,000 seconds. The importance of cache consistency was explored in this work (it turned out to be quite important, but relatively easy to enforce for the most common patterns of sharing), and the frequency of write/write sharing of files was shown to be so low that this could almost be treated as a special case. (Later, there was considerable speculation that on systems with significant database activity, this finding would have been challenged.) Moreover, considerable data were extracted on patterns of data transfer from server to client: rate of transfer, percentage of the typical file that was transferred, and so forth. Out of this work came a new generation of file systems that used closer cooperation between client and file system to exploit such patterns.

Best known among existing stateful file systems is the Windows file system, although as noted earlier, Windows is in some ways more of a stateless than a stateful system. Basically, NTFS starts with an NFS-like client/server structure, although using cryptographic authentication to prevent unauthorized file access. Layered over this basic mechanism, however, is an event notification subsystem that will notify applications when parts of the file system that they are using change. For example, a program displaying a file system directory (a folder) can register itself to receive an event notifying it if that directory changes, and then redisplay the modified contents. Moreover, the Windows file system has a coherent caching mechanism, so that a file cannot be modified by more than one program at a time without using a special locking interface, and any program reading a file will see the most current data. (This can be very irritating, of course, if a program crashes without unlocking the file). Unfortunately, however, relatively little has been written about the detailed design and performance of the Windows file system (see Vogels 1999). Rather than speculate, we will instead look closely at some other systems for which a great deal of detail is available.

Examples of well-studied file systems that employ a stateful approach to provide increased performance (as opposed to availability) are AFS (see Howard et al. 1987; Satyanarayanan et al. 1985, 1989) and Sprite (see Ousterhout et al. 1988; Srinivasan and Mogul 1989), a research file system and operating system developed at University of California, Berkeley. On the availability side of the spectrum, the Coda project (see Kistler and Satyanarayanan 1992; Mummert et al. 1995), a research effort at Carnegie Mellon University, takes these ideas one step further, integrating them into a file system specifically for use on mobile computers that operate in a disconnected, or partially connected, mode. Ficus, a project at UCLA, uses a similar approach to deal with file replication in very wide area networks with nonuniform connectivity and bandwidth properties. To varying degrees, these systems can all be viewed as stateful ones in which some of the information maintained within client workstations is guaranteed to be coherent. The term stateful is used a little loosely here, particularly in comparison with the approaches we will examine in Chap. 14. Perhaps it would be preferable to say that these systems are "more stateful" than the NFS architecture, gaining performance through the additional state. Among the four, only Sprite actually provides strong cache coherence to its clients. The other systems provide other forms of guarantees, which are used either to avoid inconsistency or to resolve inconsistencies after they occur. Finally, we will briefly discuss XFS, a file system developed at the University of California, Berkeley, which exploits the file system memory of client workstations as an extended buffer pool, paging files from machine to machine over the network to avoid the more costly I/O path from a client workstation over the network to a remote disk.

Both AFS and Sprite replace the NFS write-through caching mechanism and file handle validation protocols with alternatives that reduce costs. The basic approach in AFS is to cache entire files, informing the server that a modified version of a file may exist in the client workstation. Through a combination of features, such as whole-file transfers on file open and for write back to the server, and by having the file server actively inform client systems when their cached entries become invalid, considerable performance improvements are obtained with substantially stronger file access semantics than for NFS. Indeed, the workload on an AFS server can be an order of magnitude or more lower than that for an NFS server, and the performance observed by a client is comparably higher for many applications. AFS was commercialized subsequent to the initial research project at CMU, becoming the component technology for a line of enterprise file systems (worldwide file systems) marketed by Transarc, a subsidiary of IBM.

Sprite, which caches file system blocks (but uses a large 4 KB block size), takes the concept of coherent caching one step further, using a protocol in which the server actively tracks client caching, issuing callbacks to update cached file blocks if updates are received. The model is based on the caching of individual data blocks, not whole files, but the client caches are large enough to accommodate entire files. The Sprite approach leads to such high cache hit rates that the server workload is reduced to almost pure writes, an observation that triggered some extremely interesting work on file system organizations for workloads that are heavily biased towards writes. Similar to AFS, the technology greatly decreases the I/O load and CPU load on the servers that actually manage the disk.

Sprite is unusual in two ways. First, the system implements several different caching policies depending upon how the file is opened: One policy is for read-only access; a second and more expensive one is used for *sequential write access*, which occurs when a file is updated by one workstation and then accessed by a second one later (but in which the file is never written simultaneously from several systems); and a third policy is used for *concurrent write access*, which occurs when a file is written concurrently from several sources. This last policy is very rarely needed because Sprite does not cache directories and is not often used in support of database applications. Second, unlike NFS, Sprite does not use a write-through policy. Thus, a file that is opened for writing, updated, then closed and perhaps reopened by another application on the same machine, read, and then deleted, would remain entirely in the cache of the client workstation. This particular sequence is commonly seen in compilers that run in multiple passes and generate temporary results and in editors that operate on an intermediate copy of a file, which will be deleted after the file is rewritten and closed. The effect is to greatly reduce traffic between the client and the server relative to what NFS might have, but also to leave the server out of date with respect to a client system that may be writing cached files.

Sequential write sharing is handled using version numbers. When a client opens a file, the server returns the current version number, permitting the client to determine whether or not any cached records it may have are still valid. When a file is shared for concurrent writing, a more costly but simple scheme is used, whereby none of the clients are permitted to cache it. If the status of a file changes because a new open or close has occurred, Sprite issues a callback to other clients that have the file open, permitting them to dynamically adapt their caching policy in an appropriate manner. Notice that because a stateless file system such as NFS has no information as to its current client set, this policy would be impractical to implement within NFS. On the other hand, Sprite faces the problem that if the callback RPC fails, it must assume that the client has genuinely crashed; the technology is thus not tolerant of communication outages that can partition a file server from its clients. Sprite also incurs costs that NFS can sometimes avoid: Both *open* and *close* operations must be performed as RPCs, and there is at least one extra RPC required (to check consistency) in the case where a file is opened, read quickly, and then closed.

The recovery of a Sprite server after a crash can be complicated, because some clients may have had files opened in a cache for writing mode. To recover, the server makes use of its knowledge of the set of clients that had cached files for writing, which is saved in a persistent storage area, and of the fact that the consistency state of a file cannot change without the explicit approval of the server. This permits the server to track down current copies of the files it manages and to bring itself back to a consistent state.

The developers of Sprite commented that most of the complexity in the recovery mechanism comes in detecting crashes and reboots, rather than in rebuilding state. This is done by tracking the passage of RPC packets, and using periodic keep-alive packets to detect when a client or server has crashed or rebooted: The same mechanism also suffices to detect network partitions. There is a cost to tracking RPC packets, but a reliable crash and reboot detection mechanism is of course useful for other purposes besides recovering file server state (see Srinivasan and Mogul 1989). This may at first seem confusing, because we have seen that RPC mechanisms cannot reliably detect failures. However, Sprite is not subject to the restrictions we cited earlier because it can deny access to a file while waiting to gain access to the most current version of it. Concerns about RPC arose in trying to determine the cause of an RPC failure in real time. A system that is able to wait for a server to recover is fortunate in not needing to solve this problem: If an apparent failure has occurred, it can simply wait for the problem to be repaired if doing otherwise would violate file system consistency guarantees.

Experiments have shown the Sprite cache-consistency protocols to be highly effective in reducing traffic to the file server and preserving the illusion of a single copy of each file. Performance of the system is extremely good, utilization of servers very low, and the anomalous behaviors that can arise with NFS are completely avoided. However, the technology relies on the veracity of user-ID's, and hence suffers from some of the same security concerns that we will discuss in relation to NFS in Chap. 18.

The next file system we will consider is CODA, and was created to explore availability in disconnected mode, for example when a laptop user loads a file and then edits it while offline. It can be understood as implementing a very generalized version of the whole-file caching methods first introduced in AFS: Whereas AFS caches individual files, CODA caches groups of files and directories so as to maintain a complete cached copy of the user's entire file system or application. The idea within CODA is to track updates with sufficient precision so that the actions taken by the user while operating on a cached copy of part of the file system can be merged automatically into the master file system from which the files were copied. This merge occurs when connection between the disconnected computer and the main file system server is reestablished.

Much of the sophistication of CODA is concerned with tracking the appropriate sets of files to cache in this manner and with optimizing the merge mechanisms so that user intervention can be avoided when possible. (See Breakout 6.2) The approach was extremely successful, to the point that Microsoft apparently explored moving to a CODA-like approach for its file systems, and Doug Terry headed a group that created a candidate product intended to play this role. However, this occurred just as the cloud computing trend shifted thinking: rather than disconnect and carry files away on a laptop, more and more users began to focus on a model in which their files lived in the cloud, and could be accessed from any of a number of platforms but without really having the true location of the definitive version shift around. Microsoft never released its product (or at least, has not done so yet), and today we are watching the cloud computing storage model slowly mature, but also encounter some of the very same issues that motivated the CODA work in the first place! Thus perhaps Doug Terry's hard work will eventually pay off. If so, it will not be the first time that a major project was launched, then halted, and then much later taken off the shelves and released!

In fact CODA was not the first file system to look at versioning and related issues. The much earlier Ficus system, developed by Jerry Popek's group at UCLA (see Reiher et al. 1994), explores a similar set of issues but focuses on an enterprise computing environment similar to the world-wide file system problems to which AFS has been applied in recent years. (For brevity we will not discuss a previous system developed by the same group, Locus (see Walter et al. 1993).) In Ficus, the model is one of a large-scale file system built of file servers that logically maintain replicas of a single file system image. Communication connectivity can be lost and servers can crash—hence, at any point, a server will have replicas of some parts of the file system and will be out of touch with some other replicas for the same data. This leads to an approach in which file type information is used both to limit the updates that can be performed while a portion of the file system is disconnected from other segments, and to drive a file merge process when communication is reestablished (see Heidemann and Popek 1995). Where CODA is focused on disconnected operation, however, Ficus emphasizes support for patterns of communication seen in large organizations that experience bandwidth limits or partitioning problems that prevent servers from contacting each other for brief periods of time. The resulting protocols and algorithms are similar to the ones used in CODA, but place greater attention on file-by-file reconciliation methods, whereas CODA is oriented towards mechanisms that deal with groups of files as an ensemble.

All of these systems are known for additional contributions beyond the ones we have discussed. CODA, for example, makes use of a recoverable virtual memory mechanism, which offers a way to back out changes made to a segment of virtual memory, using a logging facility that performs replay on behalf of the user. Ficus is also known for work on stackable file systems, in which a single file system interface is used to provide access to a variety of types of file-like abstraction. These contributions, and others not cited here, are beyond the scope of our present discussion.

The last file system we will cover here is the Google File System, often referred to as GFS. This file system is used only within Google's data centers and supports all sorts of cloud computing activities. Because so many of Google's file are massive, the architecture is biased towards efficient support for very large file transfers, leading to an interesting hierarchical structure.

The basic architecture is easily summarized. At the conceptual core of GFS is a subsystem called the *master*, running as a small replicated server that can handle very large data rates, but does not deal directly with file system data at all. The requests to this server are from clients trying to open files, and the responses it sends them tell those clients where to find the file: in effect, the client is *redirected* to what GFS calls a *chunk server*.

Chunk servers manage the real data. Because files are sometimes so large at Google, the approach treats a file as a set of chunks, 64 MB in length (actual chunks can be shorter, obviously, if a file does not evenly split into 64 MB parts, and in any case this chunk size is a parameter that Google may have subsequently played with). Each chunk is replicated a minimum of three-fold for fault-tolerance, but perhaps to a greater extent if the file is heavily used in a read-intensive manner.

Thus, a client seeking a file asks the master which chunk servers have the desired content, and is granted a time-limited "lease" to read the desired chunk from a suitable chunk server. Then, as long as the lease is still valid, it fetches the content by downloading from the chunk server. At this stage it can download just portions of the chunk, or the whole thing.

File updates are handled by granting the application an *update lease* on a file. When granted, such a lease gives the user permission to update the *master* chunk for a limiter period of time (the leaser can be renewed, of course). The chunk servers themselves then collaborate to replicate the new version to the desired level, invalidating old versions if any remain.

For finer-grained synchronization, applications use the Chubby locking service. GFS is often used in conjunction with Chubby (and the GFS implementation uses Chubby internally), but locking is still treated as a separate task that occurs outside the file system itself.

In Chap. 5, when we discussed cloud computing infrastructure components, we looked at BigTable. That system layers cleanly onto GFS. Thus Google applications have choices: they can work with relatively conventional (albeit potentially enormous) files, or if they prefer, can create virtual tables using BigTable and treat their storage in a more structured manner. The popularity of BigTable at Google suggests that for many cloud computing purposes, this loosely structured approach is often the better fit to what the application developer has in mind.

6.2 Mobile File Access in CODA

The challenge faced by CODA is easily appreciated when the following example is considered. Suppose that Fred and Julia are collaborating on a major report to an important customer of their company. Fred is responsible for certain sections of the report and Julia for others, but these sections are also cited in the introductory material and boilerplate used to generate the report as a whole. As many readers of this book will appreciate, there are software tools with varying degrees of ease of use for this type of collaborative work. The most primitive tools provide only for locking of some sort, so that Julia can lock Fred out of a file while she is actually editing it. More elaborate ones actually permit multiple users to concurrently edit the shared files, annotating one another's work, and precisely tracking who changed what through multiple levels of revisions. Such tools typically view the document as a form of database and keep some type of log or history showing how it evolved through time.

If the files in which the report are contained can be copied onto portable computers that become disconnected from the network, however, these annotations will be introduced independently and concurrently on the various copies. Files may be split or merged while the systems are disconnected from each other, and even the time of access cannot be used to order these events, since the clocks on computers can drift or be set incorrectly for many reasons. Thus, when copies of a complex set of files are returned to the file system from which they were removed, the merge problem becomes a nontrivial one both at the level of the file system itself (which may have to worry about directories that have experienced both delete and add operations of potentially conflicting sorts in the various concurrent users of the directory) and at the level of the application and its concept of file semantics.

Not surprisingly, systems such as CODA and Ficus incorporate special-purpose programming tools and applications that are well matched to their styles of disconnected and partially connected operation (see Mummert et al. 1995; Reiher et al. 1994). These tools include, for example, e-mail systems that maintain logs of actions taken against mailboxes, understanding how to delete mail that has been deleted while in a disconnected mode, or merging e-mails that arrived separately in different copies of a mailbox that was split within a large-scale distributed environment. One can speculate that, over time, a small and fairly standard set of tools might emerge from such research and that developers would implement specialized disconnected applications, which rely on well-tested reconciliation methods to recorrect inconsistencies that occur during periods of disconnected interaction.

The last of the stateful file systems mentioned at the start of this section is XFS, a Berkeley project that seeks to exploit the memory of the client workstations connected to a network as a form of distributed storage region for a high-performance file server (see Anderson et al. 1995). XFS could be called a "serverless network file system," although in practice the technology would more often be paired to a conventional file system, which would serve as a backup storage region. The basic idea of XFS, then, is to distribute the contents of a file system over a set of workstations so that when a block of data is needed, it can be obtained by a direct memory-to-memory transfer over the network rather than by means of a request to a disk server, which, having much less memory at its disposal, may then need to delay while fetching it from the disk itself.

XFS raises some very complex issues of system configuration management and fault tolerance. The applications using an XFS need to know what servers belong to it, and this set changes dynamically over time. Thus, there is a membership management problem that needs to be solved in software. Workstations are reliable, but not completely reliable—hence, there is a need to deal with failures. XFS does this by using a RAID-style storage scheme in which each set of n workstations is backed by an $n + 1$ machine, which maintains a parity block. If one of the $n + 1$ machines fails, the missing data can be regenerated from the other n. Moreover, XFS is dynamically reconfigurable, creating some challenging synchronization issues. On the positive side, all of this complexity brings with it a dramatic performance improvement when XFS is compared with more traditional server architectures. It should be noted that XFS draws heavily on the log-structured file system (see Rosenblum and Ousterhout 1991), a technology that is beyond the scope of this book.

The reliability properties of these stateful file systems go well beyond those of NFS. For AFS and Sprite, reliability is limited by the manner in which the servers detect the failure of clients, since a failed client clears its cache upon recovery and the server needs to update its knowledge of the state of the cache accordingly. In fact, both AFS and Sprite detect failures through timeouts—hence, there can be patterns of failure that would cause a client to be sensed incorrectly as having failed, leaving its file system cache corrupted until some future attempt to validate cache contents occurs, at which point the problem would be detected and reported. In Sprite, network partition failures are considered unlikely because the physical network used at Berkeley is quite robust and, in any case, network partitions cause the client workstations to initiate a recovery protocol. Information concerning the precise handling of network partitions, or about methods for replicating AFS servers, was not available at the time of this writing. XFS is based on a failure model similar to that of AFS and Sprite, in which crash failures are anticipated and dealt with in the basic system architecture, but partitioning failures that result in the misdiagnosis of apparent crash failures is not an anticipated mode of failure.

CODA and Ficus treat partitioning as part of their normal mode of operation, dealing with partitioning failures (or client and server failures) using the model of independent concurrent operation and subsequent state merge that was presented earlier. Such approaches clearly trade higher availability for a more complex merge protocol and greater sophistication within the applications themselves. (See Breakout 6.3.)

6.14   Distributed Database Systems

Distributed database systems represent another use of client/server architectures in distributed systems. Unlike the case of distributed file systems, however, database technologies use a special programming model called the *transactional approach* and support this through a set of special protocols (see Gray 1978; Gray and Reuter 1993). The reliability and concurrency

6.3 Lotus Notes

The Lotus Notes system is a commercial database product that uses a client/server model to manage collections of documents, which can draw upon a great variety of applications (word processing, spreadsheets, financial analysis packages, etc.). The system is widely popular because of the extremely simple sharing model it supports and its close integration with e-mail and chat facilities, supporting what has become known as a groupware collaboration model. The term "computer-supported collaborative work," or CSCW, is often used in reference to activities that are supported by technologies such as Lotus Notes.

Notes is structured as a client/server architecture. The client system is a graphical user interface, which permits the user to visualize information within the document database, create or annotate documents, "mine" the database for documents satisfying some sort of a query, and exchange e-mail or send memos which can contain documents as attachments. A security facility permits the database to be selectively protected using passwords, so that only designated users will have access to the documents contained in those parts of the database. If desired, portions of especially sensitive documents can be encrypted so that even a database administrator would be unable to access them without the appropriate passwords.

Lotus Notes also provides features for replication of portions of its database between the client systems and the server. Such replication permits a user to carry a self-contained copy of the desired documents (and others to which they are attached) and update them in a disconnected mode. Later, when the database server is back in contact with the user, updates are exchanged to bring the two sets of documents back into agreement. Replication of documents is also possible among Notes servers within an enterprise, although the Notes user must take steps to limit concurrent editing when replication is employed. (This is in contrast with CODA, which permits concurrent use of files and works to automatically merge changes.) At the time of this writing, Notes did not support replication of servers for increased availability, but treated each server as a separate security domain with its own users and passwords. Within the terminology of this chapter, Lotus Notes is a form of partially stateful file server, although presented through a sophisticated object model and with powerful tools oriented towards cooperative use by members of workgroups. However, many of the limitations of stateless file servers are present in Notes, such as the need to restrict concurrent updates to documents that have been replicated. The Notes user environment is extremely well engineered and is largely successful in presenting such limitations and restrictions as features that the skilled Notes user learns to employ. In effect, by drawing on semantic knowledge of the application, the Lotus Notes developers were able to work around limitations associated with this style of file server. The difficulty encountered in distributed file systems is precisely that they lack this sort of semantic knowledge and are consequently forced to solve such problems in complete generality, leading to sometimes surprising or nonintuitive behavior, reflecting their distributed infrastructure.

semantics of a database are defined by this model, and its efficient implementation is a major topic of research—and an important arena for commercial competition. For the purposes of this chapter, we will simply discuss the main issues, returning to implementation issues in Chap. 20.

Transactional systems are based upon a premise that applications can be divided into client programs and server programs, such that the client programs have minimal interactions with one another. Such an architecture can be visualized as a set of wheels, with database servers forming the hubs to which client programs are connected by communication pathways—the spokes. One client program can interact with multiple database servers, but although the issues this raises are well understood, such multi-database configurations are relatively uncommon in commercial practice. Existing client/server database applications consist of some set of disjoint groups, each group containing a database server and its associated clients, with no interaction between client programs except through sharing a database, and with very few, if any, client programs that interact with multiple databases simultaneously. Moreover, although it is known how to replicate databases for increased availability and loadbalancing (see Bernstein et al. 1987; Gray and Reuter 1993), relatively little use is made of this option in existing systems. Thus, the hubs of distributed database systems rarely interact with one another.

(We will see why this is the case in Part III; ultimately, the issue turns out to be one of performance.)

A central premise of the approach is that each interaction by a client with the database server can be structured as a *begin* event, followed by a series of database operations (these would normally be database queries, but we can think of them as *read* and *update* operations and ignore the details), followed by a *commit* or *abort* operation. Such an interaction is called a *transaction*, and a client program will typically issue one or more transactions, perhaps interacting with a user or the outside world between the completion of one transaction and the start of the next. A transactional system should guarantee the persistence of committed transactions, although we will see that high-availability database systems sometimes weaken this guarantee to boost performance. When a transaction is aborted, on the other hand, its effects are completely rolled back, as if the transaction had never even been issued.

Transactional client/server systems are stateful: Each action by the client assumes that the database remembers various things about the previous operations done by the same client, such as locking information that comes from the database concurrency control model and updates that were previously performed by the client as part of the same transaction. The clients can be viewed as maintaining coherent caches of this same information during the period while a transaction is active (not yet committed).

The essential property of the transactional execution model, which is called the *serializability model*, is that it guarantees isolation of concurrent transactions. Thus, if transactions T_1 and T_2 are executed concurrently by client processes p and q, the effects will be as if T_1 had been executed entirely before T_2, or entirely after T_2—the database actively prevents them from interfering with one another. The reasoning underlying this approach is that it will be easier to write database application programs to assume that the database is idle at the time the program executed. Rather than force the application programmer to cope with real-world scenarios in which multiple applications simultaneously access the database, the database system is only permitted to interleave operations from multiple transactions if it is certain that the interleaving will not be noticeable to users. At the same time, the model frees the database system to schedule operations in a way that keeps the server as busy as possible on behalf of a very large number of concurrent clients. (See Fig. 6.11.)

Notice that simply running transactions one at a time would achieve the serializability property.[4] However, it would also yield poor performance, because each transaction may take a long time to execute. By running multiple transactions at the same time, and interleaving their operations, a database server can give greatly

---

[4]An important special case arises in settings where each transaction can be represented as a single operation, performing a desired task and then committing or aborting and returning a result. Many distributed systems are said to be transactional but, in fact, operate in this much more restrictive manner. However, even if the application perceives a transaction as being initiated with a single operation, the database system itself may execute that transaction as a series of operations. These observations motivate a number of implementation decisions and optimizations, which we discuss in Chap. 20.

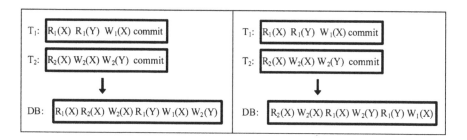

Fig. 6.11 A nonserializable transaction interleaving (*left*), and one serializable in the order T2, T1 (*right*). Each transaction can be understood as a trace, which records the actions of a program that operates on the database, oblivious to other transactions that may be active concurrently. In practice, of course, the operations become known as the transaction executes, although our example shows the situation at the time these two transactions reach their commit points. The database is presented with the operations initiated by each transaction, typically one by one, and schedules them by deciding when to execute each operation. This results in an additional trace or log, showing the order in which the database actually performed the operations presented to it. A serializable execution is one that leaves the database in a state that could have been reached by executing the same transactions one by one, in some order, and with no concurrency

improved performance, and system utilization levels will rise substantially, just as a conventional uniprocessor can benefit from multitasking. Even so, database systems sometimes need to delay one transaction until another completes, particularly when transactions are very long. To maximize performance, it is common for client/server database systems to require (or at least strongly recommend) that transactions be designed to be as short as possible. Obviously, not all applications fit these assumptions, but they match the needs of a great many computing systems.

There are a variety of options for implementing the serializability property. The most common is to use locking—for example, by requiring that a transaction obtain a read-lock on any data item that it will read, and a write-lock on any data item it will update. Read-locks are normally nonexclusive: Multiple transactions are typically permitted to read the same objects concurrently. Write-locks, however, are mutually exclusive: An object with a write lock cannot have any other locks on it (either write or read). In the most standard locking protocol, called *two-phase locking*, transactions retain all of their locks until they commit or abort, and then release them as a group. It is easy to see that this achieves serializability: If transaction T_b reads from T_a, or updates a variable after T_a does so, T_b must first acquire a lock that T_a will have held exclusively for its update operation. Transaction T_b will therefore have to wait until T_a has committed and will be serialized after T_a. Notice that the transactions can obtain read-locks on the same objects concurrently, but because read operations commute, they will not affect the serialization order (the problem gets harder if a transaction may need to upgrade some of its read-locks to write-locks).

Concurrency control (and hence locking) mechanisms can be classified as *optimistic* or *pessimistic*. The locking policy described above is a pessimistic one, because each lock is obtained before the locked data item is accessed. An optimistic policy is one in which transactions simply assume that they will be successful in acquiring locks and perform the necessary work in an opportunistic manner. At commit time, the transaction also verifies that its optimistic assumption was justified (that it got lucky, in effect), and aborts if it now turns out that some of its lock requests should in fact have delayed the computation. As one might expect, a high rate of aborts is a risk with optimistic concurrency-control mechanisms, and they can only be used in settings where the granularity of locking is small enough so that the risk of a real locking conflict between two transactions is actually very low.

The pessimistic aspect of a pessimistic concurrency-control scheme reflects the assumption that there may be frequent conflicts between concurrent transactions. This makes it necessary for a pessimistic locking scheme to operate in a more conventional manner, by delaying the transaction as each new lock request occurs until that lock has been granted; if some other transaction holds a lock on the same item, the requesting transaction will now be delayed until the lock-holding transaction has committed or aborted.

Deadlock is an important concern with pessimistic locking protocols—for example, suppose that T_a obtains a read-lock on x and then requests a write-lock on y. Simultaneously, T_b obtains a read-lock on y and then requests a write-lock on x. Neither transaction can be granted its lock, and in fact one transaction or the other (or both) must now be aborted. At a minimum, a transaction that has been waiting a very long time for a lock will normally abort; in more elaborate schemes, an algorithm can obtain locks in a way that avoids deadlock or can use an algorithm that explicitly detects deadlocks when they occur and overcomes them by aborting one of the deadlocked transactions. Deadlock-free concurrency-control policies can also be devised—for example, by arranging that transactions acquire locks in a fixed order or by using a very coarse locking granularity so that any given transaction requires only one lock. We will return to this topic, and related issues, in Chap. 20, when we discuss techniques for actually implementing a transactional system.

Locking is not the only way to implement transactional concurrency control. Other important techniques include so-called timestamped concurrency control algorithms, in which each transaction is assigned a logical time of execution, and its operations are performed as if they had been issued at the time given by the timestamp. Timestamped concurrency-control is relatively uncommon in the types of system that we consider in this book—hence, for reasons of brevity, we omit any detailed discussion of the approach. We do note, however, that optimistic timestamped concurrency control mechanisms have been shown to give good performance in systems where there are few true concurrent accesses to the same data items, and that pessimistic locking schemes give the best performance in the converse situation, where a fairly high level of conflicting operations result from concurrent access to a small set of data items. Additionally, timestamped concurrency-control is considered preferable when dealing with transactions that do a great deal of writing, while locking is considered preferable for transactions that are read-intensive. It has been demonstrated that the two styles of concurrency control cannot be mixed: One cannot use timestamps for one class of transactions and locks for another on the same database. However, a hybrid scheme, which combines features of the two approaches and works well in systems with mixtures of read-intensive and write-intensive transactions, has been proposed.

It is common to summarize the properties of a client/server database system so that the mnemonic ACID can be used to recall them:

- *Atomicity*: Each transaction is executed to completion, or not at all. The term *atomic* will be used throughout this text to refer to operations that have multiple suboperations but that are performed in an all-or-nothing manner. If a failure interrupts an atomic transaction it may be necessary to back out (roll back) any partially completed work.
- *Concurrency*: Transactions are executed so as to maximize concurrency, in this way maximizing the degrees of freedom available within the server to schedule execution efficiently (e.g., by doing disk I/O in an efficient order).
- *Independence*: Transactions are designed to execute independently from one another. Each client is written to execute as if the entire remainder of the system were idle, and the database server itself prevents concurrent transactions from observing one another's intermediate results. This is also referred to as *isolation*.
- *Durability*: The results of committed transactions are persistent.

Notice that each of these properties could be beneficial in some settings but could represent a disadvantage in others—for example, there are applications in which one wants the client programs to cooperate explicitly. The ACID properties effectively constrain such programs to interact using the database as an intermediary. Indeed, the overall model makes sense for many classical database applications, but is less suited to message-based distributed systems consisting of large numbers of servers and in which the programs coordinate their actions and cooperate to tolerate failures. All of this will add up to the perspective that complex distributed systems need a mixture of tools, which should include database technology but not legislate that databases be used to the exclusion of other technologies.

We turn now to the question raised earlier: the sense in which transactional systems are stateful, and the implications that this has for client/server software architectures.

A client of a transactional system maintains several forms of state during the period that the transaction executes. These include the transaction ID by which operations are identified, the intermediate results of the transactional operation (values that were read while the transaction was running or values that the transaction will write if it commits), and any locks or concurrency-control information that has been acquired while the transaction was active. This state is shared with the database server, which for its part must keep original values of any data objects updated by noncommitted transactions; keep updates sorted by transactional-ID to know which values to commit if the transaction is successful; and maintain read-lock and write-lock records on behalf of the client, blocking other transactions that attempt to access the locked data items while allowing access to the client holding the locks. The server thus knows which processes are its active clients, and must monitor their health in order to abort transactions associated with clients that fail before committing (otherwise, a failure could leave the database in a locked state).

The ability to use commit and abort is extremely valuable in implementing transactional systems and applications. In addition to the role of these operations in defining the scope of a transaction for purposes of serializability, they also represent a tool that can be used directly by the programmer—for example, an application be designed to assume that a certain class of operations (such as selling a seat on an airline) will succeed, and to update database records as it runs under this assumption. Such an algorithm would be optimistic in much the same sense as a concurrency-control scheme can be optimistic. If, for whatever reason, the operation encounters an error condition (no seats available on some flight, customer credit card refused, etc.), the operation can simply abort and the intermediate actions that were taken will be erased from the database. Moreover, the serializability model ensures that applications can be written without attention to one another: Transactional serializability ensures that if a transaction would be correct when executed in isolation, it will also be correct when executed concurrently against a database server that interleaves operations for increased performance.

The transactional model is also valuable from a reliability perspective. The isolation of transactions from one another avoids inconsistencies that might occur if one transaction were to see the partial results of some other transaction—for example, suppose that transaction T_a increments variable x by 1 and is executed concurrently, with transaction T_b, which decrements x by 1. If T_a and T_b read x concurrently they might base their computations on the same initial value of x. The *write* operation that completes last would then erase the other update. Many concurrent systems are prone to bugs because of this sort of mutual-exclusion problem; transactional systems avoid this issue using locking or other concurrency control mechanisms that would force T_b to wait until T_a has terminated, or the converse. Moreover, transactional abort offers a simple way for a server to deal with a client that fails or seems to hang: It can simply timeout and abort the transaction that the client initiated. (If the client is really alive, its attempt to commit will eventually fail: Transactional systems never guarantee that a commit will be successful). Similarly, the client is insulated from the effects of server failures: It can modify data on the server without concern that an inopportune server crash could leave the database in an inconsistent state.

There is, however, a negative side to transactional distributed computing. As we will see in Chap. 20, transactional programming can be extremely restrictive. The model basically prevents programs from cooperating as peers in a distributed setting, and although extensions have been proposed to overcome this limitation, none seems to be fully satisfactory—that is, transactions really work best for applications in which there is a computational master process, which issues requests to a set of slave processors on which data are stored. This is, of course, a common model, but it is not the only one. Any transactional application in which several processes know about each other and execute concurrently is difficult to model in this manner.

Moreover, transactional mechanisms can be costly, particularly when a transaction is executed on data that has been replicated for high availability or distributed over multiple servers. The locking mechanisms used to ensure serializability can severely limit concurrency, and it can be very difficult to deal with transactions that run for long periods of time, since these will often leave the entire server locked and unable to accept new requests. It can also be very difficult to decide what to do if a transaction aborts unexpectedly: Should the client retry it or report to the user that it aborted? Decisions such as these are very difficult, particularly in sophisticated applications in which one is essentially forced to find a way to roll forward.

For all of these reasons, although transactional computing is a powerful and popular tool in developing reliable distributed software systems, it does not represent a complete model or a complete solution to all reliability issues that occur.

6.15 Applying Transactions to File Servers

Transactional access to data may seem extremely well matched to the issue of file server reliability. Typically, however, file servers either do not implement transactional functionality, or do so only for the specific case of database applications. The reasons for this illustrate the sense in which a mechanism such as transactional data access may be unacceptably constraining in nontransactional settings.

General-purpose computing applications make frequent and extensive use of files. They store parameters in files, search directories for files with special names, store temporary results in files that are passed from phase to phase of a multiphase computation, implement ad hoc structures within very large files, and even use the existence or nonexistence of files and the file protection bits as persistent locking mechanisms, compensating for the lack of locking tools in operating systems such as UNIX.

As we saw earlier, file systems used in support of this model are often designed to be stateless, particularly in distributed systems—that is, each operation by a client is a complete and self-contained unit. The file system maintains no memory of actions by clients, and although the clients may cache information from the file system (such as handles pointing to open file objects), they are designed to refresh this information if it is found to be stale when referenced. Such an approach has the merit of extreme simplicity. It is certainly not the only approach: Some file systems maintain coherent caches of file system blocks within client systems, and these are necessarily stateful. Nonetheless, the great majority of distributed file systems are stateless.

The introduction of transactions on files thus brings with it stateful aspects that are otherwise avoided, potentially complicating an otherwise simple system architecture. However, transactions pose more problems than mere complexity. In particular, the locking mechanisms used by transactions are ill-matched to the pattern of file access seen in general operating systems applications.

Consider the program that was used to edit this book. When started, it displays a list of files that end with the extension ".doc," and waited for me to select the file on which I wished to work. Eventually, the file selected and opened, an extended editing session ensued, perhaps even appearing to last overnight or over a weekend if some distraction prevented me from closing the file and exiting the program before leaving for the evening. In a standard transactional model, each of the read accesses and each of the write accesses would represent an operation associated with the transaction, and transactional serialization ordering would be achieved by delaying these operations as needed to ensure that only serializable executions are permitted—for example, with locks.

This now creates the prospect of a file system containing directories that are locked against updates (because some transaction has read the contents), files that are completely untouchable (because some transaction is updating, or perhaps even deleting the contents), and of long editing sessions that routinely end in failure (because locks may be broken after long delays, forcing the client program to abort its transaction and start again from scratch). It may not seem obvious that such files should pose a problem, but suppose that a transaction's behavior was slightly different as a result of seeing these transient conditions? That transaction would not be correctly serialized if the editing transaction were now aborted, resulting in some other state. No transaction should have been allowed to see the intermediate state.

Obviously, this analysis could be criticized as postulating a clumsy application of transactional serializability to the file system. In practice, one would presumably adapt the model to the semantics of the application. However, even for the specific case of transactional file systems, the system has been less than convincing—for example, at Xerox the early versions of the Clearinghouse software (a form of file system used for e-mail and other user-profile information) offered a fully transactional interface. Over time, this was greatly restricted because of the impracticality of transactional concurrency-control in settings that involve large numbers of general-purpose applications.

Moreover, many file-based applications lack a practical way to assign a transaction-ID to the logical transaction. As an example, consider a version control software system. Such a system seems well matched to the transactional model: A user checks out a file, modifies it, and then checks it in; meanwhile, other users are prevented from doing updates and can only read old copies. Here, however, many individual programs may operate on the file over the period of the transaction. What is lacking is a practical way to associate an identifier with the series of operations. Clearly, the application programs themselves can do so, but one of the basic principles of reliability is to avoid placing excessive trust in the correctness of individual applications; in this example, the correctness of the applications would be a key element of the correctness of the transactional architecture, a very questionable design choice.

On the other hand, transactional file systems offer important benefits. Most often cited among these are the atomic update properties of a transaction, whereby a set of changes to files is made entirely, or not at all. This has resulted in proposals for file systems that are transactional in the limited sense of offering failure atomicity for updates, but without carrying this to the extreme of also providing transactional serializability. Hagmann's use of group commit to reimplement the Cedar file system (see Hagmann 1987) and IBM's QuickSilver file system (see Schmuck and Wyllie 1991) are examples of a research efforts that are viewed as very successful in offering such a compromise. However, transactional atomicity remains uncommon in the most widely used commercial file system products because of the complexity associated with a stateful file system implementation. The appeal of stateless design, and the inherent reliability associated with an architecture in which the clients and servers take responsibility only for their own actions and place limited trust in information that they do not own directly, continues to rule the marketplace.

The most popular alternative to transactions is the atomic rename operation offered by many commercially standard file systems. For complex objects represented as a single file, or as a rooted graph of files, an application can atomically update the collection by creating a new root object containing the modifications, or pointing to modified versions of other files, and then rename the result to obtain the equivalent effect of an atomic commit, with all the updates being installed simultaneously. If a crash occurs, it suffices to delete the partially modified copy; the original version will not be affected. Despite having some minor limitations, designers of fairly complex file systems applications have achieved a considerable degree of reliability using operations such as rename, perhaps together with an *fsync* operation that forces recent updates to an object or file out to the persistent disk storage area.

In conclusion, it is tempting to apply stateful mechanisms and even transactional techniques to file servers. Yet similar results can be obtained, for this particular application, with less costly and cumbersome solutions. Moreover, the simplicity of a stateless approach has enormous appeal in a world where there may be very little control over the software that runs on client computers, and in which trust in the client system will often be misplaced. In light of these considerations, file systems can be expected to remain predominantly stateless even in settings where reliability is paramount.

More generally, this point illustrates an insight to which we will return repeatedly in this book. Reliability is a complex goal and can require a variety of tools. While a stateless file system may be adequately reliable for one use, some other application may find its behavior hopelessly inconsistent and impossible to work around. A stateful database architecture works wonderfully for database applications, but it turns out to be difficult to adapt to general purpose operating systems applications that have less structure, or that merely have a nontransactional structure. Only a diversity of tools, integrated in an environment that encourages the user to match the tool to the need, can possibly lead to reliability in the general sense. No single approach will suffice.

6.16   Related Reading

A tremendous amount has been written about client/server computing, and several pages of references could easily have been included here. Good introductions into the literature, including more detailed discussions of DCE and ASN.1, can be found in Birrell and Nelson (1984), Comer and Stevens (1993), Coulouris et al. (1994), Tanenbaum (1988).

On RPC performance, the classic reference is Shroeder and Burrows (1989). Critiques of the RPC paradigm appear in Birman and van Renesse (1994, 1996, 2010), Tanenbaum and van Renesse (1988).

On the problem of inconsistent failure detection with RPC and TCP (see Birman and Glade 1995).

Other relevant publications include Bal et al. (1992), Bellovin and Merritt (1990), Berners-Lee et al. (1994, 1995), Birrell and Nelson (1984), Braun and Diot (1995), Brockschmidt (1994), Engler et al. (1995), Govindran and Anderson (1991), Heidemann and Popek (1994), Jacobson (1988, 1990), Mullender et al. (1990), Rashid (1986), Shroeder and Burrows (1989), Thekkath and Levy (1993), von Eicken et al. (1995).

A good reference to DCE is Open Software Foundation and to OLE-2 is Brockschmidt (1994). Readers interested in CORBA will find Doug Schmidt's ACE/TAO web sites useful: http://www.cs.wustl.edu/~schmidt/; these are popular CORBA platform technologies (ACE is the "distributed computing environment" and TAO is a CORBA Object Request Broker implemented over ACE).

Web Services and SOAP RPC are documented at www.w3.org and in extensive online repositories maintained by the major vendors in the field, such as IBM, Microsoft, BEA, etc.

Kerberos is discussed in Bellovin and Merritt (1990), Schiller (1994), Steiner et al. (1988).

I am not aware of any good general reference on NFS itself, although the standard is available from Sun Microsystems and is widely supported.

The definitive paper on performance of the Berkeley File System is McKusick et al. (1984), Ousterhout et al. (1988), Vogels (1999). A "contrary" view on file system performance can be found in Ganger et al. (2000).

NFS performance and access patterns is studied in Ousterhout et al. (1985) and extended to the Sprite file system in Baker et al. (1991).

References to NFS-like file systems supporting replication include Bhide et al. (1991), Digital Equipment Corporation (1995), Kronenberg et al. (1985), Ladin et al. (1992), Liskov et al. (1991), Siegal (1992).

Topics related to the CMU file system work that lead to AFS are covered in Bellovin and Merritt (1990), Birrell (1985), Howard et al. (1987), Lampson et al. (1992), Satyanarayanan et al. (1985, 1989), Schiller (1994), Spector (1985), Steiner et al. (1988).

CODA is discussed in Kistler and Satyanarayanan (1992), Mummert et al. (1995). The definitive paper on the CODA file system was published in ACM TOCS: see Kistler and Satyanarayanan (1992). Readers interested in mobile file systems should also read about the innovative work on so-called *low bandwidth* file systems, as presented at SOSP in Muthitacharoen et al. (2001). In this effort, novel compression schemes were developed to let a mobile user modify files that need to be mirrored to the main storage system. By using a non-standard file chunking approach, remarkable levels of compression were achieved.

MIT's Rover Toolkit is discussed in Joseph et al. (1995).

RAID is discussed in Patterson et al. (1988). Sprite is discussed in Nelson et al. (1987), Ousterhout et al. (1988), Srinivasan and Mogul (1989). Ficus is discussed in Reiher et al. (1994), Locus in Heidemann and Popek (1995), Walter et al. (1993).

XFS is discussed in Anderson et al. (2009).

The world's largest distributed file systems are the ones used in cloud computing systems. While there are many such file systems today (almost every cloud vendor has one of its own), Google's GFS is perhaps the best documented; readers should refer to the paper by Ghemawat et al. (2003).

Additional important work on file systems includes Ganger et al. (2000), Rosenblum and Ousterhout (1991), McKusick et al. (1984), Hartman and Ousterhout (1993) and Santry et al. (1999). A clever way to reduce the bandwidth needed by mobile file systems is described in Muthitacharoen et al. (2001). Frangiapani, a scalable distributed file system based on group communication mechanisms, is described in Thekkath et al. (1997) and is worth reading both as an interesting paper and because the Paxos mechanisms employed in the core of this system have been embraced by Microsoft Corporation for internal purposes and hence could someday become visible to developers using that company's platforms.

Work on global memory is covered in Feeley et al. (1995), Johnson et al. (1995).

Database references for the transactional approach are studied in Bernstein et al. (1987), Gray (1978), Gray and Reuter (1993).

Tandem's system is presented in Bartlett et al. (1987).

Nomadic transactional systems are covered in Alonso and Korth (1993), Amir (1995).

Transactions on file systems are discussed in Hagmann (1987), Schmuck and Wyllie (1991).

Related work is treated in Liskov and Scheifler (1983), Liskov et al. (1991), Macedo et al. (1993), Moss (1982).

CORBA: The Common Object Request Broker Architecture

7

With the emergence of object-oriented programming languages, such as Modula and C++, came a recognition that object-orientation could play a role similar to that of the OSI hierarchy for complex distributed systems. In this view, one would describe a computing system in terms of the set of objects from which it was assembled, together with the rules by which these objects interact with one another. Object-oriented system design became a major subject for research, with many of the key ideas pulled together for the first time by a British research effort, called the Advanced Network Systems Architecture group, or ANSA. In this chapter, we will briefly discuss ANSA, and then focus on CORBA, which draws on some of the ideas introduced by ANSA, and has emerged as a widely accepted standard for objected-oriented distributed computing. Finally, we touch briefly on J2EE and .NET, two modern object-oriented environments that make extensive use of ideas from CORBA.

As noted earlier, cloud computing systems generally lack anything one could view as a truly comprehensive architecture, although they do use the web services standards for requests from web clients that issue RPC-like requests, which are then dispatched to services running in the first tier of the cloud for handling. Web services, however, is still far from offering the completeness and coherent design one sees in CORBA. Indeed, a better way to think of the cloud is to view cloud platforms as building upon CORBA, or similar architectures (the other very well known one is the COM architecture used in Microsoft's .NET framework; we will say less about that because it closely resembles CORBA in most respects).

But the best examples of CORBA use cases arise in slightly smaller settings, where CORBA really shines. Many of today's distributed systems are composed of multiple subsystems that cooperate to accomplish tasks, and CORBA is ideally matched to that sort of modularity. Thus rather than approach CORBA by thinking about a massive cloud-computing system that may reflect some aspects of the CORBA architecture, it would probably be best to visualize some sort of complex but narrower system, such as the Air Traffic Control example we have used a few times. An ATC system would (obviously) have large numbers of subsystems: one doing flight tracking, one talking to the controllers, one tracking weather, etc. These

K.P. Birman, *Guide to Reliable Distributed Systems*, Texts in Computer Science, DOI 10.1007/978-1-4471-2416-0_7, © Springer-Verlag London Limited 2012

would need to talk to one-another, and that form of modularity, and that level of scale, is precisely what CORBA was invented to address.

A well known and popular implementation of the CORBA model is the TAO system, developed by Doug Schmidt. TAO runs over a remote procedure call and "execution environment" technology called ACE. Readers of this text who wish to experiment with CORBA and are using a Linux platform for development are encouraged to download ACE and TAO.

7.1   The ANSA Project

The ANSA project, headed by Andrew Herbert, was the first systematic attempt to develop technology for modeling complex distributed systems (see Architecture Projects Management Limited 1989, 1991a, 1991b). ANSA was intended as a technology base for writing down the structure of a complex application or system and then translating the resulting description into a working version of that system in a process of stepwise refinement.

Abstractly, ANSA consists of a set of models, which deal with various aspects of distributed systems design and representation problems. The *enterprise model* is concerned with the overall functions and roles of the organizational structure within which the problem at hand is to be solved—for example, an air-traffic control system would be an application within the air traffic control organization, an enterprise. The *information model* represents the flow of information within the enterprise; in an air traffic application this model might describe flight control status records, radar inputs, radio communication to and from pilots, and so forth. The *computation model* is a framework of programming structures and program development tools that are made available to developers. The model deals with such issues as modularity of the application itself, invocation of operations, parameter passing, configuration, concurrency and synchronization, replication, and the extension of existing languages to support distributed computing. The *engineering and technology models* reduce these abstractions to practice, providing the implementation of the ANSA abstractions and mapping these to the underlying run-time environment and its associated technologies.

In practical terms, most users viewed ANSA as a set of rules for system design, whereby system components could be described as objects with published interfaces. An application with appropriate permissions could obtain a handle on the object and invoke its methods using the procedures and functions defined in this interface. The ANSA environment would automatically and transparently deal with such issues as fetching objects from storage, launching programs when a new instance of an object was requested, implementing the object invocation protocols, and so forth. Moreover, ANSA explicitly included features for overcoming failures of various kinds, using transactional techniques drawn from the database community, as well as process group techniques in which sets of objects are used to implement a single highly available distributed service. We will consider both types of technology in considerable detail in Part III of the book.

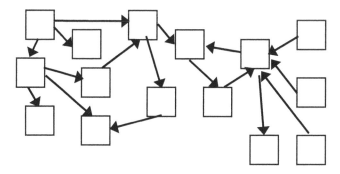

Fig. 7.1 Distributed objects abstraction. Objects are linked by object references, and the distributed nature of the environment is hidden from users. Access is uniform even if objects are implemented to have special properties or internal structure, such as replication for increased availability or transactional support for persistence. Objects can be implemented in different programming languages, but this is invisible to users

ANSA treated the objects that implement a system as the concrete realization of the enterprise computing model and the enterprise information model. These models capture the essence of the application as a whole, treating it as a single abstraction even if the distributed system as implemented necessarily contained many components. Thus, the enterprise-computing model might support the abstraction of a collision-avoidance strategy for use by an air traffic control enterprise and the enterprise data model might define the standard data objects used in support of this service. The actual implementation of the service would be reached by a series of refinements in which increasing levels of detail are added to this basic set of definitions. In effect, one passes from the abstraction of a collision-avoidance strategy to the more concrete concept of a collision-avoidance subsystem located at each set of primary sites and linked to one another to coordinate their actions (see Fig. 7.1). This concept evolved to one with further refinements, defining the standard services composing the collision-avoidance system as used on a single air traffic control workstation, and then evolved still further to a description of how those services could be implemented.

In very concrete terms, the ANSA approach required the designer to write down the sort of knowledge of distributed system structure that, for many systems, is implicit but never encoded in a machine-readable form. The argument was that by writing down these system descriptions, a better system would emerge: one in which the rationale for the structure used was self-documenting and in which detailed information would be preserved about the design choices and objectives that the system carries out; in this manner the mechanisms for future evolution could be made a part of the system itself. Such a design promotes extensibility and interoperability, and offers a path to system management and control. Moreover, ANSA designs were expressed in terms of objects, whose locations could be anywhere in the network, with the actual issues of location developing only after the design was further elaborated, or in specific situations where location of an object might matter (Fig. 7.2).

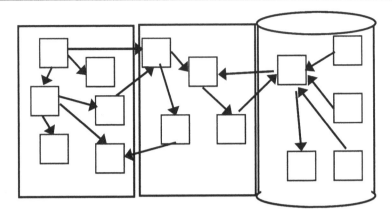

Fig. 7.2 In practice, the objects in a distributed system execute on machines or reside in storage servers. The run-time environment works to conceal movement of objects from location to location and to activate servers when they are initially referenced after having been passively stored. The environment also deals with fault-tolerance issues, the life-cycle of an object, garbage collection, and other issues that span multiple objects or sites

This type of object-oriented, location-transparent design has proved very popular with distributed systems designers.

7.2   Beyond ANSA to CORBA

While the ANSA technology per se never gained a wide following, these ideas have had a huge impact on the view of system design and function adopted by modern developers. In particular, as the initial stages of the ANSA project ended, a new project was started by a consortium of computer vendors. Called the Common Object Request Broker Architecture, CORBA defines a range of standards permitting interoperation between complex object-oriented systems potentially built by diverse vendors (see Object Management Group and X/Open 1991). CORBA has become a widely used, important platform. At the time of this writing, the J2EE and .NET platforms have become dominant, and CORBA receives somewhat less attention. Web Services are just emerging. Yet CORBA will be with us for many years into the future. Moreover, essentially all aspects of CORBA have analogs within J2EE and .NET.

CORBA represents a consensus developed within an industry standards organization called the Object Management Group, or OMG. The mission of OMG was to develop architecture standards promoting interoperability between systems developed using object-oriented technologies—the stress, then, is on getting legacy applications to talk to one-another and to new applications. In some ways, this represents a less-ambitious objective than the task with which ANSA was charged, since ANSA set out both to develop an all-encompassing architectural vision for building enterprise-wide distributed computing systems, and to incorporate reliability technologies into its solutions. However, ANSA was sometimes criticized for its emphasis on new generations of systems and its inattention to the difficulties of legacy integration. CORBA's early success was almost certainly related to the good treatment of this topic. As CORBA has evolved, it has tackled more and more of ANSA's original topics.

At the time of this writing, CORBA was basically a framework for building distributed computing environments and letting applications running in one CORBA environment issue requests to applications running in another. Notice that different vendors might offer their own CORBA solutions with differing properties. Nonetheless, adherence to the CORBA guidelines should permit such solutions to interoperate. For example, a distributed system programmed using a CORBA product from Hewlett-Packard should be useful from within an application developed using CORBA products from Sun Microsystems, IBM, or some other CORBA-compliant vendor.

Interoperability has steadily grown in importance over the decade since CORBA was first introduced. In fact, it is quite striking to discover that in some ways, J2EE and .NET have replayed the same questions that initially distinguished CORBA from ANSA. J2EE (Java version 2 Enterprise Edition) is a "commercial strength" runtime environment for Java applications—specifically, Java applications that talk to databases and other forms of servers (they are constructed using what is called the "Java Beans" component of the overall architecture). Initially, the vision of the Java community was that Java would sweep other languages to the side. As a result, much of the early effort in the Java development activities at SUN and elsewhere concentrated on pure Java applications, with interoperability arising only in the binding between a Java Bean and the server (normally, database server) to which it was connected. J2EE incorporated most aspects of the CORBA framework and all aspects of the CORBA database architecture.

J2EE was tremendously successful right from the outset, and this motivated Microsoft to fight back with a J2EE-like environment of its own. Microsoft needed a distinguishing product focus, however, hence while .NET includes analogous database and server functionality to J2EE (in the architectural framework called ADO.NET), the platform goes much further in its handling of integration issues. .NET promotes a tremendous range of integration and legacy systems features, including full language interoperability, easy mechanisms for binding a new system to a specific instance of an old system and a means for making sure that the right versions are running at the same time, cross-language debugging tools, and so forth. This position was an immediate success within the Microsoft market, and J2EE almost immediately began to lose market share. Accordingly the J2EE developers responded by developing a new "object adaptor" framework for J2EE, offering all of the kinds of interoperability available for .NET users.

J2EE is a framework aimed at Java users, and Microsoft is often portrayed as an opponent of Java. In fact, however, .NET offers reasonable support for the Java language. For users who seek to make more use of Microsoft's famework, .NET introduces a new programming language called C# (C-sharp), which builds on Java, but goes well beyond both the Java language and the associated runtime. .NET applications can be executed on Linux platforms using a complier called Mono, and the Isis[2] system presented in Appendix A was implemented in C#.

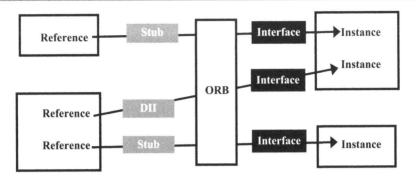

Fig. 7.3 The conceptual architecture of CORBA uses an object request broker as an intermediary that directs object invocations to the appropriate object instances. There are two cases of invocations; the static one, which we focus on in the book, and the dynamic invocation interface (DII), which is more complex to use and hence not discussed here

7.3   The CORBA Reference Model

The key to understanding the structure of a CORBA environment is the *Reference Model*, which consists of a set of components that a CORBA platform should typically provide. These components are fully described by the CORBA architecture, but only to the level of interfaces used by application developers and functionality. Individual vendors are responsible for deciding how to implement these interfaces and how to obtain the best possible performance; moreover, individual products may offer solutions that differ in offering optional properties such as security, high availability, or special guarantees of behavior that go beyond the basics required by the model.

At a minimum, a CORBA implementation must supply an *Object Request Broker*, or ORB, which is responsible for matching a requestor with an object that will perform its request, using the object reference to locate an appropriate target object (see Fig. 7.3). The implementation will also contain translation programs, responsible for mapping implementations of system components (and their IDLs) to programs that can be linked with a run-time library and executed. A set of *object services* provide the basic functionality needed to create and use objects: These include such functions as creating, deleting, copying, or moving objects; giving them names that other objects can use to bind to them; and providing security. An interesting service, which we will discuss in more detail, is the *Event Notification Service* or ENS: This allows a program to register its interest in a class of events. All events in that class are then reported to the program. It thus represents a communication technology different from the usual RPC-style or stream-style of connection. A set of *Common Facilities* contains a collection of standardized applications that most CORBA implementations are expected to support, but that are ultimately optional: These include, for example, standards for system management and for electronic mail that may contain objects. And, finally, of course, there are *Application Objects* developed by the CORBA user to solve a particular problem.

Fig. 7.4 IDL interface to a
server for a grid object coded
in Orbix, a popular
CORBA-compliant
technology

```
// grid server example for Orbix
// IDL – in file grid.idl
interface grid {
        readonly attribute short height;
        readonly attribute short width;

        void set(in short w, in short h, in long value);
        long get(in short w, in short h);
}
```

In many respects the Object Request Broker is the core of a CORBA implementation. Similar to the function of a communication network or switching system, the ORB is responsible for delivering object invocations that originate in a client program to the appropriate server program, and routing the reply back to the client. The ability to invoke an object, of course, does not imply that the object that was invoked is being used correctly, has a consistent state, or is even the most appropriate object for the application to use. These broader properties fall back upon the basic technologies of distributed computing that are the general topic of this book; as we will see, CORBA is a way of *talking about* solutions, but not a *specific set of prebuilt solutions*. Indeed, one could say that because CORBA worries about syntax but not semantics, the technology is largely superficial: a veneer around a set of technologies. However, this particular veneer is an important and sophisticated one, and it also creates a context within which a principled and standardized approach to distributed systems reliability becomes possible.

For many users, object-oriented computing means programming in Java, C++ or C#, although SmallTalk and Ada are also object-oriented languages, and one can develop object interfaces to other languages like FORTRAN and COBOL. Nonetheless, Java and C++ are the most widely used languages, and most Java programmers focus on J2EE, while C# programmers tend to use .NET. Thus for illustration of CORBA it makes sense to employ C++, since the average CORBA programmer would work in this language. Our examples are drawn directly from the programmer's guide for Orbix, an extremely popular CORBA technology at the time of this writing.

An example of a CORBA object interface, coded in the Orbix interface definition language (IDL), is shown in Fig. 7.4. This interface publishes the services available from a grid server, which is intended to manage two-dimensional tables such as are used in spreadsheets or relational databases (apologies to those who were hoping that this example is from the Grid Computing world). The server exports two read-only values, width and height, which can be used to query the size of a grid object. There are also two operations that can be performed upon the object: "set," which sets the value of an element, and "get," which fetches the value. Set is of type void, meaning that it does not return a result, get, on the other hand, returns a long integer.

To build a grid server, the user would need to write a C++ program that implements this interface. To do this, the IDL compiler is first used to transform the IDL file into a standard C++ header file in which Orbix defines the information it will need to implement remote invocations on behalf of the client. The IDL compiler

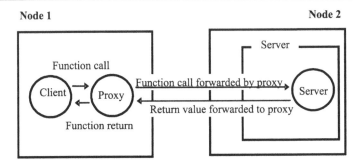

Fig. 7.5 Orbix conceals the location of objects by converting remote operations into operations on local proxy objects, mediated by stubs. However, remote access is not completely transparent in standard CORBA applications if an application is designed for reliability—for example, error conditions differ for local and remote objects. Such issues can be concealed by integrating a reliability technology into the CORBA environment, but transparent reliability is not a standard part of CORBA, and solutions vary widely from vendor to vendor

also produces two forms of stub files—one that implements the client side of the get and set operations; the other implements the server side. These stub files must be compiled and linked to the respective programs. (See Fig. 7.5.)

If one were to look at the contents of the header file produced for the grid IDL file, one would discover that width and height have been transformed into functions; that is, when the C++ programmer references an attribute of a grid object, a function call will actually occur into the client-side stub procedures, which can perform an RPC to the grid server to obtain the current value of the attribute.

We say RPC here, but in fact a feature of CORBA is that it provides very efficient support for invocations of local objects, which are defined in the same address space as the invoking program. The significance of this is that although the CORBA IDL shown in Fig. 7.4 could be used to access a remote server that handles one or more grid objects, it can also be used to communicate to a completely local instantiation of a grid object, contained entirely in the address space of the calling program. Indeed, the concept goes even further: In Orbix+Isis, a variation of Orbix, the grid server could be replicated using an object group for high availability. And in the most general case, the grid object's clients could be implemented by a server running under some other CORBA-based environment, such as IBM's DSOM product, HP's DOMF or ObjectBroker, Sun's DOE, or other object-oriented environments with which CORBA can communicate using an adapter, such as Microsoft's OLE. CORBA implementations thus have the property that object location, the technology or programming language used to build an object, and even the ORB under which it is running can be almost completely transparent to the user.

What exactly would a grid server look like? If we are working in C++, a grid would be a C++ program that includes an implementation class for grid objects. Figure 7.6 shows the code that might be used to implement this abstract data type, again drawing on Orbix as a source for our example. The "Environment" parameter is used for error handling with the client. The BOAImpl extension ("gridBOAImpl") designates that this is a Basic Object Adaptor Implementation for the grid interface.

```
// Implementation of grid class
#include "grid_i.h"

grid_i::grid_i(short h, short w) {
        m_height = h;
        m_width = w;
        m_a = new long* [h];
        for (int i = 0; i < h; i++)
                m_a[i] = new long [w];
}
grid_i::~grid_i() {
        for (int i = 0; i < m_height; i++)
                delete[ ] m_a[i];
        delete[ ] m_a;
}
short grid_i::width(CORBA::Environment &) {
        return m_width;
}
short grid_i::height(CORBA::Environment &) {
        return m_height;
}
void grid_i::set(short w, short m, long value, CORBA::Environment &) {
        m_a[n][m] = value;
}
long grid_i::get(short n, short m, CORBA::Environment &) {
        return m_a[n][m];
}
```

Fig. 7.6   Server code to implement the grid_i class in Orbix

Fig. 7.7   Enclosing program
to declare a grid object and
accept requests upon it

```
#include "grid_i.h"
#include <iostream.h>

void main() {
        grid_imyGrid(100,100);
        // Orbix objects can be named but this is not
        // needed for this example
        CORBA::Orbix.impl_is_ready();
        cout <<"server terminating" << endl;
}
```

Finally, our server needs an enclosing framework: the program itself that will execute this code. The code in Fig. 7.7 provides this; it implements a single grid object and declares itself to be ready to accept object invocations. The grid object is not named in this example, although it could have been, and indeed the server could be designed to create and destroy grid objects dynamically at run time.

The user can now declare to Orbix that the grid server is available by giving it a name and storing the binary of the server in a file, the path name of which is also provided to Orbix (see Figs. 7.8, 7.9). The Orbix life-cycle service will automatically start the grid server if an attempt is made to access it when it is not running.

Fig. 7.8 Client program for the grid object—assumes that the grid was registered under the server name "gridSrv." This example lacks error handling; an elaborated version with error handling appears in Fig. 7.10

```
#include "grid_h.h"
#include <iostream.h>

void main() {
    grid *p;

    p = grid::_bind(":gridSrv");
    cout << "height is " << p->height() << endl;
    cout << "width is " << p->width() << endl;
        p->set(2, 4, 123);
    cout << "grid(2, 4) is " << p->get(2, 4) << endl;
        p->release();
}
```

CORBA supports several concepts of reliability. One is concerned with recovering from failures—for example, when invoking a remote server. A second reliability mechanism is provided for purposes of reliable interactions with persistent objects, and is based upon what is called a transactional architecture. We discuss transactions elsewhere in this book and will not digress onto that subject at this time. However, the basic purpose of a transactional architecture is to provide a way for applications to perform operations on complex persistent data structures, without interfering with other concurrently active but independent operations, in a manner that will leave the structure intact even if the application program or server fails while it is running. Unfortunately, as we will see in Chap. 20, transactions are primarily useful in applications that are structured as database systems on which programs operate using read and update requests. Such structures are important in distributed systems, but

Fig. 7.9 Illustration of Orbix error-handling facility. Macros are used to catch errors; if one occurs, the error can be caught and potentially worked around. Notice that each remote operation can potentially fail—hence, exception handling would normally be more standardized. A handler for a high-availability application would operate by rebinding to some other server capable of providing the same functionality. This can be concealed from the user, which is the approach used in systems like Orbix+Isis or Electra, a CORBA technology layered over the Horus distributed system

```
#include "grid_h.h"
#include <iostream.h>

void main() {
    grid *p;

    TRY {
        p = grid::_bind(":gridSrv");
    }
    CATCHANY {
        cerr << "bind to object failed" << endl;
        cerror << "Fatal exception " << IT_X << endl;
        exit(1);
    }
    TRY {
        cout << "height is " << p->height() << endl;
    }
    CATCHANY {
        cerr << "call to height failed" << endl;
        cerror << "Fatal exception " << IT_X << endl;
        exit(1);
    }
    ... etc ...
}
```

there are many distributed applications that match the model poorly, and, for them, transactional reliability is not a good approach.

Outside of its transactional mechanisms, CORBA offers relatively little help to the programmer concerned with reliability or high availability. For example, Orbix can be notified that a server application can be run on one of a number of machines. When a client application attempts to use the remote application, Orbix will automatically attempt to bind to each machine in turn, selecting at random the first machine that confirms that the server application is operational. However, Orbix does not provide any form of automatic mechanisms for recovering from the failure of such a server after the binding is completed. The reason for this is that a client process that is already communicating with a server may have a complex state that reflects information specific to that server, such as cached records with record identifiers that came from the server, or other forms of data that differ in specific ways even among servers able to provide the same functionality. To rebind the client to a new server, one would somehow need to refresh, rebuild, or roll back this server-dependent state. And doing so is potentially very difficult; at a minimum, considerable detailed knowledge of the application will be required.

The same problems can also arise in the server itself. For example, consider a financial trading service, in which the prices of various stocks are presented. Now, suppose that these data are extremely dynamic due to rapidly changing market data. The server may need to have some form of setup that it uses to establish a client profile, and it may need to have an internal state that reflects the events that have occurred since the client first bound to it. Even if some other copy of the server is available and can provide the same services, there could be a substantial time lag when rebinding and there may be a noticeable discontinuity if the new server, lacking this state of the session, starts its financial computations from the current stream of incoming data. Such events will not be transparent to the client using the server and it is unrealistic to try and hide them.

The integration of a wider spectrum of reliability-enhancing technologies with CORBA represents an important area for research and commercial development, particularly if reliability is taken in the broad sense of security, fault tolerance, availability, and so forth. High-performance, commercially appealing products will be needed to demonstrate the effectiveness of the architectural features that result: When we discuss transactions on distributed objects, for example, we will see that merely supporting transactions through an architecture is not likely to make users happy. Even the execution of transactions on objects raises deeper issues that would need to be resolved for such a technology to be accepted as a genuinely valid reliability-enhancing tool—for example, the correct handling of a transactional request by a non-transactional service is unspecified in the architecture.

More broadly, CORBA can be viewed as the ISO hierarchy for object-oriented distributed computing: It provides us with a framework within which such systems can be described and offers ways to interconnect components without regard for the programming language or vendor technologies used in developing them. Exploiting this to achieve critical reliability in distributed settings, however, stands as a more basic technical challenge that CORBA does not directly address. CORBA tells us how to structure and present these technologies, but not how to build them.

Fig. 7.10 From the interface
definition, the IDL compiler
creates stub and interface
files, which are used by
clients that invoke the object
and by servers that implement
it

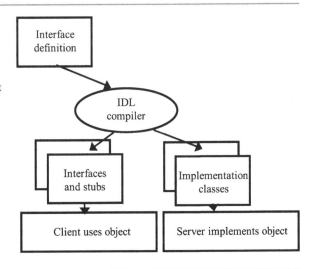

7.4   IDL and ODL

IDL is the language used to define an object interface (in the TINA standard, there is an ODL language that goes beyond IDL in specifying other attributes of the object, and in allowing each object to export more than one interface). (See Fig. 7.10.) CORBA defines an IDL for the various languages that can be supported: C++, SmallTalk, Ada95, and so forth. The most standard of these is the IDL for C++, and the examples given above are expressed in C++ for that reason. However, expanded use of IDL for other programming languages is likely in the future.

The use of C++ programs in a CORBA environment can demand a high level of sophistication in C++ programming. In particular, the operator overload functionality of C++ can conceal complex machinery behind deceptively simple interfaces. In a standard programming language one expects that an assignment statement such as $a = b$ will execute rapidly. In C++ such an operation may involve allocation and initialization of a new abstract object and a potentially costly copying operation. In CORBA such an assignment may involve costly remote operations on a server remote from the application program that executes the assignment statement. To the programmer, CORBA and C++ appear as a mixed blessing: Through the CORBA IDL, operations such as assignment and value references can be transparently extended over a distributed environment, which can seem like magic. But the magic is potentially tarnished by the discovery that a single assignment might now take seconds (or hours) to complete!

Such observations point to a deficiency in the CORBA IDL language and, perhaps, the entire technology as currently conceived. IDL provides no features for specifying *behaviors* of remote objects that are desirable or undesirable consequences of distribution. There is no possibility of using IDL to indicate a performance property (or cost, in the above example) or to specify a set of fault-tolerant guarantees for an object that differ from the ones normally provided in the environment. Synchronization requirements or assumptions made by an object, or guarantees offered by the client, cannot be expressed in the language. This missing information, potentially needed for reliability purposes, can limit the ability of the programmer to fully specify a complex distributed system, while also denying the user the basic information needed to validate that a complex object is being used correctly.

One could argue that the IDL should be limited to specification of the interface to an object and that other types of service would manage any behavioral specifications. Indeed, in the case of the life-cycle service, one has a good example of how the CORBA community approaches this problem: The life-cycle aspects of an object specification are treated as a special type of data managed by this service, and are not considered to be a part of the object interface specification. Yet this information often belongs in the interface specification, in the sense that these types of property may have direct implications for the user that accesses the object and may be information of a type that is important in establishing that the object is being used correctly. The specification of an object involves more than the specification of its interfaces, and indeed the interface specification involves more than just the manner in which one invokes the object. In contrast, the CORBA community considers behavior to be orthogonal to interface specification, and hence it relegates behavioral aspects of the object's specification to the special-purpose services directly concerned with that type of information. Unfortunately, it seems likely that much basic research will need to be done before this issue is addressed in a convincing manner.

7.5   ORB

An Object Request Broker, or ORB, is the component of the run-time system that binds client objects to the server objects they access, and that interprets object invocations at run time, arranging for the invocation to occur on the object that was referenced. (CORBA is thus the OMG's specification of the ORB and of its associated services.) ORBs can be thought of as switching systems through which invocation messages flow. A fully compliant CORBA implementation supports interoperation of ORBs with one another over TCP connections, using what is called the Internet Inter-ORB Protocol (IIOP) protocol. In such an interoperation mode, any CORBA server can potentially be invoked from any CORBA client, even if the server and client were built and are operated on different versions of the CORBA technology base.

Associated with the ORB are a number of features designed to simplify the life of the developer. An ORB can be programmed to automatically launch a server if it is not running when a client accesses it (this is called factory functionality), and can be asked to automatically filter invocations through user-supplied code that automates the handling of error conditions or the verification of security properties. The ORB can also be programmed to make an intelligent choice of an object if many objects are potentially capable of handling the same request; such a functionality would permit, for example, load-balancing within a group of servers that replicate a particular database.

7.6   Naming Service

A CORBA naming service is used to bind names to objects. Much as a file system is organized as a set of directories, the CORBA naming architecture defines a set of *naming contexts*, and each name is interpreted relative to the naming context within which that name is registered. The CORBA naming architecture is potentially a very general one, but, in practice, many applications are expected to treat it as an object-oriented generalization of a traditional naming hierarchy. Such applications would build hierarchical naming context graphs (directory trees), use ASCII style path names to identify objects, and standardize the sets of attributes stored for each object in the naming service (e.g., size, access time, modification time, owner, permissions, etc.). The architecture, however, is sufficiently flexible to allow a much broader concept of names and naming.

A CORBA name should not be confused with an object reference. In the CORBA architecture, an object reference is essentially a pointer to the object. Although a reference need not include specific location information, it does include enough information for an ORB to find a path to the object, or to an ORB that will know how to reach the object. Names, in contrast, are symbolic ways of naming these references. By analogy to a UNIX file system, a CORBA object name is similar to a path name (and, as with a path name, more than one name can refer to the same object). A CORBA object reference is similar to a UNIX *vnode* reference: a machine address and an identifier for a file *inode* stored on that machine. From the name one can lookup the reference, but this is a potentially costly operation. Given the object reference one can invoke the object, and this (one hopes) will be quite a bit cheaper.

7.7   ENS—The CORBA Event Notification Service

The CORBA Event Notification Service, or ENS, provides for notifications of asynchronous events to applications that register an interest in those events by obtaining a handle, to which events can be posted and on which events can be received. Reliability features are optionally supplied. The ENS is best understood in terms of what is called the *publish/subscribe* communication architecture[1]. In this approach, messages are produced by *publishers* that label each new message using a set of *subjects* or *attributes*. Separately, applications that wish to be informed when events occur on a given subject will *subscribe* to that subject or will poll for messages relating to the subject. The role of the ENS is to reliably bind the publishers to the subscribers, ensuring that even though the publishers do not know who the subscribers will be, and vice versa, messages are promptly and reliably delivered to them. (See Fig. 7.11.)

---

[1]It should be noted, however, that the ENS lacks the sort of subject mapping facilities that are central to many publish-subscribe message-bus architectures, and is in this sense a more primitive facility than some of the message bus technologies that will be discussed later in this book, such as the TIBCO Information Bus (TIB).

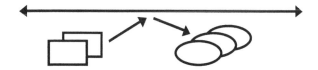

Fig. 7.11 The CORBA ENS is a form of message bus that supports a publish/subscribe architecture. The sources of events (*boxes*) and consumers (*ovals*) need not be explicitly aware of one another, and the sets can change dynamically. A single object can produce or consume events of multiple types, and, in fact, an object can be both producer and consumer

Two examples will make the value of such a model more clear. Suppose that one were using CORBA to implement a software architecture for a large brokerage system or a stock exchange. The ENS for such an environment could be used to broadcast stock trades as they occur. The events in this example would be named using the stock and bond names that they describe. Each broker would subscribe to the stocks of interest, again using these subject names, and the application program would then receive incoming quotes and display them to the screen. Notice that the publisher program can be developed without knowing anything about the nature of the applications that will use the ENS to monitor its outputs: It need not have compatible types or interfaces except with respect to the events that are exchanged between them. And the subscriber, for its part, does not need to be bound to a particular publisher: If a new data source of interest is developed, it can be introduced into the system without changing the existing architecture.

A second example of how the ENS can be useful would arise in system management and monitoring. Suppose that an application is being developed to automate some of the management functions occurring in a VLSI fabrication facility. As time goes by, the developers expect to add more and more sources of information and introduce more and more applications that use this information to increase the efficiency and productivity of the factory. An ENS architecture facilitates doing so, because it permits the developers to separate the *information architecture* of their application from its *implementation architecture*. In such an example, the information architecture is the structure of the ENS event space itself: The subjects under which events may be posted, and the types of event that can arise in each subject. The sources and consumers of the events can be introduced later, and will in general be unaware of one another. Such a design preserves tremendous flexibility and facilitates an evolutionary design for the system. After basic functionality is in place, additional functions can be introduced in a gradual way and without disrupting existing software. Here, the events would be named according to the aspect of factory function to which they relate: status of devices, completion of job steps, scheduled downtime, and so forth. Each application program would subscribe to those classes of events relevant to its task, ignoring all others by not subscribing to them.

Not all CORBA implementations include the ENS—for example, the basic Orbix product described above lacks an ENS, although the Orbix+Isis extension makes use of a technology called the Isis Message Distribution Service to implement ENS functionality in an Orbix setting. This, in turn, was implemented using the Isis Toolkit, which we will discuss in more detail in Chap. 16.

7.8 Life-Cycle Service

The Life-Cycle Service, or LCS, standardizes the facilities for creating and destroying objects, and for copying them or moving them within the system. The service includes a *factory* for manufacturing new objects of a designated type. The Life-Cycle Service is also responsible for scheduling backups, periodically compressing object repositories to reclaim free space, and initiating other life-cycle activities. To some degree, the service can be used to program object-specific management and supervisory functions, which may be important to reliable control of a distributed system.

7.9 Persistent Object Service

The Persistent Object Service, or POS, is the CORBA equivalent of a file system. This service maintains collections of objects for long-term use, organizing them for efficient retrieval and working closely with its clients to give application-specific meanings to the consistency, persistency, and access-control restrictions implemented within the service. This permits the development of special-purpose POSs—for example, to maintain databases with large numbers of nearly identical objects organized into relational tables, as opposed to file system-style storage of very irregular objects.

7.10 Transaction Service

Mentioned earlier, the transaction service is an embedding of database-style transactions into CORBA architecture. If implemented, the service provides a *concurrency control* service for synchronizing the actions of concurrently active transactions; *flat* and (optionally) *nested* transactional tools, and special-purpose persistent object services, which implement the transactional *commit* and *abort* mechanisms. The transaction service is often used with the *relationship service*, which tracks relationships among sets of objects—for example, if they are grouped into a database or some other shared data structure. We looked at the transactional execution model in Sect. 6.6, and return to it in Chap. 20.

7.11 Interobject Broker Protocol

The IOB, or Interobject Broker Protocol, is a protocol by which ORBs can be interconnected. The protocol is intended for use between geographically dispersed ORBs from a single vendor and to permit interoperation between ORBs developed independently by different vendors. The IOB includes definitions of a standard object reference data structure by which an ORB can recognize a foreign object reference and redirect it to the appropriate ORB, as well as definitions of the messages exchanged between ORBs for this purpose. The IOB is defined for use over a TCP channel; should the channel break or not be available at the time a reference is used, the corresponding invocation will return an exception.

7.12   Properties of CORBA Solutions

While the CORBA architecture is impressive in its breadth, the user should not be confused into believing that CORBA therefore embodies solutions for the sorts of problems that were raised in the first chapters of this book. To understand this point, it is important to again stress that CORBA is a somewhat superficial technology in specifying the way things *look* but not *how they should be implemented*. In language terminology, CORBA is concerned with syntax but not semantics. This is a position that the OMG adopted intentionally, and the key players in that organization would certainly defend it. Nonetheless, it is also a potentially troublesome aspect of CORBA, in the sense that a correctly specified CORBA application may still be underspecified (even in terms of the interface to the objects) for purposes of verifying that the objects are used correctly or for predicting the behavior of the application.

Another frequently cited concern about CORBA is that the technology can require extreme sophistication on the part of developers, who must at a minimum understand exactly how the various object classes operate and how memory management will be performed. Lacking such knowledge, which is not an explicit part of the IDL, it may be impossible to use a distributed object efficiently. Even experts complain that CORBA exception handling can be very tricky. Moreover, in very large systems there will often be substantial amounts of old code that must interoperate with new solutions. Telecommunication systems are sometimes said to involve millions or tens of millions of lines of such software, perhaps written in outmoded programming languages or incorporating technologies for which source code is not available. To gain the full benefits of CORBA, however, there is a potential need to use CORBA *throughout* a large distributed environment. This may mean that large amounts of old code must somehow be retrofitted with CORBA interfaces and IDLs—neither a simple nor an inexpensive proposition.

The reliability properties of a particular CORBA environment depend on a great number of implementation decisions that can vary from vendor to vendor and often will do so. Indeed, CORBA is promoted to vendors precisely because it creates a level playing field within which their products can interoperate but compete: The competition would revolve around this issue of relative performance, reliability, or functionality guarantees. Conversely, this implies that individual applications cannot necessarily count upon reliability properties of CORBA if they wish to maintain a high degree of portability: Such applications must in effect assume the least common denominator. Unfortunately, in the CORBA architectural specification this least level of guarantees is quite weak: Invocations and binding requests can fail, perhaps in inconsistent ways, corresponding closely to the failure conditions we identified for RPC protocols that operate over standard communication architectures. Security, being optional, must be assumed not to be present. Thus, CORBA creates a

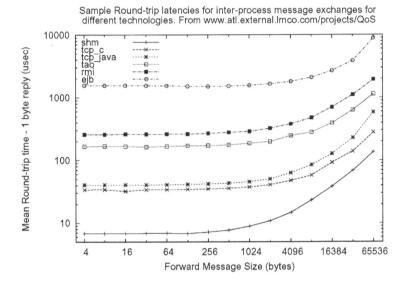

Fig. 7.12 Comparison of round-trip delay when performing a method invocation using a variety of common technologies. The graph is designed to highlight the incremental overheads associated with various technology layerings. As we work our way up to higher and higher levels of abstraction (in this graph, the extreme case is Enterprise Java Beans implemented using Jboss on the TAO CORBA object request broker), we pay higher costs but gain power and flexibility. This graph, and graphs 7.12 and 7.13, were provided by Dr. Gautam Thaker, Lockheed Martin ATL

framework within which reliability technologies can be standardized, but, as currently positioned, the technology base is not necessarily one that will encourage a new wave of reliable computing systems.

7.13   Performance of CORBA and Related Technologies

A large number of middleware, network infrastructure and operating systems choices are available to designers and builders of distributed systems. Yet there are limited data available that permit potential users and researchers to understand actual, measured real-time performance of various technologies. Lockheed Martin Advanced Technology Labs has, over many years, carried out systematic evaluations of operating system determinism, network transport behavior, and middleware performance. The company and the researcher who headed this effort, Dr. Gautam Thaker, have made their findings available to the public and also provided some representative data for use in this textbook.

Thaker's methodology has been, to the extent possible, to use identical test conditions (application, hardware etc.) which permits comparisons to reveal performance differences between various systems. The graph seen in Fig. 7.12 shows measured roundtrip latencies to exchange a "n" byte message between two processes on a 2 node SMP as one progresses from shared memory to TCP (in C and Java), ORB

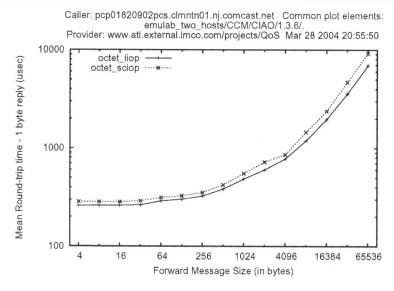

Fig. 7.13 The cost of improved fault-tolerance can be very low. Here we see that the use of STCP, a protocol that maintains duplicate TCP channels to reduce the risk of a lost connection, introduces only a negligible overhead

(TAO), RMI, and EJB. Shared memory communication, as expected, is the fastest means of message exchange as there are no protocol stacks to traverse and speed is dominated by operating system process synchronization efficiency and memcpy speed. However, shared memory architectures are inflexible, and for this reason many systems are built on top of a network transport such as TCP/IP. As we can observe in the graph, moving from shared memory to TCP/IP costs almost an order of magnitude in roundtrip latencies, although the TCP/IP configuration has increased flexibility and generality.

As we move up to higher levels of abstractions, CORBA and RMI, we see the costs associated with the extra software layers required. CORBA and RMI both utilize TCP/IP in the configuration evaluated here. Also, we note that at the TCP/IP level the difference between C and Java implementations is about 10 usec, but that the difference between TAO (an ORB implemented in C) and RMI (implemented in Java) is about 100 usec. Finally, moving to Enterprise Java Beans ("EJB"), the most popular database access technology for Java users (here, the EJB implementation was Jboss 3.2.1) adds almost another order of magnitude delay over RMI. ATL reports that these tradeoffs continue to hold as one moves from two processes on a single node to two processes on two nodes interconnected via a highspeed (100 Mbps) network.

Figure 7.13 compares a CORBA Component Model (CCM) implementation's round-trip latencies using both the TCP/IP based IIOP and SCTP/IP based SCIOP protocols mappings. Here we observe that benefits of SCTP, a specialized version of TCP that provides network fault tolerance by path multiplexing, come with just

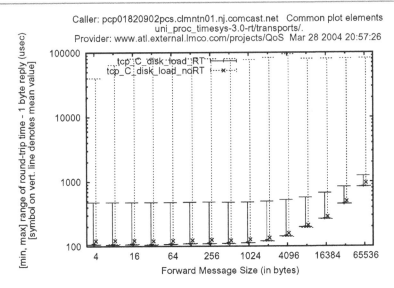

Fig. 7.14 Developers of applications that incorporate some form of responsiveness guarantee need to track not just the average response delay but also the worst case delay. Here we see that when performing method invocations on a machine with some background load (the TCP-C benchmark suite), delays can be very large. Use of an operating system with real-time scheduling capabilities reduces this delay substantially

a slight increase in latency. The ATL site includes similar studies of a great many other TCP variants.

In addition to tests under unloaded conditions, numerous tests were performed with background stress on the system, revealing some surprising problems. An example of this is seen in Fig. 7.14. Knowledge of average latencies is not always good enough. Developers of distributed, real-time, embedded systems often need to anticipate maximum latency values. Figure 7.14 shows range of latencies recorded for TCP/IP based on a Timesys RTOS node in presence of very heavy disk interrupt load. We observe that under these conditions use of real-time support from the underlying operating system makes a crucial difference in holding down the maximum latencies.

Beyond the results summarized in Figs. 7.12–7.14, a large amount of experimental data is available from ATL through a web interface to its web site (www.atl.external.lmco.com/projects/QoS). In most tests a very large number of samples (typically 1 million) were collected. Careful histograms are maintained and the website permits examination of not just the mean latencies but also entire distribution (including the maximum.) Sophisticated "Comparator" utilities (known as "MW_Comparator" and "Jitter Comparator") are available on the website. These permit the viewer to select a subset of collected data and to generate charts that overlay these results for easy visual and tabular comparison.

7.14   Related Reading

On the ANSA project and architecture (see Architecture Projects Management Limited 1989, 1991a, 1991b). Another early effort in the same area was Chronus: (see Gurwitz et al. 1986; Schantz et al. 1986).

On CORBA (see Object Management Group and X/Open 1991). Other publications are available from the Object Management Group, a standards organization; see their Web page, http://www.omg.org.

For the CORBA products cited, such as Orbix, the reader should contact the relevant vendor. Documentation for ACE and TAO, Doug Schmidt's Open Source CORBA platform, can be found at http://www.cs.wustl.edu/~schmidt/; this system is an excellent choice for readers wishing to work with a good quality CORBA implementation on Linux or other popular platforms.

System Support for Fast Client/Server Communication

8

Cloud computing systems put a tremendous amount of stress on network communication paths at every level: from the client over the Internet to the cloud provider's data center, from the point of ingress to the first-tier server that will process the request and compute a response, and internal to the data center as well. In light of this network emphasis, it may seem strange to worry about performance in client–server systems where the client is either one hop from the server or might even be on the same machine. However, it turns out that this critical path is more performance-limiting for cloud computing than any other single element of the data center architecture. Indeed, the success of object oriented systems has led developers to break many kinds of larger applications into "objects" that interact over RPC. Thus the speed of many applications, including modern desktop applications, is often a direct function of the speed of RPC.

Communication-system is typically measured in terms of the latency and throughput for typical messages that traverse that system, starting in a source application and ending at a destination application. Accordingly, these issues have received considerable scrutiny within the operating systems research community, which has developed a series of innovative proposals for improving performance in communication-oriented applications. In the following text, we review some of these proposals.

8.1   Lightweight RPC

The study of RPC performance as a research area surged in 1989 when Shroeder and Burrows undertook to precisely measure the costs associated with RPC on the Firefly operating system (see Shroeder and Burrows 1989). These researchers started by surveying the costs of RPC on a variety of standard platforms. Their results have subsequently become outdated because of advances in systems and processor speeds, but the finding that RPC performance varies enormously even in relative terms probably remains true today. In their study, the range of performance was from 1.1 ms to do a null RPC (equivalent to 4,400 instructions) on the Cedar system,

K.P. Birman, *Guide to Reliable Distributed Systems*, Texts in Computer Science,
DOI 10.1007/978-1-4471-2416-0_8, © Springer-Verlag London Limited 2012

highly optimized for the Dorado multiprocessor, to 78 ms (195,000 instructions) for a very general version of RPC running on a major vendor's top-of-the-line platform (at that time). One interesting finding of this study was that the number of instructions in the RPC code path was often high (the average in the systems they looked at was approximately 6,000 for systems with many limitations and about 140,000 for the most general RPC systems). Thus, faster processors would be expected to have a big impact on RPC performance, which is one of the reasons that the situation has improved somewhat since the time of this study.

Using a bus analyzer to pin down costs to the level of individual machine cycles, this effort led to a tenfold performance improvement in the RPC technology under investigation, which was based originally on the Berkeley UNIX RPC. Among the optimizations that had the biggest impact were the elimination of copying within the application address space by marshalling data directly into the RPC packet using an in-line compilation technique, and the implementation of an RPC fast path, which eliminated all generality in favor of a hand-coded RPC protocol using the fewest instructions possible, subject to the constraint that the normal O/S protection guarantees would be respected.

Soon after this work on Firefly RPC was completed, researchers at the University of Washington became interested in other opportunities to optimize communication paths in modern operating systems. Lightweight RPC originated with the observation that as computing systems adopt RPC-based architectures, the use of RPC in *nondistributed* settings is rising as rapidly as is RPC over a network. Unlike a network, RPC in the nondistributed case can accurately sense many kinds of failures, and because the same physical memory is potentially visible to both sender and destination, the use of shared memory mechanisms represents an appealing option for enhancing performance. Bershad and others set out to optimize this common special case (see Bershad et al. 1989).

A shared memory RPC mechanism typically requires that messages be allocated within pages, starting on page boundaries and with a limit of one message per page. In some cases, the pages used for message passing are from a special pool of memory maintained by the kernel; in others, no such restriction applies but there may be other restrictions, such as limits on passing data structures that contain pointers. When a message is sent, the kernel modifies the page table of the destination to map the page containing the message into the address space of the destination process. Depending on the operating system, the page containing the message may be mapped out of the memory of the sender, modified to point to an empty page, or marked as read-only. In this last approach (where the page is marked as read-only) some systems will trap write-faults and make a private copy if either process attempts a modification. This method is called "copy on write," and was first supported in the Mach microkernel (see Rashid 1986).

If one studies the overheads associated with RPC in the local, shared memory case, the cost of manipulating the page tables of the sender and destination and of context switching between the sending and receiving processes emerges as a major factor. The University of Washington team focused on this problem in developing what they called a *Lightweight Remote Procedure Call* facility (LRPC). In essence, this approach reduces time for local RPC both by exploiting shared memory and by avoiding excess context switches. Specifically, the messages containing the RPC arguments are placed in shared memory, while the invocation itself is done by changing the current page table and flushing the TLB so that the destination process is essentially invoked in coroutine style, with the lowest overhead possible given that virtual memory is in use on the machine. The reply from the destination process is similarly implemented as a direct context switch back to the sender process.

Although LRPC may appear to be as costly as normal RPC in the local case, the approach actually achieves substantial savings. First, a normal RPC is implemented by having the client program perform a message send followed by a separate message receive operation, which blocks. Thus, two system calls occur, with the message itself being copied into the kernel's data space, or (if shared memory is exploited) a message descriptor being constructed in the kernel's data space. Meanwhile, the destination process will have issued a receive request and would often be in a blocked state. The arrival of the message makes the destination process runnable, and on a uniprocessor this creates a scheduling decision, since the sender process is also runnable in the first stage of the algorithm (when it has sent its request and not yet performed the subsequent receive operation). Thus, although the user might expect the sender to issue its two system calls and then block, causing the scheduler to run and activate the destination process, other sequences are possible. If the scheduler runs right after the initial send operation, it could context switch to the RPC server leaving the client runnable. It is now possible that a context switch back to the client will occur, and then back to the server again, before the server replies. The same sequence may then occur when the reply is finally sent.

We thus see that a conventional operating system requires four system calls to implement an LRPC operation, and that although a minimum of two context switches must occur, it is easily possible for an additional two context switches to take place. If the execution of the operating system scheduler represents a significant cost, the scheduler may run two or more times more than the minimum. All of these excess operations are potentially costly.

LRPC is implemented using a special system call whereby the client process combines its send and receive operations into a single request, and the server (which will normally delay waiting for a new RPC request after replying to the client) issues the reply and subsequent receive as a single request. Moreover, execution of the scheduler is completely bypassed.

As in the case of RPC, the actual performance figures for LRPC are of limited value because processor speeds and architectures have been evolving so rapidly. One can get a sense of the improvement by looking at the number of instructions required to perform an LRPC. Recall that the Shroeder and Burrows study had found that thousands of instructions were required to issue an RPC. In contrast, the LRPC team calculated that only a few hundred instructions are required to perform an LRPC—a small enough number to make such factors as TLB misses (caused when the hardware cache associated with the virtual memory mapping system is flushed) emerge as important determinants of performance. LRPC was, in any case, somewhat more expensive than the theoretical minimum: about 50 percent slower measured in terms of round-trip latency or instructions executed for a null procedure call. Nonetheless, this represents a factor of at least five when compared to the performance of typical RPC in the local case, and ten or more when the approach is compared to the performance of a fairly heavyweight vendor supported RPC package.

This effect is so dramatic that some operating systems vendors began to support LRPC immediately after the work was first reported. Others limited themselves to fine-tuning their existing implementations or improving the hardware used to connect their processors to the network. At the time of this writing, RPC performances have improved somewhat, but faster processors are no longer bringing commensurate improvements in RPC performance. Vendors tend to point out that RPC performance, by itself, is only one of many factors that enter into overall system performance, and that optimizing this one case to an excessive degree can bring diminishing returns. They also argue for generality even in the local case: that LRPC is undesirable because it requires a different RPC implementation than the remote case and thus increases the complexity of the operating system for a scenario that may not be as common in commercial computing settings as it seems to be in academic research laboratories.

To some degree, these points are undoubtedly valid ones: When an RPC arrives at a server, the program that will handle it may need to be scheduled, it may experience page faults, buffering and caching issues can severely impact its performance, and so forth. On the other hand, the performance of a null RPC or LRPC is entirely a measure of operating system overhead, and hence is wasted time by any reasonable definition. Moreover, the insights gained in LRPC are potentially applicable to other parts of the operating system: Bershad, for example, demonstrated that the same idea can be generalized using a concept of *thread activations* and *continuations*, with similarly dramatic impact on other aspects of operating system performance (see Bershad et al. 1989, 1995). This work seems not to have impacted the commercial operating systems community, at least at the time of this writing.

8.2   fbufs and the *x*-Kernel Project

During the same period, the University of Arizona, under Larry Peterson, developed a series of innovative operating system extensions for high-performance communication. Most relevant to the topic of this chapter are the *x*-Kernel, a stand-alone operating system for developing high speed communication protocols, and the *fbufs* architecture (see Drushel and Peterson 1993), which is a general-purpose technique for optimizing stack-structured protocols to achieve high performance. While these extensions were developed based on the context of a particular operating system, but they are potentially applicable to most standard vendor-supported operating systems.

The *x*-Kernel (see Peterson et al. 1989b) is an operating system dedicated to the implementation of network protocols for experimental research on performance, flow control, and other issues. The assumption that *x*-Kernel applications are purely

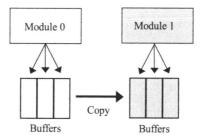

Fig. 8.1 In a conventional layered architecture, as messages pass from layer to layer (here shown from left to right), messages and headers may need to be copied repeatedly. This contributes to high overhead. In this illustration, the white and gray buffers are independent regions in virtual memory

communication-oriented greatly simplified the operating system design, which confines itself to addressing those issues encountered in the implementation of protocols, while omitting support for elaborate virtual memory mechanisms, special-purpose file systems, and many of the other operating facilities that are considered mandatory in modern computing environments.

Recall from the early chapters of this book that many protocols have a layered structure, with the different layers having responsibility for different aspects of the overall communication abstraction. In *x*-Kernel, protocols having a layered structure are represented as a partially ordered graph of modules. The application process involves a protocol by issuing a procedure call to one of the root nodes in such a graph, and control then flows down the graph as the message is passed from layer to layer. *x*-Kernel includes built-in mechanisms for efficiently representing messages and managing their headers and for dynamically restructuring the protocol graph or the route that an individual message will take, depending upon the state of the protocols involved and the nature of the message. Other *x*-Kernel features include a thread-based execution model, memory management tools, and timer mechanisms.

Using the *x*-Kernel, Peterson implemented several standard RPC and stream protocols, demonstrating that his architecture was indeed powerful enough to permit a variety of such protocols to co-exist and confirming its value as an experimental tool. Layered protocol architectures are often thought to be inefficient, but Peterson suggested a number of design practices that, in his experience, avoided overhead and permitted highly modular protocol implementations to perform as well as the original monolithic protocols on which his work was based. Later, researchers such as Tennenhouse confirmed that standard implementations of layered protocols, particularly in the UNIX stream architecture, have potentially high overheads, but also that appropriate design techniques can be used to greatly reduce these costs.

Peterson's interest in layered protocols subsequently led him to look at performance issues associated with layered or pipelined architectures, in which modules of a protocol operate in protected memory regions (Fig. 8.1). To a limited degree, systems such as UNIX and NT have an architecture similar to this—UNIX streams, for example, are based on a modular architecture, which is supported directly within the

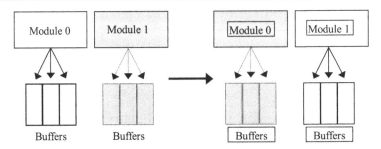

Fig. 8.2 In Peterson's scheme, the buffers are in fact shared using virtual memory, exploiting protection features to avoid risk of corruption. To pass a buffer, access to it is enabled in the destination address space and disabled in the sender's address space. (In the figure, the *white buffers* represent real pointers and the *gray* ones represent invalid page-table entries pointing to the same memory regions but with access disabled.) When the buffer finally reaches the last module in the pipeline, it is freed and reallocated for a new message arriving from the left. Such an approach reduces the overhead of layering to the costs associated with manipulation of the page table entries associated with the modules comprising the pipeline

kernel. As an example, an incoming message is passed up a stack that starts with the device driver and then includes each of the stream modules that have been pushed onto the stream connection, terminating finally in a cross-address space transfer of control to the application program. UNIX programmers think of such a structure as a form of pipe implemented directly in the kernel. Unfortunately, like a pipe, a stream can involve significant overhead.

Peterson's *fbufs* architecture focuses on the handling of memory in pipelined operating systems contexts such as these. An *fbuf* is a memory buffer for use by a protocol; it will typically contain a message or a header for a message. The architecture concerns itself with the issue of mapping such a buffer into the successive address spaces within which it will be accessed and with the protection problems that arise if modules are to be restricted so that they can only operate on data that they own. The basic approach is to cache memory bindings, so that a protocol stack that is used repeatedly can reuse the same memory mappings for each message in a stream of messages. Ideally, the cost of moving a packet from one address space to another can be reduced to the flipping of a protection bit in the address space mappings of the sending and receiving modules (Fig. 8.2). The method completely eliminates copying, while retaining a fairly standard operating system structure and protection boundaries.

8.3   Active Messages

At the University of California, Berkeley, and Cornell University, researchers explored techniques for fast message passing in parallel computing systems. Culler and von Eicken observed that operating system overheads are the dominant source of overhead in message-oriented parallel computing systems (see Thekkath and

Levy 1993; von Eicken et al. 1992). Their work resulted in an extremely aggressive attack on communication costs, in which the application interacts directly with an I/O device and the overhead for sending or receiving a message can be reduced to as little as a few instructions. The CPU and latency overhead of an operating system is slashed in this manner, with important impact on the performance of parallel applications. Moreover, as we will see, similar ideas can be implemented in general-purpose operating systems.

An *active message* is a type of message generated within a parallel application that takes advantage of knowledge that the program running on the destination node of a parallel computer is precisely the same as the program on the source node to obtain substantial performance enhancements. In this approach, the sender is able to anticipate much of the work that the destination node would normally have to do if the source and destination were written to run on general-purpose operating systems. Moreover, because the source and destination are the same program, the compiler can effectively short circuit much of the work and overhead associated with mechanisms for general-purpose message generation and for dealing with heterogeneous architectures. Finally, because the communication hardware in parallel computers does not lose messages, active messages are designed for a world in which message loss and processor failure do not occur.

The basic approach is as follows. The sender of a message generates the message in a format that is preagreed between the sender and destination. Because the destination is running the same program as the sender and is running on the same hardware architecture, such a message will be directly interpretable by the destination without any of the overhead for describing data types and layout that one sees in normal RPC environments. Moreover, the sender places the address of a handler for this particular class of message into the header of the message—that is, a program running on machine A places an address of a handler that resides within machine B directly into the message. On the reception machine, as the message is copied out of the network interface, its first bytes are already sufficient to transfer control to a handler compiled specifically to receive messages of this type. This reduces the overhead of communication from the tens of thousands of instructions common on general-purpose machines to as few as five to ten instructions. In effect, the sender is able to issue a procedure call directly into the code of the destination process, with most of the overhead associated with triggering an interrupt on the destination machine and with copying data into the network on the sending side and out of the network on the receiving side. In some situations (e.g., when the destination node is idle and waiting for an incoming request) even the interrupt can be eliminated by having the destination wait in a tight polling loop.

Obviously, active messages make sense only if a single application is loaded onto multiple nodes of a parallel computer and hence has complete trust in those programs and accurate knowledge of the memory layout of the nodes with which it communicates. In practice, the types of system that use the approach normally have identical programs running on each node. One node is selected as the master and controls the computation, while the other nodes, its slaves, take actions on the orders of the master. The actual programming model visible to the user is one

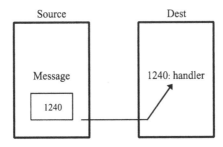

Fig. 8.3 An active message includes the address of the handler to which it should be passed directly in the message header. In contrast with a traditional message-passing architecture, in which such a message would be copied repeatedly through successively lower layers of the operating system, an active message is copied directly into the network adapter by the procedure that generates it in the application program. It is effectively transferred directly to the application-layer handler on the receiving side with no additional copying. Such a zero copy approach reduces communication latencies to a bare minimum and eliminates almost all overhead on the messages themselves. However, it also requires a high level of mutual trust and knowledge between source and destination, a condition that is more typical of parallel supercomputing applications than general distributed programs

in which a sequential program initiates parallel actions by invoking parallel operations, or procedures, which have been programmed to distribute work among the slaves and then to wait for them to finish computing before taking the next step. This model is naturally matched to active messages, which can now be viewed as optimizing normal message passing to take advantage of the huge amount of detailed information available to the system regarding the way that messages will be handled. In these systems, there is no need for generality, and generality proves to be expensive. Active messages are a general way of optimizing to extract the maximum performance from the hardware by exploiting this prior knowledge. (See Fig. 8.3.)

Active messages are useful in support of many programming constructs. The approach can be exploited to build extremely inexpensive RPC interactions, but is also applicable to direct language support for data replication or parallel algorithms in which data or computation is distributed over the modes of a parallel processor. (See Fig. 8.4) Culler and von Eicken have explored a number of such options and reported particular success with language-based embedding of active messages within a parallel version of the C programming language they call "split C," and in a data-parallel language called ID-90.

8.4   Beyond Active Messages: U-Net and the Virtual Interface Architecture (VIA)

At Cornell University, von Eicken continued the work begun in his study of active messages, looking for ways of applying the same optimizations in general-purpose operating systems connected to shared communication devices. U-Net is a communication architecture designed for use within a standard operating system such

Master

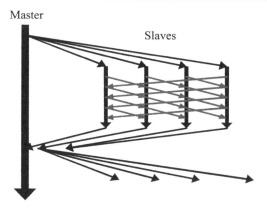

Slaves

Fig. 8.4 A typical parallel program employs a sequential master thread of control, which initiates parallel actions on slave processors and waits for them to complete before starting the next computational step. While computing, the slave nodes may exchange messages, but this too tends to be both regular and predictable. Such applications match closely with the approach to communication used in active messages, which trades generality for low overhead and simplicity

as UNIX or NT; it is intended to provide the standard protection guarantees taken for granted in these sorts of operating systems (see von Eicken et al. 1995). These guarantees are provided, however, in a way that imposes extremely little overhead relative to the performance that can be attained in a dedicated application that has direct control over the communication device interface. U-Net gains this performance using an implementation that is split between traditional software functionality integrated into the device driver and nontraditional functionality implemented directly within the communication controller interfaced to the communication device. Most controllers are programmable—hence, the approach is more general than it may sound, although it should also be acknowledged that existing systems very rarely reprogram the firmware of device controllers to gain performance!

The U-Net system (see Fig. 8.5) starts with an observation we have made repeatedly in prior chapters, namely that the multiple layers of protocols and operating system software between the application and the communication wire represent a tremendous barrier to performance, impacting both latency and throughput. U-Net overcomes these costs by restructuring the core operating system layers that handle such communication so that channel setup and control functions can operate out of band, while the application interacts directly with the device itself. Such a direct path results in minimal latency for the transfer of data from source to destination, but it raises significant protection concerns: If an application can interact directly with the device, there is no obvious reason that it will not be able to subvert the interface to violate the protection on memory controlled by other applications or break into communication channels that share the device but were established for other purposes.

The U-Net architecture is based on a concept of a *communication segment*, which is a region of memory shared between the device controller and the application program. Each application is assigned a set of pages within the segment for use in

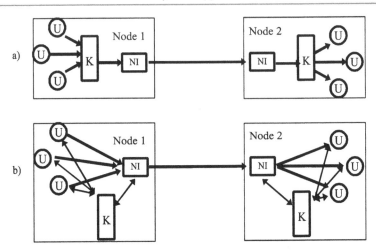

Fig. 8.5 In a conventional communication architecture, all messages pass through the kernel before reaching the I/O device (**a**), resulting in high overheads. U-Net bypasses the kernel for I/O operations (**b**), while preserving a standard protection model

sending and receiving messages, and is prevented from accessing pages not belonging to it. Associated with the application are three queues: one pointing to received messages, one to outgoing messages, and one to free memory regions. Objects in the communication segment are of fixed size, simplifying the architecture at the cost of a small amount of overhead. (See Fig. 8.6.)

Each of these communication structures is bound to a U-Net channel, which is a communication session for which permissions have been validated, linking a known source to a known destination over an established communication channel. The application process plays no role in specifying the hardware communication channels to which its messages will be sent: It is restricted to writing in memory buffers that have been allocated for its use and update the send, receive, and free queue appropriately. These restrictions are the basis of the U-Net protection guarantees cited earlier.

U-Net maps the communication segment of a process directly into its address space, pinning the pages into physical memory and disabling the hardware caching mechanisms so that updates to a segment will be applied directly to that segment. The set of communication segments for all the processes using U-Net is mapped to be visible to the device controller over the I/O bus of the processor used; the controller can thus initiate DMA or direct memory transfers in and out of the shared region as needed and without delaying any setup. A limitation of this approach is that the I/O bus is a scarce resource shared by all devices on a system, and the U-Net mapping excludes any other possible mapping for this region. However, on some machines (e.g., cluster-style multiprocessors), there are no other devices contending for this mapping unit, and dedicating it to the use of the communication subsystem makes perfect sense.

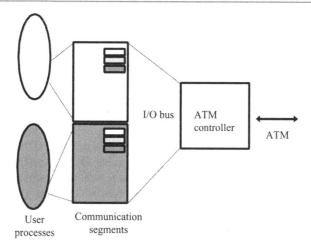

I/O bus

ATM
controller

ATM

User
processes

Communication
segments

Fig. 8.6 U-Net shared memory architecture permits the device controller to directly map a communication region shared with each user process. The send, receive and free message queues are at known offsets within the region. The architecture provides strong protection guarantees and yet slashes the latency and CPU overheads associated with communication. In this approach, the kernel assists in setup of the segments but is not interposed on the actual I/O path used for communication once the segments are established

The communication segment is directly monitored by the device controller. U-Net accomplishes this by reprogramming the device controller, although it is also possible to imagine an implementation in which a kernel driver would provide this functionality. The controller watches for outgoing messages on the send queue; if one is present, it immediately sends the message. The delay between when a message is placed on the send queue and when sending starts is never larger than a few microseconds. Incoming messages are automatically placed on the receive queue unless the pool of memory is exhausted; should that occur, any incoming messages are discarded silently. Specifically, U-Net was implemented using an ATM network controller. With this device, it only needs to look at the first bytes of the incoming message, which give the ATM channel number on which it was transmitted (this could just as easily be a MAC address in the case of Ethernet). These are used to index into a table maintained within the device controller that gives the range of addresses within which the communication segment can be found, and the head of the receive and free queues are then located at a fixed offset from the base of the segment. To minimize latency, the addresses of a few free memory regions are cached in the device controller's memory.

Such an approach may seem complex because of the need to reprogram the device controller. In fact, however, the concept of a programmable device controller is a very old one (IBM's channel architecture for the 370 series of computers already supported a similar programmable channel architecture nearly 20 years ago). Programmability such as this remains fairly common, and device drivers that download code into controllers are not unheard of today. Thus, although unconventional, the U-Net approach is not actually unreasonable. The style of programming required is similar to that used when implementing a device driver for use in a conventional operating system.

With this architecture, U-Net achieves impressive application-to-application performance. The technology easily saturates an ATM interface operating at the OC3 performance level of 155 MB/sec, and measured end-to-end latencies through a single ATM switch are as low as 26 µs for a small message. These performance levels are also reflected in higher-level protocols: Versions of UDP and TCP have been layered over U-Net and shown capable of saturating the ATM for packet sizes as low as 1 KB; similar performance is achieved with a standard UDP or TCP technology only for very large packets of 8 KB or more. Overall, performance of the approach tends to be an order of magnitude or more better than with a conventional architecture for all metrics not limited by the raw bandwidth of the ATM: throughput for small packets, latency, and computational overhead of communication. Such results emphasize the importance of rethinking standard operating system structures in light of the extremely high performance that modern computing platforms can achieve.

Vendors saw these numbers and became very interested in doing something comparable in commodity operating systems. As a result, an initiative called the VIA (Virtual Interface Architecture) effort was launched, eventually resulting in a U-Net like technology that can be hidden under conventional interfaces such as Unix or Windows sockets (although Winsock Direct, as the latter is known, loses some of the performance benefits of VIA). VIA operates today over many faster technologies, such as Infiniband, gigabit Ethernet, and fiber switches; an evaluation of the performance of the standard can be found in Liu (1998). This is a good example of a successful transition of a clever idea from research into mainstream products!

Returning to the point made at the beginning of this chapter, a technology such as U-Net also improves the statistical properties of the communication channel. There are fewer places at which messages can be lost; hence reliability increases and, in well-designed applications, may approach perfect reliability. The complexity of the hands-off mechanisms employed as messages pass from application to controller to ATM and back up to the receiver is greatly reduced—hence, the measured latencies are much tighter than in a conventional environment, where dozens of events could contribute towards variation in latency. Overall, then, U-Net is not just a higher-performance communication architecture; it is also one that is more conducive to the support of extremely reliable distributed software.

8.5   Asynchronous I/O APIs

Modern operating systems that seek to exploit some of the opportunities we've described face a problem: the cost of a system call can be high enough so that even performing a single system call per message sent and received can become a performance-limiting factor. Yet attempts to eliminate this bottleneck run up against standardization: so much code has been developed over so many years against today's standard network systems-call API that introducing a new API can be impractical. Users resist departing from the standards.

Handling of the resulting tension depends very much on the platform. In Microsoft's Windows system, the most popular approach has been to encourage developers to issue *asynchronous* I/O requests by posting message read requests and message sends in batches, arranging for the operating system to notify the application (via delivery of some form of *event upcall*, similar to the way mouse clicks are reported in a graphical GUI). This way, the application can preprovision the communication layer with large numbers of buffers and if a burst of messages arrives, the O/S can potentially deliver all of them via a single event. However, users who want to be certain that their code will port to other platforms, such as Linux, can use a more stanfard Windows version of the UNIX Socket library, called WinSock.

Linux approaches the same issue quite differently. In this and other UNIX-based operating systems, asynchronous I/O system calls are an option but are not widely popular. More common is a style of event loop in which the application places I/O sockets into non-blocking mode, then uses the `select` system call to wait until incoming packets arrive, or perhaps (if the application does both input and output), until some form of I/O is possible. Then the application will loop rapidly, doing a series of socket operations, until one of them fails, returning an EWOULDBLOCK error code. The application can then process the batch of received messages.

With modern multicore machines, a third style of application has emerged, in which separate threads are dedicated to doing receive and send operations, coupled to the threads that process data by bounded buffers; the I/O threads would generally run at high priority and in a blocking mode, potentially combining this with the multiple buffers at a time approach mentioned earlier.

None of these three options achieves the highest data rates, but they have the benefit of greater portability from platform to platform. However, they do bring considerable complexity. Accordingly, modern communication platforms such as the Isis[2] system of Appendix B often implement specialized libraries that embody all the needed logic, perhaps together with additional code to handle application-specific flow control, loss recovery, security, or other functionality. Developers who work directly with the network socket layer are thus an increasingly rare community, somewhat like those who prefer to build low-level compute loops directly in assembler language.

8.6   Related Reading

For work on kernel and microkernel architectures for high-speed communication: Amoeba (see Mullender et al. 1990; van Renesse et al. 1988, 1989), Chorus (see Armand et al. 1989; Rozier et al. 1988a, 1988b), Mach (see Rashid 1986), QNX (see Hildebrand 1992), Sprite (see Ousterhout et al. 1988).

Issues associated with the performance of threads are treated in Anderson et al. (1995).

Packet filters are discussed in the context of Mach in Mogul et al. (1987).

The classic paper on RPC cost analysis is Shroeder and Burrows (1989), but see also Clark and Tennenhouse (1987, 1990).

TCP cost analysis and optimizations are presented in Clark et al. (1989), Jacobson (1988, 1990).

Lightweight RPC is treated in Bershad et al. (1989).

Active Messages are covered in Thekkath and Levy (1993), von Eicken et al. (1992), and U-Net is discussed in von Eicken et al. (1995). An evaluation of VIA, the industry standard "Virtual Interface Architecture" based on the U-Net architecture, can be found in Liu et al. (1999).

Fbufs and the *x*-Kernel are discussed in Abbott and Peterson (1993), Drushel and Peterson (1993), Peterson et al. (1989b). A really interesting piece of follow-on work is the I/O Lite system described in Pai et al. (1999). This system implements an exceptionally efficient framework for building applications that make extensive use of message-passing.

An architecture for building very high speed Web servers and other event-driven systems is discussed in Welsh et al. (2001). Called SEDA, the approach is offered by Welsh as an alternative to extensive multi-threading and has been controversial because it requires a change in programming style on the part of developers.

Part II
Reliable Distributed Computing

In this second part of the book, we ask how distributed computing systems can be made reliable—a question motivated by our review of servers used in Web settings, but that also tries to generalize beyond the ways that today's cloud platforms implement reliability, so that what we learn might also apply to future web services that may be introduced by developers of new classes of critical distributed computing applications down the road. Our focus is on communication technologies, but we do review persistent (durable) storage technologies based on the transactional computing model, particularly as generalized to apply to objects in distributed environments. Our goals here will be to develop the core mechanisms needed; the third and final part of the book applies these mechanisms to Web Services and explores some related topics.

Earlier, we talked about the sense in which the cloud, as architected today, often makes a deliberate decision to weaken properties in order to guarantee snappy response. As we will see, the underlying tension involves the costs of reliability for a distributed application. To offer strong guarantees, such as the forms of consistency that Brewer's CAP conjecture talks about, a distributed system sometimes needs to pause while it repairs damage done by a failure. For example, if it senses that a message was lost, the system might delay subsequent updates until the missing message has been recovered through retransmissions and applied to the system state in the right order. If a server crashes, the system might pause briefly to clean up anything it was doing just at that instant, for example by rolling back a partially completed update to the service state, or by completing a multicast if the crash happened just as the multicast was being sent. These events can slow responsiveness: they put the reliability property ahead of speed of response, if you want to think about the prioritization of goals that they implicitly reflect.

Even from these simple cases we see that when a system makes promises, it also accepts obligations that can involve delayed responses. In the cloud, where fast local response is key to scalability, we can turn this around by saying that the forms of reliability meaningful in cloud services will often be limited to those that can be achieved without delay. Which properties fall into this class?

It turns out that we will be able to say a great deal about such questions. Reliable distributed computing is a much-studied topic, and while the cloud brings new challenges such as guaranteeing stability even at large scale, as the saying goes, "plus ça change; plus c'est lá meme chose". We will find that the new issues posed by the cloud do not change the foundational principles. Moreover, while not all forms of reliability scale well enough to use casually in the cloud, some consistency and reliability models We do not have all the answers yet, but can already be sure that any future science of reliable cloud computing will be an outgrowth from the more basic science of reliable distributed computing.

How and Why Computer Systems Fail

Before jumping into the question of how to make systems reliable, it will be useful to briefly understand the reasons that distributed systems fail. Although there are some widely cited studies of the consequences of failures (see, for example, Peterson 1995), causes of failure are a murkier topic. Our treatment here draws primarily from work by Jim Gray (see Gray 1990; Gray and Reuter 1993; Gray et al. 1987, 1996), who studied the question of *why* systems fail while he was working at Tandem Computers, and on presentations by Anita Borr (see Borr and Wilhelmy 1994), Joel Bartlett, a developer of Tandem's transactional system architecture (see Bartlett 1981), and Ram Chilaragee, who has studied the same question at IBM (see Chilaragee 1994). These are all fairly old papers, and one might reasonably ask if they still apply in the cloud, especially because these studies were done before strongly typed languages like Java and C# entered into widespread use; obviously, with better languages, we write better programs. Moreover, all three researchers focused on systems designed to be as robust as possible and might have drawn different conclusions had they looked at large distributed systems that incorporate technologies built with less-stringent reliability standards. To this authors's knowledge, nobody has done the sorts of updated studies of failure rates and causes that might shed light on what happens in modern cloud platforms.

Further complicating the picture, as we've seen, not only are today's cloud systems typically engineered with strong forms of reliability as a secondary goal, but they even view failure as a kind of feature, for example by literally pulling the plug on a first-tier cloud component as a part of an elasticity event, or when something might be malfunctioning. For example, many cloud platforms have a built-in cycle in which they monitor response times for important services and, if something seems slow, reboot the node or even reimage the node, and then finally take it out of service. From the perspective of the end-user, these events look like failures! The thinking is as follows: if a node is malfunctioning and we ask it to cleanup or to otherwise participate in a self-diagnostic process, we may have a long wait, and might not be able to trust it to do what we've requested. Meanwhile, as noted in Chap. 5, the cloud has many stateless components that can be shut down rather casually. Given this, it can be simpler and also safer to just kill the malfunctioning compo-

K.P. Birman, *Guide to Reliable Distributed Systems*, Texts in Computer Science, DOI 10.1007/978-1-4471-2416-0_9, © Springer-Verlag London Limited 2012

nent (if, indeed, it is malfunctioning) and then to launch a new, healthy copy. The upshot is that cloud platforms kill nodes with abandon. Thus, we know surprisingly little about the ways that cloud systems fail, although we do know that failure has become a very common event in the modern cloud; in many ways, a design element.

The situation on an end-user platform is quite different. In principle, the client runs relatively well-tested software, written in modern languages, and should be quite reliable in ways that the cloud might not be. Cloud platforms are also under more stress than client systems, most of the time. Yet client systems are sometimes under attack by viruses, and struggle with mobility that can cut the client off from needed services. Moreover, client systems deal with such issues as environmental problems (heat, humidity, being dropped), and might not be properly configured. The implications of all this haven't been carefully investigated, but must be very significant in terms of overall reliability for modern cloud applications.

9.1   Hardware Reliability and Trends

Hardware failures were a dominant consideration in architecting reliable systems until late in the 1980s. Hardware can fail in many ways, but as electronic packaging has improved and the density of integrated circuits increased, hardware reliability has grown enormously. This improved reliability reflects the decreased heat production and power consumption of smaller circuits, the reduction in the number of off-chip connections and wiring, and improved manufacturing techniques. A consequence is that hardware-related system downtime is fast becoming a minor component of the overall reliability concerns faced in a large, complex distributed system. Obviously, hardware failure does remain a factor, particularly on small handheld devices, devices dependent upon battery power, and laptop or desktop computers, all of which tend to be treated more roughly than servers. However, the frequency of hardware failures is down across the board, and dramatically so on server platforms.

To the degree that hardware failures remain a significant reliability concern today, the observed problems are most often associated with the intrinsic limitations of connectors and mechanical devices, especially when operated in humid or hot conditions, or in settings where mechanical shocks and environment interference can be significant effects. Thus, computer network problems (manifested through message loss or partitioning failures, where a component of the system becomes disconnected from some other component) are high on the list of hardware-related causes of failure for any modern system. Disk failures are also a leading cause of downtime in systems dependent upon large file or database servers, although RAID-style disk arrays can protect against such problems to a considerable degree. Of course, even RAID disks fail (rather often because of foolish repair mistakes, such as pulling the wrong module when servicing a RAID unit that has experienced a single failure). Disk failures of all kinds are down by at least an order of magnitude compared with the situation seen in the 1980s.

A common hardware-related source of downtime has very little to do with failures, although it can seriously impact system availability and perceived reliability. Any critical computing system will, over its life cycle, live through a series of hardware generations. These can force upgrades, because it may become costly and impractical to maintain old generations of hardware. Thus, routine maintenance and downtime for replacement of computing and storage components with more modern versions must be viewed as a planned activity that can emerge as one of the more serious sources of system unavailability if not dealt with through a software architecture that can accommodate dynamic reconfiguration of critical parts of the system while the remainder of the system remains on-line. This issue of planning for future upgrading, expansion, and for new versions of components extends throughout a complex system, encompassing all its hardware and software technologies.

9.2   Software Reliability and Trends

It is common to say that software reliability is best understood as a process, encompassing not just the freedom of a system from software bugs, but also such issues as the software design methodology, the testing and life-cycle quality assurance process used, the quality of self-checking mechanisms and of user interfaces, the degree to which the system implements the intended application (i.e., the quality of match between system specification and problem specification), and the mechanisms provided for dealing with anticipated failures, maintenance, and upgrades. This represents a rich, multidimensional collection of issues, and few critical systems deal with them as effectively as one might wish. Software developers, in particular, often view software reliability in simplified terms, focusing exclusively on the software specification that their code must implement and on its correctness with regard to that specification.

This narrower issue of correctness remains an important challenge; indeed, many studies of system downtime in critical applications have demonstrated that even after rigorous testing, software bugs account for a substantial fraction of unplanned downtime (figures in the range of 25 percent to 35 percent are common), and that this number is extremely hard to reduce (see, for example, Peterson 1995). Jim Gray and Bruce Lindsey, who studied reliability issues in transactional settings, once suggested that the residual software bugs in mature systems can be classified into two categories, which they called *Bohrbugs* and *Heisenbugs* (see Gray and Reuter 1993; Gray et al. 1987, 1996). (See Fig. 9.1.)

A Bohrbug is a solid, reproducible problem: If it occurs, and one takes note of the circumstances, the scenario can be reproduced and the bug will repeat itself. The name is intended to remind us of Bohr's model of the atomic nucleus: a small hard object, well localized in space. Bruce Lindsey used to comment that the whole point is that Bohrbugs are boring: you simply run the program again and again and the problem always repeats, until you've found it and fixed it. Gray and Lindsey found that as systems mature, the relative frequency of Bohrbugs drops steadily over time, although other studies (notably by Anita Borr) suggest that the population of Bohrbugs is periodically replenished when a system must be upgraded or maintained over its life cycle.

Fig. 9.1 Developers are likely to discover and fix Bohrbugs, which are easily localized and reproducible sources of errors. Heisenbugs are fuzzy and hard to pin down. Often, these bugs are actually symptoms of some other problem that occurs while the program is running, but doesn't cause an immediate crash; the developer will tend to work around them but may find them extremely hard to fix in a convincing way. The frequency of such bugs diminishes very slowly over the life cycle of an application

Heisenbugs are named for the Heisenberg model of the nucleus: a complex wave function that is influenced by the act of observation. They seem to wiggle around, are very hard to localize or reliably reproduce, and for this reason, are very hard to fix. These bugs are typically associated with concurrency, and may be side-effects of problems that occurred much earlier in an execution, such as overrunning an array or accidentally dereferencing a pointer after the object to which it points has been freed. Such errors can corrupt the application in a way that will cause it to crash, but not until the corrupted data structure is finally referenced, which may not occur until long after the bug actually was exercised. Because such a bug is typically a symptom of the underlying problem, rather than an instance of the true problem itself, Heisenbugs are exquisitely sensitive to the order of execution. Even with identical inputs, a program that crashed once may run correctly back in the laboratory.

Not surprisingly, the major source of crashes in a mature software system turns out to be Heisenbugs. Anita Borr's work actually goes further, finding that most attempts to fix Heisenbugs actually make the situation worse than it was in the first place. This observation is not surprising to engineers of complex, large software systems: Heisenbugs correspond to problems that can be tremendously hard to track down, and are often fixed by patching around them at run time. Nowhere is the gap between theory and practice in reliable computing more apparent than in the final testing and bug correction stages of a major software deployment that must occur under time pressure or a deadline.

Better programming languages can help, although language evolution in some ways lives in tension relative to the parallel evolution of the runtime environment. Starting with the introduction of Java and now continuing with languages like C#, for the first time we are seeing large numbers of programmers moving towards languages that enforce strong type-checking, automatically handle garbage collection, and will detect and flag problematic control structures and other possible signs of mistakes. Yet we are also seeing widespread adoption of multicore hardware, which can push developers towards multithreaded software designs that can be very hard to get right. Computing platforms like J2EE and .NET reach beyond the individual application by tracking dependencies upon specific versions of external services and libraries, and at runtime will enforce these dependencies. Runtime monitoring and debugging tools have taken enormous steps forward (earlier, we mentioned that Microsoft's Visual Studio .NET is an especially good example, but there are many such systems, manufactured by dozens of vendors). All of these steps really can help, yet those underlying trends towards more sophisticated hardware and multicore application designs hurt, from a reliability perspective.

Moreover, even the best languages only go so far. It is not particularly hard to make mistakes in Java or C#, or to trigger an unrecoverable runtime exception. An infinite loop is still an error, no matter what the language, and object-oriented languages bring problems of their own, such as challenges in simply making a copy of an object. As programmers familiar with these languages rapidly learn, a deep copy is made by copying the object and all other objects to which it is linked, recursively, while a shallow copy retains linked-to objects, with the effect that a single physical object may now be accessed by multiple paths, possibly including some unintended ones. In today's object oriented systems, code paths that incorrectly create shallow copies when deep copies are needed are said to account for great numbers of bugs and programming errors. Incorrectly implemented equality testing is another widespread source of mistakes (in these languages, the standard "==" operator determines whether two variables refer to the identical object; if one wants to do a value comparison, the .Equals() method must be invoked instead). New languages are not about to eliminate software reliability problems.

Particularly puzzling to the cloud computing community has been the question of how best to present cloud computing tools to developers who might need to customize those tools as part of the application-creation process. Many cloud computing applications need to leverage prebuilt solutions for data replication, synchronization, client-to-server access and load-balancing, etc. Yet we also need to control the detailed behavior of those solutions: we want data replication with such-and-such a consistency model, or load-balancing that respects some form of affinity, or fault-tolerance that behaves in such-and-such a manner. Moreover, we increasingly need to integrate those mechanisms with multithreaded application designs that leverage modern multicore platforms. Taken jointly, these goals can easily lead to very complex application designs that can break in subtle ways under conditions that don't arise often, but will still occur often enough to be disruptive causes of failure in massive cloud-scale deployments. The area is thus a fertile opportunity for researchers interested in having a real impact. We've mentioned MapReduce and some of the related back-end programming tools found in the modern cloud; it would not be at all surprising if the next edition of this text needs to dedicate a chapter to the topic, and covers not just MapReduce but a dozen other options, as well.

9.3   Other Sources of Downtime

Jointly, hardware and software downtime, including downtime for upgrades, is typically said to account for some two-thirds of system downtime in critical applications. The remaining one-third of downtime is attributable to planned maintenance, such as making backups, and environmental factors, such as power outages, air conditioning or heating failures, leaking pipes, and other similar problems.

Although there may be little hope of controlling these forms of downtime, the trend is to try and treat them using software techniques that distribute critical functionality over sufficient numbers of computers, and separate them to a sufficient degree so that redundancy can overcome unplanned outages. Having developed software capable of solving such problems, downtime for hardware maintenance, backups, or other routine purposes can often be treated in the same way as other forms of outages. Such an approach tends to view system management, monitoring, and on-line control as a part of the system itself: A critical system should, in effect, be capable of modeling its own configuration and triggering appropriate actions if critical functionality is compromised for any reason. In the chapters that follow, this will motivate us to look at issues associated with having a system monitor its own membership (the set of processes that compose it) and, dynamically, adapting itself in a coordinated, consistent manner if changes are sensed. Although the need for brevity will prevent us from treating system management issues in the degree of detail that the problem deserves, we will develop the infrastructure on which reliable management technologies can be implemented, and will briefly survey some recent work specifically on the management problem.

9.4   Complexity

Many developers would argue that the single most serious threat to distributed systems reliability is the *complexity* of today's large distributed systems: rather than coding the entire system from the ground up, to a growing degree we work by enhancing some existing (often massive) infrastructure with a bit of logic that lives around the edges and orchestrates the behavior of the rather mysterious machinery embedded into the platforms with which we work. In the past, students learned the entire software stack: the computer architecture, the compiler, the operating system. Today we learn to invoke preexisting packages of various kinds, with little deep insight into how they were created and how they might malfunction. Thus, the distributed systems used in today's systems, including many of the most critical applications often interconnect huge numbers of components using subtle protocols, and the resulting architecture may be extremely complex. The good news, however, is that when such systems are designed for reliability, the techniques used to make them more reliable may also tend to counteract this complexity.

In the chapters that follow we will be looking at replication techniques that permit critical system data and services to be duplicated as a way to increase reliability. We will also look at new-age technologies for tracking system status and reacting to problems if they arise at runtime. When these kinds of mechanism are used appropriately, the replicas will be consistent with one another and the system as a whole can be thought of as containing just a single instance of the replicated object, but one that happens to be more reliable or more secure than any single object normally would be. If the object is active (a program), it can be *actively replicated* by duplicating the inputs to it and consolidating the outputs it produces. These techniques lead to a proliferation of components but also impose considerable regularity upon the set of components. They thus embody complexity themselves, and yet they simultaneously control the complexity associated with the robustness intervention. If one believes that a platform can, over time, be hardened to a nearly arbitrary degree, the tradeoff thus shifts complexity into the platform, while reducing the complexity of the tasks confronting typical application developers, a tradeoff that favors reliability.

As just mentioned, we will also be looking at system management tools that monitor sets of related components, treating them as groups within which a common management, monitoring, or control policy can be applied. Again, by factoring out something that is true for all system components in a certain class or set of classes, these techniques reduce complexity. What were previously a set of apparently independent objects are now explicitly seen to be related objects that can be treated in similar ways, at least for purposes of management, monitoring, or control.

Broadly, then, we will see that although complexity is a serious threat to reliability, complexity can potentially be controlled by capturing and exploiting regularities in distributed system structure—regularities that are common when such systems are designed to be managed, fault tolerant, secure, or otherwise reliable. To the degree that this is done, the system structure becomes more explicit and hence complexity is reduced. In some ways, the effort of building the system will increase: This structure needs to be specified and needs to remain accurate as the system subsequently evolves. But in other ways, the effort is decreased: By managing a set of components in a uniform way, one avoids the need to do so in an on ad hoc basis, which may be similar for the members of the set but not identical if the component management policies were developed independently.

These observations are a strong motivation for looking at technologies that can support grouping of components in various ways and for varied purposes. However, they also point to a secondary consideration: Unless such technologies are well integrated with system development software tools, they will prove to be irritating and hard to maintain as a system is extended over time. As we will see, researchers have been more involved with the former problem than the latter one, but this situation has now begun to change, particularly with the introduction of CORBA-based reliability solutions, which are well integrated with CORBA development tools. For example, CORBA offers an FTOL architecture for building fault-tolerant active objects. On the downside, these kinds of feature remain rather tentative and have yet to be adopted by CORBA's siblings (progeny?), J2EE and .NET. The Web Services community seems to be at the verge of rejecting such mechanisms precisely because the CORBA community has had mixed experience with the specific versions they adopted. None of these developments is especially encouraging for those of us "in the business" of high assurance.

9.5   Detecting Failures

Surprisingly little work has been done on the problem of building failure detection subsystems. A consequence is that many distributed systems detect failures using timeouts—an error-prone approach that forces the application to overcome inaccurate failure detections in software.

Work by Vogels (see Vogels 1996) suggests that many distributed systems may be able to do quite a bit better. Vogels makes the analogy between detecting a failure and discovering that one's tenant has disappeared. If a landlord were trying to contact a tenant whose rent check is late, it would be a little extreme to contact the police after trying to telephone that tenant once, at an arbitrary time during the day, and not receiving any reply. More likely, the landlord would telephone several times, inquire of neighbors, check to see if the mail is still being collected and if electricity and water are being consumed, and otherwise check for indirect evidence of the presence or absence of the tenant. Vogels suggests that modern failure detectors operate like that extreme landlord, and that it wouldn't be hard to do far better.

Modern distributed systems offer a great number of facilities that are analogous to these physical options. The management information base of a typical computing node (its MIB) provides information on the active processes and their consumption of resources such as memory, computing time, and I/O operations. Often, the network itself is instrumented, and indeed it may sometimes be possible to detect a network partition in an accurate way by querying MIBs associated with network interface and routing nodes. If the operating system on which the application in question is running is accessible, one can sometimes ask it about the status of the processes it is supporting. In applications designed with fault-tolerance in mind, there may be the option of integrating self-checking mechanisms directly into the code, so that the application will periodically verify that it is healthy and take some action, such as resetting a counter, each time the check succeeds. Through such a collection of tactics, one can potentially detect most failures rapidly and accurately and even distinguish partitioning failures from other failures such as crashes or application termination. Vogels has implemented a prototype of a failure investigator service that uses these techniques, yielding much faster and better failure detection than is traditionally assumed possible in distributed systems. Unfortunately, however, this approach is not at all standard. Many distributed systems rely entirely on timeouts for failures; as one might expect, this results in a high rate of erroneous detections and a great deal of complexity in order to overcome their consequences.

Vogels has gone beyond this initial point in his most recent work on the problem (see Vogels and Re 2003). He is now arguing that Web Services systems should include a module, WS_MEMBERSHIP, implementing the failure detection functionality and guaranteeing system-wide consistency. As noted earlier, it is not at all clear how industry views this proposal, although he is certainly seen as a leader in the Web Services architecture community.

It is particularly interesting to realize that these forms of advice come from a person who became Amazon.com's CTO and thus oversees a cloud computing infrastructure that operates on a massive scale and, as we've noted earlier, often deliberately shuts down and then restarts components, using planned failure as a remedy for unstable behavior. Thus those who lead in the field, like Vogels, have become both pragmatists and failure experts: they use controlled failures as a tool, they are sophisticated in use of forensic tools to understand causes of uncontrolled failures, and they are elevating the notion of debugging to a new scale: debugging applications that may not exhibit problems until they are running on tens or hundreds of thousands of nodes. In single-node machines, we think of failure as something that one uses debugging tools to "eliminate" as a problem. In cloud settings, failures can only be seen as a characteristic of the environment that must be anticipated and appropriately managed.

What we lack in the cloud, at the time of this writing, but would find extremely useful, would be a standard means for the cloud management infrastructure to warn cloud applications about planning elasticity events. Suppose, for example, that before reconfiguring a first-tier or second-tier application, the management system were to issue an upcall to the application. Even a few seconds of advance notice might be enough to reconfigure data and functional mappings so that the disruption resulting from the actual elasticity event would be much reduced. Sharded data could be shifted in anticipation of the new service membership, so we wouldn't run a risk of seeing all members of a shard killed off simultaneously in an abrupt, uncontrollable manner. Of course this would cut both ways: when Amazon reconfigures a first-tier EC2 service, the platform needs to see that change occur within a short delay. So the design of such an interface would be a non-trivial task embodying some subtle tradeoffs, and would probably make a very good topic for a research paper. But with this sort of service, our options for building highly assured cloud solutions would immediately be greatly improved.

9.6 Hostile Environments

The discussion in this chapter has enumerated a great variety of reliability threats, which a typical distributed system may need to anticipate and deal with. The problems considered, however, were all of a nature that might be considered "routine," in the sense that they all fall into the category of building software and hardware to be robust against anticipated classes of accidental failures and to be self-managed in ways that anticipate system upgrades and maintenance events.

Just a few years ago, it seemed unnatural to think of the Internet as a hostile environment, and one steadily growing more so. Today, after decades of viruses and "denial of service" attacks, only a very trusting individual would still see the network as a benign place. Modern computer networks are shared with a huge population of computer-literate users, whose goals and sense of personal ethics may differ tremendously from those of the system developer. Whether intentionally or otherwise, these network users represent a diffuse threat; they may unexpectedly probe a distributed system for weaknesses or even subject it to a well-planned and orchestrated assault without prior warning. Simply visiting a standard, public, web page can leave one's computer in the hands of malefactors, who are starting to leverage cross-scripting features to hude malicious content within otherwise unremarkable content.

The intentional threat spectrum is as varied as the accidental threat spectrum reviewed earlier. The most widely known of the threats are computer viruses, which are software programs designed to copy themselves from machine to machine and to do damage to the machines on which they manage to establish themselves. (A benign type of virus that does no damage is called a *worm*, but because the mere presence of an unanticipated program can impact system reliability, it is perhaps best to take the view that all undesired intrusions into a system represent a threat to reliable behavior.) A virus may attack a system by violating assumptions it makes about the environment or the network, breaking through security codes and passwords, piggybacking a ride on legitimate messages, or any of a number of other routes. Attacks that exploit several routes at the same time are more and more common—for example, simultaneously compromising some aspect of the telecommunication infrastructure on which an application depends while also presenting the application with an exceptional condition that it can only handle correctly when the telecommunication subsystem is also functioning.

Other types of intentional threat include unauthorized users or authorized users who exceed their normal limitations. In a banking system, one worries about a rogue trader or an employee who seeks to divert funds without detection. A disgruntled employee may seek to damage the critical systems or data of an organization. In the most extreme case, one can imagine hostile actions directed at a nation's critical computing systems during a period of war or terrorism. Today, this sort of *information warfare* may seem like a suitable topic for science fiction writers, yet, as society shifts increasingly critical activities onto computing and communication technology, the potential targets for attack will eventually become rich enough to interest military adversaries. A recent non-fiction book by Richard Clarke, past national security advisor to the White House (*"Cyber War: The Next Threat to National Security and What to Do About It"* by Richard A. Clarke and Robert Knake (2010)), emphasizes this emerging reality; a second such book, by Jeffery Hunker (*"Creeping Failure: How We Broke the Internet and What We Can Do to Fix It"*, Jeffrey Hunker (2011)), a policy analyst who headed the PCCIP under the Clinton-Gore administration takes the same points even further.

A distributed denial of service (DDoS) attack occurs when a collection of machines, often subverted by hackers who have broken in over the network, are directed to barrage some server or data center with a tremendous load of costly messages, such as the first-phase messages for establishing a TCP connection. Often, origin data are concealed for such messages so as to prevent the server from using a simple filtering mechanism to weed out the bad connections. The server grinds to its knees and legitimate users are unable to connect. The basic DDoS attack has many variants, some aimed at key services such as DNS, some at routers or "weak links" in the network, and some aimed at other kinds of infrastructure or even the application itself. Moreover, DDoS attacks can be effective, but the good news is that they have limits.

For example, when Metallica unveiled its new Web site in early 2003, the band attracted the attention of the music swapping community, which had previously been attacked by Metallica and its lawyers through an organization called the RIAA.

Metallica's site fielded some 6M requests per minute for several days, until network providers worldwide devised a strategy for blocking the problematic packets. Surprisingly, though, rather few Metallica fans were actually disrupted by the event: the DDoS traffic made it hard to register with their Web site but because the actual Web content was cached on a huge data center maintained by Akamai, once a user was registered, the DDoS traffic had little impact. Thus the attackers were only able to shut down one aspect of the overall system, and only for a few days. At the other end of the spectrum, Clarke and Hunker both report cases in which entire countries were brought down, for weeks, by more sophisticated large-scale attacks that focused not on single applications, but rather on critical elements of the underlying Internet infrastructure.

Later in this part of the book we will be looking at issues of scalability, and we will see that some high availability techniques have overheads that are potentially quite significant when certain "rare" events occur. A clever attacker might even launch a denial of service attack by triggering an unusually high frequency of these kinds of event, knowing that the system will pay a steep price dealing with them. Yet because the events are normal ones, albeit normally not so frequent, the system administrator may have a tough time even noticing that a problem has occurred. For example, in a replication protocol one could repeatedly add, then remove, some process—again and again. The group membership protocol will have to run each time, and while this happens, updates can be delayed, effectively degrading the group. Peer-to-peer protocols are often sensitive to churn, the analogous problem but on a large scale. Thus an attack might not even be predicated on the use of some sort of really abnormal traffic pattern!

Clearly, no computing system can be protected against every conceivable form of internal and external threat. Distributed computing can, however, offer considerable benefits against a well-known and fully characterized threat profile. By distributing critical functionality over sets of processes that must cooperate and coordinate their actions in order to perform sensitive functions, the barrier against external threats can be formidable. For example, Metallica's decision to host content on a Web server farm maintained by Akamai meant that DDoS attacks would have had to shut down all of Akamai's thousands of computers to really shut down Metallica itself. Similarly, a terrorist who might easily overcome a system that lacks any defenses at all would face a much harder problem overcoming firewalls, breaking through security boundaries, and interfering with critical subsystems designed to continue operating correctly even if some limited number of system components crash or are compromised. Later we will discuss virtual private network technologies, which take such approaches even further, preventing all communication within the network except that initiated by authenticated users. Clearly, if a system uses a technology such as this, it will be relatively hard to break into. However, the cost of such a solution may be higher than most installations can afford.

As the developer of a critical system, the challenge is to anticipate the threats that it must overcome and to do so in a manner that balances costs against benefits. Often, the threat profile that a component subsystem may face will be localized to that component—hence, the developer may need to go to great lengths in protecting some especially critical subsystems against reliability and security threats, while using much more limited and less-costly technologies elsewhere in the same system. One goal of this part of the book involves a corresponding issue—that of understanding not just how a reliability problem can be solved, but also how the solution can be applied in a selective and localized manner, so that a developer who faces a specific problem in a specific context can draw on a solution tailored to that problem and context, without requiring that the entire system be reengineered to overcome a narrow threat.

Today, we lack a technology with these attributes. Most fault-tolerant and security technologies demand that the developer adopt a fault-tolerant or secure computing and communication architecture starting with the first lines of code entered into the system. With such an approach, fault tolerance and security become very hard to address late in the game, when substantial amounts of technology already exist. Unfortunately, however, most critical systems are built up out of preexisting technology, which will necessarily have been adapted to the new use and hence will be confronted with new types of reliability and security threat that were not anticipated in the original setting. Worse, as we saw earlier, the cloud is architected in ways that make failures more common. In the past, one thought of failure as a rare event. In cloud settings, failure is a common fact of life.

What is needed is a technology base that is flexible enough to help us how to overcome a great variety of possible threats, but that is also matched to the special conditions that arise in modern styles of computing: client computing, networks, cloud applications. Solutions must be scalable and efficient (so that these costs are as low as possible), and suitable for being introduced *late in the game*, when a system may already include substantial amounts of preexisting technology.

Can this be done? The author believes so; research is making major strides in this direction. In the following chapters, we will be looking at many of the fundamental challenges that occur in overcoming various classes of threats. We will discuss computing models that are dynamic, self-managed, and fault tolerant, and will see how a technology based on *wrapping* preexisting interfaces and components with look-alike technologies that introduce desired robustness features can be used to harden complex, pre-existing systems, albeit with many limitations. Finally, we will consider some of the large-scale system issues raised when a complex system must be managed and controlled in a distributed setting. While it would be an overstatement to claim that all the issues have been solved, it is clear that considerable progress towards an integrated technology base for hardening critical systems is being made.

But the author's view is not necessarily the prevailing one. Many cloud platform vendors see reliability as a kind of operational property, not one with a strong basis in theory or guarantees. They design systems that work pretty well, then as the systems run, improve the things that fail in annoying ways, while finding clever tricks to hide other forms of inconsistency or unreliability where the end-user will not notice. We have seen how this can lead to a view in which the cloud becomes unreliable by design, trading reliability against faster response times or other desired scalability properties. Thus, even an optimist about the technical trends should have few illusions about reliability: Critical computing systems will continue to be less reliable than they should be until the customers and societal users of such systems demand reliability, and the developers begin to routinely concern themselves with understanding the threats to reliability in a given setting—planning a strategy for responding to those threats and for testing the response. However, there is reason to believe that in those cases where this process does occur, a technology base capable of rising to the occasion can be provided.

9.7 Related Reading

On dramatic system failures and their consequences (see Gibbs 1994; Peterson 1995).

How and why systems fail and what can be done about it (see Birman and van Renesse 1996; Borr and Wilhelmy 1994; Chilaragee 1994; Gray 1990; Gray and Reuter 1993; Gray et al. 1987, 1996).

On the failure investigator (see Vogels 1996; Vogels and Re 2003).

On understanding failures (see Cristian 1996).

Overcoming Failures in a Distributed System 10

10.1 Consistent Distributed Behavior

In this and the next two chapters, we will be focused on mechanisms for *replicating data and computation* while guaranteeing some form of consistent behavior to the end-user. For example, we might desire that even though information has been replicated, some system based on that data behaves as if that information was not replicated and instead resides at a single place. This is an intuitively attractive model, because developers find it natural to think in terms of non-distributed systems, and it is reasonable to expect that a distributed system should be able to mimic the behavior of a non-distributed one. At the same time, though, it is not a minor undertaking to ensure that a distributed system will behave just like a non-distributed one.

Distributed systems are inherently concurrent: actions occur at multiple places, and if data is replicated, the possibility arises that access will occur simultaneously at more than one location, introducing synchronization challenges. Obviously, in an ideal world, actions would occur as asynchronously as possible, consistent with such pragmatic concerns as management of flow control (we would not want unbounded amounts of data to build up within the communication channels of an asynchronous system, as might occur if one node was permitted to get far ahead of others), fault-tolerance (we would not want the user to be sent a reply that reflects updates that were done at one location, only to see a crash erase those updates so that they never reach other nodes), and the selected consistency model. But taken jointly, these goals representing a surprisingly difficult objective to achieve. It is hard to visualize concurrent behaviors of a system, because one needs to think about all the things that can be happening at all the locations in the system, and the possible execution scenarios generally grow in number as the cross product of the numbers of possible local scenarios. Concurrency can be a source of serious bugs: under precisely what conditions is it safe to reply to an end-user before a set of updates have been completed? Even seemingly minor implementation issues are incredibly difficult to resolve: how threaded should a concurrent system be, and how should it use such features as thread priorities to maximize performance, and how should its

K.P. Birman, *Guide to Reliable Distributed Systems*, Texts in Computer Science,
DOI 10.1007/978-1-4471-2416-0_10, © Springer-Verlag London Limited 2012

threads do locking? These kinds of concerns often lead to very conservative (hence slow) implementations. But slow solutions, while they may be easier to debug, battle against cloud's need for rapid responses: any reply that gets delayed longer than necessary could cost the cloud enterprise revenue!

For readers who recall the introduction and first chapters of this text, it should not be hard to see how the CAP theorem and methodology emerged from such worries. After all, if data replication in the cloud turns out to be slow, it becomes very appealing to build first-tier cloud services that run on potentially stale data, as a way to avoid waiting for locks, or waiting for updates to complete. CAP can then be recognized as a pragmatic response to the complexities of building really scalable, high-speed consistency mechanisms. Accordingly, in what follows our goal will be to first see what the best that can be done might be. Can we build really fast, scalable, replication protocols? Then we can revisit design principles such as CAP and ask whether they are really the final word on consistency in cloud settings.

To simplify this thicket of complications and competing objectives, we will start by looking at models of systems that do not have any kind of replicated data, which we can then "emulate" in a distributed manner. In this way one can incrementally build towards that goal of a maximally concurrent yet always safe solution that might really be deployable at cloud-scale. Moreover, in a somewhat unexpected new twist, this way of thinking will also offer us a path towards concurrent solutions for use in multi-core settings, since to a growing degree, those systems look like small clusters of machines.

With this in mind, in what follows we will work our way up to a model in which one thinks about a system as if it is not using replicated data and does not exhibit concurrency, then shows how to implement that model in a fault-tolerant manner using a distributed system. This latter model supports a consistency model often referred to as *state machine replication*. State machine replication was introduced by Leslie Lamport in the 1970s, but at the time was really just a name he used for a very simple idea, namely that if a set of replicas for some service are deterministic[1], and if they apply the same set of actions (e.g. updates) in the same order, they will remain in the same state—what today would be called a consistent replicated state. Although the state machine model will seem somewhat trivial when stated this

---

[1]Determinism is a very unrealistic assumption for modern programs coded in languages like Java or C#, which support threads and do background garbage collection. The assumption is even more questionable if an application might receive input from multiple sources, for example by having TCP connections from multiple clients. Thus today we tend to think of the determinism assumption not as a statement about the programming language or the program "as a whole" but rather, in terms of the way some module within a program handles operations against the state maintained within that module. For example, a module might be non-threaded even if the program that uses it is multi-threaded. The module might use some form of locking to enforce ordering. In this way, we create a deterministic subsystem within which the state machine replication assumption makes sense. While one might reasonably wonder if this more restrictive notion of determinism will have to be questioned if the current trend towards highly pipelined multi-core machines continues to play out, it seems likely that future computers will still have some way to guarantee determinism no matter how complex they become in these dimensions. We literally would not know how to write programs for computing models that are non-deterministic at their core.

way, state machine replication implementations can be quite complex: they need to deal with concurrency, failures, and reconfiguration, each bringing its own set of issues. Yet, such problems can be solved, and this is why state machine replication has become the most standard way to understand the conditions under which replicated information will be updated correctly within a set of replicas even when the set experiences failures, or evolves by adding or dropping members over time (that is, what started as a definition for replication gradually became more of a model for dealing with groups of replicas that might vary in size and role dynamically). On the other hand, it took time for state machine replication to have this more general meaning. At the outset, the model assumed that the set of replicas was fixed. Moreover, the model did not evolve in a simple way: there were actually many proposals for dynamic membership management in systems that adopt the state machine approach, offered by many researchers. In what follows, we will look at several of those options.

The history in this area was quite complex; we will summarize it, but just briefly. The idea of replicating a service or system dates quite far back, it was certainly recognized before Lamport introduced the state machine replication model, and probably could be traced to the earliest days of computing. After all, the moment information was somehow moved from one computer to another, data was effectively being replicated. By the mid-1970s papers on replication despite failures had appeared. It was in the context of one such paper that Lamport suggested the state machine replication model. Although Lamport's use of the model was in a crash-failure scenario, however, many of the early papers focused on very aggressive failure models, others quickly adapted it and it became popular in connection with the Byzantine fault model, in which components of the system actively try to attack it from within. We will say more about that model below; it offers very strong assurances, but is also costly and in some ways, not very realistic (studies at Yahoo! and elsewhere suggest that real failures are rarely Byzantine). Some researchers favor this Byzantine state replication model, suggesting that even if real failures tend to be less messy, the extreme pessimism of the Byzantine model certainly covers anything a real system could possibly do. For this chapter, though, we will stick with the most widely used failure model: one in which machines fail by crashing and this is detected by timeout.

The more practical history of data replication was catalyzed by the introduction of hardware supporting a special kind of one-to-many communication option. The first use of this hardware feature was in particular networking device called the *Ethernet*, invented at Xerox Parc in the early 1980s. With an ethernet, it was easy to send one message that would be received (unreliably) by multiple receivers; basically, all the receivers just listened for some single agreed-on network address, and any message sent to that address would be accepted by all their network interfaces. Thus, a single message-send could potentially reach an unlimited number of destination machines. But hardware multicast soon morphed into a software-supported notion of network multicast, implemented by routers. Moreover, researchers began to study the use of this feature for various purposes: to find a service in a network where the location of the server might not be fixed, and to support inexpensive data replication. Papers such as the Zwaenepoel and Cheriton paper on an operating system they called V speculated about a wide variety of other possible uses for multicast. The V system itself offered a simple way to access the hardware feature, but did not really explore those applications in much detail.

This set the stage for the author's own work (with Tommy Joseph and others) in the 1985–1987 period, which yielded both a practical tool for replicating data or computation, as well as a model called virtual synchrony for explaining precisely what that guarantees this tool provides to its users. A program could count on those guarantees, and they represented a kind of virtualized execution environment, very much in the same sense that a virtual machine allows applications to run in a virtualized setting. As we will see below, virtual synchrony focuses on the communication layer, and offers a kind of distributed programming environment that supports ways to form groupings of applications (process groups), to replicate data or coordinate actions within those groups, to update data in a consistent manner, etc.

In other words, virtual synchrony formalizes a practical replication solution that guarantees a strong form of consistency, and fault-tolerance for a specified class of failures. It supports a variety of multicast protocols with varied ordering properties; the user picked whichever protocol was strong enough for the need, but cheapest within its class. The corresponding system was called the Isis Toolkit, and first entered general use around 1987. The Isis Toolit was ultimately used to create the New York Stock Exchange floor communications networking system (it ran that system for more than a decade before being replaced), the French Air Traffic Control System (which gradually spread through Europe and remains active today), the US Navy AEGIS system, and many other applications. Virtual synchrony was adopted in many other systems, including Totem, Transis, Phoenix, Horus, Ensemble and JGroups (a component of JBoss). Appendix A formalizes a modern version of the model, and the Isis^2 platform described in Appendix B implements a modern version of the virtual synchrony model, extended to work well in cloud computing environments.

But virtual synchrony was just one of several replication approaches. In 1988, Brian Oki and Barbara Liskov published a paper describing a database replication scheme called *viewstamped replication*; it uses a different protocol, of their own design, and implements a model that guarantees stronger durability properties than most of the virtual synchrony protocols[2]. They argued that these properties were ideally matched to replication scenarios that arise when supporting ACID transactions. Today, we would say that the target is replicated *hard state* in a modern cloud computing system. In contrast, the majority of the virtual synchrony replication protocols are suitable for *soft state* replication, but lack a durability property needed for hard state (the "D" in ACID). If all this seems confusing, it was even at the time: basically, from the outset, there have been a dismaying variety of options for replicating data, scaling replicated services up, and tolerating failures. All of these choices, and the subtle differences in the ways they were portrayed in papers

---

[2]We say "most" here because virtual synchrony actually had several flavors of reliable multicast; we will discuss them below.

describing them, made the early days of the field extremely chaotic; we are only starting to see real standards today.

As just mentioned, Leslie Lamport stepped into the fray in 1990, with the first paper on his Paxos protocol (the official journal publication did not appear until 1998, but the paper was in wide circulation from its first release as a technical report). Lamport's innovation was not so much the protocol itself, which contained elements familiar from his own papers and the 1988 Oki and Liskov protocol. Lamport's innovation centered on the balance he struck between offering a practical protocol side by side with a more rigorous formal analysis. Moreover, Paxos was really as much a methodology as a protocol: he offered a very elegant step-by-step way of transforming a very simple but inefficient basic Paxos protocol into a more and more efficient, optimized version that preserved the correctness of the original solution. His first papers took some initial steps along these lines, and then were followed by additional refinements over nearly a decade. Indeed, widespread interest in Paxos probably did not occur until around 2001, coinciding with a paper he entitled "Paxos made Simple," and with a few success stories on using Paxos in the Frangipani File System (1998) and the Google Chubby Lock Service (2006).

In the contemporary, fanciest, versions of Paxos one finds most features of the virtual synchrony protocols. But whereas the virtual synchrony protocol suite was hard to prove correct, these fancier versions of Paxos inherit simple correctness properties from the the less elaborate versions that from which they were derived. This was a tremendously important innovation at the time and really changed the way that people design and reason about protocols. On the negative side, that early Paxos paper was somewhat hard to read, in part because the best ways of presenting this kind of work had not yet been discovered, and in part because the paper itself made extensive use of Greek (not merely for symbols, but entire words and short phrases). The Paxos Made Simple paper did not just revisit Paxos, but went beyond the original paper by untangling and structuring the proofs and approach. Those steps transformed Paxos from being a specific protocol into more of a technique, which is the way many researchers think of it today. In effect, we tend to view Paxos as a method for starting with a simple but inefficient replication protocol, and then improving it step by step into a much more practical one, while retaining the key correctness properties in each step.

If replication ever becomes a topic for future historians, all of this may be tough going. As we have seen, many of the key ideas turn out to have been invented (and then reinvented) at least a few times, by multiple researchers. One could argue that several researchers, the author of this text included, reinvented their own ideas a few times, before finally getting the right balance between practicality, performance, and clarity of the correctness proofs. In retrospect, one can tease out elements of Paxos in both the virtual synchrony "view management" protocol, and in the Liskov and Oki work. But this is because we know what we are looking for. Readers of these three papers, at the time, would have noticed similarities but probably would not have realized that the underlying mechanisms were essentially isomorphic. More likely they would have found it all confusing, as the various authors themselves did: everyone was searching for clarity, but as it worked out, clarity emerged only after many years of research and development.

But it is interesting to realize that these and other efforts arrived at similar solutions, and did so because they were trying to solve similar problems. At the end of the day, it turns out that there are not very many ways to solve those problems. Virtual synchrony, as we will see below, was focused on what today we would call consistent data replication in the soft-state services that live in the first tier of the modern cloud. Liskov and Oki were interested in strong durability guarantees (the ACID properties needed in database systems); their solution thus aimed at consistency but in the inner hard-state tiers, to use cloud terminology. And in the first Paxos papers, Lamport was not asking about either of these applications, although in fact his model was very close to the one used by Liskov's group. Lamport's focus was on Paxos as an elegant solution to state machine replication (Lamport 1984), and on the best ways to derive the required proofs.

Further complicating the picture was an engineering issue: as mentioned, virtual synchrony was notably complicated in its early incarnation, making it hard to understand. Yet it was also real: the Isis Toolkit was in use by 1985, and the 1987 version quickly was picked up by dozens of users worldwide. The system was ultimately commercialized, which is how it came to be used in the settings listed earlier, and many others (and it was never rewritten: the commercial version was basically a very cleaned-up version of that original 1985 system). The Liskov and Oki work was used at MIT, but never adopted outside of the research project on which Oki worked. Paxos was mostly viewed as a theory and methodology contribution in the early days, but today is supported by a high quality implementation created at Microsoft Research. Turning Paxos into a really practical option, however, required a number of extensions and improvements to the original basic protocol. Nearly a decade elapsed after Paxos was first published, before practical use of the solution became an option.

During that same time period, virtual synchrony evolved by becoming more and more modular, separating concerns that in the initial protocols were mixed together. So we have a mix here of competing solutions, each evolving, and each targeting somewhat different use cases.

The story has not ended yet. In recent work, Dahlia Malkhi led an effort that managed to merge the Paxos and virtual synchrony protocols into a single model; we include it here as Appendix A. Her approach offers advantages relative to both virtual synchrony and the most current version of Paxos.

And who deserves credit for all of this? Was it Lamport, who clarified what had been very confusing? Virtual synchrony for being first to actually implement these mechanisms in a generally useable form? Liskov and Oki, for being closest to the specifics of the first version of Paxos, but predating Paxos? Any reasonable analysis would have to conclude that today's theory and practice of replicated data with strong consistency owes much to *many* researchers, including not just the ones associated with the work just mentioned, but also many others not explicitly touched upon above. A proper history would also talk about the contributions of Amir, Babaoglu, Chockler, Dolev, Guerraoui, Kaashoek, Keidar, Meliar-Smith, Moser, Moses, Schiper, Stephenson, Van Renesse and many others.

For this book, all of this forces a choice. One option would be to present the various protocols more or less as they were invented: virtual synchrony in one section, Paxos in another, the Liskov and Oki protocol in a third, etc. Such a treatment might touch upon each of the researchers just listed, explaining precisely how each contributed to an evolving but very complex, multifacted, concurrent process. After all, the community did not work on one solution; rather, dozens of contributions that overlapped in many ways slowly let us tease out today's story.

What we will do here takes the opposite approach: we will develop a single story, step by step, in a way that draws on all of this prior work and yet represents a single line of thinking, not many conflicting, concurrent lines of thought. Our treatment comes closer to Malkhi's version of virtual synchrony combined with Paxos than to any other prior approach, but what it really tries to do (hopefully, in a successful way) is to motivate each feature of the model by seeing how the need for that feature arises in real cloud settings, or in other practical contexts. We will use the term virtual synchrony for this model, but the reader should be aware that the definitions we use here are not identical to those from the earliest uses of the term.

The model we will work towards here is one that lets us substitute groups of processes or objects where we might have used a single one in our conceptual design, in effect offering the developer an incremental way to introduce replication and to achieve a high degree of concurrency. In addition to Isis[2], virtual synchrony is supported by several other popular communications packages, including the widely used JBoss and Spread technologies. Although Web Services development tools do not yet provide integrated support for these kinds of mechanism, down the road that type of integrated solution will almost certainly become available. Meanwhile, for those who need high assurance, there are practical ways to apply the ideas in this and the subsequent chapter to real systems, by using standard Web Services development tools and integrating them with communication libraries implementing the mechanisms we will be studying.

Although our "real" goal is to support replicated data and replicated computation for high availability and improved performance, we will tackle the problem a little bit at a time. In particular, the main topics on which we will focus in this chapter concerns the best options for tracking the set of members of a distributed system and on the building block primitives needed to implement those options, notably 2-phase commit and its generalization, 3-phase commit.

Monitoring membership in a system may not seem all that central to replicating data, but in fact plays a fundamental role: after all, it makes no sense to talk about replicating information unless we can explain precisely *where* the replicas are supposed to be! Moreover, it turns out that the way we solve the membership problem has stunning performance implications. Getting membership "right" can result in replicated update rates thousands of times superior to those seen in systems that approach the membership problem naively. Indeed, while there are many who would suggest that "agreeing on something" is the most fundamental distributed computing problem, the author of this text could make a pretty strong argument that agreeing on *membership* is perhaps at the real core.

Why worry about *agreement* on system membership? Why not simply trust processes to make their own decisions, in accordance with the end-to-end philosophy, perhaps using timeouts?[3] Readers may recall that in the introduction of this book, we saw that when timeout is used to detect failures, events unrelated to failure such as network congestion, brief disconnections of some computers from the network, or routing changes can trigger timeouts and thus fool the system into believing that such-and-such a node has crashed.

Worse still, this can happen in wildly inconsistent ways. Perhaps process p will conclude that processes q, r, and s are up but that process t has crashed, while process q thinks that all five are healthy, and process t believes that it is the only survivor of some sort of massive outage. Such problems can percolate up to the user, resulting in confusing or even unsafe behavior. For example, in the introduction, we saw a "split brain" scenario, where an air traffic control system might partition into two side-by-side systems, each claiming to be in control—and each unaware of the other.

It is not hard to see why confusion about membership will translate to trouble if we want to replicate data. To summarize that story from the introduction, suppose that our five processes are part of an air traffic control service that needs to maintain information about which planes are in the sky and where they are going, and the data in question is updated when controllers give instructions to the planes, or when a plane changes its course. If the system is not consistent about which members are operational, it may neglect to update one of the replicas, in which case that replica will start to give incorrect information to the pilots and controllers who are unlucky enough to query it. Conversely, if we can trust a membership service to tell us which processes "belong" to the system, we will be in a position to use that information in support of simple tools, like libraries that maintain replicated data and provide ways to lock items for exclusive use, and then in higher level algorithms, for example to rapidly "fail over" from a process that crashes to one that remains healthy so as to maintain near-continuous availability. In many ways, *agreement on membership* is thus at the center of the universe, at least insofar as high assurance computing is concerned.

Not many people build distributed air traffic control systems, so it makes sense to ask if all of this matters in the modern cloud. The answer is mixed. Today, the cloud is dominated by applications for which relatively weak consistency properties suffice. Many systems are deliberately designed to sometimes give wrong answers rather than wait for a lock or an update that might be needed in order to give the right answer: the bias, in effect, favors rapid response over correctness. Instead of offering continuous guarantees of consistency, services of this kind offer eventual consistency: they clean up the mess in the background, if anything actually goes wrong,

---

[3]Of course, one can interpret almost any distributed system built without changes to the core Internet protocols as an "end-to-end" system. But the end-to-end approach is often understood to refer to a model in which properties are enforced *pairwise*, between cooperating end-points. If we understand the model in this strong sense, the introduction of new services that play a role such as membership tracking throughout the entire system represents a major departure.

and do their best to conceal this from users. And it works. To repeat a question we posed earlier, how much consistency does YouTube or Facebook really need?

But if we begin to host high assurance systems on the cloud, this may change. Moreover, as noted earlier, many kinds of mundane system need consistency for mundane reasons. A cloud routing infrastructure that uses an inconsistent routing table, even briefly, might have loops, black holes or routing flaps. A medical record-management system that gives out inconsistent data might confuse a healthcare worker into making a dangerous mistake. A smart electric power-grid management system that behaves inconsistently could suffer blackouts. Thus if today's cloud can get away with weak consistency and eventual self-repair, it is not certain that tomorrow's cloud will have such an easy time. Fortunately, as we will see in this and the chapters that follow, we actually can build scalable consistency stories for the cloud. So the good news is that if the industry comes around to wanting to do more, no technical barriers stand in the way. For example, the CAP theorem, mentioned in the introduction, turns out to preclude scaling some forms of consistency in certain ways, but there are other forms of consistency (including virtual synchrony) that scale perfectly well. In effect, one can evade CAP, given a sufficiently sophisticated mindset.

10.1.1 Static Membership

There are many ways to obtain consistency in a distributed system, and not all boil down to the use of a group membership tracking subsystem. For example, many systems start with a list of the possible constituent computers that might be operational, and rather than continuously tracking the state of each node, deal with availability on an operation-by-operation manner. Such a system would basically have a list, readily available to all the processes in the system, listing the places where replicas *might* be found. In this "static" model, one has an unchanging list of members, but at any given point in time, only a subset of them will typically be available.

Let us think for a moment about how one might support replicated data on a static membership model. We have our five processes and we would like to maintain some sort of information—for simplicity, we will focus on just a single variable x and assume that it takes integer values. Obviously any real system might have more elaborate data structures, but it turns out that a method that works for a single integer can usually be generalized to handle more complex information in a straightforward manner.

Now, if x were a non-replicated variable, living in some place that never fails, we could track its values over time and in this manner, build a history. It might look like this: from time 0 to 20, x was zero. Then, an update occurred at time 21 and x took on the value 17. An additional update occurred at time 25, changing x to 97, and so forth. Here an "update" might overwrite x with a new value, or it might read x, perform some computation that involves the old value, and then write back a new changed value.

In our real system, processes p, q, r, s and t need to maintain replicas of x. For this purpose, let us require that each process in the system keep a single copy of x and also record the time at which it was lasted updated. When we start the system up, we will assume that all five know that at time 0, the value of x was zero. Now, at time 21, p wants to initiate an update. How should it do so?

Recall that in a static membership model, p knows the locations at which other processes in the system might be running, but does not know which ones are currently operational. It may be that if p sends an update request to each of its counterparts, asking them to record a new value for x, perhaps only some will get the message and of those, perhaps only some of the replies will get back to p. (On top of this, one needs to worry about concurrent updates, but for the purposes of this part of the chapter, one update is already quite adequate to understand the basic issues.) We also need a way to read the value of x. Suppose that s wants to read x. If it simply looks at its own value, how can it be sure that nobody else has a more "recent" update that did not get through, perhaps because of a network problem?

There is an obvious way to work around such problems, and almost all systems that use the static membership model employ it. The idea is to make sure that each operation reaches a *majority* of the processes in the system. Suppose that we know that if p wants to update x it always makes sure that at least three out of the five processes in the system record that update (since it cannot be sure how many will respond in advance of trying to do the operation, this means than an update has multiple phases—an initial attempt, then some sort of decision as to whether the operation was successful, and then a second phase in which the processes learn the outcome). If s similarly reads copies from a majority of members, at least one process is guaranteed to overlap any successful update and the read, hence at least one process will know the most current value of x!

Generalizing, this way of designing systems leads to what are called *quorum update* and *read* architectures (see Gifford 1979; Skeen 1982b; Thomas 1979). Rather than requiring that reads and updates both reach a majority, we instead define a minimum number of copies that must be read, QR, and a minimum number of copies that must be updated, QW, such that both QW + QW and QR + QW exceed the size of the system. For example, in a system with n processes, we might set QW $= n - 1$ and QR $= 2$. In this way, we can successfully update our variable even if one of the group members is faulty, and any read will definitely "see" the most current update.

Returning to our example, process p thus updates x as follows. First, it does a read operation to find the most current value of x and the associated time—and to do this, it issues an RPC-style read requests to one replica after another until it has QR replies. The current version of x will be the one with the largest time, and the value is the value associated with that version. (Several processes may report the same version and value.)

Process p now computes a time at which the new version will become active—any value will do as long as it is larger than the maximum number it read from the group, and the new value. And it issues RPCs to at least QW members, asking them to "prepare" to update x. (In practice, of course, it would probably just issue requests to all group members, but the rule allows a bit more flexibility.)

The processes in the group now respond, acknowledging that they are prepared to do the update. Process p looks to see if it has a write quorum. If the number of acknowledgements is QW or larger, p allows the update to *commit*, and otherwise, it must be *aborted*, meaning that the members do not change their replica's value. We will revisit the protocol later and pin down some of the details, but this should already give the basic sense of how it works.

Typical presentations of the Paxos protocol present this sequence in a different way, and it may be helpful to summarize that approach simply because Paxos is widely cited in the literature. Paxos works by defining a sequence of *slots* each of which can contain a message, or a null entry. Values are written into slots by *leaders*, and more than one leader can attempt to define the value for a particular slot. This is important, as we will see below.

To determine the sequence of updates to apply to the replicated state machine or database, a process must read the slots one by one, learn what the value associated with each is, and apply that value to the database or state machine. Paxos itself is concurrent and can actually define a value for, say, slot 3 when slots 1 and 2 are still being determined. Should this occur, the event associated with 3 cannot be processed until after the events associated with slots 1 and 2 (or the null events) have been processed first, since the slots determine the delivery order. Thus, the life of the database system (or whatever else uses Paxos) is to wait until the value for slot k has been decided, apply the associated value (update), if non-null, and then advance to slot $k + 1$.

Now, to delve further into Paxos, let us fix the slot number, say slot 1. The way the protocol works is to run a series of rounds (called *ballots*) that work to decide what that slot will contain, using a quorum agreement to make that decision. Ballots are associated with specific leaders: for example, perhaps one leader is assigned to use even ballot numbers, and a second leader odd ones, or perhaps the ballots use a sequential numbering rule but append the leader's IP address to avoid ties. Thus if we consider any particular slot and ballot pair, only one leader ever runs a protocol associated with that pair.

The way this occurs is as follows: a client hands the leader some sort of request: perhaps, the client has asked the leader to try and deliver message x. The leader now picks the slot it wishes to use (the next one, as far as it knows), and a ballot number larger than any it has previously used for ballots associated with this slot. It *proposes* to use value x for slot 1 on this ballot number. The group members (the term in the Paxos literature would be *acceptors*) can only agree to accept a single value for a particular slot, and only agree to do so once. The rule is that if an acceptor receives a proposal, and the slot number is larger than the largest slot number for which they have previously agreed to accept a value, and they have not previously accepted a proposal in that slot, they accept the new proposal. The value x will be successfully committed in the slot the instant that a quorum of leaders have accepted it, even before they respond to the leader: the decision to accept is what matters. Moreover, the acceptors do not worry about tabulating this: each acts separately. The threshold is thus reached "silently".

The leader, meanwhile, attempts to learn the outcome of its proposal. As we have seen, even a successful leader might not realize that it was successful, because failures, timeouts or message loss could prevent it from collecting the responses to its proposal. Thus message x could be successful in ballot 0 for slot 1, and yet it is entirely possible that nobody knows this.

In Paxos, once a message is accepted in a particular slot, no other message (value) can ever be accepted in that slot. However, the same value can be accepted again in a subsequent ballot.

If a leader believes its proposal failed (it could be wrong), it simply retries the proposal with a new slot number, but with one caveat. If an acceptor has accepted some other value in the same slot, it sends the leader the value, and a leader that learns of some other accepted value with a larger ballot number than its own must switch and begin to propose that value, instead of its own, for the slot. This way if there are two leaders contending to put two different values—to send two different messages—in slot 1, say x and y, and they actually do get responses from the acceptors, both will end up proposing the same message, albeit using different ballot numbers.

A leader stops proposing a value in a particular slot and switches to a new slot number when it discovers a failure. This occurs because some other value becomes committed in the slot, or because it discovers that no value can be committed (for example, perhaps x has been accepted by members p and q, y by members r and s, and z by member t, and this covers the full acceptor set. Here, no value can be delivered in that slot).

Ideally, in Paxos, we run with one leader at a time. Even so, it can take a long time for the status of a slot to be resolved, and for anyone to learn what the outcome was. This is because if some group members fail, we might face a situation in which there is a seeming tie between multiple outcomes for that slot: null, message x, message y, and so forth. While learning that a quorum of members accepted a given message in a given slot is definitive (and learning that a quorum did not accept it in that slot is also definitive), we may be unable to deduce this because the pattern of failures could conceal the result! This is really a concrete manifestation of the so-called *Fischer, Lynch and Patterson Impossibility Result* (FLP), which establishes that one cannot build a fault-tolerant protocol that guarantees that it will reach agreement on something (here, the contents of a particular Paxos slot) in finite time. At best we can build systems that will preserve correctness and with a little luck will also make progress.

So we have this issue of possible ambiguity. To make progress one could wait to learn the histories of all the group members, but a failure can endure for a long time. Paxos will not do anything incorrect in such cases, but will not necessarily make rapid progress either.

And to close the loop on a point made earlier: while we have described this as the Paxos protocol, it is also the Viewstamped Replication protocol, and is very similar to Herlihy's Quorum Ratchet Lock protocol, and also to the earliest group membership algorithms used in the Isis Toolkit. But if the earliest papers on Paxos were not describing a completely novel protocol, one can certainly credit Lamport for being the first to single out that protocol, and the first to explain its properties in a detailed and correct way. The first and most important correctness properly Lamport established for Paxos was his proof that when using this sort of quorum scheme, no message will be delivered anywhere unless it will become durable (quorum reads will subsequently find it), and the ordering will be unique. Every subsequent refinement of Paxos carefully preserved these properties.

Notice that in a fault-tolerant system, QW will necessarily have to be smaller than n. As a result, even if p only wants to read x it *still* needs to do an RPC to some other process, because QR > 1! This means that when using Paxos, read operations cannot run any faster than the speed of an RPC. Similarly, to do an update, p needs to perform two rounds of RPCs. Obviously, this is going to be at least as slow as the slowest respondent, and while one can shift the costs around with clever programming, static membership does tend to incur significant costs. In practice, one finds that systems built in this manner would be able to sustain tens of updates per second in a "real" group of five processes, but perhaps not much more.

Further, notice that Paxos seems to require a quorum read prior to any quorum write. If this was really needed in practical uses of Paxos, the costs of that extra read could easily be prohibitive. Fortunately, however, because Paxos is normally used with a single, stable, leader, the leader can normally do a single read when it starts execution, but subsequently retain (cache) the current values and versions of variables that are in active use. This allows the leader to optimistically skip the read step and, during the inital phase of the quorum write, one can simply validate that these optimistic values are in fact the correct versions of the corresponding data (they will be, if no other leader ran concurrently). Thus we can safely eliminate the initial quorum read in the steady state and jump directly to the quorum write step.

We will call this style of replication in a subset of a fixed list of participants the "static membership" model, although many readers might want to think of it as "basic Paxos". The set of potential system members is fixed, even though the operational subset varies, and the algorithms are quorum based. Moreover the members are typically denoted by the names of the computers on which they run, since process-ids change if a machine fails, then restarts. Obviously, networks evolve over time, and even static systems will need to update the membership list now and then, but the presumption is that this can be treated as an offline activity.

10.1.2 Dynamic Membership

When we introduce a group membership service, complexity rises, but performance also improves, and this will be important in the chapters that follow (if we were weren't aiming for blindingly fast and scalable solutions, we could already stop and just use the basic Paxos protocol outlined above). Protocols that trust such a service to monitor the system state are able to avoid doing much of the work done in the static case and this translates to dramatic speedups, at least for operations like updating replicated data. The "dynamic group membership" model is concerned with systems built this way. In experiments with one of the systems we will talk about later in this part of the book, called Horus, it was possible to send as many as 80,000 update operations per second within a group of five members—literally thousands of times faster than in the static case. The core issue here is that even for the cheapest category of operations (those that change the "internal state" of a service), a quorum-based system cannot perform an operation until a majority of its members have seen the operation, while a system like Horus can perform an operation as soon as the multicast describing it is received. This limits the quorum system: pending operations impose overhead on the initiating system. The larger such a system gets, the longer an operation will be pending before it can be executed, and the higher the impact of these overheads. Thus quorum systems will usually slow down at least linearly in the system size. In fact, the situation is often quite a bit worse: Jim Gray, winner of the ACM Turing Award, reported on studies that found the slowdown to be roughly $O(n^2)$ where n is the number of members in the service (in a more elaborated analysis that assumed a database application using the ACID model, he shows that the slowdown could rise to as much as $O(n^5)$ due to transaction rollback and redo costs). Thus, if you accept his analysis, a system with 2 nodes will be at best half as fast as one with 1 node, but a system with 4 nodes will be no better than 1/16th the speed of the single-node system, and could be hundreds of times slower if the application on top of the protocol is a transactional database using a naively implemented replication model. As a practical matter, it is extremely uncommon to talk about quorum systems having more than about 5 members[4].

To give a sense of our reasons for tackling the complexity that dynamic membership will bring, it helps to remind ourselves that Horus, in similar uses, might be thousands of times faster! Horus will also turn out to have scaling limits, but the issue is of a different nature. The Horus protocols scale well up to some bounded group size (usually around 32 members); over a multicast layer such as IP multicast, throughput may be roughly constant in this range (and similarly for other such systems, including Spread). Moreover, because Horus and Spread do not need to wait for acknowledgements on these cheapest operations, the delay seen in quorum systems is avoided. However, as Horus or Spread configurations get very large, they too begin to slow down; detailed studies suggest that this degradation in throughput is at first linear, but that eventually a quadratic factor dominates. The problem is initially one of flow control (it is easy to see why collecting acknowledgements from a set of n members should take time proportional to n if n is large enough), but then becomes more complex, involving overheads associated with retransmission of lost messages and membership health tracking. Thus, for smaller configurations, Horus and Spread will vastly outperform quorum systems, and they can also be used

---

[4]There has been recent work on so-called "Byzantine Quorum" systems, in which we think of the server as having n^2 members organized as a square array; a read quorum would be any row and a write quorum any column. Jim Gray actually argues that the costs of replication will often rise as $O(n)$ due to concurrency control conflicts and, independently, will also rise as $O(n)$ due to the cost of the quorum operations. Thus Byzantine Quorum systems, in his analysis, would slow down as $O(n^* \sqrt{n})$. This is still quite severe and any practical application would need to keep n as small as possible.

in somewhat larger group settings than can the quorum schemes. They also have a limitation: cloud computing platforms are subject to large, unpredictable scheduling and message delivery delays. Both Horus and Spread work best in systems that are lightly loaded, have very low scheduling overheads, and in which message latencies are extremely low.

In a system he called Quicksilver Scalable Multicast (QSM), Ostrowski showed how to build a hierarchical acknowledgment layer that he overlays on top of very large groups (Ostrowski et al. 2008a, 2008b), and also systems with very large numbers of overlapping groups (a pattern seen often in the cloud, where a massive number of replicas might handle some data set such as user mailboxes, but with each individual mailbox only replicated to a small number of them, perhaps 3—this is called *sharding*). QSM was successfully scaled to vastly larger configurations with thousands of group members. The Isis^2 system offers both schemes: it behaves like Horus for smaller groups, because this gives the best performance and latency. But with large groups, users can ask Isis^2 to switch to a version of the QSM protocol. Doing so allows Isis^2 to support much larger scenarios, at the price of higher latency in smaller cases where the basic groups might still have been a viable option.

In dynamic membership models, we usually assume that individual processes are the members of the system, rather than focusing on the computers hosting those processes. Processes come and go, and we will model them as "joining" and "leaving" the system. Sometimes a process fails and hence "leaves" without warning. The model is quite flexible, and in fact when working with it, one often mixes it with elements of the static approach. For example, one can build applications composed of dynamic groups, but with the restriction that no group can be formed without having members on such and such a set of servers. This flexibility, combined with the higher speed of applications built using the model, is a strong argument in its favor.

Interestingly, even the basic Paxos protocol can accommodate dynamic membership: papers by Lamport and others have shown how to do this by using a two-level quorum update scheme; one to change the membership, and the other to do quorum reads and writes during periods when membership is not changing. This strikes some as overkill: one ends up with two ways to deal with a faulty process: we could absorb it into the f parameter used in the quorum update and read protocol, or we can change membership. The argument in favor of offering both options is that some failures are transient (for example, perhaps a replica crashes and must reboot), and for those, changing membership may seem to abandon hope that the replica in question will ever resume. With Paxos such a replica can just repair itself and restart; if any updates managed to commit while it was down, they obviously will not be reflected in its durable state, but this does not matter since subsequent reads and updates need to access a quorum and will find at least one replica that knows about the event. Otherwise, it would not have been able to commit. Thus we can reserve membership changes for permanent events: the replica just went up in flames, and will definitely not be back in business, ever.

The downside, though, is that Lamport's solution for this particular case turns out to be both complex and expensive, and is also rather tricky to use: it involves something he calls a *window of concurrency* and can deliver messages that were sent during some previous, no longer active, system membership in a future membership state where those messages might not make sense. We will not discuss the details here; a more formal treatment appears in Appendix A.

These are not the only two consistency models that have been proposed. We touch on some of the others later in this chapter. For example, the static and dynamic system models assume that when a machine fails, it does so by crashing, and this of course simplifies matters in important ways. If we introduce the possibility that data is corrupt or that group members might behave maliciously, the most appropriate consistency model changes to one called the "Byzantine" model. Byzantine fault tolerance is a powerful idea and is increasingly useful in systems concerned with obtaining very strong guarantees (for example, security mechanisms), but not many developers actually work with such subsystems. For this reason, we limit ourselves to a brief mention of the Byzantine model, and similarly for several other well-known but less practically significant approaches to high assurance distributed computing.

Our basic goal, then, is to explore two kinds of system. The static ones assume a pre-specified set of servers but are able to handle failures of minority subsets. These solutions tend to be easy to describe but rather slow. The dynamic systems use a software group membership service to track membership, resulting in a more flexible but somewhat more complex architecture. The main merit of this architecture is the tremendous speedup it brings. It also brings some limitations, and we will touch on those, but in practice, they do not seem to represent real problems for users.

10.2   Time in Distributed Systems

In discussing the two views of system membership, we made casual reference to temporal properties of a system. For example, we said that processes should "agree" on the membership in a system—but when should they agree? Clearly, the concept of time represents a fundamental component of any distributed computing model. In the simplest terms, a distributed system is any set of processes that communicates by message passing and carrying out desired actions over time. Specifications of distributed behavior often include such terms as "when," "before," "after," and "simultaneously," and we will need to develop the tools to make this terminology rigorous.

In nondistributed settings, time has an obvious meaning—at least to nonphysicists. The world is full of clocks, which are accurate and synchronized to varying degrees. Something similar is true for distributed systems: All computers have some form of clock, and clock synchronization services are a standard part of any distributed computing environment. Moreover, just as in any other setting, these clocks have limited accuracy. Two different processes, reading their local clocks at the same instant in (real) time, might observe different values, depending on the quality of the clock synchronization algorithm. Clocks may also drift over long periods of time.

The use of time in a distributed system raises several problems. One obvious problem is to devise algorithms for synchronizing clocks accurately. In Chap. 19 we will look at several such algorithms, although the use of inexpensive GPS hardware may someday eliminate the need for complex protocols in many settings. However, even given very accurate clocks, communication systems operate at such high speeds that the use of physical clocks for fine-grained temporal measurements can only make sense for processes sharing the same clock—for example, by operating on the same computer. This leads to something of a quandary: In what sense is it meaningful to say that one event occurs and then another does so, or that two events are concurrent, if no means are available by which a program could label events and compare their times of occurrence?

Looking at this question in 1978, Leslie Lamport proposed a model of logical time that answers this question (see Lamport 1978a, 1984). Lamport considered sets of processes (they could be static or dynamic) that interact by message passing. In his approach, the execution of a process is modeled as a series of atomic events, each of which requires a single unit of logical time to perform. More precisely, his model represents a process by a tuple $(E_p, <_p)$, where E_p is a set of events that occurred within process p, and $<_p$ is a partial order on those events. The advantage of this representation is that it captures any concurrency available within p. Thus, if a and b are events within p, $a <_p b$ means that a happens before b, in some sense meaningful to p—for example, b might be an operation that reads a value written by a, b could have acquired a lock that a released, or p might be executing sequential code in which operation b is not initiated until after a has terminated.

Notice that there are many levels of granularity at which one might describe the events that occur as a process executes. At the level of the components from which the computer was fabricated, computation consists of concurrent events that implement the instructions or microinstructions executed by the user's program. At a higher level, a process might be viewed in terms of statements in a programming language, control-flow graphs, procedure calls, or units of work that make sense in some external frame of reference, such as operations on a database. Concurrency within a process may result from interrupt handlers, parallel programming constructs in the language or run-time system, or from the use of lightweight threads. Thus, when we talk about the events that occur within a process, it is understood that the designer of a system will typically have a granularity of representation that seems natural for the distributed protocol or specification at hand and that events are encoded to this degree of precision. In this book, most examples will be at a very coarse level of precision, in which we treat all the local computation that occurs within a process, between when it sends or receives a first message, and when it sends or receives a second message, as a single event or even as being associated with the send or receive event itself.

Lamport models the sending and receiving of messages as events. (See Fig. 10.1.) Thus, an event a could be the sending of a message m, denoted $snd(m)$; the reception of m, denoted $rcv(m)$; or the delivery of m to application code, denoted $deliv(m)$. When the process at which an event occurs is not clear from context, we will add the process identifier as a subscript: $snd_p(m)$, $rcv_p(m)$ and $deliv_p(m)$, as seen here:

Fig. 10.1 Process send, receive and deliver events

The reasons for separating receive events from delivery events are to enable us to talk about protocols that receive a message and do things to it, or delay it, before letting the application program see it. Not every message sent will necessarily be received, and not every message received will necessarily be delivered to the application; the former property depends upon the reliability characteristics of the network, and the latter upon the nature of the message.

Consider a process p with an event $snd(m)$ and a process q in which there is a corresponding event $rcv(m)$ for the same message m. Clearly, the sending of a message precedes its receipt. Thus, we can introduce an additional partial order that orders send and receive events for the same messages. Denote this communication ordering relation by $<_m$ so that we can write $snd_p(m) <_m rcv_q(m)$.

This leads to a definition of logical time in a distributed system as the transitive closure of the $<_p$ relations for the processes p that comprise the system and $<_m$. We will write $a \to b$ to denote the fact that a and b are ordered within this temporal relation, which is often called the potential causality relation for the system. In words, we will say that a happened before b. If neither $a \to b$ nor $b \to a$, we will say that a and b occur *concurrently*.

Potential causality is useful in many ways. First, it allows us to be precise when talking about the temporal properties of algorithms used in distributed systems—for example, when we have used phrasing such as "at a point in time" or "when" in relation to a distributed execution, it may not have been clear just what it means to talk about an instant in time that spans a set of processes composing the system. Certainly, the discussion at the start of this chapter, in which it was noted that clocks in a distributed system will not often be sufficiently synchronized to measure time, should have raised concerns about the concept of simultaneous events. An instant in time should correspond to a set of simultaneous events, one per process in the system, but the most obvious way of writing down such a set (namely, writing the state of each process as that process reaches some designated time) would not physically be realizable by any protocol we could implement as a part of such a system.

Consider, however, a set of concurrent events, one per process in a system. Such a set potentially represents an instantaneous snapshot of a distributed system, and even if the events did not occur at precisely the same instant in real time, there is no way to determine this from within the system, nor do we care. We will use the term *consistent cut* to refer to a set of events with this property (see Chandy and Lamport 1985). A second term, *consistent snapshot*, is commonly used in the literature to refer to the full set of events that happen before or on a consistent cut; we will not make use of snapshots here, but readers who explore the topic in more detail will want to be aware of the concept, which is a bit like a checkpoint but includes all the processes in the system and the contents of all the communications channels between them. The messages in the channels of a snapshot will be those for which the snapshot contains a *snd* event but lacks a corresponding *rcv* event.

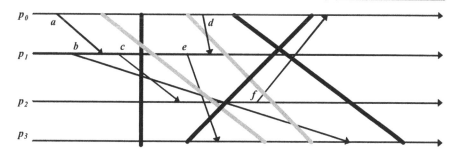

Fig. 10.2 Examples of consistent (*black*) and inconsistent (*gray*) cuts. The *gray cuts* illustrate states in which a message receive event is included but the corresponding send event is omitted. Consistent cuts represent system states that could have occurred at a single instant in real time. Notice, however, that a consistent cut may not actually capture simultaneous states of the processes in question (i.e., a cut might be instantaneous in real time, but there are many consistent cuts that are not at all simultaneous) and that there may be many such cuts through a given point in the history of a processD..

Figure 10.2 illustrates both the notion of causal time and also the concept of a consistent cut. With respect to potential causality, one can easily see that, for example, event *a* is prior (in a potentially causal sense) to events *c* and *f*, whereas events *a* and *b* are concurrent—even though *b* "looks" like it happens after *a* in the figure. The point is that, as just explained, no information could have reached *b* from *a* hence the ordering in this case is essentially arbitrary.

What about the various cuts shown in Fig. 10.2? The gray cuts are inconsistent because they include message receive events but exclude the corresponding send events. The black cuts satisfy the consistency property. If one thinks about process execution timelines as if they were made of rubber, the black cuts correspond to possible distortions of the execution in which time never flows backward; the gray cuts correspond to distortions that violate this property.

If a program or a person were to look at the state of a distributed system along an inconsistent cut (i.e., by contacting the processes one by one to check each individual state and then assembling a picture of the system as a whole from the data obtained), the results could be confusing and meaningless—for example, if a system manages some form of data using a lock, it could appear that multiple processes hold the lock simultaneously. To see this, imagine that process *p* holds the lock and then sends a message to process *q* in which it passes the lock to *q*. If our cut happened to show *q* after it received this message (and hence obtained the lock) but showed *p* before it sent it (and hence when it still held the lock), *p* and *q* would appear to both hold the lock. Yet in the real execution, this state never occurred. Were a developer trying to debug a distributed system, considerable time could be wasted in trying to sort out real bugs from these sorts of virtual bugs introduced as artifacts of the way the system state was collected!

The value of consistent cuts is that they represent states the distributed system might actually have been in at a single instant in real time. Of course, there is no way to know which of the feasible cuts for a given execution correspond to the actual real-time states through which the system passed, but Lamport's observation was that in a practical sense, to even ask this question reveals a basic misunderstanding of the nature of time in distributed systems. In his eyes, the consistent cuts for a distributed system are the *more meaningful* concept of simultaneous states for that system, while external time, being inaccessible within the system, is actually *less* meaningful. Lacking a practical way to make real-time clocks that are accurate to the resolution necessary to accurately timestamp events, he argued that real time is in fact not a very useful property for protocols that operate at this level. Of course, we can still use real time for other purposes that demand lesser degrees of accuracy, and will reintroduce it later, but for the time being, we accept this perspective. For a discussion about some uses of consistent cuts, see Babaoglu and Marzullo (1993).

Potential causality is a useful tool for reasoning about a distributed system, but it also has more practical significance. There are several ways to build logical clocks with which causal relationships between events can be detected, to varying degrees of accuracy.

A very simple logical clock can be constructed by associating a counter with each process and message in the system. Let LT_p be the logical time for process p (the value of p's copy of this counter). Then when a message is sent, LT_p is copied into the message. We will denote this by LT_m the logical time associated with message m (also called the logical timestamp of m). When m is delivered, or some other event occurs at a process p, the following rules are used to update LT_p.

1. If $LT_p < LT_m$, process p sets $LT_p = LT_m + 1$
2. If $LT_p \geq LT_m$, p sets $LT_p = LT_p + 1$
3. For important events other than reception of a message, p sets $LT_p = LT_p + 1$

The application can decide what an "important" event is—in practice, it only makes sense to track the time of events if the application needs that temporal information for some other purpose, such as concurrency control in a transactional subsystem, or deciding how to order events in ways consistent with causality. For example, some algorithms for updating replicated data generate multicasts that can be delivered out of order, and it is important to put them into timestamp order before applying the updates so as to ensure that the replicate data item ends up with the correct value. Logical timestamps turn out to be a very compact way to label the multicasts so as to achieve this goal. Similarly, some algorithms for replicating a transactional service allow operations to occur concurrently, but need to know if there *might* have been a causal relation between two events, because when this occurs the former transaction will need to be serialized before the one that may have run later. Using logical timestamps, such algorithms are able to efficiently recognize such cases. We will see additional uses for logical timestamps in the remainder of this chapter and in Chaps. 11 through 14.

We will use the notation $LT(a)$ to denote the value of LT_p when event a occurred at process p. It can easily be shown that if $a \rightarrow b, LT(a) < LT(b)$: From the definition of the potential causality relation, we know that if $a \rightarrow b$, there must exist a chain of events $a \equiv e_0 \rightarrow e_1 \cdots \rightarrow e_k \equiv b$, where each pair is related either by the event ordering $<_p$ for some process p or by the event ordering $<_m$ on messages. By construction, the logical clock values associated with these events can only increase, establishing the desired result. On the other hand, $LT(a) < LT(b)$ does not imply that $a \rightarrow b$, since concurrent events may have arbitrary timestamps. This means that in the kinds of application just mentioned, logical clocks may sometimes indicate a potential ordering relationship when none is present—and if such a situation could be costly, the developer might want a more accurate way of representing time that is not misleading in this way.

For systems in which the set of processes is static, logical clocks can be generalized in a way that permits a more accurate representation of causality. A vector clock is a vector of counters, one per process in the set (see Fidge 1988; Mattern 1989; Schiper et al. 1989, 2003). Similar to the concept of logical clocks, we will say that VT_p and VT_m represent the vector times associated with process p and message m, respectively. Given a vector time VT, the notation $VT[p]$ denotes the entry in the vector corresponding to process p.

The rules for maintaining a vector clock are similar to the ones used for logical clocks, except that a process only increments its own counter. Specifically:

1. Prior to performing an important event, process p sets $VT_p[p] = VT_p[p] + 1$
2. When sending a message, process p sets $VT_m = VT_p$
3. Upon delivering a message m, process p sets $VT_p = \max(VT_p, VT_m)$

In the third situation, the function max applied to two vectors is just the element-by-element maximum of the respective entries. We now define two comparison operations on vector times. If $VT(a)$ and $VT(b)$ are vector times, we will say that $VT(a) \leq VT(b)$ if $\forall i: VT(a)[i] \leq VT(b)[i]$. When $VT(a) \leq VT(b)$ and $\exists i: VT(a)[i] < VT(b)[i]$, we will write $VT(a) < VT(b)$.

In words, a vector time entry for a process p is just a count of the number of events that have occurred at p. If process p has a vector clock with $VT_p[q]$ set to six, and $p \neq q$, this means that some chain of events has caused p to hear (directly or indirectly) from process q subsequent to the sixth event that occurred at process q. Thus, the vector time for an event e tells us, for each process in the vector, how many events occurred at that process causally prior to when e occurred. If $VT(m) = [17, 2, 3]$, corresponding to processes $\{p, q, r\}$, we know that 17 events occurred at process p that causally precede the sending of m, two at process q, and three at process r.

It is easy to see that vector clocks accurately encode potential causality. If $a \rightarrow b$, then we again consider a chain of events related by the process or message ordering: $a \equiv e_0 \rightarrow e_1 \cdots \rightarrow e_k \equiv b$. By construction, at each event the vector time can only increase (i.e., $VT(e_i) < VT(e_{i+1})$), because each process increments its own vector time entry prior to each operation, and receive operations compute an element-by-element maximum. Thus, $VT(a) < VT(b)$. However, unlike a logical clock, the converse also holds: If $VT(a) < VT(b)$, then $a \rightarrow b$. To see this, let p be the process at which event a occurred, and consider $VT(a)[p]$. In the case where b also occurs at process p, we know that $\forall i: VT(a)[i] \leq VT(b)[i]$—hence, if a and b are not the same event, a must happen before b at p. Otherwise, suppose that b occurs at process q. According to the algorithm, process q only changes $VT_q[p]$ upon delivery of some message m for which $VT(m)[p] > VT_q[p]$ at the event of the delivery. If we denote b as e_k and $deliv(m)$ as e_{k-1}, the send event for m as e_{k-2}, and the sender of m by q', we can now trace a chain of events back to a process

q'' from which q' received this vector timestamp entry. Continuing this procedure, we will eventually reach process p. We will now have constructed a chain of events $a \equiv e_0 \rightarrow e_1 \cdots \rightarrow e_k \equiv b$, establishing that $a \rightarrow b$, the desired result.

For example, referring back to Fig. 10.2, if we follow the event chain denoted by a, b, c, e, each successive event increments one counter in the vector: a increments the counter associated with process p_0, and b, c, and e each increment the counter associated with process p_1. We will be left with a $VT = [1, 3, 0, 0]$. After events a and d at process p_0, the vector timestamp at that process is $[2, 0, 0, 0]$. And we can see that events d and e were concurrent by comparing these two vectors. Neither vector is less than the other, hence neither event preceded the other in a causal sense. In contrast, if we compare event a at process p_0 (which will have vector timestamp $[1, 0, 0, 0]$) with event d (vector timestamp $[1, 3, 0, 0]$), the latter timestamp is larger than the former, pointing to the existence of a causal path from a to d.

The key insight is that if two events are concurrent, there must be causal paths to each of them along which different vector timestamp entries will be incremented. Lacking a causal path from one to the other, neither can "learn" about the updates that occurred on the other's path. So each ends up with a vector timestamp that has some counters larger than in the other—counters for events along these disjoint parts of the causal histories. We see this when the vector timestamp associated with event d is compared with that of event e. In contrast, if an event occurred before some other event, the latter will have learned about all the counter increments that occurred up to the point that the earlier event took place. Since that time, some of these counters may have been incremented, but the resulting vector timestamp will always be recognizable as larger than the one for the earlier event. And this is the case if we compare the time at event e ($[1, 3, 0, 0]$) with that at events a ($[1, 0, 0, 0]$), b ($[1, 1, 0, 0]$) or c ($[1, 2, 0, 0]$).

This tells us that if we have a fixed set of processes and use vector timestamps to record the passage of time, we can accurately represent the potential causality relationship for messages sent and received, and other events, within that set. Doing so will also allow us to determine when events are concurrent: This is the case if neither $a \rightarrow b$ nor $b \rightarrow a$. For algorithms where we need temporal information but will pay a steep price if that information is inaccurate, vector timestamps can be a good choice. However, they also bring some costs of their own: the vectors are obviously larger than the single counter needed to implement a logical clock, and (as defined above), they only make sense for a system with static membership.

There has been considerable research on optimizing the encoding of vector time-stamps, and the representation presented above is far from the best possible in a large system (see Charron-Bost 1991). For a very large system, it is considered preferable to represent causal time using a set of event identifiers, $\{e_0, e_1, \ldots, e_k\}$ such that the events in the set are concurrent and causally precede the event being labeled (see Peterson 1987; Melliar-Smith and Moser 1993). Thus if $a \rightarrow b$, $b \rightarrow d$ and $c \rightarrow d$ one could say that event d took place at causal time $\{b, c\}$ (meaning "after events b and c"), event b at time $\{a\}$, and so forth. In practice the identifiers used in such a representation would be process identifiers and event counters maintained on a per-process basis—hence, this *precedence-order* representation is recognizable as a compression of the vector timestamp. The precedence-order representation is useful in settings where processes can potentially construct the full $\rightarrow$ relation and in which the level of true concurrency is fairly low. The vector timestamp representation is preferred in settings where the number of participating processes is fairly low and the level of concurrency may be high.

As for the membership issue, there turn out to be several ways to work around this. One obvious option is to just list the process identifier associated with each counter in the vector itself. Thus, $[1, 3, 0, 0]$ in our previous example could be written as $[p_0 : 1, p_1 : 3]$, with zero entries omitted. We will see another option in Chap. 12, when we introduce the idea of process groups that advance through a well-defined set of membership *views*. In that approach, we can associate a vector timestamp with a view; the list of members in the view then tells us which counter in the vector is associated with which process in the group.

Logical and vector clocks will prove to be powerful tools in developing protocols for use in real distributed applications. The method favored in a specific setting will typically depend upon the importance of precisely representing the potential causal order and on the overhead that can be tolerated. We will use logical clocks when possible, because the overhead is tiny. Vector clocks are useful too, but their larger size can turn out to be a serious problem, for example in systems with large groups and very small messages, where the vector timestamp itself may be much larger than the data in a message.

The remainder of this chapter focuses on problems for which logical time, represented through some form of logical timestamp, represents the most natural temporal model. In many distributed applications, however, some concept of real time is also required, and our emphasis on logical time in this section should not be taken as dismissing the importance of other temporal schemes.

10.3   The Distributed Commit Problem

An implementable way to talk about logical time represents a kind of building block that can be used in many ways in systems and protocols. We now explore a second kind of building block that addresses a classical problem seen in several of the replication methods that follow. This is the *distributed commit problem*. Distributed commit arises in many settings where one wants to perform an operation in an all-or-nothing manner (see Gray 1978; Gray and Reuter 1993). We are going to start by talking about commit in a static membership model, but in fact we will later use the commit protocol as our way to *implement* the dynamic membership model. Then we will use the resulting membership mechanisms to implement replicated data.

The commit problem arises when we wish to have a set of processes that all agree on whether or not to perform some action that may not be possible at some of the participants. To overcome this initial uncertainty, it is necessary to first determine whether or not all the participants will be able to perform the operation and then communicate the outcome of the decision to the participants in a reliable way (the assumption is that once a participant has confirmed that it can perform the operation, this remains true even if it subsequently crashes and must be restarted). We say that an operation can be *committed* if the participants can all perform it. Once a commit decision is reached, this requirement will hold even if some participants fail and later recover. On the other hand, if one or more participants are unable to perform the operation when initially queried, or some cannot be contacted, the operation as a whole *aborts*, meaning that no participant should perform it.

Consider a system composed of a static set S containing processes $\{p_0, p_1, \ldots, p_n\}$ that fail by crashing and that maintain both *volatile* data, which is lost if a crash occurs, and *persistent* data, which can be recovered after a crash in the same state they had at the time of the crash. An example of persistent data would be information in a disk file; volatile data is any information in a processor's memory, on some sort of a scratch area, that will not be preserved if the system crashes and must be rebooted. It is frequently much cheaper to store information in volatile data—hence, it would be common for a program to write intermediate results of a computation to volatile storage. The commit problem will now occur if we wish to arrange for all the volatile information to be saved persistently. The all-or-nothing aspects of the problem reflect the possibility that a computer might fail and lose the volatile data it held; in this case the desired outcome would be that no changes to *any* of the persistent storage areas occur.

As an example, we might want all of the processes in S to write some message into their persistent data storage. During the initial stages of the protocol, the message would be sent to the processes, which would each store it in their volatile memory. When the decision is made to try to commit these updates, the processes clearly cannot just modify the persistent area, because some process might fail before doing so. Consequently, the commit protocol involves first storing the volatile information into a persistent but temporary region of storage. Having done so, the participants would signal their ability to commit.

If all the participants are successful, it is safe to begin transfers from the temporary area to the real data storage region. Consequently, when these processes are later told that the operation as a whole should commit, they would copy their temporary copies of the message into a permanent part of the persistent storage area. If the operation aborts, they would not perform this copy operation. As should be evident, the challenge of the protocol will be to handle with the recovery of a participant from a failed state; in this situation, the protocol must determine whether any commit protocols were pending at the time of its failure and, if so, whether they terminated in a commit or an abort state.

A distributed commit protocol is normally initiated by a process that we will call the *coordinator;* assume that this is process p_0. In a formal sense, the objective of the protocol is for p_0 to solicit votes for or against a commit from the processes in S and then to send a *commit* message to those processes only if all of the votes are in favor of commit; otherwise an *abort* message is sent. To avoid a trivial solution in which p_0 always sends an abort, we would ideally like to require that if all processes vote for commit and no communication failures occur, the outcome should be commit. Unfortunately, however, it is easy to see that such a requirement is not really meaningful because communication failures can prevent messages from reaching the coordinator. Thus, we are forced to adopt a weaker nontriviality requirement that states that if all processes vote for commit and all the votes reach the coordinator, the protocol should commit.

For a researcher wearing a "theoretician's hat," this solves the problem by separating the obligations on the protocol from the whole question of how the network behaves. Practitioners often find such slight-of-hand annoying: all we have done is to shift any uncertainty into the network. However, one can reconcile these perspectives by recalling that our goal here is just to talk about protocol correctness—does the protocol do the right thing when the means of doing so are "placed in its hands"? A separate but equally important question is "will my network work well enough to ensure that the protocol functions in the desired manner?" Theoreticians rarely worry about that second question; practitioners will typically want to start with a correct protocol, and then take the step of engineering a network so that the overall probability that the system will be reliable satisfies some end-user objective. Thus, our non-triviality condition does not sweep the whole issue under the rug, it simply separates the issue into two aspects that can be attacked separately.

A commit protocol can be implemented in many ways. The most standard implementations are called two- and three-phase commit protocols, often abbreviated as 2PC and 3PC. In what follows, we will focus on 2PC and 3PC, but the reader should keep in mind that the commit "pattern" is sometimes concealed in a protocol that does not actually use this specific style of message exchange. When faced with such a protocol—perhaps, a protocol that sends a token twice around a ring of processes, taking actions only on the second pass—it is often helpful to realize that if the protocol "could" have been implemented using a more standard 2PC or 3PC approach, then many of the insights one can have concerning 2PC or 3PC probably apply to that protocol as well. Indeed (to pursue the analogy a little further), if one implements point to point message passing over a token ring network device, what looks to the application like a 2PC protocol might look to the network like a token circulating among a ring of processes, on which varying sets of point to point messages are piggybacked. When confronting such a duality, we should again fall back by recalling our goals.

If the goal is basically theoretical—proving correctness, or proving an impossibility result—the implementation "details" may not matter. Such results often apply to any solution to a given problem and are independent of the way a particular solution operates. If our goals are more practical, we should think of the problem statement as laying out the requirements that any implementation needs to satisfy. Within the space of possible implementations, we can then use clever engineering to maximize performance, minimize cost, and achieve other objectives. The different goals of theoreticians and engineers can sometimes create tensions, but these tensions are rarely fundamental. More often, they reflect poor communication: the theory community sometimes neglects to point out that their problem statements matter far more than the implementation of a protocol they use to illustrate a general principle. And engineers sometimes forget that no matter how a protocol is implemented, the solution may need to live within deeper constraints imposed by the nature of the problem itself. We will see several examples of this tension in the remainder of the book, including some that have provoked major debates which, seen from the perspective just outlined, turn out to be almost entirely the result of confusion and miscommunication!

10.3.1 Two-Phase Commit

A 2PC protocol operates in rounds of multicast communication. Each phase is composed of one round of messages to the participants and one round of replies from the recipients to the sender. The coordinator initially selects a unique identifier for this run of the protocol—for example, by concatenating its own process ID to the value of a logical clock. The protocol identifier will be used to distinguish the messages associated with different runs of the protocol that happen to execute concurrently, and in the remainder of this section we will assume that all the messages under discussion are labeled by this initial identifier.

The coordinator starts by sending out a first round of messages to the participants. These messages normally contain the protocol identifier, the list of participants (so that all the participants will know who the other participants are), and a message "type" indicating that this is the first round of a 2PC protocol. In a static system, where all the processes in the system participate in the 2PC protocol, the list of participants can be omitted because it has a well-known value. Additional fields can be added to this message depending on the situation in which the 2PC was needed—for example, it could contain a description of the action that the coordinator wishes to take (if this is not obvious to the participants), a reference to some volatile information that the coordinator wishes to have copied to a persistent data area, and so forth. 2PC is thus a very general tool, which can solve any of a number of specific problems sharing the attribute of needing an all-or-nothing outcome as well as the requirement that participants must be queried if they will be able to perform the operation before it is safe to assume that they can do so.

Each participant, upon receiving the first round message, takes such local actions as are needed to decide if it can vote in favor of commit—for example, a participant may need to set up some sort of persistent data structure, recording that the 2PC protocol is underway and saving the information that will be needed to perform the desired action if a commit occurs. In the previous example, the participant would copy its volatile data to the temporary persistent region of the disk and then force the records to the disk. Having done this (which may take some time), the participant sends back its vote. The coordinator collects votes, but also uses a timer to limit the duration of the first phase (the initial round of outgoing messages and the collection of replies). If a timeout occurs before the first-phase replies have all been collected, the coordinator aborts the protocol. Otherwise, it makes a commit or abort decision according to the votes it collects[5].

---

[5]As described, this protocol already violates the nontriviality goal that we expressed earlier. No timer is really safe in an asynchronous distributed system, because an adversary could just set the minimum message latency to the timer value plus one second, and, in this way cause the protocol

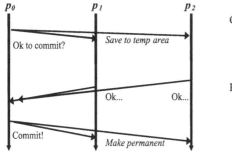

Coordinator :
  multicast: *ok to commit?*
  collect replies
    all *ok* => *send commit*
    else => *send abort*
Participant:
  ok to commit =>
    save to temp area, reply *ok*
  commit =>
    make change permanent
  abort =>
    delete temp area

Fig. 10.3   Skeleton of two-phase commit protocol

Now we enter the second phase of the protocol, in which the coordinator sends out commit or abort messages in a new round of communication. Upon receipt of these messages, the participants take the desired action or, if the protocol is aborted, they delete the associated information from their persistent data stores. Figure 10.3 illustrates this basic skeleton of the 2PC protocol.

Several failure cases need to be addressed. The coordinator could fail before starting the protocol, during the first phase, while collecting replies, after collecting replies but before sending the second-phase messages, or during the transmission of the second-phase messages. The same is true for a participant. For each case we need to specify a recovery action, which will lead to successful termination of the protocol with the desired all-or-nothing semantics.

In addition to this, the protocol described above omits consideration of the storage of information associated with the run. In particular, it seems clear that the coordinator and participants should not need to keep any form of information indefinitely in a correctly specified protocol. Our protocol makes use of a protocol identifier, and we will see that the recovery mechanisms require that some information be saved for a period of time, indexed by protocol identifier. Thus, rules will be needed for garbage collection of information associated with terminated 2PC protocols. Otherwise, the information base in which these data is stored might grow without limit, ultimately posing serious storage and management problems.

We start by focusing on participant failures, then turn to the issue of coordinator failure, and finally discuss the question of garbage collection.

Suppose that a process p_i fails during the execution of a 2PC protocol. With regard to the protocol, p_i may be in any of several states. In its initial state, p_i will be unaware of the protocol. In this case, p_i will not receive the initial vote

---

to abort despite the fact that all processes vote commit and all messages will reach the coordinator. Concerns such as this can seem unreasonably narrow-minded, but are actually important in trying to pin down the precise conditions under which commit is possible. The practical community tends to be fairly relaxed about such issues, while the theory community takes problems of this sort very seriously. It is regrettable but perhaps inevitable that some degree of misunderstanding results from these different points of view.

message; therefore, the coordinator aborts the protocol. The initial state ends when p_i has received the initial vote request and is prepared to send back a vote in favor of commit (if p_i does not vote for commit, or is not yet prepared, the protocol will abort in any case). We will now say that p_i *is prepared to commit*. In the prepared to commit state, p_i is compelled to learn the outcome of the protocol even if it fails and later recovers. This is an important observation because the applications that use 2PC often must lock critical resources or limit processing of new requests by p_i while they are prepared to commit. This means that until p_i learns the outcome of the request, it may be unavailable for other types of processing. Such a state can result in denial of services. The next state entered by p_i is called the *commit* or *abort* state, in which it knows the outcome of the protocol. Failures that occur at this stage must not be allowed to disrupt the termination actions of p_i, such as the release of any resources that were tied up during the prepared state. Finally, p_i returns to its initial state, garbage collects all information associated with the execution of the protocol, and is left in a state that retains only the effects of any committed actions.

From this discussion, we see that a process recovering from a failure will need to determine whether or not it was in a prepared to commit, commit, or abort state at the moment of the failure. In a prepared to commit state, the process will need to find out whether the 2PC protocol terminated in a commit or abort, so there must be some form of system service or protocol outcome file in which this information is logged. Having entered a commit or abort state, the process needs a way to complete the commit or abort action even if it is repeatedly disrupted by failures in the act of doing so. We say that the action must be *idempotent*, meaning that it can be performed repeatedly without ill effects. An example of an idempotent action would be copying a file from one location to another: Provided that access to the target file is disallowed until the copying action completes, the process can copy the file once or many times with the same outcome. In particular, if a failure disrupts the copying action, it can be restarted after the process recovers.

Not surprisingly, many systems that use 2PC are structured to take advantage of this type of file copying. In the most common approach, information needed to perform the commit or abort action is saved in a *log* on the persistent storage area. The commit or abort state is represented by a bit in a table, also stored in the persistent area, describing pending 2PC protocols and indexed by protocol identifier. Upon recovery, a process first consults this table to determine the actions it should take, and then uses the log to carry out the action. Only after successfully completing the action does a process delete its knowledge of the protocol and garbage collect the log records that were needed to carry it out. (See Fig. 10.4.)

Up to now, we have not considered coordinator failure—hence, it would be reasonable to assume that the coordinator itself plays the role of tracking the protocol outcome and saving this information until all participants are known to have completed their commit or abort actions. The 2PC protocol thus needs a final phase in which messages flow back from participants to the coordinator, which must retain information about the protocol until all such messages have been received.

Consider next the case where the coordinator fails during a 2PC protocol. If we are willing to wait for the coordinator to recover, the protocol requires a few changes to deal with this situation. The first change is to modify the coordinator to save its

Coordinator:	Participant:
multicast: *ok to commit?*	*ok to commit* ⇒
collect replies	save to temp area, reply *ok*
all *ok* ⇒ *log "commit"* to *"outcomes"*	*commit* ⇒
table send commit	make change permanent
else ⇒ *send abort*	*abort* ⇒
collect acknowledgments	delete temp area
garbage-collect protocol outcome	After failure:
information	*for each pending protocol*
	contact coordinator to learn outcome

Fig. 10.4   2PC extended to handle participant failures

commit decision to persistent storage *before* sending commit or abort messages to the participants[6]. Upon recovery, the coordinator is now guaranteed to have available the information needed to terminate the protocol, which it can do by simply retransmitting the final commit or abort message. A participant not in the precommit state would acknowledge such a message but take no action; a participant waiting in the precommit state would terminate the protocol upon receipt of it.

One major problem with this solution to 2PC is that if a coordinator failure occurs, the participants are blocked, waiting for the coordinator to recover. As noted earlier, preparing to commit often ties down resources or involves holding locks—hence, blocking in this manner can have serious implications for system availability. (See Fig. 10.4.) Suppose that we permit the participants to communicate among themselves. Could we increase the availability of the system so as to guarantee progress even if the coordinator crashes?

Again, there are three stages of the protocol to consider. If the coordinator crashes during its first phase of message transmissions, a state may result in which some participants are prepared to commit, others may be unable to commit (they have voted to abort and know that the protocol will eventually do so), and still other processes may not know anything at all about the state of the protocol. If it crashes during its decision, or before sending out all the second-phase messages, there may be a mixture of processes left in the prepared state and processes that know the final outcome.

---

[6]It is actually sufficient for the coordinator to save only commit decisions in persistent storage—this is called the "presumed abort" approach. After failure, a recovering coordinator can safely presume the protocol to have aborted if it finds no commit record; the advantage of such a change is to make the abort case less costly, by removing a disk I/O operation from the critical path before the abort can be acted upon. The elimination of a single disk I/O operation may seem like a minor optimization, but in fact can be quite significant in light of the tenfold latency difference between a typical disk I/O operation (10–25 ms) and a typical network communication operation (perhaps 1–4 ms latency). One does not often have an opportunity to obtain an order of magnitude performance improvement in a critical path—hence, these are the sorts of engineering decisions that can have very important implications for overall system performance. Similarly, it is possible to architect systems to "presume commit" and only log abort decisions. If aborts are very rare this can be a good option, although doing so imposes a continuous low-level of costs that can turn out to dominate the cost savings associated with the "trick."

Coordinator:	Participant: first time message received
multicast: *ok to commit?*	*ok to commit* ⇒
collect replies	save to temp area, reply *ok*
all *ok* ⇒ *log commit to outcomes table*	*commit* ⇒
wait until safe on persistent store	make change permanent
send commit	*abort* ⇒
else ⇒ *send abort*	delete temp area
collect acknowledgements	Message is a duplicate
garbage-collect protocol outcome	(recovering coordinator)
information	*send acknowledgment*
After failure:	After failure:
for each pending protocol in outcomes table	*for each pending protocol*
send outcome (commit or abort)	contact coordinator to learn outcome
wait for acknowledgements	
garbage collect outcome information	

Fig. 10.5 2PC protocol extended to overcome coordinator failures

Suppose that we add a timeout mechanism to the participants: In the prepared state, a participant that does not learn the outcome of the protocol within some specified period of time will timeout and seek to complete the protocol on its own. Clearly, there will be some unavoidable risk of a timeout occurring because of a transient network failure, much as in the case of RPC failure-detection mechanisms discussed early in the book. Thus, a participant that takes over in this case cannot safely conclude that the coordinator has actually failed. Indeed, any mechanism for takeover will need to work even if the timeout is set to 0 and even if the participants try to run the protocol to completion starting from the instant that they receive the phase-one message and enter a prepared to commit state!

Accordingly, let p_i be some process that has experienced a protocol timeout in the prepared to commit state. What are p_i's options? The most obvious would be for it to send out a first-phase message of its own, querying the state of the other p_j. From the information gathered in this phase, p_i may be able to deduce that the protocol either committed or aborted. This would be the case if, for example, some process p_j had received a second-phase outcome message from the coordinator before it crashed. Having determined the outcome, p_i can simply repeat the second phase of the original protocol. Although participants may receive as many as n copies of the outcome message (if all the participants time out simultaneously), this is clearly a safe way to terminate the protocol.

On the other hand, it is also possible that p_i would be unable to determine the outcome of the protocol. This would occur, for example, if all processes contacted by p_i, as well as p_i itself, were in the prepared state, with a single exception: process p_j, which does not respond to the inquiry message. Perhaps p_j has failed, or perhaps the network is temporarily partitioned. The problem now is that only the coordinator and p_j can determine the outcome, which depends entirely on p_j's vote. If the coordinator is itself a participant, as is often the case, a single failure can thus leave the 2PC participants blocked until the failure is repaired! This risk is unavoidable in a 2PC solution to the commit problem. (See Fig. 10.5.)

Earlier, we discussed the garbage collection issue. Notice that in this extension to 2PC, participants must retain information about the outcome of the protocol until they are certain that all participants know the outcome. Otherwise, if a participant p_j were to commit but promptly forget that it had done so, it would be unable to assist some other participant p_i in terminating the protocol after a coordinator failure.

Garbage collection can be done by adding a third phase of messages from the coordinator (or a participant who takes over from the coordinator) to the participants. This phase would start after all participants have acknowledged receipt of the second-phase commit or abort message, and it would simply tell participants that it is safe to garbage collect the protocol information. The handling of coordinator failure can be similar to that during the pending state. A timer is set in each participant that has entered the final state but not yet seen the garbage collection message. Should the timer expire, such a participant can simply echo the commit or abort message, which all other participants acknowledge. Once all participants have acknowledged the message, a garbage collection message can be sent out and the protocol state safely garbage collected.

Notice that the final round of communication, for purposes of garbage collection, can often be delayed for a period of time and then run once in a while, on behalf of many 2PC protocols at the same time. When this is done, the garbage collection protocol is itself best viewed as a 2PC protocol that executes perhaps once per hour. During its first round, a garbage collection protocol would solicit from each process in the system the set of protocols for which they have reached the final state. It is not difficult to see that if communication is first in, first out (FIFO) in the system, then 2PC protocols—even if failures occur—will complete in FIFO order. This being the case, each process need only provide a single protocol identifier, per protocol coordinator, in response to such an inquiry: the identifier of the last 2PC initiated by the coordinator to have reached its final state. The process running the garbage collection protocol can then compute the minimum over these values. For each coordinator, the minimum will be a 2PC protocol identifier, which has fully terminated at all the participant processes that can be garbage collected throughout the system.

We now arrive at the final version of the 2PC protocol shown in Fig. 10.6. Notice that this protocol has a potential message complexity which increases as $O(n^2)$ with the worst case occurring if a network communication problem disrupts communication during the three basic stages of communication. Further, notice that although the protocol is commonly called a two phase commit, a true two-phase version will always block if the coordinator fails. The version of Fig. 10.6 gains a higher degree of availability at the cost of additional communication for purposes of garbage collection. However, although this protocol may be more available than our initial attempt, it can still block if a failure occurs at a critical stage. In particular, participants will be unable to terminate the protocol if a failure of both the coordinator and a participant occurs during the decision stage of the protocol.

Coordinator:	Participant: first time message received
multicast: *ok to commit?*	*ok to commit* ⇒
collect replies	save to temp area, reply *ok*
all *ok* ⇒ *log commit to outcomes table*	*commit* ⇒
wait until safe on persistent store	log outcome, make change permanent
send commit	*abort* ⇒
else ⇒ *send abort*	log outcome, delete temp area
collect acknowledgements	Message is a duplicate (recovering
	coordinator) *send acknowledgment*
After failure:	After failure:
for each pending protocol in outcomes table	*for each pending protocol*
send outcome (commit or abort)	contact coordinator to learn outcome
wait for acknowledgements	After timeout in *prepare to commit* state:
Periodically:	query other participants about state
query each process: *terminated protocols?*	outcome can be deduced ⇒
for each coordinator: determine *fully*	*run coordinator-recovery protocol*
terminated protocols	outcome uncertain ⇒
2PC to garbage collect outcomes information	*must wait*

Fig. 10.6 Final version of 2PC commit: Participants attempt to terminate protocol without blocking periodic 2PC protocol used to garbage collect outcome information saved by participants and coordinators for recovery

10.3.2 Three-Phase Commit

In 1981, Skeen and Stonebraker studied the cases in which 2PC can block (see Skeen 1982a). Their work resulted in a protocol called *three-phase commit* (3PC), which is guaranteed to be nonblocking provided that only fail-stop failures occur. (A subsequent generalization by Keidar and Dolev weakens this requirement, making progress whenever a connected majority of processes is achieved). Before we present this protocol, it is important to stress that the fail-stop model is not a very realistic one: This model requires that processes fail only by crashing, and that such failures *be accurately detectable* by other processes that remain operational. As we will see, inaccurate failure detections and network partition failures continue to pose the threat of blocking in this protocol. In practice, these considerations limit the utility of the protocol (because we lack a way to accurately sense failures in most systems, and network partitions are a real threat in most distributed environments). Nonetheless, the protocol sheds light both on the issue of blocking and on the broader concept of consistency in distributed systems; therefore, it is presented here.

As in the case of the 2PC protocol, 3PC really requires a fourth phase of messages for purposes of garbage collection. However, this problem is easily solved using the same method presented in Fig. 10.6 for the case of 2PC. For brevity, we focus on the basic 3PC protocol and overlook the garbage collection issue.

Recall that 2PC blocks under conditions in which the coordinator crashes and one or more participants crash, such that the operational participants are unable to deduce the protocol outcome without information that is only available to the coordinator and/or these participants. The fundamental problem is that in a 2PC protocol, the coordinator can make a commit or abort decision, which would be known to

Coordinator:	Participant: logs state on each message
multicast: *ok to commit?*	*ok to commit* ⇒
collect replies	save to temp area, reply *ok*
all *ok* ⇒*log precommit*	*precommit* ⇒
send precommit	enter precommit state, *acknowledge*
else ⇒ *send abort*	*commit* ⇒
collect acks from non-failed participants	make change permanent
all *ack* ⇒*log commit*	*abort* ⇒
send commit	delete temp area
collect acknowledgements	After failure:
garbage-collect protocol outcome information	collect participant state information
	all *precommit, or any committed* ⇒
	push forward to commit
	else ⇒
	push back to abort

Fig. 10.7 Outline of a three-phase commit protocol

some participant p_j and even acted upon by p_j, and yet might be totally unknown to other processes in the system. The 3PC protocol prevents this from occurring by introducing an additional round of communication and delaying the prepared state until processes receive this phase of messages. By doing so, the protocol ensures that the state of the system can always be deduced by a subset of the operational processes, provided that the operational processes can still communicate reliably among themselves.

A typical 3PC protocol operates as shown in Fig. 10.7. As in the case of 2PC, the first-round message solicits votes from the participants. However, instead of entering a prepared state, a participant that has voted for commit enters an *ok to commit* state. The coordinator collects votes and can immediately abort the protocol if some votes are negative or if some votes are missing. Unlike for a 2PC, it does not immediately commit if the outcome is unanimously positive. Instead, the coordinator sends out a round of *prepare to commit* messages, receipt of which causes all participants to enter the prepare to commit state and to send an acknowledgment. After receiving acknowledgements from all participants, the coordinator sends *commit* messages and the participants commit. Notice that the *ok to commit* state is similar to the *prepared* state in the 2PC protocol, in that a participant is expected to remain capable of committing even if failures and recoveries occur after it has entered this state.

If the coordinator of a 3PC protocol detects failures of some participants (recall that in this model, failures are accurately detectable) and has not yet received their acknowledgements to its *prepare to commit* messages, the 3PC can still be committed. In this case, the unresponsive participants can be counted upon to run a recovery protocol when the cause of their failure is repaired, and that protocol will lead them to eventually commit. The protocol thus has the property of only committing if all operational participants are in the *prepared to commit* state. This observation permits any subset of operational participants to terminate the protocol safely after a crash of the coordinator and/or other participants.

Fig. 10.8 States for a
nonfaulty participant in 3PC
protocol

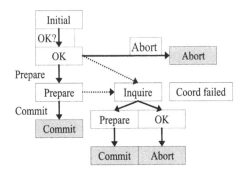

The 3PC termination protocol is similar to the 2PC protocol, and it starts by
querying the state of the participants. If any participant knows the outcome of the
protocol (commit or abort), the protocol can be terminated by disseminating that
outcome. If the participants are all in a prepared to commit state, the protocol can
safely be committed.

Suppose, however, that some mixture of states is found in the state vector. In this
situation, the participating processes have the choice of driving the protocol forward
to a commit or back to an abort. This is done by rounds of message exchange that
either move the full set of participants to *prepared to commit* and then to *commit*
or that roll them back to *ok to commit* and then abort. Again, because of the fail-
stop assumption, this algorithm runs no risk of errors. Indeed, the processes have
a simple and natural way to select a new coordinator at their disposal: Since the
system membership is assumed to be static, and since failures are detectable crashes
(the fail-stop assumption), the operational process with the lowest process identifier
can be assigned this responsibility. It will eventually recognize the situation and will
then take over, running the protocol to completion.

Notice also that even if additional failures occur, the requirement that the protocol
only commit once and that all operational processes are in a *prepared to commit*
state and only abort when all operational processes have reached an *ok to commit*
state (also called *prepared to abort*) eliminates many possible concerns. However,
this is true only because failures are accurately detectable and because processes
that fail will always run a recovery protocol upon restarting. (The "inquire" state in
Fig. 10.8.)

It is not hard to see how this recovery protocol should work. A recovering process
is compelled to track down some operational process that knows the outcome of
the protocol, and to learn the outcome from that process. If all processes fail, the
recovering process must identify the subset of processes that were the last to fail
(see Skeen 1985), learning the protocol outcome from them. In the case where the
protocol had not reached a commit or abort decision when all processes failed, it
can be resumed using the states of the participants that were the last to fail, together
with any other participants that have recovered in the interim.

Unfortunately, however, the news for 3PC is actually not quite as good as this
protocol may make it seem, because real systems do not satisfy the fail-stop failure
assumption. Although there may be some specific conditions under which failures

are detectable by crashes, these most often depend upon special hardware. In a typical network, failures are only detectable using timeouts, and the same imprecision that makes reliable computing difficult over RPC and streams also limits the failure-handling ability of the 3PC.

The problem that occurs is most easily understood by considering a network partitioning scenario, in which two groups of participating processes are independently operational and trying to terminate the protocol. One group may see a state that is entirely *prepared to commit* and would want to terminate the protocol by commit. The other, however, could see a state that is entirely *ok to commit* and would consider abort to be the only safe outcome: After all, perhaps some unreachable process voted against commit! Clearly, 3PC will be unable to make progress in settings where partition failures can occur. We will return to this issue in Sect. 11.2, when we discuss a basic result by Fisher, Lynch, and Paterson; the inability to terminate a 3PC protocol in settings that do not satisfy fail-stop failure assumptions is one of many manifestations of the so-called "FLP impossibility result" (see Fisher et al. 1985a, 1985b). For the moment, though, we find ourselves in the uncomfortable position of having a solution to a problem that is similar to, but not quite identical to, the one that occurs in real systems. One consequence of this is that few systems make use of 3PC commit protocols today: Given a situation in which 3PC is less likely to block than 2PC, but may nonetheless block when certain classes of failures occur, the extra cost of the 3PC is not generally seen as bringing a return commensurate with its cost.

Keidar and Dolev at Technion University and Hebrew University, respectfully, did some interesting work with 3PC in 1995 that illustrates a point made earlier: the theoretical structure of a problem and the engineering of a protocol sometimes lead to very different insights. In this effort, the researchers asked how one should build systems that may need to tolerate very long communication outages—extended "partitioning" events. To make the problem as interesting as possible, they focused on the most extreme scenario possible: now and then a pair of processes managed to communicate, but the system was otherwise partitioned. Thus there were never any opportunities for a majority to communicate all at the same time. On the other hand, the group eliminated the notion of communication timeout: processes were either able to communicate, or unable to "reach" one-another. Failures look like long periods of unreachability in this model.

The group was able to show that one can "simulate" a 3PC protocol by piggybacking information on messages exchanged during the brief periods when processes manage to reach one-another, and furthermore that doing so is the optimal availability strategy for replicating data under these extreme conditions. They also showed that relatively little data actually needs to be carried in the messages to accomplish this objective. Up to the present, this work has been of largely academic value. However, with the increasing interest in mobility and widespread use of ad-hoc network routing protocols, one can easily imagine situations in which a "nearly always partitioned" model for data replication could become important in a practical sense, and the Dolev, Keidar and Chockler implementation of 3PC would then be an obvious choice.

Fig. 10.9 Quorum update
algorithm uses a quorum read
followed by a 2PC protocol
for updates

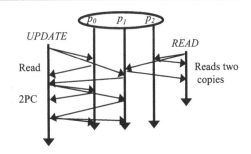

10.3.3 Quorum Update Revisited

Recall the discussion of quorum updates from the start of this chapter. The "actual"
algorithm uses 2PC, as seen in Fig. 10.9. In the example shown in the figure, we
have a group with three members, and the quorum size is set to two for both reads
and writes[7]. The read is done as a one-phase algorithm, collecting values and version numbers from two replicas, picking the correct version, and returning that to
the application. The update, in contrast, is done as a read followed by a 2-phase
commit protocol—not 3-phase commit, since we do not have an accurate way to
detect failures, so the extra phase will not bring any significant benefit. Instead, the
first phase proposes a new value, and the second phase commits or aborts depending
on the success of the first. A failed process would need to track down the outcome
of any pending commit protocol before it could resume actions in a system built this
way, presumably by contacting some form of logging service or some process that
has been up long enough to know the status of past updates.

10.4   Related Reading

On logical concepts of time (see Lamport 1978a, 1984).
  Causal ordering in message delivery (see Birman and Joseph 1987a, 1987b).
  Consistent cuts (see Babaoglu and Marzullo 1993, Chandy and Lamport 1985).
  Vector clocks (see Fidge 1988; Mattern 1989).
  Vector clocks used in message delivery (see Birman et al. 1991; Schiper et al.
1989, 2003).
  Optimizing vector clock representations (see Charron-Bost 1991; Melliar-Smith
and Moser 1993).
  Compression using topological information about groups of processes (see Bir-
man et al. 1991; Rodrigues and Verissimo 1995; Rodrigues et al. 1993, 2000).

---

[7]We have illustrated a scenario in which the read and update protocols optimistically assume that
their targets are healthy and will respond. In practice, however, lacking knowledge of the states of
the processes in the service, a quorum system might need to send additional messages simply to
maximize the likelihood of reaching a quorum of healthy group members. This, of course, makes
the protocol even more costly.

Static groups and quorum replication (see Bernstein et al. 1987; Birman and Joseph 1987a; Cooper 1985).

Two-phase commit (see Bernstein et al. 1987; Gray 1978; Gray and Reuter 1993).

Three-phase commit (see Skeen 1982a, 1985).

Method of Keidar and Dolev (see Keidar and Dolev 1995, 2000).

Dynamic Membership

11

11.1 Dynamic Group Membership

We now have the tools to develop the dynamic membership tracking service, and ultimately to build the desired high speed data replication protocols. The basic elements of the dynamic membership model are as follows. The system is initialized by starting some set of processes, perhaps by hand or on a pool of servers that have been specially designated by the system administrator—an initial bootstrapping step that we will not discuss in any detail here[1]. For the remainder of the lifetime of the system, new processes are started and *join* the system, while active processes *leave* the system when they terminate, fail, or simply chose to disconnect themselves. Of course, a dynamic membership model does not preclude having some static set of resources that play special roles; the basic idea is that the majority of the processes in the system can come and go as they like.

---

[1] Readers interested in learning more about that first step might want to look at Shlomi Dolev's work on *self-stabilization* (Dolev 2000). A self-stabilizing bootstrap algorithm would work as follows. During periods when applications can find an active membership service, they would do so. But if an application is launched and cannot find the service, it would run Dolev's self-stabilizing leader election protocol. That protocol can automatically handle various numbers of concurrent processes and is guaranteed to eventually converge to a state in which a single leader has been picked and every process knows who the leader is (the eventual convergence does require that any severe churn that may be happening settle down). At any rate, once this bootstrap step selects a leader, one would delay for a sufficient amount of time to have reasonable confidence that two leaders have not been picked (Dolev's theory lets us calculate the needed delay). Finally, the leader could boot our dynamic membership protocol. Non-leaders, in contrast, simply wait until the leader is running the membership protocol, at which point they join the now-running system. In effect, we would run the self-stabilization protocol only while no copies of the membership service are active. Thus, the normal case becomes one in which the membership service is running, and some processes either wish to join, or are terminating deliberately, or seem to have failed (other processes are reporting timeouts). We would revert to the self-stabilization approach again if all copies of the membership service crash, but otherwise will not use it again.

Notice that membership really involves dealing with two related problems. The GMS service itself needs to track its own membership, because it will not otherwise be able to provide consistent responses to applications using it. So, we need a protocol by which GMS servers talk to one-another. The second problem is that GMS servers need to track the states of other (non-GMS) processes in the system. They will use this monitoring mechanism to update their list of system members, and to report events back out to processes in the system as a whole. We end up with a 2-tier architecture.

Notice that even a static system can be treated as a special case of the dynamic membership model. For example, consider a cluster-style data center in which an instance of some database application is to be launched on every node. A static system model may seem to be a good match for such a clustered architecture, but we have seen that it brings high costs. We can just as easily adopt the view that the processes comprising the database application are launched dynamically (when the corresponding node is booted), and that they form a dynamic group whose members "own" the local database stores on their respective computers. This approach will turn out to have important benefits if the database system needs to use replicated data. Thus, our broad approach is to add a group membership service to the system, using the protocol developed below to implement it. Then we can layer groups of various kinds "over" the GMS-supported abstractions, including groups that have special relationships to various kinds of hardware.

Finally, to repeat a point made at the end of the previous chapter, some systems use both static and dynamic membership tracking. The best known example in this category is Lamport's Paxos protocol, which he derives by a series of transformations from a basic Paxos protocol that assumes static membership, using quorum operations in the manner discussed previously to ensure that updates will be durable and totally ordered. The basic scheme can tolerate some number of crashed processes: the maximum number of crashes that it can withstand is a parameter, t, and the number of replicas is required to be at least $2t + 1$. In normal operation, some replicas might lack some updates, but any read that accesses a read-quorum of replicas would see every update. Notice, though, that in a system updating an underlying database, this model is awkward: what would it mean for some databases to know that such-and-such an employee has left the company, if others do not know this? In practice, how would one query such a replicated database? For example, how would one run the query "Count employees on the payroll of the manufacturing division in North Carolina:" the query requires that we have a single relation with the correct count in one place. If we were to use Paxos in its static form, any individual database replica might have extra employee tuples, or be missing some employee tuples. Clearly, Paxos in that form is not really useful except for maintaining a list of the database updates, and even then, we can only actually know the full list if we query multiple replicas, allowing us to patch the gaps that any single replica's list of updates might contain!

From this example, we see that there are many situations in which we really would need to update *all* our replicas; doing so would let the user run a query and obtain a sensible answer from any single replica. In particular, if we are actually applying updates more or less as they occur, to a complex underlying system such as a database, the static version of Paxos (call it basic Paxos) will not be a very satisfactory option. Lamport's approach was to extend his basic Paxos scheme by adding a way to reconfigure the replica set, creating what he called a new *epoch*. This allows users to run with $f = 0$ if they prefer to avoid the case just described: with $f = 0$ every write must update every replica, and any single replica can safely be read (queried). A write would not be able to complete if a replica were to fail, but Lamport solves this by creating a new epoch each time a failure occurs. In many textbooks, this way of deriving a dynamic group communication system from a static one would be the main focus, but as we will see, we can achieve a much more efficient solution if we go about it the other way around: by creating a dynamic membership protocol that can run in a bare-bones environment, and then laying replicated update protocols *over* the dynamic layer. We will end up at the same place: we can define a version of Paxos that offers dynamic membership in this model, for example. But by approaching it in this manner, we will be able to avoid some inefficiencies that Lamport's Paxos approach encounters.

One simple way to understand the reason that a dynamic membership protocol can outperform a static approach is this: in a static scheme such as basic Paxos, we design a protocol that uses quorum methods to tolerate varying numbers of failures up to some limit f. But as we just saw, we might decide to execute it with $f = 0$, to update a database. Now one would need to go back and ask if that original protocol was as efficient as possible for this configuration. In fact, it will not be: we end up with protocol steps that can be trimmed out entirely because with $f = 0$, they never execute. The dynamic protocol we will develop in this Chapter lacks those unneeded steps. The version Malkhi developed and that we've included into Appendix A goes even further: it revists Paxos and, unlike Lamport's version (with its dual options for handling failure), simplifies Paxos by handling failure in just a single way, using reconfiguration. This leads to a faster, more optimized, Paxos, but with identical properties: the protocol Isis[2] offers as *SafeSend*.

11.1.1 GMS and Other System Processes

The interface between the GMS and other system processes provides three operations, shown in Table 11.1, and further illustrated by Fig. 11.1. The *join* operation is invoked by a process that wishes to become a system member. The *monitor* operation is used by a process to register its interest in the status of some other process; should that process be dropped from the membership, a callback will occur to notify it of the event. Such a callback is treated as the equivalent of a failure notification in the fail-stop computing model: The process is considered to have crashed, all communication links with it are severed, and messages subsequently received from it are rejected. Finally, the *leave* operation is used by a process that wishes to disconnect itself from the system, or by some other system component that has detected a fault and wishes to signal that a particular process has failed. We assume throughout this section that failure detections are inaccurate in the sense that they may result

Table 11.1 GMS operations

Operation	Function	Failure handling
Join (process-ID, callback) returns (time, GMS list)	Calling process is added to membership list of system, returns logical time of the join event and a list giving the membership of the GMS service. The callback function is invoked whenever the core membership of the GMS changes.	Idempotent: can be reissued to any GMS process with same outcome
leave (process-ID) returns void	Can be issued by any member of the system. GMS drops the specified process from the membership list and issues notification to all members of the system. If the process in question is really operational, it must rejoin under a new process-ID.	Idempotent: fails only if the GMS process that was the target is dropped from the GMS membership list
monitor (process-ID, callback) Returns callback-ID	Can be issued by any member of the system. GMS registers a callback and will invoke callback (process-ID) later if the designated process fails.	Idempotent: as for *leave*

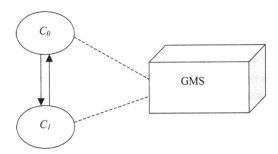

Fig. 11.1 In a system with a GMS, clients (c_0 and c_1) do not monitor one-another's health directly. Instead, they are monitored by the GMS, and trust the GMS to notify them if a counterpart fails. This ensures that members of the system will react in a consistent manner when a failure occurs. We can now separate concerns: one challenge is to build a highly available GMS, and a separate one is to implement the protocols by which clients cooperate, i.e., to replicate data or synchronize actions

from partitioning of the network, but are otherwise of sufficiently good quality as to rarely exclude an operational process as faulty.

The GMS itself will need to be highly available—hence, it will typically be implemented by a set of processes that cooperate to implement the GMS abstraction. Although these processes would normally reside on a statically defined set of server computers, so that they can readily be located by a process wishing to join the system, the actual composition of the group may vary over time due to failures within the GMS service itself, and one can imagine other ways of tracking down representatives (files, name services, the use of hardware broadcast to poll for a member, etc.). Notice that in order to implement the GMS abstraction on behalf of the rest of the system, a GMS server needs to solve the GMS problem on its own behalf. We will say that it uses a *group membership protocol*, or GMP, for this purpose. Thus, the GMP deals with the membership of a small service, the GMS, which the rest of the system (a potentially large set of processes) employs to track the composition of the system as a whole.

Similar to the situation for other system processes that do not comprise the GMS, the GMP problem is defined in terms of *join* and *leave* events; the latter being triggered by the inability of the GMS processes to communicate with one another. Clearly, such an environment creates the threat of a partitioning failure, in which a single GMS might split into multiple GMS sub-instances, each of which considers the other to be faulty. What should our goals be when such a partitioned scenario occurs?

Suppose that our distributed system is being used in a setting such as air traffic control. If the output of the GMS is treated as being the logical equivalent of a failure notification, one would expect the system to reconfigure itself after such notification to restore full air traffic control support within the remaining set of processes. If some component of the air traffic control system is responsible for advising controllers about the status of sectors of the airspace (free or occupied), and the associated process fails, the air traffic system would probably restart it by launching a new status manager process.

A GMS partition would be the likely consequence of a network partition, raising the prospect that two air traffic sector services could find themselves simultaneously active, both trying to control access to the same portions of the airspace, and neither aware of the other! Such an inconsistency would have disastrous consequences. While the partitioning of the GMS might be permissible, it is clear that at most one of the resulting GMS components should be permitted to initiate new actions.

From this example we see that although one might want to allow a system to remain operational during partitioning of the GMS, we also need a way to pick one component of the overall system as the primary one, within which authoritative decisions can be taken on behalf of the system as a whole (see Malkhi 1994; Ricciardi 1993). Nonprimary components might report information on the basis of their state as of the time when a partitioning occurred, but would not permit potentially conflicting actions (such as routing a plane into an apparently free sector of airspace) to be initiated. Such an approach clearly generalizes: One can imagine a system in which some applications would be considered primary within a component considered nonprimary for other purposes. Moreover, there may be classes of actions that are safe even within a nonprimary component; an example would be the reallocation of air traffic within sectors of the air traffic service already owned by the partition at the time the network failed. But it is clear that any GMP solution should at least track the primary component, so that actions can be appropriately limited.

The key properties of the primary component of the GMS are that its membership should overlap with the membership of a previous primary component of the GMS and that there should only be one primary component of the GMS within any partitioning of the GMS as a whole. As for the clients of the GMS, they inherit the "primaryness" property of the GMS server to which they are connected. Thus, a client connected to a GMS server in the primary component is also in the primary component, and a client connected to a GMS server that has lost contact with the primary component is itself a non-primary client (even if the vast majority of clients end up in this unhappy state).

In the beginning of this chapter, we discussed concepts of time in distributed settings. In defining the primary component of a partitioned GMS we used temporal terms without making it clear exactly what form of time was intended. In the following text, we have *logical* time in mind. In particular, suppose that process p is a member of the primary component of the GMS, but then suddenly becomes partitioned away from the remainder of the GMS, executing for an arbitrarily long period of time without sending or receiving any additional messages and finally shutting down. From the discussion up to now, it is clear that we would want the GMS to reconfigure itself to exclude p, if possible, forming a new primary GMS component, which can permit further progress in the system as a whole. But now the question occurs as to whether or not p would be aware that this has happened. If not, p might consider itself a member of the previous primary component of the GMS, and we would now have two primary components of the GMS active simultaneously.

There are two ways in which we could respond to this issue. The first involves a limited introduction of time into the model. Where clocks are available, it would be useful to have a mechanism whereby any process that ceases to be a member of the primary component of a partitioned GMS can detect this situation within a bounded period of time—for example, it would be helpful to know that within two seconds of being excluded from the GMS, p knows that it is no longer a member of the primary component. If clocks are synchronized, a process that is taking over some role would be able to delay its first action long enough to ensure that the process that previously had the role has become quiescent. For example, in an air traffic application, if process a was responsible for decisions about air-traffic sector S, and now b is informed that a has either failed or become partitioned away from the primary component, b could delay for an appropriate amount of time. During this period, we would know that a will experience a "loss of connectivity" timeout. By the time that b takes over a's role, any controller still in contact with a will be told that a has lost contact with the primary component of the system. The controller could then shift to some other, operational, machine and would find him or herself in contact with b. Notice that there would never be a point in real time where there are two processes claiming to be in control of S.

The second option involves designing our system so that if a partition does form, any process taking over some role will be able to duplicate the actions of the process that became partitioned away. In this second approach, b takes over the role of a but does so with accurate knowledge of the actions a might have taken prior to losing connectivity to the primary partition. In practice, this involves fully replicating the information a will use within the group before taking any action based on that information.

The two approaches can be combined, and for an application as "mission critical" as air traffic control, normally would be. One would arrive at a system in which, if a process fails, no process takes over from it until the failed (or disconnected) process has quiesced, and moreover, a process taking over from some other process also can reproduce the last actions taken by its quiescent counterpart prior to crashing or becoming disconnected. Of course, this is a costly approach, because every update to the group state needs to be registered with every group member before any action can be taken on the basis of that update. The delay while waiting for acknowledgements that everyone has seen the update will reduce the rate of updates we can do substantially. On the other hand, we will still be able to operate a small group at a rate of perhaps a few tens or even hundreds of events per second, and for an application like air traffic control, this may be adequate.

In addition to these considerations, we will need a way to capture the sense in which it is legal for p to lag the GMS in this manner, albeit for a limited period of time. Notice that because we wish to require that primary components of the GMS have overlapping membership, if we are given two different membership lists for the GMS, a and b, either $a \rightarrow b$, or $b \rightarrow a$. Thus, rather than say that there should be at most one primary component of the GMS active simultaneously, we will say that any two concurrently active membership lists for the GMS (in the sense that each is considered current by some process) should be ordered by causality. Equivalently, we could now say that there is at most a single sequence of GMS membership lists that is considered to represent the primary component of the GMS. We will use the term "view" of the GMS membership to denote the value of the membership list that holds for a given process within the GMS at a specified point in its execution.

If the GMS experiences a partitioning failure and the non-primary partition is permitted to remain active, steps must be taken to handle the *merging* of partitions (see Amir et al. 1992a, 1992b; Malkhi 1994; Moser et al. 1994a, 1994b). Finally, if all the members of the GMS fail, or if the primary partition is somehow lost, the GMP should provide for a restart from complete failure or for identification of the primary partition when the merge of two nonprimary partitions makes it possible to determine that there is no active primary partition within the system. We will discuss this issue at some length in Chap. 14.

The protocol that we now present is based on one that was developed as part of the Isis system in 1987 (see Birman and Joseph 1987b), but was subsequently extended by Ricciardi in 1991 as part of her Ph.D. dissertation (see Ricciardi et al. 1992; Ricciardi 1993; Ricciardi and Birman 1991). The protocol has the interesting property that all GMS members see exactly the same sequence of join and leave events. The members use this property to obtain an unusually efficient protocol execution.

To avoid placing excessive trust in the correctness or fault tolerance of the clients, our goal will be to implement a GMS for which all operations are invoked using a modified RPC protocol. Our solution should allow a process to issue requests to any member of the GMS server group with which it is able to establish contact. The protocol implemented by the group should stipulate that *join* operations are idempotent: If a joining process times out or otherwise fails to receive a reply, it can reissue its request, perhaps to a different server. Having joined the system, clients that detect apparent failures merely report them to the GMS. The GMS itself will be responsible for all forms of failure notification, both for GMS members and other clients. Thus, actions that would normally be triggered by timeouts (such as reissuing an RPC or breaking a stream connection) will be triggered in our system by a

GMS callback notifying the process doing the RPC or maintaining the stream that the party it is contacting has failed. Table 11.1 summarizes this interface.

11.1.2 Protocol Used to Track GMS Membership

We now develop the protocol used to track the core membership of the GMS service itself. These are the processes responsible for implementing the GMS abstraction, but not their clients. For simplicity, we assume that the processes all watch one another using some form of network-level ping operation, detecting failures by timeout. In practice, failure detection does not necessarily require an all-to-all pattern of monitoring, but this assumption makes the GMS protocol easier to explain. The only real requirement here is that if a process or a set of processes fail, the survivors will eventually detect all the failures.

Both the addition of new GMS members and the deletion of apparently failed members are handled by the GMS coordinator, which is the GMS member that has been operational for the longest period of time. As we will see, although the GMS protocol permits more than one process to be added or deleted at a time, it orders all add and delete events so that this concept of oldest process is well defined and consistent throughout the GMS. If a process believes the GMS coordinator has failed, it treats the next highest ranked process (perhaps itself) as the new coordinator.

Our initial protocol will be such that any process suspected of having failed is subsequently *shunned* by the system members that learn of the suspected failure. This has the effect of emulating what we called *fail-stop* behavior earlier. Upon detection of an apparent failure, a GMS process immediately ceases to accept communication from the failed process. It also immediately sends a message to every other GMS process with which it is communicating, informing them of the apparent failure; they then shun the faulty process as well. If a shunned process is actually operational, it will learn that it is being shunned when it next attempts to communicate with some GMS process that has heard of the fault; at this point it is expected that the shunned process will rejoin the GMS under a new process identifier. In this manner, a suspected failure can be treated as if it were a real one. As we've seen, this behavior is very common in cloud settings, where the cloud management infrastructure would often do precisely the same things to deal with sets of machines that have someone become partitioned away from the majority of the datacenter (e.g. a rack that suffered a network switch failure).

Having developed this initial protocol, we will discuss extensions that allow partitions to form and later merge in Sect. 11.1.5, and then will return to the topic in Chap. 14, where we present an execution model that makes use of this functionality.

Upon learning of a failure or an addition request, the GMS coordinator starts a protocol that will lead to the updating of the membership list, which is replicated among all GMS processes. The protocol requires two phases when the processes being added or deleted do not include the old GMS coordinator; a third phase is used if the coordinator has failed and a new coordinator is taking over. Any number of add operations can be combined into a single round of the protocol. A single round can also perform multiple delete operations, but here there is a limit: At most a minority of the processes present in a given view can be dropped from the subsequent view (more precisely, a majority of the processes in a given view must acknowledge the next view; obviously, this implies that the processes in question must be alive).

In the two-phase case, the first round of the protocol sends the list of add and delete events to the participants, including the coordinator itself. All acknowledge receipt. The coordinator waits for as many replies as possible, but also requires a majority response from the current membership. If less than a majority of processes are reachable it waits until communication is restored before continuing. If processes have failed and only a minority are available, a special protocol is executed.

Unless additional failures occur at this point in the protocol, which would be very unlikely, a majority of processes acknowledge the first-round protocol. The GMS coordinator now commits the update in a second round, which also carries with it notifications of any failures that were detected during the first round. Indeed, the second-round protocol can be compacted with the first round of a new instance of the deletion protocol, if desired. The GMS members update their membership view upon reception of the second-round protocol messages.

In what one hopes will be an unusual condition, it may be that a majority of the previous membership cannot be contacted because too many GMS processes have crashed. In this case, a GMS coordinator still must ensure that the failed processes did not acquiesce in a reconfiguration protocol of which it was not a part. In general, this problem may not be solvable—for example, it may be that a majority of GMS processes have crashed, and prior to crashing they could have admitted any number of new processes and deleted the ones now trying to run the protocol. Those new processes could now be anywhere in the system. In practice, however, this problem is often easy to solve: The GMS will most often execute within a static set of possible server hosts, and even if this set has some small degree of dynamicism, it is normally possible to track down any GMS server by checking a moderate number of nodes for a representative.

A three-phase protocol is employed when the current coordinator is suspected as having failed and some other coordinator must take over. The new coordinator starts by informing at least a majority of the GMS processes listed in the current membership that the coordinator has failed and then collects their acknowledgements and current membership information. At the end of this first phase, the new coordinator may have learned of pending add or delete events that were initiated by the prior coordinator before it was suspected of having failed. The first-round protocol also has the effect of ensuring that a majority of GMS processes will start to shun the old coordinator. The second and third rounds of the protocol are exactly as for the normal case: The new coordinator proposes a new membership list, incorporating any add events it has learned about, as well as all the delete events, including those it learned about during the initial round of communication and those from the prior coordinator. It waits for a majority to acknowledge this message and then commits it, piggybacking suspected failure information for any unresponsive processes.

Ricciardi has given a detailed proof that the above protocol results in a single, ordered sequence of process add and leave events for the GMS and that it is immune to partitioning (see Ricciardi et al. 1992). The key to her proof is the observation that any new membership list installed successfully necessarily must be acknowledged by a majority of the previous list, and therefore that any two concurrent protocols will be related by a causal path. One protocol will learn of the other, or both will learn of one another, and this is sufficient to prevent the GMS from partitioning. Ricciardi shows that if the ith round of the protocol starts with n processes in the GMS membership, an arbitrary number of processes can be added to the GMS and at most $\lfloor n/2 \rfloor - 1$ processes can be excluded (this is because of the requirement that a majority of processes agree with each proposed new view). In addition, she shows that even if a steady stream of join and leave or failure events occurs, the GMS should be able to continuously output new GMS views provided that the number of failures never rises high enough to prevent majority agreement on the next view. In effect, although the protocol may be discussing the proposed $i + 2$ view, it is still able to commit the $i + 1$ view.

11.1.3 GMS Protocol to Handle Client Add and Join Events

We now turn to the issues that occur if a GMS server is used to manage the membership of some larger number of client processes, which interact with it through the interface given earlier.

In this approach, a process wishing to join the system will locate an operational GMS member. It then issues a *join* RPC to that process. If the RPC times out, the request can simply be reissued to some other member. When the join succeeds, it learns its logical ranking (the time at which the join took place) and the current membership of the GMS service, which is useful in setting up subsequent monitoring operations. Similarly, a process wishing to report a failure can invoke the *leave* operation in any operational GMS member. If that member fails before confirming that the operation has been successful, the caller can detect this by receiving a callback reporting the failure of the GMS member itself and then can reissue the request.

To solve these problems, we could now develop a specialized protocol. Before doing so, however, it makes sense to ask if the GMS is not simply an instance of a service that manages replicated data on behalf of a set of clients; if so, we should instead develop the most general and efficient solutions possible for the replicated data problem, and then use them within the GMS to maintain this specific form of information. And, indeed, it is very natural to adopt this point of view.

To transform the one problem into the other, we need to understand how an RPC interface to the GMS can be implemented such that the GMS would reliably offer the desired functionality to its clients, using data replication primitives internally for this purpose. Then we can focus on the data replication problem separately and convince ourselves that the necessary primitives can be developed and can offer efficient performance.

The first problem that needs to be addressed concerns the case where a client issues a request to a representative of the GMS that fails before responding. This can be solved by ensuring that such requests are *idempotent*, meaning that the same operation can be issued repeatedly and will repeatedly return the identical result—for example, an operation that assigns the value 3 to a variable x is idempotent, whereas an operation that increments x by adding 1 to it would not be. We can make the client join operation idempotent by having the client uniquely identify itself, and repeat the identifier each time the request must be reissued. Recall that the GMS returns the time of the join operation; this can be made idempotent by arranging it so that if a client join request is received from a client already listed as a system member, the time currently listed is returned and no other action is taken.

The remaining operations are all initiated by processes that belong to the system. These, too, might need to be reissued if the GMS process contacted to perform the operation fails before responding (the failure would be detected when a new GMS membership list is delivered to a process waiting for a response, and the GMS member it is waiting for is found to have been dropped from the list). It is clear that exactly the same approach can be used to solve this problem. Each request need only be uniquely identifiable—for example, using the process identifier of the invoking process and some form of counter (for example: request 17 from process p on host h).

The central issue is thus reduced to replication of data within the GMS or within similar groups of processes. We will postpone this problem momentarily, returning later when we give a protocol for implementing replicated data within dynamically defined groups of processes.

11.1.4   GMS Notifications with Bounded Delay

If the processes within a system possess synchronized clocks, it is possible to bound the delay before a process becomes aware that it has been partitioned from the system. Consider a system in which the health of a process is monitored by the continued reception of some form of "still alive" messages received from it; if no such message is received after delay σ, any of the processes monitoring that process can report it as faulty to the GMS. (Normally, such a process would also cease to accept incoming messages from the faulty process and would also piggyback this information on messages to other processes to ensure that if p considers q to have failed, then any process that receives a message from p will also begin to shun messages from q.) Now, assume further that all processes receiving a "still alive" message acknowledge it.

In this setting, p will become aware that it may have been partitioned from the system within a maximum delay of $2\varepsilon + \sigma$, where ε represents the maximum latency of the communication channels. More precisely, p will discover that it has been partitioned from the system $2\varepsilon + \sigma$ time units after it last had contact with a majority of the previous primary component of the GMS. In such situations, it would be appropriate for p to break any channels it has to system members and to cease taking actions on behalf of the system as a whole.

Notice that the GMS may run its protocol to exclude p as early as 2ε time units before p discovers that it has been partitioned from the main system, hence there is a potentially long window of time during which the exact status of p is unknown.

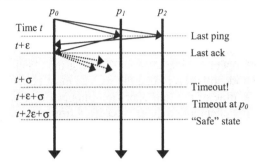

Fig. 11.2 If channel delays are bounded, a process can detect that it has been partitioned from the primary component within a bounded time interval, making it safe for the primary component to take over actions from it even if externally visible effects may be involved. The *gray region* denotes a period during which the new primary process will be unable to take over because there is some possibility that the old primary process is still operational in a nonprimary component and may still be initiating authoritative actions. At the end of the gray period a new primary process can be appointed within the primary component. There may be a period of real time during which no primary process is active, but there is very little risk that two could be simultaneously active. One can also bias a system in the other direction, so that there will always be at least one primary active provided that the rate of failures is limited

The new primary system component can safely break locks held by p or otherwise takeover actions for which p was responsible after 2ε time units have elapsed, but this event may actually follow a long period during which the system was essentially idle, waiting for this to happen. (See Fig. 11.2.) Our only options for narrowing this window are to use as fast a communication network as possible, and to detect failures aggressively, so that ε and σ will be small. If clocks are synchronized, any process q taking over from p will know how long to wait before doing so, and also will know the wall clock time for the last action that p could have initiated. In applications such as air traffic control, these guarantees are sufficient to design a safe take-over protocol.

Reasoning such as this is only possible in systems where clocks are synchronized to a known precision and in which the delays associated with communication channels are also known (if the wall-clock time issue does not arise in the application, it suffices to ensure that the various clocks advance at the same rate—that $2\varepsilon + \sigma$ time units means the same thing system-wide). In practice, such values are rarely known with any accuracy, but coarse approximations may exist. Thus, in a system where message-passing primitives provide expected latencies of a few milliseconds, one might take ε to be a much larger number: one second or ten seconds. Although extremely conservative, such an approach would in practice be quite safe. Later, we will examine real-time issues more closely, but it is useful to keep in mind that very coarse-grained real-time problems are often easy to solve in distributed systems where the equivalent fine-grained real-time problems would be very difficult or provably impossible. At the same time, even a coarse-grained rule such as this one would only be safe if there was good reason to believe that the value of ε was a safe approximation. Some systems provide no guarantees of this sort at all, in which case incorrect behavior could result if a period of extreme overload or some other unusual condition caused the ε limit to be exceeded.

To summarize, the core primary partition GMS protocol must satisfy the following properties:

- *C-GMS-1*: The system membership takes the form of system views. There is an initial system view, which is predetermined at the time the system starts. Subsequent views differ by the addition or deletion of processes.

- *C-GMS-2*: Only processes that request to be added to the system are added. Only processes that are suspected of failure or that request to leave the system are deleted.

- *C-GMS-3*: A majority of the processes in view i of the system must acquiesce in the composition of view $i + 1$ of the system.

- *C-GMS-4*: Starting from an initial system view, subsequences of a single sequence of system views are reported to system members. Each system member observes such a subsequence starting with the view in which it was first added to the system and continuing until it fails, when it either leaves the system or is excluded from the system.

- *C-GMS-5*: If process p suspects process q of being faulty, and if the core GMS service is able to report new views, either q will be dropped from the system, or p will be dropped, or both.

- *C-GMS-6*: In a system with synchronized clocks and bounded message latencies, any process dropped from the system view will know that this has occurred within bounded time.

As noted previously, the core GMS protocol will not always be able to make progress: There are patterns of failures and communication problems that can prevent it from reporting new system views. For this reason, *C-GMS-5* is a conditional liveness property: If the core GMS is able to report new views, then it eventually acts upon process add or delete requests. It is not yet clear what conditions represent the weakest environment within which liveness of the GMS can always be guaranteed. For the protocol given above, the core GMS will make progress provided that at most a minority of processes from view i fail or are suspected of having failed during the period needed to execute the two- or three-phase commit protocol used to install new views. Such a characterization may seem evasive, since such a protocol may execute extremely rapidly in some settings and extremely slowly in others. However, unless the timing properties of the system are sufficiently strong to support estimation of the time needed to run the protocol, this seems to be as strong a statement as can be made.

We note that the failure detector called $\diamond W$ in Chandra and Toueg's work is characterized in terms somewhat similar to this (see Chandra and Toueg 1991; Chandra et al. 1992). Related work by several researchers (see Babaoglu et al. 1995; Friedman et al. 1995; Guerraoui 1995) has shown that the $\diamond W$ failure detector can be adapted to asynchronous systems in which messages can be lost during failures or processes can be killed because the majority of processes in the system consider them to be malfunctioning. Although fairly theoretical in nature, these studies are shedding light on the conditions under which problems such as membership agreement can always be solved and those under which agreement may not always be possible (the theoreticians are fond of calling the latter problems "impossible"). Indeed, the protocols presented in Appendix A closely resemble a core mechanism used in the Chandra and Toueg papers; in some sense, then, the protocols in Appendix A "implement" the Chandra and Toueg scheme for achieving consensus using a weakly consistent failure detector! And the methods of Appendix A, in turn, are the basis of the protocols implemented in Isis[2]. To present this work here, however, is beyond the scope of this book.

11.1.5 Extending the GMS to Allow Partition and Merge Events

Research on the Transis system, at Hebrew University in Jerusalem, has yielded insights into the extension of protocols, such as the one used to implement our primary component GMS, so that it can permit continued operation during partitionings that leave no primary component, or allow activity in a non-primary component, reconciling the resulting system state when partitions later remerge (see Amir et al. 1992a, 1992b; Malkhi 1994). Some of this work was done jointly with the Totem project at University of California, Santa Barbara (see Moser et al. 1996).

Briefly, the approach is as follows. In Ricciardi's protocols, when the GMS is unable to obtain a majority vote in favor of a proposed new view, the protocol basically gets stuck—it ceases to make progress. This ripples up to the application layer, since the application will eventually try to send a multicast or block waiting for a message from some other process, and while the membership protocol is blocked, these operations also will block. Thus, with little delay, the entire portioned portion of the system is likely to grind to a halt waiting until a primary partition can be reestablished, or for some kind of "shut down" action initiated in the application or by a human operator. In practice, such problems should never occur in a local area network, since it is easy to design a LAN so that partitioning will only occur in situations where a small subset of the machines have somehow become isolated from the network being used by a large majority of the datacenter. However, if an application runs over wide-area links and tries to treat the entire infrastructure as a single, seamless network, partitioning failures could be common. The choice is between designing such applications differently (basically, as a set of loosely interconnected systems, with each system residing within a single LAN), or to extend the communication platform to deal with partitioning. Such an extension needs to start with a partitionable GMS.

In the extended protocol, a GMS experiencing a partitioning failure continues to produce new views, but no longer considers itself to be the primary partition of the system. Of course, there is also a complementary case in which the GMS encounters some other GMS and the two merge their membership views. It may now be the case that one GMS or the other was the primary component of the system, in which case the new merged GMS will also be primary for the system. On the other hand, perhaps a primary component fragmented in such a way that none of the surviving components considers itself to be the primary one. When this occurs, it may be that later, such components will remerge and "primaryness" can then be deduced by study of the joint histories of the two components. Thus, one can extend the GMS to make progress even when partitioning occurs.

Work at the University of Bologna, on a system named Relacs, subsequently refined this approach into one that is notable for its simplicity and clarity. Ozalp Babaoglu, working with Alberto Bartoli and Gianluca Dini, demonstrated that a very small set of extensions to a view-synchronous environment suffice to support EVS-like functionality. They call their model Enriched View Synchrony and describe it in a technical report (see Babaoglu et al. 1996). Very briefly, Enriched View Synchrony arranges to deliver only *nonoverlapping* group views within different components of a partitioned system. The reasoning behind this is that overlapping views can cause applications to briefly believe that the same process or site resides on both sides of a partition, leading to inconsistent behavior. Then, they provide a set of predicates by which a component can determine whether or not it has a quorum that would permit direct update of the global system state, as well as algorithmic tools for assisting in the state merge problem that occurs when communication is reestablished. I am not aware of any implementation of this model yet, but the primitives are simple and an implementation in a system such as Horus (Chap. 17) would not be difficult.

Having described these approaches, an important question remains: whether or not it is *desirable* to allow a GMS to make progress in this manner. We defer this point until Chap. 15, but the author's belief is that few systems require the ability to continue operation on both sides of a failure that partitions the network, and that the primary partition model (in which the non-primary partition is basically shut down until the problem has been fixed) is preferable because it is much simpler for the user to understand. In addition, as was noted in footnote 3, Keidar, Chockler and Dolev have shown that there are cases in which no component is ever the primary one for the system, and yet durable, strongly consistent actions can still be performed through a type of gossip that occurs whenever the network becomes reconnected and two nonminority components succeed in communicating. Although interesting, this protocol is costly: Prior to taking any action, a majority of all the processes in the system must be known to have seen the action. Indeed, Keidar and Dolev develop their solution for a static membership model, in which the GMS tracks subsets of a known maximum system membership. The majority requirement makes this protocol costly—hence, although it is potentially useful in the context of wide area systems that experience frequent partition failures, it is not likely that one would use it directly in the local area communication layers of a system. We will return to this issue in Chap. 14 in conjunction with the model called *Extended Virtual Synchrony*.

11.2   Replicated Data with Malicious Failures

In this and the next section we touch on two problems that are basically tangential to the overall topic of interest here, yet important enough so that a well-read student should at least be aware of them. Nonetheless, the contents of Sects. 11.2 and 11.3 are not particularly central to the remainder of the book and can be skipped by practitioners focused on building highly assured Web Services but having less of an interest in the broad area.

The discussion in the previous sections assumed a *crash-failure model*, which is approximated in most distributed systems, but may sometimes represent a risky simplification. Consider a situation in which the actions of a computing system have critical implications, such as the software responsible for adjusting the position of an aircraft wing in flight or for opening the cargo door of the Space Shuttle. In settings such as these, the designer may hesitate to simply assume that the only failures that will occur will be benign ones.

There has been considerable work on protocols for coordinating actions under extremely pessimistic failure models, centering on what is called the Byzantine generals' problem, which explores a type of agreement protocol under the assumption that failures can produce arbitrarily incorrect behavior, but that the *number* of failures is known to be bounded. Although this assumption may seem more realistic than the assumption that processes fail by clean crashes, the model also includes a second type of assumption, which some might view as unrealistically benign: It assumes that the processors participating in a system share perfectly synchronized clocks, permitting them to exchange messages in rounds that are triggered by the clocks (e.g., once every second). Moreover, the model assumes that the latencies associated with message exchange between correct processors is accurately known.

Thus, the model permits failures of unlimited severity, but at the same time assumes that the *number* of failures is limited and that operational processes share a very simple computing environment. Notice in particular that the round model would only be realistic for a very small class of modern parallel computers and is remote from the situation on distributed computing networks. The usual reasoning is that by endowing the operational computers with extra power (in the form of synchronized rounds), we can only make their task easier. Thus, understanding the minimum cost for solving a problem in this model will certainly teach us something about the minimum cost of overcoming failures in real-world settings.

We should emphasize that, to the author's knowledge, Byzantine Agreement has never been used as the basis for a GMS-like mechanism; doing so is thus an open research topic that might be worth exploring at some point. We'll report on the basics of the agreement problem itself, in this model, leaving the application of Byzantine Agreement to problems such as supporting a Byzantine-fault-tolerant GMS as an open direction for future work.

The Byzantine generals' problem is as follows (see Lynch 1996). Suppose that an army has laid siege to a city and has the force to prevail in an overwhelming attack. However, if divided, the army might lose the battle. Moreover, the commanding generals suspect that there are traitors in their midst. Under what conditions can the loyal generals coordinate their action so as to either attack in unison or not attack at all? The assumption is that the generals start the protocol with individual opinions on the best strategy: to attack or to continue the siege. They exchange messages to execute the protocol, and if they decide to attack during the ith round of communication, they will all attack at the start of round $i + 1$. A traitorous general can send out any messages he or she likes and can lie about his or her own state, but can never forge the message of a loyal general. Finally, to avoid trivial solutions, it is required that if all the loyal generals favor attacking, an attack will result, and that if all favor maintaining the siege, no attack will occur. Protocols solving this problem are generally referred to as "Byzantine Agreement" protocols.

To see why this is difficult, consider a simple case in which three generals surround the city. Assume that two are loyal, but that one favors attack and the other prefers to hold back. The third general is a traitor. Moreover, assume that it is *known that there is at most one traitor*. If the loyal generals exchange their votes, they will both see a tie: one vote for attack, one opposed. Now suppose that the traitor sends an attack message to one general and tells the other to hold back. The loyal generals now see inconsistent states: One is likely to attack while the other holds back. With the forces divided, they would be defeated in battle. The Byzantine generals' problem is thus seen to be impossible for $t = 1$ and $n = 3$.

With four generals and at most one failure, the problem is solvable, but not trivially so. Assume that two loyal generals favor attack, the third favors retreat, and the fourth is a traitor. Again, it is known that there is at most one traitor. The generals exchange messages, and the traitor sends "retreat" to one, and "attack" to two others. One loyal general will now have a tied vote: two votes to attack, two to retreat. The other two generals will see three votes for attack, and one for retreat. A second round of communication will clearly be needed before this protocol can terminate! Accordingly, we now imagine a second round in which the generals circulate messages concerning their state in the first round. Two loyal generals will start this round knowing that it is safe to attack: On the basis of the messages received in the first round, they can deduce that even with the traitor's vote, the majority of loyal generals favored an attack. The remaining loyal general simply sends out a message that it is still undecided. At the end of this round, all the loyal generals will have one undecided vote, two votes that it is safe to attack, and one message from the traitor. Clearly, no matter what the traitor votes during the second round, all three loyal generals can deduce that it is safe to attack. Thus, with four generals and at most one traitor, the protocol terminates after two rounds.

In the general case, most Byzantine Agreement algorithms operate by having some form of "witnessing" mechanism. In a typical algorithm, during the first round, each process broadcasts its proposed agreement value—its "vote." In a second round, each process broadcasts the list of votes it "witnessed" in the first round, and if a third round occurs, each processes sends messages listing the events it witnessed in the second one, and so forth. The goal is to arrive at a state in which, no matter what the faulty processes do, the correct processes are able to force a unique outcome all by themselves.

By using this model, one can prove what are called lower bounds and upper bounds on the Byzantine generals' problem. A lower bound would be a limit to the quality of a possible solution to the problem—for example, one can prove that any solution to the problem capable of overcoming t traitors requires a minimum of $3t + 1$ participants (hence: $2t + 1$ or more loyal generals). The intuition into such a bound is fairly clear: The loyal generals must somehow be able to deduce a common strategy even with t participants whose votes cannot be trusted. For the others there must be a way to identify a majority decision. However, it is surprisingly difficult to prove that this must be the case. For our purposes, such a proof would represent a digression and is omitted, but interested readers are referred to the excellent treatment in Fisher et al. (1985a). Another example of a lower bound concerns the minimum number of messages required to solve the problem: No protocol can overcome t faults with fewer than $t + 1$ rounds of message exchange, and hence $O(t * n^2)$ messages, where n is the number of participating processes.

A curious property of Byzantine protocols is the following: they normally assume that when the protocol starts, all the participants know how many processes are in the system, and have worst-case bounds on the number of failures that can occur. These protocols will typically execute to completion under those worst-case assumptions, no matter what actually transpires in a real run—no attempt is made to check for and detect faults, or to somehow exclude processes based on faulty behavior. Up to the limited number of failures that can be tolerated, these protocols simply push forward and overwhelm the attacker with the weight of correct messages they exchange. The attacker, knowing the futility of attacking, might not even bother. Thus, in some sense, these protocols kill a mosquito with a sledge-hammer: most likely, no failure even occurs, and yet the protocol grinds away under worst-case assumptions! (In fairness, we should perhaps note that there are some "early stopping" Byzantine protocols, but they tend to be slower when failures actually *do* occur—in effect, one loses performance either way!)

In practical terms, the formulas just cited represent costly findings: Recall that our 2PC protocol is capable of solving a problem much like Byzantine generals' problem in two rounds of message exchange requiring only $3n$ messages, albeit for a simpler failure model. Moreover, the quorum methods permit data to be replicated using as few as $t + 1$ copies to overcome t failures. Later in the book we will discuss even cheaper replication schemes below, albeit with slightly weaker guarantees. Thus, a Byzantine protocol is very costly, and the best solutions are also fairly complex.

An upper bound on the problem would be a demonstration of a protocol that actually solves Byzantine generals' problem and an analysis of its complexity (number of rounds of communication required or messages required). Such a demonstration is an upper bound because it rules out the need for a more costly protocol to achieve the same objectives. Clearly, one hopes for upper bounds that are as close as possible to the lower bounds, but unfortunately no such protocols have been found for the Byzantine generals' problem. The simple protocol illustrated here can easily be generalized into a solution for t failures that achieves the lower bound for rounds of message exchange, although not for numbers of messages required.

In recent years, there has been a flurry of research using Byzantine Agreement protocols as the core of practical data replication systems. Several bodies of work are worthy of special note, although both are best understood as examples of broad areas of research. The first is a project called Phalynx, in which Reiter and Malkhi combined Byzantine Agreement with quorum data replication to replicate information critical to a security architecture. Their approach assumes that each object will be replicated on k^2 nodes, for some suitable value of k (typically, 2 or 3, although larger values are certainly possible). The nodes are assigned coordinates in a $k \times k$ coordinate system. A read quorum is defined to be a row in this "array" of nodes, and a write quorum is defined to be a column. Obviously, reads and writes will overlap. Byzantine Agreement is then used to determine the value actually read or the value to be written.

Research by Castro and Liskov took Byzantine Agreement in a slightly different direction, by exploring the potential value of the protocol for file or database replication. The idea these researchers addressed involves replicating data over a set of untrusted servers, then using Byzantine Agreement to update or read the values. They actually have two versions of their basic solution: one in which agreement is performed on the entire data object, and a second in which agreement is performed only on a "digital signature," which is a type of encoded checksum that cannot be forged or guessed. By means of a clever analysis of the application, this project showed that for many purposes, one can tolerate Byzantine failures and yet incur very little overhead relative to a less secure solution. This gave rise to a whole family of practical Byzantine solutions. A group at UT Austin created one of the most efficient protocols in the series, calling it Zyzzyva with tongue-in-cheek: the term happens to be the last word in the English dictionary. Presumably they intended that particular protocol to be the last word in Byzantine Fault Tolerance (and Zyzzyva is indeed quite efficient) (Kotla et al. 2009). But there have probably been dozens of further refinements on Byzantine Agreement since Zyzzyva was published. Indeed, Quema and Guerraoui published a kind of meta-protocol shortly before this book went to press: they described it as a kind of a template for generating "the next 700 BFT protocols" (Guerraoui et al. 2010).

Yet despite these and other success stories, Byzantine Agreement remains a rather costly and relatively unpopular technology. Suppose that we wanted to use Byzantine Agreement to solve a static data replication problem in a very critical or hostile setting. To do so, it would be necessary that the setting somehow correspond to the setup of the Byzantine generals' problem itself—for example, one could imagine using this problem to control an aircraft wing or the Space Shuttle cargo door by designing hardware that carries out voting through some form of physical process. The hardware would be required to implement the mechanisms needed to write software that executes in rounds, and the programs would need to be carefully analyzed to be sure that when operational, all the computing they do in each round can be completed before that round terminates.

On the other hand, one would not want to use a Byzantine protocol in a system where, at the end of the protocol, some single program will take the output of the protocol and perform a critical action. In that sort of a setting (unfortunately, far more typical of real computer systems), all we will have done is to transfer complete trust in the set of servers within which the agreement protocol runs into a complete trust in the single program that carries out their decision.

This has resulted in quite a bit of debate between the cloud computing community and the Byzantine fault-tolerance community. The BFT community tends to argue that these days, BFT is a perfectly practical option and that cloud developers should use their BFT protocols whenever building high-assurance services, such as services that maintain security keys. The argument is that if something really matters, you should manage it using the strongest possible model. Moreover, they would argue that after all, even normal bugs might lead to data corruption or abnormal behavior. BFT protocols are provably safe when such things occur, if the frequency is low enough and the faults do not impact all the replicas at once. But the cloud community, led in this case by Ben Reed and Flavio Junqueira at Yahoo, sees things differently (these are the two inventor's of Yahoo's ZooKeeper service). They have described informal studies of how applications and machines at Yahoo failed, concluding that the frequency of Byzantine failures was extremely small relative to the frequency of crash failures. Sometimes they did see data corruption, but then they often saw it occur in a correlated way that impacted many replicas all at once. And very often they saw failures occur in the client layer, then propagate into the service. BFT techniques tend to be used only within a service, not in the client layer that talks to that service, hence offer no protection against malfunctioning clients. All of this, Reed and Junqueira conclude, lead to the realization that BFT just does not match the real needs of a cloud computing company like Yahoo, even if the data being managed by a service really is of very high importance. Unfortunately, they have not published on this study; it was reported at an "outrageous opinions" session at the ACM Symposium on Operating Systems Principles, in 2009.

The practical use of the Byzantine protocol raises another concern: The timing assumptions built into the model are not realizable in most computing environments. While it is certainly possible to build a system with closely synchronized clocks and to approximate the synchronous rounds used in the model, the pragmatic reality is that few existing computer systems offer such a feature. Software clock synchronization, on the other hand, is subject to intrinsic limitations of its own, and for this reason is a poor alternative to the real thing. Moreover, the assumption that message exchanges can be completed within known, bounded latency is very hard to satisfy in general-purpose computing environments.

Continuing in this vein, one could also question the extreme pessimism of the failure model. In a Byzantine setting the traitor can act as an adversary, seeking to force the correct processes to malfunction. For a worst-case analysis this makes a good deal of sense. But having understood the worst case, one can also ask whether real-world systems should be designed to routinely assume such a pessimistic view of the behavior of system components. After all, if one is this negative, should not the hardware itself also be suspected of potential misbehavior, as well as the compiler and the various prebuilt system components that implement message passing? In designing a security subsystem or implementing a firewall, such an analysis makes a lot of sense. But when designing a system that merely seeks to maintain availability despite failures, and is not expected to come under active and coordinated attack, an extremely pessimistic model would be both unwieldy and costly.

From these considerations, one sees that a Byzantine computing model is of value in applications (or subsystems) demanding the utmost in security provisions, and may be applicable to certain types of special-purpose hardware, but it will rarely be directly useful in more general distributed computing environments where we might raise a reliability goal. As noted above, recent work with the model (see Malkhi and Reiter 1998, 2000; Castro et al. 2003a, 2003b) focuses on such uses: in one effort, a "Byzantine Quorums" mechanism is employed to build core components of a high-security architecture (see Malkhi and Reiter 1998; Malkhi et al. 2001a, 2001b; Alvisi et al. 2001b; Abraham and Malkhi 2003), while the other uses Byzantine Agreement to ensure the integrity of data in a replicated file server where the servers themselves are not very trustworthy (see Castro and Liskov 2002). As an aside, it should be noted that Rabin has introduced a set of probabilistic Byzantine protocols that are extremely efficient, but that accept a small risk of error (the risk diminishes exponentially with the number of rounds of agreement executed) (see Rabin 1983). Meanwhile, Avlisi and Dahlin have recently proposed a fast Byzantine Agreement protocol for use in settings like the ones considered by Malkhi, Reiter, Castro and their respective colleagues. But it still is not especially fast!

11.3   The Impossibility of Asynchronous Consensus (FLP)

We now turn to the second of the two "tangential" topics mentioned at the start of Sect. 11.2, namely the "impossibility" of achieving agreement in asynchronous distributed systems. Even before tackling the topic, it may be appropriate to remind the reader that this section of the book is covering some rather theoretical material, and that the theory community sometimes defines terms in unexpected ways. In particular, as we will use it below, the term "impossible" does not mean "never possible." Rather, it means "is not always possible."

To illustrate this definition, consider the challenge of reaching the author of this book by telephone during a busy day filled with meetings, talks by students, classes to teach, and so forth. Perhaps, over the eight hours of an academic working day, I am actually at my telephone for just four hours. Is it "possible" to reach me? A pragmatic answer is that of course it is: just keep trying. If your call is timed at random, with probability roughly 1/2 you will reach me. If you make n calls at random times, the likelihood of reaching me will be $1-1/2^n$. These sound like pretty good odds. But a theoretician might not be satisfied with such an analysis. He or she would reason as follows: suppose that the caller makes n extremely brief calls at times specified by a clever adversary who is keeping one eye on my desk through the door. It will not be difficult for that adversary to steer the caller towards times when I am not at my desk. Indeed, one could formalize a model in which it is provably impossible to reach me; such a result might hold even if I am "almost always" at my desk. The impossibility result considered below is of such a nature: it has limited practical importance yet the result matters because it tells us that there are certain properties our distributed systems simply cannot be shown to possess— notably, liveness guarantees. We will be able to build systems that are safe, in the sense of "not doing bad things," and that are probabilistically live, in the sense of being "very likely to do a good thing." But we will not be able to build systems that are guaranteed to "*always* do a good thing." Such a goal would violate the theory.

Although we refer to our model as asynchronous, it is in fact more constrained. In the asynchronous model, as used by distributed systems theoreticians, processes communicate entirely by message passing and there is no concept of time. Message passing is reliable but individual messages can be delayed indefinitely, and there is no meaningful concept of failure except for a process that crashes (taking no further actions) or that violates its protocol by failing to send a message or discarding a received message. Even these two forms of communication failure are frequently ruled out.

The form of asynchronous computing environment used in this chapter, in contrast, is intended to be "realistic." This implies that there are clocks on the processors and expectations regarding typical round-trip latencies for messages. Such temporal data can be used to define a concept of reachability or to trigger a failure-detection mechanism. The detected failure may not be attributable to a specific component (in particular, it will be impossible to know if a *process* failed or just the *link* to it), but the fact that some sort of problem has occurred will be detected, perhaps very rapidly. Moreover, in practice, the frequency with which failures are erroneously suspected can be kept low.

Jointly, these properties make the asynchronous model used in this book different than the one used in most theoretical work. And this is a good thing, too: In the fully asynchronous model, it is known that the group membership problem cannot be solved, in the sense that any protocol capable of solving the problem may encounter situations in which it cannot make progress. In contrast, these problems are always solvable in asynchronous environments, which satisfy sufficient constraints on the frequency of true or incorrectly detected failures and on the quality of communication.

Fig. 11.3 The asynchronous computing model

Recall that in Sect. 11.2, we focused on the *synchronous computing model*. At the other side of the spectrum is what we call the *asynchronous* computing model (see Fig. 11.3), in which a set of processes cooperate by exchanging messages over communication links that are arbitrarily slow and balky. The assumption here is that the messages sent on the links eventually get through, but that there is no meaningful way to measure progress except by the reception of messages. Clearly such a model is overly pessimistic, but in a way that is different from the pessimism of the Byzantine model, which extended primarily to failures—here we are pessimistic about our ability to measure time or to predict the amount of time actions will take. A message that arrives after a century of delay would be processed no differently than a message received within milliseconds of being transmitted. At the same time, this model assumes that processes fail by crashing, taking no incorrect actions and simply halting silently.

One might wonder why the asynchronous system completely eliminates any physical concept of time. We have seen that real distributed computing systems lack ways to closely synchronize clocks and are unable to distinguish network partitioning failures from processor failures, so there is a sense in which the asynchronous model is not as unrealistic as it may initially appear. Real systems do have clocks and use these to establish timeouts, but generally they lack a way to ensure that these timeouts will be accurate, as we saw when we discussed RPC protocols and the associated reliability issues in Chap. 5. Indeed, if an asynchronous model can be criticized as specifically unrealistic, this is primarily in its assumption of reliable communication links: Real systems tend to have limited memory resources, and a reliable communication link for a network subject to extended partitioning failures will require unlimited spooling of the messages sent. This represents an impractical design point: A better model would state that when a process is *reachable*, messages will be exchanged reliably with it, but if it becomes *inaccessible*, messages to it will be lost and its state, faulty or operational, cannot be accurately determined. In Italy, Babaoglu and his colleagues are studying such a model, but this is recent work and the full implications of this design point are not yet fully understood (see Babaoglu et al. 1994). Other researchers, such as Cristian, are looking at models that are partially asynchronous: They have time bounds, but the bounds are large compared to typical message-passing latencies (see Cristian 1996). Again, it is too early to say whether or not this model represents a good choice for research on realistic distributed systems.

Within the purely asynchronous model, a famous theoretical result limits what we can hope to accomplish. In 1985, Fischer, Lynch, and Patterson proved that the asynchronous consensus problem (similar to the Byzantine generals' problem, but posed in an asynchronous setting; see Fig. 11.3) is impossible if even a single process can fail. Their proof revolves around the use of type of message scheduler that delays the progress of a consensus protocol and holds regardless of the way that the protocol itself works. Basically, they demonstrate that any protocol guaranteed to produce only correct outcomes in an asynchronous system can be indefinitely delayed by a complex pattern of network partitioning failures. More recent work has extended this result to some of the communication protocols we will discuss in the remainder of this chapter (see Chandra et al. 1996; Ricciardi 1996).

The Fisher, Lynch, and Paterson (FLP) proof is short but quite sophisticated, and it is common for practitioners to conclude that it does not correspond to any scenario that would be expected to occur in a real distributed system—for example, recall that 3PC is unable to make progress when failure detection is unreliable because of message loss or delays in the network. The FLP result predicts that if a protocol such as 3PC is capable of solving the consensus problem, it can be prevented from terminating. However, if one studies the FLP proof, it turns out that the type of partitioning failure exploited by the proof is at least superficially very remote from the pattern of crashes and network partitioning that forces the 3PC to block.

Thus, it is a bit facile to say that FLP predicts that 3PC will block in this specific way, because the proof constructs a scenario that seems to have relatively little to do with the one that causes problems in a protocol like 3PC. At the very least, one would be expected to relate the FLP scheduling pattern to the situation when 3PC blocks, and I am not aware of any research that has made this connection concrete.

Indeed, it is not entirely clear that 3PC *could* be used to solve the consensus problem: Perhaps the latter is actually a more difficult problem, in which case the inability to solve consensus might not imply that 3PC cannot be solved in asynchronous systems.

As a matter of fact, although it is obvious that 3PC cannot be solved when the network is partitioned, if we carefully study the model used in FLP we realize that network partitioning is not actually considered in this model: The FLP result assumes that every message sent will eventually be received, in FIFO order. Thus, FLP essentially requires that every partition eventually be fixed and that every message eventually get through. The tendency of 3PC to block during partitions, which concerned us above, is not captured by FLP because FLP is willing to wait until such a partition is repaired (and implicitly assumes that it will be), while we wanted 3PC to make progress even while the partition was present (whether or not it will eventually be repaired).

To be more precise, FLP tells us that any asynchronous consensus decision can be *indefinitely delayed*, not merely delayed, until a problematic communication link is fixed. Moreover, it says that this is true even if every message sent in the system eventually reaches its destination. During this period of delay the processes may thus be quite active. Finally, and in some sense most surprising of all, the proof does not require that any process fail at all: It is entirely based on a pattern of message delays. Thus, FLP not only predicts that we would be unable to develop a 3PC protocol guaranteeing progress despite failures, but that, in actuality, there is no 3PC protocol that can terminate at all, even if no failures actually occur and the network is merely subject to unlimited numbers of network partitioning events. We convinced ourselves that 3PC would need to block (wait) in a single situation; FLP tells us that if a protocol such as 3PC can be used to solve the consensus, then there is a sequence of communication failures that would prevent it from reaching a commit or abort point regardless of how long it executes!

11.3.1 Three-Phase Commit and Consensus

To see that 3PC solves consensus, we should be able to show how to map one problem to the other and back—for example, suppose that the inputs to the participants in a 3PC protocol are used to determine their vote, for or against commit, and that we pick one of the processes to run the protocol. Superficially, it may seem that this is a mapping from 3PC to consensus. But recall that consensus of the type considered by FLP is concerned with protocols that tolerate a single failure, which would presumably include the process that starts the protocol. Moreover, although we did not get into this issue, consensus has a nontriviality requirement, which is that if all the inputs are 1 the decision will be 1, and if all the inputs are 0 the decision will be 0. As stated, our mapping of 3PC to consensus might not satisfy non-triviality while also overcoming a single failure. Thus, while it would not be surprising to find that 3PC is equivalent to consensus, neither is it obvious that the correspondence is an exact one.

But assume that 3PC is in fact equivalent to consensus. In a *theoretical* sense, FLP would represent a very strong limitation on 3PC. In a *practical* sense, however, it is unclear whether it has direct relevance to developers of reliable distributed software. Previously, we commented that even the scenario that causes 2PC to block is extremely unlikely unless the coordinator is also a participant; thus, 2PC (or 3PC when the coordinator actually is a participant) would seem to be an adequate protocol for most real systems. Perhaps we are saved from trying to develop some other protocol to evade this limitation: FLP tells us that any such protocol will sometimes block. But once 2PC or 3PC has blocked, one could argue that it is of little practical consequence whether this was provoked by a complex sequence of network partitioning failures or by something simple and blunt, such as the simultaneous crash of a majority of the computers in the network. Indeed, we would consider that 3PC has failed to achieve its objectives as soon as the first partitioning failure occurs and it ceases to make *continuous* progress. Yet the FLP result, in some sense, has not even kicked in at this point: It relates to *ultimate* progress. In the FLP work, the issue of a protocol being blocked is not really modeled in the formalism at all, except in the sense that such a protocol has not yet reached a decision state.

We thus see that although FLP tells us that the asynchronous consensus problem cannot *always* be solved, it says nothing at all about when problems such as this actually *can* be solved. As we will see, more recent work answers this question for asynchronous consensus. However, unlike an impossibility result, to apply this new result one would need to be able to relate a given execution model to the asynchronous one and a given problem to consensus.

As noted earlier, FLP is frequently misunderstood having proved the impossibility of building fault-tolerant distributed software for realistic environments. At the risk of seeming repetitious, this is not the case at all! FLP does not say that one cannot build a consensus protocol tolerant of one failure or of many failures. It simply says that if one does build such a protocol, and then runs it in a system with no concept of global time whatsoever and no timeouts, there will be a pattern of message delays that prevents it from terminating. The pattern in question may be extremely improbable, meaning that one might still be able to build an asynchronous protocol that would terminate with overwhelming probability. Moreover, realistic systems have many forms of time: timeouts, loosely synchronized global clocks, and (often) a good idea of how long messages should take to reach their destinations and to be acknowledged. This sort of information allows real systems to evade the limitations imposed by FLP or at least to create a run-time environment that differs in fundamental ways from the FLP-style of asynchronous environment.

This brings us to the more recent work in this area, which presents a precise characterization of the conditions under which a consensus protocol *can* terminate in an asynchronous environment. Chandra and Toueg have shown how the consensus problem can be expressed using what they call "weak failure detectors," which are a mechanism for detecting that a process has failed without necessarily doing so accurately (see Chandra and Toueg 1991; Chandra et al. 1992). A weak failure detector can make mistakes and change its mind; its behavior is similar to what might result by setting some arbitrary timeout—declaring a process faulty if no communication is received from it during the timeout period, and then declaring that it is actually operational after all if a message subsequently turns up (the communication channels are still assumed to be reliable and FIFO). Using this model, Chandra and Toueg prove that consensus can be solved provided that a period of execution arises during which all genuinely faulty processes are suspected as faulty, and during which at least one operational process is never suspected as faulty by any other operational process. One can think of this as a constraint on the quality of the communication channels and the timeout period: If communication works well enough, and timeouts are accurate enough, for a long enough period of time, a consensus decision can be reached. Interested readers should also refer to Babaoglu et al. (1995), Friedman et al. (1995), Guerraoui and Schiper (1996), Ricciardi (1996). Two relatively recent papers in the area are by Babaoglu et al. (1996) and Neiger (1996).

What Chandra and Toueg have done has general implications for the developers of other forms of distributed systems that seek to guarantee reliability. We learn from this result that to guarantee progress, the developer may need to guarantee a higher quality of communication than in the classical asynchronous model, a degree of clock synchronization (lacking in the model), or some form of accurate failure detection. With any of these, the FLP limitations can be evaded (they no longer hold). In general, it will not be possible to say "my protocol always terminates" without also saying "when such and such a condition holds" on the communication channels, the timeouts used, or other properties of the environment.

This said, the FLP result does create a quandary for practitioners who hope to be rigorous about the reliability properties of their algorithms by making it difficult to talk in rigorous terms about what protocols for asynchronous distributed systems actually guarantee. We would like to be able to talk about one protocol being more tolerant of failures than another, but now we see that such statements will apparently need to be made about protocols in which one can only guarantee fault tolerance in a conditional way and where the conditions may not be simple to express or to validate.

What seems to have happened here is that we lack an appropriate concept of what it means for a protocol to be live in an asynchronous setting. The FLP concept of liveness is rigorously defined and not achievable, but does not address the more relative concept of liveness that we seek when developing a nonblocking commit protocol. As it happens, even this more relative form of liveness is not always achievable, and this coincidence has sometimes led practitioners and even theoreticians to conclude that the forms of liveness are the same, since neither is always possible. This subtle but very important point has yet to be treated adequately by the theoretical community. We need a model within which we can talk about 3PC making progress under conditions when 2PC would not do so without getting snarled in the impossibility of guaranteeing progress for all possible runs in the asynchronous model.

Returning to our data replication problem, these theoretical results do have some practical implications. In particular, they suggest that there may not be much more that can be accomplished in a static computing model. The quorum methods give us a way to overcome failures or damage to limited numbers of data objects within a set of replicas; although expensive, such methods clearly work. While they would not work with a very serious type of failure in which processes behave maliciously, the Byzantine agreement and consensus literature suggest that one cannot always solve this problem in an asynchronous model, and the synchronous model is sufficiently specialized as to be largely inapplicable to standard distributed computing systems.

Our best hope, in light of these limitations, will be to focus on the poor performance of the style of replication algorithm arrived at above. Perhaps a less-costly algorithm would represent a viable option for introducing tolerance to at least a useful class of failures in realistic distributed environments. Moreover, although the FLP result tells us that for certain categories of objectives availability must always be limited, the result does not speak directly to the sorts of tradeoffs between availability and cost seen in 2PC and 3PC. Perhaps we should talk about optimal progress and identify the protocol structures that result in the best possible availability without sacrificing consistency, even if we must accept that our protocols will (at least theoretically) remain exposed to scenarios in which they are unable to make progress.

11.4 Extending Our Protocol into a Full GMS

We have developed a protocol by which the GMS can track its own membership, converting potentially inconsistent and hence confusing timeout events into an agreed-upon sequence of join and leave events. But these events pertain only to the members of the GMS per-se. In a typical local area network, one might have a single instance of the GMS service, with perhaps three to five members belonging to it. How then should these servers handle membership information for everything else in the system?

In Chap. 12, we will tackle this problem as part of a more general one. The basic idea, though, is as follows. Each process in the system will register itself with some member of the GMS service. GMS service members *monitor* other GMS service members (since there are not very many, this is not going to be a big load), and also all members registered with them. Since few systems have more than a few thousand processes in them, a typical GMS service member might thus monitor a few hundred or even a thousand processes.

There are many ways to monitor the health of a process, and we leave it to the developer of a GMS on a given platform to pick the best option. Examples include periodically pinging the process, or having each process periodically send an "I'm still fine" event to the GMS, or watching the MIB within the operating system (the Management Information Base, or MIB, contains a variety of information, normally including the identity of currently active processes), maintaining a TCP connection to the monitored process, and so forth. In a very large system, one could use so-called gossip protocols (we will explore a number of them in our chapter on peer-to-peer techniques) to gossip about the "most recent signs of life" for processes within the system. Ideally, failure detection should be a sophisticated mechanism which reflects a keen awareness of what it means to say that the application is healthy. The outcome of all of this is that the GMS process should be able to detect, within a few seconds (or perhaps a minute or two) the failure of any of the other members or of any of the processes it as been asked to monitor.

In a system where extremely rapid crash detection is needed, and where it is acceptable to pay a high price to get fast response, one can do better. We can install a health-monitoring *agent* on each node in the system and have it open a very small shared-memory file. Each process that registers with the GMS would be assigned a slot in the shared memory file, and would begin to modify the corresponding entry at an agreed upon rate by copying clock values into that slot. The agent would then scan the file periodically, looking for entries that have not changed since the last scan, and then checking to see if the corresponding failure detection threshold has been reached yet. One could achieve failure detection speeds of a few milliseconds in such a model. As for detecting the failure of the entire operating system, such a system would need to send a steady stream of messages to the GMS server at some agreed upon rate, perhaps ten per second. In this manner, one could push failure detection times down to perhaps 200 ms.

The GMS server that detects a failure would notify other GMS members using a multicast. In Chap. 12 we will discuss various kinds of multicast, but the "flavor" required here is perhaps the most basic: a totally ordered multicast called *OrderedSend*. Technically speaking, we would want to use what is called a "strongly durable" version of this protocol, but the issue is a bit esoteric and we will not digress into it for the time being.

Upon receiving such a multicast, a member of the GMS service would relay the failure notification to the processes registered with it. They can then use these notification events as a trustworthy source of failure information, for example to disconnect TCP channels to the failed process, etc. Such events will not be very common and there is no real need to filter them prior to relaying them to the registered pool of processes, but if scalability is a major concern in a given setting, one could certainly do so.

It is useful to number the GMS events. Since each server sees the same ordering of events, this is trivial.

If a GMS server fails, the processes connected to it should probe some other GMS member to see if their failure detection is accurate. If confirmed, such a process would re-register with a different GMS member. Upon reregistering, it informs the new server that it has seen all events up to some number, and the new server forwards notifications that it may have missed. Since this should not take more than a few seconds, it suffices for each server to maintain a log of events and to keep the last few seconds of the log in memory. A process that is registering for the first time would not need to request any replay, since it will not yet be interested in the status of other processes in the system.

Thus, as we move forward in Chaps. 12 to 15, we can presume a simple mechanism for detecting failures promptly and, while mistakes can be made, we can assume that they are converted into a trustworthy input. If a process is "falsely" detected as having failed, it would be dropped from the system anyhow, and would need to reconnect. But such events should be extremely rare and in fact when they occur, would probably reflect real failures that somehow corrected themselves—a machine that hung, for example, or a network link that was broken for a while. The tradeoff evident here is between having the entire distributed application hang waiting to find out if one node has failed or not, and having the system as a whole move forward at the risk that very rarely, some application program may have to reconnect (or just shut down and be restarted from scratch). Since we would like to achieve high availability, the latter scenario is simply a small price we will have to pay for the benefits of improved responsiveness when failures do occur, which is in any case likely to be the far more common scenario.

11.5 Related Reading

Byzantine protocol (see Ben-Or 1985; Coan and Thomas 1990; Coan et al. 1986; Cristian et al. 1985, 1990; Rabin 1983; Schneider 1984).

On defense against Byzantine attacks, some interesting recent papers are Haberman's use of BFT techniques to defend against "reputation" attacks (see PeerReview (Haeberlen et al. 2007)), and Li's very clever integration of Byzantine faults with self-centered ("rational") and irrationally helpful ("altrustic") behavior, in the so-called BAR Gossip model. The SPORC project offers a generic framework for building a wide variety of collaborative applications with untrusted server, using cryptographic techniques to protect against a wide range of attack scenarios.

Byzantine quorum systems (see Malkhi and Reiter 1998, Malkhi et al. 2001a; Alvisi et al. 2001b; Abraham and Malkhi 2003).

Byzantine Agreement in servers (see Castro and Liskov 2002). Zyzzyva (see Kotla et al. 2009), the Byzantine Protocol Template idea of Guerraoui et al. (see Guerraoui et al. 2010).

Asynchronous Consensus (see Chandra and Toueg 1991; Fisher et al. 1985a, 1985b; but see also Babaoglu et al. 1995; Friedman and Birman 1996; Guerraoui and Schiper 1996; Ricciardi 1996).

The method of Chandra and Toueg (see Babaoglu et al. 1995; Chandra and Toueg 1991; Chandra et al. 1992, 1996; Friedman and Birman 1996).

Group membership (see Chockler et al. 2001; Birman and Joseph 1987a, 1987b; Chandra et al. 1996; Cristian 1991a; Melliar-Smith et al. 1991; Mishra et al. 1991; Ricciardi and Birman 1991); but see also Agarwal (1994), Anceaume et al. (1995), Babaoglu et al. (1994, 1995), Birman and Glade (1995), Chandra et al. (1996), Cristian and Schmuck (1995), Friedman et al. (1995), Golding (1992), Guerraoui and Schiper (1996), Reiter (1994b), Ricciardi et al. (1992), Ricciardi (1993, 1996), Rodrigues et al. (1993, 2000).

Partitionable membership (see Chockler et al. 2001; Fekete et al. 2001; Amir et al. 1992a, 1992b; Moser et al. 1994a, 1994b).

Fail-stop illusion (see Sabel and Marzullo 1994).

Group Communication Systems   **12**

12.1   Group Communication

As explained at the start of Chap. 10, our goal in this part of the book is to find
the very best possible way to implement high-speed data replication and other tools
needed for fault-tolerant, highly assured Web Services and other forms of distributed
computing. Given the GMS, one option would be to plunge right in and build replicated applications using the protocol directly in the application. However, as we
just saw (Sect. 11.4), rather than expect every developer to reimplement these protocols in largely identical ways, perhaps slightly tuned to reflect application-specific
optimizations, it is often preferable to implement a more general-purpose communication primitive such as the Isis[2] *OrderedSend*, and then use it to update data within
a group that maintains replicas. Doing so is more general than building a specialized
data replication scheme for our service, because that *OrderedSend* API might have
many uses. Arguing the other side of the coin, generality sometimes has a price; we
saw that in our discussion of Paxos, which has a very general reconfigurable, fault-
tolerant protocol, but turns out to be quite inefficient if a system *always* reconfigures
itself when a failure occurs, and hence never actually needs to tolerate faults.

Here, we will try and find general solutions that include a sufficient range of
options to let the developer do the most efficient thing: we will create a whole family
of primitives, with different properties matching different styles of use. We will
see that there are many possible properties that a group multicast might offer. By
supporting a few of these, we will arrive not just at a replication algorithm, but
rather at a set of tools that can easily support replicated data, while also being useful
for other purposes, such as implementing locking, or supporting fancy kinds of load-
balancing.

Readers who are not interested in details may want to skip to Chap. 14. The bottom line is that the *OrderedSend* (or *totally ordered*) virtually synchronous multicast
primitive used in Sect. 12.3 is probably all that one needs in most applications, and
Chap. 13 covers "esoteric" topics that only arise if a system supports the creation
of large numbers of groups (something platforms for group communication probably should do, but that in fact is often omitted). On the other hand, the topic of

K.P. Birman, *Guide to Reliable Distributed Systems*, Texts in Computer Science,
DOI 10.1007/978-1-4471-2416-0_12, © Springer-Verlag London Limited 2012

multicast reliability and ordering is an interesting one, and it is not all that hard to understand how the desired properties correspond to protocol mechanisms—one property requires an extra phase of communication before delivery, another requires such-and-such information in each message, etc. Indeed, one can easily come up with new mixtures of properties and can usually implement them by just composing the basic mechanisms we will explore here in a new but straightforward manner.

In this chapter, we will discuss the options for implementing quite a few forms of ordering, and some other properties as well. Here is a quick summary for those who plan to skip the details.

1. *Send*. This is a "FIFO" ordered multicast. Messages from a sender are delivered in the order they were sent. For example, if process p sends message a followed by message b, all recipients deliver a before b. Messages sent by different senders can be delivered in different orders at different recipients. In a Web Services setting, a server streaming data to a set of clients might use *Send* to do so; the multicast stream would act much like n side-by-side TCP connections, but could potentially achieve much higher throughput than is possible with TCP (for example, *Send* can exploit IP multicast, if available).

2. *CausalSend*. This is a "causally" ordered multicast (in the sense of Lamport's "causal" ordering relation, discussed in Sect. 10.2). As we will see, a *CausalSend* multicast would be an ideal way to implement data replication and locking within process groups, for example when replicating the state of a high-availability server. What makes *CausalSend* especially powerful is that it can be used in applications that need a very loosely coupled, asynchronous-style of connectivity for reasons of performance: with *CausalSend* it will turn out that we can launch an asynchronous update to a replicated data item, immediately update the local copy (without waiting for messages to be sent or delivered) and then move on to the next task without worrying about a race condition in which some application component might try to access the data and see them "before" that update has been applied. In systems that lack a *CausalSend* option, there are reasonable alternatives (one can usually do most of the same things with *Send*) but the needed code becomes more complicated).

With *CausalSend*, messages from a single thread of computation are delivered in the order they were sent, and this is true *even when that thread spans multiple processes*. For example, one could have a situation in which process p sends message a and then asks process q to do something, causing q to send message b. Notice that a and b are ordered (after all, p asked q to take the action), yet they are not ordered in the eyes of *Send*, since p and q are different processes. In object-oriented systems, such situations arise very often and may not even be obvious to the developer, since object invocation can sometimes cross a process boundary transparently. Even so, *CausalSend* would say that b came after a and deliver a before b at any destinations they have in common. Messages sent concurrently by different senders, where there is no implicit causal ordering, can be delivered in different orders at different recipients. Some people find *CausalSend* confusing, but it is easy to understand if one just thinks of it as a version of *Send* fixed to work properly in a world of remote procedure calls and cross-address space object invocations: when p asked q to perform b, this is as if the execution timeline of p extended into the address space of q, and it makes perfect sense to say that action b happens after a. For many purposes, b might not even make sense unless the receiver saw a first! Indeed, *Send* is in some ways the more confusing primitive, especially in platforms like Microsoft .NET, where object invocations can occur without the programmer even realizing that one was requested!

3. *OrderedSend*. Within any single group of processes, the system sorts messages into a total ordering and delivers them to group members in this order (historically, this primitive was also called "atomic broadcast"). The *OrderedSend* primitive is usually understood to also share the same property as *Send:* messages from a single source will be delivered in the order they were sent. In many settings, *OrderedSend* is the easiest multicast primitive to work with, although it can be slower than *CausalSend* if it is not used carefully. Just the same, if in doubt, a developer cannot really go wrong by using *OrderedSend* to send multicasts, update replicated data, inform other group members of state changes, etc.

   Token passing is a common way to actually implement a protocol such as *OrderedSend*. Without getting into the details of how failures are handled, the basic idea is to associate a token with the group. The holder of the token can take actions on behalf of the group, such as deciding the ordering to use for a set of concurrent multicasts. The idea is to have senders send their messages using *Send*. On reception, the delivery is delayed. The token holder sends an *Send* of its own from time to time, giving the official ordering to use; recipients then sort their delayed *OrderedSend* messages into order and deliver them accordingly. Of course one can make such a protocol fancier, and there are issues of how often to send the ordering messages and how to recover the token if the process holding it fails. We will tackle those later in this chapter.

   Token passing schemes require a rule for when the token should be moved. In some approaches, the token is moved on demand and remains at a sender long enough for it to send a burst of messages. This can be advantageous because the burst can then be sent using *Send*, since there is just a single sender during that period. At the other extreme, one can have a token that rotates rapidly through the entire group, permitting a sender to send a single message each time the token is in its possession. Although both approaches are useful, in what follows we'll have the former style in mind when we talk about token-based *OrderedSend* protocols.

4. *OrderedCausalSend*. There have been some suggestions that systems should actually implement *OrderedSend* with an additional causal ordering property, as if it was an extension of the *CausalSend* property into a total order. In this proposal, if the sending events for some messages are causally ordered, the messages are delivered in a total order consistent with that causal order. However, *OrderedCausalSend* is not widely used, despite the arguments suggesting that it is an even safer choice than *OrderedSend*.

5. *SafeSend*. Ordered with respect to all other kinds of communication (historically, this was also called "globally atomic broadcast"), and also durable in the sense that if any delivery occurs, every surviving group member will eventually deliver

the message. *SafeSend* is a version of Paxos: it has the identical properties to the protocols in the Paxos suite (those interested in Paxos will find that our version of *SafeSend* is most similar to what Lamport would call Faster Generalized Paxos with a leader, in a dynamic membership model). If a group of processes delivers a *SafeSend* while other multicasts are being transmitted, any given multicast is delivered entirely before or entirely after the *SafeSend*. The protocol is used within the Isis[2] system for updating the membership of a group of processes, but has many other uses as well. For example, a developer working with a database might consider employing *SafeSend* for database updates. On the other hand, after a crash followed by a recovery, a cleanup will still be needed, and for many purposes, *OrderedSend* should suffice.

6. *Failure atomicity*. This is a term that can mean different things for different communities, and to avoid the risk of confusion, we won't use in the remainder of the book. As "normally" defined, failure atomicity refers to a multicast that is delivered in the same order at all destinations, and that will be delivered to all operational processes if it is delivered to any, even in the event of a crash. For our purposes, the former property is really an ordering property—the one associated with *OrderedSend*. As for the handling of crashes, we will break this down into two cases: *strongly durable* and *non-durable* failure handling, as seen below.

7. *Durable and non-durable multicasts*. In addition to ordering, multicasts can also differ in their guarantees in the event that a failure occurs while the multicast is being delivered. A *durable* multicast guarantees that if any process delivers a message (even if it fails immediately upon doing so), all destinations that remain operational will deliver a copy of the message too. A *weakly durable multicast* would be one that achieves durability rapidly, but still has a window of vulnerability during which a multicast that has been delivered to a subset of the members of a group, but then forgotten and not delivered to other members if all of the ones that received it were to fail. Another term for this property is *amnesia freedom*, and we will show how it can be achieved and used in cloud settings when we look at multicast use cases in Chap. 15.

For example, suppose *a* sends a multicast to group *G* and process *b* receives and delivers that multicast. If *a* and *b* both crash, it is possible that the group will repair itself and resume execution, but that no other members will deliver *a*'s message! Had the multicast been strongly durable, such a condition could not arise. Weak decreability can pose problems for developers. Say that the group is implementing a replicated bank account: *a* is an application withdrawing some cash and *b* is the ATM machine. With a multicast, we could get into a situation where the customer withdraws $100 from the ATM machine, then unplugs it (very) quickly, and the main servers at the bank's data center never find out about the transaction. Using a strongly durable multicast, that kind of problem just cannot arise.

Strong durability is sometimes called *safe* delivery, in the sense that when a durable message is delivered, it is "safe" to take actions that leave externally visible effects with respect to which the remainder of the system must be consistent. However, a multicast is not necessarily *unsafe*. Often, it is perfectly safe for applications in which the action taken upon receipt of the message has only internal effects on the system state or when consistency with respect to external actions can be established in other ways—for example, from the semantics of the application. Moreover, this use of the term "safe" may confuse theoreticians, who prove protocols correct by establishing that they are "safe and live." Nonetheless, we do use this term in our *SafeSend* primitive, which is, in fact, a strongly durable protocol.

Given that it offers stronger failure guarantees, why not just insist that all multicast primitives be durable (e.g. just use *SafeSend* for everything)? Here, the right answer depends somewhat on whether one wears a theoretician's or a practitioner's hat. From a theory perspective, it makes sense to do precisely this. Strong durability is a simple property to formalize, and applications using a strongly durable multicast layer are easier to prove correct.

But the bad news is that strong durability is *very costly* when compared to non-durable protocols under conditions where performance is of the utmost importance. It should not be hard to see why this is the case: to achieve durability, we need to make sure that there is a copy of the message buffered at every group member before any member can be allowed to deliver it (otherwise, just kill all the processes with copies and clearly, the durability property will be violated, no matter what protocol we use to clean up after failure). This means that the slowest member of the group delays delivery of a message to all the other members. In cloud settings, for example, if we were to use *SafeSend* as our primary tool for replicating data, we might be unable to scale the resulting services to the desired degree. In contrast, a protocol such as *Send* or *OrderedSend* can be so fast that one could even use it for replication in the first-tier services of the cloud: doing so would give us a form of soft-state service in which there are consistency guarantees on the replicated soft-state, and yet with performance fully competitive to that of any other way of building those kinds of soft-state, first-tier solutions.

Our bias in this book is pretty practical, especially where huge performance factors arise, as turns out to be the situation here. Accordingly, we do not make much use of strong durability in the algorithms presented later in the book, and *SafeSend* won't be seen often even in the chapter where we present the Isis[2] system in greater detail. On the other hand, there are major systems (notably Paxos), for which the behavior of a *SafeSend* primitive is the default. If one does use *SafeSend*, it can be important to split the members of a group into two sets. Lamport does this; one set, the *acceptors*, are group members used to vote on ordering and durability. A second set, the *learners*, are members that will receive the ordered updates and would normally include the acceptors, but also include a great many additional non-acceptors. This way we can run *SafeSend* in a way that uses the acceptors during its first phase, and only deals with massive scale in the second phase. With a small acceptor set (in Isis[2] we often use three acceptors), the performance of the protocol is dramatically better, and yet the strong durability property still holds.

Experts in the field have debated the pros and cons of a Paxos-like guarantee of strong durability versus a weaker "Isis-like" multicast until all concerned have reached utter exhaustion. There simply is not any agreement on the matter.

Many engineers are convinced that replication is far too costly to use in settings like Web Services systems; they point to the CORBA fault tolerance standard, which was implemented using a strongly durable *SafeSend* in support of their basic point, and to database replication as further evidence supporting it. But all of these are examples in which the cost of strong durability is at the core of the performance problems they cite. In effect, durability is an appealing choice on conceptual and esthetic grounds, but once you decide to use it, you will end up using it very sparingly or rejecting it as too slow. Weakly durable or non-durable multicast can be harder to work with, but gives much faster solutions. Engineers have been quite successful using these primitives in the field; we will see examples such as the New York and Swiss Stock Exchange systems, the French Air Traffic Control system, the US Naval AEGIS warship, and many others (these are Isis success stories, but Spread has lots of stories of its own).

8. *Flush.* This is more of an algorithm than a property of a multicast primitive; we will need it as an antidote to the non-durability problems just described. In a system where multicasts are weakly durable, *flush* provides the application with a way to pause until multicasts it has sent (or received prior to calling *flush*) have actually reached their destinations and hence cannot be lost even if a failure occurs. That is, a multicast becomes durable if a receiver calls *flush* before processing (delivering) it! Thus we can have our cake (higher performance) and eat it too (achieve strong durability where we really need this costly guarantee), by using a non-durable multicast "most of the time" and calling flush now and then, when durability is really needed.

12.2   A Closer Look at Delivery Ordering Options

Let us look carefully at multicast delivery ordering, starting with a multicast that offers no guarantees whatsoever. Using such a multicast, a process that sends two messages, m_0 and m_1, concurrently would have no assurances at all about their relative order of delivery or relative atomicity—that is, suppose that m_0 was the message sent first. Not only might m_1 reach any destinations that it shares with m_0 first, but a failure of the sender might result in a scenario where m_1 was delivered atomically to all its destinations, but m_0 was not delivered to any process that remains operational (Fig. 12.1). Such an outcome would be atomic on a per-multicast basis, but might not be a very useful primitive from the perspective of the application developer! Thus, while we should ask what forms of order a multicast primitive can guarantee, we should also ask how order is connected to atomicity in our failure-atomicity model.

As just summarized, we will be studying a hierarchy of increasingly ordered delivery properties. The weakest of these is usually called "sender order" or "FIFO order" and requires that if the same process sends m_0 and m_1 then m_0 will be delivered before m_1 at any destinations they have in common (see Fig. 12.2). A slightly stronger ordering property, "causal delivery order," ensures that if $send(m_0) \rightarrow send(m_1)$, then m_0 will be delivered before m_1 at any destinations they have in common (see Fig. 12.3). Still stronger is an order whereby any processes that receive the same two messages receive them in the same order: If at process p,

Fig. 12.1 An unordered
multicast provides no
guarantees. Here, m_0 was sent
before m_1, but is received
after m_1 at destination p_0.
The reception order for m_2,
sent concurrently by process
r, is different at each of its
destinations

Fig. 12.2 Sender ordered or
FIFO multicast. Notice that
m_2, which is sent
concurrently, is unordered
with respect to m_0 and m_1

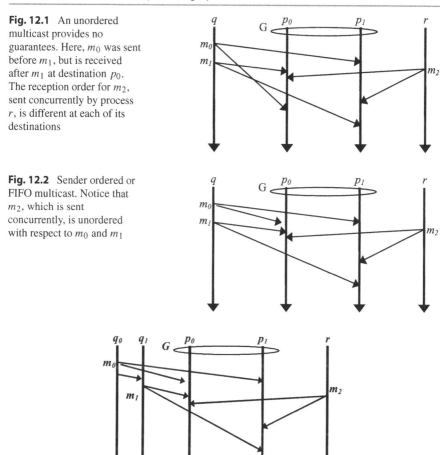

Fig. 12.3 Causally ordered multicast delivery. Here m_0 is sent before m_1 in a causal sense, because a message is sent from q_0 to q_1 after m_0 was sent, and before q_1 sends m_1. Perhaps q_0 has
requested that q_1 send m_1. m_0 is consequently delivered before m_1 at destinations that receive
both messages. Multicast m_2 is sent concurrently and no ordering guarantees are provided. In this
example, m_2 is delivered after m_1 by p_0 and before m_1 by p_1

$deliv(m_0) \rightarrow deliv(m_1)$, then m_0 will be delivered before m_1 at all destinations they
have in common. This is sometimes called a totally ordered delivery protocol, but
this is something of a misnomer, since one can imagine a number of ordering properties that would be total in this respect without necessarily implying the existence of
a single system wide total ordering on all the messages sent in the system. The reason for this is that our definition focuses on delivery orders where messages overlap,
but it does not actually relate these orders to an acyclic system wide ordering. The
Transis project calls this type of locally ordered multicast an "agreed" order, and
we like this term too: The destinations agree on the order, even for multicasts that
may have been initiated concurrently and that may be unordered by their senders

Fig. 12.4 When using a
totally ordered multicast
primitive, p_0 and p_1 receive
exactly the same multicasts,
and the message are delivered
in identical order. Hence, the
order happens to also be
causal, but this is not a
specific guarantee of the
primitive

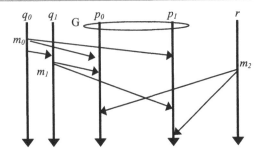

(Fig. 12.4). However, the agreed order is more commonly called a "total" order or
an "atomic" delivery order in the systems that support multicast communication and
in the literature.

One can extend the agreed order into a causal agreed order (now one requires that
if the sending events were ordered by causality, the delivery order will respect the
causal send order) or into a system-wide agreed order (one requires that there exists
a single system wide total order on messages, such that the delivery ordering used at
any individual process is consistent with the message ordering in this system's total
order). Later we will see why these are not identical orderings. Moreover, in systems
that have multiple process groups, the issue of how to extend ordering properties to
span multiple process groups will occur.

It has been proposed that total ordering be further classified as *weak* or *strong*
in terms analogous to the strongly durable and weakly durable properties. A weak
total ordering property would be one guaranteed to hold only at *correct* processes,
namely those remaining operational until the protocol terminates. A strong total
ordering property would hold even at faulty processes, namely those that fail after
delivering messages but before the protocol as a whole has terminated.

Suppose that a protocol fixes the delivery ordering for messages m_1 and m_2 at
process p, delivering m_1 first. If p fails, a weak total ordering would permit the
delivery of m_2 before m_1 at some other process q that survives the failure, even
though this order is not the one seen by p. Like strong durability, the argument
for strong total ordering is that this may be required if the ordering of messages
may have externally visible consequences, which could be noticed by an external
observer interacting with a process that later fails, and then interacts with some other
process that remained operational. Naturally, this guarantee has a price, though,
and one would prefer to use a less costly weak protocol in settings where such a
guarantee is not required.

Let us now return to the issue raised briefly above, concerning the connection
between the ordering properties for a set of multicasts and their failure-atomicity
properties. To avoid creating an excessive number of possible multicast protocols,
we will assume here that the developer of a reliable application will also want the
specified ordering property to extend into the failure-atomicity properties of the
primitives used. That is, in a situation where the ordering property of a multicast

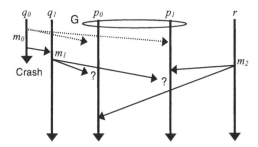

Fig. 12.5 In this undesirable scenario, the failure of q_0 leaves a causal gap in the message delivery order, preventing q_1 from communicating with members of G. If m_1 is delivered, the causal ordering property would be violated, because $send(m_0) \rightarrow send(m_1)$. But m_0 will never be delivered. Thus, q_1 is logically partitioned from G. Process r, in contrast is free to communicate with G (message m_2)

would imply that message m_0 should be delivered before m_1 if they have any destinations in common, we will require that if m_1 is delivered successfully, then m_0 must also be delivered successfully, whether or not they actually do have common destinations. This is sometimes called a *gap-freedom* guarantee: It is the constraint that failures cannot leave holes or gaps in the ordered past of the system. Such a gap is seen in Fig. 12.5.

Notice that this rule is stated so that it would apply even if m_0 and m_1 have no destinations in common. The reason is that ordering requirements are normally transitive: If m_0 is before m_1, and m_1 is before m_2, then m_0 is also before m_2, and we would like both delivery ordering obligations and failure-atomicity obligations to be guaranteed between m_0 and m_2. Had we instead required that "in a situation where the ordering property of a multicast implies that message m_0 should be delivered before m_1, then if they have any destinations in common, we will also require that if m_1 is delivered successfully, then m_0 must be too," the delivery atomicity requirement might not apply between m_0 and m_2.

Lacking a gap-freedom guarantee, one can imagine runs of a system that would leave orphaned processes that are technically prohibited from communicating with one another—for example, in Fig. 12.5, q_1 sends message m_1 to the members of group G causally after m_0 was sent by q_0 to G. The members of G are now required to deliver m_0 before delivering m_1. However, if the failure-atomicity rule is such that the failure of q_0 could prevent m_0 from ever being delivered, this ordering obligation can only be satisfied by *never* delivering m_1. One could say that q_1 has been partitioned from G by the ordering obligations of the system! Thus, if a system provides ordering guarantees and failure-atomicity guarantees, it should normally extend the latter to encompass the former.

Yet an additional question arises if a process sends multicasts to a group while processes are joining or leaving it. In these cases the membership of the group will be in flux at the time that the message is sent, and one can imagine several ways of interpreting how a system could implement group atomicity.

12.2.1 Nondurable Failure-Atomic Group Multicast

Consider the following simple, but inefficient group multicast protocol. The sender adds a header to its message listing the membership of the destination group at the time that it sends the message. It now transmits the message to the members of the group, perhaps taking advantage of a hardware multicast feature (such as IP multicast) if one is available, and otherwise transmitting the message over stream-style reliable connections to the destinations. However, unlike a conventional stream protocol, here we will assume that the connection is only broken if the GMS reports that one of the end points has left the system.

Upon receipt of a message, the destination processes deliver it immediately, but also resend it to the remaining destinations. Again, each process uses reliable stream-style channels for this retransmission stage, breaking the channel only if the GMS reports the departure of an end point. A participant will now receive one copy of the message from the sender and one from each nonfailed participant other than itself. After delivery of the initial copy, it discards any duplicates. We will now argue that this protocol is failure-atomic, although not strongly durable.

To see that it is failure-atomic, assume that some process p_i receives and delivers a copy of the message and remains operational. Failure-atomicity tells us that all other destinations that remain operational must also receive and deliver the message. It is clear that this will occur, since the only condition under which p_i would fail to forward a message to p_j would be if the GMS reports that p_i has failed, or if it reports that p_j has failed. But we assumed that p_i does not fail, and the output of the GMS can be trusted in this environment. Thus, the protocol achieves failure atomicity. To see that the protocol is not strongly durable, consider the situation if the sender sends a copy of the message only to process p_i and then both processes fail. In this case, p_i may have delivered the message and then executed for some extended period of time before crashing or detecting that it has been partitioned from the system. The message has thus been delivered to one of the destinations and that destination may well have acted on it in a visible way; however, none of the processes that remain operational will ever receive it. As we noted earlier, this often will not pose a problem for the application, but it is a behavior that the developer must anticipate and treat appropriately.

As can be seen in Fig. 12.5, this simple protocol is a costly one: To send a message to n destinations requires $O(n^2)$ messages. Of course, with hardware broadcast functions, or if the network is not a bottleneck, the cost will be lower, but the protocol still requires each process to send and receive each message approximately n times.

But now, suppose that we delay the retransmission stage of the protocol, retransmitting only if the GMS informs the participants that the sender has failed. This change yields a less-costly protocol, which requires n messages (or just one, if hardware broadcast is an option), but in which the participants may need to save a copy of each message indefinitely. They would do this just in case the sender fails.

Recall that we are transmitting messages over a reliable stream. It follows that within the lower levels of the communication system, there is an occasional acknowledgment flowing from each participant back to the sender. If we tap into this

Fig. 12.6 A very simple reliable multicast protocol. The initial round of messages triggers a second round of messages as each recipient echoes the incoming message to the other destinations

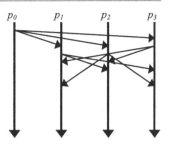

information, the sender will know when the participants have all received copies of its message. It can now send a second-phase message, informing the participants that it is safe to delete the saved copy of each message, although they must still save the message identification information to reject duplicates if the sender happens to crash midway through this stage. At this stage the participants can disable their retransmission logic and discard the saved copy of the message. Later, the sender could run still a third phase, telling the participants that they can safely delete even the message identification information, because after the second phase completes there will be no risk of a failure that would cause the message to be retransmitted by the participants.

But now a further optimization is possible. There is no real hurry to run the third phase of this protocol, and even the second phase can be delayed to some degree. Moreover, most processes that send a multicast will tend to send a subsequent one soon afterwards: This principle is well known from all forms of operating systems and database software. It can be summarized by this maxim: *The most likely action by any process is to repeat the same action it took most recently.* Accordingly, it makes sense to delay sending out messages for the second and third phase of the protocol in the hope that a new multicast will be initiated; this information can be piggybacked onto the first stage of an outgoing message associated with that subsequent protocol!

In this manner, we arrive at a solution, illustrated in Fig. 12.7, that has an average cost of n messages per multicast, or just one if hardware broadcast can be exploited, plus some sort of background cost associated with the overhead to implement a reliable stream channel. When a failure does occur, any pending multicast

Fig. 12.7 An improved three-phase protocol. Ideally, the second and third phases would be piggybacked onto other multicasts from the same sender to the same set of destinations and would not require extra messages

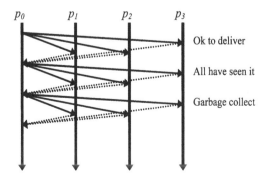

will suddenly generate as many as n^2 additional messages, but even this effect can potentially be mitigated. Since the GMS provides the same membership list to all processes and the message itself carries the list of its destinations, the participants can delay briefly in the hope that some jointly identifiable lowest-ranked participant will turn out to have received the message and will terminate the protocol on behalf of all. We omit the details of such a solution, but any serious system for reliable distributed computing would implement a variety of such mechanisms to keep costs down to an absolute minimum and to maximize the value of each message actually transmitted using piggybacking, delaying tactics, and hardware broadcast.

Notice that because the protocol in Fig. 12.7 delivers messages in the first phase, it is *non*-durable.

12.2.2 Strongly Durable Failure-Atomic Group Multicast

We can extend the above protocol to one that is strongly durable. Doing so requires that no process deliver the message until it is known the processes in the destination group all have a copy. (In some cases it may be sufficient to know that a majority have a copy, but we will not concern ourselves with these sorts of special cases now, because they are typically limited to the processes that actually run the GMS protocol.) Earlier, we mentioned the Paxos system and commented that it, and other similar systems that provide strong durability, tend to be quite slow. The problem is precisely the one just cited, namely the need to wait until a majority of processes have a copy of each message before that message can be delivered.

We could accomplish our goal with the original inefficient protocol of Fig. 12.6, by modifying the original nondurable protocol to delay the delivery of messages until a copy has been received from every destination that is still present in the membership list provided by the GMS. However, such a protocol would suffer from the inefficiencies that led us to optimize the original protocol into the one in Fig. 12.7. Accordingly, it makes more sense to focus on that improved protocol.

Here, it can be seen that an additional round of messages will be needed before the multicast can be delivered initially; the rest of the protocol can then be used without change (Fig. 12.8). Unfortunately, though, this initial round also delays the delivery of the messages to their destinations. In the original protocol, a message could be delivered as soon as it reached a destination for the first time—thus, the latency to delivery is precisely the latency from the sender to a given destination for a single hop. Now the latency might be substantially increased: For a strongly durable delivery, we will need to wait for a round trip to the slowest process in the set of destinations, and then one more hop until the sender has time to inform the destinations that it is safe to deliver the messages. In practice, this may represent an increase in latency of a factor of ten or more. Thus, while durability guarantees are sometimes needed, the developer of a distributed application should request this property only when it is genuinely necessary, or performance (to the degree that latency is a factor in performance) will suffer badly.

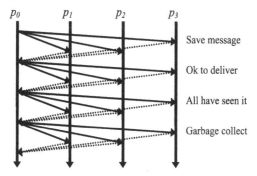

Fig. 12.8 A strongly durable version of the optimized, reliable multicast protocol. Latency to delivery may be much higher, because no process can deliver the message until all processes have received and saved a copy. Here, the third and fourth phases can piggyback on other multicasts, but the first two stages may need to be executed as promptly as possible to avoid increasing the latency still further. Latency is often a key performance factor

12.2.3 Dynamic Process Groups

When we introduced the GMS, our system became very dynamic, allowing processes to join and leave at will. But not all processes in the system will be part of the same application, and the protocols presented in the previous section are therefore assumed to be sent to groups of processes that represent subsets of the full system membership. This is seen in Fig. 12.9, which illustrates the structure of a hypothetical trading system in which services (replicated for improved performance or availability) implement theoretical pricing calculations. Here we have one big system, with many small groups in it. How should the membership of such a subgroup be managed?

In this section, we introduce a membership management protocol based on the idea that a single process within each group will serve as the coordinator for synchronizing the delivery of events reporting membership changes with the delivery of events reporting new multicast messages. If a process wishes to join the group, or voluntarily leaves the group, this coordinator will update the group membership accordingly. (The role of coordinator will really be handled by the layer of software that implements groups, so this will not be visible to the application process itself.) Additionally, the coordinator will monitor the members (through the GMS and by periodically pinging them to verify that they are still healthy), excluding any failed processes from the membership (much as in the case of a process that leaves voluntarily).

In the approach we present here, all processes that belong to a group maintain a local copy of the current membership list. We call this the "view" of the group and will say that each time the membership of the group changes, a new view of the group is reported to the members. Our protocol will have the property that all group members see the identical sequence of group views within any given component of a partitioned system. In practice, we will mostly be interested in primary component partitions, and, in these cases, we will simply say that all processes either see

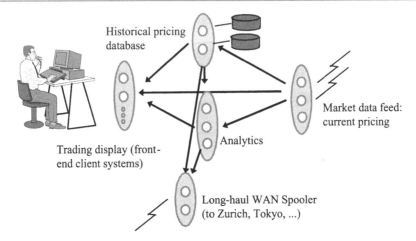

Fig. 12.9 Distributed trading system may have both static and dynamic uses for process groups. The historical database, replicated for load-balancing and availability, is tied to the databases themselves and can be viewed as static. This is also true of the market data feeds, which are often redundant for fault tolerance. Other parts of the system, however, such as the analytics (replicated for parallelism) and the client interface processes (one or more per trader), are highly dynamic groups. For durability of the model, it makes sense to adopt a dynamic group model, but to keep in mind that some of these groups manage physical resources

identical views for a group or, if excluded from the primary component, cease to see new views and eventually detect that they are partitioned, at which point a process may terminate or attempt to rejoin the system much like a new process.

The members of a group depend upon their coordinator for the reporting of new views and consequently monitor the liveness of the coordinator by periodically pinging it. If the coordinator appears to be faulty, the member or members that detect this report the situation to the GMS in the usual manner, simultaneously cutting off communication to the coordinator and starting to piggyback or gossip this information on messages to other members, which similarly cut their channels to the coordinator and, if necessary, relay this information to the GMS. The GMS will eventually report that the coordinator has failed, at which point the lowest ranked of the remaining members takes over as the new coordinator.

Interestingly, we have now solved our problem, because we can use the nondurable multicast protocol to distribute new views within the group. In fact, this hides a subtle point, to which we will return momentarily—namely, the way to deal with ordering properties of a reliable multicast, particularly in the case where the sender fails and the protocol must be terminated by other processes in the system. However, we will see below that the protocol has the necessary ordering properties when it operates over stream connections that guarantee FIFO delivery of messages, and when the failure-handling mechanisms introduced earlier are executed in the same order that the messages themselves were initially seen (i.e., if process p_i first received multicast m_0 before multicast m_1, then p_i retransmits m_0 before m_1).

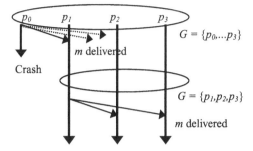

Fig. 12.10 Although m was sent when p_0 belonged to G, it reaches p_2 and p_3 after a view change reporting that p_0 has failed. The earlier (at p_1) and later (p_2, p_3) delivery events thus differ in that the recipients will observe a different view of the process group at the time the message arrives. This can result in inconsistency if, for example, the membership of the group is used to subdivide the incoming tasks among the group members

12.2.4 View-Synchronous Failure Atomicity

We have now created an environment within which a process that joins a process group will receive the membership view for that group as of the time it was added to the group. It will subsequently observe any changes that occur until it crashes or leaves the group, provided only that the GMS continues to report failure information. Such a process may now wish to initiate multicasts to the group using the reliable protocols presented earlier. But suppose that a process belonging to a group fails while some multicasts from it are pending? When can the other members be certain that they have seen all of its messages, so that they can take over from it if the application requires that they do so?

Up to now, our protocol structure would not provide this information to a group member—for example, it may be that process p_0 fails after sending a message to p_1 but to no other member. It is entirely possible that the failure of p_0 will be reported through a new process group view before this message is finally delivered to the remaining members. Such a situation would create difficult problems for the application developer, and we need a mechanism to avoid it. This is illustrated in Fig. 12.10.

It makes sense to assume that the application developer will want failure notification to represent a final state with regard to the failed process. Thus, it would be preferable for all messages initiated by process p_0 to have been delivered to their destinations before the failure of p_0 is reported through the delivery of a new view. We will call the necessary protocol a *flush* protocol, meaning that it flushes partially completed multicasts out of the system, reporting the new view only after this has been done. The reader may recall from Sect. 12.1 that *flush* is also useful in "converting" multicasts to durable ones, so as to take an external action safely. In fact the same protocol can address both requirements.

In the example shown in Fig. 12.10, we did not include the exchange of messages required to multicast the new view of group G. Notice, however, that the figure is probably incorrect if the new-view coordinator of group G is actually process p_1. To

Fig. 12.11 Process p_1
flushes pending multicasts
before initiating the new-view
protocol

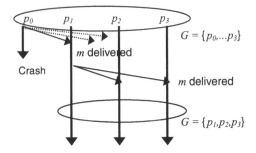

see this, recall that the communication channels are FIFO and that the termination
of an interrupted multicast protocol requires only a single round of communication.
Thus, if process p_1 simply runs the completion protocol for multicasts initiated by
p_0 before it starts the new-view multicast protocol that will announce that p_0 has
been dropped by the group, the pending multicast will be completed first. This is
shown in Fig. 12.11.

We can guarantee this behavior even if multicast m is strongly durable, simply
by delaying the new-view multicast until the outcome of the durablity protocol has
been determined.

On the other hand, the problem becomes harder if p_1 (which is the only process
to have received the multicast from p_0) is not the coordinator for the new-view protocol. In this case, it will be necessary for the new-view protocol to operate with an
additional round, in which the members of G are asked to flush any multicasts that
are as yet unterminated, and the new-view protocol runs only when this flush phase
has finished. Moreover, even if the new-view protocol is being executed to drop p_0
from the group, it is possible that the system will soon discover that some other
process, perhaps p_2, is also faulty and must also be dropped. Thus, a flush protocol
should flush messages *regardless of their originating process*, with the result that all
multicasts will have been flushed out of the system before the new view is installed.

These observations lead to a communication property that Babaoglu and his colleagues have called *view synchronous communication*, which is one of several properties associated with the *virtual synchrony model* introduced by Thomas Joseph
and the author in 1985. A view-synchronous communication system ensures that
any multicast initiated in a given view of some process group will be failure-atomic
with respect to that view and will be terminated before a new view of the process
group is installed.

One might wonder how a view-synchronous communication system can prevent
a process from initiating new multicasts while the view installation protocol is running. If such multicasts are locked out, there may be an extended delay during which
no multicasts can be transmitted, causing performance problems for the application
programs layered over the system. But if such multicasts are permitted, the first
phase of the flush protocol will not have flushed *all* the necessary multicasts!

A solution for this problem was suggested independently by Ladin and Malkhi,
working on systems called Harp and Transis, respectively. In these systems, if a
multicast is initiated while a protocol to install view i of group G is running, the

multicast destinations are taken to be the future membership of G when that new view has been installed—for example, in the Fig. 12.11, a new multicast might be initiated by process p_2 while the protocol to exclude p_0 from G is still running. Such a new multicast would be addressed to $\{p_1, p_2, p_3\}$ (not to p_0), and would be delivered only after the new view is delivered to the remaining group members. The multicast can thus be initiated while the view change protocol is running and would only be delayed if, when the system is ready to deliver a copy of the message to some group member, the corresponding view has not yet been reported. This approach will often avoid delays completely, since the new-view protocol was already running and will often terminate in roughly the same amount of time as will be needed for the new multicast protocol to start delivering messages to destinations. Thus, at least in the most common case, the view change can be accomplished even as communication to the group continues unabated. Of course, if multiple failures occur, messages will still queue up on receipt and will need to be delayed until the view flush protocol terminates, so this desirable behavior cannot always be guaranteed.

The Horus and Ensemble systems use a slightly different approach. In these systems, the sender of a message is guaranteed that the message will be delivered in the same view that it finds itself in when it performs the send operation. However, these systems also implement a form of interlock between the view installation layer and the application. When membership will be changed, the system first asks the application to stop sending new multicasts, and the application acknowledges the request. Next, the system delivers the new view. Finally, the application can resume sending multicasts, using the new view.

12.2.5   Summary of GMS Properties

The following is an informal (English-language) summary of the properties that a group membership service guarantees to members of subgroups of the full system membership. We use the term "process group" for such a subgroup. When we say "guarantees" the reader should keep in mind that a GMS service does not, and in fact cannot, guarantee that it will remain operational despite all possible patterns of failures and communication outages. Some patterns of failure or of network outages will prevent such a service from reporting new system views and will consequently prevent the reporting of new process group views. Thus, the guarantees of a GMS are relative to a constraint—namely, that the system provides a sufficiently reliable transport of messages and that the rate of failures is sufficiently low.

1. *GMS-1*: Starting from an initial group view, the GMS reports new views that differ by addition and deletion of group members. The reporting of changes is by the two-stage interface described previously, which gives protocols an opportunity to flush pending communication from a failed process before its failure is reported to application processes.

2. *GMS-2*: The group view is not changed capriciously. A process is added only if it has started and is trying to join the system, and deleted only if it has failed or is suspected of having failed by some other member of the system.

3. *GMS-3*: All group members observe continuous subsequences of the same sequence of group views, starting with the view during which the member was first added to the group and ending either with a view that registers the voluntary departure of the member from the group or with the failure of the member.
4. *GMS-4*: The GMS is fair in the sense that it will not indefinitely delay a view change associated with one event while performing other view changes. That is, if the GMS service itself is live, join requests will eventually cause the requesting process to be added to the group, and leave or failure events will eventually cause a new group view to be formed that excludes the departing process.
5. *GMS-5*: The GMS permits progress only in a primary component of a partitioned network. In fact we will see that *GMS-5* can be weakened; some group communication systems permit operation despite partitioning failures, and offer extensions to the GMS-5 property so that a recipient of a message can also learn whether it (the recipient) is still connected to the primary partition. But such extensions have not been very popular with developers, who either do not often run into partitioning scenarios or find it too difficult to work with such extensions.

Although we will not pursue these points here, it should be noted that many networks have some form of critical resources on which the processes reside. Although the protocols given above are designed to make progress when a majority of the processes in the system remain alive after a partitioning failure, a more reasonable approach would also take into account the resulting resource pattern. In many settings, for example, one would want to define the primary partition of a network to be the one that retains the majority of the servers after a partitioning event. One can also imagine settings in which the primary should be the component within which access to some special piece of hardware remains possible, such as the radar in an air traffic control application. These sorts of problems can generally be solved by associating weights with the processes in the system and redefining the majority rule as a weighted majority rule. Such an approach recalls work in the 1970s and early 1980s by Bob Thomas of BBN on weighted majority voting schemes and weighted quorum replication algorithms (see Gifford 1979; Thomas 1979).

12.2.6 Ordered Multicast

Earlier, we observed that our multicast protocol would preserve the sender's order if executed over FIFO channels and if the algorithm used to terminate an active multicast was also FIFO. Of course, some systems may seek higher levels of concurrency by using non-FIFO-reliable channels, or by concurrently executing the termination protocol for more than one multicast, but, even so, such systems could potentially number multicasts to track the order in which they should be delivered. Freedom from gaps in the sender order is similarly straightforward to ensure.

This leads to a broader issue of what forms of multicast ordering are useful in distributed systems and how such orderings can be guaranteed. In developing application programs that make use of process groups, it is common to employ what

Leslie Lamport and Fred Schneider call a *state machine* style of distributed algorithm (see Schneider 1990). Later, we will see reasons that one might want to relax this model, but the original idea is to run identical software at each member of a group of processes and to use a failure-atomic multicast to deliver messages to the members in identical order. Lamport's proposal stated that Byzantine protocols should be used for this multicast, and, in fact, he also uses Byzantine protocols on messages output by the group members. The result of this is that the group as a whole gives the behavior of a single ultra-reliable process, in which the operational members behave identically and the faulty behaviors of faulty members can be tolerated up to the limits of the Byzantine protocols. One limitation is that this method requires deterministic programs and thus could not be used in applications that are multithreaded or that accept input through an interrupt-style of event notification. Both are common in modern software, so the restriction is a serious one.

As we will use the concept, however, there is really only one aspect that is exploited—namely that of building applications that will remain in identical states if presented with identical inputs in identical orders. Here we may not require that the applications actually be deterministic, but merely that they be designed to maintain identically replicated states. This problem, as we will see, is solvable even for programs that may be very nondeterministic in other ways and very concurrent. Moreover, we will not be using Byzantine protocols, but will substitute various weaker forms of multicast protocols. Nonetheless, it has become usual to refer to this as a variation on Lamport's state machine approach, and it is certainly the case that his work was the first to exploit process groups in this manner.

FIFO Order

We have talked about the FIFO multicast protocol, *Send*. Such a protocol can be developed using the methods previously discussed, provided that the software used to implement the failure-recovery algorithm is carefully designed to ensure that the sender's order will not get lost when a crash occurs and processes other than the original sender step in to ensure that all group members will receive copies.

There are two variants on the basic *Send*: a normal *Send*, which is nondurable, and a *SafeSend*, which guarantees strong durability property at the cost of an extra round of communication. The *SafeSend* protocol is actually a version of Lamport's famous Paxos protocol.

The costs of a protocol are normally measured in terms of the latency before delivery can occur, the message load imposed on each individual participant (which corresponds to the CPU usage in most settings), the number of messages placed on the network as a function of group size (this may or may not be a limiting factor, depending on the properties of the network), and the overhead required to represent protocol-specific headers. When the sender of a multicast is also a group member, there are two latency metrics that may be important: latency from when a message is sent to when it is delivered, which is usually expressed as a multiple of the communication latency of the network and transport software, and the latency from when the sender initiates the multicast to when it learns the delivery ordering for that multicast. During this period, some algorithms will be waiting—in the sender case, the sender may be unable to proceed until it knows when its own message will be delivered (in the sense of ordering with respect to other concurrent multicasts from other senders). And in the case of a destination process, it is clear that until the message is delivered, no actions can be taken.

In all of these cases, *Send* and *SafeSend* are inexpensive protocols. The latency seen by the sender is minimal: In the case of *Send*, as soon as the multicast has been transmitted, the sender knows that the message will be delivered in an order consistent with its order of sending. Still focusing on *Send*, the latency between when the message is sent and when it is delivered to a destination is exactly that of the network itself: Upon receipt, a message is deliverable as soon as any prior messages have been delivered—hence, if message loss is rare, immediately upon receipt. The protocol requires only a single round of communication, and other costs are hidden in the background and often can be piggybacked on other traffic. And the header used for *Send* needs only to identify the message uniquely and capture the sender's order—information that may be expressed in a few bytes of storage.

For *SafeSend*, on the other hand, these costs would be quite a bit higher, because an extra round of communication is needed to find out if all the intended recipients have a copy of the message. Suppose that the network has latency σ and the slowest destination adds an additional delay of δ. Then *SafeSend* has a latency at the sender of roughly $2\sigma + \delta$. The non-sender processes need to learn that the message is safe from the sender, so they see a delay of $3\sigma + \delta$. Notice that even the fastest destinations are limited by the response times of the slowest destinations, although one can imagine partially safe implementations of the protocol in which a majority of replies would be adequate to permit progress.

Notice that although *Send* can also be converted into *SafeSend* by invoking *flush* after sending the multicast, doing so would be even more costly. Thus if *SafeSend* will be used often, one should implement the optimized version just described. The *Send* and *SafeSend* protocols can be used in a state-machine style of computing under conditions where the messages transmitted by different senders are independent of one another, and hence the actions taken by recipients will commute—for example, suppose that sender p is reporting trades on a stock exchange and sender q is reporting bond pricing information. Although this information may be sent to the same destinations, it may or may not be combined in a way that is order sensitive. When the recipients are insensitive to the order of messages that originate in different senders, *Send* is a strong enough ordering to ensure that a state machine style of computing can safely be used. However, many applications are more sensitive to ordering than this, and the ordering properties of *Send* would not be sufficient to ensure that group members remain consistent with one another in such cases.

Causal Order

An obvious question to ask concerns the maximum amount of order that can be provided in a protocol that has the same cost as *Send*. At the beginning of this chapter, we discussed the causal ordering relation, which is the transitive closure of the message send/receive relation and the internal ordering associated with processes. In 1985, Thomas Joseph and the author developed a causally ordered protocol with costs similar to that of *Send* and showed how it could be used to implement replicated data. We named the protocol *CausalSend*. Soon thereafter, Schmuck was able to show that causal order is a form of maximal ordering relation among *Send*-like protocols (see Schmuck 1988). More precisely, he showed that any ordering property that can be implemented using an asynchronous protocol can be represented as a subset of the causal ordering relationship. This proves that causally ordered communication is the most powerful protocol possible with cost similar to that of *Send*.

The basic idea of a causally ordered multicast is easy to express. Recall that a FIFO multicast is required to respect the order in which any single sender sends a sequence of multicasts. If process p sends m_0 and then later sends m_1, a FIFO multicast must deliver m_0 before m_1 at any overlapping destinations. The ordering rule for a causally ordered multicast is almost identical: if $send(m_0) \rightarrow send(m_1)$, then a causally ordered delivery will ensure that m_0 is delivered before m_1 at any overlapping destinations. In some sense, causal order is just a generalization of the FIFO sender order. For a FIFO order, we focus on events that happen in some order at a single place in the system. For the causal order, we relax this to events that are ordered under the "happens before" relationship, which can span multiple processes but is otherwise essentially the same as the send order for a single process. A causally ordered multicast simply guarantees that if m_0 is sent before m_1, then m_0 will be delivered before m_1 at destinations they have in common.

The first time one encounters the concept of causally ordered delivery, it can be confusing because the definition does not look at all like a definition of FIFO ordered delivery. In fact, however, the underlying idea is extremely similar. Most readers will be comfortable with the idea of a thread of control that moves from process to process when RPC is used by a client process to ask a server to take some action on its behalf. We can think of the thread of computation in the server as being part of the thread of the client. In some sense, a single computation spans two address spaces. Causally ordered multicasts are simply multicasts ordered along such a thread of computation—they are FIFO ordered, but along computational threads rather than by individual processes. When this perspective is adopted one sees that FIFO ordering is in some ways the less natural concept: *Send* tracks ordering of events only when they occur in the same address space. If process p sends message m_0 and then asks process q to send message m_1, it seems natural to say that m_1 was sent after m_0. Causal ordering expresses this relation, but FIFO ordering only does so if p and q are in the same address space.

There are several ways to implement multicast delivery orderings that are consistent with the causal order. We will now present two such schemes, both based on adding a timestamp to the message header before it is initially transmitted. The first uses a logical clock; the resulting change in header size is very small but the protocol itself has high latency. The second uses a vector timestamp and achieves much better performance. Finally, we discuss several ways of compressing these timestamps to minimize the overhead associated with the ordering property.

Causal Ordering with Logical Timestamps   Suppose that we are interested in preserving causal order within process groups and in doing so only during periods when the membership of the group is fixed (the flush protocol that implements view synchrony makes this a reasonable goal). Finally, assume that all multicasts are sent to the full membership of the group. By attaching a logical timestamp to each message, maintained using Lamport's logical clock algorithm, we can ensure that if $send(m_1) \rightarrow send(m_2)$, then m_1 will be delivered before m_2 at overlapping destinations. The approach is extremely simple: Upon receipt of a message m a process p_i waits until it knows that there are no messages still in the channels to it from other group members, p_j that could have a timestamp smaller than $LT(m)$.

How can p_i be sure of this? In a setting where process group members continuously emit multicasts, it suffices to wait long enough. Knowing that m will eventually reach every other group member, p_i can reason that eventually every group member will increase its logical clock to a value at least as large as $LT(m)$ and will subsequently send out a message with that larger timestamp value. Since we are assuming that the communication channels in our system preserve FIFO ordering, as soon as any message has been received with a timestamp greater than or equal to that of m from a process p_j, all future messages from p_j will have a timestamp strictly greater than that of m. Thus, p_i can for a message from every other process in the group with a timestamp greater than that of m. If there are messages with timestamps less than or equal to $LT(m)$, they can be delivered in timestamp order. If two messages have the same timestamp, they must have been sent concurrently, and p_i can either deliver them in an arbitrary order or can use some agreed-upon rule (e.g., by breaking ties using the process-ID of the sender or its ranking in the group view) to obtain a total order. With this approach, it is no harder to deliver messages in an order that is causal and total than to do so in an order that is only causal.

Of course, in many (if not most) settings, some group members will send to the group frequently while others send rarely or participate only as message recipients. In such environments, p_i might wait in vain for a message from p_j, preventing the delivery of m. There are two obvious solutions to this problem: Group members can be modified to send a periodic multicast simply to keep the channels active, or p_i can ping p_j when necessary—in this manner flushing the communication channel between them.

Although simple, this causal ordering protocol is too costly for most settings. A single multicast will trigger a wave of n^2 messages within the group, and a long delay may elapse before it is safe to deliver a multicast. For many applications, latency is the key factor that limits performance, and this protocol is a potentially slow one because incoming messages must be delayed until a suitable message is received on every other incoming channel. Moreover, the number of messages that must be delayed can be very large in a big group, creating potential buffering problems.

Causal Ordering with Vector Timestamps   If we are willing to accept a higher overhead, the inclusion of a vector timestamp in each message permits the implementation of a much more accurate message-delaying policy. Using the vector timestamp, we can delay an incoming message m_i precisely until any missing

Fig. 12.12 Upon receipt of a message with vector timestamp $[1, 1, 0, 0]$ from p_1, process p_2 detects that it is too early to deliver this message, and delays it until a message from p_0 has been received and delivered

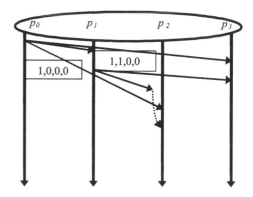

causally prior messages have been received. This algorithm, like the previous one, assumes that all messages are multicast to the full set of group members.

Again, the idea is simple. Each message is labeled with the vector timestamp of the sender as of the time when the message was sent. This timestamp is essentially a count of the number of causally prior messages that have been delivered to the application at the sender process, broken down by source. Thus, the vector timestamp for process p_1 might contain the sequence $[13, 0, 7, 6]$ for a group G with membership $\{p_0, p_1, p_2, p_3\}$ at the time it creates and multicasts m_i. Process p_1 will increment the counter for its own vector entry (here we assume that the vector entries are ordered in the same way as the processes in the group view), labeling the message with timestamp $[13, 1, 7, 6]$. The meaning of such a timestamp is that this is the first message sent by p_1, but that it has received and delivered 13 messages from p_0, seven from p_2 and six from p_3. Presumably, these received messages created a context within which m_i makes sense, and if some process delivers m_i without having seen one or more of them, it may run the risk of misinterpreting m_i. A causal ordering avoids such problems.

Now, suppose that process p_3 receives m_i. It is possible that m_i would be the very first message that p_3 has received up to this point in its execution. In this case, p_3 might have a vector timestamp as small as $[0, 0, 0, 6]$, reflecting only the six messages it sent before m_i was transmitted. Of course, the vector timestamp at p_3 could also be much larger: The only "hard" upper limit is that the entry for p_1 is necessarily 0, since m_i is the first message sent by p_1. The delivery rule for a recipient such as p_3 is now clear: It should delay message m_i until both of the following conditions are satisfied:

1. Message m_i is the *next* message, in sequence, from its sender.
2. Every causally prior message has been received and delivered to the application.

We can translate rule 2 into the following formula: If message m_i sent by process p_i is received by process p_j, then we delay m_i until, for each value of k different from i and j, $VT(p_j)[k] \geq VT(m_i)[k]$. Thus, if p_3 has not yet received any messages from p_0, it will not deliver m_i until it has received at least 13 messages from p_0. Figure 12.12 illustrates this rule in a simpler case, involving only two messages.

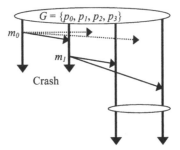

Fig. 12.13 When processes p_0 and p_1 crash, message m_1 is causally orphaned. This would be detected during the flush protocol that installs the new group view. Although m_1 has been received by the surviving processes, it is not possible to deliver it while still satisfying the causal ordering constraint. However, this situation can only occur if the sender of the message is one of the failed processes. By discarding m_1 the system can avoid causal gaps. Surviving group members will never be logically partitioned (prevented from communicating with each other)

We need to convince ourselves that this rule really ensures that messages will be delivered in a causal order. To see this, it suffices to observe that when m_i was sent, the sender had already received and delivered the messages identified by $VT(m_i)$. Since these are precisely the messages causally ordered before m_i, the protocol only delivers messages in an order consistent with causality.

The causal ordering relationship is acyclic—hence, one would be tempted to conclude that this protocol can never delay a message indefinitely. But, in fact, it can do so if failures occur. Suppose that process p_0 crashes. Our flush protocol will now run, and the 13 messages that p_0 sent to p_1 will be retransmitted by p_1 on its behalf. But if p_1 also fails, we could have a situation in which m_i, sent by p_1 causally after having received 13 messages from p_0, will never be safely deliverable, because no record exists of one or more of these prior messages! The point here is that although the communication channels in the system are FIFO, p_1 is not expected to forward messages on behalf of other processes until a flush protocol starts when one or more processes have left or joined the system. Thus, a dual failure can leave a gap such that m_i is causally orphaned.

The good news, however, is that this can only happen if the *sender of* m_i fails, as illustrated in Fig. 12.13. Otherwise, the sender will have a buffered copy of any messages that it received and that are still unstable, and this information will be sufficient to fill in any causal gaps in the message history prior to when m_i was sent. Thus, our protocol can leave individual messages that are orphaned, but it cannot partition group members away from one another in the sense that concerned us earlier.

Our system will eventually discover any such causal orphan when flushing the group prior to installing a new view that drops the sender of m_i. At this point, there are two options: m_i can be delivered to the application with some form of warning that it is an orphaned message preceded by missing causally prior messages, or m_i can simply be discarded. Either approach leaves the system in a self-consistent state, and surviving processes are never prevented from communicating with one another.

Causal ordering with vector timestamps is a very efficient way to obtain this delivery ordering property. The overhead is limited to the vector timestamp itself and to the increased latency associated with executing the timestamp ordering algorithm and with delaying messages that genuinely arrive too early. Such situations are common if the machines involved are overloaded, channels are backlogged, or the network is congested and lossy, but otherwise they would rarely be observed. In the best case, when none of these conditions are present, the causal ordering property can be assured with essentially no additional cost in latency or messages passed within the system! On the other hand, notice that the causal ordering obtained is definitely not a total ordering, as was the case in the algorithm based on logical timestamps. Here, we have a genuinely cheaper ordering property, but it is also less ordered.

Timestamp Compression   The major form of overhead associated with a vector-timestamp causality is that of the vectors themselves. This has stimulated interest in schemes for compressing the vector-timestamp information transmitted in messages. Although an exhaustive treatment of this topic is well beyond the scope of this book, there are some specific optimizations that are worth mentioning.

Suppose that a process sends a burst of multicasts—a common pattern in many applications. After the first vector timestamp, each subsequent message will contain a nearly identical timestamp, differing only in the timestamp associated with the sender itself, which will increment for each new multicast. In such a case, the algorithm could be modified to omit the timestamp: A missing timestamp would be interpreted as being the previous timestamp, incremented in the sender's field only. This single optimization can eliminate most of the vector timestamp overhead seen in a system characterized by bursty communication. More accurately, what has happened here is that the sequence number used to implement the FIFO channel from source to destination makes the sender's own vector-timestamp entry redundant. We can omit the vector timestamp because none of the other entries were changing and the sender's sequence number is represented elsewhere in the packets being transmitted.

An important case of this optimization occurs if all the multicasts to some group are sent along a single causal path—for example, suppose that a group has some form of token, which circulates within it, and only the token holder can initiate multicasts to the group. In this case, we can implement *CausalSend* using a single sequence number: the first *CausalSend*, the second *CausalSend*, and so forth. Later, this form of *CausalSend* will turn out to be important. Notice, however, that if there are concurrent multicasts from different senders (i.e., if senders can transmit multicasts without waiting for the token), the optimization is no longer able to express the causal ordering relationships on messages sent within the group.

A second optimization is to reset the vector-timestamp fields to zero each time the group changes its membership, and to sort the group members so that any passive receivers are listed last in the group view. With these steps, the vector timestamp for a message will tend to end in a series of zeros, corresponding to those processes that have not sent a message since the previous view change event. The vector timestamp can then be truncated: The reception of a short vector would imply that the missing fields are all zeros. Moreover, the numbers themselves will tend to stay smaller and hence can be represented using shorter fields (if they threaten to overflow, a flush protocol can be run to reset them). Again, a single very simple optimization would be expected to greatly reduce overhead in typical systems that use this causal ordering scheme.

A third optimization involves sending only the difference vector, representing those fields that have changed since the previous message multicast by this sender. Such a vector would be more complex to represent (since we need to know which fields have changed and by how much) but much shorter (since, in a large system, one would expect few fields to change in any short period of time). This generalizes into a run-length encoding.

This third optimization can also be understood as an instance of an ordering scheme introduced originally in the Psync, Totem, and Transis systems. Rather than representing messages by counters, a precedence relation is maintained for messages: a tree of the messages received and the causal relationships between them. When a message is sent, the leaves of the causal tree are transmitted. These leaves are a set of concurrent messages, all of which are causally prior to the message now being transmitted. Often, there will be very few such messages, because many groups would be expected to exhibit low levels of concurrency.

The receiver of a message will now delay it until those messages it lists as causally prior have been delivered. By transitivity, no message will be delivered until all the causally prior messages have been delivered. Moreover, the same scheme can be combined with one similar to the logical timestamp ordering scheme of the first causal multicast algorithm to obtain a primitive that is both causally and totally ordered. However, doing so necessarily increases the latency of the protocol.

Causal Multicast and Consistent Cuts   At the outset of Chap. 10, we discussed concepts of logical time, defining the causal relation and introducing the definition of a consistent cut. Notice that the delivery events of a multicast protocol such as *CausalSend* are concurrent and can be thought of as occurring at the same time in all the members of a process group (Fig. 12.14). In a logical sense, *CausalSend* delivers messages at what may look to the recipients like a single instant in time. Unfortunately, however, the delivery events for a single *CausalSend* do not represent a consistent cut across the system, because communication that was concurrent with the *CausalSend* could cross it. Thus, one could easily encounter a system in which a *CausalSend* is delivered at process p, which has received message m, but where the same *CausalSend* was delivered at process q (the eventual sender of m) before m had been transmitted.

With a second *CausalSend* message, it is actually possible to identify a true consistent cut, but to do so we need to either introduce a concept of an epoch number or inhibit communication briefly. The inhibition algorithm is easier to understand. It starts with a first *CausalSend* message that tells the recipients to inhibit the sending of new messages. The process group members receiving this message send back an acknowledgment to the process that initiated the *CausalSend*. The initiator, having

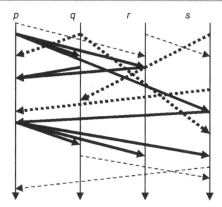

Fig. 12.14 A protocol for creating a consistent cut or snapshot. In this figure, processes are sending point-to-point messages (*dashed lines*) when process p initiates the protocol by sending a multicast to q, r, and s (*dark lines*). The delivery of the multicast is closed under causality and hence is a consistent cut. A second phase of multicasts can be used to flush communication channels (any pending message in a channel will be causally prior to the second multicast and hence delivered before it is delivered; the four messages in this category are shown in a *darker dashed line* style). Notice that during the period between delivery of the two multicasts, the sending of other messages is temporarily inhibited

collected replies from all group members, now sends a second *CausalSend* telling the group members that they can stop recording incoming messages and resume normal communication. It is easy to see that all messages that were in the communication channels when the first *CausalSend* was received will now have been delivered and that the communication channels will be empty. The recipients now resume normal communication. (They should also monitor the state of the initiator, in case it fails!) The algorithm is very similar to the one for changing the membership of a process group, discussed previously.

Noninhibitory algorithms for forming consistent cuts are also known. One way to solve this problem is to add *epoch numbers* to the multicasts in the system. Each process keeps an *epoch counter* and tags every message with the counter value. In the consistent cut protocol, the first phase message now tells processes to increment the epoch counters (and not to inhibit new messages). Thus, instead of delaying new messages, they are sent promptly but with epoch number $k + 1$ instead of epoch number k. The same algorithm now works to allow the system to reason about the consistent cut associated with its kth epoch even as it exchanges new messages during epoch $k + 1$. Another well-known solution takes the form of what is called an *echo protocol*, in which two messages traverse every communication link in the system (see Chandy and Lamport 1985). For a system with all-to-all communication connectivity, such protocols will transmit $O(n^2)$ messages, in contrast with the $O(n)$ required for the inhibitory solution.

This *CausalSend* algorithm provides a relatively inexpensive way of testing the distributed state of the system to detect a desired property. In particular, if the processes that receive a *CausalSend* compute a predicate or write down some element of their states at the moment the message is received, these states will fit together cleanly and can be treated as a glimpse of the system as a whole at a single instant in time. To count the number of processes for which some condition holds, it is sufficient to send a *CausalSend* asking processes if the condition holds and to count the number that return *true*. The result is a value that could in fact have been valid for the group at a single instant in real time. On the negative side, this guarantee only holds with respect to communication that uses causally ordered primitives. If processes communicate with other primitives, the delivery events of the *CausalSend* will not necessarily be prefix closed when the send and receive events for these messages are taken into account. Marzullo and Sabel have developed optimized versions of this algorithm.

Some examples of properties that could be checked using our consistent cut algorithm include the current holder of a token in a distributed locking algorithm (the token will never appear to be lost or duplicated), the current load on the processes in a group (the states of members will never be accidentally sampled at different times yielding an illusory load that is unrealistically high or low), the wait-for graph of a system subject to infrequent deadlocks (deadlock will never be detected when the system is in fact not deadlocked), and the contents of a database (the database will never be checked at a time when it has been updated at some locations but not others). On the other hand, because the basic algorithm inhibits the sending of new messages in the group, albeit briefly, there will be many systems for which the performance impact is too high and a solution that sends more messages but avoids inhibition states would be preferable. The epoch-based scheme represents a reasonable alternative, but we have not treated fault-tolerance issues; in practice, such a scheme works best if all cuts are initiated by some single member of a group, such as the oldest process in it, and a group flush is known to occur if that process fails and some other takes over from it.

Exploiting Topological Knowledge   Many networks have topological properties, which can be exploited to optimize the representation of causal information within a process group that implements a protocol such as *CausalSend*. Within the NavTech system, developed at INESC in Portugal, wide area applications operate over a communication transport layer implemented as part of NavTech. This structure is programmed to know of the location of wide area network links and to make use of hardware multicast where possible (see Rodriguez and Verissimo 1995; Rodrigues et al. 1993, 2000). A consequence is that if a group is physically laid out with multiple subgroups interconnected over a wide area link, as seen in Fig. 12.15, the message need only be sent once over each link.

In a geographically distributed system, it is frequently the case that all messages from some subset of the process group members will be relayed to the remaining members through a small number of relay points. Rodriguez exploits this observation to reduce the amount of information needed to represent causal ordering relationships within the process group. Suppose that message m_1 is causally dependent upon message m_0 and that both were sent over the same communication link. When these messages are relayed to processes on the other side of the link, they will appear to have been sent by a single sender and the ordering relationship between them

Fig. 12.15 In a complex network, a single process group may be physically broken into multiple subgroups. With knowledge of the network topology, the NavTech system is able to reduce the information needed to implement causal ordering

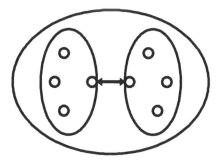

can be compressed into a single vector-timestamp entry. In general, this observation permits any set of processes that route through a single point to be represented using a single sequence number on the other side of that point.

Stephenson explored the same question in a more general setting involving complex relationships between overlapping process groups (the multigroup causality problem) (see Stephenson 1991). His work identifies an optimization similar to this one, as well as others that take advantage of other regular layouts of overlapping groups, such as a series of groups organized into a tree or some other graph-like structure.

Total Order

In developing our causally ordered communication primitive, we really ended up with a family of such primitives. The cheapest of these are purely causal in the sense that concurrently transmitted multicasts might be delivered in different orders to different members. The more costly ones combined causal order with mechanisms that resulted in a causal, total order. We saw two such primitives: One was the causal ordering algorithm based on logical timestamps, and the second (introduced very briefly) was the algorithm used for total order in the Totem and Transis systems, which extend the causal order into a total one using a canonical sorting procedure, but in which latency is increased by the need to wait until multicasts have been received from all potential sources of concurrent multicasts.[1] In this section we discuss totally ordered multicasts, known by the name *OrderedSend*, in more detail.

There are many ways to implement total ordering, and it may be best to start by just describing the most commonly used approach, partly for reasons of brevity, but partly because this has become prevalent. The idea can be traced to work by Chang and Maxemchuk, which then was simplified and refined over time by Frans Kaashoek in his PhD. thesis and finally by Robbert van Renesse in his work on the Horus system. An ordering "token" is associated with some member of the group

---

[1] Most ordered of all is the flush protocol used to install new views: This delivers a type of message (the new view) in a way that is ordered with respect to all other types of message. In the Isis Toolkit, there was actually a *SafeSend* primitive, which could be used to obtain this behavior at the request of the user, but it was rarely used and more recent systems tend to use this protocol only to install new process group views.

(usually, the first member in the current list of group members—the least ranked process in the group's current "view"). The token holder is in charge of deciding the *OrderedSend* ordering. To send an *OrderedSend* a process uses *Send* to send it out, but on receipt, members delay the message briefly. The token holder, however, sends a tiny *Send* giving ordering information: "deliver message 1234 from process p_1 as your 20th message. (Obviously, you can make this fancier by delaying the ordering message and trying to batch a few notifications up.) All recipients just follow the instructions: they reorder messages according to the specified order and then deliver them. If a failure happens, the "flush" mechanism discussed later in this chapter ensures that everyone remaining operational gets a copy of these *Send* operations. Thus, after a failure, all surviving group members will have delivered identical sequences of messages. A new token holder is selected if the old one was the process that failed, and it just takes over the role of sending ordering messages. This is a simple and efficient way to implement total ordering, and can be extremely fast if the developer takes care to optimize the critical paths. Notice also that a big message is sent directly to its destinations; some early versions of this protocol relayed all messages through the token holder, but with big messages, I/O bandwidth at that process becomes a serious bottleneck. By sending messages directly and sending ordering information separately, this can be avoided.

As described above, we end up with a version of *OrderedSend* capable of violating causal ordering. Suppose that process p_i sends an *OrderedSend*, and then sends some other point to point message or multicast (not an OrderedSend) which process p_j receives immediately. Now process p_j sends an *OrderedSend* "in response" to that message. Since the *OrderedSend* is implemented as a protocol over *Send* there is no reason to assume that the token holding process will order the one from p_i before the one from p_j. Yet the message sent by p_j could be a form of response to the one sent by p_i. For example, perhaps p_i is a message asking group members to create a new slot in the employees table for a recently hired employee, and p_j reacts by sending out some default security information. If the messages arrive out of causal order, applications may receive the "second" message, look up the employee, and then throw an exception when they are unable to find an entry for that employee in their current-employees tables. Thus we might prefer a stronger guarantee.

It is also possible to use the causally ordered multicast primitive to implement a token-based ordering scheme that is simultaneously causal and totally ordered. Such a primitive would respect the delivery ordering property of *CausalSend* when causally prior multicasts are pending in a group, similar to *OrderedSend* when two processes concurrently try to send a multicast. Rather than present this algorithm here, however, we defer it until Chap. 14, when we present it in the context of a method for implementing replicated data with locks on the data items. We do this because, in practice, token-based total ordering algorithms are more common than the other methods. The most common use of causal ordering is in conjunction with the specific replication scheme presented in Chap. 14; therefore, it is more natural to treat the topic in that setting.

Yet an additional total ordering algorithm was introduced by Leslie Lamport in his very early work on logical time in distributed systems (see Lamport 1978a) and later adapted to group communication settings by Skeen during a period when he and the author collaborated on an early version of the Isis totally ordered communication primitive. The algorithm uses a two-phase protocol in which processes vote on the message ordering to use, expressing this vote as a logical timestamp.

The algorithm operates as follows. In the first phase of communication, the originator of the multicast (we will call it the coordinator) sends the message to the members of the destination group. These processes save the message but do not yet deliver it to the application. Instead, each proposes a delivery time for the message using a logical clock, which is made unique by appending the process-ID. The coordinator collects these proposed delivery times, sorts the vector, and designates the maximum time as the *committed* delivery time. It sends this time back to the participants. They update their logical clocks (and hence will never propose a smaller time) and reorder the messages in their pending queue. If a pending message has a committed delivery time, and this time is smallest among the proposed and committed times for other messages, it can be delivered to the application layer.

This solution can be seen to deliver messages in a total order, since all the processes base the delivery action on the same committed timestamp. It can be made fault tolerant by electing a new coordinator if the original sender fails. One curious property of the algorithm, however, is that it has a ordering guarantee. To see this, consider the case where a coordinator and a participant fail and that participant also proposed the maximum timestamp value. The old coordinator may have committed a timestamp that could be used for delivery to the participant, but that will not be reused by the remaining processes, which may therefore pick a different delivery order. Thus, just as strong durability ("safety") is costly to achieve as an atomicity property, one sees that a durable ordering property may be quite costly. It should be noted that durability and total ordering tend to go together: If delivery is delayed until it is known that all operational processes have a copy of a message, it is normally possible to ensure that all processes will use identical delivery orderings

This two-phase ordering algorithm, and a protocol called the "born-order" protocol, which was introduced by the Transis and Totem systems (messages are ordered using unique message identification numbers that are assigned when the messages are first created, or "born"), have advantages in settings with multiple overlapping process groups, a topic to which we will return in Chap. 13. Both provide what is called "globally total order," which means that even *OrderedSend* messages sent in different groups will be delivered in the same order at any overlapping destinations they may have.

12.3   Communication from Nonmembers to a Group

Up to now, all of our protocols have focused on the case of group members communicating with one another. However, in many systems there is an equally important need to provide reliable and ordered communication from nonmembers into a group. This section presents two solutions to the problem—one for a situation in which the nonmember process has located a single member of the group but lacks detailed membership information about the remainder of the group, and one for the case of a nonmember that has cached group membership information.

Fig. 12.16 Nonmember of a
group uses a simple
RPC-based protocol to
request that a multicast be
done on its behalf. The ID of
the message can be assigned
by the sender. This protocol
becomes complex when
ordering considerations are
added, particularly because
the forwarding process may
fail during the protocol run

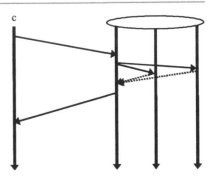

Before launching into this topic, we should note that there is a class of systems for which this problem does not really arise. When using a system such as Spread, which consists of a core set of long-running daemons to which all application processes connect (or Ensemble in its "outboard" mode), the application itself is not really responsible for group communication. Instead, all group operations are passed to the servers, which implement multicast among themselves, then relay messages up to the appropriate application processes. Since the daemons "know" the membership of the groups, communication by a non-member to a group is no different than communication from a member to a group: the request is forwarded through a daemon. However, there are performance and "single point of failure" concerns with this kind of 2-tier architecture. Many systems implement multicast directly, as an end-to-end protocol, and these are the ones for which the mechanisms described below are useful.

In the first case, our algorithm will have the nonmember process ask some group member to issue the multicast on its behalf, using an RPC for this purpose. In this approach, each such multicast is given a unique identifier by its originator, so that if the forwarding process fails before reporting on the outcome of the multicast, the same request can be reissued. The new forwarding process would check to see if the multicast was previously completed, issue it if not, and then return the outcome in either case. Various optimizations can then be introduced, so that a separate RPC will not be required for each multicast. The protocol is illustrated in Fig. 12.16 for the normal case, when the contact process does not fail. Not shown is the eventual garbage collection phase needed to delete status information accumulated during the protocol and saved for use in the case where the contact eventually fails.

Our second solution uses what is called an *iterated* approach, in which the non-member processes cache possibly inaccurate process group views. Specifically, each group view is given a unique identifier, and client processes use an RPC or some other mechanism to obtain a copy of the group view (e.g., they may join a larger group within which the group reports changes in its core membership to interested non-members). The client then includes the view identifier in its message and multicasts it directly to the group members. Again, the members will retain some limited history of prior interactions using a mechanism such as the one for the multiphase commit protocols. (See Fig. 12.17.)

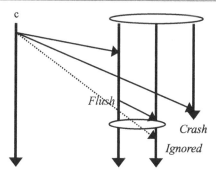

Fig. 12.17   An iterated protocol. The client sends to the group as its membership is changing (to drop one member). Its multicast is terminated by the flush associated with the new-view installation (message just prior to the new view), and when one of its messages arrives late (*dashed line*), the recipient detects it as a duplicate and ignores it. Had the multicast been so late that all the copies were rejected, the sender would have refreshed its estimate of group membership and retried the multicast. Doing this while also respecting ordering obligations can make the protocol complex, although the basic idea is quite simple. Notice that the protocol is cheaper than the RPC solution: The client sends directly to the actual group members, rather than indirectly sending through a proxy. However, while the figure may seem to suggest that there is no acknowledgment from the group to the client, this is not the case: The client communicates over a reliable FIFO channel to each member—hence, acknowledgements are implicitly present. Indeed, some effort may be needed to avoid an implosion effect, which would overwhelm the client of a large group with a huge number of acknowledgements

There are now three cases that may occur. Such a multicast can arrive in the correct view, it can arrive partially in the correct view and partially late (after some members have installed a new group view), or it can arrive entirely late. In the first case, the protocol is considered successful. In the second case, the group flush algorithm will push the partially delivered multicast to a view-synchronous termination; when the late messages finally arrive, they will be ignored as duplicates by the group members that receive them, since these processes will have already delivered the message during the flush protocol. In the third case, all the group members will recognize the message as a late one that was not flushed by the system and all will reject it. Some or all should also send a message back to the nonmember warning it that its message was not successfully delivered; the client can then retry its multicast with refreshed membership information. This last case is said to iterate the multicast. If it is practical to modify the underlying reliable transport protocol, a convenient way to return status information to the sender is by attaching it to the acknowledgment messages such protocols transmit.

This protocol is clearly quite simple, although its complexity grows when one considers the issues associated with preserving sender order or causality information in the case where iteration is required. To solve such a problem, a nonmember that discovers itself to be using stale group view information should inhibit the transmission of new multicasts while refreshing the group view data. It should then retransmit, in the correct order, all multicasts that are not known to have been successfully delivered in while it was sending using the previous group view. Some care is required in this last step, however, because new members of the group may not have sufficient information to recognize and discard duplicate messages.

To overcome this problem, there are basically two options. The simplest case occurs when the group members transfer information to joining processes, including the record of multicasts successfully received from nonmembers prior to when the new member joined. Such a state transfer can be accomplished using a mechanism discussed in the next chapter. Knowing that the members will detect and discard duplicates, the nonmember can safely retransmit any multicasts that are still pending, in the correct order, followed by any that may have been delayed while waiting to refresh the group membership. Such an approach minimizes the delay before normal communication is restored.

The second option is applicable when it is impractical to transfer state information to the joining member. In this case, the nonmember will need to query the group, determining the status of pending multicasts by consulting with surviving members from the previous view. Having determined the precise set of multicasts that was dropped upon reception, the nonmember can retransmit these messages and any buffered messages and then resume normal communication. Such an approach is likely to have higher overhead than the first one, since the nonmember (and there may be many of them) must query the group after each membership change. It would not be surprising if significant delays were introduced by such an algorithm.

12.4 Communication from a Group to a Nonmember

The discussion of the preceding section did not consider the issues raised by transmission of replies from a group to a nonmember. These replies, however, and other forms of communication outside of a group, raise many of the same reliability issues that motivated the ordering and gap-freedom protocols presented previously—for example, suppose that a group is using a causally ordered multicast internally, and that one of its members sends a point-to-point message to some process outside the group. In a logical sense, that message may now be dependent upon the prior causal history of the group, and if that process now communicates with other members of the group, issues of causal ordering and freedom from causal gaps will arise.

This specific scenario was studied by Ladin and Liskov, who developed a system in which vector timestamps could be exported by a group to its clients; the client later presented the timestamp back to the group when issuing requests to other members, and in this way the client was protected against causal ordering violations. The protocol proposed in that work used stable storage to ensure that even if a failure occurred, no causal gaps will occur.

Other researchers have considered the same issues using different methods. Work by Schiper, for example, explored the use of an $n \times n$ matrix to encode point-to-point causality information (see Schiper et al. 1989), and the Isis Toolkit introduced mechanisms to preserve causal order when point-to-point communication was done in a system. We will present some of these methods in Chap. 15.

12.5 Summary of Multicast Properties

Table 12.1 Terminology

Concept	Brief description
OrderedSend	View-synchronous totally ordered group communication. If processes p and q both receive m_1 and m_2, then either both deliver m_1 prior to m_2, or both deliver m_2 prior to m_1.
	As noted earlier, *OrderedSend* comes in several versions. Throughout the remainder of this book, we will assume that *OrderedSend* is a locally ordered but weakly durable protocol—that is, we focus on the least costly of the possible *OrderedSend* primitives, unless we specifically indicate otherwise. By weakly durable we mean that the protocol could have brief windows during which a message has been delivered to some group members and yet some pattern of failures could cause the message to be lost (forgotten, in effect). Obviously, such windows are short; typically, just a few milliseconds.
OrderedCausalSend	Totally ordered but also causal group communication. The delivery order is as for *OrderedSend*, but it is also consistent with the causal sending order (normally, an OrderedSend would be consistent with the FIFO sending order for any single source, but would not respect causal order over sets of senders that have some sort of synchronization relationship, such as passing tokens that designate permission to send). We will not say much about this protocol here.
CausalSend	Causally ordered group communication. If $send(m_1) \rightarrow send(m_2)$, then processes that receive both messages deliver m_1 prior to m_2.
Send	View-synchronous FIFO group communication. If the same process p sends m_1 prior to sending m_2, then processes that receive both messages deliver m_1 prior to m_2.
Gap freedom	The guarantee that if message m_i should be delivered before m_j and some process receives m_j and remains operational, m_i will also be delivered to its remaining destinations. A system that lacks this property can be exposed to a form of logical partitioning, where a process that has received m_j is prevented from (ever) communicating to some process that was supposed to receive m_i but will not because of failure.

Table 12.1   (Continued)

Concept	Brief description
SafeSend	A multicast having the property that if any group member delivers it, then all operational group members will also deliver it and in the same total order. This property is costly to guarantee and corresponds to a *dynamic* form of durability (that is, strong durability, but now with dynamic membership). Most multicast primitives can be implemented in a durable (safe) or weakly durable (unsafe) version; the less costly one is usually preferable. In this book, we are somewhat hesitant to use the term "safe," because a protocol lacking this property is not necessarily "unsafe." Consequently, we will normally describe a protocol as being strongly durable (safe) or nondurable (unsafe). If we do not specifically say that a protocol needs to be strongly durable, the reader should assume that we intend the nondurable case. Yet an additional option arises if a nondurable multicast is combined with a subsequent call to *Flush*; this sequence yields a form of weak durability that also goes by the name *amnesia-freedom*, and turns out to be ideally matched to replication in the first tier of cloud computing systems, which are limited to using soft-state and hence do not actually benefit from durability.
View-synchronous multicast	A way of sending a message to a process group so all the group members that do not crash will receive the message between the same pair of group views. If a process sends a multicast when the membership consists of $\{p_0, \ldots, p_k\}$ and it does not crash, the message will be delivered while the view is still $\{p_0, \ldots, p_k\}$.
Virtual synchrony	A distributed communication system in which process groups are provided, supporting view-synchronous communication and gap freedom, and in which algorithms are developed using a style of closely synchronous computing in which all group members see the same events in the same order and consequently can closely coordinate their actions. Such synchronization become virtual when the ordering properties of the communication primitive are weakened in ways that do not change the correctness of the algorithm. By introducing such weaker orderings, a group can be made more likely to tolerate failure and can gain a significant performance improvement.

12.6   Related Reading

On logical concepts of time (see Lamport 1978a, 1984).

Causal ordering in message delivery (see Birman and Joseph 1987a, 1987b).

Consistent cuts (see Babaoglu and Marzullo 1993; Chandy and Lamport 1985).

Vector clocks (see Fidge 1988; Mattern 1989).

Vector clocks used in message delivery (see Birman et al. 1991; Schiper et al. 1989, 2003).

Optimizing vector clock representations (see Charron-Bost 1991; Melliar-Smith and Moser 1993).

Compression using topological information about groups of processes (see Birman et al. 1991; Rodrigues and Verissimo 1995; Rodrigues et al. 1993, 2000).

Static groups and quorum replication (see Bernstein et al. 1987; Birman and Joseph 1987a; Cooper 1985).

Two-phase commit (see Bernstein et al. 1987; Gray 1978; Gray and Reuter 1993).

Three-phase commit (see Skeen 1982a, 1985).

Byzantine protocol (see Ben-Or 1985; Coan and Thomas 1990; Coan et al. 1986; Cristian et al. 1985, 1990; Rabin 1983; Schneider 1984).

Asynchronous Consensus (see Chandra and Toueg 1991; Fisher et al. 1985a, 1985b); but see also Babaoglu et al. (1995), Friedman et al. (1995), Guerraoui and Schiper (1996), Ricciardi (1996).

The method of Chandra and Toueg (see Babaoglu et al. 1995; Chandra and Toueg 1991; Chandra et al. 1992, 1996; Friedman et al. 1995).

Group membership (see Birman and Joseph 1987a, 1987b; Chandra et al. 1996; Cristian 1991a; Melliar-Smith et al. 1991; Mishra et al. 1991; Ricciardi and Birman 1991); but see also Agarwal (1994), Anceaume et al. (1995), Babaoglu et al. (1994, 1995), Birman and Glade (1995), Chandra et al. (1996), Cristian and Schmuck (1995), Friedman et al. (1995), Golding (1992), Guerraoui and Schiper (1996), Reiter (1994a, 1994b), Ricciardi et al. (1992), Ricciardi (1993, 1996), Rodrigues et al. (1993).

Merging the Paxos form of state machine replication with virtual synchrony to obtain a single model that spans all of these options (see Birman et al. 2010; Appendix A).

Partitionable membership (see Amir et al. 1992a; Moser et al. 1994a, 1994b).

Fail-stop illusion (see Sabel and Marzullo 1994).

Token-based total order (see Chang and Maxemchuk 1984; Kaashoek 1992).

Lamport's method (see Birman and Joseph 1987b; Lamport 1978a).

Communication from nonmembers of a group (see Birman and Joseph 1987b; Wood 1991).

Point-to-point causality (see Schiper et al. 1989, 2003).

On the timestamp technique used in Harp (see Ladin et al. 1992; Liskov et al. 1991).

On preserving causality in point-to-point message-passing systems (see Schiper et al. 1989, 2003).

On the associated controversy (see Cheriton and Skeen 1993), and on the responses (see Birman 1994; Cooper 1994; van Renesse 1993).

Point to Point and Multi-group Considerations

13

As noted at the start of Chap. 12, researchers have carried the idea of group communication to something of an extreme, although the cloud computing user community has been a bit less ambitious in its embrace of these technology. This chapter tackles some of the more esoteric topics that arise when building a group-communication platform that permits the creation of large numbers of groups without requiring (as in the Spread system) that they all be subgroups of a single encompassing group. The questions raised by such a model are quite interesting, but are not central to the use of group communication platforms for data replication, because existing platforms such as Isis², JGroups, Ensemble or Spread are more typically used in applications that employ a small number of groups. Some of these systems offer a kind of end-run around the issue, permitting the creation of subgroups within large groups; multicasts are sent to the larger group, then filtered and delivered only to the target subgroup members. Other systems, including Isis², are designed to support somewhat larger numbers of groups, but even given a system that can support many groups, restrictions often still apply. For example, with Isis², if any *individual process* were to join a genuinely large number of groups, performance problems would surely arise; thus a single application could have large numbers of groups, but any single process would need to limit itself to joining just a few of them.

With these caveats, let us look at some of the best ideas for letting applications create vast numbers of process groups, as casually as they create objects in non-distributed environments. We have already touched on some of the issues raised by this sort of aggressive multigroup scenario. The most obvious concerns are purely practical. For example, in Chap. 4 of the text we pointed out that in modern cloud computing systems, data centers use routers with a limited capacity for handling IP multicast addresses. Now, not all group communication systems require IP multicast (in Isis² the decision is controlled by a runtime parameter; if desired, the system will tunnel over TCP rather than using IP multicast). But for very large scenarios, IP multicast has obvious appeal.

The issue, as we saw in Chap. 4, is that modern data center routers represent IP multicast addresses using Bloom Filters and those filters can fill up, hence with a large number of IP multicast addresses in simultaneous use, the router algorithms

K.P. Birman, *Guide to Reliable Distributed Systems*, Texts in Computer Science,
DOI 10.1007/978-1-4471-2416-0_13, © Springer-Verlag London Limited 2012

fails, forwarding every multicast message to every multicast receiver even where the IP multicast addresses in use were very different, and even if the multicast group in which the send was done had no receivers at all! It should be easy to see how an application that works well in the lab, using a few IP multicast groups, might be deployed into a cloud setting successfully, then scaled up, gradually approaching this meltdown threshold. Once the threshold is reached, suddenly the working application will seem to collapse.

This risk of resource exhaustion forces group multicast systems to either run over a non-multicast protocol such as TCP (e.g. to emulate multicast without use of IP multicast addresses), or to run code that manages a small pool of physical IP multicast addresses. In that approach, which is implemented in Isis^2 (pioneered in a paper called the Dr. Multicast paper, by Ymir Vigfusson and others), applications use virtual IP multicast addresses, and are mapped to physical IP multicast addresses only if there are enough to go around. Otherwise, the most demanding groups get the real addresses, and other groups are either forced to share a real address (filtering and discarding unwanted traffic), or to use an emulation scheme. Thus, because Isis^2 implements Dr. Multicast, it runs no risk of meltdown unless deliberately misconfigured (the defaults it uses are very conservative). But many other platforms would lack this feature, and hence risk melting down when scaled up.

Another issue, also seen in Isis^2, is that the data structures used to implement virtual synchrony are not small or simple. Each new group brings its own copies of these structures; eventually, the sheer space required can be a serious problem. The question extends beyond data structures. For example, in Isis^2 we use multiple threads for each process group to which an application belongs: three threads (one to send multicasts, one to receive and deliver multicasts and one more to receive a deliver P2P messages). From time to time, Isis^2 even spins off additional helper threads, for example while changing membership. As a rule of thumb, one thinks of a single group has having about five associated threads, on average. In C# on .NET threads are fairly cheap, but even so, it should not be hard to see that any application using more than five or ten groups will have performance issues due to the proliferation of threads. Other per-group data overheads include lists and dictionaries of various kinds that are maintained for each group, buffering for out-of-order messages, etc.

What these observations should convey is that even if a *system* supports large numbers of process groups, it is not at all safe for individual *applications* to use many groups at one time. Developers who dream of using process groups like raindrops are probably not being at all realistic about the costs of the mechanisms they are invoking, and will surely end up with applications that either do not work at all, or perform poorly.

13.1   Causal Communication Outside of a Process Group

Although there are sophisticated protocols in guaranteeing that causality will be respected for arbitrary communication patterns, the most practical solutions generally confine concurrency and associated causality issues to the interior of a process

Client

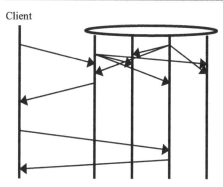

Fig. 13.1 In the replication protocol used by Ladin and Liskov in the Harp system, vector times-tamps are used to track causal multicasts within a server group. If a client interacts with a server in that group, it does so using a standard RPC protocol. However, the group timestamp is included with the reply and can be presented with a subsequent request to the group. This permits the group members to detect missing prior multicasts and to appropriately delay a request, but omits the client's point-to-point messages from the causal state of the system. Such tradeoffs between prop-erties and cost seem entirely appropriate, because an attempt to track causal order system-wide can result in significant overheads. A system such as the Isis Toolkit, which enforces causal order even for point-to-point message passing, generally do so by delaying after sending point-to-point messages until they are known to be stable—a simple and conservative solution that avoids the need to represent ordering information for such messages

group—for example, at the end of Sect. 12.3, we briefly cited the replication proto-col of Ladin and Liskov (see Ladin et al. 1992; Liskov et al. 1991). This protocol transmits a timestamp to the client, and the client later includes the most recent of the timestamps it has received in any requests it issues to the group. The group members can detect causal ordering violations and delay such a request until causally prior multicasts have reached their destinations, as seen in Fig. 13.1.

An alternative is to simply delay messages sent out of a group until any causally prior multicasts sent within the group have become stable—in other words, have reached their destinations. Since there is no remaining causal ordering obligation in this case, the message need not carry causality information. Moreover, such an ap-proach may not be as costly as it sounds, for the same reason that the *flush* protocol introduced earlier turns out not to be terribly costly in practice: Most asynchronous *CausalSend* or *Send* messages become stable shortly after they are issued—long before any reply is sent to the client. Thus, any latency is associated with the very last multicasts to have been initiated within the group, and will normally be small. We will see how this can benefit the cloud computing developer in Chap. 15, which discusses the use of group communication in support of data replication in the vari-ous tiers of cloud services. As we will see, one can use *Send* together with *Flush* for replication in the first tier of the cloud, because applications running in that tier are required to be stateless and hence the stronger guarantees one associates with *Safe-Send* (Paxos) simply do not have any value. In contrast, one would use *SafeSend* for services running deeper in the cloud that maintain durable state across failures and need to ensure that any updates are delivered in a durable manner. Interestingly,

Send with a *Flush* prior to replying to the end-user scales extremely well, and yields a way to offer consistency in the first tier: an exciting option, especially when compared with the very weak guarantees associated with the BASE alternative.

There has been some work aimed at promoting causal order as a system-wide guarantee, applying to point-to-point communication as well as multicasts. Unfortunately, representing such ordering information requires a matrix of size $O(n^2)$ in the size of the system (one for each sender-receiver pair). Moreover, this type of ordering information is only useful if messages are sent asynchronously (without waiting for replies). But, if this is done in systems that use point-to-point communication, there is no obvious way to recover if a message is lost (when its sender fails) after subsequent messages (to other destinations) have been delivered. Cheriton and Skeen discuss this form of all-out causal order in a well-known paper and conclude that it is probably not desirable (see Birman 1994; Cheriton and Skeen 1993; Cooper 1994; Schiper et al. 1989, 2003; van Renesse 1993). If point-to-point messages are treated as being causally prior to other messages, it is best to wait until they have been received before sending causally dependent messages to other destinations.[1] (We will discuss Cheriton and Skeen's paper in Chap. 15.)

Early versions of the Isis Toolkit solved this problem without actually representing causal information at all, although later work replaced this scheme with one that waits for point-to-point messages to become stable (see Birman and Joseph 1987b; Birman et al. 1991). The approach was to piggyback pending messages (those that are not known to have reached all their destinations) on *all* subsequent messages, regardless of their destination (Fig. 13.2)—that is, if process p has sent multicast m_1 to process group G and now wishes to send a message m_2 to any destination other than group G, a copy of m_1 is included with m_2. By applying this rule system-wide, p can be certain that if any route causes a message m_3, causally dependent upon m_1, to reach a destination of m_1, a copy of m_1 will be delivered too. A background garbage collection algorithm is used to delete these spare copies of messages when they do reach their destinations, and a simple duplicate suppression scheme is employed to avoid delivering the same message more than once if it reaches a destination several times.

This scheme may seem wildly expensive, but it rarely sends a message more than once in applications that operate over Isis. One important reason for this is that Isis has other options available for use when the cost of piggybacking becomes too high—for example, instead of sending m_0 piggybacked to some destination far from its true destination, q, any process can simply send m_0 to q, in this way making it stable. The system can also wait for stability to be detected by the original sender, at which point garbage collection will remove the obligation. Additionally, notice that m_0 only needs to be piggybacked once to any given destination. In Isis, which typically runs on a small set of servers, this meant that the worst case is just to

---

[1]Notice that this issue does not occur for communication to the same destination as for the point-to-point message: One can send any number of point-to-point messages or individual copies of multicasts to a single process within a group without delaying. The requirement is that messages to *other* destinations be delayed until these point-to-point messages are stable.

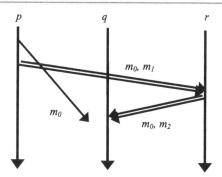

Fig. 13.2 After sending m_0 asynchronously to q, p sends m_1 to r. To preserve causality, a copy of m_0 is piggybacked on this message. Similarly, when r sends m_3 to q a copy of m_0 is included. q will receive m_0 by the first causal path to reach it. A background garbage collection algorithm cleans up copies of messages that have become stable by reaching all of their destinations. To avoid excessive propagation of messages, the system always has the alternative of sending a message directly to its true destination and waiting for it to become stable, or it can simply wait until the message reaches its destinations and becomes stable

piggyback the message once to each server. For all of these reasons, the cost of piggybacking is never excessive in the Isis Toolkit. This original Isis algorithm also has the benefit of avoiding any potential gaps in the causal communication order: If q has received a message that was causally after m_1, then q will retain a copy of m_1 until m_1 is safe at its destinations.

On the other hand, we are not aware of any system other than that early version of Isis in which piggybacking was viewed as a serious option for implementing *CausalSend*, and as noted below, many modern group communication systems (including Isis[2]) limit the developer to a choice between *Send*, *OrderedSend* and *SafeSend*, treating *CausalSend* as a kind of exotic novelty. The bottom line is that most developers understand these three options easily. No matter how one implements *CausalSend*, the issue still remains of whether end-users will find it equally easy and natural to work with, and the evidence tends to suggest that they do not.

13.2 Extending Causal Order to Multigroup Settings

Additional issues occur when groups can overlap. Suppose that a process sends or receives multicasts in more than one group—a pattern that is commonly observed in complex systems that make heavy use of group computing. Just as we asked how causal order can be guaranteed when a causal path includes point-to-point messages, we can also ask how causal and total order can be extended to apply to multicasts sent in a series of groups.

Consider first the issue of causal ordering. If process p belongs to groups g_1 and g_2, one can imagine a chain of multicasts that includes messages sent asynchronously in both groups—for example, perhaps we will have $m_1 \to m_2 \to m_3$, where m_1 and m_3 are sent asynchronously in g_1 and m_2 is sent asynchronously

Fig. 13.3 Message m_3 is
causally ordered after m_1,
and therefore may need to be
delayed upon reception if m_1
has not yet been delivered
when m_3 is received

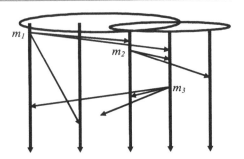

in g_2. Upon receipt of a copy of m_3, a process may need to check for and detect causal ordering violations, delaying m_3 if necessary until m_1 has been received. Actually, this example illustrates two problems, since we also need to be sure that the delivery atomicity properties of the system extend to sequences of multicasts sent in a different group. Otherwise, scenarios can occur whereby m_3 becomes causally orphaned and can never be delivered.

In Fig. 13.3, for example, if a failure causes m_1 to be lost, m_3 can never be delivered. There are several possibilities for solving the atomicity problem, which lead to different possibilities for dealing with causal order. A simple option is to delay a multicast to group g_2 while there are causally prior multicasts pending in group g_1. In the example, m_2 would be delayed until m_1 becomes stable. Most existing process group systems use this solution, which is called the *conservative scheme*. It is simple to implement and offers acceptable performance for most applications. To the degree that overhead is introduced, it occurs within the process group itself and hence is both localized and readily measured.

Less-conservative schemes are riskier in the sense that safety can be compromised when certain types of failure occur and they require more overhead; this overhead is less localized and consequently harder to quantify—for example, a *k-stability* solution might wait until m_1 is known to have been received at $k + 1$ destinations. The multicast will now be atomic provided that no more than k simultaneous failures occur in the group. However, we now need a way to detect causal ordering violations and to delay a message that arrives prematurely to overcome them.

One option is to annotate each multicast with multiple vector timestamps. This approach requires a form of piggybacking: Each multicast carries with it only timestamps that have changed or (if timestamp compression is used) only those with fields that have changed. Stephenson has explored this scheme and related ones and has shown that they offer general enforcement of causality at low average overhead. In practice, however, I am not aware of any systems that implement this method, apparently because the conservative scheme is so simple and because of the risk of a safety violation if a failure causes k processes to fail simultaneously.

Another option is to use the Isis style of piggybacking *CausalSend* implementation. Early versions of the Isis Toolkit employed this approach, and, as noted earlier, the associated overhead turns out to be fairly low. The details are essentially identi-

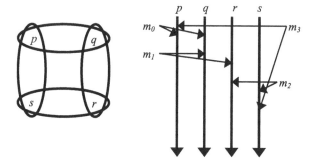

Fig. 13.4 Overlapping process groups, seen from above and in a time-space diagram. Here, m_0 was sent to $\{p, q\}$, m_1 to $\{q, r\}$ and so forth, and since each group received only one message, there is no ordering requirement within the individual groups. Thus, an *OrderedSend* protocol would never delay any of these messages. But one can deduce a global ordering for the multicasts. Process p sees m_0 after m_3, q sees m_0 before m_1, r sees m_1 before m_2, and s sees m_2 before m_3. This global ordering is thus cyclic, illustrating that many of our *OrderedSend* ordering algorithms provide locally total ordering but not globally total ordering

cal to the method presented in Sect. 12.3. This approach has the advantage of also providing atomicity, but it has the disadvantage of having unpredictable costs.

In summary, there are several possibilities for enforcing causal ordering in multi-group settings. One should ask whether the costs associated with doing so are reasonable. The consensus of the community has tended to accept costs that are limited to within a single group (i.e., the conservative mode delays) but not costs that are paid system-wide (such as those associated with piggybacking vector timestamps or copies of messages). Even the conservative scheme, however, can be avoided if the application does not actually *need* the guarantee that this provides. Thus, the application designer should start with an analysis of the use and importance of multigroup causality before deciding to assume this property in a given setting.

13.3   Extending Total Order to Multigroup Settings

The total ordering protocols presented in Sect. 12.3 guarantee that messages sent in any one group will be totally ordered with respect to one another. However, even if the conservative stability rule is used, this guarantee does not extend to messages sent in different groups but received at processes that belong to both. Moreover, the local versions of total ordering permit some surprising global ordering problems. Consider, for example, multicasts sent to a set of processes that form overlapping groups, as shown in Fig. 13.4. If one multicast is sent to each group, we could easily have process q receive m_1 followed by m_2, process r receive m_2 followed by m_3, process s receive m_3 followed by m_4, and process s receive m_4 followed by m_1. Since only a single multicast was sent in each group, such an order is total if only the perspective of the individual group is considered. Yet this ordering is clearly cyclic in a global sense.

A number of schemes for generating a globally acyclic total ordering are known, and indeed one could have qualms about the use of the term "total" for an ordering that now turns out to sometimes admit cycles. Perhaps it would be best to say that previously we identified a number of methods for obtaining *locally total* multicast ordering whereas now we consider the issue of *globally total* multicast ordering.

The essential feature of the globally total schemes is that the groups within which ordering is desired must share some resource that is used to obtain the ordering property—for example, if a set of groups shares the same ordering token, the ordering of messages assigned using the token can be made globally total as well as locally total. Clearly, however, such a protocol could be costly, since the token will now be a single bottleneck for ordered multicast delivery.

In the Psync system an ordering scheme that uses multicast labels was first introduced (see Peterson 1987; Peterson et al. 1989a); soon after, variations of this were proposed by the Transis and Totem systems (see Amir et al. 1992b; Melliar-Smith and Moser 1989). All of these methods work by using some form of unique label to place the multicasts in a total order determined by their labels. Before delivering such a multicast, a process must be sure it has received all other multicasts that could have smaller labels. The latency of this protocol is thus prone to rise with the number of processes in the aggregated membership of groups to which the receiving process belongs.

Each of these methods, and in fact all methods with which the author is familiar, has performance that degrades as a function of scale. The larger the set of processes over which a globally total ordering property will apply, the more costly the ordering protocol. When deciding if globally total ordering is warranted, it is therefore useful to ask what sort of applications might be expected to notice the cycles that a local ordering protocol would allow. The reasoning is that if a cheaper protocol is still adequate for the purposes of the application, most developers would favor the cheaper protocol. In the case of globally total ordering, there are very few applications that really need this property.

Indeed, the following explanation is the only good example of which this author is aware in which locally total order is inadequate and globally total order is consequently needed. Louise Moser and Michael Melliar Smith first suggested it. Suppose that we wish to solve the dining philosophers' problem. In this problem, which is a classical synchronization problem well known to the distributed system community, a group of philosophers gather around a table. Between each pair of philosophers is a single shared fork, and at the center of the table is a plate of pasta. In order to eat, a philosopher must have one fork in each hand. The life of a philosopher is an infinite repetition of the sequence *think, pick up forks, eat, put down forks*. Our challenge is to implement a protocol that solves this problem and avoids deadlock.

Now, imagine that the processes in our example are the forks and that the multicasts originate in philosopher processes arrayed around the table. The philosophers can thus request their forks by sending totally ordered multicasts to the process group of forks to their left and right (in effect we are creating a kind of chain of groups of 3 replicas around the table).

Before we look closely at the issue this creates, it may be helpful to understand that this specific pattern, in which we arrange a potentially large set of processes into a ring, and then replicate data or other information at subsets of three is a very common one in the cloud. As mentioned in the early chapters of the text, this arises because in many cloud systems, we need to manage really huge data sets. For fault-tolerance one needs a degree of replication, but any single data item is often safe if we just replicate it with one or two backups. In such cases cloud systems often use what they call *sharding*: each data item is considered to have some sort of name, or *key*, and we use the key to map the item to a set of 2 or 3 processes within the larger group. These sets can overlap, and the replicas do not need to be next to one-another, although in many systems, purely for convenience, they are picked to be adjacent. Thus, in a distributed hash table (DHT), we might map our processes to random locations in a virtual key-space and form it into a ring, but in a replicated process group, we could just use the index of the process within the membership list as a kind of ring-partitioning rule (in either case, when membership changes, shards often must be copied around to ensure that the right processes have the right data). However one implements, them kinds of scheme make it easy to figure out which processes to talk to when updating or querying a particular data item: with group membership, one knows immediately; with a DHT (like Chord or Amazon's Dynamo) it may require a logarithmic search.

So now we have mapped Dining Philosophers onto a shared cloud-style storage structure. In this setup, it is easy to see that if forks are granted in the order that the requests arrive, a globally total order avoids deadlock, but a locally total order is deadlock prone. Presumably, there is a family of multigroup locking and synchronization protocols for which similar results would hold. However, to repeat the point made above, the author has never encountered a *real-world* application in which globally total order is needed. This being the case, such strong ordering should perhaps be held in reserve as an option for applications that specifically request it, but not as a default. If globally total order were as cheap as locally total order, the conclusion would be reversed.

In today's cloud, with very weak consistency, this concern is hardly worth discussing. But one can imagine that in the future, if cloud systems offer stronger consistency, the question might begin to matter. After all, not every group will be huge, so while the deadlock scenario we have outlined is probably very unlikely in a large group, it is not hard to see how it could arise with, say, 3 shard groups in a ring that might have a total of perhaps just 4 or 5 processes! Thus, this is the kind of issue that future cloud developers may need to be aware of.

13.4   Causal and Total Ordering Domains

We have seen that when ordering properties are extended to apply to multiple heavy-weight groups, the costs of achieving ordering can rise substantially. Sometimes, however, such properties really are needed, at least in subsets of an application. If this occurs, one option may be to provide the application with control over these costs by introducing what are called *causal and total ordering domains*. Such a domain would be an attribute of a process group: At the time a group is created, it would be bound to an ordering domain identifier, which remains constant thereafter. We can then implement the rule that when two groups are in different domains, multicast ordering properties do not need to hold across them—for example, if group g_1 and group g_2 are members of different ordering domains, the system could ignore causal ordering between multicasts sent in g_1 and multicasts sent in g_2. More general still would be a scheme in which a domain is provided for each type of ordering: Two groups could then be in the same causal ordering domain but be in different total ordering domains. Implementation of ordering domains is simple if the corresponding multi-group ordering property is available within a system—for example, if group g_1 and group g_2 are members of different causal ordering domains, the conservative rule would be overlooked when a process switched from sending or receiving in one group to sending in the other. Delays would only occur when two groups are explicitly placed in the same ordering domain, presumably because the application actually requires multi-group ordering in this case.

It can be argued that the benefits associated with preserving causal order throughout a large system, as was done in the Isis Tookit, are significantly greater than those for supporting globally total order. The reasoning is that causal order is needed to implement asynchronous data replication algorithms, and, since these have such a large performance advantage over other schemes, the benefits outweigh the costs of needing to enforce causal order across group boundaries. However, the conservative causality scheme is an adequate solution to this particular problem, and has the benefit of providing a system-wide guarantee with a local method. When combined with causal domains, such a mechanism has a highly selective cost. This said, however, it should also be noted that the *flush* primitive proposed earlier offers the same benefits and is quite easy to use. Thus, many real systems opt for causal ordering, do not delay when sending messages outside of a group, and provide a *flush* primitive for use by the application itself when causal ordering is needed over group boundaries. Such a compromise is visible to the user and is easily understood.

Similar reasoning seems to argue against globally total order: The primitive has a significant cost (mostly in terms of latency) and limited benefit. Thus, my work has stopped providing this property, after initially doing so in the early versions of the Isis Toolkit. The costs were simply too high to make globally total ordering the default, and the complexity of supporting a very rarely used mechanism argued against having the property at all.

13.5   Multicasts to Multiple Groups

An additional multigroup issue concerns the sending of a single multicast to a set of process groups in a single atomic operation. Until now, such an action would require that the multicast be sent to one group at a time, raising issues of nonatomic delivery if the sender fails midway. One can imagine solving this problem by implementing a multigroup multicast as a form of nonblocking commit protocol; Schiper and Raynal have proposed such a protocol in conjunction with their work on the Phoenix system (see Schiper and Raynal 1996). However, there is another option, which is to create a new process group superimposed on the multiple destination groups and to send the multicast in that group. Interestingly, the best implementations of a group-creation protocol require a single *Send*—hence, if one creates a group, issues a single multicast in it, and then deletes the group, this will incur a cost comparable to doing a multiphase commit over the same set of processes and then garbage collecting after the protocol has terminated!

This last observation argues against explicit support for sending a multicast to several groups at the same time, except in settings where the set of groups to be used cannot be predicted in advance and is very unlikely to be reused for subsequent communication—that is, although the application process can be presented with an interface that allows multicasts to be sent to sets of groups, it may be best to implement such a mechanism by creating a group in the manner described previously. In the belief that most group communication patterns will be reused shortly after they are first employed, such a group could then be retained for a period of time in the hope that a subsequent multicast to the same destinations will reuse its membership information. The group can then be torn down after a period during which no new multicasts are transmitted. Only if such a scheme is impractical would one need a multicast primitive capable of sending to many groups at the same time, and I am not familiar with any setting in which such a scheme is clearly not viable.

13.6 Multigroup View Management Protocols

A final issue that occurs in systems where groups overlap heavily is that our view management and flush protocol will run once for each group when a failure or join occurs, and our state transfer protocol will only handle the case of a process that joins a single group at a time. Clearly, these will be sources of inefficiency (in the first case) and inconvenience (in the second case) if group overlap is common. This observation, combined with the delays associated with conservative ordering algorithms and the concerns raised above in regard to globally total order, has motivated research on methods of collapsing heavily overlapped groups into smaller numbers of larger groups. Such approaches are often described as resulting in *lightweight* groups, because the groups seen by the application typically map onto some enclosing set of *heavyweight* groups.

Glade explored this approach in Isis and Horus (see Glade et al. 1993). His work supports the same process group interfaces as for a normal process group, but maps multicasts to lightweight groups into multicasts to the enclosing heavyweight groups. Such multicasts are filtered on arrival, so that an individual process will only be given copies of messages actually destined for it. The approach essentially maps the fine-grained membership of the lightweight groups to a coarser-grained membership in a much smaller number of heavyweight groups.

The benefit of Glade's approach is that it avoids the costs of maintaining large numbers of groups (the membership protocols run just once if a process joins or leaves the system, updating multiple lightweight groups in one operation). Moreover, the causal and total ordering guarantees of our single-group solutions will now give the illusion of multigroup causal and total ordering, with no changes to the protocols themselves. Glade argues that when a system produces very large numbers of overlapping process groups, there are likely to be underlying patterns that can be exploited to efficiently map the groups to a small number of heavyweight ones.

13.7   Related Reading

On multiple groups in Isis (see Birman and Joseph 1987b; Birman et al. 1991, 1994, 1999, 2010).

On communication from a nonmember of a group to a group (see Birman and Joseph 1987b; Wood 1993).

On graph representations of message dependencies (see Amir et al. 1992b; Melliar-Smith and Moser 1989; Peterson 1987; Peterson et al. 1989a, 1989b).

On lightweight process groups (see Glade et al. 1993).

The Virtual Synchrony Execution Model

14

We finally have the basics out of the way and can put things together into a comprehensive platform for group communication! The process group communication primitives introduced in the previous chapters create a powerful framework for algorithmic development. When the properties of the model are combined with these primitives, we will say that a *virtually synchronous* execution environment results (see Birman and Joseph 1987a, 1987b; Birman and van Renesse 1994). In Chaps. 10–12 of the book we built up our primitives from basic message passing, but for this chapter, it is probably easier to understand the idea behind virtual synchrony in a top-down treatment. We will then use the approach to develop an extremely high performance replicated data algorithm, as well as several other tools for consistent distributed computing. Here, we explore the question in a slightly informal way; Appendix A shows how the same concepts can be expressed using a more mathematical notation.

14.1 Virtual Synchrony

Suppose that we want to use a process group (or a set of process groups) as a building block in a distributed application. The group members will join that group for the purpose of cooperation, perhaps to replicate data or to perform some operation in a fault-tolerant manner. The issue now arises of designing such algorithms with a high degree of confidence that they will operate correctly.

Recall the discussion of transactional serializability from Sects. 7.4 and 7.5. In that context, we encountered a similar problem: a set of concurrently executed programs that share files or a database and want to avoid interference with one another. The basic idea was to allow the developer to code these applications as if they would run in isolation, one by one. The database itself is permitted to interleave operations for greater efficiency, but only in ways that preserve the illusion that each transaction executes without interruption. The results of a transaction are visible only after it commits; a transaction that aborts is automatically and completely erased from the memory of the system. As we noted at the time, transactional serializability allows the developer to use a simple programming model, while offering the system

K.P. Birman, *Guide to Reliable Distributed Systems*, Texts in Computer Science,
DOI 10.1007/978-1-4471-2416-0_14, © Springer-Verlag London Limited 2012

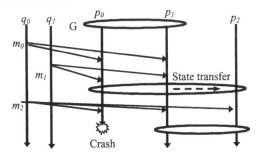

Fig. 14.1 Closely synchronous execution: All group members see the same events (incoming messages and new group views) in the same order. In this example only the nonmembers of the group send multicasts to it, but this is just to keep the picture simple. In practice, group members can also multicast to one another, and can send point-to-point messages to the nonmembers—for example, a group RPC could be performed by sending a multicast to the group, to which one or more members reply

an opportunity to benefit from high levels of concurrency and asynchronous communication.

Virtual synchrony is not based on transactions, but introduces a similar approach for developers who are programming with process groups. In the virtual synchrony model, the simplifying abstraction seen by the developer is that of a set of processes (the group members) which all see the same events in the same order. These events are incoming messages to the group and group membership changes. The key insight, is not particularly profound: Since all the processes see the same inputs, they can execute the same algorithm and in this manner stay in consistent states. This is illustrated in Fig. 14.1, which shows a process group receiving messages from several nonmembers. It then has a new member join and transfers the state of the group to this new member. Having completed the transfer, one of the old members crashes or terminates (this can accidentally, but would also occur when migrating a task from p_0 to p_2). Notice that the group members see identical sequences of events while they belong to the group. The members differ, however, in their relative ranking within the group membership. There are many possible ways to rank the members of a group, but the most common one, which is used in this chapter, assumes that the rank is based on when members joined—the oldest member having the lowest ranking, and so forth.

The State Machine approach of Lamport and Schneider first introduced this approach as part of a proposal for replicating objects in settings subject to Byzantine failures (see Schneider 1988, 1990). Lamport's work made a group of identical replicas of the object in question, and used the Byzantine protocol for all interactions with the group and to implement its interactions with the external world. However, the State Machine approach saw little use when it was first proposed for the same reason that the Byzantine protocol sees limited practical use: Few computing environments satisfy the necessary synchronous computing and communications requirements, and it is difficult to utilize a service that employs a Byzantine fault model without extending the same approach to other aspects of the environment, such as any external objects with which the service interacts and the operating systems software used to implement the communication layer.

A further concern about the State Machine approach arises because all copies of the program see identical inputs in exactly the identical order, and execute each request in exactly the same state. If one copy of a program crashes because of a software bug, so will all the replicas of that program. Unfortunately, as we saw earlier, studies of real-world computing installations reveal that even in mature software systems, bugs that crash the application remain a proportionately important cause of failures. Thus, by requiring correct processes that operate deterministically and in lockstep, the State Machine approach is unable to offer protection against software faults.

Virtual synchrony is similar to the State Machine abstraction, but it moves outside of the original Byzantine setting, while also introducing optimizations that overcome the concerns mentioned previously. The idea is to view the State Machine as a sort of reference model but to implement it in a way that yields better performance and requires less of the environment. The effect of these optimizations is that the true execution of a process group will be very far from the kind of lockstep synchrony that could cause trouble. In effect, just as transactional executions allow operations to be interleaved, provided that the behavior is indistinguishable from some serial execution, a virtually synchronous execution allows operations to be interleaved, provided that the result is indistinguishable from some closely synchronous (State Machine) execution. The benefit of this approach is that the executions of the different replicas will often be different enough to let the group as a whole tolerate software bugs that cause individual members to crash.

To take a very simple example, suppose that we wish to support a process group whose members replicate some form of database and perform load-balanced queries upon it. The operations on the service will be queries and updates, and we will overlook failures (for the time being) to keep the problem as simple as possible.

Next, suppose that we implement both queries and database updates as totally ordered multicasts to the group membership. Every member will have the same view of the membership of the group, and each will see the same updates and queries in the same order. By simply applying the updates in the order they were received, the members can maintain identically replicated copies of the database. As for the queries, an approximation of load-balancing can be had using the ranking of processes in the group view. For example, suppose that the process group view ranks the members in $[0 \ldots n - 1]$. Then the ith incoming query can be assigned to the process whose rank is ($i \bmod n$). Each query will be handled by exactly one process.

We will call this a *closely synchronous* execution. Frank Schmuck was the first to propose this term, observing that the actions of the receiving processes were closely synchronized but might be spread over a significant period of real time. The synchronous model, as discussed previously, would normally require real-time bounds on the time period over which an action is performed by the different processes. Notice that a closely synchronous execution does not require identical actions by identical processes: If we use the load-balancing idea outlined above, actions will be quite different at the different copies. Thus, a closely synchronous group is similar to a group that uses State Machine replication, but it is not identical.

Having developed this solution, however, there will often be ways to weaken the ordering properties of the protocols it uses—for example, it may be the case that updates are only initiated by a single source, in which case an *Send* protocol would be sufficient to provide the desired ordering. Updates will no longer be ordered with respect to queries if such a change is made, but in an application where a single process issues an update and follows it with a query, the update would always be received first and hence the query will reflect the result of doing the update. In a slightly fancier setting, *CausalSend* might be needed to ensure that the algorithm will operate correctly—for example, with *CausalSend* one would know that if an application issues an update and then tells some other process to do a query, that second process will see the effects of the causally prior updates. Often, an analysis such as this one can be carried very far.

Having substituted *Send* or *CausalSend* for the original *OrderedSend*, however, the execution will no longer be closely synchronous, since different processes may see different sequences of updates and queries and hence perform the same actions but in different orders. The significant point is that if the original analysis was performed correctly, the actions will produce an effect indistinguishable from what might have resulted from a closely synchronous execution. Thus, the execution appears to be closely synchronous, even though it actually is not. It is *virtually synchronous* in much the same sense that a transactional system creates the illusion of a serial execution even though the database server is interleaving operations from different transactions to increase concurrency—one might say that a transactional—system is "virtually serial."

Our transformation has the advantage of delivering inputs to the process group members in different orders, at least some of the time. Moreover, as we saw earlier, the process groups themselves are constructed dynamically, with processes joining them at different times. Also, the ranking of the processes within the group differs. Thus, there is substantial room for processes to execute in slightly different ways, affording a degree of protection against software bugs that could crash some of the members.

Recall the Gray/Lindsey characterization of Bohrbugs and Heisenbugs from Chap. 9. It is interesting to note that virtually synchronous replication can protect against many Heisenbugs (see Birman and van Renesse 1994, 1996). If a replica crashes because such a bug has been exercised, the probability that other group members will crash simultaneously is reduced by the many aspects of the execution that differ from replica to replica. Our transformation from a closely synchronous system to a virtually synchronous system increases the natural resiliency of the group, assuming that its constituent members are mature, well-debugged code. Nonetheless, some exposure to correlated failures is unavoidable, and the designer of a critical system should keep this in mind.

Additionally, notice that the *CausalSend* primitive can be used asynchronously: There is no good reason for a process that issues a *CausalSend* to perform an update to wait until the update has been completed by the full membership of the group. The properties of the *CausalSend* protocol ensure that these asynchronously transmitted messages will reliably reach their destinations and that any causally subsequent actions by the same or different processes will see the effects of the prior *CausalSends*.

In an intuitive sense, one could say that these *CausalSend* protocols look as if they were performed instantly, even when they actually execute over an extended period of time.

In practice, the most common transformation that we will make is precisely the approach just described: the replacement of a totally ordered *OrderedSend* primitive with an asynchronous, causally ordered *CausalSend* primitive. In the following sections, this pattern will occur repeatedly.

Notice that in weakening the degree of synchronization within the group, we also transformed a closely synchronous group application, in which the members operate largely in lockstep, into a very asynchronous implementation in which some members can pull ahead and others can lag behind, communication can occur concurrently with other execution, and the group may be able to tolerate software bugs that crash some of its members. Such scheduling flexibility often translates to better overall performance, and weaker multicast primitives are also much faster than the more strongly ordered ones. Thus, our solution is likely to be far faster than the original closely synchronous one.

When an application has multiple process groups in it, an additional level of analysis is often required. As we saw in the previous chapter, multigroup causal (and total) ordering is expensive. When one considers real systems, it also turns out that multigroup ordering is often unnecessary: Many applications that need multiple groups use them for purposes that are fairly independent of one another. Operations on such independent groups can be thought of as commutative, and it may be possible to use *CausalSend* to optimize such groups independently without taking the next step of enforcing causal orderings across groups. Where multigroup ordering is needed, it will often be confined to small sets of groups, which can be treated as an ordering domain. In this manner, we obtain a general solution that can scale to large numbers of groups while still preserving the benefits of the asynchronous communication pattern seen in the *CausalSend* protocol.

Our overall approach is less effective when strong durability (safe delivery) is required. The problem arises because asynchronous *CausalSend* delivers messages during its first phase of communication, pretty much as soon as the multicast can reach its destination. In contrast, a strongly durable protocol will necessarily delay delivery until a second phase because we need to be certain that all processes in the system have received a copy before any process is permitted to deliver the message. Once we have given up on quick delivery, the benefit of replacing *OrderedSend* with *CausalSend* has been lost.

Thus, one begins to see a major split between the algorithms that operate synchronously, requiring more than a single phase of message passing before delivery can occur, and those that operate asynchronously, allowing the sender of a multicast to continue computing while multicasts that update the remainder of a group or that inform the remainder of the system of some event propagate concurrently to their destinations. The split corresponds to an enormous performance difference, with asynchronous algorithms frequently outperforming their more synchronous siblings by several orders of magnitude. In effect, the asynchronous protocols can run as fast as the network is able to "pipeline" data from sources to destinations, while the synchronous ones are limited by the slowest round-trip times in the system as a whole!

The following is a summary of the key elements of the virtual synchrony model:

• *Support for process groups*: Processes can join groups dynamically and are automatically excluded from a group if they crash.

• *Identical process group views and mutually consistent rankings*: Members of a process group are presented with identical sequences of group membership, which we call *views* of that process group. If a nonprimary component of the system forms after a failure, any process group views reported to processes in that component are identified as nonprimary, and the view sequence properties will otherwise hold for all the processes in a given component. The view ranks the components, and all group members see identical rankings for identical group views.

• *State transfer to the joining process*: A process that joins a group can obtain the group's current state from some prior member or from a set of members.

• *A family of reliable, ordered multicast protocols*: We have seen a number of these, including *Send, CausalSend, OrderedSend, and SafeSend*, together with a group *Flush* primitive.

• *Gap-freedom guarantees*: After a failure, if some message, m_j, is delivered to its destinations, then any message, m_i, that the system is obliged to deliver prior to m_j will also have been delivered to its destinations.

• *View-synchronous multicast delivery*: Any pair of processes that are both members of two consecutive group views receive the same set of multicasts during the period between those views.[1]

• *Use of asynchronous, causal, or FIFO multicast*: Although algorithms will often be developed using a closely synchronous computing model, a systematic effort is made to replace synchronous, totally ordered, and strongly durable (safe) multicasts with less synchronous, less-costly alternatives—notably the *Send, CausalSend* or *OrderedSend* primitive, none of which guarantee durability, followed by a call to *Flush*, which will delay the computation until any prior multicasts have become durable. In effect, we have deconstructed *SafeSend* into one or more multicasts followed by a pause until safety is achieved. As we will see in Chap. 15, this approach is ideally matched to the needs of modern cloud computing systems.

14.2   Extended Virtual Synchrony

Even before launching into a brief discussion of tolerating partitioning events (where a group splits into two components, perhaps because of a network failure), we should warn the reader that what follows is a bit hard to understand and, in fact,

---

[1]In some systems this is interpreted so that if a process fails, but its failure is not reported promptly, it is considered to have received multicasts that would have been delivered to it had it still been operational.

is probably *not* a mechanism one would really want to use except in a small category of very demanding applications! The reader focused on high assurance Web Services might wish to skip directly to Sect. 14.3. However, other readers have now been warned, and with that out of the way, we tackle partitioning. Notice that, as presented in the previous section, the virtual synchrony model is intolerant of partitioning failures: The model was defined in terms of a single system component within which process groups reside. In this primary component approach, if a network partitioning failure occurs and splits a group into fragments, only the fragment that resides in the primary component of the system is able to continue operation. Fragments that find themselves in the nonprimary component(s) of the system are typically forced to shut down, and the processes within them must reconnect to the primary component when communication is restored.

The basis of the primary component approach lies in a subtle issue, which we first saw when discussing commit protocols. In a dynamic distributed environment there can be symmetric failure modes resulting from communication problems that mimic process failures. In such a situation perhaps process p will consider that process q has failed while process q assumes that p has failed. To make progress, one or the other (or perhaps both) of these events must become official. In a partitioned run of the system, only one of these conflicting states can become official.

At the core of this problem is the observation that if a system experiences a partitioning failure, it is impossible to guarantee that multiple components can remain operational (in the sense of initiating new actions, delivering messages, and new group views) with guarantees that also span both sides of the partition. To obtain strong system-wide guarantees a protocol must always wait for communication to be reestablished under at least some executions in at least one side of the partition. When we resolve this problem using the protocols discussed in the previous chapters, the primary component is permitted to make progress at the expense of inconsistency relative to other components: Within other components, the set of messages delivered may be different from the set in the primary component, and the order may also be different. In the case of the strongly durable protocols the guarantees are stronger, but nonprimary components may be left in a state where some strongly durable multicasts are still undelivered and where new strongly durable ones are completely blocked. The primary component, in contrast, can make progress so long as its GMS protocol is able to make progress.

Some researchers, notably those involved with the Transis and Totem projects, have pointed out that there are applications that can tolerate inconsistency of the sort that could occur if progress were permitted in a nonprimary component of a partitioned system (see Agarwal 1994; Dolev et al. 1995; Malkhi 1994). In these systems, any component that can reach internal agreement on its membership is permitted to continue operation. However, only a single component of the system is designated as the primary one. An application that is safe only in the primary component could simply shut down in nonprimary components. Alternatively, the application could remain available in nonprimary components, but buffer any update requests for delayed execution. Later, when the partition is repaired, these buffered requests would be replayed, with the effect of merging information collected by the non-primary component back into the primary component. However, not all applications can be designed in this manner—often, the user needs to see the effect of an update as soon as it is requested, in which case buffering such requests is not practical.

Carrying this observation even further, the Transis group has shown that there are distributed systems in which no component ever can be identified as the primary one, and yet every action initiated within the system can eventually be performed in a globally consistent manner (see Dolev et al. 1995; Keidar 1998, 2010; Chockler et al. 2001). However, this work involves both a static system model and a relatively costly protocol, which delays performing an action until a majority of the processes in the system as a whole have acknowledged receipt of it. The idea is that actions can be initiated within dynamically defined components, which represent subsets of the true maximal system configuration, but these actions remain in a pending state until a sufficient number of processes are known to have seen them, which occurs when communication is restored between components. Eventually, knowledge of the actions reaches enough processes so that it becomes safe to perform them. The protocol is intended for systems that operate in a partitioned mode over very long periods of time and where there is no special hurry to perform actions. Yair Amir has extended this approach to deal with more urgent actions, but his approach involves weakening global consistency properties (see Amir 1995). Thus, one is faced with a basic tradeoff between ensuring that actions will occur quickly and providing consistency between the primary component of the system and other components. We can have one or the other, but not both at once.

Cornell's Horus and Ensemble systems support an extended model of the former sort (see Malkhi 1994). (In fact, this part of Horus was actually implemented by Malkhi, who ported the associated code from Transis into Horus, and then the code was used as the basis for the Ensemble version, which is coded in the O'CaML language.) However, many users complain that the extended model is quite a bit harder to work with than the primary partition model. The merge of states when an arbitrary application resumes contact between a nonprimary and a primary component cannot, in general, be automated. In practice, such an application would use the buffered update approach just described, capturing any update actions on a queue. When a merge becomes possible, a process that joins the primary partition would replace its state with that of the primary component and then replay these updates, if any, for the benefit of the entire group. Experience with Horus and Ensemble suggests that very few applications can operate this way. Moreover, unless strongly durable protocols are employed for updates, the nonprimary component's state may be inconsistent with the primary one in significant ways.

On the other hand, the primary component model is awkward in wide area networks where partitioning events occur more easily (see Fig. 14.2). Here, the model will in effect shut down parts of the overall system that are physically remote from the main part of the system. Each time these parts manage to restart after a communication failure, a new communication problem may soon cut them off again. (See Fig. 14.3.)

Recent work, which we will not discuss in detail, points to yet a third possible mode of operation. In this mode, a computing system would be viewed as a wide area network composed of interconnected local area networks, as was first proposed

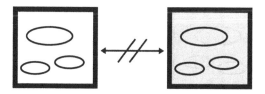

Fig. 14.2 When a partitioning failure occurs, an application may be split into two or more fragments, each complete in the sense that it may potentially have a full set of processes and groups. In the primary component model, however, only one set is permitted to remain operational—hopefully one that has a full complement of process and groups. In this figure, the white component might thus be alive after the link breaks, while the members of the gray component are prevented from continuing execution. The rationale underlying this model is that it is impossible to guarantee consistency if both sides of a partitioning failure are permitted to remain available while a communication failure is pending. Thus, we could allow both to run if we sacrifice consistency, but then we face a number of problems: Which side owns critical resources? How can the two sides overcome potential inconsistencies in their states as of the time of the partition failure event? There are no good general answers to these questions

in the Transis project. Within each of the LAN systems one would run a local subsystem: a complete primary-component system with its own sets of process groups and a self-sufficient collection of services and applications. The WAN layer of the system would be built up by superimposing a second communication structure on the aggregate of LANs and would support its own set of WAN services. At this higher level of the system, one would use a true asynchronous communication model: If a partitioning event does occur, such a WAN system would wait until the problem is resolved. The WAN system would then be in a position to make use of protocols that do not attempt to make progress while communication is disrupted, but rather wait as long as necessary until the exchange of messages resumes and the protocol can be pushed forward. The consensus protocol of Chandra and Toueg or the Paxos protocols developed by Lamport are good examples of protocols one could use at the WAN level of a system structured in this manner, while the virtual synchrony model would be instantiated multiple times separately: once for each LAN subsystem.

In this two-tiered model (see Fig. 14.4), an application would typically be implemented as a local part designed to remain available in the local component and to reconfigure itself to continue progress despite local failures. The primary component virtual synchrony model is ideal for this purpose. When an action is taken that has global implications, the local part would initiate a global action by asking the WAN architecture to communicate this message through the WAN system. The WAN system would use potentially slow protocols, which offer strong global ordering and atomicity properties at the expense of reduced progress when partitioning failures occur, delivering the resulting messages back into the various local subsystems. The local subsystems would then apply these updates to their global states.

Danny Dolev has suggested the following simple way to understand such a two-tiered system. In his view, the LAN subsystems run applications that are either entirely confined to the LAN (and have no interest in global state) or that operate by reading the *global* state but updating the *local* state. These applications do not directly update the global system state. Rather, if an action requires that the global

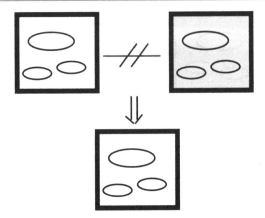

Fig. 14.3 The extended virtual synchrony model allows both white and gray partitions to continue progress despite the inconsistencies that may occur between their states. However, only one of the components is considered to be the primary one. Thus, the white partition might be considered to be authoritative for the system, while the gray partition is permitted to remain alive but is known to be potentially stale. Later, when the communication between the components is restored, the various process group components merge, resulting in a single, larger system component with a single instance of each process group (shown *at the bottom of the figure*). The problem, however, is that merging must somehow overcome the inconsistencies that may have occurred during the original partitioning failure, and this may not always be possible. Working with such a model is potentially challenging for the developer. Moreover, one must ask what sorts of applications would be able to continue operating in the gray partition knowing that the state of the system may at that point may be inconsistent—for example, it may reflect the delivery of messages in an order that differs from the order in the main partition, having atomicity errors or gaps in the message-delivery ordering

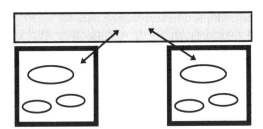

Fig. 14.4 In a two-tiered model, each LAN has its own complete subsystem and runs using its own copy of the primary-component virtual synchrony model. A WAN system (*gray*) spans the LANs and is responsible for distributing global updates. The WAN layer may block while a partitioning failure prevents it from establishing the degree of consensus needed to safely deliver updates, but the local systems continue running even if global updates are delayed. Such a mixed approach splits the concerns of the application into local ones, where the focus is on local consistency and high availability, and global ones, where the focus is on global consistency even if partitioning failures can introduce long delays. This approach is used in the Isis Toolkit's long-haul subsystem and was applied successfully in such Isis applications as its wide area publish-subscribe facility

state be updated, the LAN subsystem places the associated information on a WAN action queue, perhaps replicating this for higher availability. From that queue, the WAN protocols will eventually propagate the action into the WAN level of the system, from where it will filter back down into the LAN level in the form of an update to the global system state. The LAN layer will then update its local state to reflect the fact that the requested action has finally been completed. The LAN layer of such a system would use the primary-component virtual synchrony model, while the WAN layer employs protocols based on the method discussed by Keidar and Dolev.

First introduced in the Isis system's long-haul service by Makpangou, and then extended through Dolev and Malkhi's work on the Transis architecture (which has a "LANsys" and a "WANsys" subsystem), two-tier architectures such as this have received attention in many projects and systems (see Amir et al. 2000; Keidar et al. 2002a, 2002b; Keidar and Khazan 2002, and also Zhao et al. 2002a, 2002b, which uses a similar two-level structure, albeit for a different purpose). They are now used in Transis, Horus, NavTech, Phoenix, and Relacs. By splitting the application into the part that can be done locally with higher availability and the part that must be performed globally even if availability is limited, two-tiered architectures do not force a black or white decision on the developer. Moreover, a great many applications seem to fit well with this model. It seems likely that we will soon begin to see programming tools that encapsulate this architecture into a simple-to-use, object-oriented framework, making it readily accessible to a wide community of potential developers.

At the very end of Chap. 10, we discussed partitioning as an issue within the context of the GMS itself. At that time we observed that although a partition-tolerant GMS is certainly practical, it is not so clear that one should really expose the end-user to the resulting complexity. The same issue arises here. Yes, we can build a group communication system to tolerate partitions and support merge events—Cornell's Ensemble platform, in fact, does so. But users find this very hard to work with. Systems like Horus and Spread,[2] where the default behavior is to use the primary partition model are *much simpler* for most users. And, realistically, how often do partitioning events occur in local area networks, where these platforms are most commonly employed? The author of this text has slowly come to the conclusion that partitionable group communication is just a bit too much for the average user. Yes, there should be a way to activate such mechanisms—but only a very skilled, knowledgeable user should ever do so!

---

[2]In fact, Spread goes further and implements a single non-partitionable "group," within which the user's process groups are actually supported as subgroups. A multicast, for example, is performed by multicasting to the whole group but then filtering messages on arrival so only the appropriate subset of group members receive a copy. This proves to be an especially easy model to implement and performance is good. On the other hand, the "deliver, then filter and discard" approach imposes considerable overhead if most messages are destined for just a small subset of processes.

14.3 Virtually Synchronous Algorithms and Tools

In the following sections, we will develop a set of simple algorithms to illustrate the power and limitations of reliable multicast within dynamic process groups. These algorithms are just a small subset of the ones that can be developed using the primitives, and the sophisticated system designer may sometimes find a need for a causal and total multicast primitive (*cOrderedSend*) or one with some other slight variation on the properties we have focused on here. Happily, the protocols we have presented are easily modified for special needs, and modern group communication systems, such as the Horus system, are designed precisely to accommodate such flexibility and fine-tuning. The following algorithms, then, should be viewed as a form of template upon which other solutions might be developed through a process of gradual refinement and adaptation.

14.3.1 Replicated Data and Synchronization

When discussing the static process group model, we put it to the test by using it to implement replicated data. The reader will recall from Sect. 10.1.1 that this approach was found to have a number of performance problems. The algorithm that resulted would have forced group members to execute nearly in lockstep, and the protocols themselves were costly both in latency and messages required. Virtual synchrony, on the other hand, offers a solution to this problem that is inexpensive in all of these aspects, provided that strong durability is not required. In fact, even when strong durability is required, the cost is still lower than for the static, quorum-replication methods, but the advantage is less pronounced.

We start by describing our replication and synchronization algorithm in terms of a closely synchronous execution model. We will initially focus on the nondurable case. Suppose that we wish to support *READ*, *UPDATE*, and *LOCK* operations on data replicated within a process group. As a first approximation to a solution, we would use *OrderedSend* to implement the *UPDATE* and *LOCK* operations, while allowing any group member to perform *READ* operations using its local replica of the data maintained by the group.

Specifically, we will require each group member to maintain a private replica of the group data. When joining a group, the state transfer algorithm (developed below) must be used to initialize the replica associated with the joining process. Subsequently, all members will apply the same sequence of updates by tracking the order in which *UPDATE* messages are delivered and respecting this order when actually performing the updates. *READ* operations, as suggested above, are performed using the local replica (this is in contrast to the quorum methods, where a read must access multiple copies).

An *UPDATE* operation can be performed without waiting for the group members to actually complete the individual update actions. Instead, an *OrderedSend* is issued asynchronously (without waiting for the message to be delivered), and the individual replicas perform the update when the message arrives.

Many systems make use of nonexclusive read locks. If necessary, these can also be implemented locally. The requesting process will be granted the lock immediately unless an exclusive (write) lock is registered at this copy.

Finally, exclusive (write) *LOCK* operations are performed by issuing an *Ordered-Send* to request the lock and then waiting for each group member to grant it. A recipient of such a request waits until there are no pending read locks and then grants the request in the order it was received. The lock will later be released either with another *OrderedSend* message or upon reception of a new view of the process group reporting the failure of the process that holds the lock.

This implementation of replicated data will be tolerant of failures and guarantee the consistency of the copies. The individual replicas start in identical states because the state transfer to a joining member copies the state of the replicated data object from some existing member. Subsequent updates and lock operations behave identically at all copies. Thus, all see the same events in the same order, and all remain in identical states.

Now, let us ask how many of these *OrderedSend* operations can be replaced with asynchronous *CausalSend* operations. In particular, suppose that we replace *all* of the *OrderedSends* with asynchronous *CausalSend* operations. Remarkably, with just two small changes, the modified algorithm will be correct. The first change is that all updates must be guarded by a lock with appropriate granularity—that is, if any update might be in conflict with a concurrent update, we will require that the application must use locks to obtain mutual exclusion. On the other hand, updates that are independent can be issued concurrently—for example, updates to two different variables maintained by the same process group can be issued concurrently. In groups where all the updates for a specific type of data originate with a single process, no locks are required at all.

The second change is a bit more subtle: It has to do with the way that ordering is established when a series of write locks are requested within the group. The change is as follows. We will say that the first process to join the group, when the group is created, is its *initial writer*. This process is considered to control write access to all the data items managed by the group.

Now, before doing an update, a process will typically request a lock, sending a *CausalSend* to inform the group members of its *LOCK* request and waiting for the members to grant the request. In our original closely synchronous algorithm, a recipient of such a request granted it in first-come, first-served order when no local read-lock was pending. Our modified algorithm, however, will wait before granting lock requests. They simply pile up in a queue, ordered in whatever order the *CausalSend* messages were delivered.

When the writer for a given lock no longer needs that lock, we will say that it becomes *prepared to pass the lock*. This process will react to incoming lock requests by sending out a *CausalSend* that *grants* the first lock request on its copy of the queue. The grant message will be delivered to all group members. Once the grant message is received, a member dequeues the corresponding lock request (the causal ordering properties ensure that the request will indeed be found on the pending lock-request queue) and then grants it when any read locks present for the same item have

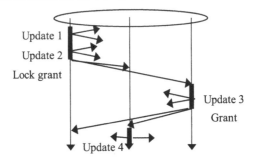

Fig. 14.5 A set of conflicting updates is ordered because only one process can write at a time. Each update, and the lock-granting message, is an asynchronous *CausalSend*. Because the causal order is in fact a total one along this causal path (shown in *bold*), all group members see the same updates in the same order. Lock requests are not shown, but they too would be issued using an asynchronous *CausalSend*. Notice that lock requests will not be seen in the same order by all processes, but this is not required for the algorithm to behave correctly. All that matters is that the grant operation grant a currently pending lock request, and, in this algorithm, all processes do have a way to track the pending requests, even though they may learn about those requests in different orders

been released. A writer grants the lock to the process that issued the oldest of the pending lock requests on its version of the lock queue.

Having obtained a grant message for its lock request, as well as individual confirmation messages from each group member that the lock has been acquired locally, the writer may begin issuing updates. In many systems the local read-lock mechanism will not be required, in which case the members need not confirm write-lock acquisition, and the writer need not wait for these messages. The members simply dequeue the pending lock request when the grant message arrives, and the writer proceeds to issue updates as soon as it receives the grant message.

It may at first seem surprising that this algorithm can work: Why should it ensure that the group members will perform the same sequence of updates on their replicas? To understand this, start by noticing that the members actually might not perform identical sequences of updates (Fig. 14.5). However, any sequence of *conflicting updates* will be identical at all replicas, for the following reason: Within the group, there can be only one writer that holds a given lock. That writer uses *CausalSend* (asynchronously) to issue updates and uses *CausalSend* (asynchronously) to grant the write lock to the subsequent writer. This establishes a total order on the updates: One can imagine a causal path traced through the group, from writer to writer, with the updates neatly numbered along it—the first update, the second, the granting of the lock to a new writer, the third update, the granting of the lock to a new writer, the fourth update, and so forth. Thus, when *CausalSend* enforces the delivery order, any set of updates covered by the same lock will be delivered in the same order to all group members.

As for the nonconflicting updates: These commute with the others and hence would have had the same effect regardless of how they were ordered. The ordering of updates is thus significant only with respect to other conflicting updates.

Finally, the reader may have noticed that lock requests are not actually seen in the same order by each participant. This is not a problem, however, because the lock-request order is not used in the algorithm. As long as the grant operation grants a request that is genuinely pending, the algorithm will work.

The remarkable thing about this new algorithm is that it is almost entirely asynchronous. Recall that our *CausalSend* protocol delivers messages in the same view of the process group as the one that was in place when the *CausalSend* was initiated. This implies that the sender of a *CausalSend* can always deliver its own copy of the multicast as soon as it initiates the message. After all, by definition, a causally prior *CausalSend* will already have been delivered to the sender, and the flush protocol enforces the view synchrony and causal gap-freedom guarantees. This means that a process wanting to issue an update can perform the update locally, sending off a *CausalSend* that will update the other replicas without delaying local computation. Clearly, a lock request will block the process that issues it—unless that process happens to hold the write lock already, as is often the case in systems with bursty communication patterns. But it is clear that this minimal delay—the time needed to request permission to write and for the grant message to travel back to the requesting process—is necessary in any system.

The algorithm can be simplified further. Although we used *CausalSend* here, one could potentially replace this with *Send* by employing a sequence number: The ith update would be so labeled, and all group members would simply apply updates in sequence order. The token would now represent permission to initiate new updates (and the guarantee that the values a process reads are the most current ones). Such a change eliminates the vector-timestamp overhead associated with *CausalSend*, and it is also recognizable as an implementation of one of the *OrderedSend* protocols we developed earlier!

From the perspective of an application, this asynchronous replication and locking scheme may seem astonishingly fast. The only delays imposed upon the application are when it requests a new write lock. During periods when it holds the lock, or if it is lucky enough to find the lock already available, the application is never delayed at all. Read operations can be performed locally, and write operations respond as soon as the local update has been completed. The *CausalSend* or *Send* (we will just call it a *CausalSend* for simplicity) will be performed asynchronously in communication subsystem. Later, we will see that the Horus system achieves performance that can reach 85,000 such updates per second. Reads are essentially free—hence, millions could be done per second. When this is compared with a quorum read and update technology, in which it would be surprising to exceed 100 reads and updates (combined) in one second, the benefits of an asynchronous *CausalSend* are nothing short of astonishing! In practice, quorum schemes are often even slower than this analysis suggests, because of the overheads built into the algorithm. Moreover, a quorum read or update forces the group members into lockstep, while our asynchronous replication algorithm encourages them to leap ahead of one another, buffering messages to be transmitted in the background.

However, this algorithm is not identical to the quorum replication scheme, because that scheme provides the equivalent of a strong durability guarantee and a strong total ordering. The algorithm described above could be modified to provide such a guarantee by using a safe *CausalSend* in place of the standard *CausalSend*. But such a change will make the protocol dramatically slower, because each *UP-DATE* will now be delayed until at least a majority of the group members acknowledge receipt of the update message. Thus, although the algorithm would continue to perform *READ* operations from local replicas, *UPDATE* operations will now be subject to the same performance limits as for a quorum update. The advantage of this scheme over a quorum scheme would be much reduced.

In the author's experience, strong durability is rarely needed. If an application is about to take an externally visible action and it is important that in the event of a failure the other replicas of the application be in a consistent state with that of the application taking the action, this guarantee becomes important. In such cases, it can be useful to have a way to *flush* communication within the group, so that any prior asynchronous multicasts are forced out of the communication channels and delivered to their destinations. A *CausalSend* followed by a *flush* is thus the equivalent of a *safe CausalSend* (stronger, really, since the *flush* will flush all prior *CausalSends*, while a safe *CausalSend* might not provide this guarantee). Many process group systems, including Horus and Ensemble, adopt this approach rather than one based on a *safe CausalSend*. The application developer is unlikely to use *flush* very frequently—hence, the average performance may approximate that of our fully asynchronous algorithm, with occasional short delays when a *flush* pushes a few messages through the channels to their destinations. Unless large backlogs develop within the system, long delays are unlikely to occur. Thus, such a compromise can be very reasonable from the perspective of the application designer.

By way of analogy, many system developers are familiar with the behavior of operating systems that buffer disk I/O. In such settings, to increase performance, it is common to permit the application to continue operation as soon as a disk write is reflected in the cache contents—without waiting for the data to be flushed to the disk itself. When a stronger guarantee is required, the application explicitly requests that the disk buffer be flushed by invoking an appropriate primitive, such as the UNIX *fsync* system call. The situation created by the asynchronous *CausalSend* is entirely analogous, and the role of the *flush* primitive is precisely the same as that of *fsync*.

What about a comparison with the closely synchronous algorithm from which ours was derived? Interestingly, the story here is not so clear. Suppose that we adopt the same approach to the strong durability issue, by using a *flush* primitive with this property if required. Now, the performance of the closely synchronous *OrderedSend* algorithm will depend entirely on the way *OrderedSend* is implemented. In particular, one could implement *OrderedSend* using the *CausalSend*-based lock and update scheme described in this section or using a rotating token (with very similar results). Indeed, if the lock (token) never moves unless the holder fails, we can use *Send* to implement the desired primitive.

Such an *OrderedSend* solution would push the logic of our algorithm into the communication primitive itself. In principle, performance could converge to that of an algorithm using *CausalSend* explicitly—this level of performance has been achieved in experiments with the Horus system. The major issues is that to use the approach just outlined, one needs to use an *OrderedSend* algorithm well matched to the communication pattern of the user, and this is not always possible: Many developers lack information at design time that would be required to predict such patterns accurately.

14.3.2 State Transfer to a Joining Process

There is often a need to transfer information about the current state of a process group to a joining member at the instant it joins. In a replicated data algorithm, for example, there is clearly a need to transfer a current copy of the data in question to the joining process.

The most appropriate representation of the state of the group, however, will be highly dependent on the application. Some forms of state may be amenable to extreme compression or may be reconstructable from information stored on files or logs using relatively small amounts of information at the time the process joins. Accordingly, we adopt the view that a state transfer should be done by the application itself. Such a transfer is requested at the time of the join. The mechanism looks very much like the creation of a checkpoint file.

The basic idea is to introduce state transfer as a mechanism within the protocol for group flush. At the time a process first requests that it be added to the group, it should signal its intention to solicit state from the members. The associated information is passed in the form a message to the group members and is carried along with the join protocol to be reported with the new group view after the members perform the flush operation.

Each member now faces a choice: It can stop processing new requests at the instant of the flush, or it can make a copy of its state as of the time of the flush for possible future use, in which case it can resume processing. The joining process will solicit state information RPC-style, pulling it from one or more of the prior members. If state information is needed from all members, they can send it without waiting for it to be solicited (Fig. 14.6), although this can create a burst of communication load just at the moment when the flush protocol is still running, with the risk of momentarily overloading some processes or the network. At the other extreme, if a transfer is needed from just a single member, the joining process should transmit an asynchronous multicast, *terminating* the transfer after it has successfully pulled the state from some member. The remaining members can now resume processing requests or discard any information saved for use during the state transfer protocol.

Perhaps the best among these options, if one single approach is desired as a default, is for the joining process to pull state from a single existing member, switching to a second member if a failure disrupts the transfer. The members should save the state in a buffer for later transfer, and should use some form of out-of-band transfer (e.g., over a specially created TCP channel) to avoid sending large state objects over the same channels used for other forms of group communication and request processing. When the transfer is completed, the joining process should send a multicast telling the other members it is safe to delete their saved state copies. This is illustrated in Fig. 14.7.

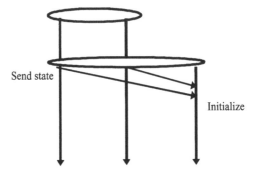

Fig. 14.6 One of several state transfer mechanisms. In this very simple scheme, the group members all send their copies of the state to the joining member and then resume computing. The method may be a good choice if the state is known to be small, since it minimizes delay, is fault tolerant (albeit sending redundant information), and is very easy to implement. If the state may be large, however, the overhead could be substantial

Fig. 14.7 A good state transfer mechanism for cases where the state is of unknown size—the joining member solicits state from some existing member and then tells the group as a whole when it is safe to delete the saved data

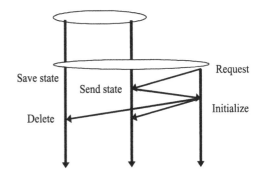

Developers should be wary of one possible problem with this approach to state transfer. In many systems, the group state can be so large that transferring it represents a potentially slow operation—for example, in a file system application, the state transferred to a joining process might need to contain the full contents of every file modified since that process was last operational. Clearly, it would be a terrible idea to shut down the request processing by existing group members during this extended period of time! Clearly, if state becomes large enough so that the system could pause for an unacceptable amount of time while recording it and reloading it at the joining member, both operations need to be forked off as asynchronous tasks that can be performed while still accepting new requests.

Such considerations lead to three broad recommendations. First, if the state is very large, it is advisable to transfer as much of it as possible before initiating the join request. A mechanism can then be implemented by which any last-minute changes are transferred to the joining process—without extended delays. Second, the state transfer should be done asynchronously—in a manner that will not lead to congestion or flow-control problems impeding the normal processing of requests by the service. A service that remains available, but is inaccessible because its communication channels are crammed with data to a joining process may seem very unavailable to other users. Finally, where possible, the approach of jotting down the state is preferable to one that shuts down a server even briefly during the transfer. Again, this reflects a philosophy whereby every effort is made to avoid delaying the response by the server to ongoing requests during the period while the join is still in progress.

14.3.3 Load-Balancing

One of the more common uses of process groups is to implement some form of load-balancing algorithm, whereby the members of a group share the workload presented to them in order to obtain a speedup from parallelism. It is no exaggeration to say that parallelism of this sort may represent the most important single property of process group computing systems: The opportunity to gain performance while also obtaining fault-tolerant benefits on relatively inexpensive cluster-style computing platforms is one of the main reasons that developers turn to such architectures.

There are several broad styles of load-balancing algorithms. The first style involves multicasting the client's request to the full membership of the group; the decision as to how the request should be processed is left for the group members to resolve. This approach has the advantage of requiring little trust in the client, but the disadvantage of communicating the full request (which may involve a large amount of data) to more processes than really need to see this information. In the second style, the client either makes a choice among the group members or is assigned a preferred group member to which its requests are issued. Here, some degree of trust in the behavior of the clients is accepted in order to reduce the communication load on the system. In this second style, the client may also need to implement a *fail-over policy* by which it reissues a request if the server to which it was originally issued turns out to be faulty or fails while processing it. A third style of load-balancing is the replicated load-balancer. Here, the server state is replicated on multiple machines and the client requests are sprayed over them, often randomly. It should perhaps be noted that in commercial practice, this third style is the most common, particularly for Web sites that have unchanging or very slowly changing content, since such content is easy to replicate.

Load-balancing algorithms of the first sort require some form of deterministic rule by which incoming requests can be assigned within the server group. As an example, if incoming requests are issued using an *OrderedSend* protocol, the group can take advantage of the fact that all members see the requests in the same order. The ith request can now be assigned to the server whose rank within the group is i (mod n), or the servers can use some other deterministic algorithm for assigning the incoming work. (See Fig. 14.8.)

If group members periodically send out load reports to one another, also using *OrderedSend*, these load measures can be used to balance work in the following manner. Suppose that the servers in the group measure their load on a simple numeric scale, with 0 representing an unloaded server, 1 representing a server currently

Fig. 14.8 Load-balancing
based on a coordinator
scheme using ranking.
Ideally, the load on the
members will be fairly
balanced

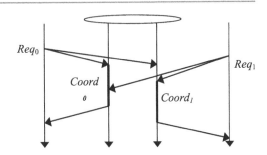

handling a single request, and so forth. The load on a group of n servers now can be
represented as a vector $[l_0, \ldots, l_n]$. Think of these load values as intervals within a
line segment of total length $L = (l_0 + \cdots + l_n)$ and assume that the group members
employ an algorithm for independently but identically generating pseudorandom
numbers—the seed of which is transferred as part of the state passed to a joining
process when it joins the group. Then, as each new request is received, the group
members can independently pick the same random number on the segment $[0, L]$,
assigning the request to the process corresponding to the interval within which that
number falls. Such an approach will tend to equalize load by randomly spreading it
within the group, and it has the benefit of working well even if the load values are
approximate and may be somewhat inaccurate.

The same methods can be used as the basis for client affinity load-balancing
schemes. In these, the group members provide the client with information that it
uses to select the server to which requests will be sent—for example, the group can
statically assign clients to particular members at the time the client first interacts
with the group. Such an approach risks overloading a server whose clients happen
to be unusually active, but it can also be advantageous if caching is a key determinate
of request processing performance, since this server is more likely to benefit from
the use of a caching algorithm. Alternatively, the client can randomly select a server
for each new request within the group membership, or it can use the same load-
balancing scheme outlined above to spread requests over the group membership
using approximate load information, which the members would periodically broadcast to the clients. Any of these methods represents a viable option for distributing
work, and the best choice for a given setting will depend on other information available only to the application designer, such as the likely size of the data associated
with each request, fault-tolerant considerations (discussed in the next section), or
issues such as the balance between queries (which can often be load-balanced) and
update requests (which generally cannot).

14.3.4 Primary-Backup Fault Tolerance

Earlier, we illustrated the concept of primary-backup fault tolerance, in which a pair
of servers are used to implement a critical service. Virtually synchronous process
groups offer a good setting within which such an approach can be used (see Budhiraja et al. 1993).

Primary-backup fault tolerance is most easily understood if one assumes that the application is completely deterministic—that is, the behavior of the server program will be completely determined by the order of inputs to it and is therefore reproducible by simply replaying the same inputs in the same order to a second copy. Under this assumption, a backup server can track the actions of a primary server by simply arranging that a totally ordered broadcast be used to transmit incoming requests to the primary-backup group. The client processes should be designed to detect and ignore duplicate replies to requests (by numbering requests and including the number in the reply). The primary server can simply compute results for incoming requests and reply normally, periodically informing the backup of the most recent replies known to have been received safely. The backup mimics the primary, buffering replies and garbage collecting them when such a status message is received. If the primary fails, the backup resends any replies in its buffer.

Most primary-backup schemes employ some form of checkpoint method to launch a new replica if the primary process actually does fail. At some convenient point soon after the failure, the backup turned primary makes a checkpoint of its state, and simultaneously launches a new backup process.[3] The new process loads its initial state from the checkpoint and joins a process group with the primary. State transfer can also be used to initialize the backup, but this is often harder to implement because many primary-backup schemes must operate with old code, which is not amenable to change and in which the most appropriate form of state is hard to identify. Fortunately, it is just this class of server that is most likely to support a checkpoint mechanism.

The same approach can be extended to work with nondeterministic primary servers, but doing so is potentially much harder. The basic idea is to find a way to *trace* (keep a record of) the nondeterministic actions of the primary, so that the backup can be forced to repeat those actions in a trace-driven mode—for example, suppose that the only nondeterministic action taken by the primary is to request the time of day from the operating system. This system call can be modified to record the value so obtained, sending it in a message to the backup. If the backup pauses each time it encounters a time-of-day system call, it will either see a copy of the value used by the primary (in which case it should use that value and ignore the value of its local clock), or it will see the primary fail (in which case it takes over as primary and begins to run off its local clock). Unfortunately, there can be a great many sources of nondeterminism in a typical program, and some will be very hard to deal with: lightweight thread scheduling, delivery of interrupts, shared memory algorithms, I/O ready notifications through system calls such as "select," and so forth. Moreover, it is easily seen that to operate a primary-backup scheme efficiently, the incoming requests, the corresponding replies, and these internal trace messages will need to be transmitted as asynchronously as possible, while respecting causality.

---

[3]Interested readers may also want to read about log-based recovery techniques, which we do not cover in this book because these techniques have not been applied in many real systems. Alvisi gives a very general log-based recovery algorithm and reviews other work in the area in his Ph.D. dissertation and in a paper with Marzullo.

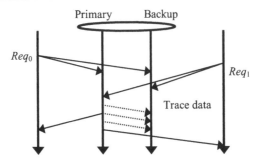

Fig. 14.9 Primary-backup scheme for nondeterministic servers requires that trace information reach the backup. The fundamental requirement is a causal gap-freedom property: If a reply or some other visible consequence of a primary's actions is visible to a client or the outside world, all causally prior inputs to the primary, as well as trace information, must also be delivered to the backup. The trace data contain information about how nondeterministic actions were performed in the primary. The ordering obligation is ultimately a fairly weak one, and the primary could run far ahead of the backup, giving good performance and masking the costs of replication for fault tolerance. The complexity of the scheme is fairly high, because it can be hard to generate and use trace information—hence, it is rare to see primary-backup fault tolerance in nondeterministic applications

(See Fig. 14.9.) Our causal ordering algorithms were oriented towards group multicast, and this particular case would demand nontrivial analysis and optimization. Thus, in practice, primary-backup replication can be very hard to implement when using arbitrary servers.

Another drawback to the approach is that it may fail to overcome software bugs. As we can see, primary-backup replication is primarily appealing for deterministic applications. But these are just the ones in which Heisenbugs would be carefully repeated by a primary-backup solution, unless the fact of starting the backup from a state checkpoint introduces some degree of tolerance to this class of failures. Thus, the approach is likely to be exposed to correlated failures of the primary and backup in the case where it can be most readily applied.

14.3.5 Coordinator-Cohort Fault Tolerance

The coordinator-cohort approach to fault tolerance generalizes the primary-backup approach in ways that can help overcome the limitations previously mentioned. In this fault-tolerant method, the work of handling requests is shared by the group members. (The same load-sharing mechanisms discussed previously are used to balance the load.) The handler for a given request is said to be the *coordinator* for processing that request and is responsible for sending any updates or necessary trace information to the other members, which are termed the *cohorts* for that request. As in the primary-backup scheme, if the coordinator fails, one of the cohorts takes over.

Unlike the primary-backup method, there may be many coordinators active in the same group for many different requests. Moreover, the trace information in a primary backup scheme normally contains the information needed for the backup

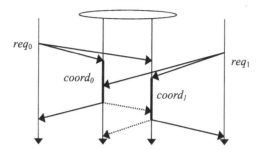

Fig. 14.10 Coordinator-cohort scheme. The work of handling requests is divided among the processes in the group. Notice that as each coordinator replies, it also (atomically) informs the other group members that it has terminated. This permits them to garbage collect information about pending requests that other group members are handling. In the scheme, each process group member is active handling some requests while passively acting as backup for other members on other requests. The approach is best suited well for deterministic applications, but it can also be adapted to nondeterministic ones

to duplicate the actions of the primary, whereas the trace data of a coordinator-cohort scheme will often consist of a log of updates the coordinator applied to the group state. In this approach, the cohorts do not actively replicate the actions of the coordinator, but merely update their states to reflect its updates. Locking must be used for concurrency control. In addition, the coordinator will normally send some form of copy of the reply to its cohorts, so that they can garbage collect information associated with the pending requests for which they are backups. The approach is illustrated in Fig. 14.10.

Some practical cautions limit the flexibility of this style of load-balanced and fault-tolerant computing (which is quite popular among users of systems such as the Isis Toolkit and Horus, we should add!). First, it is important that the coordinator selection algorithm do a good job of load-balancing, or some single group member may become overloaded with the lion's share of the requests. In addition to this, the method can be very complex for requests that involve nontrivial updates to the group state or that involve nondeterministic processing that the cohort may be expected to reproduce. In such cases, it can be necessary to use an atomic protocol for sending the reply to the requesting client and the trace information or termination information to the cohorts. Isis implements a protocol for this purpose: It is atomic and can send to the members of a group plus one additional member. However, such protocols are not common in most systems for reliable distributed computing. Given appropriate protocol support, however, and a reasonably simple server (e.g., one processing requests that are primarily queries that do not change the server state), the approach can be highly successful, offering scalable parallelism and fault-tolerance for the same price.

14.3.6 Applying Virtual Synchrony in the Cloud

One of the most exciting application areas for virtual synchrony concerns data replication within cloud settings. Here, though, we face a challenge not really discussed in this or the previous two chapters: can virtual synchrony scale?

To answer such a question, it makes sense to first think about precisely how one might want to leverage the virtual synchrony model in a cloud environment. Below are a few examples among many that we could offer. Before discussing them, however, it may be helpful to quickly recap a topic we covered in the introduction, namely the distinction between tiers within typical cloud systems, and the way that each tier's deployment model shapes the design of services for that tier.

As you will recall from Chaps. 2–6, and illustrated in Fig. 1.4, most cloud computing systems have a first tier of services that face the clients and are intended to be extremely responsive: upon receiving a request, they should ideally reply based on purely local data and without obtaining any form of locks or delaying in any way to coordinate with other replicas. These first-tier services are typically limited to soft-state: data that can be discarded if the service instance shuts down. A new instance starts in a clean state even if the node where it runs used to host an instance of the service.

Examples of soft-state include cached data that might be extracted from inner hard-state services such as databases or index files, transient information built up as the application executes such as load-balancing data, configuration data that tells this service instance what role to play right now, but that will not be relevant if the service instance shuts down (e.g. because any new instance would be given new roles), etc. A new generation of cloud-hosted systems for monitoring large collections of devices (such as sensors embedded into the environment), and use that data to control large numbers of actuators falls into this soft-state class: while they may maintain some form of audit trail for later use, such systems would often lack the capacity to log every event that occurs, and for many such applications, the fine-grained data isn't saved for offline analysis.

Examples of hard-state include a user's credit card transactions: we want the hard state to be durable and if a machine crashes and later restarts, its copy of a hard-state service should still be intact and correct up to the point when it crashed. Ideally, it would just obtain the delta between that state and the one currently in use in the system and then could resume normal operations by applying the delta.

As we saw in those early chapters, first-tier services would often consist of a web page of some kind (for example, in Microsoft's platform this might be a .ASP page, short for *Application Service Page*) bound to some kind of logic that could be a script written in a language like Javascript or Silverlight, or could be a true soft-state program. The code translates between requests originating in the client and the services within the cloud. Soft-state services are intended to be highly elastic: if a cloud platform wants to run a few thousand more instances, it just spins them up in whatever state is considered to be their initial runtime conditions, providing a small amount of configuration data through configuration services (registries). Since there is no runtime-specific initial data, the needed executables can be "predeployed" so that they are ready to launch on a moments notice and can literally transition from being idle to being fully active in milliseconds. Too many instances? The cloud platform will just shut down the unwanted ones, with no fuss (and no warning). Some degree of control is provided so that the service layer can inform the routing layer of its preferences, but that is about the extent of the configurability available.

In contrast, hard-state cloud services tend to be installed on long-running virtual partitions that have durable data associated with them. Such services are much closer to what we might think of when we visualize a large parallel Oracle deployment with a bank of machines each running a high-end database product and performing tens of thousands of transactions per second. Strong properties like snapshot isolation are common (a weak form of ACID in which reads see a virtual instant in time (the snapshot) but do not ever delay updates, while updates are ordered with respect to one-another in traditional ACID style); some services support a full ACID transactional model. Other services might have weaker models, such as the key-value stores we discussed in the early chapters (Dynamo, memcached, BigTable), but would still be viewed as hard-state services because of their long lifetimes and use of durable state.

Finally, we saw that the back-end systems in the cloud are more typical of modern kinds of batch processing system. They run applications like MapReduce or Hadoop, are hosted on massive clusters of machines and huge data sets, and often compute by crunching data for hours at a time to produce index files that can be pushed up to the first-tier so that those services can achieve their response goals.

What replication issues arise? In the first tier, we see a need for replication and consistency guarantees can be important, even though the data in question are soft state. True, we will discard any replicas that are bound to a service instance we shut down, or that crashes, but this does not mean that consistency isn't needed. Indeed, one can anticipate that many kinds of high-assurance services will be hosted mostly or even entirely in the first tier, and performing a gamut of active mission-critical tasks, in settings as sensitive as health care, operating the smart power grid, or doing or air traffic control. Consistency for such uses entails giving the right answer and is not necessarily a function of data durability. After all, will we really care which machine was controlling such and such a traffic light yesterday? Yet we might care very much that the role be owned by one machine, and that it use the correct data to decide the traffic cycle it will use.

Thus first-tier services would use replication to share control state, coherently cached data, or even active state, among counterparts. This might happen within an entire first-tier service entity, or it could occur within shards: key-value data in which each key maps to some small subset of replicas (typically three), which own the associated data item. In a database, each shard might own a separate set of rows. The database consists of the full set of rows, but no machine holds the whole thing. This pattern is very common, and notice that again, we see a need for replication.

Many kinds of inner-tier services need consistency to an even greater degree. For these services, where ACID or snapshot isolation guarantees dominate, we would often place a multicast group "in front" of a set of replicas, sending updates through the group and into the replicas. Here the challenge we face is that durability for the multicast might not be the same thing as durability for the update.

To understand this, it may be useful to appreciate that when Lamport defined Paxos, he assumed that the acceptor group for a Paxos implementation actually *is* the database, and that the database in question is managed using quorum reads and updates, as we have discussed earlier. Then he defined the learners to be an additional set of machines that monitor the acceptors, for example caching popular database records.

But if we use Paxos as a multicast protocol, this distinction does not make sense, because neither the acceptors nor the learners are the true database. More likely, the developer has replicated the database to run with one replica each on some set of nodes. Our process group has a *relaying* role: it sits in front of those nodes to pass requests into it a replicated manner, so that each replica will see the same updates in the same order (we can ignore queries for this discussion, because with Paxos or *SafeSend* each individual replica will turn out to be complete and identical, so that there is no need to multicast queries unless we want to perform a parallel read operation).

Returning to our key point, notice that if we were to claim that an update has become durable because the acceptors have logged copies of the corresponding multicast (perhaps on disk, perhaps in memory), that claim simply would not be correct. A multicast, for this particular use case, becomes durable only when the application-level update has been completed. That may happen long after the delivery of the multicast, and if a crash disrupts an update operation, the associated multicast would need to be redelivered—and redelivered again and again, if needed (always in the right order), until it can be successfully completed. Obviously, this model demands some way of filtering duplicate events; we will just have to push that into the list of things that database application needs to support.

If we consider these goals with respect to our earlier presentation of *Safe-Send*, we see that *SafeSend* was actually incomplete. Indeed, if you consult the Isis[2] manual pages for *SafeSend*, you will find an extensive discussion of just this point, culminating in an API (called g.SetDurabilityMethod) used to tell the platform how durability should work for your application. The user can also call g.SetDurabilityThreshold to specify the number of acceptors, which are taken to be the first ϕ members of the group view. In effect, to use *SafeSend* correctly, the user is required to configure the protocol, not just use it out of the box.

Two durability methods are built into Isis[2]: one, the memory logger, is default; in this, if an acceptor has a copy of a message *in memory*, it can acknowledge it, and progress will occur. Clearly, if a group experiences *total failure*, in that sense that all of its members crash and the whole group must restart from a checkpoint, this form of durability will not suffice: our database could end up in a partially updated and hence inconsistent state, at least at some replicas. Yet this behavior does match what many implementations of Paxos, as a pure multicast protocol, offer. The key insight here is that when Paxos is used purely for multicast, the durability obligation of the protocol ends, in some sense, as soon as it has done the upcalls to the application layer, thereby delivering the multicast. What happens in the application is not of interest to the multicast protocol... even if the application were to crash instantly, without even looking at the message, on all n member nodes!

This may not sound much like durability, and indeed, for applications that use *SafeSend* to maintain some form of replicated durable state, memory logging is not a sufficient story. The second option is called the *DiskLogger*. This module maintains ϕ distinct logs, each containing active multicasts: the first ϕ members of the current view each own one of the log files (if the view changes, the ownership will be remapped, hence these need to live in a globally accessible part of the file system).

Multicasts are logged (written into the log file, and then the log file is forced to disk using a disk *fsync* system call), when they first reach an acceptor, but of course at this point we lack ordering data: such a message has a unique identifier (the sender address, view id in which it was sent, and message id, which is just a counter incremented on each send, on a per-sender basis). To this the logger adds an additional id of its own, namely a receive-time logical clock (in the Lamport sense) that represents the sequence number of the message in its own local log: this is the fifth message logged by acceptor 2, this is the sixth, etc. Until the leader running the *SafeSend* protocol receives acknowledgements from all ϕ members, such a message has no ordering in the sense of the true *SafeSend* delivery order. Recall that if the desired level of acknowledgement is not reached, the leader iterates the protocol, requesting additional rounds of voting until finally the protocol succeeds.

Once the leader has acknowledgements from *all* acceptors, it uses the maximum of these logger-id values as the "time at which to deliver this message", appending the sender's address to break ties. Now it releases the message for delivery to the application, using a virtually synchronous *Send*. Receivers keep the committed messages in the same queue, but update their logical clock value and mark them committed, reordering the queue as they update the delivery time. Thus, a committed message could have a non-committed one in front of it (later that non-committed message will also receive a final committed sequence number). This puts messages in a total order, in such a way that it is always safe to deliver committed messages off the front of the pending messages queue. Notice that no message can be delivered unless it is logged in all log files, and that the delivery time can always be recomputed if all copies of the log files can be scanned.

This total-order algorithm was originally proposed by Lamport (1984), and has several nice properties. The important one is this: once a message m receives its final delivery time and reaches the front of the queue (namely, the final value for the logical clock timestamping it), no other message can be committed at an earlier delivery time! Thus it is safe to deliver messages, in committed timestamp order, from the front of the queue. It may be worthwhile for the reader to work out a small example or two to see how elegantly this works, and why. In our use, which resembles a Paxos protocol called *vertical Paxos* (Lamport et al. 2009a) it has the additional nice property that by inspection of the full set of logs a process can always reconstruct the state of the system. In fact this means that *DiskLogger* does not actually need to update the disk copy of the file, even though the commit timestamp may not be the version it initially used (perhaps one of the other proposed timestamps was the maximum and hence "won" the competition to determine the commit ordering). If needed, we could always figure this out, again, by scanning the full set of logs.

Thus, while *DiskLogger* did not know the delivery order when it first logged the message, when a message becomes committed for delivery to the application, it finally learns the committed order that was used. Up goes the message to the application, but recall from above that mere handoff to the application does not make the message durable! To achieve that form of strong application-specific durability the application may work hard for a fairly long time. Thus the *DiskLogger* awaits a downcall to *DiskLogger.Done*, allowing it to accurately sense the point when the update has finished—be that milliseconds after delivery, or twenty minutes later when a long-running Oracle update operation may finally finish. Until that "done" point is reached for every replica, the multicast is considered to still be active within the group.

Last, we have the question of failure handling. A new view will become defined, and the role of being acceptor will be remapped; current acceptors may need to close the log file they were responsible for, and to open a different one (this would happen if their ranks in the view changed: for example, the process previously functioning as acceptor number 2 and hence responsible for the second log file were now to become acceptor number 1, responsible for the first log file; the log files have distinct names, hence that acceptor would need to close the former file, then open the latter one). Meanwhile, newly assigned acceptors must open and load the log file that was previously owned and written by their predecessors. Because of the failure, some attempted *SafeSend* protocols might fail to receive ϕ acknowledgments. Those will be retried in the new view. Notice that a resent message may be present in some or even all logs but because the message identifier is constant (the sender, viewid and message id used by the sender), the duplicates are always identifiable.

We should emphasize that with less than ϕ members, the restart blocks. This style of group simply cannot do anything unless it has at least ϕ members and requires that each of the ϕ have access to the log file used by the previous acceptor with the same rank that it has now. Thus loss of a log file leaves our group wedged. (Lamport's quorum-style logging, discussed earlier, would overcome this limitation, but the Isis^2 protocol is simpler and faster and the price of speed is this slight loss of resiliency.)

Upon taking over as the new leader (the rank-0 acceptor) a process reruns the *SafeSend* protocol for any messages it finds in its log. Participants check for duplicates and use the same response as they did the first time, if a message is already known to them. Thus, if a *SafeSend* was in progress we complete it. The delivery happens, in the correct order, a second time (from the perspective of the application layer updates 1, 2, ..., 10 might be delivered, then a glitch occurs and the group repeats the delivery of 7, 8, 9, 10, but then it resumes with new messages: we can get duplicates, but every message is delivered at least once, and in the same order each time if a delivery is repeated).

The upshot of this is that after a crash, DiskLogger is able to replay, in a correct order, any pending multicasts. But to reach that guarantee, the logger pays a substantial cost, both in normal operation (where we need to incur the overhead of disk I/O (with file syncs) during the first phase), and later on recovery, when duplicates will often be presented to the application. These costs are inevitable given the split of functionality.

What about garbage collection? Here, we use a slightly awkward multiphase protocol. Once a message is *Done* at all group members, it becomes legal to garbage collect it, but care must be taken because once we delete a message from the *DiskLogger* logs, the retransmission scheme outlined above could malfunction, treating the message as new and assigning new logical timestamp values in those logs. It would then be redelivered but in a potentially different order.

Accordingly, the rank-0 member periodically runs a protocol that first queries the log states of the full set of acceptors. Perhaps in this manner it learns that message x is safe to garbage collect. It now runs a second phase protocol in which all members update their log files, marking the disk-copy of x as garbage, but retaining the identification data so that if x were ever to show up again, the participant can respond with the old timestamp information (*DiskLogger* handles this by just writing a separate message to the end of the log indicating that x, earlier in the log, is garbage; this is cheaper than actually rewriting the whole log, which may be large). Finally, in a third phase, the leader says "garbage collect x" and the log file can be replaced, atomically, with a version in which x has been removed. Ideally, the live part of the log will be so small compared to the full log that we will be replacing a huge file with a small one and the cost will be very low. The file system itself has an atomic replace operation that can be used for this.

Now we go back and revise the logic of the replay step: after failure, a new rank-0 acceptor replays only the messages that are not marked as garbage in its log. We also need to revise the garbage collection step: a member should include information about known garbage in its response on the first phase. This way, if the leader's file was garbage-collected (hence lacks x entirely), but some member has an old copy of x (marked as garbage but still in the log), the leader can include x into its third phase garbage collection message.

While *SafeSend* with a *DiskLogger* may not be a trivial protocol, we would argue that by combining virtual synchrony with Paxos in this way we have gained important benefits. One is that applications never need to read a quorum of copies: a read quorum is just a single replica of the application database, because in this scheme, if a failure occurs, the group simply reconfigures to drop the faulty member and possibly to reassign the role to some other member. A quorum write must reach every member: first, every acceptor, and then, every copy of the database; some application logic will be needed to handle this last aspect if a copy might lack a group representative for a period of time because of a failure. For example, imagine a group with 100 replicas of a database and just 3 acceptors. If the group drops to have 90 active members for a few minutes, the other 10 replicas will fall behind: they will be correct up to some point, but then will lack a series of updates, and because they are not members of the acceptor subset, *SafeSend* will not worry about replay of those missing messages to these particular replicas. Thus state transfer will need to resync the replicas: on recover, they will need to inform some group member that they have the state up to update 1234, and it should respond with updates 1235–5432, even as 5433 and subsequent updates are delivered by the communication layer. Complicated? Perhaps, a bit. But this is the price of strong durability and one of the reasons that the CAP community is convinced that strong consistency and durability, jointly, are just not adequately scalable!

With all of this context, we can finally summarize some of the opportunities for using virtual synchrony in cloud settings:

1. *Amnesia-tolerant soft-state replication using virtually synchronous ordered multicast in first-tier (soft-state) cloud services.* As we have seen, first tier services are designed to be massively replicated and must support elasticity: the degree of replication can change dramatically and without notice. To this end, most cloud platforms require that such services either be entirely stateless (e.g. the first-tier servers, when launched, have some standard initial state that can be wrapped into a virtual machine), or use only soft-state such as caches, data that can be collected while active but discarded without risk such as load-balancing information, etc.

Many cloud platforms urge the developer to use the BASE methodology when designing these soft-state services, citing the CAP theorem. The argument is fairly simple: CAP suggests that we probably cannot have consistency here anyhow, at least of the ACID database kind, hence some form of convergent model based on gossip or other eventual consistency mechanisms may represent the best tradeoff.

But virtual synchrony creates a new option. As we have seen, virtual synchrony has several levels of data durability. The basic *Send* (as well as the *CausalSend* or *OrderedSend* primitives) offers predictable ordering and synchronization with respect to group membership changes, but no durability at all. On the other hand, the developer can call *Flush* prior to interacting with an external client, in which case the computation will pause briefly until any unstable multicasts have stabilized (become permanent). Let us call this mixture of a non-durable multicast with *Flush* a guarantee of *amnesia-freedom*: once the service replies to the client, it would only forget the updates it performed in the event of some kind of total failure in which all its representatives crash simultaneously. In a modern cloud system with well-debugged and tested software, we can essentially eliminate that risk: elasticity tells us that individual replicas might come and go suddenly, but even an elastic service will still remain continually available (often we think of elastic services as if their membership can change arbitrarily, but a more typical situation would be one in which replication varies from 1000 replicas to 10,000 without ever dropping below 1000).

Thus we have two weak consistency options that might be compatible with soft-state replication in tier-one services: a completely non-durable but consistent option that could be used to share data among replicas with strong consistency but at the risk of amnesia if an update is launched but the associated server crashes immediately, and a second amnesia-free option in which we use the non-durable but consistent style of replication up to the point of interacting with an external user, but at that point first call *Flush*, as we saw early in this text in Fig. 1.7.

Amnesia-freedom may seem to be a fairly weak form of durability, in the following sense. Imagine that some update X is issued to a set of replicas. P receives X and does the update. But now a crash wipes out P and also causes the sender of X to crash, and perhaps this happens in such a way that no other group member ever saw X. X basically has been erased from the memory of the system.

Amnesia-freedom does not preclude such a sequence of events, but instead hides it: if the sender of X issued that weakly durable multicast, before replying to the external user, it would be required to call *Flush*. That call will be blocked (after all, our message has not yet reached the rest of the group). Thus X happened at P, but P has now crashed, and from the perspective of the client, the request has not completed. In fact, whichever server representative the client was talking to will time out since, in our scenario, it crashes before the *Flush* completes.

Strong durability requires that we perform updates using a substantially slower protocol, but would prevent this from happening: we would gain the guarantee that if any process delivers X (as P did), then every process also does so. Thus we will not need to do the *Flush* operation, because it will not do anything useful: once the request is delivered to any group member (and presumably we will not know what reply to send the client until at least some group member sees the request, so we will be waiting for that point to be reached), it also will reach every other group member.

Yet the interesting insight is that strong durability is pointless here. We have defined our scenario in the context of a soft-state service running in the first tier of the cloud. P crashed, and even if it were to restart on the identical node, *by definition* it restarts in a clean state. P will have no idea whether or not X was delivered and processed prior to the crash. The state updated by X would have been temporary state: used while P is up, but discarded (reconstructed from a state transfer, or by querying tier-two services) on recovery!

From this we see that while one could use *SafeSend* (Paxos) in a first-tier service, that primitive would work hard to achieve a property that, by definition, simply is not needed in soft-state services. The core strength of *SafeSend* is that every single update promises that if any replica delivers and processes an update request, then even if it crashes immediately, when it recovers *and compares its saved state with the state of other replicas*, the durable state will match the durable state of those other replicas up to the moment of the crash. This is a valuable property in a system with massive amounts of data to store but soft-state services just do not work that way, because the platform always automatically discards any local data when closing a server instance down, and every server restarts in a fresh state even if running on a node where it had previously been running and might even have been using substantial soft-state data files and other objects. In a soft-state service, the only way to recover the active state of the service is to ask some other active replica for a copy: to perform a *state transfer*. As we have just seen, that option is built into the virtual synchrony model.

Thus amnesia-freedom is as strong a guarantee of durability as one could "need" in a tier-one cloud application. This is important because whereas strongly durable protocols are typically fairly slow and may not scale very well, amnesia-free virtual synchrony is an outstanding performer and fully compatible with the performance requirements of the first-tier. For example, suppose that our service is designed to host some large number of data records, one per customer of a company. Thus there might be hundreds of millions of records. We can make the rule that from the customer-id and the group view, each record has an assigned *primary update source*, using any kind of simple hashing rule (for example, take the customer-id modulo the number of members in the view, and then assign the member with that index as the primary update source. We will route update requests to the update source and it will use *Send* to propagate the update within the replica set: this can be as cheap as a single IP multicast, if IP multicast is available; if not, a tunneled multicast that runs over some sort of point-to-point protocol like TCP will not be much slower (Isis[2] offers both options). Since updates come from only one source in any particular group view, FIFO ordering suffices: if two updates show up in inconsistent orders, they will always turn out to be updates associated with different customers and hence non-conflicting.

As for the degree of replication, this will depend upon the degree to which read-only requests are expected. For many purposes, just as we mapped the customer to a single primary update owner, we would want to map to a small number of additional read-only replicas. Thus, in a group with perhaps 10,000 members the pattern could be one in which we see perhaps 10,000 subgroups of 3 or 5 members each, with each subgroup replicating data associated with some owner, and hosting data for some subset of the customer database. Much less common would be a pattern in which all 10,000 group members host a read-only copy of all the data, but one can certainly imagine cases in which that would be desired. For the former case, read-only requests would be sprayed by a load-balancer over the appropriate subgroup of 3 to 5 members, determined by that simple hashing rule from the customer ID and the current view. For the latter, read-only requests could be sent to any member of the entire group.

Obviously, if we do just one call to *Send* and then immediately call *Flush*, this approach will not be all that fast in comparison to *SafeSend* with a small number of acceptor processes (in Isis[2], many applications run with three acceptors, irrespective of the number of group members (learners)). But if our application lends itself to parallelism, we might see a burst of concurrent *Send* operations, followed by a single *Flush* prior to the response being sent to the client that initiated the update. This will win because that single flush protocol will have its cost amortized over the burst of prior *Sends*. Moreover, the *Send* implementation will often be able to combine acknowledgements so that the stabilization step for a set of concurrent multicasts can be quite a bit cheaper than it would be had we performed stabilization on a one-by-one basis.

The actual work of computing answers to client queries will be low in this scheme. A read-only query can be performed by just reading local data at any copy that has the customer's information: there is no need for any interaction between the service replica that receives the request and its peers, at all. So this kind of request runs at the speed of that individual application on the associated machine. Hopefully, the customer data will be found in-memory and the response would then be blindingly fast.

For requests that trigger asynchronous updates, we get almost the same story. The work of doing the computation triggered by the request can be done on whichever server replica receives that request. Even the updates can be issued using asynchronous *Send* operations. Only the final *Flush* represents a delay point.

(In practice, if a request triggers multiple suboperations, since we do not want to end up with just some of them completed and others not finished in the event of a failure. we might also want to send some form of *Commit* message, but this can be done using another *Send* right before the *Flush*). Thus the cost of computing the web page or web services response for the client is determined by the local speed of the machine handling the request—in this case, the update owner for the relevant client records—and the only delay associated with replication arises when that single flush protocol occurs at the very end, before sending the reply to the client. We obtain a very fast response and yet amnesia-freedom, all within the first tier of the cloud.

Some updates need to modify durable state. Here the first-tier services would update themselves, then forward the update to whatever second-tier database is used for durable client data. Should the process performing this task crash before it finishes, the same request can be reissued if necessary. Thus a true relaying failure, from the first-tier service to the inner durable service, can only occur if all replicas fail. In a properly configured system this should not be common, but it does represent the only risk that the amnesia-freedom property might be violated.

In comparison with an approach that uses the BASE model, our solution would be expected to have similar overall cost (even BASE needs to somehow propagate updates, eventually). Yet because the replication model provides virtual synchrony, the guarantees offered to the end-user are quite strong in comparison with those of BASE, which has very weak consistency guarantees, and often entails computing a response using stale data. Thus the frequency of "mistakes" visible to the end-user will be an issue when using BASE, but should not arise at all when using virtual synchrony. For the virtual synchrony model, the only risk is that amnesia freedom could be violated if all replicas associated with some client's data shut down simultaneously (for example, if an update carries a poison pill that causes a crash, but does so after the client already has been sent a reply). BASE, in contrast, provides no real guarantees at all: while the "E" stands for "Eventual Consistency", BASE doesn't offer any assurance that eventual consistency will be achieved, or have any single standard way of implementing such a property.

2. *Virtually synchronous data replication in cloud caches.* Another scenario of interest focuses on cloud caching. Here, one has very much the same situation we have just outlined, except that whereas the external client was the source of updates in the case associated with Fig. 1.7, a cache would normally see read-only requests from the first-tier application that uses it, together with updates that propagate "up" from some underlying hard-state service running in an inner tier of the cloud. The analysis of this situation is very similar and we will not repeat it; again, the *Send* primitive should be sufficiently powerful to accomplish our goals. Here there is no risk of amnesia-freedom violations at all, because the update source is itself durable. Should some form of extreme failure occur and knock out all the first-tier service replicas associated with some client, or perhaps even the entire firs-tier service, upon restart it launches a cold (empty)

cache and then reloads cache records, as needed. The durable hard-state service just tracks the current set of cached records, and sends an update using *Send* that either updates a cached record, or invalidates it, as needed.

3. *Virtually synchronous key-value storage or sharded dataset.* We have seen in the early chapters of the text how key-value storage systems such as memcached, Dynamo, BigTable and Beehive play important roles in many cloud settings, particularly in second-tier services (see Fig. 1.4). As noted earlier, the term *sharding* is sometimes used here; it originated in the PNUTS (Cooper et al. 2008) system, where data are managed in database tuples, but each tuple is treated as having an associated key and replicated to a set of nodes (usually 3) selected using that key: a *shard*. Some cloud systems, such as FaceBook, maintain nearly all of their active data in forms of key-value store systems, using a durable logging service purely for recovery after major outages, and running entirely from the key-value service for almost all active purposes, and many Yahoo applications run entirely over PNUTS. Here the situation is actually identical to the two cases just discussed. What virtual synchrony can bring to the table is a new kind of assurance property. Whereas a key-value service such as Dynamo uses the BASE methodology and might sometimes not reflect a recent update for a "long time" (e.g. if the update somehow finds its way to the wrong nodes, which can easily occur, and then a long delay occurs before the eventual consistency reconciliation mechanism discovers and merges the data to the right place), with virtual synchrony this can never happen. Our keys would map to small groups (presumably, using exactly the same idea of hashing from the client-id into the current view to identify some subset of its members). We thus identify the correct members immediately, and then interact with the subgroup using the client-to-group protocols discussed in Chap. 13.

The costs of this approach are difficult to quantify without experiments on real clouds, and these had not yet been undertaken at the time of this writing. In their motivation for Dynamo, Amazon's research team argued that sometimes, finding the correct membership in a cloud system entails delays. Thus Dynamo would enter an inconsistent state primarily in situations where a virtual synchrony system would need to wait, presumably while tracking down the membership of the target subgroup in a larger group undergoing rapid membership changes (churn). On a large scale, membership changes certain occur fairly often, yet because one can often batch them, the pattern is typically one in which at some frequency, a batch of joins occur (the data center launches 150 new instances, for example), or a batch of leaves must be processed. Much less frequently a failure might occur. At Amazon's realistic deployment scale, would these delays really be serious enough to justify accepting inconsistency in order to respond rapidly, rather than waiting for membership to catch up? Only experiments can answer such a question (and before reaching conclusions, the associated platforms might both need some tuning: we would want to know the best-case answer, not an answer based on taking some system that has never been used in this way and doing a few quick runs that quite possibly depend on unrealistic load patterns, or that might be impacted by bugs or unoptimized code paths).

4. *Paxos style durable and strongly consistent data replication, using the virtually synchronous SafeSend in a hard-state cloud service.* For hard state services, such as databases, the world splits broadly into two categories of solutions. In the first category, the hard state service itself handles replication and uses its own methods to optimize update patterns and query workloads. Most professional databases from companies such as Oracle, Microsoft and IBM operate in this manner; true ACID semantics or variations such as snapshot isolation are common here.

The second category consists of hard-state services that were designed to run on just a single node, and that we wish to "wrap" for scalability and fault-tolerance by deploying them on multiple nodes and then delivering replicated updates to the instances by using an ordered reliable multicast as our request transport protocol. Here the need is clearly for a protocol such as *SafeSend*, and indeed one might even want to consider modifying the protocol to make sure that the first phase, in which the acceptors receive messages but only acknowledge them, actually logs those messages to disk, so as to ensure that they can be replayed after a crash and would never be lost under any conditions. Then by delivering the updates in the correct order to all the replicas, one can maintain a replicated, consistent state. In the event that some replica fails and later recovers, version numbers can be used to find the most current version of any data desired (in which case any read must access $f + 1$ replicas, if f might have been down when the update was done). Alternatively, the recovering system can transfer a log of updates that it missed while down, applying those that its local database instance lacks. For systems that have modest update rates and short downtimes, the latter scheme makes more sense; the former one might be more appropriate in hard-state services that face huge loads even after the first-tier does all it can to shield them from the full client-generated data rate.

Notice that while the virtual synchrony guarantees ease some aspects of this problem, the problem as a whole remains complex. Above we reviewed the main challenges when discussing the idea of the DiskLogger durability module in Isis[2], which automates the needed steps; lacking such a package, the task faced by the developer would be a substantial challenge and it would be fairly easy to end up with a solution that performs poorly. But with help from a well-designed package, it should be possible to achieve very high speed replication in this manner: the core protocol, *SafeSend*, performs quite well and scales surprisingly well too, provided that the acceptor set size is bounded and small (see Birman et al. 2012). The performance limiting step turns out to be the logging step, as one might expect, but with small values of ϕ is not intolerably slow. Nonetheless, one can easily see why the CAP community, with its focus on using Paxos for replication, concluded that consistent replication is too slow and not scalable enough for really ambitious scalability within the cloud, a point raised by many (Vogels 2008; Pritchett 2008).

This last point touches upon a further complication. The role of the ϕ acceptors are to ensure the durability of active multicasts, which can occur in various ways. One option is to simply use a sufficiently large number of acceptors to be sure that some will survive any possible failure. Here, if an acceptor set is kept small (perhaps three members), it becomes imperative to know that the acceptors are running on failure-independent nodes. Unfortunately, few cloud systems offer a way to accomplish this today, although perhaps demand for such a feature would lead to it being added to the management platforms on systems like Azure or Google AppEngine.

Lacking any way to know where the acceptors are running, one might be forced to use a large acceptor set: perhaps, some fraction of the group members. But with this change, the *SafeSend* protocol would slow down linearly as the size of the group increases. Notice also that with large acceptor sets, while we can dispense with the need to log updates during the accept stage, we end up displacing the question to the delivery phase of the protocol: if a major crash were to occur at this step, we could end up in a situation in which an update reaches less than a quorum of the group members. Thus recovery from a quorum loss event (a major crash of the majority of the replicas) would require some form of cleanup, potentially quite expensive. This is a common problem in the kinds of product mentioned above; many of them have very slow restarts after major crashes, although most will ride out crashes of individual server nodes without much disruption. Thus, when implementing a durable service, a protocol such as *SafeSend* really must be integrated with the underlying application to actually achieve a meaningful form of safety, and we uncover a spectrum of challenges that are not much easier than those faced by developers of commercial databases and other replicated products! Many of those cost millions of dollars to license in substantial cloud deployment scenarios.

It is interesting to reflect upon this and then reread papers about Paxos or about uses of that system, for example in Google's Chubby service, which uses Paxos to implement a lock service. It quickly becomes clear that the notion of hard failure used in most such papers is divorced from the application that would use the protocol in a way that might not always make sense. Chubby maintains its own hard-state service: a kind of customized variant on what *DiskLogger* is doing. In this sense, a service such as Chubby occupies a space somewhere between what we have called hard state and what we have called soft state! But with Paxos as the front-end to a durable service, as would arise if our locking service was built by using *SafeSend* as a front-end to a second component that actually maintains the lock state, we lose this option and are forced to integrate the acceptor phase of the protocol with whatever it means to ensure durability for an update in the application.

5. *Virtually synchronous parallel search.* Here, we use a virtually synchronous multicast to query a group. Because all the members receive the identical message in the identical group membership view, they are able to use the membership list to subdivide the work of performing the query. Obviously, if we use an ordered multicast, we get the further benefit of knowing that the query arrives in a defined state with respect to other multicasts that use a compatible ordering policy; this additional step, it will often follow that the group members are also in identical states (have consistent data), insofar as they maintain replicas of the group data.

6. *Virtually synchronous security-key management.* These same mechanisms can be used to replicate security keys, a problem first studied by Mike Reiter, and supported in the Isis[2] system via the *g.setSecure* API. Data exchanged by group members can be enciphered so that only a legitimate member in possession of the group key will be able to decipher the contents of messages and process the data. Here virtual synchrony helps us answer the fundamental question: which members should be permitted to have a copy of the key?

7. *Virtual synchrony used to develop new routing services.* A perennial problem of computer networks is that while routing tables are being updated, periods of inconsistency can arise during which routes have black holes (they lead nowhere), or cycles (packets go around and around until their TTLs expire), or might flap (switching rapidly back and forth between options in ways that destabilize applications running over the network). If we use virtual synchrony or a similar protocol suite to update routing tables, we can reduce this risk: one now can think in terms of packets that only move from one routing "epoch" to some other more current epoch, and it is easy to see that many of these routing issues immediately vanish. This topic has been explored by Arvind and Tom Anderson at the University of Washington in a paper they called Consensus Routing; it illustrates just one of many potential opportunities. Additional opportunities exist within the routers themselves: modern routers are implemented using hardware clusters and it makes sense to think about using replication to enhance the availability of routing services (see, for example, Agapi et al. 2011), to share data across router nodes as a way to promote parallelism, to support new kinds of cloud-driven routing option, etc.

14.4 Related Reading

On virtual synchrony (see Birman and van Renesse 1994, 1996; Powell 1996); but see also Birman and Joseph (1987a, 1987b), Birman and van Renesse (1996), Dolev and Malkhi (1996), Schiper and Raynal (1996).

On extended virtual synchrony (see Malkhi 1994); but see also Agarwal (1994), Amir (1995), Keidar and Dolev (2000), Moser et al. (1996). Malkhi new mode (2010)l, integrating virtual synchrony with Paxos is covered in Appendix A. Lamport and Van Renesse have both written papers that seek to make Paxos simple, see Lamport (2001), van Renesse (2011).

Security keys replicated in groups: See Reiter (1996).

On uses of the virtual synchrony model (see Birman and Joseph 1987a; Birman and van Renesse 1994).

On primary-backup schemes (see Budhiraja et al. 1993).

A discussion of other approaches to the same problems can be found in Cristian (1996).

Consistency in Distributed Systems

15

We now tackle the last of the "process group internals" topics that will be covered in this textbook. As mentioned at the start of Chap. 10, a reader focused primarily on high assurance for Web Services does not really need to read the material that follows in any detail. The questions tackled here are a bit esoteric and while they do matter, platforms like Isis^2, Horus, JGroups, Spread and Ensemble address these issues in a simple, standardized manner reflecting a sensible tradeoff between performance and guarantees. If your goal is to just use a group communication tool, it is not necessarily important to understand precisely how that tool was implemented, just as one can use TCP without understanding the details of TCP "slow start" and the so called additive-increase multiplicative-backoff congestion control used in that protocol. On the other hand, we cite TCP as an example of why readers might want to be familiar with this information just the same. If you use TCP in a mission-critical application, the behavior of the protocol might really matter; it can be hard to get good performance without understanding how TCP itself is designed. Sometimes, what you do not know can surprise you, and certainly for those readers building an elaborate or very critical application, understanding exactly how a platform behaves can avoid nasty misunderstandings. In a similar spirit, this chapter seeks to pull together what we learned in Part II into a single synthesized overview.

In the previous chapters, we examined options for implementing replicated data in various group membership models and looked at protocols for ordering conflicting actions under various ordering goals. We then showed how these protocols could be used as the basis of a computational model, virtual synchrony, in which members of distributed process groups see events that occur within those groups in consistent orders and with failure-atomicity guarantees and are consequently able to behave in consistent ways. All that is lacking is a more general synthesis, which we provide in this chapter. Key ideas underlying virtual synchrony are:

- Self-defining system and process group membership, in which processes are excluded from a system, if necessary, to permit continued progress.
- Tools for joining a group, state transfer, communication, and reporting new membership views.

- Depending on the model, a concept of primary component of the system.
- Algorithms that seek to achieve internal (as opposed to strongly durable) consistency.
- Distributed consistency achieved by ordering conflicting replicated events in consistent ways at the processes that observe those events.

The remainder of this chapter reviews these points relative to the alternatives we touched upon in developing our protocols and tools.

15.1 Consistency in the Static and Dynamic Membership Models

In the static model, the system is understood to be the set of places at which processes that act on behalf of the system execute. Here, the system is a relatively fixed collection of resources, which experience dynamic disruptions of communication connectivity, process failures, and restarts. Obviously, a static system may not be static over very long periods of time, but the time scale on which membership changes is understood to be long compared to the time scale at which these other events occur. The protocols for adding new members to the static set or dropping them are treated as being outside of the normal execution model. In cases where the system is symmetric, meaning that any correct execution of the system would also have been correct if the process identifiers were permuted, static systems rely on agreement protocols within which the majority of the statically defined composition of the full system must participate, directly or indirectly. As we have seen, the static model matches well with the Paxos protocol suite, although Paxos does include a way to reconfigure the list of places that are included in the static set (call it "mostly" static, if you wish).

The dynamic model employs a concept of system membership that is self-defined and turns out to be more complex to support but cheaper than the static one. Dynamic systems add and lose members on a very short time scale compared to static ones. In the case where the system is symmetric, the set of processes that must participate in decisions is based on a majority of a dynamically defined group; this is a weaker requirement than for the static model and hence permits progress under conditions when a static system would not make progress. (See Fig. 15.1.)

These points are already significant when one considers what it means to say that a protocol is live in the two settings. However, before focusing on liveness, we review the question of consistency.

Consistency in a static model is typically defined with regard to an external observer, who may be capable of comparing the state and actions of a process that has become partitioned from the other processes in the system with the states and actions of the processes that remained connected. Such an external observer could be a disk that contains a database that will eventually have to be reintegrated and reconciled with other databases maintained by the processes remaining in the connected portion of the system, an external device or physical process with which the system processes interact, or some form of external communication technology that

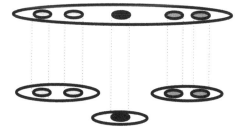

Fig. 15.1 Static and dynamic views of a single set of sites. From a static perspective, the set has fixed membership but changing connectivity and availability properties—for example, the *black nodes* may be available and the *gray ones* treated as not available. Depending upon how such a system is implemented, it may be impossible to perform certain types of operation (notably, updates) unless a majority of the nodes are available. The dynamic perspective treats the system as if it were partitioned into a set of components whose membership is self-defined. Here, the black component might be the primary one and the gray components nonprimary. In contrast to the static approach, the primary component remains available, if primaryness can be deduced within the system. If communication is possible between two components, they are expected to merge their states in this model. Neither perspective is more correct than the other: The most appropriate way to view a system will typically depend upon the application, and different parts of the same application may sometimes require different approaches to membership. However, in the dynamic model, it is frequently important to track one of the components as being primary for the system, restricting certain classes of actions to occur only in this component (or not at all, if the primaryness attribute cannot be tracked after a complex series of failures)

lacks the flexibility of message passing but may still transfer information in some way between system processes.

Consistency in a dynamic system is a more internal concept, although we have seen that the combination of a protocol like the Isis^2 *SafeSend* with a module such as the *DiskLogger* can bridge the gap from the static to the dynamic worlds (at the end of Chap. 14; see also Fig. 15.2). In essence, a dynamic form of consistency requires that processes permitted to interact with one another will never observe contradictions in their states, which are detectable by comparing the contents of messages they exchange. Obviously, process states and the system state evolve through time, but the idea here is that if process p sends a message to process q that in some way reflects state information shared by them, process q should never conclude that the message sent by process p is impossible on the basis of what q itself has seen in regard to this shared state. If the state shared by p and q is a replicated variable, and q has observed that variable to increment only by 2s from 0 to its current value of 40, it would be inconsistent if p sent a message, ostensibly reflecting a past state, in which the variable's value was 7. For q such a state would not merely be stale, it would be impossible, since q believes itself to have seen the identical sequence of events, and the variable never had the value 7 in q's history.

Although this example is unrealistic, it corresponds to more realistic scenarios in which dynamic consistency is precisely what one wants—for example, when a set of processes divides the work of performing some operation using a coordinator-cohort rule, or by exploiting a mutually perceived ranking to partition a database, dynamic

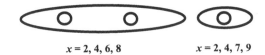

$$x = 2, 4, 6, 8 \qquad\qquad x = 2, 4, 7, 9$$

Fig. 15.2 Strong (sometimes called *interactive*) consistency is the guarantee that the members of a given system component will maintain mutually consistent states (here, by agreeing upon the sequence of values that a variable, x, has taken). If a protocol is not strongly durable, it may allow a process that becomes partitioned from a component of the system to observe events in a way that is inconsistent with the event ordering observed within that component. Thus, in this example, the component on the right (consisting of a single process) observes x to take on the values 7 and 9, while the larger component on the right sees x pass through only even values. By pronouncing at most one of these components to be the primary one for the system, we can impose a sensible interpretation on this scenario. Alternatives are to use strongly durable protocols with external consistency guarantees. Such protocols can be supported both in the dynamic membership model and the static one, where this guarantee is almost always required. However, they are far more costly than protocols that do not provide strong durability

consistency is required for the partitioning to make sense. Dynamic consistency is also what one might desire from the Web proxies and servers that maintain copies of a document: They should agree on the version of the document that is the most current one and provide guarantees to the user that the most current document is returned in response to a request.

The significance of the specific example described above is thus not that applications often care about the past state of a replicated variable, but rather that cooperation or coordination or synchronization in distributed settings all involve cases in which a process, p, may need to reason about the state and actions of some other process, q. When this occurs, p can be understood to be using a form of replicated system state that it believes itself to share with q. Our shared variable has now become the shared concept of the state of a lock or the shared list of members and ranking of members for a process group to which both belong. Inconsistency in these cases means that the system is visibly misbehaving: Two processes both think they have locked the same variable, or each thinks the other holds the lock when neither in fact holds it. Perhaps both processes consider themselves primary for some request, or perhaps neither does. Both may search the first half of a database, each thinking the other is searching the second half. These same issues only get worse if we move to larger numbers of processes.

Of course, as the system evolves through time, it may be that p once held a lock but no longer does. So the issue is not so much one of being continuously consistent, but of seeing mutually consistent and mutually evolving histories of the system state. In effect, if the processes in a system see the same events in the same order, they can remain consistent with one another. This extremely general concept is at the heart of all forms of distributed consistency.

In the purest sense, the dynamic system model is entirely concerned with freedom from detectable inconsistencies in the logically derivable system state. This concept is well defined in part because of the following rule: When a dynamic system considers some process to have failed, communication to that process is permanently severed. Under such a rule, p cannot communicate to q unless both are still within the same component of the possibly partitioned system, and the protocols for dynamic systems operate in a manner that maintains consistency within subsets of processes residing in the same component. The system may allow a process to be inconsistent with the state of the system as a whole, but it does so only when that process is considered to have failed; it will never be allowed to rejoin the system until it has done something to correct its (presumably inconsistent) state.

The ability to take such an action permits dynamic systems to make progress when a static system might have to wait for a disconnected process to reconnect itself or a failed process to be restarted. Thus, a process in the dynamic model can sometimes (often, in fact) make progress while a process in the static model would not be able to do so.

The static model, on the other hand, is in many ways a more intuitive and simpler one than the dynamic one. It is easy to draw an analogy between a static set of resources and a statically defined set of system processes. External consistency constraints, being very strong, are also easy to understand. The dynamic model is in some sense superficially easy to understand, but much harder to fathom upon close study. Suppose we are told that process p is a member of a dynamically defined system component and sets a replicated variable x to 7. In a static system we would have concluded that, since the system guarantees the consistency of this action, p was safe in taking it. In a dynamic system, it may be that it is too early to know if p is a valid member of the system and that setting x to 7 is a safe action in the broader sense. The problem is that future events may cause the system to reconfigure itself in a way that excludes p and leads to an evolution of system state in which x never does take on the value 7. Moreover, the asynchronous nature of communication means that even if in real time p sets x to 7 before being excluded by the other system members as if it were faulty, in the logical system model, p's action occurs *after* it has been excluded from the system.

Where external actions are to be taken, the introduction of time offers us a way to work around this dilemma. Recall our air traffic control example (see Sect. 11.1.5). Provided that p shares a clock with the remainder of the system, it (p) can be warned with adequate time to avoid a situation where two processes ever own the air traffic space at the same time. Of course, this does not eliminate the problem that during the period after it became disconnected and before the remainder of the system took over, p may have initiated actions. We can resolve this issue by acknowledging that it is impossible to improve on the solution and by asking the application program to take an appropriate action. In this specific example, p would warn the air traffic controller that actions taken within the past δ seconds may not have been properly recorded by the main system, and connection to it has now been lost. With a person in the loop, such a solution would seem adequate. In fact, there is little choice, for no system that takes actions at multiple locations can ever be precisely sure of its state if a failure occurs while such an action is underway.

Faced with such seemingly troubling scenarios, one asks why we consider the dynamic model at all. Part of the answer is that the guarantees it offers are almost as strong as those for the static case, and yet it can often make progress when a static solution would be unable to do so. Moreover, the static model sometimes just does not fit a problem. Web proxies, for example, are a very dynamic and unpredictable set: The truth is out there, but a server will not be able to predict in advance just where copies of its documents may end up (imagine the case where one Web proxy obtains a copy of a document from some other Web proxy!). But perhaps the best answer is, as we saw in previous chapters, that the weaker model permits dramatically improved performance, perhaps by a factor of hundreds if our goal is to replicate data.

Both the static and dynamic system models offer a strong form of consistency whereby the state of the system is guaranteed to be consistent and coordinated over large numbers of components. But while taking an action in the static model can require a fairly slow, multiphase protocol, the dynamic system is often able to exploit asynchronous single-phase protocols, such as the non-durable *Send* and *CausalSend* primitives, for similar purposes. It is no exaggeration to say that these asynchronous protocols may result in levels of performance that are hundreds of times superior to those achievable when subjected to static consistency and membership constraints—for example, as was mentioned earlier, the Horus system is able to send nearly 85,000 small multicasts per second to update a variable replicated between two processes. This figure drops to about 50 updates per second when using a quorum-style replication scheme such as the one in the Paxos system, and perhaps 1,500 per second when using an RPC scheme that is disconnected from any concept of consistency. As we have seen, the issue is not the quality of implementation (although Horus is a heavily optimized system), but rather the protocols themselves: these latter systems are limited by the need to receive acknowledgements from what may be very slow participants. The latency improvements can be even larger: In Horus, there are latency differences of as much as three orders of magnitude between typical figures for the dynamic case and typical protocols for taking actions in static, strongly durable manner. Other systems using the dynamic model, for example Ensemble or the Spread toolkit from John Hopkins University, achieve similar performance benefits.

Paxos offers an interesting illustration of this point. Lamport developed Paxos using a series of refinements on a basic protocol that was defined initially for a static membership case. If one goes back and rereads the Paxos papers in historical order, one finds that the earliest paper (The Part-Time Parliament, published in ACM TOCS in 1998, but first released as a technical report around 1990) builds on this very basic version of Paxos. It employed a simple quorum mechanism to achieve strong durability and agreed ordering. That first paper already introduced a series of optimizations aimed at improving performance without breaking the correctness of the original protocol. For example, Lamport proposed a simple form of leader election. This leader-based form of Paxos has an opportunistic feel to it: during periods when Paxos happens to have a single stable leader, Paxos never needs to retry a multicast multiple times. In contrast, with two or more concurrent leaders contending to order distinct multicasts, the protocol might fail to commit any multicast in slot after slot (think about a case in which some set of leaders run in near lock-step, each time getting some acceptors to agree on their proposals, but with none of them ever able to get a quorum: at least one will fail, and perhaps all, forcing them to loop again and again. Thus, a retry is inevitable without a single leader, but would not occur if a single leader issued all proposals). Lamport then generalized Paxos to operate on batches of messages. And only then did Lamport suggest a way to make membership dynamic, using an idea reminiscent of something called a Quorum Ratchet Scheme (the name here is a reference to work by Maurce Herlihy, done in the 1990's on this style of reconfigurable quorum system). Basically, one introduces a second level of quorum mechanism that can inhibit new multicasts and then change the agreed upon membership of the group. In this way Lamport derived the version of Paxos people use today. The fascinating innovation was that he managed to preserve the basic Paxos correctness proof as each of these steps was taken (the Paxos protocol itself, in particularly, was not all that innovative; as noted earlier, it is basically identical to a protocol called Viewstamped Replication introduced by Oki and Liskov, and also to the virtual synchrony group management protocol introduced even earlier in the first versions of the Isis system) (Birman 1985; Herlihy 1986; Oki and Liskov 1988; Lamport 1998).

At the end of Chap. 14, we basically reimplemented Paxos in a virtual synchrony setting, with a group membership service. As we saw, this can be done by combining the in-memory durability of the basic *SafeSend* protocol with a *DiskLogger* that provides durability even across failures that cause the whole group to crash. Moreover, it has the needed interlocking to deal with an external application such as a database that has been replicated on a set of nodes.

In fact the type of thing that this mixture of *SafeSend* and *DiskLogger* accomplishes was considered by Dahlia Malkhi and others in a 2010 paper (Birman et al. 2010), the contents of which have been reproduced as Appendix A in this text. In general, because a virtual synchrony system standardizes and manages membership, one can use virtual synchrony to implement a simplified version of Paxos. The resulting virtually synchronous Paxos protocol (the protocol called *SafeSend* in Isis[2]) gains a number of efficiencies over the dynamic membership versions of Paxos, but as we saw, the precise definition of durability is central to the actual safe use of this protocol: without the *DiskLogger*, *SafeSend* is durable in one sense (if any member delivers a message, all will do so) but not in a different sense (if all members crash, on recover the group has no memory of its past state). The *DiskLogger* overcomes that behavior at some cost and complexity, and yet Malkhi would view all of this as just a question of how one defines durability.

Thus for her work, the key to strong durability really centers on the use of a first phase that logs messages in a manner matched to the durability goal, but does not necessarily need to include every single group member; using an idea of Lamport's, we can run the first phase at a subset of group members (the *acceptors*), then deliver at a potentially larger set (*learners*). For example, in the Isis[2] *SafeSend*, the default is to use 3 acceptors even in a group with 1000 members. The advantages of doing this are twofold.

First, in a standard Paxos implementation, because some members might be faulty when an event occurs, updates are only guaranteed to reach $n - f$ members, where f is a fault threshold (n, of course, is the group size). With virtual synchrony, provided that the amount of group state that would need to be transferred to joining members is reasonably small, we can change the group membership inexpensively each time a failure occurs. Thus there is no need to use a quorum update in this update protocol, making it quite a bit cheaper. One also gains on read-only operations: with standard Paxos, a process must read $f + 1$ or more replicas to be sure of finding at least one replica with the most current updates. With virtually synchronous Paxos, any single replica still belonging to the group is certain to be correct. This makes reads much faster. And there is even a third benefit: with the standard form of dynamic membership for Paxos, there turns out to be some uncertainty about the outcome of pending updates that were underway when the membership was updated. Lamport introduces a parameter, call it α, and builds the protocol in such a way that when the new membership becomes defined (the new view, if you wish), at most α updates initiated in the prior view might still be delivered. But for many purposes, these late updates can be confusing, particularly because they can be delivered *arbitrarily* late. Thus, hours after a membership change, a very old update might suddenly complete (this is a side-effect of the way that future membership changes occur; they can cause an undelivered update to finally achieve the required quorum and become deliverable). With Malkhi's virtual synchronous Paxos, this cannot happen: all pending actions in a given view terminate before the next view is installed.

In practical work with dynamic system models, we typically need to assume that the system is "usually" well-behaved, despite experiencing some infrequent rate of failures. Under such an assumption, the model is easy to work with and makes sense. If a system experiences frequent failures (relative to the time it takes to reconfigure itself or otherwise repair the failures), the static model becomes more and more appealing and the dynamic one less and less predictable. Fortunately, most real systems are built with extremely reliable components, hence experience infrequent failures. This pragmatic consideration explains why dynamically consistent distributed systems have become popular: The model behaves reasonably in real environments, and the performance is superior compared to what can be achieved in the static model.

Indeed, one way to understand the performance advantage of the dynamic model is that by precomputing membership information, the dynamic algorithms represent optimizations of the static algorithms. As one looks closely at the algorithms, they seem more and more similar in a basic way, and perhaps this explains why that should be the case. In effect, the static and dynamic models are very similar, but the static algorithms (such as quorum data replication) are forced to compute the membership information they needed on each operation, while the dynamic ones precompute this information and are built using a much simpler fail-stop model.

Moreover, it is important to realize that the external concept of consistency associated with static models is in some ways much stronger, and consequently more restrictive, than is necessary for realistic applications. This can translate to periods of mandatory unavailability, where a static system model forces us to stop and wait while a dynamic consistency model permits reconfiguration and progress. Many distributed systems contain services of various kinds that have small server states (which can therefore be transferred to a new server when it joins the system) and that are only of interest when they are operational and connected to the system as a whole. Mutual consistency between the servers and the states of the applications using them is all that one needs in such internal uses of a consistency-preserving technology. If a dynamic approach is dramatically faster than a static one, so much the better for the dynamic approach!

These comments should not be taken to suggest that a dynamic system can *always* make progress even when a static one must wait. For example, Chandra, Toueg and Vassilacos established that a result similar to the FLP result holds for group membership protocols (see Chandra et al. 1996)—showing, in effect, that there are conditions under which an asynchronous system can be prevented from reaching consensus upon its own membership and therefore prevented from making progress. Other researchers have pinned down precise conditions (in various models) under which dynamic membership consensus protocols are guaranteed to make progress (see Babaoglu et al. 1995; Friedman et al. 1995; Guerraoui and Schiper 1996; Neiger 1996), and the good news is that for most practical settings the protocols make progress if the probability of failures and message loss is uniform and independent over the processes and messages sent in the system. In effect, only partitioning failures or a very intelligent adversary (one that in practice could never be implemented) can prevent these systems from making progress.

Thus, we know that *all* of these models face conditions under which progress is not possible. As a practical matter, the evidence is that all of these models are perfectly reasonable for building reliable distributed systems. The theoretical impossibility results do not appear to represent practical impediments to implementing reliable distributed software; they simply tell us that it is possible for the system to encounter complex runtime failure conditions that these reliability approaches cannot overcome. The choice, in a practical sense, is to match the performance and consistency properties of the solution to the performance and consistency requirements of the application. The weaker the requirements, the better the performance we can achieve.

Our study also revealed two other issues that deserve comment: the need, or lack thereof, for a *primary component* in a partitioned membership model and the broader but related question of how consistency is tied to ordering properties in distributed environments.

The question of a primary component is readily understood in terms of the air traffic control example we looked at earlier. In that example, there was a need to take authoritative action within a service on behalf of the system as a whole. In effect, a representative of a service needed to be sure that it could safely allow an air traffic control to take a certain action, meaning that it ran no risk of being contradicted by any other process (or, in the case of a possible partitioning failure, that before any other process could start taking potentially conflicting actions, a timeout would elapse and the air traffic controller would be warned that this representative of the service was now out of touch with the primary partition).

In the static system model, there is only a single concept of the system as a whole, and actions are taken upon the authority of the full system membership. Naturally, it can take time to obtain majority acquiescence in an action—hence, this is a model in which some actions may be delayed. However, when an action is actually taken, it is taken on behalf of the full system.

In the dynamic model we lose this guarantee and face the prospect that our concept of consistency can become trivial because of system partitioning failures—a dynamic system could partition arbitrarily, with each component having its own concept of authoritative action. All of this seems to argue that practical systems should limit themselves to supporting a single, primary component. If a partition forms and some process is operating in a non-primary component, an exception should be delivered to the application ("you have become partitioned away from the system"), and the application can deal with this, perhaps by terminating the disconnected process. Progress would be limited to the primary partition.

This is not really all that restrictive an approach. First, partitions are rare in most systems, so the whole issue of continuing execution while partitioned away from the majority of the system should be very rare. We've seen that in the cloud, such partitioning scenarios won't occur at all: if a small group of machines becomes isolated, the cloud would shut them down as soon as possible, then force them to restart in a clean state, thus mapping partitioning faults to failures. Secondly, some form of read-only behavior may suffice. A nonprimary component may, for example, continue to operate a device that it owns, but that may not be reliable for use in instructing an air traffic controller about the status of air space sectors or other global forms of state-sensitive data unless they were updated using strongly durable protocols.

Of course, a dynamic distributed system can lose its primary component, and, making matters still more difficult, there may be patterns of partial communication connectivity within which a dynamic model must block. Suppose, for example, that a system partitions so that all of its members are disconnected from one another. Now we can selectively reenable connections so that over time a majority of a static system membership set are able to vote in favor of an action. Such a pattern of communication could allow progress—for example, there is the protocol of Keidar and Dolev, cited several times previously, in which an action can be terminated entirely on the basis of point-to-point connections. However, as we commented, this protocol delays actions until a majority of the processes in the entire system know about them, which will often take a very long time.

This type of reasoning might not apply in new kinds of system that deviate from the usual behavior seen in a local network. Frequent periods of partitioned operation *could* occur in very mobile situations, such as when units are active on a battlefield. Thus, there are probably systems that should use a static model with partial communications connectivity as their basic model, systems that should use a primary component consistency model, and perhaps still other systems for which a virtual synchrony model that does not track primaryness would suffice. These represent successively higher levels of availability, and even the lowest level retains a meaningful concept of distributed consistency. At the same time, they do provide weaker forms of consistency. This suggests that there are unavoidable tradeoffs in the design of reliable distributed systems for critical applications.

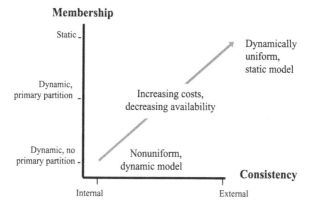

Fig. 15.3 Conceptual options for the distributed systems designer. Even when one seeks consistency, there are choices concerning how strong the consistency desired should be and which membership model to use. The least-costly and highest-availability solution for replicating data, for example, looks only for internal consistency within dynamically defined partitions of a system and does not limit progress to the primary partition. This model, as we have suggested, may be too weak for practical purposes. A slightly less available approach, which maintains the same high level of performance, allows progress only in the primary partition. As one introduces further constraints, such as strong durability or a static system model, costs rise and availability falls, but the system model becomes simpler and simpler to understand. The most costly and restrictive model sacrifices nearly three orders of magnitude of performance in some studies relative to the least-costly one. Within any given model, the degree of ordering required for multicasts introduces further fine-grained cost/benefit tradeoffs

The two-tiered architecture discussed in the previous chapter can be recognized as a response to this impossibility result. Such an approach explicitly trades higher availability for weaker consistency in the LAN subsystems, while favoring strong consistency at the expense of reduced availability in the WAN layer (which might run a protocol based on the Chandra/Toueg consensus algorithm). The LAN level of a system might use nondurable protocols for speed, while the WAN level uses tools and protocols similar to the ones proposed by the Transis effort or by Babaoglu's group in their work on Relacs.

We alluded briefly to the connection between consistency and order. This topic is perhaps an appropriate one on which to end our review of the models. Starting with Lamport's earliest work on distributed computing systems, it was already clear that consistency and the ordering of distributed events are closely linked. Over time, it has become apparent that distributed systems contain what are essentially two forms of knowledge or information. Static knowledge is that information that is well known to all of the processes in the system at the outset—for example, the membership of a static system is a form of static knowledge. Being well known, it can be exploited in a decentralized but consistent manner. Other forms of static knowledge can include knowledge of the protocol that processes use, knowledge that some processes are more important than others, or knowledge that certain classes of events can only occur in certain places within the system as a whole. (See Fig. 15.3.)

Dynamic knowledge is information that stems from unpredicted events occurring within the system—either as a consequence of nondeterminism of the members, failures or event orderings that are determined by external physical processes, or inputs from external users of the system. The events that occur within a distributed system are frequently associated with the need to update the system state in response to dynamic events. To the degree that system state is replicated, or is reflected in the states of multiple system processes, these dynamic updates of the state will need to occur at multiple places. In the work we have presented here, process groups are the places where such state resides, and multicasts are used to update such state.

Viewed from this perspective, it becomes apparent that *consistency is order*, in the sense that the distributed aspects of the system state are entirely defined by process groups and multicasts to those groups, and these abstractions, in turn, are defined entirely in terms of ordering and atomicity. Moreover, to the degree that the system membership is self-defined, as in the dynamic models, atomicity is also an order-based abstraction.

This reasoning leads to the conclusion that the deepest of the properties in a distributed system concerned with consistency may be the ordering in which distributed events are scheduled to occur. As we have seen, there are many ways to order events, but the schemes all depend upon either explicit participation by a majority of the system processes or upon dynamically changing membership, managed by a group membership protocol. These protocols, in turn, depend upon majority action (by a dynamically defined majority). Moreover, when examined closely, all the dynamic protocols depend upon some concept of token or special permission, which enables the process holding that permission to take actions on behalf of the system as a whole. One is strongly inclined to speculate that in this observation lies the grain of a general theory of distributed computing, in which all forms of consistency and all forms of progress could be related to membership and in which dynamic membership could be related to the liveness of token passing or leader election protocols. At the time of this writing, I am not aware of any clear presentation of this theory of all possible behaviors for asynchronous distributed systems, but perhaps it will emerge in the not-too-distant future.

15.2   Practical Options for Coping with Total Failure

The reader who follows the above recommendations will be guided towards a style of system in which replication is used to maintain availability in the primary partition of a system that dynamically tracks its own membership. If a machine becomes partitioned away from the primary group, it will detect this and should probably shut down.

But this recommendation raises an obvious concern. What happens if (after some sort of rare event like a power outage), the network itself shuts down, and as a result all the nodes in the system seem to be isolated from the primary partition? Should they all shut down? And more broadly, how can a system recover after a total failure? Earlier we saw one way of handling this issue, in the context of the *DiskLogger*. But what can be said about the question in the abstract?

To some extent, this problem has been solved by researchers. In a 1985 paper (see Skeen 1985), an algorithm was published for "determining the last process to fail" after a total failure. In this protocol, the processes in a system compare notes and in this way track down the last survivor of the wave of outages. That node restarts first, and the others then join. But in practice, such an approach is unlikely to be satisfactory for several reasons.

The central problem is that in most systems, not all machines are equal. Servers are more important than clients, and if a system includes a mixture (as many do), restarting the system from a client machine is often a nonsensical proposition: one restarts servers. Thus, the "last process to fail" may not be the issue. Furthermore, while an algorithm for picking the last server that failed can be designed, Skeen's solution involves waiting until all the last servers to fail are operational again. In any real-world setting, we may not want to wait so long.

This leads to the following advice. First, if possible, applications partitioned away from the majority should checkpoint their states and then either shut down (as in cloud settings), or sit idle waiting to connect with the primary partition. Thus when the network goes down, any isolated machines stop processing new operations.

There are now two cases. The easy one arises when a server in this state manages to connect to the primary partition. It should just discard the checkpointed state and "rejoin" with a state transfer. The second case arises if there is no primary partition. Here, a less than completely automated solution makes sense. The application should simply ask a human operator for help. That human operator will presumably study the system state, pick the "official" last node to fail, and tell it via command to restart (perhaps from its checkpoint). This reestablishes the primary partition and the others now follow the first rule above.

Not all problems can or should be solved in fully automated ways, and the author has become convinced that handling of severe partitionings or total failure are among them. Fortunately, such situations are infrequent, and as long as there is a simple way to restart the system, most application developers should be satisfied by the resulting mechanism.

15.3 Summary and Conclusion

There has been a great deal of debate over the concepts of consistency and reliability in distributed systems (which are sometimes seen as violating end-to-end principles) and of causal or total ordering (which are sometimes too weak or too strong for the needs of a specific application that does need ordering). See, for example, van Renesse (1993, 1994), Cheriton and Skeen (1993), Birman (1994), Cooper (1994).

Finally, although we have not focused on this here, there is the criticism that technologies such as the ones we have reviewed do not fit with standard styles of distributed systems development.

As to the first concern, the best argument for consistency and reliability is to simply exhibit classes of critical distributed computing systems that will not be sufficiently "assured" unless data are replicated and will not be trustworthy unless the data is replicated consistently. One would not want to conclude that *most* distributed applications need these properties: Today, the ones that do remain a fairly small subset of the total. However, with the advent of Web Services, this subset is poised for rapid growth. Moreover, even if one believed that consistency and reliability are extremely important in a great many applications, one would not want to impose potentially costly communication properties system-wide, especially in applications with very large numbers of overlapping process groups. To do so is to invite poor performance, although there may be specific situations where the enforcement of strong properties within small sets of groups is desirable or necessary.

Turning to the second issue, it is clearly true that different applications have different ordering needs. The best solution to this problem is to offer systems that permit the ordering and consistency properties of a communication primitive or process group to be tailored to their needs. If the designer is concerned about paying the minimum price for the properties an application really requires, such a system can then be configured to only offer the requested properties. Later in the book, will see that the Horus and Ensemble systems adopt this approach, while others (notably Spread) simply adopt an easily understood multicast and focus on making it as fast as possible. Both approaches make sense, and users seem to find both rather easy to use.

Finally, as to the last issue, it is true that we have presented a distributed computing model that, so far, may not seem very closely tied to the software engineering tools normally used to implement distributed systems. In the next chapter we study this practical issue, looking at how group communication tools and virtual synchrony can be applied to real systems that may have been implemented using other technologies.

15.4   Related Reading

On concepts of consistency in distributed systems (see Birman and van Renesse 1994, 1996); in the case of partitionable systems (see Amir 1995; Keidar and Dolev 1995, 2000; Malkhi 1994; Moser et al. 1996). For Malkhi's integration of virtual synchrony with Paxos, see Birman and Joseph (1987a) and Malkhi (1994).

On the causal controversy (see van Renesse 1993).

On the dispute over CATOCS (see Cheriton and Skeen 1993); but see also Birman (1994), Cooper (1994), van Renesse (1994) for responses.

The end-to-end argument was first put forward in Saltzer et al. (1990).

Regarding theoretical work on tradeoffs between consistency and availability (see Babaoglu et al. 1995; Chandra et al. 1996; Fisher et al. 1985a, 1985b; Friedman et al. 1995). The survey of group communication systems in Vitenberg et al. (2001) is considered to be a classic treatment of the topic, looking at a wide range of group multicast models, with a focus on placing them into a standard theoretical framework and on comparing their failure assumptions and guarantees.

Part III
Applications of Reliability Techniques

In this third part of the book, we apply the techniques developed in Part III to real problems seen in a wide variety of systems, including Web Services. The techniques on which we focus are fairly practical and a talented student should not have much trouble employing them in conjunction with a platform such as Spread or Ensemble. We pick problems that are interesting in their own terms, but are also representative of broader classes of issues seen in a wide range of settings and systems, in the hope that the examples developed here might serve as templates for developers working on mission-critical problems in production settings.

In fact at the end of Chap. 14 we see some preliminary ideas along these lines, when asking how one might use virtual synchrony in the first tier services of a cloud system, or as a front-end to a replicated and durable database; we wo will not repeat that material here, although the reader of this chapter should certainly review those options if he or she has not already done so. Particularly important is the discussion of how the Isis[2] *SafeSend* protocol must be used with its *DiskLogger* component if placed in front of a durable database, and even then, an appropriate application-layer state transfer might be needed (would be needed, in fact, if the *SafeSend* parameter ϕ has a value smaller than n). By working out that detailed case we intended both to show how the problem can be solved, but also to make it clear that doing so is not trivial even with a powerful tool at one's disposal! These are just not simple problems to solve, although tools of that kind do make them simpler than they would be without such help.

Retrofitting Reliability into Complex Systems 16

In this chapter, we explore options for presenting group computing tools to the application developer. Two broad approaches are considered: those involving wrappers that encapsulate an existing piece of software in an environment that transparently extends its properties—for example, by introducing fault tolerance through replication or security—and those based upon toolkits that provide explicit procedure-call interfaces. We will not examine specific examples of such systems now, but will instead focus on the advantages and disadvantages of each approach and on their limitations. At the time of this writing, it remains unclear how best to integrate reliability mechanisms with Web Services, although it *is* clear that doing so would be feasible (and also of considerable commercial value).

Down the road, it seems likely that we will see a third and perhaps more prevalent option: platforms that include reliability functionality as an integral component. For example, when doing cloud programming on Microsoft platforms, the developer works with an environment called Azure that integrates with the Visual Studio product, an editing and debugging framework with support for many languages. In Visual Studio, one can literally drag-and-drop complex functionality into an application. To turn a C# application into a Web Services program, in Azure, one basically extends a stylized template that starts by using an ASP.NET template to define a web page or web-services API, then grafts application-specific logic to it. The develop essentially fills in the contents of a kind of dialog box to define this logic, which can be as simple as a script written in a language like SilverLight, or as complex as a full-fledged C# application program. Further dialog boxes allow the user to specify which classes should be exported, and to control such aspects as how the interface will appear in a UDDI-compliant name server. Through a combination of dialog boxes associated with the template and implementation of any application-specific methods, the user is led rather directly to a working Web Services program. A similar approach (a bit less automated) is used by Google's AppEngine; FaceBook and Force.com and Yahoo each offer substantial packages to their users, etc.

Thus one could imagine a path by which industry would embrace the kinds of solutions discussed in this book and even package them to a point where by dragging "replication" onto a Visual Studio application (or doing the analogous action

K.P. Birman, *Guide to Reliable Distributed Systems*, Texts in Computer Science, 473
DOI 10.1007/978-1-4471-2416-0_16, © Springer-Verlag London Limited 2012

in some other development platform, since many share this style of intentional programming), group communication technology, security tools, or other specialized reliability mechanisms could be requested. All that we really need is to see broad demand emerge for such functionality, and this may finally be occurring as the Web Services community begins to roll out an increasingly critical class of applications and to encounter the reliability and availability limitations of the initial Web Services architecture and platform technologies.

16.1   Wrappers and Toolkits

The introduction of reliability technologies into a complex application raises two sorts of issues. One is that many applications contain substantial amounts of preexisting software or make use of off-the-shelf components (the military and government favor the acronym COTS for this), meaning "commercial off the shelf." In these cases, the developer is extremely limited in terms of the ways that the old technology can be modified. A *wrapper* is a technology that overcomes this problem by intercepting events at some interface between the unmodifiable technology and the external environment (see Jones 1993), replacing the original behavior of that interface with an extended behavior, which confers a desired property on the wrapped component, extends the interface itself with new functionality, or otherwise offers a virtualized environment within which the old component executes. Wrapping is a powerful technical option for hardening existing software, although it also has some practical limitations. In this section, we will review a number of approaches to performing the wrapping operation itself, as well as a number of types of intervention that wrappers can enable.

Wrapping is not trivial. Returning to our earlier example, while it may seem natural to wrap a replicated database by just putting a group that uses the durable *SafeSend* in front of the replicas, that solution would not actually be correct. Only by instantiating *SafeSend* with the appropriate durability option (the *DiskLogger*), setting a suitable durability threshold value (ϕ), and then making certain to call the *DiskLogger.Done* API after the application-layer updates complete can we achieve the desired robustness. Moreover, even that was not the whole story: we also needed a fairly elaborate state transfer capable of bringing a replica up to date if it missed a series of updates. Often this will cause the application to maintain a duplicate of the same log files that the *DiskLogger* employs! The point of this chapter, then, is that we need to move towards a day when tools like the Azure/VisualStudio automate enough of these steps to make it easy for a typical developer to understand the sequence and to carry it out (and then to debug and test the resulting system). The steps are far easier than they would be without help, but still daunting for a developer working in today's versions of these kinds of cloud development platform, which entirely lack this sort of support.

On the positive side of the coin, the notion of wrapping as we use it here should not seem unfamiliar; what we lack is really the specific wrappers that might yield reliability and other forms of high assurance. Many developers view Web Services as wrappers, because the Web Services model and interfaces are often used as a gateway between a "new" application and a legacy server to which the Web Services dispatcher has been linked. Unfortunately, however, the notion of wrapping is not currently a first-class part of the Web Services architecture, and wrapping an entire Web Services system is not (yet) a straightforward action. Additionally, because the Web Services request dispatch and routing component often runs on a different computer than does the back-end server, the extra layer between the client and the server can raise availability and reliability issues of its own, for example because it might experience a crash even when the client and server both remain operational; the client would then lose connectivity to the server even though the server is still healthy. As we saw in Part I of the book, the reliability mechanisms of the Web Services architecture focus on this problem but address it in a way that favors a pipelined, very asynchronous style of interaction with the back-end server. High availability for Web Services applications is just not anticipated in the initial architectural designs for the technology.

An alternative to wrapping is to explicitly develop a new application program designed from the outset with the reliability technology in mind—for example, we might set out to build an authentication service for a distributed environment that implements a particular encryption technology and uses replication to avoid denial of service when some of its server processes fail. Such a program would be said to use a *toolkit* style of distributed computing, in which the sorts of algorithms developed in the previous chapter are explicitly invoked to accomplish a desired task. A toolkit approach packages potentially complex mechanisms, such as replicated data with locking, behind easy-to-use interfaces (in the case of replicated data, *LOCK, READ* and *UPDATE* operations). The disadvantage of such an approach is that it can be hard to glue a reliability tool into an arbitrary piece of code, and the tools themselves will often reflect design tradeoffs that limit generality. Thus, toolkits can be very powerful in the hands of a developer with the freedom to use them in the intended manner, and who understands their limitations, but they are also inflexible: They adopt a programming paradigm, and, having done so, it is potentially difficult to use the functionality encapsulated within the toolkit in a setting other than the one envisioned by the tool designer.

Toolkits can also take other forms—for example, one could view a firewall, which filters messages entering and exiting a distributed application, as a tool for enforcing a limited security policy. When one uses this broader interpretation of the term, toolkits include quite a variety of presentations of reliability technologies— even a Web Services system is a toolkit in this very broad sense. In addition to the case of firewalls, a toolkit could package a reliable communication technology as a message bus, a system monitoring and management technology, a fault-tolerant file system or database system, or a wide area name service (Table 16.1). Moreover, one can view a programming language that offers primitives for reliable computing as a form of toolkit.

As we see in Table 16.1, each toolkit would address a set of application-specific problems, presenting an API specialized to the programming language or environment within which the toolkit will be used and to the task at hand. While it is also

Table 16.1 Types of toolkit useful in building or hardening distributed systems

Toolkit	Description
Server replication	Tools and techniques for replicating data to achieve high availability, load-balancing, scalable parallelism, very large memory-mapped caches, and so forth. Cluster APIs for management and exploitation of clusters.
Video server	Technologies for striping video data across multiple servers, isochronous replay, and single replay when multiple clients request the same data.
WAN replication	Technologies for data diffusion among servers that make up a corporate network.
Client groupware	Integration of group conferencing and cooperative work tools into Java agents, TCL/TK, or other GUI builders and client-side applications.
Client reliability	Mechanisms for transparently fault-tolerant RPC to servers, consistent data subscription for sets of clients that monitor the same data source, and so forth.
System management	Tools for instrumenting a distributed system and performing reactive control. Different solutions might be needed when instrumenting the network itself, cluster-style servers, and user-developed applications.
Firewalls and containment tools	Tools for restricting the behavior of an application or for protecting it against a potentially hostile environment-for example, such a toolkit might provide a bank with a way to install a partially trusted client/server application in order to permit its normal operations while preventing unauthorized ones.

possible to develop extremely general toolkits, which seek to address a great variety of possible types of user, doing so can result in a presentation of the technology that is architecturally weak and does not guide users to the best system structure for solving their problems. In contrast, application-oriented toolkits often reflect strong structural assumptions, which are known to result in solutions that perform well and achieve high reliability.

In practice, many real-world distributed applications are so large and so complex that they require a mixture of toolkit solutions and wrappers. To the degree that a system has new functionality, which can be developed with a reliability technology in mind, the designer is afforded a great deal of flexibility and power through the execution model supported (e.g., transactional serializability or virtual synchrony) and may be able to provide sophisticated functionality that would not otherwise be feasible. On the other hand, in any system that reuses large amounts of old code, wrappers can be invaluable by shielding the previously developed functionality from the programming model and assumptions of the toolkit.

16.1.1 Wrapper Technologies

In our usage, a wrapper is any technology that intercepts an existing execution path in a manner transparent to the wrapped application or component. By wrapping a component, the developer is able to virtualize the wrapped interface, introducing an extended version with new functionality or other desirable properties. In particular, wrappers can be used to introduce various robustness mechanisms, such as replication for fault tolerance or message encryption for security. A wrapper may be quite a non-trivial component; the database wrapper of Chap. 14 makes that clear: while its way of dealing with *SafeSend* and the *DiskLogger* is fairly simple (it receives messages and called *DiskLogger.Done* when finished with updates), understanding that *SafeSend* needs to be configured this way, and why, and implementing the needed state transfer code to bring a lagging replica back up to date without discarding its state entirely (the easy way out) will be a challenge. Moreover, for many kinds of application, knowing when they have finished doing an update is not so easy. With disk I/O in an operating system, an update has not occurred until the file has been synced (flushed) to disk. With a database, an update is not final unless the database has done a strong form of update commit. A wrapper, in effect, needs to stick its fingers into the state of the application it wraps, and this may not be trivial to do. But often it is possible, and that leads to the following possible use cases.

Wrapping at Object Interfaces

Object-oriented interfaces are the best example of a wrapping technology (Fig. 16.1), and systems built using CORBA or OLE-2 are, in effect, pre-wrapped in a manner that makes it easy to introduce new technologies or to substitute a hardened implementation of a service for a nonrobust one. Suppose, for example, that a CORBA implementation of a client/server system turns out to be unavailable because the server has crashed. Earlier, when discussing CORBA, we pointed out that the CORBA architectural features in support of dynamic reconfiguration or fail-over are difficult to use. If, however, a CORBA service could be replaced with a process group (object group) implementing the same functionality, the problem becomes trivial. This is the main insight underlying the CORBA Fault Tolerant Objects standard (FTOL), and has been implemented by researchers at UCSD as part of a system they call Eternal. The approach is an older one; technologies such as Orbix+Isis and Electra, described in Chap. 17, also provided this ability; on the other hand, the CORBA standard was the first time that replication was embraced by a major standards body. In effect, the CORBA interface wraps a service in such a manner that any other service providing a compatible interface can be substituted for the original one transparently.

Moreover, the CORBA Fault Tolerance standard has not been widely popular. Early in this book, we alluded to the distinction between a standard, and a widely accepted standard. Simply standardizing a technology does not mean that the technology will ever become widely used, or even that it works well—all it tells us is that some community saw value in sitting down and hammering out a political document expressing their agreement as to the interfaces to the technology, its functionality, and the appropriate patterns of use. Only if the standard is embodied into products that become popular does the term take on real importance. On the other hand, commercial users often reject complex, non-standard technologies. Industry needs standards, even though many proposed standards are quickly abandoned.

In the case of CORBA, users apparently find that the standard, which provides for state-machine replication of active (server) objects and the data they maintain, and requires that the server code be completely deterministic, is overly restrictive.

Fig. 16.1   Object-oriented
interfaces permit the easy
substitution of a reliable
service for a less- reliable
one. They represent a simple
example of a wrapper
technology. However, one can
often wrap a system
component even if it were not
built using object-oriented
tools

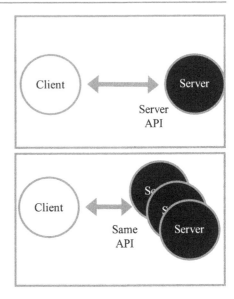

Thus while the associated wrapper technology is extremely simple to use and highly transparent, the "positioning" of this standard seems not to accord with a large market. It seems likely that any Web Services High Availability standard would need to offer greater flexibility to the user (perhaps, integrated with a comprehensive development environment) to gain wider acceptance.

Wrapping by Library Replacement

Even when we lack an object-oriented architecture, similar ideas can often be employed to achieve the same sorts of objectives. As an example, one can potentially wrap a program by relinking it with a modified version of a library procedure that it calls. In the relinked program, the code will still issue the same procedure calls as it did in the past. But control will now pass to the wrapper procedures, which can take actions other than those taken by the original versions. In this sense, an RPC stub is a wrapper.

In practice, this specific wrapping method would only work on older operating systems, because of the way that libraries are implemented on typical modern operating systems. Until fairly recently, it was typical for linkers to operate by making a single pass over the application program, building a *symbol table* and a list of *unresolved external references*. The linker would then make a single pass over the library (which would typically be represented as a directory containing object files or as an archive of object files), examining the symbol table for each contained object and linking it to the application program if the symbols it declares include any of the remaining unresolved external references. This process causes the size of the program object to grow, and it results in extensions both to the symbol table and, potentially, to the list of unresolved external references. As the linking process continues, these references will in turn be resolved, until there are no remaining external

Fig. 16.2   A linker
establishes the
correspondence between
procedure calls in the
application and procedure
definitions in libraries, which
may be shared in some
settings

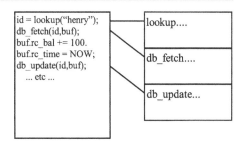

```
id = lookup("henry");
db_fetch(id,buf);
buf.rc_bal += 100.
buf.rc_time = NOW;
db_update(id,buf);
... etc ...
```

lookup....

db_fetch....

db_update...

references. At that point, the linker assigns addresses to the various object modules and builds a single program file, which it writes out. In some systems, the actual object files are not copied into the program, but are instead loaded dynamically when first referenced at run time. (See Fig. 16.2.)

Operating systems and linkers have evolved, however, in response to pressure for more efficient use of computer memory. Most modern operating systems support some form of shared (also called "dynamically linked") libraries. In the shared library schemes, it would be impossible to replace just one procedure in the shared library. Any wrapper technology for a shared library environment would then involve reimplementing all the procedures defined by the shared library—a daunting prospect if the library is large enough, especially if the documentation available was not designed for the developer of such a wrapper. Indeed, many libraries have important but undocumented internal interfaces.

Wrapping by Object Code Editing

Object code editing is an example of a wrapping technology that has been exploited in a number of research and commercial application settings. The approach was originally developed by Wahbe, Lucco, Anderson, and Graham and involves analysis of the object code files before or during the linking process. A variety of object code transformations are possible. Lucco, for example, used object code editing to enforce type safety and to eliminate the risk of address boundary violations in modules that will run without memory protection—a software fault isolation technique. Object code editors for languages such as C# and Java, which compile into an intermediate representation, should be even easier to build, since so much information is preserved about object types and uses.

For purposes of wrapping, object code editing would permit the selective remapping of certain procedure calls into calls to wrapper functions, which could then issue calls to the original procedures if desired (see Fig. 16.3). In this manner, an application that uses the UNIX *send to* system call to transmit a message could be transformed into one that calls *filter_sendto* (perhaps even passing additional arguments). This procedure, presumably after filtering outgoing messages, could then call *sendto* if a message survives its output filtering criteria. Notice that an approximation to this result can be obtained by simply reading in the symbol table of the application's object file and modifying entries prior to the linking stage. Of course, this can only be done if the object file format is well documented and is not protected against such tampering. Unfortunately, modifying programs in this manner

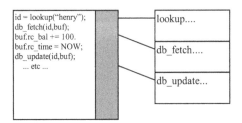

Fig. 16.3 A wrapper (*gray*) intercepts selected procedure calls or interface invocations, permitting the introduction of new functionality transparently to the application or library. The wrapper may itself forward the calls to the library, but it can also perform other operations. Wrappers are an important option for introducing reliability into an existing application, which may be too complex to rewrite or to modify easily with explicit procedure calls to a reliability toolkit or some other new technology

could also be done for purposes of attacking a system, hence it is less and less practical to take such a step—many operating systems now support some form of cryptographic signature scheme to detect evidence of "tampering" and will refuse to run a program that has been modified in this manner.

On the other hand, some systems exploit object code editing as a way to secure themselves against a threat. For example, one important application of object code editing, discussed earlier, involves importing untrustworthy code into a client's Web browser. When we discussed this option in Sect. 3.4, we described it simply as a security enhancement tool. Clearly, however, the same idea could be useful in many other settings. Thus, it makes sense to understand object code editing as a wrapping technology and how specific use of it in Web browser applications might permit us to increase our level of trust in applications that would otherwise represent a serious security threat.

Because programming languages such as C# and Java are compiled into an intermediary language, then "JIT" compiled, they offer new opportunities for code transformation and rewriting. Indeed, Java environments often include powerful rewriters. These would appear to offer substantial opportunities for those seeking ways to automatically introduce replication or fault-tolerance mechanisms.

Wrapping with Interposition Agents and Buddy Processes

Until now, we have focused on wrappers that operate directly upon the application process and that live in its address space. However, wrappers need not be so intrusive.

Interposition involves placing some sort of object or process in between an existing object or process and its users, much as in our recurring database replication example from Chap. 14. An interposition architecture based on what are called "co-processes" or "buddy processes" is a simple way to implement this approach, particularly for developers familiar with UNIX pipes (Fig. 16.4). Such an architecture involves replacing the connections from an existing process to the outside world with an interface to a buddy process that has a much more sophisticated view of the

Fig. 16.4 A simple way to wrap an old program may be to build a new program, which would control the old one through a pipe. The buddy process now acts as a proxy for the old process. Performance of pipes is sufficiently high in modern systems to make this approach surprisingly inexpensive. The buddy process is typically very simple and hence is likely to be very reliable; a consequence is that the reliability of the pair (if both run on the same processor) is typically the same as that of the old process

external environment—for example, perhaps the existing program is basically designed to process a pipeline of data, record by record, or to process batch-style files containing large numbers of records. The buddy process might employ a pipe or file system interface to the original application, which will often continue to execute as if it were still reading batch files or commands typed by a user at a terminal; therefore, it may not need to be modified. To the outside world, however, the interface seen is the one presented by the buddy process, which may now exploit sophisticated technologies such as CORBA, Web Services, Spread or Horus, a message bus, and so forth. (One can also imagine imbedding the buddy process directly into the address space of the original application, coroutine style, but this is likely to be much more complex and the benefit may be small unless the connection from the buddy process to the older application is known to represent a bottleneck.) The pair of processes would be treated as a single entity for purposes of system management and reliability: They would run on the same platform and be set up so that if one fails, the other automatically fails too.

Interposition is easier in some settings than in others. In CORBA, for example, any object can be replaced by a link to a remote object, accessed via the CORBA remote object invocation protocol (IIOP). The ability to make this replacement turns out to be the "hook" that permitted developers of the CORBA Fault Tolerance specification to slide group replication into CORBA in a relatively clean manner. Windows, similarly, includes a fairly general way to interpose an object providing identical interfaces where some existing object is used in the system; the author is not aware of that ability having been exploited to introduce high assurance properties, but it is used for other purposes (indeed, within the operating system itself, the Windows virtual memory subsystem is interposed under a number of other mechanisms, including the file system, permitting the developers of the system to reuse functionality and simplifying the core of the operating system). This, then, could be an attractive development path for future work on high assurance Windows-based applications. On the other hand, it would result in proprietary solutions that depend upon features of Windows.

Interposition wrappers may also be supported as a general capability provided by the operating system. Many operating systems provide some form of packet filter capability, which would permit a user-supplied procedure to examine incoming or outgoing messages, selectively operating on them in various ways. Clearly, a packet filter can implement wrapping. The streams communication abstraction in UNIX and Linux supports a related form of wrapping, in which stream modules are pushed and popped from a protocol stack. Pushing a stream module onto the stack is a way of wrapping the stream with some new functionality implemented in the module. The stream still looks the same to its users, but its behavior changes.

Interposition wrappers were elevated to a real art form in the Chorus operating system (see Rozier et al. 1988a, 1988b), which is object oriented and uses object invocation for procedure and system calls. In Chorus, an object invocation is done by specifying a procedure to invoke and providing a handle referencing the target object. If a different handle is specified for the original one, and the object referenced has the same or a superset of the interface of the original object, the same call will pass control to a new object. This object now represents a wrapper. Chorus uses this technique extensively for a great variety of purposes, including the sorts of security and reliability objectives discussed above.

What systems like Chorus failed to recognize however, and what we've now seen in the database example, is the sense in which a wrapper needs to extend the reliability semantics it offers the user deep into the things it wraps. If the end-user is expecting to see a high-assurance, secure, durable version of such-and-such a functionality, our wrapper will need to understand the corresponding properties within the wrapped object, so as to correctly translate between the two works. This may not always be easy, and when we can do it, may not always be the most efficient solution to the problem at hand. Our challenge, as wrapper-designers, is to bridge the two worlds. Work on this topic in systems such as Chorus often focused on the bridging of two software worlds ("how can object A invoke object B given that they run in different operating systems?") without tackling this deeper question ("A needs to know that B has made such-and-such a part of its state durable. How can it sense that?")

This last point is somewhat discouraging, because there is little agreement on the necessary steps for building a highly assured applications, much less on standardizing them, so that a term like "durability" would have a standard meaning and applications would offer standard APIs for requesting durability, sensing that it has been achieved, etc. Object orientation of the kind seen in Chorus without standard interfaces is just glue without any kind of rationale for precisely how and when to glue things together: a recipe for chaos.

Wrapping Communication Infrastructures: Generalized Virtual Private Networks

Sometime in the near future, it may become possible to wrap an application by replacing the communication infrastructure it uses with a virtual infrastructure. A great deal of work on the Internet and on telecommunication information architectures is concerned with developing a technology base that can support virtual private networks, having special security or quality-of-service guarantees. A virtual network could also wrap an application—for example, by imposing a firewall interface between certain classes of components or by encrypting data so that intruders can be prevented from eavesdropping.

The concept of a generalized virtual private network runs along the following lines. In Sect. 3.4 we saw how cross-scripting languages permit a server to download special-purpose display software into a client's browser. One could also imagine doing this in the network communication infrastructure itself, so that the network routing and switching nodes would be in a position to provide customized behavior on behalf of specialized applications needing particular, non-standard communication features. We call the resulting structure a generalized virtual private network (GVPN)[1] because, from the perspective of each individual user, the network seems to be a dedicated one with precisely the properties needed by the application. This is a virtual behavior, however, in the sense that it is superimposed on a physical network of a more general nature. Uses to which a GVPN could be put include the following:

- Support for a security infrastructure within which only legitimate users can send or receive messages. This behavior might be accomplished by requiring that messages be signed using some form of GVPN key, which the GVPN itself would validate. This is the most common meaning for the term "GVPN."
- Communication links with special video transmission properties, such as guarantees of limited loss rate or real-time delivery (so-called "isochronous" communication).
- Tools for stepping down data rates when a slow participant conferences to individuals who all share much higher-speed video systems. Here, the GVPN would filter the video data, sending through only a small percentage of the frames to reduce load on the slow link.
- Concealing link-level redundancy from the user. In current networks, although it is possible to build a redundant communication infrastructure that will remain connected even if a link fails, one often must assign two IP addresses to each process in the network, and the application itself must sense that problems have developed and switch from one to the other explicitly. A GVPN could hide this mechanism, providing protection against link failures in a manner transparent to the user.

16.1.2 Introducing Robustness in Wrapped Applications

Our purpose in this text is to understand how reliability can be enhanced through the appropriate use of distributed computing technologies. How do wrappers help in this undertaking? Examples of robustness properties that wrappers can introduce into an application include the following:

---

[1]This uses the term somewhat loosely: a VPN, in platforms like Windows and Linux, is a fairly specific technology packaging focused on providing secure remote access to a corporate network by tunneling through the firewall using a shared-key cryptographic scheme. In contrast, here we are employing the same term to connote a more general idea of overlaying a network with "other properties" on a base network with "base properties." Others might call this an overlay network— but, overlay networks, like VPNs, also have come to have a fairly specific meaning, associated with end-to-end implementations of routing. Rather than invent some completely new term, the book uses VPN in a generalized way.

- *Fault tolerance*: Here, the role of the wrapper is to replace the existing I/O interface between an application and its external environment with one that replicates inputs so that each of a set of replicas of the application will see the same inputs. The wrapper also plays a role in collating the outputs, so that a replicated application will appear to produce a single output, albeit more reliably than if it were not replicated. To the author's knowledge, the first such use was in a protocol proposed by Anita Borg as part of a system called Aurogen (see Borg et al. 1983, 1985), and the approach was later generalized by Eric Cooper in his work at Berkeley on a system called Circus (see Cooper 1985), and in the Isis system, which I developed at Cornell University (see Birman and Joseph 1987a). Generally, these techniques assume that the wrapped application is completely deterministic, although later we will see an example in which a wrapper can deal with nondeterminism by carefully tracing the non-deterministic actions of a primary process and then replaying those actions in a replica. Obviously, our wrapped database example from Chap. 14 falls squarely intro this category.
- *Caching*: Many applications use remote services in a client/server pattern, through some form of RPC interface. Such interfaces can potentially be wrapped to extend their functionality—for example, a database system might evolve over time to support caching of data within its clients in order to take advantage of patterns of repeated access to the same data items, which are common in most distributed applications. To avoid changing the client programs, the database system could wrap an existing interface with a wrapper that manages the cached data, satisfying requests out of the cache when possible and otherwise forwarding them to the server. Notice that the set of clients managing the same cached data item represents a form of process group, within which the cached data can be viewed as a form of replicated data. Indeed, the Java Jini architecture allows a server stub to specify its own transport protocol for talking to the server, in effect, "wrapping" the notion of communication from client to server. On the other hand, this option has not been used very actively, and Jini itself seems to have never gained the degree of acceptance of J2EE, in which such wrapping is impractical.
- *Security and authentication*: A wrapper that intercepts incoming and outgoing messages can secure communication by, for example, encrypting those messages or adding a signature field as they depart and decrypting incoming messages or validating the signature field. Invalid messages can either be discarded silently, or some form of I/O failure can be reported to the application program. This type of wrapper needs access to a cryptographic subsystem for performing encryption or generating signatures. Notice that in this case, a single application may constitute a form of *security enclave*, having the property that all components of the application share certain classes of cryptographic secrets. It follows that the set of wrappers associated with the application can be considered as a form of process group, despite the fact that it may not be necessary to explicitly represent that group at run time or communicate to it as a group.
- *Firewall protection*: A wrapper can perform the same sort of actions as a firewall, intercepting incoming or outgoing messages and applying some form of filtering to them—passing only those messages that satisfy the filtering criteria. Such a

wrapper would be placed at each of the I/O boundaries between the application and its external environment. As in the case of the security enclave just mentioned, a firewall can be viewed as a set of processes surrounding a protected application or encircling an application to protect the remainder of the system from its potentially unauthorized behavior. If the ring contains multiple members (multiple firewall processes) the structure of a process group is again present, even if the group is not explicitly represented by the system—for example, all firewall processes need to use consistent filtering policies if a firewall is to behave correctly in a distributed setting.

- *Monitoring and tracing or logging*: A wrapper can monitor the use of a specific interface or set of interfaces and can trigger certain actions under conditions that depend on the flow of data through those interfaces. A wrapper could be used, for example, to log the actions of an application for purposes of tracing the overall performance and efficiency of a system, or, in a more active role, it could be used to enforce a security policy under which an application has an associated behavioral profile and in which deviation from that profile of expected behavior potentially triggers interventions by an oversight mechanism. Such a security policy would be called an *in-depth security mechanism*, meaning that, unlike a security policy applied merely at the perimeter of the system, it would continue to be applied in an active way throughout the lifetime of an application or its access to the system.

- *Quality-of-service negotiation*: A wrapper could be placed around a communication connection for which the application has implicit behavioral requirements, such as minimum performance, throughput, loss rate requirements, or maximum latency limits. The wrapper could then play a role either in negotiation with the underlying network infrastructure to ensure that the required quality of service is provided or in triggering reconfiguration of an application if the necessary quality of service cannot be obtained. Since many applications are built with *implicit* requirements of this sort, such a wrapper would really play the role of making *explicit* an existing (but not expressed) aspect of the application. One reason such a wrapper might make sense would be that future networks may be able to offer guarantees of quality of service even when current networks do not. Thus, an existing application might in the future be wrapped to take advantage of those new properties with little or no change to the underlying application software itself.

- *Language-level wrappers*: Wrappers can also operate at the level of a programming language or an interpreted run-time environment. Fault tolerance and load-balancing can often be introduced into object-oriented programming languages, such as C++, C#, Java, or SmallTalk, by introducing new object classes that are transparently replicated or that use other transparent extensions of their normal functionality. An existing application can then benefit from replication by simply using these objects in place of the ones previously used.

The above list is at best very partial. What it illustrates is that given the idea of using wrappers to reach into a system and manage or modify it, one can imagine a great variety of possible interventions that would have the effect of introducing fault tolerance or other forms of robustness, such as security, system management, or explicit declaration of requirements that the application places on its environment.

Wrappers do not always require process group support, but the two technologies are well matched to one another. Where a process group technology is available, the developer of a wrapper can potentially benefit from it to provide sophisticated functionality, which would otherwise be difficult to implement. Moreover, some types of wrapper are only meaningful if process group communication is available.

16.1.3 Toolkit Technologies

In the introduction to this chapter, we noted that wrappers will often have limitations—for example, although it is fairly easy to use wrappers to replicate a completely deterministic application to make it fault tolerant, it is much harder to do so if an application is not deterministic. And, unfortunately, many applications are nondeterministic for obvious reasons—for example, an application that is sensitive to time (e.g., timestamps on files or messages, clock values, timeouts) will be nondeterministic to the degree that it is difficult to guarantee that the behavior of a replica will be the same without ensuring that the replica sees the same time values and receives timer interrupts at the same point in its execution. The UNIX *select* system call is a source of nondeterminism, since even identically replicated programs presented with identical inputs might detect the availability of data at different times in their execution and thus follow differing execution paths. Interactions with devices are notorious sources of nondeterminism. Any time an application uses *ftell* to measure the amount of data available in an incoming communication connection, this introduces a form of nondeterminism. Asynchronous I/O mechanisms, common in many systems, are also potentially nondeterministic. Parallel or preemptive multithreaded applications are potentially the most nondeterministic of all.

More than twenty years ago, researchers confronted by this problem began to explore mechanisms that would transform nondeterministic inputs into events fielded by one copy of a replicated program, which could then record enough information to allow other replicas to reproduce its actions accurately. For example, suppose that process p issues a *select* system call and discovers that I/O is ready on channel 6. It can record this in a message and send it to process q. If q has the same data available on its 6th channel, and knows when the *select* call returned this value, it can wait until its own code issues that same call and then return the same result that p saw, without even needing to ask the operating system to actually perform the *select* operation. By carrying this concept further, to include thread scheduling, and having q lag the execution of p so that these messages always warn it of future events, q should be in a position to take precisely the same actions that p took. There will still be some cases such an approach cannot cover—for example, if p and q try to replicate the behavior of a UDP socket on which incoming packets are received, it can be tricky to deal with cases where a packet is dropped by one but not the other, or where the order of the packets differs. But the vast majority of applications could certainly be replicated in this manner.

Today, as communication systems continue to improve in performance, it may make sense to adopt such an approach. However, the general sense at the time of these early studies was that this form of intervention is simply too costly, in which

Table 16.2   Typical interfaces in toolkits for process group computing[a]

Tool	Description
Load-balancing	Provides mechanisms for building a load-balanced server, which can handle more work as the number of group members increases.
Guaranteed execution	Provides fault tolerance in RPC-style request execution, normally in a manner that is transparent to the client.
Locking	Provides synchronization or some form of token passing.
Replicated data	Provides for data replication, with interfaces to read and write data, as well as selectable properties, such as data persistence, strong durability, and the type of data integrity guarantees supported.
Logging	Maintains logs and checkpoints and provides playback.
Wide area spooling	Provides tools for integrating LAN systems into a WAN solution.
Membership ranking	Within a process group, provides a ranking on the members that can be used to subdivide tasks or load-balance work.
Monitoring and control	Provides interfaces for instrumenting communication into and out of a group and for controlling some aspects of communication.
State transfer	Supports the transfer of group state to a joining process.
Bulk transfer	Supports out-of-band transfer of very large blocks of data.
Shared memory	Tools for managing shared memory regions within a process group. The members can then use these tools for communication that is difficult or expensive to represent in terms of message passing.

[a]In typical practice, a set of toolkits is sometimes be needed, each aimed at a different class of problems. The components listed above would be typical for a server replication toolkit, but might not be appropriate for building a cluster-style multimedia video server or a caching Web proxy with dynamic update and document consistency guarantees

case there may be no obvious way that a wrapper could be introduced to transparently confer the desired reliability property. Alternatively, it may be possible to do so but impractical in terms of cost or complexity. In such cases, it is sometimes hard to avoid building a new version of the application in question, in which explicit use is made of the desired reliability technology. Generally, such approaches involve what is called a *toolkit* methodology. The Isis^2 system is a library, but not a toolkit in this sense. Readers who skim Appendix B will see that although the system does include some functionality that would fit the notion of toolkit as described below, mostly the Isis^2 system limits itself to the formation of groups and their use for high-speed communication with various reliability properties. The few exceptions (the built-in shared DHT, for example) are few, and are really just presentations of communication functionality through other APIs.

A toolkit typically tries to go further, building a wider range of sophisticated, prepackaged technology that one accesses through some form of procedure calls (Table 16.2). These provide the functionality needed by the application, but without requiring that the user understand the reasoning that lead the toolkit developer to decide that in one situation *CausalSend* was a good choice of communication primitive, but that in another *OrderedSend* was a better option, or that *SafeSend* can be used to update a durable database, but that ϕ should be set to 3 and the *DiskLog-*

ging durability method selected: choices that require some deeper understanding of the model. A toolkit for managing replicated data might offer an abstract data type called a replicated data item, perhaps with some form of name and some sort of representation, such as a vector or an *n*-dimensional array. Operations appropriate to the data type would then be offered: *UPDATE, READ*, and *LOCK* being the obvious ones for a replicated data item (in addition to such additional operations that might be needed to initialize the object, detach from it when no longer using it, etc.). Other examples of typical toolkit functionality might include transactional interfaces, mechanisms for performing distributed load-balancing or fault-tolerant request execution, tools for publish/subscribe styles of communication, tuple-space tools implementing an abstraction similar to the one in the Linda tuple-oriented parallel programming environment, and so forth. The potential list of tools is really unlimited, particularly if such issues as distributed system security are also considered.

Toolkits often include other elements of a distributed environment, such as a name space for managing names of objects, a concept of a communication end point object, process group communication support, message data structures and message manipulation functionality, lightweight threads or other event notification interfaces, and so forth. Alternatively, a toolkit may assume that the user is already working with a distributed computing environment, such as the DCE environment or Sun Microsystem's ONC environment. The advantage of such an assumption is that it reduces the scope of the toolkit itself to those issues explicitly associated with its model; the disadvantage being that it compels the toolkit user to also use the environment in question, thus reducing portability.

16.1.4 Distributed Programming Languages

Agent programming languages and other *fourth-generation languages* (4GLs) package powerful computing tools in the form of special-purpose programming environments. Unlike general purpose programming languages such as C# or Java, these languages play specific roles. For example, Java Script is a well known language intended for use in building sophisticated Web Pages. The language (related to Java but quite different in the details) is intended for a setting in which reliability is taken primarily to mean security of the user's system against viruses, worms, and other forms of intrusion. Web Browsers support Java Script because the browser development community has satisfied itself that there are few security issues created by such scripts. Other types of agent-oriented programming language include TCL/TK (see Ousterhout 1994) and TACOMA (see Johansen et al. 1995a). Very good examples of cloud-computing 4GLs include the Dryad/Linq language created by Yuan Yu and Mike Isard at Microsoft Research (Yu et al. 2008) and the Singularity and Orleans languages created by that company's extreme computing group under the leadership of Jim Larus (Bykov et al. 2011).

Although most existing distributed programming languages lack group communication features and few make provisions for reliability or fault tolerance, one can extend many such languages without difficulty, Dryad/Linq and Orleans both do so.

The resulting enhanced language can be viewed as a form of distributed computing toolkit in which the tools are tightly integrated with the language. However, neither of these has the degree of uptake (as of now) seen for tools like MapReduce (the main competitor for Dryad/Linq) or C# 5.0 in Azure, the competition for Orleans. If we focus on very widely used technologies, one sees that Java users are fond of a communications package called JBOSS, within which JavaGroups provides group communication functionality that seems natural and quite easy to use in a Java Enterprise context. Of course, JBOSS is more of a package than a language, but it represents a major step in the direction of embedding group communication functionality into a Java context—and this is, after all, the way that one "extends" the Java platform. Indeed there have been programming languages in which group communication was offered as a basic language primitive. If language extension can solve the problem, designing a language around a computational abstraction is perhaps overkill. On the other side of the coin, by extending a language, one can incorporate such ideas as "location" and "replication" into the underlying type system, a fascinating opportunity. As networks continue to spread and non-distributed computing eventually becomes the exception rather than the norm, it is entirely possible that both approaches will become common: in object oriented languages like C# and Java, these sorts of technologies will be available as class libraries (so that the developer who wants to replicate information will simply use a replication class and extend it with the specific methods and data appropriate to the need), while the type theory community slowly presses forward on logical foundations of replication and the mathematics of correctness for highly available applications.

16.2 Wrapping a Simple RPC Server

To illustrate the idea of wrapping for reliability, consider a simple RPC server designed for a financial setting. A common problem that occurs in banking is to compute the theoretical price for a bond; this involves a calculation that potentially reflects current and projected interest rates, market conditions and volatility (expected price fluctuations), dependency of the priced bond on other securities, and myriad other factors. Typically, the necessary model and input data is tracked by a server, which clients access using RPC. Note that RPC underlies the Web Services remote method invocation model, hence what follows is also relevant to Web Services design. However, notice also that in a bond pricing setting, each request—each RPC—can be reissued as often as necessary: The results may not be identical (because the server is continuously updating the parameters to its model), but any particular result should be valid for at least a brief period of time. We will exploit that property below.

To start, suppose that we have developed a bond pricing server using standard out of the box technologies such as the TAO CORBA package or one of the Web Services platforms. Only after putting it into operation do we begin to be concerned about its availability. A typical scenario might be that the server has evolved over time, so that although it was really quite simple and easy to restart after crashes

Fig. 16.5   A client/server
application can be wrapped to
introduce fault tolerance and
load-balancing with few or no
changes to the existing code

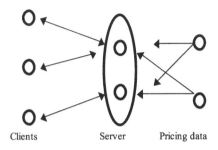

Clients   Server   Pricing data

when first introduced, it now uses a large database and restarting after failures it can
take twenty minutes or longer. The server does not fail often, but when it does, the
disruption could be extremely costly.

An analysis of the causes of failure is likely to reveal that the server itself is
fairly stable, although a low residual rate of crashes is observed. Perhaps there is a
lingering suspicion that some changes introduced to handle the unification of European currencies into the euro are buggy and are causing crashes. The development
team is rewriting the entire euro package, and expects to have a new version in a
few months, but management, being pragmatic, doubts that this will be the end of
the software-reliability issues for this server. Meanwhile, however, routine maintenance and communication link problems are known to be at least as serious a source
of downtime. Finally, although the server hardware is relatively robust, it has definitely caused at least two major outages during the past year, and loss of power
associated with a minor electrical problem triggered additional downtime recently.

In such a situation, it may be extremely important to take steps to improve server
reliability. But rebuilding a server from scratch is often impractical, particularly in
light of the evolutionary nature of such software. The rebuilding effort could take
months or years, and when traders perceive a problem, they are rarely prepared to
wait years for a solution. Management is now demanding that something be done.
(If you have not been in this situation, you have not worked in the industry!)

The introduction of reliable hardware and networks could improve matters substantially. A dual network connection to the server, for example, would permit messages to route around problematic network components such as faulty routers or
damaged bridges. One can purchase off-the-shelf routers with this capability, and
they are known to achieve extremely high levels of network robustness. But the software and management failures would remain an issue. Upgrading to a fault-tolerant
hardware platform on which to run the server would clearly improve reliability, but
only to a degree. If the software is in fact responsible for many of the failures that are
being observed, all of these steps will only eliminate some fraction of the outages.

An approach that replicates the server using wrappers might be very appealing
in this setting. As stated, the server state seems to be dependent on pricing inputs
to it, but not on queries. Thus, a solution such as the one illustrated in Fig. 16.5
can be considered. Here, the inputs that determine server behavior are replicated
using broadcasts to a process group. The queries are load-balanced by directing the
queries for any given client to one or another member of the server process group.

The architecture has substantial design flexibility in this regard: The clients can be managed as a group, with their queries carefully programmed to match each client to a different, optimally selected server. Alternatively, the clients can use a random policy to issue requests to the servers. If a server is unreasonably slow to respond, or has obviously failed, the same request could be reissued to some other server (or, if the request itself may have caused the failure, a slightly modified version of the request could be issued to some other server). Moreover, the use of wrappers makes it easy to see how such an approach can be introduced transparently (without changing existing server or client code). Perhaps the only really difficult problem would be to restart a server while the system is already active.

In fact, even this problem may not be so difficult to solve. The same wrappers that are used to replace the connection from the data sources to the server with a broadcast to the replicated server group can potentially be set up to log input to the server group members in the order that they are delivered. To start a new server, this information can be transferred to it using a *state transfer* from the old members, after which any new inputs can be delivered. After the new server is fully initialized, a message can be sent to the client wrappers informing them that the new server is able to accept requests. To optimize this process, it may be possible to launch the server using a checkpoint, replaying only those logged events that changed the server state after the checkpoint was created. If updates are not all that common and the associated log files can be kept small, these steps would have the effect of minimizing the impact of the slow server restart on perceived system performance.

This discussion is not entirely hypothetical. The author is aware of a number of settings in which problems such as this were solved precisely in this manner. The use of wrappers is clearly an effective way to introduce reliability or other properties (such as load-balancing) transparently, or nearly so, in complex settings characterized by substantial preexisting applications.

16.3   Wrapping a Web Site

The techniques of the preceding section could also be used to develop a fault-tolerant version of a Web server (the kind that serves requests for documents). However, whereas the example presented above concerned a database server used only for queries, many Web servers also offer applications that become active in response to data submitted by the user through a form-fill, a "cgi" script, or some similar interface. To wrap such a server for fault tolerance, one would need to first confirm that its implementation is deterministic. That is, if these operations are invoked in the same order at the replicas, one would need to know that the resulting states would be identical. Given such information, the *OrderedSend* protocol could be used to ensure that the replicas all see the same inputs in the same order. Since the replicas would now take the same actions against the same state, the first response received could be passed back to the user; subsequent duplicate responses can be ignored.

A slightly more elaborate approach is commonly used to introduce load-balancing within a set of replicated Web servers for query accesses, while fully replicating update accesses to keep the copies in consistent states. The HTTP protocol is sufficiently sophisticated to make this an easy task: For each retrieval (*get*) request received, a front-end Web server simply returns a different server's address from which that retrieval request should be satisfied, using a temporary redirection error code. This requires no changes to the HTTP protocol, Web browsers, or Web servers, and although purists might consider it to be a form of hack, the benefits of introducing load-balancing without having to redesign HTTP are so substantial that within the Web development community, the approach is viewed as an important design paradigm. In the terminology of this chapter, the front-end server wraps the cluster of back-end machines.

16.4   Hardening Other Aspects of the Web

A wrapped Web server just hints at the potential that group communication tools may have in future enterprise uses of the Web. As seen in Table 16.3 and Figs. 16.6 and 16.7, the expansion of the Web into groupware applications and environments, computer-supported cooperative work (CSCW), and dynamic information publication applications create challenges that the tools we developed in previous chapters could be used to solve. Web Services bring new requirements and new challenges, and indeed represent a fascinating potential area for research.

Today, a typical enterprise that makes use of a number of Web servers treats each server as an independently managed platform and has little control over the cache coherency policies of the Web proxy servers residing between the end user and the Web servers; those policies depend on a mixture of parameter settings that the enterprise *does* control and document properties, which are controlled by the servers that produced the documents. With group replication and load-balancing, we could transform these Web servers into fault-tolerant, parallel processing systems. Such a step would bring benefits such as high availability and scalable performance, enabling the enterprise to reduce the risk of server overload when a popular document is under heavy demand. Web servers will increasingly be used as video servers, capturing video input (such as conferences and short presentation by company experts on topics of near-term interest, news stories off the wire, etc.), in which case such scalable parallelism may be critical to both data archiving (which often involves computationally costly techniques such as compression) and playback.

Wide area group tools could also be used to integrate these servers into a wide area architecture that would be seamless, presenting users with the abstraction of a single, highly consistent, high-availability Web service—yet internally self-managed and structured. Such a multi-server system might implement data migration policies, moving data to keep them close to the users who demand data most often, and wide area replication of frequently requested critical information, while also providing guarantees of rapid update and consistency. Later, we will be looking at security technologies that could also be provided through such an enterprise architecture, permitting a company to limit access to its critical data to just those users who have been authorized.

Table 16.3 Potential uses of groups in Internet systems

Application domain	Uses of process groups
Server replication	• High availability, fault-tolerance • State transfer to restarted process • Scalable parallelism and automatic load-balancing • Coherent caching for local data access • Database replication for high availability
Data dissemination	• Dynamic update of documents in the Web or of fields in documents • Video data transmission to group conference browsers with video viewers • Updates to parameters of a parallel program • Updates to spreadsheet values displayed to browsers showing financial data • Database updates to database GUI viewers • Publish/subscribe applications
System management	• Propagate management information base (MIB) updates to visualization systems • Propagate knowledge of the set of servers that compose a service • Rank the members of a server set for subdividing the work • Detect failures and recoveries and trigger consistent, coordinated action • Coordinate actions when multiple processes can all handle some event • Rebalance of load when a server becomes overloaded, fails, or recovers
Security applications	• Dynamically updating firewall profiles • Updating security keys and authorization information • Replicating authorization servers or directories for high availability • Splitting secrets to raise the barrier faced by potential intruders • Wrapping components to enforce behavior limitations (a form of firewall that is placed close to the component and monitors the behavior of the application as a whole)

Turning to the caching Web proxies, group communication tools would permit us to replace the standard caching policy with a stateful coherent caching mechanism. In contrast with the typical situation today, where a Web page may be stale, such an approach would allow a server to reliably send out a message that would invalidate or refresh any cached data that has changed since the data was copied. Moreover, by drawing on CORBA functionality, one could begin to deal with document groups (sets of documents with hyperlinks to one another) and over multidocument structures in a more sophisticated manner. Earlier, we mentioned that one study by IBM researchers C. Mohan and G. Cuomo revealed that Web Services systems are likely to exploit caching in dozens of ways. One common property of all of these mechanisms is that they replicate information, hence group communication tools could be valuable in implementing such structures.

Fig. 16.6 Web server transmits continuous updates to documents or video feeds to a group of users. Depending upon the properties of the group-communication technology employed, the users may be guaranteed seeing identical sequences of input, seeing data synchronously, security from external intrusion or interference, and so forth. Such a capability is most conveniently packaged by integrating group communication directly into a Web agent language such as Java or Visual BASIC-for example, by extending the browser with group communication protocols that could then be used through a groupware API

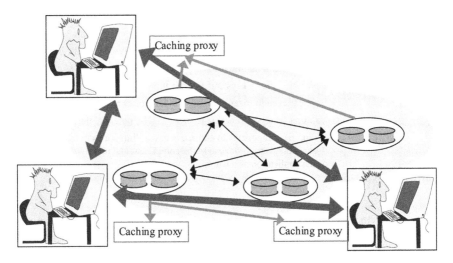

Fig. 16.7 Potential group communication uses in Web applications occur at several levels. Web servers can be replicated for fault tolerance and load-balancing or integrated into wide-area structures, which might span large corporations with many sites. Caching Web proxies could be fixed to provide guarantees of data consistency, and digital encryption or signatures could be used to protect the overall enterprise against intrusion or attack. Moreover, one can foresee integrating group communication directly into agent languages such as Java, thereby creating a natural tool for building cooperative groupware applications. A key to successfully realizing this vision will be to design wrappers or toolkit APIs that are both natural and easy to use for the different levels of abstraction and purposes seen here: Clearly, the tools one would want to use in building an interactive multimedia groupware object would be very different from those one would use to replicate a Web server

In fact there has been research on "cooperative caching," with very promising initial results. A system called Squirrel, developed using the Pastry platform (a peer-to-peer file sharing service developed at Rice University and Microsoft Research in Cambridge, England) tracks information within client caches and allows one client system to look up objects in the caches of other clients. At Cornell University, the Kelips peer-to-peer indexing technology has been applied to the same problem, again with very encouraging results. However (we will see this in the chapter on peer-to-peer technologies) neither system implements a true coherent cache, since neither maintains an accurate list of which objects are in which cache—both track this information with a kind of loose consistency guarantee, stemming from the lack of any sort of interlock between the update stream as objects move around and the query stream of requests to find copies of objects. Thus, there is considerable potential to apply group communication mechanisms having stronger guarantees to the problem. Success would enable a style of Web server that deliberately "manages" the caches of its clients, just as the distributed file systems we looked at early in the book manage file caches and buffer pools of their clients to ensure consistency.

Web Services applications using event notification products conforming to the new WS_Eventing specification (basically, a publish-subscribe specification compatible with most publish-subscribe products) can be understood as exploiting a form of group multicast to stream updates to groups of clients who share an interest in some form of dynamically updated data. This raises the question of whether one might build a single basic technology layer offering primitive services such as groups, group communication, overlay routing infrastructures, and event logging, and then employ that single layer to offer a range of technical mechanisms aimed at server availability, system monitoring, event notification, publish-subscribe, system monitoring and management, and so forth. By standardizing the basic layers, the Web Services community could encourage the emergence of a variety of platforms all sharing the same APIs and yet implemented in different ways. The resulting mechanisms could be valuable in a tremendous number of settings. Web Services implementations of financial systems could use them to notify client systems as stock prices change, triggers are reached, or when important news is released. E-commerce systems could use them to notify customers of pricing or availability changes. Large data centers could use these technologies to adjust parameters that client systems employ when talking to the center: the rate at which data should be polled, for example, or security settings, or even security keys.

The same platform might also open the door to new kinds of application. For example, suppose that a group of soldiers is operating in a dangerous environment. Streams of updates could be used to keep their maps updated about enemy troop movements and activities, or to keep the soldiers current as their orders and mission status evolves. But the same style of system could also be used to inform real-time routing software in our cars as congestion occurs and then clears during rush hour, opening the door to much smarter choices of routes during rush hour. A person shopping in a big city could be sent advertising reporting sales of interesting items in stores within a few blocks walking distance.

We may not perceive these as group communication tools: their presentation will cover a spectrum ranging from monitoring and system management interfaces, to replication for mission-critical components, to publish-subscribe notification architectures. And yet group communication is there, just below the service. These communication patterns will be common in Web Services systems, even if the Web Services architecture lacks explicit support for such patterns.

Obviously, our wrapped Web server represents just the tip of a potentially large application domain. While it is difficult to say with any certainty that this type of system will ever be of commercial importance, or to predict the timeframe in which it might become operational, it seems plausible that the pressures that today are pushing more and more organizations and corporations onto the Web will tomorrow translate into pressure for consistent, predictable, and rapidly updated groupware tools and objects. The match of the technologies we have presented with this likely need is good, although the *packaging* of group communication tools to work naturally and easily within such applications will certainly demand additional research and development. In particular, notice that the tools and APIs one might desire at the level of a replicated Web server will look completely different from those that would make sense in a multimedia groupware conferencing system. This is one reason that systems such as Horus need flexibility, both at the level of how they behave and how they look. Nonetheless, the development of appropriate APIs ultimately seems like a small obstacle.

16.5   Unbreakable Stream Connections

The surging interest in high availability Web platforms justifies revisiting of material we covered covered briefly in Chap. 4. Recall that most applications that use the Web connect to the services on which they depend using TCP connections. Those terminate in tier-one cloud service entities that are prone to sudden redeployments due to elasticity decisions by the framework: they may be replicated to larger numbers of nodes, or removed from current nodes, with no warning at all. Thus the application using the service may experience connectivity disruptions and be forced to reconnect.

For many uses this is just not a problem. For example, a video streaming system will often have a built-in reconnection layer that just re-requests the identical movie from a few seconds before the point where the playback suddenly stopped. Whatever server gets this new request tracks down the identical movie, seeks to the appropriate spot, and then starts playing. The end user experiences an annoying but hopefully brief disruption.

But there are cases where the disruption is more costly. In Chap. 4 the problem we looked at closely involved BGP on a cluster-style router running in the core of the Internet, where even brief protocol disruptions can trigger waves of routing issues: black holes, incorrect or slow routes, route flaps, routing loops. However the same issues arise in situations where a web-hosted service monitors a sensor or actuator and needs to provide some form of continuous, high-integrity control. Applications of this kind will be common in cloud-hosted health-care systems, the future smart electric power grid, transportation control systems (e.g. the ones that operate traffic lights), etc.

The common feature of these examples is that there is a form of mutual state present: the cloud-hosted services have a notion of state that matches with the state of the remote client system, which is often quite simple and best seen as a worker controlled by the cloud server that operates it. This use of cloud systems is somewhat at odds with the requirement that the first tier of the cloud be stateless, but perhaps less so with soft-state replication: we can adopt the view that whereas some uses of the cloud require strong forms of durability and hard state (see Fig. 2.1) others can get by with replicated soft state (see Fig. 2.2) provided that the soft-state service maintains at least some live members to continue to play the required role. This makes good sense: a cloud might elastically vary the number of members of some service so that sometimes, it has 10,000 representatives and at other times, 100,000 of them, yet without ever dropping below 10,000. Such a service has a form of durability and for a task such as monitoring a device, stronger durability might not matter (who would ever want to know why a traffic-light controlling program used a 30 second cycle instead of a 45 second cycle last week on Wednesday last week?)

These kinds of application need a form of durability that really adds up to state replication of a current state in combination with the assurance that connections will not break unless something goes very wrong, like the loss of regional power and networking support because of a major weather event. We know how to do replicated data in the soft-state tier of the cloud: the match is with the *amnesia-freedom* properties obtained by using virtually synchronous protocols such as *Send* in conjunction with a *Flush* prior to sending data to the external client. But how can we avoid connectivity disruptions if a server shuts down while handling a TCP endpoint?

For this, the same "reliable TCP connections" approach discussed in Chap. 4 is really an ideal fit. As we saw there, Robert Surton and others have looked at ways to build a form of network address translator that also can update the TCP byte counts (the technical term is frame counters) in the messages that travel between a client and a server, in a way that is completely transparent to both ends. By interposing TCPR between client and server when a connection is first made, it becomes possible to seamlessly graft a new endpoint to the existing, open, channel, provided that the application that will host the new endpoint is in the identical state to the application that previously played that role. Soft-state replication with strong consistency properties offers us precisely this mix of guarantees! In fact, as this chapter was being revised in 2011, work was underway to integrate TCPR with Isis[2] so that this kind of continuous availability for stream connections would become a standard tool within the Isis[2] options.

TCPR failover is extremely lightweight: a few milliseconds. The overhead is essentially neglible, and comparable to that of any network address translation device. In fact there have been other solutions to the same problem; notable is the work of Bressoud and Schneider (1995), which uses state machine replication to replicate the entire TCP state machine between a primary and backup. But TCPR is much simpler and for that reason, quite a bit faster. Moreover, unlike prior solutions, TCPR requires no changes to the actual TCP implementation or operating system; it operates purely as a kind of network appliance and merely needs to be interposed on the path between the client and the server as a kind of application-provided router. Note that the server here must use a kind of virtual IP address that can be shifted from node to node; a system call for doing this exists in Windows or Linux today, and there is nothing especially difficult or constraining about the use of the method.

16.5.1 Discussion

Although we presented the unbreakable stream problem as a concrete example of how a service might offer continuous availability a remote client, it is important to realize that TCP is not the only protocol used in the Internet, and that streams of videos or data between a web client and a web service are not the only cases in which such issues arise. One of the main challenges is that some of these services are not easily able to satisfy the determinism rules outlined above: we need the new service instance that takes over to do so from the identical state that the failed one was in immediately before it terminated. In the use case presented in Chap. 4, where TCPR was used to replicate a BGP session, this was solved by having BGP checkpoint every incoming BGP update received into the replicated (soft) state shared by primary and backup before processing the BGP update, and then replicating the response before sending any form of data to the remote client; *Flush* is used to ensure that these updates have become durable. TCPR itself cooperates by blocking TCP-level acknowledgments for bytes that have not yet been securely checkpointed, so that if a failure occurs, we can be certain that every single byte is either still in the sender's TCP stack, or safely duplicated. This made it possible for the BGP shim to literally resume where the BGP that failed was interrupted, byte for byte. Moreover, it does not really require BGP determinism, per-se: only that the new BGP be willing to pick up from the same state that the previous BGP instance was in.

One can use similar tricks in many kinds of service. For example, Cho focused on the case of TCP channels to mobile users, whose handheld computers might need to connect to a succession of base stations as the computer was moved around (see Cho and Birman 1994). Cited earlier, Alvisi et al. (2001a) and Ekwall et al. (2002) explore related solutions to the basic unbreakable stream problem. All find that performance is quite good.

16.6   Reliable Distributed Shared Memory

During much of the 1990s, distributed shared memories were a "hot topic" in the distributed system research community. Although the enthusiasm ultimately ebbed as the Internet boom gained momentum, the subject remains interesting. Accordingly, in this section we will look at the idea of implementing a wrapper for the UNIX *mmap* (or *shrmem*) functions, which are used to map files and memory regions into the address space of user applications and shared between concurrently executing processes. The extension we consider here provides for the sharing of memory-mapped objects over a virtually synchronous communication architecture running on a high-speed communication network. One might use such a system as a repository for rapidly changing visual information in the form of Web pages: The provider of the information would update a local mapped copy directly in memory, while the subscribers could map the region directly into the memory of a display device and in this way obtain a direct I/O path between the data source and the remote display. Other uses might include parallel scientific computations, in which the shared memory represents the shared state of the parallel computation; a collaborative workplace or virtual reality environment shared between a number of users; a simulation of a conference or meeting room populated by the participants in a teleconference; or some other abstraction.

As noted, this topic emerges from an area of research in which many operating systems groups worldwide participated (see Ahamad et al. 1991; Carter 1993; Feeley et al. 1995; Felton and Zahorjan 1991; Gharachorloo et al. 1990; Johnson et al. 1995; Li and Hudak 1989). Our goals here are simply to look at how a DSM might be implemented in a highly assured manner using process group technology. The resulting solution is interesting for pedagogical reasons, but would certainly not offer performance and latency properties comparable to hardware solutions.

16.6.1 The Shared Memory Wrapper Abstraction

As with the unbreakable TCP connection, our solution will start with an appropriate wrapper technology. In many UNIX-like operating systems (including Linux and Microsoft Windows) there is a mechanism available for mapping a file into the memory of a process, sharing memory between concurrently executing processes or doing both at the same time. The UNIX system calls supporting this functionality are called *shrmem* or *mmap*, depending on the version of UNIX one is using; a related interface called *semctl* provides access to a semaphore-based mutual-exclusion mechanism. By wrapping these interfaces (e.g., by intercepting calls to them, checking the arguments and special-casing certain calls using new code, and passing other calls to the operating system itself), the functionality of the shared memory subsystem can potentially be extended. Our design makes use of such a wrapper.

In particular, if we assume that there will be a *distributed shared memory daemon* process (DSMD) running on each node where our extended memory-mapping functionality will be used, we can adopt an approach whereby certain mapped-memory operations are recognized as being operations on the DSM and are handled through cooperation with the DSMD. The recognition that an operation is remote can be supported in either of two ways. One simple option is to introduce a new file system object called a DSM object, which is recognizable through a special file type, filename extension (such as .dsm), or some other attribute. The file contents can then be treated as a handle on the DSM object itself by the DSM subsystem. A second option is to extend the options field supported by the existing shared memory system calls with extra bits, one of which could indicate that the request refers to a region

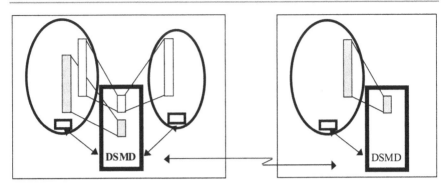

Fig. 16.8 Two machines share memory through the intermediary of a distributed shared memory daemon that runs on each. On the left we see that more than one process might employ the same DSMD and might even share memory with one-another (and with remote processes) through it. A wrapper (shown as *small boxes*) intercepts memory mapping and semaphore system calls, redirecting DSM operations to the DSMD. The DMSD processes sharing a given region of memory belong to a process group and cooperate to provide coherent, fault-tolerant behavior. The best implementation of the abstraction depends upon the expected pattern of sharing and the origin of updates

of the DSM. In a similar manner, we can extend the concept of semaphore names (which are normally positive integers in UNIX) to include a DSM semaphore name space for which operations are recognizable as being distributed synchronization requests.

Having identified a DSM request, that request can then be handled through a protocol with the DSMD process. In particular, we can adopt the rule that all distributed shared memory is implemented as locally shared memory between the application process and the DSMD process, which the DSMD process arranges to maintain in a coherent manner with regard to other processes mapping the same region of memory. The DSMD process thus functions as a type of server, handling requests associated with semaphore operations or events that involve the mapped memory and managing the mapped regions themselves as parts of its own address space. It will be the role of the DSMD servers as a group to cooperate to implement the DSM abstractions in a correct manner; the system call wrappers are thereby kept extremely small and simple, functioning mainly by passing requests through to the DSMD or to the local copy of the operating system, depending on the nature of the system call that was intercepted. This is illustrated in Fig. 16.8.

It would be inefficient to require that our wrapper see every memory reference to the mapped region. Accordingly, the architecture we favor operates at the granularity of pages and makes use of memory protection features of the hardware, as explained below, to trap operations on pages. The basic idea is to map the full set of pages desired by a process into memory, but to disable access (perhaps just write access, or perhaps both read and write access). If a process does not actually access the pages in question, nothing happens. But on its "first" access after a page is locked, a trap will occur. The application catches these events through the wrapper interface.

The wrapper can now forward information to the DSMD, for example asking it to make sure the page is current. Once the DSMD indicates that it is safe to do so, the wrapper unlocks the page and permits the application to resume execution. The sequence of events is exactly the same as when a page fault occurs for a virtual memory region, except that we are handling the fault ourselves in the wrapper and the DSMD, rather than asking the kernel to do it for us.

The sequence of events just described can be implemented more easily on some operating systems than on others. Thus the form of distributed shared memory we will describe might require kernel changes in some settings, while it could be implemented entirely in the user's address space in others. However, let us view this as an implementation detail. It will not really change the distributed communication issues seen in implementing the DSMD, which is the focus of attention in this book. Indeed, a kernel implementation of a DSM would surely yield material for a fascinating research paper. A paper design, such as the one in this chapter, is mostly interesting as an academic exercise!

For design simplicity, it will be helpful to consider the DSM architecture as being volatile: DSM regions exist only while one or more processes are mapping them, and there is no persistent disk storage associated with them, except perhaps for purposes of paging if the region is too large to maintain in memory. We can view the DSM as a whole as being a collection of objects or *regions*, each having a base address within the DSM, a size, and perhaps access restrictions and security properties. A region might be associated with a file system name, or could be allocated using some form of DSM region manager server; we will not address this issue here.

Our design reduces the issue to one of maintaining replicated data and performing synchronization with a collection of superimposed process groups (one on behalf of each shared memory region). The DMSD processes that map a given region would also belong to the corresponding process group. The properties of that process group and the algorithms used to maintain the data in it can now be tuned to match the patterns of access expected from the application processes using it.

16.6.2 Memory Coherency Options for Distributed Shared Memory

In any distributed memory architecture, memory coherence is one of the hardest issues to address. Abstractly, the coherence properties of memory characterize the degree to which that memory is guaranteed to behave like a single, nonshared memory that handles every memory access directly. Because our memory is not resident at any single location, but is shared among the processes that happen to be mapping it at a given time, there are a number of options in regard to the degree to which these copies should be coherent. The choices correspond to the options for shared memory on parallel processors, and consist of the following:

- *Strong consistency*: In this model, the DSM is expected to behave precisely as a single nonreplicated memory might have behaved. In effect, there is a single global serialization order for all read and write operations.

- *Weak consistency*: In this model, the DSM can be highly inconsistent. Updates propagate after an unspecified and possibly long delay, and copies of the mapped region may differ significantly for this reason.
- *Release consistency* (*DASH project*): This model assumes that conflicting read or update accesses to memory are always serialized (protected) using mutual-exclusion locks, such as the semaphore system calls intercepted by our wrapper. The model requires that if process p obtains a lock associated with a region from process q, then p will also observe the results of any update that q has performed. However, if p tries to access the DSM without properly locking the memory, the outcome can be unpredictable.
- *Causal consistency (Neiger and Hutto)*: In this model, the causal relationship between reads and updates is tracked; the memory must provide the property that if access b occurs after access a in a causal sense, then b will observe the results of access a.

The developer who implements an application (or a parallel computing platform, like PVM or MPI) needs to be aware of the consistency properties of the shared memory, and to code accordingly. Strongly consistent memory can be accessed very much in the same way that memory is shared by concurrent threads running in a single address space on a multiprocessor system. This turns out to be an unrealistically expensive "positioning" in the technology stack because strong consistency is hard to implement efficiently, whether in hardware or, as in our case, in software. Weak consistency suffers from the opposite problem. Here, applications just cannot trust the data they read from the shared memory: someone wrote the values, but there is no way to be certain that they are at all consistent from copy to copy. Of course, weak consistency is easy to implement, but it is not very useful. Release consistency turns out to be the most popular option: it fits well with a style of programming in which the application knows about page boundaries and locks each page before modifying the data within it (some models use read and write locks; others only have write locks). Finally, causal consistency offers an interesting extension to the release consistency model, but has not been adopted by developers; apparently, release consistency is "good enough."

This list is not comprehensive, but these four options already represent a sufficient variety of options to present us with some reasonable design choices. To implement strong consistency, it will be necessary to order all update operations, raising the question of how this can be accomplished. The memory protection mechanisms of a virtual memory system offer the needed flexibility: by write-protecting pages managed by the DSMD, we can force an interrupt when those pages are updated and the DSMD can then take any needed action to gain exclusive access. Similarly, by read-protecting a page, we can give the DSMD an opportunity to fetch a current copy if that page might be stale.

For example, to implement strong consistency, we can just protect all the mapped pages against both read and write access. Each time a read or write occurs, we intercept the resulting page fault. The DSMD can then use the replication protocol developed in Sect. 14.3 to manage the pages, obtaining read and write locks and unprotecting pages at a process during periods of time when that process holds the lock on that page. In effect, we have "wrapped" the mapped file and turned it into a shared memory. However, the solution could be costly. (Without locks, the solution gets much cheaper... but only provides weak consistency.)

The release consistency model can be implemented in a similar manner, except that in this case, we only need to protect pages against writes. We use *CausalSend* to implement semaphore operations in the manner of Sect. 14.3, and also to send updated copies of pages. Notice that there is no need to communicate changes to a page until the corresponding semaphore is released, hence those update messages can be delayed, and only one will need to be sent even if many writes are done on a page (keep in mind that we have one semaphore for each page). Of course, there may be performance considerations that favor transmitting updates *before* the semaphore is released, but the release consistency model itself does not require us to do so.

Asynchronous *CausalSend* is a fast protocol: very efficient, suitable for implementations that stream messages without delaying the sender, and yet delaying a process precisely when needed to prevent violations of causal order. Thus we end up with quite an efficient DSMD in this case. Moreover, if the application obtains read as well as write locks, this implementation will satisfy the causal consistency properties!

Consider now the degree of match between these design options and the expected patterns of use for a DSM. It is likely that a DSM will either be updated primarily from one source at a time or in a random way by the processes that use it, simply because this is the pattern seen for other types of distributed application that maintain replicated data. For the case where there is a primary data source, both the strong and release consistency models will work equally well: The update lock will tend to remain at the site where the updates are done, and other copies of the DSM will passively receive incoming updates. If the update source moves around, however, there may be advantages to the release consistency implementation: Although the programmer is compelled to include extra code (to lock objects in a way that guarantees determinism), these locks may be obtained more efficiently than in the case of strong consistency, where the implementation we proposed might move the update lock around more frequently than necessary, incurring a high overhead in the process. Further, the release consistency implementation avoids the need to trap page faults in the application, and in this manner avoids a potentially high overhead for updates. (See Fig. 16.9.)

These considerations make release consistency an appealing model for our DSM, despite its dependence on the use of semaphore-style locking. Of course, should an application desire a weak consistency model or need strong consistency, we now know how both models can be implemented.

However, there are also issues that the consistency model overlooks and that could be quite important in a practical DSM. Many applications that operate on shared memory will be sensitive to the latency with which updates are propagated, and there will be a subset in which other communication patterns and properties are needed—for example, video algorithms will want to send a full frame at a time and will need guarantees of throughput and latency from the underlying communication architecture. Accordingly, our design should include one additional interface

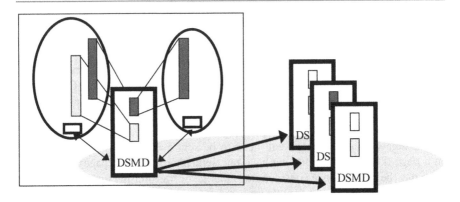

Fig. 16.9 The proposed solution maps the DSM problem to a more familiar one: replicated data with locking within a virtually synchronous process group. Only one of several overlapped groups is shown; another group would be used for the dark gray memory region, another for the white one, and so forth. Virtual synchrony provides us with simple solutions for what would otherwise be tricky problems, such as ensuring the coherence of the distributed memory, handling failures and dynamic join events, and dealing with protection

by which a knowledgeable application can specify the desired update properties to the DSM. This *dsmctl* system call would be used to specify both the pattern of updates that the application will generate (random, page based, isochronous) and also the maximum latency and other special requirements for acceptable performance. The DSMD can then use this information to schedule its communication appropriately. If available, the *page dirty bit* provided by the virtual memory hardware can be checked periodically by the DSMD; if not available, shared regions that are mapped for update can be transmitted in their entirety at the frequency requested by the user.

16.6.3 False Sharing

False sharing is a phenomenon seen on parallel shared memory machines that triggers a form of thrashing, similar to the kind of thrashing sometimes seen in a virtual memory architecture. False sharing arises when multiple logically unrelated objects are mapped to the same shared memory region or page by an accident of storage allocation. When these objects are updated in parallel, the memory subsystem is unable to detect that the updates are independent ones and treats the situation as one in which the processes doing the updates are contending for the same object. In our implementation of strong consistency, the update token would bounce around in this case, resulting in a huge overhead for token passing and page fault handing on the client systems. Yet the problem also points to an issue in our proposed release consistency scheme—the *granularity of locking*. In particular, it becomes clear that the semaphores used for locking must have the same granularity as the objects the DSMD transmits for updates—most likely a page. Otherwise, because the DSMD lacks a fine-grained concept of data access, when an object is updated on a page and the semaphore locking that object is released, the entire page will be transmitted to other processes mapping the page, potentially overwriting parts of the page that the semaphore was not considered to lock and which are in fact not even up-to-date on the node that held the lock.

Our DSM architecture can only work if the granularity of locking is at the page level or region level, and, in either case, false sharing could now occur as a visible problem for the developer. Rather than trying to overcome this problem, it may be best to simply caution the user: The DSM architecture we have proposed here will perform poorly if an application is subject to false sharing; hence, such applications may need to be redesigned to arrange for concurrently updated but logically unrelated objects to reside in different regions or at least on different pages, and in the case of release consistency, must be locked by separate semaphores.

16.6.4 Demand Paging and Intelligent Prefetching

We cited the case of frequent and time-critical updates, but there is another style of DSM use that will require more or less the opposite treatment. Suppose that the DSM region is extremely large and most applications access it in a sparse manner. Then, even if a region is mapped by some process, it may not be necessary or even desirable to actively update that region each time some process updates some part of the data area. In such cases, a demand paging model, whereby a portion of the DSM is maintained as current only if the process holding that region is actually accessing it, makes more sense.

Although we will not tackle the problem here, for reasons of brevity, it would be desirable for large regions to be managed as multiple subregions, shrinking the process group for a given subregion to include only those processes that are actively updating it or reading it. With such an approach, one arrives at a form of *demand paging*, in which a process, upon attempting to access a subregion not currently mapped into its address space, experiences a page fault. To resolve the fault the DSMD would join the process group for that subregion, transferring the current state of the subregion (or just those updates that have occurred since the process was last a memory) and then enabling read or update access to the subregion and resuming local computation.

Notice that the virtual synchrony properties of the state transfer make it easy to describe a solution to what would otherwise be a tricky synchronization problem! Lacking the virtual synchrony model, it would not be at all simple to coordinate the addition of a new memory to a subregion group and to integrate the state transfer operation with updates that may be occurring dynamically. The virtual synchrony model makes it easy to do so and still be able to guarantee that release consistency or strong consistency will be observed by the DSM user. On the other hand, recall that virtual synchrony comes with no guarantees of real-time performance, and hence support for dynamically adjusting the members of a process group that maps a given region or subregion may be incompatible with providing real-time performance and latency guarantees. For situations in which such guarantees are desired, it may be wise to disable this form of dynamicism unless the requirements are fairly weak ones.

Demand paging systems perform best if the relatively costly operations involved in fetching a page are performed shortly before the page fault actually takes place, so as to overlap useful computation with the paging-in activity and to minimize the delay associated with actually servicing the page fault when it occurs. Accordingly, it would be advisable to implement some form of prefetching policy, whereby the DSMD, recognizing a pattern of access (such as sequential access to a series of subregions), would assume that this pattern will continue into the future and would join subregion groups in anticipation of the future need. For example, the DSMD could include one or more "prefetchers": threads that wait for a pattern of accesses to occur that seems to predict some future access, and then acquire the corresponding semaphore in anticipation that it may soon be needed. Our architecture creates a convenient context within which to implement such a policy.

16.6.5 Fault Tolerance Issues

A DSM implemented by a process group has a natural form of fault tolerance, arising directly from the fault tolerance of the virtual synchrony model used by the DSMD processes to form process groups and propagate updates. The issues that arise are primarily ones associated with the possibility of a failure by a process while it is doing an update. Such an event might leave the DSM corrupted and a semaphore in the locked state (the token for the group would be at the process that failed).

A good way to solve this problem would be to introduce a new kind of page fault exception into the DSM model; this could be called a *page corruption* exception. In such an approach, when a process holding an update lock or semaphore for a page or region fails, any subsequent access by some other process mapping that region would result in a corruption trap. The handler for such a trap would be granted the update lock or semaphore and would be required to restore the page to a consistent state. The next update would be understood to clear the corruption bit, so that processes not attempting to access the page during the period of corruption would be completely unaware that a problem had occurred.

16.6.6 Security and Protection Considerations

The reliability of a DSM should extend beyond issues of fault tolerance and detecting potential corruption to also include guarantees of protection and security or privacy if desired. We have not yet treated security issues in this book and defer discussion of the options until later. In brief, one could arrange for the data on the wire to be encrypted so that eavesdroppers lacking an appropriate key would be unable to map a protected segment and unable to make sense of any intercepted updates. Depending on the degree to which the system implementing virtual synchrony is trusted, weaker security options might include some form of user-ID-based access control in which unauthorized users are prevented from joining the group. Because the DSMD must join a process group to gain access to a DSM segment, the group join operation can include authorization keys for use in determining whether or not access should be granted. Alternatively, if the DSMD process itself can be trusted, it can perform a mapping from local user-IDs on the host machine where it is running to global user-IDs in a protection domain associated with the DSM, permitting access under UNIX-style restrictions.

To some extent, communication tools like Isis[2] address this issue: in the Isis[2] approach, one simply uses *g.SetSecure(key)* to associate an AES cryptographic key with a group, and then the system will encrypt all data sent within it. Yet this may not be as strong a guarantee as one would desire, since those AES keys themselves can potentially be stolen. Far preferable would be an approach in which the keys used for this purpose are somehow integrated with hardware-managed keys, using a Hardware Root of Trust module. Moreover, in cloud settings, where virtualization is common, there are several studies pointing to new kinds of risk that involve cohosted platforms that share a single hardware system with one or more untrusted virtual machines; the upshot is that there are many ways that information can potentially leak from VMM to VMM in such settings and little is known about providing very strong security guarantees, at least for standard operating systems such as Windows or Linux. Thus, this form of sharing is powerful, but one would want to think about who might be using the same hardware, and what they might be up to.

16.6.7 Summary and Discussion

The previous examples in this chapter illustrated some of the challenges that can be encountered when using group structures in implementing a distributed system. We have seen that not all problems lend themselves to elegant solutions: nondeterminism, for example, seems to create a great deal of complexity in replication algorithms. In contrast, replicating a deterministic state machine can be child's play. We saw that where there is a close match between the application programming model and our primitives, as in the case of "release consistency" and *CausalSend*, one can sometimes map even a fairly elaborate programming model into a simple and elegant solution. Moreover, these solutions turn out to be easy to understand when the match of problem and tool is close, although they become complex when that is not the case.

With respect to the DSM architecture, it seems clear that the practicality of the proposed solution depends upon having a suitable shared memory subsystem available for use between the DSMD and its clients. The scheme discussed above would be easy to implement on Unix or Linux but less so on Windows, where access to the memory protection mechanisms is not as simple in the case of shared memory regions. Perhaps this explains why distributed shared memory is such an uncommon computing tool; after all, one would expect the simplicity of the abstraction to carry tremendous end-user appeal. The area certainly seems ripe for further research.

16.7   Related Reading

On wrappers and technologies that can support them (see Jones 1993; Rozier et al. 1988a, 1988b; Wahbe et al. 1993).

On wrapping TCP (see Birman and van Renesse 1996; Alvisi et al. 2001a; Ekwall et al. 2002).

On the Isis Toolkit (see Birman and Joseph 1987a; Birman and van Renesse 1994). (Information on the most current APIs should be obtained directly from the company that markets the Isis product line; their Web page is http://www.isis.com.)

On agents (see Gosling and McGilton 1995a, 1995b; Johansen et al. 1995a; Ousterhout 1994).

On virtual fault tolerance (see Bressoud and Schneider 1995).

On shared memory (see Ahamad et al. 1991; Carter 1993; Feeley et al. 1995; Felton and Zahorjan 1991; Gharachorloo et al. 1990; Johnson et al. 1995; Li and Hudak 1989). Tanenbaum also discusses shared memory (see Tanenbaum 1988), and Coulouris treats the topic as well (see Coulouris et al. 1994).

Software Architectures for Group Communication

17

The purpose of this chapter is to shift our attention away from protocol issues to architectural considerations associated with the implementation of process group computing solutions. Although there has been a great deal of work in this area, we focus on the Horus system, because that system is well matched to the presentation of this book.

The Isis[2] system borrows many of these ideas; we will not discuss it in detail here, for reasons of brevity and because it does not really break new ground on the topics outlined below. Robbert van Renesse has recently created a new very minimal group communication solution coded in about 100 lines of Erlang; for some purposes, this is ideal since "real systems" like Isis[2] are enormous and complex (roughly 25,000 lines of C# at last count), dealing with all sorts of practical issues, but with the core protocols buried in masses of code. Thus, a researcher hoping to use a theorem prover to prove that a particular varient of these ideas is correct would be far wiser to start with this small Erlang implementation (it does not even have a name) than to try and work with Isis[2]. In contrast, a developer hoping to build something real would be much more likely to succeed by using Isis[2] as their platform of choice.

It should be stressed that Isis[2] is just one of many systems a developer might consider working with. At Cornell, the Ensemble system was developed as a successor to Horus and is available for free download too; unlike Horus, Ensemble had an active user community for many years, and while it is no longer supported, was quite stable and mature when work on it ended (http://www.cs.cornell.edu/Info/Projects/Ensemble). Indeed, one developer (Mark Hayden) created a series of commercial follow-on products for the system. Ensemble became more widely used than Horus, despite being coded in the O'CaML language, a variant of ML which is widely praised for its elegant handling of mathematical constructs and its powerful type system. Users, of course, should not be aware of the underlying language—they can work in C, C++, C#, or whatever. Our focus on Isis[2] in prior chapters is a reflection of the current options at the time this text was being revised in 2011. This said, we are currently supporting Isis[2] and are

K.P. Birman, *Guide to Reliable Distributed Systems*, Texts in Computer Science, DOI 10.1007/978-1-4471-2416-0_17, © Springer-Verlag London Limited 2012

hoping that it will have a long lifetime and enter wide use. We also see it as an active research vehicle for cloud consistency for at least a few years into the future.

Mentioned earlier, the Spread Toolkit, built by a great team at John Hopkins University (http://www.spread.org/), is another good option for those who seek to build real systems, particularly if support is required. Spread is simpler than Ensemble, is supported commercially and offers many advantages, notably exceptional efficiency and simplicity of the user interface. Users concerned about the complexity of group communication will find a happy option in Spread, which was deliberately designed to be as foolproof as possible. Still other options include Eternal, a technology developed at UCSB in support of the CORBA fault-tolerance architecture and JavaGroups (JGroups), a part of the JBOSS communications platform.

Our decision to drill down on Horus, then, is not a judgment about the relative merits of the various options available to the developer. We do so simply because Horus was a real system, remains available for users willing to invest the time needed to recompile it, was rather elegantly structured, and widely known as the first system to offer a valuable form of design flexibility, on which the remainder of this chapter will be focused.

17.1   Architectural Considerations in Reliable Systems

The reader may feel that Part II of this book and the first chapters of Part III have lost one of the important themes of Part I—namely, the growing importance of architectural structure and modularity in reliable distributed systems and, indeed, in structuring distributed systems of all types. Our goal in this chapter, in part, is to reestablish some of these principles in the context of the group computing constructs introduced in Part III. Specifically, we will explore the embedding of group communication support into a modular systems architecture.

Historically, group computing and data replication tools have tended to overlook the importance of architectural structure. These technologies have traditionally been presented in what might be called a flat architecture: one in which the APIs provided by the system are fixed, correspond closely to the group construct and associated communication primitives, and less uniformly accessible from any application making use of the group communication environment anywhere in the system.

In practice the use of group communication will vary considerably depending upon what one is attempting to do. Consider the examples that arose in Chap. 16, when we discussed group computing in the context of enterprise Web applications:

- Groups used to replicate a Web server for load-balancing, fault tolerance, or scalable performance through parallelism.
- Groups used to interconnect a set of Web servers, giving the illusion of a single, corporate-wide server within which objects might migrate or be replicated to varying degrees, depending on usage patterns.
- Groups corresponding to the set of Web proxy servers that cache a given data item and are used to invalidate those cached copies or to refresh them when they change.

- Groups used to distribute Java applets to users cooperating in conferencing applications or other groupware applications (we gave a number of examples in Chap. 16 and will not repeat them here).
- Groups used to distribute updates to documents, or other forms of updates, to Java applets running close to the client browsers.
- Groups formed among the set of Java applets, running on behalf of clients, for the purpose of multicasting updates or other changes to the state of the group session among the participants.
- Groups associated with security keys employed in a virtual private network.

Clearly, these uses correspond to applications that would be implemented at very different levels of programming abstraction and for which the most appropriate presentation of the group technology would vary dramatically. Several of these represent potential uses of wrappers, but others would match better with toolkit interfaces and still others with special-purpose, high-level programming languages. Even within those subclasses, one would expect considerable variation in terms of what is wrapped, the context in which those tools or languages are provided, and the nature of the tools themselves. No single solution could possibly satisfy all of these potential types of developer and types of use. On the contrary, any system that offers just a single interface to all of its users is likely to confuse its users and to be perceived as complex and difficult to learn, because that API is unlikely to match with the other APIs and major programming paradigms used in the parts of the system where one might want to exploit groups. For example, if one developer is thinking about publish-subscribe, and another about replicating a server, neither may see a group join/leave/multicast interface as a "natural" fit to their needs. If one steps back and looks at the broad history of the field, the tendency to offer group communication tools through a flat interface (one that looks the same to all applications and that offers identical capabilities no matter where it is used in the system) has proved to be an obstacle to the adoption of these technologies, because the resulting tools tend to be conceptually mismatched with the developer's goals and mindset.

The insight here recalls the point made by Cheriton and Skeen in their criticism of "causal and total ordering." Not all applications need all properties. The list of properties that a group *could* offer is almost endless. By picking this one and deciding not to offer that one, the developer of a platform gradually disenfranchises larger and larger subgroups of the potential user community.

Indeed, the lesson goes further than this. Although we have presented group communication as a natural and elegant step, the experience of programming with groups can be more challenging. Obtaining good performance is not always an easy thing, and the challenge of doing so increases greatly if groups are deployed in an unstructured way, creating complex patterns of overlap within which the loads placed on individual group members may vary widely from process to process. Thus, what may seem elegant to the reader, can start to seem clumsy and complex to the developer, who is struggling to obtain predictable performance and graceful scalability.

Cheriton and Skeen concluded from this that one should build systems around a loosely coupled paradigm such as publish-subscribe, without any built-in consistency (reliability, durability or ordering) guarantees. In keeping with this philosophy, their recommended technology does not provide any form of strong guarantee in the usual case, although a "logged" event stream is available as a more costly option for those who need absolute reliability. Thus they prefer a positioning in which the basic primitive offered to the user is rather weak (a best-effort publish-subscribe mechanism), and anything stronger is achieved through end-to-end mechanisms. The Isis Toolkit went the other way, offering publish-subscribe interfaces to group communication tools, so that one could exploit the stronger properties of those tools as needed.

Stepping back, the author's research group concluded that these observations argue for a more *structured* presentation of group computing technologies: one in which the tools and APIs provided are aimed at a specific class of users and will guide those users to a harmonious and simple solution to the problems anticipated for that class of users. If the same technology will also support some other community of users, a second set of tools and APIs should be offered to them. Thus, the tools provided for developers of highly assured Web Services might look very different from those available to the developer of a highly assured database system, even if both are basically forms of replication similar to the functionally found group communication subsystems. I believe that far too little attention has been given to this issue up to the present and that this has emerged as a significant obstacle to the widespread use of reliability technologies.

At a minimum, focusing only on issues associated with communication (as opposed to security, system management, or real time), it would appear that three layers of APIs are needed (Fig. 17.1). The lowest layer is the one aimed at uses within servers, the middle layer focuses on interconnection and management of servers within a WAN setting, and the third layer focuses on client-side issues and interfaces. Such layers may be further subdivided: Perhaps the client layer offers a collection of transactional database tools and a collection of C# or Java groupware interfaces, while the server layer offers tools for multimedia data transmission, consistent replication and coordinated control, and fault tolerance through active replication. This view of the issues now places unusual demands upon the underlying communication system: not only must it potentially look different for different classes of users, but it may also need to offer very different properties for different classes of users. Security and management subsystems would introduce additional APIs, which may well be further structured. Real-time subsystems are likely to require still further structure and interfaces.

17.2   Horus: A Flexible Group Communication System

The observations in the preceding section may seem to yield an ambiguous situation. On the one hand, we have seen that process group environments for distributed computing represent a promising step toward robustness for mission-critical distributed applications. Process groups have a natural correspondence with data or services that have been replicated for availability or as part of a coherent cache, such as might be used to ensure the consistency of documents managed by a set

---

Functionality of a client-level API:
Fault-tolerant remote procedure call
Reliable, unbreakable streams to servers
Publish-subscribe interfaces, with the possibility of guaranteed reliability or ordering
Tools for forming groupware sessions involving other client systems
Functionality of a WAN server API:
Tools for consistently replicating data within wide area or corporate networks
Technology for updating global state and for merging after a partitioning failure is corrected
Security tools for creating virtual private networks
Management tools for control and supervision
Functionality of a cluster-server API:
Tools for building fault-tolerant servers (ideally, as transparently as possible)
Load-balancing and scalable parallelism support
Management tools for system servicing and automatic reconfiguration
Facilities for on-line upgrade
Other cases that might require specialized APIs:
Multimedia data transport protocols (special quality-of-service or real-time properties)
Security (key management and authentication APIs)
Debugging and instrumentation
Very large scale data diffusion

Fig. 17.1   Different levels of a system may require different styles of group computing support. A simple client/server architecture gives rise to three levels of API (levels in the sense that we start with client issues, then push closer and closer to a server and finally to "platform" uses internal to the operating system and network). Further structure might be introduced in a multimedia setting (where special protocols may be needed for video data movement or to provide time-synchronous functionality), in a transactional database setting (where client's may expect an SQL-oriented interface), or in a security setting (where APIs will focus on authentication and key management)

of Web proxies. They can been used to support highly available security domains. Also, group mechanisms fit well with an emerging generation of intelligent network and collaborative work applications.

Yet we have also seen that there are many options concerning how process groups should look and behave. The requirements that applications place on a group infrastructure vary and there may be fundamental tradeoffs between semantics and performance. Even the most appropriate way to present the group abstraction to the application depends on the setting.

The Horus system responds to this observation by providing an unusually flexible group communication model to application developers. This flexibility extends to system interfaces; the properties provided by a protocol stack; and even the configuration of Horus itself, which can run in user space, in an operating system kernel or microkernel, or be split between them. Horus can be used through any of several application interfaces. These include toolkit-style interfaces and wrappers, which hide group functionality behind UNIX communication system calls, the TCL/TK programming language, and other distributed computing constructs. The intent is that it be possible to slide Horus beneath an existing system as transparently as possible—for example, to introduce fault tolerance or security without requiring substantial changes to the system being hardened (see Bressoud and Schneider 1995).

For example, one could slide Horus beneath a publish-subscribe API of the sort favored by Cheriton and Skeen. To do this, we use a hashing function to map subjects into a smaller set of process groups (the objective being to limit the number of groups; systems like Horus scale to tens of groups but not tens of thousands). A publish event becomes a multicast to the appropriate group. A subscriber joins the group or group to which their subscription hashes ("groups" in the case of wildcard subscription patterns).

A basic goal of Horus is to provide efficient support for the virtually synchronous execution model. However, although often desirable, properties such as virtual synchrony may sometimes be unwanted, introduce unnecessary overheads, or conflict with other objectives such as real-time guarantees. Cheriton and Skeen, for example, would grimace at the concept of a publish-subscribe system that offers any properties at all, beyond a best effort delivery guarantee and some end-to-end mechanism for recovering data if an application really needs to do so. So while we can map publish-subscribe onto groups, it is not obvious that we would want those groups to run over the protocols we have developed so painstakingly over the past five chapters of the book! Yet we would not want to be too quick to dismiss the value of causal or total order, or virtual synchrony, either: a publish-subscribe system in which processes are replicating system state and want strong guarantees would obviously need stronger group communication properties.

Moreover, the optimal implementation of a desired group communication property sometimes depends on the run-time environment. In an insecure environment, one might accept the overhead of data encryption but wish to avoid this cost when running inside a firewall. On a platform such as an IBM SP scalable supercomputer, which has reliable message transmission, protocols for message retransmission would be superfluous.

Accordingly, Horus provides an architecture whereby the protocol supporting a group can be varied, at run time, to match the specific requirements of its application and environment. Virtual synchrony is only one of the options available, and, even when it is selected, the specific ordering properties that messages will respect, the flow-control policies used, and other details can be fine-tuned. Horus obtains this flexibility by using a structured framework for protocol composition, which incorporates ideas from systems such as the UNIX stream framework and the x-Kernel, but replaces point-to-point communication with group communication as the fundamental abstraction. In Horus, group communication support is provided by stacking protocol modules having a regular architecture, where each module has a separate responsibility. A process group can be optimized by dynamically including or excluding particular modules from its protocol stack.

17.2.1 A Layered Process Group Architecture

It is useful to think of Horus's central protocol abstraction as resembling a Lego block; the Horus system is thus similar to a box of Lego blocks. Each type of block implements a microprotocol, which provides a different communication feature. To

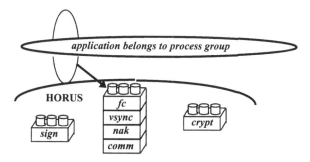

Fig. 17.2 Group protocol layers can be stacked at run time like Lego blocks and support applications through one of several application programmer interfaces. Shown is an application program belonging to a single process group, supported by a Horus protocol stack of four layers: "*fc*," the flow-control layer; "*vsync*," the layer implementing virtually synchronous process group views; "*nak*," a layer using negative acknowledgements to overcome communication failures; and "*comm*," which interfaces Horus to a network. The application would often use Horus through a wrapper, which might conceal this group functionality, but it can also do so using a toolkit. The layers illustrated here are imaginary; some real layers are shown in Table 17.1. Horus supports many layers, but not all need be used in any particular stack: Shown here are two security layers (one for signing messages and one for encrypting their contents), which were not used for this particular application

promote the combination of these blocks into macroprotocols with desired properties, the blocks have standardized top and bottom interfaces, which allow them to be stacked on top of each other at run time in a variety of ways (see Fig. 17.2). Obviously, not every sort of protocol block makes sense above or below every other sort. But the conceptual value of the architecture is that where it makes sense to create a new protocol by restacking existing blocks in a new way, doing so is straightforward.

Technically, each Horus protocol block is a software module with a set of entry points for downcall and upcall procedures—for example, there is a downcall to send a message and an upcall to receive a message. Each layer is identified by an ASCII name and registers its upcall and downcall-handlers at initialization time. There is a strong similarity between Horus protocol blocks and object classes in an object-oriented inheritance scheme, and readers may wish to think of protocol blocks as members of a class hierarchy.

To see how this works, consider the Horus *message_send* operation. It looks up the message send entry in the topmost block and invokes that function. This function may add a header to the message and will then typically invoke *message_send* again. This time, control passes to the message send function in the layer below it. This repeats itself recursively until the bottommost block is reached and invokes a driver to actually send the message.

The specific layers currently supported by Horus solve such problems as interfacing the system to varied communication transport mechanisms, overcoming lost packets, encryption and decryption, maintaining group membership, helping a process that joins a group obtain the state of the group, merging a group that has parti-

Table 17.1 Microprotocols available in Horus

Layer	Description
COM	The COM layer provides the Horus group interface to such low-level protocols as IP, UDP, and some ATM interfaces
NAK	This layer implements a negative acknowledgement-based message retransmission protocol
CYCLE	Multimedia message dissemination using Smith's cyclic UDP protocol
PARCLD	Hierarchical message dissemination (parent-child layer)
FRAG	Fragmentation and reassembly of large messages
MBRSHIP	This layer provides each member with a list of end-points believed to be accessible. It runs a group membership consensus protocol to provide its users with a virtually synchronous execution model
FC	Flow-control layer
TOTAL	Totally ordered message delivery
STABLE	This layer detects when a message has been delivered to all destination end-points and can consequently be garbage collected
CRYPT	Encryption and decryption of message body
MERGE	Location and merging of multiple group instances

tioned, flow control, and so forth. Horus also includes tools to assist in the development and debugging of new layers.

Each stack of blocks is carefully shielded from other stacks. It has its own prioritized threads and has controlled access to available memory through a mechanism called *memory channels*. Horus has a memory scheduler, which dynamically assigns the rate at which each stack can allocate memory, depending on availability and priority, so that no stack can monopolize the available memory. This is particularly important inside a kernel or if one of the stacks has soft real-time requirements.

Besides threads and memory channels, each stack deals with three other types of objects: end-points, groups, and messages. The end-point object models the communicating entity. Depending on the application, it may correspond to a machine, a process, a thread, a socket, a port, and so forth. An end-point has an address and can send and receive messages. However, as we will see later, messages are not addressed to end-points, but to groups. The end-point address is used for membership purposes.

A *group object* is used to maintain the local protocol state on an end-point. Associated with each group object is the *group address*, to which messages are sent, and a *view*: a list of destination end-point addresses believed to be accessible group members. An end-point may have multiple group objects, allowing it to communicate with different groups and views. A user can install new views when processes crash or recover and can use one of several membership protocols to reach some form of agreement on views between multiple group objects in the same group.

The message object is a local storage structure. Its interface includes operations to push and pop protocol headers. Messages are passed from layer to layer by passing a pointer and never need be copied.

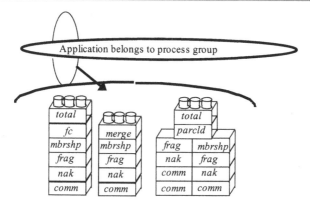

Fig. 17.3 The Horus stacks are shielded from each other and have their own threads and memory, each of which is provided through a scheduler. Each stack can be thought of as a small program executing inside Horus. Although this feature is not shown, a stack can be split between the user's address space and the kernel, permitting the user to add customized features to a stack while benefiting from the performance of a kernel-based protocol implementation

A thread at the bottom-most layer waits for messages arriving on the network interface. When a message arrives, the bottom-most layer (typically COM) pops off its header and passes the message on to the layer above it. This repeats itself recursively. If necessary, a layer may drop a message or buffer it for delayed delivery. When multiple messages arrive simultaneously, it may be important to enforce an order on the delivery of the messages. However, since each message is delivered using its own thread, this ordering may be lost, depending on the scheduling policies used by the thread scheduler. Therefore, Horus numbers the messages and uses *event count* synchronization variables (see Reed and Kanodia 1979) to reconstruct the order where necessary.

17.3 Protocol Stacks

The microprotocol architecture of Horus would not be of great value unless the various classes of process group protocols we might wish to support could be simplified by being expressed as stacks of layers perform well and share significant functionality. The experience with Horus in this regard has been very positive.

The stacks shown in Fig. 17.3 all implement virtually synchronous process groups. The left-most stack provides totally ordered, flow-controlled communication over the group membership abstraction. The layers FRAG, NAK, and COM, respectively, break large messages into smaller ones, overcome packet loss using negative acknowledgements, and interface Horus to the underlying transport protocols. The adjacent stack is similar, but provides weaker ordering and includes a layer supporting state transfer to a process joining a group or when groups merge after a network partition. To the right is a stack that supports scaling through a hierarchical structure, in which each parent process is responsible for a set of child processes.

The dual stack illustrated in this case represents a feature whereby a message can be routed down one of several stacks, depending on the type of processing required. Additional protocol blocks provide functionality such as data encryption, packing small messages for efficient communication, isochronous communication (useful in multimedia systems), and so forth.

In order for Horus layers to fit like Lego blocks, they each must provide the same downcall and upcall interfaces. A lesson learned from the x-Kernel is that if the interface is not rich enough, extensive use will be made of general-purpose control operations (similar to *ioctl*), which reduce configuration flexibility. (Since the control operations are unique to a layer, the Lego blocks would not fit as easily.) The *Horus Common Protocol Interface* (HCPI), therefore supports an extensive interface, which supports all common operations in group communication systems, going beyond the functionality of earlier layered systems such as the x-Kernel. Furthermore, the HCPI is designed for multiprocessing and is completely asynchronous and reentrant.

Broadly, the HCPI interfaces fall into two categories. Those in the first group are concerned with sending and receiving messages and the stability of messages.[1] The second category of Horus operations is concerned with membership. In the down direction, it lets an application or layer control the group membership used by layers below it. As upcalls, these report membership changes, communication problems, and other related events to the application.

While supporting the same HCPI, each Horus layer runs a different protocol—each implementing a different property. Although Horus allows layers to be stacked in any order (and even multiple times), most layers require certain semantics from layers below them, imposing a partial order on the stacking. Given information about the properties of the network transport service, and the properties provided by the application, it is often possible to automatically generate a minimal protocol stack to achieve a desired property. Indeed, one of the major reasons that Cornell developed Ensemble, the successor to Horus, was that by reimplementing the system in the O'CaML language, it became possible to use a single mathematical formalism to express constraints, properties, and protocols, enabling the use of mathematical theorem proving tools to establish the correctness of the system in a formal way (see Liu et al. 1999).

Layered protocol architectures sometimes perform poorly: the layering limits opportunities for optimization and imposes excessive overhead. Clark and Tennenhouse have suggested that the key to good performance rests in *Integrated Layer Processing* (ILP) (see Abbott and Peterson 1993; Braun and Diot 1995; Clark and Tennenhouse 1987, 1990; Karamcheti and Chien 1994; Kay and Pasquale 1993). Systems based on the ILP principle avoid interlayer ordering constraints and

---

[1]It is common to say that a message is *stable* when processing has completed and associated information can be garbage collected. Horus standardizes the handling of stability information, but leaves the actual semantics of stability to the user. Thus, an application for which stability means "logged to disk" can share this Horus functionality with an application for which stability means "displayed on the screen."

can perform as well as monolithically structured systems. Horus is consistent with ILP: There are no intrinsic ordering constraints on processing, so unnecessary synchronization delays are avoided. Moreover, as we will see, Horus supports an optional protocol accelerator, which greatly improves the performance of the layered protocols making use of it.

17.4   Using Horus to Build a Publish-Subscribe Platform and a Robust Groupware Application

Earlier, we commented that Horus can be hidden behind standard application programmer interfaces, giving the example of a publish-subscribe "mapping" of subjects down to groups. Clearly, the core issue in implementing such a publish-subscribe system involves the mapping itself. If we map each subject to a distinct group, we get a very natural implementation of publish-subscribe, but run into the problem that Horus itself was not implemented with membership in large numbers of groups as one of its primary goals. The software would "bog down" when a process joins or leaves the system and triggers membership changes in large numbers of groups nearly simultaneously.

If we want to pursue such a mapping, the most obvious idea is to just simplify the job Horus is faced with by applying some sort of a function to reduce the size of the group space. For example, suppose that each subject is somehow hashed to a small space of (just for the sake of argument) about 75 groups, e.g., by taking the first alphanumeric character of the subject name as the group name. Thus "/equities/nyse/ibm" would be mapped to group "e" while "/bonds/fixed/..." to group "b". (Obviously this is not a particularly intelligent mapping since all the equity symbols end up in one group, but that is a technicality.) A subscription would be implemented by a join; a subscription to a pattern such as "/equities/nyse/*" by joining all the groups that the pattern might match.

Now, this subscription scheme is inefficient, since a subscriber might end up receiving some publications not intended for it. But the data rates would presumably be 75-times reduced relative to the full flow of data into the system, and the extra cost of reevaluating the match and tossing out non-matching incoming events should not be prohibitive. All that remains is to pick an appropriate Horus stack for these groups, and voila: instant publish-subscribe. In the example given, Horus could be configured without the virtual synchrony and ordering layers if one accepts the Cheriton and Skeen argument, or could be set up with stronger ordering and reliability guarantees if the setting demands them.

A second way of exploiting group communication involves the use of groups as a more basic distributed computing "architectural element." Here, the groups become a structural construct visible in the application itself.

A good illustration of this second idea arose some years ago, when colleagues at Cornell interfaced the TCL/TK graphical programming language to Horus. A challenge posed by running systems such as Horus side by side with a package such as X Windows or TCL/TK is that such packages are rarely designed with threads or Horus communication stacks in mind. To avoid a complex integration task, we therefore chose to run TCL/TK as a separate thread in an address space shared with Horus. Horus intercepts certain system calls issued by TCL/TK, such as the UNIX *open* and *socket* system calls. We call this resulting mechanism an *intercept proxy*; it is a special type of wrapper oriented toward intercepting this type of system call. The proxy redirects the system calls, invoking Horus functions, which will create Horus process groups and register appropriate protocol stacks at run time. Subsequent I/O operations on these group I/O sockets are mapped to Horus communication functions.

To make Horus accessible within TCL applications, two new functions were registered with the TCL interpreter. One creates end-point objects, and the other creates group addresses. The end-point object itself can create a group object using a group address. Group objects are used to send and receive messages. Received messages result in calls to TCL code that typically interpret the message as a TCL command. This yields a powerful framework: a distributed, fault-tolerant, whiteboard application can be built using only eight short lines of TCL code over a Horus stack of seven protocols.

To validate the approach, we ported a sophisticated TCL/TK application to Horus. The Continuous Media Toolkit (CMT) (see Rowe and Smith 1992) is a TCL/TK extension providing objects that read or output audio and video data. These objects can be linked together in pipelines and are synchronized by a *logical timestamp* object. This object may be set to run slower or faster than the real clock or even backwards. This allows stop, slow motion, fast forward, and rewind functions to be implemented.

Architecturally, CMT consists of a multimedia server process, which multicasts video and audio to a set of clients. We decided to replicate the server using a primary-backup approach, where the backup servers stand by to back up failed or slow primaries.

The original CMT implementation depends on extensions to TCL/TK. These implement a master-slave relationship between the machines, provide for a form of logical timestamp synchronization between them, and support a real-time communication protocol called Cyclic UDP. The Cyclic UDP implementation consists of two halves: a sink object, which accepts multimedia data from another CMT object, and a source object, which produces multimedia data and passes it on to another CMT object (see Fig. 17.4a). The resulting system is distributed but intolerant of failures and does not allow for multicast.

By using Horus, it was straightforward to extend CMT with fault tolerance and multicast capabilities. Five Horus stacks were required. One of these is hidden from the application and implements a clock synchronization protocol (see Cristian 1989). It uses a Horus layer called MERGE to ensure that the different machines will find each other automatically (even after network partitions), and it employs the virtual synchrony property to rank the processes, assigning the lowest-ranked machine to maintain a master clock on behalf of the others. The second stack synchronizes the speeds and offsets with respect to real time of the logical timestamp objects. To keep these values consistent, it is necessary that they be updated in the

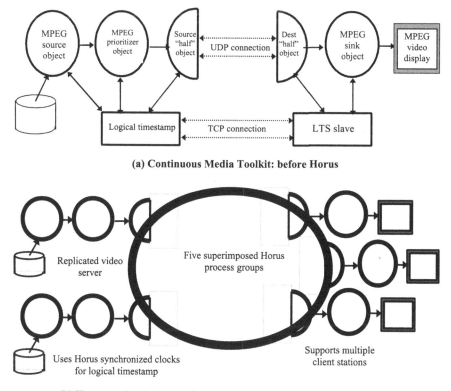

(a) Continuous Media Toolkit: before Horus

(b) Horus used to introduce fault tolerance and groupware capabilities

Fig. 17.4   This illustrates an example of a video service implemented using the Continuous Media Toolkit. MPEG is a video compression standard. In (**a**), a standard, fault-intolerant set-up is depicted. In (**b**), Horus was used to implement a fault-tolerant version that is also able to multicast to a set of clients

same order. Therefore, this stack is similar to the previous one, but includes a Horus protocol block, which places a total order on multicast messages delivered within the group.[2] The third stack tracks the list of servers and clients. Using a deterministic rule based on the process ranking maintained by the virtual synchrony layer, one server is selected to multicast the video, and one server, usually the same, is picked to multicast the audio. This setup is shown in Fig. 17.4b.

To disseminate the multimedia data, we used two identical stacks—one for audio and one for video. The key component in these is a protocol block, which implements a multimedia generalization of the cyclic UDP protocol. The algorithm is

---

[2]This protocol differs from the *Total* protocol in the Trans/Total (see Moser et al. 1996) project in that the Horus protocol only rotates the token among the current set of senders, while the Trans/Total protocol rotates the token among all members.

similar to FRAG, but it will reassemble messages arriving out of order and drop messages with missing fragments.

One might expect that a huge amount of recoding would have been required to accomplish these changes. However, all of the necessary work was completed using 42 lines of TCL code. An additional 160 lines of C code support the CMT frame buffers in Horus. Two new Horus layers were needed, but were developed by adapting existing layers; they consist of 1,800 lines of C code and 300 lines of TCL code, respectively (ignoring the comments and lines common to all layers). Moreover, performance of the resulting system was quite good; the primary bottleneck at the time was associated with the Internet itself, not the protocols, and a substantial user community emerged over a period of a few years before the developers moved on to other challenges and the software fell into disrepair. Thus, with relatively little effort and little code, a complex application written with no expectation that process group computing might later be valuable was modified to exploit Horus functionality.

17.5   Using Electra to Harden CORBA Applications

The introduction of process groups into CMT required sophistication with Horus and its intercept proxies. Many potential users would lack the sophistication and knowledge of Horus required to do this; hence, we recognized a need for a way to introduce Horus functionality in a more transparent way. This goal evokes an image of plug-and-play robustness; it leads one to think in terms of an object-oriented approach to group computing.

Early in this book, we looked at CORBA, noting that object-oriented distributed applications that comply with the CORBA RB specification and support the IOP protocol can invoke one another's methods with relative ease. This work resulted in a CORBA-compliant interface to Horus, which we call Electra (see Maffeis 1995). Electra can be used without Horus, and vice versa, but the combination represents a more complete system. This work preceded the development of the CORBA Fault Tolerance architecture, and differs from what the CORBA community ultimately opted to do in many details—the Eternal ORB is a much more "faithful" implementation of the CORBA specification. However, Electra is interesting in part because it has more flexibility than the CORBA specification allows, and we will present it here in that spirit. (Readers who might consider working with CORBA and using Eternal should keep in mind that the standard is quite a bit more restrictive, and that this code long ago ceased to be supported.)

In Electra, applications are provided with ways to build Horus process groups and to directly exploit the virtual synchrony model. Moreover, Electra objects can be aggregated to form object groups, and object references can be bound to both singleton objects and object groups. An implication of the interoperability of CORBA implementations is that Electra object groups can be invoked from *any* CORBA-compliant distributed application, regardless of the CORBA platform on which it is running, without special provisions for group communication. This means that a service can be made fault tolerant without changing its clients.

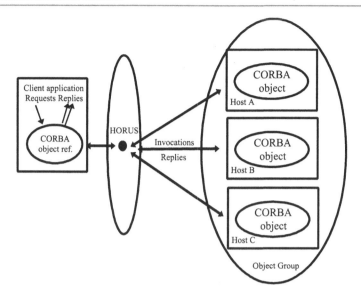

Fig. 17.5 Object-group communication in Electra, a CORBA-compliant ORB, which uses Horus to implement group multicast. The invocation method can be changed depending on the intended use. Orbix+Isis and the COOL-ORB are examples of commercial products that support object groups

When a method invocation occurs within Electra, object-group references are detected and transformed into multicasts to the member objects (see Fig. 17.5). Requests can be issued either in transparent mode, where only the first arriving member reply is returned to the client application, or in non-transparent mode, permitting the client to access the full set of responses from individual group members. The transparent mode is used by clients to communicate with replicated CORBA objects, while the nontransparent mode is employed with object groups whose members perform different tasks. Clients submit a request either in a synchronous, asynchronous, or deferred-synchronous way.

The integration of Horus into Electra shows that group programming can be provided in a natural, transparent way with popular programming methodologies. The resulting technology permits the user to plug in group communication tools anywhere that a CORBA application has a suitable interface. To the degree that process group computing interfaces and abstractions represent an impediment to their use in commercial software, technologies such as Electra suggest a possible middle ground, in which fault tolerance, security, and other group-based mechanisms can be introduced late in the design cycle of a sophisticated distributed application.

17.6 Basic Performance of Horus

A major concern of the Horus architecture is the overhead of layering. Layering was the key to most of the applications described above, and the essence of our response to the Cheriton and Skeen criticism. To paraphrase them, the criticism is that no matter what standard properties a system elects to offer, individual developers may object to some of those properties (and hence will pay an undesired cost) while needing others (and hence need an end-to-end mechanism of their own, anyhow). Horus responds by offering a framework for building the software implementing properties (layers) and allowing the user to mix and match so that the application runs over precisely the protocol stack it prefers. Most developers should agree that in doing so, Horus offers a good response to the criticism. But this flexibility would be far less interesting if it brings excessive costs.

This section presents the overall performance of Horus on a system of Sun SPARC10 workstations running SunOS 4.1.3, communicating through a loaded Ethernet. We used two network transport protocols: normal UDP and UDP with the Deering IP multicast extensions (see Deering 1988) (shown as "Deering"). These performance figures are fairly old, and were one to re-run the same experiments today, hardware advances would certainly result in better raw numbers—a Sparc 10 was a 100MIP processor, and the Ethernet on which Horus was tested ran at 10 Mbits/second (the ATM was about ten times faster). Thus, a ten-fold performance increase should be possible today. Yet these figures also represent a kind of "speed record," in the sense that Horus was (and perhaps still is) the fastest of the group communication systems. Subsequent to the development of this technology, the academic research community moved on to other topics, and there has been little attention to multicast performance over the ensuing five years—perhaps because there are not any obvious ways to take dramatic steps beyond the performance levels achieved in the work described below.

To highlight some of the performance numbers: Horus achieves a one-way latency of 1.2 ms over an unordered virtual synchrony stack (over ATM, this dropped to 0.7 ms) and, using a totally ordered layer over the same stack, 7,500 one-byte messages per second. Given an application that can accept lists of messages in a single receive operation, we can drive up the total number of messages per second to over 75,000 using the FC flow-control layer, which buffers heavily using the message list capabilities of Horus (see Friedman and van Renesse 1995b). Horus easily reached the Ethernet 1,007 KB/sec maximum bandwidth with a message size smaller than 1 KB.

The performance test program has each member do exactly the same thing: Send k messages and wait for $k * (n - 1)$ messages of size s, where s is the number of members. This way we simulate an application that imposes a high load on the system while occasionally synchronizing on intermediate results.

Figure 17.6 depicts the one-way communication latency of one-byte Horus messages. As can be seen, hardware multicast is a big win, especially when the message size goes up. In this figure, we compare Send to OrderedSend. For small messages we get a FIFO one-way latency of about 1.5 ms and a totally ordered one-way latency of about 6.7 ms. A problem with the totally ordered layer is that it can be inefficient when senders send single messages at random, and with a high degree of concurrent sending by different group members. With just one sender, the one-way latency drops to 1.6 ms. Of course, as noted earlier, computers are much faster than

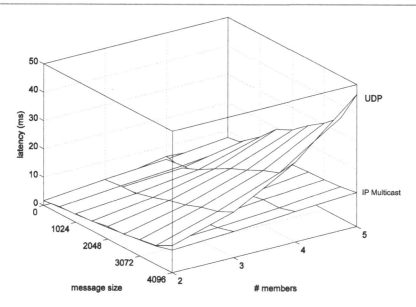

Fig. 17.6 Performance of the Horus system, with/without IP multicast

when these experiments were performed in 1996; today, a ten-fold or better speedup would be likely, simply because the hardware has become faster.

Figures 17.7 and 17.8 show the number of one-byte messages per second that can be achieved for three cases. For normal UDP and Deering UDP the throughput is fairly constant. For totally ordered communication we see that the throughput becomes better if we send more messages per round (because of increased concurrency). Perhaps surprisingly, the throughput also becomes better as the number of members in the group goes up. The reason for this is threefold. First, with more members there are more senders. Second, with more members it takes longer to order messages, and thus more messages can be packed together and sent out in single network packets. Third, the ordering protocol allows only one sender on the network at a time, thus introducing flow control and reducing collisions.

In the text, we noted several times that Horus has been "clocked" at 80,000 small multicasts per second in a four-process group. Here we can see how that figure came about. With each packet carrying a separate multicast, Horus is already running at approximately 1,000 multicasts per second. But when Horus has an opportunity to pack multiple small messages into a single packet, it will do so. A stream of asynchronous multicasts can easily achieve a packing ratio of 30 or 40 multicasts per packet, and when conditions are optimal (very small messages, sent with almost no delay at all) the ratio can reach 250 to one. Again, the numbers are bit old, and merely by moving to modern hardware we could easily obtain a ten-fold speedup. Thus, at least for small asynchronous messages, we may be entering an era in which data rates of 1,000,000 messages per second will be achievable. It is not obvious what applications can be expected to generate small messages at these data rates, but the capability is there.

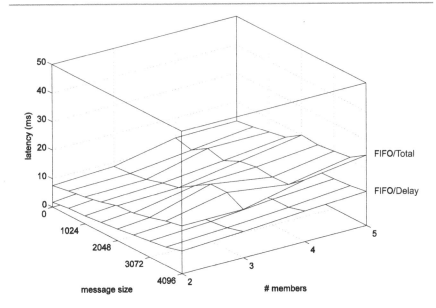

Fig. 17.7 Figure 17.6 compares the one-way latency of one-byte FIFO Horus messages over straight UDP and IP multicast. This figure compares the performance of OrderedSend and Send in Horus, both over IP multicast. Technology has advanced since this experiment was run; on modern machines a ten-fold (or more) speedup would be expected

In contrast, protocols seeking "safe" (strong durability) guarantees will not benefit as much from the technology advances of the past decade, which have yielded much higher bandwidths and processor speed, but not reduced latency all that much. These protocols are limited by worst-case latency and worst-case processing delay, and while their first phase can exploit IP multicast, the acknowledgement phase will still be a many-to-one protocol using point-to-point messages. Thus while our "hundred events a second" estimate for such protocols may be conservative on modern hardware, it is not excessively so.

17.7   Masking the Overhead of Protocol Layering

Although layering of protocols can be advocated as a way of dealing with the complexity of computer communication, it is also criticized for its performance overhead. Work by van Renesse yielded considerable insight regarding best way to mask the overhead of layering in Horus. The fundamental idea is very similar to client caching in a file system. With these new techniques, he achieves an order of magnitude improvement in end-to-end message latency in the Horus communication framework, compared to the best latency possible using Horus without these optimizations. Over an ATM network, the approach permits applications to send and deliver messages with varied properties in about 85 μs, using a protocol stack written in ML, an interpreted functional language. In contrast, the performance figures

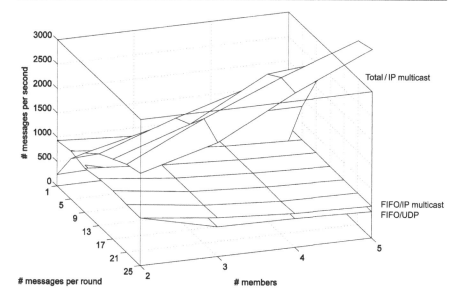

Fig. 17.8 This graph depicts the message throughput for virtually synchronous, FIFO-ordered communication (Send) over normal UDP and IP multicast, as well as for totally ordered communication (OrderedSend) over IP multicast. The number of application messages packed into each network message is shown on the "z" axis. If very small multicasts are sent in an asynchronous stream, Horus can pack as many as 250 multicasts into each message and hence can achieve throughputs as much as ten times that seen in the single message case. Today one might anticipate throughputs approaching 1,000,000 small, asynchronous messages per second

given in the previous section were for a version of Horus coded in C—carefully optimized by hand but without use of the protocol accelerator.[3]

Having presented this material in seminars, the author has noticed that the systems community seems to respond to the very mention of the ML language with skepticism, and it is perhaps appropriate to comment on this before continuing. First, the reader should keep in mind that a technology such as Horus is simply a tool used to harden a system. It makes little difference whether such a tool is internally coded in C, assembly language, LISP, or ML if it works well for the desired purpose. The decision to work with a version of Horus coded in ML is not one that would impact the *use* of Horus in applications that work with the technology through wrappers or toolkit interfaces. However, as we will see here, it does bring some important benefits to Horus itself, notably the potential for us to harden the system using formal software analysis tools. Moreover, although ML is often viewed as obscure and of academic interest only, the version of ML used in our work on Horus is not really so different from LISP or C++ once one becomes accustomed to the syntax. Finally, as we will see here, the performance of Horus coded in ML is actually better than

---

[3]This version of Horus ultimately evolved into the Ensemble system, but the two are not identical. Ensemble was a complete rewrite by Mark Hayden and Ohad Rodeh.

that of Horus coded in C, at least for certain patterns of communication. Thus, we would hope that the reader will recognize that the work reported here is in fact very practical.

As we saw in earlier chapters, modern network technology allows for very low latency communication—for example, the U-Net (see von Eicken et al. 1995) interface to ATM achieves 75 μs round-trip communication as long as the message is 40 bytes or smaller. Technologies such as Infiniband, switched fiber-optic Ethernet, and other ultra-high speed communication devices have pushed well beyond these limits. On the other hand, focusing just on ATM, if a message is larger, it will not fit in a single ATM cell, significantly increasing the latency. This points to two basic concerns: first, that if you really want to squeeze overhead to a minimum, systems such as Horus need to be designed to take full advantage of the potential performance of the communication technology on which they run, and, second, that to do so, it may be important to use small headers and introduce minimal processing overhead. Perhaps these observations are less important in a world of faster and faster processors and communications devices. Yet for those concerned with performance, dismissing the issue makes little sense: new generations of technology should open the door to new applications, not simply serve to paper over the costs and overheads of inefficient software!

Unfortunately, these properties are not typical of the protocol layers needed to implement virtual synchrony. Many of these protocols are complex, and layering introduces additional overhead of its own. One source of overhead is interfacing: crossing a layer costs some CPU cycles. The other is header overhead. Each layer uses its own header, which is prepended to every message and usually padded so that each header is aligned on a four- or eight-byte boundary. Combining this with a trend to very large addresses (of which at least two per message are needed), it is impossible to have the total amount of header space be less than 40 bytes.

The Horus Protocol Accelerator (Horus PA) eliminates these overheads almost entirely and offers the potential of one to three orders of magnitude of latency improvement over the protocol implementations described in the previous subsection—for example, we looked at the impact of the Horus PA on an ML (see Milner et al. 1990) implementation of a protocol stack with five layers. The ML code is interpreted (Ensemble, its successor, is compiled) and is therefore relatively slow compared to compiled C code. Nevertheless, between two SunOS user processes on two SPARC20s connected by a 155 MB/sec ATM network, the Horus PA permits these layers to achieve a roundtrip latency of 175 μs, down from about 1.5 ms in the original Horus system (written in C).

The Horus PA achieves its results using three techniques. First, message header fields that never change are only sent once. Second, the rest of the header information is carefully packed, ignoring layer boundaries, typically leading to headers that are much smaller than 40 bytes and thus leaving room to fit a small message within a single U-Net packet. Third, a semiautomatic transformation is done on the send and delivery operations, splitting them into two parts: one that updates or checks the header but not the protocol state, and the other vice versa. The first part is then executed by a special packet filter (both in the send and the delivery path) to circumvent the actual protocol layers whenever possible. The second part is executed, as much as possible, when the application is idle or blocked.

17.7.1 Reducing Header Overhead

In traditional layered protocol systems, each protocol layer designs its own header data structure. The headers are concatenated and prepended to each user message. For convenience, each header is aligned to a four- or eight-byte boundary to allow easy access. In systems such as the x-Kernel or Horus, where many simple protocols may be stacked on top of each other, this may lead to extensive padding overhead.

Some fields in the headers, such as the source and destination addresses, never change from message to message. Yet, instead of agreeing on these values, they are frequently included in every message and used as the identifier of the connection to the peer. Since addresses tend to be large (and they are getting larger to deal with the rapid growth the Internet), this results in significant use of space for what are essentially constants of the connection. Moreover, notice that the connection itself may already be identifiable from other information. On an ATM network, connections are named by a small four-byte VPI/VCI pair, and every packet carries this information. Thus, constants such as sender and destination addresses are implied by the connection identifier, and including them in the header is superfluous.

The Horus PA exploits these observations to reduce header sizes to a bare minimum. The approach starts by dividing header fields into four *classes*:

- *Connection identification*: Fields that never change during the period of a connection, such as sender and destination.
- *Protocol-specific information*: Fields that are important for the correct delivery of the particular message frame. Examples are the sequence number of a message, or the message type (Horus messages have types, such as "data," "ack," or "nack"). These fields must be deterministically implied by the protocol state—not on the message contents or the time at which it was sent.
- *Message-specific information*: Fields that need to accompany the message, such as the message length and checksum or a timestamp. Typically, such information depends only on the message—not on the protocol state.
- *Gossip*: Fields that technically do not need to accompany the message but are included for efficiency.

Each layer is expected to declare the header fields that it will use during initialization, and it subsequently accesses fields using a collection of highly optimized functions implemented by the Horus PA. These functions extract values directly from headers, if they are present, or otherwise compute the appropriate field value and return that instead. This permits the Horus PA to precompute header templates that have optimized layouts, with a minimum of wasted space.

Horus includes the protocol-specific and message-specific information in every message. Currently, although not technically necessary, gossip information is also included, since it is usually small. However, since the connection identification fields never change, they are only included occasionally, since they tend to be large.

A 64-bit miniheader is placed on each message to indicate which headers it actually includes. Two bits of this are used to indicate whether or not the connection identification is present in the message and to destinate the byte ordering for bytes in the message. The remaining 62 bits are a *connection cookie*, which is a magic number established in the connection identification header, selected randomly, to identify the connection.

The idea is that the first message sent over a connection will be a connection identifier, specifying the cookie to use and providing an initial copy of the connection identification fields. Subsequent messages need only contain the identification field if it has changed. Since the connection identification fields tend to include very large identifiers, this mechanism reduces the amount of header space in the normal case significantly—for example, in the version of Horus that van Renesse used in his tests, the connection identification typically occupies about 76 bytes. It is interesting to note that a similar style of header compression has become common in adapting the IP protocol stack for communication over slow wireless links (see RFC 2507 for details).

17.7.2 Eliminating Layered Protocol Processing Overhead

In most protocol implementations, layered or not, a great deal of processing must be done between the application's send operation and the time that the message is actually sent out onto the network. The same is true between the arrival of a message and the delivery to the application. The Horus PA reduces the length of the critical path by updating the protocol state only after a message has been sent or delivered and by precomputing any statically predictable protocol-specific header fields, so that the necessary values will be known *before* the application generates the next message (Fig. 17.9). These methods work because the protocol-specific information for most messages can be predicted (calculated) before the message is sent or delivered. (Recall that, as noted above, such information must not depend on the message contents or the time on which it was sent.) Each connection maintains a predicted protocol-specific header for the next send operation and another for the next delivery (much like a read-ahead strategy in a file system). For sending, the gossip information can be predicted as well, since this does not depend on the message contents. The idea is a bit like that of prefetching in a file system.

Thus, when a message is actually sent, only the message-specific header will need to be generated. This is done using a *packet filter* (see Mogul et al. 1987), which is constructed at the time of layer initialization. Packet filters are programmed using a simple programming language (a dialect of ML), and they operate by extracting information from the message information needed to form the message-specific header. A filter can also hand-off a message to the associated layer for special

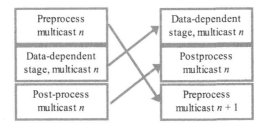

Fig. 17.9 Restructuring a protocol layer to reduce the critical path. By moving data-dependent code to the front, delays for sending the next message are minimized. Post-processing of the current multicast and preprocessing of the next multicast (all computation that can be done before seeing the actual contents of the message) are shifted to occur after the current multicast has been sent and hence concurrently with application-level computing

handling—for example, if a message fails to satisfy some assumption that was used in predicting the protocol-specific header. In the usual case, the message-specific header will be computed, other headers are prepended from the precomputed versions, and the message transmitted with no additional delay. Because the header fields have fixed and precomputed sizes, a header template can be filled in with no copying, and scatter-send/scatter-gather hardware used to transmit the header and message as a single packet without copying them first to a single place. This reduces the computational cost of sending or delivering a message to a bare minimum, although it leaves some background costs in the form of prediction code, which must be executed before the next message is sent or delivered.

17.7.3 Message Packing

The Horus PA as described so far will reduce the latency of individual messages significantly, but only if they are spaced out far enough to allow time for postprocessing. If not, messages will have to wait until the postprocessing of every previous message completes (somewhat like a process that reads file system records faster than they can be prefetched). To reduce this overhead, the Horus PA uses *message packing* (see Friedman and van Renesse 1995b) to deal with backlogs. The idea is a very simple one. After the postprocessing of a send operation completes, the PA checks to see if there are messages waiting. If there are more than one, the PA will pack these messages together into a single message. The single message is now processed in the usual way, which takes only one preprocessing and postprocessing phase. When the packed message is ready for delivery, it is unpacked and the messages are individually delivered to the application.

Returning to our file system analogy, the approach is similar to one in which the application could indicate that it plans to read three 1 KB data blocks. Rather than fetching them one by one, the file system can now fetch them all at the same time. Doing so amortizes the overhead associated with fetching the blocks, permitting better utilization of network bandwidth.

17.7.4 Performance of Horus with the Protocol Accelerator

The Horus PA dramatically improved the performance of the system over the base figures described earlier (which were themselves comparable to the best performance figures cited for other systems). With the accelerator, one-way latencies dropped to as little as 85 μs (compared to 35 μs for the U-Net implementation over which the accelerator was tested). As many as 85,000 one-byte messages could be sent and delivered per second over a protocol stack of five layers implementing the virtual synchrony model within a group of two members. For RPC-style interactions, 2,600 round-trips per second were achieved. These latency figures, however, represent a best-case scenario in which the frequency of messages was low enough to permit the predictive mechanisms to operate; when they become overloaded, latency increases to about 425 μs for the same test pattern. This points to a strong dependency of the method on the speed of the code used to implement layers.

The Horus PA does suffer from some limitations. Message fragmentation and reassembly is not supported by the PA—hence, the preprocessing of large messages must be handled explicitly by the protocol stack. Some technical complications result from this design decision, but it reduces the complexity of the PA and improves the maximum performance achievable using it. A second limitation is that the PA must be used by all parties to a communication stack. However, this is not an unreasonable restriction, since Horus has the same sort of limitation with regard to the stacks themselves (all members of a group must use identical or at least compatible protocol stacks).

17.8   Scalability

Up to the present, this book has largely overlooked issues associated with protocol scalability. Although a serious treatment of scalability in the general sense might require a whole book in itself, the purpose of this section is to set out some general remarks on the subject, as we have approached it in the Horus project. It is perhaps worthwhile to comment that, overall, surprisingly little is known about scaling reliable distributed systems.

For example, we commented earlier that Horus does not scale well if a system uses large numbers of overlapping process groups (e.g., a typical process might join ten or even a hundred groups, and the system as a whole might include tens of thousands of them). The Isis Toolkit was an even worse choice for such configurations; indeed, both systems offer a mechanism in which a large group can be presented to users as a collection of smaller ones (multicasts are sent in the large group and then filtered prior to delivery—a simple hack that works, but imposes high overhead). The problem with this approach, needless to say, is that group overlap will not always yield a simple containment pattern, and the overhead of receiving and discarding unwanted multicasts could become prohibitive.

It is not just Horus and Isis that work this way. Ensemble and Spread also address the multiple group scalability problem in the same manner. Thus there are dimensions in which Isis, Horus, Ensemble and Spread do not scale—not because the problem cannot be solved, but because we simply have not explored the dimension carefully yet!

But what of scalability in a single group? If one looks at the scalability of Horus protocols, as we did earlier in presenting some basic Horus performance figures, it is clear that Horus performs well for groups with small numbers of members and for moderately large groups when IP multicast is available as a hardware tool to reduce the cost of moving large volumes of data to large numbers of destinations. Yet although these graphs are correct, they may be misleading. In fact, as systems like Horus are scaled to larger and larger numbers of participating processes, they experience steadily growing overheads in the form of acknowledgements and negative acknowledgements from the recipient processes to the senders. A consequence is that if these systems are used with very large numbers of participating processes, the backflow associated with these types of messages and with flow control becomes a serious problem.

A simple thought experiment suffices to illustrate that there are probably fundamental limits on reliability in very large networks. Suppose that a communication network is extremely reliable, but that the processes using it are designed to distrust that network and to assume that it may actually malfunction by losing messages. Moreover, assume that these processes are in fact closely rate-matched (the consumers of data keep up with the producers), but again that the system is designed to deal with individual processes that lag far behind. Now, were it not for the backflow of messages to the senders, this hypothetical system might perform very well near the limits of the hardware. It could potentially be scaled just by adding new recipient processes and, with no changes at all, continue to provide a high level of reliability.

However, the backflow messages will substantially impact this simple and rosy scenario. They represent a source of overhead, and, in the case of flow-control messages, if they are not received, the sender may be forced to stop and wait for them. Now, the performance of the sender side is coupled to the timely and reliable reception of backflow messages, and, as we scale the number of recipients connected to the system, we can anticipate a traffic jam phenomenon at the sender's interface (protocol designers call this an acknowledgement "implosion"), which will cause traffic to get increasingly bursty and performance to drop. In effect, the attempt to protect against the mere risk of data loss or flow-control mismatches is likely to slash the maximum achievable performance of the system. Now, obtaining a stable delivery of data near the limits of our technology will become a tremendously difficult juggling problem, in which the protocol developer must trade the transmission of backflow messages against their performance impact.

Graduate students Guerney Hunt and Michael Kalantar have studied aspects of this problem in their Ph.D. dissertations at Cornell University—both using special-purpose experimental tools (i.e., neither actually experimented on Horus or a similar system; Kalantar, in fact, worked mostly with a simulator). Hunt's work was on flow control in very large scale system. He concluded that most forms of backflow were unworkable on a large scale, and he ultimately proposed a rate-based flow-control scheme in which the sender limits the transmission rate for data to match what the receivers can accommodate (see Hunt 1995). Kalantar looked at the impact of multicast ordering on latency, asking how frequently an ordering property such as causal or total ordering would significantly impact the latency of message delivery (see Kalantar 1995). He found that although ordering had a fairly small impact on latency, there were other, much more important, phenomena that represented serious potential concerns.

In particular, Kalantar discovered that as he scaled the size of his simulation, message latencies tended to become unstable and bursty. He hypothesized that in large-scale protocols, the domain of stable performance becomes smaller and smaller. In such situations, a slight perturbation of the overall system—for example, because of a lost message—could cause much of the remainder of the system to block due to reliability or ordering constraints. Now, the system would shift into what is sometimes called a *convoy* behavior, in which long message backlogs build up and are never really eliminated; they may shift from place to place, but stable, smooth delivery is generally not restored. In effect, a bursty scheduling behavior represents a more stable configuration of the overall system than one in which message delivery is extremely regular and smooth, at least if the number of recipients is large and the presented load is a substantial percentage of the maximum achievable (so that there is little slack bandwidth with which the system can catch up after an overload develops).

Hunt and Kalantar's observations are not really surprising ones. It makes sense that it should be easy to provide reliability or ordering when far from the saturation point of the hardware and much harder to do so as the communication or processor speed limits are approached.

Over many years of working with Isis and Horus, the author has gained considerable experience with these sorts of scaling and flow-control problems. Realistically, the conclusion can only be called a mixed one. On the positive side, it seems that one can fairly easily build a reliable system if the communication load is not expected to exceed, say, 20 percent of the capacity of the hardware. With a little luck, one can even push this to as high as perhaps 40 percent of the hardware. However, as the load presented to the system rises beyond this threshold, or if the number of destinations for a typical message becomes very large (hundreds), it becomes increasingly difficult to guarantee reliability and flow control. The good news is that in most settings, a shared switched Ethernet is so much faster than any computer's interface that these properties are easily achievable. The bad news, however, is that even in such configurations one observers infrequent conditions under which a few machines essentially jam the medium and disrupt performance to such a degree that only the epidemic protocols we will discuss in Chap. 17 have any hope of overcoming the problem.

A fundamental tradeoff seems to be present: One can send data and hope that these data will arrive, and, by doing so, one may be able to operate quite reliably near the limits of the hardware. But, of course, if a process falls behind, it may lose large numbers of messages before it recovers, and no mechanism is provided to let it recover these messages from any form of backup storage. On the other hand, one can operate in a less demanding performance range and in this case provide reliability, ordering, and performance guarantees. In between the two, however, lies a domain

Fig. 17.10 The Spread
client-daemon architecture

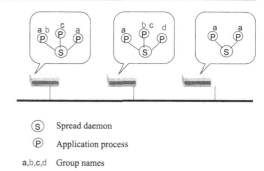

that is extremely difficult in an engineering sense and often requires a very high level of software complexity, which will necessarily reduce reliability. Moreover, one can raise serious questions about the stability of message-passing systems that operate in this intermediate domain, where the load presented is near the limits of what can be accomplished. The typical experience with such systems is that they perform well, most of the time, but that once something fails, the system falls so far behind that it can never again catch up—in effect, any perturbation can shift such a system into the domain of overloads and hopeless backlogs.

17.9   Performance and Scalability of the Spread Toolkit

The Spread toolkit is a group communication system available from www.spread.org. Spread provides a range of reliability, ordering and stability guarantees for message delivery. Spread supports a rich fault model that includes process crashes and recoveries and network partitions and merges under the extended virtual synchrony semantics. The standard virtual synchrony semantics are also supported.

Spread is highly configurable, allowing the user to tailor it to their needs. Spread can be configured to use a single daemon in the network or to use one daemon in every computer running group communication applications. Figure 17.10 illustrates a case where each computer executes one Spread daemon. As can be seen in the figure, all the physical communication is handled by the daemon. The Spread daemons keep track of the computers' heavyweight membership. Each daemon keeps track of processes residing on its machine and participating in group communication. This information is shared between the daemons, creating the lightweight process group membership. The benefits of this client-daemon architecture are significant:

- The membership algorithm is invoked only if there is a change in the daemons' membership. Otherwise, when a process joins or leaves a group, the Spread daemon sends a notification message to the other daemons. When this message is ordered, the daemons deliver a membership notification containing the new group membership to the members of the group.

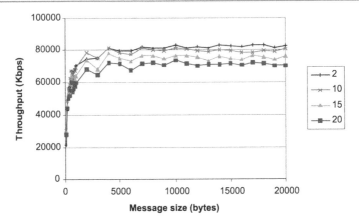

Fig. 17.11 Throughput (large messages)

- Order is maintained at the daemons' level and not on a group basis. Therefore, for multi-group systems, message ordering is more efficient in terms of latency and excessive messages. Moreover, message ordering across groups is trivial since only one global order at the daemons' level is maintained.

- Implementing open groups, where processes that are not members of a group can multicast messages to the group is easily supported.

- Flow control is maintained at the daemons' level rather than at the level of the individual process group. This leads to better overall performance in multi-group systems.

  Several performance and scalability evaluations of the Spread toolkit are included below. The tests were conducted by the developers of the system (Yair Amir and his team) on 20 Pentium III 850 MHz Linux computers connected by a 100 Mbps Fast Ethernet network. Figure 17.11 presents the total order throughput achieved by Spread as a function of the size of the network (number of daemons, each running on a separate computer) and the size of the multicast messages. Note that in all of these graphs, the curves "stack" quite nicely and the key is ordered to correspond to the curves: the top-most curve matches the top-most key entry, etc. In this experiment, half of the participating daemons serve a single local process each that multicasts to a specific group. Each of the other daemons serves a single local process that is a member of that group. For configurations ranging from 2 to 20 computers and message size above 1 Kbytes a throughput of 60–80 Mbits is achieved with a slight degradation as the number of participating computers is increased. Figure 17.12 presents the same experiment focusing on small messages. It is interesting to note the performance dip for messages around 700 Bytes that happens when messages can no longer be packed into one network packet. Similar but less pronounced fragmentation effects can also be noticed in Fig. 17.12 for larger message sizes.

  In a different experiment, Spread was run on 20 computers. On each computer a receiving application joins a certain number of groups, from 1 to 10,000. All the receiving applications on the different computers join the same set of groups. On one

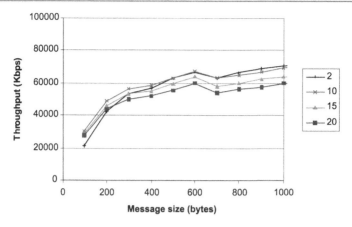

Fig. 17.12   Throughput (small messages)

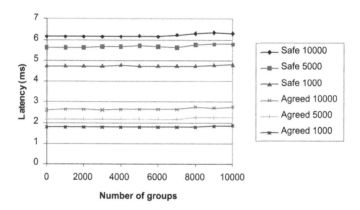

Fig. 17.13   Message latency

of the computers, a test application sends messages at a constant rate of 500 Kbps, each message to a different group joined by the receiving applications. The one-way latency of each message received is recorded by the receiving applications. The clocks of the computers are accurately synchronized through a separate process similar to NTP. Figure 17.13 presents the message latency as a function of the number of groups joined by the receiving applications, the size of the multicast messages, and the type of the service (Agreed delivery for total order, or Safe delivery for stability). The latency of Agreed delivery (total order) ranges between 1.7 ms to 2.8 ms depending on the size of the message (1000, 5000 and 10000 bytes). The latency for Safe delivery (stability) ranges between 4.7 ms to 6.4 ms. The higher latency incurred by larger messages is mostly attributed to the time it takes to send them on a 100 Mbits network. The figure shows that the number of groups in the system does not affect the message latency much. This is achieved thanks to a skip list data structure that provides $\log(n)$ access to the lightweight group structures in Spread.

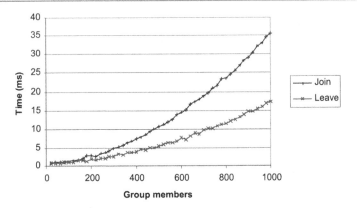

Fig. 17.14 Lightweight membership latency

In the last experiment, Spread runs on 20 computers. Each computer runs between 1 and 50 instances of a test application, each joining the same group. Therefore, in the group communication system as a whole there are between 20 to 1000 participating processes. A separate application joins and leaves the same group 100 times and the latency of each join and leave operation is measured. Figure 17.14 presents the average latency of the join and leave operations as a function of the group size. This experiment shows that joining a group that has 1000 members takes less than 40 ms (including membership notifications to all 1000 members). As the number of members in the group increases, the size of the membership notification increases linearly (each member contributes about 32 bytes to the size of the notification), and the number of notifications per daemon also increases linearly. This explains the quadratic shape of the graph. The scalability with the number of groups and number of group participants in the system is attributed to the client-daemon architecture of Spread.

Note: In all of the above figures, the ordering of items in the key matches the ordering of the curves. For example, in Fig. 17.14 the top curve corresponds to "Join" and the one below it to "Leave".

17.10 Related Reading

Chapter 23 includes a review of related research activities, which we will not duplicate here.

On the Horus system: (see Birman and van Renesse 1996; Friedman and van Renesse 1995b; van Renesse et al. 1995, 1996). Rodrigues et al. (2000) tackled the overlapping groups problem in Horus, but Glade et al. (1993) was probably the first to propose the "lightweight" group mechanism described here.

On Horus used in a real-time telephone switching application (see Friedman and Birman 1996).

On virtual fault tolerance (see Bressoud and Schneider 1995).

On layered protocols (see Abbott and Peterson 1993; Braun and Diot 1995; Clark and Tennenhouse 1987, 1990; Karamcheti and Chien 1994; Kay and Pasquale 1993).

On event counters (see Reed and Kanodia 1979).

On the Continuous Media Toolkit (see Rowe and Smith 1992).

On U-Net (see von Eicken et al. 1995).

Part IV
Related Technologies

In this fifth and final part of the book, we review additional technologies relevant to our broad reliability theme: security mechanisms, transactions, and real-time systems. This part of the book also surveys some of the research under way in academic and commercial laboratories world-wide.

There is a tremendous degree of interest in peer-to-peer computing today, and we treat the topic in Chap. 20. However, our review is tempered by some skepticism about the field. Much of the work being done related to file sharing of the type done in Gnutella and Napster, an application that violates intellectual property laws and hence is illegal. On the other hand, there are some exciting non-filesharing applications for these kinds of protocols; these are of interest because peer-to-peer technologies permit a degree of scalability never previously available and also offer reliability guarantees that can help the developer ensure that solutions will be stable even under stress and may actually be able to self-reorganize and self-repair ("regenerate") if a disruption occurs. Accordingly, our emphasis in the chapter will be on the power of peer-to-peer protocols in these kinds of unconventional setting.

With one eye on length, we will draw the line at the network layer, although one can make a very strong argument that developers who seek to build secure, reliable applications over the current Internet will ultimately be frustrated by the experience. The author has been promoting a type of overlay network architecture recently, in which the Internet is more or less partitioned into multiple side-by-side networks, only one of which would actually run the Internet protocols. Other networks could run different routing and security protocols, dedicate resources for specific needs, and even implement different queuing policies in the router layer.

Security Options for Distributed Settings 18

18.1 Security Options for Distributed Settings

The use of distributed computing systems for storage of sensitive data and in commercial applications has created significant pressure to improve the security options available to software developers. Yet distributed system security has many possible interpretations, corresponding to very different forms of guarantees, and even the contemporary distributed systems that claim to be secure often suffer from basic security weaknesses. In Chap. 3, we pointed to some of these limitations. The current chapter looks at the available security technologies, the nature of their guarantees and their limitations and discusses some of the issues raised when we require that a security system also guarantee high availability.

The constraints of brevity make it difficult to do justice to security in a setting such as ours; the topic is deserving of entire textbooks in its own right. Yet it is also difficult to treat security as a problem orthogonal to reliability: if a system is designed to withstand failures, one must anticipate the possibility that those failures will be provoked by an attacker, or by a software bug or operator error that can seem like an attack from within the system. Similarly, while there is a long tradition of tackling security and ignoring reliability, it makes little sense to talk about securing a system if reliability is not addressed. Is a system "secure" if the attacker can shut it down by crashing a component? Accordingly, the text adopts a middle ground: we have treated reliability in detail, and now offer a very skimpy review of security, not so much with the intent that a reader could learn the area from this single chapter, but just to expose the reader to some of the major options and issues.

We should perhaps comment here on the linkage between the kind of security available in a system like Isis[2] (via the g.*SetSecure*(key) API) and the issues treated below. When a user of Isis[2] puts a group into secure mode, that user either asks the system to create a group key (in which case the key ends up stored in a file accessible only under the user's login credentials), or supplies a key obtained from some form of credential source. Only processes with a valid key can make sense of traffic within the group (see Reiter and Birman 1994; Rodeh et al. 2002).

K.P. Birman, *Guide to Reliable Distributed Systems*, Texts in Computer Science, DOI 10.1007/978-1-4471-2416-0_18, © Springer-Verlag London Limited 2012

Now this is a perfectly reasonable security options, and they certainly protect against certain kinds of threat, such as spies capable of monitoring network traffic. Yet there are many reasons to object that this sort of scheme might be breakable in today's cloud platforms, particularly in a cloud owned by a less trusted entity. For example, trusting file system security is risky if the file system is actually owned and operated by a cloud provider. And while it may seem secure to store credentials in a certificate repository, on a cloud system that virtualizes applications, anything in main memory can potentially be accessed by administrators. They would simply freeze or copy the virtual machine, attach a debugger, and then hunt around until they find the key. Thus real security raises deeper issues.

The technologies we consider here span a range of approaches. At the low end of the spectrum are firewall technologies (often with an integrated network address translation capability, which will block access to machines behind the wall unless a mapping is established first) and other *perimeter defense mechanisms*, which operate by restricting access or communication across specified system boundaries. These technologies are extremely popular and clearly necessary, but very limited in their capabilities. Once an intruder has found a way to work around the firewall or to log into the system, the protection benefit is lost. For example, a common kind of computer virus operates by relaying messages received on a non-traditional path into the local area network behind a firewall. Once a machine becomes infected, such a virus permits intruders to tunnel through the firewall, opening the door to unrestricted access to data within the local area network and permitting the intruder to work on breaking into machines on that network. Worse still, machines behind a firewall are sometimes poorly protected; presumably, the administrators reason that since the firewall deals with security issues, within the firewalled environment there is no need to fuss over it!

Internal to a distributed system one typically finds *access control mechanisms*, which are often based on user and group IDs employed to limit access to shared resources such as file systems. When these are used in stateless settings, serious problems occur, and we will touch upon several of them here. Access control mechanisms rarely extend to communication, and this is perhaps their most serious security exposure. In fact, many communication systems are open to attack by a clever intruder able to guess what port numbers will be used by the protocols within the system: Secrecy of port numbers is a common security dependency in modern distributed software. Security by secrecy is always a poor idea: far preferable are schemes that can be openly described, and yet retain their security because the mechanism is simply very difficult to break. As we will see, Unix and Linux systems are particularly vulnerable in this regard because of their continued use of a stateless file system technology, NFS.

Stateful protection mechanisms operate by maintaining strong concepts of session and channel state and authenticating use at the time that communication sessions are established. These schemes adopt the approach that after a user has been validated, the difficulty of breaking into the user's session will represent an obstacle to intrusion. Microsoft's Windows systems are an example of an architecture based on a form of stateful protection. (As often happens, Windows remains vulnerable in other ways, even if the Windows file system is relatively more secure than NFS.)

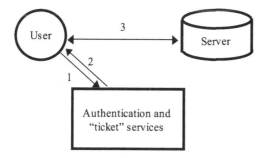

Fig. 18.1   MIT's Project Athena developed the Kerberos security architecture. Kerberos or a similar mechanism is found at the core of many distributed system security technologies today. In this approach, an authentication service is used as a trusted intermediary to create secure channels, using DES or public key encryption for security. During step 1, the user employs a password or a secret key to sign a request that a connection be established to the remote server. The authentication server, which knows the user's password or key, constructs a session key, which is sent back in duplicated form—one copy by the user and one encrypted with the server's secret key (step 2). The session key is now used between the user and server (step 3), providing the server with trusted information about user identification. In practice, Kerberos avoids the need to keep user passwords around by trading the user's password for a session to the "ticket granting service," which then acts as the user's proxy in establishing connections to necessary servers, but the idea is unchanged. Kerberos session keys expire and must be periodically renewed—hence, even if an intruder gains physical access to the user's machine, the period during which illicit actions are possible is limited. Kerberos originally used DES throughout, but later was extended to exploit public-key cryptography

Authentication-based security systems employ some scheme to authenticate the user running each application; the method may be highly reliable or less so, depending on the setting (see Denning 1984; Needham and Schroeder 1988). Individual communication sessions are protected using a key, which is negotiated using a trusted agent. Messages may be encrypted or signed in this key, resulting in very strong security guarantees. However, the costs of the overall approach can also be high, because of the intrinsically high costs of data encryption and signature schemes. Moreover, such methods may involve nontrivial modifications of the application programs being used, and they may be unsuitable for embedded settings in which no user would be available to periodically enter passwords or other authentication data. The best-known system of this sort is Kerberos, developed by MIT's Project Athena, and our review will focus on the approaches used in that system (see Schiller 1994; Steiner et al. 1988). (See Fig. 18.1.) Initially Kerberos was based on shared secrets (DES keys), but it evolved over time to exploit public keys where those were available.

Today, echoes of this second-generation Kerberos architecture can be seen in many settings: In the Internet's SSL security architecture, a system can use built-in keys to request help in establishing a secured connection to a target platform. The basic idea is that the pre-installed key allows the system to talk to a directory server and to establish a trust relationship with it, and the server then generates a certificate containing the information the client needs to create a secure channel. In a modern elaboration of the ideas seen in Kerberos, authentication servers can also vouch for one-another. Thus the user purchasing cheese from www.Fromages.com places trust in Microsoft, which vouches for Verisign's certificate directory, which has a representative at such and such a machine operated by Verisign, from which the user's computer obtained a certificate giving a public key for Fromages.com. We call this a "chain of trust." In the Internet, such chains usually are one-way structures: I can trust Fromages.com to a sufficient degree to convince me that it is safe to provide my credit card information (after all, I can always contest any false charges). Fromages.com, however, is not given any sort of strong information about my identity, although for practical reasons it may require that I provide a user-name and password. But the possession of a password is not proof that the customer is me. Indeed, the company cannot even trust data it generated previously and left on my computer: the cookies on my hard drive might have been moved there from some other machine! Even my IP address may change from time to time.

The broad picture is evolving, particular because of wider availability of hardware security modules that encapsulate security keys and can do simple security operations without leaking those keys, yet not much use has been made of these options in commercial platforms, and it is not clear that major changes are in store anytime soon. For example, if we focus on hardware roots of trust, these define an architecture in which keys can be sealed into the hardware and used to countersign messages or to unseal sensitive data, a step that would let a site produce an object that can only be accessed on a specified platform, and perhaps only by a specified application. Such an architecture can help a media company enforce copyrights on digital content, at least to a degree, and this has been a main use of the technology. Yet even with keys in the hardware, it is not hard to imagine counterattacks whereby a determined user might steal protected information; short of securing the TV monitor and the speakers, there is always a boundary to the protected realm. Moreover, because hardware trust modules are fairly slow, the operating system must use them with great care to maintain good performance. A great example of how one can walk this fine line arises in the Nexus system, created by Sirer and Schneider (see Schneider et al. 2011); it leverages hardware security to secure higher level abstractions, including a simple BGP routing service. Yet there is a great deal left to be done, and Nexus is at best a first step in the right direction.

One of the challenges for any form of security system is that once the user's identity is known, a scheme is needed for determining the appropriate set of policies to enforce. Should "Ken Birman" be permitted to order raw-milk Brie for shipment into the United States? Should FBI agent "Bob Anthony" be permitted to review the hospital records for patient Jane Jones? Notice that many factors enter into answering such policy questions: policies associated with the user, with the parties to the transaction, and with their respective countries. In a microcosm, this points to one of the more difficult issues seen even in mundane business-to-business transactions: corporation A has one set of policies, corporation B a second set, and now users a and b wish to share information. Should this be allowed? How can we write down the rules and verify that the desired transaction is safe under both sets? Best known among the security policy languages is a logic-based language called SPKI/SDSI, which uses a kind of deductive reasoning to manage trust and permission relationships. However, for practical reasons, SPKI/SDSI is not nearly elaborate enough to solve the full range of problems seen in real settings. We will touch on these issues below; they point to an exciting research opportunity.

Multilevel distributed system security architectures are based on a government security standard developed in the mid-1980s. The basic idea is to emulate the way that secrets are handled in the military and in other government settings. This security model is very strong, but it has proven to be difficult to implement and it requires extensive effort on the part of application developers. Perhaps for these reasons, the approach has not been widely successful. Moreover, the pressure to use off-the-shelf technologies made it difficult for the government to build systems that enforce multilevel security. Accordingly, we will not discuss this issue here.

Traditional security technologies have not considered availability when failures occur, creating exposure to attacks whereby critical system components are shut down, overloaded, or partitioned away from application programs that depend upon them. However, when one considers failures in the context of a security subsystem, the benign failure models of earlier chapters must be called into question. Thus, work in this area has included a reexamination of Byzantine failure models, questioning whether extremely robust authentication servers can be built that will remain available even if Byzantine failures occur. Researchers are actively working to overcome these concerns, and one can now see the first signs of a new generation of highly available security technologies (the BASE system, which employs a "practical" form of Byzantine replication (see Castro and Liskov 2002) is most often cited in this context, but the Byzantine Quorum approach of Malkhi and Reiter is also noteworthy). Interestingly, these projects use process groups, although do not employ the virtual synchrony model.

In the future, technologies supporting digital cash and digital commerce are likely to be of increasing importance and will often depend upon the use of trusted banking agents and strong forms of encryption, such as the RSA or DES standards (see Desmedt 1988; Diffie and Hellman 1979; Rivest et al. 1978). Progress in this area has been very rapid and we will review some of the major approaches. Another area in which there has been a great deal of progress recently involves secured peer-to-peer file sharing mechanisms, used in settings ranging from storage and sharing of music (often illegally) to long-term archival preservation in digital library systems. Here, security involves such topics as hiding the identity of the individual who stored or who retrieves a file, hiding the contents of the file, or overcoming "bit rot" that might occur over long periods of time in library settings where files could be preserved for decades.

Yet, if the progress in distributed system security has been impressive, the limitations on such systems remain quite serious. We saw this in Chap. 3, when first reviewing security requirements for future Web sites and Web Services systems. We identified a wide range of problems that fall outside of the prevailing security model for existing distributed systems, and as a result, are in essence not solvable today. Many of these related to representation of security policy or associating other kinds of "meaning" with security mechanisms; other limitations stem from such issues as security rules that depend upon the roles an individual is playing, or that arise when corporations collaborate in some ways while competing in others. Yet as noted above, policy languages are a weak point of modern security architectures.

On the whole, it remains difficult to secure a distributed system and very hard to add security to a technology that already exists and must be treated as a form of black box. The best-known technologies, such as Kerberos, are still used only sporadically. SSL security will let user *a* make a secure connection to company *b*, but really does not tackle problems outside of that narrow domain. This makes it hard to implement customized security mechanisms, very difficult to deal with issues of policy representation and enforcement, and leaves the average distributed system quite open to attack.

Break-ins and security violations are extremely common in the most standard distributed computing environments and if anything, each new wave of advances in operating systems and environments has made the security situation worse than in the previous generation of systems: Clearly, the very mechanisms that make it possible for systems to cooperate and interoperate also expose them to attack. Until distributed system security is difficult to *disable*, as opposed to being difficult to enable, we may continue to read about intrusions of increasingly serious nature, and will continue to be at risk for serious intrusions into our personal medical records, banking and financial systems, and personal computing environments.

18.2   Perimeter Defense Technologies

It is common to protect a distributed system by erecting barriers around it. Examples include the password control associated with dial-in ports; dial-back mechanisms, which some systems use to restrict access to a set of predesignated telephone numbers; and firewalls through which incoming and outgoing messages must pass. Each of these technologies has important limitations.

Password control systems are subject to attack by password-guessing mechanisms and by intruders who find ways to capture packets containing passwords as they are transmitted over the Internet or some other external networking technology. So-called password "sniffers" became a serious threat to system security in the mid-1990s and illustrate that the general Internet is not the benign environment it was in the early days of distributed computing, when most Internet users knew each other by name. Typical sniffers operate by exhibiting an IP address for some other legitimate machine on the network or by placing their network interfaces into a special mode, in which all passing packets will be accepted. They then scan the traffic captured for packets that might have originated in a log-in sequence. With a bit of knowledge about how such packets normally look, it is not hard to reliably capture passwords as they are routed through the Internet. Sniffers have also been used to capture credit card information and to break into e-mail correspondence.

In a world that makes increasing use of wireless connectivity and broad-band technologies, it may seem strange to talk about dial-up connections. Yet dial-up systems are often perceived as being more secure than direct network connections, presumably because the user cannot establish the connection without authenticating him or herself at the time it is established. For many reasons, dial-up security is ultimately illusory. The major problem is that many systems use their dial-up connections for data and file transfer and as a sending and receiving point for fax communications—hence, the corresponding telephone numbers are stored in various standard data files, often with connection information. An intruder who breaks into one system may in this manner learn dial-up numbers for other systems and may even find log-ins and passwords, which will make it easy to break in to them, as well. Moreover, the telephone system itself is increasingly complex and, as an unavoidable side-effect, increasingly vulnerable to intrusions. There have been many break-ins in which intruders started by wiretapping a dialup communications link, then dialed in and established a connection by replaying pre-recorded authentication information. The telephone system itself is wide-open to clever hackers, and treating the telephone network as a form of secure perimeter can be dangerously naïve if enough is at stake. Worst of all, even a system in which high speed network access has long been the norm may still have a bank of old dialup modems connected to it somewhere down in the basement. The best firewall in the world will not help if a hacker stumbles on a telephone number and password combination that will permit him to dial in.

Dial-back mechanisms, whereby the system calls the user back, clearly increase the hurdle an intruder must cross to penetrate a system relative to one in which the caller is assumed to be a potentially legitimate user. However, such systems also depend for their security upon the integrity of the telephone system, which, as we have noted, can be subverted. In particular, the emergence of mobile telephones and the introduction of mobility mechanisms into telephone switching systems create a path by which an intruder can potentially redirect a telephone dial-back to a telephone number other than the intended one. Such a mechanism is a good example of a security technology that can protect against benign attacks but would be considerably more exposed to well-organized malicious ones.

Firewalls (often integrated with network address translators) have become popular as a form of protection against communication-level attacks on distributed systems. This technology operates using *packet filters* and must be instantiated at all the access points to a distributed network. Each copy of the firewall will have a *filtering control policy* in the form of a set of rules for deciding which packets to reject and which to pass through; although firewalls that can check packet content have been proposed, typical filtering is on the basis of protocol type, sender and destination addresses, and port numbers. Thus, for example, packets can be allowed through if they are addressed to the e-mail or FTP server on a particular node; otherwise they are rejected. Often, firewalls are combined with *proxy* mechanisms, which permit file transfer and remote log in through an intermediary system enforcing further restrictions. The use of proxies for the transfer of public Web pages and FTP areas has also become common: In these cases, the proxy is configured as a mirror of some protected internal file system area, copying changed files to the less-secure external area periodically.

Other technologies commonly used to implement firewalls include application-level proxies and routers. With these approaches, small fragments of user-supplied code (or programs obtained from the firewall vendor) are permitted to examine the incoming and outgoing packet streams. These programs run in a loop, waiting for the next incoming or outgoing message, performing an acceptance test upon it, and then either discarding the message or permitting it to continue. The possibility of logging the message and maintaining additional statistics on traffic, or routing certain messages to specialized systems designed to diagnose and protect against intrusions, are also commonly supported.

Yet this cuts both ways. Network address translation is sometimes claimed to increase security, because NATs make it physically hard for an intruder to access machines behind the NAT interface. However, once an intruder breaks into a system through a NAT, that security evaporates: it then suffices to introduce an application-level "router" and, in effect, tunnel messages through the NAT and then retransmit them from behind it. Thus, while a NAT does secure a system in some ways, once a chink in the security architecture has been identified, the NAT protection may collapse.

For example, a common pattern of intrusion starts when the user downloads some form of application. This happens all the time: we extend our web browser with a codec, or download a file decompression utility, or a child who shares the computer downloads a game. Suppose that in additional to doing the tasks that program was designed to do, it also makes a connection out through the network filewall. That connection can now function as a tunnel by which an intruder can gain access to the local network and subvert the system. Yet as long as the downloaded code functions normally, the user may be completely unaware that his or her system has been compromised! This type of "Trojan horse" technique has become very common.

The major problem associated with firewall technologies is that they represent a single point of compromise: If the firewall is breached, the intruder essentially could gain free run of the enclosed system. And yet there are a tremendous number of ways to break through even the best firewall. Firewalls are thus central to modern distributed systems security architectures, and yet are simultaneously the weakest point in many systems.

The need to support remote connectivity through firewalls is leading many corporations to implement what are called *virtual private networks* (see Fig. 18.2). In the most general case, a VPN is a kind of network in which communication is authenticated (typically using a digital signature scheme) so that all messages originating outside of the legitimately accepted sources will be rejected. The idea is that one can run a VPN on top of a public network without fear; intruders will not be able to compromise packets and may not even be able to read them.

More often, VPN security is used to create a secure tunnel through a firewall, as a way to allow a mobile user to connect to his home network. In this common use, the VPN becomes a surprisingly serious security *risk*, because it makes it so easy for a machine that often lives outside the corporate firewall to tunnel through from time to time. Suppose that Dr. Welby is given a PC for home use by the hospital at which he works. At home, his son sometimes uses it to connect to the Internet, and

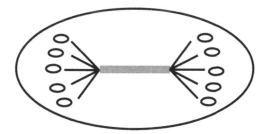

Fig. 18.2 A long-haul connection internal to a distributed system (*gray*) represents a potential point of attack. Developers often protect systems with firewalls on the periphery but overlook the risk that the communication infrastructure itself may be compromised, offering the intruder a backdoor approach into the protected environment. Although some corporations are protecting themselves against such threats by using encryption techniques to create virtual private networks, most mundane communication systems are increasingly at risk

the machine becomes infected with a virus. Dr. Welby may be completely unaware that his computer is compromised, but the next time he uses his machine at work, or connects to the hospital with a VPN connection, any viruses on his machine can gain access to the internal LAN.

Thus, while the prospects for strong security may be promising in certain settings, such as military systems or electronic banking systems, the more routine computing environments, on which the great majority of sensitive applications run, remain open to a great variety of attacks and are likely to continue to have such exposure well into the next decade, if not indefinitely. The core problem is really a social one: the ways we use computers are at odds with strong security.

This situation may seem pessimistic; however, in many respects, the other shoe has not even fallen. Although it may seem extremely negative to think in such terms, it is probable that future information terrorists and warfare tactics will include some of these forms of attack and perhaps others that are hard to anticipate until they have first been experienced. One day, terrorist hackers may manage to do significant damage through a coordinated cyber-attack, for example using a virus that spreads rapidly and also wipes disks. Up to the time of this writing, we have seen nasty viruses and we have seen viruses that spread quickly, but not both at once. Perhaps for this reason, our exposure to such risks is only increasing.

Although we will now move on to other topics in security, we note that defensive management techniques can be coupled with security-oriented wrappers to raise the barriers in systems that use firewall technologies for protection.

18.3   Access Control Technologies

Access control techniques operate by restricting use of system resources on the basis of user or group identifiers, which are typically fixed at log-in time—for example, by validation of a password. It is typical that these policies trust the operating system, its key services, and the network. In particular, the log-in program is trusted to obtain the password and correctly check it against the database of system passwords, granting the user permission to work under the user-ID or group-ID only if a match is detected. The log-in system trusts the file server or Network Information Server to respond correctly with database entries that can be used safely in this authentication process, and the resource manager (typically, an NFS server or database server) trusts the ensemble, believing that all packets presented to it as "valid NFS packets" or "valid XYZbase requests" originated at a trusted source.[1] (Microsoft's PC File System uses a stronger model and is not quite as "trusting" in this respect.)

These dependencies are only rarely enforced rigorously. Thus, one could potentially attack an access control system by taking over a computer, rebooting it as the root or superuser, directing the system to change the user-ID to any desired value, and then starting work as the specified user. An intruder could replace the standard log-in program with a modified one—introducing a false NIS, which would emulate the NIS protocol but substitute invalid password records. One could even code one's own version of the NFS client protocol, which, operating from user space as a normal RPC application, could misrepresent itself as a trusted source of NFS requests. All these attacks on the NFS have been used successfully at one time or another, and many of the loopholes have been closed by one or more of the major vendors. Yet the fact remains that file and database servers continue to be largely trusting of the major operating system components on the nodes where they run and where their clients run.

Perhaps the most serious limitation associated with access control mechanisms is that they generally do not extend to the communication subsystem: typically, any process can issue an RPC message to any address it wishes to place in a message and can attempt to connect to any stream end point for which it possesses an address. In practice, these exposures are hard to exploit, because a process that undertakes to do so will need to guess the addresses and ports being used by the applications it attacks. Precisely to reduce this risk, many applications exploit *randomly generated* end-point addresses, so that an intruder would be forced to guess a pseudorandom number to break into a critical server. However, pseudorandom numbers may be less random than intended. Moreover, an intruder with a packet sniffer may be able to pull all sorts of "secrets" off the wire: MAC addresses of trusted computers, port numbers, etc.

Such break-ins are more common than one might expect—for example, in 1994 an attack on X11 servers was discovered in which an intruder found a way to deduce the connection port number that would be used. Sending a message that would cause the X11 server to prepare to accept a new connection to a shell command window, the intruder managed to connect to the server and to send a few commands to it. Not surprisingly, this proved sufficient to open the door to a full-fledged penetration. Moreover, the attack was orchestrated in such a manner as to trick typical firewalls

---

[1]Not all file systems are exposed to such problems—for example, the AFS file system has a sophisticated stateful client/server architecture, which is also much more robust to attack. AFS has become popular, but it is less widely used than NFS.

Table 18.1   NFS security assumptions

NFS assumption	Dependent on...
O/S integrity	NFS protocol messages originate only in trusted subsystems or the kernel
	Attacks: Introduce a computer running an open operating system; modify the NFS subsystem. Develop a user-level program to implement the NFS client protocol; use it to emulate a legitimate NFS client issuing requests under any desired user-ID.
Authentication	Assumes that user- and group-ID information is valid
	Attacks: Spoof the Network Information Server or NFS response packets so that authentication will be done against a falsified password database. Compromise the log-in program. Reboot the system or log-in using the root or superuser account; then change the user-ID or group-ID to the desired one and issue NFS requests.
Network integrity	Assumes that communication over the network is secure
	Attacks: Intercept network packets, reading file system data and modifying data written. Replay NFS commands, perhaps with modifications.

into forwarding these poisoned messages, even though the normal firewall protection policy should have required that they be rejected. Until the nature of the attack was understood, the approach permitted intrusion into a wide variety of firewall-protected systems. In 2003, a rather similar attack occurred, but this time involved the Microsoft remote procedure call mechanism at the center of the Windows implementation of distributed object invocations. In both cases, the core problem is that it is difficult to inexpensively validate a packet as it arrives on a machine, hence a faked packet may sometimes slip through.

To give a sense of how exposed typical distributed systems currently are, Table 18.1 presents some of the assumptions made by the NFS file server technology when it is run without the security technology available from some vendors (in practice, NFS security is rarely enabled in systems that are protected by firewalls; the security mechanisms are hard to administer in heterogeneous environments and can slow down the NFS system significantly). We have listed typical assumptions of the NFS, the normal reason that this assumption holds, and one or more attacks that operate by emulation of the normal NFS environment in a way that the server is unable to detect. The statelessness of the NFS server makes it particularly easy to attack, but most client/server systems have similar dependencies and are similarly exposed.

One can only feel serious concern when these security exposures are contemplated against the backdrop of increasingly critical applications that trust client/server technologies such as NFS—for example, it is very common to store sensitive files on unprotected NFS servers. As we noted, there is an NFS security standard, but it is vendor-specific and may be impractical to use in heterogeneous environments. A hospital system, for example, is necessarily heterogeneous: The workstations used in such systems must interoperate with a great variety of special-purpose devices and peripherals, produced by many vendors. Thus, in precisely the setting one might hope would use strong data protection, one typically finds propri-etary solutions or unprotected use of standard file servers! Indeed, many hospitals might be prevented from using a strong security policy, because, since so many in-dividuals need access to a patient's record, any form of restriction would effectively be nullified.

Thus, in a setting where protection of data is not just important but is actually legally mandated, it may be very easy for an intruder to break in. While such an individual might find it hard to walk up to a typical hospital computing station and break through its password protection, by connecting a portable laptop computer to the hospital Ethernet (potentially a much easier task), it would be easy to gain access to the protected files stored on the hospital's servers. Such security exposures are already a potentially serious issue, and the problem will only grow more serious with time.

When we first discussed the NFS security issues, we pointed out that there are other file systems that do quite a bit better in this regard. The Microsoft NT File Sys-tem protocol is far more secure than NFS. The AFS system, developed originally at Carnegie Mellon University and then commercialized by Transarc (an IBM divi-sion) has been widely adopted. But most systems combine these kinds of secured technology with other less secure ones. Attackers simply focus on the weakest link that they can find, and since few system operators can even account for the majority of programs running in the background on the typical computer in their installation, the intruder will often have many options to pick from!

18.4   Authentication Schemes, Kerberos, and SSL

The weak points of typical computing environments are readily seen to be their authentication mechanisms and their blind trust in the security of the communica-tion subsystem. Best known among the technologies that respond to these issues is MIT's Kerberos system, developed as part of Project Athena, and SSL security, the standard used in the Internet.

Both schemes make use of encryption, albeit in slightly different ways, hence we start by reviewing the existing encryption technologies and their limitations. Although a number of encryption schemes have been proposed, the most popular ones at the time of this writing are the RSA public key algorithms and a version of the DES encryption standard in which one creates 3 DES keys and then encrypts information three times (called triple DES, the effect is comparable to DES with a single triple-length key). Kerberos was originally designed to use (single) DES, then extended to use triple-DES and finally "ported" to run on RSA. SSL, in contrast, was designed to use RSA but with provisions for the use of other non-RSA schemes; to the author's knowledge, SSL over RSA is far more prevalent than any other mix.

The cryptographic community has generated far more "tools" than these basic schemes, including message digest and signature algorithms, ways of splitting se-crets into n portions so that any k out the n can be used to reconstruct the secret (but fewer "shares" are inadequate to do so), techniques for hiding information so that a third-party can counter-sign it without actually seeing it, etc. However, none of these are widely used in the Internet today, and hence they are beyond the limited scope of the present chapter.

18.4.1   RSA and DES

RSA (see Rivest et al. 1978) is an implementation of a public key cryptosystem (see Diffie and Hellman 1979), which exploits properties of modular exponentiation. In practice, the method operates by generating pairs of *keys*, which are distributed to the users and programs within a distributed system. One key within each pair is the *private* key and is kept secret. The other key is *public*, as is an encryption function, *crypt(key, object)*. The encryption function has a number of useful properties. Suppose that we denote the public key of some user as K and the private key of that user as K^{-1}. Then $crypt(K, crypt(K^{-1}, M)) = crypt(K^{-1}, crypt(K, M)) = M$—that is, encryption by the public key will decrypt an object encrypted previously with the private key and vice versa. Moreover, even if keys A and B are unrelated, encryption is commutative: $crypt(A, crypt(B, M)) = crypt(B, crypt(A, M))$.

Although a number of mechanisms can be used to implement RSA, the scheme actually used is based on modular exponentiation and is secure under the assumption that very large composite integers are computationally hard to factor. In the scheme, if one knows the factors of a large integer, it is easy to decode messages. The public key is the large integer itself, and the private key is its factorization. RSA keys are typically very large, indeed—512 or 1024 bits are common at the time of this writing. With the best known factoring algorithms, a 512-bit key would still require some six months of computer time on a grid of processors to factor, and a 1024-bit key is effectively impossible to factor. However, a 512 bit key seemed absurdly long even a few years ago, hence one must wonder if this implementation of RSA has a limited lifetime and, if so, it is not at all clear what might replace it!

At any rate, in typical use, public keys are published in some form of trusted directory service (see Birrell 1985). If process A wants to send a secure message to process B (this message could only have originated in process A and can only be read by process B), A sends $crypt(A^{-1}, crypt(B, M))$ to B, and B computes $crypt(B^{-1}, crypt(A, M))$ to extract the message. Here, we have used A and A^{-1} as shorthand for the public and private keys of processes A and B. A can send a message that only B can read by computing the simpler $crypt(B, M)$ and can sign a message to prove that the message was seen by A by attaching $crypt(A^{-1}, digest(M))$ to the message, where $digest(M)$ is a function that computes some sort of small number reflecting the contents of M, perhaps using an error-correcting code for this purpose. Upon reception, process B can compute the digest of the received message and compare this with the result of decrypting the signature sent by A using A's public key. This message can be validated by verifying that these values match (see Denning 1984).

A process can also be asked to encrypt or sign a blinded message when using the RSA scheme. To solve the former problem, process A is presented with $M' = crypt(B, M)$. If A computes $M'' = crypt(A^{-1}, M')$, then $crypt(B^{-1}, M'')$ will yield *crypt*(A^{-1}, M) without A having ever seen M. Given an appropriate message digest function, the same approach also allows a process to sign a message without being able to read that message.

In contrast, the DES standard (see *Data Encryption Standard* 1977; Diffie and Hellman 1979) is based on shared secret keys, in which two users or process exchanging a message will both have a copy of the key for the messages sent between them. Separate functions are provided for encryption and decryption of a message. Similar to the RSA scheme, DES can also be used to encrypt a digest of a message as proof that the message has not been tampered with. However, there is no standard blinding mechanism for DES.

DES is the basis of a government standard, which specifies a standard key size and can be implemented in hardware. Although the standard key size is large enough to provide security for most applications, the key is still small enough to permit it to be broken using a supercomputing system or a large number of powerful workstations in a distributed environment. This is viewed by the government as a virtue of the scheme, because it provides the possibility of decrypting messages for purposes of criminal investigation or national security. When using DES, it is possible to convert plain text (such as a password) into a DES key; in effect, a password can be used to encrypt information so that it can only be decrypted by a process that also has a copy of that password. As will be seen, this is the central feature that makes possible DES-based authentication architectures such as Kerberos (see Schiller 1994; Steiner et al. 1988).

One way to work within the DES standard and yet avoid the weakness of the 48-bit key standard is to apply DES three times to each message, using different keys. This approach, called "triple DES," is believed to offer roughly the same cryptographic security as would DES with a single triple-length key.

During the early 1990s, a security standard was proposed for use in telecommunication environments. This standard, Capstone, was designed for telephone communication but is not specific to telephony; it involves a form of key for each user and supports what is called *key escrow*, whereby the government is able to reconstruct the key by combining two portions of it, which are stored in secure and independent locations (see Denning and Branstad 1996). The objective of this work was to permit secure and private use of telephones while preserving the government's right to wiretap with appropriate court orders. A product called the Clipper chip, which implements Capstone in hardware, was eventually produced, and incorporated into some secure telephones. The same mechanism was also adapted for use in computer networks and implemented in a PCMCIA card called Fortezza. However, after a brief period of experimentation with the card, the commercial sector lost interest in it, making it harder and harder for the government to procure Capstone-based solutions. The stunning advances in wireless communication and telephony created a tough choice for the government: either to go it alone, at great cost, or to accept defeat and simply work with commercially available off-the-shelf technologies, layering mechanisms "over" the COTS base to harden it. Faced with a mixture of budget stress and the impossibility of competing for "lowest cost bidder" contracts, both Clipper and Fortezza vanished from the market. At the time of this writing, a number of mobile telephone security products can be found, but there seem to be no generally accepted security standards. On the other hand, a new computer security architecture called Palladium, based on the idea of hard-wiring a security key into a protected read-only register internal to an Intel CPU, is gaining considerable attention, and may eventually offer some of the same opportunities.

Setting aside their limited commercial impact, both DES and Capstone security standard remain the subjects of vigorous debate. On the one hand, such methods limit privacy and personal security, because the government is able to break both schemes and indeed may have taken steps to make them easier to break than is widely known. On the other hand, the growing use of information systems by criminal organizations clearly poses a serious threat to security and privacy as well, and it is obviously desirable for the government to be able to combat such organizations. Meanwhile, the fundamental security of methods such as RSA and DES is not known—for example, although it is conjectured that RSA is very difficult to break, in 1995 it was shown that in some cases, information about the amount of time needed to compute the *crypt* function could provide data that substantially reduce the difficulty of breaking the encryption scheme. Moreover, clever uses of large numbers of computers have made it possible to break DES encryption. For example, when the first version of this textbook came out in 1997, a "state of the art" DES key seemed fairly secure. Today, most DES systems use triple DES.

Thus we face many kinds of challenge. Should systems be "genuinely" secure, or should they have weaknesses that would allow intelligence agencies to crack messages? Is security even possible? And to the extent that it is, will the commercial sector embrace the needed technologies? Up to the present, we lack a compelling story that addresses all of these issues at the same time.

18.4.2 Kerberos

The Kerberos system is a widely used implementation of secure communication channels, based on the DES encryption scheme (see Schiller 1994; Steiner et al. 1988). Integrated into the DCE environment, Kerberos is quite popular in the UNIX community. The approach genuinely offers a major improvement in security over that which is traditionally available within UNIX. Its primary limitations are, first, that SSL security dominates in the Internet and Web, making Kerberos increasingly "non-standard." Secondly, applications using Kerberos must be modified to create communication channels using the Kerberos secure channel facilities. Although this may seem to be a minor point, it represents a surprisingly serious one for potential Kerberos users, since application software using Kerberos is not yet common. Nonetheless, Kerberos has had some important successes.

In what follows, we will discuss the original DES-based Kerberos protocol, although an RSA version of Kerberos was introduced many years ago. Kerberos per-se is perhaps less important than the basic ideas it illustrates. The basic Kerberos protocols revolve around the use of a trusted authentication server, which creates session keys between clients and servers upon demand. The basic scheme is as follows. At the time the user logs in, he or she presents a name and password to a log-in agent, which runs in a trusted mode on the user's machine, and establishes a secured channel to the Kerberos authentication server at boot time. Having logged in, the user is able to connect securely to various applications using Kerberos as an intermediary. The role of Kerberos is to mediate during connection setup, helping the client and server to authenticate one-another and to agree on a key for use to protect their shared communication channel.

Suppose that a user wants to connect to Fromages.com to purchase a wheel of finest French brie cheese. The first step is to request help from Kerberos. The agent on the user's machine creates a "connection request" message (it says, more or less, that "Ken Birman wishes to connect to Fromages.com"), signs this message using the user's password, encrypts it using the authentication server's key, and sends it to the server. (A few extra pieces of information are used to avoid "replay" attacks, such as the time of the request and a randomly generated number—a "nonce" in the parlance of the cryptographic community).

The Kerberos authentication server keeps a database of user names and passwords, and of course also remembers the key it negotiated with the log-in agent at boot time. It decrypts the request, verifies that Ken Birman's password was really used to sign it, and then creates a "certificate" containing information by which each end-point can validate the other, encrypting the piece destinated for use by Fromages.com with a secret key known only to Fromages.com, and the piece destinated for the user's computer with the session key employed by the log-in agent. It sends this back to the log-in agent, which decrypts it and extracts the two pieces of the certificate.

Now the user's computer presents the remote half of the certificate to Fromages.com. The Fromages.com server can easily validate the request, since it has been encrypted with its own secret key, which could only have been done by the authentication server. The session key also contains trustworthy information concerning the identification of the person who is making the request (in our example, me), the workstation-ID, and the expiration time of the key itself. Thus, the server knows that it is being used by someone with my password, knows which machine I'm on, and knows how long the session can remain open without a refreshed session key.

In UNIX, a "super user" with access to the debugger can potentially read information out of memory, including the memory of the log-in agent. Thus a risk associated with this method is that it needs the user's password as an encryption key and hence must keep it in the memory of the agent for a long period of time. Kerberos tries to minimize this threat by exchanging the user's password for a type of one-time password, which has a limited lifetime and is stored only at a *ticket granting service* with which a session is established as soon as the user logs in. In effect, the user's password is only employed very briefly, to obtain a temporary "one-time" password that will be employed on the user's behalf for a little while. The human user will be prompted to re-enter his or her password if the session lasts very long, or if the machine goes idle for more than a few minutes.

Once a session exists, communication to and from the file server can be done in the clear, in which case the file server can use the user-ID information established during the connection setup to authenticate file access, or it can be signed, giving a somewhat stronger guarantee that the channel protocol has not been compromised in any way, or even encrypted, in which case data exchange are only accessible by the user and the server. In practice, the initial channel authentication, which also provides strong authentication guarantees for the user-ID and group-ID information to be employed in restricting file access, suffices for most purposes. An overview of the protocol is seen in Fig. 18.1 on p. 545.

The Kerberos protocol has been proven secure against most forms of attack (see Lampson et al. 1992); one of its few dependencies is its trust in the system time servers, which are used to detect expiration of session keys (see Gong 1989). Moreover, the technology has been shown to scale to large installations using an approach whereby authentication servers for multiple protection domains can be linked to create session keys spanning wide areas. Perhaps the most serious exposure of the technology is that associated with partitioned operation. If a portion of the network is cut off from the authentication server for its part of the network, Kerberos session keys will begin to expire, and it will be impossible to refresh them with new keys. Gradually, such a component of the network will lose the ability to operate, even between applications and servers residing entirely within the partitioned component. In applications requiring support for mobility, with links forming and being cut very dynamically, the Kerberos design would require additional development.

A less obvious exposure to the Kerberos approach is that associated with active attacks on its authentication and ticket granting server. The server is a software system operating on standard computing platforms, and those platforms are often subject to attack over the network. A knowledgeable user might be able to concoct a poison pill by building a message, which will look sufficiently legitimate, to be passed to a standard service on the node; this message will then provoke the node into crashing by exploiting some known intolerance to incorrect input. The fragility of contemporary systems to this sort of attack is well known to protocol developers, many of whom have the experience of repeatedly crashing the machines with which they work during the debugging stages of a development effort. Thus, one could imagine an attack on Kerberos or a similar system aimed not at breaking through its security architecture, but rather at repeatedly crashing the authentication server, with the effect of denying service to legitimate users.

Kerberos supports the ability to prefabricate and cache session keys (tickets) for current users, and this mechanism would offer a period of respite to a system subjected to a denial of service attack. However, after a sufficient period of time, such an attack would effectively shut down the system.

Within military circles, there is an old story (perhaps not true) about an admiral who used a new generation of information-based battle management system in a training exercise. Unfortunately, the story goes, the system had an absolute requirement that all accesses to sensitive data be logged on an audit trail, which for that system was printed on a protected line printer. At some point during the exercise the line printer jammed or ran low on paper, and the audit capability shut down.

The admiral's command was crippled by shutdown of the computer system, and the admiral himself developed such a dislike for computers that henceforth, he decreed, no computing system could be installed in his unit without first having its security subsystem disabled. Basically, he felt that having access to data when he needed them was a far higher priority than ensuring that bad guys would be kept away from those data.

And this illustrates an important point. The developer of a secure system often thinks of his or her task as being that of protecting critical data from the "bad guys." But any distributed system has a more immediate obligation, which is to make data and critical services available to the "good guys." Denial of service in the name of security may be far worse than providing service to an unauthorized user!

As noted earlier, Kerberos has been extended to also run over RSA. In this approach, the server becomes a directory managing public keys for applications in the system. Knowing a public key, it is possible to make a secure connection to that server. Of course, one can argue that such a system is no longer Kerberos, but we will leave semantics to the experts and simply observe that Kerberos, and its progeny, have been hugely important systems.

18.4.3 ONC Security and NFS

Sun Microsystems, Inc., has developed an RPC standard, which it calls Open Network Computing (ONC), around the protocols used to communicate with NFS servers and similar systems. ONC includes an authentication technology, which can protect against most of the spoofing attacks previously described. Similar to a Kerberos system, this technology operates by obtaining unforgeable authorization information at the time a user logs into a network. The NFS is able to use this information to validate accesses as being from legitimate workstations and to strengthen its access control policies. If desired, the technology can also encrypt data to protect against network intruders who monitor passing messages.

ONC security shares the strengths and weaknesses of Kerberos, but is also considered to have suffer from some important practical limitations. For example, a set of restrictions limits export of strong cryptographic-based security. As a result, it is impractical for Sun to enable the NFS protection mechanisms by default or to envision an open standard, allowing complete interoperability between client and server systems from multiple vendors (the major benefit of NFS), which, at the same time, would be secure. A second worry related to heterogeneity: Sun systems need to "play" in settings where hardware and software from other vendors will also be used. Security can be a barrier to setting up such configurations, and when this happens, the user often disables security. He or she may never get around to figuring out how to re-enable it.

Beyond the heterogeneity issue is the problem of management of a security technology in complex settings. Although ONC security works well for NFS systems in fairly simple systems based entirely on Sun products, serious management challenges occur in complex system configurations, where users are spread over a large physical area, or in systems using heterogeneous hardware and software sources. With security disabled, these problems vanish. Finally, the same availability issues raised in our discussion of Kerberos pose a potential problem for ONC security. Thus, it is perhaps not surprising that these technologies have not been adopted on a widespread basis. Such considerations raise the question of how one might wrap a technology such as NFS, which was not developed with security in mind, so that security can be superimposed without changing the underlying software. One can also ask about monitoring a system to detect intrusions as a proactive alternative to hardening a system against intrusions and then betting that the security scheme will in fact provide the desired protection. We discuss these issues further in Chap. 22.

18.4.4 SSL Security

The Secure Sockets Layer (SSL) standard defines a scheme for obtaining security over a TCP channel, typically between a Web browser and a secure Web server to which it connects. SSL consists of two elements: a chain of trust model used to find a trustworthy authentication server, and a protocol by which a client system can obtain security certificates containing a security key (normally, an RSA public key) from that authentication server and then use it to create a secured TCP connection to the target platform. In the SSL model, unlike Kerberos, the focus is on establishing trust in the client that it is talking to the correct server; the server is expected to authenticate the client using some other end-to-end mechanism (a password, or a visa card, etc.).

The chain of trust model works as follows. A client system is pre-loaded with a security key and network address for an initial directory server. For example, the Microsoft Windows platform has a preinstalled public key and network address by which it can contact a Microsoft security directory service, and the Netscape browser has a preinstalled key and address for a Netscape directory service. This information is maintained using a mechanism designed to be as tamper-proof as possible.

Microsoft (and Netscape) maintains a directory of trusted authentication servers: Verisign, for example. And Verisign can maintain a directory of its own—perhaps, machines within its data center. Thus through a chain of authorizations, we can work our way down from Microsoft to a company that makes part of its money by maintaining a database of certificates on behalf of corporate clients. Our client system, seeking a secured connection to Fromages.com, determines from Fromages.com that it uses Verisign as a directory server, then traverses the chain to establish contact with a Verisign authentication server, and then retrieves a trusted certificate for Fromages.com from that server.

The certificate, as might be expected, includes identification information for the issuer of the certificate and for the target server, expiration time, a public key for the target, and perhaps additional information concerning the possible uses of the key. In effect, the client system learns that "Microsoft trusts Verisign, and Verisign vouches for this certificate for the Fromages.com secure transactional server." Unlike a Kerberos certificate, the SSL one does not include information about the specific client; this is either a strength of the scheme or a weakness, depending upon one's priorities.

Given the public key of the target server, the client system can now create a secure connection to the target system. It does this by creating a TCP connection but then exchanging a series of messages over that connection, using the public key of the server to ensure that the endpoint of the channel is in possession of the same private key that it held when the certificate for the server was first registered. In principle, SSL can use RSA keys, DES keys, or other cryptographic systems, and can sign or encrypt messages. The "mode" of connection is negotiated by the client and server in the first messages of the authentication handshake.

Why do we need to exchange messages at all, given the certificate? It turns out there even with keying information for the target system, a bit more work must be done. To illustrate both the protocol and these additional issues, we will imagine a dialog between two people, Alice and Bob, who wish to create a connection. Bob has a pair of keys, one public and one private. Bob's public key has been obtained by Alice from a trustworthy third party. Suppose that Alice tackles this problem by first generating a random message and sending it to Bob:

```
A->B  random-message
```

In an SSL-like protocol, Bob could use his private key to encrypt Alice's message and return the encrypted result:

```
B->A  {random-message}bobs-private-key
```

Alice receives this message and decrypts it by using Bob's previously published public key. She compares the decrypted message with the one she originally sent to Bob; if they match, she knows she's talking to Bob. As long as Alice does not reuse the same random message, an imposter lacking Bob's private key would be unable to properly encrypt the random message for Alice to check.

There is a problem with the above protocol. Bob may not be comfortable simply signing an unknown message with his key, because keys are often used for many purposes and Alice may be trying to trick Bob into signing something he did not intend to sign, like a loan guarantee. Thus we need to enhance this simple protocol to offer Bob a bit more protection. Here is a modified protocol in which Bob generates the messages he signs (hence he does not need to trust Alice), and uses digital signatures instead of outright encryption. (We will represent a signature as an encrypted message digest):

```
A->B  ''Hello, are you Bob?''
B->A  ''Alice, This Is Bob'' {digest[Alice, This Is Bob]}
      bobs-private-key
```

When he uses this protocol, Bob knows what message he is sending to Alice, and he does not mind signing it. He sends the unencrypted version of the message first, "Alice, This Is Bob." Then he sends a signature: a digest of the string, encrypted with his private key. Alice can easily verify that Bob is Bob, and Bob has not signed anything he does not want to. Recall that in the certificate for Bob, Alice has a secure version of Bob's name, and she can check this against the name in the message to make sure everything matches up. She needs to trust the source of the certificate, of course, but if that source hands out legitimate certificates, Alice has a secure way to convince herself she is talking to Bob.

Once Alice has authenticated Bob, she can send Bob a message that only Bob can decode:

```
A->B {secret}bobs-public-key
```

The only way to find the secret is by decrypting the above message with Bob's private key. Exchanging a secret is another powerful way of using public key cryptography. Even if the communication between Alice and Bob is being observed, nobody but Bob can get the secret.

When working with SSL, the secret is typically a freshly generated key that will now be used between Alice and Bob to sign or encrypt subsequent data on their shared connection. This technique strengthens Internet security by allowing Alice and Bob to switch from RSA to a symmetric cryptographic algorithm (such as triple-DES, RC4, or IDEA). The advantage here is that symmetric cryptography is *much faster* than public-key cryptography. Alice knows the secret because she generated it before sending it to Bob. Bob knows the secret because Bob has the private key and can decrypt Alice's message. Because they both know the secret, they can both initialize a symmetric cipher algorithm and then start sending messages encrypted with it.

SSL includes one extra mechanism, intended to prevent an intruder from interposing himself between Alice and Bob and interfering with their connection. This is done by introducing what is called a message authentication code (MAC) into the protocol. A MAC is a piece of data that is computed by using a secret and some transmitted data. The digest algorithm described earlier has just the right properties for building a MAC function that can defend against an intruder:

```
MAC := Digest[some message, secret]
```

Because the intruder does not know the secret, he cannot compute the right value for the digest. Even if the intruder randomly garbles messages, his chance of success is small if the digest data are large. For example, by using MD5 (a good cryptographic digest algorithm invented by RSA), Alice and Bob can send 128-bit MAC values with their messages. No intruder could guess such a large, essentially random, number.

Here is the SSL protocol as Netscape implements it, with all of these refinements:

```
A->B    hello
B->A    Hi, I'm Bob, bobs-certificate (the certificate
        contains bob's key, and is signed by a CA
        that Alice trusts)
A->B    Prove it
B->A    Alice, This Is Bob {digest[Alice, This Is Bob]}
```

```
          bobs-private-key
A->B      Bob, here is a secret {secret} bobs-public-key
          {some message}secret-key
```

Finally, SSL protects against "playback" attacks, in which an intruder does not try to understand messages or to modify them, but just passively replays them in the hope of getting something to happen. For example, if the intruder can capture a sequence by which Alice asks Bob to unlock a door, the intruder might replay the sequence later without needing to understand the details, in the hope that Bob will unlock the door again. The solution is to introduce random elements, called "nonce" values, from both sides of the conversation. Thus, each interaction between Alice and Bob will be different from any previous one, and any replay attack will fail almost immediately.

If the SSL protocol is placed side-by-side with the Kerberos protocol, one can see that the SSL approach is simultaneously similar and different from the Kerberos one. Both rely upon a trusted certificate authority, which provides certificates that can be used to establish connections to a server whose identity can be trusted, to the extent that the CA itself can be trusted. In Kerberos, the client authenticates itself to the CA, and the resulting certificate allows the server to authenticate the client as well as vice versa. SSL does not worry about this, and in fact does not bother to authenticate the client at all: the goal is to convince a human client that it is safe to give his or her credit card information to Fromages.com. If we are in a situation where the identity of the client is also an issue, the server might require a login prior to permitting transactions, so we can enhance the basic SSL guarantees fairly easily.

One interesting question concerns the way that hardware like the Intel Palladium architecture, in which the processor itself possesses a secret key, could integrate with SSL security. With this type of hardware, it becomes feasible for the client to "prove" to the server that he or she is using such-and-such a platform. The server could then use this information as part of its policies, for example by granting access to certain media files and denying access to others, on the basis of the client's previously negotiated access permissions and the rules applicable to that particular platform. Exploiting this option opens all sorts of avenues for the research community, and one can anticipate a flurry of results over the next few years.

18.5   Security Policy Languages

An important and active research topic concerns the challenge of representing a nontrivial *security policy* and using it to determine whether or to authorize an action at runtime. To understand this issue, consider the way that security works in the real world, say in a hospital. Certain people are authorized to access the pharmacy stockroom, for example. These people were first cleared by the hospital security manager, who issued them with an appropriate badge. The manager reports to the Vice President for Operations, and this person reports to the CEO and Board of Directors. They, in turn, have legal responsibilities defined under the state charter that incorporated the hospital as a non-profit health center.

This example traces just one chain of authority within the organization – from the top down, we could say that the state gave the hospital certain rights, such as the right to stockpile medications, and the right to authorize individuals to access that stockpile. The hospital delegated rights in a chain that ultimately authorizes such and such a pharmacist to enter that room to retrieve a needed medication.

Complex organizations have many forms of trust. In addition to the hierarchical trust delegation example we have just seen, many organizations have an internal structure in which divisions have distinct roles. Perhaps, the consulting division is allowed to make stock evaluations, but must be kept completely independent of the investment division, which invests in stocks. In our hospital, the records-keeping division should not be accessible to the computer systems used by patients, visitors and volunteers for routine tasks such as finding out what room a patient is in and when she can be visited.

When organizations compete in some spheres of activity while cooperating on others, we get even more complex kinds of rule. IBM competes with SAP in some respects, but perhaps SAP runs IBM computers internally and needs to allow IBM service representatives in to service those systems, run diagnostic tests on them, etc. Chapter 3 illustrated some of the subtle issues raised by such situations. Is this service representative here for a legitimate reason? Did IBM really designate him to repair the problem? Is he doing the appropriate thing and nothing else?

Existing security policy languages are far more useful for representing and dealing with chains of authorization than with these complex security scenarios. To represent a chain of authority or a delegation of rights we can use what are called "authentication logics." A well-known example is Rivest's SPKI/SDSI language (pronounced "spooky and sudsy"). The language allows one to write down simple rules such as "John is authorized to open the safe," or "John trusts Sally to operate the cash register." SPKI/SDSI also allows inference—given an elaborate rules database, one can ask a question such as "Should John open the safe for Sally to deposit the cash receipts for the evening?" and arrive at a sensible answer (hopefully, "yes"). However, SPKI/SDSI has limitations (for example, it does not deal all that well with situations involving mutually distrustful organizations that must cooperate for a specific task without revealing more about their security policy than desired or authorizing one-another to have broader rights than intended), and in any case has not been accepted by any very large community as a standard.

Making matters far more complex, many organizations are reluctant to share their security policies except on a need to know basis. Suppose that John presents himself at the FBI and states that he works for the CIA and has been asked to review the FBI's records associated with a terrorism investigation. Not only do we see all the issues just mentioned, but this "disclosure" question now also arises. The CIA will have a mechanism by which the FBI can confirm that John is a legitimate CIA representative and has been tasked to perform the study in question, but will not want to disclose other "unrelated" information, such as John's roles within the CIA, or those of other CIA agents unrelated to John. SPKI/SDSI, however, and other security languages too, assumes that the policy "database" will be placed into the public. Applied to our situation, the CIA would need to publish a complete list of all its agents and all their security permissions. Clearly, such an approach will not fly—yet we do not have any real alternatives today.

We run into the problem that unless a technology is very powerful, very sensitive to the possible concerns of its users, and also widely used as a standard, it will not be all that useful. After all, any one developer, say of a Web Services application, deals with just a tiny corner of the system. Unless everyone uses the same security language and standards, nobody will have the ability to even express their little corner of the security requirements and policies. At the time of this writing, any comprehensive security policy language seems remote.

Readers interested in learning more about SPKI/SDSI should consult the Web Site maintained by the MIT group that developed the system: http://theory.lcs.mit.edu/~cis/sdsi.html.

18.6   On-The-Fly Security

A rather popular style of security applies some form of security policy on the fly. We see this in a firewall, where as messages travel in or out of a system, the firewall checks them against a database of security rules and decides, on-the-fly, whether to allow the message through or to block it. Similarly, languages such as Java and C# enforce security rules at runtime, limiting the active program to only access objects for which it has valid handles. These mechanisms can be quite effective in dealing with what might be called low-level security considerations. They are less useful in dealing with complex requirements arising from the security needs of the application itself. For example, if an application is allowed to create files, one could run into a security issue if some kinds of file, such as files with an extension named ".lock," have a special meaning for some programs. Particularly if the security concern arises from an application that was developed by a third party, one runs into problems using vendor-supplied security mechanisms to enforce the special rules associated with the application's security needs.

Some researchers have begun to experiment with tackling this problem by extending the mechanisms seen in firewalls for use in running programs. The idea can be traced to work by Steve Lucco and Brian Bershad. Lucco's work was concerned with editing already compiled programs at the object code layer to insert behavioral checks, for example to prevent a piece of code from accessing objects outside its legitimate address space. Brian Bershad's project, SPIN, was concerned with protecting the operating system from malicious (or buggy) behavior by applications that need to be downloaded into the kernel, such as a device driver. Both systems aim at allowing the user to benefit from high performance by loading untrusted code right into the address space of some sort of sensitive system service and yet protecting themselves against undesired behavior.

Fred Schneider has taken this idea even further in work underway at Cornell. Schneider's approach is to represent security policy in a simple database that can be used to insert protective mechanisms (firewall style) right into applications, intervening at the layer where the application interacts with the network or the surrounding environment. If the policy says, for example, that users lacking security clearance must not access classified documents, Schneider would modify the program itself, at runtime, to ensure that each operation that accesses any kind of object is filtered to ensure that if the actor lacks a clearance, the object is not a classified one. Since the program was built without knowledge of the security policy and protective mechanisms, the belief is that this sort of fine-grained firewall can give a degree of customized protection not otherwise feasible.

Combined with work on security policy languages and inference systems, like SPKI/SDSI, one can see hope for a truly comprehensive approach to security policy management and enforcement at some point in the future. We are beginning to understand the mechanisms and beginning to sort out the complexity of simply representing security policy and desires. Yet we are also very far from having the whole story in hand. Developer's of Web Services systems will find themselves in the thick of it: They will often need to enforce corporate security policies, but will lack the kind of standardized, powerful, and widely used mechanisms that might make this straightforward. As a result the developer will be on his or her toes, and in fact is likely to overlook important issues. Even if not, security is an evolving concept: the security policy for a small company doing military development under a classified contract may change drastically when that company is acquired by Boeing, a large company doing many kinds of work. An application built by the small company may not be so easily extended to cover the complex scenarios that can arise at the large one later. Thus, new exposures can creep in, even when a system is initially extremely secure. Schneider's approach, in some future mature and widely used form, could address such a need—but again, we are probably decades from that point today.

18.7   Availability and Security

Research on the introduction of availability guarantees into Kerberos-based (or SSL-based) architectures has revealed considerable potential for overcoming the availability limitations of the basic Kerberos approach. As we have seen, Kerberos and SSL are both dependent on the availability of their authentication servers for the generation of new protection keys. Should a server fail or become partitioned away from the applications depending on it, the establishment of new channels and the renewal of keys for old channels will cease to be possible, eventually shutting down the system.

In a Ph.D. dissertation based on an early version of the Horus system, Reiter showed that process groups could be used to build highly available authentication servers (see Reiter 1993, 1994a, 1994b; Reiter et al. 1992, 1994). His work included a secure join protocol for adding new processes to such a group; methods for securely replicating data and for securing the ordering properties of a group communication primitive (including the causal property); and an analysis of availability issues, which occur in key distribution when such a server is employed. Interestingly, Reiter's approach does not require that the time service used in a system such as Kerberos be replicated: His techniques have a very weak dependency on time.

Process group technologies permitted Reiter to propose a number of exotic new security options as well. Still working with Horus, he explored the use of split secret mechanisms to ensure that in a group of n processes (see Desmedt 1988; Desmedt et al. 1992; Frankel 1989; Frankel and Desmedt 1992; Herlihy and Tygar 1987; Laih and Harn 1991), the availability of any $n - k$ members would suffice to maintain secure and available access to that group. In this work, Reiter uses a state machine approach: The individual members have identical states and respond to incoming requests in an identical manner. Accordingly, his focus was on implementing state machines in environments with intruders and on signing responses in such a way that $n - k$ signatures by members would be recognizable as a group signature carrying the authority of the group as a whole.

A related approach can be developed in which the servers split a secret in such a manner that none of the servers in the group has access to the full data, and yet clients can reconstruct these data provided that $n - k$ or more of the servers are correct. Such a split secret scheme might be useful if the group needs to maintain a secret that none of its individual members can be trusted to manage appropriately.

Techniques such as these can be carried in many directions. Reiter, after leaving the Horus project, started work on a system called Rampart at AT&T (see Reiter 1996). Rampart provides secure group functionality under assumptions of Byzantine failures and is used to build extremely secure group-based mechanisms for use by less stringently secured applications in a more general setting—for example, Rampart could be the basis of an authentication service, a service used to maintain billing information in a shared environment, a digital cash technology, or a strongly secured firewall technology.

More recently, Reiter and Malkhi have worked with Byzantine Quorum methods. These approaches form a group of N processes in such a way that data can be read or updated using just $O(sqrt(N))$ members, and are also able to tolerate Byzantine failures. Authentication services stand out as one of the first settings that could benefit from such a technology.

Cooper, also working with Horus, has explored the use of process groups as a blinding mechanism. The concept here originated with work by Chaum, who showed how privacy can be enforced in distributed systems by mixing information from many sources in a manner that prevents an intruder from matching an individual data item to its source or tracing a data item from source to destination (see Chaum 1981). Cooper's work shows how a replicated service can actually mix up the contents of messages from multiple sources to create a private and secure e-mail repository (see Cooper 1994). In his approach, the process group-based mail repository service stores mail on behalf of many users. A protocol is given for placing mail into the service, retrieving mail from it, and for dealing with vacations; the scheme offers privacy (intruders cannot determine sources and destinations of messages) and security (intruders cannot see the contents of messages) under a variety of attacks and can also be made fault tolerant through replication. More recently, Mazieres developed a peer-to-peer system using similar ideas. His *Tangler* system mixes data together in ways that maintain privacy of the publisher, privacy of access and security of the data itself.

Intended for large-scale mobile applications, Cooper's work would permit exchanging messages between processes in a large office complex or a city without revealing the physical location of the principals—however, this type of communication is notoriously insecure. Maziere's Tangler system aims at individuals concerned about their right to free speech (and also at individuals hoping to share files in ways that the government might find very hard to regulate). And these are hardly the only such efforts. The emergence of digital commerce may expose technology users to very serious intrusions on their privacy and finances. Work such as that done by Reiter, Chaum, Mazieres and Cooper suggests that security and privacy should be possible even with the levels of availability that will be needed when initiating commercial transactions from mobile devices.

Later in this book we will discuss some recent work on using Byzantine Agreement protocols to achieve security in certain types of replicated service, and also work on security in peer-to-peer systems. To avoid repetition, we defer these topics until later sections.

18.8 Related Reading

Chapter 3 reviewed limitations of existing security models. See also *Trust in Cyberspace*, a National Academy of Sciences report edited by F. Schneider, which discusses capabilities and limitations of modern security architectures.

On Kerberos (see Schiller 1994; Steiner et al. 1988).

On authorization, we highly recommend reading the paper by Mitchell et al. (Li et al. 2002) in which John Mitchell (Stanford) and two colleagues create and then demonstrate a very simple and elegant credentials-based authorizaton logic.

On associated theory (see Bellovin and Merritt 1990; Lampson et al. 1992).

On RSA and DES (see Denning 1984; Desmedt 1988; Diffie and Hellman 1979; Rivest et al. 1978).

On Rampart (see Reiter 1993, 1994a; Reiter et al. 1992, 1994).

On split-key cryptographic techniques and associated theory (see Desmedt 1988; Desmedt et al. 1992; Frankel 1989; Frankel and Desmedt 1992; Herlihy and Tygar 1987; Laih and Harn 1991).

On mixing techniques (see Chaum 1981; Cho and Birman 1994; Cooper 1994).

On the Secure Socket Layer protocol: Netscape originally developed this protocol and maintains very clear materials online. The protocol itself is defined by RFC 2246 (Transport Layer Security) and RFC 2818 (HTTPS over TLS).

Interested readers should also revisit Chap. 10, where we discussed Castro and Liskov's recent work on introducing Byzantine fault tolerance in data replication systems. (See Castro and Liskov 2002.)

Clock Synchronization and Synchronous Systems

19

Previous chapters of this book have made a number of uses of clocks or time in distributed protocols. In this chapter, we look more closely at the underlying issues. Our focus is on aspects of real-time computing that are specific to distributed protocols and systems.

19.1 Clock Synchronization

Clock synchronization is an example of a topic that until the recent past represented an important area for distributed system research (see Clegg and Marzullo 1996; Cristian 1989; Cristian and Fetzer 1994; Kopetz and Ochsenreiter 1987; Lamport 1984; Lamport and Melliar-Smith 1985; Marzullo 1984; Srikanth and Toueg 1987; Verissimo 2003); overviews of the field can be found in Liskov (1993), Simons et al. (1990). The introduction of the global positioning system, in the early 1990s, greatly changed the situation. As recently as five years ago, a book such as this would have treated the problem in considerable detail, to the benefit of the reader, because the topic is an elegant one and the clock-based protocols that have been proposed are interesting to read and analyze. Today, however, it seems more appropriate to touch only briefly on the subject.

The general problem of clock synchronization occurs because the computers in a distributed system typically use internal clocks as their primary time source. On most systems, these clocks are accurate to within a few seconds per day, but there can be surprising exceptions to the rule. PCs, for example, may operate in power-saving modes, in which even the clock is slowed down or stopped, making it impossible for the system to gauge real time reliably. At the other end of the spectrum, the global positioning system (GPS) has introduced an inexpensive way to obtain accurate timing information using a radio receiver; time obtained in this manner is accurate to within a few milliseconds unless the GPS signal itself is distorted by unusual atmospheric conditions or problems with the antenna used to receive the signal. Many systems connect to some source of accurate time on the Internet, then use a protocol such as NNTP (an Internet standard for time synchronization)

K.P. Birman, *Guide to Reliable Distributed Systems*, Texts in Computer Science, DOI 10.1007/978-1-4471-2416-0_19, © Springer-Verlag London Limited 2012

Fig. 19.1 The global
positioning system is a
satellite network that
broadcasts highly accurate
time values worldwide.
Although intended for
accurate position location,
GPS systems are also making
accurate real-time
information available at low
cost

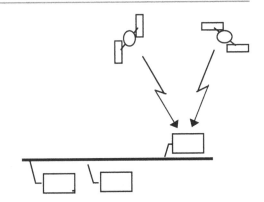

to obtain further accuracy, yielding synchronization to within a few tens of milliseconds. This level of synchronization is adequate for a great many embedded systems
uses. For example, Break-out 19.1 discusses the MARS system, which uses clock
synchronization for real-time control. We cite MARS because the work focused on
distributed coordination with time-based protocols, but there is a huge body of research around the broader issues associated with time-driven computing; indeed, far
more than we can really cover in the space available in this text.

Traditionally, clock synchronization was treated in the context of a group of
peers, each possessing an equivalent local clock, with known accuracy and drift
properties. The goal in such a system was typically to design an agreement protocol
by which the clocks could be kept as close as possible to real time and with which
the tendency of individual clocks to drift (either from one another and/or relative
to real time) could be controlled. To accomplish this, processes would periodically
exchange time readings, running a protocol by which a software clock could be
constructed having substantially better properties than that of any of the individual
participating programs—with the potential to overcome outright failures whereby a
clock might drift at an excessive rate or return completely erroneous values.

Key parameters to such a protocol are the expected and maximum communication latencies of the system. It can be shown that these values limit the quality
of clock synchronization achievable in a system by introducing uncertainty in the
values exchanged between processes—for example, if the latency of the communication system between p and q is known to vary in the range $[0, \varepsilon]$, any clock
reading that p sends to q will potentially be aged by ε time units by the time q
receives it. When latency is also bounded below, a method developed by Verissimo
(briefly presented here) can achieve clock precisions bounded by the *variation* in
latency. In light of the high speed of modern communication systems, these limits
represent a remarkably high degree of synchronization: It is rarely necessary to time
events to within accuracies of a millisecond or less, but these limits tell us that it
would be possible to synchronize clocks to that degree if desired. Indeed, we will
see precisely how it could be done shortly.

19.1 MARS: A Distributed System for Real-Time Control

The MARS system uses clock synchronization as the basis of an efficient fault tolerance method, implemented using pairs of processing components interconnected by redundant communication links. The basic approach is as follows (see Damm et al. 1989; Kopetz and Ochsenreiter 1987; Kopetz and Verissimo 1993).

A very high quality of clock synchronization is achieved using a synchronization method that resides close to the hardware (a broadcast-style bus). Implemented in part using a special-purpose device controller, clocks can be synchronized to well under a millisecond and, if a source of accurate timing information is available, can be both precise and accurate to within this degree of precision.

Applications of MARS consist of directly controlled hardware, such as robotic units or components of a vehicle. Each processor is duplicated, as is the program that runs on it, and each action is taken redundantly. Normally, every message will be sent four times: once by each processor on each message bus. The architecture is completely deterministic in the sense that all processes see the same events in the same order and base actions on synchronized temporal information in such a way that even clock readings will be identical when identical tasks are performed. Software tools for scheduling periodic actions and for performing actions after a timer expires are provided by the MARS operating system, which is a very simple execution environment concerned primarily with scheduling and message passing.

MARS is designed for very simple control programs and assumes that these programs fail by halting (the programs are expected to self-check their actions for sanity and shut down if an error is detected). In the event that a component does fail, this can be detected by the absence of messages from it or by their late arrival. Such a failed component is taken off-line for replacement and reintegrated into the system the next time it is restarted from scratch. These assumptions are typical of in-flight systems for aircraft and factory-floor process control systems.

Although MARS is not a particularly elaborate or general technology, it is extremely effective within its domain of intended use. The assumptions made are felt to be reasonable ones for this class of application, and although there are limitations on the classes of failures that MARS can tolerate, the system is also remarkably simple and modular, benefiting from precisely those limitations and assumptions. The performance of the system is extremely good for the same reasons.

Modern computing systems face a form of clock synchronization problem that is easier to solve than the most general version of the problem. If such systems make use of time at all, it is common to introduce two or more GPS receivers—in this manner creating a number of system time sources. Devices consisting of

Accuracy is a characterization of the degree to which a correct clock can differ from an external clock that gives the true time. A clock synchronization protocol guaranteeing highly accurate clocks thus provides the assurance that a correct clock will return a value within some known maximum error of the value that the external clock would return. In some settings, accuracy is expressed as an absolute bound; in others, accuracy is expressed as a maximum rate of drift-in this case, the accuracy of the clock at a given time is a function of how long the clock has been free-running since the last round of the synchronization protocol.

Skew is a measure of the difference between clock readings for a pair of processes whose clocks have been sampled at the same instant in real time.

Precision is a characterization of the degree to which any pair of correct clocks can differ over time. As with accuracy, a precision may be given as a constant upper bound on the skew or as a maximum rate of drift of the skews for pairs of correct clocks.

Fig. 19.2 Definitions of accuracy, skew, and precision for synchronized clocks in distributed settings

nothing more than a GPS receiver and a network interface can, for example, be placed directly on a shared communication bus. The machines sharing that bus will now receive time packets at some frequency, observing identical values at nearly identical time. (See Fig. 19.1.)

If the device driver associated with the network device is able to identify these incoming time packets, it can be used to set the local clock of the host machine to extremely high precision; if not, an application should be able to do so with reasonable accuracy. Given data for the average access and propagation delays for packets sent over the communication hardware, the associated latency can be added to the incoming time value, producing an even more accurate result. In such a manner, systems in which real time is important can synchronize processor clocks to within fractions of a millisecond, obviating the need for any sophisticated application-level synchronization algorithm. After all, the delays associated with passing a message through an operating system up to the application, scheduling the application process if it were in a blocked state, and paging in the event of a possible page fault are substantial compared with the clock accuracy achievable in this manner. Moreover, it is very unlikely that a GPS time source would fail other than by crashing. If noncrash failures are a concern, a simple solution is to collect sets of readings from three GPS sources, exclude the outlying values, and take the remaining value as the correct one. (See Fig. 19.2 for definitions of some useful terms.)

In light of this development, it has become desirable to consider distributed computing systems as falling into two classes. Systems in which time is important for reliability can readily include accurate time sources and should do so. Systems in which time is not important for reliability should be designed to avoid all use of workstation clock values, using elapsed time on a local clock to trigger timer-based events such as retransmission of messages or timeout, but not exchanging time values between processes or making spurious use of time. For the purposes of such elapsed timers, the clocks on typical processors are more than adequate: A clock that is accurate to a few seconds per day will measure a 100 ms timeout with impressive accuracy.

Where clocks are known to drift, Verissimo and Rodrigues have suggested an elegant method for maintaining very precise clocks (see Verissimo and Rodrigues 1992); see also Clegg and Marzullo (1996). This protocol, call *a-posteriori clock synchronization*, operates roughly as follows. A process other than the GPS receiver initiates clock synchronization periodically (for fault tolerance, two or more processes can run the algorithm concurrently). Upon deciding to synchronize clocks, this process sends out a *resynchronize* message, including its own clock value in the message and setting this value as close as possible to when the message is transmitted on the wire—for example, the device driver can set the clock field in the header of an outgoing message just before setting up the DMA transfer to the network.

Upon arrival in destination machines, each recipient notes its local clock value, again doing this as close as possible to the wire. The recipients send back messages containing their clock values at the time of the receipt. The difference between these measured clock values and that of the initiator will be latency from the initiator to the receivers plus the drift of the recipient's clock relative to the clock of the initiator. For example, suppose the initiator believes it to be three o'clock. It sends out this value over the LAN to a nearby machine. After a latency (communication delay) of 1 ms, that machine receives the clock value and compares it with its own clock, discovering its clock to be smaller by 31 ms. If we "knew" the latency (and we do not), we could now deduce that the recipients clock is running 30 ms slower than that of the initiator. Similarly, a computed difference of 121 ms would correspond to a recipient running 120 ms "ahead" of the initiator, assuming that the latency from initiator to recipient was still 1 ms. Of course in a real LAN, communication latency is somewhat variable. Thus successive runs of the protocol might result in computed "clock skews" varying slightly from these nominal values: perhaps -31.050 ms, or 120.980 ms. And making matters worse, clocks may be drifting as our protocol executes.

In the protocol proposed by Verissimo and Rodriguez, the synchronization algorithm selects one of the participants as the official clock of the system. It does so either by selecting a value returned from a process with a GPS receiver, if one is included, or by sorting the returned differences and selecting the median. It subtracts this value from the other differences. The vector will now have small numbers in it if, as assumed, the latency from initiator to participants if fairly constant over the set. The values in the vector will represent the distance that the corresponding participant's clock has drifted with respect to the reference clock. Given an estimate of the message latency between the reference process and the initiator, the initiator can also compute the drift of its own clock—for example, a process may learn that its clock has drifted by -32 ms since the last synchronization event. Any sort of reliable multicast protocol can be used to return the correction factors to the participants.

To actually correct a clock that has drifted, it is common to use an idea introduced by Srikanth and Toueg. The approach involves gradually compensating for the drift under the assumption that the rate of drift is constant. Thus, if a process has drifted 120 ms over a one-minute period, the clock might be modified in software to introduce a compensating drift rate of -240 ms over the next minute, in this manner correcting the original 120 ms and overcoming the continuing 120 ms drift of its clock during the period. Such an adjustment occurs gradually, avoiding noticeable jumps in the clock value that might confuse an application program.

The above discussion has oversimplified the protocol: The method is actually more complicated because it needs to account for a variety of possible failure modes; this is done by running several rounds of the protocol and selecting, from among the candidate clocks appearing best in each round, that round and clock for which the overall expected precision and accuracy is likely to be best.

Verissimo and Rodrigues's algorithm is optimally precise but not necessarily the best for obtaining optimal accuracy: The best-known solution to that problem is the protocol of Srikanth and Toueg mentioned above. However, when a GPS receiver is present in a distributed system having a standard broadcast-style LAN architecture, the a-posteriori method will be optimal in both respects—accuracy and precision—with clock accuracies comparable in magnitude to the variation in message latencies from initiator to recipients. These variations can be extremely small: Numbers in the tens of microseconds are typical. Thus, in a worldwide environment with GPS receivers, one can imagine an inexpensive software and hardware combination permitting processes anywhere in the world to measure time accurately to a few tens of microseconds. Accuracies such as this are adequate for even very demanding real-time uses.

Unfortunately, neither of these methods is actually employed by typical commercial computing systems. At the time of this writing, the situation is best characterized as a transitional one. There are well-known and relatively standard software clock synchronization solutions available for most networks, but the standards rarely span multiple vendor systems. Heterogeneous networks are thus likely to exhibit considerable time drift from processor to processor. Moreover, the clock synchronization mechanisms built into standard operating systems often run over the Internet, where latencies between the user's computer and a trusted clock can range from tens to hundreds of milliseconds. A result is that the average PC or workstation has a clock that can be trusted at a resolution of seconds or tens of seconds, but not to a higher resolution. This turns out to be fine for such uses as remembering to renew a lease on a network resource or a lock on a file, or timestamping a file when it is accessed or modified; developers tackling problems in which finer-grained temporal information is needed should consider adding GPS units to their machines.

19.2   Timed-Asynchronous Protocols

Given a network of computers that share an accurate time source, it is possible to design broadcast protocols to simultaneously guarantee real-time properties as well as other properties, such as failure-atomicity or totally ordered delivery. The best-known work in this area is that of Cristian, Aghili, Strong, and Dolev and is widely cited as the CASD protocol suite or the Δ-T atomic broadcast protocols (see Cristian et al. 1985, 1990). These protocols are designed for a static membership model, although Cristian later extended the network model to dynamically track the formation and merging of components in the event of network partitioning failures, again with real-time guarantees on the resulting protocols. In the remainder of this section, we present these protocols in the simple case where processes fail only by crashing or by having clocks that lie outside of the acceptable range for correct clocks—where messages are lost but not corrupted. The protocols have often been called synchronous, but Cristian currently favors the term "timed asynchronous" (see Cristian and Schmuck 1995), and this is the one we use here.

The CASD protocols seek to guarantee that in a time period during which a set of processes is *continuously operational* and *connected*, this set will deliver the same messages at the same time and in the same order. Two caveats apply. First, "same time" must be understood to be limited by the clock skew: Because processor clocks may differ by as much as ε, two correct processors undertaking to perform the same action at the same time may in fact do so as much as ε time units apart. Additionally, and this may seem a bit confusing on first reading, a process may not be able to detect that its own clock is incorrect. In effect, a process may be considered "faulty" by the system and yet has no way to know that this is the case (in contrast, if a virtual synchrony system considers a process faulty, that process is excluded from the system and will certainly find out). The importance of this is that when a process is faulty, the guarantees of the protocol no longer apply to it. So, if process a receives a message m we know that if the system considers a to be healthy, m was delivered to a at the same time that it was delivered to any other healthy process. But if a is considered unhealthy (and as noted before, a has no way to detect this), all bets are off. We will see how this can complicate the job of the developer who works with CASD shortly.

We start by considering the simple scenario of a network consisting of a collection of n processes, k of which may be faulty. The CASD protocol is designed for a network in which packets must be routed; the network diameter, d, is the maximum number of hops a packet may have to take to reach a destination node from a source node. It is understood that failures will not cause the network to become disconnected. Although individual packets can be lost in the network, it is assumed that there is a known limit on the number of packets that will actually be lost in any single run of the protocol. Finally, multicast networks are not modeled as such: An Ethernet or FDDI is treated as a set of point-to-point links.

The CASD protocol operates as follows. A process (which may itself be faulty) creates a message and labels it with a timestamp, t (from its local clock), and its process identifier. It then forwards the message to all processors reachable over communication links directly connected to it. These processes accept incoming messages. A message is *discarded* if it is a duplicate of a message that has been seen previously or if the timestamp on the message falls outside a range of currently feasible valid timestamps. Otherwise, the incoming message is *relayed* over all communication links except the one on which it was received. This results in the exchange of $O(n^2)$ messages, as illustrated in Fig. 19.3.

A process holding a message waits until time $t + \Delta$ on its local clock (here, t is the time when the message was sent) and then delivers it in the order determined by the sender's timestamp, breaking ties using the processor ID of the sender. For suitable validity limits and Δ, this protocol can be shown to overcome crash failures,

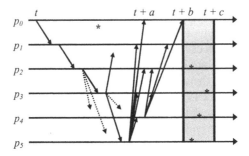

Fig. 19.3 In the CASD protocol, messages are delivered with real-time guarantees despite a variety of possible failures. In this example for a fully connected network ($d = 1$), processes p_0 and p_1 are faulty and send the message only to one destination each. p_2 and p_3 are correct but experience communication failures, which prevent the message from being forwarded to the full set of correct processors. Eventually, however, the full set of possible failures has been exhausted and the message reaches all correct destinations even if the execution is a worst-case one. In this example, the message finally reaches its last destination at time $t + a$. The processors now delay delivery of the message under a best-case/worst-case analysis, whereby each process reasons that it may have received the message in the minimum possible time but that others may receive it after the maximum possible time and yet assume that they too had received the message after a minimal delay. When this delay has elapsed, all correct processes know that all other correct processes have the message and are prepared to deliver it; delivery then takes place during a period bounded above and below by the clock synchronization constant e (shown as $[t + b, t + c]$ in the figure). Incorrect processes may fail to deliver the message, as in the case of p_1; may deliver outside of the window, as does p_0; or may deliver messages rejected by all correct processes

limited numbers of communication failures, and incorrect clock values on the part of the sender or intermediary relay processes.

The calculation of the parameter Δ is based on the following reasoning: For the range of behaviors possible in the system, there is a corresponding maximum latency after which a message that originates at a faulty process and that has been forwarded only by faulty processes finally reaches a correct process and is accepted as valid. From this point forward, there is an additional maximum latency before the message has reached all correct processes, limited by the maximum number of network packet losses that can occur. Finally, any specific recipient may consider itself to be the earliest of the correct processes to have received the message and will assume that other correct processes will be the last to receive a copy. From this analysis, a value can be assigned to Δ such that at time $t + \Delta$, every correct process will have a copy of the message and will know that all other correct processes also have a copy. It is therefore safe to deliver the message at time $t + \Delta$: The other processes will do so as well, within a time skew of ε, corresponding to the maximum difference in clock values for any two correct processes. This is illustrated in Fig. 19.3, where time $t + b$ corresponds to $t + \Delta - \varepsilon/2$ and $t + c$ to $t + \Delta + \varepsilon/2$.

Although we will not develop the actual formulas here, because the analysis would be fairly long, it is not hard to develop a basic intuition into the reasoning behind this protocol. If we are safe in assuming that there are at most f faulty processes in the network and that the network itself loses no more than k packets during

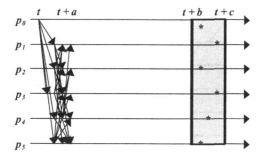

Fig. 19.4 A run of the CASD protocol in which no failures occur. After a flurry of message exchanges during which $O(n^2)$ messages are sent and received, the protocol lies quiescent until delivery occurs. The delay to delivery is unaffected by the good fortune of the protocol in having reached all the participants so rapidly. Notice that as normally presented, the protocol makes no use of broadcast hardware

Fig. 19.5 More aggressive parameter settings and assumptions can substantially reduce the delay before delivery occurs

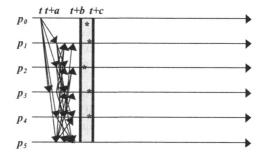

a run of the protocol, it must follow that a broadcast will reach at least one operational process, which will forward it successfully to every other operational process within $f + k$ rounds. A process using the protocol simply waits long enough to be able to deduce that every other process must have a copy of the message, after which it delivers the message in timestamp order.

Because all the operational processes will have received the same messages and use the same timestamp values when ordering them for delivery, the delivered messages are the same and in the same order at all correct processes. However, this may not be the case at *incorrect* processes—namely, those for which the various temporal limits and constants of the analysis do not hold or those that failed to send or receive messages the protocol requires them to send or receive. (We will say more about this in a moment, but an illustration of the problem can be seen in Fig. 19.4.)

Clearly, when a protocol such as this one is used in a practical setting, it will be advantageous to reduce the value of Δ as much as possible, since Δ is essentially a minimum latency for the protocol. For this reason, the CASD protocol is usually considered in a broadcast network for which the network diameter, d, is 1; processes and communication are assumed to be quite reliable (hence, these failure limits are reduced to numbers such as 1); and clocks are assumed to be very closely synchronized for the operational processes in the network. With these sorts of assumptions,

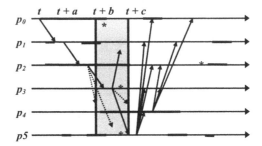

Fig. 19.6 In this case, overly aggressive parameter settings have caused many processes to be incorrect in the eyes of the protocol, illustrated by bold intervals on the process timelines (each process is considered incorrect during a bold interval-for example, because its clock has drifted too far from the global mean). The real-time and atomicity properties are considerably weakened; moreover, participating processes have no way to determine if they were correct or incorrect on a given run of the protocol. Here, the messages that arrive prior to time $t + c$ are considered as valid by the protocol; the others arrive too late and are ignored by correct processes

Δ, which would have a value of about three seconds in the local area network used by the Computer Science Department at Cornell, can be reduced into the range of 100–150 ms. Such a squeezing of the protocol leads to runs such as the one shown in Fig. 19.5.

We noted that there is a subtle issue associated with the definition of "operational" in the goals of the CASD protocol. The problem occurs when we consider a process that is technically faulty because its clock has drifted outside the limits assumed for a correct process; with the clock synchronization methods reviewed above, this is an unavoidable risk, which grows as the assumed limits become tighter. This is also true when using Cristian's recommended clock synchronization protocol (see Cristian 1989)—that is, the same actions that we took to reduce Δ also have the side-effect of making it more likely that a process will be considered faulty.

Such a process is only faulty in a technical sense. Viewed from above, we can see that its clock is slightly too fast or too slow, perhaps only five or ten milliseconds from the admissible range. Internally, the process considers itself quite operational and would be unable to detect this type of fault even if it tried to do so. Yet, because it is faulty in the formal sense of violating our conditions on correct processes, the guarantees of the protocol may no longer hold for such a process: It may deliver messages that no other process delivered, fail to deliver messages that every other process delivered successfully, or deliver messages outside the normal time range within which delivery should have occurred. Even worse, the process may then drift back into the range considered normal and hence recover to an operational state immediately after this condition occurs. The outcome might be a run more like the one shown in Fig. 19.6.

Thus, although the CASD protocol offers strong temporal and fault-tolerant properties to correct processes, the guarantees of these protocols may appear weaker to a process using them, because such a process has no way to know, or to learn, whether or not it is one of the correct ones. In some sense, the protocol has a concept of system membership built into it, but this information is not available to the processes

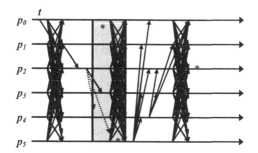

Fig. 19.7 In the NavTech protocol suite developed by Almeida and Verissimo, periodic background exchanges of state (*dark intervals*) cut through the normal message traffic, permitting such optimizations as early message delivery and offering information for use in overcoming inconsistency. However, short of running a group membership protocol in the background communication channel, there are limits to the forms of inconsistency that this method can actually detect and correct

in the system. The effect is to relax all the properties of the protocol suite, which is perhaps best understood as being probabilistically reliable for this reason.

A stronger statement could be made if failures were detectable so that such a process could later learn that its state was potentially inconsistent with that of other processes. There has been some encouraging work on strengthening the properties of this protocol by layering additional mechanisms over it. Gopal et al., for example, have shown how the CASD protocols can be extended to guarantee causal ordering and to overcome some forms of inconsistency (see Gopal et al. 1990). This, however, slows the protocol down so drastically as to be useless. Another option, explored in Chap. 21, simply embraces the idea of a protocol that gives probabilistic guarantees to its users.

In the Portuguese NavTech project, Almeida and Verissimo have explored a class of protocols that superimpose a background state exchange mechanism on a CASD-like protocol structure (see Fig. 19.7). In this approach, processes within the system periodically send snapshots of aspects of their state to one another using unreliable all-to-all message exchanges over dedicated but low bandwidth links. The resulting n^2 message exchange leaves the correct processes with accurate information about one another's states prior to the last message exchange and with partially accurate information as of the current exchange (the limitation is due to the possibility that messages may be lost by the communication subsystem). In particular, the sender of a CASD-style broadcast may now learn that it has reached all its destinations. During the subsequent exchange of messages, information gained in the previous exchange can be exploited—for example, to initiate an early delivery of a timed broadcast protocol. Unfortunately, however, the mechanism does not offer an obvious way to assist the correct processes in maintaining mutually consistent knowledge concerning which processes are correct and which are not: To accomplish that goal, one would need to go further by implementing a process group membership service superimposed on the real-time processes in the system. This limitation is apparent when one looks at possible uses for information that can be gathered through such a message exchange: It can be used to adjust protocol parameters in limited ways, but generally cannot be used to solve problems in which the correct processes must have mutually consistent views of shared parameters or other forms of replicated state.

It would be interesting to explore an architecture in which real-time protocols are knowingly superimposed on virtually synchronous process groups, using a high-priority background channel such as the one introduced in Almeida's work to support the virtually synchronous group. With such a hybrid approach, it would be possible to exclude faulty processes from a system within a known delay after the fault occurs; adjust protocol parameters such as the delay to delivery by correct processes, so that the system will adaptively seek out the best possible delay for a given configuration; or combine the use of coherently replicated data and state with real-time updates to other forms of data and state. An approach that uses reserved-capacity, high-priority channels, such as the ones introduced by Almeida, could be used to support such a solution. At the time of this writing, however the author is not aware of any project that has implemented such an architecture.

This brings us back to the normal implementation of the CASD protocol suite. The user of such a protocol must expect that the distributed system as a whole contains processes that have become contaminated—they did not realize it, but their clocks had drifted outside of the legal bounds, and as a result messages were delivered differently than at the correct processes. Such a process may have missed some updates to a replicated object, or seen updates out of order.

Now, keep in mind that nobody "knows" which processes are suffering from such problems. CASD does not exclude a faulty process from the system in the manner of the virtual synchrony protocols. Accordingly, a process in an incorrect state can still initiate new messages, and those will be delivered just like any other multicasts would be. Indeed, over time, almost any process may be viewed as incorrect for one or another run of the protocol; hence, contamination is likely to be pervasive and is capable of spreading. Mechanisms for ensuring that such a system will converge back into a mutually consistent state should a divergence of states occur are needed when these protocols are used. However, this problem has never received careful study. The most common approach is to simply restrict the use of CASD protocols to forms of information that need not be absolutely correct, or as input to algorithms that are tolerant of some degree of inconsistency. One should never use them as the basis of a safety critical decision that must be made consistently at multiple locations in a system.

The CASD protocols represent an interesting contrast with the virtual synchrony protocols we discussed earlier in this book. The virtual synchrony protocols tolerate similar types of failure, but lack any concept of time and offer no temporal delivery guarantees. On the other hand, they do offer strong logical guarantees. CASD, as we have now seen, lacks this concept of consistency, but has a very strong temporal guarantee when used by processes that are operational within its model. Thus, we have what appears to be a basic tradeoff between logical guarantees and temporal ones. It is intriguing to speculate that such tradeoffs may be fundamental ones.

The tradeoff is also noticeable in the delay of the protocol. For large values of Δ the CASD protocol provides very strong guarantees, but also has a very large latency to delivery. This is the converse of the situation for the virtually synchronous *Send* or *OrderedSend* protocol, which does provide very strong guarantees and yet has very low latency to delivery in the usual case. On the other hand, *OrderedSend* does not offer any kind of rigorously specified real-time guarantees, and can sometimes be slow (e.g., if a view change is occurring when the protocol runs, or if some process is very slow to acknowledge receipt of messages). CASD, in contrast, is normally slow to deliver messages but one can formalize its real-time properties. The only way to *guarantee* that *OrderedSend* runs quickly involves classifying many processes as faulty—a high cost. Similarly, if we try to force CASD to deliver messages rapidly by using a small value of Δ, many processes end up inconsistent—also a high cost.

One might characterize the basic difference here as one of pessimism versus optimism. The *OrderedSend* style of protocols is generally optimistic in its expectations from the system: It is expected that failures will be relatively uncommon events and will be optimized for the earliest possible delivery if a failure does occur. These protocols can give extremely low latency (two or more orders of magnitude better than the CASD style of protocol) and can be extremely predictable in their behavior provided that the network load is light, paging and other delays do not occur, and failures are genuinely infrequent. Indeed, if one could be *certain* that these conditions held, a protocol such as *OrderedSend* could be the basis of a real-time system, and it would perform perhaps thousands of times better than the timed-asynchronous style of system. But hoping that a condition holds and proving that it holds are two different matters.

The CASD suite of protocols and other work by Cristian's group on the timed-asynchronous model can be viewed as relatively pessimistic, in the sense that for a given set of assumptions, these protocols are designed to expect and to overcome a worst-case execution. If CASD is used in a setting where it is known that the number of failures will be low, the protocol can be optimized to benefit from this. As we have seen, however, the protocol will only work to the degree that the assumptions are valid and that most operational processes will be considered as correct. When this ceases to be the case, the CASD protocols break down and will appear to behave incorrectly from the point of view of processes that, in the eyes of the system model, are now considered to flicker in and out of the zone of correct behavior. But the merit of this protocol suite is that if the assumptions are valid ones, the protocols are *guaranteed* to satisfy their real-time properties.

As noted above, Cristian has also worked on group membership in the timed-asynchronous model. Researchers in the Delta-4 project in Europe have also proposed integrated models in which temporal guarantees and logical guarantees were integrated into a single protocol suite (see Powell 1991; Rodrigues and Verissimo 1989; Rodrigues et al. 1993, 2000; Verissimo 1993, 1994). For brevity, however, we will not present these protocols here.

19.3   Adapting Virtual Synchrony for Real-Time Settings

Friedman has developed a real-time protocol suite for Horus, which works by trying to improve the expected behavior of the virtually synchronous group protocols rather than by starting with temporal assumptions and deriving provable protocol behaviors as in the case of CASD (see Friedman and van Renesse 1995a). Friedman's approach yielded a novel extension to the view installation and message-delivery architecture for Horus, loosely motivated by the Transis idea of distinguishing safe from unsafe message delivery states. In Friedman's protocols, "safe" states are those for which the virtual synchrony properties hold, while "unsafe" ones are states for which real-time guarantees can be offered but in which weaker properties than the usual virtual synchrony properties hold.

One way to understand Friedman's approach is to think of a system in which each message and view is delivered twice (the data in a message are only copied to the user's address space a single time). The initial delivery occurs with real-time guarantees of bounded latency from sending to reception or bounded delay from when an event that will change the group view occurs to when that view is delivered. However, the initial delivery may occur before the virtually synchronous one. The second delivery has the virtual synchrony properties and may report a group view different from the initial one, albeit in limited ways (specifically, such a view can be smaller than the original one but never larger—processes can fail but not join). The idea is that the application can now select between virtual synchrony properties and real-time ones, using the real-time delivery event for time-critical tasks and the virtually synchronous event for tasks in which logical consistency of the actions by group members are critical. Notice that a similar behavior could be had by placing a Horus protocol stack running a real-time protocol side by side in the same processes with a Horus protocol stack supporting virtual synchrony and sending all events through both stacks. Friedman's scheme also guarantees that event orderings in the two stacks will be the same, unless the time constraints make this impossible; two side-by-side stacks might differ in their event orderings or other aspects of the execution.

In support of the effort to introduce real-time protocols into Horus, Vogels and Mosse have investigated the addition of real-time scheduling features to Horus, message and thread priorities, and preallocation mechanisms whereby resources needed for a computation can be pinned down in advance to avoid risk of delay if a needed resource is not available during a time-critical task.

One possible application of this real-time, fault-tolerant technology addresses the problem of building a telecommunication switch in which a cluster of computers control the actions taken as telephone calls are received (Fig. 19.8). Such an application has a very simple architecture: The switch itself (based on the SS7 architecture) sees the incoming call and recognizes the class of telephone numbers as one requiring special treatment, as in the case of an 800 or 900 number in the United States. The switch creates a small descriptive message, giving the caller's telephone number, the destination, billing information, and a call identification number, and forwards this to a what is called an *intelligent network coprocessor*, or IN coprocessor. The coprocessor (traditionally implemented using a fault-tolerant computer

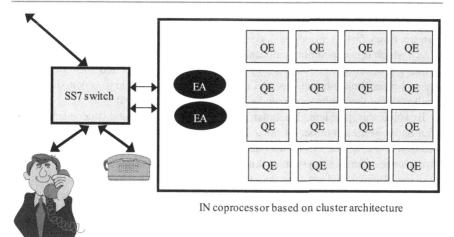

IN coprocessor based on cluster architecture

Fig. 19.8 Friedman has experimented with the use of a cluster of computing systems in support of a demanding real-time telecommunication application. On the left is a single switch, which handles telephone calls in the SS7 switching architecture. Somewhat simplifying the actual setup, we see local telephones connected to the switch from below and lines connecting to other switches above. SS7-compatible switches can be connected to adjunct processors, called IN coprocessors, which provide intelligent routing functionality and implement advanced services on behalf of the switch—for example, if an 800-number call is received, the coprocessor would determine which line to rout the call on, and, if call forwarding were in use, the coprocessor would reroute forwarded calls. Friedman's architecture uses Horus to support a cluster configuration within the IN coprocessor, an approach that provides very large scalable memory for the query elements (which would typically map a telephone directory into memory), load-balancing, and fault tolerance

system) is expected to perform a database query based on the telephone numbers and to determine the appropriate routing for the call, responding within a limited amount of time (typically, 100 ms). Typically, the switch will need to handle as many as 10,000 to 20,000 calls per second, dropping no more than some small percentage, and do this randomly even during periods when a failure is being serviced. The switch must never be down for more than a few seconds per year, although an individual call may sometimes have a small chance of not going through and may need to be redialed.

The argument in favor of using a cluster of computers for this purpose is that such a system potentially has greater computing power (and much more aggregate main memory) than any single processor could have. This may translate to the ability to keep a very large database in memory for rapid access (spread among the nodes) or of executing a more sophisticated query strategy. Moreover, whereas the upgrading of a fault-tolerant coprocessor may require that the switch be shut down, one can potentially upgrade a cluster-style computer one node or one program at a time.

Without getting into the details, Friedman has demonstrated that systems such as Horus can indeed be used to support such a model. He reports on a system emulating this configuration of telephone switch, servicing 22,000 calls per second while dropping no more than 1 to 3 percent even when a failure or recovery is actually being serviced (and this was back in 1988—today's hardware is more than ten times faster). Friedman's design involves a pair of external adapter nodes (EAs), which sense incoming calls and dispatch the corresponding query onto pairs of query-processing nodes (QEs). Friedman batches requests and uses an innovative real-time, fault-tolerant protocol to optimize for the very high processing loads characterizing the application (see Friedman and Birman 1996).

To solve this problem, Friedman's work combines the real-time mechanisms cited above with a number of other innovations, and it is fair to say that the application is not a straightforward one. However, the benefits of being able to use a cluster-style computing system in this manner could be dramatic: Such systems are quite inexpensive, and yet they may bring a great deal of performance and flexibility to the application, which would otherwise be very constrained by the physical limitations typical of any single-processor solution.

Although cast in the context of a telephone switching application, it should be noted that the type of real-time, client/server architecture being studied in Friedman's work is much more general. We have seen in earlier chapters of this book that the great majority of distributed systems have a client/server architecture, and this is also true for real-time systems, which typically look like client/server systems with time-critical response deadlines superimposed upon an otherwise conventional architecture. Thus, Friedman's work on telephone switching could also be applicable to process control systems, air traffic control systems, and other demanding applications that combine fault tolerance and real-time constraints.

Other work in this area includes Marzullo's research on the CORTO system, which includes such features as *periodic process groups*. These are process groups whose members periodically and within a bounded period of real time initiate synchronized actions. Marzullo has studied minimizing the communication overhead required in support of this periodic model, integrating real-time communication with other periodic or real-time actions, priority inversion in communication environments, and other topics in the area.

19.4 Related Reading

On clock synchronization, see the review in Simons et al. (1990); other references include Cristian (1989), Kopetz and Ochsenreiter (1987), Lamport (1984), Lamport and Melliar-Smith (1985), Marzullo (1984), Srikanth and Toueg (1987).

On the a-posteriori method (see Clegg and Marzullo 1996; Verissimo and Rodrigues 1992).

On the CASD protocol (see Cristian 1996; Cristian and Schmuck 1995; Cristian et al. 1985, 1990, Gopal et al. 1990).

On the MARS system (see Damm et al. 1989; Kopetz and Ochsenreiter 1987; Kopetz and Verissimo 1993).

On Delta-4 (see Powell 1991, 1994; Rodrigues and Verissimo 1989; Rodrigues et al. 1993, 2000; Verissimo 1993, 1994).

On real-time work with Horus (see Friedman and Birman 1996; Friedman and van Renesse 1995a).

Transactional Systems

20

20.1 Review of the Transactional Model

We first encountered the transactional execution model in Chap. 7, in conjunction with client/server architectures. As noted at that time, the model draws on a series of assumptions to arrive at a style of computing that is especially well matched to the needs of applications operating on databases. In this chapter we consider some of the details that Chap. 7 did not cover: notably the issues involved in implementing transactional storage mechanisms and the problems that occur when transactional architectures are extended to encompass transactional access to distributed objects in a reliable distributed system.

Without repeating the material covered earlier, it may be useful to start by reviewing the transactional model in light of what we have subsequently learned about other styles of distributed computing and distributed state. Notice first that the assumptions underlying the transactional approach are quite different from those underlying the virtual synchrony model. Transactional applications are expected to be structured in terms of the basic transactional constructs: *begin, read, update*, and *commit* or *abort*. They are assumed to have been written in isolation, so that they will operate correctly when applied to an idle database system in an initially consistent state. Each transaction, in effect, is a function transforming the database from a consistent state into a new consistent state. The database, for its part, is a well-defined entity: It manages data objects, has a limited interface by which transactions operate on it, and manages information using operations with well-understood semantics.

General-purpose distributed systems, and many client/server applications, match such a model only to a limited degree. The computations performed may or may not act upon saved data in a database, and even when they do, it will be difficult to isolate data access operations from other types of message-based interaction and other types of operation.

The basic reliability goals of the transactional model are tied closely to its programming model. The transactional reliability guarantees are basically this: If a server or client crashes, prior to the commit point of a transaction, a complete rollback of the server state will occur—it is as if the transaction had never been exe-

K.P. Birman, *Guide to Reliable Distributed Systems*, Texts in Computer Science,
DOI 10.1007/978-1-4471-2416-0_20, © Springer-Verlag London Limited 2012

cuted. There is a strong emphasis on recoverability of the database contents after a crash: Any committed transaction will have effects that survive repeated server crashes and restarts. This strong separation of computation from data, coupled with an emphasis on recoverability (as opposed, for example, to continuous availability), distinguishes the transactional approach from the process group replication schemes we have studied in the preceding chapters of this book.

One could ask whether general-purpose distributed programs could not be considered as transactional programs, in this manner mapping the general case to the transactional one. This turns out to be very hard to do. General purpose distributed programs lack a well-defined *begin* or *commit* point, and it would not always be practical to introduce such a structure—sometimes one could do so, but often it would be difficult. These programs lack a well-defined separation of program (transactional client) from persistent state (database); again, some applications could be represented this way, but many could not. Indeed, it is not unreasonable to remark that because of the powerful support that exists for database programming on modern computer systems, most database applications are, in fact, implemented using database systems. The applications that are left over are the ones where a database model either seems unnatural, fails to match some sort of external constraint, or would lead to extremely inefficient execution. This perspective agues that the distributed applications of interest to us will probably split into the transactional ones and others, which are unlikely to match the transactional model even if one tries to force them into it.

Nonetheless, the virtual synchrony model shares some elements of the transactional one: The serialization ordering of the transactional model is similar to the view-synchronous addressing and ordered delivery properties of a multicast to a process group.[1] Virtual synchrony can be considered as having substituted the concept of a multicast for the concept of the transaction itself: In virtual synchrony one talks about a single operation that affects multiple processes, while in transaction systems one talks about a sequence of *read* and *update* operations that are treated as a single atomic unit. The big difference is that whereas explicit data semantics are natural in the context of a database, they are absent in the communication-oriented world we considered when studying the virtual synchrony protocols.

As we examine the transactional approach in more detail, it is important to keep these similarities and differences in mind. One could imagine using process groups and group multicast to implement replicated databases, and there have been several

---

[1]One can imagine doing a multicast by *reading the view of the group and then writing to the group members* and updating the view of the group by *writing to the group view*. Such a transactional implementation of virtual synchrony would address some aspects of the model, such as view synchronous addressing, although it would not deal with others, such as the ordered gap-freedom requirement (Chap. 12). More to the point, it would result in an extremely inefficient style of distributed computing, because every multicast to a process group would now require a database update. The analogy, then, is useful because it suggests that the fundamental approaches are closely related and differ more at the level of how one engineers such systems to maximize performance than in any more basic way. However, it is not an architecture one would want to implement!

research projects that have done just this. A great many distributed systems combine transactional aspects with nontransactional ones, using transactions where a database or persistent data structure is present and using virtual synchrony to maintain consistently replicated in-memory structures to coordinate the actions of groups of processes and so forth. The models are different in their assumptions and goals, but are not incompatible. Indeed, there has been work on merging the execution models themselves, although we will not discuss this here.

Perhaps the most important point is the one stated at the start of this chapter: Transactions focus primarily on recoverability and serializability, while virtual synchrony focuses primarily on order-based consistency guarantees. This shift in emphasis has pervasive implications, and even if one could somehow merge the models, it is likely that they would still be used in different ways. Indeed, it is not uncommon for distributed system engineers to try to simplify their lives, by using transactions throughout a complex distributed system as its sole source of reliability, or by using virtual synchrony throughout, exploiting strongly durable protocols as the sole source of external consistency. Such approaches are rarely successful.

20.2 Implementation of a Transactional Storage System

In this section we briefly review some of the more important techniques used in implementing transactional storage systems. Our purpose is not to be exhaustive or even try to present the best techniques known; there are several excellent books dedicated to the subject (see Bernstein et al. 1987; Gray 1978; Gray and Reuter 1993). Rather, we focus on basic techniques with the purpose of building insight into the reliability mechanisms needed when implementing transactional systems.

20.2.1 Write-Ahead Logging

A *write-ahead log* is a data structure used by a transactional system as a form of backup for the basic data structures that compose the database itself. Transactional systems *append* to the log by writing *log records* to it. These records can record the operations that were performed on the database, their outcome (commit or abort), and can include before or after images of data updated by an operation. The specific content of the log will depend upon the transactional system itself.

We say that a log satisfies a *write-ahead property* if there is a mechanism by which records associated with a particular transaction can be safely and persistently flushed to disk before (ahead of) updates to data records being done by that transaction. In a typical use of this property, the log will record before images (old values) before a transaction updates and commits records for that transaction. When the transaction does an update, the database system will first log the old value of the record being updated and then update the database record itself on disk. Provided that the write-ahead property is respected, the actual order of I/O operations done can potentially be changed to optimize use of the disk. Should the server crash, it

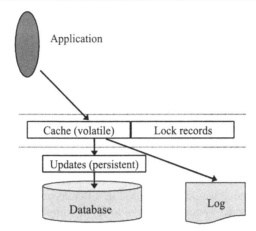

Fig. 20.1 Overview of a transactional database server. Volatile data are used to maintain a high-speed cache of database records and for storage of lock records for uncommitted transactions. An updates list and the database itself store the data, while a write-ahead log is used to enable transactional rollback if an abort occurs and to ensure that updates done by committed transactions will be atomic and persistent. The log saves before or after images of updated data and lock records associated with a transaction running its commit protocol. Log records can be garbage collected after a transaction commits or aborts and the necessary updates to the database have been applied or rolled out

can recover by reviewing the uncommitted transactions in the log and reinstalling the original values of any data records these had modified. The transactions themselves will now be forced to abort, if they have not already done so. Such an event rolls back the transactions that have not committed, leaving the committed ones in place. Later, the log can be garbage collected by cleaning out records for committed transactions (which will never need to be rolled back) and those for uncommitted transactions that have been successfully aborted (and hence need not be rolled back again). (See Fig. 20.1.)

Although a write-ahead log is traditionally managed on the disk itself, there has been recent research on the use of nonvolatile RAM memory or active replication techniques to replace the log with some form of less-expensive structure (see Liskov et al. 1991). Such trends are likely to continue as the relative performance gap between disks (which seems to have reached a performance limit of approximately 10 ms per disk access for a fast disk and as much as 40 to 50 ms per access for a slow one) and communication continue to grow.

20.2.2 Persistent Data Seen Through an Updates List

Not all transactional systems perform updates to the persistent database at the time they are first issued. The decision to do updates directly depends on several factors; among these are the frequency with which transactions are expected to abort and the likelihood that the transaction will rewrite the same record repeatedly. The major alternative to performing direct updates on the database itself is to maintain some form of *updates list* in which database records that have been updated are saved. Each access to the database is first filtered through this updates storage object, and if the record being accessed has changed, the changed version is returned. The database itself is only accessed if the updates list does not contain the desired item, and any update made to the database is instead applied to this updates list.

The advantage of such a structure is that the database itself can be maintained in a very efficient search and access structure without requiring costly structural updates as each operation occurs. Periodically, the database can be updated to merge the committed updates from the updates list into the persistent part of the database, but this does not need to be done until there is a convenient time, perhaps while the database as a whole is under very light load. Moreover, as we will see shortly, the updates list can be generalized to deal with the nested transactions that occur when transactional databases are constructed using abstract data types.

The updates list data structure, if present, should not be confused with a cache or buffer pool. A database cache is a volatile data structure used to accelerate access to frequently used data items by maintaining them in high-speed memory. The updates list is a persistent data structure, which is logically part of the database itself. Its role is to provide the database system with a way of doing database updates without reorganizing the secondary index and other access structures needed to rapidly access items in the main portion of the database.

20.2.3 Nondistributed Commit Actions

To commit a transaction, it is necessary to ensure that its effects will be atomic even if the database server or client program fails during the commit procedure. In the nondistributed case, the required actions are as follows. First, all log records associated with updates done by the transaction are forced to the disk, as are *lock records* recording the locks currently held by the transaction. Once these actions are taken, the transaction is *prepared to commit*. A log record containing the *commit bit* is now written to disk; once it is recorded in a persistent manner in the log, the transaction is said to have *committed*.

Next, updates done by the transaction are applied to the updates list or database. In many transactional systems, this updating is done while the transaction is running, in which case this step (and the forcing of log records to disk) may have already occurred before the transaction reached the commit point.

Finally, when the updates have all been performed, the locks associated with the transaction are released and any log records associated with the transaction are freed for reuse by other transactions. The transaction is now said to be *stable*.

To abort a transaction, the log records associated with it are scanned and used to roll back any updates that may have been performed. All locks associated with the transaction are released, and the log records for the transaction are freed.

In the event that the client process should crash before requesting that the transaction commit or abort, the database server may *unilaterally abort* the transaction. This is done by executing the abort algorithm and later, if the client ever presents additional requests to the server, refusing them and returning an *already aborted* exception code.

Finally, in the event that the database server should crash, when it recovers it must execute a log-recovery procedure before reenabling access to the database. During this process, any transactions that are not shown as committed are aborted, and any updates that may have been done are backed out. Notice that if the log stored before images, backing out updates can be done by simply reinstalling the previous values of any records that were written by the transaction; this operation can be done as many times as necessary if the database server crashes repeatedly before recovering (i.e., the recovery operation is *idempotent*, meaning that it can be performed repeatedly with the same effect as if it had been performed only once).

For transactions shown as committed in the log, the database server recovers by completing the commit procedure and then freeing the log records. Abstractly, the database server can be thought of as recovering in a state where the committed transactions continue to hold any locks that they held at the time of the commit; this will be useful in the case of a distributed transaction on multiple databases.

20.3   Distributed Transactions and Multiphase Commit

When a transaction operates on multiple databases, it is said to be a *distributed transaction*. The commit problem now becomes the multiphase commit problem we discussed in Sect. 10.3. To commit, each participating database server is first asked to *prepare to commit*. If the server is unable to enter this state, it votes for abort; otherwise, it flushes log records and agrees that it is prepared. The transaction commits only if all the participating servers are prepared to commit; otherwise, it aborts. For this purpose, the transactional commit protocols presented earlier can be used without any modifications at all.

In the case of a database server recovery to the prepared state of a transaction, it is important for the server to act as if that transaction continues to hold any locks it held at the time it first became prepared to commit (including read locks, even if the transaction were a read-only one from the perspective of the database server in question). These locks should continue to be held until the outcome of the commit protocol is known and the transaction can complete by committing or aborting. When a transaction has read data at a server that subsequently crashed, upon recovery any read locks it held at that server will be lost. This means the server might grant read or update lock requests that it should have delayed pending the commit or abort of the earlier transaction, a situation easily seen to result in nonserializable executions. Accordingly, the transaction that lost its locks would need to abort. From this we can see that a distributed transaction must include all database servers it has accessed in its commit protocol, not just the ones at which it performed updates, and must verify that locks are still intact at the time of commit, even read locks.

20.4 Transactions on Replicated Data

A transactional system can replicate data by applying updates to all copies of a database, while load-balancing queries across the available copies (in a way that will not change the update serialization order being used). In the most standard approach, each database server is treated as a separate database, and each update is performed by updating at least a quorum of replicas. The transaction aborts if fewer than a quorum of replicas are operational. It should be noted, however, that this method of replication, although much better known than other methods, performs poorly in comparison with the more-sophisticated method described in Sect. 20.7.

The reality is that few existing database servers make use of replication for high availability; therefore, the topic is primarily of academic interest. Transactional systems that are concerned with availability more often use primary-backup schemes in which a backup server periodically is passed a log of committed action performed on a primary server. Such a scheme is faster (because the backup is not included in the commit protocol), but it also has a window during which updates by committed transactions can be temporarily lost (e.g., if the log records for a committed transaction have not yet reached the backup when the primary crashes). When this occurs, the lost updates are rediscovered later, after the primary recovers, and are either merged into the database or, if this would be inconsistent with the database state, user intervention is requested.

Another popular option is to use a spare computer connected by a dual-ported disk controller to a highly reliable RAID-style disk subsystem. If the primary computer on which the database is running fails, it can be restarted on the backup computer with little delay. The RAID disk system provides a degree of protection against hardware failures of the stored database in this case.

Although database replication for availability remains uncommon, there is a small but growing commercial market for systems that support distributed transactions on data spread over multiple sites within an enterprise. The limiting factor for widespread acceptance of these technologies remains performance. Whereas a non-replicated, nondistributed transactional system may be able to achieve thousands or tens of thousands of short update and read transactions per second, distributed transactional protocols and replication slow such systems to perhaps hundreds of updates per second. Although the resulting performance is adequate to sustain a moderately large market of customers, provided that they value high availability or distributed consistency more than performance, the majority of the database marketplace remains focused on scalable, high-performance systems. Such customers are apparently prepared to accept the risk of downtime because of hardware or software crashes to gain an extra factor of 10 to 100 in performance. However, it should again be noted that process group technology may offer a compromise: combining high performance with replication for increased availability or scalable parallelism. We will return to this issue in Sect. 20.7.

20.5   Nested Transactions

Recall that at the beginning of this book, we suggested that object-oriented distributed system architectures are a natural match with client/server distributed system structures. This raises the question of how transactional reliability can be adapted to object-oriented distributed systems.

As we saw in Chap. 7, object-oriented distributed systems are typically treated as being composed of *active objects*, which invoke operations on *passive objects*. To some degree, of course, the distinction is an artificial one, because some passive objects have active computations associated with them—for example, to rearrange a data structure for better access behavior. However, to keep this section simple, we will accept the division. We can now ask if the active objects should be treated as transactional processes and the passive objects as small database servers.

This perspective leads to what are called *nested transactions* (see Moss 1982). The sense in which the transactions are nested is that when an active object invokes an operation on an abstract object stored within an object-oriented database, that object may implement the operation by performing a series of operations on some other, more primitive, database object. An operation that inserts a name into a list of names maintained in a name server, for example, may be implemented by performing a series of updates on a file server in which the name list and associated values are actually stored. One now will have a tree-structured perspective on the transactions themselves, in which each level of object performs a transaction on the objects below it.

In this a tree, the topmost level corresponds to an active object or program in the conventional sense. The intermediate levels of code correspond to the execution of methods (procedures) defined by the passive objects in the database. For these passive objects, transactions begin with the operation invocation by the invoking object and end when a result is returned—that is, procedure executions (operation invocations) are treated as starting with an implicit *begin* and ending with an implicit *commit* in the normal return case. Error conditions can be mapped to an *abort* outcome. The active object at the very top of the tree, in contrast, is said to *begin* a *top-level transaction* when it is started and to *commit* when it terminates normally. A nested transaction is shown in Fig. 20.2.

The nested transaction model can be used for objects that are colocated on a single object repository or for objects distributed among multiple repositories. In both cases, the basic elements of the resulting system architecture resemble that of a single-level transaction system. The details differ, however, because of the need to extend the concurrency control mechanisms to deal with nesting.

The easiest way to understand nested transactions is to view each subtransaction as a transaction that runs in a context created by its parent transaction and any committed sibling subtransactions the parent executed prior to it. Thus, operation op_{21} in Fig. 20.2 should see a database state that corresponds to having executed the subtransaction below op_1 and committing it, even though the effects of that subtransaction will not become permanent and globally visible until the main transaction commits. This approach can be extended to deal with internal concurrency—for example, if op_1 were executed in parallel with op_2.

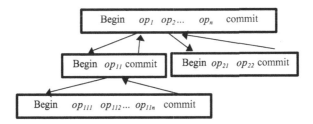

Fig. 20.2 Nested transaction. The operations are numbered hierarchically: op_{ijk} thus represents the kth suboperation initiated by the jth suboperation initiated by operation i at the top level. Commit and abort becomes relative in this model, which is the result of work done by Moss and Liskov

Moss proposed a concept of lock and data version inheritance to accomplish this goal. In his approach, each subtransaction operates by creating new versions of data items and acquiring locks, which are *inherited* by the subtransaction's immediate parent when the subtransaction commits or which return to the state prior to when the subtransaction began if it aborts. These inherited locks and data values are accessible to other subtransactions of the parent that now retains them, but they remain inaccessible to transactions outside of its scope. Moss's Ph.D. dissertation includes proof that this approach yields a nested version of two-phase locking, which guarantees serializable executions.

To implement a nested transaction system, it is usual to start by extending the updates list and locking subsystems of the database so that it will know about transactional nesting. Abstracting, the resulting architecture is one in which each lock and each data item are represented as a *stack* of locks or data items. When a new subtransaction is spawned, the abstract effect is to push a new copy of each lock or data item onto the top of the stack. Later, as the subtransaction acquires locks or updates these data items, the copy at the top of the stack is changed. Finally, when the subtransaction aborts, the topmost stack element is discarded; if it commits, the topmost stack item is popped, as well as the one below it, and then the topmost item is pushed back onto the stack. In a similar manner, the stack of lock records is maintained; the one difference is that if a subtransaction obtains a different class of lock than that held by the parent transaction, the lock is left in the more restrictive of the lock modes.

In practice, nested transactional systems are designed to be lazy, so the creation of new versions of data items or new lock records is delayed until absolutely necessary. Thus, the stack of data items and lock records is not actually generated unless it is needed to perform operations.

A similar abstraction is used to handle the commit and abort mechanisms. Abstractly, as a nested transaction executes, each level of the transaction tracks the data servers it visits, maintaining a list of *commit participants*. In order to commit or abort, the transaction will interact with the servers on this list. In practice, however, such an approach would require repeated execution of the multiphase commit protocols, which will have to run once for each internal node in the transaction tree and one more time for the root! Clearly, this would be prohibitively expensive.

To avoid this problem, Liskov's Argus group proposed an approach in which commit decisions are *deferred*, so that only the top-level commit protocol is actually executed as a multiphase protocol (see Ladin et al. 1990; Liskov and Scheifler 1983; Liskov et al. 1987). Intermediate commits are optimistically assumed successful, while aborts are executed directly by informing the commit participants of the outcome. Now, the issue arises of how to handle an access by a subtransaction to a lock held by a sibling subtransaction or to a data item updated by a sibling. When this occurs, a protocol is executed by which the server tracks down a mutual parent and interrogates it about the outcomes, commit or abort, of the full transaction stack separating the two subtransactions. It then updates the stacks of data items and locks accordingly and allows the operation to proceed. In the case where a transaction rarely revisits data items, the strategy reduces the cost of the nest transactional abstraction to the cost of a flat one-level transaction; the benefit is smaller as the degree of interference increases.

The reader may recall that Liskov's group also pioneered in the use of optimistic (or lazy) concurrency control schemes. These approaches, which are analogous to the use of asynchronous communication in a process group environment, allow a system to achieve high levels of internal concurrency, improving performance and processor utilization time by eliminating unneeded wait states—much as an asynchronous multicast eliminates delay when a multicast is sent in favor of later delays if a message arrives out of order at some destination. At the limit, they converge towards an implementation in which transactions on nonreplicated objects incur little overhead beyond that of the commit protocol run at the end of the top level transaction, while transactions on replicated objects can be done largely asynchronously but with a similar overhead when the commit point is reached. These costs are low enough to be tolerable in many distributed settings, and it is likely that at some future time, a commercially viable, high-performance, object-oriented transaction technology will emerge as a serious design option for reliable data storage in distributed computing systems.

20.5.1 Comments on the Nested Transaction Model

Nested transactions were first introduced in the Argus project at MIT (see Moss 1982) and were rapidly adopted by several other research projects, such as Clouds at the Georgia Institute of Technology and CMU's TABS and Camelot systems (see Spector 1985) (predecessors of Encina, a commercial product marketed by Transarc). The model proved elegant but also difficult to implement efficiently and sometimes quirky. The current view of this technology is that it works best on object-oriented databases, which reside mostly on a single-storage server, but that it is less effective for general-purpose computing in which objects may be widely distributed and in which the distinction between active and passing objects can become blurred.

It is worthy of note that the same conclusions have been reached about database systems. During the mid-1980s, there was a push to develop database operating systems in which the database would take responsibility for more and more of the

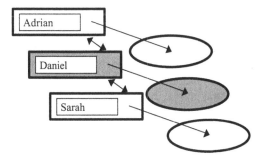

Fig. 20.3   While a directory is being updated (in this case, the entry corresponding to "Daniel"), other transactions may be prevented from scanning the associated directory node by locks upon it, even if they are searching for some other record, such as the one corresponding to "Sarah" or "Adrian." Although a number of schemes can be used to work around such problems, they require sophistication by the developer, who must consider cases that can occur because of concurrency and arrange for concurrent transactions to cooperate implicitly to avoid inefficient patterns of execution. Such metadesign considerations run counter to the principle of independent design on which transactions are based and make the overall approach hard to use in general-purpose operating system settings

tasks traditionally handled by a general-purpose operating system. This trend culminated in systems such as IBM's AS/400 database server products, which achieve an extremely high level of integration between database and operation system functionality. Yet there are many communication applications that suffer a heavy performance penalty in these architectures, because direct point-to-point messages must be largely replaced by database updates followed by a read. While commercial products that take this approach offer optimizations capable of achieving the performance of general-purpose operating systems, users may require special training to understand how and when to exploit them. The trend at the time of this writing seems to be to integrate database servers into general-purpose distributed systems by including them on the network, but running nondatabase operating systems on the general-purpose computing nodes that support application programs.

The following example illustrates the sort of problems that can occur when transactions are applied to objects that fit poorly with the database computing model. Consider a file system directory service implemented as an object-oriented data structure: In such an approach, the directory would be a linked list of named objects, associating a name with some sort of abstract object corresponding to what would be a file in a conventional file system. Operations on a directory include searching it, scanning it sequentially, deleting and inserting entries, and updating the object nodes. Such a structure is illustrated in Fig. 20.3.

A typical transaction in such a system might be a program that displays a graphical interface by which the user enters a name and then looks up the corresponding object. The contents of the object could then be displayed for the user to edit, and the changes, if any, saved into the object when the user finishes. Interfaces such as this are common in modern operating systems, such as Microsoft's Windows or some of the more advanced versions of UNIX.

Viewed as an instance of a nested transaction, this program begins a transaction and then reads a series of directory records looking for the one that matches the name the user entered. The corresponding node would then be locked for update while the user scrutinizes its contents and updates it. The transaction commit would occur when the record is saved in its changed state. An example of such a locked record is highlighted in gray in Fig. 20.3.

But now consider the situation if the system has any concurrency at all. While this process is occurring, the entire data structure may potentially be locked against operations by other transactions, even if they are not interested in the same record as the user is preparing to update! The problem is that any simplistic application of the nested transaction concurrency control rules will leave the top-level records that bind names to objects locked for either read or update and will leave all the directory records scanned while searching for the name entered by the user locked for reads. Other transactions will be unable to acquire conflicting forms of locks on these records and may thus be delayed until the user (who is perhaps heading down the hall for a cup of coffee!) terminates the interaction.

Many extensions to the nested transaction model have been proposed to cope with this sort of problem. Argus, for example, offers a way to perform operations outside the scope of a transaction and includes a way for a transaction to spawn new top-level transactions from deep within a nested execution. Weihl argues for a relaxation of the semantics of objects such as directory servers: In his view, over-specification of the interface of the directory service is the cause of this sort of problem, and he suggests extensions, such as unordered queues and nondeterministic interfaces, which correspond to implementations that give better performance. In this approach one would declare the directory to be an unordered semiqueue (an unordered set) and would implement a nontransactional search mechanism in which the search order is nondeterministic and does not need to involve an access to the locked record until all other records have been scanned. Shasha has developed families of concurrent data structures, in which semantic information is exploited to obtain highly concurrent transactional implementations of operations specific to the data type. Still other researchers have proposed that such problems be addressed by mixing transactional and nontransactional objects and have offered various rules to adapt the ACID properties to such an environment.

The example we gave above occurs in a data structure of unsurpassed simplicity. Similar issues would also be encountered in other data structures, such as doubly linked lists where order *does* matter, trees, hash tables, stacks, and so forth. In each case, a separate set of optimizations is needed to achieve optimal levels of concurrency.

Those who have worked with transactions have concluded that although the model works very well for databases, there are problems for which the transactional model is poorly matched. The argument is basically this: Although the various solutions suggested in the literature do work, they have complicated side-effects (interested readers may want to track down the literature concerned with terminating what are called "orphans of an aborted nested transaction," a problem that occurs when a nested transaction having active subtransactions aborts, eliminating the database state in which those subtransactions were spawned and exposing them to various forms of inconsistency). The resulting mechanisms are complex to work with, and many users might have problems using them correctly; some developers of nested transaction systems have suggested that only experts would be likely to actually build transactional objects, while most real users would work with libraries of preconstructed objects. Thus, even if mechanisms for overcoming these issues do exist, it seems clear that nested transactions do not represent an appropriate general-purpose reliability solution for nondatabase applications.

The commercial marketplace seems to have reached a similar decision. Transactional systems consist largely of relational databases (which may be used to store abstract data types, but in which the relationships between the objects are represented in the transactional tables) or transactional file-structured systems. Although many distributed, object-oriented, transactional systems have been developed, few seem to have made the transition from research prototype to commercial use.

Intriguingly, many of the problems that are most easily solved using process groups are quite hard to solve using transactional solutions. The isolation property of transactions runs counter to the idea of load-balancing in a service replicated at several nodes or of passing a token within a group of cooperating processes. Conversely, however, transactional mechanisms bring a considerable infrastructure to the problem of implementing the ACID properties for applications that act upon persistent data stored in complex data structures, and this infrastructure is utterly lacking in the virtual synchrony model.

The implication is that while both models introduce reliability into distributed systems, they deal with very different reliability goals: recoverability on the one hand and availability on the other. While the models can be integrated so that one could use transactions within a virtual synchrony context and vice versa, there seems to be little hope that they could be merged into a single model that would provide all forms of reliability in a single, highly transparent environment. Integration and coexistence are, therefore, a more promising goal, which seems to be the one favored by industry and research groups.

20.6   Weak Consistency Models

There are some applications in which one requires most aspects of the transactional model, but where serializability in the strict sense is not practical to implement. Important among these are distributed systems in which a database must be accessed from a remote node, which is sometimes partitioned away from the system. In this situation, even if the remote node has a full copy of the database, it is potentially limited to read-only access. Even worse, the impossibility of building a nonblocking commit protocol for partitioned settings potentially prevents these read-only transactions from executing on the most current state of the database, since a network partitioning failure can leave a commit protocol in the prepared state at the remote site.

In practice, many distributed systems treat remote copies of databases as a form of second-class citizen. Such databases are often updated by periodic transfer of the log of recently committed transactions and are used only for read-only queries.

Update transactions execute on a *primary copy* of the database. This approach avoids the need for a multiphase commit but has limited opportunity to benefit from the parallelism inherent in a distributed architecture. Moreover, the delay before updates reach the remote copies may be substantial, so that remote transactions will often execute against a stale copy of the database, with outcomes that may be inconsistent with the external environment—for example, a remote banking system may fail to reflect a recent deposit for hours or days.

In the following text, we briefly present some of the mechanisms that have been proposed as extensions to the transactional model to improve its usefulness in settings such as these.

20.6.1 Epsilon Serializability

Originally proposed by Pu, *epsilon serializability* is a model in which a preagreed strategy is used to limit the possible divergence between a primary database and its remote replicas (see Pu 1993). The epsilon is supposed to represent the degree to which reported data may depart from the "actual" result, and is best understood where the database contains numeric data. In this case, the model guarantees that any value read by a transaction will be within ε of the exact answer.

Suppose, for example, that a remote transaction is executed to determine the current value of a bank balance, and the result obtained is $500. If $\varepsilon = \$100$, the model allows us to conclude that the exact balance in the database (in the primary database server for the bank) is no less than $400 and no more than $600. The benefit of this approach is that it relaxes the need to run costly synchronization protocols between remote copies of a database and the primary: Such protocols are only needed if an update might violate the constraint.

Continuing with our example, suppose we know that there are two replicas and one primary copy of the database. We can now allocate ranges within which these copies can independently perform update operations without interacting with one another to confirm that it is safe to do so. Thus, the primary copy and each replica might be limited to a maximum cumulative update of $50 (larger updates would require a standard locking protocol). Even if the primary and one replica perform maximum increments to the balance of $50, respectively, the remaining replica would still see a value within $100 of the true value, and this remains true for any update that the third replica might undertake. In general, the minimum and maximum cumulative updates done by other copies must be bounded by ε, to ensure that a given copy will see a value within ε of the exact answer.

20.6.2 Weak and Strong Consistency in Partitioned Database Systems

During periods when a database system may be completely disconnected from other replicas of the same database, we will in general be unable to determine a safe serialization order for transactions originating at that disconnected copy.

Suppose that we want to implement a database system for use by soldiers in the field, where communication may be severely disrupted. The database could be a map showing troop positions, depots, the state of roads and bridges, and major targets. In such a situation, one can imagine transactions of varying degrees of urgency. A fairly routine transaction might be to update the record showing where an enemy outpost is located, indicating that there has been no change in the status of the outpost. At the other extreme would be an emergency query seeking to locate the closest medic or supply depot capable of servicing a given vehicle.

Serializability considerations underlie the consistency and correctness of the real database, but one would not necessarily want to wait for serializability to be guaranteed before making an informed guess about the location of a medical team. Thus, even if a transactional system requires time to achieve a completely stable ordering on transactions, there may be cases in which one would want it to process at least certain classes of transactions against the information presently available to it.

In his Ph.D. dissertation, Amir addressed this problem using the Transis system as a framework within which he constructed a working solution (see Amir 1995); see also Amir et al. (1992b, 1994), Davidson et al. (1985), Terry et al. (1995). His basic approach was to consider only transactions that can be represented as a single multicast to the database, which is understood to be managed by a process group of servers. (This is a fairly common assumption in transactional systems, and in fact most transactional applications indeed originate with a single database operation, which can be represented in a multicast or remote procedure call.) Amir's approach was to use *OrderedSend* (the strongly durable or safe form) to distribute update transactions among the servers, which were designed to use a serialization order deterministically related to the incoming *OrderedSend* order. Queries were implemented as local transactions requiring no interaction with remote database servers.

As we saw earlier, strongly durable *OrderedSend* protocols must wait during partitioning failures in all but the primary component of the partitioned system. Thus, Amir's approach is subject to blocking in a process that has become partitioned away from the main system. Such a process may, in the general case, have a queue of undeliverable and partially ordered *OrderedSends*, which are waiting either for a final determination of their relative ordering or for a guarantee that dynamic uniformity will be achieved. Each of these *OrderedSends* corresponds to an update transaction, which could change the database state, perhaps in an order-sensitive way, and which cannot be safely applied until this information is known.

What Amir does next depends on the type of request presented to the system. If a request is urgent, it can be executed either against the last known completely safe state (ignoring these incomplete transactions) or against an approximation to the correct and current state (by applying these transactions, evaluating the database query, and then aborting the entire transaction). A non-urgent update, on the other hand, can simply wait until the safe and global ordering for the corresponding transaction is known, which may not occur until communication has been reestablished with remote sites. As mentioned when we discussed the commit problem, Keidar and Dolev later showed that it is not necessary to achieve simultaneously connectivity in order to push such a protocol forward; it suffices that over a period of time, a majority of processes in the system manage to exchange enough messages to discover a safe event ordering.

Amir's work is not the only effort to have arrived at this solution to the problem. Working independently, a group at Xerox PARC developed a very similar approach to disconnected availability in the Bayou system (see Petersen et al. 1997). Their work is not expressed in terms of process groups and totally ordered, strongly durable, multicast, but the key ideas are the same. In other ways, the Bayou system is more sophisticated than the Transis-based one: It includes a substantial amount of constraint checking and automatic correction of inconsistencies that can creep into a database if urgent updates are permitted in a disconnected mode. Bayou is designed to support distributed management of calendars and scheduling of meetings in large organizations: a time-consuming activity, which often requires approximate decision making because some participants may be on the road or otherwise unavailable at the time a meeting must be scheduled.

20.6.3 Transactions on Multidatabase Systems

The Phoenix system (see Malloth 1996), developed by Malloth, Guerraoui, Raynal, Schiper, and Wilhelm, adopts a similar philosophy but considers a different aspect of the problem. Starting with the same model used in Amir's work and in Bayou, where each transaction is initiated from a single multicast to the database servers, which form a process group, this effort asked how transactions operating upon multiple objects could be accommodated. Such considerations led them to propose a generalized multigroup atomic broadcast, which is totally ordered, strongly durable, and failure-atomic over multiple process groups to which it is sent (see Schiper and Raynal 1996). The point of using this approach is that if a database is represented in fragments managed by separate servers, each of which is implemented in a process group, a single multicast would not otherwise suffice to do the desired updates. The Phoenix protocol used for this purpose is similar to the extended three-phase commit developed by Keidar for the Transis system and is considerably more efficient than sending multiple concurrent and asynchronous multicasts to the process groups and then running a multiphase commit on the full set of participants. Moreover, whereas such as multistep protocols would leave serious unresolved questions insofar as the view-synchronous addressing aspects of the virtual synchrony model are considered, the Phoenix protocol can be proved to guarantee this property within all of the destination groups.

20.6.4 Linearizability

Herlihy and Wing studied consistency issues from a more theoretical perspective (see Herlihy and Wing 1990). In a paper on the *linearizability* model of database consistency, they suggested that object-oriented systems may find the full nested serializability model overly constraining, and yet could still benefit from some forms of ordering guarantees. A nested execution is *linearizable* if the invocations of each object, considered independently of other objects, leave that object in a state that could have been reached by some sequential execution of the same operations, in an order consistent with the causal ordering on the original invocation sequence. In other words, this model says that an object may reorder the operations upon it and interleave their execution provided that it behaves as if it had executed operations one by one, in an order consistent with the (causal) order in which the invocations were presented to it.

Linearizability is thus a sort of stripped down transactional property. In fact, once one gets used to the definition, the property is rather simple and almost obvious. Nonetheless, there are many distributed systems in which servers might not be guaranteed to respect this property. Such servers can allow concurrent transactions to interfere with one another or may reorder operations in ways that violate intuition (e.g., by executing a read-only operation on a state that is sufficiently old to be lacking some updates issued before the read by the same source). At the same time, notice that traditional serializability can be viewed as an extension of linearizability (although serializability does not require that the causal order of invocations be respected, few database systems intentionally violate this property). Herlihy and Wing argue that if designers of concurrent objects at least prove them to achieve linearizability, the objects will behave in an intuitive and consistent way when used in a complex distributed system; should one then wish to go further and superimpose a transactional structure over such a system, doing so simply requires stronger concurrency control.

20.6.5 Transactions in Real-Time Systems

The option of using transactional reliability in real-time systems has been considered by a number of researchers, but the resulting techniques have apparently seen relatively little use in commercial products. There are a number of approaches that can be taken to this problem. Davidson is known for work on transactional concurrency control subject to real-time constraints; her approach involves extending the scheduling mechanisms used in transactional systems (notably, timestamped transactional systems) to seek to satisfy the additional constraints associated with the need to perform operations before a deadline expires.

Broadly, the complexity of the transactional model makes it ill-suited for use in settings where the temporal constraints have fine granularity with regard to the time needed to execute a typical transaction. In environments where there is substantial breathing room, transactions may be a useful technique even if there are real-time constraints to take into account, but as the temporal demands on the system rise, more and more deviation from the pure serializability model is typically needed in order to continue to guarantee timely response.

20.7   Advanced Replication Techniques

Although the need for brevity precludes a detailed treatment of the topic, readers of this text may be interested to know that there has been a flurry of research on combining various group replication techniques with transactional database systems to obtain scalable high performance database servers (see Holliday et al. 1999, 2002; Pedone et al. 1998). To the author's taste, the most interesting work in the area uses an idea originating in what has come to be known as "optimistic" concurrency control, an approach in which a transaction is permitted to execute without locks or with only some of the locks it needs, and then subjected to a "validation" test before being permitted to commit.

In this approach, a database is replicated at multiple servers, each of which has a full copy. Each server is willing to perform transactions against its local replica, with locking performed locally and reads and writes served entirely from the local replica. Later, as each transaction reaches its commit point, any updates performed by the transaction are propagated to other copies. Prior to letting the transaction commit, a test is performed to validate that transactions can commit in the order of delivery of the first-phase commit message, which is transmitted using a totally ordered multicast. This validation test involves applying the same updates and checking to make sure that the reads would be valid against the local committed replica. Agarwal has explored this technique in some detail and his results suggest that it could be quite effective. The commercial community is only beginning to take a serious look at the approach.

For example, suppose that the transactional server manages two variables, x and y and supports transactions that read and write these variables. Now suppose that we replicate the server on nodes a and b so that each has a full copy of the database.

When a read request is received, say at server a, it can be processed in the same manner as if a was the sole server in the system. The transaction obtains local read locks on the variables it accesses (waiting, if necessary, for write locks to be released if a desired data object is locally write-locked), then computes the desired result and returns.

An update transaction, however, is handled in a slightly more elaborate manner. Suppose that at server a an update transaction reads y and then modifies x and at server b a concurrent transaction reads x and then modifies y. Each is executed *locally* at the corresponding server. That is, write locks are acquired at that server, and a log is maintained of the changes made by the transaction (the new value of x in the case of the transaction on a, and of y in the case of the transaction on b). When the two transactions are preparing to commit, the system can be understood as including the locking information and the update logs in the commit messages and using *OrderedSend* to transmit them. Thus, both servers will see these commit requests in an identical order and will process them, one by one, in that order.

Notice that if nothing else is happening in the system, these transactions will be mutually exclusive. They need to be serialized, and because we have allowed them to run concurrently against different copies of the database, one or the other will now need to be aborted.

The commit requests are evaluated relative to the committed system state to determine whether or not any committed transaction may have "invalidated" the read or write set of the transaction under consideration. The issue is as follows. While the transaction that updated x was running on server a some other transaction could have been running at server b and performing an action that would invalidate the transactional serialization order presumed at a. For example, perhaps the update transaction reads y. Recall that at server b we assumed a transaction was updating y, and its commit request may have been ordered by *OrderedSend* ahead of that of the update to x. If that transaction committed successfully, all servers will now have updated y in their committed database. When validating the update to x we now discover that subsequent to the "time" when the x transaction was executed at a, an update to y was committed, and that the x update read the old copy of y. Agarwal suggests a very simple way to test for validity based on a notion of virtual time and an inexpensive mechanism that tracks read and write sets for transactions. At any rate, the update to x is thus discovered to have been invalidated by the concurrent update of y which already committed, and the x update is therefore aborted and forced to re-execute.

Had the *OrderedSend* delivered the commit requests in the opposite order, the converse outcome would have occurred. Notice that because the servers ignore the currently active transactions and use only the committed database state to make decisions, and because the *OrderedSend* ordering is the same at all replicas, all servers reach the same decision when validating each transaction. At server a we discover that the transaction to update x has aborted, roll it back, and restart it. At server b the cost is lower: upon receiving the *OrderedSend*, that server just tests for validity, discovers that the transaction is invalid, and ignores it. Had the transaction committed, we would have applied its updates to the committed database state. Any transaction running locally that read one of these updated variables will later abort, when its own commit request is multicast to the server group.

The costs of this basic scheme, then, are rather low: we need to track the lock set (both read and write), maintain an update log, and transmit copies of this information in the commit request. And, of course, we do need to roll back and restart transactions invalidated by concurrent activity at some other server.

How well would the basic scheme scale? Here, the answer depends entirely on the mix of updates and read-only transactions, and on the amount of data each update produces. If the system sees rather few updates, and they do not touch a tremendous amount of data, Agarwal's replication algorithm will scale almost linearly in the number of servers. The cost of the commit requests would, in this case, be negligible.

On the other hand, if a large amount of data are modified by the update, transmitting the log could be a problem; in such cases, executing the same transaction in parallel on the various servers would be a much more efficient strategy. Worse still, if transactions often conflict and aborts become common, the scheme would face a high overhead—and in such a scenario, it seems likely that the rate of conflicts would rise roughly linearly in the number of servers. This is because one would normally assume that each server sees essentially the identical workload; thus, the more servers we add, the more transactions will be at risk of conflict.

Beyond Agarwal's basic idea one could do more. For example, a smart load-balancing system might try to partition update transactions, so that transactions likely to experience concurrency control conflicts go to the same server, and only transactions likely to be independent are dispatched to different servers. Although such a load-balancing agent would need to look "inside" each request to make an appropriate guess, for many applications it should be possible to do this. The frequency of update conflicts would drop accordingly.

We could do still better. Suppose that while transactions run, we use an asynchronous multicast to *lazily* inform replicas of locks held locally and to pretransmit update logs. For example, long before the transaction to update x tries to commit, we might already have informed the other servers that the transaction has a read lock on y and a write-lock on x, and has modified x to new value 24. When this information arrives, the server receiving it can stash the log of updates for later use at commit time, but can also try and obtain the identical locks locally. If no other transaction holds locks on x and y this will register the corresponding locks, with the effect that when the transaction finally tries to commit, it is far more likely to succeed. Moreover, having pretransmitted its updates, the commit message itself will be far smaller, hence faster to send. (One could even go further and pre-apply the log of updates.)

In this modified scheme, we reduce the window during which a conflict can arise. However, we do not close it, since server b may learn of the activity at server a only to find that a conflicting activity has already started locally; server a will, symmetrically, discover this shortly after. But keep in mind that not all transactions commit in any case, and of course we can ultimately trust the *OrderedSend* ordering to pick a winner if a true conflict arises and persists to commit time.

With such extensions, it seems possible that at least for databases with a mostly read workload, a replicated system could perform read-only transactions at close to the speed of a non-replicated database, while performing updates only slightly slower. This holds the promise of near linear speedup in the sustainable read load as the database is run on more and more compute nodes, with relatively minor degradation as a function of scale (since multicast performance for small process groups of the size this might yield tends to be relatively independent of group size—up to a group of perhaps 32 members, that is). Of course, once the server pool gets large enough, the costs of transmitting update logs and handling aborts become to dominate, but this would already represent a substantial opportunity for speedup!

20.8 Snapshot Isolation

Although the need for brevity makes it difficult to do justice to every important topic, the use of *snapshot isolation* has become so important in cloud systems and other scalable database settings that we really must at least touch upon the technique.

Snapshot isolation was first proposed in connection with multiversion database systems, where instead of overwriting one value with a subsequent value, the database system keeps old values, tracking the period of time during which each value was active. This enables modern databases to use a form of timestamped concurrency control for read-only applications: rather than force a read to wait until a current write finishes, or allow a read to delay a write, as a transaction executes the system defines a window of validity, so that reads often execute in the recent past, but against a consistent "snapshot" of the database or transactional application. Update transactions are serialized with respect to one another in a normal ACID-style, but by removing reads from the mix, performance is hugely enhanced.

Modern cloud computing systems tend to use snapshot isolation for transactions that run on hard-state services in the inner tiers of the cloud. First-tier systems generally shard data and use some form of mostly consistent caching scheme, detecting and resolving errors (if any) using background mechanisms that run periodically and try to clean up any noticeable inconsistencies. Thus one has an outer tier that offers either inconsistency or at best a form of snapshot-isolation for reads, and then as we push deeper into the cloud, we find applications that offer stronger properties and assurance guarantees.

20.9 Related Reading

Chapter 23 includes a review of some of the major research projects in this area, which we will not attempt to duplicate here. For a general treatment of transactions (see Bartlett et al. 1987; Gray and Reuter 1993).

On the nested transaction model (see Moss 1982).

On disconnected operation in transactional systems (see Amir 1995; Amir et al. 1992a, 1992b, 1994, 1995, 2000; Davidson et al. 1985; Terry et al. 1995).

On log-based transactional architectures (see Birman and van Renesse 1994; Joseph 1986; Liskov et al. 1991; Seltzer 1993).

As part of Cornell's course on "Advanced Replication Techniques", CS734, offered in Fall of 2001, Alan Demers assembled an outstanding bibliography of techniques for replicating database systems (www.cs.cornell.edu/courses/cs734/2001fa).

Peer-to-Peer Systems and Probabilistic Protocols

21

In this chapter, we consider a number of protocols representative of a wave of research and commercial activity in distributed computing. The protocols in question share two characteristics. First, they exploit what are called *peer-to-peer* communication patterns. Peer-to-peer computing is in some ways a confusing categorization, since all of the protocols we have discussed in this book involve direct exchanges of messages between "peers." A better term might be "client to client" protocols, because most peer-to-peer systems emerge from a world of client/server computing, but replace some or all functions of the servers by functionality hosted on the clients themselves. For example, in what has become the most standard example of peer-to-peer computing, individuals willing to share music might copy MP3 files onto their machines, then advertise their availability in some form of directory that others can query. To obtain a song, one would look for someone with a copy, then download the file from that machine. Space permitting, the user who downloads a song would then become an alternative source for the file, so that over time, a great many copies would become available. The benefit is that the workload of serving files will be spread over a number of machines proportional to the popularity of each file, so that the system should scale well (although we will soon need to qualify this statement with all sorts of caveats!).

P2P communication arises in many settings other than this canonical file-sharing one. In Chap. 4 we discussed some examples of this class of system, including peer-to-peer file sharing technologies and peer-to-peer indexing. Here we look at additional peer-to-peer use cases, focusing on peer-to-peer multicast and data mining.

21.1 Bimodal Multicast Protocol

In this section, we shift our focus and look at a class of multicast protocols that use P2P techniques to achieve a high degree of scalability. They are also *probabilistically reliable*. Unlike the protocols presented previously, they are based on a probabilistic system model somewhat similar to the synchronous model, which we

K.P. Birman, *Guide to Reliable Distributed Systems*, Texts in Computer Science, DOI 10.1007/978-1-4471-2416-0_21, © Springer-Verlag London Limited 2012

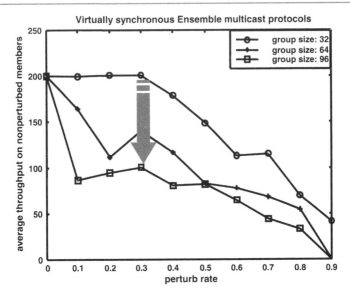

Fig. 21.1 Throughput of a virtually synchronous process group suffers when even a single member is perturbed, and the problem gets worse as the group size increases. This suggests that traditional ways of implementing virtual synchrony scale poorly

considered in our discussion of real-time protocols. In contrast to the asynchronous model, no mechanism for detecting failure is required. Virtual synchrony is not supported "directly" on this model, but we do note that Gupta has shown how to implement a scalable virtual synchrony protocol over the Bimodal Multicast (Birman 1999), obtaining a solution that is always safe, but may report new views after a delay that rises slowly in group size.

Figure 21.1 illustrates the type of scalability problem we are trying to overcome. In this figure, we have graphed the "steady state" throughput of the basic *Ordered-Send* protocol implemented in the Ensemble system. Each line on the graph corresponds to a different group size: 32, 64, and 96 members. The x axis shows how performance is impacted by a "perturbation" at a single member within the overall group, where we stole cycles by forcing the process to sleep for brief intervals of time, thus mimicking the behavior one might see if the process shared the computer with some other workload. With $x = 0$, the process was unperturbed, with $x = 0.3$, 30% of the time it was sleeping, and so forth.

As can be seen in the figure, this rather minor intervention causes the sustainable throughput to collapse. We should note that the actual throughput numbers are not very important here—the experiment was performed more than a decade ago, ran on an IBM SP2 cluster and used rather large messages, but similar graphs can be obtained for almost any size of message and on any platform.

The problem may at first glance seem specific to the implementation of the protocol: it turns out that when this experiment is running, the sender is forced to choke back (to perform flow control) because messages are piling up in the buffer it uses

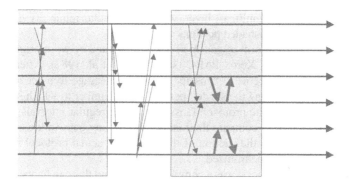

Fig. 21.2 A push gossip multicast protocol. Multicast uses a flooding-style of distribution mechanism, with no effort to achieve reliability (perhaps, IP multicast, perhaps some other scheme). Periodically, each process shares state information with a randomly selected peer, allowing each to catch up with any missed messages that the other received, and within a few rounds, the gaps are filled. Bimodal Multicast will reissue an (unreliable) multicast within a region where it seems likely that several receivers are missing copies, so this gap fill mechanism is used to clean up just the last few gaps in the message sequence

to retransmit lost messages in the event of a communication problem. As the group gets bigger the percentage of messages for which an acknowledgement arrives only after a long delay seems to grow, hence the sender exhausts its buffering space. Studies have shown, however, that this kind of problem is anything but unique to the virtual synchrony reliability model or its implementation in Ensemble. In fact, the great majority of "reliable" multicast protocols share such behavior—regardless of their particular reliability goals. The reasons for the collapse vary from protocol to protocol, but the collapse of achievable throughput seems to be a common phenomenon.

In contrast, the P2P multicast protocols we will now discuss are scalable in two senses. First, message costs and latencies grow slowly with system size. Second, reliability (the probability of non-atomic delivery of a multicast) falls to 0 exponentially as group size increases. This scalable reliability is achieved through a form of "gossip" protocol, which is strongly self-stabilizing. By this we mean that if the system is disrupted, it will repair itself given a sufficient period of time without failures. Our protocols (particularly for handling replicated data) also have this property.

The basic idea we will work with is illustrated in Fig. 21.2, which shows a possible execution for a protocol we call Bimodal Multicast, but also known by the names *ProbabilisticSend* and *pbcast*. Bimodal multicast combines a message distribution phase with a *gossip* repair phase, and we see both types of event in the figure (the figure makes it look as if the system runs in synchronous rounds, but that is just to make it clear how things work; the actual protocol is not at all synchronous and both kinds of round are superimposed). The basic idea is as follows. To send a multicast, a process transmits it with some form of quick but not necessarily reliable transport layer, like IP multicast. (If IP multicast is not available, as is the case in the modern Internet, we can use Scribe trees—a type of overlay built on the Pastry system, or some similar hand-built multicast layer, with no particular reliability guarantees.) So this is shown in the unshaded portions of Fig. 21.2.

Next, we introduce a form of gossip protocol motivated by work originally done by Demers and others at Xerox PARC (see Demers et al. 1987). After a process receives a message, it begins to "gossip" about the message to a set of peers (in Fig. 21.2 this occurs during the shaded periods). The number to which it gossips is said to be the *fanout* of the protocol. Gossip occurs at regular intervals, and offers the members a chance to compare their states and fill any gaps in the message sequence. As mentioned in the caption of the figure, the actual protocol runs gossip continuously and is unsynchronized.

Even if the initial multicast was a complete failure (and this can happen, although it is unlikely), gossip protocols will typically flood the network within a logarithmic number of rounds. This behavior is very similar to that of a biological epidemic; hence, such protocols are also known as *epidemic* ones (see Bailey 1975). Notice that although each process may hear about a message many times, it does not need to receive multiple copies of the message: the gossip messages typically are very compact lists of messages available at the sender, and the actual copies must be retrieved in a separate RPC-style interaction. In fact, the cost of gossip is basically constant. The randomness of the protocols has the benefit of overcoming failures of individual processes, in contrast with protocols where each process has a specific role to play and must play it correctly, or fail detectably, for the protocol itself to terminate correctly. We say that a gossip *push* occurs if a process, picking some peer, sends information to it, and a gossip *pull* occurs if the peer sends information back. Bimodal Multicast uses a *push-pull epidemic*, in which both forms of exchange occur.

Demers and his colleagues have provided an analysis of the convergence and scaling properties of gossip protocols based on pushing, pulling, and combined mechanisms and have shown how these can overcome failures. They prove that both classes of protocols converge toward flooding at an exponential rate and demonstrate that they can be applied to real problems. The motivation for their work was a scaling problem, which occurred in the wide area mail system developed at PARC in the 1980s. As this system was used on a larger and larger scale, it began to exhibit consistency problems and had difficulties in accommodating mobile users. Demers and his colleagues showed that by reimplementing the e-mail system to use a gossip broadcast protocol they could overcome these problems, helping ensure timely and consistent e-mail services that were location independent and inexpensive. Thus, in their system, the "multicast" is a very slow action—a replicated database update that occurs rarely. We will focus on the use of gossip in systems running at much higher speeds here, where multicast runs at network speeds and gossip may occur many times per second.

21.1.1 Bimodal Multicast

In the style of protocol explored at Xerox, the actual rate with which messages will flood the network is not guaranteed, because of the risk of failures. Instead, these protocols guarantee that, given enough time, eventually either all or no correct processes will deliver a message. This property is called *eventual convergence*. Although eventual convergence is sufficient for many uses, the property is weaker than the guarantees of the protocols we used earlier to replicate data and perform synchronization, because eventual convergence does not provide bounds on message latency or ordering properties. Hayden was the first to suggest that gossip protocols can be extended to have these properties (see Birman et al. 1999), and in this section we present the protocol he developed for this purpose. As mentioned above, Hayden calls this protocol Bimodal Multicast and uses *pbcast* as a shorthand for it, but for similarity to the protocol names we have used elsewhere in this book, we will call it *ProbabilisticSend*.

Specifically, *ProbabilisticSend* is designed for a static set of processes, which communicate synchronously over a fully connected, point-to-point network. The processes have unique, totally ordered identifiers and can toss weighted, independent random coins. Runs of the system proceed in a sequence of rounds in which messages sent in the current round are delivered in the next round. The protocol is basically the same as the one shown in Fig. 21.2, but it incorporates a number of optimizations intended to retransmit a multicast quickly using IP multicast if several processes may have dropped their copies, and also to deal with a peculiarity of link load seen in wide-area settings. We will discuss these optimizations below.

Hayden was able to analyze the behavior of his solution, and this is part of what makes it such an interesting protocol. His model assumes that there are two types of failure. The first is process failure. Hayden assumes an independent, per-process probability of at most f_p that a process has a crash failure during the finite duration of a protocol. Such processes are called faulty. The second type of failure is message omission failure. There is an independent, per-message probability of at most f_m that a message between nonfaulty processes experiences a send omission failure. The union of all message omission failure events and process failure events is mutually independent. In this model, there are no malicious faults, spurious messages, or corruption of messages. We expect that both f_p and f_m are small probabilities (e.g., unless otherwise stated, the values used in the graphs in this chapter are $f_m = 0.05$ and $f_p = 0.001$).

The impact of the failure model can be visualized by thinking of the power that would be available to an adversary seeking to cause a run of the protocol to fail by manipulating the system within the bounds of the model. Such an adversary has these capabilities and restrictions:

- An adversary cannot use knowledge of future probabilistic outcomes, interfere with random coin tosses made by processes, cause correlated (nonindependent) failures to occur, or do anything not enumerated below.
- An adversary has complete knowledge of the history of the current run of the protocol.
- At the beginning of a run of the protocol, the adversary has the ability to individually set process failure rates, within the bounds $[0 \ldots f_p]$.
- For faulty processes, the adversary can choose an arbitrary point of failure.
- For messages, the adversary has the ability to individually set send omission failure probabilities within the bounds of $[0 \ldots f_m]$.

Note that although probabilities can be manipulated by the adversary, doing so can only make the system more reliable than the bounds, f_p and f_m.

Using this model, Hayden developed recurrence relations and solved them to derive predictions of how *ProbabilisticSend* would behave with various parameter settings. We will review some of his findings momentarily.

Hayden's probabilistic analysis of the properties of the *ProbabilisticSend* protocol is only valid in runs of the protocol in which the system obeys the model. In particular, the independence properties of the system model are quite strong and are not likely to be continuously realizable in an actual system—for example, partition failures in the sense of correlated communication failures do not occur in this model. Partitions can be simulated by the independent failures of several processes, but they are of low probability. However, the protocols we develop using *ProbabilisticSend*, such as our replicated data protocol, remain safe even when the system degrades from the model. In addition, *ProbabilisticSend*-based algorithms can be made self-healing—for instance, our replicated data protocol has guaranteed eventual convergence properties similar to normal gossip protocols: If the system recovers into a state that respects the model and remains in that state for sufficiently long, the protocol will eventually recover from the failure and reconverge to a consistent state.

At the same time, Hayden's analysis is in some ways very pessimistic. For example, he found that *ProbabilisticSend* is so reliable if IP multicast succeeds that he ended up focused on the case where IP multicast is sometimes a complete failure and nobody receives the initial multicast. This leads to a sort of extreme scenario in which some messages are essentially delivered reliably system-wide in the first phase, while others are not delivered at all until the gossip mechanism kicks in. Realistic runs of *ProbabilisticSend* live somewhere in between these extremes, but are hard to analyze using the style of closed form recurrence relations Hayden employed in his investigation. As a result, in what follows we will use Hayden's analysis to derive worst case bounds, and experimental studies to understand the normal case that might be seen in real deployments of *ProbabilisticSend*.

21.1.2 Unordered ProbabilisticSend Protocol

We begin with an unordered version of *ProbabilisticSend* with static membership (the protocol shown in Fig. 21.3). The protocol consists of a fixed number of rounds, in which each process participates in at most one round. A process initiates a *ProbabilisticSend* by sending a message to a random subset of other processes using an unreliable multicast primitive such as IP multicast, or a flooding scheme implemented over UDP. No effort is made to detect packet loss or repair missing packets, but obviously, one would hope that many of the packets get through. Notice, though, that the cost of initially disseminating the packet is unrelated to network load or congestion, since the protocol starts with just a single attempt to send each message and never sends extra messages no matter what fate befalls that first attempt.

When other processes receive a message, they begin to gossip about it to their peers for a period of time called the "fanout" of the protocol. Gossip occurs at a constant frequency in this system: each process maintains a timer and at some rate

(* State kept per *pbcast*: have I received a message regarding this *pbcast* yet? *)
let received_already = false

(* Initiate a *pbcast*. *)
to *pbcast*(msg):
  deliver_and_gossip(msg,k)

(* Handle message receipt. *)
on receive gossip(msg,round):
  deliver_and_gossip(msg,round)

(* Auxiliary function. *)
to deliver_and_gossip(msg,round):
  (* Do nothing if already received it. *)
  if received_already then return

(* Mark the message as being seen and deliver. *)
received_already := true
deliver(msg)

(* If last round, don't gossip. *)
if round = 0 then return

for each *p* in P:
  do with probability *r*:
    sendto *p* gossip(msg,round-1)

Fig. 21.3 Unordered *ProbabilisticSend* protocol. The function time() returns the current time expressed in rounds since the first round. Message receipt and *ProbabilisticSend* are executed as atomic actions

(say, ten times per second), picks a peer and sends it a gossip message. There is no need to synchronize gossip or synchronize clocks, and gossip messages are treated as unreliable, asynchronous packets. Presumably, many will get through, but no attempt is made to detect loss or retransmit a lost packet.

The content of a gossip packet is a *digest* of the state of the sender. This typically includes membership information (thus, as nodes join or leave, information about those events will spread through the system) and also a summary of multicasts that the sender of the gossip message has received. The receiver of a gossip message can react in two ways: it can request a copy of a message it lacks, pulling it from the sender of the gossip message, or can send a copy of a message it received that the sender seems to be missing. (In practice, it can react in a third way, too: by re-multicasting a message, unreliably, if there is evidence that a few processes in the region are missing it; this is done cautiously, but with the goal of ensuring that most processes receive each message in an unreliable multicast, and gossip is used just to plug the last few gaps.)

For purposes of analysis, the parameters of the protocol are as follows:

- *P*: the set of processes in the system: $n = |P|$
- *k*: the number of rounds of gossip to run

- r: the probability that a process gossips to each other process (the weighting of the coin mentioned earlier)

The behavior of the gossip protocol mirrors a class of disease epidemics, which nearly always infects either almost all of a population or almost none of it. In the following text, we will show that *ProbabilisticSend* has a bimodal delivery distribution, which stems from the epidemic behavior of the gossip protocol. The normal behavior of the protocol is for the gossip to flood the network in a random but exponential fashion. If r is sufficiently large, most processes will usually receive the gossip within a logarithmic number of rounds.

21.1.3 Weaking the Membership Tracking Rule

One objection that some researchers raised about the original Bimodal Multicast protocol centered on selection of peers for the gossip step of the protocol. The issue here is that Hayden's analysis assumes that each group member knows the full membership of the group, and can exchange messages with every other member. In many systems these assumptions would not hold: tracking the full membership might be very costly in a large system where membership evolves steadily, and in many settings, firewalls and network address translation components create barriers that prevent certain group members from communication with one-another. In fact, the Bimodal Multicast paper does touch upon this issue, suggesting that Bimodal Multicast can run on subsets of the membership that satisfy certain mathematical properties (the requirement is that the communication graph satisfy a mathematical property called *expansion*), but the paper did not explore the best solutions to actually implement this approach. This problem was addressed by Guerraoui, Kermarrec and a group of their students in a protocol they called the Lightweight Probabilistic Broadcast protocol (often shortened to *lbpbcast*; similarly, Hayden uses *pbcast* as a shorthand name for the Bimodal Multicast) (Eugster et al. 2003).

The basic idea in this variation on the protocol is to allow each member to track just a subset of the other members of the system, but to do so in a way designed to be safe. For example, a developer might want group members to only peer with other members that are close in terms of network latency, or those with which it can communicate without needing to tunnel through firewalls; Lightweight Probabilistic Broadcast allows this sort of subset selection provided, however, that enough long-distance links remain to ensure the connectivity of the resulting communication graph, which obviously must have adequate ways of reaching all members of the system. Thus, while process p might not know about process s in a direct sense, p should know q which knows of r which knows of s, etc. One then runs the basic Bimodal Multicast algorithm but with gossip occurring only between neighbors in which one knows the other: p gossips with its neighbors (including q), q gossips with r, etc. The research team showed that the resulting solution converges just as rapidly as Hayden's more costly full-membership solution, and offers equally good robustness.

Hayden had previously pointed to the mathematical property called graph expansion, but this research showed precisely how one can achieve that goal. First, they observed that in the ideal case one wants the communication graph to have the properties of what are called *Small Worlds Graphs*, meaning that the overall graph diameter is logarithmic in the system size, but in practice most random peer selection schemes are adequate. Although a highly biased peer selection scheme can reduce the speed of convergence or reliability of the protocol, it turns out to be relatively easy to avoid this risk, a topic the same team explored in Jelasity et al. (2007). Indeed, this latter paper shows that the same idea can be applied in very general ways, yielding a general methodology for designing gossip protocols in which one starts by assuming a uniform and random peer selection scheme over the full membership of the system, and then plugs in a lightweight peer selection algorithm. Most gossip research uses this approach today.

21.1.4 Adding CASD-Style Temporal Properties and Total Ordering

In the protocol shown in Fig. 21.3, the *ProbabilisticSend* messages are unordered. However, because the protocol runs in a fixed number of rounds of fixed length, it is trivial to extend it using the same method as was proposed in the CASD protocols (see Fig. 21.4). By delaying the delivery of a message until it is known that all correct processes have a copy of that message, totally ordered delivery can be guaranteed. This yields a protocol similar to *OrderedSend* in that it has totally ordered message delivery and probabilistically good reliability within the fixed membership of the process group invoking the primitive. It would not be difficult to introduce a further extension of the protocol for use in dynamic process groups, but we will not address that issue here.

21.1.5 Scalable Virtual Synchrony Layered over ProbabilisticSend

Indranil Gupta has shown that virtual synchrony can be layered over the *ProbabilisticSend* protocol. Without getting into the details, he does this using a scheme that probabilistically selects a small set of leader processes, which are responsible for deciding on the ordering of messages relative to view changes. Multicasts are sent to the full group "directly," but membership events vector through these processes, which then use the *ProbabilisticSend* protocol to report each new view and its sequencing relative to the message stream. This permits him to support a token-based *OrderedSend* protocol: total ordering, but not the CASD-style temporal properties of Hayden's method.

Gupta shows that he can preserve the scalability of *ProbabilisticSend* and yet get the strong guarantees of virtual synchrony in this manner, at the cost of some delay before messages can be delivered. His experiments showed that at least in the range of group sizes seen earlier in Fig. 21.1, where virtual synchrony "melted down" under stress, virtual synchrony over *ProbabilisticSend* should continue to perform quite well.

```
(* Local state: message buffer and counter for generating unique identifiers. *)
let buffer = {}
let id_counter = 0

(* Initiate a pbcast. *)
to pbcast(msg):
    (* Create unique id for each message. *)
    let id = (my_id, id_counter)
    id_counter := id_counter + 1


    do_gossip(time(),id,msg,k)

(* Handle message receipt. *)
on receive gossip (timesent, id, msg, round):
    do_gossip(timesent, id, msg, round)

(* Handle timeouts. *)
on timeout(time):
    (* Check for messages ready for delivery. Assumes buffer is
     * scanned in lexicographic order of (sent, id). *)
    for each (sent, id, msg) in buffer:
        if sent + k + 1 = time then
            buffer := buffer \ (sent, id, msg)
            deliver(msg)

(* Auxiliary function. *)
to do_gossip(timesent, id, msg, rnd):
    (* If have seen message already, do nothing. *)
    if (timesent, id, msg) in buffer then
        return

(* Buffer the message for later delivery, and then gossip. *)
buffer := buffer ∪(timesent, id, msg)
set_timer timesent + k + 1

(* If last round, do nothing more. *)
if rnd = 0 then return

foreach p in P
    with probability r
        send p gossip(timesent, id, msg, rnd-1)
```

Fig. 21.4 Ordered *ProbabilisticSend* protocol, using the method of CASD

21.1.6 Probabilistic Reliability and the Bimodal Delivery Distribution

Hayden has demonstrated that when the system respects the model, a *ProbabilisticSend* is almost always delivered to most or to few processes and almost never to some processes. Such a delivery distribution is called a "bimodal" one and is depicted in Fig. 21.5. The graphs show that varying numbers of processes will deliver *ProbabilisticSend*—for instance, the probability that 26 out of the 50 processes will deliver a *ProbabilisticSend* is around 10^{-28}. Such a probabilistic guarantee is, for most practical purposes, a guarantee that the outcome cannot occur. The bimodal

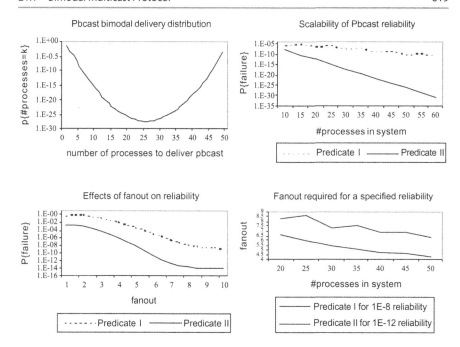

Fig. 21.5 A set of graphs illustrating the manner in which the analysis of *ProbabilisticSend* can be used to predict its reliability and to select parameter settings matched to desired behavior. The graph is drawn from Birman and van Renesse (1996)

distribution property is presented here informally, but later we discuss the method used by Hayden to calculate the actual probability distributions for a particular configuration of *ProbabilisticSend*.

The *ProbabilisticSend* protocol also has a second bimodal characteristic: delivery delays (latency) tends to be bimodal, with one distribution of very low latencies for messages that arrive without packet loss using the basic IP multicast, and a second distribution with higher latencies for messages that had to be remulticast or repaired using the gossip-driven gap-filling mechanism. Hayden's analysis does not focus on this aspect and in fact had he done so, his model would do a poor job of predicting the observed behavior. However, the actual implementation of *ProbabilisticSend* reported by Hayden et al. did explore this question (see Birman et al. 1999). One finds that the degree to which *ProbabilisticSend* latencies are bimodal is very much a function of parameter settings; with aggressive settings the protocol overhead is still rather low, and latencies can be squeezed down to within a small constant factor of the average network latency. This is quite an encouraging result.

Most important of all, *ProbabilisticSend* overcomes the scalability problems we saw in Fig. 21.1, where virtual synchrony seemed to melt down. Under precisely the same experimental conditions, *ProbabilisticSend* is known to continue to deliver messages at a steady rate even while as many as 25% of the participants are intermittently perturbed. Indeed, a tremendously disruptive scenario is required to overload the protocol, and even then, it has been shown to degrade rather gracefully.

The basic reliability of *ProbabilisticSend* is often all that one needs in an application, in which case it offers a uniquely scalable and stable way to disseminate information. Indeed, studies have shown that *ProbabilisticSend* will scale essentially without limit, imposing constant cost on the participants (here we assume a constant rate of new multicasts), and with essentially identical latency distributions throughout the system if we factor out the delay of the initial unreliable multicast itself. Indeed, in a healthy network, *ProbabilisticSend* is so reliable that it can often be substituted for *Send* or, when totally ordered, for *OrderedSend*. Nonetheless, there are circumstances under which gaps will not be repaired, and *Probabilistic-Send* does not support virtually synchronous group membership reporting unless Gupta's extensions are employed.

In practice, one finds that most systems that include a version of *Probabilistic-Send* integrate the protocol with a form of logging service that captures messages and archives them. Such a service can be used by *ProbabilisticSend* to overcome failures but can also be used by the application itself, to fill gaps in the delivery sequence not repaired by the protocol itself. For example, at Cornell there has been some recent work on implementing a publish-subscribe system over *Probabilistic-Send*. In this system, the logging servers are also used by applications that join the system: they can check for "back postings" on subjects of interest, and then are given a stream of updates. The guarantees of this publish-subscribe implementation approximate those of virtual synchrony: the application will see every posting on the subjects of interest to it, both archived and new, will not see any duplicates, and will see events in the same order as everyone else did. QuickSilver, a new multicast platform including this functionality (unrelated to the file system with the same name), should be available for download from Cornell in 2005.

Gupta's work, and Hayden's prior work, point to the other major way of using these protocols. A bimodal distribution is particularly useful for voting-style protocols where, as an example, updates must be made at a majority of the processes to be valid; we saw examples of such protocols when we discussed quorum replication. Problems do occur in these sorts of protocols when failures cause a large number of processes, but not a majority, to carry out an update. *ProbabilisticSend* overcomes this difficulty through its bimodal delivery distribution by ensuring that votes will almost always be weighted strongly for or against an update, and will very rarely be evenly divided. By counting votes, it can almost always be determined whether an update was valid or not, even in the presence of some failed processes. Gupta carries this quite far, developing an entire methodology for building solutions to "classical" distributed computing problems over *ProbabilisticSend* and a few other probabilistic peer-to-peer protocols of his own design.

With *ProbabilisticSend*, the bad cases are when "some" processes deliver the *ProbabilisticSend*; these are the cases that *ProbabilisticSend* makes unlikely to occur. We will call *ProbabilisticSends* that are delivered to "some" processes *failed ProbabilisticSends* and *ProbabilisticSends* delivered to "few" processes *invalid ProbabilisticSends*. The distinction anticipates the replicated data protocol presented in the following text, in which invalid *ProbabilisticSends* are inexpensive events and failed *ProbabilisticSends* are potentially costly.

To establish that *ProbabilisticSend* does indeed have a bimodal delivery distribution, Hayden used a mixture of symbolic and computational methods. First, he computed a recurrence relation, which expresses the probability that a *ProbabilisticSend* will be received by a processes at the end of round j, given that the message had been received by b processes at the end of round $j - 1$, c of these for the first time. In the terminology of a biological infection, b denotes the number of processes that were infected during round $j - 1$ and hence are infectious; the difference between a and b thus represents the number of *susceptible* processes that had not yet received a gossip message and that are successfully infected during round j.

The challenge aspect of this analysis is to deal with the impact of failures, which has the effect of making the variables in the recurrence relation random ones with binomial distributions. Hayden arrives at a recursive formula but not a closed form solution. However, such a formula is amenable to computational solutions and, by writing a program to calculate the various probabilities involved, he is able to arrive at the delivery distributions shown in Fig. 21.2.

A potential risk in the analysis of *ProbabilisticSend* is to assume, as may be done for many other protocols, that the worst case occurs when message loss is maximized. *ProbabilisticSend*'s failure mode occurs when there is a partial delivery of a *ProbabilisticSend*. A pessimistic analysis must consider the case where local increases in the message-delivery probability decrease the reliability of the *overall ProbabilisticSend protocol*. This makes the analysis quite a bit more difficult than the style of worst-case analysis used in protocols such as the CASD one, where the worst case is the one in which the maximum number of failures occurs.

21.1.7 Evaluation and Scalability

The evaluation of *ProbabilisticSend* is framed in the context of its scalability. As the number of processes increases, *ProbabilisticSend* scales according to several metrics. First, the reliability of *ProbabilisticSend* grows with system size. Second, the cost per participant, measured by number of messages sent or received, remains at or near constant as the system grows. Having made these claims, it must be said that the version of *ProbabilisticSend* presented and analyzed for a network makes assumptions that become less and less realizable for large systems. In practice, this issue could be addressed with a more hierarchically structured protocol, but Hayden's analysis has not been extended to such a protocol. In this section, we will address the scaling characteristics according to the metrics previously listed and then discuss informally how *ProbabilisticSend* can be adapted for large systems.

Reliability
ProbabilisticSend has the following property: As the number of processes participating in a *ProbabilisticSend* grows, the protocol becomes more reliable. In order to demonstrate this, we present a graph, Fig. 21.5(b), of *ProbabilisticSend* reliability as the number of processes is varied between 10 and 60, fixing fanout and failure rates—for instance, the graph shows that with 20 processes the reliability is about

10^{-13}. The graph almost fits a straight line with slope $= -0.45$, thus the reliability of *ProbabilisticSend* increases almost tenfold with every two processes added to the system.

Message Cost and Fanout

Although not immediately clear from the protocol, the message cost of the *ProbabilisticSend* protocol is roughly a constant multiple of the number of processes in the system. In the worst case, all processes can gossip to all other processes, causing $O(n^2)$ messages per *ProbabilisticSend*. r will be set to cause some expected *fanout* of messages, so that on average a process should gossip to about *fanout* other processes, where *fanout* is some constant, in practice at most 10 (unless otherwise stated, *fanout* $= 7$ in the graphs presented in Fig. 21.5). Figure 21.5(c) shows a graph of reliability versus *fanout* when the number of processes and other parameters held is constant—for instance, the graph shows that with a fanout of 7.0, *ProbabilisticSend*'s reliability is about 10^{-13}. In general, the graph shows that the fanout can be increased to increase reliability, but eventually there are diminishing returns for the increased message cost.

On the other hand, *fanout* (and hence cost) can be decreased as the system grows, keeping the reliability at a fixed level. In Fig. 21.5(d), reliability of at least "twelve nines" (i.e., the probability of a *failed ProbabilisticSend* is less than or equal to 10^{-12}) is maintained, while the number of processes is increased. The graph shows that with 20 processes a *fanout* of 6.63 achieves "twelve nines" reliability, while with 50 processes a *fanout* of 4.32 is sufficient.

21.1.8 Experimental Results

For reasons of brevity we omit detailed experimental data from the evaluation of *ProbabilisticSend* reported in Birman et al. (1999). To summarize quickly, this work showed that with appropriate parameter settings *ProbabilisticSend* was able to achieve a message throughput similar to that of the Horus or Ensemble *OrderedSend* protocol *in cases where the sender of the message does not hold the group's ordering token*. However, *ProbabilisticSend* is much slower than *OrderedSend* in small configurations where the application exploits *OrderedSend* in a near-optimal manner. Thus in situations where *OrderedSend* can achieve thousands or tens of thousands of multicasts per second to a group of perhaps 8 to 10 members, *ProbabilisticSend* rates of one tenth those figures are probably the best that can be expected (both kinds of protocol can benefit from message packing, so we will set the associated "speedup" to the side here).

The experimental work showed that *ProbabilisticSend* delivery latency is comparable to that of the Horus *OrderedSend* protocol; both need to repair lost messages, and the bottom line is that both do so with comparable mechanisms. Finally, as noted earlier, under large-scale networking conditions where *OrderedSend* performance collapses, *ProbabilisticSend* performance remains quite stable.

These findings suggest that production-quality systems may need to implement a protocol like *ProbabilisticSend* side by side with a more traditional virtual synchrony stack, switching from the traditional stack to the bimodal one when the system size exceeds about 32 members, a point at which *OrderedSend* starts to exhibit pronounced instability. Such an approach should give almost unlimited scalability, stability under all sorts of stresses, and bounded overhead even when the network is exhibiting extreme problems. As mentioned before, Cornell is employing *ProbabilisticSend* in a new publish-subscribe platform called QuickSilver. The approach just outlined is likely to be the one implemented in the system. The need for Gupta's probabilistic virtual synchrony mechanisms is still being evaluated; it is unclear at the time of this writing that virtual synchrony is really needed on a very large scale, although total ordering and the ability to find missing messages in a logging server does appear to be quite useful.

21.2 Astrolabe

We conclude this chapter with a brief look at a system called Astrolabe (van Renesse et al. 2003), a system that uses P2P protocols to build a scalable system monitoring, management, control and data-mining framework that has strong probabilistic convergence guarantees. Astrolabe builds a form of virtual database—one that does not really exist on a physical server, and yet can be accessed by an application in a manner not unlike a normal database on a real server. This database is structured hierarchically and can be queried using SQL. Astrolabe automatically populates the database with data drawn from the nodes in a distributed system and will automatically update the database as conditions change. The peer-to-peer protocols used by the system scale extremely well and are stable under conditions that would cripple systems built in other ways. Astrolabe is intended for use in monitoring, managing or controlling a system that could have hundreds, thousands or even millions of nodes. Moreover, Astrolabe is well matched to the needs of "data mining" applications, in which a large system is searched for desired data or for the resources best matched to some requirement.

We will focus on a data mining scenario later in this section as a way to illustrate the power of the system. The basic idea involves configuring Astrolabe to continuously track information of interest to the data miner (perhaps, the team responsible for managing a data center or a set of them, or even the client systems connected to a Web Services platform). The collection of data will occur on the end-nodes, and might even involve asking those nodes to check for something—files matching a search criteria, for example. However, this work is spread over vast numbers of machines, and hence is extremely decentralized and parallel. Astrolabe then combines the information discovered out at the "edges" by continuously computing summaries using on-the-fly *aggregation*. Aggregation is similar to performing a query on a large database, and yields a smaller result that the user can see (or monitor, because the aggregate will be updated regularly as changes occur in the underlying data). The entire protocol has a very light, near-constant, communication and computational overhead on the nodes in the system.

For example, suppose that the manager of a large network notices that performance for a major application has begun to degrade, but has no idea why. Traditionally, she would have little recourse except to run whatever monitoring tools are available in the application. With Astrolabe, as we will see, she can dynamically change the way the system is instrumented and the way the findings are reported, thus forming a theory, evaluating it (the system can be reconfigured in a few tens of seconds, even on a massive scale), and then perhaps setting that idea to the side and pursuing some other angle. Moreover, rather than being limited to whatever instrumentation was provided by the vendor, she can pursue all sorts of possibilities, even including contents of configuration files, page fault rates, or other kinds of indirect indicator.

To take another example, consider an intelligence analyst working for a government who becomes suspicious that a group of terrorists may be trying to infiltrate chemical or fertilizer supply depots somewhere in Iraq. If monitoring systems have been put in place, he can rapidly configure Astrolabe to look for unusual patterns of activity, then zero in to try and find out who is responsible and precisely what they are up to. Astrolabe offers the analyst a way to search data residing on thousands of computer without downloading all of that data (potentially, terabytes) to a central location. Moreover, the massive parallelism of the network of machines permits him to perform queries that, on any single machine, might take hours to complete. By doing the work out at the edges, the same tasks are finished in seconds.

The need for this type of data mining seems to be increasing rapidly. Corporations and other enterprises cannot avoid having large numbers of data centers scattered throughout their organizations: such an approach puts computing where it is needed and administers data close to where it was gathered. Making a centralized copy for purposes of data mining can be very inefficient, and may simply create an overloaded central resource.

Moreover, as the Web Services architecture rolls out, we are starting to see companies that hope to use Web Services to open up their data centers for use in a new kind of 4-tier architecture. Suppose that Amazon.com were to hand out small "serverlets" to assist application developers in embedding point-and-click purchase functionality into their applications. For example, a hospital computing system developer could use these serverlets to integrate the medical system with Amazon's purchasing and delivery mechanisms, so that when the hospital orders supplies, Amazon fills the order. It is not hard to see why both Amazon.com and the developer might view this as an advantageous arrangement: the developer does not need to duplicate Amazon's computing systems (or their network of warehouses and supplier relationships), and Amazon itself gains increased sales volumes. The hospital benefits too, since they are using a widely used supply intermediary that may be able to negotiate volume discounts and other special deals.

But now if a problem occurs—say that hospitals in Pennsylvania suddenly are unable to connect to Amazon's data center in Chicago, we will need ways to diagnose the problem, to get those serverlets to "fail over" to a different center (maybe New York) in a coordinated way, and to orchestrate the repair. The more one studies such a scenario the more it looks like a decentralized data mining problem. Client systems (serverlets) want to share their current status, diagnose and react in a consistent way, etc. Administrators want to pin down the origin of the problem; perhaps, a problem in the Internet, or in the firewall configuration at the hospital, or at the Amazon data center.

Underlying Astrolabe's powerful data mining and monitoring mechanisms is a principle called *peer-to-peer aggregation*. Aggregation is analogous to computing a dependent cell in a spreadsheet. When the underlying information changes, Astrolabe will automatically and rapidly recompute the associated aggregates and report the changes to applications that have registered their interest. What makes this an aggregation problem is that the underlying data was gathered from many machines in a large networked setting. Astrolabe's protocols ensure that even in huge networks, any change is soon visible everywhere. For example, Astrolabe aggregation can be used to identify sets of sensors which have made related observations—biothreat sensors reading low levels of toxins, coastal traffic sensors reporting vessels matching an Interpol profile of potential concern, and so forth. As a user's needs evolve, Astrolabe can be reconfigured on the fly by changing the set of aggregation queries. Astrolabe uses peer-to-peer protocols to implement aggregation, and this is the "secret" of its power, flexibility and robustness.

21.2.1 How It Works

Astrolabe is best understood as a relational database built through a peer-to-peer protocol running between the applications or computers on which Astrolabe is installed. Like any relational database, the fundamental building block employed by Astrolabe is a tuple (a row of data items) into which values can be stored. For simplicity in this paper, we will focus on the case where each tuple contains information associated with some computer. The technology is quite general, however, and can be configured with a tuple per application, or even with a tuple for each instance of some type of file or database.

Modern computing platforms, such as Microsoft's .NET and J2EE, provide a wealth of instrumentation options. Astrolabe is designed to tap into these. Basically, there are two forms of data available, although both are presented to the user through a single API.

One option is to extract information from the management information base (MIB) of a computer. A MIB is a standardized database maintained by the computer itself, containing such information as load, currently active processes, machine name and IP address, etc. The MIB is an extremely powerful and general source of information, and for a user with appropriate permissions, gives access to almost anything the operating system "knows." On systems such as Linux and Microsoft .NET, the MIB is provided by a server object that can be accessed using an RPC protocol, and Astrolabe taps into this interface to extract data of the type desired by the user, then to monitor that data for changes at a frequency the user controls.

The second major source of data for Astrolabe consists of information that the system extracts directly from a file, database, spreadsheet, or application program. Astrolabe is able to perform this operation by exploiting a recent set of standards

Fig. 21.6   Three Astrolabe domains

Name	Load	Weblogic?	SMTP?	Version

Name	Load	Weblogic?	SMTP?	Version

Name	Load	Weblogic?	SMTP?	Version
swift	2.0	0	1	6.2
falcon	1.5	1	0	4.1
cardinal	4.5	1	0	6.0

(ODBC, JDBC) whereby an application with appropriate permissions can treat the objects on a computer much like databases. For example, Astrolabe could be asked to count the number of image files containing possible matches with a picture of a wanted criminal, or even to report the name of the file having the best match (the image itself would be too large to export into Astrolabe, which limits the data extracted to a few k-bytes per computer). The match with databases or spreadsheets is especially good; in such cases, Astrolabe can perform a "query" on the underlying object and report the result through its own tuple data structure (assuming, that is, that the result can be represented as a single tuple).

Like most modern systems, Astrolabe is flexible about data types, supporting the usual basic types but also allowing the application to supply arbitrary information encoded with XML. The only requirement is that the total size of the tuple be no more than a few k-bytes; much larger objects can be identified by some form of URL or other reference but the data would not reside directly in Astrolabe itself.

The specific data to be pulled into Astrolabe is specified in a *configuration certificate*. Should the needs of the user change, the configuration certificate can be modified and, within a few seconds, Astrolabe will reconfigure itself accordingly. This action is, however, restricted by a security policy.

Astrolabe groups small sets of tuples into relational tables. Each such table consists of perhaps 30 to 60 tuples containing data from sources physically close to one-another in the network; we call this a "zone." This grouping (a database administrator would recognize it as a form of schema) can often be created automatically, using latency and network addresses to identify nearby machines. However, the system administrator can also specify a desired layout explicitly.

Where firewalls are present, Astrolabe employs a tunneling method to send messages to machines residing behind the firewall and hence not directly addressable. This approach also allows Astrolabe to overcome most restrictions associated with network address translation (NAT) filters.

The data collected by Astrolabe evolves as the underlying information sources report updates, hence the system constructs a continuously changing database using information that actually resides on the participating computers. Figure 21.6 illustrates this: we see a collection of small database relations, each tuple corresponding to one machine, and each relation collecting tuples associated with some set of nearby machines. In this figure, the data stored within the tuple includes the name of the machine, its current load, an indication of whether or not various servers are running on it, and the "version" for some application. Keep in mind that this selection of data is completely determined by the configuration certificate. In principle,

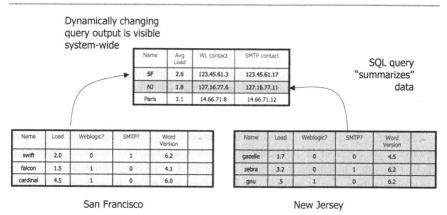

Fig. 21.7 Hierarchy formed when data-mining with an aggregation query fuses data from many sources

any data available on the machine or in any application running on the machine can be exported. In particular, spreadsheets and databases can easily be configured to export data to Astrolabe.

An application using Astrolabe can access this local data (that is, data associated with machines in its own zone) just as it might access any other table, database or spreadsheet. As updates are reported through Astrolabe, the application receives a form of event notifying it that the table should be rescanned. For example, Astrolabe data can be dragged into a local database, spreadsheet, or even onto a web page. As the data changes, the application will receive refresh events.

Astrolabe is intended for use in very large networks, hence this form of direct access to local data cannot be used for the full dataset: while the system does capture data throughout the network, the amount of information would be unwieldy and the frequency of updates excessive. Accordingly, although Astrolabe does provide an interface with which a remote zone's data can be accessed, the normal way of monitoring remote data is through aggregation queries.

As the name suggests, an aggregation query is just an SQL query that operates on these leaf relations, extracting a single summary tuple from each which reflects the globally significant information within the zone. Sets of summary tuples are concatenated by Astrolabe to form summary relations (again, the size is typically 30 to 60 tuples each), and if the size of the system is large enough so that there will be several summary relations, this process is repeated at the next level up, and so forth. Astrolabe is thus a hierarchical relational database. Each of the summaries is updated, in real-time, as the leaf data from which it was formed changes. Even in networks with thousands or millions of computers, updates are visible system-wide within a few tens of seconds (Fig. 21.7).

A computer using Astrolabe will, in general, have a local copy of the data for its own zone and for aggregation (summary) data for zones above it on the path to the root of this hierarchy. As just explained, the system maintains the abstraction of a hierarchical relational database. Notice that in a physical sense, this hierarchy is an illusion, constructed using a peer-to-peer protocol of our own design, somewhat like a jig-saw puzzle in which each computer has copies of some of the pieces. The protocols permit the system to assemble the puzzle as a whole when needed. Thus, while the user thinks of Astrolabe as a somewhat constrained but rather general database residing on a conventional server, accessed using conventional programmer APIs and development tools, and updated as information changes, in reality there is no server. The user abstraction is created on the fly.

The peer-to-peer protocol used for this purpose is, to first approximation, easily described. We consider first the case of a single zone. Each Astrolabe system keeps track of the other machines in its zone, and of a subset of *contact* machines in other zones. This subset is selected in a pseudo-random manner from the full membership of the system (a peer-to-peer gossip protocol is used to track approximate membership). At some fixed frequency, typically every 2 to 5 seconds, each participating machine sends a concise state description to a randomly selected destination within this set of neighbors and remote contacts. The state description is very compact and consists of identification of objects available on the system and their timestamps. We call such a message a *gossip* event, because it behaves much like the gossip exchanges described in connection with the *ProbabilisticSend* protocol. Unless an object is very small, the gossip event contains version information, not actual data.

Upon receiving such a gossip message, an Astrolabe system is in a position to identify information which may be stale at the sender's machine (because timestamps are out of date) or that may be more current at the sender than on its own system. We say *may* because time elapses while messages traverse the network, hence no machine actually has current information about any other. Our protocols are purely asynchronous: when sending a message, the sender does not pause to wait for it to be received and, indeed, the protocol makes no effort to ensure that gossip gets to its destinations.

Through exchanges of gossip messages and data, information should propagate within a network over an exponentially increasing number of randomly selected paths among the participants. That is, if a machine updates its own row, after one round of gossip, the update will probably be found at two machines. After two rounds, the update will probably be at four machines, etc. In general, updates propagate in log of the system size—seconds or tens of seconds in our implementation. In practice, we configure Astrolabe to gossip rapidly within each zone (to take advantage of the presumably low latency) and less frequently between zones (to avoid overloading bottlenecks such as firewalls or shared network links). The effect of these steps is to ensure that the communication load on each machine using Astrolabe and also each communication link involved is bounded and independent of network size.

We have said that Astrolabe gossips about *objects*. In our work, a tuple is an object, but because of the hierarchy used by Astrolabe, a tuple would only be of interest to a receiver in the same region as the sender. In general, Astrolabe gossips about information of *shared interest* to the sender and receiver. This could include tuples in the regional database, but also membership data, and aggregation results for aggregation zones which are common ancestors to the sender and receiver.

So far we have discussed the behavior of Astrolabe within a single zone. To compute the contents of internal zones containing aggregation results, each zone "elects" (using an aggregation query) a small number of representatives to run the Astrolabe gossip protocol on its behalf in the next higher-level zone within the zone hierarchy. These spawn an additional instance of the gossip protocol and, before gossiping, recomputed the zone's contribution to the aggregate. Thus, the average machine within a zone will gossip only with other machines in the same zone, not with representatives of remote zones. Thus, a computer may run gossip on behalf of 1, 2, or as many as $\log_{\text{zone-size}}(N)$ simultaneous gossip protocols. The zone size in Astrolabe is large (often 64 or 100) hence this will be a small number, rarely more than 3 or 4.

After a round of gossip or an update to its own tuple, Astrolabe informs any local readers of the Astrolabe database that its value has changed, and the associated application rereads the object and refreshes its state accordingly. For example, if an Astrolabe aggregation output is pulled from Astrolabe into a web page, that web server would refresh that page each time it changes. The change would be expected to reach the server within a delay logarithmic in the size of the network, and proportional to the gossip rate. Using a 2-second gossip rate, an update would thus reach all members in a system of 10,000 computers in roughly 25 seconds. Of course, the gossip rate can be tuned to make the system run faster, or slower, depending on the importance of rapid responses and the amount of bandwidth available for our protocols.

Additional details of how Astrolabe is implemented and how it performs can be found in van Renesse et al. (2003).

21.2.2 Peer-to-Peer Data Fusion and Data Mining

Astrolabe is a powerful, flexible technology for data fusion and data mining. The system can be understood as performing data fusion in a continuous manner, since the basic Astrolabe data structure *fuses* designated data into a virtual database for use by the application. The SQL aggregation mechanism permits additional data fusion, and also permits the user to perform a wide variety of data mining actions.

The power of these mechanisms is, however, limited by the physical layout of the Astrolabe database and by our need, as builders of the system, to provide a solution which is secure and scalable. The focus of this section is not so much on the basic ideas but on these limitations and their implications for the Astrolabe user.

Consistency

Although Astrolabe is best understood as a form of hierarchical database, the system does not support the transactional consistency model employed by databases. Astrolabe is accessible by read-only operations on the local zone and aggregation zones on the path to the root. Update operations can only be performed by a machine on the data stored in its own tuple. Moreover, the ACID properties do not apply; for example, two different observers will often see updates in different orders and may not even see the identical updates.

If Astrolabe is imagined as a kind of replicated database, a further distinction arises. In a replicated database each update will be reflected at each replica. Astrolabe offers a weaker guarantee: if a participating computer updates its tuple and then leaves the tuple unchanged for a sufficiently long period of time, there is a very high probability that the update will become visible to all non-faulty computers. Indeed, this probability converges to 1.0 in the absence of network partitioning failures. Astrolabe gains a great deal by accepting this weaker probabilistic property: the system is able to scale with constant loads on computers and links, and is not forced to stop and wait if some machine fails to receive an update. In contrast, there is a well-known impossibility result that implies that a database system using the serializability model may need to pause and wait for updates to reach participating nodes, and indeed that a single failure could prevent a replicated database from making progress. Jointly, these results limit the performance and availability of a replicated database. Astrolabe, then, offers a weaker consistency property but gains availability and very stable, predictable performance by so doing.

Aggregation raises a different kind of consistency issue. Suppose that an aggregation query reports some property of a zone, such as the least loaded machine, the average humidity in a region, etc. Recall that aggregates are recomputed each time the Astrolabe gossip protocol runs. One could imagine a situation in which machine A and machine B concurrently update their own states; perhaps, their loads change. Now suppose that an aggregation query computes the average load. A and B will both compute new averages, but the values are in some sense unordered in time: A's value presumably reflects a stale version of B's load, and vice versa. Not only does this imply that the average computed might not be the one expected, it also points to a risk: Astrolabe (as described so far) might report aggregates that bounce back and forth in time, first reflecting A's update (but lacking B's more current data), then changing to reflect B's update but "forgetting" A's change. The fundamental problem is that even if B has an aggregation result with a recent timestamp, the aggregate could have been computed from data which was, in part, more stale than was the data used to compute the value it replaces.

To avoid this phenomenon, Astrolabe tracks minimum and maximum timestamp information for the inputs to each aggregation function. A new aggregate value replaces an older one only if the minimum timestamp for any input to that new result is at least as large as the maximum timestamp for the one it replaces. It can be seen that this will slow the propagation of updates but will also ensure that aggregates advance monotonically in time. Yet this stronger consistency property also brings a curious side-effect: if two different Astrolabe users write down the series of aggregate results reported to them, those sequences of values could advance very differently; perhaps, A sees its own update reflected first, then later sees both its own and B's; B might see its update first, then later both, and some third site, C, could see the system jump to a state in which both updates are reflected. Time moves forward, but different users see events in different order and may not even see the identical events! This tradeoff seems to be fundamental to our style of distributed data fusion.

Security Model and Mechanisms

A related set of issues surround the security of the Astrolabe technology. We noted earlier that many peer-to-peer systems suffer from insecurity and are easily incapacitated or attacked by malfunctioning or malicious users. Astrolabe is intended to run on very large numbers of machines, hence the system itself could represent a large-scale security exposure.

To mitigate such concerns, we have taken several steps. First, Astrolabe reads but does not write data on the machines using it. Thus, while Astrolabe can pull a great variety of data into its hierarchy, the system does not take the converse action of reaching back onto the participating machines and changing values within them, except to the extent that applications explicitly read data from Astrolabe.

The issue thus becomes one of trustworthiness: can the data stored in Astrolabe be trusted? In what follows, we assume that Astrolabe is correctly implemented, but that the computers on which it runs could fail, and software bugs (hopefully, rare) could corrupt individual Astrolabe instances. To overcome such problems, Astrolabe includes a public-key infrastructure (PKI) which is built into the code. We employ digital signatures to authenticate data. Although machine B may learn of machine A's updates through a third party, unless A's tuple is correctly signed by A's private-key, B will reject it. Astrolabe also limits the introduction of configuration certificates and aggregation queries by requiring keys for the parent zones within which these will have effect; by controlling access to those keys, it is possible to prevent unauthorized users from introducing expensive computations or configuring Astrolabe to pull in data from participating hosts without appropriate permissions. Moreover, the ODBC and JDBC interfaces by means of which Astrolabe interfaces itself to other components offer additional security policy options.

A limitation on the Astrolabe security mechanism is evident when one considers the way that aggregates are computed. As noted earlier, each zone elects some representatives to run the gossip protocol for the next higher level zone, and this continues up to the layer below the root. Those representatives compute the zone's aggregate function and then gossip about this value, and other cached values from other sibling zones, and in this manner the value of an aggregate zone is assembled.

Now suppose that some node aggregates incorrectly, or even maliciously. For example, it could proclaim itself to have the lowest load in the region and thereby elect itself as the regional aggregation contact, and then incorrectly claim that the region is not reporting and denial of service problems, when in fact many machines are complaining about overloads. The "false" aggregation information might be trusted by other nodes and this can cause problems system-wide. At the time of this writing, work was underway on a type of attestation scheme similar to the one we discussed in conjunction with Byzantine Agreement. The idea (being developed by Kevin Walsh and others) is to require that aggregations be countersigned by multiple nodes; with k counter-signatures, up to k failures can be tolerated.

In fact this idea is harder to put into practice than to describe. For example, Astrolabe's consistency model is not strong enough to ensure that a node selected to countersign a value can actually do so. To address this, Walsh was forced to add a history mechanism to Astrolabe, whereby each participant would accumulate a history of values for each row. An aggregate can then be pinned down by specifying the row versions used to compute it.

Query Limitations

A final set of limitations arises from the lack of a join feature in the aggregation query mechanism. As seen above, Astrolabe performs data mining by computing summaries of the data in each zone, then gluing these together to create higher level zones on which further summaries can be computed. The approach lacks a way to compute results for queries that require cross-zone joins.

For example, suppose that Astrolabe were used as the basis for a sensor network in a military targeting setting. One might want to express a data fusion query along the following lines: "for each incoming threat, report the weapons system best positioned to respond to that threat." The natural way to express this as a query in a standard database would involve a join. In Astrolabe, one would need to express this as two aggregation queries, one to compute a summary of threats and the other, using output from the first as an input, tracking down the response options. In general, this points to a methodology for dealing with joins by "compiling" them into multiple current aggregation queries. However, at present, we have not developed this insight into a general mechanism; users who wish to perform joins would need to break them up in this manner, by hand. Moreover, it can be seen that while this approach allows a class of join queries to compile into Astrolabe's aggregation mechanism, not all joins can be so treated: the method only works if the size of the dataset needed from the first step of the join, and indeed the size of the final output, will be sufficiently small.

Configuring Astrolabe so that one query will use the output of another as part of its input raises a further question: given that these queries are typically introduced into the system while it is running, how does the user know when the result is "finished"? We have a simple answer to this problem, based on a scheme of counting the number of sub-zones reflected in an aggregation result. The idea is that as a new aggregate value is computed, a period passes during which only some of the leaf zones have reported values. At this stage the parent aggregation zone is not yet fully populated with data. However, by comparing a count of the number of reporting child zones with a separately maintained count of the total number of children, applications can be shielded from seeing the results of an aggregation computation until the output is stable. By generalizing this approach, we are also able to handle failures or the introduction of new machines; in both cases, the user is able to identify and disregard outputs representing transitional states. The rapid propagation time for updates ensures that such transitional conditions last for no more than a few seconds.

21.3   Other Applications of Peer-to-Peer Protocols

This chapter has limited itself to scraping the surface of a thriving area. Recent work suggests that peer-to-peer protocols may also be useful in building scalable publish-subscribe systems, improving the reliability of very large "chat" systems, in managing caches for large Web sites and Web Service applications, and in increasing the robustness of mobile, wireless computing platforms, which often suffer from brief disconnections and other disruptive outages. One very exciting piece of work, by Ion Stoica at Berkeley, proposes to replace the entire Internet with an architecture (called the Internet Indirection Infrastructure, or I3) in which a DHT is used to deliver packets, substituting this for the traditional Internet routing mechanism. Stoica shows that his scheme is able to accommodate such functions as multicast and anycast efficiently, can implement various kinds of packet transformation and pipeline processing, and is even able to provide mobile packet routing under conditions where the standard Internet incurs high overhead.

The author's recent work in this area included a collaborative effort to build an efficient *distributed slicing* protocol (called Sliver, this protocol organizes the data in a large P2P system into k sets, or slices, so that after $O(\log(N))$ delay each node learns the slice to which it belongs. Thus for $k = 2$ we divide the nodes into two sets: those with big values and those with small ones, of roughly the same size; for $k = 4$ we generate quartiles, $k = 10$ yields deciles, etc. This notion of slicing was pioneered by Kermarrec, and in fact the Sliver protocol uses elements of protocols she developed previously, but that had cases in which convergence might be slow. Sliver is quite simple, and has been shown to outperform even highly efficient parallel sorting algorithms, which also have complexity $O(N)$: parallel sort has large constants in front of the N that $O(N)$ brushes to the side; for Sliver, the relevant constant is very small.

A second collaboration between the author's group and Kermarrec's group resulted in a small operating system for supporting gossip and P2P applications, called Gossip Objects or GO. Here, the key idea is that if an operating system sends the actual gossip messages on behalf of a set of objects that are hosted on it and all use gossip communication patterns, there might be opportunities to combine multiple gossip messages into a single larger one that can carry data on behalf of many applications. Ymir Vigfusson showed that this formulation leads to a very practical optimization challenge, which he solves using a greedy algorithm that performs well and even manages to route gossip traffic opportunistically along indirect paths. For example, a node gossiping from p to q might carry a gossip message actually intended for r in the hope that q will get a chance to pass it along to r soon. Experiments with GO confirm that there can be substantial opportunity for benefit with this approach in applications where there are multiple, heavily overlapping, gossip objects. In his Ph.D. thesis, Vigfusson shows that if overlap arises at all, that pattern of extensive overlap should be common.

While it does seem safe to say that peer-to-peer computing is solidly established as an important technology area, it is also important to realize that like most technologies in this third part of the book, peer-to-peer applications remain a somewhat marginalized technology. Only Napster, Gnutella and Kazaa have achieved much success, and of course that was in support of what turns out to have been an illegal application. Whether peer-to-peer solutions ever gain a "first class" role in modern operating systems platforms remains to be determined.

21.4   Related Reading

Peer-to-peer computing is a new and very active area. By far the best way to get the sense of the scope of activities and to learn about some of the very best work is to consult the proceedings of the Workshop on Future Directions in Distributed Computing (see Schiper et al. 2003), the International Workshop on Peer-to-Peer Computing, which was held at MIT in 2002 and at Berkeley in 2003. Other major outlets for peer-to-peer research include the SIGCOM conference, INFOCOM, and OSDI. Some notable recent papers include (see Andersen et al. 2001a, 2001b; Balakrishnan et al. 2003; Bhagwan et al. 2003; Castro et al. 2003a; Gribble et al. 2001; Iyer et al. 2002; Kermarrec et al. 2001; Kubiatowicz et al. 2000a, 2000b; Kubiatowicz 2003; Muthitacharoen et al. 2002; Weatherspoon and Kubiatowicz 2002; Zhao et al. 2002a, 2002b).

One important problem in P2P systems is that poor choice of peers can warp the otherwise clean convergence behavior of these protocols in ways that cause sharp degradation in performance, loss of connectivity, or similar issues. Moreover, because of network address translation and firewalls, situations can arise in which process p learns of some peer q and yet is unable to communicate directly with q. Even worse, churn can contaminate membership lists with stale entries corresponding to dead processes. As a result, one can build a high-quality P2P routing overlay only to discover that it malfunctions badly by becoming disconnected, has connectivity to all members but with inadequate bandwidth for some, etc. Quite a bit of theoretical work has been done on this topic; one sees that the real need is for a so-called expander graph (see Hoory et al. 2006) (one in which, with probability 1, all members have paths to all other members) and that the optimal expander graph is what we call a *Small Worlds Graph* (see Kleinberg 2000b), exhibiting a specific rather simple connectivity pattern. and logarithmic diameter. Peer selection algorithms and the effects of bias has been explored in Kermarrec et al. (2009) and Guerraoui (1995). Qi Huang has developed a number of tools for automatically sensing the state of a graph such as this (see Huang et al. 2010), and Vivien Quema has shown how one can work around obstacles using indirection (see Kermarrec et al. 2009).

On gossip protocols (see Alon et al. 1987; Demers et al. 1987; Golding 1991; Golding and Taylor 1992). For Sliver, see Gramoli et al. (2009). For Gossip Objects (GO), see Vigfusson et al. (2009). For Vigfusson's thesis, see Vigfusson (2009).

On the underlying theory (see Bailey 1975).

Hayden's work (see Birman 1999), draws on Chandra and Toueg (1990) and Cristian et al. (1985).

Appendix A: Virtually Synchronous Methodology for Building Dynamic Reliable Services

22

Ken Birman, Dahlia Malkhi, and Robbert Van Renesse

The general style of this text has been, up to now, fairly informal by the standards of the distributed computing community, which has a substantial and very active theoretical arm (the author of this text, in contrast, is more typical of the engineering side of the community). Yet for readers or instructors who cross over by teaching a distributed engineering course from time to time while doing their own research primarily on theoretical topics, this style can be frustrating because of its imprecision.

The motivation for creating a more formal model of dynamic membership in a fault-prone distributed setting is as follows. In designing and building distributed systems, it is common engineering practice to separate steady-state ("normal") operation from abnormal events such as recovery from failure. This way the normal case can be optimized extensively while recovery can be amortized. However, integrating the recovery procedure with the steady-state protocol is often far from obvious, and can present subtle difficulties. This issue comes to the forefront in modern data centers, where applications are often implemented as elastic sets of replicas that must reconfigure while continuing to provide service, and where it may be necessary to install new versions of active services as bugs are fixed or new functionality is introduced. This appendix explores the question in the context of a dynamic reconfiguration model of our own design that unifies two widely popular prior approaches to the problem: *virtual synchrony*, a model and associated protocols for reliable group communication, and *state machine replication* (Lamport 1978a, 1978b; Schneider 1990) (in particular, Paxos (Lamport 1998)), a model and protocol for replicating some form of deterministic functionality specified as an event-driven state machine.

K. Birman · R. Van Renesse
Cornell University, Ithaca, USA

D. Malkhi
Microsoft Research Silicon Valley, Mountain View, USA

K.P. Birman, *Guide to Reliable Distributed Systems*, Texts in Computer Science,
DOI 10.1007/978-1-4471-2416-0_22, © Springer-Verlag London Limited 2012

22.1   Introduction

Our work deals with a style of distributed services that uses elastic sets of replicas to achieve availability, scalability, and long term durability. These replica sets can vary widely over time: expanding as the service confronts load surges or replaces failed server instances, and contracting as load drops or members crash. Thus, the contemporary distributed systems developer, or service developer, is unavoidably faced with issues of dynamic service replication.

Service replication and reconfiguration confront the developer with a series of tough choices. One can evade these choices by abandoning consistency, but there are many kinds of service for which consistency guarantees are important and must not be violated simply because the service replica set is elastic. For services of this type, reconfiguration remains a murky black art, error prone and associated with complex, subtle bugs. Moreover, among the correct, rigorously analyzed solutions there are all sorts of hidden tradeoffs, representing deliberate compromises between performance and complexity during steady-state operation of the service (when reconfiguration is not happening) and the complexity of the reconfiguration event itself, which may also entail some period of service unavailability.

Our treatment of this problem is tutorial in style, but aimed at a sophisticated audience. We suspect that any developer confronting this topic will have had a considerable amount of experience with distributed systems. Accordingly, we target a reader who knows how one creates distributed services, has some familiarity with the classical papers on asynchronous consensus and communication protocols and impossibility results such as the FLP theorem, and who may even have worked with the virtual synchrony (Birman and Joseph 1987a) or the state machine replication methodologies (Lamport 1978a, 1998; Schneider 1990). Our premise is that even knowledgeable readers be surprised to learn of some of the pitfalls, anomalies and tradeoffs that the prevailing methodologies tacitly accept. Our work unifies what had previously been different models using a single overarching methodology and formalism which we name Dynamic Service Replication (DSR).

Our goal will be to design services that can be reconfigured without disrupting correctness, up to some maximum tolerable rate of service membership changes, beyond which it becomes unavailable. We assume that reconfiguration is triggered by a *reconfiguration command,* issued by the system management layer, and either removing some members from a service, or adding some, or perhaps doing both at once. Reconfiguration could also change application parameters, or even be used to upgrade to a new version of an application or a protocol while keeping the service as available as possible.

Building a reliable service using the DSR approach entails three fundamental steps.

Safety   The first is to provide a service-oriented *safety* definition. A good specification must abstract away from implementation details, and describe the service using the methods clients can access, and expressing properties in terms of guarantees that those methods will offer. Two example services are interwoven throughout the body of this chapter. The first example is a Reliable Multicast service, for which we give a service-oriented description. Our definition exposes a **Get**() API call that provide clients with a full, consistent history of messages that clients **Add**(). This definition lets us focus on the matter of preserving service state consistently while transitioning through configuration changes. Conversely, it is stripped of internal details such as clients joining and departing the service, delivery duplication, etc.; those can be added as various filters and add-ons, as discussed below. We use the well known State Machine Replication (SMR) problem (Lamport 1978a, 1978b; Schneider 1990) as our second primary example. For completeness, in Sect. 22.8 we also briefly flesh out an Atomic Read/Write Storage service.

Liveness The second ingredient of our treatment is an appropriate failure model. In the distributed computing arena, reliability is often expressed as the requirement to tolerate a threshold t failures out of an initial system of n processes. This classical fault model ignores the ability of a dynamic system to out-live such an initial setting via administrative decrees, e.g., to deploy new processes, or to remove faulty ones from consideration. For example, an initial system configuration of four processes, $\{A, B, C, D\}$, may tolerate a single failure. However, through an administrative decree to reconfigure, say removing A after a failure, the remaining set $\{B, C, D\}$ can tolerate an additional single failure. But as this example suggests, although we have increased the overall fault tolerance through dynamism, we cannot simply say that we have a system of four processes, any two of which may crash at any time. We need a more subtle condition that gives the system "sufficient time" to reconfigure. In our example, two crashes can be tolerated over the total period the system is running, but during the early part, before the system had been reconfigured, only one of $\{A, B, C, D\}$ may fail. This notion of a dynamically defined majority appeared implicitly in various prior works, including Ricciardi and Birman (1991), Ricciardi (1993), Yeger-Lotem et al. (1997), Lamport (1998), Lynch and Shvartsman (2002), Martin and Alvisi (2004), but the conditions always involved solution-specific details. Here, we adopt the principles of the DynaStore liveness model (Aguilera et al. 2009a), which gives an opaque **Reconfig**() handle for (administrative) clients. We then enhance this model to suit our more general framework.

Reconfiguration Recipe The third component is an algorithmic foundation for our solution. Briefly, a DSR epoch-by-epoch reconfiguration starts with a consensus decision *by the current configuration* (say, C_1) on a new configuration (C_2). The reconfiguration procedure proceeds with a transfer of control from C_1 to C_2, which entails (a) a decision to suspend C_1; (b) a snapshot of completed and potentially completed operations in C_1; (c) a state transfer of the snapshot to C_2. The reconfiguration completes with a decision to enable C_2 for processing new operations, with the initial state of C_2 determined by step b.

In our methodology, the developer deals with one epoch at a time. An epoch terminates with a configuration change decision. The next configuration is uniquely determined in the current epoch, and transition to it is irreversible. When an epoch ends, a new epoch starts a new incarnation of the same algorithm (albeit with a non-empty initial service state), whose participants and messages do not mix with the current epoch. If an epoch starts in a configuration that already includes some failed nodes, it might make progress in that state, or it might initiate a further round of reconfiguration to remove those nodes; indeed, it can initiate reconfiguration as its first action. The new configuration operates completely separately from the current one; the messages in it are not confused with messages in the current configuration; and it can consist of an entirely new set of machine. Any number of reconfigurations can be chained in this manner.

Solutions   While the general framework—decide, suspend, state transfer, resume —may appear obvious, there are numerous design choices and potential pitfalls when realizing any specific service. Underlying any choice of reconfiguration solution are inherent tradeoffs. One wants to maximize availability and performance, but without violating safety, and it is not easy to accomplish all of these simultaneously. This does not mean that protocols need to be overly cumbersome. To the contrary, in six figures, Figs. 22.3–22.9, we give succinct pseudo-code solutions for six service variants, each frame containing a entire solution including precise safety and liveness definitions.

We'll see that we can trade steady-state simplicity with continuous availability: A *fault-recovery* approach utilizes servers in steady-state in an uncomplicated manner, disregarding the possibility of failure. It can be highly optimized, but requires reconfiguration to unblock the service in case of a failure. Figure 22.3 illustrates this methodology within the context of Reliable Multicast and Fig. 22.7 does so for SMR. The alternative is a *fault-masking* methodology, which crafts steady-state protocols with built-in redundancy for high availability; it adds reconfiguration functionality for even greater agility in a long-lived system. Figures 22.4, 22.5, 22.8 and 22.9 demonstrate fault-masking for multicast, SMR and read/write storage, respectively.

Reconfiguration itself presents another interesting design tradeoff. The reconfiguration procedure entails forming two consensus decisions—one on the next configuration and another on the closing state of the current. These may be obtained either among the group of servers themselves, or using a separate consensus engine. Even the latter case requires careful integration with the steady-state protocol, and we give the recipes for doing so in Figs. 22.3 and 22.7. Fully distributed reconfiguration protocols are detailed in Figs. 22.5, 22.9 and 22.8.

In general, any new members will need to catch up: for this we use the term *state transfer*; it entails packaging the state of the service into some sort of external representation, copying that data to the new member(s), and them loading the state before starting to process new requests. The benefit of forming agreement on a closing state is explained below in Sect. 22.6, using a novel formulation of an old idea, virtual synchrony. Without agreement, we'll see that a service might exhibit various forms of unexpected behavior. For example, one standard approach leads to services that are correct, but in which unfinished operations can linger in a concealed form, suddenly becoming complete "retroactively" arbitrarily far in the future, as discussed in Sect. 22.9. An alternative approach to this problem was explored in systems like RAMBO (Lynch and Shvartsman 2002) which seek to offer continuous availability, to do so they must keep both the old and the new configurations active for a potentially extended period until the new one can take over entirely. Our methodology explains such behaviors, clarifies the associated design choices, and offers simple tradeoffs that let the developer select the properties needed, and to understand the associated costs and implementation issues.

We also explore a number of misconceptions regarding reconfigurable SMR. For example, when using the reconfigurable Paxos protocol, developers find themselves forced to choose between a simple solution with poor performance and a far more complex one that runs at higher speed (corresponding to the choice of value for the Paxos concurrency window parameter). However, a higher concurrency window may result in undesirable behavior where the sequence of state machine commands contains a mix of decisions out of their intended order. In fact, the treatment presented here grew out of a project to create a new "Virtually Synchronous Paxos" protocol, and our dynamically reconfigurable version of state machine replication in Sect. 22.7.2 achieves this objective (in particular, Fig. 22.8 can be recognized as a virtually synchronous version of the Paxos protocol).

More pitfalls and anomalies of existing approaches are discussed in Sect. 22.9. This section contrasts our DSR method with respect to the three most relevant methodologies, namely, implementations of *virtually synchronous* protocols, implementations of the Paxos protocol for state machine replication, and dynamic atomic storage protocols.

Finally, we briefly sketch a correctness argument for a sample of our solutions in the Appendix.

Contribution   While some methodologies lead the developer to some single best solution, that will not be the case here; not only will the solutions we develop be incomparable in some ways, they even include application-specific considerations: the best protocols for implementing a reconfigurable reliable multicast turn out not to be directly mappable to state machine replication solution, and this illustrates just one of many such examples. Thus, readers of this appendix will draw different conclusions based on the utility they individually assign to the various tradeoffs involved. Our contribution is not some single answer, but rather a more principled treatment of the question. The methodology we offer here offers confidence in correctness, and for any given set of application-specific goals, enables steady-state performance similar to the best known hand-crafted solutions to the same problems. Also, our solution assumes less than is assumed when creating state machine solutions, and for this reason may be applicable to problems for which state machine replication is inappropriate.

In summary, this appendix offers an overarching and unified reconfiguration framework, which reveals relationships between a number of prior works that led to correct and yet seemingly incomparable reconfigurable solutions in this space. Doing so helps the developer understand reconfiguration against a broad spectrum of choices, to understand the implications of those choices, and also makes it possible to see protocols that might previously have been portrayed as competing options as different realizations of a single overall goal.

22.2   Liveness Model

Our aim is to provide services in asynchronous systems whose set of servers is changed through explicit reconfigurations. We assume an additional set, potentially overlapping, of clients. We do not assume any bounds on message latencies or message processing times (i.e., the execution environment is asynchronous), and messages may get lost, re-ordered, or duplicated on the network. However, we assume that a message that is delivered was previously sent by some live member and that correct members can eventually communicate any message.

In order to capture a formal execution model with changing memberships, we borrow concepts which express explicit dynamism from Aguilera et al. (2009a), but modify the treatment for weaker requirements. We proceed with a formal definition, and follow with examples.

A fixed system *membership* consists of some set of servers and liveness conditions. As usual, our goal is to build systems that are guaranteed to make progress as long as the conditions on the servers hold. If too many servers fail (violating the conditions for liveness), safety will not be impaired, but the system might need to stop responding to client requests until reconfiguration occurs. We further refine our liveness conditions by breaking them into two parts, one for performing read requests, and one for performing updates; by doing so, we can sometimes continue to support one kind of operation even if the other kind is temporarily unavailable. Example memberships are '$f + 1$ servers, f may crash on any read, no crash tolerance on update', and 'n servers, any minority of which may fail for either read or write tolerance'.

We assume an initial membership M_0. Clients are provided with a membership-changing API function **Reconfig**(M), where M is a new membership. A call to **Reconfig**(M) must eventually complete, and returns an ACK response some time after its invocation. Clients might issue concurrent **Reconfig**(M) calls, and when this occurs, the protocol orders the reconfigurations through the sequence of ACK responses. Thus, a system might perform $M_0, M_1, M_2, \ldots$ even though **Reconfig**(M_2) was invoked before **Reconfig**(M_1). We will view issues such as pre-conditions for invoking **Reconfig**, and any access restrictions (e.g., to designated administrative users) on using the **Reconfig** API as falling outside of the scope of our treatment.

In our model, two execution events are associated with each **Reconfig** call, marking its invocation and its completion. Both events change the liveness conditions, so they could be thought of as 'model-changing' events in that they transform a fixed liveness-condition into another liveness-condition. For clarity, we will continue referring to them as **Reconfig** invocation and response events. The first event occurs upon invocation of **Reconfig**. It changes the current liveness condition to incorporate the requested new membership, including its set of servers and its corresponding liveness conditions. The second event in our model marks a completion of a **Reconfig** call. This event signifies that the system has re-organized to switch the service to the new set of servers and transferred all necessary information to it, so that the old membership may be garbage collected.

We define the *startup* of a membership M_k to begin with the **Reconfig**(M_k) invocation and end with its response event (for M_0, this is defined as the point the system starts). We define the *lifetime* of a membership M_k to begin with the **Reconfig**(M_k) invocation (or with the start time of the system, for M_0) and end when the succeeding reconfiguration **Reconfig**(M_{k+1}) startup is completed.

Liveness We use the notation X-resilience condition (where X is read or update) to refer to the liveness condition that must hold for operations of type X to complete. For every membership M_k in the sequence of **Reconfig** calls, the following holds:
1. Throughout the *lifetime* of M_k, its **read**-resilience is not violated.
2. There exists a future membership M_ℓ, where $\ell > k$, such that the **update**-resilience condition of M_ℓ holds throughout the *startup* of **Reconfig**(M_ℓ).

Note that it follows inductively from the definitions above that memberships $M_{k+1}, \ldots, M_{\ell-1}$ maintain their read-resilience condition until the response event of **Reconfig**(M_ℓ).

To illustrate the features of our liveness model, let us apply it in three simple scenarios. In the first, we have a system implemented by a single server which may be replaced as needed. Each membership consists of a singleton set. The read and update resilience conditions are identical here: Zero failures. Plugging these bounds into our liveness condition implies that, not surprisingly, a server must remain alive until a new one is installed. Moreover, the new server must be alive during its startup procedure. For example, say that initially we have M_0, which contains a singleton set of servers $\{q_0\}$. A client wishes to replace q_0 with an upgraded server q_1 by invoking **Reconfig**(M_1), with M_1 containing the set of servers $\{q_1\}$. Internally, the startup procedure of **Reconfig**(M_1) suspends q_0, copies data from q_0 to q_1, and redirects clients to q_1. Note that this startup procedure will be successful under the assumptions of our liveness model, because both q_0 and q_1 remain alive while **Reconfig**(M_1) is in progress. Once q_1 stores the system state, the **Reconfig**(M_1) procedure completes and we model this as an abstract response event. From here on, q_0 may safely shut down.

The second example is a service implemented by $N = F + 1$ servers for F-tolerance, such as a primary-backup setup. Here, the read and the update thresholds are substantially different. The update-threshold is $F + 1$. That is, in order for the service to store updates durably, it requires participation of all servers. In case of a failure, updates become stalled, and we use the reconfiguration manager to facilitate progress. Such a service must include another system component in charge of reconfiguration, because it impossible to form a consensus decision on the next membership among the $F + 1$ processes alone. To reconfigure, we need both one server to be available, in order to persist the service state; and the reconfiguration manager must be available in order to initiate the **Reconfig** procedure.

For example, say that M_0 has a set of servers S_0 and M_1 has S_1, each consisting of $F + 1$ servers. Upon invocation of **Reconfig**(M_1), our liveness requires read availability in both S_0 and S_1 and that some later membership has update availability. More specifically, our model says that at most F out of each of the sets S_0, S_1 fail. This suffices to suspend M_0 and transfer the closing state of M_0 to at least one server in S_1. When the closing state of M_0 has been transferred to all $F + 1$ servers of M_1 our model schedules the **Reconfig**(M_1) response event. At that time, our liveness model changes: it drops any resilience assumption on M_0. Indeed, it would be safe for all servers of S_0 (that are not in S_1) to shut down.

To re-iterate a point made above, **Reconfig** calls may overlap. Hence, this scenario could develop quite differently. Say that there is a failure in S_1 before we complete the state transfer to it. Hence, a client may issue **Reconfig**(M_2) to remedy this, before **Reconfig**(M_1) completes. In our formal model, another event occurs, marking the invocation of **Reconfig**(M_2) and changing the liveness assumption to 'F out of each of the sets S_0, S_1 and S_2 may fail'. Now servers in S_2 suspend M_1 and obtain its state. Note that our read-resilience assumption implies that this is possible, despite having failures in M_1 already. When all $F + 1$ servers in S_2 obtained their state, **Reconfig**(M_2) becomes completed. In this case, the completion of **Reconfig**(M_2) also pertinently marks the completion of **Reconfig**(M_1). Consequently, both M_0 and M_1 will be retired by this completion.

In our last example, a membership consists of a set of $N = 2F + 1$ servers, F of which may crash for either read or update. Here, the read and update resilience thresholds are identical. The liveness condition is simple here: During the lifetime of a membership, at most F of its servers may crash. A membership M_k ends with the completion of **Reconfig**(M_{k+1}), when the closing state of M_k is stored on $F + 1$ members of M_{k+1}. At that time, M_k may be retired.

Finally, we note that in order to reach a unique **Reconfig** decision, we are obviously bound by the impossibility of consensus: in order to guarantee termination for **Reconfig** decisions, we require an eventual leader with timely communication to a majority of the membership.

22.3   The Dynamic Reliable Multicast Problem

Let us jump in by exploring the reconfiguration question in the context of a simple but general form of reliable multicast. A reliable multicast protocol is simply a service (perhaps implemented by a library that its clients employ), which allows clients to *send* new multicast messages to groups of receivers, and to *receive* messages within groups. Multicast is a popular technology, both in the explicit form just described, and also in implicit forms, such as publish-subscribe or content-based communication infrastructures, so called *enterprise message bus* technologies, and many kinds of data replication and caching technology. In accompanying break-out boxes (Figs. 22.1 and 22.2) we discuss the possible mappings of our simple multicast API to more standard ones that might be used in such services.

Reliable multicast is a good place to start because many distributed systems rely on some form of multicast-like mechanism at a basic level, perhaps presenting it as a multicast, or perhaps hiding it in a data or file replication mechanism. But whatever form the end-user functionality takes, the multicast communication pattern arises. If we can understand reconfiguration in a multicast protocol, we will have taken a big step towards understanding reconfiguration as a general computing paradigm.

The Multicast API   Our proposed service offers two interfaces to its clients, **Add**() and **Get**(). The **Add**() primitive sends a new message and returns an ACK.

How can our service model be made available through a more standard multicast package? Our multicast API is pull-based, but one could change it into a notification API by supporting an explicit group join operation. The join itself would change the group membership using a reconfiguration command, and we will discuss these below. The Send operation maps directly to our **Add()** interface. Receive would then be supported as a callback from the multicast library into the application. When a process joins a multicast group for the first time, our durability rule requires it to learn the state of the group. Thus the first event that occurs upon joining would be a **Get()** of the sort we have included in our model: the **Get()**, in effect, embodies the state transfer. Subsequent receive operations, in contrast, would be modeled as **Get()** operations that omit messages that were previously delivered to the caller. View notification, if desired, would be implemented as an upcall that occurs when a new membership is initiated.

A real implementation would also garbage collect durable multicast messages once they are processed by the group members and reflected into the group state. The needed mechanisms complicate the protocol, but have no fundamental bearing on the reconfiguration problem, hence we omit discussion of them here.

Fig. 22.1 Our simple multicast service abstracts classical ones

A **Get()** call returns a set of messages. A message m of a completed **Add()** or **Get()** operation becomes *durable*. The main requirement we have of a **Get()** call is:

Definition (Multicast Durability) A **Get()** call returns a set of messages that contains all messages which have become durable when the call was invoked.

In practice, **Get()** returns all durable messages of completed **Add()** operations and possibly also some additional messages associated with concurrently executing **Add()** operations. If a message m is returned by **Get**, it becomes durable; hence every subsequent call to **Get** will also return m.

We do not require any particular order on operations; in particular, two concurrent calls to **Get()** may return disjoint sets of durable messages, and might order messages differently. Thus, the model could be used with *Send, OrderedSend, CausalSend*, etc. However, notice that because of the emphasis on durability, our treatment in this Appendix really applies only to the *safe* versions of those protocols, which do provide strong durability. The model can be extended to deal with amnesia-freedom of the kind needed in the first tier of the cloud, but doing so is beyond the scope of our treatment here.

Epoch-by-Epoch Solution   Our approach for dynamically reconfigurable reliable multicast has two parts: A *steady-state* protocol for sending and delivering messages during normal, stable periods; and a *reconfiguration* protocol. Each of these proto-

Readers familiar with protocols such as IP multicast, or gossip-based multicast, might be surprised to see durability even considered as a property that a multicast protocol should offer. In many settings, durability is viewed strictly as an end-to-end question, not something that belongs in a multicast layer. Moreover, there are many ways for an application to satisfy objectives such as durability. For example, while our discussion looks at multicasts that only deliver messages when they are safe in the sense of durable, there are some kinds of application that operate optimistically, accepting messages instantly upon reception, but then rolling back if necessary to back out of unsafe states (Patino-Martinez et al. 2005). Why, then, are we treating durability as a multicast property?

Recall, however, that our overarching goal is to drill down on the question of *reconfiguring a durable service*, with the hope of teasing out essential aspects of the required solution. We are looking at multicast simply because multicast is the communication pattern underlying data replication, hence applications that perform durable data replication can be understood as if they were using a multicast for the data updates. By modeling the multicast protocol as the source of durability, we avoid needing to explicitly model the application, and can isolate the interplay between durability within the multicast protocol and reconfiguration of the multicast group membership.

Fig. 22.2 Durablity can be defined in application-specific terms (for example, by requiring that a database retain an update), or in protocol specific terms (for example, by requiring that if any multicast delivery occurs, every member learns the multicast). As discussed in connection with the SafeSend logging problem in Sect. 15.2, the definition one selects has important implications. In this Appendix, we've adopted a definition that focuses purely on the multicast protocol itself, for clarity of the presentation

cols is defined relative to a single *epoch*, which begins when a configuration of the system becomes live and ends by running the epoch termination protocol given below. After the current epoch ends, a new epoch starts, and we can understand it as hosting a completely new incarnation of this algorithm, whose newly added messages do not mix with the previous epoch. Indeed, when changing epochs a system could modify protocol parameters or even switch to a new protocol stack entirely incompatible with the prior one, reinitialize data, agree upon new security keys (in a secured group (Reiter 1994a, 1994b)), and so forth.

A Single Server Solution   It may be helpful to begin with a degenerate solution that employs just a single server, because by doing so, we create a form of reference implementation. Later when we explore distributed solutions, we can reason about their correctness by asking ourselves what properties it shares with the single server solution.

To implement **Add**(), the client in the single-server case locates the server and sends it a **store** request for whatever message m is being sent. The server adds m to the message history and acknowledges, and the client considers the **Add**() complete when the acknowledgment is received.

To implement **Get**(), the client contacts the server and the server sends back the entire current message history. Notice that this history will contain every completed **Add**(), and perhaps also a few more messages that were recently stored but for which the corresponding client has not yet received the acknowledgment. These requests are, in a technical sense, incomplete, although the associated messages will in fact be durable. In particular, notice that once a **Get**() includes m into a response, every future **Get**() will also include m.

Finally, how might we reconfigure the single-server implementation? The simplest solution would be as follows. A membership tracking module would receive a reconfigure command, specifying that henceforth, server s' will run the service. The membership service determines that s is currently running the service, and sends a message to s that causes it to enter what we will call a *wedged* state, meaning that no further operations will be accepted. Server s now transmits its final state to the membership service, which now sends s' a message that includes the final state. Having initialized itself from this transferred state, s' becomes operational, accepting new store operations. Meanwhile, s can terminate, discarding its state. The protocol, of course, is not tolerant of failures: if s fails before the state is transferred, s' will be unable to enter the normal operational state.

Notice that we passed the new epoch state via the membership service. If this state is large, doing so might be undesirable, because during the period between when s transmits the state and when s' loads it, the service will be unavailable. However, there are ways to reduce this gap. For example, we might have s' speculatively copy the state from s using **Get**() operations, before the reconfiguration is even initiated. Now only the recent delta of messages that reached s subsequent to that preliminary transfer will be needed to bring s' into sync with s. Indeed, one could iterate, such that the membership service forms the new epoch, in which s' is the new server, only when the remaining delta is small enough; this way, if s' tries to join during a burst of activity, it is delayed slightly (during which it will continue to transfer chunks of state), until finally a brief moment of reduced load occurs, when s' can finally catch up relatively rapidly.

To use the terminology introduced above, we now have a fault-intolerant solution in which each epoch is associated with some single server, begins with the initialization of that server, runs in a steady state by storing messages, and ends when the next server takes over, wedging the previous one. The previous server can shut down entirely once the state transfer has been carried out.

Fault-Recovery Versus Fault-Masking Steady State   We are now in a position to replicate our service to achieve such benefits as higher availability, load balancing of **Get**() operations over its members, etc. In what follows, we start by designing the steady-state protocols and only then consider the protocol needed to reconfigure. Two principal strategies suggest themselves:

1. The first is a *fault-recovery* approach, in which we store messages at *all* of the servers. If some server is unresponsive, this version will become blocked until a reconfiguration occurs.

2. The second is a *fault-masking* algorithm, in which we store messages at a majority of the servers. We deliver messages by reading from a majority and storing back messages at a majority. This version can continue to complete operations of both types as long as no more than a minority of servers become unresponsive. We need a majority of servers to remain available in order to transfer the state of the current configuration to any future one, but after reconfiguration, the old configuration may be retired completely.

In the coming two sections, we first flesh out a fault-recovery solution (Sect. 22.4), then a fault-masking one (Sect. 22.5).

22.4 Fault-Recovery Multicast

We start with the fault-recovery solution. The advantage of the a fault-recovery approach to the reliable multicast problem is that it requires just $N = F + 1$ servers and maintains data durability in the face of up to F failures. In case of a failure, we employ an auxiliary *consensus engine* to facilitate reconfiguration.

Figure 22.3 gives a succinct summary of the entire problem definition and its fault-recovery solutions. We elaborate further on them below.

22.4.1 Fault-Recovery Add/Get Implementation

Add   A client that wants to send a message m sends a **store** message containing m to all servers in a configuration. A server that receives the update inserts m to its local messages set (unless the server is wedged—see Reconfiguration below). Each server acknowledges the **store** message to the client, and the **Add** call completes when acknowledgments have been received from all servers.

Get   When a client invokes **Get()**, it sends a **collect** message to all servers in a configuration. A server that receives a collect command returns its locally stored messages to the client (again, unless it is wedged). The client waits to receive responses from all servers, and computes an intersection set S of message which appear in all of these histories (message order is unimportant). The **Get** call returns the set S.

22.4.2 Reconfiguration Protocol

Recall that participants initiate reconfiguration by issuing a **Reconfig** command. Reconfiguration entails these steps:

1. The issuing client sends a *wedge* request to servers in the current epoch. As in our single-server solution, such a request causes a receiving server to become wedged (it may already be wedged from another **Reconfig** command), and to return a representation of its state.

2. Since as many as F servers could be faulty, the client waits for just one response, but this response will contain all durable messages (and possibly more). These messages are used for the initial state of each server in the next epoch.

API:

> **Add**(m): return(ACK)
> **Get**(): return(S), such that:
> > if **Add**(m) completed before **Get**() was invoked, $m \in S$
> > if $S' = $ **Get**() completed before invocation, $S' \subseteq S$
>
> **Reconfig**(M): return(ACK)

Liveness condition:

> throughout the *lifetime* of M, at least one server is correct; and
> there exists a future membership M' in which all servers are correct throughout the *startup*
> of **Reconfig**(M')

Operation **Add**(m) at client:
  send($\langle$**store**, $m\rangle$) to servers
  wait for replies from all servers
  return(ACK)
	Upon $\langle$**store**, $m\rangle$ request at server and not wedged:
	  save m to local store and return ACK

Operation **Get**() at client:
  send($\langle$**collect**$\rangle$) to servers
  wait for reply S_q from each server q
  return($\cap_q S_q$)
	Upon $\langle$**collect**$\rangle$ request at server and not wedged:
	  return all locally stored messages

Operation **Reconfig**(M):
  Send($\langle$**wedge**$\rangle$) request to servers
  Wait for reply $\langle$**suspended**, $S_q\rangle_q$
    from any server q
  Invoke consensus engine $decide(M, S_q)$
  When all servers of new epoch have
      started
    return(ACK)
	Upon $\langle$**wedge**$\rangle$ request at server q:
	  stop serving **store/collect** commands
	  return $\langle$**suspended**, $S_q\rangle$ where
	    S_q contains all locally stored messages
	
	At any server of new membership M'
	Upon learning $(M', S) \leftarrow decide()$:
	  store S locally and start service

Fig. 22.3 Single epoch fault-recovery reliable multicast solution

3. **Reconfig** employs some kind of a consensus engine to form a decision both on the next membership M and on the set S of durable messages. For example, the consensus engine could be implemented by a centralized authority, which itself could be made reliable by running Paxos among replicated state machines (Lamport 1998).

4. Servers s' in a new membership M' learn the reconfiguration decision either directly from the auxiliary authority, or indirectly from other members. Either way, they learn both the membership M' of the new configuration and its initial message store S'. The initial state could also include application-specific information, or even specify an upgrade to a new version of the application or the protocols it uses. As in the single-server case, note that there are many ways to optimize state transfer so that the amount of information actually passed through the membership service could be quite small. What matters here is that a server

s' in the new epoch should only process new requests after it has initialized itself appropriately.

After completing state transfer, the server enables itself for handling normal client requests in the new epoch. Of course, if the server was also present in an earlier epoch, it remains wedged with respect to that epoch.

5. The **Reconfig** command is considered completed when all servers in the new configuration have enabled themselves. Note that **Reconfig** may never complete. In that case, yet a further reconfiguration command would be needed before system availability is restored.

The reader may wonder about reconfigurations that occur in response to a failure. In such cases, one or more servers in the current epoch will be unresponsive. However, any durable message will have been stored in all histories, and hence will be included in the initial state of all servers in the new epoch. On the other hand, consider an uncompleted operation, corresponding to a message stored in just a subset of the histories. At this stage, depending on the pattern of failures, that message could be missing from some of the surviving histories and dropped. But it could also turn out to be included in the history of the server whose state is used for the next configuration, in which case it would become durable even though the associated **Add()** operation may not have completed.

It is not difficult to see that such problems are unavoidable. In effect, the outcome of a **Add()** that was pending at the time of a reconfiguration is determined by the membership service: if the message is included into the new epoch state, the **Add()** should be construed as successful, and if the message is not included, the **Add()** has failed and should be reissued in the new epoch. The client can learn this outcome from any server in the new epoch, or from the membership service itself. We leave the details of returning these out-of-band responses to clients out of the discussion here.

The reader may also wonder why a **Get()** operation collects messages from all servers instead of just one. It is instructive to see what would go wrong if a **Get()** operation reads from a single server. Suppose a client invokes **Add(x)** to send a message. Say that server X has received the message, but server Y hasn't yet. Now one client that invokes **Get()** happens to read from server X and obtains the message. Later, still before server Y has received the message, another client happens to read from server Y and does not obtain the message. This scenario violates the durability property. This is not possible if clients read from all servers and intersect the responses. If the first **Get()** returns a certain message, subsequent **Get()** operations would now be certain to return that message as well.

22.5   Fault-Masking Multicast

We continue with a fault-masking, majorities-based solution. The majorities-based fault-masking approach to the reliable multicast problem deploys $N = 2F + 1$ servers to maintain both data durability and non-disrupted operation in face of up to F failures. Figure 22.4 gives a succinct summary.

API:

    Add(m): return(ACK)

    Get(): return(S), such that:

            if **Add**(m) completed before **Get**() was invoked, $m \in S$

            if $S' =$ **Get**() completed before invocation, $S' \subseteq S$

    Reconfig(M): return(ACK)

Liveness condition:

    throughout the lifetime of a membership M, a majority of servers are correct

---

Operation **Add**(m) at client:
    send($\langle$**store**, $m\rangle$) to servers
    wait for replies from a majority servers
    return(ACK)
	Upon $\langle$**store**, $m\rangle$ request at server and not wedged:
	    save m to local store and return ACK

Operation **Get**() at client:
    send($\langle$**collect**$\rangle$) to servers
    wait for replies S_q from a majority of
        servers q
    send ($\langle$**store**, $\cup_q S_q\rangle$) to servers
    wait for replies from a majority of
        servers
    return($\cup_q S_q$)
	Upon $\langle$**collect**$\rangle$ request at server and not wedged:
	    return all locally stored messages

Operation **Reconfig**(M):
    Send($\langle$**wedge**$\rangle$) request to servers
    Wait for reply $\langle$**suspended**, $S_q\rangle_q$
        from a majority of servers q
    Invoke consensus engine
        $decide(M, \cup_q S_q)$
    When a majority of servers in M have
        started
    return(ACK)
	Upon $\langle$**wedge**$\rangle$ request at server q:
	    stop serving **store**/**collect** commands
	    return $\langle$**suspended**, $S_q\rangle$ where
	        S_q contains all locally stored messages
	
	At any server of new membership M'
	Upon learning $(M', S) \leftarrow decide()$:
	    store S locally and start service

Fig. 22.4 Majority-based reliable multicast solution

22.5.1 Majorities-Based Tolerant Add/Get Implementation

The steady-state fault-masking solution for Reliable Multicast works as follows.

Add A client that wants to send a message m sends a **store** message containing m to all servers in a configuration. A server that receives the update and is not wedged inserts m to its local messages set. Each server acknowledges the **store** message to the client, and the **Add** call completes when a majority of acknowledgments have been received.

Get When a client invokes **Get**(), it sends a **collect** message to all servers in a configuration. A server that receives a collect command and is not wedged returns its locally stored messages to the client. The client waits to receive responses from a majority, and computes a union set S of messages which appear in any of these histories. The client then stores back the set S at a majority by issuing a **store** message and waiting for acknowledgement from a majority.[1] The **Get** call returns the set S.

22.5.2 Reconfiguration Protocol for Majorities-Based Multicast

The same reconfiguration protocol as the fault-recovery one can be used in this case, but with a minor modification to the rule used to compute the initial state of the new epoch.

Now, the issuing client must contact a majority of servers to discover all successful multicasts. Such a server enters the wedged state, and then sends the message history to the client, as above. This was why we required that, for the fault-masking case, the service include at least $2F + 1$ servers: if F fail, $F + 1$ will still be operational, and for any durable message, at least one of them will know of it. This, then, permits the client to include all durable messages in the initial state of the new epoch.

Again, after completing state transfer, a server of the new membership enables itself for handling normal client requests in the new epoch. However, it suffices for a majority of servers of the new configuration to become enabled for the **Reconfig** operation to be considered completed. And just as we saw above, state transfer can be optimized to transfer much of the data through an out-of-band channel, directly from the servers in the current epoch to the ones that will be members of the next epoch.

22.5.3 Reconfiguration Agreement Protocol

We now "open" the consensus engine and flesh out a procedure that unifies forming agreement on the next epoch with state transfer. Figure 22.5 summarizes a multicast solution that uses $N = 2F + 1$ servers and contains a detailed reconfiguration decision protocol combined with state transfer. (Only the **Reconfig** part is changed from Fig. 22.4, but for completeness, Fig. 22.5 gives a full solution.)

The combined reconfiguration and state transfer protocol is based on the well-known Synod algorithm (Lamport 1998). It is triggered by a client **Reconfig** command and uses a set of $N = 2F + 1$ servers of the current epoch. The **Reconfig** procedure makes use of a uniquely chosen *stake* (for example, an integer or some other ordered type). Clients invoking reconfiguration may repeatedly try increasingly higher stakes until a decision is reached. The protocol of a particular stake has two phases. Although we could wait for the consensus decision and then perform state transfer, it turns out that we can make efficient use of message exchanges inside the protocol to accomplish state transfer at the same time.

---

[1]Clearly, we can optimize to store S only at sufficiently many servers to guarantee that S is stored at a majority.

API:

    Add(m): return(ACK)
    Get(): return(S), such that:
        if **Add**(m) completed before **Get**() was invoked, $m \in S$
        if $S' = $ **Get**() completed before invocation, $S' \subseteq S$
    Reconfig(M): return(ACK)

Liveness condition:
    throughout the lifetime of a membership M, a majority of servers are correct

---

Operation **Add**(m) at client:
    send(⟨**store**, m⟩) to servers
    wait for replies from a majority of
        servers
    return(ACK)

Upon ⟨**store**, m⟩ request at server and not
    wedged:
    save m to local store and return ACK

Operation **Get**() at client:
    send(⟨**collect**⟩) to servers
    wait for replies S_q from a majority of
        servers q
    send(⟨**store**, $\cup_q S_q$⟩) to servers
    wait for replies from a majority of
        servers
    return($\cup_q S_q$)

Upon ⟨**collect**⟩ request at server and not
    wedged:
    return all locally stored messages

Operation **Reconfig**(M):
    Choose unique *stake*
    Send(⟨**wedge**, *stake*⟩) request to
        servers
    Wait for replies
        ⟨**suspended**, *stake*, ⟨*st*, *RC*⟩, S_q⟩$_q$
        from a majority of servers q
    if any (*st*, *RC*) is non-empty
        choose *RC* of highest (*st*, *RC*)
            pair;
    else
        let $RC \leftarrow (M, \cup_q S_q)$
    Send(⟨**accept**, *stake*, *RC*⟩)
    When a majority of servers in *RC* have
        started
    return(ACK)

Upon ⟨**wedge**, *st*⟩ request at server q:
    stop serving **store/collect** commands
    unless accessed by higher-stake leader
        already return
    ⟨**suspended**, *st*, ⟨*highst*, *highRC*⟩, S_q⟩

Upon ⟨**accept**, *st*, *RC*⟩⟩ request at server q:
    unless accessed by higher-stake leader
        already
    store *highst* $\leftarrow$ *st*, *highRC* $\leftarrow$ *RC*
    send ⟨**start**, *st*, *RC*⟩ to servers in *RC*

At any server in *RC*
    Upon obtaining ⟨**start**, *st*, *RC* = (*M*, *S*)⟩
        from a majority of previous
        epoch
    store *S* locally and start service

Fig. 22.5 Majority-based reliable multicast with $2F + 1$ servers: full solution

More specifically, in **Phase 1**, a client performs one exchange with a majority of servers. When the client hears back from a majority, it learns:

(1) Either a reconfiguration command *RC*, which might have been chosen. In case of multiple possibly chosen *RC*'s, the one whose stake is highest is selected.

(2) Or that no reconfiguration command was chosen.

This exchange also tells the servers to ignore future proposals from any client that precedes it in the stake-order.

Coupled into this (standard) Phase 1 of consensus protocol is the collect phase of our state transfer. Namely, the same exchange marks the servers wedged, which is done by obtaining a commitment from the servers not to respond to any **store** or **collect** request from processes. In their responses in Phase 1, the client collects from each server the set of messages it stores.

In **Phase 2**, the client performs another single exchange with a majority of servers. If case (1) applies, then it tells servers to choose RC. Otherwise, in case (2), it proposes a new reconfiguration decision RC. The new RC contains the configuration that the client requested, as well as a union of the messages it collected in the first phase.

The server's protocol is to respond to client's messages, unless it was contacted by a higher-stake client already:

- In Phase 1, it responds with the value of a reconfiguration proposal RC of the highest-stake it knows of, or an empty RC. It also incorporates into the response the set of messages it stores locally, and commits to ignore future client **store/collect** requests.
- In Phase 2, it acknowledges a client's proposal and stores it.

Each server in the new membership waits to collect **start** messages with the same stake from a majority of servers of the previous epoch. In this way, it learns about the next epoch decision, which includes the new configuration and the set of messages that are now durable. It stores these messages in its message history and becomes enabled for serving clients in the new epoch. Once a majority of servers in the new epoch are enabled, the **Reconfig**() operation completes.

As an example scenario, consider a system with three servers $\{1, 2, 3\}$. Assume message a reaches $\{1, 2\}$, b reaches $\{2, 3\}$ and c reaches server 3. During Phase 1 of reconfiguration, a client sends **wedge** messages to the servers. In response, server 2 suspends itself and sends $\{a, b\}$, and server 3 sends $\{b, c\}$. The client collects these responses, and enters Phase 2, proposing a new epoch configuration consisting of server-set $\{4, 5, 6\}$ and message set $\{a, b, c\}$. Although this set contains more than the set of completed messages (c's **Add**() not having completed), those extra messages pose no problem; in effect, they complete and become durable as part of reconfiguration. Again, here we ignore the matter of sending out of band responses to the client which invoked **Add**(c).

Servers $\{4, 5\}$ in the new epoch each learns the decision, stores $\{a, b, c\}$ locally and become enabled. At this point, it is possible that all the servers in the previous epoch are shut down. This poses no risk, as no information is lost. In particular, every **Get**() request in the new epoch returns $\{a, b, c\}$.

Another possibility is that the client collects information from servers $\{1, 2\}$, and the reconfiguration decision includes only messages $\{a, b\}$. In this case, message c disappears. This is legitimate, as no **Add**() or **Get**() with c ever completes, in the past or in the future.

22.6   Coordinated State Transfer: The Virtual Synchrony Property

Consider what would happen in the Reliable Multicast service if we did not include in the reconfiguration decision the set S of messages ever completed in the current configuration. Instead, imagine a protocol in which every server in the new membership independently obtains the state from a read-set of the current configuration. For those messages M whose **Add** or **Get** have completed, there will be no difference. That is, every server in the new membership will obtain M before starting the new epoch. However, messages with partially completed **Add/Get** may or may not be obtained by the new servers, depending on which member(s) of the current configuration they query. Such messages could later become durable, by being transferred to all servers some epoch. Let us study this case in more detail by revisiting our fault-recovery approach.

For example, suppose that **Add**(a) has arrived at both servers $\{1, 2\}$ of some initial epoch. Say that **Add**(b) has reached $\{1\}$ so far, and **Add**(c) has reached $\{2\}$. Let the reconfiguration manager establish a decision on a new epoch set $\{3, 4, 5\}$. We may have server 3 suspend and pull messages $\{a, b\}$ from $\{1\}$. Note that message a was completed, and b may yet complete in the future; however, we cannot distinguish between these two situations. If servers $4, 5$ were to do the same state transfer, it would then be possible for a client to perform a **Get**() in the new epoch, and return $\{a, b\}$. This is the only safe response, as **Add**(b) could complete meanwhile.

Alternatively, servers $4, 5$ might pull $\{a, c\}$ from $\{2\}$. At this point, because both 1 and 2 are wedged and will not acknowledge further **store** requests, neither b nor c may ever complete in the current configuration. However, this situation cannot be distinguished by the servers. Hence, when a client requests **Get**() in the new epoch, server 3 must respond with $\{a, b\}$, while $4, 5$ must respond with $\{a, c\}$. This is fine, since the client will return the intersection $\{a\}$ in response to **Get**().

The service remains correct with such 'uncoordinated state transfer'. However, in some future epoch, events might transpire in a way that causes all the servers to pull b and c from the preceding configuration. Suddenly, b and c will become durable, and all future **Get**() requests will include them. We believe that this behavior is undesirable. Indeed, in DSR we prevented such outcome by including in the consensus reconfiguration decision a set of messages from the current configuration, such that no other messages may appear later. The connection of the DRS approach to reconfiguration with the virtual synchrony approach to group communication may now become apparent to readers familiar with that literature: DRS guarantees to terminate operations within the lifetime of their invoking configuration. We now give a new formal definition of this old idea.

We will start by explicitly modeling the configuration visible to a client when it invokes an operation. Notice that this is a reasonable addition to our model, since any client-side library must locate and interact with servers of the configuration, and hence it makes sense to rigorously specify the behavior of the associated interface. In addition to **Reconfig** invoke and response events, we model **Reconfig** *notification* events, which arrive at clients individually. Clients may be notified at different times about the same configuration.

Definition We say that a client invokes operation o *in configuration* C if C is the latest **Reconfig**-notification event at this client preceding o's invocation, or, in case no **Reconfig**-notification event has occurred, if C is the initial configuration C_0.

For example, for some client, we may have the following sequence of events: invoke **Add**(m_1), response from **Add**(m_1), invoke **Add**(m_2), **Reconfig**(C_1) notification, response from **Add**(m_2), invoke **Add**(m_3), response from **Add**(m_3). In this sequence, the **Add**() operations of m_1 and m_2 are invoked in the initial configuration (C_0), and that of m_3 is invoked in C_1.

Now for Reliable Multicast, virtual synchrony requires the following:

Definition (Virtually Synchronous Multicast) If **Add**(m) was invoked in configuration C_k, then if ever **Get**() returns m, then for all configurations C_ℓ, where $\ell > k$, a **Get**() invoked in C_ℓ returns m.

It is not hard to see that our Multicast reconfiguration strategy satisfies this condition, because whether or not m is stored in future configuration is determined by the reconfiguration decision itself.

For arbitrary services, we would consider operations which *have an effect* on others. In the Multicast case, **Add** operations change the behavior of future **Get** requests: **Get**() must return all previously sent messages. More generally, an operation o of type O which has an effect on operations o' of type O' changes the outcome of o' if the response event for o occurs before o' is invoked. Conversely, we say that o' *reflects* o.

The Virtual Synchrony guarantee implies the following:

Definition (Virtual Synchrony) Consider an operation o of type O which has an effect on operations of type O'. If o was invoked in configuration C_k, then if any operation o' of type O' reflects o, then for all configurations C_ℓ, where $\ell > k$, operations w' of type O' invoked in C_ℓ reflect o.

22.7   Dynamic State Machine Replication and Virtually Synchronous Paxos

In this section, we take our Dynamic Service Replication (DSR) epoch-changing approach into the generic realm of State Machine Replication (SMR). In the state machine replication approach, replicas are implemented as deterministic state machines. The state machines start with a common initial state and apply commands in some sequential order. This approach yields a protocol we refer to as *Virtually Synchronous Paxos*[2]. Paxos users will recognize the close similarity of the protocol

---

[2]This is a good juncture at which to note that Leslie Lamport was involved in an earlier stage of this research. Although he is not a co-author on this chapter, his help in the initial formulation of our problem was invaluable, and this choice of protocol name is intended to acknowledge the strong roots of our protocol in his earlier work.

to the standard Paxos, yet in contrast with Reconfigurable Paxos and other reconfigurable SMR implementations, this solution achieves higher steady state performance with less complexity around the handling of reconfiguration.

22.7.1 On Paxos Anomalies

Our goal in this section is to highlight some rarely appreciated issues that arise when working with Paxos. Before doing so, we should remind the reader of an issue we touched upon in Sect. 15.2, where we explained the role of the Isis[2] *DiskLogger* durability method. As the reader may recall, the issue concerns the application's definition of durability and the possible mismatch between that definition, and the one used in the multicast protocol (*SafeSend*, in that case). As we defined this property at the outset of Part II, durability was taken to have an inward-looking definition: a message is durable if delivery to any group member (even one that promptly crashes) creates an obligation for the protocol to delivery that same multicast, in the same order (both with respect to other messages and with respect to the delivery of new view events), to all group members that do not crash first. This is achievable with an in-memory copy of each message, but in-memory logging is not sufficient to ensure that after a total failure of a group, durable data managed by the application would reflect the updates the protocol "delivered". Note that, in our model, delivery occurs in two possible ways: either by a delivery event, or by inclusion of a message into the initial state used for a new group configuration. This is important; if the requirement were expressed purely in terms of message delivery events and new view notification events, durability of this kind would not be achievable.

The extensions associated with the Isis[2] durability method, the *DiskLogger*, eliminated most aspects of this issue by ensuring that the state of the group would be preserved on disk even across a complete failure of its members. With this change, *SafeSend* becomes a true implementation of Paxos (most Paxos implementations would similarly maintain state on a disk). The single caveat is that with Isis[2] and the *DiskLogger*, some members might deliver a message prior to a complete failure of the group, while others deliver it after the group restarts from a total failure of all members. This violates virtual synchrony and occurs because Isis[2] lacks direct access to the application state and hence has no way to apply a message to an application state other than by delivery, and because recovery from a total failure necessarily defines a new group view (after all, the entire membership of the group will have changed). We have used the term *strong durability* earlier in the text to evoke the disk-storage of the property: a strongly durable multicast protocol is one that preserves a history of delivered multicasts on disk until the application program using the protocol has explicitly confirmed successful delivery (with Isis[2] and the *DiskLogger*, via a call to *DiskLogger.Done*()).

Even with strong durability, Paxos can exhibit other unexpected behaviors. In the remainder of this section we touch upon those. Our model eliminates these risks, and we will see how that occurs.

Fig. 22.6 Anomalous Paxos
behavior

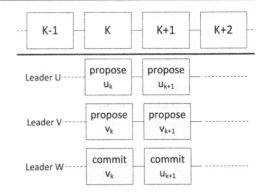

SMR operates on an infinite sequence of commands. Even though the sequence of commands is logically active all the time, in reality, systems progress in epochs: During each epoch, a fixed leader chooses a dense sequence of commands. Then, the leader is replaced, and a new epoch starts. The new leader starts where the previous leader stopped, and passes another subsequence of commands. And so on. If we envision the sequence of commands as a horizontal axis, then each leader-epoch lasts a contiguous segment along the horizontal axis. Nevertheless, abstractly, the same consensus protocol runs in the entire infinite sequence of commands, ignoring epoch and leader changes. Each instance vertically runs a succession of leaders, though each leader takes actual actions only in some instances, and none in others. The consensus-based point of view makes arguing correctness easy.

Unfortunately, the seemingly obvious intuition about epochs is wrong, and may lead to undesirable effects. Consider the scenario depicted in Fig. 22.6. We have two Leaders U and V contending for the same pair of offsets, k and $k + 1$. U proposes u_k at k and u_{k+1} at $k + 1$, intending that u_k executes before u_{k+1}. V proposes v_k and v_{k+1} for these offsets. Consider the case where neither Leader U nor V obtains acceptance of a majority to their proposals. Hence, a third Leader W, starts after U and V are both retired. W finds traces of the command u_{k+1}, proposed by U, at offset $k + 1$, and of the command v_k, proposed by V, at offset k. Paxos mandates W to re-propose v_k and u_{k+1} at k and $k + 1$, respectively. If W is a stable leader, then indeed v_k and u_{k+1} will be chosen. But this violates the intended ordering constraint of the proposers!

In the above situation, Paxos permits the intended ordering of commands to be violated. As noted by the engineers who designed and built the Yahoo! ZooKeeper service (Junqueira et al. 2009), there are real-life situations in which leaders intend for their proposed $k + 1$ command to be executed only if their proposed k command is done first. To achieve high performance many such systems are forced to pipeline their proposals, so a leader might propose command $k + 1$ without waiting for a decision on command k. Paxos is quite capable of choosing $k + 1$ but not k, and (as just noted) there are conditions under which it might choose both, but each one from a different leader. This particular case was sufficiently troublesome to convince the ZooKeeper engineers to move away from Paxos and to implement a virtually synchronous, epoch-by-epoch type of leader election in their system.

So far, we have only discussed simple leader-changes. Our scenario turns out to have even more serious ramifications for previous reconfigurable SMR solutions. Recall that vanilla Paxos allows reconfiguration of the system that implements the state machine by injecting configuration-changing commands into the sequence of state machine commands. This is a natural use of the power of consensus inherent in the implementation of SMR. It entails a concurrency barrier on the steady-state command path: Suppose we form a reconfiguration command, for example, at index y in the sequence of commands. The command determines how the system will form the agreement decision on subsequent commands, for example, at index $y + 1$ and subsequently. More generally, the configuration-changing command at y may determine the consensus algorithm for commands starting at index $y + \alpha$, for some pre-determined concurrency parameter α. We must wait for a reconfiguration decision at y to complete before we inject additional command requests to the system, at index $y + 1$ in the case where $\alpha = 1$ and subsequently (or $y + \alpha$ in the general case). This barrier effectively reduces the system to one-by-one execution of commands, hence if reconfigurable Paxos is used, it would normally be deployed with α greater than 1 (Lorch et al. 2006).

But, now consider the behavior of a Paxos-based SMR solution with $\alpha > 1$. Recall the scenario of contending leaders in Fig. 22.6, and suppose that commands v_k and u_{k+1} are reconfiguration commands, which are mutually incompatible. This may cause the current configuration to issue two (or more) Reconfig commands, up to the maximum of α commands. Suppose that all of these were intended to apply to the configuration in which they were issued. The first to be chosen will update the configuration as usual. But what are we to do when a second or subsequent command is chosen? These commands may no longer make sense. For example, a pending request to remove a faulty server from the configuration might be chosen after one that switches to a configuration in which that server is no longer a member. Executing these reconfigurations one after another is nonsensical. Likewise, a command to change a protocol parameter might be executed in a context where the system has reconfigured and is now using some other protocol within which that parameter has a different meaning, or no meaning at all.

If we use a window α larger than 1, then such events will be possible. An approach that seeks to prevent these commands from being chosen once they are no longer meaningful would require us to implement complex semantic rules. Allowing them to be chosen forces the application designer to understand that a seemingly "buggy" behavior is actually permitted by the protocol. In practice, many Paxos implementations (indeed, all that we know of) either do not support reconfiguration at all, or set α to 1, thus serializing command processing: only one command can be performed at a time. Batching commands can alleviate this cost: rather than one command at a time, the system might perform β at a time, for some parameter β. But this can help only to a limited degree: even with batching the protocol has little opportunity for true parallelism.

Our remarks may come as a surprise to readers familiar with SMR and Paxos, because many published presentations of the model and protocols omit any discussion of the complexities introduced by reconfiguration. These remarks are not entirely new, and summarize several recent works which allude to these difficulties: The causality-violating scenario has been pointed out in Junqueira et al. (2009), and Paxos reconfiguration idiosyncracies were discussed in Lamport et al. (2009a, 2009b).

22.7.2 Virtually Synchronous SMR

We now give a full solution to the dynamic SMR problem which avoids the above undesired behavior. As for the multicast service, we flesh out two approaches, a fault-recovery solution and a fault-masking one. The latter we also call "Virtually Synchronous Paxos" because of its resemblance to the Paxos protocol.

We model an SMR service as providing clients with a **Submit**(op) API to atomically perform op on a shared object obj. Below, we denote by obj^k the object state after k operations. For durability, we store obj at a group of servers: $F + 1$ in the fault-recovery approach, and $2F + 1$ for fault-masking. We denote by obj_q the copy stored by server q. As usual, we provide a **Reconfig** API in order to reconfigure the service.

It is worth noting that our model is slightly different from the standard SMR model, in which there is a distributed engine for forming total order on commands and a separate one for execution. In most deployments, the same set of servers is used for both roles, and this simplifies our exposition.

Fault-Recovery Virtually Synchronous SMR

We begin with a fault-recovery approach, which utilizes only $F + 1$ state machine servers for F-tolerance. As usual, this means that an auxiliary configuration engine is responsible for forming a consensus decision on the next configuration. This captures the classical primary-backup approach for replication, and extends it with a precise treatment of reconfiguration. Figure 22.8 describes the problem definition and gives a full solution in pseudo-code. We give one reconfiguration procedure for all cases, though specific scenarios may be further optimized, e.g., single backup failure, deploying a new secondary without failures, etc. Our formulation follows precisely the *Vertical Paxos* protocol (Lamport et al. 2009b), and we repeat it here for completeness.

The steady-state solution designates one server as *primary*. The primary obtains command requests from clients. For each request, it picks the next unused index k in the sequence of commands and requests the servers to accept the new command as the k'th. (If computing an operation is a heavy burden, the primary may opt to precompute the next state obj^k and send it to servers for efficiency, instead of sending the operation itself. This trick may also be used in case non-deterministic operations are to be supported.) A command is completed when the client received a (deterministic) response from all servers.

We put our DSR methodology to action in order to reconfigure state machines by having a reconfiguration decision that stops the sequence of state machine commands. The reconfiguration procedure first wedges (at least) one server. Here, the

---

API:

> **Submit**(*op*): execute *op* atomically on object and return result $r = apply(op, obj)$
> **Reconfig**(*M*): return(ACK)

Liveness condition:

> throughout the *lifetime* of a membership M, one server is correct and
> there exists a future membership M' in which all servers are correct throughout the *startup*
> of **Reconfig**(*M'*)

Operation **Submit**(*op*) at client:
  send ⟨*op*⟩ to designated primary
  wait for responses *r* from all servers
  return(*r*)
	Upon ⟨*op*⟩ request at primary:
	  send ⟨**submit**, *k*, *op*⟩ to servers
	  increment *k*
	    possibly optimize:
	      $r^k \leftarrow apply(op, obj^{k-1})$
	      send ⟨**submit**, *k*, *obj^k*, r^k⟩

	Upon ⟨**submit**, *k*, *op*⟩ request at server and
	not wedged:
	  let $r^k \leftarrow apply(op, obj^{k-1})$
	  store *k*, *obj^k*
	  send r^k to client

Operation **Reconfig**(*M*):
  Send ⟨**wedge**⟩ request to servers
  Wait for reply ⟨**suspended**, k_q, obj_q⟩$_q$
    from any server *q*
  Invoke consensus engine
    $decide(M, k_q, obj_q)$
  When all servers of new epoch have
      started
    return(ACK)
	Upon ⟨**wedge**⟩ request at server *q*:
	  stop serving **submit** commands
	  return ⟨**suspended**, k_q, obj_q⟩
	
	At any server in M'
	  Upon learning $(M', k_q, obj_q) \leftarrow decide()$:
	    initialize local *k*, *obj* from k_q, obj_q and
	    start service

Fig. 22.7 Fault-recovery virtually synchronous SMR with $F + 1$ servers (vertical Paxos)

server's protocol is to respond to client's **wedge** messages with the latest object state and its index obj_q, k_q. The initiating client then lets the consensus engine form a decision on the next configuration. Crucially, the consensus decision contains the new configuration as well as the closing state of the current configuration. The decision value determines the configuration used in the next SMR instance and its initial object state. This decision effectively completes operations up to the k'th (and as usual, results of uncompleted operations are returned to their clients).

Once a decision is formed on both the new configuration and on its closing state, we can start the new state machine. However, in order for the new configuration to uphold linearizability (Herlihy and Wing 1990), the sequence of commands in the new configuration must follow those of the current configuration. We achieve this by initializing the servers of the new configuration with the closing state of the object from the current configuration. Any server in the new membership M' that learns the decision (M', k_q, obj_q) can start the new configuration by (i) initializing its local state to k_q, obj_q and becoming enabled for normal command processing. Our liveness condition guarantees that the transfer can complete before reconfiguration is done to at least one server in the next configuration, and that some future configuration can become completely enabled. Accordingly, only upon receiving acknowledgement from all servers of that configuration, the **Reconfig** response event occurs.

Fault-Masking Virtually Synchronous SMR

We continue in Fig. 22.8 with a fault-masking virtually synchronous SMR solution, which we call *Virtually Synchronous Paxos*. Although we could use the Paxos Synod protocol even in steady-state mode, we present a simpler version that uses a fixed primary. When the primary fails, we simply reconfigure to facilitate progress. Reconfiguring upon primary replacement in this manner alleviates the anomalous behavior related with primary transition in Paxos pointed above in Fig. 22.6. Leader election of our Virtually Synchronous Paxos within a fixed configuration is similar to the leader change protocol of ZooKeeper (Junqueira and Reed 2009; Junqueira et al. 2009).

Steady state operation is done as follows. The primary obtains command requests from clients. For each request, it picks the next unused index k in the sequence of commands and requests the servers to accept the new command as the k'th. (The same optimization of pre-computing the resulting state is possible in case computing is expensive or non-deterministic, but not shown in the code.) A command is completed when the client received a (deterministic) response from majority of servers.

Recall that when reconfiguration is desired, we need to form agreement both on the next configuration and on the closing state of the current configuration. A client that wishes to reconfigure chooses a unique stake and performs the following two phases.

Phase 1: The client performs one exchange with a majority of servers. When it hears back from servers, it learns the latest computed state of the object obj^k known to servers. This reflects a prefix of the commands sequence proposed by the primary, whose tail may not have been completed yet. It also learns with respect to the configuration-changing decision either: (1) A reconfiguration command RC that might have been chosen, or (2) that no command was chosen. In this exchange, the client also obtains a commitment from the servers to ignore future messages from any lower stake client.

Phase 2: The client performs another single exchange with a majority of servers. If case (1) applies, then it tells servers to choose RC. Otherwise, in case (2), it proposes a new RC which contains the new membership and the closing state (k, obj^k). In either case, a client may propose only one reconfiguration for a particular stake.

The server's protocol is to respond to client's messages, unless it was instructed by a higher-stake client to ignore this client: In phase 1, server q responds with the latest object state obj_q; and with the value of a reconfiguration proposal RC of the highest-ranking client it knows of, or empty if none. In phase 2, it stores a client's

---

API:
Submit(op): execute op atomically on object and return result $r = apply(op, obj)$
Reconfig(M): return(ACK)

Liveness condition:
throughout the lifetime of a membership M, a majority of servers are correct

---

Operation **Submit**(op) at client:
   send $\langle op \rangle$ to designated primary
   wait for responses r from a majority of servers
   return(r)

Upon $\langle op \rangle$ request at primary:
   send $\langle$submit$, k, op \rangle$ to servers
   increment k

Upon $\langle$submit$, k, op \rangle$ request at server and not wedged:
   let $r^k \leftarrow apply(op, obj^{k-1})$
   store k, obj^k
   send r^k to client

Operation **Reconfig**(M):
   choose unique *stake*
   send $\langle$wedge$, stake \rangle$ request to servers
   wait for replies
   $\langle$wedged$, (st, RC), k_q, obj_{j_q} \rangle$
    from each server q in a majority
   if any (st, RC) is non-empty
    choose RC of highest (st, RC)
     pair;
   else
    let $RC \leftarrow (M, k_q, obj_{j_q})$ of highest
     k_q
   send $\langle$accept$, stake, RC \rangle$

   when a majority of servers in RC
    have started
    return(ACK)

Upon $\langle$wedge$, st \rangle$ request at server q:
   stop serving **submit** commands
   unless accessed by higher-stake leader already
   return $\langle$wedged$, st_q, RC_q, k_q, obj_{j_q} \rangle$

Upon $\langle$accept$, st, RC \rangle$ request at server q:
   unless accessed by higher-stake leader already
   store st, RC
   send $\langle$start$, st, RC \rangle$ to servers in RC

At any server in RC
Upon obtaining $\langle$start$, st, RC =$
   $(M, k_q, obj_{j_q}) \rangle$
   from a majority of previous
    epoch
   initialize obj state from RC and start
    service

Fig. 22.8 Fault-masking virtually synchronous SMR with $2F + 1$ servers (Virtually Synchronous Paxos)

proposal and acknowledges it in the form of a **start** message to the servers of the new configuration.

Any server in the new membership that learns the decision RC from a majority of servers in the current configuration (directly or indirectly) can start the new configuration by (i) initializing its local object to $RC.obj$ and becoming enabled for normal command processing. Our liveness condition guarantees that the transfer can complete before reconfiguration is done. Accordingly, only upon receiving acknowledgement from a majority of servers in $RC.M$, the **Reconfig** response event occurs.

22.8   Dynamic Read/Write Storage

In this section, we complement our arsenal of dynamic services with a solution to the dynamic Read/Write storage problem. A Read/Write Storage service provides two API methods, **Read** and **Write**, which execute atomically. This classical problem received much attention in the literature, starting with the seminal fault tolerant solution for static environments by Attiya et al. (1995), and continuing with several recent storage systems for dynamic settings (Lynch and Shvartsman 2002; Gilbert et al. 2003; Chockler et al. 2005; Aguilera et al. 2009a, 2009b; Shraer et al. 2010). The full problem description and pseudo-code solution are given in Fig. 22.9 below. The solution resembles the RDS protocol of Chockler et al. (2005), but differs in that it maintains the virtual synchrony property and uses fewer phases. Although the solution approach is very similar to the Reliable Multicast one, we discuss it here for completeness. However, we only describe one flavor, a fault-masking protocol; the reader can complete the other variants based on the Multicast example. The fault-masking solution employs $2F + 1$ servers, each of which stores a copy of a shared object obj along with a logical update timestamp t. We denote by obj_q, t_q, the local copies stored at server q.

22.9   DSR in Perspective

Although our development portrays reconfiguration as a relatively linear task that entails making a series of seemingly straightforward decisions, there exist many incorrect or inefficient reconfiguration solutions in the published literature. In this section, we discuss the reasoning that can lead to complexity in dynamic membership protocols, and because of that complexity, expose the solution to potential bugs. As a first step it may be helpful to express our solution as a high-level recipe. Abstractly, the DSR epoch-by-epoch reconfiguration strategy entails the steps listed below. We have numbered the steps as either A.n or B.n to indicate that steps A/B may intermix in any order: in effect, the protocol consists of two threads, A and B, that execute concurrently (below, step A.2/B.4 occurs after the two join).

A.1   In the current configuration, form a **consensus** decision on the next configuration.

B.1   Suspend the current configuration from serving new requests (in progress requests may continue to completion, or die).

B.2   Take a snapshot of the current configuration's closing state. A legitimate (non-unique) snapshot must contain all operations *ever to complete*.

B.3   Form **consensus** on a legitimate closing state. In fault-recovery solutions, this agreement must be carried by the configuration manger, or in the next configuration (after the configuration manager has designated one). In a fault-masking solution, it may be carried by either the current configuration or the next one, but we must a-priori designate which one has the responsibility.

A.2/B.4   Enable servers in the next configuration initialized with the consensus snapshot state formed in step B.3.

API:
  Write(v): execute write(v) atomically on *obj* and return(ACK)
  Read(): execute read() atomically on *obj* and return(u)
  Reconfig(M): return(ACK)

Liveness condition:
  throughout the lifetime of a membership M, a majority of servers are correct

---

Operation **Write**(v) at client:
  send($\langle$**writequery**$\rangle$) to servers
  wait for replies $\langle t_q \rangle$ from a majority of
    servers q
  choose t greater than all t_q
  send($\langle$**store**, $v, t\rangle$) to servers
  wait for replies from a majority of
    servers
  return(ACK)
Operation **Read**() at client:
  send($\langle$**collect**$\rangle$) to servers
  wait for replies $\langle v_q, t_q \rangle$ from a majority
    of servers q
  let $\langle v, t \rangle$ be the pair of highest
    timestamp
  send($\langle$**store**, $v, t\rangle$) to servers
  wait for replies from a majority of
    servers
  return(v)

Upon $\langle$**writequery**$\rangle$ request at server q and not
    wedged:
  return $\langle t_q \rangle$

Upon $\langle$**store**, $v', t'\rangle$ request at server q and
    not wedged:
  if $t' > t_q$ save v', t' to obj_q, t_q
  return ACK

Upon $\langle$**collect**$\rangle$ request at server q and not
    wedged:
  return $\langle obj_q, t_q \rangle$

Operation **Reconfig**(M):
  Choose unique *stake*
  Send($\langle$**wedge**, *stake*$\rangle$) request to servers
  Wait for replies
    $\langle$**suspended**, *stake*, $\langle st, RC\rangle, obj_q, t_q\rangle_q$
    from a majority of servers q
  if any (st, RC) is non-empty
    choose RC of highest (st, RC)
      pair;
  else
    let $RC \leftarrow (M, obj_q, t_q)$ of highest
      t_q
  Send($\langle$**accept**, *stake*, $RC\rangle$)
  When a majority of servers in RC have
    started
    return(ACK)

Upon $\langle$**wedge**, *st*$\rangle$ request at server q:
  stop serving **store/collect/writequery**
    commands
  unless accessed by higher-stake leader
    already
  return $\langle$**suspended**, *st*, $\langle$*highst*,
    highRC$\rangle, obj_q, t_q\rangle$

Upon $\langle$**accept**, *st*, $RC\rangle$ request at server q:
  unless accessed by higher-stake leader
    already
  store *highst* $\leftarrow st$, *highRC* $\leftarrow RC$
  send $\langle$**start**, *st*, $RC\rangle$ to servers in RC

At any server in RC
  Upon obtaining $\langle$**start**, *st*, $RC =$
    $(M, obj_q, t_q)\rangle$
      from a majority of previous
        epoch
  store v, t, locally and start service

Fig. 22.9 Majority-based atomic read/write storage with $2F + 1$ servers: full solution

With this in mind, we pause to highlight some of the more common pitfalls that have traditionally led researchers (including the authors of the current chapter to propose less than ideal solutions.

22.9.1 Speculative-Views

One design decision that we recommend against arises when a service is optimized for high availability by adding a mechanism that will copy state and enable activity in a new epoch that has been proposed, but not finalized, for example during intermediate steps of the agreement protocol. Much prior work in the group communication literature falls in this category (Birman 1985; Amir et al. 1992b, 1995; van Renesse et al. 1996, 1998; Babaoglu et al. 1995); a significant body of PhD dissertations and published papers on *transient/ambiguous configurations*, *extended/weak virtual synchrony*, and others, were devoted to this strategy (Amir 1995; Friedman 1994; Keidar 1998; Montresor 2000). Many other works in the group-communication area are covered in the survey by Chockler et al. (2001).

The group communication approach essentially performs the task of steps A.1 and B.1–B.3 *inside a speculative next configuration*, in an attempt to optimize and transfer-state while forming agreement on it. This works roughly as follows.

A.1   In the current configuration, form a **proposal** on the next configuration.

A.2(B.1) Suspend those members of the next configuration which persist from the current one from serving new requests.

A.3(B.2-3) Among the members of the proposed next configuration, form agreement on both the transition itself, and on a legitimate snapshot of the current configuration's closing state. The snapshot decision incorporates input from those members which persist from the current configuration and from previously attempted *proposed* configurations.

A.4   If the next configuration fails to reach consensus, go back to step A.1.

A.5(B.4) Enable servers in the next configuration (their state is already initialized with the consensus snapshot state formed in step A.3).

While the resulting solutions can certainly be implemented and proved correct, they require protocol steps in which the members of a new epoch collect information from every view in which operations might have been performed, so that the view that will ultimately be used has full knowledge of the service state. Such solutions can embody substantial complexity, and this of course means that implementations will often be quite hard to debug.

As an example scenario, let us revisit the scenario explored above, with an initial membership $\{1, 2, 3\}$. During reconfiguration, a client could propose a new epoch configuration consisting of server-set $\{2, 3, 4\}$. A typical complication here was for servers $\{2, 3, 4\}$ to form a "transient" configuration without waiting for a majority of the previous epoch to acknowledge it. They perform a state transfer and start serving client requests immediately. Thus, servers $\{3, 4\}$ might respond to a **Get()** request with a message-set containing $\{b, c\}$. In the end, we may form consensus on a different configuration, say $\{1, 2, 5\}$. If we only collect information from a majority of the previous epoch, say $\{1, 2\}$, we might "forget" message c. Note that we intentionally chose a new server-set that intersects with a majority of the members of the previous epoch. We did so to illustrate that there are situations in which a set large enough to reach agreement could nonetheless not suffice if a system needs to discover every durable message.

We therefore need to collect information from the transient configuration, so as not to lose message c. This is not only complex, but there is no guarantee that we will find traces of the transient epoch, unless we enforce additional constraints, the dynamic-quorum rule, as we now show.

22.9.2 Dynamic-Quorums and Cascading Changes

The above scenario leads us to another common pitfall. In essence, it requires that cascading epoch changes jointly have a non-empty intersection. This guarantees that speculative epochs all intersect and become aware of one another. In the example above, server 2 is in the intersection of all attempted changes, and so we rely on information collected from it to discover the transient epoch, and collect information from its majority as well. More generally, a line of related works emanating from those with speculative configurations was devoted to the issue of handling "cascading reconfigurations", and to quorum intersection rules that guarantee to maintain a unique primary quorum through such cascading changes, e.g., Birman (1985), Ricciardi and Birman (1991), Yeger-Lotem et al. (1997). This constraint is unnecessary.

In our method, consensus is reached by a majority in the current epoch; the next epoch need not share any servers with the previous one. More generally, our epoch-by-epoch approach emphasizes that one only needs to deal with one epoch at a time, and that cascading or chained epochs just are not necessary (nor do they have any performance or code complexity benefit; indeed, quite the opposite). The correct algorithmic foundation we establish terminates an epoch with a configuration-changing decision. It does not matter if we have a centralized configuration manager, or run a distributed consensus protocol; both are part of the current epoch, and it is well defined who determines the next configuration. The next epoch is uniquely determined in the current epoch, and transition to it is irreversible. When an epoch ends, a new epoch starts a new incarnation of the same algorithm (albeit with a non-empty initial service state), whose participants and messages do not mix with the current epoch. The new epoch may itself decide to reconfigure, and we iterate through epoch changes again. Any number of reconfigurations can be chained in this manner, with no difficulty at all.

In the example above, either we decide to transition to $\{2, 3, 4\}$ or not. If a decision is made, it is irreversible. A future decision to switch to $\{1, 2, 5\}$ must be taken by the new epoch, after it is enabled. It is achieved with the normal decision and state transfer mechanism. Conversely, if there is no decision on $\{2, 3, 4\}$, then no client operation executes in that epoch. Later, when a different decision is reached the new epoch starts with servers $\{1, 2, 5\}$.

22.9.3 Off-line Versus On-line Reconfiguration

We need to comment briefly on our decision to use an off-line reconfiguration strategy. A recent line of works, pioneered by the RAMBO project (Lynch and Shvartsman 2002) and continued in Rambo II (Gilbert et al. 2003), RDS (Chockler et al. 2005), DynaStore (Aguilera et al. 2009a) and DynaDisk (Shraer et al. 2010), emphasize the importance of non-blocking reconfiguration. These systems tackle dynamic **Read/Write** storage services, but the same design issues occur in Reliable Multicast and other, similar services.

In the "RAMBO" approach, the solution is further optimized by mechanisms that prevent a client from ever encountering a suspended service. This *on-line* transition comes, however, at the cost of greater system complexity. RAMBO clients continue accessing the **Read/Write** objects by interacting both with the current and the next epoch. Every **Read** operation copies the object it accesses from one epoch to the next. Every **Write** operation also accesses a majority in the previous epoch, but no copying of data is necessary. Even if clients access objects which have already been copied to the new epoch (which would be the common case for "hot objects"), they still need to access majorities in *all* active configurations. The advantage is that RAMBO never blocks any client request, even momentarily, but the disadvantage is the complication of sorting through responses from two epochs and figuring out which one is more current.

Even more importantly, the on-line reconfiguration approach prevents a client from ever "sealing" partially completed operations which were initiated in the current epoch. Traces of those may transfer to later epochs, and become durable arbitrarily far in the future. Such behavior may not be desirable for applications engineered with a Reliable Multicast (or Read/Write) infrastructure, as we saw earlier in our discussion of Virtual Synchrony (Sect. 22.6).

By comparison, the advantage of off-line reconfiguration is simplicity: clients only deal with a single system view at a time. We therefore see the off-line reconfiguration strategy above as occupying an attractive sweet-spot, despite the need to briefly block the service while switching from the old to the new configuration. On the other hand, off-line reconfiguration comes with its own form of complexity: the need to think hard about state transfer. If the service state might become large (for example, if the server is an entire file system or database) state transfer may entail moving a huge amount of data from the old to the new servers. Blocking the service while this occurs can be prohibitive, and even doing it rapidly may degrade the responsiveness of a service to an unacceptable degree. Thus our suggestion that state be transferred in advance of the reconfiguration, as much as possible, is important and may be key to using this approach in settings where service unavailability must be minimized.

By pre-transferring server state, the amount of state actually moved in the last steps of the procedure can be minimized and clients prevented from seeing much of a disruption. Moreover, the actual mechanism needed for this sort of anticipatory state transfer is fairly simple; the new server needs to fetch and load the state, and also needs some way to compute the delta between the loaded state and the initial state assigned to it in the new epoch, which will reflect operations that completed after it fetched that preloaded state and before the consensus decision was made.

22.9.4 Paxos Anomaly

The anomalous behavior we encountered when discussing Paxos reconfiguration illustrated a different kind of problem. Recall that vanilla Paxos is quite simple but runs in a fixed configuration. In contrast, reconfigurable Paxos introduced not just a leader-changing procedure, but also a set of secondary issues that represent side-effects of the way in which reconfiguration is supported. Although the per-command leader transition in Paxos entails a virtually synchronous reconfiguration, the actions of a new leader are made independently for each command. In this way, leader W in our example above could not know that leader V's proposal to command $k + 1$ implies that no command was committed by its predecessor, leader U, at command k.

Reconfigurable Paxos with $\alpha > 1$ indeed forms an orderly succession of configurations, but suffers from the same leader-change anomaly above within the window of α commands.

22.10 Correctness

Our goal in this section is to give a flavor of the correctness argument regarding our DSR epoch-by-epoch reconfiguration methodology. We view a formal specification and correctness proofs as being outside the scope of this chapter. In this section, we provide sketch arguments on two sample solutions, the fault-recovery Reliable Multicast solution (Fig. 22.3) and the fault-masking Reliable Multicast solution (Fig. 22.5). The proof arguments for our other protocols, for SMR and for Read/Write storage, are similar in their core arguments concerning reconfiguration. They differ mostly in details regarding the specific problem models, namely, consensus and atomic Read/Write storage, which are well studied in the literature.

22.10.1 Correctness of Fault-Recovery Reliable Multicast Solution

In this section, we show that our fault-recovery protocol of Fig. 22.3 maintains *Multicast Durability* (see Definition 22.3) and *Virtual Synchrony* (see Definition 22.6). Our proof shows that these conditions hold from one configuration to the next; proving that it holds for a sequence of reconfigurations follows by induction.

Refer to a current, initial configuration as C_0 and a new configuration as C_1. Recall that a message is durable if it belongs to a completed **Add**() or **Get**() operation.

Claim 1 *If a message m ever becomes durable by **Add**(m) or **Get**() operations in C_0, and a server q that learns about C_1 transfers to C_1 a set S_0 of messages, then $m \in S_0$.*

Proof This claim is the core of the correctness claim. Although it is simple to prove given our algorithmic foundation, it is crucial to note that the set of messages sent/delivered in C_0 may continue changing after a decision on C_1 was made, and also subsequent to a state transfer. Nevertheless, the precise statement of this claim is in fact *stable*: Any message m which is **ever** sent/delivered in C_0 is included in S_0. We now prove it.

Since m is in a **Add**(m) or **Get**() which completes in C_0, every process in C_0 performs the $\langle$**store**, $m\rangle$ request and acknowledges it. Since wedged servers do not respond to **store** requests, q has responded to the **store** request before it became wedged for state transfer. Therefore, at step 2 of the state transfer, q already stores m, and includes it in the set S_0 which it transfers to C_1.   □

Claim 2 *If a message m becomes durable by* **Add**(m) *or* **Get**() *operations in C_0 and a subsequent* **Get**() *command completes at some process p, then p's response contains m.*

Proof A **Get**() request which is subsequent to the completion of the **Add**(**Get**) command containing m may either occur in C_0 or in C_1. In C_0, every process already acknowledged $\langle$**store**, $m\rangle$. Hence, every server contacted by the requesting client will include m in the delivery response. In C_1, by Claim 1 above, every server also stores m by the time state transfer has completed. Therefore, **Get**() in C_1 also includes m.   □

Claim 3 *If a message m becomes durable by* **Add**(m) *or* **Get**() *operations in C_1 and a subsequent* **Get**() *command completes at some process p, then p's delivery response contains m.*

Proof We first note that a **Get**() request that arrives at C_0 after m was sent/delivered in C_1 is not served by any server that participated in reconfiguration, because they are wedged; hence, the deliver request does not complete in C_0, and is deferred to C_1. In C_1, every process stores already acknowledged $\langle$**store**, $m\rangle$. Hence, every server contacted by the requesting client will include m in the delivery response. □

Claim 4 *The fault-recovery protocol maintains Multicast Durability (Definition 22.3); that is, if a message m becomes durable by* **Add**(m) *or* **Get**() *operations, and a subsequent* **Get**() *command completes at some process p, then p's delivery response contains m.*

Proof By Claims 2 and 3, after m is completely sent/delivered, a subsequent **Get**() request invoked at any process p includes m in the delivery response.   □

Claim 5 *The fault-recovery protocol maintains Multicast Virtual Synchrony (Definition 22.6); that is, If* **Add**(m) *was invoked in configuration C_k, then if ever* **Get**() *returns m, then for all configurations C_ℓ, where $\ell > k$,* **Get**() *returns m.*

Proof By Claim 1, if **Get**() ever returns m in C_0, then m is included in the set S_0 of messages transferred to C_1. Hence, any **Get**() request in C_1 will return m.

Otherwise, suppose that no **Get**() in C_0 returns m, but there exists a **Get**() call in C_1 which returns m. Since m was sent to C_0, there exists a server q in C_1 which obtained m in a state transfer. But since state transfer passes a message-set determined by a consensus decision, every server in C_1 stores m before it becomes enabled for service in C_1. Hence, every **Get**() call in C_1 must return m.

We have shown that the claim holds for C_1. Using C_1 as the initial view, we obtain the result by induction for any subsequent view following C_1. ☐

22.10.2 Correctness of Fault-Masking Reliable Multicast Solution

In this section, we show that our fault-masking protocol of Fig. 22.5 maintains Multicast Durability and Virtual Synchrony. Our proof shows that these conditions hold from one configuration to the next; proving that it holds for a sequence of reconfigurations follows by induction.

Refer to a current, initial configuration as C_0 and a new configuration as C_1. Recall that a message is durable if it belongs to a completed **Add**() or **Get**() operation.

Claim 6 *If a message m ever becomes durable by **Add**(m) or **Get**() operations in C_0, and a client collects **suspended** responses to a* wedge *request from a majority of servers in C_0 into a set S_0 of messages, then $m \in S_0$.*

Proof Since m is in an **Add**(m) or **Get**() which completes in C_0, a majority of servers in C_0 perform the $\langle$store, $m\rangle$ request and acknowledge it. Since wedged servers do not respond to **store** requests, every server in this majority has responded to the **store** request before it became wedged for state transfer. There exists a server q in the intersection of this majority and the majority of servers responding to the client *wedge* request. Therefore, q already stores m when it sends its **suspended** response to the client, and m is included in S_q. Since the client takes a union of the sets S_q contained in all the server responses, $m \in S_0$. ☐

Claim 7 *If a message m ever becomes durable by **Add**(m) or **Get**() operations in C_0, then the set S_0 of the consensus decision on the next configuration contains m, i.e., $m \in S_0$.*

Proof By Claim 6 above, any client which proposes input to the consensus engine regarding reconfiguration includes m in its proposed message-set. Hence, any decision S_0 contains m. ☐

Claim 8 *If a message m becomes durable by **Add**(m) or **Get**() operations in C_0 and a subsequent **Get**() command completes at some process p, then p's response contains m.*

Proof A **Get**() request which is subsequent to the completion of the **Add**(**Get**) command containing m may either occur in C_0 or in C_1.

In C_0, a majority of servers already acknowledged $\langle$store, $m\rangle$. There exists a server q in the intersection of this majority and the majority of servers responding to the client's *collect* request. Therefore, q already stores m when it sends its response to the client's collect request, and m is included in the response S_q. Since the client takes a union of the sets S_q contained in all the server responses, m is returned in the return-set of the **Get**() call.

In C_1, by Claim 7 above, a majority of servers also stores m by the time state transfer has completed. Therefore, **Get**() in C_1 also includes m by the same argument as in C_0. $\qquad\Box$

Claim 9 *If a message m becomes durable by* **Add**(m) *or* **Get**() *operations in C_1 and a subsequent* **Get**() *command completes at some process p, then p's delivery response contains m.*

Proof We first note that a **Get**() request that arrives at C_0 after m was sent/delivered in C_1 is not served by any server that participated in reconfiguration, because they are wedged; hence, the deliver request does not complete in C_0, and is deferred to C_1. In C_1, a majority of servers already acknowledged $\langle$store, $m\rangle$. Hence, by the same argument as in Claim 7 above, a **Get**() call in C_1 returns m. $\qquad\Box$

Claim 10 *If a message m becomes durable by* **Add**(m) *or* **Get**() *operations, and a subsequent* **Get**() *command completes at some process p, then p's delivery response contains m.*

Proof By Claims 8 and 9, after m is completely sent/delivered, a subsequent **Get**() request invoked at any process p includes m in the delivery response. $\qquad\Box$

Claim 11 *The fault-masking protocol maintains Multicast Virtual Synchrony (Definition 22.6); that is, If* **Add**(m) *was invoked in configuration C_k, then if ever* **Get**() *returns m, then for all configurations C_ℓ, where $\ell > k$,* **Get**() *returns m.*

Proof By Claim 6, if **Get**() ever returns m in C_0, then m is included in the set S_0 of messages transferred to C_1. Hence, any **Get**() request in C_1 will return m.

Otherwise, suppose that no **Get**() in C_0 returns m, but there exists a **Get**() call in C_1 which returns m. Since m was sent to C_0, there exists a server q in C_1 which obtained m in a state transfer. But since state transfer passes a message-set determined by a consensus decision, every server in C_1 stores m before it becomes enabled for service in C_1. Hence, every **Get**() call in C_1 must return m.

We have shown that the claim holds for C_1. Using C_1 as the initial view, we obtain the result by induction for any subsequent view following C_1. $\qquad\Box$

22.11 Further Readings

Our primary contribution in this chapter is to offer a unifying framework for the problem of dynamic service reconfiguration. We are not aware of any prior work on this question. Closest was the survey of Chockler et al. (2001), which offers a very interesting review of group communication systems in a single model. However, the main objective in that work was to contrast the guarantees offered by each category of solution and to categorize the weakest progress (liveness) assumptions made in each. In particular, the model used did not formalize the reconfiguration topic as a separate mechanism, and hence does not get at the kinds of fine-grained choice, and their consequences, explored here.

Our epoch-by-epoch approach draws heavily on prior work on group communication. As mentioned, a good survey of group communication specifications appears in Chockler et al. (2001). The approach resembles virtual synchrony (Birman 1985; Birman and Joseph 1987a), but unlike our approach these early papers on Virtual Synchrony did not provide linearizability. The approach also resembles Reconfigurable Paxos (as worked out in SMART (Lorch et al. 2006)), but as pointed out in Sect. 22.7 this approach allows anomalous behavior. Approaches like Boxwood (MacCormick et al. 2004) and Chain Replication (van Renesse and Schneider 2004) allow reconfiguration with the help of an external configuration service.

There has also been considerable work on reconfigurable read/write stores, such as RAMBO (Lynch and Shvartsman 2002) Dynamic Byzantine Storage (Martin and Alvisi 2004), and DynaStore (Aguilera et al. 2009a). Our approach allows more general operations. Our liveness model is entirely based on that of DynaStore, however.

This review of prior work could cite a huge number of papers on specific multicast protocols, message-queuing middleware products, publish-subscribe products, enterprise service buses and related technologies. However, we concluded that to do so would be tangential and perhaps even confusing to the reader. First, only some of these prior technologies offered durability, and among the ones that did (such as message-queuing middleware), some accomplished that goal using non-reconfigurable databases or logging servers. Thus, while the area is rich in prior work, the prior work on durability across reconfigurations is much scantier, and we believe the key works on that specific topic are precisely the ones we looked at closely in the body of this chapter.

Appendix B: Isis² API

23

Readers of this text will have learned a great deal about Cornell's Isis² platform, available for download from Cornell (under freeBSD licensing) from the web site http://www.cs.cornell.edu/ken/isis2.

Isis² is just one of many possible tools to which a practitioner in this area might turn; we created it at Cornell as a research vehicle to explore scalable consistency in cloud settings, and are not in any way suggesting that it would be a superior choice to other options (notably commercially supported solutions such as JGroups, Spread, C-Ensemble) for those creating real products.

It is important to appreciate that Isis² is not a product and is better understood as a research prototype developed almost entirely by the author of this text, Ken Birman, with help from some of his students. Neither Springer Verlag, the publisher of this text, and Cornell University, as Professor Birman's primary employer, participated in the development of Isis², and neither has any active role in distributing or supporting the system. Neither company endorses its use, vouches for its correctness, or recommends it for any particular project. The views and expressions contained within this text are those of the author, not of Springer Verlag or Cornell.

Users who decide to download and work with Isis² should understand themselves to be working with an experimental research prototype. No guarantees of support are available, and it is very likely that the system includes a large number of bugs and deficiencies, and has many kinds of problem that might represent serious issues in commercial settings that have genuine high assurance needs and where there might be liability implications in the event of failure. For these reasons, *it is not appropriate to use this free version of Isis² in production settings*. Only a system that underwent a professional quality-assurance and testing process and that has a professional support organization behind it should ever be placed into high-assurance settings. This public, open source version of Isis² does not rise to the necessary standard at the present time.

On the other hand, we do believe the system is a very good platform for creating research prototypes of distributed system, and we hope to do so ourselves at Cornell and to continue to enhance and improve the platform itself over an extended period. To this end, Professor Birman is providing best-effort support for the system and

K.P. Birman, *Guide to Reliable Distributed Systems*, Texts in Computer Science,   673
DOI 10.1007/978-1-4471-2416-0_23, © Springer-Verlag London Limited 2012

hopes to do so in an ongoing basis well into the future. Moreover, as an open source system, it is hoped that a community of users capable of supporting one-another will emerge over time. Details of how to access the support forum are available on the download web site.

In this appendix we provide a very abbreviated summary of the Isis^2 API. A full discussion of the platform and its use model can be found in the user manual on the download web site, which also will have a growing collection of demonstration solutions to simple problems over time. The hope is that eventually, most potential users will find a prebuild demonstration solution that matches their needs fairly closely. Readers of this textbook who create high quality Isis^2 applications and wish to share them should contact the author about contributing to the public repository, ideally using the same freeBSD licensing employed for the main system.

For this Appendix we focus on the use of the system from within the C# programming language, which evolved from the Java language under the leadership of researchers and developers at Microsoft Corporation. C# can be cross-compiled using Mono to run on Linux platforms, and because Isis^2 is a library, it can be used from any of the 40 or so programming languages supported by .NET, including C, C++, Visual Basic, Python, OĆaML, Fortan, Basic, etc. Users who are working on Linux platforms in languages like C or C++ may, however, find it awkward to link directly to Isis^2 because the system operates in a managed framework, relying upon .NET garbage collection. Thus in a language such as C, where memory is not managed automatically, we run into the issue that when an object is passed to a managed language, the managed library has no standard way to indicate the number of active references it might have maintained to that object, and similarly when a message is delivered by Isis^2 (by upcall), if the receiving system is unmanaged, it may be impossible to avoid making a copy of the data. Otherwise, after the upcall returns, .NET might garbage collect the incoming message without warning.

Thus, to use Isis^2 directly, one should either work in one of the managed .NET languages, or consider building some form of interposition layer that accepts RPC or web services requests, calls Isis^2, then passes back the results. In this way a program external to the managed framework can access the Isis^2 services without needing to worry about memory management conflicts of these kinds.

There are two main ways to build Isis^2 applications. Stand-alone applications would be launched with command-line arguments on one or more machines and form groups that cooperate to do whatever the command request (the command, that is, being designed by the developer as part of the application). Such groups might also have some members maintain console or GUI APIs that let the end user interact with the group, or could even be linked to the powerful *Live Distributed Objects* framework, also available from Cornell, which makes it easy to create live graphical applications such as multiuser games that employ Isis^2 groups for communication and state sharing.

The second main option is to build a web service, for example in Azure, and then have a helper application associated with the server instances, using Isis^2 within the helper program. We have experimented with this option mostly on Azure but it also works on Amazon's EC2 and other major cloud platforms. For such uses, the system may need to be configured to run over TCP, since Azure and EC2 both disallow UDP and IP multicast communication. The user's manual includes an example that shows exactly how to do this.

23.1 Basic Data Types

Isis^2 has the following basic data types:
1. *Address*. Represents an endpoint address, be that a process or a group.
2. *Group*. A handle on an object used by the platform to maintain the state of a group.
3. *View*. An object that reports on the membership of a group, listing a unique counter (the view-id), the members, and indicating which members joined or left the group since the previous view.
4. *Msg*. Mostly used internally in the Isis^2 platform, the Msg object encapsulates a message containing strongly typed objects. Users would more often deal with messages indirectly, by invoking the Isis^2 multicast or point-to-point send APIs, and then by receiving upcalls to handlers that have a matching type signature.

We should emphasize that there are many additional data types that might be visible to more sophisticated users of the platform. Actual use of Isis^2 requires consulting the user manual; this summary is intended just to give a sense of the system, not as substitute for the user's manual.

23.2 Basic System Calls

The Isis^2 system is launched by calling *Isis.Start();*. Using parameters pulled from the runtime environment of the process and documented in the user manual, the platform seeks out other applications that are running Isis^2 using the same rendezvous configuration (a mixture of port numbers and some additional information, such as the name of a rendezvous machine or machines, if IP multicast is not available in support of the protocol that seeks out peers).

Having started the system, the user can set up one or more process groups:
1. *Group g = new Group("name");* Creates a group object (a local endpoint) and specifies a name for the group.
2. *g.SetSecure([key]);* Puts this group into secure mode. An optional AES key can be provided; if none is supplied, a new 256-bit random AES key is used. All data will be encrypted prior to transmission.
3. *g.ViewHandlers += (ViewHandler)method;* Registers a handler that will receive upcalls notifying it when the view of the group changes.
4. *g.Handlers[REQUEST_CODE] += requestHandler;* Registers a request handler; messages that have a matching request code (a small integer) and type signature will be delivered to it.

5. *g.MakeChkpt +=* *(Isis.ChkptMaker)method;* Registers a method that will make a checkpoint or state transfer on behalf of a new member joining the group. It issues zero or more calls to *g.SendChkpt(data);* and then a final call to *g.EndOfChkpt();.* The *data* is any list of typed data objects.

6. *g.LoadChkpt +=* *loadMethod;* Registers a method that can receive a checkpoint that has a matching type signature and will load (initialize) the group using those data.

7. *g.Persistent("file name")* Allow a group to retain its state across invocations. Checkpoint will be stored into the file name. Details on the frequency of check-pointing and on triggering the creation of a new checkpoint can be found in the user manual. On restart after all members have been down, the first member to restart will reload the checkpoint.

8. *g.Join();* Connects this local endpoint to the other group members, if any.

9. *g.Leave();* Leaves the group (use with care: this member will not be allowed to rejoin for a few minutes). A flush is issued, then the leave occurs, and then a final view is delivered in which the member sees itself leaving.

10. *g.Terminate();* Issued by some member, this closes the entire group (use with care: the group cannot be recreated for a few minutes). A flush will occur and then a final view will be delivered to each member. *Caution: If process p issues a Terminate() just as process q is starting a multicast, the outcome is unpredictable.*

Again, these are just a subset of the available options; a more complete list is available in the user's manual. In particular, the system has a number of batch start methods for working with very large groups; these avoid the huge overloads that can occur if thousands of members try to join one by one and are highly recommended in groups of more than about 50 members. Type checking will throw exceptions if an attempt is made to join a group by a process that has configured the group differently than the existing members did.

Having created a group object, attached the needed handlers, and joined the group, the application can initiate multicasts to it:

1. *g.Send(REQUEST_CODE, arg0, arg1, ...);* Sends a new message containing the typed arguments arg0, ... argn to the group. In this case a virtually synchronous FIFO send is requested. The matching handler will be invoked in all members (including the sender, since the sender itself must be a member).

2. *g.CausalSend(REQUEST_CODE, arg0, arg1, ...);* Sends a virtually synchronous and causally ordered multicast to the group.

3. *g.OrderedSend(REQUEST_CODE, arg0, arg1, ...);* Sends a virtually synchronous and totally ordered multicast to the group.

4. *g.Flush();* Terminates any unstable (still active) multicasts that have been sent or received in the group prior to when *Flush* was invoked. Normally, used after a burst of amnesia-free but weakly durable *Send*, *CausalSend* or *OrderedSend* operations before sending data to a client external to the group.

5. *g.SafeSend(REQUEST_CODE, arg0, arg1, ...);* Sends a Paxos-style "safe" (strongly durable, totally ordered) multicast to the group. The user should also configure the group by setting the number of acceptors using *g.SetSafeSend-*

Threshold(phi); and, if desired, configure the group to use the *g.setDurability-Method(DiskLogger);* durability method (by default, memory logging is employed; this may not suffice for some uses, as we saw in Chap. 14).

Type checking will throw exceptions if an attempt is made to multicast to a group using a type signature that does not match some existing type signature for a handler within the group.

Point to point communication is also possible:

1. *g.P2PSend(member, REQUEST_CODE, arg0, arg1, ...);* Sends a new message containing the typed arguments arg0, ... argn to the designated group member (obtained from the view).

To query a group, a member that receives a request (e.g. from a human user of a GUI, or from an incoming web services request) can just read the local state, compute a response, and send it. But if desired, a group member can share a request out for parallel execution using the following methods:

1. *nr = g.Query(ALL, REQUEST_CODE, arg0, arg1, ..., EOL, res0, res1, ...);* Sends a new message containing the typed arguments arg0, ... argn to the group, but now the recipient is expected to send a typed *g.Reply(res0, res1, ...);* The results are unpacked into the lists *resp0, resp1, ...* The matching handler will be invoked in all members (including the sender, since the sender itself must be a member), the replies collected, and then the total number of replies is returned to the caller, which can iterate over the response lists.

2. *nr = g.CausalQuery(ALL, REQUEST_CODE, arg0, arg1, ..., EOL, res0, res1, ...);* Same, but sends the query with *CausalSend.*

3. *nr = g.OrderedQuery(ALL, REQUEST_CODE, arg0, arg1, ..., EOL, res0, res1, ...);* Same, but sends the query with *OrderedSend.*

4. *nr = g.SafeQuery(ALL, REQUEST_CODE, arg0, arg1, ..., EOL, res0, res1, ...);* Same, but sends the query with *SafeSend.*

Again, there is also a point to point option:

1. *g.P2PQuery(member, REQUEST_CODE, arg0, arg1, ..., EOL, res0, res1, ...);* Sends a new message containing the typed arguments arg0, ... argn to the designated group member (obtained from the view). Unpacks the response into the result list objects (which obviously will end up with just zero or one replies each: zero if the destination crashed, one if not).

Notice the code ALL in the multicast queries: this signifies that all current group members, in the view to which the message was delivered, will reply to the request. You can also wait for just 1 reply, or any constant number of members. One warning here: the query may not occur in the same group view in which it was issued, since membership can change at any time. Thus a group might have five members when a Query is sent, and yet seven by the time delivery occurs.

Not all systems use quorum methods, but if you do want to implement such a method, how would majority operations be coded correctly? The simple and correct solution is to just have the receivers determine how which, and how many, should reply. At the time a query is delivered, the members will have identical views. Thus on receipt of a given request every member can check *g.GetNMembers()* and learn their individual rank using *g.GetMyRank()* (or these can be obtained during a new view upcall and cached). The seven members can thus compute that a read quorum should have, perhaps, three members, that a write quorum should have four members, and then on that basis can implement some sort of rule for which members will play each role. Had the sender tried to guess in advance, it might have believed that a read quorum would be two and a write quorum, three members. This, of course, would have resulted in errors.

There are actually three ways to send a reply:

1. *Reply(res0, res1, ...);* Send a reply to the current query.
2. *AbortReply("reason");* Abort this query. *IsisAbortReply* exception will be thrown in the caller, giving the reason.
3. *NullReply();* Indicates that this caller will not be replying to this query. Useful in the sort of quorum settings mentioned above (otherwise, if one of the selected respondents crashes the request will time out; with a NullReply(), the system knows which members are participating and will not wait for the other non-participants to respond). Note that an actual message is sent from the member to the query source; it will be small, but it does need to be transmitted.

A non-member of a group can also register as a client of the group *g* = *Client("name");*, in which case some existing member will be selected (automatically) and designated as a proxy for the non-member. The non-member can then send P2P messages (via *g.P2PSend*) or queries (via *g.P2PQuery*), but not multicasts. If the proxy fails or leaves, the *Client* layer will automatically select some other proxy.

23.3   Timeouts

The query calls all have a default timer associated with them, running in the background, and will time out and give up on a member if it does not respond in a timely manner. The default can be overridden by specifying a *new Isis.Timeout(milliseconds, action)* timeout object after the request code giving the delay before a timeout should go off, and the action desired (ignore this reply, which is the default, cause the query to throw an exception, or treat the delayed responder as a faulty process, causing it to be excluded from the system. There are also ways to explicitly tell Isis[2] that some member of some group is faulty.

23.4   Large Groups

We note that for very large groups (more than a hundred or so members), some of these APIs will start to perform poorly because the recipients of a request, in effect, begin to "attack" the sender with bursts of huge numbers of acknowledgments or query replies. (Imagine trying to collect 10,000 20 KB replies that arrive, all at once, at a single UDP socket). For these larger-scaled groups the Isis[2] user should use *g.SetLarge()* to place the group into large-group mode, but will then need to work with a subset of the normal functionality. In large groups, Isis^2 favors an aggregated method for collecting replies, if a query will be processed by all members. Information on this technique appears in the user manual.

23.5 Threads

Isis^2 itself is a highly concurrent system, and each group will typically have 3–5 active threads. When you down call into Isis^2, you should expect that the upcalls triggered by your requests will occur on different threads than on the one that did the downcall. Thus, even if you are not fond of multithreaded coding styles, Isis^2 forces them upon you.

In particular, you should be aware that point to point calls are done on one upcall thread, in sequential (FIFO) order, and that all multicasts and view notifications occur on a second thread. Locking must be used if multiple, concurrently active threads share memory, but notice that you should be able to determine this from the rules we have summarized.

23.6 Debugging

When using a debugger with an Isis^2 application, keep in mind that many calls to your code occur from within the platform. Thus do not be surprised to see fairly deep call stacks listing methods with names that may look like gibberish to you. Those are just our internal method names. Because we make heavy use of a form of inline method declaration supported by C# called delegate() creation (anonymous methods) many of our methods have names assigned by the compiler, and hence that do not print in a very nice format.

If something illegal happens or something goes very wrong, Isis^2 throws exceptions. These have string values that explain what happened. For example, if using a configuration of the platform that has only been tested on 100 nodes at a time, and you try to launch it on 500 nodes, 400 of them will throw an *IsisException("Isis was launched on too many nodes.")*. Such an event will come from inside our library, but it was your mistake that caused the issue, not ours.

When logging is enabled, the Isis^2 will create a log file into which it can print information such as complaints about problems it senses. If you wish to do so, you may call *IsisSystem.WriteLine(something)* to add information to the Isis^2 log for your application. A very useful report, at least for us, is produced by running with logging enabled and calling *IsisSystem.WriteLine(IsisSystem.GetState());*. This will dump all of the internal Isis^2 data structures in a pretty-printed form and can sometimes help us assist you with bugs or other problems.

Our system does depend upon many timers and real-time features. If you use a debugger to pause an Isis^2 application, it will probably throw an exception if you then try and restart execution.

If your application seems to hang, Isis[2] will "poison" it and you will see an exception to this effect. Such events are a very common problem for users just learning to work with the system, especially if they write code that runs very slowly or that sometimes pauses, e.g. to wait for user input. If you prevent progress in the threads that keep Isis[2] alive, your application will surely fail.

Appendix C: Problems

24

This book is intended for use by professionals or advanced students, and the material presented is at a level for which simple problems are not entirely appropriate. Accordingly, most of the problems in this appendix are intended as the basis for essay-style responses or for programming projects, which might build upon the technologies we have treated up to now. Some of these projects are best undertaken as group exercises for a group of three or four students; others could be undertaken by individuals.

A number of platforms are suitable for the types of programming problem presented below. At Cornell University, we initially taught this course using Unix or Linux systems, and the students were encouraged to work in C or C++. However, with the creation of the Isis^2 system, which was built in C# and is very easy to use on Windows, we are starting to focus on C# as our recommended programming language. In fact Isis^2 can be used easily from C++ or C, or from Java, but crossing language barriers does demand a kind of sophistication that one avoids by just working in the same language we used. On Windows, Visual Studio is probably the best development environment and debugging tool. For Linux users, we cross-compile the system with Mono. Our experience with the Mono version is very positive and we see no downside to that approach at all.

Professionals may find these problems interesting from a different perspective. Many of them are the sorts of questions that one would want to ask about a proposed distributed solution and hence could be useful as a tool for individuals responsible for the development of a complex system. I am sometimes asked to comment on proposed system designs, and, like many others, have found that it can be difficult to know where to start when the time for questions finally arrives after a two-hour technical presentation. A reasonable suggestion is to begin to pose simple questions aimed at exposing the reliability properties and nonproperties of the proposed system, the assumptions it makes, the dependencies embodied in it, and the cost/benefit tradeoffs reflected in the architecture. Such questions may not lead to a drastically changed system, but they do represent a path toward understanding the mentality of the designer and the philosophical structure of the proposed system. Many of the questions below are of a nature that might be used in such a situation.

K.P. Birman, *Guide to Reliable Distributed Systems*, Texts in Computer Science,
DOI 10.1007/978-1-4471-2416-0_24, © Springer-Verlag London Limited 2012

1. Make a list of five cloud-hosted services that support applications running on your iPhone or Android phone or pad. These can be services that you are sure exist, or can be services that you believe must exist on the basis of things these devices allow you to do. Now, for each of these services, ask yourself what the weakest assurance properties that would completely eliminate any possible risk of client annoyance would be. Do not be wildly unrealistic: networks will still fail or have poor connectivity; users will still be mobile, loads are still hard to predict. But are there assurance properties that would really be desirable for the services you have listed? Do you see ways that they could be implemented?

2. What sorts of assurance properties would matter most in a system designed to deliver video content (television shows, for example) over the web?

3. Imagine that a small medical office has purchased a cloud-hosted medical system designed to allow them to monitor large numbers of home-care patients. They keep an eye on their patients and perhaps step in to update prescriptions or even to adjust devices like insulin pumps, from time to time. What kinds of assurance property would such an application require?

   Sticking with this same example, we clearly will need to ensure that it behaves in a fail-safe manner: if something critical goes down (like a network link), it should sound the alarm in the doctor's office or perhaps in the manager's office of the building where the patient lives. Is it possible to solve this problem? How would you go about it?

4. Suppose that a law was written whereby if a network were to carry illegal content (such as child pornography), the network operator would be liable for large fines or other significant legal sanctions. Would it be technically feasible to implement such a policy? What challenges can you identify? (This is not a completely speculative question; there have been a number of proposals along these lines in the US Congress.)

5. Write a program to experimentally characterize the packet loss rate, frequency of out-of-order delivery, send-to-receive latency, and byte throughput of the UDP and TCP transport protocols available on your computer system. Evaluate both the local case (source and destination on the same machine) and the remote case (source and destination on different machines).

6. In the Introduction, in Fig. 3.1, we saw an illustration of network loads oscillating because of a broadcast storm. Compare this with the TCP sawtooth throughput graph in Fig. 3.1 that we discussed in Chap. 4, stemming from the TCP flow-control policy (linear increase, multiplicative decrease). Both figures show a kind of oscillation. Briefly explain why the first kind was considered so bad that IP multicast is now banned in most data centers, and yet the second kind is completely acceptable and, in fact, most data centers require that TCP be used for everything!

7. One of the examples in the Isis^2 user's manual lets you create a very simple cloud-hosted web service that uses Isis^2 to replicate data. Build such a service, run it on a real cloud platform such as Amazon EC2 or Microsoft Azure (you'll need to apply for a free account; you will not need very many nodes or a lot of computing time). Now use this service to measure simple RPC-style requests

from your client platform to the service that are load-balanced over its members, then "relayed" by the service instance that receives the request. Relay the data using *OrderedSend* and call *Flush* before replying to the external client. Now, measure:

   a. The cost of doing a "null" operation on the Web Service (one with no arguments and no return value).

   b. The per-byte cost of including a byte-string argument. (Graph the result for byte strings of length 10 bytes, 100, 1000, 10,000 and 50,000.)

   c. The per-byte cost if your procedure returns a byte-string result.

   d. The cost of including a vector of n 32-bit integers. (Again, graph results for various argument lengths.)

   e. The cost of including a vector of double-precision floating point numbers in the argument or result. Does it change the answer if the numbers have simple integer values like 1.0 or 0.0, relative to random double-precision numbers over a large range of values? Why?

   f. Design your Web Service so that some member, picked at random (perhaps using the group view) will crash with a zero-divide. Now, have your client application call the Web Service. How long does it take for the failure to be detected? What information is available to the client program? Do you get the same results if the client and Web Service run on different machines?

   g. Same as (f), but now have your Web Service application "freeze up" by calling sleep and never returning a result. What happens?

 8. (A substantial O/S level challenge). We discussed the role of the Dr. Multicast algorithm in taming the broadcasts storms that gave rise to Fig. 3.1. Could Dr. Multicast be implemented within an operating system? Modify the network device driver for Linux to implement Dr. Multicast directly at that level, maintaining complete transparency for the end-user applications. Note: If properly evaluated, a paper on this could certainly be published in a major conference such as HotOS, HotNets, or even OSDI or NSDI.

 9. Devise a method for rapidly detecting the failure of a process on a remote machine and implement it. How rapidly can your solution detect a failure without risk of inaccuracy? Your work should consider one or more of the following cases: a program that runs a protocol you have devised and implemented over UDP, a program that is monitored by a parent program, and a program on a machine that fails or becomes partitioned from the network. For each case, you may use any system calls or standard communication protocols that are available to you.

10. Suppose that it is your goal to develop a *network radio service*, which transmits identical data to a large set of listeners, and that you need to pick the best communication transport protocol for this purpose (there are many products of this kind in the market, you should browse a few product web pages to see how such radios look and feel to their users). Evaluate and compare the UDP, TCP, and IP multicast transport protocols on your computer (you may omit IP multicast if this is not available in your testing environment). Your evaluation should look at throughput and latency (focusing on variability of these as a function of

throughput presented to the transport). Can you characterize a range of performance within which one protocol is superior to the others in terms of loss rate, achievable throughput, and consistently low latency? Your results will take the form of graphs showing how these attributes scale with increasing numbers of destinations.

11. Develop a simple Isis[2] ping-pong program that bounces a small packet back and forth between a source and destination machine, using the *P2PSend* or *P2PQuery* API. One would expect such a program to give extremely consistent latency measurements when run on idle workstations. In practice, however, your test is likely to reveal considerable variation in latency. Track down the causes of these variations and suggest strategies for developing applications with highly predictable and stable performance properties.

12. One challenge to timing events in a distributed system is that the workstations in that system may be running some form of clock synchronization algorithm, which is adjusting clock values even as your test runs—leading to potentially confusing measurements. From product literature for the computers in your environment or by running a suitable experiment, determine the extent to which this phenomenon occurs in your testing environment. Can you propose ways of measuring performance that are immune to distortions of this nature?

13. Suppose you wish to develop a *topology service* for a local area network, using *only* two kinds of information as input with which to deduce the network topology: IP addresses for machines and measured point-to-point latency (for lightly loaded conditions, measured to a high degree of accuracy). How practical would it be to solve this problem? Ideally, a topology service should be able to produce a map showing how your local area network is interconnected, including bridges, individual Ethernet segments, and so forth.

14. (Moderately Difficult.) If you concluded that you should be able to do a good job on the previous problem, implement such a topology service using your local area network. What practical problems limit the accuracy of your solution? What forms of use could you imagine for your service? Can information available within the MIBs of the machines of your network be used to improve the quality of the topological map?

15. (A current topic of research.) In many cloud settings, applications must run on virtualized machines that could be stacked many-to-one on the same physical machines. How might this be detected? Could you design an application capable of sensing collocation rapidly? How might such an application be extended to sense other properties of the cloud runtime environment, such as the best options for replicas to talk to one-another (e.g. via shared memory-mapped files, TCP, UDP, IPMC, and for the latter, with what size packets)?

16. (A current topic of research.) In many applications, it would be helpful to be able to anticipate the costs of operations so as to make intelligent decisions. For example, if a data object can be downloaded from multiple places, one would like to download from the one that will give the fastest transfer, and so forth. Our goal in this problem is to provide an application with a way to estimate such costs. Suppose that your software will be installed in a set of *agent* programs at

a large number of nodes in a network (namely, the places where the application in question is running). By looking at IP addresses and measuring round-trip delays for messages exchanged by these agents, as well as the transfer speeds for moving larger amounts of data between them, is it possible to arrive at a reasonably good way to *estimate performance* for operations that the system may wish to do in the future? Develop the least costly mechanism you can (in terms of network load, etc.) for tracking the underlying network so that an application running from the same end-points can anticipate the costs associated with its communication events. Since your solution will be used as a kind of "library" by the application, you should provide access to it from a clean, simple API that will be easy for application developers to use.

17. Stream protocols like TCP can fail in inconsistent ways. Develop an application that demonstrates this problem by connecting two programs with multiple TCP streams, running them on multiple platforms and provoking a failure in which some of the streams break and some remain connected. To do this test you may need to briefly disconnect one of the workstations from the network; hence, you should obtain the permission of your network administration staff. Now, develop a wrapper for TCP that disables the TCP KEEPALIVE function and uses your mechanism to break channels. Your wrapper should mimic the API normally supported by TCP; indeed, you might even consider using the "library wrapper" methods discussed in Sect. 16.1 if you work on UNIX or Linux.

18. Suppose one were building a cloud-hosted runtime environment for very long-lived applications. The applications will be ones that need to remain *continuously operational* for years at a time in support of physics and astronomy experiments. For example, your technology might be used to build a control system for a satellite. Obviously, some downtime will be inevitable in any solution, but assume that the price of outages is considered very high and must be driven absolutely as low as possible. Would Isis[2] be a suitable platform for this purpose? Analyze the limitations of the system for uses such as this one, and then propose a set of extensions that might overcome the problems you identified. (Hint: Read about the highly available router research discussed in Chap. 4.)

19. (A good project for classes in which a large project is required from each student or group.) Suppose that a Web Services system is required to cache information from some underlying database server. Using the Isis[2] system, implement a coherent caching scheme and measure its performance and scalability in a real cloud setting such as Amazon's EC2 or Microsoft's Azure (cloud computing resources often have programs to allow students to get slices of compute time to run experiments such as this).

   Cloud computing systems would often wish to customize routing in ways matched to their application needs. Design a possible new Internet routing service that could be deployed in today's real Internet without disrupting or changing any existing routing technology or hardware, and yet that would give the cloud companies greatly enhanced control over their own private data streams.

20. (A good project for a class in which a large project is required from each student or group.) Develop a small library for use in a Web Services setting that

provides *secure, replicated keys* shared between a Web Services platform and its clients. The package should have a way to authenticate the identity of the client, and should implement two kinds of key. One form of key would be a symmetric key shared by the Web Service and exactly one client, and used to perform encryption or to sign data in messages transmitted between them. The second form of key, also symmetric, should support a "group" mode in which all clients running under the same ID share the same key. Can you support key refresh, whereby the key currently in use is replaced with a new key, in such a manner that even if the old key is later cracked, and even if the intruder has a complete record of all messages ever sent on the network, the new key will not be compromised?

21. This project uses a popular Cornell created package called *Live Distributed Objects* with which it is easy to create cloud-hosted visualization applications such as multiuser games or sharable data "dashboards" that have live content. Download this freeBSD package and, following the online manual, develop a game that leverages existing content such as Google's Maps database to support a kind of global chase, in which one character flees within a real urban setting and others chase him or her firing various kinds of weapon. You may want to consider combining the Live Objects solution with multicast solutions built over Isis[2] to achieve very high data rates for the movement events, weapons firing, etc.

22. Discuss options for building a kind of software development tool that will help students transform transactional Web Services applications into a less transactional, weakly consistent versions that can in the first-tier of the cloud. For example, you could start with an application that books an airline ticket, hotel room and vehicle for each stage of a multi-country trip. For ideas on how to go about this task we recommend reading Pritchett's classic paper on the BASE methodology (see Pritchett 2008). In effect, your software engineering solution would automate as much of BASE as possible, and then make it easy for the end user to take the steps that cannot be fully automated.

23. We discussed the need for a "security rules and policies" management mechanism, whereby the security rules and policies enforced by a system might be stored in a database, then used at runtime to decide whether specific actions should be authorized. Reach about the DL security policy "delegation" language by Feigenbaum (Delegation Logic) or the RT Role-Based Trust Language proposed by Stanford's John Mitchell and his colleagues. You can download implementations of both off the web, for example the RT implementation available from Berkeley's DETER laboratory. Now design a mechanism that uses these sorts of policies for use in Web Services settings that might support medical records on behalf of a hospital or some other medical practice. The rules should be of the form "client so-and-so is permitted/not-permitted to perform action so-and-so on Web Service such-and-such." How hard would it be to implement the solution you have designed? Give some examples of problems which this mechanism would solve, and some examples of problems it is not powerful enough to solve.

24. Suppose that a *rebinding* mechanism is to be used to automatically rebind a Web Services or CORBA applications to a working server if the server being used fails. What constraints on the application would make this a safe thing to do without notifying the application when rebinding occurs? Would this form of complete transparency make sense, or are the constraints too severe to use such an approach in practice?

25. A protocol that introduces tolerance to failures will also make the application using it more complex than one making no attempt to tolerate failures. Presumably, this complexity carries with it a cost in decreased application reliability. Discuss the pros and cons of building systems to be robust, in light of the likelihood that doing so will increase the cost of developing the application, the complexity of the resulting system, and the challenge of testing it. Can you suggest a principled way to reach a decision on the appropriateness of hardening a system to provide a desired property?

26. Consider an air traffic control system in which each flight is under the control of a specific individual at any given point in time. Suppose the system takes the form of a collection of client/server distributed networks—one for each of a number of air traffic control centers. Design a protocol for handing off a flight from one controller to another, considering first the case of a single center and then the case of a multicenter system. Now, analyze the possible failure modes of your protocol under the assumption that client systems, server systems, and the communication network may be subject to failures. Keep in mind that your goal is to ensure that the system is fail-safe but not necessarily to accomplish that goal in a completely automated manner. If the system sometimes needs to ask for help from the human air-traffic controllers or system operators, doing so is perfectly appropriate.

27. Suppose that a large city has decided to manage all of its traffic flow on a cloud platform. Data collected will include estimates for traffic volumes on each road (obtained from detection devices of various kinds, programs that collect photos from skyscrapers at a few strategic locations and then use image processing to determine how many vehicles are on each street and how fast they are moving, etc.). Actions are to adjust the timing cycles for the traffic lights to optimize traffic flow. How would you solve this problem? What assurance properties would it need, if any?

28. Focusing on the case of a medical computing system used to monitor at-home patients and that can take actions, such as adjusting an insulin pump, make a list of ten or fifteen distinct tasks (roles) that such a system might play. Now, for each, develop a breakdown of the associated security and consistency requirements, fault-tolerance needs, etc. Given an application of this kind, where one sees a mix of needs, would you recommend using the worst-case requirements as an overall goal (e.g. implement everything to satisfy the worst-case assurance needs, even if some subsystem does not need those worst-case guarantees)? From the insights you gain in answering this question, develop an overall rule of thumb that a developer of a high-assurance system might use in deciding how to define and implement the various subsystems that arise. (E.g. your goal

here is to generalize from a specific medical case to the more general world of high assurance financial systems, traffic control systems, smart power grid applications, and so forth.)

29. (Term project; team of two or more.) Use $Isis^2$ to build a high-assurance replicated database that can tolerate various patterns of failures include unexpected sudden outages of the full set of machines on which the application is running. What limits the performance of your solution?

30. Suppose that you were to use the $Isis^2$ system to implement the CASD protocol we looked at in the chapter on real-time protocols (e.g. you would implement CASD over the basic $Isis^2$ *Send* and *P2PSend* primitives). Would the analysis of correctness used in the CASD proofs still apply, or would the layering complicate that analysis in some way? What about the converse question: would the solution be a virtually synchronous version of the CASD real-time protocols?

31. Suppose that you were to use the $Isis^2$ system to implement the Zyzzva Byzantine Fault Tolerance protocol (Kotla et al. 2009), a fancier and more complete protocol than the simple BFT protocol we looked at in Sect. 11.2. That is, you would implement Zyzzva over the basic $Isis^2$ *Send* and *P2PSend* primitives. Would the analysis of correctness used in the Zyzzva proofs still apply, or would the layering complicate that analysis in some way? What about the converse question: would the solution be a virtually synchronous Byzantine Agreement solution? For example, would it be safe to make use of the $Isis^2$ group views within the services that use this BFT technology? How would it perform relative to a hand-coded version of Zyzzva?

32. Some authors consider RPC to be an extremely successful protocol, because it is highly transparent, reasonably robust, and can be optimized to run at very high speed—so high that if an application wants stronger guarantees, it makes more sense to layer a protocol over a lower-level RPC facility than to build it into the operating system at potentially high cost. Discuss the pros and cons of this point of view. In the best possible world, what primitives do you believe should be included into the vendor-supplied communication subsystem, and what primitives should be implemented by the application in an end-to-end manner?

33. Research the *end-to-end argument*. Now, suppose that you are working with mobile computers that use relatively low-reliability wireless links to connect to the Internet, and then run TCP to download Web pages. Does the end-to-end argument suggest that the wireless link should be treated just like the wired part of the Internet? Explain how best to handle such a link, if our goal is rapid download speeds.

34. Review flow-control options for environments in which a Web Service is sending streams of data to large numbers of receivers. Today, TCP does not coordinate the actions of one stream relative to those of any other. Yet the one Web Service may be connected to hundreds of clients, and if congestion occurs, there is a good chance that it will impact sets of clients (all of them if the problem is close to the server, and if the problem occurs close to a client, it will probably impact other clients at the same place). Can you suggest ways that a TCP

protocol might be modified to make use of this kind of information? (If you are a real hacker, consider using NS/2, which has very accurate TCP simulations built in, to simulate such scenarios and explore the likely impact of your proposed scheme.)

35. A protocol is said to be "acky" if most packets are acknowledged immediately upon reception. Discuss some of the pros and cons of this property. Suppose that a stream protocol could be switched in and out of an acky mode. Under what conditions would it be advisable to operate that protocol with frequent acks?

36. Suppose that a streaming style of multidestination information service, such as the Internet radio service we discussed in an earlier problem, is to be used in a setting where a small subset of the application programs can be unresponsive for periods of time. A good example of such a setting would be a network in which the client systems run on PCs, because the most popular PC operating systems allow applications to preempt the CPU and inhibit interrupts—a behavior that can delay the system from responding to incoming messages in a timely manner. This might also arise if a client is connected over a wireless link that sometimes "burps." What options can you propose for ensuring that data delivery will be reliable and ordered *in all cases*, but that small numbers of briefly unresponsive machines will not impact performance for the much larger number of highly responsive machines?

37. (Term project.) Suppose you were building a large-scale distributed system for video playback of short video files on demand—for example, such a system might be used in a large bank to provide brokers and traders with current projections for the markets and trading instruments tracked by the bank. Assume that videos are often updated. Design a scheme for getting data to the display servers so as to avoid overloading servers while also giving the best possible user experience. Your solution will probably need to track copies of each video, so that any machine with a copy can be treated as a possible data source (more or less in the style of Napster and other P2P file sharing protocols). You should provide for a way to update the database of available videos and to play a video on an end-user "playback unit"; beyond this, include such additional functionality as is needed to achieve a high availability, high performance solution.

38. Consider the Group Membership Protocol discussed in Sect. 11.1. Suppose that this protocol was implemented in the address space of an application program and that the application program contained a bug causing it to infrequently but randomly corrupt a few cells of memory. To what degree would this render the assumptions underlying the GMS protocol incorrect? What behaviors might result? Can you suggest practical countermeasures that would overcome such a problem if it were indeed very infrequent?

39. (Difficult.) Again, consider the Group Membership Protocol discussed in Sect. 11.1. This protocol has the following property: All participating processes observe *exactly the same sequence* of membership views. The coordinator can add unlimited numbers of processes in each round and can drop any minority of the members each time it updates the system membership view; in both cases,

the system is provably immune from partitioning. Would this protocol be simplified by eliminating the property that processes must observe the same view sequence? (Hint: Try to design a protocol that offers this "weaker" behavior. Do not worry about network partitioning failures.)

40. (A real problem that has caused outages in several major cloud systems.) Suppose that the processes in a process group are managing replicated data using some technique (perhaps gossip, perhaps virtually synchronous data replication) to propagate updates. Due to a lingering bug, it is known that although the group seems to work well for periods of hours or even days, over very long periods of time the replicated data can become slightly corrupted so that different group members have different values. For example, perhaps sometimes the amount of free space for one of the storage servers tends to show a random number instead of the correct value. Discuss the pros and cons of introducing a stabilization mechanism, whereby the members would periodically crash themselves, then restart and rejoin the system as a "new" member. What issues might this raise in the application program, and how might they be addressed?

41. Same question, but now assume that your cloud system is having this problem because it is coming under attack by the competing company that operates the cloud platform up the block. Apparently they have found a sneaky way to send data on your corporate network. How would you protect the solution from the previous question against attack?

42. Implement a very simple Web Services banking application supporting accounts into which money can be deposited and withdrawals can be made. (You can easily do this using Visual Studio for .NET with the ASP.NET project design and working in a language such as C# with Isis^2 at the backend, or even with some simple SQL backend.) Have your application support a form of *disconnected operation* based on the two-tiered architecture, in which each branch system uses its own set of process groups and maintains information for local accounts. Your application should simulate partitioning failures through a command interface. If branches cache information about remote accounts, what options are there for permitting a client to withdraw funds while the local branch at which the account really resides is unavailable? Consider both the need for safety by the bank and the need for availability, if possible, for the user—for example, it would be silly to refuse a user $250 from an account that had thousands of dollars in it moments earlier when connections were still working! Can you propose a policy that is always safe for the bank and yet also allows remote withdrawals during partition failures? (Hint: this question is motivated by research undertaken by Professor Calton Pu on "epsilon serializability." Although this work was not covered in the textbook in the interest of brevity, you might find it useful to track down Pu's publications on the Web.)

43. Design a protocol by which a process group implemented using Isis^2 can solve the asynchronous consensus problem. Assume that the environment is one in which Isis^2 can run correctly, processes only fail by crashing, and the network only fails by losing messages with some low frequency. Your processes should be assumed to start with a variable, *input$_i$*, which, for each process, p_i, is initially 0 or 1. After deciding, each process should set a variable, *output$_i$*, to its

decision value. The solution should be such that the processes all reach the same decision value, v, and this value is the same as at least one of the inputs.

44. In regard to your solution to problem 37, discuss the sense in which your solution solves the asynchronous consensus problem. Would any distributed programming tool (e.g. Isis^2, JGroups, Ensemble or Spread) be guaranteed to make progress under the stated conditions? Do these conditions correspond to the conditions of the asynchronous model used in the FLP and Chandra/Toueg results?

45. Can the virtual synchrony protocols of a system such as Isis^2, Horus, Ensemble or Spread be said to guarantee safety and liveness in the general asynchronous model of FLP or the Chandra/Toueg results?

46. Group communication systems such as Isis^2, JGroups, Ensemble and Spread are usually designed to operate under the conditions seen in clustered computing systems on a local area network. That is, the protocols basically assume low latency, high throughput, and infrequent network disconnections or partitioning events. But cloud systems are so massive that rare things happen all the time, somewhere in the cloud. Consider the challenges of running a group communication platform in a *wireless ad-hoc network*, where connectivity is often disrupted, power considerations may be a factor, and messages need to be relayed to reach their destination, introducing significant latency variations. What sorts of group communication protocols might work best in this setting? If you find it helpful to imagine an application, assume that your solution is aimed at supporting rescue workers who are entering a region that recently experienced a flood or earthquake and need to coordinate their actions, or fire fighters working in a mountainous forest threatened by a fire.

47. Suppose that a process group is created in which three member processes each implement different algorithms for performing the same computation (so-called "implementation redundancy"). You may assume that these processes interact with the external environment *only using message send and receive primitives*. Design a wrapper that compares the actions of the processes, producing a single output if two of the three or all three processes agree on the action to take for a given input and signaling an exception if all three processes produce different outputs for a given input. Implement your solution using Isis^2 or some other technology and demonstrate it for a set of fake processes that usually copy their input to their output, but that sometimes make a random change to their output before sending it.

48. A set of processes in a group monitors devices in the external environment, detecting *device service requests* to which they respond in a load-balanced manner. The best way to handle such requests depends upon the frequency with which they occur. Consider the following two extremes: requests that require long computations to handle but that occur relatively infrequently and requests that require very short computations to handle but that occur frequently on the time scale with which communication is done in the system. Assuming that the processes in a process group have identical capabilities (any can respond to any request), how would you solve this problem in the two cases?

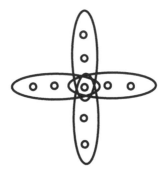

Fig. 24.1 Overlapping process groups for problem 47. In this example there is only a single process in the overlap region; the problem concerns state transfer if we wanted to add another process to this region. Assume that the state of the processes in the overlap region reflects messages sent to it by the outer processes, which belong to the "petals" but not the overlap area. Additionally, assume that this state is not cleanly decomposed group by group and that it is necessary to implement a single state transfer for the entire structure

49. Design a locking protocol for a virtually synchronous process group (read about the Google Chubby service to better understand the goal: See Burrows 2006). Your protocol should allow a group member to *request* a lock, specifying the name of the object to be locked (the name can be an integer to simplify the problem), and to *release* a lock that it holds. What issues occur if a process holding a lock fails? Recommend a good, general way of dealing with this case and then give a distributed algorithm by which the group members can implement the *request* and *release* interfaces, as well as your solution to the broken lock case.

50. (Suggested by Jim Pierce.) Suppose we want to implement a system in which n process groups will be superimposed—much like the petals of a flower. Some small set of k processes will belong to all n groups, and each group will have additional members that belong only to it. The problem now occurs of how to handle *join* operations for the processes that belong to the overlapping region and in particular how to deal with state transfers to such a process. Assume that the group states are only updated by "petal" processes, which do not belong to the overlap region. Now, the virtually synchronous state transfer mechanisms we discussed in Sect. 14.3 would operate on a group-by-group basis, but it may be that the states of the processes in the overlap region are a mixture of information arriving from all of the petal processes. For such cases one would want to do a *single* state transfer to the joining process, reflecting the *joint state* of the overlapped groups. Propose a fault-tolerant protocol for joining the overlap region and transferring state to a joining process that will satisfy this objective. (Refer to Fig. 24.1.)

51. Discuss the pros and cons of using an *inhibitory* protocol to test for a condition along a consistent cut in a process group. Describe a problem or scenario where such a solution might be appropriate and one where it would not be.

52. In Lamport's Paxos protocol, the number of acceptors plays an important role in both performance and durability. It can be appealing to use a small number of acceptors (like 3) because this maximizes performance. But what issues can arise if a group has a large number of learners and a much smaller number of acceptors?

     Look closely at the Isis[2] *Send* protocol. Describe a sequence of events that can cause a *Send* to be delivered to at least one group member, and yet not be delivered (ever) at other group members. Could an external user of a service ever glimpse such a situation if *Flush* is called after the *Send*, before sending messages to the external user?

     Give an example of a simple data replication protocol that will guarantee consistency if implemented using *CausalSend* and yet is incorrect when implemented using *Send* (recall that the former offers a causal delivery ordering, while the latter is only FIFO).

     Give an example of a data replication approach that behaves identically whether *CausalSend* or *SafeSend* is used. Can you describe a general principle that would tell a person who is not sure which primitive to use whether they need *CausalSend* or not? When working with very large groups that are only updated rarely, what overheads will result if your system uses *CausalSend* just to be on the safe side? How do these overheads scale as a group grows larger?

53. Suppose that the processes in a distributed system share a set of resources, which they lock prior to using and then unlock when finished. If these processes belong to a process group, how could deadlock detection be done within that group? Design your deadlock detection algorithm to be completely idle (with no background communication costs) when no deadlocks are suspected; the algorithm should be one that can be launched when a timeout in a waiting process suggests that a deadlock may have occurred. For bookkeeping purposes, you may assume that a process waiting for a resource calls the local procedure *waiting_for(resource)*, a process holds exclusive access to a resource calls the procedure *holding(resource)*, and a process releasing a resource calls the procedure *release(resource)*, where the resources are identified by integers. Each process thus maintains a local database of its resource status. Notice that you are not being asked to implement the actual mutual-exclusion algorithm here: Your goal is to devise a protocol that can interact with the processes in the system as needed to accurately detect deadlocks. Prove that your protocol detects deadlocks if, and only if, they are present.

54. Suppose you wish to monitor a distributed system for an overload condition, defined as follows. The system state is considered normal if no more than one-third of the processes signal that they are overloaded, heavily loaded if more than one-third but less than two-thirds of the processes signal that they are overloaded, and seriously overloaded if two-thirds or more of the processes are overloaded. Assume further that the loading condition does not impact communication performance. If the processes belong to a process group, would it be sufficient to simply send a multicast to all members asking their states and then to compute the state of the system from the vector of replies so obtained?

What issues would such an approach raise, and under what conditions would the result be correct?

55. (Joseph and Schmuck.) What would be the best way to implement a *predicate addressing* communication primitive for use within virtually synchronous process groups (assume that the group primitives are already implemented and available for you). Such a primitive sends a message to *all the processes in the group for which some acceptance criteria hold* and does so *along a consistent cut.* You may assume that each process contains a predicate, *accept()*, which, at the time it is invoked, returns *true* if the process wishes to accept a copy of the message and *false* if not. (Hint: It is useful to consider two separate cases here—one in which the criteria that determine acceptance change slowly and one in which they change rapidly, relative to the speed of the multicasting in the system.)

56. (Term project.) Implement Agarwal's architecture, and experimentally evaluate its behavior with a small cluster of side-by-side PC's on a high speed LAN, using a simple hand-built database instead of a full-scale transactional database as the underlying database "system" (for example, you might use a file 100 blocks in length and generate transactions at random to read or write segments of the file, locking each record as it is first accessed).

57. (Schneider.) We discussed two concepts of clock synchronization: *accuracy* and *precision.* Consider the case of aircraft operating under *free-flight* rules, where each pilot makes routing decisions on behalf of his or her plane, using a shared trajectory mapping system. Suppose that you faced a fundamental tradeoff between using clocks with high accuracy for such a mapping system or clocks with high precision. Which would you favor and why? Would it make sense to implement two such solutions, side by side?

58. Suppose that a-posteriori clock synchronization using GPS receivers becomes a worldwide standard in the coming decade. The use of temporal information now represents a form of communication channel that can be used in indirect ways— for example, process p, executing in Lisbon, can wait until process q performs a desired operation in New York (or fails) using timer events. Interestingly, such an approach communicates information faster than messages can. What issues do these sorts of hidden information channels raise in regard to the protocols we explored in the book? Could temporal information create hidden causality relationships?

59. Show how tightly synchronized real-time clocks can be made to reflect causality in the manner of Lamport's logical clocks. Would such a clock be preferable in some ways to a purely logical clock? Explain, giving concrete examples to illustrate your points.

60. (Difficult.) In discussion of the CASD protocols, we saw that if such protocols were used to replicate the state of a distributed system, a mechanism would be needed to overcome inconsistencies occurring when a process is technically considered incorrect according to the definitions of the protocols and therefore does not benefit from the normal guarantees of atomicity and ordering seen by correct processes. In an IBM technical report, Skeen and Cristian once suggested that the CASD protocols could be used in support of an abstraction called

Δ-*common storage*; the basic idea is to implement a distributed shared memory, which can be read by any process and updated using the CASD style of broadcast protocol. Such a distributed shared memory would reflect an update within Δ time units after it is initiated, plus or minus a clock skew factor of ε. How might the inconsistency issue of the CASD protocol be visible in a Δ-common storage system? Propose a method for detecting and eliminating such inconsistencies. (Note: This issue was not considered in the technical report.)

61. (Marzullo and Sabel.) Suppose you wish to monitor a distributed system to detect situations in which a logical predicate defined over the states of the member processes holds. The predicate may state, for example, that process p_i holds a token and that process p_j is waiting to obtain the token. Under the assumption that the states in question change very slowly in comparison to the communication speeds of the system, design a solution to this problem. You may assume that there is a function, *sample_local_state()*, that can be executed in each process to sample those aspects of its local state referenced in the query, and when the local states have been assembled in one place, a function, *evaluate*, can determine if the predicate holds or not. Now, discuss the modifications needed if the rate of state changes is increased enough so that the state can change in the same order of time as your protocol needs to run. How is your solution affected if you are required to detect *every state in which the predicate holds*, as opposed to just detecting *states in which the predicate happens to hold when the protocol is executed*. Demonstrate that your protocol cannot falsely detect satisfying states.

62. There is increasing interest in building small multiprocessor systems for use in inexpensive communication satellites. Such systems might look similar to a rack containing a small number of conventional workstations or PCs, running software that handles such tasks as maintaining the proper orientation of the satellite by adjusting its position periodically, turning on and off the control circuits that relay incoming messages to outgoing channels, and handling other aspects of satellite function. Now, suppose that it is possible to put highly redundant memory modules on the satellite to protect extremely critical regions of memory, but that it is costly to do so. However, unprotected memory is likely to experience a low level of corruption as a result of the harsh conditions in space, such as cosmic rays and temperature extremes. What sorts of programming considerations would result from using such a model? Propose a software architecture that minimizes the need for redundant memory, but also minimizes the risk that a satellite will be completely lost (e.g., a satellite might be lost if it erroneously fires its positioning rockets and thereby exhausts its supply of fuel). You may assume that the actual rate of corruption of memory is low, but not completely insignificant, and that program instructions are as likely as data to be corrupted. Assume that the extremely reliable memories, however, never experience corruption.

63. Continuing with the topic of problem 62 there is debate concerning the best message-routing architecture for these sorts of satellite systems. In one approach, the satellites maintain a routing network among themselves; a relatively

small number of ground stations interact with whatever satellite happens to be over them at a given time, and control and data messages are then forwarded satellite to satellite until they reach the destination. In a second approach, satellites communicate only with ground stations and mobile transmitter/receiver units: Such satellites require a larger number of ground systems, but they do not depend upon a routing transport protocol, which could be a source of unreliability. Considering the conditions cited in problem 59 and your responses, what would be the best design for a satellite-to-satellite routing network? Can you suggest a scientifically sound way to make the design tradeoff between this approach and the one using a larger number of potentially costly ground stations?

64. We noted that the theoretical community considers a problem to be impossible in a given environment if, for all proposed solutions to the problem, there exists at least one behavior consistent with the environment that would prevent the proposed solution from terminating or would lead to an incorrect outcome. Later we considered probabilistic protocols, which may be able to guarantee behaviors to very high levels of reliability—higher, in practice, than the reliability of the computers on which the solutions run. Suggest a definition of *impossible* that might reconcile these two perspectives on computing systems.

65. Suppose that a system is using Chord and has access to the finger tables used by the Chord technology. Devise an efficient protocol for counting the number of nodes actually in the system. How costly is your protocol?

66. Suppose that we wanted to enumerate all (*key, value*) pairs within some range of keys (here, we mean the actual key, not the hashed key). Is there an efficient way to do this using Chord? Explain why or why not.

67. Suppose that we want to do an inverted lookup—for a given value, we would like to find the corresponding key or keys. Can this be done efficiently using Chord? Can you suggest a way to modify Chord to support such an operation?

68. A stock exchange typically reports two kinds of event: actual trades that are completed, and bid-offered pricing. The latter is less important, since bid-offered prices change all the time, whereas information on trades that are consummated is of very high value, because applications predicting pricing trends tend to weight such events very heavily. Which multicast properties would be most appropriate for reporting each kind of event?

69. Suppose that for reasons of scalability, you are building a stock exchange system that will use bimodal multicast (*ProbabilisticSend*) for all event reporting. Can you suggest ways to extend the basic protocol so that if a node can tell whether a missing message is one of the "important" ones mentioned in question 64, as opposed to one of the less critical kinds of event?

70. Can Astrolabe aggregators be used to "count" objects in a distributed setting?
   a. Show how Astrolabe can be used to count the number of computers running it (that is, count the number of machines in its own table).
   b. How can Astrolabe be used to count the number of machines reporting load > 10.0?

    c. Could Astrolabe be used to count the number of machines having connectivity problems? What issues arise if we try to base an aggregate on data being reported by a machine suffering intermittent connectivity failures?

    d. Suppose that a virus is actively spreading through a network. It modifies a file called C:\FooBar.exe on machines running version 2.1 of Microsoft "Age of Mythology." Can Astrolabe be used to count the number of infected machines? To list them? How would Astrolabe behave if these numbers are changing even as the system operator is looking at the output?

71. Your boss has asked you to estimate the number of downloaded music files on the computers in your company, a multinational corporation with some 25,000 machines on its corporate network. Astrolabe is running on all of these machines.

    a. Would you use a "configuration certificate" or an "aggregation function" to ask each machine to count the files in the "myDownloadedMusic" folder and report the count into Astrolabe?

    b. Assume that Astrolabe is structured with 100 machines per zone and that one gossip message is sent by each participant in a gossip epidemic every 5 seconds. Further, assume that it takes 10 seconds for a machine to count the number of music files it has, once it has been asked to do so. You initiate the action you recommended in (a). How long will it take before all the machines in the network start to report their counts of music files?

    c. How would you design an aggregation query to count the number of files in the system as a whole? Suppose that a time t you ask Astrolabe to begin to compute this aggregate. What issues arise during the period when the aggregation query is known at some machines but not all of them? Could this result in an incorrect reported count? Explain.

    d. Is there a way to set this query up so that you will know how long to wait until the exact count has been computed? Suppose that starting at time $t + \delta$ the correct count is reported by Astrolabe. Why might the count continue to change long after time $t + \delta$ is reached?

    e. What if you now want to identify the employee with the largest number of downloaded music files. How could you solve this problem with Astrolabe?

72. The corporate database center in your company has become overloaded and you want to improve the use of caching by allowing client systems to share their cache contents with one-another. This way, if machine a can obtain a database record from the cache of machine b it will do so, rather than downloading a copy from the database. Assume that staleness of the cached records is not a concern. Which is the best technology for solving this problem: a DHT such as Chord or Pastry, a one-hop DHT such as Kelips, a scalable database-like system such as Astrolabe, or a scalable event reporting system such as a publish-subscribe technology or Bimodal Multicast (*ProbabilisticSend*)?

73. In a caching architecture we may want to maintain *coherent caches* by having the server notify nodes that have cached copies of a given record in the event that the record changes. They can then discard or refresh the stale copy. Of course, cache records can also be discarded for other reasons, such as timing considerations or a need to reuse the space for some other purpose. Which

would be the best way for the server to track the set of clients that have a given record in their caches? Your answer should focus on the cost of the mechanism and also on how well it is likely to work:

   a. Maintain a collection of dynamic process groups, one group per record.

   b. Use Kelips to advertise copies of the cached record and also to announce that a cached copy has been discarded.

   c. Use some other DHT, such as Pastry, for the same purpose as in (b).

   d. Use Astrolabe for this purpose. One column of the Astrolabe data structure would list the cached records at a given machine, represented as a string of record identifiers separated by semicolons. (Astrolabe would just think of it as a fairly long string.)

   e. When downloading a record, tell the server if it will be cached. If so, do an RPC to the server to notify it if and when the cached record is discarded.

   f. Do not explicitly track caching. Use Bimodal Multicast (*pbcast*) to notify all the client systems when a record changes. If a large number of records change, the notifications can be packed into very large messages for greater efficiency.

74. We are building a military system to monitor the health of soldiers on the battlefield. Each soldier's equipment includes some number of sensors. Although the maximum number of sensors is known and is not unreasonably large, the actual set of active sensors varies from soldier to soldier.

   a. We would like to use Astrolabe in such a setting, but we do not want its aggregation mechanism to be confused by the cases where a given soldier is not reporting the sensor value that a given aggregate reads. For example, we might want to list the soldiers who have the lowest reserves of ammunition, but we do not want our list to include a huge number of individuals who either do not have an ammunition counting sensor, or for whom that sensor is not currently working.

   b. Suppose that one of the sensors is capable of detecting even traces of VX nerve gas. How might Astrolabe be used to identify the soldiers whose sensors are detecting more than some specified threshold level of VX?

   c. What if we wanted to use *ProbabilisticSend* to send a message to all soldiers within 100 meters of any soldier whose VX sensor is reporting an over-threshold level of the gas, for example to warn those soldiers to immediately put on a gas mask. How could we solve this problem? Assume that all soldiers have a GPS location sensor reporting their current coordinates.

75. OfficeStuff corporation just called to warn that users of OfficeStuff version 2.1 may be at risk of attack by the NimbleFrog virus. Your virus scanning software is not able to detect this problem, hence you decide to use Astrolabe to do so. How might you tackle this challenge?

76. Astrolabe can identify machines that match a pattern, as in problem 69, but does not take actions on those machines. Suppose that you build an "AstroActor" application intended to run on the same client nodes that use Astrolabe. Its job is to take the actions Astrolabe cannot take. For example, in problem 69, AstroAction might be used to initiate a software upgrade to OfficeStuff version 2.2.

    a. How might you design AstroAction?

    b. What security issues are raised by such a capability? Keep in mind that Astrolabe and AstroAction may be running on all nodes in a corporate network.

    c. How might you address these security concerns?

77. The Kelips and Pastry systems both include mechanisms to track and use the cheapest possible links. For example, Pastry constantly probes the nodes to which its finger tables point, and will substitute a cheaper and more responsive node if one turns out to be slow. Kelips similarly changes the affinity group contacts list to try and use inexpensive contacts that are known to be responsive. What are the pros and cons of such a policy? Think both about the expected performance of the DHT itself and also about the performance overhead of the mechanism.

78. Suppose that a very large information management system is being designed for surveillance of the airports, train stations, bus stations and borders of a large country. It will have millions of digital camera systems, each associated with a storage device for archival recording of images captured. Now we would like to make this information accessible to authorized law enforcement officials. A small number of locations will be permitted to query the overall system. A typical query involves providing the system with some number of digital pictures of individuals suspected of trying to gain entry into the country, and the goal is to retrieve any possible matches from the archived databases of all of those computers. You can assume that the picture-matching operation is built into the image server, and can be accessed via a secured Web Services interface.

    a. Would this problem be better matched to a client/server architecture, a peer-to-peer architecture, or a virtual synchrony process group approach? Why?

    b. Suppose that you decide to use a peer-to-peer technology. How could you chose between Astrolabe, Kelips and Chord for the kind of search operation just described? Is one of these a much better "match" with the need than the others? Why?

    c. Analyze the ways that a terrorist group might try to compromise the correct behavior of the solution you advocate in part (b). Assume that the group has one person working with them who has gained access to the network on which the system runs, and who is in a position to change the behavior of a few of the nodes collecting data—but just a few. Could such an intruder bring the whole system down? Could he cause the system to report a false result, such as to claim that there have been no sightings of such and such an individual?

79. If a message must take d hops to reach its destination and the worst-case delay for a single link is δ, it is common to assume that the worst-case transit time for the network will be $d * \delta$. However, a real link will typically exhibit a distribution of latencies, with the vast majority clustered near some minimum latency, δ_{min}, and only a very small percentage taking as long as δ_{max} to traverse the link. Under the assumption that the links of a routed network provide statistically independent and identical behavior, derive the distribution of expected latencies for a message that must traverse d links of a network. You may assume that the

distribution of delays has a convenient form for your analysis. (This problem is hard to solve in closed form, but using MathLab you should be able to define a regression formula and solve it numerically, then graph the results.)

80. A network address translation box increases the size of the network name space. Suppose that addresses consist of a 32-bit address and a 16-bit port number and that network address translation is used as aggressively as possible. Also, assume that on the average, each application has a single open connection to some remote computer (this is just the average; some may have far more connections and some might not have any connections at all).

   a. Characterize this "extreme translation" scenario. How many computers could be connected to the network before we run into situations where some computer. *a* cannot communicate with some other computer *b* because we have exhausted the address space?

   b. How is your answer impacted if each application has, on the average, 10 open connections?

   c. Network address translation is unidirectional: a client behind a NAT can connect to a server on the public Internet, but the server cannot initiate a connection from outside the NAT back through it. How is this reflected in your answer to (a)?

   d. Does the answer to this problem change if we allow multiple levels of NAT boxes? E.g., "LayersCorp" might have some application running behind two NAT boxes, so that connection requests must pass through first one, then the other.

   e. Many people consider NAT boxes as a form of security mechanism. What kinds of protection can a NAT provide?

81. (Ethical problem.) Suppose that a medical system does something a person would not be able to do, such as continuously monitoring the vital signs of a patient and continuously adjusting some form of medication or treatment in response to the measured values. Now, imagine that we want to attach this device to a distributed system so that physicians and nurses elsewhere in the hospital can remotely monitor the behavior of the medical system and so that they can change the rules that control its actions if necessary (e.g., by changing the dosage of a drug). In this book we have encountered many practical limits to security and reliability. Identify some of the likely limits on the reliability of a technology such as this. What are the ethical issues that need to be balanced in deciding whether or not to build such a system?

82. (Ethical problem.) You have been asked to participate on a government panel evaluating research proposals submitted to a major funding agency. One of the very strong proposals is focused on a new peer-to-peer file sharing technology with the following properties. First, content is completely anonymous: it is impossible to determine who uploaded a given file into the system. Second, downloads are anonymous: you can tell that data are being accessed, but the underlying system mixes files together in such a way that it is very hard to tell *which* data are being accessed. And third, the identity of the individual downloading the file is also anonymous. (Note: such technologies do exist;

they have been developed by a number of researchers and tend to be based on so-called cryptographic "Mixes" (Chaum 1981) and either strong encryption or some other form of steganographic storage (see Cooper and Birman 1995; Waldman and Mazières 2001).) The proposal claims that this system is for use by individuals who wish to exchange e-mail and engage in discussions that the government might find objectionable or that might result in discrimination against them by others, and the research group also states that the technology will be available to pro-democracy dissidents in foreign countries. But such a technology could also be used for theft of IP, coordination of spying or terrorist activities, and even for distribution of child pornography. Do you recommend that this work be funded? How would you convince the remainder of the committee to accept your position on the matter?

83. (Ethical dilemma.) The home of an individual suspected of involvement in terrorist activities is searched. No clearly compromising materials are found, but on his laptop computer the investigators discover a program built along the lines discussed in problem 77. The program has created some large files, but they are illegible and, as discussed in problem 77, presumably contain a mixture of encrypted data from many sources. Without the user's cooperation, it is impossible to launch the program or retrieve the files the user himself has stored into the system, or to make sense of any of these data. Should it be possible to compel such an individual to reveal his passwords and access codes? Keep in mind that if such a law were in place and the individual were to refuse, he would be subject to fines, imprisonment or other penalties. If you find it helpful to do so, you may assume that it is very likely that this individual is guilty, but not certain.

84. (Ethical problem.) An *ethical theory* is a set of governing principles or rules for resolving ethical conflicts such as the one in the previous problem—for example, an ethical theory might stipulate that decisions should be made to favor the maximum benefit for the greatest number of individuals. A theory governing the deployment of technology could stipulate that machines must not replace people if the resulting system is at risk of making erroneous decisions that a person would have avoided. Notice that these particular theories could be in conflict—for example, if a technology that is normally beneficial develops occasional life-threatening complications. Discuss the issues that might occur in developing an ethical theory for the introduction of technologies in life- or safety-critical settings and, if possible, propose such a theory. What tradeoffs are required, and how would you justify them?

References

Abbott, M., Peterson, L.: Increasing network throughput by integrating protocol layers. IEEE/ACM Trans. Netw. **1**(5), 600–610 (1993)

Abraham, I., Malkhi, D.: Probabilistic quorums for dynamic systems. In: The 17th International Symposium on Distributed Computing (DISC 2003), Sorento, Italy, October 2003

Agapi, A., Birman, K., Broberg, R., Cotton, C., Kielmann, T., Millnert, M., Payne, R., Surton, R., van Renesse, R.: Routers for the cloud: Can the Internet achieve 5-nines availability? IEEE Internet Comput. **15**(5), 72–77 (2011)

Agarwal, D.A.: Totem: A reliable ordered delivery protocol for interconnected local area networks. Ph.D. diss., Department of Electrical and Computer Engineering, University of California, Santa Barbara (1994)

Aguilera, M.K., Strom, R.E., Sturman, D.C., Astley, M., Chandra, T.D.: Matching events in a content-based subscription system. In: 18th ACM Symposium on Principles of Distributed Computing (PODC), Atlanta, GA (1999)

Aguilera, M., Keidar, I., Malkhi, D., Shraer, A.: Dynamic atomic storage without consensus. In: Proceedings of the ACM Symposium on Principles of Distributed Computing (PODC) (2009a)

Aguilera, M.K., Merchant, A., Shah, M., Veitch, A., Karamanolis, C.: Sinfonia: A new paradigm for building scalable distributed systems. ACM Trans. Comput. Syst. **27**(3), 5 (2009b)

Ahamad, M., Burns, J., Hutto, P., Neiger, G.: Causal memory. Technical Report, College of Computing, Georgia Institute of Technology, July (1991)

Alon, N., Barak, A., Manber, U.: On disseminating information reliably without broadcasting. In: Proceedings of the Seventh International Conference on Distributed Computing Systems, Berlin, September, pp. 74–81. IEEE Computer Society Press, New York (1987)

Alonso, R., Korth, F.: Database issues in nomadic computing. In: Proceedings of the ACM SIG-MOD International Conference on Mannagement of Data, Washington, DC, May 1993, pp. 388–392 (1993)

Alvisi, L., Bressoud, T., El-Khasab, A., Marzullo, K., Zagorodnov, D.: Wrapping server-side TCP to mask connection failures. In: INFOCOMM 2001, Anchorage, Alaska, 22–26 April 2001, vol. 1, pp. 329–337 (2001a)

Alvisi, L., Malkhi, D., Pierce, E., Reiter, M.: Fault detection for byzantine quorum systems. IEEE Trans. Parallel Distrib. Syst. **12**(9), 996–1007 (2001b)

Amir, Y.: Replication using group communication over a partitioned network. Ph.D. diss., Hebrew University of Jerusalem (1995)

Amir, Y., Dolev, D., Kramer, S., Malkhi, D.: Membership algorithms in broadcast domains. In: Proceedings of the Sixth WDAG, Israel, June 1992. Lecture Notes in Computer Science, vol. 647, pp. 292–312. Springer, Berlin (1992a)

Amir, Y., Dolev, D., Kramer, S., Malkhi, D.: Transis: A communication subsystem for high availability. In: Proceedings of the Twenty-Second Symposium on Fault-Tolerant Computing Systems, Boston, July 1992, pp. 76–84. IEEE Computer Society Press, New York (1992b)

Amir, O., Amir, Y., Dolev, D.: A highly available application in the Transis environment. In: Proceedings of the Workshop on Hardware and Software Architectures for Fault Tolerance. Lecture Notes in Computer Science, vol. 774, pp. 125–139. Springer, Berlin (1994)

Amir, Y., Moser, L.E., Melliar-Smith, P.M., Agarwal, D.A., Ciarfella, P.: The totem single-ring ordering and membership protocol. Trans. Comput. Syst. **13**(4), 311–342 (1995)

Amir, Y., Danilov, C., Stanton, J.: A low latency, loss tolerant architecture and protocol for wide area group communication. In: International Conference on Dependable Systems and Networks (DCCA-8), New York, June 25–28, 2000

Anceaume, E., Charron-Bost, B., Minet, P., Toueg, S.: On the formal specification of group membership services. Technical Report 95-1534, Department of Computer Science, Cornell University, August (1995)

Andersen, D., Balakrishnan, H., Kaashoek, M.F., Morris, R.: Resilient overlay networks. In: Proceedings of the 8th Workshop on Hot Topics in Operating Systems (HotOS-VIII), Schloss Elmau, Germany, May 2001a

Andersen, D., Balakrishnan, H., Kaashoek, M.F., Morris, R.: Resilient overlay networks. In: Proceedings of the Symposium on Operating Systems Principles 17, Vancouver, CA, Oct. 2001, pp. 131–145 (2001b)

Anderson, D., Franklin, J., Kaminsky, M., Phanishayee, A., Tan, L., Vasudevan, V.: FAWN: A fast array of wimpy nodes. In: Proc. 22nd ACM Symposium on Operating Systems Principles (SOSP), Big Sky, MT, October 2009

Anderson, T., et al.: Serverless network file systems. In: Proceedings of the Fifteenth Symposium on Operating Systems Principles, Copper Mountain Resort, CO, December 1995, pp. 109–126. ACM Press, New York (1995). Also ACM Trans. Comput. Syst. **13**(1) (1996)

Armand, F., Gien, M., Herrmann, F., Rozier, M.: Revolution 89, or distributing UNIX brings it back to its original virtues. Technical Report CS/TR-89-36-1, Chorus Systemes, Paris, France, August (1989)

Architecture Projects Management Limited: The advanced networked systems architecture: An engineer's introduction to the architecture. Technical Report TR-03-02, November (1989)

Architecture Projects Management Limited: The advanced networked systems architecture: A system designer's introduction to the architecture. Technical Report RC-253-00, April (1991a)

Architecture Projects Management Limited: The advanced networked systems architecture: An application programmer's introduction to the architecture. Technical Report TR-017-00, November (1991b)

Attiya, H., Bar-Noy, A., Dolev, D.: Sharing memory robustly in message-passing systems. J. ACM **42**(1), 124–142 (1995)

Babaoglu, O., Marzullo, K.: Consistent global states of distributed systems: Fundamental concepts and mechanisms. In: Mullender, S.J. (ed.) Distributed Systems, 2nd edn. Addison-Wesley/ACM Press, Reading (1993)

Babaoglu, O., Davoli, R., Giachini, L.A., Baker, M.B.: RELACS: A communications infrastructure for constructing reliable applications in large-scale distributed systems. BROADCAST Project Deliverable Report, Department of Computing Science, University of Newcastle upon Tyne, United Kingdom (1994)

Babaoglu, O., Davoli, R., Montresor, A.: Failure detectors, group membership, and view-synchronous communication in partitionable asynchronous systems. Technical Report UBLCS-95-19, Department of Computer Science, University of Bologna, November (1995)

Babaoglu, O., Bartoli, A., Dini, G.: Enriched view synchrony: A paradigm for programming dependable applications in partitionable asynchronous distributed systems. Technical Report, Department of Computer Science, University of Bologna, May (1996)

Bailey, N.: The Mathematical Theory of Epidemic Diseases, 2nd edn. Charles Griffen and Company, London (1975)

Baker, M.G., et al.: Measurements of a distributed file system. In: Proceedings of the Thirteenth ACM Symposium on Operating Systems Principles, Orcas Island, WA, November 1991, pp. 198–212 (1991)

Bal, H.E., Kaashoek, M.F., Tanenbaum, A.S.: Orca: A language for parallel programming of distributed systems. IEEE Trans. Softw. Eng. 190–205 (1992)

Balakrishnan, H., Katz, R.H., Padmanbhan, V.N.: The effects of asymmetry on TCP performance. Mob. Netw. Appl. **4**(3), 219–241 (1999)

Balakrishnan, H., Kaashoek, M.F., Karger, D., Morris, R., Stoica, I.: Looking up data in P2P systems. Commun. ACM 46(2), 43–48 (2003)

Balakrishnan, M., Marian, T., Birman, K., Weatherspoon, H., Vollset, E.: Maelstrom: Transparent error correction for lambda networks. In: NSDI 2008: Fifth Usenix Symposium on Networked Systems Design and Implementation, April 2008

Bartlett, J.F.: A nonstop kernel In: Proceedings of the Eighth ACM Symposium on Operating Systems Principles, Pacific Grove, CA, December 1981, pp. 22–29. ACM Press, New York (1981)

Bartlett, J., Gray, J., Horst, B.: Fault tolerance in tandem computing systems. In: Evolution of Fault-Tolerant Computing, pp. 55–76. Springer, Berlin (1987)

Bellovin, S.M., Merritt, M.: Limitations of the Kerberos authentication system. Comput. Commun. Rev. 20(5), 119–132 (1990)

Ben-Or, M.: Fast asynchronous byzantine agreement. In: Proceedings of the Fourth ACM Symposium on Principles of Distributed Computing, Minaki, Canada, August 1985, pp. 149–151 (1985)

Berners-Lee, T., et al.: The World Wide Web. Commun. ACM 37(8), 76–82 (1994)

Berners-Lee, T., et al.: Hypertext Transfer Protocol—HTTP 1.0. IETF HTTP Working Group Draft 02 (Best Current Practice), August (1995)

Bernstein, P.E., Hadzilacos, V., Goodman, N.: Concurrency Control and Recovery in Database Systems. Addison-Wesley, Reading (1987)

Bershad, B., Anderson, T., Lazowska, E., Levy, H.: Lightweight remote procedure call. In: Proceedings of the Eleventh ACM Symposium on Operating Systems Principles, Litchfield Springs, AZ, December 1989, pp. 102–113 (1989). Also ACM Trans. Comput. Syst. 8(1), 37–55 (1990)

Bershad, B., et al.: Extensibility, safety, and performance in the SPIN operating system. In: Proceedings of the Fifteenth Symposium on Operating Systems Principles, Copper Mountain Resort, CO, December 1995, pp. 267–284 (1995)

Bhagwan, R., Moore, D., Savage, S., Voelker, G.M.: Replication strategies for highly available peer-to-peer storage. In: Future Directions in Distributed Computing, pp. 153–158. Springer, Berlin (2003)

Bhide, A., Elnozahy, E.N., Morgan, S.P.: A highly available network file server. In: Proceedings of the USENIX Winter Conference, Austin, December 1991, pp. 199–205 (1991)

Birman, K.P.: Replication and availability in the ISIS system. In: Proc. of the 10th ACM Symp. on Operating Systems Principles, Orcas Island, WA, December 1985, pp. 79–86 (1985)

Birman, K.P.: A response to Cheriton and Skeen's criticism of causal and totally ordered communication. Oper. Syst. Rev. 28(1), 11–21 (1994)

Birman, K.P.: A review of experiences with reliable multicast. Softw. Pract. Exp. 29(9), 741–774 (1999)

Birman, K.P.: The league of SuperNets. IEEE Internet Comput. 7(5), 93–96 (2003)

Birman, K.P., Glade, B.B.: Consistent failure reporting in reliable communications systems. IEEE Softw., Special Issue on Reliability (1995)

Birman, K.P., Joseph, T.A.: Exploiting virtual synchrony in distributed systems. In: Proceedings of the Eleventh Symposium on Operating Systems Principles, Austin, November 1987, pp. 123–138. ACM Press, New York (1987a)

Birman, K.P., Joseph, T.A.: Reliable communication in the presence of failures. ACM Trans. Comput. Syst. 5(1), 47–76 (1987b)

Birman, K.P., van Renesse, R. (eds.): Reliable Distributed Computing with the Isis Toolkit. IEEE Computer Society Press, New York (1994)

Birman, K.P., van Renesse, R.: Software for reliable networks. Sci. Am. 274(5), 64–69 (1996)

Birman, K.P., van Renesse, R.: A history of the virtual synchrony replication model. In: Charron-Bost, B., Pedone, F., Schiper, A. (eds.) Replication: Theory and Practice. Chap. 6. Lecture Notes in Computer Science, vol. 5959, pp. 91–120. Springer, Berlin (2010)

Birman, K.P., Schiper, A., Stephenson, P.: Lightweight causal and atomic group multicast. ACM Trans. Comput. Syst. 9(3), 272–314 (1991)

Birman, K.P., Malkhi, D., Ricciardi, A., Schiper, A.: Uniform action in asynchronous distributed systems. Technical Report TR 94-1447, Department of Computer Science, Cornell University (1994)

Birman, K.P., Hayden, M., Ozkasap, O., Xiao, Z., Budiu, M., Minsky, Y.: Bimodal multicast. ACM Trans. Comput. Syst. **17**(2), 41–88 (1999)

Birman, K., Cantwell, J., Freedman, D., Huang, Q., Nikolov, P., Ostrowski, K.: Edge mashups for service-oriented collaboration. IEEE Comput. **42**(5) (2010)

Birman, K.P., Freedman, D.F., Huang, Q.: Overcoming CAP with consistent soft-state replication. IEEE Comput. Soc. Mag., special issue on the growing importance of the CAP conjecture, January/February 2012

Birrell, A.: Secure communication using remote procedure calls. ACM Trans. Comput. Syst. **3**(1), 1–14 (1985)

Birrell, A., Nelson, B., Implementing remote procedure call. ACM Trans. Program. Lang. Syst. **2**(1), 39–59 (1984)

Borg, A., Baumbach, J., Glazer, S.: A message system for supporting fault tolerance. In: Proceedings of the Ninth Symposium on Operating Systems Principles, Bretton Woods, NH, October 1983, pp. 90–99 (1983)

Borg, A., et al.: Fault tolerance under UNIX. ACM Trans. Comput. Syst. **3**(1), 1–23 (1985)

Borr, A., Wilhelmy, C.: Highly available data services for UNIX client/server networks: Why fault-tolerant hardware isn't the answer. In: Banatre, M., Lee, P. (eds.) Hardware and Software Architectures for Fault Tolerance. Lecture Notes in Computer Science, vol. 774, pp. 385–404. Springer, Berlin (1994)

Braun, T., Diot, C.: Protocol implementation using integrated layer processing. In: Proceedings of SIGCOMM-95, September 1995

Bressoud, T.C., Schneider, F.B.: Hypervisor-based fault tolerance. In: Proceedings of the Fifteenth Symposium on Operating Systems Principles, Copper Mountain Resort, CO, December 1995, pp. 1–11. ACM Press, New York (1995). Also ACM Trans. Comput. Syst. **13**(1) (1996)

Brewer, E.: Towards robust distributed systems. Keynote talk, ACM PODC (2000). Available as http://www.cs.berkeley.edu/~brewer/cs262b-2004/PODC-keynote.pdf

Brockschmidt, K.: Inside OLE-2. Microsoft Press, Redmond (1994)

Broder, A.Z., Frieze, A.M., Upfal, E.: Static and dynamic path selection on expander graphs: A random walk approach. J. Random Struct. Algorithms **14**(1), 87–109 (1999)

Budhiraja, N., et al.: The primary-backup approach. In: Mullender, S.J. (ed.) Distributed System, 2nd edn. Addison-Wesley/ACM Press, Reading (1993)

Burrows, M.: The Chubby lock service for loosely-coupled distributed systems. In: Proceedings of the 7th Symposium on Operating Systems Design and Implementation (OSDI '06), pp. 335–350. USENIX Association, Berkeley (2006)

Bykov, S., Geller, A., Kliot, G., Larus, J., Pandya, R., Thelin, J.: Orleans: Cloud computing for everyone. In: ACM Symposium on Cloud Computing (SOCC 2011), October 2011. ACM, New York (2011)

Carter, J.: Efficient distributed shared memory based on multi-protocol release consistency. Ph.D. diss., Rice University, August (1993)

Carzaniga, A., Rosenblum, D., Wolf, A.: Design and evaluation of a wide-area event notification service. ACM Trans. Comput. Syst. **19**(3) (2001)

Castro, M., Liskov, B.: Practical Byzantine fault tolerance and proactive recovery. ACM Trans. Comput. Syst. **20**(4), 398–461 (2002)

Castro, M., Druschel, P., Hu, Y.C., Rowstron, A.: Topology-aware routing in structured peer-to-peer overlay networks. In: Future Directions in Distributed Computing 2003, pp. 103–107. Springer, Berlin (2003a)

Castro, M., Rodrigues, R., Liskov, B.: BASE: Using abstraction to improve fault tolerance. ACM Trans. Comput. Syst. **21**(3), 236–269 (2003b)

Chandra, T., Toueg, S.: Time and message efficient reliable broadcasts. Technical Report TR 90-1094, Department of Computer Science, Cornell University, February (1990)

Chandra, T., Toueg, S.: Unreliable failure detectors for asynchronous systems. J. ACM (in press). Previous version in ACM Symposium on Principles of Distributed Computing (Montreal, 1991), pp. 325–340

Chandra, T., Hadzilacos, V., Toueg, S.: The weakest failure detector for solving consensus. In: ACM Symposium on Principles of Distributed Computing, August 1992, pp. 147–158 (1992)

Chandra, T., Hadzilacos, V., Toueg, S., Charron-Bost, B.: On the impossibility of group membership. In: Proceedings of the ACM Symposium on Principles of Distributed Computing, Vancouver, May 1996

Chandy, K.M., Lamport, L.: Distributed snapshots: Determining global states of distributed systems. ACM Trans. Comput. Syst. 3(1), 63–75 (1985)

Chang, M., Maxemchuk, N.: Reliable broadcast protocols. ACM Trans. Comput. Syst. 2(3), 251–273 (1984)

Chang, F., Dean, J., Ghemawat, S., Hsieh, W.C., Wallach, D.A., Burrows, M., Chandra, T., Fikes, A., Gruber, R.E.: Bigtable: A distributed storage system for structured data. ACM Trans. Comput. Syst. 26(2), 4 (2008), 26 pages

Charron-Bost, B.: Concerning the size of logical clocks in distributed systems. Inf. Process. Lett. 39(1), 11–16 (1991)

Chaum, D.: Untraceable electronic mail, return addresses, and digital pseudonyms. Commun. ACM 24(2), 84–88 (1981)

Cheriton, D., Skeen, D.: Understanding the limitations of causally and totally ordered communication. In: Proceedings of the Thirteenth ACM Symposium on Operating Systems Principles, Asheville, NC, December 1993, pp. 44–57. ACM Press, New York (1993)

Chilaragee, R.: Top five challenges facing the practice of fault tolerance. In: Banatre, M., Lee, P. (eds.) Hardware and Software Architectures for Fault Tolerance. Lecture Notes in Computer Science, vol. 774, pp. 3–12. Springer, Berlin (1994)

Cho, K., Birman, K.P.: A group communication approach for mobile computing. Technical Report TR94-1424, Department of Computer Science, Cornell University, May (1994)

Chockler, G., Keidar, I., Vitenberg, R.: Group communication specifications: A comprehensive study. ACM Comput. Surv. 33(4), 1–43 (2001)

Chockler, G., Gilbert, S., Gramoli, V.C., Musial, P.M., Shvartsman, A.A.: Reconfigurable distributed storage for dynamic networks. In: 9th International Conference on Principles of Distributed Systems (OPODIS'05), December 2005

Chockler, G., Laden, G., Vigfusson, Y.: Design and implementation of caching services in the cloud. IBM J. Res. Dev. (2011, to appear). Special Issue on Cloud Computing

Clark, D., Tennenhouse, M.: Architectural considerations for a new generation of protocols. In: Proceedings of SIGCOMM-87, August 1987, pp. 353–359 (1987)

Clark, D., Tennenhouse, D.L.: Architectural considerations for a new generation of protocols. In: Proceedings of the 1990 Symposium on Communication Architectures and Protocols, Philadelphia, September 1990, pp. 200–208. ACM Press, New York (1990)

Clark, D., Jacobson, V., Romkey, J., Salwen, H.: An analysis of TCP processing overhead. IEEE Commun. 27(6), 23–29 (1989)

Clarke, R., Knake, R.: Cyber War: The Next Threat to National Security and What to Do About It. HarperCollins e-books (April 20, 2010)

Clegg, M., Marzullo, K.: Clock synchronization in hard real-time distributed systems. Technical Report, Department of Computer Science, University of California, San Diego, March (1996)

Coan, B., Thomas, G.: Agreeing on a leader in real time. In: Proceedings of the Eleventh Real-Time Systems Symposium, December 1990, pp. 166–172 (1990)

Coan, B., Oki, B.M., Kolodner, E.K.: Limitations on database availability when networks partition. In: Proceedings of the Fifth ACM Symposium on Principles of Distributed Computing, Calgary, August 1986, pp. 187–194 (1986)

Comer, D.E.: Internetworking with TCP/IP. Principles, Protocols, and Architecture, vol. I. Prentice Hall, Englewood Cliffs (1991)

Comer, D.E., Stevens, D.L.: Internetworking with TCP/IP. Design, Implementation, and Internals, vol. II. Prentice Hall, Englewood Cliffs (1991)

Comer, D.E., Stevens, D.L.: Internetworking with TCP/IP. Client/Server Programming and Applications, vol. III. Prentice Hall, Englewood Cliffs (1993)

Cooper, E.: Replicated distributed programs. In: Proceedings of the Tenth ACM Symposium on Operating Systems Principles, Orcas Island, WA, December 1985, pp. 63–78. ACM Press, New York (1985)

Cooper, R.: Experience with causally and totally ordered group communication support—A cautionary tale. Oper. Syst. Rev. **28**(1), 28–32 (1994)

Cooper, D.A., Birman, K.P.: The design and implementation of a private message service for mobile computers. Wirel. Netw. **1**(3), 297–309 (1995)

Cooper, B.F., Ramakrishnan, R., Srivastava, U., Silberstein, A., Bohannon, P., Jacobsen, H.A., Puz, N., Weaver, D., Yerneni, R.: PNUTS: Yahoo!'s hosted data serving platform. In: Proc. 34th VLDB, August 2008, vol. 1, 2, pp. 1277–1288 (2008)

Coulouris, G., Dollimore, J., Kindberg, T.: Distributed Systems: Concepts and Design. Addison-Wesley, Reading (1994)

Cristian, F.: Probabilistic clock synchronization. Distrib. Comput. **3**(3), 146–158 (1989)

Cristian, F.: Reaching agreement on processor group membership in synchronous distributed systems. Distrib. Comput. **4**(4), 175–187 (1991a)

Cristian, F.: Understanding fault-tolerant distributed systems. Commun. ACM **34**(2), 57–78 (1991b)

Cristian, F.: Synchronous and asynchronous group communication. Commun. ACM **39**(4), 88–97 (1996)

Cristian, F., Delancy, R.: Fault tolerance in the advanced automation system. IBM Technical Report RJ7424, IBM Research Laboratories, San Jose, CA, April (1990)

Cristian, F., Fetzer, C.: Fault-tolerant internal clock synchronization. In: Proceedings of the Thirteenth Symposium on Reliable Distributed Systems, October 1994

Cristian, F., Schmuck, F.: Agreeing on process group membership in asynchronous distributed systems. Technical Report CSE95-428, Department of Computer Science and Engineering, University of California, San Diego (1995)

Cristian, F., Aghili, H., Strong, R., Dolev, D.: Atomic broadcast: From simple message diffusion to byzantine agreement. In: Proceedings of the Fifteenth International Symposium on Fault-Tolerant Computing, pp. 200–206. IEEE Computer Society Press, New York (1985). Revised as IBM Technical Report RJ5244

Cristian, F., Dolev, D., Strong, R., Aghili, H.: Atomic broadcast in a real-time environment. In: Fault-Tolerant Distributed Computing. Lecture Notes in Computer Science, vol. 448, pp. 51–71. Springer, Berlin (1990)

Dabek, F., Cox, R., Kaashoek, F., Morris, R.: Vivaldi: A decentralized network coordinate system. In: Proceedings of the 2004 Conference on Applications, Technologies, Architectures, and Protocols for Computer Communications (SIGCOMM '04), pp. 15–26. ACM, New York (2004)

Damm, A., Reisinger, J., Schwabl, W., Kopetz, H.: The real-time operating system of mars. ACM Oper. Syst. Rev. **22**(3), 141–157 (1989)

Davidson, S., Garcia-Molina, H., Skeen, D.: Consistency in a partitioned network: A survey. ACM Comput. Surv. **17**(3), 341–370 (1985)

Deering, S.E.: Multicast routing in internetworks and extended LANs. Comput. Commun. Rev. **18**(4), 55–64 (1988)

Demers, A., et al.: Epidemic algorithms for replicated data management. In: Proceedings of the Sixth Symposium on Principles of Distributed Computing, Vancouver, August 1987, pp. 1–12 (1987). Also Oper. Syst. Rev. **22**(1), 8–32 (1988)

Denning, D.: Digital signatures with RSA and other public-key cryptosystems. Commun. ACM **27**(4), 388–392 (1984)

Denning, D., Branstad, D.A.: Taxonomy for key escrow encryption systems. Commun. ACM **39**(3), 34–40 (1996)

Desmedt, Y.: Society and group-oriented cryptography: A new concept. In: Advances in Cryptology—CRYPTO'87 Proceedings. Lecture Notes in Computer Science, vol. 293, pp. 120–127. Springer, Berlin (1988)

Desmedt, Y., Frankel, Y., Yung, M.: Multi-receiver/multi-sender network security: Efficient authenticated multicast/feedback. In: Proceedings of the IEEE INFOCOM, May 1992

Diffie, W., Hellman, M.E.: Privacy and authentication: An introduction to cryptography. Proc. IEEE **673**, 397–427 (1979)

Diffie, W., Landau, S.: Privacy on the Line: The Politics of Wiretapping and Encryption. MIT Press, Cambridge (2007). Updated and expanded edition. ISBN-10: 0262042401

Digital Equipment Corporation: A technical description of the DECsafe available server environment (ASE). Digit. Tech. J. **7**(4), 89–100 (1995)

Dolev, S.: Self-stabilization. MIT Press, Cambridge (2000)

Dolev, D., Malkhi, D.: The Transis approach to high availability cluster communication. Commun. ACM **39**(4), 64–70 (1996)

Dolev, D., Malkhi, D., Strong, R.: A framework for partitionable membership service. Technical Report TR 95-4, Institute of Computer Science, Hebrew University of Jerusalem, March (1995)

Drushel, P., Peterson, L.L.: Fbufs: A high-bandwidth cross-domain transfer facility. In: Proceedings of the Thirteenth ACM Symposium on Operating Systems Principles, Pacific Grove, CA, December 1993, pp. 189–202. ACM Press, New York (1993)

Ekwall, R., Urbán, P., Schiper, A.: Robust TCP connections for fault tolerant computing. In: Proceedings of the 9th International Conference on Parallel and Distributed Systems (ICPDS), Taiwan ROC, Dec. 2002

Engler, D.R., Kaashoek, M.F., O'Toole, J.: Exokernel: An operating system architecture for application-level resource management. In: Proceedings of the Fifteenth Symposium on Operating Systems Principles, Copper Mountain Resort, CO, December 1995, pp. 251–266. ACM Press, New York (1995)

Eugster, P., Guerraoui, R., Handurukande, S.B., Kouznetsov, P., Kermarrec, A.-M.: Lightweight probabilistic broadcast. ACM Trans. Comput. Syst. **21**(4), 341–374 (2003)

Feeley, M., et al.: Implementing global memory management in a workstation cluster. In: Proceedings of the Fifteenth ACM SIGOPS Symposium on Operating Systems Principles, Copper Mountain Resort, CO, December 1995, pp. 201–212 (1995)

Fekete, A., Lynch, N., Shvartsman, A.: Specifying and using a partitionable group communication service. ACM Trans. Comput. Syst. **19**(2), 171–216 (2001)

Felton, E., Zahorjan, J.: Issues in the implementation of a remote memory paging system. Technical Report 91-03-09, Department of Computer Science and Engineering, University of Washington, March (1991)

Fidge, C.: Timestamps in message-passing systems that preserve the partial ordering. In: Proceedings of the Eleventh Australian Computer Science Conference (1988)

Fisher, M.J., Lynch, N.A., Merritt, M.: Easy impossibility proofs for distributed consensus problems. In: Proceedings of the Fourth Annual ACM Symposium on Principles of Distributed Computing, Minaki, Canada, August 1985. ACM Press, New York (1985a)

Fisher, M.J., Lynch, N.A., Paterson, M.S.: Impossibility of distributed computing with one faulty process. J. ACM **32**(2), 374–382 (1985b)

Frankel, Y.: A practical protocol for large group-oriented networks. In: Advances in Cryptology—EUROCRYPT '89. Lecture Notes in Computer Science, vol. 434, pp. 56–61. Springer, Berlin (1989)

Frankel, Y., Desmedt, Y.: Distributed reliable threshold multisignature. Technical Report TR-92-0402, Department of EECS, University of Wisconsin, Milwaukee, June (1992)

Freedman, D., Marian, T., Lee, J.H., Birman, K., Weatherspoon, H., Xu, C.: Exact temporal characterization of 10 Gbps optical wide-area network. In: Proceedings of the 10th ACM SIGCOMM Internet Measurement Conference (IMC), Melbourne, Australia, November 2010

Friedman, R.: Consistency conditions for distributed shared memories. Ph.D. thesis, Technion (1994)

Friedman, R., Birman, K.P.: Using group communication technology to implement a reliable and scalable distributed IN coprocessor. In: TINA'96: The Convergence of Telecommunications and Distributed Computing Technologies, Heidelberg, September 1996, pp. 25–42. VDE-Verlag, Berlin (1996). Also Technical Report, Department of Computer Science, Cornell University, March (1996)

Friedman, R., van Renesse, R.: Strong and weak virtual synchrony in Horus. Technical Report 95-1537, Department of Computer Science, Cornell University, August (1995a)

Friedman, R., van Renesse, R.: Packing messages as a tool for boosting the performance of total ordering protocols. Technical Report 95-1527, Department of Computer Science, Cornell University, July (1995b). IEEE Trans. Netw. (submitted)

Friedman, R., Keider, I., Malkhi, D., Birman, K.P., Dolev, D.: Deciding in partitionable networks. Technical Report 95-1554, Department of Computer Science, Cornell University, October (1995)

Ganger, G., McKusick, M., Soules, C., Patt, Y.: Soft updates: A solution to the metadata update problem in file systems. ACM Trans. Comput. Syst. **18**(2), 127–153 (2000)

Garbinato, B., Guerraoui, R.: Using the strategy pattern to compose reliable distributed protocols. In: Proceedings of 3rd USENIX COOTS, Portland, Oregon, June 1997

Gharachorloo, K., et al.: Memory consistency and event ordering in scalable shared-memory multiprocessors. In: Proceedings of the Seventeenth Annual International Symposium on Computer Architecture, Seattle, May 1990, pp. 15–26 (1990)

Ghemawat, S., Gobioff, H., Leung, S.T.: File and storage systems: The Google file system. In: 19th ACM Symposium on Operating Systems Principles (SOSP), Bolton Landing, NY, October 2003

Gibbs, B.W.: Software's chronic crisis. Sci. Am. (1994)

Gifford, D.: Weighted voting for replicated data. In: Proceedings of the Seventh ACM Symposium on Operating Systems Principles, Pacific Grove, CA, December 1979, pp. 150–162. ACM Press, New York (1979)

Gilbert, S., Lynch, N.: Brewer's conjecture and the feasibility of consistent, available, partition-tolerant web services. ACM PODC (2002), published as ACM SIGACT News **33**(2), 51–59 (2002)

Gilbert, S., Lynch, N., Shvartsman, A.: Rambo II: Rapidly reconfigurable atomic memory for dynamic networks. In: Proc. of the 17th Intl. Symp. on Distributed Computing (DISC), June 2003, pp. 259–268 (2003)

Glade, B.B., Birman, K.P., Cooper, R.C., van Renesse, R.: Lightweight process groups in the Isis system. Distrib. Syst. Eng. J. (1993)

Golding, R.A.: Distributed epidemic algorithms for replicated tuple spaces. Technical Report HPL-CSP-91-15, June (1991). Concurrent systems project, Hewlett-Packard Laboratories

Golding, R.A.: Weak consistency group communication and membership. Ph.D. diss., Computer and Information Sciences Department, University of California, Santa Cruz (1992)

Golding, R., Taylor, K.: Group membership in the epidemic style. Technical Report UCSC-CRL-92-13, University of California, Santa Cruz, May (1992)

Gong, L.: Securely replicating authentication services. In: Proceedings of the Ninth International Conference on Distributed Computing Systems, August 1989, pp. 85–91 (1989)

Gopal, A., Strong, R., Toueg, S., Cristian, F.: Early-delivery atomic broadcast. In: Proceedings of the Ninth ACM Symposium on Principles of Distributed Computing, Toronto, August 1990, pp. 297–309. ACM Press, New York (1990)

Gosling, J., McGilton, H.: The Java language environment: A white paper. Sun Microsystems, Inc., October (1995a). Available as http://java.sun.com/langEnv/index.html

Gosling, J., McGilton, H.: The Java programmer's guide: A white paper. Sun Microsystems, Inc., October (1995b). Available as http://java.sun.com/progGuide/index.html

Govindran, R., Anderson, D.P.: Scheduling and IPC mechanisms for continuous media. In: Proceedings of the Twelfth ACM Symposium on Operating Systems Principles, Asilomar, CA, October 1991, pp. 68–80. ACM Press, New York (1991)

Gramoli, V., Vigfusson, Y., Birman, K., Kermarrec, A.-M., van Renesse, R.: Slicing distributed systems. IEEE Trans. Comput. **58**(11), 1444–1455 (2009)

Gray, J.: Notes on database operating systems. In: Operating Systems: An Advanced Course. Lecture Notes in Computer Science, vol. 60, pp. 393–481. Springer, Berlin (1978)

Gray, J.: A census of tandem system availability between 1985 and 1990. Technical Report 90.1, Tandem Computer Corporation, September (1990)

Gray, J., Reuter, A.: Transaction Processing: Concepts and Techniques. Morgan Kaufmann, San Mateo (1993)

Gray, J., Bartlett, J., Horst, R.: Fault tolerance in tandem computer systems. In: Avizienis, A., Kopetz, H., Laprie, J.C. (eds.) The Evolution of Fault-Tolerant Computing. Springer, Berlin (1987)

Gray, J., Helland, P., Shasha, D.: Dangers of replication and a solution. In: ACM SIGMOD International Conference on Management of Data, Montreal, Quebec, Canada, June 1996

Gribble, S., et al.: The Ninja architecture for robust Internet-scale systems and services. Comput. Netw. **35**(4), 473–497 (2001)

Guerraoui, R.: Revisiting the relationship between nonblocking atomic commitment and consensus. In: International Workshop on Distributed Algorithms, September 1995, pp. 87–100 (1995)

Guerraoui, R., Schiper, A.: Gamma-accurate failure detectors. Technical Report APFL, Lausanne, Switzerland: Départment d'Informatique (1996)

Guerraoui, G., Felber, P., Garbinato, B., Mazouni, K.: System support for object groups. In: OOPSLA '98: Proceedings of the 13th ACM SIGPLAN Conference on Object-oriented Programming, Systems, Languages, and Applications, October 1998

Guerraoui, R., Knežević, N., Quéma, V., Vukolić, M.: The next 700 BFT protocols. In: Proceedings of EuroSys, Paris, France, April 2010, pp. 363–376 (2010)

Gupta, I., Birman, K.P., Linga, P., Demers, A., van Renesse, R.: Kelips: Building an efficient and stable P2P DHT through increased memory and background overhead. In: Proc. 2nd International Workshop on Peer-to-Peer Systems (IPTPS '03), Oakland, CA (2003)

Gurwitz, R.F., Dean, M., Schantz, R.E.: Programming support in the Chronus distributed operating system. In: Proceedings of the Sixth International Conference on Distributed Computing Systems, pp. 486–493. IEEE Computer Society Press, New York (1986)

Haeberlen, A., Kuznetsov, P., Druschel, P.: PeerReview: Practical accountability for distributed systems. In: Proceedings of the 21st ACM Symposium on Operating Systems Principles (SOSP '07), Stevenson, WA, October 2007

Hagmann, R.: Reimplementing the cedar file system using logging and group commit. In: Proceedings of the Eleventh ACM Symposium on Operating Systems Principles, Austin, November 1987, pp. 155–171. ACM Press, New York (1987)

Hall, R., Mathur, A., Jahanian, F., Prakash, A., Rassmussen, C.: Corona: A communication service for scalable, reliable group collaboration systems. In: Ackerman, M.S. (ed.) Proceedings of the ACM Conference on Computer Supported Cooperative Work (CSCW '96), pp. 140–149. ACM, New York (1996)

Halpern, J.Y., Moses, Y.: Knowledge and common knowledge in a distributed environment. J. ACM **37**(3), 549–587 (1990)

Hartman, J.H., Ousterhout, J.K.: The Zebra striped network file system. In: Proceedings of the Thirteenth ACM Symposium on Operating Systems Principles, Asheville, NC, December 1993, pp. 29–43. ACM Press, New York (1993)

Heidemann, J., Popek, G.: File system development with stackable layers. Commun. ACM **12**(1), 58–89 (1994)

Heidemann, J., Popek, G.: Performance of cache coherence in stackable filing. In: Proceedings of the Fifteenth ACM Symposium on Operating Systems Principles, Copper Mountain Resort, CO, December 1995, pp. 127–142 (1995)

Herlihy, M.: A quorum-consensus replication method for abstract data types. ACM Trans. Comput. Syst. **4**(1), 32–53 (1986)

Herlihy, M.P., Tygar, J.D.: How to make replicated data secure. In: Advances in Cryptography—CRYPTO'87 Proceedings. Lecture Notes in Computer Science, vol. 293, pp. 379–391. Springer, Berlin (1987)

Herlihy, M., Wing, J.: Linearizability: A correctness condition for concurrent objects. ACM Trans. Program. Lang. Syst. **12**(3), 463–492 (1990)

Hildebrand, D.: An architectural overview of QNX. In: Proceedings of the First USENIX Workshop on Microkernels and Other Kernel Architectures, Seattle, April 1992, pp. 113–126 (1992)

Holliday, J., Agrawal, D., El Abbadi, A.: The performance of database replication with group multicast. In: FTCS 1999, pp. 158–165 (1999)

Holliday, J., Agrawal, D., El Abbadi, A.: Partial database replication using epidemic communication. In: ICDCS 2002, p. 485 (2002)

Hoory, S., Linial, N., Widgerson, A.: Expander graphs and their applications. Bull. Am. Math. Soc. **43**(4), 439–561 (2006). doi:10.1090/S0273-0979-06-01126-8

Howard, J., et al.: Scale and performance in a distributed file system. In: Proceedings of the Eleventh ACM Symposium on Operating Systems Principles, Austin, November 1987. ACM Press, New York (1987). Also ACM Trans. Comput. Syst. **5**(1) (1988)

Huang, Q., Birman, K., Vigfusson, Y., Li, H.: Quilt: A patchwork of multicast regions. In: 4th ACM International Conference on Distributed Event-Based Systems (DEBS2010), Cambridge, United Kingdom, July 2010

Hunker, J.: Creeping Failure: How We Broke the Internet and What We Can Do to Fix It. McClelland and Stewart, Toronto (2011). Reprint edition (September 27). ISBN-10: 0771040245

Hunt, G.D.: Multicast flow control on local area networks. Ph.D. diss., Department of Computer Science, Cornell University, February (1995). Also available as Technical Report TR-95-1479

Iyer, S., Rowstron, A., Druschel, P.: Squirrel: A decentralized peer-to-peer web cache. In: Principles of Distributed Computing (PODC), pp. 213–222 (2002)

Jacobson, V.: Congestion avoidance and control. In: Proceedings of the ACM SIGCOMM '88, Palo Alto (1988)

Jacobson, V.: Compressing TCP/IP headers for low-speed serial links. Technical Report RFC 114, Network Working Group, February (1990)

Jelasity, M., Babaoglu, O.: T-Man: Gossip-based overlay topology management. In: European Workshop on Engineering Self-organising Systems, pp. 1–15 (2005)

Jelasity, M., Voulgaris, S., Guerraoui, R., Kermarrec, A.M., van Steen, M.: Gossip-based peer sampling. Trans. Comput. Syst. **25**(3) (2007)

Jelasity, M., Montresor, A., Babaoglu, O.: T-Man: Gossip-based fast overlay topology construction. Comput. Netw. **53**(13) (2009)

Johansen, H., Allavena, A., van Renesse, R.: An introduction to the TACOMA distributed system (Version 1.0). Computer Science Technical Report 95-23, University of Tromsö, June (1995a)

Johansen, H., Allavena, A., van Renesse, R.: Fireflies: Scalable support for intrusion-tolerant network overlays. In: Proceedings of the 1st ACM SIGOPS/EuroSys European Conference on Computer Systems 2006 (EuroSys '06), pp. 3–13. ACM, New York (2006)

Johnson, K., Kaashoek, M.F., Wallach, D.: CRL: High-performance all software distributed shared memory. In: Proceedings of the Fifteenth ACM Symposium on Operating Systems Principles, Copper Mountain Resort, CO, December 1995, pp. 213–228 (1995)

Jones, M.B.: Interposition agents: Transparent interposing user code at the system interface. In: Proceedings of the Fourteenth ACM Symposium on Operating Systems Principles, Asheville, NC, December 1993, pp. 80–93. ACM Press, New York (1993)

Joseph, T.A.: Low cost management of replicated data. Ph.D. diss., Cornell University (1986). Also Technical Report, Department of Computer Science, Cornell University

Joseph, A., de Lespinasse, A., Tauber, J., Gifford, D., Kaashoek, F.K.: Rover: A toolkit for mobile information access. In: 15th ACM Symposium on Operating Systems (SOSP), Copper Mountain, CO, December 1995

Junqueira, F., Reed, B.: The life and times of a ZooKeeper. In: ACM Symposium on Parallel Algorithms and Architectures (SPAA) (2009). Also published as a "brief announcement" in the Symposium on Principles of Distributed Computing (PODC)

Junqueira, F., Hunt, P., Konar, M., Reed, B.: The ZooKeeper coordination service (poster). In: Symposium on Operating Systems Principles (SOSP) (2009)

Kaashoek, F.: Group communication in distributed computer systems. Ph.D. diss., Vrije Universiteit (1992)

Kalantar, M.: Issues in ordered multicast performance: A simulation study. Ph.D. diss., Department of Computer Science, Cornell University, August (1995). Also Technical Report TR-95-1531

Karamcheti, V., Chien, A.A.: Software overhead in messaging layers: Where does the time go? In: Proceedings of the Sixth ACM Symposium on Principles of Programming Languages and Operating Systems, San Jose, CA, October 1994. ACM Press, New York (1994)

Kay, J., Pasquale, J.: The importance of nondata touching processing overheads. In: Proceedings of SIGCOMM-93, August 1993, pp. 259–269 (1993)

Keidar, I.: Consistency and high availability of information dissemination in multi-processor networks. Ph.D. thesis, Hebrew University of Jerusalem, October (1998)

Keidar, I.: Challenges in evaluating distributed algorithms. In: Future Directions in Distributed Computing. Lecture Notes in Computer Science, vol. 2584, pp. 40–44 (2010)

Keidar, I., Dolev, D.: Increasing the resilience of atomic commit at no additional cost. In: Proceedings of the 1995 ACM Symposium on Principles of Database Systems, May 1995, pp. 245–254 (1995)

Keidar, I., Dolev, D.: Totally ordered broadcast in the face of network partitions. Exploiting group communication for replication in partitionable networks. In: Avresky, D. (ed.) Dependable Network Computing, pp. 51–75. Kluwer Academic, Dordrecht (2000). Chap. 3

Keidar, I., Khazan, R.: A virtually synchronous group multicast algorithm for WANs: Formal approach. SIAM J. Comput. 32(1), 78–130 (2002)

Keidar, I., Khazan, R., Lynch, N., Shvartsman, A.: An inheritance-based technique for building simulation proofs incrementally. ACM Trans. Softw. Eng. Methodol. 11(1), 63–91 (2002a)

Keidar, I., Sussman, J., Marzullo, K., Dolev, D.: Moshe: A group membership service for wans. ACM Trans. Comput. Syst. 20(3), 1–48 (2002b)

Kermarrec, A.M., Rowstron, A., Shapiro, M., Druschel, P.: The IceCube approach to the reconciliation of divergent replicas. In: Principles of Distributed Computing, pp. 210–218 (2001)

Kermarrec, A.M., Pace, A., Quéma, V., Schiavoni, V.: NAT-resilient gossip peer sampling. In: Proceedings of the International Conference on Distributed Computing Systems (ICDCS), Montreal, Canada, June 2009, pp. 360–367 (2009)

Kistler, J.J., Satyanarayanan, M.: Disconnected operation in the Coda file system. ACM Trans. Comput. Syst. 10(1), 3–25 (1992)

Kleinberg, J.: Navigation in a small world. Nature 406, 845 (2000a)

Kleinberg, J.: The small-world phenomenon: An algorithmic perspective. In: Proc. 32nd ACM Symposium on Theory of Computing (2000b). Also appears as Cornell Computer Science Technical Report 99-1776 (October 1999)

Kleinberg, J.: Small-world phenomena and the dynamics of information. Adv. Neural Inf. Process. Syst. 14 (2001)

Kleinberg, J.: The small-world phenomenon and decentralized search. A short essay as part of Math Awareness Month 2004. SIAM News 37(3) (2004)

Kopetz, H., Ochsenreiter, W.: Clock synchronization in distributed real-time systems. IEEE Trans. Comput. C36(8), 933–940 (1987)

Kopetz, H., Verissimo, P.: Real-time dependability concepts. In: Mullender, S.J. (ed.) Distributed Systems, 2nd edn., pp. 411–446. Addison-Wesley/ACM Press, Reading (1993)

Kotla, R., Alvisi, L., Dahlin, M., Clement, A., Wong, E.: Zyzzyva: Speculative byzantine fault tolerance. ACM Trans. Comput. Syst. 27(4) (2009)

Kronenberg, N., Levy, H., Strecker, W.: VAXClusters: A closely-coupled distributed system. In: Proceedings of the Tenth ACM Symposium on Operating Systems Principles, Orcas Island, WA, December 1985. Also ACM Trans. Comput. Syst. 4(2), 130–146 (1986)

Kubiatowicz, J.: Extracting guarantees from chaos. Commun. ACM 46(2), 33–38 (2003)

Kubiatowicz, J., Bindel, D., Chen, Y., Czerwinski, S., Eaton, P., Geels, D., Gummadi, R., Rhea, S., Weatherspoon, H., Weimer, W., Wells, C., Zhao, B.: OceanStore: An architecture for global-scale persistent storage. In: Proceedings of ACM, ASPLOS (2000a)

Kubiatowicz, J., et al.: OceanStore: An architecture for global-scale persistent storage. In: Proceedings of Architectural Support for Programming Languages and Systems (ASPLOS), pp. 190–201 (2000b)

Ladin, R., Liskov, B., Shrira, L., Ghemawat, S.: Lazy replication: Exploiting the semantics of distributed services. In: Proceedings of the Tenth ACM Symposium on Principles of Distributed Computing, Quebec, August 1990, pp. 43–58. ACM Press, New York (1990)

Ladin, R., Liskov, B., Shrira, L., Ghemawat, S.: Providing availability using lazy replication. ACM Trans. Comput. Syst. **10**(4), 360–391 (1992)

Laih, C.S., Harn, L.: Generalized threshold cryptosystems. In: Proceedings of ASIACRYPT '91 (1991)

Lakshman, A., Malik, P.: Cassandra: A structured storage system on a P2P network. In: Proceedings of the Twenty-First Annual Symposium on Parallelism in Algorithms and Architectures (SPAA '09), pp. 47. ACM, New York (2009)

Lamport, L.: Time, clocks, and the ordering of events in a distributed system. Commun. ACM **21**(7), 558–565 (1978a)

Lamport, L.: The implementation of reliable distributed multiprocess systems. Comput. Netw. **2**, 95–114 (1978b)

Lamport, L.: Using time instead of timeout for fault-tolerant distributed systems. ACM Trans. Program. Lang. Syst. **6**(2), 254–280 (1984)

Lamport, L.: The part-time parliament. ACM Trans. Comput. Syst. **16**, 133–169 (1998)

Lamport, L.: Paxos made simple. Distrib. Comput. Column ACM SIGACT News **32**(4), 51–58 (2001)

Lamport, L., Melliar-Smith, P.M.: Synchronizing clocks in the presence of faults. J. ACM **32**(1), 52–78 (1985)

Lamport, L., Malkhi, D., Zhou, L.: Vertical Paxos and primary-backup replication. In: Proceedings of the 28th ACM Symposium on Principles of Distributed Computing (PODC'09), pp. 312–313 (2009a)

Lamport, L., Malkhi, D., Zhou, L.: Reconfiguring a state machine. Technical report, Microsoft Research (2009b)

Lampson, B., Abadi, M., Burrows, M., Wobber, E.: Authentication in distributed systems: Theory and practice. ACM Trans. Comput. Syst. **10**(4), 265–434 (1992)

Lee, E., Seshia, S.: Introduction to Embedded Systems, A Cyber-Physical Systems Approach. http://LeeSeshia.org. ISBN 978-0-557-70857-4 (2011)

Lessig, L.: Code and Other Laws of Cyberspace. Basic Books, New York (1999). ISBN 046503912X

Leveson, N.: Safeware: System safety and computers. Addison-Wesley, Reading (1995)

Li, K., Hudak, P.: Memory coherence in a shared virtual memory system. ACM Trans. Comput. Syst. **7**(4), 321–359 (1989)

Li, N., Mitchell, J.C., Winsborough, W.H.: Design of a role-based trust management framework. In: Proceedings of the 2002 IEEE Symposium on Security and Privacy, May 2002, pp. 114–130. IEEE Computer Society Press, Los Alamitos (2002)

Liskov, B.: Practical uses of synchronized clocks in distributed systems. Distrib. Comput. **6**(4), 211–219 (1993)

Liskov, B., Scheifler, R.: Guardians actions: Linguist support for robust, distributed programs. ACM Trans. Program. Lang. Syst. **5**(3), 381–404 (1983)

Liskov, B., Curtis, D., Johnson, P., Scheifler, R.: Implementation of Argus. In: Proceedings of the Eleventh ACM Symposium on Operating Systems Principles, Austin, November 1987, pp. 111–122. ACM Press, New York (1987)

Liskov, B., et al.: Replication in the Harp file system. In: Proceedings of the Twelfth ACM Symposium on Operating Systems Principles, Asilomar, CA, October 1991, pp. 226–238. ACM Press, New York (1991)

Liu, X.: Evaluation of the virtual interface architecture (VIA). Tech Report, UCSD, June (1998)

Liu, X., Kreitz, C., van Renesse, R., Hickey, J., Hayden, M., Birman, K.P., Constable, R.: Building reliable, high-performance communication systems from components. In: Proc. of the 17th ACM Symposium on Operating System Principles, Kiawah Island Resort, SC, December 1999

Lorch, J.R., Adya, A., Bolosky, W.J., Chaiken, R., Douceur, J.R., Howell, J.: The SMART way to migrate replicated stateful services. In: Proc. of the 1st Eurosys Conference, Leuven, Belgium, April 2006, pp. 103–115 (2006)

Lynch, N.: Distributed Algorithms. Morgan Kaufmann, San Mateo (1996)

Lynch, N., Shvartsman, A.A.: RAMBO: A reconfigurable atomic memory service for dynamic networks. In: Proc. of the 16th International Symposium on Distributed Computing, Toulouse, France, October 2002, pp. 173–190 (2002)

MacCormick, J., Murphy, N., Najork, M., Thekkath, C.A., Zhou, L.: Boxwood: Abstractions as the foundation for storage infrastructure. In: Symposium on Operating System Design and Implementation (OSDI), pp. 105–120. USENIX, Berkeley (2004)

Macedo, R.A., Ezhilchlvan, P., Shrivastava, S.: Newtop: A total order multicast protocol using causal blocks. BROADCAST Project Technical Reports, vol. I, Department of Computer Science, University of Newcastle upon Tyne, October (1993)

Maffeis, S.: Adding group communication and fault tolerance to CORBA. In: Proceedings of the 1995 USENIX Conference on Object-Oriented Technologies, Monterey, CA, June 1995

Malkhi, D.: Multicast communication for high availability. Ph.D. diss., Hebrew University of Jerusalem (1994)

Malkhi, D., Reiter, M.K.: Byzantine quorum systems. Distrib. Comput. 11(4), 203–213 (1998)

Malkhi, D., Reiter, M.K.: An architecture for survivable coordination in large distributed systems. IEEE Trans. Knowl. Data Eng. 12(2), 187–202 (2000)

Malkhi, D., Reiter, M., Wool, A., Wright, R.: Probabilistic quorum systems. Inf. Comput. J. 170(2) (2001a)

Malkhi, D., Reiter, M.K., Tulone, D., Ziskind, E.: Persistent objects in the Fleet system. In: Proceedings of the 2nd DARPA Information Survivability Conference and Exposition (DISCEX II), June 2001, vol. II, pp. 126–136 (2001b)

Malloth, C.: Conception and implementation of a toolkit for building fault-tolerant distributed applications in large-scale networks. Ph.D. diss., Swiss Federal Institute of Technology, Lausanne (EPFL) (1996)

Martin, J.-P., Alvisi, L.: A framework for dynamic byzantine storage. In: Proc. of the Intl. Conf. on Dependable Systems and Networks, pp. 325–334 (2004)

Marzullo, K.: Maintaining the time in a distributed system. Ph.D. diss., Department of Electrical Engineering, Stanford University, June (1984)

Marzullo, K.: Tolerating failures of continuous valued sensors. ACM Trans. Comput. Syst. 8(4), 284–304 (1990)

Mattern, F.: Time and global states in distributed systems. In: Proceedings of the International Workshop on Parallel and Distributed Algorithms. North-Holland, Amsterdam (1989)

McKusick, M.K., Joy, W., Leffler, S., Fabry, R.S.: A fast file system for UNIX. Comput. Syst. 2(3), 181–197 (1984). Retrieved 2008-12-30

Melliar-Smith, P.M., Moser, L.E.: Fault-tolerant distributed systems based on broadcast communication. In: Proceedings of the Ninth International Conference on Distributed Computing Systems, June 1989, pp. 129–133 (1989)

Melliar-Smith, P.M., Moser, L.E.: Trans: A reliable broadcast protocol. IEEE Trans. Commun. 140(6), 481–493 (1993)

Melliar-Smith, P.M., Moser, L.E., Agrawala, V.: Membership algorithms for asynchronous distributed systems. In: Proceedings of the IEEE Eleventh ICDCS, May 1991, pp. 480–488 (1991)

Milner, R., Tofte, M., Harper, R.: The Definition of Standard ML. MIT Press, Cambridge (1990)

Mishra, S., Peterson, L.L., Schlichting, R.D.: A membership protocol based on partial order. In: Proceedings of the IEEE International Working Conference on Dependable Computing for Critical Applications, February 1991, pp. 137–145 (1991)

Mogul, J., Rashid, R., Accetta, M.: The packet filter: An efficient mechanism for user-level network code. In: Proceedings of the Eleventh ACM Symposium on Operating Systems Principles, Austin, November 1987, pp. 39–51. ACM Press, New York (1987)

Montresor, A.: System support for programming object-oriented dependable applications in partitionable systems. Ph.D. thesis, University of Bologna, Italy (2000)

Moser, L.E., Amir, Y., Melliar-Smith, P.M., Agarwal, D.A.: Extended virtual synchrony. In: Proceedings of the Fourteenth International Conference on Distributed Computing Systems, June 1994, pp. 56–65. IEEE Computer Society Press, New York (1994a). Also Technical Report TR-93-22, Department of ECE, University of California, Santa Barbara, December (1993)

Moser, L.E., Melliar-Smith, P.M., Agarwal, U.: Processor membership in asynchronous distributed systems. IEEE Trans. Parallel Distrib. Syst. **5**(5), 459–473 (1994b)

Moser, L.E., Melliar-Smith, P.M., Agarwal, D.A., Budhia, R.K., Lingley-Papadopoulos, C.A.: Totem: A fault-tolerant multicast group communication system. Commun. ACM **39**(4), 54–63 (1996)

Moss, J.E.: Nested transactions and reliable distributed computing. In: Proceedings of the Second Symposium on Reliability in Distributed Software and Database Systems, pp. 33–39 (1982)

Mullender, S.J., et al.: Amoeba—A distributed operating system for the 1990s. IEEE Comput. **23**(5), 44–53 (1990)

Mummert, L.B., Ebling, M.R., Satyanarayanan, M.: Exploiting weak connectivity for mobile file access. In: Proceedings of the Fifteenth Symposium on Operating Systems Principles, Copper Mountain Resort, CO, December 1995, pp. 143–155. ACM Press, New York (1995). Also ACM Trans. Comput. Syst. **13**(1) (1996)

Muthitacharoen, A., Chen, B., Mazieres, D.: A low-bandwidth network file system. In: 18th ACM Symposium on Operating Systems Principles (SOSP '01), Chateau Lake Louise, Banff, Canada, October 2001

Muthitacharoen, A., Morris, R., Gil, T., Ivy, B. Chen: A read/write peer-to-peer file system. In: Proceedings of the 5th USENIX Symposium on Operating Systems Design and Implementation (OSDI '02), Boston, Massachusetts, December 2002

National Bureau of Standards: Data Encryption Standard. Federal Information Processing Standards Publication, vol. 46. Government Printing Office, Washington (1977)

Needham, R.M., Schroeder, M.D.: Using encryption for authentication in large networks of computers. Commun. ACM **21**(12), 993–999 (1988)

Neiger, G.: A new look at membership services. In: Proceedings of the Fifteenth ACM Symposium on Principles of Distributed Computing, Vancouver (1996). In press

Nelson, M., Welsh, B., Ousterhout, J.: Caching in the Sprite network file system. In: Proceedings of the Eleventh ACM Symposium on Operating Systems Principles, Austin, November 1987. ACM Press, New York (1987). Also ACM Trans. Comput. Syst. **6**(1) (1988)

Object Management Group and X/Open: Common Object Request Broker: Architecture and Specification. Reference OMG 91.12.1 (1991)

Oki, B., Liskov, B.: Viewstamped replication: A new primary copy method to support highly-available distributed systems. In: Proceedings of the Seventh Annual ACM Symposium on Principles of Distributed Computing (PODC '88), pp. 8–17. ACM, New York (1988)

Oki, B., Pfluegl, M., Siegel, A., Skeen, D.: The information bus-an architecture for extensible distributed systems. In: Proceedings of the Thirteenth ACM Symposium on Operating Systems Principles, Asheville, NC, December 1993, pp. 58–68. ACM Press, New York (1993)

Ostrowski, K., Birman, K.: Storing and accessing live mashup content in the cloud. SIGOPS Oper. Syst. Rev. **44**(2) (2009)

Ostrowski, K., Birman, K., Dolev, D.: QuickSilver scalable multicast (QSM). In: 7th IEEE International Symposium on Network Computing and Applications (IEEE NCA 2008), Cambridge, MA, July 2008a

Ostrowski, K., Birman, K., Dolev, D., Ahnn, J.H.: Programming with live distributed objects. In: Vitek, J. (ed.) 22nd European Conference on Object-Oriented Programming (ECOOP 2008), Paphos, Cyprus, July 7–11, 2008. Lecture Notes in Computer Science, vol. 5142, pp. 463–489. Springer, Berlin (2008b)

Ousterhout, J.: Why aren't operating systems getting faster as fast as hardware. In: USENIX Summer Conference Proceedings, Anaheim, CA, pp. 247–256 (1990)

Ousterhout, J.: TCL and the TK Toolkit. Addison-Wesley, Reading (1994)

Ousterhout, J., Da Costa, H., Harrison, D., Kunze, J.A., Kupfer, M., Thompson, J.G.: A trace-driven analysis of the UNIX 4.2 BSD file system. In: Proceedings of the Tenth ACM Symposium on Operating Systems Principles, Orcas Island, WA, December 1985, pp. 15–24. ACM Press, New York (1985)

Ousterhout, J., et al.: The sprite network operating system. Computer **21**(2), 23–36 (1988)

Pai, V.S., Druschel, P., Zwaenepoel, W.: IO-Lite: A unified I/O buffering and caching system. In: 3rd Symposium on Operating Systems Design and Implementation (OSDI), New Orleans, LA, February 1999

Patino-Martinez, M., Jimenez-Peris, R., Kemme, B., Alonso, G.: MIDDLE-R: Consistent database replication at the middleware level. Trans. Comput. Syst. **23**(4) (2005)

Patterson, D., Gibson, G., Katz, R.: A case for redundant arrays of inexpensive disks (RAID). In: Proceedings of the 1988 ACM Conference on Management of Data (SIGMOD), Chicago, June 1988, pp. 109–116 (1988)

Pedone, F., Guerraoui, R., Schiper, A.: Exploiting atomic broadcast in replicated databases. In: Proceedings EuroPar 98 (1998)

Petersen, K., Spreitzer, M., Terry, D., Theimer, M., Demers, A.: Flexible update propagation for weakly consistent replication. In: Proceedings of the 16th ACM Symposium on Operating Systems Principles (SOSP-16), Saint Malo, France, October 5–8, pp. 288–301 (1997)

Peterson, L.: Preserving context information in an IPC abstraction. In: Proceedings of the Sixth Symposium on Reliability in Distributed Software and Database Systems, March 1987, pp. 22–31. IEEE Computer Society Press, New York (1987)

Peterson, I.: Fatal Defect: Chasing Killer Computer Bugs. Time Books/Random House, New York (1995)

Peterson, L., Buchholz, N.C., Schlicting, R.D.: Preserving and using context information in interprocess communication. ACM Trans. Comput. Syst. **7**(3), 217–246 (1989a)

Peterson, L., Hutchinson, N., O'Malley, S., Abbott, M.: RPC in the x-kernel: Evaluating new design techniques. In: Proceedings of the Twelfth Symposium on Operating Systems Principles, Litchfield Park, AZ, November 1989, pp. 91–101. ACM Press, New York (1989b)

Powell, D. (ed.): Delta-4: A Generic Architecture for Dependable Distributed Computing. Springer-Verlag ESPRIT Research Reports, vol. I, Project 818/2252 (1991)

Powell, D.: Lessons learned from Delta-4. IEEE MICRO **14**(4), 36–47 (1994)

Powell, D.: Introduction to special section on group communication. Commun. ACM **39**(4), 50–53 (1996)

Pritchett, D.: BASE: An acid alternative. Queue **6**(3), 48–55 (2008)

Pu, D.: Relaxing the limitations of serializable transactions in distributed systems. Oper. Syst. Rev. **27**(2), 66–71 (1993). (Special issue on the Workshop on Operating Systems Principles at Le Mont St. Michel, France)

Rabin, M.: Randomized Byzantine generals. In: Proceedings of the Twenty-Fourth Annual Symposium on Foundations of Computer Science, pp. 403–409. IEEE Computer Society Press, New York (1983)

Rashid, R.F.: Threads of a new system. UNIX Rev. **4**, 37–49 (1986)

Reed, D.P., Kanodia, R.K.: Synchronization with eventcounts and sequencers. Commun. ACM **22**(2), 115–123 (1979)

Reiher, P., et al.: Resolving file conflicts in the ficus file system. In: Proceedings of the Summer USENIX Conference, June 1994, pp. 183–195 (1994)

Reiter, M.K.: A security architecture for fault-tolerant systems. Ph.D. diss., Cornell University, August (1993). Also Technical Report, Department of Computer Science, Cornell University

Reiter, M.K.: Secure agreement protocols: Reliable and atomic group multicast in rampart. In: Proceedings of the Second ACM Conference on Computer and Communications Security, Oakland, November 1994, pp. 68–80 (1994a)

Reiter, M.K., A secure group membership protocol. In: Proceedings of the 1994 Symposium on Research in Security and Privacy, Oakland, May 1994, pp. 89–99. IEEE Computer Society Press, New York (1994b)

Reiter, M.K.: Distributing trust with the Rampart toolkit. Commun. ACM **39**(4), 71–75 (1996)

Reiter, M.K., Birman, K.P.: How to securely replicate services. ACM Trans. Program. Lang. Syst. **16**(3), 986–1009 (1994)

Reiter, M.K., Birman, K.P., Gong, L.: Integrating security in a group-oriented distributed system. In: Proceedings of the IEEE Symposium on Research in Security and Privacy, Oakland, May 1992, pp. 18–32. IEEE Computer Society Press, New York (1992)

Reiter, M., Birman, K.P., van Renesse, R.: A security architecture for fault-tolerant systems. Trans. Comput. Syst. **12**(4), 340–371 (1994)

Ricciardi, A.M.: The group membership problem in asynchronous systems. Ph.D. diss., Cornell University, January (1993)

Ricciardi, A.: The impossibility of (repeated) reliable broadcast. Technical Report TR-PDS-1996-003, Department of Electrical and Computer Engineering, University of Texas, Austin, April (1996)

Ricciardi, A., Birman, K.P.: Using process groups to implement failure detection in asynchronous environments. In: Proceedings of the Eleventh ACM Symposium on Principles of Distributed Computing, Quebec, August 1991, pp. 341–351. ACM Press, New York (1991)

Ricciardi, A., Birman, K.P., Stephenson, P.: The cost of order in asynchronous systems. In: WDAG 1992. Lecture Notes in Computer Science, pp. 329–345. Springer, Berlin (1992)

Ritchie, D.M.: A stream input-output system. AT&T Bell Lab. Tech. J. **63**(8), 1897–1910 (1984)

Rivest, R.L., Shamir, A., Adleman, L.: A method for obtaining digital signatures and public key cryptosystems. Commun. ACM **22**(4), 120–126 (1978)

Rodeh, O., Birman, K., Dolev, D.: Using AVL trees for fault-tolerant group key management. Int. J. Inf. Secur. **1**(2), 84–99 (2002)

Rodrigues, L., Verissimo, P.: xAMP: A MultiPrimitive group communications service. In: Proceedings of the Eleventh Symposium on Reliable Distributed Systems, Houston, October 1989. IEEE Computer Society Press, New York (1989)

Rodrigues, L., Verissimo, P.: Causal separators for large-scale multicast communication. In: Proceedings of the Fifteenth International Conference on Distributed Computing Systems, May 1995, pp. 83–91 (1995)

Rodrigues, L., Verissimo, P., Rufino, J.: A low-level processor group membership protocol for LANs. In: Proceedings of the Thirteenth International Conference on Distributed Computing Systems, May 1993, pp. 541–550 (1993)

Rodrigues, L., Guo, K., Verissimo, P., Birman, K.P.: A dynamic light-weight group service. J. Parallel Distrib. Comput. **60**, 1449–1479 (2000)

Rosenblum, M., Ousterhout, J.K.: The design and implementation of a log-structured file system. In: Proceedings of the Twelfth ACM Symposium on Operating Systems Principles, Asilomar, CA, October 1991, pp. 1–15. ACM Press, New York (1991). Also ACM Trans. Comput. Syst. **10**(1), 26–52 (1992)

Rowe, L.A., Smith, B.C.: A continuous media player. In: Proceedings of the Third International Workshop on Network and Operating Systems Support for Digital Audio and Video, San Diego, CA, November 1992

Rozier, M., et al.: Chorus distributed operating system. Comput. Syst. J. **1**(4), 305–370 (1988a)

Rozier, M., et al.: The Chorus distributed system. Comput. Syst. 299–328 (1988b)

Sabel, L., Marzullo, K.: Simulating fail-stop in asynchronous distributed systems. In: Proceedings of the Thirteenth Symposium on Reliable Distributed Systems, Dana Point, CA, October 1994, pp. 138–147. IEEE Computer Society Press, New York (1994)

Saltzer, J.H., Reed, D.P., Clark, D.D.: End-to-end arguments in system design. ACM Trans. Comput. Syst. **39**(4) (1990)

Santry, D.S., Feeley, M.J., Hutchinson, N.C., Veitch, A.C., Carton, R.W., Ofir, J.: Deciding when to forget in the Elephant file system. In: Proceedings of the Seventeenth ACM Symposium on Operating Systems Principles, SOSP '99, Charleston, South Carolina, United States, pp. 110–123. ACM, New York (1999)

Satyanarayanan, M., et al.: The ITC distributed file system: Principles and design. In: Proceedings of the Tenth ACM Symposium on Operating Systems Principles, Orcas Island, WA, December 1985, pp. 35–50. ACM Press, New York (1985)

Satyanarayanan, M., et al.: Integrating security in a large distributed system. ACM Trans. Comput. Syst. **7**(3), 247–280 (1989)

Schantz, R.E., Thomas, R.H., Bono, G.: The architecture of the Chronus distributed operating system. In: Proceedings of the Sixth International Conference on Distributed Computing Systems, New York, June 1986, pp. 250–259. IEEE Computer Society Press, New York (1986)

Schiller, J.I.: Secure distributed computing. Sci. Am. 72–76 (1994)

Schiper, A., Raynal, M.: From group communication to transactions in distributed systems. Commun. ACM **39**(4), 84–87 (1996)

Schiper, A., Eggli, J., Sandoz, A.: A new algorithm to implement causal ordering. In: Proceedings of the Third International Workshop on Distributed Algorithms. Lecture Notes in Computer Science, vol. 392, pp. 219–232. Springer, Berlin (1989)

Schiper, A., Shvartsman, A.A., Weatherspoon, H., Zhao, B.: Future Directions in Distributed Computing, Research and Position Papers. Springer, Berlin (2003)

Schmuck, F.: The use of efficient broadcast primitives in asynchronous distributed systems. Ph.D. diss., Cornell University, August (1988). Also Technical Report, Department of Computer Science, Cornell University

Schmuck, F., Wyllie, J.: Experience with transactions in quicksilver. In: Proceedings of the Twelfth ACM Symposium on Operating Systems Principles, Asilomar, CA, October 1991, pp. 239–252. ACM Press, New York (1991)

Schneider, F.B.: Byzantine generals in action: Implementing fail-stop processors. ACM Trans. Comput. Syst. **2**(2), 145–154 (1984)

Schneider, F.B.: The StateMachine approach: A tutorial. In: Proceedings of the Workshop on Fault-Tolerant Distributed Computing, Asilomar, CA. Lecture Notes on Computer Science, vol. 448, pp. 18–41. Springer, Berlin (1988)

Schneider, F.B.: Implementing fault-tolerant services using the StateMachine approach. ACM Comput. Surv. **22**(4), 299–319 (1990)

Schneider, F.B., Walsh, K., Sirer, E.G.: Nexus authorization logic (NAL): Design rationale and applications. ACM Trans. Inf. Syst. Secur. **14**(1), 8 (2011). 28 pages

Seltzer, M.: Transaction support in a log-structured file system. In: Proceedings of the Ninth International Conference on Data Engineering, April 1993

Shieh, A., Sirer, E.G., Schneider, F.B.: NetQuery: A knowledge plane for reasoning about network properties. In: Proceedings of the ACM SIGCOMM 2011 Conference on SIGCOMM (SIGCOMM '11), pp. 278–289. ACM, New York (2011)

Shraer, A., Martin, J.-P., Malkhi, D., Keidar, I.: Data-centric reconfiguration with network-attached disks. In: Large-Scale Distributed Systems and Middleware (LADIS 2010), July 2010

Shroeder, M., Burrows, M.: Performance of firefly RPC. In: Proceedings of the Eleventh ACM Symposium on Operating Systems Principles, Litchfield Springs, AZ, December 1989, pp. 83–90 (1989). Also ACM Trans. Comput. Syst. **8**(1), 1–17 (1990)

Siegal, A.: Performance in flexible distributed file systems. Ph.D. diss., Cornell University, February (1992). Also Technical Report TR-92-1266, Department of Computer Science, Cornell University

Siegel, A., Birman, K.P., Marzullo, K.: Deceit: A flexible distributed file system. Technical Report 89-1042, Department of Computer Science, Cornell University (1989)

Simons, B., Welch, J.N., Lynch, N.: An overview of clock synchronization. In: Simons, B., Spector, A. (eds.) Fault-Tolerant Distributed Computing. Lecture Notes in Computer Science, vol. 448, pp. 84–96. Springer, Berlin (1990)

Skeen, D.: Crash recovery in a distributed database system. Ph.D. diss., Department of EECS, University of California, Berkeley, June (1982a)

Skeen, D.: A quorum-based commit protocol. In: Proceedings of the Berkeley Workshop on Distributed Data Management and Computer Networks, Berkeley, CA, February 1982, pp. 69–80 (1982b)

Skeen, D.: Determining the last process to fail. ACM Trans. Comput. Syst. **3**(1), 15–30 (1985)

Spasojevic, M., Satyanarayanan, M.: An empirical study of a wide area distributed file system. ACM Trans. Comput. Syst. **14**(2) (1996)

Spector, A.: Distributed transactions for reliable systems. In: Proceedings of the Tenth ACM Symposium on Operating Systems Principles, Orcas Island, WA, December 1985, pp. 12–146 (1985)

Srikanth, T.K., Toueg, S.: Optimal clock synchronization. J. ACM **34**(3), 626–645 (1987)

Srinivasan, V., Mogul, J.: Spritely NFS: Experiments with cache consistency protocols. In: Proceedings of the Eleventh ACM Symposium on Operating Systems Principles, Litchfield Springs, AZ, December 1989, pp. 45–57 (1989)

Steiner, J.G., Neuman, B.C., Schiller, J.I.: Kerberos: An authentication service for open network systems. In: Proceedings of the 1988 USENIX Winter Conference, Dallas, February 1988, pp. 191–202 (1988)

Stephenson, P.: Fast causal multicast. Ph.D. diss., Cornell University, February (1991). Also Technical Report, Department of Computer Science, Cornell University

Stoica, I., Morris, R., Karger, D., Kaashoek, M.F., Balakrishnan, H.: Chord: A scalable peer-to-peer lookup service for Internet applications. In: ACM SIGCOMM 2001, San Diego, CA, August 2001, pp. 149–160 (2001)

Strom, R.E., Banavar, G., Chandra, T.D., Kaplan, M., Miller, K., Mukherjee, B., Sturman, D.C., Ward, M.: Gryphon: An information flow based approach to message brokering. CoRR (1998)

Tanenbaum, A.: Computer Networks, 2nd edn. Prentice Hall, Englewood Cliffs (1988)

Tanenbaum, A., van Renesse, R.: A critique of the remote procedure call paradigm. In: Proceedings of the EUTECO '88 Conference, Vienna, April 1988, pp. 775–783 (1988)

Terry, D.B., et al.: Managing update conflicts in a weakly connected replicated storage system. In: Proceedings of the Fifteenth Symposium on Operating Systems Principles, Copper Mountain Resort, CO, December 1995, pp. 172–183. ACM Press, New York (1995)

Thekkath, C.A., Levy, H.M.: Limits to low-latency communication on high-speed networks. ACM Trans. Comput. Syst. **11**(2), 179–203 (1993)

Thekkath, C., Mann, T., Lee, E.: Frangipani: A scalable distributed file system. In: 16th ACM Symposium on Operating Systems Principles (SOSP), Saint-Malo, France, October 1997

Thomas, T.: A majority consensus approach to concurrency control for multiple copy databases. ACM Trans. Database Syst. **4**(2), 180–209 (1979)

Tock, Y., Naaman, N., Harpaz, A., Gershinsky, G.: Hierarchical clustering of message flows in a multicast data dissemination system. In: IASTED PDCS (2005)

van Renesse, R.: Causal controversy at Le Mont St.-Michel. Oper. Syst. Rev. **27**(2), 44–53 (1993)

van Renesse, R.: Why bother with CATOCS? Oper. Syst. Rev. **28**(1), 22–27 (1994)

van Renesse, R.: Paxos made moderately simple. Technical report, Cornell University, March (2011)

van Renesse, R., Schneider, F.B.: Chain replication for supporting high throughput and availability. In: Sixth Symposium on Operating Systems Design and Implementation (OSDI '04), San Francisco, CA, December 2004

van Renesse, R., van Staveren, H., Tanenbaum, A.: Performance of the world's fastest operating system. Oper. Syst. Rev. **22**(4), 25–34 (1988)

van Renesse, R., van Staveren, H., Tanenbaum, A.: The performance of the Amoeba distributed operating system. Softw. Pract. Exp. **19**(3), 223–234 (1989)

van Renesse, R., Birman, K.P., Friedman, R., Hayden, M., Karr, D.: A framework for protocol composition in Horus. In: Proceedings of the Fourteenth Symposium on the Principles of Distributed Computing, Ottawa, August 1995, pp. 80–89. ACM Press, New York (1995)

van Renesse, R., Birman, K.P., Maffeis, S.: Horus: A flexible group communication system. Commun. ACM **39**(4), 76–83 (1996)

van Renesse, R., Birman, K.P., Hayden, M., Vaysburd, A., Karr, D.: Building adaptive systems using Ensemble. In: Software—Practice and Experience, August 1998

van Renesse, R., Birman, K.P., Vogels, W.: Astrolabe: A robust and scalable technology for distributed system monitoring, management, and data mining. ACM Trans. Comput. Syst. **21**(2), 164–206 (2003)

Verissimo, P.: Real-time communication. In: Mullender, S.J. (ed.) Distributed Systems, 2nd edn., pp. 447–490. Addison-Wesley/ACM Press, Reading (1993)

Verissimo, P.: Ordering and timeliness requirements of dependable real-time programs. J. Real-Time Syst. **7**(2), 105–128 (1994)

Verissimo, P.: Uncertainty and predictability: Can they be reconciled. In: Future Directions in Distributed Computing, pp. 108–113. Springer, Berlin (2003)

Verissimo, P., Rodrigues, L.: A-posteriori agreement for fault-tolerant clock synchronization on broadcast networks. In: Proceedings of the Twenty-Second International Symposium on Fault-Tolerant Computing, Boston, July 1992

Vigfusson, Y.: Affinity in distributed systems. PhD dissertation. Cornell University, Sept. (2009). (Degree conferred Feb. 2010)

Vigfusson, Y., Birman, K., Huang, Q., Nataraj, D.P.: GO: Platform support for Gossip applications. In: IEEE P2P 2009, Seattle, WA, September 9–11, pp. 222–231 (2009)

Vigfusson, Y., Abu-Libdeh, H., Balakrishnan, M., Birman, K., Burgess, R., Li, H., Chockler, G., Tock, Y.: Dr. Multicast: Rx for data center communication scalability. In: Eurosys, ACM SIGOPS, Paris, France, April 2010, pp. 349–362 (2010)

Vitenberg, R., Chockler, G.V., Keidar, I.: Group communication specifications: A comprehensive study. ACM Comput. Surv. **33**(4) (2001)

Vogels, W.: The private investigator. Technical Report, Department of Computer Science, Cornell University, April (1996)

Vogels, W.: File system usage in Windows NT 4.0. In: Proceedings of the Seventeenth ACM Symposium on Operating Systems Principles, SOSP'99, Charleston, South Carolina, United States, pp. 93–109. ACM, New York (1999)

Vogels, W.: Eventually consistent—Revisited. http://www.allthingsdistributed.com/2008/12/eventually_consistent.html. Dec (2008)

Vogels, W., Re, C.: WS-membership—failure management in a Web-Services World. In: 12th International World Wide Web Conference, Budapest, Hungary, May 2003

von Eicken, T., Culler, D.E., Goldstein, S.C., Schauser, K.E.: Active messages: A mechanism for integrated communication and computation. In: Proceedings of the Nineteenth International Symposium on Computer Architecture, May 1992, pp. 256–266 (1992)

von Eicken, T., Basu, A., Buch, V., Vogels, W.: U-Net: A user-level network interface for parallel and distributed computing. In: Proceedings of the Fifteenth Symposium on Operating Systems Principles, Copper Mountain Resort, CO, December 1995, pp. 40–53. ACM Press, New York (1995)

Voulgaris, S., van Steen, M.: Epidemic-style management of semantic overlays for content-based searching. In: Euro-Par 2005, pp. 1143–1152 (2005)

Voulgaris, S., Kermarrec, A.M., Massoulié, L., van Steen, M.: Exploiting semantic proximity in peer-to-peer content searching. In: FTDCS 2004, pp. 238–243 (2004)

Voulgaris, S., van Steen, M., Iwanicki, K.: Proactive gossip-based management of semantic overlay networks. Concurr. Comput. **19**(17), 2299–2311 (2007)

Wahbe, R., Lucco, S., Anderson, T., Graham, S.: Efficient software-based fault isolation. In: Proceedings of the Thirteenth ACM Symposium on Operating Systems Principles, Asheville, NC, December 1993, pp. 203–216. ACM Press, New York (1993)

Waldman, M., Mazières, D.: Tangler: A censorship-resistant publishing system based on document entanglements. In: Proceedings of the 8th ACM Conference on Computer and Communications Security, November, pp. 126–135 (2001)

Walter, B., et al.: The locus distributed operating system. In: Proceedings of the Ninth ACM Symposium on Operating Systems Principles, Bretton Woods, NH, October 1993, pp. 49–70 (1993)

Wang, Y., Keller, E., Biskeborn, B., van der Merwe, J., Rexford, J.: Virtual routers on the move: Live router migration as a network-management primitive. In: Proc. ACM SIGCOMM, August 2008

Weatherspoon, H., Kubiatowicz, J.: Erasure coding vs. replication: A quantitative comparison. In: IPTPS 2002, pp. 328–338 (2002)

Weatherspoon, H., Ganesh, L., Marian, T., Balakrishnan, M., Birman, K.: Smoke and mirrors: Reflecting files at a geographically remote location without loss of performance. In: Proceedings of the 7th USENIX Conference on File and Storage Technologies (FAST), February 2009

Welsh, M., Culler, D., Brewer, E.: SEDA: An architecture for well-conditioned, scalable Internet services. In: 18th Symposium on Operating Systems Principles (SOSP), Banff, Canada, October 2001

Wilkes, J., et al.: The HP AutoRAID hierarchical storage system. In: Proceedings of the Fifteenth Symposium on Operating Systems Principles, Copper Mountain Resort, CO, December 1995, pp. 96–108. ACM Press, New York (1995). Also ACM Trans. Comput. Syst. **13**(1) (1996)

Wong, B., Slivkins, A., Sirer, E.G.: Meridian: A lightweight network location service without virtual coordinates. In: Proceedings of the 2005 Conference on Applications, Technologies, Architectures, and Protocols for Computer Communications (SIGCOMM '05), pp. 85–96. ACM, New York (2005)

Wood, M.D.: Fault-tolerant management of distributed applications using a reactive system architecture. Ph.D. diss., Cornell University, December (1991). Also Technical Report TR 91-1252, Department of Computer Science, Cornell University

Wood, M.D.: Replicated RPC using Amoeba closed-group communication. In: Proceedings of the Twelfth International Conference on Distributed Computing Systems, Pittsburgh (1993)

Yeger-Lotem, E., Keidar, I., Dolev, D.: Dynamic voting for consistent primary components. In: 16th ACM Symposium on Principles of Distributed Computing (PODC'97), pp. 63–71 (1997)

Yu, Y., Isard, M., Fetterly, D., Budiu, M., Erlingsson, U., Gunda, P., Currey, J.: DryadLINQ: A system for general-purpose distributed data-parallel computing using a high-level language. In: ACM Symposium on Operating System Design and Implementation (OSDI), San Diego, CA, December 8–10, 2008

Zagorodnov, D., Marzullo, K., Alvisi, L., Bressoud, T.C.: Practical and low-overhead masking of failures of TCP-based servers. ACM Trans. Comput. Syst. **27**(2) (2009)

Zhao, B., Duan, Y., Huang, L., Joseph, A.D., Kubiatowicz, J.: Brocade: Landmark routing on overlay networks. In: IPTPS 2002, pp. 34–44 (2002a)

Zhao, Duan, B.Y., Huang, L., Joseph, A.D., Kubiatowicz, J.D.: Brocade: Landmark routing on overlay networks. In: First International Workshop on Peer-to-Peer Systems (IPTPS), Cambridge, MA, March 2002b

Index